PRENTICE HALL

African-American History

PRENTICE HALL

African-American History

DARLENE CLARK HINE
Northwestern University

WILLIAM C. HINE
South Carolina State University

STANLEY HARROLD
South Carolina State University

PEARSON
Prentice Hall

Upper Saddle River, New Jersey 07458

Library of Congress Cataloging-in-Publication Data

Hine, Darlene Clark.
   The African-American odyssey/Darlene Clark Hine, William C. Hine, Stanley Harrold.—2nd ed.
      p. cm.
   Includes bibliographical references and index.
   ISBN 0-13-192217-3
   1. African Americans. 2. African Americans—History. I. Hine, William C. II. Harrold, Stanley. III. Title.
E185.H533 2002
973.04'96073—dc21   2002017052

Vice President/Editorial Director: Charlyce Jones Owen
Supervisor/Assistant: Maureen Diana
Associate Editor: Emsal Hasan
Editor-in-Chief/Development: Rochelle Diogenes
Development Editor: Gerald Lombardi
Media Editor: Deborah O'Connell
Director of Production and Manufacturing: Barbara Kittle
Managing Editor: Joanne Riker
Production Liaison: Louise Rothman
Prepress and Manufacturing Manager: Nick Sklitsis
Prepress and Manufacturing Buyer: Benjamin D. Smith
Director of Marketing: Heather Shelstad
Creative Design Director: Leslie Osher
Cover and Interior Design: Anne DeMarinis, Kathy Mrozek, and Rosemary Ross
Electronic Artist: Mirella Signoretto
Cartographer: International Mapping
Cover Art: "The 1920's . . . The Migrants Arrive And Cast Their Ballots," Jacob Lawrence. Silkscreen print,
      32″ × 25″. The Newark Museum/Art Resource, NY. © 2005 The Estate of Jacob
      Lawrence/Artists Rights Society (ARS), New York
Director, Image Resource Center: Melinda Reo
Manager, Visual Research: Beth Brenzel
Color Scanning Service: Joe Conti, Greg Harrison, Cory Skidds, Rob Uibelhoer, Ron Walko
Cover Image Specialist: Karen Sanatar
Photo Researcher: Steven Forsling
Image Coordinator: Craig Jones
Composition and Full-Service Vendor: GGS Book Services
Printer/Binder: Courier Kendallville
Cover Printer: Phoenix Color Corporation

Credits and acknowledgments for materials borrowed from other sources and reproduced, with permission,
   in this textbook, appear on pages 933–935.

Pearson Education Ltd.
Pearson Education Australia Pty. Ltd.
Pearson Education Singapore, Pte. Ltd.
Pearson Education North Asia Ltd.
Pearson Education Canada Ltd.
Pearson Educación de Mexico, S.A. de C.V.
Pearson Education–Tokyo, Japan
Pearson Education Malaysia, Pte. Ltd.
Pearson Education Upper Saddle River, New Jersey

10 9 8 7 6 5 4 3 2 1

Student Edition ISBN 0-13-194725-7
Teacher's Edition ISBN 0-13-194731-1

To

CARTER G. WOODSON & BENJAMIN QUARLES

About the Authors

Darlene Clark Hine

Darlene Clark Hine is Board of Trustees Professor of African American Studies and Professor of History at Northwestern University. She is past-president of the Organization of American Historians (2001–2002) and of the Southern Historical Association (2002–2003). Hine received her BA at Roosevelt University in Chicago, and her MA and Ph.D. from Kent State University, Kent, Ohio. Hine has taught at South Carolina State University, Purdue University, and at Michigan State University. In 2000–2001 she was a fellow at the Center for Advanced Study in the Behavioral Sciences at Stanford University, and in 2002–2003 she was a fellow at Radcliffe Institute for Advanced Studies. She is the author and/or editor of fifteen books, most recently with David Barry Gaspar, *Beyond Bondage: Free Women of Color in the Americas* (Urbana: University of Illinois Press, 2004), and *The Harvard Guide to African American History* (Cambridge: Harvard University Press, 2000) coedited with Evelyn Brooks Higginbotham and Leon Litwack. She coedited a two volume set with Earnestine Jenkins, A *Question of Manhood: A Reader in Black Men's History and Masculinity* (Bloomington: Indiana University Press, 1999, 2001); and with Jacqueline McLeod, *Crossing Boundaries: Comparative History of Black People in Diaspora* (Bloomington: Indiana University Press, 2000pk). With Kathleen Thompson she wrote *A Shining Thread of Hope: The History of Black Women in America* (New York: Broadway Books, 1998), and edited with Barry Gaspar, *More Than Chattel: Black Women and Slavery in the Americas* (Bloomington: Indiana University Press, 1996). She won the Dartmouth Medal of the American Library Association for the reference volumes coedited with Elsa Barkley Brown and Rosalyn Terborg-Penn, *Black Women in America: An Historical Encyclopedia* (New York: Carlson Publishing, 1993). She is the author of *Black Women in White: Racial Conflict and Cooperation in the Nursing Profession, 1890–1950* (Bloomington: Indiana University Press, 1989). Her forthcoming book is entitled *Black Professional Class and Race Consciousness: Physicians, Nurses, Lawyers, and the Origins of the Civil Rights Movement, 1890–1955.*

William C. Hine

William C. Hine received his undergraduate education at Bowling Green State University, his master's degree at the University of Wyoming, and his Ph.D. at Kent State University. He is a professor of history at South Carolina State University. He has had articles published in several journals, including *Agricultural History, Labor History*, and the *Journal of Southern History*. He is currently writing a history of South Carolina State University.

Stanley Harrold

Stanley Harrold, Professor of History at South Carolina State University, received his bachelor's degree from Allegheny College and his master's and Ph.D. degrees from Kent State University. He is coeditor with Randall M. Miller of *Southern Dissent*, a book series published by the University Press of Florida. He received during the 1990s two National Endowment for the Humanities Fellowships to pursue research dealing with the antislavery movement. His books include: *Gamaliel Bailey and Antislavery Union* (Kent, Ohio: Kent State University Press, 1986), *The Abolitionists and the South* (Lexington: University Press of Kentucky, 1995), *Antislavery Violence: Sectional, Racial, and Cultural Conflict in Antebellum America* (co-edited with John R. McKivigan, Knoxville: University of Tennessee Press, 1999), *American Abolitionists* (Harlow, U.K.: Longman, 2001); *Subversives: Antislavery Community in Washington, D.C., 1828–1865* (Baton Rouge: Louisiana State University Press, 2003), and *The Rise of Aggressive Abolitionism: Addresses to the Slaves* (Lexington: University Press of Kentucky, 2004). He has published articles in *Civil War History, Journal of Southern History, Radical History Review*, and *Journal of the Early Republic.*

Acknowledgments

We are grateful to the reviewers who devoted valuable time to reading and commenting on *The African-American Odyssey* from which *African-American History* is adapted: Shadrach Henry, Everglades High School, Miami, FL; Dana King, Philadelphia School District; Lori Lachowsky, Jacksonville Junior High School, Jacksonville, AR; Bobbie Owensby, Marion High School, Marion, IN; Carole Ann Provin, Northwood Middle School, North Little Rock, AR; Barbara Riebau, Custer High School, Milwaukee, WI. A special thanks to Jacquelin McCord, Chicago Public Schools, Barbara Riebau, Custer High School, Milwaukee, WI; Carol Ann Provin, Northwood Middle School, North Little Rock, AR, Whitney Orwig, John Reisbord, and Dr. Larry Ross, Lincoln University, Missouri for their contributions to the student and teacher materials that accompany the text. We also owe a special thanks to Andrew Workman, Mills College, for his valuable assistance with the revision of *The African-American Odyssey*.

Each of us also enjoyed the support of family members, particularly Barbara A. Clark, Robbie D. Clark, Emily Harrold, Judy Harrold, Carol A. Hine, Peter J. Hine, Thomas D. Hine, and Alma J. McIntosh. Finally, we gratefully acknowledge the essential help of the superb editorial and production team at Prentice Hall: Charlyce Jones Owen, Vice President and Editorial Director for the Humanities, whose vision got this project started and whose unwavering support saw it through to completion; Leslie Osher, Creative Design Director; Anne DeMarinis, who created the book's handsome design; Kathy Mrozek and Rosemary Ross for their adaptation of the original design; Louise Rothman, Production Editor, who saw it efficiently through production; Donna Lee Lurker and Cindy Miller at GGS Book Services for their superb attention to the production of the text, Benjamin D. Smith, Manufacturing Buyer, for getting the best schedule possible, and Joanne Riker, Managing Editor, who kept the whole team together.

Contents

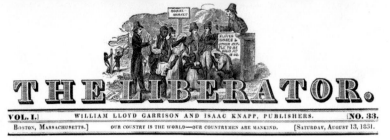

THE LIBERATOR.

VOL. I.] WILLIAM LLOYD GARRISON AND ISAAC KNAPP, PUBLISHERS. [NO. 33.

BOSTON, MASSACHUSETTS.] OUR COUNTRY IS THE WORLD—OUR COUNTRYMEN ARE MANKIND. [SATURDAY, AUGUST 13, 1831.

UNIT 2 ~ SLAVERY, ABOLITION, AND THE QUEST FOR FREEDOM 176

Anthony Burns

UNIT 3 ～ THE CIVIL WAR, EMANCIPATION, AND BLACK RECONSTRUCTION 346

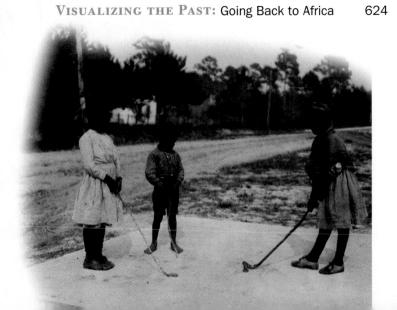

Special Features

Primary Source Documents

Profiles

Maps

Figures and Tables

Map and Data Explorations

Skills for Life

Step-by-step lessons to learn and practice important skills

Reading Informational Texts

Reading a newspaper, a magazine, an Internet page, or a textbook is not the same as reading a novel. The purpose of reading nonfiction texts is to acquire new information. Researchers have shown that the Target Reading Skills presented below will help you get the most out of reading informational texts. You'll have chances to practice these skills and strategies throughout the book. Good luck!

Before You Read

Before you read an informational text, it's important to take the time to do some pre-reading. Here are some strategies for pre-reading an informational text.

Set a Purpose for Reading

It's important to have a goal in mind when you're reading your text. Preview the section you're about to read by reading the objectives and looking at the illustrations. Then write down a purpose for your reading such as "I'll learn about the history of ___, " or "I'll find out about the causes of ___."

Predict

Another pre-reading strategy is to make a prediction about what you're preparing to learn. Do this by scanning the section headings and visuals. Then write down a prediction such as "I will find out what caused the American Revolution."

Ask Questions

Before you read a section ask a few questions that you'd like to answer while reading. Scan the section headings and illustrations and then jot down a few questions in a table. As you read, try to fill in answers to your questions. You don't need to use complete sentences.

Question	Answer
1. Why do people emigrate from their home country?	War, poverty, lack of food or jobs, persecution
2. What challenges do many immigrants face?	New language, new customs, finding jobs

Use Prior Knowledge

Research shows that if you connect the new information you're reading about to something you already know—your prior knowledge—you'll be more likely to remember the new information. After previewing a section, create a table like the one at right. Complete the chart as you read the section.

What I Know	What I Want to Know	What I Learned
Women have the right to vote.	When did women win the right to vote?	The 19th Amendment, guaranteeing women the right to vote, was ratified in 1920.

As You Read

It's important to be an active reader. Here are some strategies to use while you're reading an informational text.

Reread or Read Ahead

If you don't understand a certain passage, reread it to look for connections among the words and sentences. Or try reading ahead to see if the ideas are clarified further on.

Paraphrase

To paraphrase is to restate information in your own words. Paraphrasing is a good way to check that you understand what you've read.

Original Paragraph	Paraphrase
Latin America's northern edge is marked by the boundary between the United States and Mexico. To the south, the region extends to the tip of the continent of South America.	Latin America extends from the U.S.-Mexico border in the north all the way to the southern tip of South America.

Reading and Writing Handbook

Summarize

Summarizing is another good way to check that you understand what you've read. To summarize is to restate the main ideas of a passage.

Original Paragraph	Summary
Electricity made from water power is called hydroelectricity. One way to build a hydroelectric plant is to dam a river. This creates a huge lake. When the dam gates open, water gushes from the lake to the river, turning a wheel that creates electricity.	Hydroelectricity is created when rushing water turns a wheel.

Identify Main Ideas and Details

A main idea is the most important point in a paragraph or section of text. Sometimes a main idea is stated directly, but other times you must determine it yourself by reading carefully. Main ideas are supported by details. Good readers pause occasionally to make sure they can identify the main idea. You can record main ideas and details in an outline format like the one shown here.

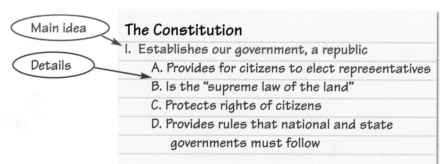

Main idea

The Constitution establishes our form of government, a republic. A republic is a government in which citizens elect their representatives. As the "supreme law of the land," the Constitution protects the rights of citizens by providing general rules that the national government and the state governments must follow.

Main idea

Details

The Constitution

I. Establishes our government, a republic
   A. Provides for citizens to elect representatives
   B. Is the "supreme law of the land"
   C. Protects rights of citizens
   D. Provides rules that national and state governments must follow

Use Context Clues

When you come across an unfamiliar word, you can sometimes figure out its meaning from clues in the surrounding words. For example, in the sentence "Some vendors sold bottled water," the word *sold* is a clue indicating that a vendor is someone who sells things.

Analyze Word Parts

When you come across an unfamiliar word, sometimes it's helpful to break the word into parts—its root, prefix, or suffix. For example, the prefix *in-* means "not." The word *injustice* means something that is "not just." Create a reference chart indicating the meanings of common prefixes and suffixes.

Recognize Word Origins

Another way to figure out the meaning of an unfamiliar word is to understand the word's origins, or where it comes from. For example, the words *import* and *export* contain the Latin root *–port,* which means "to carry." Imports are goods carried into a country and exports are goods carried out of a country.

Analyze the Text's Structure

In a social studies text, the author frequently uses one of the structures at right to organize the information in a section. Research shows that if you identify a text's overall structure, you're more likely to remember the information you're reading.

Compare and Contrast—the author points out the similarities and differences between two or more things such as people or places.

Sequence—the author tells the order in which events took place or the steps someone took to accomplish something.

Cause and Effect—the author points out the main causes and/or effects of an event.

Analyze the Author's Purpose

Different types of materials are written with different purposes in mind. For example, a textbook is written to teach students information about a subject. The purpose of a technical manual is to teach someone how to use something, such as a computer. A newspaper editorial might be written to persuade the reader to accept a particular point of view.

A writer's purpose influences how the material is presented. Sometimes an author states his or her purpose directly. More often the purpose is only suggested, and you must use clues to identify the author's purpose.

Reading and Writing Handbook

Distinguish Between Facts and Opinions and Recognize Bias

It's important when reading informational texts to read actively and remember to distinguish between fact and opinion. A fact can be proven or disproven. An opinion reveals someone's personal viewpoint or evaluation.

For example, the editorial pages in a newspaper offer opinions on topics that are currently in the news. You need to read newspaper editorials with an eye for bias and faulty logic. For example, the newspaper editorial shown here shows factual statements highlighted in blue and opinion statements in red. The underlined words are examples of highly charged words. They reveal bias on the part of the writer.

> More than 5,000 people voted last week in favor of building a new shopping center, but the opposition won out. The margin of victory is irrelevant. Those <u>radical</u> voters who opposed the center are obviously <u>self-serving elitists</u> who do not care about anyone but themselves.
>
> This month's unemployment figures for our area are 10 percent, which represents an increase of about 5 percent over the figures for last year. These figures mean that unemployment is worsening. But the people who voted against the mall probably do not care about creating new jobs.

Identify Evidence

Before you accept an author's conclusion, you need to make sure that the author has based the conclusion on enough evidence and on the right kind of evidence. An author may present a series of facts to support a claim, but the facts may not tell the whole story. For example, what evidence does the author of the newspaper editorial above provide to support his or her claim that the new shopping center would create more jobs? Is it possible that the shopping center might have put many small local businesses out of business, thus increasing unemployment rather than decreasing it?

Evaluate Credibility

Whenever you read informational texts you need to assess the credibility of the author. This is especially true of sites you may visit on the Internet. All Internet sources are not created equal. Here are some questions to ask yourself when evaluating the credibility of a Web site.

◆ What is the source of the information? Is the Web site created by a respected organization, a discussion group, or an individual?

◆ Does the Web site creator include his or her name as well as credentials and the sources he or she used to write the material?

◆ Is the information on the site balanced or biased?

◆ Can you verify the information using two other sources?

◆ Is the information up-to-date? Is there a date on the Web site telling you when the Web site was created or last updated?

After You Read

Test yourself to find out what you learned from reading the text. Go back to the questions you asked yourself before you read the text. You should be able to give more complete answers to these questions:

◆ What is the text about?
◆ What is the purpose of the text?
◆ How is the text structured?

You should also be able to make connections between the new information you learned and what you already knew about the topic.

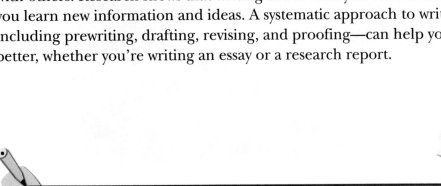

Reading and Writing Handbook

Writing for Social Studies

Writing is one of the most powerful communication tools you will use today and for the rest of your life. You will use it to share your thoughts and ideas with others. Research shows that writing about what you read actually helps you learn new information and ideas. A systematic approach to writing—including prewriting, drafting, revising, and proofing—can help you write better, whether you're writing an essay or a research report.

Narrative Essays

Writing that tells a story about a personal experience

❶ Select and Narrow Your Topic

A narrative is a story. In social studies, it might be a narrative essay about how a historical event affected you or your family. The focus of your essay should be a special event of significance to you.

❷ Gather Details

Brainstorm a list of details you'd like to include in your narrative. Keep in mind who your audience will be.

❸ Write a First Draft

Start by writing a simple opening sentence that will catch your reader's attention. Continue by writing a colorful story that has a beginning, middle, and end. Write a conclusion that sums up the significance of the event or situation described in your essay.

❹ Revise and Edit

Consider adding dialogue to convey a person's thoughts or feelings in his or her own words. Check to make sure you have not begun too many sentences with the word I. If you have, revise the sentences. Replace general words with more specific, colorful ones.

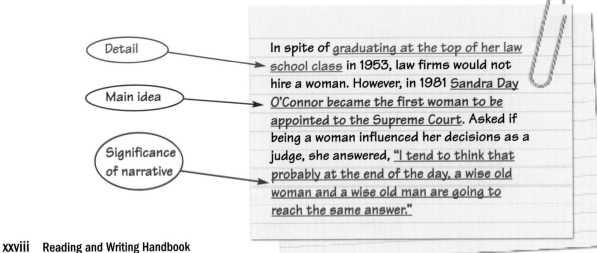

Detail → In spite of graduating at the top of her law school class in 1953, law firms would not hire a woman. However, in 1981 Sandra Day

Main idea → O'Connor became the first woman to be appointed to the Supreme Court. Asked if being a woman influenced her decisions as a judge, she answered,

Significance of narrative → "I tend to think that probably at the end of the day, a wise old woman and a wise old man are going to reach the same answer."

Persuasion

Writing that supports an opinion or position

1 Select and Narrow Your Topic

Choose a topic that provokes an argument and has at least two sides. If there are too many pros and cons for the argument, consider narrowing your topic to cover only part of the debate.

2 Consider Your Audience

The argument that you make in your writing should be targeted to the specific audience for your writing. Which argument is going to appeal most to your audience and persuade them to understand your point of view?

3 Gather Evidence

You'll need to include convincing examples in your essay. Begin by creating a graphic organizer that states your position at the top. Then in two columns list the pros and cons for your position. Consider interviewing experts on the topic. Even though your essay may focus on the pro arguments, it's important to predict and address the strongest arguments against your stand.

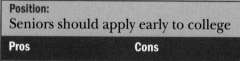

Position: Seniors should apply early to college	
Pros	**Cons**
◆ Improves your chances of acceptance ◆ Reduces stress ◆ Allows more time for friends and family	◆ Less time to decide which school to apply to

4 Write a First Draft

Begin by writing a strong thesis statement that clearly states the position you will prove. Continue by presenting the strongest arguments in favor of your position and acknowledging and refuting opposing arguments. Build a strong case by including facts, statistics, and comparisons, and by sharing personal experiences.

5 Revise and Proof

Check to make sure you have made a logical argument and that you have not oversimplified the argument. Try adding the following transition words to make your reasoning more obvious:

To show a contrast—*however, although, despite*
To point out a reason—*since, because, if*
To signal a conclusion—*therefore, consequently, so, then*

Not Now, but Right Now!

It sneaks up on you at all hours of the day or night, a floating cloud of angst. Suddenly, a feeling bubbles up from the pit of your stomach, an achy, acidic feeling of panic. "Which college is the right college? Can I get in?" These fears are definitely part of your senior year experience, but two simple words hold the secret to reduced stress: Apply early. It is as simple as that. Apply early for college admissions and you will sleep easier at night.

Think for a moment of how the college admissions process works. Like a thousand cattle trying to pass through the same gate at once, vast numbers of people across the nation apply each year for a limited number of places at college. Academic records of applicants aside, admissions boards work on a first come, first served basis. The longer you wait to apply, the less likely you are to make the cut, no matter how qualified you may be.

Your senior year is a time of closing chapters, a time to enjoy the last days at home with friends and family, a time to remember the joys of childhood before jumping into the great unknown, adulthood. While waiting until the last minute to apply to college may give you more time to decide which schools to apply to, it will dramatically increase your stress. Take some pressure off yourself by getting applications in early. With just two simple words in mind, you can enjoy the sweet pleasures of the last year of high school in peace: Apply early.

Adapted from an essay by Jason Heflin, Lakeland, Florida

Reading and Writing Handbook

Exposition

Writing that explains a process, compares and contrasts, explains causes and effects, or explores solutions to a problem

1 Identify and Narrow Your Topic

Expository writing is writing that explains something in detail. An essay might explain the similarities and differences between two or more subjects (compare and contrast), it might explain how one event causes another (cause and effect), or it might explain a problem and describe a solution.

2 Gather Evidence

Create a graphic organizer that identifies details to include in your essay. Create a Venn Diagram for a compare-and-contrast essay, a diagram showing multiple causes and effects for a cause-and-effect essay, or a web for defining all the aspects of a problem and the possible solutions.

3

Kennedy
- Democrat
- Cuba Crisis

- President
- Vietnam War
- Term of office ends early

Nixon
- Republican
- China Relations

Write Your First Draft

Write a strong topic sentence and then organize the body of your essay around your similarities and differences, causes and effects, or problem and solutions. Be sure to include convincing details, facts, and examples.

4 Revise and Proof

Be sure you've included transition words between sentences and paragraphs:

Transitions to show similarities—*all, similarly, both, in the same way, closely related, equally*

Transitions that show differences—*on the other hand, in contrast, however, instead, yet*

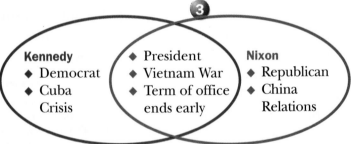

John F. Kennedy and Richard Nixon ran for president of the United States against each other, yet both became president. Kennedy, a Democrat, was elected in 1960. He dealt with crises in Cuba and saw the beginnings of the Vietnam War. He was assassinated in 1963.

Nixon, a Republican, was elected in 1968. He opened relations with China and saw the end of the Vietnam War. Because of the Watergate scandal, he resigned from office in 1974.

Research Writing

Writing that presents research about a topic

1 Identify and Narrow Your Topic

Choose a topic you're interested in and make sure that it is not too broad a topic. For example, instead of writing a report on Panama, write about the Panama Canal. Ask yourself, What do I want to know about the topic?

2 Acquire Information

Locate and use several sources of information about the topic from the library, Internet, or an interview with someone knowledgeable. Before you use a source make sure that it is reliable and up-to-date. Take notes using an index card for each detail or subtopic and note which source the information was taken from. Use quotation marks when you copy the exact words from a source. Create a source index card for each resource, listing the author, the title, the publisher, and the place and date of publication.

3 Make an Outline

Use an outline to decide how to organize your report. Sort your index cards into the same order.

4 Write a First Draft

Write an introduction, body, and conclusion. Leave plenty of space between lines so you can go back and add details that you may have left out.

5 Revise and Proof

Be sure to include transition words between sentences and paragraphs.

To show a contrast–*however, although, despite*

To point out a reason–*since, because, if*

To signal a conclusion–*therefore, consequently, so, then*

Introduction
Building the Panama Canal
Ever since Christopher Columbus first explored the Isthmus of Panama, the Spanish had been looking for a water route through it. They wanted to be able to sail west from Spain to Asia without sailing around South America. However, it was not until 1914 that the dream became a reality.

Conclusion
It took eight years and more than 70,000 workers to build the Panama Canal. It remains one of the greatest engineering feats of modern times.

PRENTICE HALL

African-American History

UNIT 1

Becoming African American

	to 1500	1500–1700

Religion

300s CE Axum adopts Christianity

750s Islam begins to take root in West Africa

1300s–1500s Timbukto flourishes as a center of Islamic learning

1324 Mansa Musa's pilgrimage to Mecca

c.1500 Portuguese convert Kongo kings to Christianity

Culture

1600s African versions of English and French—Gullah, Geechee, and Creole—begin to develop

1600s–1700s African-American folk culture appears among the slaves

Politics & Government

c.3150–30 BCE Independence of Ancient Egypt

1st century CE Fall of Kush

8th century CE Decline of Axumite Empire in Ethiopia

c.750–1076 Empire of Ghana

1230–1468 Empire of Mali

1400s–1700s Expansion of Benin

1468–1571 Empire of Songhai

1500s Rise of Akan states

1607 Jamestown founded

1696 South Carolina Slave Code enacted

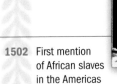

Society & Economy

10th century Islamic slave trade across the Sahara and Central Africa begins

1472 First Portuguese slave traders in Benin

1481 First "slave factory" in Elmira on the Guinea coast

1502 First mention of African slaves in the Americas

1518 Spanish *Asiento* begins

c.1520 Sugar plantations begin in Brazil

1619 First African slaves arrive in Jamestown

1620s Chesapeake tobacco plantations increase the demand for slaves

1624 First black child reported born in British North America

1660s Chattel slavery emerges in the southern colonies

Phillis Wheatley

Elizabeth Freeman

James Forten

1700–1800	1800–1820	Key People
c.1738 First Great Awakening: George Whitefield preaches to African Americans	1808 Abyssinian Baptist Church organized in New York City	**King Piankhy of Kush** (r. c.750 BCE)
1780 Lemuel Haynes becomes first ordained black Congregationalist Minister	1811 African Presbyterian Church established in Philadelphia under Samuel E. Cornish	**Sudiata of Mali** (c.1235 CE)
1794 Mother Bethel Church founded in Philadelphia St. Thomas's Episcopal Church established under Absalom Jones	1816 African Methodist Episcopal Church established	**Emperor Mansa Musa of Mali** (r. 1312–1337)

King Sunni Ali of Songhai (r. 1464–1492)

1740s Lucy Terry Prince publishes poetry	1818 Mother Bethel Church establishes the Augustine School	**King Askia Muhammed Toure of Songhai** (r. 1492–1528)
1760 Jupiter Hammon publishes a book of poetry		**King Nzmiga Mbembba (Affonso I) of Kongo** (r. 1506–1543)
1773 Phillis Wheatley's *Poems on Various Subjects*		
1775 Prince Hall founds first African-American Masonic Lodge		**Ayubu Sulieman Diallo of Bondu** (c.1701–1773)
1780 First African-American mutual aid society founded in Newport Rhode Island		**Jupiter Hammon** (1711–c.1806)
1787 Free African Society founded in Philadelphia		**Crispus Attucks** (1723–1770)
1791–1795 Benjamin Banneker's *Almanac* published		**Benjamin Banneker** (1731–1806)
1793 Philadelphia's Female Benevolent Society of St. Thomas founded		

Prince Hall (1735–1807)

1773 Massachusetts African Americans petition the legislature for freedom	1807 Britain abolishes the Atlantic slave trade	**Elizabeth Freeman** (1744–1811)
1775 Black militiamen fight at Lexington and Concord	1808 U.S. abolishes the Atlantic slave trade	**Absalom Jones** (1746–1818)
1776 Declaration of Independence	1820 Missouri Compromise	**Olaudah Equiano** (c.1745–1797)
1777 Vermont prohibits slavery	First settlement of Liberia by African Americans	**James Forten** (1746–1818)
1782 Virginia allows manumission		**Peter Salem** (1750–1816)
1783 Massachusetts allows male black taxpayers to vote		
1787 Congress bans slavery in the Northwest Territory		**Phillis Wheatley** (c.1753–1784)
1789 U.S. Constitution includes the Three-Fifths clause		**Richard Allen** (1760–1831)
1793 Congress passes First Fugitive Slave Act		**Paul Cuffe** (1759–1817)

1712 New York City slave rebellion	1800 Gabriel's rebellion in Charleston	**Daniel Coker** (1780–1846)
1739 Stono slave revolt in South Carolina	1811 Deslondes's rebellion in Louisiana	**Gabriel** (d. 1800)
1776–1783 100,000 slaves flee southern plantations		**Charles Deslondes** (d. 1811)
1781–1783 20,000 black Loyalists depart with British troops		
1793 Eli Whitney invents the cotton gin		

CHAPTER 1

Africa

ca. 6000 BCE–ca. 1600 CE

Section 1
Africa

Section 2
West Africa

Section 3
West African Society and Culture

This Benin bronze plaque portrays a king on horseback
flanked by two attendants.

Chapter 1

A **wall painting** from an Egyptian tomb shows Nubians carrying baskets and beads. Nubia had close cultural ties to ancient Egypt.

These [West African] nations think themselves the foremost men in the world, and nothing will persuade them to the contrary. They imagine that Africa is not only the greatest part of the world but also the happiest and most agreeable.

—Father Cavazzi, 1687

 Why do you think Africans impressed the writer as he described them?

Chapter Preview

The ancestral homeland of most African Americans is West Africa. Other regions—Angola and East Africa—were caught up in the great Atlantic slave trade that carried Africans to the New World during a period stretching from the sixteenth to the nineteenth century. But West Africa, known to the Arab and European world as the center of trade for gold, salt, ivory and pepper, would become the center for the trading of human beings. Knowing the history of West Africa, therefore, is important for understanding the people who became the first African Americans.

That history is best understood within the larger context of the history and geography of the whole African continent. This chapter begins with a survey of the larger context, emphasizing the aspects of the broader African experience that shaped life in West Africa before the arrival of Europeans in that region. It then explores West Africa's unique heritage and the facets of its culture that have influenced the lives of African Americans from the Diaspora—the original forced dispersal of Africans from their homeland—to the present.

▶▶ **Witnessing History**

He did not expect Africans to be so proud of their homeland.

Section 1

Africa

A Huge and Diverse Land

Africa, the second largest continent in the world (only Asia is larger), is bounded by the Mediterranean Sea to the north, the Atlantic Ocean to the west, and the Indian Ocean and the Red Sea to the east. A narrow strip of land in its northeast corner connects it to the Arabian Peninsula and beyond that to Asia and Europe.

From north to south, Africa is divided into a succession of climatic zones (see Map 1–1). With the exception of a fertile strip along the Mediterranean coast and the agriculturally rich Nile River valley, most of the northern third of the continent consists of the Sahara Desert. For thousands of years, the Sahara had limited contact between the rest of Africa—known as sub-Saharan Africa—and the Mediterranean coast, Europe, and Asia. South of the Sahara is a semidesert region known as the Sahel, and south of the Sahel is a huge grassland, or **savannah**, stretching from Ethiopia westward to the Atlantic Ocean. Arab adventurers named this savannah *Bilad es Sudan*, meaning "land of the black people," and the term **Sudan** designates this entire region, rather than simply the modern East African nation of Sudan. Much of the habitable part of West Africa falls within the savannah. The rest lies within the northern part of a rain forest that extends eastward from the Atlantic coast over most of the central part of the continent. Another region of savannah borders the rain forest to the south, followed by another desert—the Kalahari—and another coastal strip at the continent's southern extremity.

 **Reading Check** What are the geographical characteristics of Africa?

The Birthplace of Humanity

Paleoanthropologists—scientists who study the evolution and prehistory of humans—have concluded that the origins of humanity lie in the savannah regions of Africa. All people today, in other words, are very likely descendants of beings who lived in Africa millions of years ago.

GUIDE TO READING

▶ What are the geographical characteristics of Africa?

▶ Why is Africa considered the "birthplace of humanity"?

▶ Where and how did humans originate?

▶ Why are ancient African civilizations important?

KEY TERMS

▶ savannah, p. 7

▶ Sudan, p. 7

▶ hominids, p. 8

▶ *Homo erectus*, p. 9

▶ ancient Egypt, p. 9

▶ pharaoh, p. 10

▶ **Guide to Reading/Key Terms**

For answers, see the *Teacher's Resource Manual*.

▶ **Reading Check**

With the exception of the Mediterranean coast and the Nile River valley, most of the northern third of the continent consists of the Sahara Desert. South of the Sahara is a semi-desert region known as the Sahel. South of the Sahel is a huge grassland, or savannah. A rain forest covers much of the center of the continent. The rain forest is bordered by savannah to the south, followed by the Kalahari Desert and another coastal strip.

▶ **Recommended Reading**

John Reader. *Africa: A Biography of the Continent.* New York: Knopf, 1998. The most up-to-date account of early African history, emphasizing the ways the continent's physical environment shaped human life there.

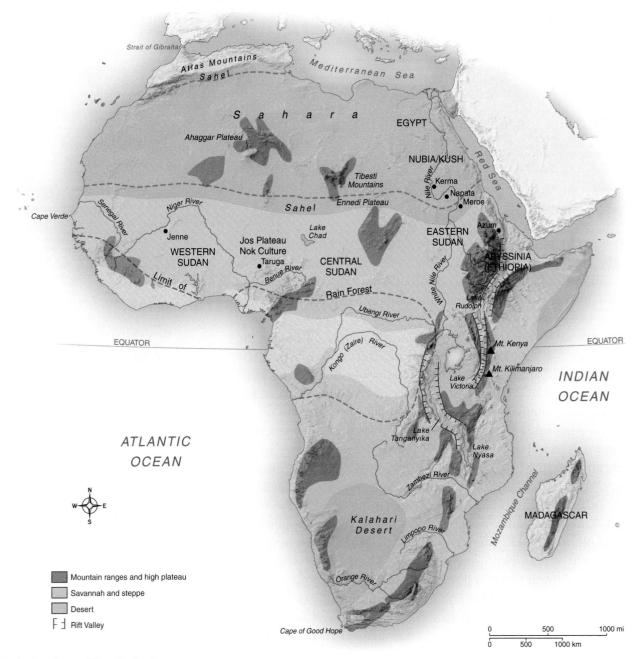

MAP 1–1 Africa: Climatic Regions and Early Sites

Africa is a large continent with several climatic zones. It is also the home of several early civilizations.

 What impact did the variety of climatic zones have on the development of civilization in Africa?

Explore this map online at www.prenhall.com/aah.map1.1

Fossil and genetic evidence suggests that humans descended from a common ancestry who lived in Africa about five to ten million years ago. The African climate was growing drier at that time, as it has continued to do into the present. Forests gave way to spreading savannahs dotted with isolated groups of trees.

The earliest known **hominids** (the term designates the biological family to which humans belong) were the *australopithecines*, who emerged about four million years ago. The first stone tools are associated with the emergence—about 2.4 million years ago—of *Homo habilis*, the earliest creature designated as within the *homo* (human) lineage. Individuals of the *Homo habilis* species had larger brains than the australopithecines. They butchered meat with stone cutting and chopping tools and built shelters with stone foundations. Like people in hunting and gathering societies today, they probably lived in small bands in which women foraged for plant food and men hunted and scavenged for meat.

Homo erectus, who emerged in Africa about 1.6 million years ago, is associated with the first evidence of human use of fire. *Homo erectus*, spread even farther from Africa, reaching eastern Asia and Indonesia.

Paleoanthropologists agree that modern humans, Homo sapiens evolved from Homo erectus, but they disagree on how. According to the out of Africa model, modern humans emerged in Africa some 200,000 years ago and began migrating to the rest of the world about 100,000 years ago, eventually replacing all other existing hominid populations. According to the multiregional model, modern humans evolved throughout Africa, Asia, and Europe from ancestral regional populations of Homo erectus and archaic Homo sapiens. According to this model, a continuous exchange of genetic material allowed archaic human populations in Africa, Asia, and Europe to evolve simultaneously into modern humans. Although, both of these models are consistent with recent genetic evidence, and both indicate that all living peoples are closely related, the prevailing consensus in anthropology is that Africa is the birthplace of all humankind. The "Eve" hypothesis, which supports the out-of-Africa model, suggests that all modern humans are descended from a single African woman. The multiregional model maintains that a continuous exchange of genetic material allowed archaic human populations in Africa, Asia, and Europe to evolve simultaneously into modern humans.

 Reading Check   Where and how did humans originate?

Ancient Civilizations

The earliest civilization in Africa and one of the two earliest civilizations in world history is that of **ancient Egypt** (see Map 1–1), which emerged in the Nile River valley in the fourth millennium BCE. Civilization appeared at the end of a long process in which hunting and gathering gave way to agriculture. The settled village life that resulted from this transformation permitted society to become increasingly hierarchical and specialized. Similar processes gave rise to civilization in the Indus valley in India around 2300 BCE, in China—with the founding of the Shang dynasty—around 1500 BCE, and in Mexico and Andean South America during the first millennium BCE.

The race of the ancient Egyptians and the extent of their influence on Western civilization have long been sources of controversy. It is a con-

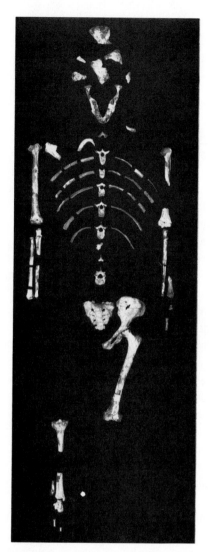

Anthropologists discovered these fossilized bones, nicknamed "Lucy," in 1974 at Hadar, Ethiopia.

▶▶ **Map 1-1, p. 8**

Such distinct environments, savannah and forest, resulted in very different and distinct cultures.

▶ **Reading Check**

The earliest known hominids emerged about 4 million years ago. The first use of stone tools is associated with *homo habilis* (about 2.5 million years ago) and the first use of fire is associated with *homo erectus* (about 1.6 million years ago). *Homo sapiens* evolved from *homo erectus*.

▶ **Recommended Reading**

Christopher Stringer and Robin McKie. *African Exodus: The Origins of Modern Humanity*. New York: Henry Holt, 1997. A very clearly written account favoring the "out of Africa model."

▶ **Map 1-2, p. 11**

Egypt was much more established than Nubia/
Kush, with many more city centers and pyramids.

▶ **Teaching Notes**

According to Dr. John Henrik Clarke, the racial
history of the ancient Egyptians is a dilemma
created in Western historiography dating back
200 years, when some historians stated that
Egyptians were non-African. Although these
accounts were challenged, the most noted
challenge came from Drs. Cheik Ante Diop and
Theophile Obenga. Diop answered the question,
"Who were the Egyptians of the ancient world?"
at the 1974 symposium sponsored by the
United Nations Educational, Scientific and
Cultural Organization (UNESCO). This
symposium, which was held in Cairo, Egypt,
attracted twenty prominent Egyptologists from
around the world who debated the race of the
ancient Egyptians. Dr. Diop's presentation
included his development of the "melanin
dosage test," which "provided the means by
which one could determine the phenotype of the
Egyptian royal mummies by examining the
melanin content present in their skin"

According to Professor Anthony Browder, in
his book, *Nile Valley Contributions to
Civilizations*: "The general consensus reached at
the Cairo Symposium was that there was no
evidence that the ancient Egyptians were white,
and Egypt was not influenced by Mesopotamia,
but by peoples from "the Great Lakes region in
inner-equatorial Africa." Anthony Browder, further
states that despite the fact that the research of
Drs. Diop and Obenga addressed numerous
issues concerning the ethnicity of the ancient
Egyptians, the Egyptians' contributions to
civilization continue to be discussed and
debated. The works of white and black
historians such as Gerald Massey, Martin Bernal,
Carter G. Woodson, W.E.B. Du Bois, J.A. Rogers,
John Jackson, Yosef Ben-Jochannan and
Chancellor Williams have recognized Egypt's
contribution to the spread of civilization not only
throughout the Mediterranean region but
throughout the history of the world.

Egyptian wall paintings from ancient tombs show skilled carpenters at work.

troversy that reflects more about racial politics since the eighteenth century than about the Egyptians themselves. Ethnically the Egyptians were
an African people related to other African peoples across that continent. They had early cultural associations with people to their south in
Nubia and in the "Great Lakes region." They were, nevertheless,
engaged in cultural exchanges with early civilizations in southeastern
Asia. In addition, many scholars have recognized that Egypt as an African
nation influenced the spread of civilization to Greece and throughout
the world. In religion, commerce, philosophy, art, science, and mathematics Egypt played a founding role in what became Western Civilization.

Egyptian Civilization

Egypt was, as the Greek historian Herodotus observed 2,500 years ago,
the "gift of the Nile." It was the Nile that allowed Egyptians to cultivate
wheat and barley and herd goats, sheep, pigs, and cattle in an otherwise
desolate region. The Nile also provided the Egyptians with a transportation and communications artery, while its desert surroundings protected them from foreign invasion.

Egypt was unified into a single kingdom in about 3150 BCE and was
ruled by a succession of thirty-one dynasties until its incorporation into
the Roman Empire in the first century BCE. Historians have divided this
immensely long span into several epochs. During the early dynastic
period (3100–2700 BCE) and Old Kingdom (2700–2200 BCE), Egypt's
kings consolidated their authority and claimed the status of gods. After
a period of instability following the end of the Old Kingdom, royal
authority was reestablished during the Middle Kingdom (2050–1650).

During the New Kingdom (1550–1100), Egypt expanded beyond the Nile valley to establish an empire over coastal regions of southwest Asia as well as Libya and Nubia in Africa. It was in this period that Egypt's kings began using the title **pharaoh**, which means "great house." During the Post-Empire period (1100–30 BCE), Egypt fell prey to a series of outside invaders—Assyrians, Persians, Greeks, Romans, and Arabs. (see Map 1–2).

The way of life that took shape during the Old Kingdom, however, had resisted change for most of ancient Egypt's history. Kings presided over a strictly hierarchical society. Beneath them were classes of warriors, priests, merchants, artisans, and peasants. A class of scribes, who were masters of Egypt's complex hieroglyphic writing, staffed a comprehensive bureaucracy.

Egyptian society was strictly patrilineal and patriarchal. Kings and other men could take additional wives if the first wife failed to produce children. Egyptian women held a high status compared with women in much of the rest of the ancient world. They owned property independently of their husbands, oversaw household slaves, controlled the education of their children, held public office, served as priests, and operated businesses. There were several female rulers, one of whom, Hatshepsut, reigned for twenty years (1478–1458 BCE). She is depicted in carvings and monuments, however, wearing the regalia of male rulers, including the tradtional false beard.

Religion shaped every facet of Egyptian life. Although there were innumerable gods, two of the more important were the sun god Re (or Ra), who represented the immortality of the Egyptian state and Osiris, the god of the Nile, who embodied each individual's personal immortality.

Personal immortality and the immortality of the state merged in the person of the king. The Great Pyramids at Giza near the modern city of Cairo, were built more than 4,500 years ago to protect the bodies of three prominent kings of the Old Kingdom so that their souls might successfully enter the life to come. The pyramids also dramatically symbolized the power of the Egyptian state and have endured as symbols of the grandeur of Egyptian civilization.

Kush

To the south of Egypt, in what is today the nation of Sudan, lay the ancient region known as Nubia. As early as the fourth millennium BCE, the indisputably black people who lived there

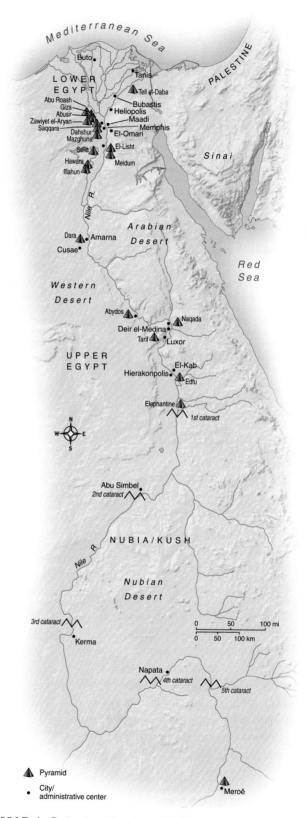

MAP 1–2 Ancient Egypt and Nubia

 What does this map indicate about the relationship between ancient Egypt and Nubia/Kush?

The ruined pyramids of Meroë on the banks of the upper Nile River are examples of the cultural connections between Meroë and Egypt.

▶ **Teaching Notes**

In Egyptian myth Osiris was murdered by his evil brother Seth and resurrected by his sister and wife Isis. This myth, originally an allegory for the seasonal rebirth of vegetation brought by the Nile's annual flooding, came to symbolize the possibility of individual immortality. Egyptians came to regard Osiris as the judge of the worthiness of souls.

▶ **Retracing the Odyssey**

African Collection, National History Museum of Los Angeles County, Los Angeles, CA. This collection includes about five thousand objects representing African cultures.

interacted with the Egyptians. Recent archaeological evidence suggests that grain production and the concept of monarchy may have arisen in Nubia and then spread northward to Egypt. But Egypt's population was always much larger than that of Nubia. During the second millennium BCE, Egypt used its military power to make Nubia an Egyptian colony and control Nubian copper and gold mines. Egyptians also imported ivory, ebony, leopard pelts, and slaves from Nubia and required the sons of Nubian nobles to live in Egypt as hostages.

The hostages served as ambassadors of Egyptian culture when they returned home. As a result, Egyptian religion, art, hieroglyphics, and political structure became firmly established in Nubia. Then, with the decline of Egypt's New Kingdom at the end of the second millennium BCE, the Nubians established an independent kingdom known as Kush, which had its capital at Kerma on the upper Nile River. During the eighth century BCE, the Kushites took control of upper Egypt, and in about 750 the Kushite king Piankhy added lower Egypt to his realm. Piankhy made himself pharaoh and founded Egypt's twenty-fifth dynasty, which ruled until the Assyrians, who invaded Egypt from southwest Asia, drove the Kushites out in 663 BCE.

Meroë

Kush itself remained independent for another thousand years. Its kings continued for centuries to call themselves pharaohs and had themselves buried in pyramid tombs covered with Egyptian hieroglyphics. They and the Kushite nobility practiced the Egyptian religion and spoke the Egyptian language. But a resurgent Egyptian army destroyed Kerma in 540 BCE and the Kushites moved their capital southward to Meroë. The new capital was superbly located for trade with East Africa, with regions to the west across the Sudan, and with the Mediterranean world by way of the Nile River. Trade made Meroë wealthy, and the development of a smelting technology capable of exploiting local deposits of iron transformed the city into Africa's first industrial center.

As Meroë's economic base expanded, the dependence of Kushite civilization on Egyptian culture declined. By the second century CE, the Kushites had developed their own phonetic script to replace hieroglyphics. An architecture derived from that of Egypt gave way to an eclectic style that included Greek, Indian, and sub-Saharan African motifs, as well as Egyptian.

Axum

Because of its commerce and wealth, Kush attracted powerful enemies, including the Roman Empire. By 31 BCE the Roman Empire controlled all the lands bordering the Mediterranean Sea. A Roman army, for example, invaded Kush in 23 BCE. But it was actually the decline of Rome and its Mediterranean economy that were the chief factors in Kush's destruction. As the Roman Empire grew weaker and poorer, its trade with Kush declined, and Kush, too, grew weaker. During the early fourth century CE, Kush fell to the neighboring Noba people, who in turn fell to the nearby kingdom of Axum, whose warriors destroyed Meroë.

Located in what is today Ethiopia, Axum emerged as a nation during the first century BCE. Semitic people from the Arabian Peninsula, who were influenced by Hebrew culture, settled among a local black population. By the time it absorbed Kush during the fourth century CE, Axum had become the first Christian state in sub-Saharan Africa. By the eighth century, shifting trade patterns, environmental depletion, and Islamic invaders combined to reduce Axum's power. It nevertheless retained its unique culture and its independence.

 Reading Check Why are ancient African civilizations important?

This giant stele at Axum demonstrates the spread of Egyptian architecture into what is today Ethiopia.

▶ **Reading Check**

Egypt played a key role in the spread of civilization throughout the Mediterranean region. Egyptian religion, commerce, and art all influenced the development of Greece and subsequent Western civilizations.

▶ **Document**

1-1 *Herodotus on Carthaginian Trade and on the City of Meroë*
In these two passages, Herodotus reports (in about 430 BCE) on the trading practices along the Atlantic coast of Africa as gleaned from the Carthaginian traders who passed beyond the Strait of Gibraltar and describes what he knows of the country, known to him as the land of the Ethiopians.

KEY TERMS

► **Guide to Reading/Key Terms**

For answers, see the *Teacher's Resource Manual*.

► *Living Words* **Audio Clips**

Track 1   Ghana: Ewe-Atsiagbekor

► **Recommended Reading**

Robert W. July. *A History of the African People*, 5th ed. Prospect Heights, IL: Waveland, 1998. A comprehensive and current social history with good coverage of West Africa and West African women.

► **Teaching Notes**

The Soninke succeeded in dominating their neighbors and forging an empire through constant warfare and the possession of superior iron weapons. Ghana's boundaries reached into the Sahara desert to its north and modern Senegal to its south. But the empire's real power lay in commerce.

Section 2
West Africa

West African Civilizations

Like Africa as a whole, West Africa is physically, ethnically, and culturally diverse. Much of West Africa south of the Sahara Desert falls within the great savannah that spans the continent from east to west. West and south of the savannah, however, in Senegambia (modern Senegal and Gambia), stretching along the southwestern coast of West Africa, and in the lands located along the coast of the Gulf of Guinea, there are extensive forests. These two environments—savannah and forest—were home to a great variety of cultures and languages. Patterns of settlement in the region ranged from isolated homesteads and hamlets through villages and towns to cities.

West Africans began cultivating crops and tending domesticated animals between 1000 BCE and 200 CE. Those who lived on the savannah usually adopted settled village life well before those who lived in the forests. The early farmers produced millet, rice, and sorghum while tending herds of cattle and goats. By 500 BCE, beginning with the Nok people of the forest region, some West Africans were producing iron tools and weapons.

From early times, the peoples of West Africa traded among themselves and with the peoples who lived across the Sahara Desert in North Africa. This extensive trade became an essential part of the region's economy and formed the basis for the three great western Sudanese empires that successively dominated the region from before 800 CE to the beginnings of the modern era.

Ancient Ghana

The first known kingdom in the western Sudan was Ghana (see Map 1–3). Founded by the Soninke people in the area north of the modern republic of Ghana, its origins are unclear. Its name comes from the Soninke word for king.

Ghana's kings were known in Europe and southwest Asia as the richest of monarchs, and the source of their wealth was trade. The key to this trade was the Asian camel, which was introduced into Africa during the first century CE. With its ability to endure long journeys on small amounts of water, the camel dramatically increased trade across the Sahara between the western Sudan and the coastal regions of North Africa.

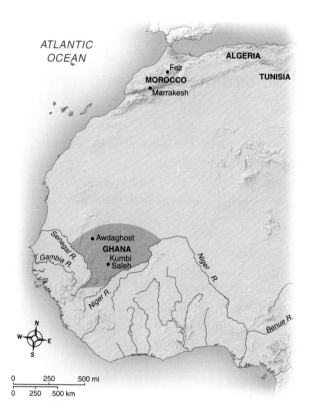

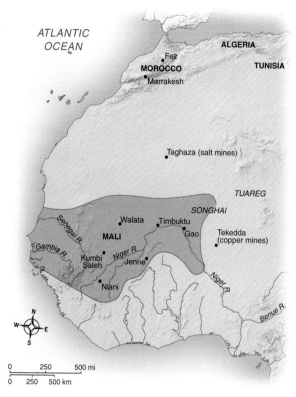

MAP 1–3 The Empires of Ghana and Mali

The western Sudanese empires of Ghana and Mali helped shape West African culture.

 What does this map suggest about the historical relationship between ancient Ghana and Mali?

Ghana traded in several commodities. From North Africa came silk, cotton, glass beads, horses, mirrors, dates, and, especially, salt, which was a scarce necessity in the torridly hot western Sudan. In return, Ghana exported pepper, slaves, and, especially, gold. The slaves were usually war captives, and the gold came from mines in the Wangara region to the southwest of Ghana. The Soninke did not mine the gold themselves, but the kings of Ghana grew rich by taxing it as it passed through their lands.

Before the fifth century CE, when the Roman Empire dominated the Mediterranean region, Roman merchants and **Berbers**—the indigenous people of western North Africa—were West Africa's chief partners in the trans-Sahara trade. After the fifth century, as Roman power declined and Islam spread across North Africa, Arabs replaced the Romans. Arab merchants settled in Saleh, the Muslim part of Kumbi Saleh, Ghana's capital. This was an impressive city, with stone houses and tombs, and as many as twenty thousand people. Visitors remarked the splendor of Kumbi Saleh's royal court. Some Soninke converted to Islam. Moslems dominated the royal bureaucracy and in the process introduced Arabic writing to the region.

A combination of commercial and religious rivalries finally destroyed Ghana during the twelfth century. The Almorvids, who were Islamic Berbers, had been Ghana's principal competitors for control of the trans-Sahara trade. In 992 Ghana's army captured Awdaghost, the Almorvid trade center northwest of Kumbi Saleh. Driven as much by

▶ Map 1-3

Mali had a larger territory that provided more trading advantages than Ghana.

▶ Documents

1-2 *A Tenth-Century Arab Description of the East African Coast*

This selection is from the famous Baghdadi scholar, al-Mas'udi, who died in Cairo about 956 CE. He describes the coastal region of East Africa from the Horn down to Mozambique, a region that he visited on a voyage from Oman.

1-3 *Ghana and Its People in the Mid-Eleventh Century*

This excerpt is from the geographical work of the Spanish Muslim geographer al-Bakri (d. 1094). He describes with great precision some customs of the ruler and the people of the capital of Ghana gleaned from other Arabic sources and travelers.

Al Bakri Describes Kumbi Saleh and Ghana's Royal Court

Nothing remains of the documents compiled by Ghana's Islamic bureaucracy. As a result, accounts of the civilization are all based on the testimony of Arab or Berber visitors. In this passage, written in the eleventh century, Arab geographer Al Bakri describes the great wealth and power of the king of Ghana.

The city of Ghana [Kumbi Saleh] consists of two towns lying in a plain. One of these towns is inhabited by Muslims. It is large and possesses twelve mosques. . . . There are imams and muezzins, and assistants as well as jurists and learned men. Around the town are wells of sweet water from which they drink and near which they grow vegetables. The town in which the king lives is six miles from the Muslim one, and bears the name Al Ghaba [the forest]. The land between the two towns is covered with houses. The houses of the inhabitants are of stone and acacia wood. The king has a palace and a number of dome-shaped dwellings, the whole surrounded by an enclosure like the defensive wall of a city. In the town where the king lives, and not far from the hall where he holds his court of justice, is a mosque where pray the Muslims who come on diplomatic missions. Around the king's town are domed buildings, woods, and copses where live the sorcerers of these people, the men in charge of the religious cult. . . .

Of the people who follow the king's religion, only he and his heir presumptive, who is the son of his sister, may wear sewn clothes. All the other people wear clothes of cotton, silk, or brocade, according to their means. All men shave their beards and women shave their heads. The king adorns himself like a woman, wearing necklaces and bracelets, and when he sits before the people he puts on a high cap decorated with gold and wrapped in a turban of fine cotton. The court of appeal [for grievances against officials] is held in a domed pavilion around which stand ten horses with gold embroidered trappings. Behind the king stand ten pages holding shields and swords decorated with gold, and on his right are the sons of the subordinate kings of his country, all wearing splendid garments and their hair mixed with gold. . . . When the people professing the same religion as the king approach him, they fall on their knees and sprinkle their heads with dust, for this is their way of showing him their respect. As for the Muslims, they greet him only by clapping their hands.

What Do You Think?

▶ What does this passage indicate about life in ancient Ghana?

▶ According to Al Bakri, in what ways do customs in Kumbi Saleh differ from customs in Arab lands?

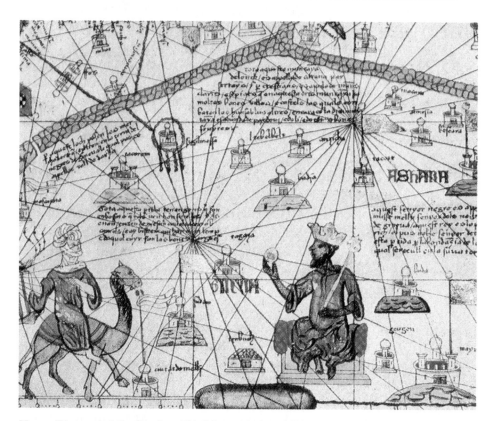

Mansa Musa ruled the Empire of Mali from 1312 to 1337.

religious fervor as by economic interest, the Almorvids retaliated in 1076 by conquering Ghana. The Soninke regained their independence in 1087, but a little over a century later fell to the Sosso, a previously tributary people, who destroyed Kumbi Saleh.

The Empire of Mali, 1230–1468

Following the defeat of Ghana by the Almorvids, many western Sudanese peoples competed for political and economic power. This contest ended in 1235 when the Mandinka, under their legendary leader Sundiata (c. 1210–1260), defeated the Sosso at the Battle of Kirina. Sundiata went on to forge the Empire of Mali.

Mali, which means "where the emperor resides," was socially, politically, and economically similar to Ghana. Stretching 1,500 miles from the Atlantic coast to the region east of the Niger River, Mali was centered farther south than Ghana, in a region of greater rainfall and more abundant crops. Sundiata gained direct control of the gold mines of

▶ **What Do You Think**

· Religious tensions between the King's religion, Islam, and the indigenous religion of the Soninke, were a part of everyday life in ancient Ghana.

· All men shave their beards and women shave their heads. Also, the Ghana King wears ornate clothing and jewelry.

▶ Map 1-4

Being on the Atlantic Ocean made them susceptible to slave trading.

Wangara, making his empire wealthier than Ghana had been. As a result, Mali's population grew, reaching a total of eight million.

Sundiata was also an important figure in western Sudanese religion. According to legend, he wielded magical powers to defeat his enemies. But Sundiata was a Muslim and helped make Mali—at least superficially—a Muslim state. West Africans had been converting to Islam since Arab traders began arriving in the region centuries before. By Sundiata's time, most merchants and bureaucrats were Muslims, and the empire's rulers gained stature among Arab states by converting to Islam.

To administer their vast empire at a time when communication was slow, Mali's rulers relied heavily on personal and family ties with local chiefs. Mali's most important city was Timbuktu, which had been established during the eleventh century beside the Niger River near the southern edge of the Sahara Desert.

By the thirteenth century, Timbuktu was a major hub for trade in gold, slaves, and salt. It attracted merchants from throughout the Mediterranean world and became a center of Islamic learning. There were several mosques in the city, 150 Islamic schools, a law school, and many book dealers. It supported a cosmopolitan community and impressed visitors with its absence of religious and ethnic intolerance. Even though Mali enslaved war captives and traded slaves, an Arab traveler noted in 1352–1353, "the Negroes possess some admirable qualities. They are seldom unjust, and have a greater abhorrence of injustice than any other people."

The Mali Empire reached its peak during the reign of Mansa Musa (1312–1337). One of the wealthiest rulers the world has known, Musa made himself and Mali famous when in 1324 he undertook a pilgrimage across Africa to the Islamic holy city of Mecca in Arabia. With an entourage of sixty thousand, a train of one hundred elephants, and a propensity for distributing huge amounts of gold to those who greeted him along the way, Musa amazed the Islamic world. After Musa's death, however, Mali declined. In 1468, one of the most powerful of its formerly subject peoples, the Songhai, captured Timbuktu. Their leader, Sunni Ali, founded a new West African empire.

The Empire of Songhai, 1464–1591

The Songhai were great traders and warriors. They had seceded from Mali in 1375. Under Sunni Ali, who reigned from 1464 to 1492, they built the last and largest of the western Sudanese empires (see Map 1–4). Sunni Ali required conquered peoples to pay tribute, but otherwise let them run their own affairs.

When Sunni Ali died by drowning, Askia Muhammad Toure led a successful revolt against Ali's son to make himself king of Songhai. The new king, who reigned from 1492 to 1528, extended the empire northward

MAP 1–4 West and Central Africa, c. 1500

This map shows the Empire of Songhai (1464–1591), the Kongo kingdom (c. 1400–1700), and the major kingdoms of the West African forest region.

 How did the Western Sudanese empires' geographical location make them susceptible to slave trading?

into the Sahara, westward into Mali, and eastward to encompass the trading cities of Hausaland. He centralized the administration of the empire, replacing local chiefs with members of his family, substituting taxation for tribute, and establishing a bureaucracy to regulate trade.

A devout Muslim, Muhammad Toure used his power to spread the influence of Islam within the empire. During a pilgrimage to Mecca in 1497 he established diplomatic relations with Morocco and Egypt and recruited Moslem scholars to serve at the Sankore Mosque at Timbuktu. Despite these efforts, by the end of Muhammad Toure's reign (the aging ruler, senile and blind, was deposed by family members), Islamic culture was still weak in West Africa outside urban areas. Peasants, who made up 95 percent of the population, spoke a variety of languages, continued to practice indigenous religions, and remained loyal to their local chiefs.

Songhai reached its peak of influence under Askia Daud between 1549 and 1582. But the political balance of power in West Africa was changing rapidly, and Songhai failed to adapt. Since the 1430s, adventurers from Portugal had been establishing trading centers along the Guinea coast seeking gold and diverting it from the trans-Sahara trade. Their success threatened the Arab rulers of North Africa, Songhai's traditional partners in the trans-Sahara trade. In 1591 the king of Morocco, hoping to regain access to West African gold, sent an army of mercenaries armed with muskets and cannons across the Sahara to attack Gao, Songhai's capital. The Songhai forces were armed only with bows and lances, which were no match for firearms. Its army destroyed, the Songhai empire fell apart. West Africa was without a government powerful enough to intervene when the Portuguese, other Europeans, and the African kingdoms of the Guinea Coast became more interested in trading for human beings than for gold.

The West African Forest Region

The area called the **forest region** of West Africa, which includes stretches of savannah, extends two thousand miles along the Atlantic coast from Senegambia in the northwest to the former kingdom of Benin (modern Cameroon) in the east. Among the early settlers of the forest region were the Nok, who around 500 BCE, in what is today southern Nigeria, created a culture noted for its iron working technology and its terracotta sculptures. But significant migration into the forests began only after 1000 CE, as the western Sudanese climate became increasingly dry.

The peoples of the forest region are of particular importance for African-American history because of the role they played in the Atlantic slave trade as both slave traders and as victims of the trade.

Because people migrated southward from the Sudan in small groups over an extended period, the process brought about considerable cultural diversification. A variety of languages, economies, political systems, and traditions came into existence. Some ancient customs survived, such as dividing types of agricultural labor by gender and living in villages composed of

▶ **Documents**

1-4 *Muslim Reform in Songhai*
Around 1500 Askia Muhammad al-Turi, the first Muslim among the rulers of Songhai, wrote to the North African Muslim theologian Muhammad al-Maghili (d. 1504) with a series of questions about proper Muslim practices.

1-5 *Job Hortop and the British Enter the Slave Trade, 1567*
In 1567, a British admiral seized 500 Africans in Sierre Leone and set off across the ocean, but the Spanish fleet captured him in a Mexican port and destroyed many of his ships. Although he escaped, 100 of his men were left in the Bay of Mexico; only three eventually returned to England. One of those was 17-year-old Job Hortop, who wrote this narrative after 23 years in Spanish captivity.

The Nok people of what is today Nigeria produced terra-cotta sculptures like this one during the first millennium BCE.

The great mosque at the West African city of Jenne was first built during the fourteenth century CE.

This life-size bust of a Yoruba king — perhaps Obalufon II—is one of fifteen found in the city of Ife.

extended families. The forest region became a patchwork of diverse ethnic groups with related, but sometimes quite different, ways of life.

Colonizing a region covered with thick vegetation was hard work. In some portions of the forest, agriculture did not supplant hunting and gathering until the fifteenth and sixteenth centuries. In more open parts of the region, however, several small kingdoms emerged centuries earlier. Benin City, for example, dates to the thirteenth century and life in Nigeria to the eleventh. Although none of these kingdoms ever grew as large as the empires of the western Sudan, some were powerful. They were ruled by kings who claimed semi divine status. Their power was limited by local nobility and urban elites. Kings sought to extend their power by conquering neighboring peoples. Secrecy and elaborate ritual marked royal courts, which were also centers of support for art and religion.

Senegambia and the Akan States

The inhabitants of Senegambia shared a common history and spoke closely related languages, but they were not politically united. Parts of the region had been incorporated within the empires of Ghana and Mali and had been exposed to Islamic influences. Senegambian society was strictly hierarchical, with royalty at the top and slaves at the bottom. Most people were farmers, growing rice, millet, sorghum, plantains, beans, and bananas. They supplemented their diet with fish, oysters, rabbits, and monkeys.

To the southeast of Senegambia were the Akan states. They emerged during the sixteenth century as the gold trade provided local rulers with the wealth they needed to clear forests and initiate agricultural economies. To accomplish this, the rulers traded gold from mines under their control for slaves, who did the difficult work of cutting trees and burning refuse. Then settlers received open fields from the rulers in return for a portion of their produce and services. When Europeans arrived, they traded guns for gold. The guns in turn allowed the Akan states to expand, and during the late seventeenth century, one of them, the Ashante, created a well-organized and densely populated kingdom, comparable in size to the modern country of Ghana. By the eighteenth century, this kingdom not only dominated the central portion of the forest region, but also used its army extensively to capture slaves for sale to European traders.

To the east of the Akan states (in modern Benin and western Nigeria) lived the people of the Yoruba culture, who gained ascendancy in the area as early as 1000 CE by trading kola nuts and cloth to the peoples of the western Sudan. The artisans of the Yoruba city of Ife gained renown for their fine bronze, brass, and terra-cotta sculptures. Ife was also notable for the prominent role of women in conducting its profitable commerce. During the seventeenth century, the Oyo people, employing a well-trained cavalry, imposed political unity on part of the Yoruba region. They, like the Ashante, became extensively involved in the Atlantic slave trade.

Located to the west of the Oyo were the Fon people, who formed the Kingdom of Dahomey, which rivaled Oyo as a center for the slave trade. The king of Dahomey was an absolute monarch who took thousands of wives for himself from leading Fon families as a way to assure the loyalty of potential rivals.

The Kingdom of Benin

At the eastern end of the forest region was the Kingdom of Benin, which controlled an extensive area in what is today southern Nigeria. The people of this kingdom shared a common heritage with the Yoruba, who played a role in its formation during the thirteenth century. Throughout its history, Benin's politics were marked by a struggle for power between the Oba (king), who claimed divine status, and the kingdom's hereditary nobility.

During the fifteenth century, after a reform of its army, Benin began to expand to the Niger River in the east, to the Gulf of Guinea to the south, and into Yoruba country to the west. The kingdom reached its apogee during the late sixteenth century. European visitors at that time remarked on the size and sophistication of its capital, Benin City, which was a center for the production of the fine bronze sculptures for which the region is still known. The wealthy people of the city dined on beef, mutton, chicken, and yams. Its streets, unlike those of European cities of the time, were free of beggars.

Benin remained little influenced by Islam or Christianity, but like other coastal kingdoms, it became increasingly involved in the Atlantic slave trade. Beginning in the late fifteenth century, the Oba of Benin allowed Europeans to enter the country to trade for gold, pepper, ivory, and slaves. Initially, the Oba forbade the sale of his own subjects, but his large army—the first in the forest region to be provided with European firearms—captured others for the trade as it conquered neighboring regions. By the seventeenth century, Benin's prosperity depended on

This carved wooden ceremonial offering bowl is typical of a Yoruba art form that has persisted for centuries.

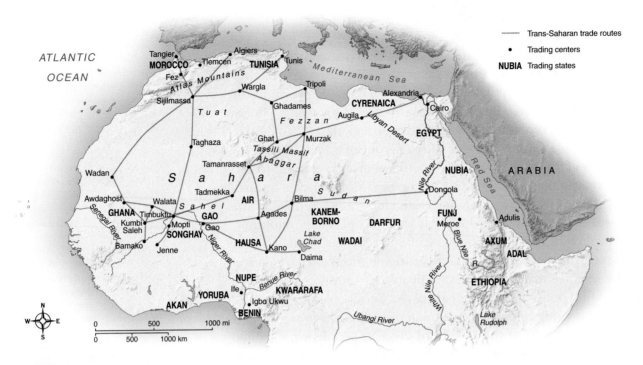

——	Trans-Saharan trade routes
●	Trading centers
NUBIA	Trading states

MAP 1–5 Trans-Saharan Trade Routes

Ancient trade routes connected sub-Saharan West Africa to the Mediterranean coast.

 What was the significance of the trans-Sahara trade in West African history?

▶ Reading Check

West Africans, particularly the peoples of the forest region, played an important role in the Atlantic slave trade, both as slave traders and as victims of the trade. Thus, the region's history and culture are closely tied to the forced migration of Africans to North America and to the culture African Americans developed in their new environment.

▶ Retracing the Odyssey

African Gallery, University of Pennsylvania Museum of Archaeology and Anthropology, Philadelphia. The gallery includes a collection of Benin bronzes.

▶ Map 1-5

Trans-Sahara trade became an essential part of the region's economy and formed the basis for the three great western Sudanese empires that dominated the region.

the slave trade. As the kingdom declined during the eighteenth century, it began to sell some of its own people to European slave traders.

To Benin's east was Igboland, a densely populated but politically weak region stretching along the Niger River. The Igbo people lived in one of the stateless societies common in West Africa. In these societies, families rather than central authorities governed. Village elders provided local government and life centered on family homesteads. Igboland had for many years exported field workers and skilled artisans to Benin and other kingdoms. When Europeans arrived, they expanded this trade, which brought many Igbos to the Americas (see Map 1–5).

 Reading Check   Why is West Africa significant for African-American history?

Kongo and Angola

Although the forebears of most African Americans came from West Africa, many also came from Central Africa, in particular the region around the Congo River and its tributaries and the region to the south that the Portuguese called Angola. The people of these regions had much in common with those of the Guinea Coast. They divided labor by gender, lived in villages composed of extended families, and accorded semidivine status to their kings. Like the people of West Africa, they were ensnared in the Atlantic slave trade as it grew to immense proportions after 1500.

During the fourteenth and fifteenth centuries, much of the Congo River system, with its fertile valleys and abundant fish, came under the control of the Kingdom of Kongo. The wealth of this kingdom also derived from its access to salt and iron and its extensive trade with the interior of the continent. Nzinga Knuwu, who was *Mani Kongo* (the Kongolese term for king) when Portuguese expeditions arrived in the region in the late fifteenth century, surpassed other African rulers in welcoming the intruders. His son Nzinga Mbemba tried to convert the kingdom to Christianity and remodel it along European lines. The resulting unrest, combined with Portuguese greed and the effects of the slave trade, undermined royal authority and ultimately led to the breakup of the kingdom and the social disruption of the entire Kongo-Angola region.

▶ **Retracing the Odyssey**

National Museum of African Art, Smithsonian Institution, Washington, D.C. The museum exhibits visual art from African regions south of the Sahara Desert. It includes art from ancient Benin and ancient Kerma in Nubia. There is also an exhibit of African musical instruments.

PROFILE ❖ Nzinga Mbemba of Kongo

Nzinga Mbemba, baptized Dom Affonso, ruled as the Mani Kongo from about 1506 to 1543 CE. Mbemba was a son of Nzinga Knuwu, who, as Mani Kongo, established diplomatic ties with Portugal. Amid considerable ceremony, Knuwu converted to Christianity because conversion gave him access to Portuguese musketeers he needed to put down a rebellion.

By 1495, Knuwu's inability to accept Christian monogamy led him to renounce his baptism and to banish Christians—both Portuguese and Kongolese—from Mbanza Kongo. Mbemba, who was a sincere Christian, became their champion in opposition to a traditionalist faction headed by his half brother Mpanza. Following Knuwu's death in 1506, the two princes fought over the succession. The victory of Mbemba's forces led to his coronation as Affonso and the execution of Mpanza.

By then Mbemba had gained at least outward respect from the Portuguese monarchy as a ruler and devout Christian missionary. In 1516 a Portuguese priest described Mbemba as "not . . . a man but an angel sent by the Lord to this kingdom to convert it." Mbemba destroyed fetishes and shrines associated with Kongo's traditional religion. He replaced them with crucifixes and images of saints and built several Christian churches.

Mbemba hoped also to modernize his nation on a European model. He dressed in Portuguese clothing, sent young men to Portugal to be educated, and began schools to educate the children of Kongo's nobility. His son Dom Henrique, who became a Christian bishop, briefly represented Kongo at the Vatican.

Mbemba put too much faith in his Portuguese patrons and too little in the traditions of his people. By 1508, Portuguese priests were trading in slaves and living with Kongolese mistresses. He was supposed to have a monopoly over the slave trade, and increasingly his own people were subjected to that trade.

Mbemba's complaints led to a formal agreement in 1512 called the *Regimento*, which actually worsened matters. It placed restrictions on the priests and pledged continued Portuguese military assistance. But it also recognized the right of Portuguese merchants to trade for copper, ivory, and slaves and exempted Portuguese from punishment under local law. Soon the trade and related corruption increased, and so did unrest among Mbemba's increasingly unhappy subjects. In 1526, Mbemba begged the Portuguese king that "in these kingdoms there should not be any trade in slaves or market for slaves."

In 1568—a quarter-century after his death—Kongo became a client state of Portugal, and the slave trade expanded.

23

▶▶ **Guide to Reading/Key Terms**

For answers, see the *Teacher's Resource Manual*.

▶▶ **Recommended Reading**

Roland Oliver. *The African Experience: Major Themes in African History from Earliest Times to the Present.* New York: HarperCollins, 1991. Short, innovative, and insightful analysis of cultural relationships.

Section 3

West African Society and Culture

West Africa's great ethnic and cultural diversity makes it hazardous to generalize about the social and cultural background of the first African Americans. But historians have pieced together a broad understanding of the way the people of West Africa lived at the beginning of the Atlantic slave trade.

Families and Villages

By the early sixteenth century, most West Africans were farmers. They usually lived in hamlets or villages composed of extended families and clans called **lineages**. Depending on the ethnic group involved, extended families and lineages were either **patrilineal** or **matrilineal**. In patrilineal societies, social rank and property passed in the male line from fathers to sons. In matrilineal societies, rank and property, although controlled by men, passed from generation to generation in the female line. A village chief in a matrilineal society was succeeded by his sister's son, not his own. But many West Africans lived in stateless societies with no government other than that provided by extended families and lineages.

In extended families, nuclear families (husband, wife, and children) or in some cases polygynous families (husband, wives, and children) acted as economic units. Both kinds of family units existed in the context of the broader family community composed of grandparents, aunts, uncles, and cousins. Elders in the extended family had great power over the economic and social lives of its members. In contrast with ancient Egypt, strictly enforced incest taboos prohibited people from marrying within their extended family.

Village Life

Villages tended to be larger on the savannah than in the forest. In both regions, people used forced earth or mud to construct small houses, which were round or rectangular in shape, depending on local tradition. The houses usually had thatched roofs, or, sometimes in the forest, they had palm roofs. In both savannah and forest, mud or mud-brick walls up to 10 feet high surrounded villages. A nuclear or polygynous family unit might have several houses. In nuclear households, the husband occupied the larger house and his wife the smaller. In **polygynous** households, the husband had the largest house, and his wives lived in smaller ones.

Villagers' few possessions included cots, rugs, stools, and wooden storage chests. Their tools and weapons included bows, spears, iron axes, hoes, and scythes. Households used grinding stones, woven baskets, and a variety of ceramic vessels to prepare and store food. Villagers in both the savannah and forest regions produced cotton for clothing, but their food crops were quite distinct. West Africans in the savannah cultivated millet, rice, and sorghum as their dietary staples; kept goats and cattle for milk and cheese; and supplemented their diets with peas, okra, watermelons, and a variety of nuts. Yams, rather than grains, were the dietary staple in the forest region. Other important forest region crops included bananas and coco yams, both ultimately derived from far-off Indonesia.

Farming in West Africa was not easy. Drought was common on the savannah. In the forest, where diseases carried by the tsetse fly sickened draft animals, agricultural plots were limited in size, because they had to be cleared by hand. The fields surrounding forest villages averaged just two or three acres per family.

Although there was private ownership of land in West Africa, people generally worked land communally, dividing tasks by gender. Among the Akan of the Guinea coast, for example, men were responsible for clearing the land of trees and underbrush while women tended the fields (planting, weeding, harvesting, and carrying in the harvested produce). Women also took care of children, prepared meals, and manufactured household pottery.

Women

In general, men dominated women in West Africa. As previously noted, it was common for men to take two or more wives, and, to a degree, custom held women to be the property of men. But West African women also enjoyed a relative amount of freedom that impressed Arab and European visitors. In ancient Ghana, women sometimes served as government officials. Later, in the forest region, women sometimes inherited property and owned land—or at least controlled its income. Women—including enslaved women—in the royal court of Dahomey held high government posts. Ashante noblewomen could own property, although they themselves could be considered inheritable property. The Ashante queen held her own court to administer women's affairs.

Women retained far more freedom in West Africa than was the case in Europe or southwest Asia. Ibn Battuta, a Muslim Berber from North Africa who visited Mali during the fourteenth century, was shocked to discover that in this Islamic country "women show no bashfulness before men and do not veil themselves, though they are assiduous in attending prayer." Battuta was even more dumbfounded to learn that in West

▶ **Retracing the Odyssey**

Chattanooga African American Museum, Chattanooga, TN. The museum includes an exhibit dealing with African culture and history.

Africa women could have male friends and companions other than their husbands or relatives.

Throughout the region secret societies instilled in men and women ethical standards of personal behavior. The most important secret societies were the women's *Sande* and the men's *Poro*. They initiated boys and girls into adulthood. They also established standards for personal conduct, especially in regard to issues of gender, by emphasizing female virtue and male honor. Other secret societies influenced politics, trade, medical practice, recreation, and social gatherings.

Class and Slavery

Although many West Africans lived in stateless societies, most lived in hierarchically organized states headed by monarchs who claimed divine or semidivine status. These monarchs were far from absolute in the power they wielded, but they commanded armies, taxed commerce, and accumulated considerable wealth. Beneath the royalty were classes of landed nobles, warriors, peasants, and bureaucrats. Lower classes included blacksmiths, butchers, weavers, woodcarvers, tanners, and the oral historians called *griots*.

Slavery had been part of this hierarchical social structure since ancient times. Although it was very common throughout West Africa, slavery was less so in the forest region than on the savannah. It took a wide variety of forms and was not necessarily a permanent condition. Like people in other parts of the world, West Africans held war captives—including men, women, and children—to be without rights and suitable for enslavement. In Islamic regions, masters had obligations to their slaves similar to those of a guardian for a ward and were responsible for their slaves' religious well-being. In non-Islamic regions, the children of slaves acquired legal protections, such as the right not to be sold away from the land they occupied.

Slaves who served either in the royal courts of West African kingdoms or in the kingdoms' armies often exercised power over free people and could acquire property. Also, the slaves of peasant farmers often had standards of living similar to those of their masters. Slaves who worked under overseers in gangs on large estates were far less fortunate. However, even for such enslaved agricultural workers, the work and privileges accorded to the second and third generations became little different from those of free people. Regardless of their generation, slaves retained a low social status, but in many respects slavery in West African societies functioned as a means of assimilation.

Religion

There were two religious traditions in fifteenth-century West Africa: Islamic and **indigenous**. Islam, which was introduced into West Africa by Arab traders and took root first in the Sudanese empires, was most prevalent in the more cosmopolitan savannah. Even there it was stronger in

▶ Recommended Readings

John Thornton. *Africa and Africans in the Making of the Atlantic World, 1400–1689.* New York: Cambridge University Press, 1992. A thorough consideration of West African culture and its impact in the Americas.

John S. Mbiti. *An Introduction to African Religion.* London: Heinemann, 1975.

cities than in rural areas. Islam was the religion of merchants and bureaucrats. It fostered literacy in Arabic, the spread of Islamic learning, and the construction of mosques in the cities of West Africa.

West Africa's indigenous religions remained strongest in the forest region. They were polytheistic and animistic, recognizing a great number of divinities and spirits. Beneath an all-powerful, but remote, creator god were lesser gods who represented the forces of nature. Other gods were associated with particular mountains, rivers, trees, and rocks. Indigenous West African religion saw the force of God in all things.

Practitioners of West African indigenous religions believed the spirits of their direct and remote ancestors could influence their lives. Therefore, ceremonies designed to sustain ancestral spirits and their power over the earth were a central part of traditional West African religions. These rituals were part of everyday life, making organized churches and professional clergy rare. Instead, family members assumed religious duties and encouraged their relatives to participate actively in ceremonies that involved music, dancing, and animal sacrifices in honor of deceased ancestors. Funerals were especially important because they symbolized the linkage between living and dead.

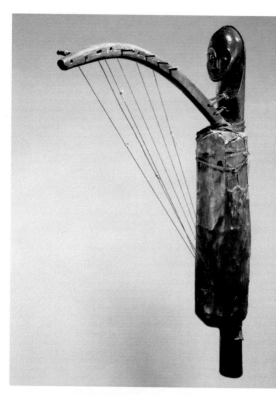

This six-string wooden harp is a rare example of the type of instrument West African musicians and storytellers used to accompany themselves.

Art and Music

West African art was intimately related to religious practice. West Africans, seeking to preserve the images of their ancestors, excelled in woodcarving and sculpture in terra-cotta, bronze, and brass. Throughout the region, artists produced wooden masks representing in highly stylized manners ancestral spirits as well as various divinities. Wooden and terra-cotta figurines, sometimes referred to as "fetishes," were also extremely common. West Africans used them in funerals, in rituals related to ancestral spirits, in medical practice, and in coming-of-age ceremonies.

West African music also served religion. Folk musicians employed such instruments as drums, xylophones, bells, flutes, and mbanzas (predecessor to the banjo) to produce a highly rhythmic accompaniment to the dancing that was an important part of religious rituals. A call-and-response style of singing also played a vital role in ritual. Vocal music style was characterized by polyphonic textures and sophisticated rhythms.

Literature: Oral Histories, Poetry, and Tales

West African literature was part of an oral tradition that passed from generation to generation. At its most formal, this was a literature developed by specially trained poets and musicians who served kings and nobles. But West African literature was also a folk art that expressed the views of the common people.

At a king's court there could be several poet-musicians who had high status and specialized in poems glorifying rulers and their ancestors by link-

▶▶ **Recommended Readings**

Werner Gillon. *A Short History of African Art.* New York: Viking, 1984.

J. H. Kwabena Nketia. *The Music of Africa.* New York: Norton, 1974.

Centuries-old rituals and traditions continue today in African life.

▶ **Reading Check**

West African social norms were recreated in the Americas. The emphasis on the importance of extended families is a good example of this phenomenon. Moreover, elements of West African culture survived to shape the unique culture of African Americans.

▶ **Recommended Readings**

Oyekan Owomoyela. *Yoruba Trickster Tales.* Lincoln, NE: University of Nebraska Press, 1977.

Ruth Finnegan. *Oral Literature in Africa.* 1970; reprint, Nairobi: Oxford University Press, 1976.

▶ **Teaching Notes**

In recent years, paleoanthropologists, archaeologists, and historians have revealed much about Africa's history and prehistory, but much remains to be learned concerning the past of this vast and diverse continent. The evolution of humans, the role of ancient Egypt in world history, and Egypt's relationship to Nubia and Kush are all topics that continue to attract wide interest.

Yet the history of African Americans begins in West Africa, the region from which the ancestors of most of them were unwillingly wrested. Historians have discovered, as subsequent chapters will show, that West Africans taken to America and their descendants in America were able to preserve much more of their ancestral way of life than scholars once believed possible. West African family organization, work habits, language structures and some words, religious beliefs, legends and stories, pottery styles, art, and music all made it to America. These African legacies, although often attenuated, influenced the way African Americans and other Americans lived in their new land and continue to shape American life.

ing fact and fiction. Recitations of these poems were often accompanied by drums and horns. Court poets also used their trained memories to recall historical events and precise genealogies. The self-employed poets, called **griots**, who traveled from place to place were socially inferior to court poets, but they functioned in a similar manner. Both court poets and griots were men. It was in the genre of folk literature that women excelled. They joined men in the creation and performance of work songs and led in creating and singing dirges, lullabies, and satirical verses. Often these forms of literature used a call-and-response style similar to that of religious songs.

Just as significant for African-American history were the West African prose tales. Like similar stories told in other parts of Africa, these tales took two forms: those with human characters and those with animal characters who represented humans. The tales involving human characters dealt with such subjects as creation, the origins of death, paths to worldly success, and romantic love. Such tales often involved magic objects and potions.

The animal tales aimed both to entertain and to teach lessons. They focused on small creatures, often referred to as "trickster characters," which are pitted against larger beasts. Among the heroes were the hare, the spider, and the mouse. Plots centered on the ability of these weak animals to outsmart larger and meaner antagonists, such as the snake, leopard, and hyena. In all instances, the animal characters had human emotions and goals.

In West Africa, these tales represented the ability of common people to counteract the power of kings and nobles. When the tales reached America, they became allegories for the struggle between enslaved African Americans and their powerful white masters.

 **Reading Check**   How did the legacies of West African society and culture influence the way African Americans lived?

Analyzing Timelines

A timeline is a visual representation of events shown in the order in which they happened. Timelines can help you understand historical events and their relationships to each other.

By the early 1600s, Europe's major powers were scrambling to establish colonies in North America and fighting to secure their claims against rivals—both European and Native American. The two timelines below set out in chronological order a number of events relating to this struggle. The upper timeline is a standard timeline: it covers major events within a broad time frame. The lower timeline is similar to the inset on a map and works something like a microscope. It magnifies a short time segment from the standard timeline and reveals more details of a series of related events.

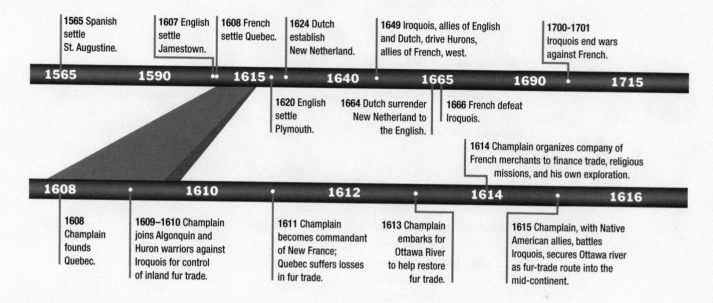

1565 Spanish settle St. Augustine.

1607 English settle Jamestown.

1608 French settle Quebec.

1624 Dutch establish New Netherland.

1649 Iroquois, allies of English and Dutch, drive Hurons, allies of French, west.

1700-1701 Iroquois end wars against French.

1565 | 1590 | 1615 | 1640 | 1665 | 1690 | 1715

1620 English settle Plymouth.

1664 Dutch surrender New Netherland to the English.

1666 French defeat Iroquois.

1614 Champlain organizes company of French merchants to finance trade, religious missions, and his own exploration.

1608 | 1610 | 1612 | 1614 | 1616

1608 Champlain founds Quebec.

1609–1610 Champlain joins Algonquin and Huron warriors against Iroquois for control of inland fur trade.

1611 Champlain becomes commandant of New France; Quebec suffers losses in fur trade.

1613 Champlain embarks for Ottawa River to help restore fur trade.

1615 Champlain, with Native American allies, battles Iroquois, secures Ottawa river as fur-trade route into the mid-continent.

LEARN THE SKILL

Use the following steps to analyze timelines:

1. **Identify the time period covered by each timeline.** Study the timelines to discover the span of history each covers.

2. **Determine how each timeline has been divided.** Timelines are divided into equal periods of time, such as 10-year, 25-year, or 100-year intervals.

3. **Study the timelines to see how events in one are related to events in the other.** Note which time span is magnified by the lower timeline. Explore the possible relationship between events on the two timelines.

PRACTICE THE SKILL

Answer the following questions:

1. **(a)** What are the earliest and the latest dates shown on the upper timeline? **(b)** How many years does it cover? **(c)** What are the earliest and the latest dates on the lower timeline? **(d)** How many years does it cover?

2. **(a)** Into what intervals is the upper timeline divided? **(b)** Into what intervals is the lower timeline divided?

3. **(a)** What general topic does the lower timeline examine in detail? **(b)** When and why did hostilities between the French and the Iroquois begin? Which timeline shows this? **(c)** How does the lower timeline help explain the 1649 entry on the standard timeline? **(d)** How long did hostilities between the French and the Iroquois last?

▶ **Skills for Life**

For answers, see *Teacher's Resource Manual*.

Chapter Timeline

EVENTS IN AFRICA

WORLD EVENTS

10 million years ago

5–10 million years ago

Separation of hominids from apes

4 million years ago

Emergence of *australopithecines*

2.4 million years ago

Emergence of *Homo habilis*

1.7 million years ago

Emergence of *Homo erectus*

1.6 million years ago

Homo erectus beginning to spread through Eurasia

1.5 million years ago

100,000–200,000 years ago

Appearance of modern humans

6000 BCE

Beginning of Sahara Desert formation

8000 BCE

Appearance of the first agricultural settlements in southwest Asia

5000 BCE

5000 BCE

First agricultural settlements in Egypt

3800 BCE

Predynastic period in Egypt

c. 3150 BCE

Unification of Egypt

3500 BCE

Sumerian civilization in Mesopotamia

2500 BCE

2700–2150 BCE

Egypt's Old Kingdom

2100–1650 BCE

Egypt's Middle Kingdom

2300 BCE

Beginning of Indus Valley civilization

1500 BCE

1550–700 BCE

Egypt's New Kingdom

1600–1250 BCE

Mycenaean Greek civilization

c. 1500

Beginning of Shang dynasty in China

1000 BCE

750–670 BCE
Rule of Kushites over Egypt

600–336 BCE
Classical Greek civilization

540 BCE
Founding of Meroë

c. 500 BCE
Beginning of iron smelting in West Africa

50 CE
Destruction of Kush

500 CE

632–750 CE
Islamic conquest of North Africa

204 BCE–476 CE
Domination of Mediterranean by Roman Republic and Empire

c. 750–1076 CE
Empire of Ghana; Islam begins to take root in West Africa

500–1350 CE
European Middle Ages

c. 570 CE
Birth of Muhammad

1200 CE

1230–1468 CE
Empire of Mali

c. 1300 CE
Rise of Yoruba states

1400 CE

1434 CE
Start of Portuguese exploration and establishment of trading outposts on West African coast

1492 CE
Christopher Columbus and European encounter of America

c. 1450 CE
Centralization of power in Benin

1517
Reformation begins in Europe

1464–1591 CE
Empire of Songhai

1600 CE

c.1650 CE
Rise of Kingdom of Dahomey and the Akan states

1610
Scientific Revolution begins in Europe

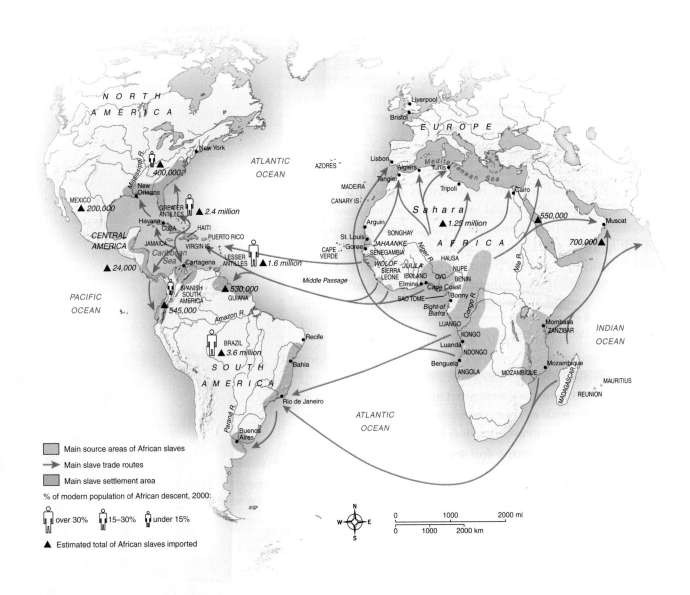

Main source areas of African slaves

→ Main slave trade routes

Main slave settlement area

% of modern population of African descent, 2000:

over 30%   15–30%   under 15%

▲ Estimated total of African slaves imported

MAP 2–1 The Atlantic and Islamic Slave Trades

The Atlantic slave trade reached the proportions of the Islamic slave trade in 1600.

 According to this map, which region in the Americas imported the most slaves?

Explore this map online at www.prenhall.com/aah/map.2.1

countrymen that I was first kidnapped and betrayed by [those of] my own complexion."

Until the early sixteenth century, Portuguese seafarers conducted the Atlantic slave trade on a tiny scale to satisfy a limited market for domestic servants on the Iberian Peninsula (Portugal and Spain). Other European countries had no demand for slaves because their own workforces were already too large. But the impact of Columbus's voyages drastically changed the trade. The Spanish and the Portuguese—followed by the Dutch, English, and French—established colonies in the Caribbean, Mexico, and Central and South America. As the numbers of American Indians in these regions rapidly declined, Europeans relied on the Atlantic slave trade to replace them as a source of slave labor (see Map 2–1). As early as 1502, African slaves lived on the island of Hispaniola—modern Haiti and the Dominican

Republic (see Map 2–2). During the sixteenth century, gold and silver mines in Spanish Mexico and Peru and especially sugar plantations in Portuguese Brazil produced an enormous demand for labor. The Atlantic slave trade grew to huge and tragic proportions to meet that demand (see Table 2–1).

 Reading Check How did the slave trade in Africa differ from the Atlantic slave trade?

Growth of the Atlantic Slave Trade

Because Europe provided an insatiable market for sugar, cultivation of this crop in the Americas became extremely profitable. Sugar plantations employing slave labor spread from Brazil to the Caribbean islands (West Indies). Later the cultivation of tobacco, rice, and indigo in British North America added to the demand for African slaves, although far more Africans went to Brazil than ever reached North America. By 1510 Spain had joined Portugal in the enlarged Atlantic slave trade, and a new, harsher form of slavery had become established in the Americas. Unlike slavery in Africa, Asia, and Europe, slavery in the Americas was based on race; most of the enslaved were males, and they were generally employed as agricultural laborers rather than soldiers or domestic servants. The enslaved also became **chattel**—meaning personal property—of their masters and lost their customary rights as human beings. Men and boys predominated in part because

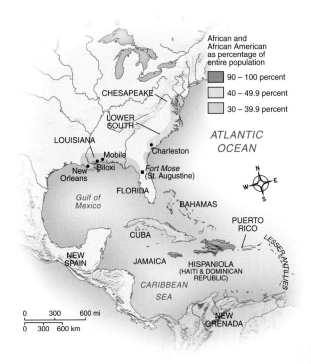

MAP 2–2 Slave Colonies of the Seventeenth and Eighteenth Centuries
This map indicates regions in North America, the West Indies, and South America that had significant populations of enslaved people of African descent.

 What European powers controlled the regions of North America and the Caribbean islands shown in this map?

TABLE 2–1 Estimated Slave Imports by Destination, 1451–1870

Destination	Total Slave Imports
British North America	500,000
Spanish America	2,500,000
British Caribbean	2,000,000
French Caribbean	1,600,000
Dutch Caribbean	500,000
Danish Caribbean	28,000
Brazil	4,000,000
Old World	200,000

Source: Hugh Thomas, *The Slave Trade: The Story of the Atlantic Slave Trade, 1440–1870* (New York: Simon & Schuster, 1997), 804.

➤➤ **Map 2-1**
South America (Brazil)

➤➤ **Map 2-2**
England, Portugal, Spain, France, The Netherlands

➤➤ **Reading Check**
Race was not a major factor in the African slave trade. The trade dealt mainly with women and children, destined to live as concubines and domestic servants. The men enslaved in this trade were most often used as soldiers.

Europeans believed they were stronger laborers than women and girls. Another factor was that West Africans preferred to have women do agricultural work and therefore tended to withhold them from the Atlantic trade.

Portugal and Spain

Portugal and Spain dominated the Atlantic slave trade during the sixteenth century. They shipped about two thousand Africans per year to their American colonies, with by far the most going to Brazil. From the beginning of the trade until its nineteenth-century abolition, approximately 6,500,000 of the approximately 11,328,000 Africans taken to the Americas went to Portugal's and Spain's colonies. Both of these monarchies granted monopolies over the trade to private companies. In Spain

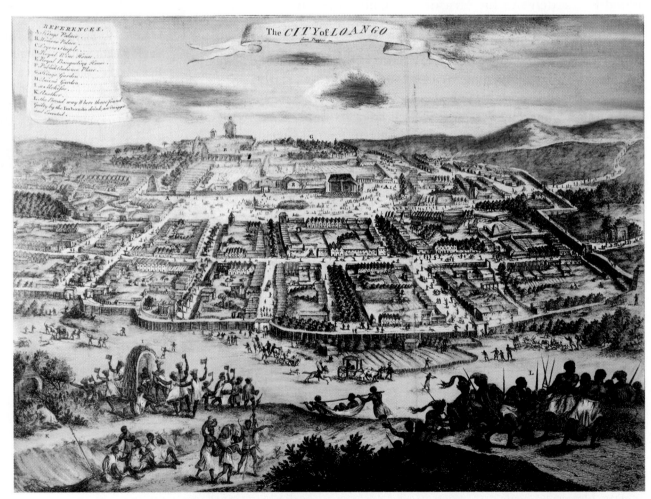

The Portuguese established the city of Luanda in 1575 as a center for the shipment of enslaved Africans to Brazil.

this monopoly became known in 1518 as the *Asiento* (meaning contract). The profits from the slave trade were so great that by 1550 the Dutch, French, and English were becoming involved. During the early seventeenth century, the Dutch drove the Portuguese from the West African coast and became the principal European slave-trading nation. For the rest of that century, most Africans came to the Americas in Dutch ships—including a group of twenty in 1619 who until recently were considered to have been the first of their race to reach British North America.

The Dutch

The Dutch also shifted the center of sugar production to the West Indies. England and France followed, with the former taking control of Barbados and Jamaica and the latter taking Saint Domingue (Haiti), Guadeloupe, and Martinique. With the development of tobacco as a cash crop in Virginia and Maryland during the 1620s and with the continued expansion of sugar production in the West Indies, the demand for African slaves grew. The result was that England and France competed with the Dutch to control the Atlantic slave trade. After a series of wars, England emerged supreme. It had driven the Dutch out of the trade by 1674. Victories over France and Spain led in 1713 to English control of the *Asiento*, which allowed English traders the exclusive right to supply slaves to all of Spain's American colonies. After 1713 English ships dominated the slave trade, carrying about twenty thousand slaves per year from Africa to the Americas. At the peak of the trade during the 1790s, they transported fifty thousand per year.

Africans working on a sugar plantation in the West Indies.

▶ **Document**

2-1 *England Asserts Her Dominion through Legislation in 1660*
England sought to strengthen the American colonies' dependence on her for trade goods. British Parliament's passage of the Navigation Act of 1660 made it necessary for all trade goods bound for the colonies to enter England first and, likewise, for all goods sent to market from the colonies to travel through England. Although the Navigation Act was not strictly enforced, it set the basis for the increasingly constrictive British trade practices that led to the American Revolution. The document outlines the main points of the legislation.

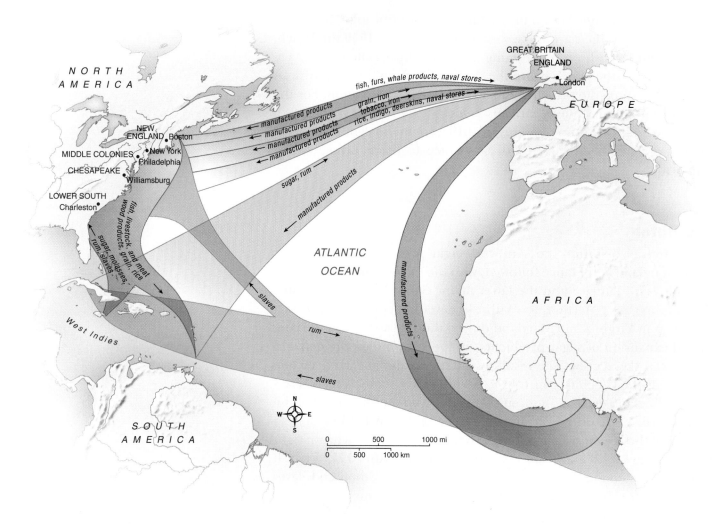

Labels on map:
NORTH AMERICA

GREAT BRITAIN
ENGLAND
London
EUROPE

fish, furs, whale products, naval stores →
grain, iron
tobacco, iron
rice, indigo, deerskins, naval stores →

NEW ENGLAND • Boston
manufactured products ←
manufactured products ←
manufactured products ←
manufactured products ←

MIDDLE COLONIES • New York
• Philadelphia

CHESAPEAKE
• Williamsburg

LOWER SOUTH
Charleston •

sugar, rum

manufactured products ←

fish, livestock, and wood products, grain, rice
sugar, molasses, rum, slaves

ATLANTIC OCEAN

manufactured products

AFRICA

West Indies

slaves

rum →

slaves ←

manufactured products

SOUTH AMERICA

N
W E
S

0   500   1000 mi
0 500 1000 km

MAP 2–3 Atlantic Trade among the Americas, Great Britain, and West Africa during the seventeenth and eighteenth centuries

Often referred to as a triangular trade, this map shows the complexity of early modern Atlantic commerce, of which the slave trade was a major part.

 What does this map suggest about the economy of the Atlantic world between 1600 and 1800?

▶▶ Map 2-3

It was dependent on a triangular trade system that involved British manufactured goods, slaves, sugar and rum.

Economics of the Slave Trade

The profits from the Atlantic slave trade, together with those from the sugar and tobacco produced in the Americas by slave labor, were invested in England and consequently helped fund the industrial revolution during the eighteenth century. In turn, Africa became a market for cheap English manufactured goods (see Map 2–3). Eventually, two **triangular trade systems** developed. In one, traders carried English goods to West Africa and exchanged the goods for slaves. Then the traders carried the slaves to the West Indies and exchanged them for sugar, which they took back to England on the third leg of the triangle. In the other triangular trade, white Americans from Britain's New England colonies carried rum to West Africa to trade for slaves. From Africa they took the slaves to the West Indies to exchange for sugar or molasses—sugar syrup—which they then took home to distill into rum.

Section 2
From Capture to Destination

The Capture of Africans

Recent scholarship indicates that the availability of large numbers of slaves in West Africa resulted from the warfare that accompanied the formation of states in that region. Captives suitable for enslavement were a by-product of these wars. Senegambia and nearby Sierra Leone, then Oyo, Dahomey, and Benin became, in turn, centers of the trade. Meanwhile, on the west coast of Central Africa, slaves became available as a result of the conflict between the expanding Kingdom of Kongo and its neighbors. The European traders provided the aggressors with firearms but did not instigate the wars. Instead they used the wars to enrich themselves.

Sometimes African armies enslaved the inhabitants of conquered towns and villages. At other times, raiding parties captured isolated families or kidnapped individuals. As warfare spread to the interior, captives had to march for hundreds of miles to the coast where European traders awaited them. The raiders tied the captives together with rope or secured them with wooden yokes about their necks. It was a shocking experience, and many captives died from hunger, exhaustion, and exposure during the journey. Others killed themselves rather than submit to their fate, and the captors killed those who resisted.

Once the captives reached the coast, those destined for the Atlantic trade went to fortified structures called **factories**. Portuguese traders constructed the first factory at Elmina on the Guinea Coast in 1481—the Dutch captured it in 1637. Such factories contained the headquarters of the traders, warehouses for their trade goods and supplies, and dungeons or outdoor holding pens for the captives. In these pens, slave traders divided families and—as much as possible—ethnic groups to prevent rebellion. The traders stripped the captives naked and inspected them for disease and physical defects. Those considered fit for purchase were then branded like cattle with a hot iron bearing the symbol of a trading company.

The Crossing

After being held in a factory for weeks or months, captives faced the frightening prospect of leaving their native land for a voyage across the ocean in European ships called **slavers**. This voyage became known as

GUIDE TO READING

▶ How did Africans come to be enslaved?

▶ What happened to Africans between capture and departure for the Americas?

▶ What was the "middle passage"?

▶ What happened to Africans during the voyage across the Atlantic?

▶ How did Africans attempt to resist captivity at sea?

▶ What were voyages on slave ships like for African women?

KEY TERMS

▶ factories, p. 45

▶ slavers, p. 45

▶ middle passage, p. 46

▶ *Brookes*, p. 47

▶ Olaudah Equiano, p. 48

▶ indentured servant, p. 50

▶ **Guide to Reading/Key Terms**

For answers, see the *Teacher's Resource Manual*.

▶ **Document**

2-2 *A Slave Tells of His Capture in Africa in 1798*

One of the few surviving slave narratives of the colonial period of American history, Ventura Smith's story gives us valuable insight as to how Africans were captured by black slave traders and transported.

African slave traders march a group of bound captives from the interior of Africa toward European trading posts.

▶▶ Document

2-4 *An African Captive Tells the Story of Crossing the Atlantic in a Slave Ship*
This passage describes Equiano's trip from Africa to America.

▶▶ Recommended Reading

Paul Edwards, ed. *Equiano's Travels.* London: Heinemann, 1967.

Herbert S. Klein. *The Middle Passage: Comparative Studies in the Atlantic Slave Trade.* Princeton, NJ: Princeton University Press, 1978.

the **middle passage**. Sailors rowed them out in large canoes to slave ships offshore. One English trader recalled that during the 1690s "the negroes were so wilful and loth to leave their own country, that they often leap'd out of the canoos, boat and ship, into the sea, and kept under water till they were drowned."

Once at sea, the slave ships followed the route established by Columbus during his voyages to the Americas: from the Canary Islands off West Africa to the Windward Islands in the Caribbean. Because ships taking this route enjoyed prevailing winds and westward currents, the passage normally lasted between two and three months. But the time required for the crossing varied widely. The larger ships were able to reach the Caribbean in forty days, but voyages could take as long as six months.

Both human and natural causes accounted for such delays. During the three centuries that the Atlantic slave trade endured, Western European nations were often at war with each other, and slave ships became prized targets. As early as the 1580s, English "sea dogs," such as John Hawkins and Sir Francis Drake, attacked Spanish ships to steal their valuable human cargoes. Outright piracy peaked between 1650 and 1725 when demand for slaves in the West Indies greatly increased.

There were also such potentially disastrous natural forces as doldrums—long windless spells at sea—and hurricanes, which could destroy ships, crews, and cargoes.

The Slavers

Slave ships were usually small and narrow. A ship's size, measured in tonnage, theoretically determined how many slaves it could carry, with the formula being two slaves per ton. A large ship of three hundred tons, therefore, was expected to carry six hundred slaves. But captains often ignored the formula. Some kept their human cargo light, calculating that smaller loads lowered mortality and made revolt less likely. But most captains were "tight packers," who squeezed human beings together in hope that large numbers would offset increased deaths. For example, the 120-ton *Henrietta Marie*, a British ship that sailed from London on its final voyage in 1699, should have been fully loaded with 240 slaves. Yet it carried 350 from West Africa when it set out for Barbados and Jamaica. Another ship designed to carry 450 slaves usually carried 600.

The cargo space in slave ships was generally only five feet high. Ships' carpenters halved this vertical space by building shelves, so slaves might be packed above and below on planks that measured only 5.5 feet long and 1.3 feet wide. Consequently, slaves had only about 20 to 25 inches of headroom. To add to the discomfort, the crews chained male slaves together in pairs to help prevent rebellion and lodged them away from women and children.

The most frequently reproduced illustration of a slaver's capacity for human cargo comes from the *Brookes*, which sailed from Liverpool, England, during the 1780s. At three hundred tons, the *Brookes* was an exceptionally large ship for its time, and the diagrams show how tightly packed the slaves were who boarded it. Although those who wished to abolish the Atlantic slave trade created the diagrams, their bias does not make the diagrams less accurate. In fact, as historian James Walvin points out in his study of the trade, the precise, unemotional renderings of the *Brookes*'s design scarcely indicate the physical suffering it caused. The renderings do not show the constant shifting, crushing, and chafing among the tightly packed human cargo caused by the movement of the ship at sea.

Mortality rates were high because the crowded, unsanitary conditions encouraged seaboard epidemics. Between 1715 and 1775, slave deaths on French ships averaged 15 percent. The highest recorded mortality rate was 34 percent. By the nineteenth century, the death rate had declined to 5 percent. Overall, one-third of the Africans subjected to the trade perished between their capture and their embarkation on a slave ship. Another third died during the middle passage or during "seasoning" on a Caribbean island. It would have been slight consolation to the

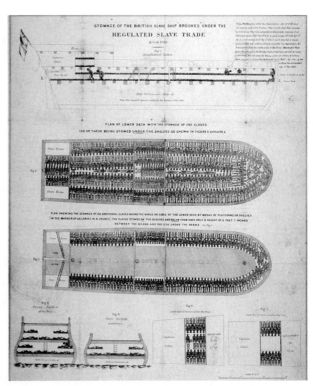

Plan of the British slave ship *Brookes*, 1788 shows how tightly Africans were packed aboard slave ships.

▶ **Retracing the Odyssey**

The Henrietta Marie. This is a slave ship placed on traveling display by the Museum of Southern Florida in Miami. The *Henrietta Marie* sank in 1701 after delivering slaves to Jamaica.

▶ **Recommended Reading**

Lief Svalesen. *The Slave Ship Fredensborg.* Bloomington, IN: Indiana University Press, 2000.

▶ **Teaching Notes**

During storms the crew often neglected to feed the slaves, empty the tubs used for excrement, take slaves on deck for exercise, tend to the sick, or remove the dead.

enslaved to learn that because of the epidemics, the rate of death among slaver crews was proportionally higher than their own.

 Reading Check   What was the "Middle Passage"?

An Enslaved African's Story

In his book *The Interesting Narrative of the Life of Olaudah Equiano or Gustavus Vassa*, published in 1789, **Olaudah Equiano** provides a vivid account of his capture, sale, and voyage to America in 1755. Equiano was an Igbo, the dominant group in what is today southern Nigeria. When he was ten years old, African slave raiders captured him and forced him to march along with other captives to the Niger River or one of its tributaries, where they traded him to other Africans. His new captors took him to the coast and sold him to European slave traders whose ships sailed to the West Indies.

Equiano's experience at the coastal slave factory convinced him he had entered a sort of hell, peopled by evil spirits. The stench caused by forcing many people to live in close confinement made him sick to his stomach and emotionally agitated. His African and European captors tried to calm him with liquor. But because he was not accustomed to alcohol, he became disoriented and more convinced of his impending doom. When the sailors lodged him with others below deck on the ship, he was so sick that he lost his appetite and hoped to die. Instead, because he refused to eat, the sailors took him on deck and whipped him. Later Equiano witnessed the flogging of one of the white crew members. The man died, and the sailors threw his body into the sea just as they disposed of dead Africans.

During the time the ship was in port awaiting a full cargo of slaves, Equiano spent much time on its deck. After putting to sea, however, he usually remained below deck with the other slaves where "each had scarcely room to turn himself." There, the smells of unwashed bodies and of the toilet tubs, "into which the children often fell and were almost suffocated," created a loathsome atmosphere. The darkness, the chafing of chains on human flesh, the shrieks and groans of the sick and disoriented created "a scene of horror almost inconceivable."

When slaves were allowed to get some fresh air and exercise on deck, the crew strung nets to prevent them from jumping overboard. Even so, Equiano observed two Africans, who were chained together, evade the nets and jump into the ocean, preferring drowning to staying on board. Equiano shared their desperation. He recalled that as the ship left the sight of land, "I now saw myself deprived of all chance of returning to my native country, or even the least glimpse of hope of [re]gaining the shore." Equiano insisted that "many more" would have jumped overboard "if they had not been prevented by the ship's crew."

Attempts to keep the slaves entertained and in good humor seldom succeeded. Crews sometimes forced the slaves to dance and sing, but

▶ **Reading Check**

The middle passage was the middle leg in a triangular trade that linked Europe, Africa, and the Americas. On this leg, slaves purchased with European finished products were transported to the Americas. Once there, the vast majority worked as agricultural slaves producing commodities for the European market.

▶ **Interactive Activity**

Racism in American History
This activity examines the connection between slavery and race. Written accounts, including the writings of Olaudah Equiano and George Fitzhugh, depict the brutal treatment Africans received in the slave trade. Visual images portray the ways in which slaves were treated as commodities in a marketplace. Interactive maps and a chronology provide space and time contexts. Print documents illuminate the issues over racism that emerged during the revolutionary period.

their songs, as slave-ship surgeon Alexander Falconbridge testified, were "melancholy lamentations, of their exile from their native country." Depression among the Africans led to a catatonia that contemporary observers called melancholy or extreme nostalgia. Falconbridge noted that the slaves had "a strong attachment to their native country" and a "just sense of the value of liberty."

Although the traders, seeking to lessen the possibility of shipboard conspiracy and rebellion, separated individuals who spoke the same language, Equiano managed to find comfort in hearing others speak Igbo. They explained to him the purpose of the voyage, which he came to understand was to go to the white people's country to labor for them rather than to be eaten by them. He did not realize that work on a West Indian island could be a death sentence.

PROFILE ❖ Olaudah Equiano

Olaudah Equiano was probably born in 1745 in what is today eastern Nigeria. Local slave raiders captured Equiano when he was ten years old. They sold him to African traders who sold him to Europeans on the coast. They, in turn, shipped him on a slaver to Barbados in the West Indies. After about two weeks on Barbados, Equiano was sent to Virginia on another slave ship. There he spent "a few weeks weeding grass and gathering stones in a plantation."

Equiano's luck improved when a visiting sea captain named Michael Henry Pascal purchased him to become his personal servant. Pascal renamed him Gustavus Vassa (after the king of Sweden), which name Equiano kept for the rest of his life.

Pascal and Equiano traveled extensively and served together in North America during the French and Indian War. Equiano also lived in England where he received the schooling that allowed him to work as "a shipping clerk and amateur navigator on the ship of his second [third] master, the Quaker Robert King of Philadelphia, trading chiefly between [North] America and the West Indies."

Equiano purchased his freedom for forty pounds sterling in 1766, when he was about twenty-one years old. This was a considerable amount of money, amounting to more than most eighteenth-century British laborers earned in a year. Thereafter, Equiano toured the Mediterranean, sailed to the Arctic and Central America, converted to Calvinism, and joined the British antislavery movement.

It was as an opponent of slavery that Equiano helped organize a colony for emancipated British slaves at Sierra Leone in West Africa in 1787. Shortly thereafter, he wrote his autobiography and supported himself for the rest of his life by selling copies of it in conjunction with the antislavery movement.

In April 1792 Equiano married "a Miss Susan or Susanna Cullen" at Cambridge, England. Whether Equiano and his wife had children is in dispute. He probably died in April 1797. At that time, British abolitionist Granville Sharp wrote a brief eulogy for Equiano, noting that he "was a sober, honest man."

Equiano

A Captain's Story

Another perspective on the middle passage is provided by white slave-ship captain John Newton, who was born in London in 1725. In 1745 Newton, as an **indentured servant**, joined the crew of a slaver bound for Sierra Leone. Indentured servants lost their freedom for a specified number of years, either because they sold it or because they were being punished for debt or crime. In 1748, on the return voyage to England, Newton survived a fierce Atlantic storm and, thanking God, became an evangelical Christian. Like most people of his era, Newton saw no contradiction between his newfound faith and his participation in the enslavement and ill treatment of men, women, and children. When he became a slaver captain in 1750, he read Bible passages to his crew twice each Sunday and forbade swearing on board his vessel. But he treated his slave cargoes as harshly as any other slaver captain.

Newton was twenty-five years old when he became captain of the *Duke of Argyle*, an old 140-ton vessel that he converted into a slaver after it sailed from Liverpool on August 11, 1750. Near the Cape Verde Islands, off the coast of Senegambia, carpenters began making the alterations required for packing many Africans below deck. Newton also put the ship's guns and ammunition in order to protect against pirates or African resistance. On October 23 the *Duke of Argyle* reached Frenchman's Bay, Sierra Leone, where Newton observed other ships from England, France, and New England anchored offshore. Two days later, Newton purchased two men and a woman from traders at the port, but he had to sail to several other ports to accumulate a full cargo. Leaving West Africa on May 23, 1751, for the open sea, the ship reached Antigua in the West Indies on July 3 to deliver its slaves.

Poor health forced Newton to retire from the slave trade in 1754. Ten years later he gained ordination as an Anglican priest. In 1779 he became rector of St. Mary Woolnoth Church in London and served there until his death in 1807. By the late 1770s, Newton had repented his involvement in the slave trade and had become one of its leading opponents. Together with William Cowper—a renowned poet—Newton published the *Olney Hymns* in 1779. Among the selections included in this volume was "Amazing Grace," which Newton wrote as a reflection on divine forgiveness for his sins. For several reasons, Newton and other religious Britons had begun to perceive an evil in the slave trade that, despite their piety, they had failed to see earlier.

Provisions for the Middle Passage

Slave ships left Liverpool and other European ports provisioned with food supplies for their crews. These included beans, cheese, beef, flour, and grog, a mixture of rum and water. When the ships reached the Guinea Coast in West Africa, their captains began purchasing pepper, palm oil, lemons, limes, yams, plantains, and coconuts. Because slaves

Africans are sold to English colonists at Jamestown by a Dutch captain on the outskirts of the 17th century village.

▶ **Document**

2-3 *A Slave Ship Surgeon Writes about the Slave Trade in 1788*
Alexander Falconbridge was forced through poverty to work as a surgeon on slave ships. Witnessing the horrors of the trade, Falconbridge became an advocate for the slaves. He went on to become involved in Sierra Leone, a British antislavery resettlement colony in West Africa. This passage outlines how slaves were obtained in Africa by kidnapping and examined by traders before being sold.

were not accustomed to European foods, the ships needed these staples of the African diet. Meat and fish were rare luxuries on board, and crews did not share them with slaves. Equiano recalled that, at one point during the passage, crew members caught far more fish than they could eat but threw what was left overboard, instead of giving it to the Africans who were exercising on deck. "We begged and prayed for some as well as we could," Equiano noted, "but in vain." The sailors whipped those Africans who filched a few fish for themselves.

The crew usually fed the slaves twice per day in shifts. Cooks prepared vegetable pulps, porridge, and stews for the crew to distribute in buckets as the slaves assembled on deck during good weather or below deck during storms. At the beginning of the voyage, each slave received a wooden spoon for dipping into the buckets, which were shared by about ten individuals. But in the confined confusion below deck, slaves often lost their spoons. In such cases, they had to eat from the buckets with their unwashed hands, a practice that spread disease.

Although slaver captains realized it was in their interest to feed their human cargoes well, they often skimped on supplies to make room for more slaves. Some captains calculated how the eventual profits from an increased human cargo would offset the losses from inevitable deaths during a voyage. Therefore, the food on a slave ship was often too poor and insufficient to prevent malnutrition and weakened immune systems among people already traumatized by separation from their families and homelands. As a result, many Africans died during the middle passage from diseases amid the horrid conditions that were normal aboard the slave ships. Others died from depression: they refused to eat, despite the crews' efforts to force food down their throats.

Sanitation, Disease, and Death

Diseases such as malaria, yellow fever, measles, smallpox, hookworm, scurvy, and dysentery constantly threatened African cargoes and European crews during the middle passage. Death rates were astronomical on board the slave ships before 1750. Mortality dropped after that date because ships became faster and ships' surgeons knew more about hygiene and diet. There were also early forms of vaccinations against smallpox, which may have been the worst killer of slaves on ships.

Usually slavers provided only three or four toilet tubs below deck for enslaved Africans to use during the middle passage. They had to struggle among themselves to get to the tubs, and children had a particularly difficult time. Those who were too ill to reach the tubs excreted where they lay, and diseases such as dysentery, which are spread by human waste, thrived. Dysentery, known by contemporaries as the bloody flux, vied with smallpox to kill the most slaves aboard ships. Alexander Falconbridge reported that during one dysentery epidemic, "The deck, that is, the floor of [the slaves'] rooms, was so covered with blood and mucus which had proceeded from them in

▶▶ **Document**

2-4 *An African Captive Tells the Story of Crossing the Atlantic in a Slave Ship*
This passage from Equiano's autobiography describes the trip from Africa to America.

▶▶ **Teaching Notes**

Even after 1750 poor sanitation led to many deaths. It is important to remember that before the early twentieth century, no civilization had developed a germ theory of disease. Physicians blamed human illnesses on poisonous atmospheres and imbalances among bodily fluids.

The Journal of a Dutch Slaver

The following account of slave trading on the West African coast is from a journal kept on the Dutch slaver St. Jan *between March and November 1659. Although it is written from a European point of view, it clearly indicates the sort of conditions Africans faced on board such ships.*

We weighed anchor, by the order of the Hon'ble Director, Johan Valckenborch, and the Hon'ble Director, Jasper van Heussen to proceed on our voyage to Rio Reael [on the Guinea Coast] to trade for slaves for the hon'ble company.

March 8. Saturday. Arrived with our ship before Ardra, to take on board the surgeon's mate and a supply of tamarinds for refreshment for the slaves; sailed again next day on our voyage to Rio Reael.

17. Arrived at Rio Reael in front of a village called Bany, where we found the company's yacht, named the *Vrede*, which was sent out to assist us to trade for slaves.

In April. Nothing was done except to trade for slaves.

May 6. One of our seamen died. . . .

22. Again weighed anchor and ran out of Rio Reael accompanied by the yacht *Vrede*, purchased there two hundred and nineteen head of slaves, men, women, boys and girls, and set our course for the high land of Ambosius, for the purpose of procuring food there for the slaves, as nothing was to be had at Rio Reael.

June 29. Sunday. Again resolved to proceed on our voyage, as there also but little food was to be had for the slaves in consequence of the great rains which fell every day, and because many of the slaves were suffering from the bloody flux in consequence of the bad provisions we were supplied with at El Mina. . . .

July 27. Our surgeon, named Martyn de Lanoy, died of the bloody flux.

Aug. 11. Again resolved to pursue our voyage towards the island of Annebo, in order to purchase there some refreshments for the slaves. . . .

Aug. 15. Arrived at the island Annebo, where we purchased for the slaves one hundred half tierces of beans, twelve hogs, five thousand coconuts, five thousand sweet oranges, besides some other stores.

Sept. 21. The skipper called the ships officers aft, and resolved to run for the island of Tobago and to procure water there; otherwise we should have perished for want of water, as many of our water casks had leaked dry.

24. Friday. Arrived at the island of Tobago and hauled water there, also purchased some bread, as our hands had had no ration for three weeks.

Nov. 1. Lost our ship on the Reef of Rocus [north of Caracas], and all hands immediately took to the boat, as there was no prospect of saving the slaves, for we must abandon the ship in consequence of the heavy surf.

4. Arrived with the boat at the island of Curaco; the Hon'ble Governor Beck ordered two sloops to take the slaves off the wreck, one of which sloops with eighty four slaves on board, was captured by a privateer [pirate vessel].

What Do You Think?

▶ What dangers did the slaves and crew on board the *St. Jan* face?

▶ What is the attitude of the author of the journal toward slaves?

consequence of the flux, that it resembled a slaughter-house. It is not in the power of human imagination, to picture to itself a situation more dreadful or disgusting."

John Newton's stark, unimpassioned records of slave deaths aboard the *Duke of Argyle* indicate even more about how the Atlantic slave trade devalued human life. Newton recorded deaths at sea only by number. He wrote in his journal, "Bury'd a man slave No. 84 . . . bury'd a woman slave, No. 47." Yet Newton probably was more conscientious than other slave-ship captains in seeking to avoid disease. During his 1750 voyage, he noted only eleven deaths. Compared with the usual high mortality rates, this was an achievement.

What role ships' surgeons—general practitioners in modern terminology—played in preventing or inadvertently encouraging deaths aboard slave ships is difficult to determine. Some of them were outright frauds. Even the best were limited by the primitive medical knowledge that existed between the fifteenth and nineteenth centuries. Captains rewarded the surgeons with "head money" for the number of healthy slaves who arrived in the Americas, but the surgeons could also be blamed for deaths at sea that reduced the value of the human cargo.

Many surgeons recognized that African remedies were more likely than European medications to alleviate the slaves' illnesses. The surgeons collected herbs and foods along the Guinea Coast. They also learned African nursing techniques, which they found more effective in treating on-board diseases than European procedures. What the surgeons did not understand, and regarded as superstition, was the holistic

▶ **What do You Think?**

· Lack of food and water, diseases, shipwrecks due to storms, and piracy.

· The author is indifferent to the slaves' suffering.

nature of African medicine. African healers maintained that body, mind, and spirit were interconnected elements of the totality of a person's well-being.

The enslaved Africans, of course, were often just as dumbfounded by the beliefs and actions of their captors. Equiano and others thought they had entered a world of bad spirits when they boarded a slave ship, and they attempted to counteract the spirits with rituals from their homeland.

PROFILE ❖ Ayuba Sulieman Diallo

Ayuba Sulieman Diallo, known to Europeans as Job ben Solomon, was one of the many West Africans caught up in the Atlantic slave trade. Diallo was born in about 1701 at the village of Marsa located in the eastern Senegambian region of Bondu. His father, the imam of the local mosque and village head, taught him Arabic and the Koran when he was a child and prepared him to become a merchant. Diallo, following Muslim and West African custom, had two wives.

In February 1730 Diallo was on his way to sell two slaves to an English trader when he was captured by Mandingo warriors and sold as well. Although the English slaver captain was willing to ransom Diallo, his ship sailed before Diallo's father could send the money. As a result, Diallo was shipped with other Africans to Annapolis, Maryland, and delivered to a London merchant. Shortly thereafter, Diallo was sold to a Mr. Tolsey who operated a tobacco plantation on Maryland's Eastern Shore.

Diallo's "religious abstinence" and the difficulties he had experienced during the middle passage unsuited him for field work. Therefore, Tolsey assigned him to tending cattle. In June 1731, Diallo escaped to Dover, Delaware, where he was apprehended and jailed. There, Thomas Bluett, who in 1734 published an account of Diallo's adventures, discovered that Diallo was literate in Arabic, pious in his religious devotions, and—according to Bluett's stereotypical notions—"no common slave." Bluett provided this information to Tolsey, who on Diallo's return allowed him a quiet place to pray and permitted him to write a letter in Arabic to his father.

The letter reached James Oglethorpe, the director of England's slave-trading Royal African Company, who arranged to purchase Diallo from Tolsey and in March 1733 transport him by ship to England. Accompanied by Bluett, Diallo learned during the long voyage to speak, read, and write English. In London, Bluett contacted several well-to-do gentlemen who raised sixty pounds to secure Diallo's freedom. With the aid of the Royal African Company, he returned to Senegambia.

Diallo's wives and children greeted him upon his return to his village, but otherwise much had changed during his absence. Futa Toro had conquered Bondu, Diallo's family had suffered economically as a result, the slave trade in Senegambia had intensified, and Morocco had begun to interfere militarily in the region. Grateful to his English friends, Diallo used his influence in these difficult circumstances to help the Royal African Company hold its share of the trade in slaves and gold until the company disbanded in 1752. Quite able to differentiate between his fortunes and those of others, he retained commercial ties to the British until his death in 1773.

John Newton noted that during one voyage he feared slaves had tried to poison the ship's drinking water. He was relieved to discover that they were only putting what he called "charms" in the water supply. In fact, such fetishes, representing the power of spirits, were important in West African religions.

 Reading Check What happened to Africans during the voyage across the Atlantic?

Resistance and Revolt at Sea

Because many enslaved Africans refused to accept their fate, slaver captains had to be vigilant. Uprisings were common, and Newton himself had to put down a potentially serious one aboard the *Duke of Argyle*. Twenty men had broken their chains below deck, but they were apprehended before they could assault the crew.

Most such rebellions took place while a ship prepared to set sail, the African coast was in sight, and the slaves could still hope to return home. But some revolts occurred on the open sea where it was unlikely the Africans, even if their revolt succeeded, would be able to return to their homes or regain their freedom. Both sorts of revolt indicate that not even capture, forced march to the coast, imprisonment, branding, and sale could break the spirit of many captives. These Africans preferred to face death rather than accept bondage.

John Atkins, an English slave-ship surgeon who made many voyages between Africa and the Americas during the 1720s, noted that although the threat of revolt diminished on the high seas, it never disappeared:

> When we are slaved and out at sea, it is commonly imagined that the *Negroes*['] Ignorance of Navigation, will always be a Safeguard [against revolt]; yet, as many of them think themselves bought to eat, and more, that Death will send them into their own Country, there has not been wanting Examples of rising and killing a Ship's Company, distant from Land, though not so often as on the Coast: But once or twice is enough to shew, a Master's Care and Diligence should never be over till the Delivery of them.

Later in the eighteenth century, a historian used the prevalence of revolt to justify the harsh treatment of Africans on slave ships. Edward Long wrote that "the many acts of violence they [the slaves] have committed by murdering whole crews and destroying ships when they had it left in their power to do so, have made this rigour wholly chargeable on their own bloody and malicious disposition, which calls for the same confinement as if they were wolves or wild boars."

Failed slave mutineers could expect harsh punishment, although profit margins influenced sentences. Atkins chronicled how the captain of the *Robert*, which sailed from Bristol, England, punished the ringleaders,

▶ **Reading Check**

Slaves endured horrendous conditions on the voyage to the Americas. Disease and poor sanitation resulted in countless deaths. Revolt and suicide led to still more casualties. In addition, female slaves were subject to sexual predation by the ship's crew.

who were worth more, less harshly than their followers who were not as valuable. Atkins related that

> Captain Harding, weighing the Stoutness and Worth of the two [ringleaders], did, as in other Countries they do by Rogues of Dignity, whip and scarify them only; while three others, Abettors, but not Actors, nor of Strength for it, he sentenced to cruel Deaths; making them first eat the Heart and Liver of one of them killed. The Woman [who had helped in the revolt] he hoisted up by the Thumbs, whipp'd and slashed her with Knives, before the other Slaves, till she died.

Other slaves resisted their captors by drowning or starving themselves. Thomas Phillips, captain of the slaver *Hannibal* during the 1690s, commented, "We had about 12 negroes did wilfully drown themselves and others starved themselves to death; for 'tis their belief that when they die they return home to their own country and friends again." As we previously indicated, captains used nets to prevent deliberate drowning. To deal with starvation, they used hot coals or a metal device called a *speculum oris* to force individuals to open their mouths for feeding.

 Reading Check How did Africans attempt to resist captivity at sea?

Cruelty

The Atlantic slave trade required more capital than any other maritime commerce during the seventeenth and eighteenth centuries. The investments for the ships, the exceptionally large crews they employed, the navigational equipment, the armaments, the purchase of slaves in Africa, and the supplies of food and water to feed hundreds of passengers were phenomenal. The aim was to carry as many Africans in healthy condition to the Americas as possible in order to make the large profits that justified such expenditures. Yet, as we have indicated, conditions aboard the vessels were abysmal.

Scholars have debated how much deliberate cruelty the enslaved Africans suffered from ships' crews. The West Indian historian Eric Williams asserts that the horrors of the middle passage have been exaggerated. Many writers, Williams contends, are led astray by the writings of those who, during the late eighteenth and early nineteenth centuries, sought to abolish the slave trade. In Williams's view—and that of other historians as well—the difficulties of the middle passage were similar to those experienced by European indentured servants who suffered high mortality rates on the voyage to America.

From this perspective the primary cause of death at sea on all ships carrying passengers across the Atlantic Ocean to the Americas was epidemic disease, against which medical practitioners had few tools before the twentieth century. Contributing factors included inadequate means of preserv-

▶ **Reading Check**

Resistance and rebellion occurred sometime when ships had not yet left Africa since Africans were still close to home were they able to escape. On the open sea, uprisings were common. Captured Africans mutinied, attempted to kill their captors or tried to resist their captors by drowning or starving themselves. Because of their value on the slave market, leaders of mutinies were dealt with more harshly than their followers and those who tried to jump into the sea or not eat were saved and force fed.

▶ **Teaching Notes**

Such observations help place conditions aboard the slave ships in a broader perspective. Cruelty and suffering are, to some degree, historically relative in that practices that were acceptable in the past are now considered inhumane. Yet cruelty aboard slavers must also be placed in a cultural context. Cultures distinguish between what constitutes acceptable behavior to their own people, on the one hand, and to strangers, on the other.

Several European slave traders capture Africans as a schooner waits in the harbor.

ing food from spoilage and keeping fresh water from becoming contaminated during the long ocean crossing. According to Williams, overcrowding by slavers was only a secondary cause for the high mortality rates.

For Europeans, Africans were cultural strangers, and what became normal in the Atlantic slave trade was in fact exceptionally cruel in comparison to how Europeans treated each other. Slaves below deck, for example, received only one-half the space allocated on board to European soldiers, free emigrants, indentured servants, and convicts. Europeans regarded slavery itself as a condition suitable only for non-Christians. And as strangers, Africans were subject to brutalization by European crew members who often cared little about the physical and emotional damage they inflicted.

African Women on Slave Ships

For similar reasons, African women did not enjoy the same protection against European men that European women received. Consequently, sailors during long voyages attempted to abuse enslaved women. African women caught in the Atlantic slave trade were worth half the price of African men in Caribbean markets. As a result, captains took fewer of them on board their vessels. Perhaps because the women were less valuable commodities, crew members felt they had license to abuse them. The separate below-deck compartments for women on slave ships also made them easier targets than they otherwise might have been.

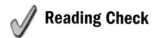 **Reading Check** What were voyages on slave ships like for African women?

▶ **Reading Check**
African women were viewed as worth less on the slave market than African men and were therefore treated even less humanely during the voyage. They were subject to sexual abuse by the crew of slave ships and isolated from men on the ships.

▶ **Guide to Reading/Key Terms**

For answers, see the *Teacher's Resource Manual.*

▶ **Recommended Reading**

Clarence J. Munford. *The Black Ordeal of Slavery and Slave Trading in the French West Indies, 1625–1715.* Lewiston, NY: Mellen, 1991.

Keith Albert Sandiford. *The Cultural Politics of Sugar: Caribbean Slavery and Narratives of Colonialism.* New York: Cambridge University Press, 2000. The Granger Collection, New

Section 3

Landing and Sale in the West Indies

The Selling of Africans

As slave ships neared their West Indian destinations, the crew prepared the human cargo for landing and sale. They allowed the slaves to shave, wash with fresh water, and take more vigorous exercise. Those bound for the larger Caribbean islands or for the British colonies of southern North America were often given some weeks to rest in the easternmost islands of the West Indies. French slave traders typically rested their slave passengers on Martinique. The English preferred Barbados. Sale to white plantation owners followed, and then began a period of what the **planters** called **seasoning**, a period of up to two years of acculturating slaves and breaking them in to plantation routines.

The process of landing and sale that ended the middle passage was often as protracted as the events that began it in Africa. After anchoring at one of the Lesser Antilles Islands—Barbados, St. Kitts, or Antigua— English slaver captains haggled with the agents of local planters over numbers and prices. They then determined whether to sell all their slaves at their first port of call, sell some of them, sail to another island, or sail to such North American ports as Charleston, Williamsport, or Baltimore. If the market looked good in the first port, the captain might still take a week or more to sell his cargo. The captain of the *James*, who landed at Barbados in 1676, just as the cultivation of cane sugar there was becoming extremely profitable, sold most of his slaves in three days. "May Thursday 25th . . . sold 163 slaves. May Friday 26th. We sold 70 slaves. May Saturday 27th. Sold 110 slaves," he recorded in his journal.

Often, captains and crew had to do more to prepare slaves for sale than allow them to clean themselves and exercise. The ravages of cruelty, confinement, and disease could not be easily remedied. According to legend, young African men and women arrived in the Americas with gray hair, and captains used dye to hide such indications of age before the slaves went to market. Slaves were also required to oil their bodies to conceal blemishes, rashes, and bruises. Ships' surgeons used hemp with those suffering from dysentery in order to block the bloody discharge the disease caused.

This nineteenth-century engraving suggests the humiliation Africans endured as they were subjected to physical inspections before being sold.

The humiliation continued as the slaves went to market. Once again they suffered close physical inspection from potential buyers, which—according to Equiano—caused "much dread and trembling among us" and "bitter cries." Unless a single purchaser agreed to buy an entire cargo of slaves, auctions took place either on deck or in sale yards on shore. However, some captains employed "the scramble." In these barbaric spectacles, the captain established standard prices for men, women, and children, herded the Africans together in a corral, and then allowed buyers to rush pell-mell among them to grab and rope together the slaves they desired.

 Reading Check What happened to Africans after they crossed the Atlantic?

Seasoning

Seasoning followed sale. On Barbados, Jamaica, and other Caribbean islands, planters divided slaves into three categories: **Creoles** (slaves born in the Americas), old Africans (those who had lived in the Americas for some time), and **new Africans** (those who had just survived the middle passage). For resale, Creole slaves were worth three times the value of unseasoned new Africans, whom planters and Creole slaves called "salt-water Negroes" or "Guinea-birds." Seasoning was the beginning of the process of making new Africans more like Creoles.

▶ **Reading Check**

As ships neared their destinations, the crews prepared the human cargo for sale. The crew then attempted to find the best price for their slaves. Once in the marketplace, slaves were subjected to the humiliation of examination and sale.

▶ **Teaching Notes**

Historian James Walvin estimates that one-third of the new Africans died during their first three years in the West Indies. African men died at a greater rate than African women, perhaps because they did the more arduous fieldwork.

▶ **Recommended Reading**

Barbara Bush. *Slave Women in Caribbean Society, 1650–1838.* Bloomington, IN: University of Indiana Press, 1990. The book contains an insightful discussion of African women, their introduction to slavery in the Americas, and their experience on sugar plantations.

Edward Brathwaite. *The Development of Creole Society in Jamaica, 1770–1820.* New York: Oxford University Press, 1971.

In the West Indies, this process involved not only an apprenticeship in the work routines of the sugar plantations on the islands. It was also a means of preparing many slaves for resale to North American planters, who preferred "seasoned" slaves to "unbroken" ones who came directly from Africa. In fact, most of the Africans who ended up in the British colonies of North America before 1720 had gone first to the West Indies. By that date, the demand for slave labor in the islands had become so great that they could spare fewer slaves for resale to the North American market. Thereafter, as a result, slave imports into the tobacco-, rice-, and later cotton-growing regions of the American South came directly from Africa and had to be seasoned by their American masters.

In either case, seasoning was a disciplinary process intended to modify the behavior and attitude of slaves and make them effective laborers. As part of this process, the slaves' new masters gave them new names: Christian names, generic African names, or names from classical Greece and Rome (such as Jupiter, Achilles, or Plato).

The seasoning process also involved slaves learning European languages. Masters on the Spanish islands of the Caribbean were especially thorough in this regard. Consequently, the Spanish of African slaves and their descendants, although retaining some African words, was easily understood by any Spanish-speaking person. In the French and English Caribbean islands and in parts of North America, however, slave society produced Creole dialects that in grammar, vocabulary, and intonation had distinctive African linguistic features. These Africanized versions of French and English—including the Gullah dialect still prevalent on South Carolina's sea islands and the Creole spoken today by most Haitians—were difficult for those who spoke more standardized dialects to understand.

Seasoning varied in length from place to place. Masters or overseers broke slaves into plantation work by assigning them to one of several work gangs. The strongest men joined the first gang, or **great gang**, which did the heavy fieldwork of planting and harvesting. The second gang, including women and older men, did lighter fieldwork, such as weeding. The third gang, composed of children, worked shorter hours and did such tasks as bringing food and water to the field gangs. Other slaves became domestic servants. New Africans served apprenticeships with old Africans from their same ethnic group or with Creoles.

Some planters looked for cargoes of young people, anticipating that they might be more easily acculturated than older Africans. One West Indian master in 1792 recorded his hopes for a group of children: "From the late Guinea sales, I have purchased altogether twenty boys and girls, from ten to thirteen years old." He emphasized that "it is the practice, on bringing them to the estate, to distribute them in the huts of Creole blacks, under their direction and care, who are to feed them, train them to work, and teach them their new language."

Planters had to rely on old Africans and Creoles to train new recruits because white people were a minority in the Caribbean. Later, a similar demographic pattern developed in parts of the cotton-producing

American South. As a result, in both regions African custom shaped the cooperative labor of slaves in gangs. But the use of old Africans and Creoles as instructors and the appropriation of African styles of labor should not suggest leniency. Although the plantation overseers, who ran day-to-day operations, could be white, of mixed race, or black, they invariably imposed strict discipline. **Drivers**, who directed the work gangs, were almost always black, but they carried whips and frequently punished those who worked too slowly or showed disrespect. Planters assigned the more difficult new Africans to the strictest overseers and drivers.

Planters housed slaves undergoing seasoning with the old Africans and Creoles who were instructing them. The instructors regarded such additions to their households as economic opportunities. The new Africans provided extra labor on the small plots of land that West Indian planters often allocated to slaves. Slaves could sell surplus root vegetables, peas, and fruit from their gardens and save to purchase freedom for themselves or others. Additional workers helped produce larger surpluses to sell at local markets, thereby cutting the amount of time required to accumulate a purchase price.

New Africans also benefited from this arrangement. They learned how to build houses in their new land and to cultivate vegetables to supplement the food the planter provided. Even though many Africans brought building skills and agricultural knowledge with them to the Americas, old Africans and Creoles helped teach them how to adapt what they knew to a new climate, topography, building materials, and social organization.

Slaves in this nineteenth-century painting are preparing a field for cultivation on the island of Antigua, a British possession in the West Indies.

 Reading Check What was seasoning and why was it used?

Masters and Slaves in the Americas

By what criteria did planters assess the successful seasoning of new Africans? The first criterion was survival. Already weakened and traumatized by the middle passage, many Africans did not survive seasoning.

A second criterion was that the Africans had to adapt to new foods and a new climate. The foods included salted codfish traded to the West Indies by New England merchants, Indian corn (maize), and varieties of squash not available in West Africa. The Caribbean islands like West Africa were tropical, but North America was much cooler.

A third criterion was learning a new language. Planters did not require slaves to speak the local language, which could be English, French, Spanish, Danish, or Dutch, perfectly. But slaves had to speak a Creole dialect well enough to obey commands. A final criterion was psychological. When new Africans ceased to be suicidal, planters assumed they had accepted their status and their separation from their homeland.

▶ Reading Check

Seasoning was a disciplinary process designed to modify the behavior and attitude of slaves. Seasoning was meant to break connections with Africa. It was also designed, in the minds of slaveholders, to produce efficient and effective laborers.

▶ Recommended Reading

John Thornton. *Africa and Africans in the Making of the Atlantic World, 1400–1800.* 2d ed. New York: Cambridge University Press, 1998. Thornton emphasizes the contributions of Africans, slave and free, to the economic and cultural development of the Atlantic world during the slave-trade centuries.

> ► **Reading Check**

While there was some variation from master to master, all slaves could expect to face a constant, heavy workload. Fear of slave uprisings and the belief that Africans would only work hard under the threat of physical pain, spurred masters to use harsh and frequent punishments.

> ► **Reading Check**

Disgust at the cruelties associated with the trade contributed to its abolition. More important, England grew less dependent on the plantation system. Thus, a combination of morals and economic self-interest led to the trade's abolition.

> ► **Skills for Life**

For answers, see the *Instructor's Resource Manual.*

> ► **Chapter 2 Teaching Summary**

Over more than three centuries, the Atlantic slave trade brought more than eleven million Africans to the Americas. Several millions more died in transit. Of those who survived, most came between 1701 and 1810, when more Africans then Europeans were reaching the New World. Most Africans went to the sugar plantations of the Caribbean and Brazil. Only 500,000 reached the British colonies of North America, either directly or after seasoning in the West Indies. From them have come the more than thirty million African Americans alive today.

This chapter has described the great forced migration across the Atlantic that brought Africans into slavery in the Americas. We still have much to learn about the origins of the trade, its relationship to the earlier trans-Sahara trade, and its involvement with state formation in West and western Central Africa. Historians continue to debate just how cruel the trade was, the ability of transplanted Africans to preserve their cultural heritage, and why Britain abolished the trade in the early nineteenth century.

We are fortunate that a few Africans, such as Olaudah Equiano, who experienced the middle passage, recorded their testimony. Otherwise, we would find its horror even more difficult to comprehend. But, just as important, Equiano, in overcoming his fears, in surviving the slave trade and ten years of enslavement, and in finally regaining his freedom, testifies to the human spirit that is at the center of the African-American experience.

It would have suited the planters if their slaves had met all these criteria. Yet that would have required the Africans to have been thoroughly desocialized by the middle passage, and they were not. As traumatic as that voyage was, most of the Africans in the Americas had not been stripped of their memories or their culture. When their ties to their villages and families were broken, they created bonds with shipmates. Such bonds became the basis of new extended families.

As this suggests, African slaves did not lose all their culture during the middle passage and seasoning in the Americas. Their value system never totally replicated that of the plantation. Despite their ordeal, the Africans who survived the Atlantic slave trade and slavery in the Americas were resilient. Seasoning did modify behavior, but it did not obliterate African Americans' cultural roots.

 Reading Check   How did masters treat slaves in the Americas?

The Ending of the Atlantic Slave Trade

The cruelties associated with the Atlantic slave trade contributed to its abolition in the early nineteenth century. During the late 1700s, English abolitionists led by Thomas Clarkson, William Wilberforce, and Granville Sharp began a religiously oriented moral crusade against both slavery and the slave trade. Because the English had dominated the Atlantic trade since 1713, Britain's growing antipathy became crucial to the trade's destruction. But it is debatable whether moral outrage alone prompted this humanitarian effort. By the late 1700s, England's economy was less dependent on the slave trade and the entire plantation system than it had been previously. To maintain its prosperity, England needed raw materials and markets for its manufactured goods. Slowly but surely its industrialists realized it was more profitable to invest in industry and other forms of trade and to leave Africans in Africa.

So morals and economic self-interest were combined when Great Britain abolished the Atlantic slave trade in 1807 and tried to enforce that abolition on other nations through a naval patrol off the coast of Africa. The U.S. Congress joined Britain in outlawing the Atlantic trade the following year. Although American, Brazilian, and Spanish slavers continued to defy these prohibitions for many years, the forced migration from Africa to the Americas dropped to a tiny percentage of what it had been at its peak. Ironically, it was the coastal kingdoms of Guinea and western Central Africa that fought most fiercely to keep the trade going because their economies had become dependent on it. This persistence gave the English, French, Belgians, and Portuguese an excuse to establish colonial empires in Africa during the nineteenth century in the name of suppressing the slave trade.

 Reading Check   Why did the Atlantic slave trade end?

Generalizing From Multiple Sources

A generalization is a broad statement based on multiple examples or facts, often from various sources. Valid generalizations are useful for summing up information. The illustration and the quotation below relate to the experience of Africans being sold at auction after arriving in the West Indies on slave ships. In the excerpt from his autobiography, Olaudah Equiano described one such experience, called a "scramble."

This nineteenth-century engraving suggests the humiliation Africans endured as they were subjected to physical inspections before being sold.

LEARN THE SKILL

Use the following steps to make generalizations:

1. **Learn the main ideas of each source.** Consider both the information and the time period. Look at the illustration as a whole; then study the details. Refer to the caption for more information.

2. **List relevant facts.** Determine which facts in the sources support each main idea. Note how the illustration conveys information and how it creates a mood or an emotion.

3. **Find a common element.** Look for general trends, or a common thread, in the ideas stated in the sources. Also look for patterns or trends in the details and facts.

4. **Make a generalization.** "Add up" the facts and ideas in your sources to make a general statement. Be sure that you can support your generalization with facts and that it is not too broad. Valid generalizations often include words such as *many, most, often, usually, some, few,* and *sometimes*. Faulty generalizations may include words such as *all, none, always, never,* and *every*.

PRACTICE THE SKILL

Answer the following questions:

1. **(a)** What is the main idea of the excerpt? **(b)** What time period does it cover? **(c)** What is the main idea of the illustration? **(d)** What time period does the illustration refer to?

From *The Interesting Narrative of the Life of Olaudah Equiano or Gustavus Vassa,* 1789

"We were conducted immediately to the merchant's yard, where we were all pent up together like so many sheep in a fold without regard to sex or age . . . we were sold after their usual manner, which is this: On a signal given, (as the beat of a drum) the buyers rush at once into the yard where the slaves are confined, and make choice of that parcel they like best. The noise and clamor with which this is attended and the eagerness visible in the countenances of the buyers serve not a little to increase the apprehensions of the terrified Africans."

2. **(a)** What main idea do both sources share? **(b)** How does the illustration support the quotation and vice versa? In other words, what is the benefit of having these two kinds of sources?

3. What valid generalizations can you make about **(a)** slave auctions, **(b)** the experience of Olaudah Equiano, and **(c)** the experience of Africans?

Climatic change and warfare destroyed the Mississippian culture during the fourteenth century, and only remnants of it existed when Europeans and Africans arrived in North America. By that time, a diverse variety of Indian cultures existed in what is today the eastern portion of the United States. People resided in towns and villages, supplementing their agricultural economies with fishing and hunting. They held land communally, generally allowed women a voice in ruling councils, and—although warlike—regarded battle as an opportunity for young men to prove their bravery rather than as a means of conquest. Gravely weakened by diseases that settlers unwittingly brought from Europe, the woodlands Indians of North America's coastal regions were ineffective in resisting British settlers during the seventeenth century. Particularly in the Southeast, the British developed an extensive trade in Indian slaves.

But because the Indians were experts at living harmoniously with the natural resources of North America, they influenced the way people of African and European descent came to live there as well. Indian crops, such as corn, potatoes, pumpkins, beans, and squash, became staples of the newcomers' diets. On the continent's southeastern coast, British cultivation of tobacco, an Indian crop, secured the economic survival of the Chesapeake colonies and led directly to the enslavement in them of Africans. The Indian canoe became a means of river transportation for black and white people, and Indian moccasins became common footwear for everyone.

▶▶ **Living Words**

Track 3 *"Bars Fight"*: poem by Lucy Terry Prince; read by Arna Bontemps

▶▶ **Document**

3-6 *Lucy Terry Prince, "Bars Fight," 1746*
Stories about Indians kidnapping women and children were quite popular during the colonial period. As a distinct genre known today as "captivity narratives" they provide historians with firsthand accounts of Native American life. "Bars Fight" recounts the death of two families who were killed in an Indian attack at Deerfield, Massachusetts on August 26, 1646. Composed by Lucy Terry Prince, who was only 22-years-old when the attack occurred, "Bars Fight" marked her as the first black woman to write a poem. For decades the poem was recited or sung before it was finally published in 1855. The original meaning of the word "bars" is lost on modern readers, but in colonial America it meant meadows.

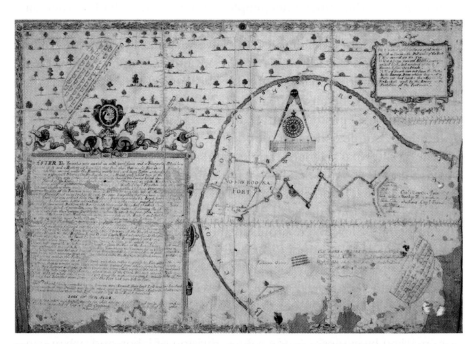

Escaping slaves in the Carolinas sometimes found shelter with the Tuscaroras and other Indian tribes. This map shows a Tuscarora fort that escaped slaves probably helped design and build.

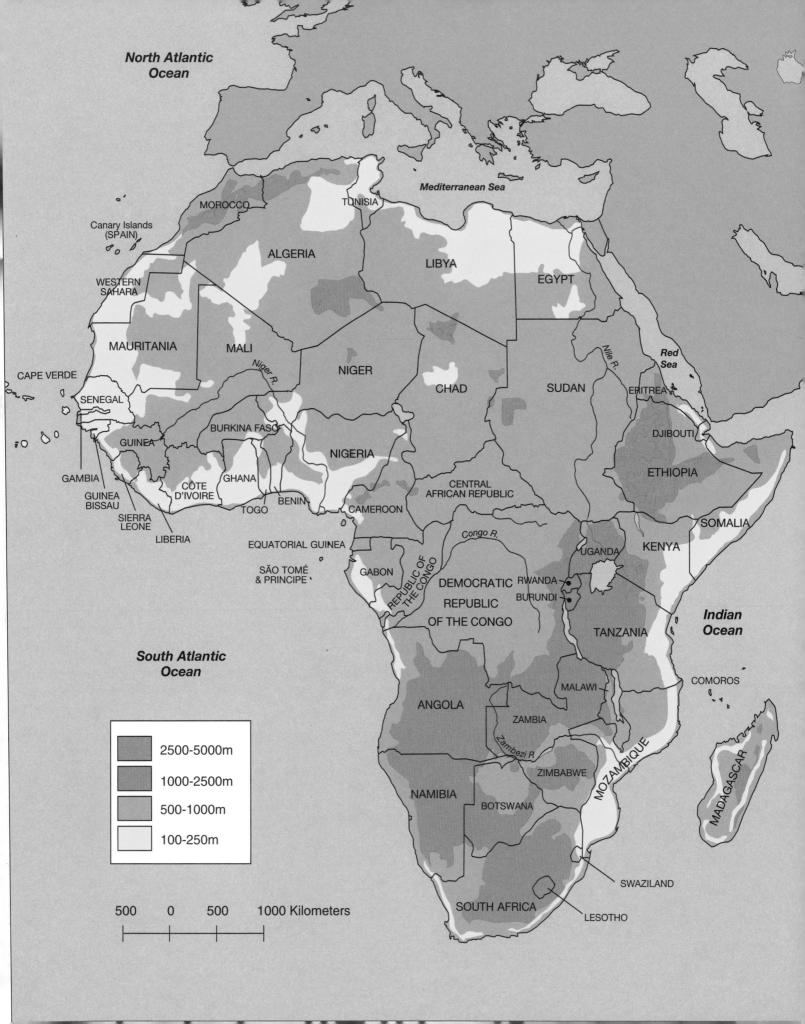

North Atlantic Ocean

MOROCCO

TUNISIA

Canary Islands (SPAIN)

ALGERIA

LIBYA

Mediterranean Sea

EGYPT

WESTERN SAHARA

MAURITANIA

MALI

NIGER

CHAD

SUDAN

Nile R.

Red Sea

ERITREA

CAPE VERDE

SENEGAL

Niger R.

DJIBOUTI

BURKINA FASO

GAMBIA

GUINEA

NIGERIA

ETHIOPIA

GUINEA BISSAU

CÔTE D'IVOIRE

GHANA

SIERRA LEONE

TOGO

BENIN

CENTRAL AFRICAN REPUBLIC

SOMALIA

LIBERIA

CAMEROON

KENYA

EQUATORIAL GUINEA

Congo R.

UGANDA

SÃO TOMÉ & PRINCIPE

GABON

REPUBLIC OF THE CONGO

DEMOCRATIC REPUBLIC OF THE CONGO

RWANDA

BURUNDI

Indian Ocean

South Atlantic Ocean

TANZANIA

MALAWI

COMOROS

ANGOLA

ZAMBIA

Zambezi R.

ZIMBABWE

MADAGASCAR

NAMIBIA

MOZAMBIQUE

BOTSWANA

	2500–5000m
	1000–2500m
	500–1000m
	100–250m

SWAZILAND

500   0   500   1000 Kilometers

SOUTH AFRICA

LESOTHO

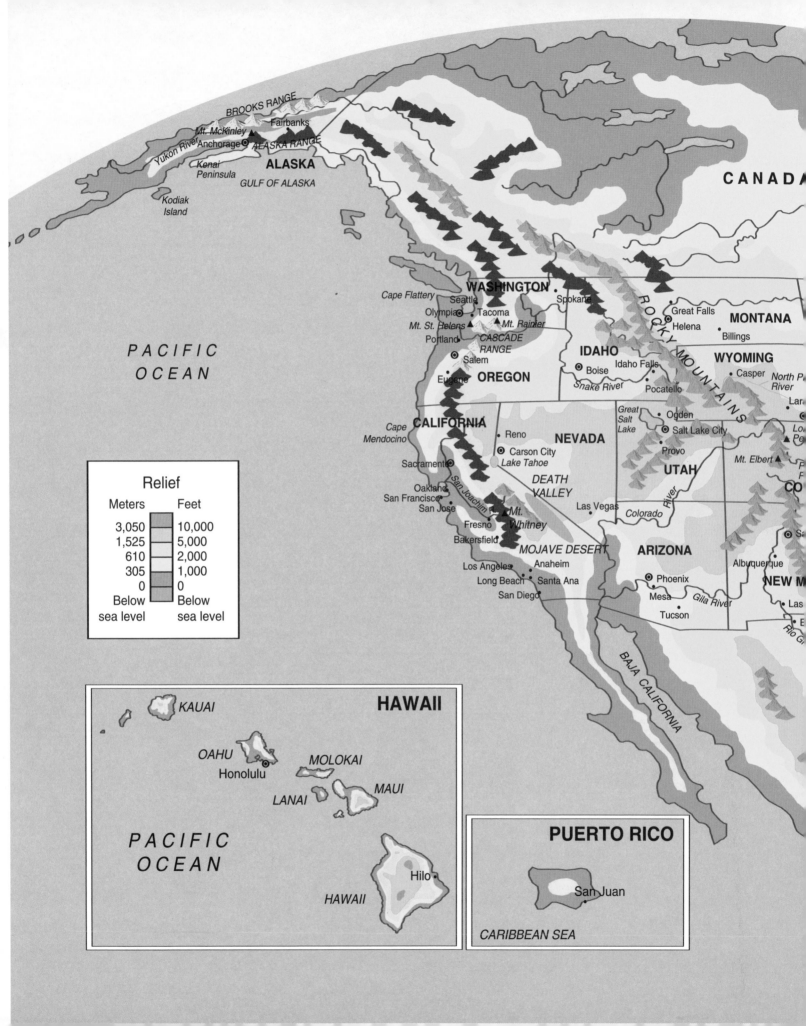

1600

SLAVE TRADE	WORLD EVENTS
1610	**1607**
Dutch drive Portuguese from Africa's west coast	Founding of Jamestown
1619	**1620**
Africans reported to be in British North America	Pilgrims reach New England

1650

1662	**1688**
Portuguese destroy Kongo Kingdom	England's Glorious Revolution
1674	
England drives the Dutch out of the slave trade	

1700

1713	**1728**
England begins its domination of the slave trade	Russian exploration of Alaska begins
c. 1745	
Olaudah Equiano born	

1750

1752	**1776**
British Royal African Company disbands	American Declaration of Independence
	1789
	United States Constitution ratified

1800

1807	**1815**
Great Britain abolishes the Atlantic slave trade	Napolean defeated at the Battle of Waterloo
1808	
United States abolishes the Atlantic slave trade	

Chapter Review and Assessment

SUMMARY

Section 1 European Exploration And Colonization, p. 37

▶ The Atlantic slave trade has its origins in Western Europe's expansion that began in the fifteenth century.

▶ When Portuguese travellers arrived in West Africa, they found a thriving slave trade, fuelled by demand for slaves in Muslim countries.

▶ Europeans became a new set of consumers in this trade.

▶ The cultivation of sugar in the New World provided an important stimulus for the rapid expansion of the slave trade between Africa and the Americas.

Section 2 From Capture To Destination, p. 45

▶ Many of the Africans who were shipped to the Americas were enslaved as a result of the warfare that accompanied the formation of West African states.

▶ Captured slaves were marched to coastal factories where they were processed before transportation to the Americas.

▶ Conditions on board slavers were horrible and many slaves died during the long voyage, most from disease.

▶ In addition, female slaves were subject to the sexual predation of sailors. Slaves frequently rebelled or committed suicide, taking one last opportunity to control their own fate.

Section 3 Landing and Sale in the West Indies, p. 58

▶ As slave ships arrived at their destinations, crews prepared their human cargo for sale, doing what they could to make the slaves look as strong and healthy as possible.

▶ Once sold, slaves were assigned to work gangs and endured seasoning, a disciplinary process designed to turn them into compliant and effective laborers.

▶ Despite the best efforts of planters, slaves were not completely desocialized by transportation and seasoning. They retained elements of their culture and reinforced these elements through the building of relationships with their fellow slaves.

▶ The Atlantic slave trade did not come to an end until the early nineteenth century, when a combination of moral and economic factors led to its abolition by Britain and the United States.

REVIEWING KEY TERMS

1. Atlantic slave trade, p. 37
2. chattel, p. 41
3. *Asiento*, p. 43
4. triangular trade systems, p. 44
5. factories, p. 45
6. slavers, p. 45
7. middle passage, 46
8. *Brookes*, p. 47
9. Olaudah Equiano, p. 48
10. indentured servant, p. 50
11. planters, p. 58
12. seasoning, p. 58
13. Creoles, p. 59
14. new Africans, p. 59
15. great gang, p. 60
16. drivers, p. 61

REVIEWING MAIN IDEAS

17. How did the Atlantic slave trade reflect the times during which it existed?

18. Think about Olaudah Equiano's experience as a young boy captured by traders and brought to a slave ship. What new and strange things did he encounter? How did he explain these things to himself? What kept him from descending into utter despair?

19. How could John Newton reconcile his Christian faith with his career as a slave-ship captain?

20. What human and natural variables could prolong the middle passage across the Atlantic Ocean? How could delay make the voyage more dangerous for slaves and crew?

21. How could Africans resist the dehumanizing forces of the middle passage and seasoning and use their African cultures to build black cultures in the New World?

ANALYZING DOCUMENTS

England Asserts Her Dominion through Legislation in 1660

. . . no goods or commodities whatsoever shall be imported into or exported out of any lands, islands, plantations or territories to his Majesty belonging or in his possession, or which may hereafter belong unto or be in the possession of his Majesty, his heirs, and successors, in *Asia*, *Africa* or *America*, in any other ship or ships, vessel or vessels, whatsoever, but in such ships or vessels as do truly and without fraud belong only to the people of *England* . . . From the *Navigation Act of 1660*.

Making Inferences: Based on this brief passage, for whom and why do you think England created the Navigation Act? What affect did it have on England's control of the slave trade?

WRITING ACTIVITY

In a short report or research paper, consider these questions:

Why was the history of slavery repressed for so long? Why has interest in the subject grown in the past quarter of a century?

STUDY ONLINE!

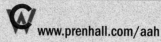 **www.prenhall.com/aah**

Additional study resources are available for this chapter on the *Companion Website*.

▶▶ **Review and Assessment**

For answers, see the *Teacher's Resource Manual*.

Enslaved black men, women, and children engage in curing tobacco.

Chapter 3

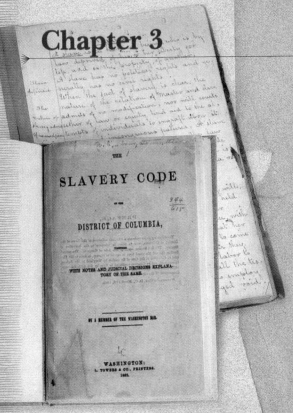

Whereas, the plantations and estates of this Province [of South Carolina] cannot be well and sufficiently managed and brought into use, without the labor and service of negroes and other slaves; and forasmuch as the said negroes and other slaves brought unto the People of the Province for that purpose, are of barbarous, wild, savage natures, and such as renders them wholly unqualified to be governed by the laws, customs, and practices of this Province; . . . it is absolutely necessary, that such other constitutions, laws and orders, should in this Province be made and enacted, for the good regulating and ordering of them, as may restrain the disorderly rapines and inhumanity, to which they are naturally prone and induced; and may also tend to the safety and security of the people of this Province and their estates.

—From the introduction to the original South Carolina Slave Code of 1696.

Slavery codes regulated slaves and asserted the rights of slave owners.

 Why were codes such as those described in this excerpt created?

Chapter Preview

The passage that begins this chapter is an excellent example of what we can learn about African-American history by reading between the lines in the official publications of the colonial governments. It reveals the willingness of British and other European settlers in North America to brand Africans and their American descendants as "barbarous, wild, [and] savage." Although real cultural differences underlay such negative perceptions, white people used them to justify oppressing black people. Black people by the 1640s could be enslaved for life. Black people did not enjoy the same legal protection as white people and were punished more harshly.

This chapter describes the history of African-American life in colonial North America from the early sixteenth century to the end of the French and Indian War in 1763. It briefly covers the black experience in Spanish Florida, in New Spain's borderlands in the Southwest, and in French Louisiana, but concentrates on the British colonies that stretched along the eastern coast of the continent. During the seventeenth century, the plantation system took shape in the Chesapeake tobacco country and in the low country of South Carolina and Georgia.

▶ **Witnessing History**

Slave owners believed that they needed the labor of enslaved Africans for their colony to prosper. They feared Africans, and the codes were a way to control them.

Section 1

The Peoples of North America

GUIDE TO READING

▶ Who were the peoples of colonial North America?

▶ What was the relationship between black people and Indians during the colonial period?

▶ Why did white labor produce most of the tobacco in the Chesapeake colonies until 1700?

KEY TERMS

▶ indigenous peoples, p. 71

▶ Indians, p. 71

▶ Cahokia, p. 71

In the North American colonies during the seventeenth and eighteenth centuries, African immigrants gave birth to a new African-American people. Born in North America and forever separated from their ancestral homeland, they preserved a surprisingly large core of their African cultural heritage. Meanwhile, a new natural environment and contacts with people of American Indian and European descent helped African Americans shape a way of life within the circumstances that slavery forced on them. To understand the early history of African Americans, we must first briefly discuss the other peoples of colonial North America.

American Indians

Historians and anthropologists group the original inhabitants of North America together as American Indians. But when the British began to colonize the coastal portion of this huge region during the early seventeenth century, the **indigenous peoples** who lived there had no such all-inclusive name. They spoke many different languages, lived in diverse environments, and considered themselves distinct from one another. Europeans called them **Indians** as a result of Christopher Columbus's mistaken assumption in 1492 that he had landed on islands near the "Indies," by which he meant near Southeast Asia.

In Mexico, Central America, and Peru, American Indian peoples developed complex, densely populated civilizations with hereditary monarchies, formal religions, armies, and social classes. The peoples of what is today the United States were influenced by cultural developments in Mexico and by the northerly spread of the cultivation of maize (corn). In what is today the American Southwest, the Anasazi, Hopi, and later Pueblo peoples developed sophisticated farming communities. In the region east of the Mississippi River, known as the Eastern Woodlands, the Adena culture, which flourished in the Ohio River valley as early as 1000 BCE, had attained the social organization required to construct large burial mounds. Between the tenth and fourteenth centuries CE, what is known as the Mississippian culture established a sophisticated civilization, marked by extensive trade routes, division of labor, and urban centers. The largest such center was **Cahokia**—located near modern St. Louis—which at its peak had a population of about thirty thousand.

▶▶ Guide to Reading/Key Terms

For answers, see the *Teacher's Resource Manual.*

▶▶ **Teaching Notes**

Like other Indian peoples of the western hemisphere, these indigenous peoples are believed to have descended from Asians who had migrated eastward across a land bridge connecting Siberia and Alaska at least 12,000 years ago.

Climatic change and warfare destroyed the Mississippian culture during the fourteenth century, and only remnants of it existed when Europeans and Africans arrived in North America. By that time, a diverse variety of Indian cultures existed in what is today the eastern portion of the United States. People resided in towns and villages, supplementing their agricultural economies with fishing and hunting. They held land communally, generally allowed women a voice in ruling councils, and—although warlike—regarded battle as an opportunity for young men to prove their bravery rather than as a means of conquest. Gravely weakened by diseases that settlers unwittingly brought from Europe, the woodlands Indians of North America's coastal regions were ineffective in resisting British settlers during the seventeenth century. Particularly in the Southeast, the British developed an extensive trade in Indian slaves.

But because the Indians were experts at living harmoniously with the natural resources of North America, they influenced the way people of African and European descent came to live there as well. Indian crops, such as corn, potatoes, pumpkins, beans, and squash, became staples of the newcomers' diets. On the continent's southeastern coast, British cultivation of tobacco, an Indian crop, secured the economic survival of the Chesapeake colonies and led directly to the enslavement in them of Africans. The Indian canoe became a means of river transportation for black and white people, and Indian moccasins became common footwear for everyone.

▶▶ **Living Words**

Track 3   *"Bars Fight"*: poem by Lucy Terry Prince; read by Arna Bontemps

▶▶ **Document**

3-6   *Lucy Terry Prince, "Bars Fight," 1746*
Stories about Indians kidnapping women and children were quite popular during the colonial period. As a distinct genre known today as "captivity narratives" they provide historians with firsthand accounts of Native American life. "Bars Fight" recounts the death of two families who were killed in an Indian attack at Deerfield, Massachusetts on August 26, 1646. Composed by Lucy Terry Prince, who was only 22-years-old when the attack occurred, "Bars Fight" marked her as the first black woman to write a poem. For decades the poem was recited or sung before it was finally published in 1855. The original meaning of the word "bars" is lost on modern readers, but in colonial America it meant meadows.

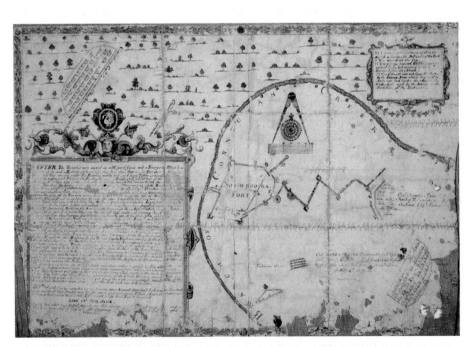

Escaping slaves in the Carolinas sometimes found shelter with the Tuscaroras and other Indian tribes. This map shows a Tuscarora fort that escaped slaves probably helped design and build.

The relationships between black people and Indians during colonial times were complex. Although Indian nations often provided refuge to escaping black slaves, Indians sometimes became slaveholders and on occasion helped crush black revolts. Some black men assisted in the Indian slave trade and sometimes helped defend European colonists against Indian attacks. Nevertheless, people of African and Indian descent frequently found themselves in similarly oppressive circumstances in Britain's American colonies.

The Spanish Empire

Following Christopher Columbus's voyage in 1492, the Spanish rapidly built a colonial empire in the Americas. Mining of gold and silver, as well as the production of sugar, tobacco, and leather goods, provided a firm economic foundation. Spain's colonial economy rested on the forced labor of the Indian population. When the Indian population declined from disease and overwork, they turned to enslaved Africans. Overseers in the mines and fields often brutally worked Africans and Indians to death. But because the Spanish were few, some of the Africans and Indians who survived were able to gain freedom and become tradesmen, small land-holders, and militiamen. Often they were of mixed race and identified with their former masters rather than with the oppressed people beneath them in society. African, Indian, and Spanish customs intermingled in what became a multicultural colonial society. Its center was in the West Indian islands of Cuba and Santo Domingo, Mexico, and northern South America. On its northern periphery were lands that are now part of the United States: Florida, Texas, Arizona, New Mexico, and California.

Africans came early to these borderlands. In 1526 Luis Vasquez de Ayllon brought one hundred African slaves with him from Hispaniola (modern Haiti and the Dominican Republic) in an attempt to establish a Spanish colony near what is now Georgetown, South Carolina. A decade later, slaves, who were either African or of African descent, accompanied Hernando de Soto on a Spanish expedition from Florida to the Mississippi River. In 1565 Africans helped construct the Spanish settlement of St. Augustine in Florida, which is now the oldest city in the continental United States. In 1528 a Spanish expedition that departed Cuba to search for gold in western Florida and the Gulf Coast included a slave of African descent named Esteban. Following a shipwreck, Esteban reached the coast of Texas. After a brief captivity among the local Indians, he and other survivors made their way southward to Mexico City.

The British and Jamestown

The British, like the Africans and the American Indians, were not a single nation. The British Isles—consisting principally of Britain and Ireland and located off the northwest coast of Europe—were the homeland

▶▶ **Recommended Reading**

Winthrop D. Jordon. *White over Black: American Attitudes toward the Negro, 1550-1812.* Chapel Hill, NC: University of North Carolina Press, 1968. This classic study provides a probing and detailed analysis of the cultural and psychological forces that led white people to enslave black people in early America.

Alan Gallay. *The Indian Slave Trade: The Rise of the English Empire in the American South, 1670-1717.* New Haven: Yale University Press, 2002.

John L. Kessell. *Spain in the Southwest: A Narrative History of Colonial New Mexico, Arizona, Texas, and California.* Norman: University of Oklahoma Press, 2002.

▶▶ **Teaching Notes**

While the powerful Spanish Empire colonized warm, populous, and wealthy regions of the Americas, the relatively less powerful British acquired lands that were cooler, less populous, and deficient in easily acquired wealth.

of the English, Welsh, Scots, and Irish. At that time, the Kingdom of England was, compared to Spain, a poor country notable mainly for producing wool.

England's claim to the east coast of North America rested on the voyage of John Cabot, who sailed in 1497, just five years after Columbus's first westward voyage. But, unlike the Spanish who rapidly created an empire in the Americas, the English were slow to establish themselves in the region Cabot had discovered. This was partly because of the harsher North American climate, with winters much colder than in England, but also because the English monarchy was too poor to finance colonizing expeditions and because the turmoil associated with the Protestant Reformation absorbed the nation's energies.

It took the English naval victory over the Spanish Armada in 1588 and money raised by joint-stock companies to produce in 1607 at Jamestown the first permanent British colony in North America. This settlement was located in the Chesapeake region the British called Virginia—after Queen Elizabeth I (r. 1558–1603), the so-called Virgin Queen of England. The company hoped to make a profit at Jamestown by finding gold, trading with the Indians, cutting lumber, or raising crops, such as rice, sugar, or silk, that could not be produced in Britain.

None of these schemes was economically viable. There was no gold, and the climate was unsuitable for rice, sugar, and silk. Because of disease, hostility with the Indians, and especially economic failure, the settlement barely survived into the 1620s. By then, however, the experiments begun in 1612 by the English settler John Rolfe to cultivate a mild strain of tobacco that could be grown on the North American mainland began to pay off. Tobacco was in great demand in Europe where smoking was becoming popular. Soon growing tobacco became the economic mainstay in Virginia and the neighboring colony of Maryland.

The sowing, cultivating, harvesting, and curing of tobacco were labor intensive. Yet colonists in the Chesapeake could not follow the Spanish example and enslave the Indians to produce the crop. Rampant disease had reduced the local Indian population, and those who survived eluded British conquest by retreating westward.

Unlike the West Indian sugar planters, however, the North American tobacco planters did not immediately turn to Africa for laborers. British advocates of colonizing North America had always promoted it as a solution to unemployment, poverty, and crime in England. The idea was to send England's undesirables to America, where they could provide the cheap labor tobacco planters needed. Consequently, until 1700, white labor produced most of the tobacco in the Chesapeake colonies.

✓ Reading Check   Who were the peoples of colonial North America?

▶ **Reading Check**

American Indians made up the indigenous population of the continent. The Spanish arrived in the late fifteenth century. They were joined by the French and the English and by African slaves.

▶ **Interactive Activity**

Jamestown

Historians have suggested that early and long-lasting frontier struggles for survival left an imprint on American folklore, heritage, and national character that distinguish the United States from older nations. An early example of this frontier struggle is the settlement of Jamestown. This activity focuses on important individuals who contributed to the colony's development. Primary source documents, visual images, and the narrative introductions bring the historical figures to life.

Section 2

Africans Arrive in the Chesapeake

Africans in Jamestown

By the early months of 1619, there were thirty-two people of African descent—fifteen men and seventeen women—living in the English colony at Jamestown. Nothing is known concerning when they had arrived or from where they had come. They were all "in the service of sev[er]all planters." The following August a Dutch warship, carrying seventeen African men and three African women from Angola, moored at Hampton Roads at the mouth of the James River. The Dutch warship, with the help of an English ship, had attacked a Portuguese slaver, taken most of its human cargo, and brought these twenty Angolans to Jamestown. The Dutch captain traded them to local officials in return for provisions.

The Angolans became servants to the Jamestown officials and to favored planters. The colony's inhabitants, for two reasons, regarded the new arrivals and those black people who had been in Jamestown earlier to be *unfree*, but not slaves. First, unlike the Portuguese and the Spanish, the English had no law for slavery. Second, at least the Angolans, who bore such names as Pedro, Isabella, Antoney, and Angelo, had been converted by the Portuguese to Christianity. According to English custom and morality in 1619, Christians could not be enslaved. So, once these individuals had worked off their purchase price, they could regain their freedom. In 1623, Antoney and Isabella married. The next year they became parents of William, whom their master had baptized in the local Church of England. William may have been the first black person born in English America. He was almost certainly born free.

During the following years, people of African descent remained a small minority in the expanding Virginia colony. A 1625 census reported only twenty-three black people living in the colony, compared with a combined total of 1,275 white people and Indians. This suggests that many of the first black inhabitants had either died or moved away. By 1649 the total Virginia population of about 18,500 included only 300 black people. The English, following the Spanish example, called them **negroes**. (The word "negro" means black in Spanish.) In neighboring Maryland, which was established as a haven

GUIDE TO READING

▶ How did black servitude develop in the Chesapeake?

▶ What role did indentured servitude play in the early economy of the Chesapeake colonies?

▶ What economic and demographic developments led to the enslavement of people of African descent in the British tobacco colonies?

KEY TERMS

▶ negroes, p. 75

▶ indentured servants, p. 76

▶ chattel slavery, p. 76

▶ House of Burgesses, p. 79

▶ Bacon's rebellion, p. 80

▶▶ **Guide to Reading/Key Terms**

For answers, see the *Teacher's Resource Manual*.

▶▶ **Teaching Notes**

For many years, historians believed that the Angolans were the first black people in British North America. They were part of a group of over 300 who had been taken from Angola by a Portuguese slaver that had set sail for the port city of Vera Cruz in New Spain (Mexico).

▶▶ **Recommended Reading**

Philip D. Morgan. *Slave Counterpoint: Black Culture in the Eighteenth-Century Chesapeake and Lowcountry.* Chapel Hill, NC: University of North Carolina Press, 1998. Comparative history at its best, this book illuminates the lives of black people in important parts of British North America.

in 1632 for persecuted English Catholics, the black population also remained small. In 1658 only 3 percent of Maryland's population was of African descent.

Black Servitude in the Chesapeake

During the early years of the Chesapeake colonies, black people represented a small part of a labor force composed mainly of white **indentured servants**. From the 1620s to the 1670s, black and white people worked in the tobacco fields together, lived together, and slept together (and also did these things with American Indians). As members of an oppressed working class, they were all unfree indentured servants.

Indentured servitude had existed in Europe for centuries. In England, parents indentured—or, in other words, apprenticed—their children to "masters," who controlled their lives and had the right to their labor for a set number of years. In return, the masters supported the children and taught them a trade or profession.

As the demand for labor to produce tobacco in the Chesapeake expanded, indentured servitude came to include adults who sold their freedom for two to seven years in return for the cost of their voyage to North America. Instead of training in a profession, the servants could improve their economic standing by remaining as free persons in America after completing their period of servitude.

When Africans first arrived in Virginia and Maryland, they entered into similar contracts, agreeing to work for their masters until the proceeds of their labor recouped the cost of their purchase. Such indentured servitude could be harsh in the tobacco colonies because masters sought to get as much labor as they could from their servants before the indenture ended. Most indentured servants died from overwork or disease before regaining their freedom. But those who survived, black people as well as white people, could expect eventually to leave their masters and seek their fortunes as free persons.

During the seventeenth century, free black men living in the Chesapeake participated fully in the commercial and legal life of the colony. They owned land, farmed, lent money, sued in the courts, served as jurors and as minor officials, and at times voted.

Prior to the 1670s the English in the Chesapeake did not draw a strict line between white freedom and black slavery. Yet the ruling elite had from the early 1600s treated black servants differently from white servants. Over the decades, the region's British population gradually came to assume that persons of African descent were alien. This sentiment did not become universal among the white poor during the colonial period. It was a foundation for what historian Winthrop D. Jordan calls the "unthinking decision" among the British in the Chesapeake to establish **chattel slavery**, in which slaves were legally private property on a level with livestock, as the proper condition for Africans and those of African descent.

▶ Recommended Readings

Oscar Reiss. *Blacks in Colonial America.* Jefferson, NC: McFarland, 1997. Although short on synthesis and eccentric in interpretation, this book is packed with information about black life in early America.

Donald R. Wright. *African Americans in the Colonial Era: From African Origins through the American Revolution*, 2d edition. Arlington Heights, IL: Harlan Davidson, 2000. Wright provides a brief but well-informed survey of black history during the colonial period.

Race and the Origins of Black Slavery

Between 1640 and 1700, the British tobacco-producing colonies stretching from Delaware to northern Carolina underwent a social and demographic revolution. An economy based primarily on the labor of white indentured servants became an economy based on the labor of black slaves. In Virginia, for example, the slave population in 1671 was less than 5 percent of the colony's total non-Indian population. White indentured servants outnumbered black slaves by three to one. By 1700, however, slaves constituted at least 20 percent of Virginia's population. Probably most agricultural laborers were now slaves.

Although historians still debate how this extraordinary change occurred, several interrelated factors brought it about. Some of these factors are easily understood. Others are more complicated and profound, because they involve basic assumptions about the American nation.

PROFILE ❖ Anthony Johnson

Little is known of the individual Africans and African Americans who lived in North America during the seventeenth and eighteenth centuries. In rare instances, however, black people emerge from the bits and pieces of information preserved in court records. This is the case for Anthony Johnson and his family.

Anthony Johnson arrived at Jamestown in 1621 from England, but his original home may have been Angola. On the Bennett plantation, where he labored, he was one of four out of fifty-six inhabitants to survive. He was also lucky to wed "Mary a Negro Woman," who in 1625 was the only woman residing at Bennett's.

In 1635 Johnson's master, Nathaniel Littleton, released him from further service. He received his own 250-acre plantation in 1651 under the "headright system" by which the colonial government encouraged population growth by awarding fifty acres of land for every new servant a settler brought to Virginia.

This meant that Johnson had become the master of five servants, some of them white. His estate was in Northampton County. A few years later, his relatives, John and Richard Johnson, also acquired land in this area.

The Johnson estates existed among white-owned properties in the same area. Like their white neighbors, the Johnsons were not part of the planting elite, but they owned their own land, farmed, and had social, economic, and legal relations with other colonists. Anthony Johnson in particular engaged in litigation that tells us much about black life in early Virginia.

In 1654 his lawsuit against his black servant John Casor and a white neighbor set a precedent in favor of black slavery but also revealed Johnson's legal rights. Casor claimed that Johnson "had kept him his serv[an]t seven years longer than hee should or ought." Johnson momentarily relented when he realized that if he persisted in his suit, Casor could win damages against him. Shortly thereafter, however, Johnson brought suit against his white neighbor Robert Parker, whom Johnson charged had detained Casor "under pretense [that] the s[ai]d John Casor is a freeman." This time the court ruled in Johnson's favor. It returned Casor to him and required Parker to pay court costs.

During the 1660s, the extended Johnson family moved to Somerset, Maryland. They were still prospering as planters during the early eighteenth century. Some family members moved on to New Jersey and others to Delaware, where some of them intermarried with the Nanticoke Indians.

Johnson

Among the economic and demographic developments that led to the enslavement of people of African descent in the tobacco colonies was the precedent for enslaving Africans set in the British Caribbean sugar colonies during the second quarter of the seventeenth century. Also, Britain was gaining more control over the Atlantic slave trade at a time when fewer English men and women were willing to indenture themselves in return for passage to the Chesapeake. Poor white people found better opportunities for themselves in other regions of British North America, driving up the price of European indentured servants in the tobacco colonies. Meanwhile, British control of the slave trade made African laborers cheaper in those colonies.

These changing circumstances provide the context for the beginnings of black slavery in British North America. Yet race and class played the crucial role in shaping the *character* of slavery in the British mainland colonies. From the first arrival of Africans in the Chesapeake, those English who exercised authority made decisions that qualified the apparent social mobility the Africans enjoyed. The English had historically made distinctions between how they treated each other and how they treated those who were physically and culturally different from them. Such discrimination had been the basis of their colonial policies toward the Irish, whom the English had been trying to conquer for centuries, and the American Indians. Because they considered Africans even more different from themselves than either the Irish or the Indians, the English assumed from the beginning that Africans were generally inferior to themselves.

Therefore, although black and white servants residing in the Chesapeake during the early seventeenth century had much in common, their masters immediately made distinctions between them based on race. The few women of African descent who arrived in the Chesapeake during those years worked in the tobacco fields with the male servants, whereas most white women were assigned domestic duties. Also, unlike white servants, black servants usually did not have surnames, and early census reports listed them separately from whites. By the 1640s, black people could not bear arms, and during the same decade, local Anglican priests (although not those in England itself) maintained that persons of African descent could not become Christians.

These distinctions suggest that the status of black servants had never been the same as that of white servants. But only starting in the 1640s do records indicate a predilection toward making black people slaves rather than servants. During that decade, courts in Virginia and Maryland began to reflect an assumption that it was permissible for persons of African descent to serve their master for life rather than for a set term.

One court case, which was heard in 1640, involved the escape of three servants from Virginia to Maryland. One of the escapees was Dutch, another was a Scot, and the third—named John Punch—was of African descent. Following their capture and return to Virginia, a court ruled that all three should be whipped, that the Scot and Dutchman should have their terms of service extended for four years, and that Punch "being a

▶▶ **Documents**

3-1 *Maryland Addresses the Status of Slaves in 1664*
Although slavery dates back before 2000 BCE to the Sumerians, the status of black slaves in the early years of colonization in Maryland was unclear. Were they to serve a limited number of years? Were they the property of their owners to do with as they saw fit? This excerpt is from the *Maryland Statute on Negroes and Other Slaves*, which established that all blacks, as well as their children and their families, would be slaves *durante vita*, that is, for their entire lives.

negro . . . serve his said master or his assigns for the time of his natural life." By mid-decade, black men, women, and children were often sold for higher prices than their white counterparts on the explicit provision that the black people would serve "for their Life tyme," or "for ever."

The Emergence of Chattel Slavery

Legal documents and statute books reveal that, during the 1660s, other aspects of chattel slavery emerged in the Chesapeake colonies. Bills of sale began to stipulate that the children of black female servants would also be servants for life. In 1662 Virginia's **House of Burgesses** decreed that a child's condition—free or unfree—followed that of the mother. This ran counter to English common law, which assumed that a child's status derived from the father. The change permitted masters to exploit their black female servants without having to acknowledge the children who might result from such contacts. Just as significant, by the mid-1660s statutes in the Chesapeake colonies assumed servitude to be the natural condition of black people.

With these laws, slavery in British North America emerged in the form that it retained until the American Civil War: a racially defined system of perpetual involuntary servitude that compelled almost all black people to work as agricultural laborers. Slave codes enacted between 1660 and 1710 further defined American slavery as a system that sought as much to control persons of African descent as to exploit their labor. Slaves could not testify against white people in court, own property, leave their master's estate without a pass, congregate in groups larger than three or four, enter into contracts, marry, or, of course, bear arms. Profession of Christianity no longer protected a black person from enslavement nor was conversion a cause for manumission. In 1669 the House of Burgesses exempted from felony charges masters who killed a slave while administering punishment.

By 1700, just as the slave system began to expand in the southern colonies, enslaved Africans and African Americans had been reduced legally to the status of domestic animals except that, unlike animals (or masters when it came to abusing slaves), the law held slaves to be strictly accountable for their transgressions.

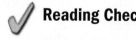 **Reading Check**   How did black servitude develop in the Chesapeake?

Bacon's Rebellion and American Slavery

The series of events that led to the enslavement of black people in the Chesapeake tobacco colonies preceded their emergence as the great majority of laborers in those colonies. The dwindling supply of white indentured servants, the growing availability of Africans, and preexisting white racial biases affected this transformation. But the key event in bringing it about was the rebellion led by Nathaniel Bacon in 1676.

▶▶ **Reading Check**

In the early years, black people represented a small part of the labor force in the Chesapeake. White indentured servants made up the majority of the labor force. During this period, Africans worked as indentured servants and free black men participated fully in the life of the colony. However, as white laborers found better opportunities, and demand for tobacco increased, a shift to black slave labor occurred.

▶▶ **Documents**

3-2   *The Selling of Joseph, 1700*
In addition to being an important merchant in Boston, Massachusetts, Samuel Sewell had also been a judge during the Salem witch trials, which he later regretted and made a public apology. In 1697 he wrote a tract against the slave trade, making *The Selling of Joseph* one of the first antislavery publications in America.

3-3   *A Virginian Describes the Difference between Servants and Slaves in 1722*
Robert Beverly, who wrote *The History and Present State of Virginia* in 1705, worked at various government positions in the early Virginia colony before being dismissed for criticizing several public events. Beverly published a revised version in 1722, from which this passage is taken. In the excerpt he tries to distinguish between the role of servants and slaves and outlines some of the legal rights accorded servants, which, by omission, also illustrates the legal rights that were denied slaves.

▶▶ **Retracing the Odyssey**

Colonial Williamsburg, Williamsburg, Virginia. The "Enslaving Virginia Tour" allows visitors to "explore [the] conditions that led to slavery's development in the Jamestown/Virginia colony."

Bacon's Rebellion. Nathaniel Bacon (center) and his followers at the burning of Jamestown, Virginia on 19 September 1676. Illustration by Howard Pyle.

Bacon was an English aristocrat who had recently migrated to Virginia. The immediate cause of **Bacon's rebellion** was a disagreement between him and the colony's royal governor William Berkeley over Indian policy. Bacon's followers were mainly white indentured servants and former indentured servants who resented the control exercised by the tobacco-planting elite over the colony's resources and government. That Bacon also appealed to black slaves to join his rebellion indicates that poor white and black people still had a chance to unite against the master class.

Before such a class-based, biracial alliance could be realized, Bacon died of dysentery, and his rebellion collapsed. But the uprising convinced the colony's elite that continuing to rely on white agricultural laborers, who could become free and get guns, was dangerous. By switching from indentured white servants to an enslaved black labor force that would never become free or control firearms, the planters hoped to avoid class conflict among white people. Increasingly thereafter, white Americans perceived that both their freedom from class conflict and their prosperity rested on denying freedom to black Americans.

Section 3

Plantation Slavery, 1700–1750

GUIDE TO READING

▶ What were the characteristics of plantation slavery from 1700 to 1750?

▶ Under what conditions did enslaved black laborers in the tobacco colonies work before 1750?

▶ What were the defining characteristics of low-country slavery?

▶ What were the material conditions of slave life in Early America?

KEY TERMS

▶ low country, p. 83

▶ miscegenation, p. 87

▶ creolization, p. 87

▶ mulattoes, p. 87

The reliance of Chesapeake planters on slavery to meet their labor needs was thus the result of racial prejudice, the declining availability of white indentured servants, the increasing availability of Africans, and fear of white class conflict. When the demand for tobacco in Europe increased sharply, the newly dominant slave labor system expanded rapidly.

Tobacco Colonies

Between 1700 and 1770, some 80,000 Africans arrived in the tobacco colonies, and even more African Americans were born into slavery there (see Figure 3–1). Tobacco planting spread from Virginia and Maryland to Delaware and North Carolina and from the coastal plain to the foothills of the Appalachian Mountains. In the process, American slavery began to assume the form it kept for the next 165 years.

By 1750, 144,872 slaves lived in Virginia and Maryland, accounting for 61 percent of all the slaves in British North America. Another 40,000 slaves lived in the rice-producing regions of South Carolina and Georgia, accounting for 17 percent. Unlike the sugar colonies of the Caribbean, where whites were a tiny minority, whites remained a majority in the tobacco colonies and a large minority in the rice

From Servitude to Slavery

1619 Thirty-two Africans reported to be living at Jamestown. Twenty more arrive

1621 Anthony Johnson arrives at Jamestown

1624 First documented birth of a black child occurs at Jamestown

1640 John Punch is sentenced to servitude for life

1651 Anthony Johnson receives estate of 250 acres

1661 House of Burgesses (the Virginia colonial legislature) recognizes that black servants would retain that status throughout their life

1662 House of Burgesses affirms that a child's status—slave or free— follows the status of her or his mother

▶▶ Guide to Reading/Key Terms

For answers, see the *Teacher's Resource Manual*.

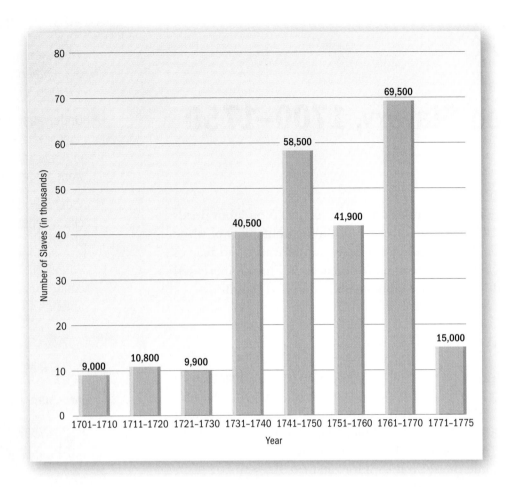

FIGURE 3–1 Africans Brought as Slaves to British North America, 1701–1775.

The rise in the number of captive Africans shipped to British North America during the early eighteenth century reflects the increasing dependence of British planters on African slave labor.

Source: R. C. Simmons, *The American Colonies: From Settlement to Independence* (New York: David McKay, 1976).

▶ Map 3-1

The French and Spanish slaves had easier routes to freedom than slaves in the British colonies, which provided African Americans in the British colonies with examples of hope for future freedoms.

colonies. Also, most southern whites did not own slaves. Nevertheless, the economic development of the region depended on enslaved black laborers.

The conditions under which those laborers lived varied. Most slaveholders farmed small tracts of land and owned fewer than five slaves. These masters and their slaves worked together and developed close personal relationships. Other masters owned thousands of acres of land and rarely saw most of their slaves. During the early eighteenth century, the great planters divided their slaves among several small holdings. They did this to avoid concentrating potentially rebellious Africans in one area. As the proportion of newly arrived Africans in the slave population declined later in the century, larger concentrations of slaves became more common.

Before the mid-eighteenth century, nearly all slaves—both men and women—worked in the fields. On the smaller farms, they worked with their master. On larger estates, they worked for an overseer, who was usually white. Like other agricultural workers, enslaved African Americans normally worked from sunup to sundown with breaks for food and rest. Even during colonial times, they usually had Sunday off.

From the beginnings of slavery in North America, masters tried to make slaves work harder and faster while the slaves sought to conserve their energy, take breaks, and socialize with each other. African men regarded field labor as women's work and tried to avoid it if possible. But, especially if they had incentives, enslaved Africans could be efficient workers.

Not until after 1750 did some black men begin to hold such skilled occupations on plantations as carpenter, smith, carter, cooper, miller, sawyer, tanner, and shoemaker. Black women had less access to such occupations. When they did not work in the fields, they were domestic servants in the homes of their masters, cooking, washing, cleaning, and caring for children. Such duties could be extremely taxing, because, unlike field-work, they did not end when the sun went down.

Low-Country Slavery

South of the tobacco colonies, on the coastal plain, or **low country**, of Carolina and Georgia a distinctive slave society developed (see Map 3–1). The influence of the West Indian plantation system was much stronger here than in the Chesapeake, and rice, not tobacco, became the staple crop.

The first British settlers who arrived in 1670 at Charleston (in what would later become South Carolina) were mainly immigrants from Barbados, rather than England. Many of them had been slaveholders on that island and brought slaves with them. In the low country, black people were chattel from the start. The region's subtropical climate discouraged white settlement and encouraged dependence on black labor the way it did in the sugar islands. During the early years of settlement, nearly one-third of the immigrants were African, most of them males. By the early eighteenth century, more Africans were arriving than white people.

Carolina Low Country

By 1740 the Carolina low country had 40,000 slaves, who constituted 90 percent of the population in the region around Charleston. In all, 94,000 Africans arrived at Charleston between 1706 and 1776, which made it North America's leading port of entry for Africans during the eighteenth century. A Swiss immigrant commented in 1737 that the region "looks more like a negro country than like a country settled by white people."

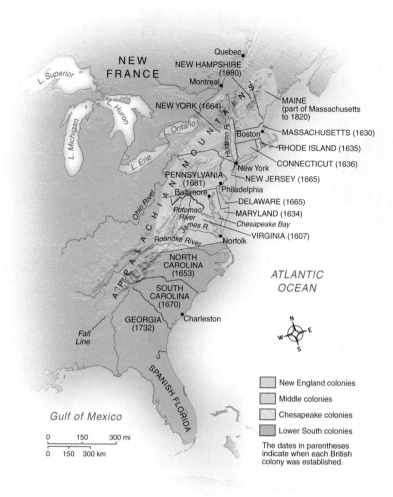

MAP 3–1 Regions of Colonial North America, 1683–1763.

The British colonies on the North American mainland were divided into four regions. They were bordered on the south by Spanish Florida and to the west by regions claimed by France.

 How did African Americans in the British colonies benefit from the close proximity of regions controlled by France and Spain?

Explore this map online at www.prenhall.com/aah/map3.1

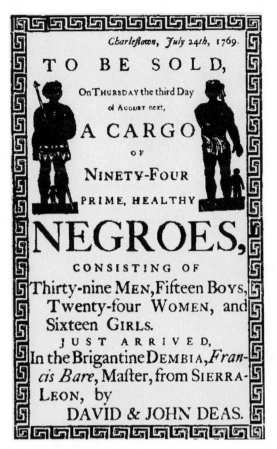

Sales like the one announced in this 1769 broadside were common in the low country.

▶ **Teaching Notes**

White Carolinians also enslaved more Indians than other British colonists did, and during the early 1700s approximately one-quarter of the colony's slave population was Indian. Carolina was also the center of an Indian slave trade. Although official colonial policy was to keep Africans and Indians apart, black slaves sometimes helped acquire and transport Indian slaves. Carolina exported Indian slaves to the West Indies and to other mainland British colonies.

▶ **Recommended Readings**

Peter H. Wood. *Black Majority: Negroes in Colonial South Carolina from 1670 through the Stono Rebellion.* New York: Norton, 1974. This is the best account available of slavery and the origins of African-American culture in the colonial low country.

Alan Gallay. *The Indian Slave Trade: The Rise of the English Empire in the American South, 1670–1717.* New Haven: Yale University Press, 2002.

During its first three decades, Carolina supplied Barbados with beef and lumber. Because West Africans from the Gambia River region were skilled herders, white settlers sought them out as slaves. Starting around 1700, however, the low-country planters concentrated on growing rice. Rice had been grown in West Africa for thousands of years, and many of the enslaved Africans who reached Carolina had the skill required to cultivate it in America. Economies of scale, in which an industry becomes more efficient as it grows larger, were more important in the production of rice than tobacco. Although tobacco could be profitably produced on small farms, rice required large acreages. Therefore, large plantations on a scale similar to those on the sugar islands of the West Indies became the rule in the low country.

Georgia Low Country

In 1732 King George II of England chartered the colony of Georgia to serve as a buffer between South Carolina and Spanish Florida. James Oglethorpe, who received the royal charter, wanted to establish a refuge for England's poor, who were expected to become virtuous through their own labor. Consequently, in 1734 he and the colony's other trustees banned slavery in Georgia. But economic difficulties combined with land hunger among white South Carolinians soon led to the ban's repeal. During the 1750s, rice cultivation and slavery spread into Georgia's coastal plain. By 1773 Georgia had as many black people—15,000—as white people.

As on Barbados, absentee plantation owners became the rule in South Carolina and Georgia because planters preferred to live in Charleston or Savannah where sea breezes provided relief from the heat. Enslaved Africans on low-country plantations suffered from a high mortality rate from diseases, overwork, and poor treatment just as did their counterparts on Barbados and other sugar islands. Therefore, unlike the slave population in the Chesapeake colonies, the slave population in the low country did not grow by reproducing itself—rather than through continued arrivals from Africa—until shortly before the American Revolution.

Slave Society

This low-country slave society produced striking paradoxes in race relations during the eighteenth century. As the region's black population grew, white people became increasingly fearful of revolt, and by 1698 Carolina had the strictest slave code in North America. In 1721, Charleston organized a "Negro watch" to enforce a curfew on its black population, and watchmen could shoot Africans and African Americans on sight. Black people in Carolina faced the quandary of being both feared and needed by white people. Even as persons of European descent grew fearful of black revolt, the colony in 1704 authorized the arming of enslaved black men when needed for defense against Indian and Spanish raids.

Of equal significance was the appearance in Carolina and to some extent in Georgia of distinct classes among people of color. Like the low-country society itself, such classes were more similar to those in the Caribbean sugar islands than in the mainland colonies to the north. A creole population that had absorbed European values lived in close proximity to white people in Charleston and Savannah. Members of this creole population were frequently mixed-race relatives of their masters and enjoyed social and economic privileges denied to slaves who labored on the nearby rice plantations. Yet this urban mixed-race class was under constant white supervision.

In contrast, slaves who lived in the country retained considerable autonomy in their daily routines. The intense cultivation required to produce rice encouraged the evolution of a "task system" of labor on the low-country plantations. Rather than working in gangs as in the tobacco colonies, slaves on rice plantations had daily tasks. When they completed these tasks, they could work on plots of land assigned to them or do what they pleased without white supervision. Because black people were the great majority in the low-country plantations, they also preserved more of their African heritage than did black people who lived in the region's cities or in the more northerly British mainland colonies.

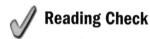 **Reading Check** What were the characteristics of plantation slavery from 1700 to 1750?

Slave Life in Early America

Little evidence survives of the everyday lives of enslaved Africans and African Americans in colonial North America. This is because they, along with Indians and most white people of that era, were poor. They had few possessions, lived in flimsy housing, and kept no records. Yet recent studies provide a glimpse of their material culture.

Eighteenth-century housing for slaves was minimal and often temporary. In the Chesapeake, small log cabins with dirt floors, brick fireplaces, wooden chimneys, and few, if any, windows were typical. African styles of architecture were more common in coastal South Carolina and Georgia. In these regions, slaves built the walls of their houses with tabby—a mixture of lime, oyster shells, and sand—or, occasionally, mud. In either case, the houses had thatched roofs. Early in the eighteenth century, when single African men made up the mass of the slave population, these structures were used as dormitories. Later they housed generations of black families.

The amount of furniture and cooking utensils the cabins contained varied from place to place and according to how long the cabins were occupied. In some cabins, the only furniture consisted of wooden boxes for both storage and seating and planks for beds. But a 1697 inventory of items contained in a slave cabin in Virginia includes chairs, a bed, a large iron kettle, a brass kettle, an iron pot, a frying pan, and a "beer barrel."

▶ **Reading Check**

Before the mid-eighteenth century, nearly all slaves worked in the fields. On smaller farms, they worked with their master. On larger farms, they worked under an overseer. African-American slaves worked from sunup to sundown with breaks for food and rest.

Slave quarters and the master's house at Mulberry Plantation, located near Charleston, South Carolina.

Enslaved black people, like contemporary Indians and white people, used hollowed-out gourds for cups and carted water in wooden buckets for drinking, cooking, and washing. As the eighteenth century progressed, slave housing on large plantations became more substantial, and slaves acquired tables, linens, chamber pots, and oil lamps. Yet primitive, poorly furnished log cabins persisted in many regions even after the abolition of slavery in 1865.

At first, slave dress was minimal during summer. Men wore breechcloths, women wore skirts, leaving their upper bodies bare, and children went naked until puberty. Later men wore shirts, trousers, and hats while working in the fields. Women wore shifts (loose, simple dresses) and covered their heads with handkerchiefs. In winter, masters provided more substantial cotton and woolen clothing and cheap leather shoes. In the early years, much of the clothing, or at least the cloth used to make it, came from England. Later, as the account of George Mason's Gunston Hall plantation indicates, homespun made by slaves replaced English cloth. From the seventeenth century onward, slave women brightened clothing with dyes made from bark, decorated clothing with ornaments, and created African-style headwraps, hats, and hairstyles. In this manner, African Americans retained a sense of personal style compatible with West African culture.

Food consisted of corn, yams, salt pork, and occasionally salt beef and salt fish. Slaves also caught fish and raised chickens and rabbits. When farmers in the Chesapeake began planting wheat during the eighteenth century, slaves baked biscuits. In the South Carolina low country, rice became an important part of African-American diets. During colonial times, slaves occasionally supplemented this limited diet with vegetables that they raised in their own gardens.

Miscegenation and Creolization

When Africans first arrived in the Chesapeake during the early seventeenth century, they interacted culturally and physically with white indentured servants and with American Indians. This mixing of peoples changed all three groups. Interracial sexual contacts—**miscegenation**—produced people of mixed race. Meanwhile, cultural exchanges became an essential part of the process of **creolization** that led African parents to produce African-American children. When, as often happened, miscegenation and creolization occurred together, the change was both physical and cultural. However, the dominant British minority in North America during the colonial period defined persons of mixed race as black. Although enslaved **mulattoes**—those of mixed African and European ancestry—enjoyed some advantages over slaves who had a purely African ancestry, mulattoes as a group did not receive enhanced legal status.

Miscegenation

Miscegenation between blacks and whites and blacks and Indians was extensive throughout British North America during the seventeenth and eighteenth centuries. But it was less extensive and accepted than it was in the European sugar colonies in the Caribbean, in Latin America, or in French Canada, where many French men married Indian women. British North America was exceptional because many more white women migrated there than to Canada or the Caribbean, so that white men did not have to take black or Indian wives and concubines.

Miscegenation between blacks and Indians was extensive, and striking examples of black-white marriage also occurred in seventeenth-century Virginia. For example, in 1656 in Northumberland County, a mulatto woman named Elizabeth Kay successfully sued for her freedom and immediately thereafter married her white lawyer. In Norfolk County in 1671, Francis Skiper had to pay a tax on his wife Anne because she was black. In Westmoreland County in 1691, Hester Tate, a white indentured servant, and her husband James Tate, a black slave, had four children; one was apprenticed to her master, and the other three to his.

Colonial assemblies banned such interracial marriages mainly to keep white women from bearing mulatto children. The assemblies feared that having free white mothers might allow persons of mixed race to sue and gain their freedom, thereby creating a legally recognized mixed-race class. Such a class, wealthy white people feared, would blur the distinction between the dominant and subordinate races and weaken white supremacy. The assemblies did little to prevent white male masters from exploiting their black female slaves—although they considered such exploitation immoral—because the children of such liaisons would be slaves.

▶ **Guide to Reading/Key Terms**

For answers, see the *Teacher's Resource Manual.*

▶ **Recommended Reading**

Peter Kolchin. *American Slavery, 1619–1877.* New York: Hill and Wang, 1993. This is the best brief study of the development of slavery in America. It is particularly useful on African-American community and culture.

Section 4

The Origins of African-American Culture

Families

Creolization and miscegenation transformed the descendants of the Africans who arrived in North America into African Americans. Historians long believed that in this process the creoles lost their African heritage. But scholars have found many African legacies not only in African-American culture but in American culture in general.

The second generation of people of African descent in North America did lose their parents' native languages and their ethnic identity as Igbos, Angolas, or Senegambians. But they retained a generalized West African heritage and passed it on to their descendants. Among the major elements of that heritage were family structure and notions of kinship, religious concepts and practices, African words and modes of expression, musical style and instruments, cooking methods and foods, folk literature, and folk arts.

The preservation of the West African extended family was the basis of African-American culture. Because most Africans imported into the British colonies during the late seventeenth and early eighteenth centuries were males, most black men of that era could not have wives and children. It was not until the Atlantic slave trade declined briefly during the 1750s that sex ratios became more balanced and African-American family life began to flourish. Without that family life, black people could not have maintained as much of Africa as they did.

Even during the middle passage, enslaved Africans created **fictive kin relationships** for mutual support, and in dire circumstances, African Americans continued to improvise family structures. By the mid-eighteenth century, however, extended black families based on biological relationships were prevalent. These extended families were rooted in Africa, but were also a result of—and a reaction to—slavery. West African incest taboos encouraged slaves to pick mates who lived on different plantations from their own. The sale of slaves away from their immediate families also tended to extend families over wide areas. Once established, such far-flung kinship relationships made it easier for others, who were forced to leave home, to adapt to new conditions under a new master. Kinfolk also sheltered escapees.

This eighteenth-century painting of slaves on a South Carolina plantation shows the continuities between West African and African-American culture.

Extended families influenced African-American naming practices, which reinforced family ties. Africans named male children after close relatives. This custom survived in America because boys were more likely to be separated from their parents by being sold than girls were. Having one's father's or grandfather's name preserved one's family identity. Also when, early in the eighteenth century, more African Americans began to use surnames, they clung to the name of their original master. This reflected a West African predisposition to link a family name with a certain location. Like taking a parent's name, it helped maintain family relationships despite repeated scatterings.

Bible names did not become common among African Americans until the mid-eighteenth century. This was because masters often refused to allow their slaves to be converted to Christianity. As a result, African religions—both indigenous and Islamic—persisted in parts of America well into the nineteenth century. The indigenous religions in particular maintained a premodern perception of the unity of the natural and the supernatural, the secular and the sacred, and the living and the dead. Black Americans continued to perform an African circle dance known as the "ring shout" at funerals, and they decorated graves with shells and pottery in the West African manner. They looked to recently arrived Africans for religious guidance, held bodies of water to be sacred,

▶ **Teaching Notes**

African Americans preserved given and family names over many generations. Black men continued to bear such African names as Cudjo, Quash, Cuffee, and Sambo, and black women such names as Quasheba and Juba. Even when masters imposed demeaning classical names, such as Caesar, Pompey, Venus, and Juno, black Americans passed them on from generation to generation.

George Whitefield, a founder of the Methodist Church and an emotional preacher, addressed black as well as white audiences during his 1739 tour of Britain's North American colonies. John Wollaston "George Whitefield" ca. 1770. By courtesy of the National Portrait Gallery, London. © 2004 Artist Rights Society (ARS), New York/ADAGP, Paris.

▶ **Interactive Activity:** *The Great Awakening*

This activity includes first-hand accounts with commentary on the first major religious revival in America. The comments of such figures as Benjamin Franklin and the responses of people from various backgrounds act as a debate over the Great Awakening and the style of religion that resulted from it. The map of settlement patterns of the ethnic and racial groups comprising the colonial population offers insight into which groups were most supportive of the Great Awakening.

remained in daily contact with their ancestors through spirit possession, and practiced divination and magic. When they became ill, they turned to "herb doctors" and "root workers." Even when many African Americans began to convert to Christianity during the mid-eighteenth century, West African religious thought and practice shaped their lives.

The Great Awakening

The major turning point in African-American religion came in conjunction with the religious revival known as the **Great Awakening**. This extensive social movement of the mid- to late-eighteenth century grew out of growing dissatisfaction among white Americans with a deterministic and increasingly formalistic style of Protestantism that seemed to deny most people a chance for salvation. During the early 1730s in western Massachusetts, a Congregationalist minister named Jonathan Edwards began an emotional and participatory ministry aimed at bringing more people into the church. Later that decade, George Whitefield, an Englishman who with John Wesley founded the Methodist Church, carried a similarly evangelical style of Christianity to the mainland colonies. In his sermons, Whitefield appealed to emotions, offered salvation to all who believed in Christ, and—although he did not advocate emancipation—preached to black people as well as white people.

Some people of African descent had converted to Christianity before Whitefield's arrival in North America. But two factors had prevented widespread black conversion. First, most masters feared that converted slaves would interpret their new religious status as a step toward freedom and equality. Second, many slaves continued to derive spiritual satisfaction from their ancestral religions and were not attracted to Christianity.

With the Great Awakening, however, a process of general conversion began. African Americans did indeed link the spiritual equality preached by evangelical ministers with a hope for earthly equality. They tied salvation for the soul with liberation for the body. They recognized that the preaching style Whitefield and other evangelicals adopted had much in common with West African "spirit possession." As in West African religion, eighteenth-century revivalism in North America emphasized personal rebirth, singing, movement, and emotion. The practice of total body immersion during baptism in rivers, ponds, and lakes that gave the Baptist church its name paralleled West African water rites.

Because it drew African Americans into an evangelical movement that helped shape American society, the Great Awakening increased mutual black-white acculturation. Revivalists appealed to the poor of all races and emphasized spiritual equality. Evangelical Anglican, Baptist, Methodist, and Presbyterian churches welcomed black people. Members of these biracial churches addressed each other as *brother* and *sister*. Black members took communion with white members, served as

church officers, and both groups were subject to the same church discipline. By the late eighteenth century, black men were being ordained as priests and ministers and—often while still enslaved—preached to white congregations. They thereby influenced white people's perception of how services should be conducted.

Other factors, however, favored the development of a distinct African-American church. From the start, white churches seated black people apart from white people, belying claims to spiritual equality. Black members took communion *after* white members. Masters also tried to use religion to instill in their chattels such self-serving Christian virtues as meekness, humility, and obedience. Consequently, African Americans established their own churches when they could. Dancing, shouting, clapping, and singing became especially characteristic of their religious meetings. Black spirituals probably date from the eighteenth century, and like African-American Christianity itself, they blended West African and European elements.

African Americans also retained the West African assumption that the souls of the dead returned to their homeland and rejoined their ancestors. Reflecting this family-oriented view of death, African-American funerals were often loud and joyous occasions with dancing, laughing, and drinking. Perhaps most important, the emerging black church reinforced black people's collective identity and helped them persevere in slavery.

Language, Music, and Folk Literature

Although African Americans did not retain their ancestral languages, those languages contributed to the pidgins and creolized languages that became Black English by the nineteenth century. It was in the low country, with its large and isolated black populations, that African-English creoles lasted the longest. The Gullah and Geechee dialects of the sea islands of South Carolina and Georgia, which combine African words and some African grammatical elements with a basically English structure, are still spoken today. In other regions, where black people were less numerous, the creoles were less enduring. Nevertheless, they contributed many words to American—particularly southern—English. Among them are *yam, banjo* (from mbanza), *tote, goober* (peanut), *buckra* (white man), *cooter* (tortoise), *gumbo* (okra), *nanse* (spider), *samba* (dance), *tabby* (a form of concrete), and *voodoo.*

Music was another essential part of West African life, and it remained so among African Americans, who preserved an antiphonal, call-and-response style of singing with an emphasis on improvisation, complex rhythms, and a strong beat. They sang while working and during religious ceremonies. Early on, masters banned drums and horns because of their potential for long-distance communication among slaves. But the African banjo survived in America, and African

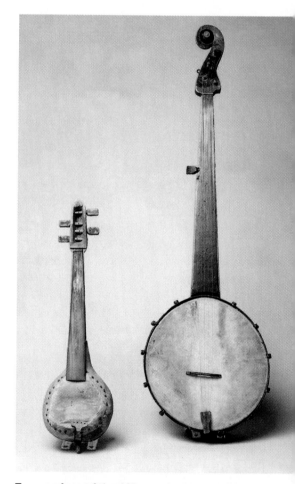

Two versions of the African *mbanza,* instruments that became known as banjos in America.

Enslaved Africans often used music and other aspects of West African culture as a way to endure life under slavery.

▶ **Reading Check**

African-Americans held on to elements of West African family structure and notions of kinship, religious concepts and practices, words, music, cooking methods, folk literature, and folk art. Collectively these elements amounted to a generalized version of West African culture that survived the process of transplantation in North America.

▶ **Recommended Readings**

Michael Gomez. *Exchanging Our Country Marks: The Transformation of African Identities in the Colonial and Antebellum South.* Chapel Hill, NC: University of North Carolina Press, 1998.

Sheila S. Walker, ed. *African Roots/American Culture: Africa and the Creation of the Americas.* Lanham, MD: Rowman and Littlefield, 2001.

Americans quickly adopted the violin and guitar. At night, in their cabins or around communal fires, slaves accompanied these instruments with bones and spoons. Music may have been the most important aspect of African culture in the lives of American slaves. Eventually African-American music influenced all forms of American popular music.

West African folk literature also survived in North America. African tales, proverbs, and riddles—with additions from American Indian and European stories—entertained, instructed, and united African Americans. Just as the black people on the sea islands of South Carolina and Georgia were most able to retain elements of African language, so did their folk literature remain closest to its African counterpart. Africans used tales of how weak animals like rabbits outsmarted stronger animals like hyenas and lions to symbolize the power of the common people over unjust rulers. African Americans used similar tales to portray the ability of slaves to outsmart and ridicule their masters.

 **Reading Check** What major elements of West African culture were retained and passed on by the second generation of people of African descent in North America?

A Poem by Jupiter Hammon

Jupiter Hammon (1711–1806?) was a favored slave living on Long Island, New York, when on Christmas day 1760 he composed "An Evening Thought. Salvation by Christ with Penitential Cries," an excerpt of which appears below. A Calvinist preacher and America's first published black poet, Hammon was deeply influenced by the Great Awakening's emphasis on repentance and Christ's spiritual sovereignty.

Salvation comes by Jesus Christ alone,
    The only Son of God;
Redemption now to every one,
    That love his holy Word.
Dear Jesus we would fly to Thee,
    And leave off every Sin,
Thy tender Mercy well agree;
    Salvation from our King.

Salvation comes from God we know,
    The true and only One;
It's well agreed and certain true,
    He gave his only Son.
Lord hear our penitential Cry:
    Salvation from above
It is the Lord that doth supply,
    With his Redeeming Love.

Dear Jesus let the Nations cry,
    And all the People say,
Salvation comes from Christ on high,
    Haste on Tribunal Day.
We cry as Sinners to the Lord,
    Salvation to obtain;
It is firmly fixt his holy Word,
    Ye shall not cry in vain.

What Do You Think?

▶ What elements in Hammon's poem might appeal to African Americans of his time?

▶ Does Hammon suggest a relationship between Christ and social justice?

▶ **What Do You Think?**

· African Americans of this time might find the concept that Jesus Christ gives salvation and redemption to everyone appealing.

· Hammon does suggest a relationship between Christ and social justice. In the last passage of the poem, he indicates that his people are crying to Christ, and Christ has promised that these cries will not be in vain.

The African-American Impact on Colonial Culture

African Americans also influenced the development of white culture. As early as the seventeenth century, black musicians performed English ballads for white audiences in a distinctively African-American style. They began to shape American music. In the northern and Chesapeake colonies, people of African descent helped determine how all Americans celebrated. By the eighteenth century, slaves in these regions organized black election or coronation festivals that lasted for several days. Sometimes called *Pinkster* and ultimately derived from Dutch-American pre-Easter celebrations, these festivities included parades, athletics, food, music, dancing, and mock coronations of kings and governors. Although dominated by African Americans, they attracted white observers and a few white participants.

The African-American imprint on southern diction and phraseology is especially clear. Generations of slaveholders' children, who were often raised by black women, were influenced by African-American speech patterns and intonations. Black people also influenced white notions about portents, spirits, and folk remedies. Seventeenth- and eighteenth-century English lore about such things was not that different from West African lore, and white Americans consulted black conjurers and "herb doctors." Black cooks in early America influenced both white southern and African-American eating habits. Preferences for barbecued pork, fried chicken, black-eyed peas, and collard and mustard greens owed much to West African culinary traditions.

African Americans also used West African culture and skills to shape the way work was done in the American South during and after colonial times. Africans accustomed to collective agricultural labor imposed the **gang system** on most American plantations. Masters learned that their slaves would work harder and longer in groups. Their work songs were also an African legacy, as was the slow, deliberate pace of their labor. By the mid-eighteenth century, masters often employed slaves as builders. As a result, African styles and decorative techniques influenced southern colonial architecture. Black builders introduced African-style high-peaked roofs, front porches, woodcarvings, and elaborate ironwork.

 Reading Check In what ways did African-American culture develop in America?

▶▶ **Reading Check**

Creolization and miscegenation transformed Africans into African Americans. The second generation of people of African descent in North America retained a generalized West African heritage. The preservation of the West African extended family was the basis of African-American culture.

▶▶ **Retracing the Odyssey**

Charles H. Wright Museum of African American History, Detroit. The "Of the People: The African American Experience" exhibit includes material dealing with the memory of Africa and the "survival of the spirit."

Section 5

Slavery in Colonial America

Slavery in the Northern Colonies

The British mainland colonies north of the Chesapeake had histories, cultures, demographics, and economies that differed considerably from those of the southern colonies. Organized religion was much more important in the foundation of most of the northern colonies than those of the South (except for Maryland). In New England, where the Pilgrims settled in 1620 and the Puritans in 1630, religious utopianism shaped colonial life. The same was true in the West Jersey portion of New Jersey, where members of the English pietist Society of Friends, or Quakers, began to settle during the 1670s, and Pennsylvania, which William Penn founded in 1682 as a Quaker colony. Quakers, like other pietists, emphasized nonviolence and a divine spirit within all humans, both of which beliefs disposed some of them to become early opponents of slavery.

Even more important than religion in shaping life in northern British North America were a cooler climate, sufficient numbers of white laborers, lack of a staple crop, and a diversified economy. All these circumstances made black slavery in the colonial North less extensive than and different from its southern counterparts.

By the end of the colonial period during the 1770s, only 50,000 African Americans lived in the northern colonies in comparison to 400,000 in the southern colonies. In the North, black people were 4.5 percent of the total population, compared with 40 percent in the South. But, as in the South, the northern black population varied in size from place to place. By 1770 enslaved African Americans constituted 10 percent of the population of Rhode Island, New Jersey, New York, and Pennsylvania. New York City had a particularly large black population, 20 percent of its total by 1750 (see Figure 3–2).

Like all Americans during the colonial era, most northern slaves were agricultural laborers. But, in contrast to those in the South, slaves in the North typically lived in their master's house and worked with their master, his family, and one or two other slaves on a small farm. In northern cities, which were often homeports for slave traders, enslaved people of African descent worked as artisans, shopkeepers, messengers, domestic servants, and general laborers.

GUIDE TO READING

▶ How did the experience of African Americans under French and Spanish rule in North America compare to that in the British colonies?

▶ How did slavery affect black women in colonial America?

▶ How did African Americans resist slavery?

KEY TERMS

▶ slave codes, p. 96

▶ assimilation, p. 96

▶ outliers, p. 101

▶ maroons, p. 101

▶ acculturation, p. 101

▶▶ **Guide to Reading/Key Terms**
For answers, see the *Teacher's Resource Manual*.

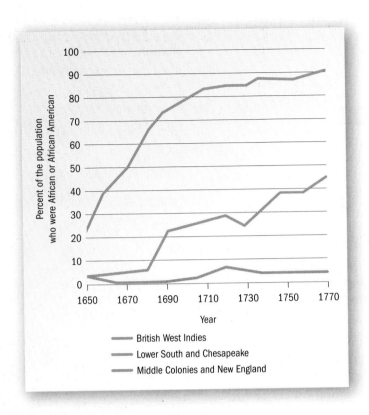

FIGURE 3–2 Africans as a Percentage of the Total Population of the British American Colonies, 1650–1770.

From *Time on the Cross: The Economics of Negro Slavery* by Robert W. Fogel and Stanley L. Engerman. Copyright © 1974 by Robert W. Fogel and Stanley L. Engerman. Reprinted by permission of W. W. Norton & Company, Inc.

▶ **Teaching Notes**

There was an increase in African customs among black northerners between 1740 and 1770. Before that time, most northern slaves had been born or "seasoned" in the South or West Indies. During the middle decades of the eighteenth century, direct imports of African slaves into the North temporarily increased. With them came knowledge of African life.

Consequently, most northern African Americans led different lives from those in the South. Mainly because New England had so few slaves, but also because of Puritan religious principles, slavery there was least oppressive. White people had no reason to suspect that the small and dispersed black population posed a threat of rebellion. The local **slave codes** were milder and, except for the ban on miscegenation, not rigidly enforced. New England slaves could legally own, transfer, and inherit property. From the early seventeenth century onward, Puritans converted to Christianity the Africans and African Americans who came among them, recognizing their spiritual equality before God.

In the middle colonies of New York, New Jersey, and Pennsylvania, where black populations were larger and hence perceived by white people to be more threatening, the slave codes were stricter and penalties harsher. But even in these colonies, the curfews imposed on Africans and African Americans and restrictions on their ability to gather together were less well enforced than they were further south.

These conditions encouraged rapid **assimilation**. Because of their small numbers, frequent isolation from others of African descent, and close association with their masters, northern slaves had fewer opportunities to preserve an African heritage. The less harsh and more peripheral nature of slavery in this region limited the retention of African perspectives, just as it allowed the slaves more freedom than most of their southern counterparts enjoyed.

Slavery in Spanish Florida and French Louisiana

Just as slavery in Britain's northern colonies differed from slavery in its southern colonies, slavery in Spanish Florida and French Louisiana—areas that would later become parts of the United States—had distinctive characteristics. People of African descent, brought to Florida and Louisiana during the sixteenth, seventeenth, and eighteenth centuries, had different experiences from those who arrived in the British colonies. They and their descendants learned to speak Spanish or French rather than English, and they became Roman Catholics rather than Protestants. In addition, the routes to freedom were more plentiful in the Spanish and French colonies than they were in Britain's plantation colonies.

The Spanish monarchy regarded the settlement it established at St. Augustine in 1565 as primarily a military outpost, and plantation agriculture was not significant in Florida under Spanish rule. Therefore, the

Philadelphia's London Coffee House suggests the routine nature of slave auctions in early America.

number of slaves in Florida remained small, and black men were needed more as soldiers than as field workers. As militiamen, they gained power that eluded slaves in most of the British colonies, and as members of the Catholic Church, they acquired social status. When the British took control of Florida in 1763, these local people of African descent retreated along with the city's white inhabitants to Cuba. It was with the British takeover that plantation slavery began to grow in Florida.

When the French in 1699 established their Louisiana colony in the lower Mississippi River valley, their objective, like that of the Spanish in Florida, was primarily military. In 1720 few black people (either slave or free) lived in the colony. During the following decade, Louisiana imported about six thousand slaves, most of whom were male and from Senegambia. Although conditions were harsh and many died, by 1731 black people outnumbered white people in the colony. Most lived in the port city of New Orleans, where many became skilled artisans, lived away from their masters, became Roman Catholics, and gained freedom. Unfortunately, New Orleans early in its history also became a place where it was socially acceptable for white men to exploit black women. This custom eventually created a sizable mixed-race population

with elaborate social gradations based on the amount of white ancestry a person had and the lightness of his or her skin. Unlike the case in Florida, Louisiana's distinctive black and mixed-race population did not leave when the colony became part of the United States in 1803.

African Americans in New Spain's Northern Borderlands

What is today the southwestern portion of the United States was from the sixteenth century to 1821 the northernmost part of New Spain. Centered on Mexico, this Spanish colony reached into Texas, California, New Mexico, and Arizona. The first people of African descent who entered this huge region were members of Spanish exploratory expeditions. The best known of them was Esteban, an enslaved *Moor*, which was the Spanish term for a dark-skinned Muslim, who survived a shipwreck on the Texas coast in 1529 and joined Spanish explorer Alva Núñez Cabeza de Vaca in an arduous seven-year trek from Texas to Mexico City. Esteban, a skilled interpreter, later explored regions in what are today New Mexico and Arizona. During the seventeenth century, black soldiers participated in the Spanish conquest of Pueblo Indians. Some black or mulatto women also joined in Spanish military expeditions. The best known of them was Isabel de Olvena, who traveled with an expedition through New Mexico in 1600.

During the colonial era, however, New Spain's North American borderlands had far fewer black people than there were in the British colonies. In part this was because the total non-Indian population in the borderlands was extremely small. As late as 1792, for example, only

▶▶ **Teaching Notes**

Black men also accompanied Francisco Vasquez de Coronado's 1540–1542 search across the Southwest for the mythical Seven Cities of Cibola, as well as in Spanish expeditions along the upper regions of the Rio Grande in 1593 and 1598. Black men in the borderlands gained employment as sailors, soldiers, tradesmen, cattle herders, and day laborers. In the borderlands some black men held responsible positions at Roman Catholic missions. A few acquired large land holdings called "ranchos."

Men and women of African descent often labored at Spanish mission churches in New Spain's northern borderlands.

This detail of a mural located in the Arizona capitol building shows, on its extreme right, the former slave Esteban, who wears a blue turban.

around 3,000 colonists lived in Texas, including about 450 described as black or mulatto. There were even fewer colonists in New Mexico and California where people of mixed African, Indian, and Spanish descent were common. Some of them were slaves, but others had limited freedom. In contrast to the British colonies, in New Spain's borderlands most slaves were Indians. They worked as domestics and as agricultural laborers or were marched south to Mexico where they labored in gold and silver mines.

Also in contrast to the British mainland colonies, where no formal aristocracy existed but where white insistence on racial separation gradually grew in strength, there were in New Spain's borderlands both hereditary rank and racial fluidity. In theory throughout the Spanish Empire in the Americas, "racial purity" determined social status, with Spaniards of "pure blood" at the top and Africans and Indians at the bottom. In Texas, for example, free black people and Indians suffered legal disabilities. They paid special taxes and could not own guns or travel freely. But almost all of the Spaniards who moved north from Mexico were themselves of mixed race, and people of African and Indian descent could more easily acquire status than was the case in the British colonies. In 1783 Spain's royal government began to allow black people and Indians to elevate themselves legally by paying between seven hundred and one thousand pesos, a substantial sum at the time. By this means they could acquire hereditary rank and great power over those who labored for them.

 **Reading Check** How did the experience of African Americans under French and Spanish rule in North America compare to that in the British colonies?

▶ **Reading Check**

People of African descent brought to Florida and Louisiana during the sixteenth, seventeenth, and eighteenth centuries, learned Spanish and French. They became Roman Catholics rather than Protestants. Moreover, the routes to freedom were more plentiful in the Spanish and French colonies than they were in British colonies.

▶ **Recommended Reading**

Quintard Taylor. *In Search of the Racial Frontier: African Americans in the American West, 1528-1990.* New York: Norton, 1998.

Black Women in Colonial America

The lives of black women in early North America varied according to the colony in which they lived. The differences between Britain's New England colonies and its southern colonies are particularly clear. In New England, where religion and demographics made the boundary between slavery and freedom permeable, black women distinguished themselves in a variety of ways. The thoroughly acculturated Lucy Terry Prince of Deerfield, Massachusetts, published poetry during the 1740s and had gained her freedom by 1756. Other black women succeeded as bakers and weavers. But in the South, where most black women of the time lived, they had few opportunities for work beyond the tobacco and rice fields and domestic labor in the homes of their masters.

During the late seventeenth and the eighteenth centuries, approximately 90 percent of southern black women worked in the fields, as was customary for women in West Africa. White women sometimes did field-work as well, but masters considered black women to be tougher than white women and therefore able to do more hard physical labor. Black women also mothered their children and cooked for their families, a chore that involved lugging firewood and water and tending fires as well as preparing meals. Like other women of their time, colonial black women suffered from inadequate medical attention while giving birth. But because black women worked until the moment they delivered, they were more likely than white women to experience complications in giving birth and to bear low-weight babies.

As the eighteenth century passed, more black women became house servants. Yet most jobs as maids, cooks, and body servants went to the young, the old, or the infirm. Black women also wet-nursed their master's children. None of this was easy work; those who did it were under constant white supervision.

Masters and overseers used their power to force themselves on female slaves. The results were evident in the large mixed-race populations in the colonies and in the psychological damage it inflicted on African-American women and their mates. In particular, the abuse of black women by white men disrupted the emerging black families in North America because black men usually could not protect their wives from it.

 Reading Check How did slavery affect black women in colonial America?

Black Resistance and Rebellion

Slavery in America was always a system that relied ultimately on physical force to deny freedom to enslaved Africans. From its start, black men and women responded by resisting their masters as well as they could.

▶ **Reading Check**

The lives of black women in early North America varied from colony to colony. During the seventeenth and eighteenth centuries, about 90 percent of southern black women worked in the fields. Over the course of the eighteenth century, more black women became house servents. Female black slaves were subject to the sexual predation of masters and overseers.

▶ **Teaching Notes**

Although black women were more expensive than white indentured servants—because, unlike the children of white indentured servants, their children would become their master's property—slave traders and slaveholders never valued black women as highly as they did black men. Until 1660, British mainland colonies imported twice as many African men as women. Thereafter, the ratio dropped to three African men for every two women, and by the mid-eighteenth century, natural population growth among African Americans had corrected the sexual imbalance.

▶ **Recommended Reading**

Joan Rezner Gunderson, "The Double Bonds of Race and Sex: Black and White Women in a Colonial Virginia Parish," in Darlene Clark Hine, Wilma King, and Linda Reed, eds. *We Specialize in the Wholly Impossible: A Reader in Black Women's History.* Brooklyn, NY: Carlson, 1995.

Jenny Sharpe. *Ghosts of Slavery: A Literary Archaeology of Black Women's Lives.* Minneapolis: University of Minnesota Press, 2003.

Such resistance ranged from sullen goldbricking (shirking assigned work) to sabotage, escape, and rebellion. Before the late eighteenth century, however, resistance and rebellion were not part of a coherent antislavery effort. Slave resistance and revolt did not aim to destroy slavery as a social system. Africans and African Americans resisted, escaped, and rebelled not as part of an effort to free all slaves. Instead, in the case of resistance, they aimed to force masters to make concessions within the framework of slavery. In the case of escape and rebellion, they aimed to relieve themselves, their friends, and their families from intolerable disgrace and suffering.

African men and women newly arrived in North America were most open in defying their masters. They frequently refused to work and often could not be persuaded by punishment to change their behavior. "You would really be surpris'd at their Perseverance," one frustrated master commented. "They often die before they can be conquered." Africans tended to escape in groups of individuals who shared a common homeland and language. When they succeeded, they usually became **outliers**, living nearby and stealing from their master's estate. Less frequently, they headed west where they found a degree of safety among white frontiersmen, Indians, or interracial banditti. In 1672, Virginia's colonial government began paying bounties to anyone who killed outliers, and six decades later, the governor of South Carolina offered similar rewards. In some instances, escaped slaves, known as **maroons**—a term derived from the Spanish word *cimarron*, meaning wild—established their own settlements in inaccessible regions.

The most durable of such maroon communities in North America existed in the Spanish colony of Florida. In 1693 the Spanish king officially made this colony a refuge for slaves escaping from the British colonies, although he did not free slaves who were already there. Many such escapees joined the Seminole Indian nation and thereby gained protection during the period between 1763 and 1783 when the British ruled Florida and after 1821 when the United States took control. It was in part to destroy this refuge for escaped slaves that the United States fought the Seminole War from 1835 to 1842. Although some continued to head for maroon settlements, most sought safety among relatives, in towns, or in the North Carolina piedmont where there were few slaves.

As slaves became acculturated, forms of slave resistance changed. To avoid punishment, African Americans replaced open defiance with more subtle day-to-day obstructionism. They malingered, broke tools, mistreated domestic animals, destroyed crops, poisoned their masters, and stole. Not every slave who acted this way, of course, was consciously resisting enslavement, but masters assumed that they were. **Acculturation** also brought different escape patterns. Increasingly, it was the more assimilated slaves who escaped. They were predominantly young men who left on their own and relied on their knowledge of American society to pass as free.

▶ **Document**

3-4 *Runaway Notices from The South Carolina Gazette, 1732 and 1737*
Southern newspapers were replete with advertisements for runaway slaves. These examples show the lengths that slave owners went to retrieve them.

▶ **Recommended Reading**

Ira Berlin. *Many Thousands Gone: The First Two Centuries of Slavery in North America.* Cambridge, MA: Belknap Press, 1998. Berlin presents an impressive synthesis of black life in slavery during the seventeenth and eighteenth centuries that emphasizes the ability of black people to shape their lives in conflict with the will of masters.

As it turned out, however, Parliament had repealed the Townshend duties, except the one on tea, before the massacre. This parliamentary retreat and a reaction against the bloodshed in Boston reduced tension between the colonies and Britain. A period of calm lasted until May 1773 when Parliament passed the Tea Act.

 Reading Check What British policies in the 1760s led to rising resentment and resistance in the colonies?

The Tea Act

The **Tea Act** gave the British East India Company a monopoly over all tea sold in the American colonies. A huge but debt-ridden entity, the East India Company governed India for the British Empire. At the time, Americans drank a great deal of tea and Parliament hoped the tea monopoly would save the company from bankruptcy. But American merchants assumed the act was the first step in a plot to bankrupt them. Because it had huge tea reserves, the East India Company could sell its tea much more cheaply than colonial merchants could. Other Americans believed the Tea Act was a trick to get them to pay the tax on tea by lowering its price. They feared that once Americans paid the tax on tea, British leaders would use it as a precedent to raise additional taxes.

To prevent this from happening, in December 1773 Boston's radical Sons of Liberty dumped a shipload of tea into the harbor. Britain then sent more troops to Boston in early 1774 and punished the city economically. This action sparked resistance throughout the colonies and led eventually to American independence. Patriot leaders organized the **Continental Congress**, which met in Philadelphia in September 1774 and demanded the repeal of all "oppressive" legislation. By November, Massachusetts Minutemen—members of an irregular militia—had begun to stockpile arms in the villages surrounding Boston.

In April 1775 Minutemen clashed with British troops at Lexington and Concord near Boston. This was the first battle in what became a war for independence. Shortly thereafter, Congress appointed George Washington commander in chief of the Continental Army. Before he took command, however, the American and British forces at Boston fought a bloody battle at Bunker Hill. After a year during which other armed clashes occurred and the British rejected a compromise, Congress in July 1776 declared the colonies to be independent states, and the war became a revolution.

 Reading Check What was the main provision of the Tea Act of 1773? Why did some colonists object to it?

▶ **Reading Check**

The Proclamation Line of 1763 forbid American settlement west of the crest of the Appalachian Mountains. The Sugar Act of 1764 levied import duties on sugar. The Stamp Act of 1765 taxed printed material.

▶ **Reading Check**

The Tea Act gave the British East India Company a monopoly on tea sold in the American colonies. American merchants saw it as an effort to bankrupt them. Other colonists saw the Tea Act as a first step toward the imposition of a tea tax.

▶ **Interactive Activity**

The Stamp Act

In 1765, Great Britain set about putting its imperial house in order. Retiring debt was a major priority. The Stamp Act was one of several revenue measures designed to get the colonies to pay a greater share of the costs of the empire. This activity examines the emotions stimulated by the Stamp Act, arguments that illuminate both sides of the taxation issue, and later debates that culminated in the American Revolution.

Section 2

The Declaration of Independence and African Americans

GUIDE TO READING

▶ What did the Declaration of Independence mean to African Americans?

▶ What influence did the ideas of John Locke have on the ideology of the American Revolution?

▶ What role did African Americans play in the events and debate that led to the American Revolution?

KEY TERMS

▶ Declaration of Independence, p. 115

▶ Enlightenment, p. 116

▶ natural laws, p. 116

Drafting the Declaration

The **Declaration of Independence** that the Continental Congress adopted on July 4, 1776, was drafted by a slaveholder in a slaveholding country. When Thomas Jefferson wrote "that all men are created equal; that they are endowed by their Creator with certain unalienable rights; that among these are life, liberty, and the pursuit of happiness," he was not supporting black claims for freedom. Men like Jefferson and John Adams, who served on the drafting committee with Jefferson and Ben Franklin, frequently distinguished between the rights of white men of British descent and a lack of rights for people of color. So convinced were Jefferson and his colleagues that black people could not claim the same rights as white people that they felt no need to qualify their words proclaiming universal liberty.

The draft declaration that Jefferson, Adams, and Benjamin Franklin submitted to Congress for approval did denounce the Atlantic slave trade as a "cruel war against human nature itself, violating its most sacred rights of life and liberty in the persons of a distant [African] people." But Congress deleted this passage because delegates from the deep South objected to it. The final version of the Declaration referred to slavery only to accuse the British of arousing African Americans to revolt against their masters.

Jefferson and the other delegates did not mean to encourage African Americans to hope the American War for Independence could become a war against slavery. But that is what African Americans believed. Black people were in attendance when Patriot speakers made unqualified claims for human equality and natural rights; they read accounts of such speeches and heard white people discuss them. In response African Americans began to assert that such principles logically applied as much to them as to the white population. They forced white people to confront the contradiction between the new nation's professed ideals and its reality.

▶ **Guide to Reading/Key Terms**

For answers, see the *Teacher's Resource Manual.*

▶ **Document**

4-9 *The Declaration of Independence*

▶ **Recommended Reading**

Jack P. Greene. *All Men Are Created Equal: Some Reflections on the Character of the American Revolution.* Oxford: Clarendon, 1976.

The Impact of the Enlightenment

At the center of that ideology was the European **Enlightenment**. The roots of this intellectual movement, also known as the Age of Reason, lay in Renaissance secularism and humanism dating back to the fifteenth century. Isaac Newton's *Principia Mathematica*, published in England in 1687 shaped a new way of perceiving human beings and their universe. Newton used mathematics to portray an orderly, balanced universe that ran according to natural laws that humans could discover through reason.

What made the Enlightenment of particular relevance to the Age of Revolution was John Locke's application of Newton's ideas to politics. In his essay "Concerning Human Understanding," published in 1690, Locke maintained that human society—like the physical universe—ran according to **natural laws**. He contended that at the base of human laws were natural rights all people shared. Human beings, according to Locke, created governments to protect their natural individual rights to life, liberty, and private property. If a government failed to perform this basic duty and became oppressive, he insisted, the people had the right to overthrow it. Locke also maintained that the human mind at birth was a *tabula rasa* (i.e., knowledge and wisdom were not inherited, but were acquired through experience). Locke saw no contradiction between these principles and human slavery. During the eighteenth century that contradiction became increasingly clear.

Most Americans became acquainted with Locke's ideas through pamphlets that a radical English political minority produced during the early eighteenth century. This literature portrayed the British government of the day as a conspiracy aimed at depriving British subjects of their natural rights, reducing them to slaves, and establishing tyranny. After the French and Indian War, during the 1760s, Americans, both black and white, interpreted British policies and actions from this same perspective.

The influence of such pamphlets is clear between 1763 and 1776 when white Patriot leaders charged that the British government sought to enslave them by depriving them of their rights as Englishmen. When they made these charges, they had difficulty denying that they themselves deprived African Americans of their natural rights. George Washington, for example, declared in 1774 that "the crisis is arrived when we must assert our rights, or submit to every imposition, that can be heaped upon us, till custom and use shall make us tame and abject, as the blacks we rule over with such arbitrary sway."

African Americans in the Revolutionary Debate

During the 1760s and 1770s when powerful slaveholders such as George Washington talked of liberty, natural rights, and hatred of enslavement, African Americans listened. Most of them had been born in America,

▶▶ **Teaching Notes**

Newton's insights supported the rationalized means of production and commerce associated with the Industrial Revolution that began in England during the early eighteenth century. An emerging market economy required the same sort of rational use of resources that Newton discovered in the universe.

▶▶ **Recommended Readings**

David Brion Davis. *The Problem of Slavery in the Age of Revolution, 1770–1823.* Ithaca, NY: Cornell University Press, 1975. This magisterial study discusses the influence of the Enlightenment and the industrial revolution on slavery and opposition to slavery in the Atlantic world.

Bernard Bailyn. *The Ideological Origins of the American Revolution.* Cambridge, MA: Harvard University Press, 1967.

they had absorbed English culture, they were united as a people, and they knew their way in colonial society. Those who lived in or near towns and cities had access to public meetings and newspapers. They were aware of the disputes with Great Britain and the contradictions between demanding liberty for oneself and denying it to others. They understood that the ferment of the 1760s had shaken traditional assumptions about government, and many of them hoped for more changes.

The greatest source of optimism for African Americans was the expectation that white Patriot leaders would realize their revolutionary principles were incompatible with slavery. Those in England who believed white Americans must submit to British authority pointed out the contradiction. Samuel Johnson, the most famous writer in London, asked, "How is it that we hear the loudest yelps for liberty among the drivers of negroes?" But white Americans made similar comments. As early as 1763, James Otis of Massachusetts warned that "those who every day barter away other mens['] liberty, will soon care little for their own." Thomas Paine, whose pamphlet *Common Sense* rallied Americans to endorse independence in 1776, asked them to contemplate "with what consistency, or decency they complain so loudly of attempts to enslave them, while they hold so many hundred thousands in slavery; and annually enslave many thousands more."

Such principled misgivings among white people about slavery helped improve the situation for black people in the North and upper South during the war, but African Americans acting on their own behalf were key. In January 1766 slaves marched through Charleston, South Carolina, shouting "Liberty!" In the South Carolina and Georgia low country and in the

A black youngster joins in a Boston demonstration against the Stamp Act of 1765.

▶ **Recommended Readings**

Gary B. Nash. *Forging Freedom: The Formation of Philadelphia's Black Community, 1720–1840.* Cambridge, MA: Harvard University Press, 1988.

Benjamin Quarles. *The Negro in the American Revolution.* 1961; reprint, New York: Norton, 1973. This classic study remains the most comprehensive account of black participation in the War for Independence. It also demonstrates the impact of the war on black life.

The title page of the 1795 edition of Benjamin Banneker's *Almanac* includes his portrait.

▶ Reading Check

The Enlightenment helped to develop the careers of the first black intellectuals. Some African Americans became scientists and authors. Phillis Wheatley and Benjamin Banneker, the most famous intellectuals, contributed the first published works by African Americans. Most African Americans who gained intellectual distinction in this period owed more to the Great Awakening than to Enlightenment.

Benjamin Banneker

In the breadth of his achievement, Benjamin Banneker is even more representative of the Enlightenment than Phillis Wheatley. Like hers, his life epitomizes a flexibility concerning race that the revolutionary era briefly promised to expand.

Banneker was born free in Maryland in 1731 and died in 1806. The son of a mixed-race mother and an African father, he inherited a farm near Baltimore from his white grandmother. As a child, Banneker, whose appearance was described by a contemporary to be "decidedly Negro," attended a racially integrated school. His farm gave him a steady income and the leisure to study literature and science. With access to the library of his white neighbor George Ellicott, Banneker "mastered Latin and Greek and had a good working knowledge of German and French."

By the 1770s he had a reputation as a man "of uncommonly soft and gentlemanly manners and of pleasing colloquial powers." Like Jefferson, Franklin, and others of his time, Banneker was fascinated with mechanics and in 1770 constructed his own clock. However, he gained international fame as a mathematician and astronomer. Because of his knowledge in these disciplines, he became a member of the survey commission for Washington, D.C. This made him the first black civilian employee of the U.S. government. Between 1791 and 1796, he published an almanac based on his observations and mathematical calculations.

Like Wheatley, Banneker had thoroughly assimilated white culture and was keenly aware of the fundamental issues of human equality associated with the American Revolution. In 1791 he sent Thomas Jefferson, who was then U.S. secretary of state, a copy of his almanac to refute Jefferson's claim in *Notes on the State of Virginia* that black people were inherently inferior intellectually to white people. Noting Jefferson's commitment to the biblical statement that God had created "us all of one flesh," and Jefferson's words in the Declaration of Independence, Banneker called the great man to account concerning slavery.

Referring to the Declaration, Banneker wrote, "You were then impressed with proper ideas of the great valuation of liberty, and the free possession of those blessings, to which you were entitled by nature; but, Sir, how pitiable is it to reflect, that altho you were so fully convinced of the benevolence of the Father of Mankind, and of his equal and impartial distribution of these rights and privileges . . . that you should at the Same time counteract his mercies, in detaining by fraud and violence so numerous a part of my brethren, under groaning captivity and cruel oppression."

 **Reading Check**   How did African Americans contribute to the Enlightenment?

Section 4

African Americans in the War for Independence

The Revolutionary War

When it came to fighting between Patriots on one side and the British and their **Loyalist** American allies on the other, African Americans joined the side that offered freedom. In the South, where the British held out the promise of freedom in exchange for military service, black men eagerly fought on the British side as Loyalists. In the North, where white Patriots were more consistently committed to human liberty than in the South, black men just as eagerly fought on the Patriot side (see Map 4–2).

The war began in earnest in August 1776 when the British landed a large army at Brooklyn, New York, and drove Washington's Continental Army across New Jersey into Pennsylvania. The military and diplomatic turning point in the war came the following year at Saratoga, New York, when a poorly executed British strategy to take control of the Hudson River led British general John Burgoyne to surrender his entire army to Patriot forces. This victory led France and other European powers to enter the war against Britain. Significant fighting ended in October 1781 when Washington forced Lord Cornwallis to surrender another British army at Yorktown, Virginia.

When Washington had organized the Continental Army in July 1775, he forbade the enlistment of new black troops and the reenlistment of black men who had served at Lexington and Concord, Bunker Hill, and other early battles. Shortly thereafter, all thirteen states followed Washington's example. Several reasons account for Washington's decision and its ratification by the Continental Congress. Patriot leaders feared that if they enlisted African-American soldiers, it would encourage slaves to leave their masters without permission. White people—especially in the South—also feared that armed black men would endanger the social order. Paradoxically, white people simultaneously believed black men were too cowardly to be effective soldiers. Although apparently contradictory, these last two beliefs persisted into the twentieth century.

Black Loyalists

Because so many Patriot leaders resisted employing black troops, by mid-1775 the British had taken the initiative in recruiting African Americans. From Maryland southward, during the spring of that year,

A young French officer named Jean-Baptiste-Antoine Deverger painted this watercolor of American foot soldiers who served during the Yorktown campaign of 1781.

When the conflict with Great Britain made human rights a political as well as a religious issue, Woolman and Benezet carried their abolitionist message beyond the Society of Friends. They thereby merged their sectarian crusade with the rationalist efforts of such northern white revolutionary leaders as former slaveholder Benjamin Franklin of Philadelphia and John Jay and Alexander Hamilton—who continued to own slaves—of New York. Under Quaker leadership, **antislavery societies** came into existence in both the North and the Chesapeake. By 1774 such societies had joined African Americans in petitioning northern legislatures and, in one instance, the Continental Congress to act against slavery or the slave trade.

The Revolutionary Impact

In calling for emancipation, the antislavery societies emphasized black service in the war against British rule and the religious and economic progress of northern African Americans. They also contended that emancipation would prevent black rebellions. As a result, by 1784 all the northern states except New Jersey and New York had undertaken either immediate or gradual abolition of slavery. Delaware, Maryland, and Virginia made manumission easier. Even the deep South saw efforts to mitigate the most brutal excesses that slavery encouraged among masters. Many observers believed the Revolution had profoundly changed the prospects for African Americans.

In fact, the War for Independence dealt a heavy, although not mortal, blow to slavery (see Figure 4–1). While northern states prepared to abolish involuntary servitude, an estimated 100,000 slaves escaped from their masters in the South. In South Carolina alone, approximately 25,000 escaped—about 30 percent of the state's black population. Twenty thousand black people left with the British at the end of the war (see Map 4–3). Meanwhile, numerous escapees found their way to southern cities or to the North, where they became part of a rapidly expanding free black class.

FIGURE 4–1 The Free Black Population of the British North American Colonies in 1750, and of the United States in 1790 and 1800.

The impact of revolutionary ideology and a changing economy led to a great increase in the free black population during the 1780s and 1790s.

Source: *A Century of Population Growth in the United States. 1790–1900* (1909), p. 80. Data for 1750 estimated.

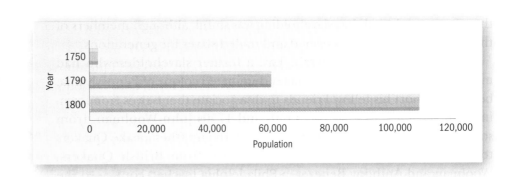

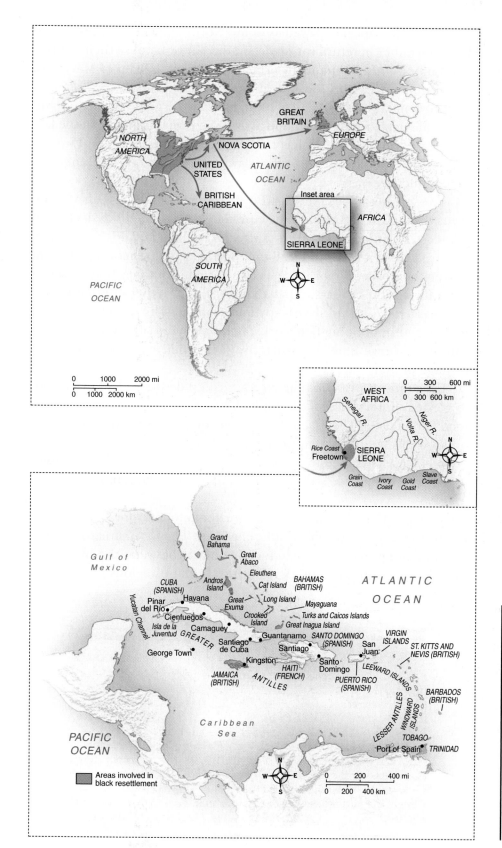

⏩ **Map 4-3**

Due in large part to the dedication of black slaves to the Loyalist cause, Great Britain had begun to recognize slaves as worthy of their freedom.

MAP 4–3 The Resettlement of Black Loyalists after the American War for Independence

Many black Loyalists left with the British following the Patriot victory. Most of those who settled in Nova Scotia soon moved on to Great Britain or the British free black colony of Sierra Leone. Some black migrants to the British Caribbean were reenslaved.

 What does the arrival of some black Loyalists in Sierra Leone indicate about Great Britain's changing attitudes toward slavery?

In the Chesapeake, as well as in the North, individual slaves gained freedom either in return for service in the war or because their masters had embraced Enlightenment principles. Philip Graham of Maryland, for example, freed his slaves, commenting that holding one's "fellow men in bondage and slavery is repugnant to the gold law of God and the unalienable right of mankind as well as to every principle of the late glorious revolution which has taken place in America." The Virginia legislature ordered masters to free slaves who had fought for American independence.

Those Chesapeake slaves who did not become free also made gains during the Revolution because the war hastened the decline of tobacco raising. As planters switched to wheat and corn, they required fewer year-round, full-time workers. This encouraged them to free their excess labor force or to negotiate contracts that let slaves serve for a term of years rather than for life. Another alternative was for masters to allow slaves—primarily males—to practice skilled trades instead of doing fieldwork. Such slaves were often hired out or "hired their own time" in return for giving their masters a large percentage of their wages.

Even those slaves who remained agricultural workers had more time to garden, hunt, and fish to supply themselves and their families with food and income. They gained more freedom to visit relatives who lived on other plantations, attend religious meetings, and interact with white people. Masters tended to refrain from the barbaric punishments used in the past, to improve slave housing, and to allow slaves more access to religion.

In South Carolina and Georgia, greater autonomy for slaves during the revolutionary era took a different form. The war increased absenteeism among masters and reduced contacts between the black and white populations. The black majorities in these regions grew larger,

▶ **Retracing the Odyssey**

Colonial Williamsburg, Williamsburg, Virginia. This is the largest historical restoration site in America. It emphasizes the period on the "eve of the American Revolution." Take the "Other Half Tour," which deals with "the lives and livelihoods of eighteenth-century African Americans."

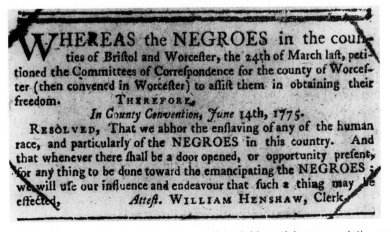

WHEREAS the NEGROES in the counties of Briftol and Worcefter, the 24th of March laft, petitioned the Committees of Correfpondence for the county of Worcefter (then convencd in Worcefter) to affift them in obtaining their freedom. THEREFORE,

In County Convention, June 14th, 1775.

RESOLVED, That we abhor the enflaving of any of the human race, and particularly of the NEGROES in this country. And that whenever there fhall be a door opened, or opportunity prefent, for any thing to be done toward the emancipating the NEGROES; we will ufe our influence and endeavour that fuch a thing may be effected. Atteft. WILLIAM HENSHAW, Clerk.

The Patriot newspaper *Massachusetts Spy* published this antislavery resolution on June 21, 1775.

more isolated, and more African in culture as both South Carolina and Georgia imported more slaves from Africa. The constant arrival of Africans helped the region's African-American population retain a distinctive culture and the Gullah dialect. The increase in master absenteeism also permitted the task system of labor to expand.

The Revolutionary Promise

Even though the northern states were moving toward general emancipation during the revolutionary era, most newly free African Americans lived in the Chesapeake. They gained their freedom by serving in the war or escaping or because of economic and ideological change. As a result, a substantial free black population emerged in the Chesapeake after the war. In 1782 Virginia had only 1,800 free people within a total black population of 220,582. By 1790 the state had 12,766 free people within a total black population of 306,193. By 1810 it was 30,570 within 423,088. Free black populations also grew in Delaware and Maryland, where—unlike Virginia—the number of slaves began a long decline. (See Map 4–4.)

But in South Carolina and Georgia, the free black class remained tiny. Most low-country free black people were the children of white slave owners. They tended to be less independent of their former masters than their Chesapeake counterparts and lighter complexioned because their freedom was often a result of a family relationship to their masters.

In the North and the Chesapeake, free African Americans frequently moved to cities. Boston, New York, Philadelphia, Baltimore, Richmond, and Norfolk gained substantial free black populations after the Revolution. Black women predominated in this migration because they could more easily find jobs as domestics in the cities than in rural areas. Cities also offered free black people opportunities for community development that did not exist in thinly settled farm country. Although African Americans often used their new mobility to reunite families disrupted by slavery, relocating to a city could disrupt families that had survived enslavement. It took about a generation for stable, urban, two-parent households to emerge.

Newly freed black people also faced economic difficulty, and their occupational status often declined. Frequently they emerged from slavery without the economic resources needed to become independent farmers, shopkeepers, or tradespeople. In the North such economic restraints sometimes forced them to remain with their former masters long after formal emancipation. To make matters worse, white artisans used legal and extralegal means to protect themselves from black competition so African Americans who had learned trades as slaves had difficulty employing their skills in freedom.

▶ **Reading Check, p.132**

The willingness of African Americans to fight for the Patriot cause encouraged northern legislatures to consider emancipation. Moreover, economic changes encouraged such considerations. As a result, in the North emancipation made steady progress.

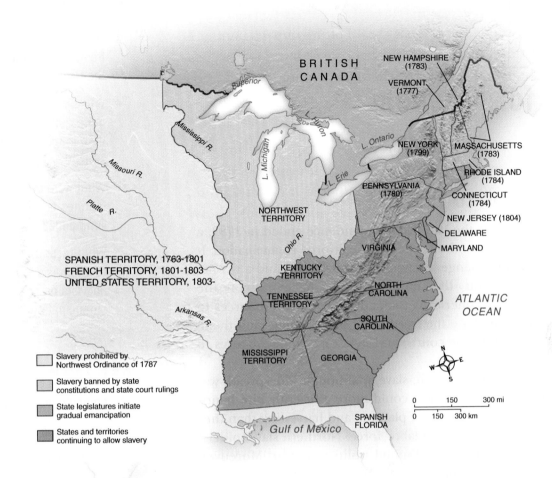

MAP 5–1 Emancipation and Slavery in the Early Republic

This map indicates the abolition policies adopted by the states of the Northeast between 1777 and 1804, the antislavery impact of the Northwest Ordinance of 1787, and the extent of slavery in the South during the early republic.

 Why did the states and territories shown in this map adopt different policies toward African Americans?

▶▶ **Map 5-1**

Varying regional economic factors, including the northern market economy based on wage labor versus the southern economy based on the production of cotton and slave labor, resulted in different territorial policies toward African Americans.

residents agreed. The struggle against slavery in the middle states was longer and harder because more white people there had a vested interest in maintaining it.

The New England States

Vermont and Massachusetts, certainly, and New Hampshire, probably, abolished slavery immediately during the 1770s and 1780s. Vermont, where there had never been more than a few slaves, prohibited slavery in the constitution it adopted in 1777. Massachusetts, in its constitution of 1780, declared "that all men are born free and equal; and that every subject is entitled to liberty." Although this constitution did not specifically ban slavery, within a year Elizabeth Freeman and other slaves in Massachusetts sued under it for their freedom.

Meanwhile, another slave, Quok Walker, left his master and began living as a free person. In response, Walker's master sought a court order to force Walker to return to slavery. This case led in 1783 to a Massachusetts Supreme Court ruling that "slavery is . . . as effectively abolished as it can be by the granting of rights and privileges wholly

incompatible and repugnant to its existence." At the same time, another judge used similar logic to grant Freeman her liberty. These decisions encouraged other Massachusetts slaves to sue for their freedom or—like Walker—to leave their masters because the courts had ruled the law did not recognize the right of slaveholders to their human chattel.

As a result, the first U.S. census in 1790 found no slaves in Massachusetts. Even before then, black men in the state had gained the right to vote. In 1780 Paul and John Cuffe, free black brothers who lived in the town of Dartmouth, protested with five other free black men to the state legislature that they were being taxed without representation. After several setbacks, the courts finally decided in 1783 that African-American men who paid taxes in Massachusetts could vote there.

▶▶ **Document**

5-1 *John Wesley, "Thoughts Upon Slavery" 1774* John Wesley distributed this anti-slavery tract in England and America under his own name. However, it is a short piece from an earlier work entitled, *Some Historical Accounts of Guinea*, published in Philadelphia in 1771 by Anthony Benezet, an American Quaker. Today's students will find it interesting to know that in the eighteenth century, people considered literary "borrowing" as an endorsement and not plagiarism.

PROFILE ❖ Elizabeth Freeman

Known as Mum Bett, Elizabeth Freeman showed a strength of character that impressed everyone she met. Although records are contradictory, she was probably born in 1744 in Claverack, New York. Because her parents were African slaves, she was also a slave. On the death of her first master in 1758, Freeman and her sister became the property of Colonel John Ashley, a court of common pleas judge, in Sheffield, Massachusetts. She married while quite young, gave birth to her only child—a daughter—and became a widow when her husband was killed fighting on the Patriot side in the War for Independence.

Freeman, who was illiterate, may have first learned of natural rights when in 1773 a group of men met at Ashley's home to draft a protest against British policies in the American colonies. "Mankind . . . have a right to the undisturbed Enjoyment of their lives, their Liberty and Property," the document declared. She took these words to heart, and when she learned while serving as a waitress in 1780 that the state of Massachusetts had adopted a bill of rights asserting that all people were born free and equal, she was ready to apply the doctrine.

In 1781 Freeman received "a severe wound" to her arm when she attempted to protect her sister from Ashley's wife, who "in a fit of passion" was threatening her with a hot kitchen shovel.

Outraged at this attack, Freeman left the Ashley home and refused to return. Instead, she engaged the legal assistance of Theodore Sedgwick Sr. in a suit for her freedom on the basis of Massachusetts's new bill of rights. The jury found in Freeman's favor and required Ashley to pay her thirty shillings in damages. It was at this point that Mum Bett changed her name legally to Elizabeth Freeman. Shortly thereafter, the Massachusetts Supreme Court declared slavery unconstitutional throughout the state.

For the remainder of her active life, Freeman worked as a paid domestic servant in the Sedgwick household and moved with the Sedgwicks to Stockbridge in 1785. Freeman earned enough while employed by the Sedgwicks to purchase her own home and retire. When she died she left a small estate to her daughter, grandchildren, and great grandchildren. Charles Sedgwick had the following lines inscribed on Freeman's gravestone: "She never violated a trust, nor failed to perform a duty. In every situation of domestic trial, she was the most efficient helper, and the tenderest friend. Good mother fare well."

The Abolition of Slavery in the North

1777 Vermont constitutional convention prohibits slavery within what becomes the fourteenth state

1780 Pennsylvania begins gradually abolishing slavery within its borders

1783 Massachusetts's supreme court abolishes slavery there

1784 Connecticut and Rhode Island adopt gradual abolition plans

1785 New Jersey and New York legislatures defeat gradual abolition plans

1799 The New York legislature provides for gradual abolition within its jurisdiction

1804 New Jersey becomes the last northern state to initiate gradual abolition

New Hampshire's record on emancipation is less clear than that of Vermont and Massachusetts. In 1779 black residents petitioned the New Hampshire legislature for freedom. Evidence also indicates that court rulings based on New Hampshire's 1783 constitution, which was similar to Massachusetts's constitution, refused to recognize human property. Nevertheless, New Hampshire still had about 150 slaves in 1792, and slavery may have simply withered away there rather than having been abolished by the courts.

In Connecticut and Rhode Island, the state legislatures, rather than individual African Americans, took the initiative against slavery. In 1784 these states adopted gradual abolition plans, which left adult slaves in bondage but proposed to free their children over a period of years. In Connecticut all children born to enslaved mothers after March 1, 1784, were to become free at age twenty-five. Rhode Island's plan was less gradual. Beginning that same March 1, it freed the children of enslaved women at birth. By 1790 only 3,763 slaves remained in New England out of a total black population there of 16,882. By 1800 only 1,339 slaves remained in the region, and by 1810 only 418 were left (108 in Rhode Island and 310 in Connecticut).

The Mid-Atlantic States

In New Jersey, New York, and Pennsylvania, the investment in slaves was much greater than in New England. After considerable debate, the

► Teaching Notes

In comparison to other parts of the Atlantic world, emancipation in the northern portion of the United States began early. Its first stages preceded the revolt that had, by 1804, ended slavery in Haiti, the first independent black republic. It preceded by a much greater margin the initiation in 1838 of peaceful, gradual abolition of slavery in the British Empire and the termination in 1848 of slavery in the French Empire. Northern emancipation was exceptional in that it was not the result of force or outside intervention by an imperial power. Although free black communities were emerging throughout the western hemisphere, those in the North were distinctive because they included the bulk of the region's black population.

This engraving suggests the progress African Americans had made in the North but also the contempt in which many white northerners held them.

TABLE 5–1 Slave Populations in the Mid-Atlantic States, 1790–1860

	1790	1800	1810	1820	1830	1840	1850	1860
New York	21,324	20,343	15,017	10,888	75	4		
New Jersey	11,432	12,343	19,851	7,557	2,243	674	236	18
Pennsylvania	3,737	1,706	795	211	403	64		

Source: Philip S. Foner, *History of Black Americans, from Africa to the Emergence of the Cotton Kingdom*, vol. 1 (Westport, CT: Greenwood, 1975), 374.

Pennsylvania legislature in 1780 voted that the children of enslaved mothers would become free at age twenty-eight. Under this scheme, Pennsylvania still had 403 slaves in 1830 (see Table 5–1). But many African Americans in the state gained their freedom much earlier by lawsuits or by simply leaving their masters. Emancipation came even more slowly in New York and New Jersey. In 1785 their legislatures *defeated* proposals for gradual abolition. White revolutionary leaders, such as Alexander Hamilton and John Jay, worked for abolition in New York, and Quakers had long advocated it in New Jersey. But these states had relatively large slave populations, powerful slaveholders, and white workforces fearful of free black competition.

In 1799 the New York legislature finally agreed that male slaves born after July 4 of that year were to become free at age twenty-eight and females at age twenty-five. In 1804 New Jersey adopted a similar law that freed male slaves born after July 4 of that year when they reached age twenty-five and females when they reached age twenty-one. Under this plan, New Jersey still had eighteen slaves in 1860.

The Northwest Ordinance of 1787

During the 1780s, Congress drew its authority from a constitution known as the **Articles of Confederation**. The Articles created a weak central government that lacked power to tax or to regulate commerce. Despite its weaknesses, this government acquired jurisdiction over the region west of the Appalachian Mountains and east of the Mississippi River, where several states previously had conflicting land claims.

During the War for Independence, increasing numbers of white Americans had migrated across the Appalachians into this huge region. Some of the migrants brought slaves with them. The migrants also provoked hostilities with Indian nations. Those migrants who moved into the Northwest faced British opposition, and those who moved into the Southwest contested with Spanish forces for control of that area. In response to these circumstances, Congress formulated policies to protect the migrants and provide for their effective government. The new nation's leaders were also concerned with the expansion of slavery, and

▶ **Teaching Notes**

Even in parts of the Old Northwest, some African Americans remained unfree after 1787. The first governor of the territory forced those who had been slaves before the adoption of the ordinance to remain slaves. In 1803, when Ohio became a state, the remainder of the Northwest Territory legalized indentured servitude. The result was that in southern parts of what became Illinois and Indiana, a few African Americans remained in involuntary servitude well into the nineteenth century.

▶ **Retracing the Odyssey**

Monticello, Charlottesville, Virginia. One hundred and thirty African Americans worked on this plantation during the late eighteenth century and early nineteenth century.

Amherst History Museum, Amherst, Massachusetts. Includes an exhibit on free black people who lived in eighteenth-century Amherst.

Thomas Jefferson sought to deal with both issues. First, he suggested that the western region be divided into separate territories and prepared for statehood. Second, he proposed that after 1800 slavery be banned from the entire region stretching from the Appalachians to the Mississippi River and from Spanish Florida (Spain had regained Florida in 1783) to British Canada.

In 1784 Jefferson's antislavery proposal failed by a single vote to pass Congress. Three years later, Congress adopted the **Northwest Ordinance**. This legislation applied the essence of Jefferson's plan to the region north of the Ohio River—what historians call the Old Northwest. The ordinance provided for the orderly sale of land, support for public education, territorial government, and the eventual formation of new states. Unlike Jefferson's plan, the ordinance banned slavery immediately. But, because it applied only to the Northwest Territory, the ordinance left the huge region south of the Ohio River open to slavery expansion.

Yet, by preventing slaveholders from taking slaves legally into areas north of the Ohio River, the ordinance set a precedent for excluding slavery from U.S. territories. Whether Congress had the power to do this became an issue after President Jefferson divided the huge Louisiana Territory in 1803 (see p. 152). The issue continued to divide northern and southern politicians until the Civil War.

Antislavery Societies in the North and the Upper South

While African Americans participated in the destruction of slavery in the northeastern states and Congress blocked its advance into the Old Northwest, a few white people organized to spread antislavery sentiment. In 1775 Quaker **abolitionist** Anthony Benezet organized the first **antislavery society** in the world. It became the Pennsylvania Society for Promoting the Abolition of Slavery in 1787, and Benjamin Franklin became its president. Similar societies were founded in Delaware in 1788 and Maryland in 1789. By the end of the eighteenth century, there were societies in New Jersey, Connecticut, and Virginia. Organized antislavery sentiment also quickly rose in the new slave states of Kentucky and Tennessee. However, such societies never appeared in the deep South.

From 1794 to 1832, antislavery societies cooperated within the loose framework of the American Convention for Promoting the Abolition of Slavery and Improving the Condition of the African Race. Only white people participated in these Quaker-dominated organizations, although members often cooperated with black leaders. As the northern states adopted abolition plans, the societies focused their attention on Delaware, Maryland, and Virginia. They aimed at gradual, **compensated emancipation**, encouraged masters to free their slaves, attempted to protect free black people from reenslavement, and frequently advocated sending freed black people out of the country.

▶▶ **Document**

5-4 Congress Prohibits Importation of Slaves, 1807

President Thomas Jefferson strongly supported the congressional bills to prohibit the importation of slaves. The bills were an outgrowth of the section of the Constitution that stated "The importation of persons as any of the States shall think proper to admit, shall not be prohibited by the Congress prior to the year 1808. . . ." At Jefferson's behest, both the House of Representatives and the Senate introduced bills outlawing the importation of slaves. This excerpt outlines the law and the penalties regarding the importation of slaves.

Experience with emancipation in the northern states encouraged the emphasis on gradual abolition. So did the reluctance of white abolitionists to challenge the property rights of masters. Abolitionists also feared that immediate emancipation might lead masters to abandon elderly slaves and assumed that African Americans would require long training before they could be free. Yet gradualism played into the hands of slaveholders who, like Thomas Jefferson, opposed slavery in the abstract but had no intention of freeing their own slaves.

The antislavery societies of the upper South tended to be small and short lived. A Wilmington, Delaware, society established in 1788 peaked at 50 members and ceased to exist in 1800. The Maryland society organized in 1781 with 6 members grew to 250 in 1797 but disbanded in 1798.

Manumission and Self-Purchase

Another hopeful sign for African Americans was that after the Revolution most southern states liberalized their **manumission laws**. In general, masters could free individual slaves by deed or will. They no longer had to go to court or petition a state legislature to prove that an individual they desired to manumit had performed a "meritorious service." Virginia led the way in 1782 by repealing its long-standing ban on private manumissions. Delaware in 1787, Maryland in 1790, Kentucky in 1792, and the slaveholding territory of Missouri in 1804 followed.

As a result, hundreds of slaveholders in the upper South began freeing slaves. Religious sentiment and natural rights principles motivated many of these masters. Even though most of them opposed general emancipation, they considered the slave system immoral. Yet noble motives were not always the most important. Masters often negotiated self-purchase agreements with slaves that, although ending in manumission, gave masters a profit. To purchase their freedom, or that of loved ones, slaves raised money over a number of years by marketing farm produce or through outside employment. This allowed masters to enjoy income in addition to the slave's labor over the period of time the slave needed to raise the entire purchase price.

Masters also sometimes manumitted slaves who were no longer profitable investments. A master might be switching from tobacco to wheat or corn—crops that did not need a year-round workforce. Or a master might manumit older slaves whose best years as workers were behind them. Frequently, however, slaves, usually young men, presented masters with the alternative of manumitting them after a term of years or seeing them escape immediately.

Self-purchase often left African Americans in precarious financial condition. Sometimes they used up their savings to buy their freedom. In other instances, they went into debt to their former masters, to white lawyers who acted as their agents, or to other white people who had

▶▶ **Document**

5-3 *Venture Smith Narrative, 1798*
Venture Smith was born in Africa but was captured and enslaved when he was 8 years old. He was named Broteer by his father, a "Prince of the tribe of Dukandarra" in Guinea. He was reported to be a giant of a man, weighing more than 300 pounds. Smith believed his ancestors were "very large, tall and stout race of beings, much larger than the generality of people in other parts of the globe." It comes as no surprise to learn that Smith's size and his refusal to suffer insults caused great difficulties for his owners. He was sold several times before he was able to purchase his freedom in 1765, at the age of thirty-six. Smith believed he had "lost much by misfortunes and paid an enormous sum for my freedom." He told his story to a local schoolteacher, which was published in 1798. On September 19, 1805, Smith died; he was 77.

▶▶ **Recommended Reading**

Ira Berlin. *Slaves Without Masters: The Free Negro in the Antebellum South*. New York: New Press, 1974. The early chapters of this classic study indicate the special difficulties the first large generation of free black southerners faced.

Humanitarian opposition to the Atlantic slave trade had mounted during the revolutionary era. Under pressure from black activists, such as Prince Hall of Boston, and Quakers, northern state legislatures during the 1780s forbade their citizens to engage in the slave trade. Rhode Island led the way in 1787. Massachusetts, Connecticut, and Pennsylvania followed in 1788. Economic change in the upper South also prompted opposition to the trade. Virginia, for example, banned the importation of slaves from abroad nearly a decade before Rhode Island.

Yet convention delegates from South Carolina and Georgia maintained that their states had an acute labor shortage. They threatened that citizens of these states would not tolerate a central government that could stop them from importing slaves—at least not in the near future. Torn between these conflicting perspectives, the convention compromised by including a provision in the Constitution that prohibited Congress from abolishing the trade until 1808. During the twenty years prior to 1808, when Congress banned the trade, thousands of Africans were brought into the southern states. Between 1804 and 1808, for example, forty thousand entered through Charleston. Overall, more slaves entered the United States between 1787 and 1808 than during any other twenty years in American history. Such huge numbers helped fuel the westward expansion of the slave system.

▶▶ **Document**

The United States Constitution
This annotated version provides insight and
analysis of the various amendments.
To access this document go to PHSchool.com,
enter the Webcode lif-0001.

▶▶ **Interactive Activity**

Ratification of the Constitution
This activity offers both a general discussion and
a case study of the debate over the Constitution,
indicating that ratification was an arduous
struggle. The narrative provides a structure for
the extensive primary source excerpts that set
the positions for and against the Constitution.

▶▶ **Recommended Reading**

Sidney Kaplan and Emma Nogrady Kaplan. *The
Black Presence in the Era of the American
Revolution.* Rev. ed. Amherst, MA: University
of Massachusetts Press, 1989. This
delightfully written book provides informative
accounts of black leaders who lived during
the early American republic.

Proslavery and the Constitution

Other proslavery clauses of the U.S. Constitution aimed to counteract slave rebellion and escape. The Constitution gave Congress power to put down "insurrections" and "domestic violence." It also provided that persons "held to service or labour in one State, escaping into another . . . shall be delivered up on claim of the party to whom such service or labour may be due." This clause was the basis for the **Fugitive Slave Act** of 1793, which allowed masters or their agents to pursue slaves across state lines, capture them, and take them before a judge. There, on presentation of satisfactory evidence, masters could regain legal custody of the person they claimed. This act did not stop slaves from escaping from Virginia and Maryland to Pennsylvania. But it did extend the power of masters into the North. It forced the federal and northern state governments to uphold slavery, create personal tragedies for those who were recaptured, and encourage the kidnapping of free black northerners falsely claimed as escapees.

Finally, the Constitution strengthened the political power of slaveholders through the **Three-Fifths Clause**. This clause was also a compromise between northern and southern delegates at the Convention. Southern delegates desired slaves to be counted toward representation in the national government but not counted for purposes of taxation. Northern delegates desired just the opposite. The Three-Fifths Clause provided that a slave be counted as three-fifths of a free person in determining a state's representation in the House of

Representatives and in the electoral college. Slaves would be counted similarly if and when Congress instituted a **per capita tax**.

This gave southern slaveholders increased representation on the basis of the number of slaves they owned—slaves who, of course, had no vote or representation. The South gained enormous political advantage from it. If not for the Three-Fifths Clause, for example, northern nonslaveholder John Adams would have been reelected president in 1800 instead of losing the presidency to southern slaveholder Thomas Jefferson. For many years, this clause contributed to the domination of the U.S. government by slaveholding southerners, although the South's population steadily fell behind the North's.

Four other factors, however, were more important than constitutional provisions in fostering the continued enslavement of African Americans in the new republic: increased cultivation of cotton, the Louisiana Purchase, declining revolutionary fervor, and intensified white racism.

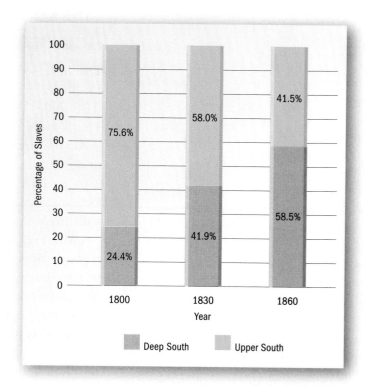

FIGURE 5–1 Distribution of the Southern Slave Population, 1800–1860.

The demand for slaves in the cotton-growing deep South produced a major shift in the distribution of the slave population.

Cotton

By the late eighteenth century, Britain was the world's leading textile producer. As mechanization made the spinning of cotton cloth more economical, Britain's demand for raw cotton increased dramatically. The United States took the lead in filling that demand as a result of Eli Whitney's invention of the **cotton gin** in 1793. This simple machine provided an easy and quick way to remove the seeds from the type of cotton most commonly grown in the South.

British demand combined with the cotton gin encouraged cotton production in the United States to rise from 3,000 to 178,000 bales between 1790 and 1810. Cotton became by far the most lucrative U.S. export. Southern cotton production also encouraged the development of textile mills in New England, thereby creating a proslavery alliance between the "lords of the lash and the lords of the loom."

Cotton reinvigorated the slave-labor system, which spread rapidly across Georgia and later into Alabama, Mississippi, Louisiana, and Texas. Cotton was also cultivated in South Carolina, North Carolina, and parts of Virginia and Tennessee. To make matters worse for African Americans, the westward expansion of cotton production encouraged an **internal slave trade**. Masters in the old tobacco-growing regions of Maryland, Virginia, and other states began to support themselves by selling their slaves to the new cotton-growing regions (see Figure 5–1).

The Louisiana Purchase and African Americans in the Lower Mississippi Valley

The Jefferson administration's purchase of Louisiana from France in 1803 accelerated the westward expansion of slavery and the domestic slave trade. The purchase nearly doubled the area of the United States. That slavery might extend over this entire vast region was an issue of great importance to African Americans. The purchase also brought under American sovereignty those black people, both free and slave, who lived in the portion of the territory that centered on the city of New Orleans. As Chapter 3 indicates, black life in this region had developed a distinctive pattern under French and Spanish rule from 1699 to 1803.

Although people of African descent constituted a majority of the region's population, they were divided into two groups. First were the free people of color who referred to themselves as Creoles. They were craftsmen and shopkeepers in New Orleans and other port cities. They spoke French, belonged to the Roman Catholic Church, and aspired to equal rights with other free inhabitants. Some of them bought and sold slaves. Their numbers had increased under Spanish rule as urban slaves purchased their freedom. This route to freedom became more difficult under American sovereignty, but, as a group, Louisiana's free people of color remained optimistically integrationist in outlook.

The second group was growing more rapidly. It consisted of plantation slaves, most of whom had come directly from Africa and worked on the region's plantations. Spain had encouraged white Americans to settle in the lower Mississippi Valley. The Americans, in turn, demanded more strictly enforced slave codes and the expansion of the external slave trade. At first the slaves continued to produce tobacco and indigo, but by the 1790s sugar and cotton had emerged as the crops of the future. As demand for these crops grew, conditions for slaves in Louisiana became increasingly harsher. The slaves' rural location, their predominantly African culture, and, eventually, their Protestant religion cut them off from free people of color. In 1770 Louisiana's slave population was 5,600. By 1810 it was 34,660. By 1820 it was 149,654. This tremendous growth, involving an extremely harsh form of slavery in a huge region, constituted a warning to all opponents of that institution. The notorious slave markets of New Orleans became the dreaded destination of thousands of African Americans "sold south" by their masters in the domestic slave trade.

Conservatism and Racism

The waning of revolutionary humanitarianism and the rise of a more intense racism among white people were less tangible forces than cotton production and the Louisiana Purchase. But they were just as important in strengthening slavery. They also made life more difficult for free African Americans.

By the 1790s white Americans had begun a long retreat from the egalitarianism of the revolutionary era. In the North and Chesapeake, most white people became less willing to challenge the prerogatives of slaveholders and more willing to accept slavery as suitable for African Americans. Most Marylanders and Virginians came to think of emancipation as best left to the distant future. This outlook strengthened the slaveholders and their nonslaveholding white supporters in the deep South who had never embraced the humanitarian ideals of the Enlightenment and Great Awakening.

Increasing proslavery sentiment among white Americans stemmed, in part, from revulsion against the radicalism of the French Revolution that had begun in 1789. Reports of bloody class warfare, disruption of the social order, and redistribution of property in France led most Americans to value property rights—including human property—and order above equal rights. In addition, as cotton production spread westward and the value of slaves soared, rationalist and evangelical criticism of human bondage withered. Antislavery sentiment in the upper South became increasingly confined to African Americans and Quakers. By the early 1800s, manumissions began a long decline.

Using race to justify slavery was an important component of this conservative trend. Unlike white people, the argument went, black people were unsuited for freedom or citizenship. The doctrines embodied in the Declaration of Independence were, therefore, not applicable to them. A new scientific racism supported this outlook. As early as the 1770s, scholars began to propose that black people constituted a separate species as close to the great apes as to white people. During the 1780s Thomas Jefferson reflected this view when he argued that "scientific observation" supported the conclusion that black people were inherently "inferior to whites in the endowments of both body and mind."

Such views were common among white northerners and white southerners and had practical results. During the 1790s Congress expressed its determination to exclude African Americans from the benefits of citizenship in "a white man's country." A 1790 law limited the granting of naturalized citizenship to "any alien, being a white person." Two years later, Congress limited enrollment in state militias to "each and every free, able-bodied white male citizen." These laws implied that African Americans had no place in the United States except as slaves. In other words, the free black class was an anomaly and, in the opinion of most white people, a dangerous anomaly.

 Reading Check Why did slavery survive in the new United States?

▶▶ **Reading Check**

The Constitution supported the interests of slave owners. Moreover, the emergence of the cotton industry created enormous demand for slave labor. Finally, the expansion of the United States added to the territory in which slavery could grow and survive.

▶▶ **Recommended Reading**

Donald R. Wright. *African Americans in the Early Republic, 1789–1831*. Arlington Heights, IL: Harlan Davidson, 1993. This is a brief but comprehensive account that reflects recent interpretations.

GUIDE TO READING

▶ What were the characteristics of early free black communities?

▶ What role did mutual aid societies play in African-American society?

▶ What place did black churches have in African-American communities?

KEY TERMS

▶ mutual aid societies, p. 154

▶ Free African Society, p. 154

▶ freemasonry, p. 155

▶ Prince Hall , p. 155

▶ Prince Hall Masons, p. 155

▶▶ **Guide to Reading/Key Terms**

For answers, see the *Teacher's Resource Manual.*

▶▶ **Document**

5-2 *Preamble of the Free Africa Society, 1787*

▶▶ **Recommended Reading**

Gary B. Nash. *Forging Freedom: The Formation of Philadelphia's Black Community, 1720–1840.* Cambridge, MA: Harvard University Press, 1988. This path-breaking study of a black community analyzes the origins of separate black institutions.

Section 3

The Emergence of Free Black Communities

Black Community Life

The competing forces of slavery and racism, on one hand, and freedom and opportunity, on the other, shaped the growth of African-American communities in the early American republic. A distinctive black culture had existed since the early colonial period. But enslavement had limited black community life. The advent of large free black populations in the North and upper South after the Revolution allowed African Americans to establish autonomous and dynamic communities. They appeared in Philadelphia, Baltimore, Newport (Rhode Island), Richmond, Norfolk, New York, and Boston. Although smaller and less autonomous, there were also free black communities in such deep South cities as Charleston, Savannah, and New Orleans. As free black people in these cities acquired a modicum of wealth and education, they established institutions that have shaped African-American life ever since.

A combination of factors encouraged African Americans to form these distinctive institutions. First, as they emerged from slavery, they realized they would have inferior status in white-dominated organizations or not be allowed to participate in them at all. Second, black people valued the African heritage they had preserved over generations in slavery. They wanted institutions that would perpetuate their heritage.

Black Societies

The earliest black community institutions were **mutual aid societies**. Patterned on similar white organizations, these societies were like modern insurance companies and benevolent organizations. They provided for their members' medical and burial expenses and helped support widows and children. African Americans in Newport, Rhode Island, organized the first such black mutual aid society in 1780. Seven years later, Richard Allen and Absalom Jones established the more famous **Free African Society** in Philadelphia.

Most early free black societies admitted only men, but similar organizations for women appeared during the 1790s. For example, in 1793 Philadelphia's Female Benevolent Society of St. Thomas took over the welfare functions of the city's Free African Society. Other black women's organizations in Philadelphia during the early republic included the

Benevolent Daughters—established in 1796 by Richard Allen's wife Sarah—Daughters of Africa established in 1812, the American Female Bond Benevolent Society formed in 1817, and the Female Benezet begun in 1818.

These ostensibly secular societies maintained a decidedly Christian moral character. They insisted that their members meet standards of middle-class propriety. In effect, they became self-improvement as well as mutual aid societies. By the early 1800s, such societies also organized resistance to kidnappers who sought to recapture fugitive slaves or enslave free African Americans.

Because such societies provided real benefits and reflected black middle-class aspirations, they spread to every black urban community. More than one hundred such organizations existed in Philadelphia alone by 1830. These societies were more common in the North than in the South.

Black Freemasons

Of particular importance were the black freemasons because, unlike other free black organizations, the masons united black men from several northern cities. Combining rationalism with secrecy and obscure ritual, **freemasonry** was a major movement among European and American men during the late eighteenth and early nineteenth centuries. Opportunities for male bonding, wearing fancy regalia, and achieving prestige in a supposedly ancient hierarchy attracted both black and white men. As historians James Oliver Horton and Lois E. Horton suggest, black people drew special satisfaction from the European-based order's claims to have originated in ancient Egypt, which black people associated with their own African heritage.

The most famous black mason of his time was **Prince Hall**, the Revolutionary War veteran and abolitionist. During the 1770s he founded what became known as the African Grand Lodge of North America, or, more colloquially, the **Prince Hall Masons**. In several respects, Hall's relationship to masonry epitomizes the free black predicament in America.

In 1775 the local white masonic lodge in Boston rejected Hall's application for membership because of his black ancestry. Instead, Hall, who was a Patriot, got a limited license for what was called African Lodge No. 1 from a British lodge associated with the British Army that then occupied Boston. The irony of this situation was compounded when, after the War for Independence, American masonry refused to grant the African Lodge a full charter. Hall again had to turn to the British masons who approved his application in 1787. It was under this British charter that Hall in 1791 became provincial grand master of North America and began authorizing black lodges in other cities, notably Philadelphia, Pennsylvania, and Providence, Rhode Island.

A former slave, a skilled craftsman and entrepreneur, an abolitionist, and an advocate of black education, Prince Hall is best remembered as the founder of the African Lodge of North America, popularly known as the Prince Hall Masons.

The Origins of Independent Black Churches

Black churches emerged at least a decade later than black benevolent associations and quickly became the core of African-American communities. Not only did these churches attend to the spiritual needs of free black people and—in some southern cities—slaves, their pastors also became the primary African-American leaders. Black church buildings housed schools, social organizations, and antislavery meetings.

During the late eighteenth century, separate, but not independent, black churches appeared in the South. The biracial churches spawned by the Awakening had never embraced African Americans on an equal basis with white people. As time passed white people denied black people significant influence in church governance and subjected them to segregated seating, communion services, Sunday schools, and cemeteries. Separate black congregations, usually headed by black ministers but subordinate to white church hierarchies, were the result of these policies. The first such congregations appeared during the 1770s in South Carolina and Georgia.

The First Independent Black Church

In contrast to these subordinate churches, a truly independent black church emerged gradually in Philadelphia between the 1780s and the early 1800s. The movement for such a church began within the city's white-controlled St. George's Methodist Church. The movement's leaders were Richard Allen and Absalom Jones, who could rely on the Free African Society they had established to help them.

These men were former slaves who had purchased their freedom: Allen in 1780 and Jones in 1783. Allen, a fervent Methodist since the 1770s, had received permission from St. George's white leadership to preach to black people in the evenings in what was then a simple church building. By the mid-1780s, Jones had joined Allen's congregation, and soon they and other black members of St. George's chafed under policies they considered unchristian and insulting. But Allen's and Jones's faith that Methodist egalitarianism would prevail over racial discrimination undermined their efforts during the 1780s to create a separate black Methodist church.

The break finally came in 1792 when St. George's white leaders grievously insulted the church's black members. An attempt by white trustees to prevent Jones from praying in what the trustees considered the white section of the church led black members to walk out. "We all went out of the church in a body," recalled Allen, "and they were no more plagued with us in the church."

St. George's white leaders fought hard and long to control the expanding and economically valuable black congregation. Yet other white Philadelphians, led by abolitionist Benjamin Rush, applauded the concept of an independent "African church." Rush and other sympathetic

▶▶ **Document**

5-5 *Absalom Jones, Sermon on the Abolition of the International Slave Trade, 1808*
Congress outlawed the importation of slaves into the United States, effective January 1, 1808. To mark the occasion, Absalom Jones, co-founder and first pastor of Philadelphia's African Methodist Episcopal Church, preached a sermon in which he expressed his hope that each year this day would be remembered and "our children, to the remotest generations" would learn "the history of the sufferings of our brethren, and of their deliverance [from] the trade which dragged your fathers from their native country, and sold them as bond men in the United States of America."

▶▶ **Retracing the Odyssey**

Afro-American Historical and Cultural Museum, Philadelphia, Pennsylvania. Includes an exhibit on the rise of black churches, 1740–1977.

Richard Allen on the Break with St. George's Church

It took an emotionally wrenching experience to convince Richard Allen, Absalom Jones, and other black Methodists that they must break their association with St. George's Church. Allen published the following account in 1831 as part of his autobiography, The Life Experiences and Gospel Labors of the Rt. Rev. Richard Allen. *Although many years had passed since the incident, Allen's account retains a strong emotional immediacy.*

A number of us usually attended St. George's church in Fourth street; and when the colored people began to get numerous in attending the church, they moved us from the seats we usually sat on, and placed us around the wall, and on Sabbath morning, we went to the church and the sexton stood at the door, and told us to go in the gallery. He told us to go, and we would see where to sit. We expected to take the seats over the ones we formerly occupied below, not knowing any better. We took those seats. Meeting had begun and they were nearly done singing, and just as we got to the seats, the elder said, "Let us pray." We had not been long upon our knees before I heard considerable scuffling and low talking. I raised my head up and saw one of the trustees, H M, having hold of the Rev. Absalom Jones, pulling him up off his knees, and saying, "You must get up—you must not kneel here." Mr. Jones replied, "Wait until prayer is over." Mr. H M said, "No, you must get up now, or I will call for aid and force you away." Mr. Jones said, "Wait until prayer is over, and I will get up and trouble you no more." With that he [H M] beckoned to one of the other trustees, Mr. L S to come to his assistance. He came, and went to William White to pull him up. By this time prayer was over, and we all went out of the church in a body, and they were no more plagued with us in the church. . . . We then hired a storeroom, and held worship by ourselves. Here we were pursued with threats of being disowned, and read publicly out of meeting if we did continue worship in the place we had hired; but we believed the Lord would be our friend. We got subscription papers out to raise money to build the house of the Lord.

What Do You Think?

▶ What appears to have sparked the confrontation Allen describes?

▶ How did white church leaders respond to the withdrawal of the church's black members?

▶ **What Do You Think?**

· Racial prejudice appears to have sparked the confrontation.

· White church leaders threatened to ban them publicly from the church if they continued to hold their own services.

▶ **Document**

7-2 Richard Allen, "Address to the Free People of Colour of these United States," 1830 American Methodist Episcopal Bishop Richard Allen and other free blacks issued a call for a Negro convention. In September 1830 free blacks throughout the country arrived in Philadelphia to discuss forming the American Society of Free Persons of Colour. For four days, more than three-dozen delegates representing eight states met at Bethel AME Church debated ways that would improve their lives. Although the Society denounced African colonization, the organization did have plans for "purchasing land, and locating a settlement in the Province of Upper Canada." In addition, Allen wanted to establish auxiliary societies across the nation that would aid in establishing a Canadian colony. Fifteen delegates from five states returned to Philadelphia's Wesleyan Church the following year to discuss obstacles that plagued black freedom. The meeting marked the beginning of Negro Conventions that would meet before and after the Civil War as black people sought ways of coping with white America.

Philadelphia's Bethel African Methodist Episcopal Church was built in 1793 under the direction of Richard Allen, the first bishop of the AME denomination.

white people contributed to the new church's building fund. When construction began in 1793, Rush and at least one hundred other white people joined with African Americans at a banquet to celebrate the occasion.

However, the black congregation soon split. When the majority determined that the new church would be Episcopalian rather than Methodist, Allen and a few others refused to join. The result was *two* black churches in Philadelphia. St. Thomas's Episcopal Church, with Jones as priest, opened in July 1794 as an African-American congregation within the white-led national Episcopal Church. Then Allen's Mother Bethel congregation got under way as the first truly independent black church. The white leaders of St. George's tried to control Mother Bethel until 1816. That year Mother Bethel became the birthplace of the African Methodist Episcopal (AME) Church. Allen became the first bishop of this organization, which quickly spread to other cities in the North and the South.

New Black Churches Emerge

The more significant among the other AME congregations were Daniel Coker's in Baltimore, the AME Zion in New York, and those in Wilmington, Delaware; Salem, New Jersey; and Attleboro, Pennsylvania. Additional independent black churches formed at this time out of similar conflicts with white-led congregations. Among them were the African Baptist Church established in Boston in 1805 and led by Thomas Paul from 1806 to 1808, the Presbyterian Evangelical Society founded in 1811 by John Gloucester, the Abyssinian Baptist Church organized in New York City in 1808 by Paul, and the African Presbyterian Church, established in Philadelphia by Samuel E. Cornish in 1822.

The First Black Schools

Schools for African-American children, slave and free, date to the early 1700s. In both North and South, white clergy, including Cotton Mather, ran the schools. So did Quakers, early abolition societies, and missionaries acting for the Anglican Society for the Propagation of the Gospel in Foreign Parts. But the first schools established by African Americans to instruct African-American children arose after the Revolution. The new black mutual aid societies and churches created and sustained them.

Schools for black people organized or taught by white people continued to flourish. But in other instances, black people founded their own schools because local white authorities regularly refused either to admit black children to public schools or to maintain adequate separate schools for them. For example, in 1796, when he failed to convince Boston's city council to provide a school for black students, Prince Hall had the children taught in his own home and that of his son Primus. By

▶▶ What do You Think?

· Lack of food and water, diseases, shipwrecks due to storms, and piracy.

· The author is indifferent to the slaves' suffering.

1806 the school was meeting in the basement of the new African Meeting House, which housed Thomas Paul's African Baptist Church.

Hall was not the first to take such action. As early as 1790, Charleston's Brown Fellowship operated a school for its members' children. Free black people in Baltimore supported schools during the same decade, and during the early 1800s, similar schools opened in Washington, D.C. Such schools frequently employed white teachers. Not until Philadelphia's Mother Bethel Church established the Augustine School in 1818 did a school entirely administered and taught by African Americans for black children exist.

These schools faced great difficulties. Many black families could not afford the fees, but rather than turn children away, the schools strained their meager resources by taking charity cases. Some black parents also believed education was pointless when African Americans often could not get skilled jobs. White people feared competition from skilled black workers, believed black schools attracted undesirable populations, and, particularly in the South, feared that educated free African Americans would encourage slaves to revolt.

Threats of violence against black schools and efforts to suppress them were common. The case of Christopher McPherson exemplifies these dangers. McPherson, a free African American, established a night school for black men at Richmond, Virginia, in 1811 and hired a white teacher. All went well until McPherson advertised the school in a local newspaper. In response, white residents forced the teacher to leave the city, and local authorities had McPherson committed to the state lunatic asylum. Nevertheless, similar schools continued to operate in both the North and upper South, producing a growing class of literate African Americans.

 Reading Check What were the characteristics of early free black communities?

"ZION" SCHOOL FOR COLORED CHILDREN, CHARLESTON, SOUTH CAROLINA.—From a Sketch by A. R. Waud.—[See Page 790.]

▶▶ **Reading Check**

The advent of large free black populations in the North allowed for the creation of autonomous and dynamic black communities. Conscious of their disadvantages in a society dominated by whites and desirous of preserving their African heritage, free blacks developed their own community institutions.

▶ How would you characterize free black leaders in the early nineteenth century?

▶ What practical obstacles stood in the way of mass black migration to Africa?

▶ What role did the principles of the American and French Revolutions play in the slave uprisings of Gabriel and Desmondes?

▶ How did fear of slave uprisings shape white southern attitudes toward slavery?

▶ **Guide to Reading/Key Terms**

For answers, see the *Teacher's Resource Manual.*

▶ **Teaching Notes**

Other influential black ministers of the late eighteenth and early nineteenth centuries were Jupiter Hammon, Daniel Coker of Baltimore, John Chavis of Virginia, and Lemuel Haynes of New England. Hammon, who is quoted at the beginning of this chapter, became a well-known poet. Coker, who was of mixed race, conducted a school, cofounded the AME Church, and advocated black migration to Africa. Chavis also combined preaching and teaching. Born free, he served on the Patriot side in the War for Independence and entered the College of New

Section 4

Black Leaders and Choices

Early Black Leaders

By the 1790s an educated black elite that was well able to provide leadership for African Americans had come into existence in the North and Chesapeake. Experience had driven members of this elite to a contradictory perception of themselves and of America. They were acculturated, patriotic Americans who had achieved some personal well-being and security. But they were well aware that American society had not lived up to its revolutionary principles.

Prominent among these leaders were members of the clergy. Two of the most important of them were Richard Allen and Absalom Jones. Besides organizing his church, Allen opened a school in Philadelphia for black children, wrote against slavery and racial prejudice, and made his home a refuge for fugitive slaves. A year before his death in 1831, Allen presided over the first national black convention. Jones, too, was an early abolitionist. In 1797 his concern for fugitives facing reenslavement led him to become the first African American to petition Congress. His petition anticipated later abolitionists in suggesting that slavery violated the spirit of the U.S. Constitution and that Congress could abolish it.

Vying with clergy for influence were African-American entrepreneurs. Prince Hall, for example, owned successful leather dressing and catering businesses in Boston, and Peter Williams, principal founder of New York's AME Zion church, was a prosperous tobacco merchant. Another prominent black entrepreneur was James Forten of Philadelphia, described as "probably the most noteworthy free African-American entrepreneur in the early nineteenth century." Born to free parents in 1766, Forten was a Patriot during the War for Independence and became the owner of his own business in 1798. For the rest of his life, he advocated equal rights and abolition.

American patriotism, religious conviction, organizational skill, intellectual inquisitiveness, and antislavery activism delineate the lives of most free black leaders in this era. Yet these leaders often were torn in their perceptions of what was best for African Americans. Some were accommodationist about slavery and racial oppression. They condemned slavery and lauded human liberty, but they were not activists.

Others such as Allen, Jones, Hall, and Forten were more optimistic about the ability of African Americans to mold their own destiny in the

United States. They believed that, despite setbacks, the egalitarian principles of the American Revolution would prevail if black people insisted on liberty. Forten never despaired that African Americans would be integrated into the larger American society on the basis of their individual talent and enterprise. Although he was often frustrated, Hall for four decades pursued a strategy based on the assumption that white authority would reward black protest and patriotism. Allen and Jones put more emphasis on separate black institutions. Yet they were just as willing to organize, protest, and petition to establish the rights of black people as American citizens.

Jersey (Princeton) in 1792. Thereafter he became a Presbyterian missionary among African Americans in Virginia, Maryland, and North Carolina and gained a wide reputation as a biblical scholar. Haynes was perhaps even better known for his intellectual accomplishments. The son of a white mother and black father, Haynes served with the Minutemen and Continental Army, spoke against slavery, and in 1780, became the first ordained black Congregationalist minister, serving as pastor to several white congregations.

PROFILE ❖ James Forten

James Forten was one of the few black leaders of the early American republic to live well beyond that era. From the 1790s until his death in 1842, Forten used his wealth and organizational talents to build a cohesive black community in Philadelphia. But he also struggled to create a broader American community based on merit rather than on racial privilege.

Forten was born in Philadelphia in 1766. His paternal grandfather was one of the first Pennsylvania slaves to purchase his freedom. As a child, Forten learned to read and write at a school run by Quaker abolitionist Anthony Benezet. In 1781 Forten volunteered to serve as a powder boy on board the American privateer *Royal Louis*. He proved himself a brave sailor in battle. When taken prisoner and offered special treatment, Forten declared, " No, NO! I am here a prisoner for the liberties of my country; I *never, NEVER, shall prove a traitor to her interests.*" Forten spent seven months on a rotting prison ship in New York harbor.

After his release Forten walked back to Philadelphia and became an apprentice sail maker. He became foreman in 1786 and bought the business in 1798. By 1807 he employed an interracial work force of thirty, and by 1832 had acquired a fortune of about $100,000—a large sum at the time.

In 1797 he emerged as an active black leader. At that time he joined Richard Allen and Absalom Jones in establishing the African Masonic Lodge of Pennsylvania. Forten then joined eighty other Philadelphia African Americans to petition Congress to repeal the Fugitive Slave Law of 1793.

By 1817 Forten had become a major opponent of black migration to Africa. He had come to believe such efforts were racist because they assumed black people were not suited for American citizenship. He was determined to improve their standing in the United States. In 1809 he had joined Allen and Jones in creating a self-improvement organization, the Society for the Suppression of Vice and Immorality. By 1830 he hoped to use the newly organized Black National Convention movement to train young black men for skilled trades.

At about the same time, Forten became an important influence on the white abolitionist leader William Lloyd Garrison. Forten introduced Garrison to other black leaders, and helped finance his antislavery newspaper, the *Liberator*. In 1833 Forten joined Garrison, Arthur Tappan, Lewis Tappan, and other white and black abolitionists in organizing the American Antislavery Society. He also helped establish the American Moral Reform Society. He demonstrated his commitment to women's rights in the way he raised his daughters, Sarah, Margaretta, and Harriet, who carried on his activism.

Raphaelle Peale completed this oil portrait of the Reverend Absalom Jones in 1810.

Migration

African Americans, however, had another alternative: migration from the United States to establish their own society free from white prejudices. In 1787 British philanthropists, including Olaudah Equiano, had established **Freetown** in Sierra Leone on the West African coast as a refuge for former slaves. Some African Americans who had been Loyalists during the American Revolution settled there. Other black and white Americans proposed that free black people should settle western North America or in the Caribbean islands. There were great practical obstacles to mass black migration to each of these regions. Migration was extremely expensive, difficult to organize, and involved long, often fruitless, negotiations with foreign governments. But no black leader during the early national period was immune to the appeal of such proposals.

In 1787 Hall petitioned the Massachusetts legislature to support efforts by black Bostonians to establish a colony in Africa. Although he recognized black progress in Massachusetts, Hall maintained that he and others found themselves "in many respects, in very disagreeable and disadvantageous circumstances; most of which must attend us so long as we and our children live in America." By the mid-1810s, a few influential white Americans had also decided there was no place in the United States for free African Americans. In 1816 they organized the **American Colonization Society**. Under its auspices, Daniel Coker in 1820 led the first party of eighty-six African Americans to the new colony of **Liberia** on the West African coast.

The major black advocate of migration to Africa during this period, however, was Paul Cuffe, the son of an Ashante (in modern Ghana) father and Wampanoag Indian mother. He became a prosperous New England sea captain and, by the early 1800s, cooperated with British humanitarians and entrepreneurs to promote migration. He saw African-American colonization in West Africa as a way to end the Atlantic slave trade, spread Christianity, create a refuge for free black people, and make profits.

Slave Uprisings

While black northerners became increasingly aware of the limits to their freedom after the Revolution, black southerners saw the perpetuation of their enslavement. As cotton production expanded westward, as new slave states entered the Union, and as masters in such border slave states as Maryland and Virginia turned away from the revolutionary commitment to gradual emancipation, slaves faced several choices.

Some lowered their expectations and loyally served their masters. Most continued patterns of day-to-day resistance. Mounting numbers of men and women escaped. A few risked their lives to join revolutionary movements to destroy slavery violently. When just several hundred out of hundreds of thousands of slaves rallied behind Gabriel in 1800 near Richmond or Charles Deslondes in 1811 near New Orleans, they frightened white southerners and raised hopes for freedom among countless African Americans.

The egalitarian principles of the American and French revolutions influenced Gabriel and Deslondes. Unlike earlier slave rebels, they acted not to revenge personal grievances or to establish maroon communities but to destroy slavery because it denied natural human rights to its victims. The American Declaration of Independence and the legend of Haiti's **Toussaint Louverture** provided the intellectual foundations for their efforts. Louverture, against great odds, had led the enslaved black people of the French sugar colony of Saint Domingue—modern Haiti—to freedom and independence. This bitter and bloody struggle lasted from 1791 to 1804. Many white planters fled the island with their slaves to take refuge in Cuba, Jamaica, South Carolina, Virginia, and, somewhat later, Louisiana. The Haitian slaves carried the spirit of revolution with them to their new homes.

Toussaint Louverture led the rebellion that resulted in the creation of the independent black republic of Haiti in 1804. Stock Montage, Inc./Historical Pictures Collection

Gabriel's Conspiracy

During the early 1790s, black unrest and rumors of pending revolt mounted in Virginia. The state militia arrested suspected plotters, who got off with whippings. In this revolutionary atmosphere, Gabriel, the human property of Thomas Prosser Sr., prepared to lead a massive slave insurrection. Gabriel was an acculturated and literate blacksmith who was well aware of the rationalist and revolutionary currents of his time. He was also a large and powerful man with a violent temper. In the fall of 1799, for example, a local court convicted him of "'biting off a considerable part of [the] left Ear' of a white neighbor."

The ideology of the American Revolution shaped Gabriel's actions. He was also aware that white people were politically divided and distracted by an undeclared naval war with France. He enjoyed some secret white support and hoped that poor people generally would rally to his cause as he and his associates planned to kill those who supported slavery and take control of central Virginia.

But on August 30, 1800—the day the uprising was to occur—two slaves revealed the plan to white authorities while a tremendous thunderstorm prevented Gabriel's followers from assaulting Richmond. Then governor—and future U.S. president—James Monroe quickly had suspects arrested. Gabriel, who relied on white allies to get to Norfolk, was among the last captured. In October he and twenty-six others, convicted of "conspiracy and insurrection," were hanged. By demonstrating that slaves could organize for large-scale rebellion, they left a legacy of fear among slaveholders and hope for liberation among southern African Americans.

The Louisiana Rebellion

The far less famous **Louisiana Rebellion** took place under similar circumstances. By the early 1800s, refugees from Haiti had settled with their slaves in what was then known as Orleans Territory. As they arrived,

▶ **Recommended Reading**

Douglas R. Egerton. *Gabriel's Rebellion: The Virginia Slave Conspiracies of 1800 and 1802.* Chapel Hill, NC: University of North Carolina Press, 1993. This most recent account of Gabriel's conspiracy emphasizes both the revolutionary context within which he acted and his legacy.

rumors of slave insurrection spread across the territory. The rumors became reality on January 8, 1811, when Deslondes, a Haitian native and slave driver on a plantation north of New Orleans, initiated a massive revolt in cooperation with maroons.

Although no record of Deslondes's rhetoric survives and his goals may have been less ideologically coherent than Gabriel's, he organized a force of at least 180 men and women. They marched south along the Mississippi River toward New Orleans, with leaders on horseback, and with flags and drums, but few guns. The revolutionaries plundered and burned plantations but killed only two white people and one recalcitrant slave. They were overwhelmed on January 10 by a force of about seven hundred territorial militia, slaveholding vigilantes, and U.S. troops. The "battle" was a massacre. The well-armed white men slaughtered sixty-six of the rebels and captured twenty-one, including Deslondes. These captives were tried without benefit of counsel, found guilty of rebellion, and shot. The white authorities cut off each executed rebel's head and displayed it on a pike to warn other African Americans of the consequences of revolt.

The White Southern Reaction

Although Deslondes's uprising was one of the few major slave revolts in American history, Gabriel's conspiracy and events in Haiti left the more significant legacy. For generations, enslaved African Americans regarded Louverture as a black George Washington and recalled Gabriel's revolutionary message. The networks among slaves that Gabriel established continued to exist after his death. As the external slave trade carried black Virginians southwestward, they took his promise of liberation with them.

The fears that the Haitian revolution and Gabriel's conspiracy raised among white southerners deepened their reaction against the egalitarian values of the Enlightenment. Because they feared race war and believed emancipation would encourage African Americans to begin such a war, most white people in Virginia and throughout the South determined to make black bondage stronger, not weaker.

Beginning with South Carolina in December 1800, southern states outlawed assemblies of slaves, placed curfews on slaves and free black people, and made manumissions more difficult. The old colonial practice of white men on horseback patrolling slave quarters revived. Assuming that revolutionaries like Gabriel received encouragement from white abolitionists as well as free African Americans, white southerners became suspicious of such outsiders as Yankee peddlers, evangelicals, and foreigners. Forcing free black people out of southern states became more attractive to some white southerners and brought about the odd alliance between them and black advocates of emigration to Africa.

 **Reading Check** How did fear of slave uprisings shape white southern attitudes toward slavery?

▶ **Reading Check**

Fear of slave uprisings deepened white southerners distrust and dislike of Enlightenment principles. They feared a race war and believed emancipation would help spark such a war. As a result, white southerners became even more committed to the continuation of slavery.

Section 5

War and Politics

The War of 1812

Many of the themes developed in this chapter—African-American patriotism, opportunities for freedom, migration sentiment, and influences pushing slaves toward revolutionary action—are reflected in the black experience during the U.S. war with Great Britain that began in 1812. The roots of this conflict lay in a massive military and economic struggle between Britain and France for mastery over the Atlantic world. The struggle lasted from 1793, during the French Revolution, to the defeat of Napoleon Bonaparte by a British-led coalition in 1815.

British military support for American Indian resistance in the Old Northwest, an American desire to annex Canada, and especially Britain's interference with American ships trading with Europe drew the United States into the war, which lasted until early 1815. Although the United States won some important victories, it failed to achieve its major objective—the conquest of Canada—and the war ended in a draw. Yet many Americans regarded the war as a second struggle for independence and, as had been the case during the American Revolution, black military service and white fear of slave revolt played important roles (see Map 5–2).

When the war began, white prejudice and fear of black revolt had nearly nullified memories of the service of black Patriot soldiers during the Revolution. The **Militia Act** of 1792 had eliminated armed black participation in all state militias except that of North Carolina. The secretary of the navy ended black service on American warships in 1798. White southerners joined John Randolph of Virginia in regarding African Americans as "an internal foe." When the war with Great Britain began, therefore, the southern states refused to enlist black men for fear they would use their guns to aid slave revolts. Meanwhile the lack of enthusiasm for the war among many northerners, combined with the absence of a British threat to their part of the country, kept northern states from mobilizing black troops during 1812 and 1813.

Southern fears of slave revolt mounted in the spring of 1813 when the British invaded the Chesapeake. As they had during the Revolution, British generals offered slaves freedom in Canada or the British West Indies in return for help. In response, African Americans joined the British army that burned Washington, D.C., in 1814 and attacked Baltimore.

GUIDE TO READING

▶ What factors led to the War of 1812?

▶ How did the War of 1812 affect African Americans?

▶ What was the Missouri Compromise?

▶ What impact did the Missouri Compromise have on African Americans?

KEY TERMS

▶ Militia Act, p. 165

▶ Black Brigade, p. 166

▶ Put-in-Bay, p. 166

▶ Battle of New Orleans, p. 166

▶ Federalist, p. 167

▶ Republican, p. 167

▶ Missouri Territory, p. 167

▶ Missouri Compromise, p. 168

▶ **Guide to Reading/Key Terms**

For answers, see the *Teacher's Resource Manual*.

MAP 5–2 War of 1812

African Americans fought on both sides during the War of 1812. Some joined the British army that burned Washington, D.C. Others helped the United States win control of Lake Erie in 1813 and stop the British invasion of Louisiana at the Battle of New Orleans in 1815.

 What was at stake for African Americans in the War of 1812?

➤ **Map 5-2**

White people across the country were fearful of black military service, as they were concerned blacks would use their weapons to revolt against slavery. If this occurred, white people would use this as an argument to fuel proslavery sentiment.

The threat this British army posed to Philadelphia and New York led to the first active black involvement in the war on the American side. The New York state legislature authorized two black regiments, offered freedom to slaves who enlisted, and promised compensation to their masters. Meanwhile, African Americans in Philadelphia and New York City volunteered to help build fortifications. In Philadelphia, James Forten, Richard Allen, and Absalom Jones patriotically raised a **Black Brigade**, which never saw action because the British halted when they failed to capture Baltimore.

African-American men did fight, however, at two of the war's most important battles. During the naval engagement at **Put-in-Bay** on Lake Erie in September 1813 that secured control of the Great Lakes for the United States, one-quarter of Commandant Oliver Hazard Perry's four hundred sailors were black. Although Perry had been staunchly prejudiced against using these men, after the battle he praised their valor.

At the **Battle of New Orleans**—fought in January 1815, about a month after a peace treaty had been negotiated (news of peace had not yet reached the area)—African Americans also fought bravely. Yet white memories of

Deslondes's recent uprising almost prevented them from being allowed to fight on the American side. Many white people feared that, if mobilized, the local free black militia—which dated back to the Spanish occupation of Louisiana from 1763 to 1801—would make common cause with slaves and the British rather than take the American side. In defiance of such fears, General Andrew Jackson included the black troops in his force defending New Orleans and offered them equal pay and benefits. At least six hundred free black men fought on the American side at the Battle of New Orleans. Jackson lived up to his promise of equal treatment. It was a choice, he later informed President James Monroe, between having the free African Americans "in our ranks or . . . in the ranks of the enemy."

The Battle of Put-in Bay, fought on Lake Erie in September 1813, was a notable American victory during the War of 1812.

 Reading Check How did the War of 1812 affect African Americans?

The Missouri Compromise

During the years following 1815, sectional issues between the North and South revived. The nation's first political parties—the **Federalist** and the **Republican**—had failed to confront slavery as a national issue. The northern wing of the modernizing Federalist Party had abolitionist tendencies. But during the 1790s when they controlled the national government, the Federalists did not raise the slavery issue. Then the victory of the state-rights-oriented Republican Party in the election of 1800 fatally weakened the Federalists as a national organization. The Republicans brought a series of implicitly proslavery administrations to power in Washington.

Innovations in transportation and production during the 1810s, as well as the continuing disappearance of slavery in the northern states transformed the North into a region at odds with the South's traditional culture and slave-labor economy. The first major expression of intensifying sectional differences over slavery and its expansion came in 1819 when the slaveholding **Missouri Territory**, which had been carved out of Louisiana Territory, applied for admission to the Union as a slave state. Northerners expressed deep reservations about the creation of a new slaveholding state, which threatened to destroy the political balance between the sections and the expansion of slavery in general. Thomas Jefferson called this negative northern reaction a "fire bell in the night." It awakened slaveholders to an era in which slavery could no longer be avoided as an issue in national politics.

▶ **Reading Check**

African Americans fought in the War of 1812. As in the War of Independence, the war brought southern fears of slave revolt to the surface, fears that made them resistant to the use of armed black soldiers. However, once again, military necessity overruled such fears.

▶ **Document**

5-6 *Missouri Admitted to Statehood, Slavery at Issue, 1820*

The Missouri Compromise, as this bill came to be known, was moved through Congress by Speaker of the House, Henry Clay. Slavery would be prohibited north of a line drawn at 36 degrees, 30 minutes latitude. These excerpts are the sections from the bill admitting Missouri to statehood outline the relevant parts pertaining to slavery.

▶ **Map 5-3, p. 168**

The Missouri Compromise banned slavery to the north in the unorganized portion of the old Louisiana Territory, while maintaining slavery to the south.

BRITISH NORTH AMERICA (Canada)

Hudson Bay

OREGON COUNTRY (U.S. and Great Britain)

Continental Divide

UNORGANIZED TERRITORY

Arkansas R.

SPANISH TERRITORY

Red R.

Rio Grande

PACIFIC OCEAN

Gulf of Mexico

NEW HAMPSHIRE
VERMONT
MAINE (admitted as free state, 1821)
MICHIGAN TERR.
NEW YORK
MASSACHUSETTS
RHODE ISLAND
CONNECTICUT
NEW JERSEY
DELAWARE
MARYLAND
PENNSYLVANIA
ILLINOIS
INDIANA
OHIO
MISSOURI (admitted as slave state, 1821)
Missouri Compromise line 36° 30'
KENTUCKY
VIRGINIA
ARKANSAS TERRITORY
TENNESSEE
NORTH CAROLINA
SOUTH CAROLINA
MISSISSIPPI
ALABAMA
GEORGIA
LOUISIANA
FLORIDA TERRITORY

ATLANTIC OCEAN

0   250   500 mi
0   250   500 km

MAP 5–3 **The Missouri Compromise of 1820.**

Under the Missouri Compromise, Missouri entered the Union as a slave state, Maine entered as a free state, and Congress banned slavery in the huge unorganized portion of the old Louisiana Territory.

 Which section of the United States did the Missouri Compromise favor?

Explore this map online at **www.prenhall.com/aah.map5.3.**

Suggested answer is on page 167.

Concerned African Americans were also aware of the significance of the Missouri crisis. Black residents of Washington, D.C. crowded into the U.S. Senate gallery as that body debated the issue. Finally, Henry Clay of Kentucky, the slaveholding Speaker of the House of Representatives, directed an effort that produced in 1820 a compromise that temporarily quieted discord. This **Missouri Compromise** (see Map 5–3) permitted Missouri to become a slave state and maintained a sectional political balance by admitting Maine, which had been part of Massachusetts, as a free state. It banned slavery north of the 36° 30′ line of latitude in the old Louisiana Territory. Yet sectional relations would never be the same, and a new era of black and white antislavery militancy soon confronted the South.

 Reading Check What impact did the Missouri Compromise have on African Americans?

Using Population Density Maps

A population density number represents the average number of persons living in a given area—usually a square mile or a square kilometer. Population density maps can show density for a small area, such as a city, or for a very large area, such as a continent or the entire world. Historians use population density maps to see patterns of human settlement at a particular period of time or changes in population over time.

The maps below represent the population densities in the United States in 1790 and 1830. The figures are based on United States census counts, which, at that time, included whites and African Americans but not Native Americans.

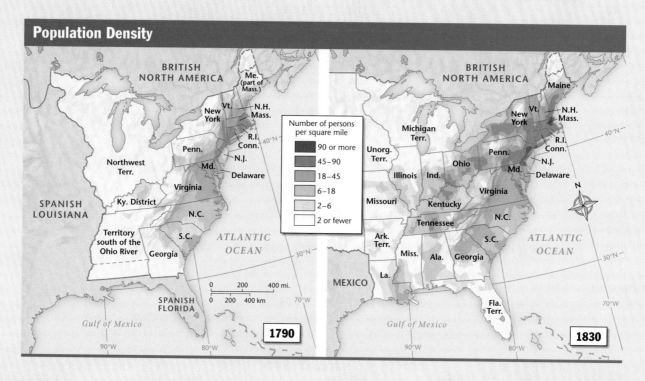

LEARN THE SKILL
Use the following steps to interpret population density maps:

1. **Determine what information each map provides.** Look at the map title and key; then study the map.

2. **Determine the population density of different regions.** Use the map key as your guide.

3. **Analyze population density patterns.** Note where density is the highest and the lowest, and where changes have occurred over time.

4. **Study the maps to draw conclusions.** Relate what you already know about history to what you see on the maps.

PRACTICE THE SKILL
Answer the following questions:

1. **(a)** What kind of information is represented by the colors? **(b)** What do the darkest and lightest colors represent?

2. **(a)** What was the population density of the Northwest Territory in 1790? **(b)** Which states on each map had population densities of 45 or more persons per square mile?

3. **(a)** In general, where was most of the population concentrated in 1790? **(b)** Which was the most densely populated state in 1790? **(c)** Do you think this state also had the largest total population of any state? Explain. **(d)** Which states experienced the greatest and most widespread increase in population density between 1790 and 1830?

4. **(a)** What economic factors do you think accounted for the difference in the population densities of the North and the South, in 1790 and 1830? **(b)** What geographical factors probably contributed to the overall pattern of settlement in 1830? Explain.

▶ **Skills for Life**

For answers, see *Teacher's Resource Manual.*

Chapter Timeline

1775

1775
First antislavery society formed

1776
Declaration of Independence

1777
Vermont bans slavery

1777
Battle of Saratoga

1780

1780
Pennsylvania begins gradual emancipation

1781
Articles of Confederation ratified

17811783
Elizabeth Freeman begins her legal suit for freedom

Great Britain recognizes independence of the United States

1782
Virginia repeals its ban on manumission

1783
Massachusetts bans slavery and black men gain the right to vote there

1784
Connecticut and Rhode Island begin gradual abolition

1785

1785
New Jersey and New York defeat gradual emancipation

1786
Shays's Rebellion

1787
Northwest Ordinance bans slavery in the territory north of the Ohio River

1787
Constitutional Convention

1789
Constitution ratified; George Washington becomes president

1790

1793
Congress passes Fugitive Slave Law

1794
Mother Bethel Church established in Philadelphia
New York adopts gradual abolition plan

1795

1796

John Adams elected president of United States

1799

Undeclared war against France

1800

1800

Gabriel's revolt conspiracy

1800

Thomas Jefferson elected president

1803

Louisiana Purchase

1805

1808

Congress bans the external slave trade

1808

James Madison elected president of United States

1810

1811

Louisiana slave rebellion

1812

War of 1812 begins

1815

1815

AME Church formally established

1815

War of 1812 ends

1819

Panic of 1819

1820

1820

Daniel Coker leads first black settlers to Liberia

1820

Missouri Compromise

Chapter Review and Assessment

SUMMARY

Section 1 Forces for Freedom, p. 141

- After 1783, strong trends in the North and the Chesapeake favored emancipation.
- The process moved quickly in New England, but more slowly in the mid-Atlantic states where a greater number of whites were invested in the continuation of slavery.
- Liberalization of manumission laws and the possibility of self-purchase opened up the promise of freedom to African Americans living in the southern states.
- Over time, a free black class emerged in the South.

Section 2 Forces for Slavery, p. 149

- A number of factors strengthened slavery in the decades after the Revolution.
- First, the U.S. Constitution was a major force in favor of the continuation of slavery. Key clauses maintained and strengthened the enslavement of African Americans in the southern states.
- Second, the emergence of the cotton industry dramatically increased demand for slaves and spurred the development of the internal slave market.
- Third, the Louisiana Purchase opened a vast new territory to slavery.
- Finally, the white population gradually became more conservative and more committed to race-based arguments in favor of slavery.

Section 3 The Emergence of Free Black Communities, p. 154

- Free black communities developed a number of institutions to help strengthen their communities.
- The earliest were mutual aid societies.
- Black freemason lodges were particularly important.
- The church was the core of the black community.
- Black schools were supported by both churches and mutual aid societies.

Section 4 Black Leaders and Choices, p. 160

- By the 1790s an educated black elite had come into existence in the North and Chesapeake.
- These leaders responded in a variety of ways to the failure of American society to live up to its revolutionary principles, including advocating migration from the United States.

- In the South, some blacks responded to the perpetuation of slavery with acquiescence, many with day-to-day resistance, and others with open rebellion.
- Slave uprisings deepened white southerners' fears of race war and intensified their support for the institution of slavery.

Section 5 War and Politics, p. 165

- British invasion during the War of 1812 renewed southern fears of slave revolt.
- Despite such anxieties, black soldiers fought in the two most important battles of the war.
- In the years following the end of the war, sectional differences over slavery and its expansion gained greater prominence in national politics.
- The Missouri Compromise (1820) was an effort to maintain sectional balance by allowing Missouri to enter the Union as a slave state and Maine to enter as a free state, while banning slavery north of the 36° 30′ line of latitude in the old Louisiana Territory.

REVIEWING KEY TERMS

1. emancipation, p. 141
2. transatlantic immigration, p. 141
3. Articles of Confederation, p. 145
4. Northwest Ordinance, p. 146
5. abolitionist, p. 146
6. antislavery society, p. 146
7. compensated emancipation, p. 146
8. manumission, p. 147
9. U.S. Constitution, p. 149
10. sovereignty, p. 149
11. Shays's Rebellion, p. 149
12. Fugitive Slave Act, p. 150
13. Three-Fifths Clause, p. 150
14. per capita tax, p. 151
15. cotton gin, p. 151
16. internal slave trade, p. 151
17. mutual aid societies, p. 154
18. Free African Society, p. 154
19. freemasonry, p. 155
20. Prince Hall, p. 155
21. Prince Hall Masons, p. 155

REVIEWING MAIN IDEAS

35. Which were stronger in the era of the early American republic, the forces in favor of black freedom or those in favor of continued enslavement?

36. How were African Americans able to achieve emancipation in the North?

37. How was the United States Constitution, as it was drafted in 1787, proslavery? How was it antislavery?

38. How important were separate institutions in shaping the lives of free black people during the late eighteenth and early nineteenth centuries?

39. What led Gabriel to believe that he and his followers could abolish slavery in Virginia through armed uprising?

ANALYZING DOCUMENTS

Absalom Jones Petitions Congress on Behalf of Fugitives Facing Reenslavement

That, being of African descent, the late inhabitants and natives of North Carolina, to you only, under God, can we apply with any hope of effect, for redress of our grievances, having been compelled to leave the State wherein we had a right of residence, as freemen liberated under the hand and seal of humane and conscientious masters, the validity of which act of justice in restoring us to our native right of freedom, was confirmed by judgment of the Superior Court of North Carolina. . . . yet, not long after this decision, a law of that State was enacted, under which men of cruel disposition, and void of just principle, received countenance and authority in violently seizing, imprisoning, and selling into slavery,

such as had been so emancipated; . . . We beseech your impartial attention to our hard condition, . . .

If, notwithstanding all that has been publicly avowed as essential principles respecting the extent of human right to freedom; notwithstanding we have had that right restored to us, so far as was in the power of those by whom we were held as slaves, we cannot claim the privilege of representation in your councils, yet we trust we may address you as fellow-men, who, under God, the sovereign Ruler of the Universe, are intrusted with the distribution of justice, . . . susceptible of benevolent feelings and clear conception of rectitude to a catholic extent, who can admit that black people . . . have natural affections, social and domestic attachments and sensibilities; and that, therefore, we may hope for a share in your sympathetic attention while we represent that the unconstitutional bondage in which multitudes of our fellows in complexion are held, is to us a subject sorrowfully affecting; . . . May we not be allowed to consider this stretch of power, morally and politically, a Governmental defect, if not a direct violation of the declared fundamental principles of the Constitution; and finally, is not some remedy for an evil of such magnitude highly worthy of the deep inquiry and unfeigned zeal of the supreme Legislative body of a free and enlightened people?

—From *Annals of Congress,* 4 Cong., 2 sess. (January 23, 1797), 2015–18.

Thinking Critically: 1. On what principles does Jones believe the United States government is bound to act? 2. What does Jones's petition indicate concerning the status of African Americans before the law?

WRITING ACTIVITY

In a short report or research paper, consider this question:

How did the Missouri Compromise shape the lives of African Americans in the decades after its passage?

STUDY ONLINE!

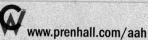

www.prenhall.com/aah

Additional study resources are available for this chapter on the *Companion Website.*
For answers, see the *Teacher's Resource Manual.*

The Voyage to Slavery

The voyage to slavery often began with captured Africans shackled together at the head. They were forced to march to factories where they were held in dungeons or outdoor holding pens. Many captives died from hunger, exhaustion, and exposure during the journey. Others killed themselves rather than submit to their fate, or were killed if they resisted. Families and ethnic groups were divided. Once considered fit for purchase, captives were branded like cattle with a hot iron bearing the symbol of a trading company. Those sent to the Atlantic slave trade continued the journey in the cargo space of slave ships that were only five feet high. Crews often neglected to feed slaves, empty the tubs used for excrement, take slaves on deck for exercise, tend to the sick, or remove the dead.

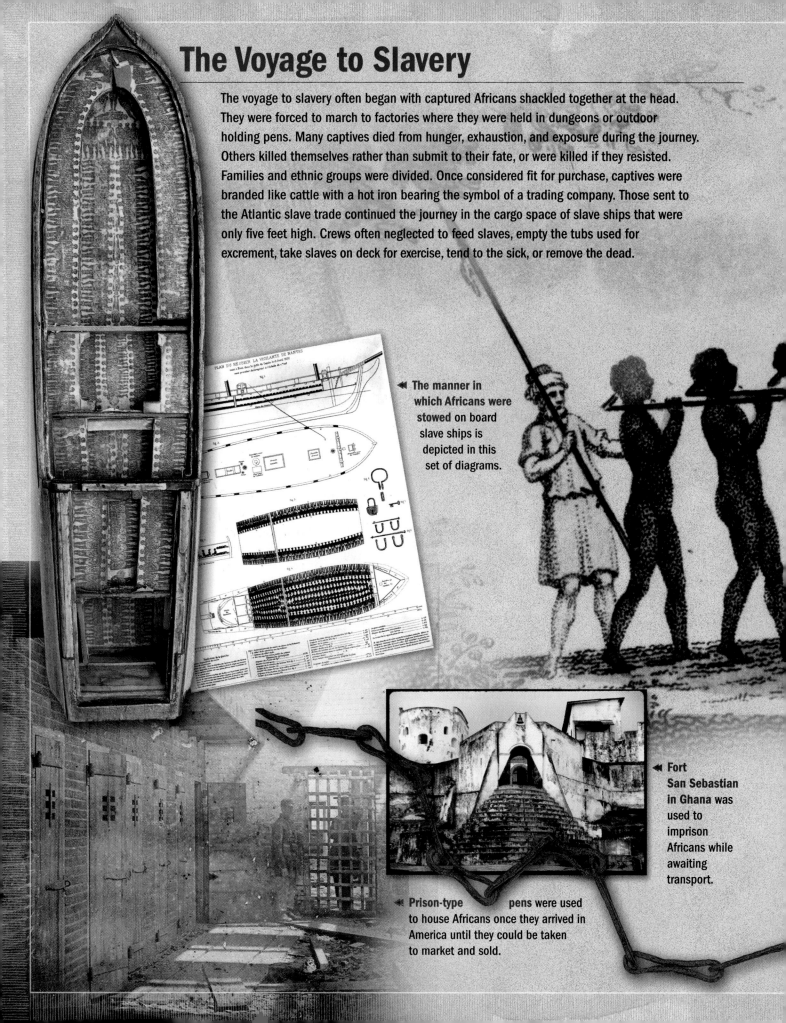

◄ The manner in which Africans were stowed on board slave ships is depicted in this set of diagrams.

◄ Fort San Sebastian in Ghana was used to imprison Africans while awaiting transport.

◄ Prison-type pens were used to house Africans once they arrived in America until they could be taken to market and sold.

◄ Slave traders branded Africans with the symbol of the trading company that bought and would eventually sell them.

◄ Physical torture included beatings with whips.

The first step of the voyage from Africa was called a slave coffle, a parade of Africans tied together in chains after being captured by slave traders. ▼

TO BE SOLD & LET
BY PUBLIC AUCTION,
On MONDAY the 18th of MAY, 1829,
UNDER THE TREES,
FOR SALE,
THE THREE FOLLOWING
SLAVES,
TO BE LET,
MALE AND FEMALE
SLAVES,
Also for Sale, at Eleven o'Clock, Fine Rice, Gram, Paddy, Books, Muslins, Needles, Pins, Ribbons &c. &c.
AT ONE O'CLOCK, THAT CELEBRATED ENGLISH HORSE,
BLUCHER.

Charlestown, July 24th, 1769.
TO BE SOLD,
On THURSDAY the third Day of AUGUST next,
A CARGO
OF
NINETY-FOUR
PRIME, HEALTHY
NEGROES,
CONSISTING OF
Thirty-nine MEN, Fifteen Boys, Twenty-four WOMEN, and Sixteen GIRLS.
JUST ARRIVED,
In the Brigantine DEMBIA, Francis Bare, Master, from SIERRA-LEON, by
DAVID & JOHN DEAS.

◄ The arrival of Africans for sale or auction was often advertised in handbills or printed notices.

Enslaved Africans ► were sent to auction houses such as this one to be sold.

◄ Shackles were used to restrain Africans.

AUCTION & NEGRO SALES.

VISUALIZING THE PAST

UNIT 2

Slavery, Abolition, and the Quest for Freedom

	1770–1820	1820–1830
Religion 	**1775** Philadelphia Quakers organize first antislavery society in America **late 1700s–1830s** Second Great Awakening **1819** Episcopal Diocese of New York excludes black delegates from annual conventions	**1820s** Semisecret churches spread among slaves **1829** Oblate Sisters of Providence founded in Baltimore, first African-American order of Roman Catholic nuns
Culture 	**Early 1800s** Growth of folk tales among slaves	**1820s–1830s** Numerous black literary societies established in northern cities 
Politics & Government 	**1804–1849** Black laws in midwestern states restrict rights of African Americans **1807** New Jersey disfranchises black voters **1818** Connecticut bans new black voters	**1820** Missouri Compromise **1821** New York retains property qualification for black voters **1822** Rhode Island disfranchises black voters 
Society & Economy	**1784** Society for the Promotion of the Abolition of Slavery founded **1800** Gabriel's conspiracy **1812** African schools become part of Boston's public schools **1816** American Colonization Society founded	**1822** Denmark Vesey's conspiracy **1827** *Freedom's Journal* begins publication

Harriet Tubman

Frederick Douglass

Sojourner Truth

1830–1850	1850–1870	Key People

1830–1850

1840s Mother Bethel Church in Philadelphia has largest black congregation in the United States

1840s–1850s Paintings of Robert Duncannon

1845 *Narrative of the Life of Frederick Douglass* published

1848 Okah Tubee's fictionalized autobiography published

1832 Virginia rejects gradual emancipation

1836–1841 "Gag rule" prohibits Congress from considering petitions regarding slavery

1838 Pennsylvania disfranchises black voters

1846–1848 Mexican War

1846 Wilmot Proviso

1847 Liberia becomes an independent republic

1848 Free Soil party founded

1831 Nat Turner's revolt

William Lloyd Garrison begins publication of *The Liberator*

1832 First black women's abolitionist organization founded

1833 American Anti-Slavery Society founded

1834 African Free Schools become part of New York's public schools

1835 Abolitionist postal campaign begins

1836 Elijah P. Lovejoy killed by antiabolitionist mob

1839 *Amistad* mutiny

1843 Henry H. Garnet's *Appeal to the Slaves*

1847 Frederick Douglass begins publication of the *North Star*

Missouri bans education of free blacks

1850–1870

1853 Episcopal Diocese of New York readmits black delegates

1852 *Uncle Tom's Cabin* published

1853 William W. Brown, first African-American novelist, publishes *Clotel*

Elizabeth Taylor Greenfield makes her singing debut in New York before a white audience

Solomon Northup publishes *Twelve Years as a Slave*

1854 Frances Ellen Watkins Harper publishes *Poems*

1855 William C. Nell publishes *The Colored Patriots of the American Revolution*

1859 Harriet Wilson publishes first novel by an African-American woman

1850 Compromise of 1850 includes stronger Fugitive Slave Act

1851 Indiana bans African Americans from residing in the state

1855–1856 "Bleeding Kansas"

1857 Dred Scott decision

1858 Arkansas reenslaves free blacks who refuse to leave the state

1859 John Brown raids Harper's Ferry

1860 Lincoln elected president

1860–1861 Eleven southern states secede and form the Confederacy

1861 Civil War begins

1851 "Battle" of Christiana

1853 Rochester Convention

1854 Ashmun Institute, first black institution of higher education in the U.S., founded

1860 U.S. slave population put at 3,953,760

Key People

Denmark Vesey (c.1767–1822)

Benjamin Lundy (1789–1839)

April Ellison (1790–1861)

Samuel Cornish (1795–1858)

Dred Scott (c. 1795–1858)

Daniel Walker (c. 1796–1830)

Sojourner Truth (c. 1797–1883)

Nat Turner (1800–1831)

Maria W. Stewart (1803–1879)

William Lloyd Garrison (1805–1879)

Solomon Northup (c. 1808–1863)

Robert Purvis (1810–1898)

Harriet Beecher Stowe (1811–1896)

Martin R. Delany (1812–1885)

Henry H. Garnet (1815–1882)

Frederick Douglass (1817–1895)

Harriet Tubman (1820–1883)

Robert Duncannon (c. 1821–1872)

Frances Ellen Watkins Harper (1825–1911)

Harriet E. Wilson (1828–1863)

Anthony Burns (c. 1829–1862)

Edmonia Lewis (1845–c. 1911)

UNCLE TOM'S CABIN

Slaves in the Old South produced a variety of crops, including wheat, corn, and sweet potatoes.

Chapter 6

A slave buyer offers cash for men, women, and children in this 1835 advertisement.

In Their Own Words . . .

There may be humane masters, as there certainly are inhumane ones; there may be slaves well-clothed, well-fed, and happy, as there surely are those half-clad, half-starved and miserable; nevertheless, the institution that tolerates such wrong and inhumanity . . . is a cruel, unjust, and barbarous one.

—Solomon Northup, *Twelve Years a Slave: Narrative of Solomon Northup*

 How would you interpret Northup's feelings about slavery?

Chapter Preview

Solomon Northup, a free black man, had been kidnapped into slavery during the 1840s. After twelve years in bondage, he finally escaped. In this passage he identifies the central cruelty of slavery. It was not that some masters failed to provide slaves with adequate food, clothing, and shelter while others did. Nor was it that some masters treated their slaves brutally while others did not. The central cruelty of slavery was that it gave masters nearly absolute power over their slaves. The sufferings of African Americans in slavery were not caused by abuses in an otherwise benevolent institution. They were caused by the institution itself.

In this chapter we describe the life of black people in the slave South from the rise of the Cotton Kingdom to the eve of the Civil War. As we have indicated in previous chapters, African Americans suffered brutal oppression on southern plantations. But they also developed means of coping with that oppression, resisting it, and escaping. Between 1820 and 1861, slavery in the South was at its peak as a productive system and a means of white control of black southerners. We seek to explain the extent of that slave system, how it varied across the South, and how it operated. We also investigate the slave communities that African-American men, women, and children built.

▶▶ **Witnessing History**

He feels that slavery cannot be justified under any circumstances.

American Women in New York City in May 1837. At the second convention, Susan Paul became a vice president, and Douglass became treasurer.

The main task of all the women's antislavery societies was fund-raising. They held bake sales, organized antislavery fairs and bazaars, and sold antislavery memorabilia with the proceeds going to the AASS or to antislavery newspapers. But the separate women's societies also inspired the birth of feminism by creating an awareness that women had rights and interests that a male-dominated society had to recognize. By writing essays and poems on political subjects and making public speeches, black and white female abolitionists challenged a culture that relegated respectable women to domestic duties. By the 1850s the famous African-American speaker Sojourner Truth was emphasizing that all black women through their physical labor and the pain they suffered in slavery had earned equal standing with both men and their more favored white sisters.

Black men and women also formed auxiliaries during the early 1830s to the Quaker-initiated **Free Produce Association**, which tried to put economic pressure on slaveholders by boycotting agricultural products produced by slaves. James Cornish led the Colored Free Produce Society of Pennsylvania, which marketed meat, vegetables, cotton, and sugar

PROFILE ❖ Sojourner Truth

Sojourner Truth does not fit easily into the history of the antislavery movement. She did not identify with a particular group of abolitionists. Instead, as her biographer Nell Irvin Painter points out, Truth served the cause by transforming herself into a symbol of the strength of all black women.

Originally named Isabella, Truth was born a slave—probably in 1797—in a Dutch-speaking area north of New York City. She had several masters, one of whom beat her brutally. In 1827 Truth escaped to an antislavery family who purchased her freedom. Two years later, she became a powerful revivalist preacher in New York City. Later she joined a communal religious cult, became an ardent millenarian—predicting that Judgment Day was rapidly approaching. In 1843 took the name Sojourner Truth. A few years later, while working at a commune in Northampton, Massachusetts, she met abolitionists Frederick Douglass and David Ruggles. This meeting led to her career as a champion of abolition and women's rights.

She lectured across the North and as far west as Kansas during the late 1840s and the 1850s. She was blunt, but eloquent, and used common sense to argue that African Americans and women deserved the same rights as white men. They did so, she insisted, because they could work as hard as white men. Truth almost always addressed white audiences and made a strong impression on them. During the Civil War, she volunteered to work among black Union troops. President Lincoln invited her to the White House in 1864. She continued to advocate black and women's rights until her death in 1883.

produced by free labor. Judith James and Laetitia Rowley organized the Colored Female Free Produce Society of Pennsylvania with a similar aim. Other black affiliates to the Free Produce Association existed in New York and Ohio, and black abolitionist William Whipper operated a free produce store in Philadelphia in 1834. During the 1850s Frances Ellen Watkins Harper, one of the few prominent black female speakers of the time, always included the free produce movement in her abolitionist lectures and wrote newspaper articles on its behalf.

The Black Convention Movement

The dozens of local, state, and national black conventions held in the North between 1830 and 1864 were further removed from the AASS. They did, nevertheless, provide an independent forum for the more prominent black male abolitionists, such as Henry Highland Garnet, Frederick Douglass, and, later, Martin R. Delany. They also provided a setting in which abolitionism could grow and change its tactics to meet the demands of the sectionally polarized and violent 1840s.

Hezekiah Grice, a young black man who had worked with Benjamin Lundy and William Lloyd Garrison in Baltimore during the 1820s, organized the first Black National Convention. It met on September 24, 1830, at the Bethel Church in Philadelphia with the venerable churchman Richard Allen presiding. The national convention became an annual event for the next five years and then met irregularly in such cities as Philadelphia, New York, Buffalo, Rochester, Syracuse, and Cleveland into the Civil War years. Meanwhile, many state and local black conventions also met across the North. By current standards, these conventions were small and informal—particularly those at the local level—and had no strict guidelines for choosing delegates. These characteristics, however, did not prevent the conventions from becoming effective forums for black concerns. They invariably called for the abolition of slavery and for improving the conditions of northern African Americans. Among other reforms, the conventions called for integrated public schools and the right of black men to vote, serve on juries, and testify against white people in court.

During the 1830s the conventions also stressed black self-help through temperance, sexual morality, education, and thrift. These causes remained important parts of the conventions' agenda throughout the antebellum years. But by the early 1840s, politics and the active resistance to oppression that Garnet called for in the speech quoted at the start of this chapter received more emphasis. By the late 1840s, assertions of black nationalism and endorsements of black migration to Africa or Latin America had become common.

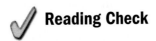 **Reading Check** How did the American Anti-Slavery Society influence the creation of black antislavery groups?

▶ **Reading Check**

While the AASS was committed to bridging the gap between blacks and whites, its white leaders were not fully comfortable with their black counterparts. Blacks participated in the organization, but few held important offices. Under these circumstances, black abolitionists chose to form their own auxiliaries to the AASS.

▶ **Recommended Readings**

R. J. Young. *Antebellum Black Activists: Race, Gender, Self.* New York: Garland, 1996. A sophisticated study of the motivation of black abolitionists.

Section 1

The Expansion of Slavery

GUIDE TO READING

▶ Why did slavery expand in the cotton kingdom?

▶ How was the slave population distributed across the South?

▶ Why did a small number of free blacks purchase slaves?

KEY TERMS

▶ bondage, p. 181

▶ manumit, p. 183

Slave Population Growth

Eli Whitney's invention of the cotton gin in 1793 made the cultivation of cotton profitable on the North American mainland. It was the key to the rapid and extensive expansion of slavery from the Atlantic coast to Texas. By 1811 cotton cultivation had spread across South Carolina, Georgia, and parts of North Carolina and Virginia. By 1821 it had crossed Alabama and reached Mississippi, Louisiana, and parts of Tennessee. It then expanded again into Arkansas, Florida, and eastern Texas (see Map 6–1). Enslaved black labor cleared forests and drained swamps to make these lands fit for cultivation.

In the huge region stretching from the Atlantic coast to Texas, however, a tremendous increase in the number of African Americans in **bondage** accompanied territorial expansion. The slave population of the United States grew almost sixfold between 1790 and 1860, from 697,897 to 3,953,760 (see Table 6–1). Agricultural laborers constituted 75 percent of the South's slave population. But slaves were not equally distributed across the region. In western North Carolina, eastern Tennessee, western Virginia, and most of Missouri, for example, there were never many slaves. The slave population grew fastest in the newer cotton-producing states, such as Alabama and Mississippi (see Map 6–2).

Virginia had the largest slave population throughout the period. But between 1820 and 1860, that population increased by only 15 percent, from 425,153 to 490,865. During the same forty years, the slave population of Louisiana increased by 209 percent, from 149,654 to 462,198, and that of Mississippi by 1,231 percent, from 32,814 to 436,631. By 1860 Mississippi had joined South Carolina as the only states that had more slave than free inhabitants.

Ownership of Slaves in the Old South

Slaveholders were as unevenly distributed as the slaves. Unlike slaves, they were declining in number. In 1830, 1,314,272 white southerners (36 percent), out of a total white southern population of 3,650,758,

▶ **Guide to Reading/Key Terms**

For answers, see the *Teacher's Resource Manual*.

▶ **Interactive Activity**

de Tocqueville

Alexis de Tocqueville's *Democracy in America* accurately discusses the rapid growth of the country and how sectional tensions might endanger the Union.

▶ **Recommended Reading**

Peter Kolchin. *American Slavery, 1619–1877*. New York: Hill and Wang, 1993. The bulk of this book deals with slavery during the antebellum period. It provides a brief but comprehensive introduction to the subject.

olomon Northup was born free at Minerva, New York, in about 1808. His parents were prosperous farmers, and he became a farmer as well. He also worked occasionally as a violinist. He lived in Saratoga Springs with his wife and three children. His aspirations as a musician led in 1841 to his kidnapping and sale into slavery. For twelve years, he labored in the cotton and sugar regions of Louisiana, interacted with slaves and masters, and experienced firsthand what it was like to be caught up in a brutal labor system. In March 1841 two white men suggested that he become a musician in their circus, which was performing in Washington, D.C.

Enticed by the prospect of good wages and a chance to perform, Northup left with the two men without informing his wife or anyone else. Within two days of arriving in Washington, he was drugged, robbed of his money and free papers, chained, and sold to slave traders. Northup was shipped to New Orleans and sold to William Ford, who owned a cotton plantation and sawmill in Louisiana's Red River region.

As Ford's slave, Northup worked at the mill "piling lumber and chopping logs." Northup liked Ford and regarded him to be a "model master," who treated his slaves well and read scripture to them each Sunday. But when Ford became insolvent and sold his slaves, Northup had to deal with a series of brutal masters. They employed him as a carpenter, as a field hand on cotton and sugar plantations, and finally as a slave driver.

At one point when he was cutting lumber and building cabins, Northup was surprised to have several "large and stout" black women join in the forestry work. Later he observed women engaged in other demanding physical labor. "There are lumberwomen as well as lumbermen in the forests of the South," he reported. "In fact . . . they perform their share of all the labor required by the planters. They plough, dray, drive team, clear wild lands, work on the highway and so forth."

Northup spent ten years as a slave of Edwin Epps, a cotton planter. When he was drunk, Epps enjoyed forcing his slaves to dance. Northup noted that Epps's slaves received a meager diet of corn and bacon. They slept in crude, crowded cabins on planks of wood. During harvest season "it was rarely that a day passed by without one or more whippings" as slaves failed to pick their quota. During harvest season "it was rarely that a day passed by without one or more whippings" when slaves failed to pick their quota. During a three-year period, Epps hired Northup out to sugar plantations for $1.00 per day.

By 1852 Northup had become Epps's slave driver. He was finally able to set in motion the events that led to his rescue. Deeply disturbed by being forced to whip other slaves, he conspired with a Canadian carpenter to smuggle a letter to two white businessmen in Saratoga Springs. The letter led the governor of New York to send Henry B. Northup to Louisiana to present evidence that Solomon Northup was a free man. Northup was a member of the family that had once owned Solomon Northup's father.

By January 1853 Northup had been reunited with his family in New York. In July of that year he published *Twelve Years a Slave*, which sold over 30,000 copies. He earned enough money to purchase a home for his family in Glens Falls, New York, where he died in 1863.

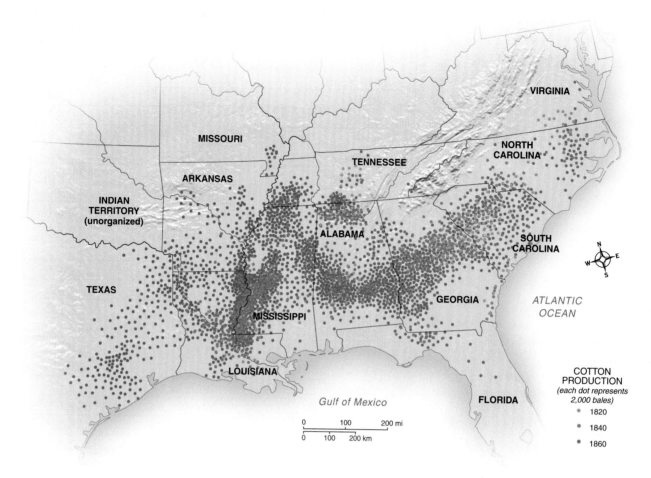

COTTON
PRODUCTION
(each dot represents
2,000 bales)
• 1820
• 1840
• 1860

**MAP 6–1 Cotton Production
in the South, 1820–1860**

Cotton production expanded westward
between 1820 and 1860 into Alabama,
Mississippi, Louisiana, Texas, Arkansas,
and western Tennessee.

Source: Sam Bowers Hilliard, *Atlas of Antebellum Southern
Agriculture* (Louisiana State University Press, 1984) pp. 67–71.

 **Why did cotton production spread
westward?**

owned slaves. In 1860 only 383,673 white southerners (4.7 percent), out
of a total white southern population of 8,097,463, owned slaves. Even
counting the immediate families of slaveholders, only 1,900,000 (or less
than 25 percent of the South's white population) had a direct interest in
slavery in 1860.

Almost half of the South's slaveholders owned fewer than 5 slaves,
only 12 percent owned more than 20 slaves, and just 1 percent owned
more than 50 slaves. Yet more than half the slaves belonged to masters
who had 20 or more slaves. So although the typical slaveholder owned
few slaves, the typical slave lived on a sizable plantation.

Black Slaveholders

Since the mid-1600s, a few black people had been slaveholders, and
this class continued to exist. In 1830 only 2 percent, or 3,775 free
African Americans, owned slaves. Many of them became slaveholders
to protect their families from sale and disruption. This was because, as

⏵ **Map 6-1**

Eli Whitney's invention of the cotton gin made
the cultivation of cotton profitable and therefore
lead to its westward expansion.

⏵ **Retracing the Odyssey**

William Johnson House and **Melrose
Plantation**, Natchez, Mississippi. Johnson was
one of the rare black slaveholders and John T.
McMurrin, the owner of Melrose Plantation, was
a northern white man who became a slaveholder.

TABLE 6–1 U.S. Slave Population, 1820 and 1860

	1820	1860
United States	1,538,125	3,953,760
North	19,108	64
South	1,519,017	3,953,696
Upper South	965,514	1,530,229
Delaware	4,509	1,798
Kentucky	127,732	225,483
Maryland	107,397	87,189
Missouri	10,222	114,931
North Carolina	205,017	331,059
Tennessee	80,107	275,719
Virginia	425,153	490,865
Washington, D.C.	6,377	3,185
Lower South	553,503	2,423,467
Alabama	41,879	435,080
Arkansas	1,617	111,115
Florida	*	61,745
Georgia	149,654	462,198
Louisiana	69,064	331,726
Mississippi	32,814	436,631
South Carolina	258,475	402,406
Texas	*	182,566

*Florida and Texas were not states in 1820.

Source: Ira Berlin, *Slaves without Masters: The Free Negro in the Antebellum South* (New York: New Press, 1974), 396–97.

▶ **Reading Check**

The invention of the cotton gin made the cultivation of cotton profitable. This was the key to the rapid expansion of slavery in cotton-growing regions. Demand for cotton by the textile industry drove up prices, encouraging the expansion of cotton cultivation and slavery.

▶ **Teaching Notes**

The expansion of the cotton culture led to the removal of the American Indians—some of them slaveholders—who inhabited this vast region. During the 1830s the United States Army forced the Cherokee, Chickasaw, Choctaw, Creek, and most Seminole to leave their ancestral lands for Indian Territory in what is now Oklahoma. Many Indians died during this forced migration, and the Cherokee remember it as "The Trail of Tears." Yet the Cherokees created in Oklahoma an economy dependent on black slave labor. By 1860 there were seven thousand slaves there, amounting to 14% of the population.

Far fewer slaves lived in the other western territories. There were never more than a few dozen slaves in Kansas during the 1850s and none after 1858. In New Mexico in 1850 there were about forty black slaves and 3,000 American Indian slaves. When Utah Territory legalized slavery in 1852, only about twenty-six enslaved black people were living there. By 1860 Utah still had just twenty-nine black people. Although California entered the Union as state in 1850 under a constitution that banned slavery, two years later it had more than 300 illegally held slaves working as prospectors or domestics.

the nineteenth century progressed, southern states made it more difficult for masters to **manumit** slaves and for slaves to purchase their freedom. The states also threatened to expel former slaves from their territory. In response to these circumstances black men and women sometimes purchased relatives who were in danger of sale to traders and who—if legally free—might be forced by white authorities to leave a state.

Some African Americans purchased slaves for financial reasons and passed those slaves on to their heirs. Most black people who became masters for financial reasons owned five or fewer slaves. But William Johnson, a wealthy free black barber of Natchez, Louisiana, owned many slaves whom he employed on a plantation he purchased. Some black women, such as Margaret Mitchell Harris of South Carolina and Betsy Somayrac of Natchitoches, Louisiana, also became slaveholders

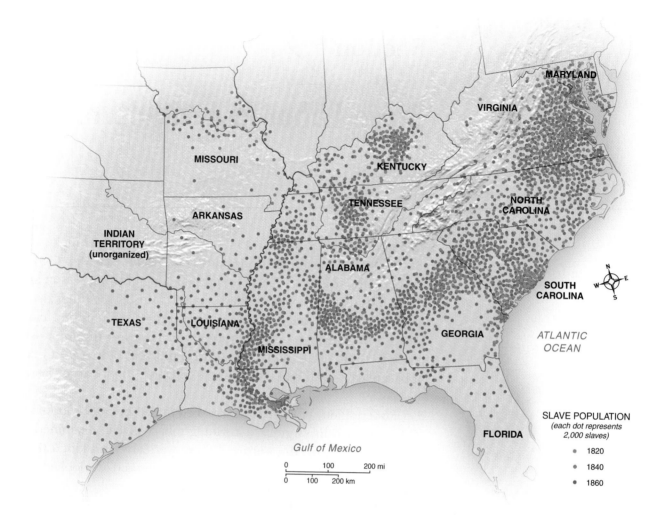

MAP 6–2 Slave Population, 1820–1860

Slavery spread southwestward from the upper South and the eastern seaboard following the spread of cotton cultivation.

Source: Sam Bowers Hilliard, *Atlas of Antebellum Southern Agriculture* (Louisiana State University Press, 1984), pp. 29-34.

 What does this map suggest concerning black life in the South?

for economic reasons. Harris was a successful rice planter who inherited twenty-one slaves from her white father. She prospered by carefully managing her resources in land and slaves. By 1849, when she sold out, she had more than forty slaves and nearly a thousand acres, which produced 240,000 pounds of rice per year.

Somayrac's case shows that economic considerations could override emotional ties between black women and their bond people. In her will, recorded in January 1845, Somayrac wrote that she intended to pass her human property on to her children. She required that "my negro woman named Jane" labor to pay off family debts. She stipulated that one of her sons must own any children that Jane might produce. She even provided that a "negro boy named Solomon," who was her godson, not be manumitted until he had reached the relatively old age of thirty-five.

 Reading Check   Why did slavery expand in the cotton kingdom?

▶▶ **Map 6-2**

Black life in the south was dictated by cotton production; as slavery spread southwestward following the spread of cotton cultivation.

GUIDE TO READING

▶ What types of crops did slaves cultivate in the South?

▶ Why did slaves fear being sent to work on sugar plantations?

▶ What was a typical day like for a slave working in the cotton fields?

KEY TERMS

▶ cotton culture, p. 187

▶ hemp, p. 189

Section 2

Slave Labor in Agriculture

Tobacco

Tobacco remained important in Virginia, Maryland, Kentucky, and parts of North Carolina and Missouri during the 1800s (see Map 6–3). A difficult crop to produce, tobacco required a long growing season and careful cultivation. In the spring slaves had to transfer seedlings from sterilized seed beds to well-worked and manured soil. Then they had to hoe weeds, pick off insects, and prune lower leaves so the topmost leaves grew to their full extent. Slaves also built scaffolds used to cure the tobacco leaves and made the barrels in which the tobacco was shipped to market.

Robert Ellett, a former slave, recalled that when he was just eight years old he worked in Virginia "a-worming tobacco." He "examined tobacco leaves, pull[ed] off the worms, if there were any, and killed them." He claimed that if an overseer discovered that slaves had overlooked worms on the tobacco plants, the slaves were whipped or forced to eat the worms. Nancy Williams, another Virginia slave, recalled that sometimes as a punishment slaves had to inhale burning tobacco until they became nauseated.

Rice

Unlike the cultivation of tobacco, which spread westward and southward from Maryland and Virginia, rice production remained confined to the coastal waterways of South Carolina and Georgia. As they had since colonial times, slaves in these regions worked according to task systems that allowed them considerable independence. Because rice fields needed to be flooded for the seeds to germinate, slaves maintained elaborate systems of dikes and ditches. Influenced by West African methods, they sowed, weeded, and harvested the rice crop.

Rice cultivation was labor intensive. Rice plantations needed large labor forces to grow and harvest the crop and maintain the fields. By 1860 twenty rice plantations had 300 to 500 slaves, and eight others had between 500 and 1,000. The only American plantation employing more than 1,000 slaves was in the rice-producing region. These vast plantations represented sizable capital investments. Masters or overseers carefully monitored slave productivity. Slaves enjoyed considerable leeway in

▶▶ **Guide to Reading/Key Terms**

For answers, see the *Teacher's Resource Manual.*

▶▶ **Teaching Notes**

About 55 percent of the slaves in the South cultivated cotton; 10 percent grew tobacco; and 10 percent produced sugar, rice, or hemp. About 15 percent were domestic servants, and the remaining 10 percent worked in trades and industries.

how they performed their assigned duties. However those who missed a day's work risked forfeiting their weekly allowance "of either bacon, sugar, molasses, or tobacco."

Sugar

Another important crop that grew in a restricted region was sugar, which slaves cultivated on plantations along the Mississippi River in southern Louisiana. Commercial production of sugarcane did not begin in Louisiana until the 1790s. It required a consistently warm climate, a long growing season, and at least sixty inches of rain per year.

Raising sugarcane and refining sugar also required constant labor. Together with the great profitability of the sugar crop, these demands encouraged masters to work their slaves hard. Slave life on sugar plantations was extremely harsh, and African Americans across the South feared being sent to labor on them.

Slaves did this work in hot and humid conditions, adding to the toll it took on their strength and health. Because cane could not be allowed to stand too long in the fields, harvesttime was hectic. As one former slave recalled, "On cane plantations in sugar time, there is no distinction as to the days of the week. They [the slaves] worked on the Sabbath as if it were Monday or Thursday."

Cotton

Although tobacco, rice, and sugar were economically significant, cotton was by far the South's and the country's most important staple crop. By 1860 cotton exports amounted to more than 50 percent annually of the dollar value of all U.S. exports (see Figure 6–1). This was almost ten times the value of its nearest export competitors—wheat and wheat flour.

Cotton as a crop did not require cultivation as intensive as that needed for tobacco, rice, or sugar. But the **cotton culture** was so extensive that cotton planters as a group employed the most slave labor. By 1860 out of the 2,500,000 slaves employed in agriculture in the United States, 1,815,000 were producing cotton. Cotton drove the South's economy and its westward expansion. Even in rice-producing South Carolina and sugar-producing Louisiana, cotton was dominant. Cotton plantations employed the bulk of the slave populations.

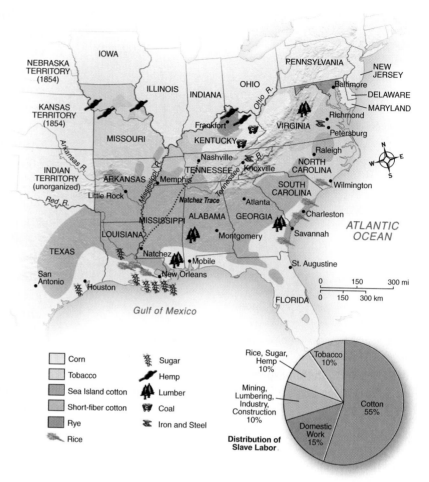

MAP 6–3 Agriculture, Industry, and Slavery in the Old South, 1850.

The experience of African Americans in slavery varied according to their occupation and the region of the South in which they lived.

 What does this map suggest concerning slave labor?

Explore this map online at www.prenhall.com/aah/map6.3

▶▶ **Map 6-3**

Slave labor in 1850 was varied according to occupation and region of the South, however it was largely dominated by agriculture.

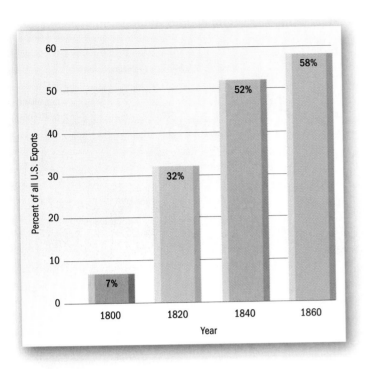

FIGURE 6–1 Cotton Exports as a Percentage of All U.S. Exports, 1800–1860

Cotton rapidly emerged as the country's most important export crop after 1800 and key to its prosperity.

Most American cotton was the more hardy short staple variety that flourished over much of the South. Demand for cotton fiber in the textile mills of Britain and New England stimulated the westward spread of cotton cultivation. This demand increased by at least 5 percent per year between 1830 and 1860. In response—and with the essential aid of Whitney's cotton gin—American production of cotton rose from 10,000 bales in 1793 to 500,000 annually during the 1820s to 4,491,000 bales in 1860. The new states of Alabama, Louisiana, and Mississippi led this mounting production.

Potential profits drew white farmers to the rich Black Belt lands of Mississippi and Alabama during the early nineteenth century. Rapid population growth allowed Mississippi to gain statehood in 1817 and Alabama in 1819. White men with few slaves led the way into this southwestern cotton belt. Its frontier social structure allowed them to become plantation owners. Their success was not certain and many of them failed. Those who succeeded created large agricultural units because profits were directly related to the amount of cotton harvested. As a result, Mississippi and Alabama—the leading producers of cotton—had by 1860 the greatest concentration of plantations with one hundred or more slaves. Twenty-four of Mississippi's slaveholders each owned between 308 and 899 slaves.

▶ **Retracing the Odyssey**

Hampton Plantation State Park, McClellanville, South Carolina. The plantation house dates to about 1750, and the outbuildings include slave cabins.

Magnolia Mound Plantation, Baton Rouge, Louisiana. This historic site includes a plantation house, outbuildings, an overseer's house, and a separate kitchen building.

Zephaniah Kingsley Plantation, Fort George Island, Florida. Kingsley's was an interracial family. Buildings on the plantation include the oldest standing plantation house in Florida and thirty-two slave quarters.

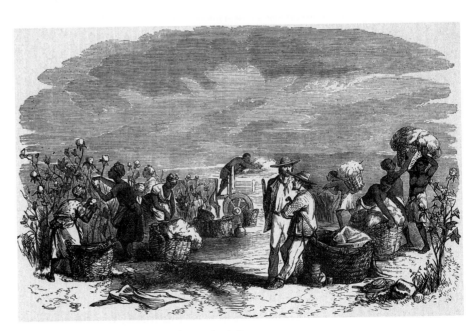

Slaves harvest cotton on a southern plantation.

As these large agricultural units drew in labor, the price of slaves increased. During the 1830s, for example, a prime male field hand sold for $1,250 (about 21,000 current dollars) in the New Orleans slave market. Prices dipped during the hard times of the early 1840s. But by the 1850s, such slaves cost $1,800 (about 33,000 current dollars). Young women usually sold for up to $500 less than young men. Prices for elderly slaves dropped off sharply unless they were highly skilled.

The enslaved men and women who worked in the cotton fields rose before dawn when the master or overseer sounded the plantation bell or horn. They ate breakfast and then assembled in work gangs of twenty or twenty-five under the control of black slave drivers. They plowed and planted in the spring. They weeded with heavy hoes in the summer and harvested in the late fall. During harvest season, adult slaves picked about two hundred pounds of cotton per day. Regardless of the season, the work was hard, and white overseers frequently whipped those who seemed to be lagging. Slaves usually got a two-hour break at midday in the summer and an hour to an hour and a half in the winter. Then they returned to the fields until sunset, when they went back to their cabins for dinner and an early bedtime enforced by the master or overseer.

 Reading Check Why did slaves fear being sent to work on sugar plantations?

Other Crops

Slaves in the Old South produced other crops, including hemp, corn, wheat, oats, rye, white potatoes, and sweet potatoes. They also raised cattle, hogs, sheep, and horses. The hogs, and corn and other grains, were mainly for consumption on the plantations themselves. But all the hemp, and much of the livestock and wheat, were raised for the market. In fact wheat replaced tobacco as the main cash crop in much of Maryland and Virginia. The transition to wheat encouraged many planters to substitute free labor for slave labor, but slaves grew wheat in the South until the Civil War.

Kentucky was the center of the **hemp** industry. Before the Civil War, Americans used hemp to make rope and bagging for cotton bales. As a result, hemp production tied Kentucky economically to the deep South. Hemp also led to a distinctive system of slavery in Kentucky because it required much less labor than rice, sugar, or cotton. Because three slaves could tend fifty acres of hemp, slave labor forces in Kentucky were much smaller than elsewhere. Robert Wickliffe, who was the largest slaveholder in the state during the 1840s, owned just two hundred slaves—a large number, but far fewer than his counterparts in the Cotton Belt.

 Reading Check What types of crops did slaves cultivate in the South?

▶▶ **Reading Check**

Sugar requires a warm climate, a long growing season, and abundant rain. These same conditions took their toll on the health of slaves sent to work on sugar plantations. Moreover, sugarcane cultivation and processing requires constant work, particularly at harvest time.

▶▶ **Reading Check**

Slaves cultivated tobacco, rice, sugarcane, cotton, a variety of other crops. Of these, cotton cultivation claimed the single largest portion of the slave population.

▶ **Guide to Reading/Key Terms**

For answers, see the *Teacher's Resource Manual.*

Section 3

Other Types of Slave Labor

House Servants and Skilled Slaves

About 75 percent of the slave workforce in the nineteenth century consisted of field hands. But because masters wanted to make their plantations as self-sufficient as possible, they employed some slaves as house servants and skilled craftsmen. Slaves who did not have to do field labor were an elite. Those who performed domestic duties, drove carriages, or learned a craft considered themselves privileged. However, they were also suspended between two different worlds.

House Slaves

House slaves worked as cooks, maids, butlers, nurses, and gardeners. Their work was less physically demanding than fieldwork. They often received better food and clothing. Nevertheless, nineteenth-century kitchen work could be grueling. Maids and butlers were on call at all hours. House servants' jobs were also more stressful than field hands' jobs because the servants were under closer white supervision.

In addition, house servants were by necessity cut off from the slave community centered in the slave quarters. Nevertheless house servants rarely sought to become field hands. Conversely, field hands had little desire to be exposed to the constant surveillance house servants had to tolerate. As Frederick Law Olmsted, a northern traveler, put it,

> Slaves brought up to housework dread to be employed at field-labor; and those accustomed to the comparatively unconstrained life of the Negro-settlement detest the close control and careful movements required of the house-servants. It is a punishment of a lazy field hand to employ him in menial duties at the house . . . and it is equally a punishment to a neglectful house-servant, to banish him to the field-gangs.

Skilled Slaves

Skilled slaves tended to be even more of a slave elite than house slaves. As had been true earlier, black men had a decided advantage over black women—apart from those who became seamstresses—in becoming

skilled. Slave carpenters, blacksmiths, and millwrights built and maintained plantation houses, slave quarters, and machinery. Because they might need to travel to get tools or spare parts, such skilled slaves gained a broader outlook than field hands or house servants. They got a taste of freedom, which from the masters' point of view was dangerous.

As plantation slavery declined in the Chesapeake, skilled slaves were able to leave their master's estate to "hire their time." Either they or their masters negotiated labor contracts with employers who needed their expertise. In effect, these slaves worked for money. Although masters often kept all or most of what they earned, some of these skilled slaves merely paid their master a set rate and lived as independent contractors.

Hauling the Whole Week's Picking, painted in 1842 by William Henry Brown, shows slaves at work on a Mississippi cotton plantation.

Urban and Industrial Slavery

Most skilled slaves, who hired their time, lived in the South's towns and cities where they interacted with free black communities. Many of them resided in Baltimore and New Orleans, which were major ports and the Old South's largest cities. But there were others in such smaller southern urban centers as Richmond and Norfolk, Virginia; Atlanta and Augusta, Georgia; Washington, D.C.; Charleston, South Carolina; Louisville, Kentucky; and Memphis, Tennessee.

Slave populations in southern cities were often large, although they tended to decline between 1800 and 1860. In 1840 slaves were a majority of Charleston's population of 29,000. They nearly equaled white residents in Memphis and Augusta, which had total populations of 14,700 and 6,000, respectively. Slaves were almost one-quarter of New Orleans's population of 145,000 (see Map 6–4).

Urban Slaves

Life in a city could be much more complicated for a slave than life on a plantation. When urban slaves were not working for their masters, they could earn money for themselves. As a result, masters had a harder time controlling their lives. Those who contracted to provide their masters with a certain amount of money per year could live on their own, buying their own food and clothing. "You couldn't pay me," observed one slave woman, "to live at home if I could help myself."

Urban slaves served as domestics, washwomen, waiters, artisans, stevedores, drayers, hack drivers, and general laborers. In general, they did the urban work that foreign **immigrants** undertook in northern cities. If urban slaves purchased their freedom, they usually continued in the same line of work they had done as slaves. Particularly in border

▶ **Recommended Reading**

Charles B. Dew. *Bonds of Iron: Masters and Slaves at Buffalo Forge.* New York: Norton, 1994. Dew offers an excellent account of one type of industrial slavery in the Old South.

▶ Recommended Reading

Michael P. Johnson and James L. Roark. *Black Masters: A Free Family of Color in the Old South.* New York: Norton, 1984. This book provides a full account of William Ellison and his slaveholding black family.

cities like Baltimore, Louisville, and Washington urban slaves increasingly relied on their free black neighbors and sympathetic white people to escape north. Urban masters often let slaves purchase their freedom over a term of years to keep them from leaving. In Baltimore, during the early nineteenth century, this sort of **term slavery** was gradually replacing slavery for life.

PROFILE ❖ William Ellison

William Ellison was born a slave in the Fairfield district of South Carolina in 1790. Named *April* by his master, he was a skilled slave. He used that skill to accumulate enough savings to purchase his freedom and subsequently became a slaveholder himself. His story came to light in 1935 when three white children, playing in the crawlspace under his former home, discovered his personal papers.

The son of a slave mother and an unknown white father, Ellison received special treatment from his owner. He was apprenticed at age twelve to a white craftsman named William McCreight. Ellison learned carpentry, blacksmithing, and how to repair cotton gins. He also learned how to conduct a business. He did so well that in 1816, when he was 26, he purchased himself and became a free man.

Once free, Ellison petitioned a court to change his name to *William*, in honor of his mentor—or perhaps his father. With freedom, skills, and a new name, Ellison opened a gin-making and gin-repair shop in Statesburg, South Carolina. Ellison achieved a respectable reputation among his white clients and neighbors as a churchgoing businessman. His ties to his slave past diminished as he prospered. Because his income depended on white slaveholders, he did nothing to antagonize them.

As a result, Ellison became one of the wealthiest owners of real and personal property in the South. He owned hundreds of acres of farmland and woodland. By 1860 he owned sixty-three slaves and was worth in personal property alone $53,000 (about 954,000 current dollars).

Ellison assigned tasks to his slaves according to their gender and age. The field hands were mostly women and children. The gin shop workers—men and adolescent boys—worked as blacksmiths, carpenters, and mechanics.

When the Civil War began in 1861, Ellison and his family were caught between two contradictory forces. Ellison, who died on December 5, 1861, did not live to see the emancipation of his slaves in 1865. But his children did. They also saw the destruction of his business when its newly emancipated workers refused to continue to work for the Ellisons as free men and women.

◀ William Ellison's house near Columbia, South Carolina.

This 1831 lithograph portrays a demonstration of Cyrus McCormick's automatic reaper. It shows the adaptability of slave labor to new technology.

Industrial Slaves

Industrial slavery overlapped with urban slavery, but southern industries that employed slaves were often in rural areas. By 1860 about 5 percent of southern slaves—approximately 200,000 people—worked in industry. Enslaved men, women, and children worked in textile mills in South Carolina and Georgia, sometimes beside white people. In Richmond and Petersburg, Virginia, during the 1850s, about six thousand slaves, most of whom were male, worked in factories producing chewing tobacco. Richmond's famous Tredegar Iron Works also employed a large slave workforce. So did earlier southern ironworks in Virginia, Maryland, northern Tennessee, and southern Kentucky.

The bulk of the sixteen thousand people who worked in the South's lumber industry in 1860 were slaves. Under the supervision of black drivers, they felled trees, operated sawmills, and delivered lumber. Slaves also did most of the work in the naval stores industry of North Carolina and Georgia, manufacturing tar, turpentine, and related products. In western Virginia, they labored in the salt works of the Great Kanawha River Valley, producing the salt used to preserve meat—especially the southern mainstay salt pork. During the 1820s the Maryland Chemical Works in Baltimore, which manufactured industrial chemicals, pigments, and medicines, included many slaves among its workers.

Most southern industrialists hired slaves from their masters rather than buy them themselves. The work slaves performed for them was

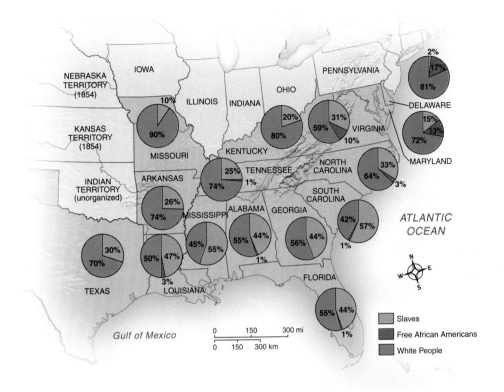

often dangerous, as well as physically tiring. Slaves came to prefer industrial jobs to plantation labor. Like urban slaves, industrial slaves had more opportunities to advance themselves, enjoyed more independence, and were often paid cash incentives. Industrial labor, like urban labor, was a path to freedom for some.

 Reading Check What types of labor did slaves perform in the South?

▶▶ **Map 6-4**

Due to the need for labor in cotton producing states, black majorities existed in Mississippi and South Carolina.

▶ **Reading Check**

While most slaves worked in the fields, some worked as house servants. Still others acquired skills. Such slaves were often hired out by their masters.

Punishment

Those who used slave labor, whether on plantations, small farms, in urban areas, or industry, frequently offered incentives to induce slaves to perform well. Yet slave labor by definition is forced labor based on the threat of physical punishment. Masters denied that this brutal aspect detracted from what they claimed was the essentially benign and paternalistic character of the South's "peculiar institution." After all, Christian masters found support in the Bible for using corporal punishment to chastise servants.

IN THEIR OWN WORDS . . .

Frederick Douglass on the Readiness of Masters to Use the Whip

This passage from the Narrative of the Life of Frederick Douglass, An American Slave, *published in 1845, suggests the volatile relationship between slaves and masters that could quickly result in violence. As Douglass makes clear, masters and overseers used the whip not just to force slaves to work but also to enforce a distinction between what was proper for white men and what was forbidden behavior for slaves.*

It would astonish one, unaccustomed to a slaveholding life, to see with what wonderful ease a slaveholder can find things of which to make occasion to whip a slave. A mere look, word, or motion—a mistake, accident, or want of power—are all matters for which a slave may be whipped at any time. Does a slave look dissatisfied? It is said, he has the devil in him, and it must be whipped out. Does he speak loudly when spoken to by his masters? Then he is getting high-minded, and should be taken down a button-hole lower. Does he forget to pull off his hat at the approach of a white person? Then he is wanting in reverence, and should be whipped for it. Does he ever venture to vindicate his conduct, when censured for it? Then he is guilty of impudence—one of the greatest crimes of which a slave can be guilty. Does he ever venture to suggest a different mode of doing things from that pointed out by his master? He is indeed presumptuous, and getting above himself; and nothing less than a flogging will do for him. Does he, while plowing, break a plough—or, while hoeing, break a hoe? It is owing to his carelessness, and for it a slave must always be whipped.

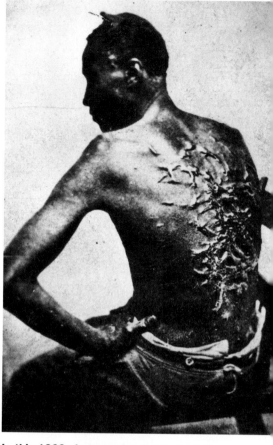

In this 1863 photograph a former Louisiana slave displays the scars that resulted from repeated whippings.

What Do You Think?

▶▶ What does Douglass imply are some of the motives that led masters and overseers to whip slaves?

▶▶ Given the behavior by masters that Douglass describes, how were slaves likely to act around white people?

Source: Roy Finkenbine, ed., *Sources of the African-American Past* (New York: Longman, 1997), 43–44.

▶▶ **What Do You Think?**

· Douglass implies that masters and overseers could conger any reason whatsoever to whip slaves.

· Slaves were likely to act in fear around white people, as they never knew what small thing might provoke a whipping.

Southern whites believed that African Americans would not work unless they were threatened with beatings. One observer reported that in Mississippi he had observed a young girl subjected to "the severest corporal punishment" he had ever seen. The white overseer had administered the flogging with a rawhide whip because the girl had been shirking her duties. He claimed that "if I hadn't [punished her so hard] she would have done the same thing again tomorrow, and half the people on the plantation would have followed her example. . . They'd never do any work at all if they were not afraid of being whipped."

Fear of the lash drove slaves to do their work and to cooperate among themselves for mutual protection. Black parents and other older relatives taught slave children how to avoid punishment and still resist masters and overseers. They worked slowly—but not too slowly. They faked illness to maintain their strength. They broke tools and injured mules, oxen, and horses to tacitly protest their condition. This pattern of resistance and physical punishment caused anxiety for both masters and slaves. Resistance often forced masters to reduce work hours and improve conditions. Yet few slaves escaped being whipped at least once during their lives in bondage.

 Reading Check Why was physical punishment so widely used by slaveholders?

The Domestic Slave Trade

The expansion of the cotton kingdom south and west combined with the decline of slavery in the Chesapeake to stimulate the **domestic slave trade**. As masters in Delaware, Maryland, Virginia, North Carolina, and Kentucky trimmed excess slaves from their workforces—or switched entirely from slave to wage labor—they sold men, women, and children to slave traders. The traders in turn shipped these unfortunate people to the slave markets of New Orleans and other cities for resale. Masters also sold slaves as punishment. Fear of being "sold down river" led many slaves in the Chesapeake to escape. A vicious circle resulted: masters sold slaves south to prevent their escape and slaves escaped to avoid being sold south.

The number of people traded was huge and, considering that many of them were ripped away from their families, tragic. Starting in the 1820s, about 150,000 slaves per decade moved toward the southwest either with their masters or traders. Between 1820 and 1860, an estimated 50 percent of the slaves of the upper South moved involuntarily into the Southwest.

Traders operated compounds called slave prisons or **slave pens** in Baltimore, Maryland; Washington, D.C.; Alexandria and Richmond, Virginia; Charleston, South Carolina; and in smaller cities as well. Most of the victims of the trade moved on foot in groups called **coffles**,

▶ Document

6-7 *A Slave Tells of His Sale at Auction, 1848*
The auctioning of slaves, the separation of mothers from their children, men from their families, was one of the most inhumane aspects of slavery. The account of one slave's auction is captured in a passage from Henry Watson's *Narrative of Henry Watson, A Fugitive Slave. Written by Himself,* which was published in 1848.

▶ Reading Check

Slave labor by definition is forced labor. Moreover, southern whites believed that African-Americans would not work unless threatened with beatings. Slaves learned how to resist masters while still avoiding punishment.

chained or roped together. From the 1810s onward, northern and European visitors to Washington noted the coffles passing before the U.S. Capitol. There was also a considerable coastal trade in slaves from Chesapeake ports to New Orleans. By the 1840s, some slave traders were carrying their human cargoes in railroad cars.

The domestic slave trade demonstrated the falseness of slaveholders' claims that slavery was a **benign institution**. Driven by economic necessity, by profit, or by a desire to frustrate escape plans, masters in the upper South separated husbands and wives, mothers and children, brothers and sisters. Traders sometimes tore babies from their mothers' arms. The journey from the Chesapeake to Mississippi, Alabama, or Louisiana could be long and hard. Some slaves died along the way. A few managed to keep in touch with those they had left behind through letters and travelers. But most could not. After the abolition of slavery in 1865, many African Americans used their new freedom to travel across the South looking for relatives from whom they had been separated long before.

This woodcut portrays a slave coffle—a group of slaves bound together—passing the Capitol Building in about 1815.

 Reading Check   What was the domestic slave trade?

This woodcut of a black father being sold away from his family appeared in *The Child's Anti-Slavery Book* in 1860.

▶▶ **Recommended Reading**

Norrece T. Jones Jr. *Born a Child of Freedom, Yet a Slave: Mechanisms of Control and Strategies of Resistance in Antebellum South Carolina.* Middleton, CT: Wesleyan University Press, 1990. This book explores how masters controlled slaves and how slaves resisted.

▶▶ **Reading Check**

The domestic slave trade was the trade in slaves within the United States. Often this involved the sale of slaves in the mid-Atlantic states to masters in the southern states. The volume of the trade was enormous. It resulted in incredible hardships for the slaves involved and the destruction of countless families.

▶▶ **Document**

6-10   *A Slave Girl Tells of Her Life, 1861*
Harriet Jacobs's *Life of a Slave Girl*, first published in 1861, has become one of the classic narratives of slavery, told from a woman's view. The book's authenticity was under question for many years, as it was heavily edited by white abolitionists and published under a pen name. But its later authentication and compelling account mark it as one of the best slave narratives and necessary for comprehending the fear that was the life of slaves, particularly the women.

GUIDE TO READING

▶ What was life like for African Americans under slavery?

▶ What was life like for children under slavery?

▶ How did white southerners justify the sexual abuse of black women?

▶ What factors affected the health of slaves?

▶ **Guide to Reading/Key Terms**

For answers, see the *Teacher's Resource Manual*.

Section 4

Slave Life

Slave Families

The families that enslaved African Americans sought to preserve had been developing in America since the seventeenth century. However, such families had no legal standing. Most enslaved men and women could choose their own mates, although masters sometimes arranged such things. Masters encouraged pairings among female and male slaves because they assumed correctly that black husbands and fathers would be less rebellious than single men. Masters were also aware that they would benefit if their human chattel reproduced. As Thomas Jefferson put it, "I consider a [slave] woman who brings [gives birth to] a child every two years as more profitable than the best man on the farm. What she produces is an addition to the capital, while his labors disappear in mere consumption."

Marriage

Families were also the core of the African-American community in slavery. Even though no legal sanctions supported slave marriages and the domestic slave trade could sunder them, many such marriages endured. Before they wed, some couples engaged in courting rituals. Similarly, slave weddings ranged from simply "taking up" to religious ceremonies replete with food and frolics.

Jumping the broom was often part of these ceremonies, although this custom was not African but European. During the 1930s former slave Tempie Herndon recalled her wedding ceremony conducted by "de nigger preacher dat preached at de plantation church." In particular, she remembered that after the religious ceremony, "Marse George got to have his little fun" by having the newlyweds jump backward over a broomstick. "You got to do dat to see which one gwine be boss of your household," she commented. "If both of dem jump over without touchin' it, dey won't gwine be no bossin', dey just gwine be congenial." In fact, more equality existed between husbands and wives in slave marriages than in those of the masters. Southern white concepts of **patriarchy** required male dominance. But because black men lacked power, their wives were more like partners than servants.

Slave couples usually lived together in cabins on their master's property. They had little privacy. Slave cabins were rude, small one-room

dwellings that two families might have to share. But couples who shared cabins were generally better off than husbands and wives who were the property of different masters and lived on different plantations. In these cases, children lived with their mother. Their father visited when he could in the evenings. Work patterns that changed with the seasons or with the mood of a master could interfere with such visits. So could the requirement that slaves have passes to leave home.

Children

Despite these difficulties, slave parents were able to instruct their children in family history, religion, and the skills required to survive in slavery. They sang to their children and told them stories full of folk wisdom. In particular, they impressed on them the importance of extended family relationships. The ability to rely on grandparents, aunts and uncles, cousins, and honorary relatives was a hedge against the family disruption that the domestic slave trade might inflict. The extended black family became the core of the black community. It provided slaves with the independent resources they needed to avoid complete physical, intellectual, cultural, and moral subjugation to their masters.

During an age when infant mortality rates were much higher than they are today, those for black southerners were even higher than they were for white people. There were several reasons for this. Enslaved black women usually had to do field labor up to the time they delivered a child, and their diets lacked necessary nutrients. Consequently, they tended to have babies whose weights at birth were less than normal. In addition, black infants were more likely to be subject to such postpartum maladies as rickets, tetany, tetanus, high fevers, intestinal worms, and influenza. More than 50 percent of slave children died before the age of five.

Slaveholders contributed to high infant mortality rates probably more from ignorance than malevolence. It was, after all, in the master's economic self-interest to have slave mothers produce healthy children. Masters often allowed mothers a month to recuperate after giving birth and time off from fieldwork to nurse their babies for several months thereafter. Although this reduced the mother's productivity, the losses would be made up by the children's labor when they entered the plantation workforce. Unfortunately, many infants needed more than a few months of breast-feeding to survive.

The care of slave children varied with the size of a slaveholder's estate, the region it was in, and the mother's work. House servants could carry their babies with them while they did their work. On small farms, slave women strapped their babies to their backs or left them at the edge of fields, so they could nurse them periodically. The latter practice risked exposing an infant to ants, flies, or mosquitoes. On larger plantations, mothers could leave a child with an elderly or infirm adult. This encouraged a sense of community and a shared responsibility among the slaves for all black children on a plantation.

▶▶ **Document**

6-6 *Frederick Douglass, Excerpt from Narrative of the Life, 1845*
An excerpt from the *Narrative of the Life of Frederick Douglass* that describes life for slaves, especially children.

▶▶ **Recommended Reading**

Wilma King. *Stolen Childhood: Slave Youth in Nineteenth-Century America.* Bloomington, IN: Indiana University Press, 1995. This is the most up-to-date account of enslaved black children. It is especially useful concerning the children's work.

exploitation on black women. They failed to note that the rape of black women by white men emphasized in the most degrading manner the inability of black men to protect their wives and daughters.

Health and Welfare

A typical plantation's weekly ration of one peck of cornmeal and three to four pounds of salt pork or bacon was enough to maintain an adult's body weight and, therefore, appeared to be adequate. But even when black men and women added vegetables and poultry that they raised or fish and small game that they caught, this diet was deficient in calcium, vitamin C, riboflavin, protein, and iron. Because these vitamins and nutrients were essential to the health of people who performed hard labor in a hot climate, slaves frequently suffered from chronic illnesses.

Yet masters and white southerners generally consumed the same sort of food that slaves ate. In comparison to people in other parts of the Atlantic world, enslaved African Americans were not undernourished. Although adult slaves were on average an inch shorter than white northerners, they were three inches taller than new arrivals from Africa, two inches taller than slaves who lived in the West Indies, and one inch taller than British Royal Marines.

African-American cooks, primarily women, developed a distinctive cuisine based on African culinary traditions. They seasoned foods with salt, onions, pepper, and other spices and herbs. They fried meat and fish, served sauce over rice, and flavored vegetables with bits of smoked meat. The availability in the South of such African foods as okra, yams, benne seeds, and peanuts strengthened their culinary ties to that continent. Cooking also gave black women the ability to control part of their lives and to demonstrate their creativity.

Clothing

Slaves in general rarely had the time or skill to make their own clothes. They went barefoot during the warm months and wore cheap shoes, usually made by local cobblers, in the winter. Slaveholding women, with the help of trained female house servants, sewed the clothes slaves wore. This clothing was usually made of homespun cotton or wool.

Slaves usually received clothing allotments twice a year. At the fall distribution, slave men received two outfits for the cold weather along with a jacket and a wool cap. At the spring distribution, they received two cotton outfits. Slave drivers wore garments of finer cloth and greatcoats during the winter. Butlers and carriage drivers wore liveries appropriate to their public duties. Slave women received at each distribution two simply cut dresses of calico or homespun. In the winter they wore capes or cloaks and covered their heads with kerchiefs or bonnets.

Because masters gave priority to clothing adult workers, small children often went naked during the warm months. Depending on their ages and the season, children received garments called *shirts* if worn by boys and *shifts* if worn by girls. This garb lasted until children reached "about twelve or fourteen," when they began doing the work of adults.

Although they received standard-issue clothing, black women particularly sought to individualize what they wore. They changed the colors of clothes with dyes they extracted from roots, berries, walnut shells, oak leaves, and indigo. They wove threads of different color into their clothes to make "checkedy" and other patterns.

To further adorn themselves, young women wore hoops under their skirts fashioned from grapevines, stiffly starched petticoats, intricately arranged turbans, and colorful kerchiefs. On special occasions they braided or twisted their hair, used rouge made from berries, eye shadow made from soot, and perfume derived from honeysuckle. Urban slaves had access to commercial products. Plantation slaves often bought clothes, shoes, ribbons, and kerchiefs at local stores or from peddlers.

Health

Low birth weight, diet, and clothing all affected the health of slaves. Before the 1830s various diseases were endemic among bond people, and death could come quickly. Much of this ill health resulted from overwork in the South's hot, humid summers, from exposure to cold during the winter, and from poor hygiene. Slave quarters, for example, rarely had privies. Drinking water could become contaminated. Food was prepared under less than healthy conditions. Dysentery, typhus, food poisoning, diarrhea, hepatitis, typhoid fever, salmonella, and intestinal worms were common and sometimes fatal maladies.

The South's warm climate encouraged mosquito-borne diseases, the growth of bacteria, and the spread of viruses. Some diseases were passed from one race to another. Smallpox, measles, and gonorrhea were European diseases; malaria, hookworm, and yellow fever came from Africa. The sickle-cell blood trait protected people of African descent from malaria but could cause **sickle-cell anemia**, a painful, debilitating, and fatal disease. African Americans were also more susceptible to other afflictions than were persons of European descent.

They suffered from **lactose intolerance**, which greatly limited the amount of calcium they could absorb from dairy products, and from a limited ability to acquire enough vitamin D from the sunlight in temperate regions. Because many slaves also lost calcium through perspiration while working, these characteristics led to a high incidence of debilitating diseases. These included, according to historian Donald R. Wright, "blindness or inflamed and watery eyes; lameness or crooked limbs; loose, missing or rotten teeth; and skin sores. Also, they made African Americans much more apt than whites to suffer

from a number of often fatal diseases—tetanus, intestinal worms, diphtheria, whooping cough, pica (or dirt eating), pneumonia, tuberculosis, and dysentery."

However, black southerners constituted the only New World slave population that grew by natural reproduction. Although the death rate among slaves was higher than among white southerners, it was similar to that of Europeans. Slave health also improved after 1830 when their economic value increased. Masters improved slave quarters, provided warmer winter clothing, reduced overwork, and hired physicians to care for bond people. During the 1840s and 1850s, slaves were more likely than white southerners to be cared for by a physician.

Enslaved African Americans also used traditional remedies—derived from Africa and passed down by generations of women—to treat the sick. Wild cherry bark and herbs like pennyroyal or horehound went into teas to treat colds. Slaves used jimsonweed tea to counter rheumatism and chestnut leaf tea to relieve asthma. One former slave recalled that her grandmother dispensed syrup to treat colic and teas to cure fevers and stomachaches. Nineteenth-century medical knowledge was so limited that some of these folk remedies were more effective than those prescribed by white physicians. This was especially true of kaolin, a white clay also used in ceramics, which black women used to treat dysentery.

 Reading Check What was life like for African Americans under slavery?

▶ **Reading Check**

Working long hours, constant threat of physical torture and punishment, sexual exploitation, poor diet and separation from family are some of the many hardships and obstacles of slave life. Inspite of these hardships, slaves strove to preserve a sense of community and family. In fact, family was the core of slave communities.

The physical toll of slave life is captured in this painting of workers picking cotton in a field in Georgia.

Section 5

The Socialization of Slaves

Surviving Slavery

African Americans had to acquire the skills needed to protect themselves and their loved ones from a brutal slave system. Folktales often derived from Africa, but on occasion from American Indians, helped pass such skills from generation to generation. Parents, other relatives, and elderly slaves generally told such tales to teach survival, mental agility, and self-confidence.

The heroes of the tales are animal tricksters with human personalities. Most famous is Brer Rabbit who in his weakness and cleverness represents African Americans in slavery. Although the tales portray Brer Rabbit as far from perfect, he uses his wits to overcome threats from strong and vicious antagonists, principally Brer Fox, who represents slaveholders. By hearing these stories and rooting for Brer Rabbit, slave children learned how to conduct themselves in a difficult environment.

They learned to watch what they said to white people, not to talk back, to withhold information about other African Americans, to dissemble. In particular, they refrained from making antislavery statements and camouflaged their awareness of how masters exploited them. As Henry Bibb, who escaped from slavery, put it, "The only weapon of self defense that I could use successfully was that of deception." Another former slave, Charshee Charlotte Lawrence-McIntyre, summed up the slave strategy in rhyme: "Got one mind for the boss to see; got another for what I know is me."

Masters tended to miss the subtlety of the divided consciousness of their bond people. When slaves refused to do simple tasks correctly, masters saw it as black stupidity rather than resistance. Sometimes outsiders, such as white northern missionary Charles C. Jones, understood more clearly what was going on. In 1842 Jones observed,

> Persons live and die in the midst of Negroes and know comparatively little of their real character. The Negroes form a distinct class in the community, and keep themselves very much to themselves. They are one thing before the whites and another before their own color. Deception towards the former is characteristic of them, whether bond or free. . . . It is habit—long established custom, which descends from generation to generation.

GUIDE TO READING

▶ How did African Americans adapt to life under slavery?

▶ What were characteristics of the semisecret black churches that slaves created?

▶ How have historians evaluated slavery and slaves?

KEY TERMS

▶ paternalism, p. 207

▶ peculiar institution, p. 208

▶▶ **Guide to Reading/Key Terms**

For answers, see the *Teacher's Resource Manual.*

▶▶ **Document**

6-3 *Southern Novel Depicts Slavery, 1832* John P. Kennedy wrote a novel, *Swallow Barn,* which depicted an imaginary plantation with an exemplary slave owner. The excerpt paints an idyllic picture of happy slaves and kind masters with little mention of the poverty and drudgery of plantation work by slaves.

Living Words Audio Clip

Track 6 Come by Hyar, traditional; sung by Bernice Reagon

Track 7 Go Down Moses, sung by Bill McAdoo

Recommended Reading

6-5 *Charles C. Jones, The Religious Instruction of the Negroes In the United States, 1842* In this passage, Rev. Charles Colcock Jones Sr., warns against the dangers of religious instruction of slaves. A graduate of Princeton College, Jones published several books on the subject of preaching to slaves. During the 1830s and 40s he was a professor at the Presbyterian Theological Seminary in Columbia, South Carolina.

Religion

Along with family and socialization, religion helped African Americans cope with slavery. Some masters denied their slaves access to Christianity, and some slaves ignored the religion. In New Orleans, Baltimore, and a few other locations there were Roman Catholic slaves, who were usually the human property of individual Roman Catholic masters. In Maryland during the 1830s the Jesuits, an order of Roman Catholic priests and brothers, collectively owned approximately three hundred slaves. But by the mid-nineteenth century, the overwhelming majority of American slaves practiced a Protestantism similar, but not identical, to that of most white southerners.

Biracial Baptist and Methodist congregations persisted in the South longer than they did in northern cities. The southern congregations usually had racially segregated seating, but blacks and whites joined in communion and church discipline, and they shared cemeteries. Many masters during the nineteenth century sponsored plantation churches for slaves, and white missionary organizations also supported such churches.

British artist John Antrobus' painting, named *Plantation Burial,* suggests the importance of religion among enslaved African Americans.

In the plantation churches, white ministers told their black congregations that Christian slaves must obey their earthly masters as they did God. This was not what slaves wanted to hear. Cornelius Garner, a former slave, recalled that "dat ole white preacher jest was telling us slaves to be good to our marsters. We ain't keer'd a bit 'bout dat stuff he was telling us 'cause we wanted to sing, pray, and serve God in our own way." At times slaves walked out on ministers who preached obedience.

Instead of services sponsored by masters, slaves preferred a semi-secret black church they conducted themselves. This was a church characterized by self-called, often illiterate black preachers. It emphasized Moses and deliverance from bondage rather than a consistent theology or Christian meekness. Services were quite emotional and involved singing, dancing, shouting, moaning, and clapping. Mixed in with this black Christianity were, according to historian Peter Kolchin, African "potions, concoctions, charms, and rituals [used] to ward off evil, cure sickness, harm enemies, and produce amorous behavior."

 Reading Check How did African Americans adapt to life under slavery?

The Character of Slavery and Slaves

For over a century, historians have debated the character of the Old South's slave system and the people it held in bondage. During the 1910s southern historian Ulrich B. Phillips portrayed slavery as a benign, paternalistic institution in which Christian slaveholders cared for largely content slaves. Slavery, Phillips argued—as had the slaveholders themselves—rescued members of an inferior race from African barbarism. It permitted them to rise as far as they possibly could toward civilization. With a much different emphasis, historian Eugene D. Genovese has, since the 1960s, seen **paternalism** at the heart of southern plantation slavery.

Other historians, however, have denied that paternalism had much to do with a system that rested on force. Since the 1950s historians have contended that slaveholders exploited their bond people in a selfish quest for profits. Although some slaveholders were concerned about the welfare of their slaves, this brutal portrait of slavery is persuasive at the dawn of the twenty-first century. Many masters never met their slaves face to face. Most slaves experienced whipping at some point in their lives, and over half the slaves caught up in the domestic slave trade were separated from their families.

There is also a scholarly tradition of comparing slavery in the American South with its counterpart in Latin America. Historians note that slaves in Latin American countries influenced by Roman law and the Roman Catholic Church enjoyed more protection from abusive

▶ **Reading Check**
African Americans acquired the skills they needed to survive a brutal system. They learned to watch what white people said, not talk back, and to withhold information. At the same time, they engaged in subtle acts of resistance.

MAP 7–1 The Slave, Free Black, and White Population of the United States in 1830

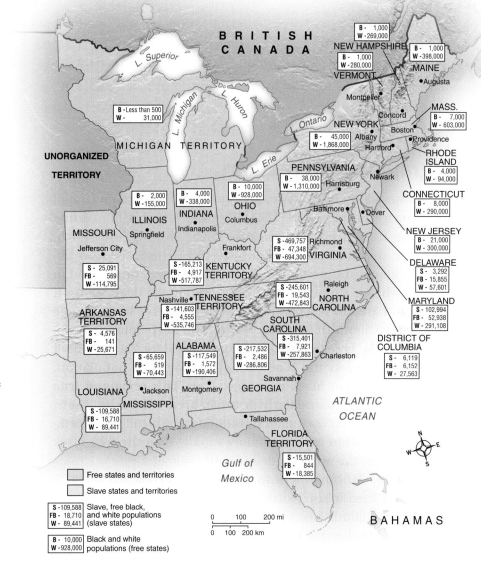

Although the process of gradual emancipation in several northeastern states was still underway, some black northerners remained enslaved.

Source: For slave states, Ira Berlin, *Slaves without Masters: The Free Negro in the Antebellum South* (New York: New Press, 1971); for free states, *Historical Statistics of the United States* (Washington: GPO, 1960). Note: Figures for free states are rounded to the nearest thousand.

 Which states had the largest and the smallest free black populations in 1830?

Explore this map online at www.prenhall.com/aah/map7.1

Map legend:

Free states and territories	
Slave states and territories	
S -109,588 FB - 18,710 W - 89,441	Slave, free black, and white populations (slave states)
B - 10,000 W -928,000	Black and white populations (free states)

0 100 200 mi
0 100 200 km

State population boxes:

- NEW HAMPSHIRE: B - 1,000 / W - 269,000
- VERMONT: B - 1,000 / W - 280,000
- MAINE: B - 1,000 / W - 398,000
- MASS.: B - 7,000 / W - 603,000
- NEW YORK: B - 45,000 / W - 1,868,000
- RHODE ISLAND: B - 4,000 / W - 94,000
- CONNECTICUT: B - 8,000 / W - 290,000
- PENNSYLVANIA: B - 38,000 / W - 1,310,000
- NEW JERSEY: B - 21,000 / W - 300,000
- MICHIGAN TERRITORY: B - Less than 500 / W - 31,000
- OHIO: B - 10,000 / W - 928,000
- INDIANA: B - 4,000 / W - 338,000
- ILLINOIS: B - 2,000 / W - 155,000
- MISSOURI: S - 25,091 / FB - 569 / W - 114,795
- DELAWARE: S - 3,292 / FB - 15,855 / W - 57,601
- VIRGINIA: S - 469,757 / FB - 47,348 / W - 694,300
- MARYLAND: S - 102,994 / FB - 52,938 / W - 291,108
- KENTUCKY: S - 165,213 / FB - 4,917 / W - 517,787
- TENNESSEE TERRITORY: S - 141,603 / FB - 4,555 / W - 535,746
- NORTH CAROLINA: S - 245,601 / FB - 19,543 / W - 472,843
- DISTRICT OF COLUMBIA: S - 6,119 / FB - 6,152 / W - 27,563
- ARKANSAS TERRITORY: S - 4,576 / FB - 141 / W - 25,671
- SOUTH CAROLINA: S - 315,401 / FB - 7,921 / W - 257,863
- ALABAMA: S - 117,549 / FB - 1,572 / W - 190,406
- MISSISSIPPI: S - 65,659 / FB - 519 / W - 70,443
- LOUISIANA: S - 109,588 / FB - 16,710 / W - 89,441
- GEORGIA: S - 217,532 / FB - 2,486 / W - 286,806
- FLORIDA TERRITORY: S - 15,501 / FB - 844 / W - 18,385

BRITISH CANADA

UNORGANIZED TERRITORY

ATLANTIC OCEAN

Gulf of Mexico

BAHAMAS

▶▶ Map 7-1

The state with the smallest free black population was Mississippi. Maryland maintained the largest free black population.

▶▶ Reading Check

In 1820 there were 233,504 free black people living in the United States. Slightly more free black people lived in the upper South than in the North. More black women than black men were free. By 1860, the number of free African Americans had increased to 488,070, but free blacks made up a smaller percentage of the overall population.

The black populations of such important northern cities as New York, Boston, Providence, New Haven, and Cincinnati were considerably smaller than Philadelphia's, but they were still large enough to develop dynamic communities. In Baltimore, Richmond, Norfolk, and other cities of the upper South, free African Americans interacted with enslaved populations to create black communities embracing both groups.

 Reading Check What were the demographics of black freedom?

The Jacksonian Era

After the War of 1812, free African Americans—like other Americans of the time—witnessed rapid economic, social, and political change. Between 1800 and 1860, a **market revolution** transformed the North into a modern industrial society. An economy based on subsistence farming, goods produced by skilled artisans, and local markets grew into one marked by commercial farming, factory production, and national markets. The industrial revolution that had begun in Britain a century earlier set the stage for these changes. But transportation had to improve enormously to allow for such a revolution in America. After Robert Fulton demonstrated the practicality of steam-powered river vessels in 1807, steamboats speeded travel on the country's inland waterways. By the 1820s a system of turnpikes and canals began to unite the North and parts of the South. Of particular importance were the National Road extending westward from Baltimore and the **Erie Canal** that in 1825 opened a water route from New York City to the Old Northwest. By the 1830s railroads began to link urban and agricultural regions.

As faster transportation revolutionized trade, as a factory system began to replace small shops run by artisans, and as cities expanded, northern society changed in profound ways. A large urban working class arose. Artisans and small farmers feared for their future. Entrepreneurs began to replace the traditional social elite. The North also became increasingly different from a still largely premodern South. By the 1820s the northern states were bristling with reform movements designed to deal with the social dislocations the market revolution had caused.

The market revolution also helped create mass political parties. By 1810 states across the country began dropping the traditional property qualifications that had limited citizens' right to vote. One by one, they moved toward universal white manhood **suffrage**. This trend doomed the openly elitist Federalist Party and disrupted its foe, the Republican Party. As the market revolution picked up during the 1820s, unleashing hopes and fears among Americans, politicians recognized the need for more broadly based political parties.

A turning point came in 1825 when Congress chose Secretary of State John Quincy Adams of Massachusetts to become president over war hero Andrew Jackson of Tennessee, after no candidate received a majority of the electoral votes. As president, Adams paradoxically represented both the old elitist style of politics and the entrepreneurial spirit

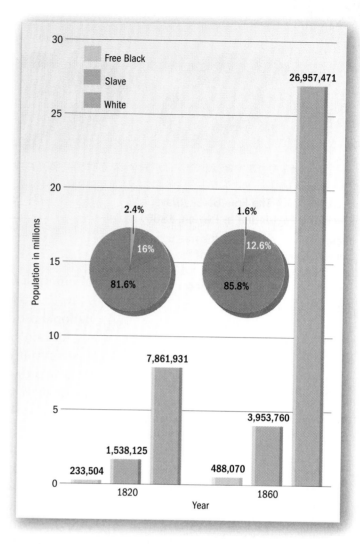

FIGURE 7–1 The Free Black, Slave, and White Population of the United States in 1820 and 1860.

The bar graph shows the relationship among free African-American, slave, and white populations in the United States in the years 1820 and 1860.

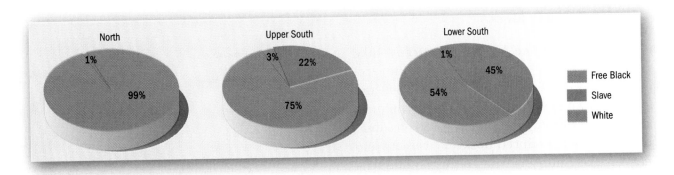

FIGURE 7–2 The Free Black, Slave, and White Population by Region, 1860.

These pie charts compare the free black, slave, and white populations of the North, upper South, and lower South in 1860. Note the near balance of the races in the lower South.

of emerging northern capitalism. Adams, along with his secretary of state, Henry Clay, hoped to promote **industrialization** through a national program of federal government aid.

Jackson's supporters, led by Martin Van Buren of New York, organized a new **Democratic Party** to counter Adams's and Clay's program by making Jackson president. By appealing to slaveholders, who feared that economic nationalism would favor the North over the South, and to "the common man" throughout the country, the Democrats elected Jackson in 1828.

Jackson was a strong but controversial president. During the **Nullification Crisis** of 1832–1833 he acted as a nationalist in facing down the attempt of South Carolina to nullify—to block—the collection of the U.S. tariff (tax) on imports within the state. Otherwise, Jackson, who owned many slaves, promoted states' rights, economic localism, and the territorial expansion of slavery. In opposition to Jackson, Henry Clay, a Kentucky slaveholder, and others formed the **Whig Party** during the early 1830s.

A national organization that fought the Democrats for power from 1834 to 1852, the Whig Party mixed traditional and modern politics. It was a mass political party, but many of its leaders questioned the legitimacy of mass parties. It favored a nationalist approach to economic policy, which made it more successful in the North than in the South, opposed territorial expansion, worried about the growing number of immigrants, and endorsed the moral values of evangelical Protestantism. In contrast to Democratic politicians who increasingly made racist appeals to antiblack prejudices among white voters, Whigs generally adopted a more conciliatory tone regarding race. By the late 1830s, a few northern Whigs believed their party actually opposed slavery and racial oppression. They were, however, exaggerating. The Whigs constantly nominated slaveholders for the presidency, and few Whig politicians defended the rights of African Americans.

 Reading Check How did the policies of the Jacksonian Democrats favor slaveholders?

▶ **Reading Check**

Jackson and Democrats promoted states' rights and economic localism. They also supported the expansion of the territory in which slavery was legal. Racist appeals to antiblack prejudices became a mainstay of Democratic political rhetoric.

▶ **Document**

7-5 *A Senator Sees Slavery as a "Positive Good" in 1837*
Senator John C. Calhoun made these remarks in the United States Senate on February, 6, 1837.

Section 2

Limits of Freedom

GUIDE TO READING

▶ How was black freedom limited in the North?

▶ What were black laws and why were they enacted?

▶ What steps did northern states take to deny free African Americans the right to vote?

KEY TERMS

▶ black laws, p. 222

▶ disfranchisement, p. 223

▶ franchise, p. 223

▶ Jim Crow, p. 225

▶ segregation, p. 225

The North

Addressing an interracial audience in Boston, white abolitionist Joseph C. Lovejoy in 1846 described the North as a land "partially free." Lovejoy was especially concerned that the Fugitive Slave Law of 1793 extended into the northern states the power of southern slaveholders to enslave African Americans. But white northerners also limited black freedom by enacting black laws, by rarely allowing black men to vote, by advocating segregated housing, schools, and transportation, and by limiting African Americans' employment opportunities.

The Fugitive Slave Law endangered the freedom of northern black men, women, and children. Those who had escaped from slavery, of course, lived in fear that as long as they stayed in the United States they might be seized and returned to their erstwhile masters. In fact, any black northerner could be kidnapped, taken to a southern state, and enslaved under the aegis of this law. Even such black leaders as Richard Allen and David Ruggles faced this threat. Ruggles, a prominent northern-born abolitionist, author, and lecturer during the 1830s and 1840s, barely escaped an attempt to haul him before a judge so he could be transported to the South. Others were less lucky. Vigilance against kidnapping became important in African-American community life in the North throughout the antebellum period.

Black Laws

As white Americans began to perceive self-reliance, intellectual curiosity, the capacity for self-government, military valor, and an energetic work ethic as inherently "Anglo-Saxon" characteristics, they began to believe other racial groups lacked these virtues. As Samuel Cornish suggested, even those white people who befriended black people considered them outsiders in a "white man's country."

Most white northerners wanted nothing to do with African Americans. Like white southerners, they considered black people inferior in every way. They paradoxically dismissed black people as incapable of honest work and feared black competition for jobs. Contact

▶ **Guide to Reading/Key Terms**

For answers, see the *Teacher's Resource Manual.*

▶ **Recommended Reading**

James Oliver Horton and Lois E. Horton. *In Hope of Liberty: Culture, Community, and Protest among Northern Free Blacks, 1700–1860.* New York: Oxford University Press, 1997. The authors focus on how the black community responded to difficult circumstances, especially during the antebellum decades.

Eliza, Nellie, and Margaret Copeland in an 1854 portrait by W. M. Prior. The Copeland family was one of the few African-American families in antebellum America affluent enough to commission such a portrait. Reproduced with permission. © 2001 Museum of Fine Arts, Boston. All Right Reserved.

with African Americans, they believed, had degraded white southerners and would also corrupt white northerners if they permitted it. Therefore, as historian Leon Litwack puts it, "Nearly every northern state considered, and many adopted, measures to prohibit or restrict the further immigration of Negroes" into its jurisdiction.

Such measures were adopted more often in the Old Northwest than in the Northeast. In 1821 a bill to restrict black people from entering Massachusetts failed to reach a vote in the state legislature on the grounds that it was inconsistent with "love of humanity." In Pennsylvania, which had a much larger influx of southern African Americans than did Massachusetts, the legislature defeated attempts to limit their entry to the state. But Ohio, Illinois, Indiana, Michigan, Iowa, and Wisconsin all limited or banned black immigration and discriminated against black residents.

Between 1804 and 1849, Ohio's **black laws** required that African Americans entering the state produce legal evidence that they were free, register with a county clerk, and post a $500 bond "to pay for their support in case of want." State and local authorities rarely enforced these provisions, and when the Ohio Free Soil Party brought about their repeal in 1849, Ohio had about 25,000 African Americans. But these rules certainly made black people insecure. In 1829, for example, Cincinnati used them to force between 1,100 and 2,200 black residents to depart. Moreover, other provisions of Ohio's black laws were rigorously enforced, including those that prohibited black testimony against white people, black service on juries, and black enlistment in the state militia.

In 1813 the Illinois Territory threatened that African Americans who tried to settle within its borders would be repeatedly whipped until they left. In 1847, long after it had become a state, Illinois updated this pro-

TABLE 7–1 Black Population in the States of the Old Northwest, 1800–1840

	1800	1810	1820	1830	1840
Ohio	337	1,899	4,723	9,574	17,345
Michigan		144	174	293	707
Illinois		781	1,374	2,384	3,929
Indiana	298	630	1,420	3,632	7,168
Iowa					188

Source: Horton and Horton, *In Hope of Liberty: Culture, Community, and Protest among Northern Free Blacks, 1700–1860* (Oxford University Press, 1997), 104.

vision by mandating that African Americans who sought to become permanent residents could be fined. Those who could not pay the fine could be sold at public auction into indentured servitude. Indiana citizens ratified a state constitution in 1851 that explicitly banned all African Americans from the state, and Michigan, Iowa, and Wisconsin followed Indiana's example. These laws testify to white prejudice and fear. They suggest how uncomfortable African Americans felt in the Old Northwest. Yet, as in Ohio, these states rarely enforced such restrictive laws. As long as they did not feel threatened, white people were usually willing to tolerate a few black people (see Table 7–1).

Disfranchisement

The **disfranchisement** of black voters was, excepting most of New England, common throughout the North during the antebellum decades. The same white antipathy to African Americans that led to exclusionary legislation supported the movement to deny the right to vote to black men (no women could vote anywhere in the United States during most of the nineteenth century). Because northern antiblack sentiment was strongest in the Old Northwest, prior to the Civil War no black men were allowed to vote in Ohio, Indiana, Illinois, Michigan, Wisconsin, and Iowa. But the older northern states had allowed black male suffrage, and efforts to curtail it were by-products of Jacksonian democracy.

During the eighteenth and early nineteenth centuries, the dominant elite in the northeastern states had used property qualifications to prevent both poor black and poor white men from voting. Because black people were generally poorer than white people, these property qualifications gave most white men the right to vote but denied it to most black men. Under such circumstances white people saw no danger in letting a few relatively well-to-do black men exercise the **franchise**.

Both advocates and opponents of universal white male suffrage argued it would be dangerous to extend the same privilege to black men. They alleged that in certain places black men would be elected to office, and morally suspect African Americans would corrupt the political process. Black people would be encouraged to try to mix socially with white people and that justifiably angry white people would react violently. The movement for universal white manhood suffrage transformed a class issue into a racial one. Although a few white politicians opposed disfranchisement of black voters, the outcome was predictable.

New Jersey stopped allowing black men to vote in 1807 and in 1844 adopted a white-only suffrage provision in its state constitution. In 1818 Connecticut determined that, although black men who had voted before that date could continue to vote, no new black voters would be allowed. At the other extreme, Maine, New Hampshire, Vermont, and Massachusetts—none of which had a significant African-American minority—made no effort to deprive black men of the vote. In the middle were Rhode Island, New York, and Pennsylvania, which had protracted struggles over the issue.

In 1822 Rhode Island denied that black men were eligible to vote in its elections. In 1842 a popular uprising against the state's conservative government extended the franchise to all men, black as well as white. In New York an 1821 state constitutional convention defeated an attempt to disfranchise all black men. Instead, it raised the property qualification for black voters while eliminating it for white voters. To vote in New York, black men had to have property worth $250 (approximately 3,000 current dollars) and pay taxes, whereas white men simply had to pay taxes or serve in the state militia. This provision denied the right to vote to nearly all of the ten thousand black men who had previously voted in the state. African Americans nevertheless remained active in New York politics. As supporters of the Liberty Party in 1844, the Whig Party in 1846, and of the Free-Soil Party in 1848, they fought unsuccessfully to regain equal access to the polls.

A similar protracted struggle in Pennsylvania resulted in a more absolute elimination of black suffrage. From 1780 to 1837, black men who met property qualifications could vote in some of this state's counties but not in others. Then, in 1838, a convention to draft a new state constitution enfranchised all white men and disfranchised all black men. As late as 1855, black Pennsylvanians argued that without the right to vote they faced mounting repression. They petitioned Congress to help them gain equal access to the polls. But their efforts failed. During the years before the Civil War, 93 percent of northern black people lived in states where black men's right to vote was either denied or severely limited.

Segregation

Exclusionary legislation was confined to the Old Northwest, and not all northern states disfranchised black men. But no black northerner could avoid being victimized by a pervasive determination among white people to segregate society.

This nineteenth-century lithograph depicts a street scene in the Five-Points neighborhood of New York City. Amid deteriorating buildings, black people are shown to be victims of poverty, crime, and immorality.

Northern hotels, taverns, and resorts turned black people away unless they were the servants of white guests. African Americans were either banned from public lecture halls, art exhibits, and religious revivals or could attend only at certain times. When they were allowed in churches and theaters, they had to sit in segregated sections. Ohio excluded African Americans from state-supported poorhouses and insane asylums. In relatively enlightened Massachusetts, prominent black abolitionist and orator Frederick Douglass was "within the space of a few days . . . turned away from a menagerie on Boston Common, a lyceum and revival meeting in New Bedford, [and] an eating house."

African Americans faced special difficulty trying to use public transportation. They could ride in stagecoaches only if there were no white passengers. As rail travel became more common during the late 1830s, companies set aside special cars for African Americans. In Massachusetts in 1841, a railroad first used the term *Jim Crow*, which derived from a blackface minstrel act, to describe these cars. Later the term came to define other forms of racial **segregation** as well. In cities, many omnibus

and streetcar companies barred African Americans entirely, even though urban black people had little choice but to try to use them anyway. Steamboats accepted black passengers but refused to rent them cabins.

All African Americans, regardless of their wealth or social standing, were treated this way. Frederick Douglass, who made a point of challenging segregation, refused to ride in Jim Crow train cars unless physically forced to do so. He once clung so tightly to the arms of his seat when several white men attempted to move him that the seat ripped away from its supports. In 1854, in New York City, a black public school teacher named Elizabeth Jenkins was beaten by a white streetcar conductor who tried to expel her from his vehicle. All black people, regardless of their class, were also frequently insulted in public by white adults and children.

In this atmosphere, African Americans learned to distrust white people. A correspondent of Douglass's newspaper, the *North Star*, wrote in 1849 that there seemed "to be a fixed determination on the part of our oppressors in this country to destroy every vestige of self-respect, self-possession, and manly independence left in the colored people." Even when African Americans interacted with white people on an ostensibly equal basis, there were underlying tensions. James Forten's wealthy granddaughter Charlotte Forten, who attended an integrated school in Boston, wrote in her diary, "It is hard to go through life meeting contempt with contempt, hatred with hatred, fearing with too good reason, to love and trust hardly any one whose skin is white—however lovable, attractive, and congenial."

African Americans moving to northern cities, therefore, were not surprised to find segregated black neighborhoods. A few wealthy northern black people lived in white urban neighborhoods, and a few northern cities, such as Cleveland and Detroit, had no patterns of residential segregation. But in most northern cities, the white belief that black neighbors led to lowered property values produced such patterns. There were "Nigger Hill" in Boston, "Little Africa" in Cincinnati, "Hayti" in Pittsburgh, and Philadelphia's Southside. Conditions in these ghettoes were often dreadful, but they provided a refuge from constant insult and places where black institutions could develop.

Because African Americans representing all social and economic classes lived in these segregated neighborhoods, the quality of housing in them varied. But, at its worst, housing was bleak and dangerous. One visitor called the black section of New York City's Five Points "the worst hell of America," and other black urban neighborhoods were just as bad. People lived in unheated shacks and shanties, in dirt-floored basements, or in houses without doors and windows. These conditions nurtured disease, infant mortality, alcoholism, and crime. Southern visitors to northern cities blamed the victims, insisting that the plight of many urban black northerners proved that African Americans were better off in slavery.

 Reading Check   How was black freedom limited in the North?

▶ Reading Check

The Fugitive Slave Law endangered the freedom of blacks living in the North. Not only could escaped slaves be recaptured, free blacks were often kidnapped into slavery. Black laws limited the migration of free blacks. With exception of New England, disfranchisement of black voters was common. Finally, segregation was the norm throughout the North.

▶ Retracing the Odyssey

Boston African-American National Historic Site: Black Heritage Trail and Museum of Afro-American History, Boston. Visitors may follow the Black Heritage Trail to historic locations located in Boston's antebellum black community on Beacon Hill. Of particular interest are the African Meeting House and the Abiel Smith School.

Section 3

Black Communities in the Urban North

The Black Family

Urban neighborhoods, with their more concentrated black populations, nurtured black community life (see Table 7–2). African-American urban communities of the antebellum period developed from the free black communities that had emerged from slavery in the North during the late eighteenth century. The communities varied from city to city and from region to region. Yet they had much in common and interacted with each other. They were characterized by resilient families, poverty, class divisions, active church congregations, the continued development of voluntary organizations, and concern for education.

As they became free, northern African Americans left their masters and established their own households. By the 1820s the average black family in northern cities had two parents and between two and four children. However, in both the Northeast and Northwest, single-parent black families, usually headed by women, became increasingly common during the antebellum period. In Cincinnati, for example, black families headed by women increased from 11 percent in 1830 to more than

GUIDE TO READING

▶ What were the characteristics of Northern black communities?

▶ Describe the typical free black family living in a northern city during the antebellum period.

▶ How did the northern black elite gain financial security during the antebellum period?

TABLE 7–2   Free Black Population of Selected Cities, 1800–1850

City	1800	1850
Baltimore	2,771	25,442
Boston	1,174	1,999
Charleston	951	3,441
New Orleans	800 (estimated)	9,905
New York	3,499	13,815
Philadelphia	4,210	10,736
Washington	123	8,158

Source: Leonard P. Curry, *The Free Black in Urban America, 1800–1850: The Shadow of the Dream* (Chicago: University of Chicago Press, 1981), 250.

▶ **Guide to Reading/Key Terms**

For answers, see the *Teacher's Resource Manual.*

▶ **Recommended Reading**

Leon F. Litwack. *North of Slavery: The Negro in the Free States, 1790–1860.* Chicago: University of Chicago Press, 1961. This book emphasizes how northern white people treated African Americans. It is an essential guide to the status of African Americans in the antebellum North.

▶ **Recommended Readings**

Philip S. Foner. *History of Black America: From the Emergence of the Cotton Kingdom to the Eve of the Compromise of 1850.* Westport, CT: Greenwood Press, 1983. This second volume of Foner's three-volume series presents a wealth of information about African-American life between 1820 and 1861, especially about the northern black community.

W. Jeffrey Bolster. *Black Jacks: African American Seamen in the Age of Sail.* Cambridge, MA: Harvard University Press, 1997. Black Jacks explores the lives of black seamen between 1740 and 1865.

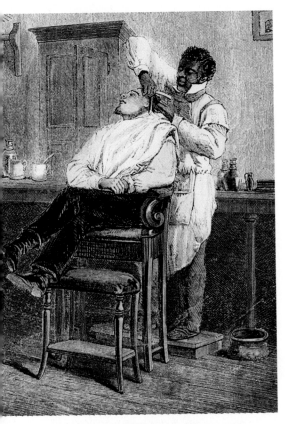

Barbering was one of the skilled trades open to black men during the antebellum years. Several wealthy African Americans began their careers as barbers.

22 percent in 1850. This trend may have been influenced by the difficulty black men had gaining employment. It certainly was a function of a high mortality rate among black men, which made many black women widows during their forties.

Both financial need and African-American culture encouraged black northerners to take in boarders and create extended families. By 1850 approximately one-third of black adults in such cities as Boston, Buffalo, Chicago, Detroit, and Cincinnati boarded. Economic considerations were implicit in such arrangements, but friendship and family relationships also played a part. Sometimes entire nuclear families boarded, but most boarders were young, single, and male. As historians James Oliver Horton and Lois E. Horton put it, "The opportunity to rely on friends and family for shelter enhanced the mobility of poor people who were often forced to move to find employment. It provided financial assistance when people were unemployed; it provided social supports for people who faced discrimination; and it saved those who had left home or run away from slavery from social isolation."

The Struggle for Employment

The rising tide of immigration from Europe hurt northern African Americans economically. Before 1820 black craftsmen had been in demand but, given the choice, white people preferred to employ other white people, and black people suffered. To make matters worse for African Americans, white workers excluded young black men from apprenticeships, refused to work with black people, and used violence to prevent employers from hiring black workers when white workers were unemployed. By the 1830s these practices had driven African Americans from the skilled trades. For the rest of the antebellum period, most northern black men performed menial day labor, although a few worked as coachmen, teamsters, waiters, barbers, carpenters, masons, and plasterers. By the 1850s black men were losing to Irish immigrants unskilled work as longshoremen, drayers, railroad workers, hod-carriers, porters, and shoe-shiners as well as positions in such skilled trades as barbering.

By 1847 in Philadelphia, for example, 80 percent of employed black men did unskilled labor. Barbers and shoemakers predominated among those black workers with skills. Only one-half of 1 percent held factory jobs. Among employed black women, 80 percent either washed clothes or worked as domestic servants. Three-quarters of the remaining 20 percent were seamstresses. By the 1850s black women, too, were losing work to Irish immigrants. A few became prostitutes. About 5 percent of black men and women were self-employed, selling food or secondhand clothing.

Unskilled black men were often unable to find work. When they did work, they received low wages. To escape such conditions in Philadelphia and other port cities, they became sailors. By 1850 about

50 percent of the crewmen on American merchant and whaling vessels were black. Not only did these sailors have to leave their families for months at a time and endure brutal conditions at sea, but they also risked imprisonment if their ship anchored at southern ports.

The Northern Black Elite

Despite the poor prospects of most northern African Americans, a northern black elite emerged during the first six decades of the nineteenth century. Membership in this elite could be achieved through talent, wealth, occupation, family connections, complexion, and education. The elite led in the development of black institutions and culture, in the antislavery movement, and in the struggle for racial justice. It was also the bridge between the black community and sympathetic white people.

Although few African Americans achieved financial security during the antebellum decades, black people could become rich in many ways. Segregated neighborhoods gave rise to a black professional class of physicians, lawyers, ministers, and undertakers who served an exclusively black clientele. Black merchants could gain wealth selling to black communities. Other relatively well-off African Americans included skilled tradesmen, such as carpenters, barbers, waiters, and coachmen, who generally found employment among white people.

Although less so than among African Americans in the South, complexion influenced social standing among African Americans in the North, especially in cities like Cincinnati that were close to the South. White people often preferred to hire people of mixed race, successful black men often chose light-complexioned brides, and African Americans generally accepted white notions of human beauty.

By the 1820s the black elite was becoming better educated and more socially polished than its less wealthy black neighbors, yet it could never disassociate itself from them. Segregation and discriminatory legislation in the North applied to all African Americans regardless of class and complexion, and all African Americans shared a common culture and history.

Black sailors were rarely allowed the command of ships, but Captain Absalom Boston was the master of the *Industry*, a whaling ship that sailed out of Nantucket in 1822.

Entrepreneurs

Conspicuous among the black elite were entrepreneurs who, against considerable odds, gained wealth and influence in the antebellum North. As we noted in Chapter 5, James Forten was one of the first of them, but several other examples indicate the character of such people. John Remond—who as a child migrated from Curacao, a Dutch-ruled island in the Caribbean, to Salem, Massachusetts—and his wife, Nancy Lenox Remond, became prosperous restaurateurs, caterers, and retailers, whose fortune subsidized the abolitionist career of their son Charles Lenox Remond. Louis Hayden, who escaped from slavery in Kentucky in 1845, had become a successful haberdasher and an abolitionist in Boston by

▶ **Retracing the Odyssey**

The Kendall Whaling Museum, Sharon, Massachusetts. Exhibits include "Heroes in the Ships: African Americans in the Whaling Industry, 1840–1900."

Chattanooga African American Museum, Chattanooga, TN. A major exhibit focuses on free black businessmen in antebellum Chattanooga.

1849. Henry Boyd, like Hayden a native of Kentucky, built and operated a steam-powered furniture factory in Cincinnati during the 1840s and 1850s.

Perhaps most successful was Stephen Smith, who owned a lumber and coal business in Lancaster County, Pennsylvania, and speculated in real estate. In 1849 Smith and his partner William Whipper owned, in addition to a huge inventory of coal and lumber, twenty-two railroad cars and

PROFILE ❖ Stephen Smith & William Whipper

African-American entrepreneurs faced limited educational opportunities, inequality before the law, disfranchisement, and pervasive antiblack prejudice. To make their fortunes, they had to compete in a marketplace dominated by white people. Yet a few African Americans, aided by skill, determination, and luck, acquired great wealth. Some used their affluence to better conditions for other African Americans. Black Pennsylvanians Stephen Smith and William Whipper, who linked their commercial success to reform efforts, illustrate this point.

Both Smith and Whipper were children of black mothers and white fathers. Both of their mothers were domestic servants in white households. Smith was born unfree in Dauphin County in south central Pennsylvania in about 1795. Whipper was born free in nearby Lancaster, Pennsylvania, in about 1804. Nothing suggests that either of them had a formal education.

When Smith was five years old, his master apprenticed him to Thomas Boule, who owned a lumber business at Columbia in Lancaster County. During his late teens, Smith became manager of Boule's business. In 1816 he purchased his freedom, married, and began his own lumber company. Shortly thereafter, he began purchasing real estate. Not far away, Whipper grew up and struck out on his own. During the 1820s he worked as a steam scourer in Philadelphia. There in 1834 he opened a grocery store.

The two men became partners in 1835. They had phenomenal success despite a mob attack that same year on their office. They operated one of the largest lumbering businesses in southeastern Pennsylvania. They expanded into selling coal. Smith continued to excel in real estate acquisition, owning at one point fifty-two brick houses in Philadelphia. He was, perhaps, the richest African American in antebellum America.

The two men were partners in reform as well as in business. Early on, Whipper made his grocery a center for temperance and antislavery activities. He became a leader at the Black National Conventions. Meanwhile Smith became an AME minister and builder of churches. They both engaged in Underground Railroad activities and opened their homes to people escaping from slavery. Despite their own success, however, they grew during the 1850s more pessimistic regarding peaceful reform as a means of gaining black rights in the United States. Whipper began to promote black migration to Canada. In 1858 Smith hosted a meeting at which white antislavery activist John Brown discussed his plan to incite slave revolt in the South. Clearly Smith and Whipper as African Americans experienced the double consciousness that W.E.B. Du Bois later identified so eloquently.

◀ William Whipper, ca. 1835.

Smith & Whipper

230

bank stock worth $9,000 (about 175,000 current dollars). They grossed $100,000 (nearly 2,000,000 current dollars) per year, and by 1860 Smith owned real estate in Lancaster and Philadelphia worth $23,000 (about 420,000 current dollars).

Black Professionals

The northern black elite also included physicians and lawyers. Among the physicians, some, such as James McCune Smith and John S. Rock, received medical degrees. Smith, the first African American to earn a medical degree, graduated from the University of Glasgow in Scotland in 1837 and practiced in New York City until his death in 1874. Rock, who had been a dentist in Philadelphia, graduated from the American Medical College in 1852 and practiced medicine in Boston until 1860 when he undertook the study of law. In 1865 he became the first African American to argue a case before the U.S. Supreme Court.

Either because they had been forced out of medical school or they chose not to go, other prominent black physicians practiced medicine without having earned a degree. (This was legal in the nineteenth century.) James Still of Medford, New Jersey, had meager formal education but used natural remedies to develop a successful practice among both black and white people. The multitalented Martin R. Delany, who had been born free in Charles Town, Virginia, in 1812, practiced medicine in Pittsburgh after having been expelled from Harvard Medical School at the insistence of two white classmates.

Prominent black attorneys included Macon B. Allen, who was admitted to the Maine bar in 1844, and Robert Morris, who qualified to practice law in Massachusetts in 1847. Both Allen and Morris apprenticed with white attorneys, and Morris had a particularly successful and lucrative practice. Yet white residents thwarted his attempt to purchase a mansion in a Boston suburb.

Educated at Oberlin College, Edmonia Lewis (1843–1911?) studied sculpture in Rome and emerged as one of the more prolific American artists of the late nineteenth century.

Artists and Musicians

Although they rarely achieved great wealth and fame, black artists and musicians were also part of the northern African-American elite. Among the best-known artists were Robert S. Duncanson, Robert Douglass, Patrick Reason, and Edmonia Lewis. Several of them supported the antislavery movement through their artistic work.

Douglass, a painter who studied in England before establishing himself in Philadelphia, and Reason, an engraver, created portraits of abolitionists during the 1830s. Reason also etched illustrations of the sufferings of slaves. Duncanson, who was born in Cincinnati and worked in Europe between 1843 and 1854, painted landscapes and portraits. Lewis, the daughter of a black man and a Chippewa woman, was admitted with abolitionist help to Oberlin College in Ohio and studied sculpture in Rome. Her works, which emphasized African-American themes, came into wide demand after the Civil War.

Frances Ellen Watkins Harper (1825–1911) was born free in Baltimore. During the 1850s, she published antislavery poetry and traveled across the North as an antislavery speaker.

▶ **Reading Check**

Black communities varied from city to city, but had much in common with each other. They were characterized by resilient families, poverty, class divisions, active church congregations, the development of voluntary organizations, and concern for education.

▶ **Document**

7-8 *An African American Novel Critiques Racism in the North in 1859*
Excerpt from *Our Nig; or, Sketches from the Life of a Free Black, in a Two-Story White House, North: Showing That Slavery's Shadows Fall Even There.*

Jefferson and Sally Hemings to explore in fiction the moral ramifications of slaveholders who fathered children with their bondwomen. Another black novelist of the antebellum years was Martin R. Delany. His *Blake, or the Huts of America,* a story of emerging revolutionary consciousness among southern slaves, ran as a serial in the *Weekly Anglo-African* during 1859. Black poets included George M. Horton, a slave living in North Carolina, who in 1829 published *The Hope of Liberty,* and James W. Whitfield of Buffalo who in 1853 lampooned the song "My Country 'tis of Thee" when he wrote the following:

> America, it is to thee
> Thou boasted land of liberty,—
> Thou land of blood, and crime, and wrong.

African-American women who published fiction during the period included Frances Ellen Watkins Harper and Harriet E. Wilson. Harper was born free in Baltimore in 1825. Associated with the antislavery cause in Pennsylvania and Maine, she published poems that depicted the sufferings of slaves. Her first collection, *Poems on Various Subjects,* appeared in 1854. Wilson published *Our Nig: Or, Sketches from the Life of a Free Black, in a Two-Story White House, North* in 1859. This was the first novel published by a black woman in the United States. It was autobiographical fiction and compared the lives of black domestic workers in the North with those of southern slaves. Wilson's book, however, received little attention during her lifetime, and until the 1980s critics believed a white author had written it. In the following excerpt, Wilson describes Mag's loneliness.

> Such was Mag's experience; and disdaining to ask favor or friendship from a sneering world, she resolved to shut herself up in a hovel she had often passed in better days, and which she knew to be untenanted. She vowed to ask no favors of familiar faces; to die neglected and forgotten before she would be dependent on any. Removed from the village, she was seldom seen except as upon your introduction, gentle reader, with downcast visage, returning her work to her employer, and thus providing herself with the means of subsistence. In two years many hands craved the same avocation; foreigners who cheapened toil and clamored for a livelihood, competed with her, and she could not thus sustain herself. She was now above no drudgery. Occasionally old acquaintances called to be favored with help of some kind, which she was glad to bestow for the sake of the money it would bring her, but the association with them was such a painful reminder of by-gones, she returned to her hut morose and revengeful, refusing all offers of a better home than she possessed. Thus she lived for years, hugging her wrongs, but making no effort to escape.

At about the same time that Wilson wrote *Our Nig,* Hanna Crafts, who had recently escaped from slavery in North Carolina, wrote *The Bondwoman's Narrative.* Unpublished until 2002, this melodramatic autobiographical novel tells the story of a house slave and her escape.

 Reading Check What were the characteristics of Northern black communities?

Section 4

African-American Institutions

Black Churches

The black institutions that had appeared during the revolutionary era became stronger, more numerous, and more varied. This was the result of growing black populations, the exertions of the African-American elite, and the persistence of racial exclusion and segregation. Black institutions of the time included schools, mutual aid organizations, benevolent and fraternal societies, self-improvement and temperance associations, literary groups, newspapers and journals, and theaters. But, aside from families, the most important black community institution remained the church.

Black church buildings were community centers. They housed schools and were meeting places for a variety of organizations. Antislavery societies often met in churches, and the churches harbored fugitive slaves. This went hand in hand with the community leadership black ministers provided. They began schools and various voluntary associations. They spoke against slavery, racial oppression, and what they considered weaknesses among African Americans. However, black ministers never spoke with one voice. Throughout the antebellum decades, many followed Jupiter Hammon in admonishing their congregations that preparing one's soul for heaven was more important than gaining equal rights on earth.

By 1846 the independent African Methodist Episcopal (AME) Church had 296 congregations in the United States and Canada with 17,375 members. In 1848 Frederick Douglass maintained that the AME Mother Bethel Church in Philadelphia was "the largest church in this Union," with between two and three thousand worshippers each Sunday. The AME Zion Church of New York City was probably the second largest black congregation with about two thousand members.

Most black Baptist, Presbyterian, Congregationalist, Episcopal, and Roman Catholic congregations remained affiliated with white denominations, although they were rarely represented in regional and national church councils. For example, the Episcopal Diocese of New York in 1819 excluded black ministers from its annual conventions. Not until 1853 was white abolitionist William Jay able to convince New York Episcopalians to admit black representatives.

Many northern African Americans continued to attend white churches. To do so, they had to submit to the same second-class status that had driven Richard Allen and Absalom Jones to establish separate

▶ What institutions did African Americans rely on most?

▶ What role did black churches play in free black communities?

▶ Why did most black children receive an inadequate education in the antebellum period?

KEY TERMS

▶ temperance, p. 238

▶ African Dorcas Associations, p. 239

This lithograph depicts the bishops of the AME church and suggests both the church's humble origins and its remarkable growth during the antebellum years. Founder Richard Allen is portrayed at the center.

black churches in Philadelphia during the 1790s. Throughout the antebellum years, northern white churches required their black members to sit in special sections during services, provided separate Sunday schools for black children, and insisted that black people take communion after white people. Even Quakers, who spearheaded white opposition to slavery in the North and South, often provided separate seating for black people at their meetings.

By the 1830s and 1840s, some black leaders had begun to criticize the existence of separate black congregations and denominations. Frederick Douglass called them "Negro pews, on a higher and larger scale." Such churches, Douglass and others maintained, were part and parcel of a segregationist spirit that divided America according to complexion. Douglass also denounced what he considered the illiteracy and anti-intellectual bias of most black ministers. Growing numbers of African Americans, nevertheless, regarded such churches as sources of spiritual integrity and legitimate alternatives to second-class status among white Christians.

Schools

Education, like religion, was racially segregated in the North between 1820 and 1860. Tax-supported compulsory public education for children in the United States began in Massachusetts in 1827 and spread throughout the Northeast and Old Northwest during the 1830s. Some public schools, such as those in Cleveland, Ohio, during the 1850s, were racially integrated. But usually, as soon as twenty or more African-American children appeared in a school district, white parents demanded that black children attend separate schools. White people claimed that black children lacked mental capacity and lowered the quality of education. White people also feared that opening schools to black children would encourage more black people to live in the school district.

Across the North, white people were reluctant to use tax dollars to fund education for African Americans. As a result, appropriations for black public schools lagged far behind those for public schools white children attended. This tendency extended to cities where African-American leaders and white abolitionists had created private schools for black children. In 1812 the African School established by Prince Hall in 1798 became part of Boston's public school system. As a result, it began to suffer from inadequate funding and a limited curriculum. The

In 1834 a white mob in Canterbury, Connecticut attacked a school for "colored girls" that had been established by a white woman named Prudence Crandall. This drawing, published in 1839 by abolitionists, dramatizes the incident.

African Free Schools, begun in New York City in 1787 by the New York Society for Promoting the Manumission of Slaves, had a similar fate. In 1834, when these schools became part of New York's public school system, funding and attendance declined. By the 1850s public support for the city's black schools had become negligible.

Woefully inadequate public funding resulted in poor education or none at all for most black children across the North. The few black schools were dilapidated and overcrowded. White teachers who taught in them received lower pay than those who taught in white schools, and black teachers received even less, so teaching was generally poor. Black parents, however, were often unaware that their children received an inadequate education. Even black and white abolitionists tended to expect less from black students than from white students.

Some black leaders defended segregated schools as better for black children than integrated ones. They probably feared that the real choice was between separate black schools or none at all. But, by the 1830s, most northern African Americans favored racially integrated public education. During the 1840s Frederick Douglass became a leading advocate for such a policy. Douglass, other black leaders, and their white abolitionist allies made the most progress in Massachusetts, where by 1845 all public schools, except for those in Boston, had been integrated. After a ten-year struggle, the Massachusetts legislature finally ended segregated schools in that city too. This victory encouraged the opponents of segregated public schools across the North. By 1860 integration had advanced among the region's smaller school districts. But, except for those in Boston, urban schools remained segregated on the eve of the Civil War.

The black elite had more success gaining admission to northern colleges during the antebellum period than most African-American children had in gaining an adequate primary education. Some colleges were exclusively for African Americans. Ashmum Institute in Oxford, Pennsylvania, was founded in 1854 to prepare black missionaries who would go to Africa. Ashmum, later renamed Lincoln University, was the first black institution of higher learning in the United States. Another exclusively black college was Wilberforce University, founded by the AME church in 1855 near Columbus, Ohio. Earlier some northern colleges had begun to admit a few black students. They included Bowdoin in Maine, Dartmouth in New Hampshire, Harvard and Mount Pleasant in Massachusetts, Oneida Institute in New York, and Western Reserve in Ohio. Because of its association with the antislavery movement, Oberlin College in Ohio became the most famous biracial institution of higher learning during the era. By 1860 many northern colleges, law schools, medical schools, and seminaries admitted black applicants, although not on an equal basis with white applicants.

 **Reading Check** Why did most black children receive an inadequate education in the antebellum period?

▶ **Reading Check**

Inadequate public funding was the basic cause of poor education for most black children. The few black schools were dilapidated and overcrowded. Teachers received lower pay than those who taught in white schools, contributing to poor teaching.

Voluntary Associations

The African-American mutual aid, benevolent, self-improvement, and fraternal organizations that originated during the late eighteenth century proliferated during the antebellum decades. So did black literary and **temperance** associations. Mutual aid societies became especially attractive to black women. For example, in 1830 black women in Philadelphia had 27 such organizations compared with 16 for black men. By 1855 Philadelphia had 108 black mutual aid societies, enrolling 9,762 members.

Among black benevolent societies, **African Dorcas Associations** were especially prevalent. Originally organized in 1828 in New York City by black women, these societies distributed used clothing to the poor, especially poor schoolchildren. During the early 1830s, black women also began New York City's Association for the Benefit of Colored Orphans, which operated an orphanage that by 1851 had helped 524 children. Other black benevolent organizations in New York maintained the Colored Seaman's Home and a home for the elderly.

Meanwhile, the Prince Hall Masons created new lodges in the cities of the Northeast and the Chesapeake. Black Odd Fellows lodges also became common from the 1840s on. But more prevalent were self-improvement, library, literary, and temperance organizations. These were manifestations of the reform spirit that swept the North and much of the upper South during the antebellum decades. Closely linked to evangelical Protestantism, reformers maintained that the moral regeneration of individuals was essential to perfecting society. African Americans shared this belief and formed myriad organizations to put it into practice.

Among the societies for black men were the Phoenix Literary Society established in New York City in 1833, the Philadelphia Library Company of Colored Persons begun in 1833, Pittsburgh's Theban Literary Society founded in 1831, and Boston's Adelphi Union for the Promotion of Literature and Science established in 1836. Black women had the Female Literary Society of Philadelphia begun in 1831, New York City's Ladies Literary Society founded in 1834, the Ladies Literary Society of Buffalo, which emerged in the mid-1830s, and Boston's Afric-American Female Intelligence Society begun in 1832.

Black temperance societies were even more widespread than literary and benevolent organizations, although they also tended to be more short lived. Like their white counterparts, black temperance advocates were members of the middle class who sought to stop the abuse of alcoholic beverages by those lower on the social ladder. The temperance societies organized lecture series and handed out literature that portrayed the negative physical, economic, and moral consequences of liquor. Whether such societies were effective is debatable, but they helped unite black communities.

 Reading Check What institutions did African Americans rely on most?

▸ **Reading Check**

Black institutions included schools, mutual aid organizations, benevolent and fraternal societies, self-improvement and temperance associations, literary groups, newspapers, and theaters. However, the institutions they relied on most were churches.

▸ **Document**

7-6 *Sarah Mapps Douglass, Letter to William Basset, 1837*
In December 1837 Sarah Douglass sent a letter to Quaker abolitionist William Basset of Lynn, Massachusetts, telling him about the racism black people encountered at the Quaker Arch Street meeting she had attended as a child.

► How did free African Americans live in the South and in the West?

► What were the most important differences between free black communities in the North and those in the upper South?

► Describe the three-caste system in the deep South.

KEY TERMS

► free papers, p. 240

► tenant farmers, p. 241

► Oblate Sisters, p. 242

► three-caste system, p. 243

►► Guide to Reading/Key Terms

For answers, see the *Teacher's Resource Manual.*

►► Recommended Reading

Leonard Curry. *The Free Black in Urban America, 1800– 1850: The Shadow of the Dream.* Chicago: University of Chicago Press, 1981. Curry provides a comprehensive account of urban African-American life in the antebellum period.

►► Teaching Notes

Life for free black people in the South during the antebellum period was different from that in the North. The free black experience in the upper South was also different from what it was in the deep South. In general free African Americans in the North, despite the limits on their liberty, had opportunities their southern counterparts did not enjoy. Each of the southern regions, nevertheless, offered advantages to free black residents.

Section 5

Free African Americans

The Upper South

The free black people of the upper South had much in common with their northern counterparts. In particular, African Americans in the Chesapeake cities of Baltimore, Washington, Richmond, and Norfolk had many ties to black northerners, ranging from family and church affiliations to business connections and membership in fraternal organizations. But significant differences, which resulted from the South's agricultural economy and slavery, set free people of color in the upper South apart from those in the North. Although nearly half of the free black population in the North lived in cities, only one-third did so in the upper South, hampering the development of black communities there.

Freedom

A more important difference was the impact of slavery on the lives of free African Americans in the upper South. Unlike black northerners, free black people in the upper South lived alongside slaves. Many had family ties to slaves and were more directly involved than black northerners in the suffering of the enslaved. Free black people of the upper South often tried to prevent the sale south of relatives or friends. They paid for manumissions and freedom suits and earned a reputation among white southerners as inveterate harborers of escaped slaves. Southern white politicians and journalists used this close connection between free black southerners and slaves to justify limiting the freedom of the former group.

Free black people of the upper South were also more at risk of being enslaved than were black northerners. Except for Louisiana, with its French and Spanish heritage, all southern states assumed African Americans were slaves unless they could prove otherwise. Free black people had to carry **free papers**, which they had to renew periodically. They could be enslaved if their papers were lost or stolen, and sheriffs in the upper South routinely arrested free black people on the grounds they might be fugitive slaves. Even when those arrested proved they were free, they were sometimes sold as slaves to

pay the cost of imprisoning them. Free African Americans who got into debt in the South risked being sold into slavery to pay off their creditors.

As the antebellum period progressed, the distinction between free and enslaved African Americans narrowed in the upper South. Although a few northern states allowed black men to vote, no southern state did after 1835 when North Carolina followed Tennessee—the only other southern state to allow black suffrage—in revoking the franchise of property-owning black men. Free black people of the upper South also had more problems in traveling, owning firearms, congregating in groups, and being out after dark than did black northerners. Although residential segregation was less pronounced in southern cities than in the North, African Americans of the upper South were more thoroughly excluded from hotels, taverns, trains and coaches, parks, theaters, and hospitals.

Work

Free black people in the upper South also experienced difficulties in earning a living, although, during the nineteenth century, their employment expanded as slavery declined in Maryland and northern Virginia. Free persons of color in rural areas were generally **tenant farmers**. Some of them had to sign labor contracts that reduced them to semislavery. But others owned land and a few owned slaves. Free African Americans also worked in rural areas as miners, lumberjacks, and teamsters. In upper South urban areas, most free black men were unskilled day laborers, waiters, whitewashers, and stevedores. Free black women worked as laundresses and domestic servants.

As in the North, the most successful African Americans were barbers, butchers, tailors, caterers, merchants, and those teamsters and hack drivers who owned their own horses and vehicles. Before 1850 free black people in the upper South faced less competition from European immigrants for jobs than those did who lived in northern cities. Therefore, although the upper South had fewer factories than the North, more free black men worked in them. This changed during the 1850s when Irish and German immigrants competed against free black people in the upper South just as they did in the North for all types of employment. As was the case in the North, immigrants often used violence to drive African Americans out of skilled trades.

Community Life

These circumstances made it more difficult for free black people in the upper South to maintain community institutions. In addition, the measures white people adopted out of fear of slave revolt greatly limited free

▶▶ **Document**

7-7 *North Carolina Codes, 1855*
These codes were several of many statutes prohibiting interaction between free African Americans and slaves. Inviting slaves to social gatherings, playing cards or games of chance, and even marrying or cohabitation with a slave was illegal, thus undermining a number of the liberties free African Americans had.

Chapter Review and Assessment

SUMMARY

Section 1 Freedom, p. 219

- In 1820 free black people made up 2.4 percent of the American population.
- By 1860, the free black population had more than doubled, but had fallen to 1.6 percent of the total population.
- In 1860 almost half of the free black population lived in cities. The market revolution in the North helped create mass political parties.
- The Democratic Party, led by Andrew Jackson, pursued policies that favored slaveholders.

Section 2 Limits of Freedom, p. 223

- Even in the North, whites limited black freedom in important ways.
- Black laws restricted the migration of blacks.
- Except in New England, the disfranchisement of blacks was common throughout the North.
- Whites enforced racial segregation everywhere.

Section 3 Black Communities in the Urban North, p. 229

- Black urban communities were characterized by resilient families, poverty, class divisions, active church congregations, the development of voluntary organizations, and concern for education.
- Economic and cultural factors encouraged the formation of extended families.
- Competition with European immigrants for employment contributed to high unemployment rates among blacks and loss of access to skilled trades.
- Despite the challenges faced by all free African Americans, a northern black elite emerged in the six decades leading up to the Civil War.

Section 4 African-American Institutions, p. 237

- African-American institutions became stronger, more numerous, and more varied in the first half of the nineteenth century.
- Black churches served as community centers.
- Despite the best efforts of black community leaders, inadequate public funding resulted in poor or no education for most black children.

- Black voluntary associations provided a variety of services and did much to strengthen black communities.

Section 5 Free African Americans, p. 242

- Although free black people in the upper South had much in common with their northern counterparts, there were important differences.
- Free blacks in the upper South lived alongside slaves, faced the danger of enslavement themselves, had difficulty finding economic opportunities.
- These conditions made it difficult for them to maintain community institutions.
- A three-caste system developed in the deep South made up of white people, free black people, and slaves. In the trans-Mississippi West, free black people were rare.

REVIEWING KEY TERMS

1. market revolution, p. 219
2. Erie Canal, p. 219
3. suffrage, p. 219
4. industrialization, p. 220
5. Democratic Party, p. 220
6. Nullification Crisis, p. 220
7. Whig Party, p. 220
8. black laws, p. 222
9. disfranchisement, p. 223
10. franchise, p. 223
11. Jim Crow, p. 225
12. segregation, p. 225
13. temperance, p. 238
14. African Dorcas Associations, p. 239
15. free papers, p. 240
16. tenant farmers, p. 241
17. Oblate Sisters, p. 242
18. three-caste system, p. 243

REVIEWING MAIN IDEAS

18. How was black freedom in the North limited in the antebellum decades?
19. How did northern African Americans deal with these limits?

20. What was the relationship of the African-American elite to urban black communities?

21. How did African-American institutions fare between 1820 and 1861?

22. Compare black life in the North to free black life in the upper South, deep South, and the West.

ANALYZING DOCUMENTS

The Constitution of the Pittsburgh African Education Society

Whereas, ignorance in all ages has been found to debase the human mind, and to subject its votaries to the lowest vices, and most abject depravity—and it must be admitted, that ignorance is the sole cause of the present degradation and bondage of the people of color in these United States—that the intellectual capacity of the black man is equal to that of the white, and that he is equally susceptible of improvement, all ancient history makes manifest; and even modern examples put beyond a single doubt.

We, therefore, the people of color, of the city and vicinity of Pittsburgh, and State of Pennsylvania, for the purpose of dispersing the moral gloom that has so long hung around us, have, under Almighty God, associated ourselves together, which association shall be known by the name of the *Pittsburgh African Education Society.* . . .

It shall be the duty of the Board of Managers . . . to purchase such books and periodicals as the Society may deem it expedient, they shall have power to raise money by subscription or otherwise, to purchase ground, and erect thereon a suitable building or buildings for the accommodation and education of youth, and a hall for the use of the Society. . . .

—From Dorothy Porten, ed., *Early Negro Writing, 1760–1837* (1971; reprint, Baltimore: Black Classics, 1995), 120–22.

 Drawing Conclusions: Based on the group's stated reasons for establishing a society and school, why was the Pittsburgh African Education Society necessary?

WRITING ACTIVITY

In a short report or research paper, consider these questions:

 Compare and contrast the lives of free blacks in the North and the South. What key differences do you note?

STUDY ONLINE!

www.prenhall.com/aah

Additional study resources are available for this chapter on the *Companion Website.*

In this contemporary drawing Nat Turner's personal dignity is apparent during his capture for leading a slave uprising in August, 1831.

Chapter 8

TOUSSAINT L'OUVERTURE.

Haitian independence movement leader Touissant Louverture fought successfully against the French and British and provided inspiration for leaders of slave uprisings in America.

Beloved brethren—here let me tell you, and believe it, that the Lord our God, as true as he sits on his throne in heaven, and as true as our Savior died to redeem the world, will give you a Hannibal [an ancient Carthaginian general], and when the Lord shall have raised him up, and given him to you for your possession, O my suffering brethren! . . . Read the history particularly of Hayti, and see how they were butchered by the whites, and do you take warning. The person whom God Shall give you, give him your support and let him go his length, and behold in him the salvation of your God. God will indeed, deliver you through him from your deplorable and wretched condition under the Christians of America.

—David Walker's *Appeal*

 Why was Louverture an inspiration to advocates of slave revolts in America?

Chapter Preview

Witnessing History

Louverture led a successful revolt against French and British oppression in Haiti.

Black abolitionist David Walker wrote these words in Boston in 1829. They suggest both the sense early-nineteenth-century Americans had of the nearness of God and the anguish a free black man felt about his brothers and sisters in bondage.

In his harsh language and demands for action, Walker was a precursor of the militant black and white abolitionists of the 1830s, 1840s, and 1850s. He bluntly portrayed the oppression suffered by African Americans. He urged black men to redeem themselves by defending their loved ones from abuse. If that led to violence and death, he asked, "Had you not rather be killed than be a slave to a tyrant, who takes the life of your mother, wife and dear little children?" Through his provocative language and his efforts to have his *Appeal to the Colored Citizens of the World* distributed in the South, Walker became a prophet of violent revolution against slaveholders.

Walker's *Appeal* was not just a reaction to slavery; it was also a response to a conservative brand of antislavery reform. This chapter explores the emergence, during the years between Gabriel's conspiracy in 1800 and the organization of the American Anti-Slavery Society in 1833, of a radical antislavery movement in the United States. We first discuss the turmoil of the period, the Second Great Awakening, the related social reform efforts, the two strains within the abolition movement, and the black response to African colonization. We then describe how Walker, Denmark Vesey, Nat Turner, other black leaders, and white abolitionist William Lloyd Garrison radicalized the abolition movement during the late 1820s and early 1830s. Chapter 9 traces the development of abolitionism from 1833 into the 1850s.

Section 1

A Country in Turmoil

GUIDE TO READING

▶ What impact did the Second Great Awakening have on black leaders?

▶ How did the Democratic Party support the interests of the South's slaveholding elite?

▶ What was the Benevolent Empire and what causes did it champion?

KEY TERMS

▶ money power, p. 256

▶ slave power, p. 256

▶ Trail of Tears, p. 256

▶ conservatives, p. 256

▶ expansionism, p. 256

▶ revivalism, p. 257

▶ Second Great Awakening, p. 257

▶ practical Christianity, p. 258

▶ Benevolent Empire, p. 258

▶ Jacksonian reform, p. 258

▶ abolitionists, p. 258

When David Walker wrote his *Appeal*, the United States was in economic, political, and social turmoil. The invention of the cotton gin in 1793 led to a vast westward expansion of cotton cultivation. Where cotton went, so did slavery. By the late 1820s, southern slaveholders and their slaves had pushed into what was then the Mexican province of Texas.

The states of the Old Northwest were passing from frontier conditions to commercial farming. By 1825 the Erie Canal, between the Great Lakes and the Hudson River, had linked this region economically to the Northeast. Later, railroads carried the Old Northwest's agricultural products to East-Coast cities. An enormous amount of grain and meat also flowed down the Ohio and Mississippi Rivers encouraging the growth of such cities as Pittsburgh, Cincinnati, Louisville, St. Louis, Memphis, and New Orleans.

In the North, the transportation and market revolutions changed how people lived and worked. As steamboats became common and as networks of macadam turnpikes (paved with crushed stone and tar), canals, and railroads spread, travel time diminished. As Americans began to move from one region to another, families became more scattered, and ties to local communities became less permanent. For African Americans, subject to the domestic slave trade, mobility came with a high price.

Political Paranoia

The Jacksonian Era began with charges leveled by Andrew Jackson's supporters that John Quincy Adams and Henry Clay had conspired to cheat Jackson out of the presidency in 1824. Jackson had won a plurality of the popular vote but failed to get a majority in the electoral college. Congress chose Adams to be president. These charges and the belief that Adams and his political allies represented the interests of rich businessmen and intellectuals, rather than those of the common people, led to the organization of the Democratic Party to contest the national election of 1828. The Democrats claimed to stand for the natural rights and economic well-being of American workers and farmers against what they

▶▶ **Guide to Reading/Key Terms**

For answers, see the *Teacher's Resource Manual*.

This drawing appeared in Henry Highland Garnet's 1848 edition of David Walker's *Appeal . . . to the Colored Citizens of the World.* It portrays a black Moses receiving divine laws guaranteeing liberty and justice.

called the **money power**, a conspiratorial alliance of bankers and businessmen.

Yet, from its start, the Democratic Party also represented the interests of the South's slaveholding elite. Democratic politicians from both the North and South favored a states' rights doctrine that protected slavery from interference by the national government. They sought through legislation, judicial decisions, and diplomacy to make the right to hold human property inviolate. They became the most ardent supporters of expanding slavery into new regions, leading their opponents to claim they were part of a **slave power** conspiracy. Most Democratic politicians also openly advocated white supremacy. Although their rhetoric demanded equal rights for all and special privileges for none, they were really concerned only with the rights of white men.

This was clear in their outlook toward American Indians, women, and African Americans. Democratic politicians were in the forefront of those who demanded the removal of Indians to the area west of the Mississippi River, which culminated in the Cherokee **Trail of Tears** in 1838. Generally, Democrats were also traditionalists concerning the role of women in society. They supported patriarchy and a subservient role for women in both the family and the church. Finally, almost all Democratic leaders in both the North and the South believed God and nature had designed African Americans to be slaves. Yet, during the 1820s and early 1830s, only a few radicals like Walker saw the hypocrisy of the Democrats' outlook and contended that real democracy would embrace all men, regardless of race. Reformers did not even begin to propose equal rights for women until the late 1830s.

By the mid-1830s, those Americans who favored a more enlightened social policy than the Democrats offered turned—often reluctantly—to the Whig Party, which opposed Jackson and the Democrats. The Whigs also attracted those who had supported the Anti-Masonic Party during the early 1830s. This small party epitomized political paranoia by contending that the Freemasons were a vast conspiracy to subvert republican government. From the late 1820s onward, politicians such as Henry Clay, Daniel Webster, William H. Seward, and John Quincy Adams, who identified with the Whig Party, placed much more emphasis on Christian morality and an active national government than the Democrats did. They regarded themselves as **conservatives**, did not seek to end slavery in the southern states, and included many wealthy slaveholders within their ranks. But in the North, the party's moral orientation and its opposition to territorial expansion by the United States made it attractive to slavery's opponents.

The Whig Party also served as the channel through which evangelical Christianity influenced politics. In the North, Whig politicians appealed to evangelical voters. Distrustful of slaveholders and **expansionism**, some northern Whig politicians and journalists defended the human rights of African Americans and American

The Trail of Tears, painted in 1942 by Robert Lindneux, dramatizes the westward journey of Cherokees from their homeland in Georgia to what is now Oklahoma. The Democratic party, which championed the rights of white men, was chiefly responsible for the forced westward relocation of the Cherokees and other southeastern Indian peoples.

Indians. They criticized the inhumanity of slaveholders and tried to limit the federal government's support for the peculiar institution. When and where they could, black men voted for Whig candidates.

The Second Great Awakening

Evangelicals were motivated to carry their Christian morality into politics by a new era of **revivalism** in America. Like David Walker, they saw the hand of God everywhere. Religion, of course, had always been important in America. During the 1730s and 1740s, the widespread religious revival known as the Great Awakening had used emotional preaching and hymn singing to bring men and women to embrace God and reform their lives. African Americans helped shape this emphasis on emotion. American churches had first made a concerted effort to convert black people at that time. Then a new wave of emotional revivalism began at the end of the eighteenth century. Known as the **Second Great Awakening**, it lasted into the 1830s. The new evangelicalism led ordinary black and white Americans to try to take control of religion from the established clergy and to impose moral order on an increasingly turbulent American society.

The Second Great Awakening influenced Richard Allen and Absalom Jones's efforts to establish separate black churches in Philadelphia during

the 1790s. It helped shape the character of other black churches that emerged during the 1800s and 1810s. These black churches became an essential part of the antislavery movement. However, the Second Great Awakening did not reach its peak until the 1820s. With particular force in the North and Northwest, Charles G. Finney, a white Presbyterian, and other revivalists helped democratize religion in America. At camp meetings that lasted for days, Finney and other revivalists preached that all men and women—not just a few—could become faithful Christians and save their souls. Just as Jacksonian democracy revolutionized politics in America, the Second Great Awakening revolutionized the nation's spiritual life and led many Americans to join reform movements.

 Reading Check   What impact did the Second Great Awakening have on black leaders?

The Benevolent Empire

Evangelicals—both black and white—emphasized **practical Christianity**. Those who were saved, they maintained, would not be content with their own salvation. Instead, they would help save others. Black evangelicals, in particular, called for "a *liberating* faith" that would advance material and spiritual well-being. An emphasis on action led to what became known during the 1810s and 1820s as the **Benevolent Empire**, a network of church-related voluntary organizations designed to fight sin and save souls. The Benevolent Empire launched what is now known as antebellum or **Jacksonian reform**.

This social movement flourished from the 1810s through the 1850s. It consisted of voluntary associations dedicated to a host of causes: public education, self-improvement, limiting or abolishing alcohol consumption (the temperance movement), prison reform, and aid to the mentally and physically handicapped. Members of the movement were also involved in distributing Bibles and religious tracts, funding missionary activities, discouraging prostitution, seeking health through diet and fads, improving conditions for seamen, and—by the 1840s—seeking rights for women. The self-improvement, temperance, and missionary associations that free black people—and sometimes slaves—formed in conjunction with their churches in urban areas were part of this movement.

The most important of these societies, however, were those dedicated to the problem of African-American bondage in the United States. At first called societies for promoting the abolition of slavery, they later became known as antislavery societies. Whatever they called themselves, their members were **abolitionists**, people who favored doing away with or abolishing slavery in their respective states and throughout the country. To understand American abolitionism in the 1820s, we must return to the first abolitionist organizations that arose during the revolutionary era.

▶ **Reading Check**

The new evangelicalism led both black and white Americans to try to take control of religion from the established clergy and impose moral order on American society. Black elites were inspired to establish separate black churches and to join reform movements.

Section 2

Abolitionism Begins in America

The Antislavery Movement

The **antislavery movement** in its broadest context reflected economic, intellectual, and moral changes that affected the Atlantic world during the Age of Revolution. In the United States that age forged *two* antislavery movements that continued to exist until the end of the Civil War. Although different, the two movements constantly influenced each other. The first of these movements existed in the South among slaves with the help of free African Americans and a few sympathetic white people. As we mentioned in earlier chapters, from the seventeenth century onward, enslaved African Americans individually and in groups sought their freedom through both violent and nonviolent means. Before the revolutionary era, however, these slaves only wanted to free themselves and did not seek to destroy slavery as a social system.

The second antislavery movement consisted of black and white abolitionists in the North, with outposts in the upper South. Far more white people were in this movement than in the one southern slaves conducted. In the North, white people controlled the larger antislavery organizations, although African Americans led in direct action against slavery and its influences in the North. In the upper South, African Americans could not openly establish or participate in antislavery organizations, but they cooperated covertly and informally with white abolitionists.

The Quakers

This second and essentially northern movement took root during the 1730s when white Quakers in New Jersey and Pennsylvania became convinced that slaveholding contradicted their belief in spiritual equality. For the rest of the eighteenth century, they advocated the abolition of slavery—at least among their fellow Quakers—in their home states and in the Chesapeake. Quakers always remained prominent in the northern antislavery movement. As members of a denomination that emphasized nonviolence, they generally expected slavery to be abolished peacefully and gradually.

GUIDE TO READING

▶ Why and how did abolitionism begin in America?

▶ What of the early abolition movement limited its effectiveness?

▶ How did the revolts of Gabriel and Denmark Vesey affect African Americans?

KEY TERMS

▶ antislavery movement, p. 259

▶ Gabriel's conspiracy, p. 260

▶▶ **Guide to Reading/Key Terms**

For answers, see the *Teacher's Resource Manual.*

▶ **Retracing the Odyssey**

National Afro-American Museum and Cultural Center, Wilberforce, Ohio. Exhibits on African-American history include the antislavery struggle. **The Amistad Research Center**, Tulane University, New Orleans. This institution maintains the archives of the American Missionary Association, the largest American antislavery organization of the 1840s and 1850s.

Philadelphia Quakers in 1775 organized what became the first antislavery society. But when it was reorganized in 1784 as the Society for the Promotion of the Abolition of Slavery, it attracted non-Quakers. Among the first of these were Benjamin Rush and Benjamin Franklin, both of whom were influenced by natural rights doctrines. Revolutionary principles also influenced Alexander Hamilton and John Jay, who helped organize New York's first antislavery society. Prince Hall, the most prominent black abolitionist of his time, also based his effort to abolish slavery in Massachusetts on universal natural rights. He contended that African Americans "have in common with all other men a natural right to our freedom."

Northern Abolitionists

The efforts of northern black and white abolitionists were instrumental in abolishing slavery in the North. However, the early northern antislavery movement had several limiting features. First, black and white abolitionists had similar goals but worked in separate organizations. Even white Quaker abolitionists were reluctant to mix socially with African Americans or welcome them to their meetings. Second, except in parts of New England, abolition in the North proceeded *gradually* to protect the economic interests of slaveholders. Third, white abolitionists did not advocate equal rights for black people. In most northern states, laws kept black people from enjoying full freedom after their emancipation. Fourth, early northern abolitionists did little to bring about abolition in the South where most slaves lived.

All this indicates that neither Quaker piety nor natural rights principles created a truly egalitarian or sectionally aggressive northern abolitionism. It took the moralistic emotionalism of the Second Great Awakening combined with the activism of the Benevolent Empire to establish the framework for a more biracial and wide-ranging antislavery movement. Even more important in providing a prod were southern slaves and their free black allies, who had their own plans for emancipation.

 Reading Check Why and how did abolitionism begin in America?

Gabriel's Conspiracy

Gabriel's abortive slave revolt of 1800 owed as much to revolutionary ideology as did the northern antislavery movement. The arrival of Haitian refugees in Virginia had led to slave unrest throughout the 1790s. Gabriel himself hoped to attract French revolutionary support. **Gabriel's conspiracy**, though, was betrayed, and he and twenty-six of his followers were executed. But the revolutionary spirit and network Gabriel established lived on (see Map 8–1). Virginia authorities had to

▶ **Reading Check**

There were two early antislavery movements in the United States. The white northern abolition movement began among the Quakers of New Jersey and Pennsylvania during the 1730s. Many Quakers were convinced that slaveholding contradicted their belief in spiritual equality. In addition, from the seventeenth century onward, slaves, with the help of free blacks and few whites, worked to gain their freedom.

suppress another slave conspiracy in 1802, and sporadic minor revolts erupted for years.

Gabriel's conspiracy had two unintended consequences. First, the Quaker-led antislavery societies of the Chesapeake declined rapidly. They had always been small and weak compared with antislavery societies in the North. They were more effective helping free black people who were illegally held as slaves than promoting emancipation. After Gabriel's conspiracy, these organizations either became dormant, were suppressed, or withered under pressure from public opinion. The chance all but vanished that Maryland, Virginia, and North Carolina would follow the northern example by gradually abolishing slavery.

Second, white southerners and many white northerners became convinced that, as long as black people lived among them, a race war like the one in Haiti could erupt in the United States. Slaveholders and their defenders argued that this threat did not result from the oppressiveness of slavery. On the contrary, they maintained, the slaves were naturally suited for and content in bondage. It was the growing class of free black people, they asserted, who instigated otherwise passive bondpeople to revolt.

Free African Americans were, slavery's defenders contended, a dangerous, criminal, and potentially revolutionary class that had to be regulated, subdued, and ultimately expelled from the country. No system of emancipation that would increase the number of free black people in the United States could be tolerated. Slaveholders who had never shown a willingness to free their slaves began to claim they would favor emancipation if it were not for fear of enlarging such a dangerous group. As an elderly Thomas Jefferson put it, white southerners had a wolf by the ears: once they had enslaved black people, it was impossible to free them safely. Unless African Americans were restrained by slavery, southern politicians and journalists argued, they would become an economic threat to white workers, a perpetual criminal class, and a revolutionary enemy of white rule.

MAP 8–1 Slave Conspiracies and Uprisings, 1800–1831

Major slave conspiracies and revolts were rare between 1800 and 1860. This was in part because those that took place frightened masters and led them to adopt policies aimed at preventing recurrences.

 What factors account for the distribution of black conspiracies and revolts?

Explore this map online at **www.prenhall.com/aah.map8.1**

Denmark Vesey's Revolt

In 1822 black informants revealed a conspiracy for a massive slave revolt. A free black man named Denmark Vesey had carefully organized it. Like Gabriel before him, Vesey could read and was well aware of the revolutions that had shaken the Atlantic world. Vesey was born

▶ **Map 8-1**

Slave conspiracies and revolts were rare and scattered across the U.S. in part because after one took place, policies were adopted aimed at preventing recurrence.

Julianne Jane Tillman was one of the few women of her time to be employed as an AME preacher.

▶ **Reading Check**

First, Quaker-led antislavery societies in the Chesapeake declined rapidly. Second, many whites became convinced that the existence of free blacks would lead eventually to a race war. Thus, they became the objects of intensified fear and efforts at control.

▶ **Recommended Readings**

Merton L. Dillon. *Slavery Attacked: Southern Slaves and Their Allies, 1619–1865.* Baton Rouge, LA: Louisiana State University Press, 1990. Integrates slave resistance and revolt with the northern abolitionist movement.

Eugene D. Genovese. *From Rebellion to Revolution: Afro-American Slave Revolts in the Making of the Modern World.* Baton Rouge, LA: Louisiana State University Press, 1979. Places the major American slave revolts and conspiracies in an Atlantic context.

most likely on the Caribbean island of St. Thomas. A carpenter by trade and a former sailor who had been to Haiti, Vesey hoped for Haitian aid for an antislavery revolution in the South Carolina low country. He understood the significance of the storming of the Bastille on July 14, 1789, that marked the start of the French Revolution and planned to start his revolution on July 14, 1822. Vesey was also familiar with the antislavery speeches of northern members of Congress during the 1820 debates over the admission of Missouri to the Union and may have hoped for northern aid.

Religious influence was more prominent in Vesey's plot than in Gabriel's. Vesey was a Bible-quoting Methodist who conducted religious classes. Like other free black people and slaves in Charleston, he deeply resented attempts by the white authorities to suppress the city's AME church in 1818. Vesey also used aspects of African religion that had survived among low-country slaves to promote his revolutionary efforts. To reach slaves whose Christian convictions were blended with West African spiritualism, he relied on his closest collaborator, Jack Pritchard. Known as Gullah Jack, a "conjure-man" who had been born in East Africa, Pritchard distributed charms and cast spells that he claimed would make revolutionaries invincible.

Vesey and his associates planned to capture arms and ammunition and seize control of Charleston. About a month before the revolt was to begin, the arrest of one of Vesey's lieutenants put local authorities on guard. Vesey moved the date of the uprising to June 16. But on June 14 a house servant revealed the conspiracy to his master. The local government called in the state militia and arrests were made. Over several weeks, the authorities rounded up 131 suspects. The accused received public trials, and juries convicted seventy-one. Thirty-five, including Vesey and Gullah Jack, were hanged. Thirty-seven were banished. Four white men—three of them foreigners—were convicted of inciting slaves to revolt. They were imprisoned and fined.

After the executions, Charleston's city government destroyed what remained of the local AME church, and white churches assumed responsibility for supervising other black congregations. The state legislature outlawed assemblages of slaves and banned teaching slaves to read. Local authorities jailed black seamen whose ships docked in Charleston until the ships were ready to leave port. Assuming that free black and white abolitionists inspired slave unrest, white South Carolinians became increasingly suspicious of local free African Americans, as well as of white Yankees who visited their state.

 **Reading Check** How did the revolts of Gabriel and Denmark Vesey affect African Americans?

Section 3

Colonization

The American Colonization Society

Fear of free African Americans as a subversive class shaped the program of the most significant white antislavery organization of the 1810s and 1820s—but whether its aim was actually abolition is debatable. In late 1816 concerned white leaders met in Washington, D.C., to form the American Society for Colonizing Free People of Colour of the United States, usually known as the **American Colonization Society** (ACS). Among its founders were such prominent slaveholders as Bushrod Washington—a nephew of George Washington—and Henry Clay. In 1821 the ACS, with the support of the U.S. government, established the colony of **Liberia** in West Africa as a prospective home for African Americans.

The ACS had a twofold program. First, it proposed to abolish slavery gradually in the United States, perhaps giving slaveholders financial compensation for their human property. Second, it proposed to send emancipated slaves and free black people to Liberia. The founders of the ACS believed that masters would never emancipate their slaves if they thought emancipation would increase the free black population in the United States. Moral and practical objections to this program were not immediately clear to either black or white abolitionists. In fact, the ACS became an integral part of the Benevolent Empire and commanded widespread support among many who regarded themselves friends of humanity.

Although the ACS was always strongest in the upper South and enjoyed the support of slaveholders, including Francis Scott Key, Andrew Jackson, John Tyler, and John Randolph, by the 1820s it had branches in every northern state. Such northern white abolitionists as Arthur and Lewis Tappan, Gerrit Smith, and William Lloyd Garrison initially supported **colonization**. They tended to emphasize the abolitionist aspects of the ACS and clung to a belief that free and soon-to-be-emancipated African Americans could choose whether to stay in the United States or go to Liberia. In either case, they hoped, black people would be free.

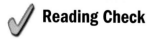 **Reading Check** What were the goals of the American Colonization Society?

GUIDE TO READING

▶ What were the goals of the American Colonization Society?

▶ What elements of the argument in favor of colonization appealed to some African Americans?

▶ Why did many African Americans oppose colonization?

KEY TERMS

▶ American Colonization Society (ACS), p. 263

▶ Liberia, p. 263

▶ colonization, p. 263

▶ black nationalist tradition, p. 264

▶ voluntary colonization, p. 265

▶▶ **Guide to Reading/Key Terms**

For answers, see the *Teacher's Resource Manual.*

▶▶ **Reading Check**

First, the ACS wanted to abolish slavery gradually in the United States. Slaveholders would be compensated for the loss of their human property. Second, the ACS wanted to transport emancipated slaves and free blacks to Liberia.

► **Recommended Reading**

P. J. Staudenraus. *The American Colonization Movement, 1816–1865*. New York: Columbia University Press, 1961. Although published in the 1960s, the most recent account of the American Colonization Society.

Black Nationalism and Colonization

Prominent black abolitionists initially shared this positive assessment of the ACS. They were part of a **black nationalist tradition** dating back at least to Prince Hall that endorsed black American migration to Africa. During the early 1800s, the most prominent advocate of this point of view was Paul Cuffe of Massachusetts. In 1811, six years before the ACS organized, Cuffe, a Quaker of African and American Indian ancestry, addressed Congress on the subject of African-American Christian colonies in Africa.

The ACS argument that appealed to Cuffe and many other African Americans was that white prejudice would never allow black people to enjoy full citizenship, equal protection under the law, and economic success in the United States. Black people born in America, went the argument for African colonization, could enjoy equal rights only in the continent of their ancestors. In the spirit of American evangelicalism, African Americans were also attracted by the prospect of bringing Christianity to African nations. Like white people, many African Americans considered Africa a pagan, barbaric place that could benefit from their knowledge of Christianity and republican government. Other black leaders who favored colonization objected to this view of Africa. They considered African cultures superior to those of America and Europe. They were often Africans themselves, the children of African parents, or individuals who had been influenced by Africans.

In 1815 Cuffe, who was the captain of his own ship, took thirty-four African-American settlers to the British free black colony of Sierra Leone, located just to the north of present-day Liberia. Cuffe himself would probably have later settled in Liberia if his American Indian wife had not refused to leave her native land. So it was the AME bishop Daniel Coker who led the first eighty-six African-American colonists to Liberia in 1820–1821. Pro-ACS sentiment was especially strong among African Americans in Coker's home city of Baltimore and other Chesapeake urban areas. By 1838 approximately 2,500 colonists had made the journey and were living less than harmoniously with Liberia's 28,000 indigenous inhabitants (see Map 8-2).

In 1847 Liberia became an independent republic. But despite the efforts of such Black Nationalist advocates as Henry Highland Garnet and Alexander Crummel, only about ten thousand African-American immigrants had gone there by 1860. This amounted to just .3 percent of the increase of the black population in the United States since 1816. Well before 1860 it was clear African colonization would never fulfill the dreams of its black or white advocates.

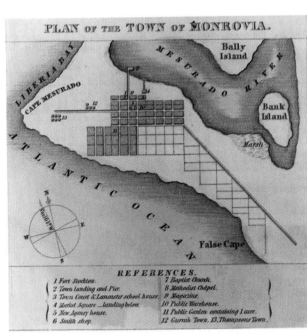

Monrovia, Liberia, ca. 1830. This map shows the American Colonization Society's main Liberian settlement as it existed about ten years after its founding.

Other African Americans saw Haiti as a potential refuge from the oppression they suffered in the United States. Haiti was especially attractive to those whose ancestors had lived in the Caribbean and to those who admired its revolutionary history. In 1824 about two hundred men, women, and children from Philadelphia, New York City, and Baltimore went to Haiti. By the end of the 1820s, between eight and thirteen thousand African Americans had arrived there, but African Americans found Haitian culture to be more alien than they had anticipated. They had difficulty learning French and distrusted the Roman Catholic Church. By 1826 about one-third of the emigrants had returned to the United States.

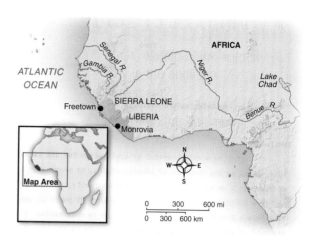

✔ **Reading Check** What elements of the argument in favor of colonization appealed to some African Americans?

Black Opposition to Colonization

Some African Americans had always opposed overseas colonization. As early as 1817, such influential black leaders as James Forten were wavering in their support of the ACS. Although Forten continued to support colonization in private, he led a meeting that year of three thousand black Philadelphians to denounce it. By the mid-1820s, many black abolitionists in East Coast cities from Richmond to Boston were criticizing colonization in general and the ACS in particular.

Among them was Samuel Cornish, who with John Russwurm began publication of *Freedom's Journal* in New York City in 1827 as the first African-American newspaper. Cornish, a young Presbyterian minister and a fierce opponent of the ACS, called for independent black action against slavery. The *Journal*—reflecting the values of antebellum reform—encouraged self-improvement, education, black civil rights in the North, and sympathy among black northerners for slaves in the South. Russwurm, however, was less opposed to the ACS than was Cornish. This disagreement helped lead to the suspension of the newspaper in 1829. That same year Russwurm, who was one of the first African Americans to earn a college degree, moved to Liberia.

People like Cornish regarded themselves as Americans, not Africans, and wanted to improve their condition in this country. They considered Liberia foreign and unhealthy. They had no desire to go there themselves or send other African Americans there. They feared that ACS talk about *voluntary* colonization was misleading. They knew that nearly every southern state required the expulsion of slaves individually freed by their masters. They were also aware of efforts in the

MAP 8–2 The Founding of Liberia
British abolitionists established Sierra Leone as a colony for former slaves in 1800. The American Colonization Society established Liberia for the same purpose in 1821.

 Why were Sierra Leone and Liberia established in West Africa?

▶▶ **Map 8-2**

They were established as colonies for former slaves.

▶▶ **Reading Check**

Supporters of colonization believed that whites in America would never grants blacks equal rights and full citizenship. Blacks would only enjoy such rights in the land of their ancestors. Moreover, African American evangelicals were attracted to the idea of bringing Christianity to Africa.

such hostility from the black community that in September 1833 she retired as a public speaker. Henceforth, she labored in more conventional and respectable female ways for the antislavery cause.

Many African-American women (as well as many white women), however, did not fit the early nineteenth-century criteria for respectability that applied to the Fortens, Stewart, and others in the African-American elite. Most black women were poor. They lacked education. They had to work outside their homes. Particularly in the upper South, these women were **practical abolitionists**.

PROFILE ❖ Maria Stewart

Maria W. Stewart had a brief but striking career as an abolitionist, feminist, and advocate of racial justice. She was born Maria Miller in Hartford, Connecticut, in 1803 to free parents, and she was orphaned at age five. Raised in the home of a minister, she had little formal education until she began attending "sabbath schools" when she was fifteen. In 1826 she married James W. Stewart, a successful Boston businessman who died in 1829.

In 1830 Maria W. Stewart determined to dedicate herself to Christian benevolence. In 1831 William Lloyd Garrison published her pamphlet *Religion and Pure Principles of Morality, the Sure Foundation on Which We Must Build*, in which she advocated abolition and black autonomy. The following year, Garrison published her second and last pamphlet, which dealt more narrowly with religion.

Meanwhile, Stewart began speaking to black organizations. In early 1832 she addressed Boston's Afric-American Female Intelligence Society. She noted that the world had entered a revolutionary age. She called on African-American women to influence their husbands and children in behalf of the cause of black freedom, equality, education, and economic advancement in America. In regard to African colonization, she said, "before I go, the bayonet shall press me through."

When in February 1833 she addressed Boston's African Masonic Lodge, Stewart over-played her role as a prophet. She invoked the glories of ancient Africa as well as black service in the American Revolution in order to chastise black men of her time for not being more active in behalf of the liberty of their people. By claiming that black men lacked "ambition and requisite courage," she provoked her audience to respond with hoots, jeers, and a barrage of rotten tomatoes.

Daunted by this stunning rejection, Stewart determined to leave Boston for New York City. In her farewell address of September 1833, she asserted that her advice had been rejected because she was a woman. Nevertheless, while acknowledging that black men must lead, she called on black women to promote themselves, their families, and their race.

During the rest of her life, Stewart sought to fulfill that role in a less flamboyant manner. In New York she joined the Female Literary Society and became for many years a public school teacher. She moved to the slaveholding city of Baltimore in 1852 to start a school for black children. During the Civil War, with the assistance of black seamstress Elizabeth Keckley, she organized a black school in Washington. Later she worked as a matron at that city's Freedmen's Hospital and organized a Sunday school for poor black children. She died at Freedmen's Hospital in December 1879.

Stewart

From the revolutionary era onward, countless anonymous black women, both slave and free, living in such southern border cities as Baltimore, Louisville, and Washington risked everything to harbor fugitive slaves. Other heroic women saved their meager earnings to purchase freedom for themselves and their loved ones. Among them was Alethia Tanner of Washington, who purchased her own freedom in 1810 for $1,400 (about 16,000 current dollars). During the 1820s she also purchased the freedom of her sister, her sister's ten children, and her sister's five grandchildren. During the 1830s Tanner purchased the freedom of seven more slaves. Meanwhile, according to an account written in the 1860s, "Mrs. Tanner was alive to every wise scheme for the education and elevation of her race."

 Reading Check What role did black women play in the abolition movement?

The Baltimore Alliance

Among the stronger black abolitionist opponents of the ACS were William Watkins, Jacob Greener, and Hezekiah Grice, associates in Baltimore of Benjamin Lundy, a white Quaker abolitionist who published an antislavery newspaper named the *Genius of Universal Emancipation*. By the mid-1820s, Watkins, a schoolteacher, had emerged, in a series of letters he published in *Freedom's Journal* and in Lundy's paper, as one of the more articulate opponents of colonization. Greener, a whitewasher and schoolteacher, helped Lundy publish the *Genius* and promoted its circulation. Grice, who later changed his mind and supported colonization, became the principal founder of the National Black Convention Movement, which during the 1830s, 1840s, and 1850s became a forum for black abolitionists.

In 1829 in Baltimore, Watkins, Greener, and Grice profoundly influenced a young white abolitionist and temperance advocate named William Lloyd Garrison, who later became the most influential of all the American antislavery leaders. Lundy had convinced Garrison to leave his native Massachusetts to come to Baltimore as the associate editor of the *Genius*. Garrison, a deeply religious product of the Second Great Awakening and a well-schooled journalist, had already decided before he came to Baltimore that *gradual* abolition was neither practical nor moral. Gradualism was impractical, he said, because it continually put off the date of general emancipation. It was immoral because it encouraged slaveholders to go on sinfully and criminally oppressing African Americans.

Garrison, however, tolerated the ACS until he came under the influence of Watkins, Greener, and Grice. They set Garrison on a course that transformed the abolitionist movement in the United States during the early 1830s. They also initiated a bond between African

▶ **Document**

8-8 *A Black Feminist Speaks Out in 1851* Having addressed the first National Women's Rights Convention in 1850 at Worcester, Massachusetts, Sojourner Truth was met with hisses by the women at the Ohio Woman's Rights Convention the following year. The women were afraid of getting involved with the abolitionist movement and confusing their own women's issues. However, after Sojourner's speech, she was met with applause and accolades from the audience.

▶ **Reading Check**

The first formal abolitionist groups of black women operated within norms of elite respectability. They were active in education, making speeches, and furthering the abolitionist cause. Otherwise black women were active as practical abolitionists, working in a variety of informal ways—harboring and helping escaped slaves, saving to purchase freedom for themselves and others and furthering the cause of emancipation and equal rights.

William Lloyd Garrison (1805–1879) sat in 1833 for this oil portrait by renowned artist Nathaniel Jocelyn.

A Black Woman Speaks Out on the Right to Education

Historians generally believe the antebellum women's rights movement emerged from the antislavery movement during the late 1830s. But as the following letter, published in Freedom's Journal *on August 10, 1827, indicates, some black women advocated equal rights for women much earlier:*

Messrs. Editors,

Will you allow a female to offer a few remarks upon a subject that you must allow to be all-important? I don't know that in any of your papers, you have said sufficient upon the education of females. I hope you are not to be classed with those, who think that our mathematical knowledge should be limited to "fathoming the dish-kettle," and that we have acquired enough of history, if we know that our grandfather's father lived and died. . . . The diffusion of knowledge has destroyed those degraded opinions, and men of the present age, allow, that we have minds that are capable and deserving of culture. There are difficulties . . . in the way of our advancement; but that should only stir us to greater efforts. We possess not the advantages with those of our sex, whose skins are not coloured like our own, but we can improve what little we have, and make our one talent produce two-fold. . . . Ignorant ourselves, how can we be expected to form the minds of our youth, and conduct them in the paths of knowledge? I would address myself to all mothers. . . . It is their bounden duty to store their daughters' minds with useful learning. They should be made to devote their leisure time to reading books, whence they would derive valuable information, which could never be taken from them. . . .

MATILDA

What Do You Think?

▶ How does MATILDA use sarcasm to make her point?

▶ What special difficulties did black women like MATILDA face in asserting their rights?

Source: Herbert Aptheker, ed., *A Documentary History of the Negro People in the United States*, 7 vols. (1951; reprint, New York: Citadel, 1990), 1: 89.

▶▶ **Document**

8-6 *Angelina E. Grimké, Appeal To The Christian Women of the South, 1836*

▶▶ **Recommended Reading**

Benjamin Quarles. *Black Abolitionists.* New York: Oxford University Press, 1969. A classic study that emphasizes cooperation between black and white abolitionists.

▶▶ **What Do You Think?**

· MATILDA uses sarcasm to make her point by asking whether female knowledge should be limited to that of dish kettles and knowing when their grandfather's died.

· Women like MATILDA had three strikes against them in asserting their rights: they were black, female, and largely uneducated.

The Radical Turn in the Abolition Movement

JULY 1829	William Lloyd Garrison joins Benjamin Lundy in Baltimore as associate editor of the *Genius of Universal Emancipation*.
SEPTEMBER 1829	David Walker's *Appeal* is published in Boston and then circulated in the South.
NOVEMBER 1829	William Watkins's anticolonization letters first appear in the *Genius*.
JUNE 1830	Garrison is sentenced to jail in Baltimore for libeling a slave trader.
AUGUST 1830	Walker dies of tuberculosis in Boston.
JANUARY 1831	Garrison begins publication of *The Liberator* in Boston.
AUGUST 1831	Nat Turner's revolt occurs.

▶ **Document**

8-4 *Abolitionist Demands Immediate End to Slavery, 1831*
This document is the prospectus which appeared in the first issue of the Liberator.

▶ **Recommended Reading**

Peter P. Hinks. *To Awaken My Afflicted Brethren: David Walker and the Problem of Antebellum Slave Resistance.* University Park, PA: Pennsylvania State University Press, 1997. The most recent biography of Walker, which places him within the black abolitionist movement and attempts to clarify what little we know about his life.

Americans and Garrison that—although strained at times—shaped the rest of his antislavery career. That bond intensified in 1830 when Garrison was imprisoned in Baltimore jail for forty-nine days on charges he had libeled a slave trader. While in jail, Garrison met imprisoned fugitive slaves and denounced—to their faces—masters who came to retrieve them.

In 1831 when he began publishing his own abolitionist newspaper, **The Liberator**, in Boston, Garrison led the antislavery movement in a new, more radical direction. Although Garrison had called for the *immediate*, rather than the *gradual*, abolition of slavery before he arrived in Baltimore, he was not the first to make that demand or to oppose compensating masters who liberated their slaves. What made Garrison's brand of abolitionism revolutionary was the insight he gained from his association with African Americans in Baltimore: that immediate emancipation must be combined with a commitment to racial justice in the United States. Watkins and Greener were especially responsible for convincing Garrison that African Americans must have equal rights in America and not be sent to Africa after their emancipation. Immediate emancipation without compensation to slaveholders and without **expatriation** of African Americans became the core of Garrison's program for the rest of his long antislavery career.

David Walker's *Appeal*

Two other black abolitionists shaped Garrison's brand of abolitionism. They were David Walker and Nat Turner. This chapter begins with a quote from David Walker's *Appeal . . . to the Colored Citizens of the World*, which Walker published in 1829. As historian Clement Eaton commented in 1936, this *Appeal* was "a dangerous pamphlet in the Old

Well before this illustration of a man escaping from slavery appeared on the cover of *The Anti-Slavery Record* in 1837, fugitive slaves helped shape the development of the sectional controversy over slavery.

8-3 *An African American Advocates Radical Action in 1829*

This account, from Walker's pamphlet *An Appeal to Blacks* illustrates a small rebellion that Walker proposed for the entire South. Fear by slaveholders in the South brought the banning of the pamphlet, and even the closing of black churches for fear the slaves would hear Walker's ideas and take them to heart.

South." In aggressive language, Walker furiously attacked slavery and white racism. He suggested that slaves use violence to secure their liberty. "I do declare," he wrote, "that one good black can put to death six white men." This especially frightened white southerners because Walker's *Appeal* circulated among slaves in southern ports.

The *Appeal* shaped the struggle over slavery in three ways. First, although Garrison was committed to peaceful means, Walker's aggressive writing style influenced the tone of Garrison and other advocates of immediate abolition. Second, Walker's desperate effort

PROFILE ❖ David Walker

David Walker was born free in Wilmington, North Carolina, in 1796 or 1797. We know nothing of his early life except that he learned to read and write. As a young man, he traveled widely. According to his *Appeal*, he spent time in Charleston, South Carolina, where he attended a religious camp meeting in 1821. This has led historians to conjecture that Walker knew something about Denmark Vesey's conspiracy or if he was still in Charleston in 1822 that he may even have participated in it.

By 1825 Walker was in Boston dealing in secondhand clothes. He had his own shop, and lived in the city's black neighborhood. He was married and had a daughter and a son. At a time when many occupations were closed to African Americans, Walker was doing relatively well. He associated with well-established local black people, including Thomas Paul, an abolitionist minister, and

William C. Nell, a foe of Boston's segregated public schools. During the late 1820s, Walker served as a circulation agent in Boston for John Russwurm and Samuel Cornish's *Freedom's Journal.*

Walker also wrote for the *Journal.* He was as conscious of the legal disabilities African Americans faced in Boston as he was of the oppressiveness of slavery. In December 1828 he addressed the Massachusetts General Colored Association on the topic of black cooperation with white abolitionists to improve the conditions of free black people and to liberate the slaves.

Not long after this, Walker became more radical. He wrote his *Appeal* and in September 1829 implemented a clandestine method to circulate it among slaves. He had black and white sailors, to whom he sold used clothes in Boston, take copies of the pamphlet to southern ports and distribute them to African Americans.

When white southerners discovered that slaves had copies of the pamphlet, southern officials demanded that the mayor of Boston stop Walker from publishing. When the mayor refused, rumors circulated that a group of white southerners had offered a reward for Walker, dead or alive. It was not surprising, therefore, that when Walker's daughter and then Walker himself died during the summer of 1830, many assumed they had been poisoned. The most recent biography of Walker, however, indicates that they both died of tuberculosis.

WALKER'S

APPEAL,

IN FOUR ARTICLES,

TOGETHER WITH

A PREAMBLE

TO THE

COLORED CITIZENS OF THE WORLD,

BUT IN PARTICULAR AND VERY EXPRESSLY TO THOSE OF THE

UNITED STATES OF AMERICA.

Written in Boston, in the State of Massachusetts, Sept. 28th, 1829.

Boston:

to instill hope and pride in an oppressed people inspired an increasingly militant black abolitionism. Third, Walker's pamphlet and its circulation in the South made white southerners fearful of encirclement from without and subversion from within. This fear encouraged southern leaders to make demands on the North that helped bring on the Civil War.

 Reading Check What was David Walker's *Appeal* and why was it important?

▶▶ **Reading Check**

David Walker's *Appeal* was a pamphlet that aggressively attacked slavery and white racism. The *Appeal* influenced the tone of future abolitionists. It inspired an increasingly militant black abolitionism. And, it raised intense anxieties among white southerners.

Nat Turner

In this last respect, Nat Turner's contribution was even more important than Walker's. Slave conspiracies had not ended with Denmark Vesey's execution in 1822. But in 1831 Turner, a privileged slave from eastern Virginia, became the first African American actually to initiate a large-scale slave uprising since Charles Deslondes had done so in Louisiana in 1811. As a result Turner inspired far greater fear among white southerners than Walker had.

During the late 1820s and early 1830s, unrest among slaves in Virginia had increased. Walker's *Appeal*, which was circulating among some southern free black people by late 1829, may have contributed to this increase. Meanwhile divisions among white Virginians encouraged slaves to seek advantages for themselves. In anticipation of a state constitutional convention in 1829, white people in western Virginia, where there were few slaveholders, called for emancipation. Poorer white men demanded an end to the property qualifications that denied them the vote. As the convention approached, a "spirit of dissatisfaction and insubordination" became manifest among slaves. Some armed themselves and escaped northward. As proslavery white Virginians grew fearful, they demanded further restrictions on the ability of local free black people and northern abolitionists to influence slaves.

Yet no evidence indicates that Nat Turner or any of his associates had read Walker's *Appeal*, had contact with northern abolitionists, or were aware of divisions among white Virginians. Although Turner knew about the successful slave revolt in Haiti, he was more of a religious visionary than a political revolutionary. Born in 1800 he learned to read as a child, and as a young man, he spent much of his time studying and memorizing the Bible. He became a lay preacher and a leader among local slaves. By the late 1820s, he had begun to have visions that convinced him God intended him to lead his people to freedom through violence.

Despite their knowledge of slave resistance and revolt, white abolitionists in particular tended to portray slaves as peacefully begging for deliverance.

A nineteenth-century engraving shows Nat Turner talking with his men.

▶ **Reading Check**

Turner's revolt of 1831 was the first large-scale slave uprising since 1811. The bloodshed that accompanied the revolt inspired general revulsion. White southerners accused abolitionists of inspiring Turner. Abolitionists asserted their commitment to nonviolence, but nonetheless respected Turner. This ambivalence about violence against slavery characterized the abolitionist movement of the next thirty years.

▶ **Document**

8-5 *The Confessions of Nat Turner, 1831*
As details of Nat Turner's Rebellion in August 1831 became known, southern white people shudder in fear at the prospects of slave uprisings. David Walker's Appeal, and growing northern threat against the South's peculiar institution only added to southern apprehension. Turner's Rebellion led to increased slave patrols. Across the South, state legislatures met in special sessions to deal with a possible emergency. Even the Virginia legislature would soon consider abolishing slavery. Many states fortified their Slave Codes. In this excerpt, Turner explains the motivating factors that led the uprising.

After considerable planning, Turner began his uprising on the evening of August 21, 1831. His band, which numbered between sixty and seventy, killed fifty-seven white men, women, and children—the largest number of white Americans ever killed by slave rebels—before militia put down the revolt the following morning. In November, Turner and seventeen others were found guilty of insurrection and treason and were hanged. Meanwhile panicked white people in nearby parts of Virginia and North Carolina killed more than one hundred African Americans whom they—almost always wrongly—suspected of being in league with the rebels.

Turner, like Walker and Garrison, shaped a new era in American abolitionism. The bloodshed in Virginia inspired general revulsion. White southerners—and some northerners—accused Garrison and other abolitionists of inspiring the revolt. In response, northern abolitionists of both races asserted their commitment to a peaceful struggle against slavery. Yet both black and white abolitionists respected Turner. Black abolitionists accorded him the same heroic stature they gave Toussaint Louverture and Gabriel. Garrison and other white abolitionists compared Turner to George Washington and other leaders of national liberation movements. This tension between lip service to peaceful means and admiration for violence against slavery characterized the antislavery movement for the next thirty years.

 Reading Check   What was the significance of Nat Turner's revolt?

Creating an Oral or Visual Presentation

How can you make a historical event come alive for an audience? One way is to synthesize several kinds of sources to create an oral or visual presentation. Suppose your topic is an overview of the Abolitionist movement. Although there are no photographs or recordings from that time, you can show maps, diagrams, paintings, and drawings, or you can read aloud from primary sources such as newspaper accounts, letters, and journals. The two sources are ads that take pro- and anti-slavery views.

LEARN THE SKILL

Use the following steps to create an oral or visual presentation:

1. **Explore a variety of sources.** Use a reliable secondary source for general information. Consider the topic: Are there likely to be letters or diaries? What visual depictions might be useful?

2. **Select and evaluate your sources.** Knowing the background of a writer or the source of a map helps you evaluate the information. For balance, try to select sources representing different points of view. Also vary the types of sources.

3. **Draw conclusions.** Determine the main points of each source. Combine different pieces of information to present and support your conclusions.

4. **Give life to your presentation.** Read excerpts from primary sources aloud as though you were the historical person who wrote them, show a variety of illustrations depicting the event, or combines oral and visual presentations for a more dramatic effect.

PRACTICE THE SKILL

Answer the following questions:

1. **(a)** Who published these ads? **(b)** When were they published? **(c)** What is the message of the ads? **(d)** Who is the likely audience for the ads?

2. **(a)** What propaganda technique is used in the ads? **(b)** What does the writer hope to persuade the reader to think or to do? **(c)** What is the writer's point of view in each ad?

3. **(a)** What message do the words in the ads give? **(b)** Are these ads propoganda? Explain.

4. Find other sources, illustrations, or letters/diaries that expand on the themes of these ads. Create a presentation that traces the development of pro- or anti-slavery literature.

▶ **Skills for Life**

For answers, see the *Teacher's Resource Manual.*

Chapter Timeline

AFRICAN-AMERICAN EVENTS		NATIONAL AND WORLD EVENTS
	1790	
		1791 Haitian Revolution begins
	1795	
1796 or 1797 David Walker born		**1796** John Adams elected U.S. president **1798** Undeclared Franco-American war
	1800	
1800 Gabriel's conspiracy is exposed **1803** Maria W. Stewart born		**1800** Thomas Jefferson elected U.S. president **1803–1806** Lewis and Clark Expedition
	1805	
1805 William Lloyd Garrison born		**1807** Britain bans Atlantic slave trade **1808** United States bans Atlantic slave trade
	1810	
1811 Louisiana Slave Revolt		**1812** War of 1812 begins

1815

1815
Paul Cuffe leads African Americans to Sierra Leone

1816
American Colonization Society is formed

1815
War of 1812 ends

1816
James Madison elected U.S. president

1820

1822
Denmark Vesey's conspiracy is exposed

1824
Benjamin Lundy comes to Baltimore

1820
Missouri Compromise passed

1824
John Quincy Adams is elected U.S. president

1825

1827
Freedom's Journal begins publication

1829
William Lloyd Garrison comes to Baltimore; David Walker's *Appeal*

1828
Andrew Jackson is elected U.S. president

1830

1831
Nat Turner's Revolt is suppressed

1830
Indian Removal Act passed by Congress

1832
Great increase in migration to U.S. begins

1835

Chapter Review and Assessment

SUMMARY

Section 1 A Country in Turmoil, p. 255

▶ The Democratic Party represented the interests of the South's slaveholding white male elite. This was made clear by their outlook toward American Indians, women, and African Americans.

▶ By the mid-1830s, Americans who favored a more enlightened social policy turned to the Whig Party, a party that served as the conduit through which evangelical Christianity influenced politics.

▶ Evangelicals, stirred by the Second Great Awakening, sought to bring Christian ideals to the political world. Through the Benevolent Empire, they launched what is now known as Jacksonian reform.

Section 2 Abolitionism Begins in America, p. 259

▶ The antislavery movement was really two movements. The movement in the South existed among slaves with the help of free blacks and a few sympathetic whites. The movement in the North was made up of black and white abolitionists.

▶ The Quakers played a key role in initiating antislavery organizations in the North, but the movement they inspired had severe limitations.

▶ Southern slaves and their free black allies played a key role in the development of a more wide-ranging antislavery movement.

▶ Efforts by Gabriel and Denmark Vesey to launch slave revolts led to the decline of the Quaker-led antislavery movement and hardened the proslavery positions of many whites.

Section 3 Colonization, p. 263

▶ Fear of free African Americans shaped the most significant white antislavery organization of the 1810s and 1820s, the American Colonization Society (ACS).

▶ The twin goals of the ACS were to abolish slavery gradually in the United States and to send emancipated free blacks to Liberia.

▶ Opinion among African Americans was split over the issue of colonization.

▶ Some black abolitionists believed that African Americans would never achieve equal status in the United States and must, therefore, look overseas.

▶ Others saw themselves as, first and foremost, Americans, not Africans, and had no wish to go to a place they saw as foreign and dangerous.

Section 4 Black Abolitionists, p. 267

▶ Black women joined black men in opposing slavery.

▶ Female members of the black elite were active in the movement. Many more black women were practical abolitionists.

▶ An alliance of abolitionists in Baltimore pushed the movement in a new, more radical direction.

▶ David Walker's *Appeal* aggressively attacked slavery and white racism. His writing influenced the abolitionist movement and helped galvanize proslavery feeling in the South, a position that was further cemented by Nat Turner's slave revolt.

REVIEWING KEY TERMS

1. money power, p. 256
2. slave power, p. 256
3. Trail of Tears, p. 256
4. conservatives, p. 256
5. expansionism, p. 256
6. revivalism, p. 257
7. Second Great Awakening, p. 257
8. practical Christianity, p. 258
9. Benevolent Empire, p. 258
10. Jacksonian reform, p. 258
11. abolitionists, p. 258
12. antislavery movement, p. 259
13. Gabriel's conspiracy, p. 260
14. American Colonization Society (ACS), p. 263
15. colonization, p. 263
16. Liberia, p. 263
17. black nationalist tradition, p. 264
18. voluntary colonization, p. 265
19. Philadelphia Female Anti-slavery Society, p. 267
20. practical abolitionists, p. 268
21. *The Liberator*, p. 271
22. expatriation, p. 271

REVIEWING MAIN IDEAS

23. What did the program of the ACS mean for African Americans? How did they respond to this program?

24. Analyze the role in abolitionism played (1) by Christianity and (2) by the revolutionary tradition in the Atlantic world. Which was most important in shaping the views of black and white abolitionists?

25. Evaluate the interaction of black and white abolitionists during the early nineteenth century. How did their motives for becoming abolitionists differ?

26. How did Gabriel, Denmark Vesey, and Nat Turner influence the northern abolitionist movement?

27. What risks did Maria W. Stewart take when she called publicly for antislavery action?

ANALYZING DOCUMENTS

William Watkins Opposes Colonization

[The Reverend Mr. Hewitt says] "Let us unite into select societies for the purpose of digesting a plan for raising funds to be appropriated to this grand object" [African colonization]. This we cannot do; we intend to let the burden of this work rest upon the shoulders of those who wish us out of the country. We will, however, compromise the matter with our friend. We are willing and anxious to "unite into select societies for the purpose of digesting a plan": for the improvement of our people in science, morals, domestic economy, &c. We are willing and anx-

ious to form union societies . . . that shall discountenance and destroy, as far as possible, those unhappy schisms which have too long divided us, though we are brethren. We are willing to unite . . . in the formation of temperance societies . . . that will enable us to exhibit to the world an amount of moral power that would give new impetus to our friends and "strike alarm" into the breasts of our enemies, if not wholly disarm them of the weapons they are hurling against us.

—From "A Colored American [Watkins] to Editors," n.d., in *Genius of Universal Emancipation* , December 18, 1829.

 Making Inferences What difficulties does Watkins believe African Americans must overcome to make themselves stronger in the United States?

WRITING ACTIVITY

In a short report or research paper, consider these questions.

 What forces and events fueled the antislavery movement? What role did antislavery advocates see free blacks playing in America after slavery was abolished?

STUDY ONLINE!

www.prenhall.com/aah

Additional study resources are available for this chapter on the *Companion Website.*

In this 1867 oil painting by Theo Kaufman, a group of women and children prepare to ford a river as they escape from slavery.

Chapter 9

Fugitive slaves aim guns at slave-catchers in an attempt to preserve their freedom.

Witnessing History . . .

It is in your power to torment the God-cursed slaveholders, that they would be glad to let you go free. . . . But you are a patient people. You act as though you were made for the special use of these devils. You act as though your daughters were born to pamper the lusts of your masters and overseers. And worse than all, you tamely submit, while your lords tear your wives from your embraces, and defile them before your eyes. In the name of God we ask, are you men? . . . Heaven, as with a voice of thunder, calls on you to arise from the dust. Let your motto be RESISTANCE! RESISTANCE! RESISTANCE! No oppressed people have ever secured their Liberty without resistance.

—Henry Highland Garnet, "Address to the Slaves of the United States of America."

 What kind of resistance is Garnet suggesting of African Americans?

Chapter Preview

When black abolitionist Henry Highland Garnet spoke these words at the National Convention of Colored Citizens, held in Buffalo, New York, on August 16, 1843, he caused a tremendous stir among those assembled. Garnet had escaped with his family from slavery in Maryland in 1824 when he was a boy. He had received an excellent education while growing up in New York and was a powerful speaker. But some of the delegates pointed out that he was far away from the slaves he claimed to address. Others believed he had called for a potentially disastrous slave revolt, and, by a narrow margin, the convention refused to endorse his speech.

Rather than a bloody revolt like Nat Turner's, Garnet advocated a general strike among slaves. This, he contended, would put the onus of initiating violence on the masters. Nevertheless, Garnet's speech reflected a growing militancy among black and white abolitionists that shaped the antislavery movement during the two decades before the Civil War.

In this chapter we investigate the causes of that militancy and explore the role of African Americans in the antislavery movement from the establishment of the American Anti-Slavery Society in 1833 to the Compromise of 1850. Largely in response to changes in American culture, unrest among slaves, and sectional conflict between North and South, the biracial northern antislavery movement during this period became splintered and diverse, but also more powerful.

▶ **Witnessing History**

Garnet is suggesting that African Americans use any means necessary to fight against slavery and violence used against them, principally to refuse to be slaves.

Section 1

A Rising Tide of Racism and Violence

GUIDE TO READING

► When did antiblack mob violence reach its peak? Why did it taper off?

► What was the goal of the Compromise of 1850 and what consequences did it have for African Americans?

KEY WORDS

► manifest destiny, p. 283

► nativism, p. 283

► annexation, p. 284

The growing militancy among abolitionists occurred within a context of increasing racism and violence in the United States, lasting from the 1830s through the Civil War. By the 1840s white Americans had embraced an exuberant nationalism called **manifest destiny** that defined political and economic progress in racial terms and legitimized war to expand the boundaries of the United States.

During this same period, American ethnologists—scientists who studied racial diversity—maintained that white people—particularly white Americans—were a superior race culturally, physically, economically, politically, and intellectually. This theory provided white Americans with an apparently scientific justification for the continued enslavement of African Americans and extermination of American Indians, as both these groups were deemed inferior. Prejudice against European immigrants to the United States also increased. By the late 1840s, a movement known as **nativism** pitted native-born Protestants against foreign-born Roman Catholics, whom the natives saw as competitors for jobs and as culturally subversive.

Accompanying these broad intellectual and cultural developments was a wave of racially motivated violence committed by the federal and state governments, as well as by white vigilantes. Antiblack riots became common in urban America. From 1829 until the Civil War, white mobs led by "gentlemen of property and standing" attacked abolitionist newspaper presses and wreaked havoc in African-American neighborhoods.

Antiblack and Anti-Abolitionist Riots

Antiblack urban riots predated the start of immediate abolitionism during the late 1820s. But such riots became more common as abolitionism gained strength during the 1830s and 1840s (see Figure 9–1 and Map 9–1). Although few northern cities escaped racist mob attacks on African Americans and their property, riots in Cincinnati, Providence, New York City, and Philadelphia were infamous.

In 1829 a three-day riot instigated by local politicians led many black people in Cincinnati to flee to Canada. In 1836 and 1841 mob attacks on the *Philanthropist,* Cincinnati's white-run abolitionist newspaper, expanded into attacks on African-American homes and businesses. Both times, black residents defended their property with guns. In 1831 white

▶▶ **Guide to Reading/Key Terms**

For answers, see the *Teacher's Resource Manual.*

▶▶ **Interactive Activity**

Angelina Grimké

On May 17, 1838, an anti-abolition mob in Philadelphia attacked and destroyed Pennsylvania Hall. The speaker who provoked their fury was a young woman named Angelina Grimké. This activity explores the hostility to Grimké's speech and antislavery activism. It also shows the important role women played in reform movements.

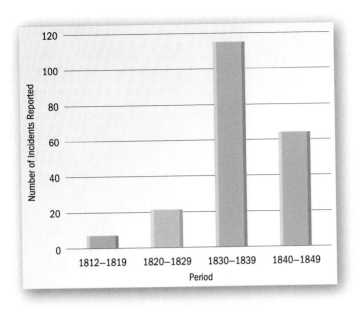

FIGURE 9-1 Mob Violence in the United States, 1812-1849.

This graph illustrates the rise of mob violence in the North in reaction to abolitionist activity. Attacks on abolitionists peaked during the 1830s and then declined as antislavery sentiment spread in the North.

sailors led a mob in Providence that literally tore that city's black neighborhood to pieces. With spectators cheering them on, rioters first pulled down the chimneys of black residences and then "with a fire hook and plenty of axes and iron bars" tore down the buildings themselves and dragged the occupants into the streets. The Rhode Island militia finally had to stop the mayhem.

In New York City in 1834, a mob destroyed twelve houses owned by black residents, a black church, a black school, and the home of white abolitionist Lewis Tappan. But no city had worse race riots than Philadelphia. In 1820, 1829, 1834, 1835, 1838, 1842, and 1849, antiblack riots broke out there. In 1838 a white mob in Philadelphia burned Pennsylvania Hall, which abolitionists had just built and dedicated to free discussion. But the ugliest riot came in 1842 when Irish immigrants led a mob that assaulted members of a black temperance society, who were commemorating the abolition of slavery in the British colony of Jamaica. When African Americans defended themselves with muskets, the mob looted and burned Philadelphia's principal black neighborhood. Among those who successfully defended their homes was Robert Purvis, the abolitionist son-in-law of James Forten.

Texas and the War against Mexico

Violence was not confined to northern cities. Under President James K. Polk, the United States adopted a belligerent foreign policy that culminated in a war against Mexico that lasted from 1846 to 1848. During the 1820s slaveholding Americans had begun to settle in Texas, which was then part of the Republic of Mexico. In 1822 Mexico had gained its independence from Spain and in 1829 had abolished slavery within its borders. At the time, Mexico also included the gigantic region that now comprises the states of California, Arizona, New Mexico, Utah, and part of Colorado. In 1836 the Americans in Texas won independence from Mexico. Once Texas had become an independent slaveholding republic, its leaders immediately applied for **annexation** to the United States. They were rebuffed for nine years because Democratic and Whig Party leaders recognized that adding a large new slave state to the Union would divide the country along North-South sectional lines. But the desire for new territory encouraged by Manifest Destiny and an expanding slave-labor economy could not be denied. In 1844 Polk, the Democratic presidential candidate, called for the annexation of Texas and Oregon, a huge territory in the Pacific Northwest that the United States and Great Britain had been jointly administering. When Polk defeated the Whig candidate Henry Clay, who favored delaying annexation, Congress in early 1845 annexed Texas by joint resolution. This vastly expanded the area within the United States that was open to slavery.

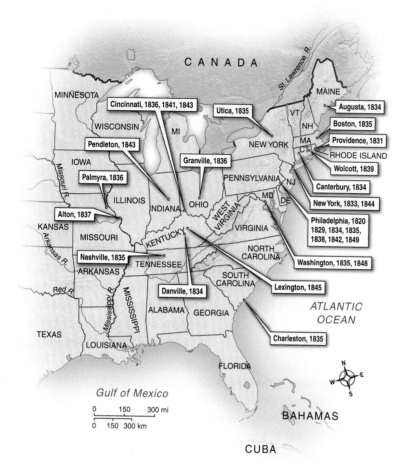

CANADA

MINNESOTA

WISCONSIN

MI

Cincinnati, 1836, 1841, 1843

Utica, 1835

Pendleton, 1843

IOWA

Granville, 1836

Palmyra, 1836

ILLINOIS

INDIANA   OHIO

Alton, 1837

KANSAS

MISSOURI

KENTUCKY

Nashville, 1835

TENNESSEE

ARKANSAS

Danville, 1834

ALABAMA   GEORGIA

TEXAS

LOUISIANA

MAINE

VT

NH

Augusta, 1834

Boston, 1835

Providence, 1831

RHODE ISLAND

Wolcott, 1839

NEW YORK

MA

CT

PENNSYLVANIA   NJ

Canterbury, 1834

MD   DE

New York, 1833, 1844

WEST
VIRGINIA

VIRGINIA

Philadelphia, 1820
1829, 1834, 1835,
1838, 1842, 1849

NORTH
CAROLINA

Washington, 1835, 1848

SOUTH
CAROLINA

Lexington, 1845

ATLANTIC
OCEAN

Charleston, 1835

FLORIDA

Gulf of Mexico

0   150   300 mi
0 150 300 km

BAHAMAS

CUBA

MAP 9–1 Antiabolitionist and Antiblack Riots during the Antebellum Period

African Americans faced violent conditions in both the North and South during the antebellum years.

 Why did most of these riots occur in the Northeast?

In early 1846 Polk backed away from a confrontation with Great Britain over Oregon. A few months later, however, he provoked a war with Mexico that by 1848 had forced that country to recognize American sovereignty over Texas and to cede what were then the Mexican provinces of New Mexico and California (see Map 10–1 on page 315). Immediately, the question of whether slavery would expand into these southwestern territories became a burning issue. Many white northerners assumed that slaveholders, by creating slave states out of the new territories, would dominate the federal government and enact policies detrimental to white workers and farmers.

As these sentiments spread across the North, slaveholders became fearful they would be excluded from the western lands they had helped take from Mexico. The resulting Compromise of 1850 (see Chapter 10) attempted to satisfy both sections. But it subjected African Americans to additional violence because part of the Compromise met slaveholders' demands for a stronger fugitive slave law. Not only did this law make it easier for masters to recapture bondpeople who had escaped to the North, but it also caused an increase in attempts to kidnap free black northerners into slavery.

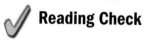 **Reading Check** What was the goal of the Compromise of 1850 and what consequences did it have for African Americans?

▶▶ **Map 9-1**

Most of these riots occurred in the Northeast as this section of the country had the strongest and largest population of abolitionists.

▶▶ **Reading Check**

The Compromise of 1850 was meant to satisfy sectional interests in both the North and South. It subjected blacks to additional violence because it created a stronger fugitive slave law. It also caused an increase in attempts to kidnap free northern blacks into slavery.

▶▶ **Documents**

9-5   *The Fugitive Slave Act, 1850*
10-1   *The Compromise of 1850*
The Missouri Compromise permitted Missouri to become a slave state, maintained political balance by admitting Maine as a free state, and banned slavery north of the 36°30′ line of latitude in the old Louisiana Territory.

KEY WORDS

▶ American Anti-Slavery Society (AASS), p. 286

▶ Free Produce Association, p. 289

▶ **Guide to Reading/Key Terms**

For answers, see the *Teacher's Resource Manual*.

▶ **Document**

9-1 *The American Anti-Slavery Society Declares its Sentiments, 1833*
At its founding in 1833, the American Anti-Slavery Society adopted this Declaration of Sentiments. William Lloyd Garrison condemned slavery and set forth the new organization's principles and proposed activities.

9-3 *An Abolitionist Lecturer's Instructions*
In 1834 the American Anti-Slavery Society commissioned Theodore Dwight Weld to serve as an abolitionist agent in Ohio. These are his instructions.

Section 2

The Response of the Antislavery Movement

The American Anti-Slavery Society

The **American Anti-Slavery Society** (AASS)—the most significant abolitionist organization—emerged from a major turning point in the abolitionist cause. This was William Lloyd Garrison's decision in 1831 to create a movement dedicated to immediate, uncompensated emancipation and to equal rights for African Americans in the United States. To reach these goals, abolitionists led by Garrison organized the AASS in December 1833 at Philadelphia's Adelphi Hall. Well aware of the fears raised by Nat Turner's revolt, those assembled declared, "The society will never, in any way, countenance the oppressed in vindicating their rights by resorting to physical force."

No white American worked harder than Garrison to bridge racial differences. He spoke to black groups, stayed in the homes of African Americans when he traveled, and welcomed them to his home. Black abolitionists responded with affection and loyalty. They provided financial support for his newspaper, *The Liberator*, worked as subscription agents, paid for his speaking tour in England in 1833, and served as his bodyguards. But Garrison, like most other white abolitionists, remained stiff and condescending in conversation with his black colleagues, and the black experience in the AASS reflected this.

On one hand, it is remarkable that the AASS allowed black men to participate in its meetings without formal restrictions. At the time, no other American organization did so. On the other hand, that black participation was paltry. Three African Americans—James McCrummell, Robert Purvis, and James G. Barbadoes—helped found the AASS, and McCrummell presided at its first meeting. Throughout the history of the AASS, black people rarely held positions of authority.

As state and local auxiliaries of the AASS organized across the North during the early 1830s, this pattern repeated itself. Black men participated but did not lead, although a few held prominent offices. In 1834 Barbadoes and Joshua Easton joined the board of directors of the Massachusetts Anti-Slavery Society. In 1837 seven black men, including James Forten, helped organize the Pennsylvania Anti-Slavery Society. With some exceptions, black and white women could observe, but not participate in, the proceedings of these organizations. It took a three-

year struggle between 1837 and 1840 over "the woman question" before an AASS annual meeting elected a woman to a leadership position, and that victory helped split the organization.

Black and Women's Antislavery Societies

In these circumstances, black male, black female, and white female abolitionists formed their own auxiliaries to the AASS. Often African Americans belonged to both all-black and to integrated predominantly

▶ **Recommended Reading**

Shirley J. Yee. *Black Women Abolitionists: A Study of Activism.* Knoxville, TN: University of Tennessee Press, 1992. Discusses the activities of black women abolitionists in both white and black organizations.

PROFILE ❖ Henry Highland Garnet

Henry Highland Garnet rivaled Frederick Douglass as a black leader during the antebellum decades. While Douglass emphasized assimilation, Garnet emerged as an advocate of black nationalism. The two men had much in common, however, and by the time of the Civil War were almost indistinguishable in their views.

In 1824, when Garnet was nine, his family struck out from a Maryland plantation for freedom in the North. His father led the family to New York City, where Garnet enrolled in the Free African School. In 1835 Garnet was among twelve black students admitted to Noyes Academy in Canaan, New Hampshire. The following year he enrolled at Oneida Theological Institute located near Utica, New York. There, guided by white abolitionist Beriah Green, Garnet prepared for the Presbyterian ministry. In 1842 he became pastor of the black Presbyterian church in Troy, New York.

By that time, he had been an active abolitionist for several years. He worked closely with Gerrit Smith's radical New York wing of the Liberty Party. He also became a strong advocate of independent antislavery action among African Americans. Referring to white abolitionists, he said, "They are our allies—*Ours* is the battle." Garnet delivered his famous "Address to the Slaves" at the 1843 National Convention of Colored Citizens. By demanding what amounted to a general strike by slaves and acknowledging that violence could

result, Garnet highlighted his differences with Frederick Douglass and other African Americans who remained dedicated to nonviolence.

Garnet's conviction that African Americans ultimately must free themselves led him to promote migration to Africa. By 1848 he had come to believe African colonization could become a powerful adjunct to the struggle for emancipation in the United States. Garnet's years abroad during the early 1850s strengthened him in this outlook. He served as a delegate to the World Peace Conference in Frankfort, Germany, in 1850, spent 1851 in Great Britain, and lived in Jamaica from 1853 to 1856 as a Presbyterian missionary. Garnet returned to the United States in 1856. In 1858 he organized the African Civilization Society designed to build a strong, independent Africa through black emigration from America and the cultivation of cotton. But Garnet's views remained very much in the minority among African-American leaders. The Civil War effectively ended his nationalist efforts.

In 1863 he became pastor of the 15th Street Presbyterian Church in Washington, D.C., and in 1865 became the first African American to deliver a sermon in Congress. In January 1882 Garnet became the ambassador to Liberia. He died there a month later.

Garnet

Wealthy black abolitionist **Robert Purvis** is at the very center of this undated photograph of the Philadelphia Anti-Slavery Society. The famous Quaker abolitionist Lucretia Mott and her husband James Mott are seated to Purvis's left.

▶ **Document**

9-2 *A Call for Women to Become Abolitionists*
This essay is one of the earliest appeals to women. It also shows that women's participation in the movement was sometimes opposed even by women themselves. The excerpt is a response to a woman who objected to other women publicly advocating emancipation.

▶ **Recommended Readings**

Benjamin Quarles. *Black Abolitionists*. New York: Oxford University Press, 1969. A classic study that emphasizes cooperation between black and white abolitionists.

Jane H. Pease and William H. Pease. *They Who Would Be Free: Blacks' Search for Freedom, 1830–1861*. New York: Athenaeum, 1974. Deals with cooperation and conflict between black and white abolitionists. The book emphasizes conflict.

white organizations. Black men's auxiliaries to the AASS were formed across the North during the mid-1830s.

The black organizations arose both because of racial discord in the predominantly white organizations and because of a black desire for racial solidarity. But historian Benjamin Quarles makes an essential point when he writes that during the 1830s "the founders of Negro societies did not envision their efforts as distinctive or self-contained; rather they viewed their role as that of a true auxiliary—supportive, supplemental, and subsidiary." Despite their differences, black and white abolitionists were still members of a single movement.

Although racially integrated female antislavery societies did not entirely overcome the racism of their time, they elevated more African Americans to prominent positions than their male counterparts did. Black abolitionist Susan Paul became a member of the board of the Boston Female Anti-Slavery Society when it was established in 1833. Later that year, Margaretta Forten became recording secretary of the Female Anti-Slavery Society of Philadelphia, founded by white Quaker abolitionist Lucretia Mott. Black Quaker Sarah M. Douglass of Philadelphia and Sarah Forten— Margaretta's sister—were delegates to the First Anti-Slavery Convention of

Section 3

Black Community Institutions

GUIDE TO READING

▶ What roles did black institutions play in the antislavery movement?

▶ What role did black ministers play in the antislavery movement?

▶ What difficulties did black newspapers face?

KEY WORDS

▶ *Freedom's Journal*, p. 292

▶ *North Star*, p. 292

Although the persistence of slavery and oppression helped shape the agenda of the Black Convention Movement, the movement itself was a product of a maturing African-American community. Free black people in the United States grew from 59,000 in 1790 to 319,000 in 1830. The growing free black population was concentrated in such large cities as New York, Philadelphia, Baltimore, Boston, and Cincinnati. These cities had enough free African Americans to provide the resources that built the churches, schools, benevolent organizations, and printing presses that created a self-conscious black community.

Black Churches in the Antislavery Cause

Black churches were especially significant for the antislavery movement. With a few major exceptions, the leading black abolitionists were ministers. Among them were Garnet, Jehiel C. Beman, Samuel E. Cornish, Theodore S. Wright, Charles B. Ray, James W. C. Pennington, Nathaniel Paul, Alexander Crummell, Daniel A. Payne, and Samuel Ringgold Ward. Some of these men led congregations affiliated with separate African-American churches, such as the African Baptist Church or the African Methodist Episcopal (AME) Church. Others preached to black congregations affiliated with predominantly white churches. A few black ministers, such as Amos N. Freeman of Brooklyn, New York, served white antislavery congregations. These clergy used their pulpits to attack slavery, racial discrimination, proslavery white churches, and the American Colonization Society (ACS). Black churches also provided forums for abolitionist speakers, such as Frederick Douglass and Garrison, and meeting places for predominantly white antislavery organizations, which were frequently denied space in white churches.

Black Newspapers

Less influential than black churches in the antislavery movement, black newspapers still played an important role, particularly by the 1840s. Abolitionist newspapers, whether owned by black or white people, almost always faced financial difficulties. Few survived for more than a few years.

▶▶ **Guide to Reading/Key Terms**

For answers, see the *Teacher's Resource Manual*.

▶▶ **Recommended Reading**

Harry Reed. *Platforms for Change: The Foundations of the Northern Free Black Community, 1776–1865.* East Lansing, MI: Michigan State University Press, 1994. Places black abolitionism and black nationalism within the context of community development.

Reform, as opposed to *commercial*, newspapers were a luxury that many subscribers both black and white could not afford. Black newspapers faced added difficulties finding readers because most African Americans were poor, and many were illiterate. Moreover, white abolitionist newspapers, such as the *Liberator*, served a black clientele. They published speeches by black abolitionists and reported black convention proceedings. Some black abolitionists argued, therefore, that a separate black press was unnecessary. An additional, self-imposed, burden was that publishers eager to get their message out almost never required subscribers to pay in advance, thereby compounding their papers' financial instability.

Nevertheless several influential black abolitionist newspapers were in existence between the late 1820s and the Civil War. The first black newspaper, **Freedom's Journal**, owned and edited by Samuel Cornish and John B. Russwurm, lasted only from 1827 to 1829. It showed, nevertheless, that African Americans could produce interesting and competent journalism and attract both black and white subscribers. The *Journal* also established a framework for black journalism during the antebellum period by emphasizing antislavery, racial justice, and Christian and democratic values.

Black journalist Philip A. Bell was either publisher or co-publisher of the *New York Weekly Advocate* in 1837, the *Colored American* from 1837 to 1842, and two San Francisco newspapers, the *Pacific Appeal* and the *Elevator*, during the 1860s. Black clergyman Charles B. Ray of New York City was the spirit behind the *Colored American*. Well aware of the need for financial success, Ray declared in 1838, "If among the few hundred thousand free colored people in the country—to say nothing of the white population from whom it ought to receive a strong support—a living patronage for the paper cannot be obtained, it will be greatly to their reproach."

Among other prominent, if short-lived, black newspapers of the 1840s and 1850s were Garnet's *United States Clarion*, published in his home city of Troy, New York; Stephen Myers's *Northern Star and Freeman's Advocate*, which was published in Albany, New York, and had many white, as well as black, subscribers; Samuel Ringgold Ward's *True American*, of Cortland, New York, which in 1850 became the *Impartial Citizen*; Martin Delany's *Mystery*, published in Pittsburgh during the 1840s; and Thomas Van Rensselaer's *Ram's Horn*, which appeared in New York City during the 1850s.

However, Frederick Douglass's **North Star** and its successor *Frederick Douglass' Paper* were the most influential black antislavery newspapers of the late 1840s and the 1850s. Heavily subsidized by Gerrit Smith, a wealthy white abolitionist, and attracting more white than black subscribers, Douglass's weeklies were supported by many black abolitionist organizations. The papers were extremely well edited and attractively printed. They also employed able assistant editors, including Martin R. Delany during the late 1840s, and insightful correspondents, such as William J. Wilson of Brooklyn and James McCune Smith of New York City.

 **Reading Check** What roles did black institutions play in the antislavery movement?

▶ **Reading Check**

Black institutions played an important role in creating a self-conscious black community. Black churches and newspapers articulated the case against slavery and disseminated the abolitionist message.

Section 4

The Changing Abolitionist Movement

Moral Suasion

During the 1830s the AASS adopted a reform strategy based on **moral suasion**—what we would call moral *persuasion* today. This was an appeal to Americans to support abolition and racial justice on the basis of their Christian consciences and concern for their immortal souls. Slaveholding, the AASS argued, was a sin and a crime that deprived African Americans of the freedom of conscience they needed to save their souls. Slaveholding, according to the AASS, also led white masters to eternal damnation through indolence, sexual exploitation of black women, and unrestrained brutality. In addition, abolitionists argued slavery was an inefficient labor system that enriched a few masters but impoverished most black and white southerners and hurt the economy of the United States as a whole.

Abolitionists, however, did not restrict themselves to criticizing white southerners. They noted that northern industries thrived by manufacturing cloth from cotton produced by slave labor. The U.S. government protected the interests of slaveholders in the District of Columbia, in the territories, in the interstate slave trade, and through the Fugitive Slave Act of 1793. Northerners who profited from slave labor and supported the national government with their votes and taxes, therefore, bore their share of guilt for slavery and faced divine punishment.

The AASS sought to use these arguments to convince masters to free their slaves and to persuade northerners and nonslaveholding white southerners to put moral pressure on slaveholders. To reach a southern audience, the AASS in 1835 launched the **Great Postal Campaign**, designed to send antislavery literature to southern post offices and individual slaveholders. At about the same time, the AASS organized a massive petitioning campaign aimed to introduce the slavery issue into Congress. Antislavery women led in circulating and signing the petitions. In 1836 over thirty thousand of the petitions reached Washington.

In the North, AASS agents gave public lectures against slavery and distributed antislavery literature. Often a pair of agents—one black and one white—traveled together on speaking tours. Ideally, the black agent would be a former slave, so he could attack the brutality and immorality of slavery from personal experience. During the early 1840s, the AASS paired fugitive slave Frederick Douglass with William A. White, a young

▶▶ **Guide to Reading/Key Terms**

For answers, see the *Teacher's Resource Manual.*

white Harvard graduate, in a tour through Ohio and Indiana. In 1843 the Eastern New York Anti-Slavery Society paired white Baptist preacher Abel Brown with "the noble colored man," Lewis Washington. At first, all the agents were men. Later, the abolitionist organizations also employed women as agents.

The reaction to these efforts in both the North and the South was not what the leaders of the AASS anticipated. Speaking of racial justice and exemplifying inter-racial cooperation, the abolitionists were treading new ground. In doing so, they created awkward situations that are—in retrospect—humorous. But their audiences often reacted violently. Southern postmasters burned antislavery literature when it arrived at their offices, and southern states censored the mail. Vigilantes drove off white southerners who openly advocated abolition. Black abolitionists, of course, did not even attempt openly to denounce slavery while in the South.

In Congress, southern representatives and their northern allies passed the **Gag Rule** in 1836. It required that no petition related to slavery could be introduced in the House of Representatives. In response, the AASS sent 415,000 petitions in 1838, and Congressman John Quincy Adams (a former president) launched his long struggle against the Gag. Technically not an abolitionist, but a defender of the First Amendment right to petition Congress, Adams succeeded in having the Gag Rule repealed in 1844.

Meanwhile, in the North, mobs attacked abolitionist agents, disrupted their meetings, destroyed their newspaper presses, and burned black neighborhoods. In 1837 a proslavery mob killed Elijah P. Lovejoy, a white abolitionist newspaper editor, when he tried to defend his printing press in Alton, Illinois. On another occasion, Douglass, White, and an older white abolitionist named George Bradburn were conducting antislavery meetings in the small town of Pendleton, Indiana, when an enraged mob attempted to kill Douglass.

The American and Foreign Anti-Slavery Society

In 1840 the AASS splintered. Most of its members left to establish the **American and Foreign Anti-Slavery Society** (AFASS) and the **Liberty Party**, the first antislavery political party. On the surface, the AASS broke apart over long-standing disagreements about the role of women in abolitionism and William Lloyd Garrison's broadening radicalism. Garrison seemed to many to be losing sight of the AASS's main concern. But the failure of moral suasion to make progress against slavery—particularly in the South—and the question of how abolitionists should respond to the increasing signs of slave unrest also helped fracture the AASS.

Garrison and a minority of abolitionists, who agreed with his radical critique of American society and were centered in New England, retained control of what became known as the "Old Organization." By

1842 they had deemphasized moral suasion and had begun calling for **disunion**—the separation of the North from the South—as the only means of ending northern support for slavery. The U.S. Constitution, Garrison declared, was a thoroughly proslavery document that had to be destroyed before African Americans could gain their freedom.

The Liberty Party

Those who withdrew from the AASS took a more traditional stand on the role of women, believed the country's churches could be converted to abolitionism, and asserted the Constitution could be used in behalf of abolitionism. Under the leadership of Lewis Tappan, a wealthy white New York City abolitionist, some of them formed the church-oriented AFASS. Others created the Liberty Party and nominated James G. Birney, a slaveholder-turned-abolitionist, as their candidate in the 1840 presidential election. Birney received only 7,069 votes out of a total cast of 2,411,187, and William Henry Harrison, the Whig candidate, became president. But the Liberty Party constituted the beginning of an increasingly powerful political crusade against slavery.

Black abolitionists joined in the disruption of the Old Organization. Only in New England did most black abolitionists remain loyal to the AASS. Frederick Douglass, William Wells Brown, Robert Purvis, Charles L. Remond, Susan Paul, and Sarah Douglass were notable Garrison loyalists. As might have been expected, most black clerical abolitionists joined the AFASS. Eight, including Jehiel C. Beman and his son Amos G. Beman, Christopher Rush, Samuel E. Cornish, Theodore S. Wright, Stephen H. Gloucester, Henry Highland Garnet, and Andrew Harris, were among the new organization's founders. After 1840 African Americans were always more prominent as leaders in the AFASS than the AASS.

The Liberty Party also attracted black support, although few black men could vote. Particularly appealing to black abolitionists was the platform of the radical New York wing of the party led by Gerrit Smith. Philip A. Bell, Charles B. Ray, Samuel E. Cornish, Henry Highland Garnet, and Jermain Wesley Loguen endorsed the New York Liberty Party because, of all the antislavery organizations, it advocated the most aggressive action against slavery in the South and was most directly involved in helping slaves escape.

A More Aggressive Abolitionism

The New York Liberty Party maintained that the U.S. Constitution, interpreted in the light of the Bible and natural law, outlawed slavery throughout the country—not only in the District of Columbia and in

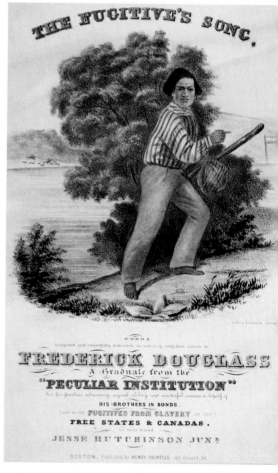

An increase in slave escapes helped inspire the more aggressive abolitionist tactics of the 1840s and 1850s. In this 1845 cover illustration for sheet music composed by white antislavery minstrel Jesse Hutchinson Jr., Frederick Douglass is shown in an idealized rendition of his escape from slavery in Maryland.

the territories, which were governed by the federal government, but in the states as well. This, the party's leaders asserted, meant Congress could abolish slavery in the southern states. More practically it meant that for slaves to escape and for others to help them escape were perfectly legal actions. Some argued that neither northern state militia nor the U.S. Army should help suppress slave revolts.

This body of thought, which dated to the late 1830s, supported growing northern abolitionist empathy with the slaves as they struggled for freedom against their masters. While the AASS disintegrated, escapes and minor rebellions proliferated in the border slave states of Maryland, Virginia, Kentucky, and Missouri as enslaved black people reacted to worsening conditions there. Throughout this region black families were being torn apart by the domestic slave trade, which was funneling black workers into the newly opened cotton-producing areas of the Southwest. In response, the radical wing of the Liberty Party cited the Constitution in support of slave resistance to this brutal traffic. It also encouraged black and white northerners to go south to help slaves escape.

The *Amistad* and the *Creole*

Two maritime slave revolts were crucial in encouraging rising militancy among northern abolitionists. The first of these revolts, however, did not involve enslaved Americans. In June 1839 fifty-four African captives aboard the Spanish schooner *Amistad*, meaning "friendship," successfully rebelled under the leadership of Joseph Cinque and attempted to sail to Africa. When a U.S. warship recaptured the *Amistad* off the coast of Long Island, New York, the Africans attracted the support of Lewis Tappan and other abolitionists. As a result of the abolitionists' efforts and arguments presented by Congressman Adams, the U.S. Supreme Court ruled in November 1841 that Cinque and the others were free.

▶ **Recommended Reading**

Stanley Harrold. *The Abolitionists and the South, 1831-1861*. Lexington, KY: University Press of Kentucky, 1995. Emphasizes the formative impact of slave resistance on northern abolitionism and the aggressiveness of that movement toward the South.

***Mutiny*, painted by Hale Woodruff** in 1939, provides a dramatic and stylized portrayal of the successful uprising of African slaves on board the Spanish schooner *Amistad* in 1839.

Later that same month, Madison Washington led a revolt aboard the brig *Creole*, which was transporting 135 American slaves from Richmond, Virginia, to the slave markets of New Orleans. Washington had earlier escaped to Canada from slavery in Virginia. When he returned to rescue his wife, he was captured, reenslaved, and shipped aboard the *Creole*. Once at sea, Washington and about a dozen other black men seized control of the vessel and sailed it to the British colony of the Bahamas. There local black fishermen surrounded the *Creole* with their boats to protect it, and most of the people on board immediately gained their freedom under British law. A few days later, so did Washington and the other rebels. Although Washington soon vanished, the *Creole* revolt made him a hero among abolitionists and a symbol of black bravery.

Cinque and Washington inspired others to risk their lives and freedom to help African Americans escape bondage. The New York Liberty Party reinforced this commitment by maintaining that what they did was both divinely ordained and strictly legal.

The Underground Railroad

The famous underground railroad must be placed within the context of increasing southern white violence against black families, slave resistance, and aggressive northern abolitionism. Because the underground railroad had to be secret, few details of how it operated are known. We do not even know the origin of the term **underground railroad**. Slaves had always escaped from their masters, and free black people and some white people had always assisted them. But the organized escape of slaves

Charles T. Weber painted *The Underground Railroad* in about 1893. It shows fugitive slaves arriving in winter at Quaker abolitionist Levi Coffin's Indiana farm. The painting misleadingly suggests that white abolitionists were primarily responsible for helping slaves escape.

▶ **Retracing the Odyssey**

"Free at Last: A History of the Abolition of Slavery in America." A "National Touring Exhibition" sponsored by the Lincoln Home National Historic Site, Springfield, Illinois, that shows how "abolition became a national issue, how the slavery issue drew politicians and moral reformers together, [and] how the efforts of escaped slaves contributed a human face to the horrors of slavery."

National Underground Railroad Freedom Center Cincinnati. Exhibits, programs, and events dealing with "slavery and freedom," with emphasis on the underground railroad.

National Underground Railroad Museum, Maysville, Kentucky. Houses artifacts associated with and provides information on the underground railroad.

MAP 9–2 The Underground Railroad

This map illustrates *approximate* routes traveled by escaping slaves through the North to Canada. Although some slaves escaped from the deep South, most who utilized the underground railroad network came from the border slave states.

By what means did escaping slaves travel the routes shown on this map?

Explore this map online at www.prenhall.com/aah/map9.2

▶ Map 9-2

Slaves escaped through a network of predetermined routes organized by free black people and white people, who assisted slaves in their path to freedom.

from the Chesapeake, Kentucky, and Missouri along predetermined routes to Canada became much more common after the mid-1830s. A united national underground railroad with a president or unified command never existed. Instead there were different organizations separated in both time and space from one another (see Map 9–2). Even during the 1840s and 1850s, most of the slaves who escaped did so on their own.

The best documented underground railroad organizations were centered in Washington, D.C., and Ripley, Ohio. In Washington Charles T. Torrey, a white Liberty Party abolitionist from Albany, New York, and Thomas Smallwood, a free black resident of Washington, began in 1842 to help slaves escape along a predetermined northward route. Between March and November of that year, they sent at least 150 enslaved men, women, and children to Philadelphia. From there, a local black vigilance committee provided the fugitives with transportation to Albany, New York, where a local, predominantly white, vigilance group smuggled them to Canada. In southern Ohio, some residents, black and white, had for years helped fugitive slaves as they headed north from the slaveholding state of Kentucky. The most well known of these early underground railroad operatives was John Rankin, a white Presbyterian minister who lit a lantern each night at his home in Ripley, Ohio, which was located on a hill above the north shore of the Ohio River, to serve as a beacon for escaping slaves. From the late 1840s into the Civil War years, former slave John P. Parker made the Ripley-based underground railroad more aggressive. With Rankin's support, Parker, who had purchased his own freedom in 1845, repeatedly went into Kentucky to lead others to freedom.

The escapees, however, were by no means passive "passengers" in the underground railroad network. They raised money to pay for their transportation northward, recruited and helped other escapees, and sometimes became underground railroad agents themselves. This was not an easy journey, and the underground railroad was always a risky business. In 1843 Smallwood had to flee to Canada as Washington police closed in on his home. In 1846 Torrey died of tuberculosis in a Maryland prison while serving a six-year sentence for helping slaves escape. Parker recalled "real warfare" in southern Ohio between underground railroad operators and slaveholders from Kentucky. "I never thought of going uptown without a pistol in my pocket, a knife in my belt, and a blackjack handy," he later recalled.

By the early 1850s, Harriet Tubman, a fugitive slave herself, had become the most active worker on the eastern branch of the underground railroad. Her master abused her, but she did not escape until he threatened to sell her and her family south. After her escape in 1849, Tubman returned about thirteen times to Maryland to help others flee. She had the help of Thomas Garrett, a white Quaker abolitionist who lived in Wilmington, Delaware, and William Still, the black leader of the Philadelphia Vigilance Association. Still, who as a child had been a fugitive slave himself, coordinated the work of many black and white underground agents between Washington and Canada.

Harriet Tubman, standing at the left, is shown in this undated photograph with a group of people she helped escape from slavery. Because she worked in secret during the 1850s, she was known only to others engaged in the underground railroad, the people she helped, and a few other abolitionists.

 Reading Check How did the underground railroad work?

Canada West

The ultimate destination for many African Americans on the underground railroad was **Canada West**—present-day Ontario—between Buffalo and Detroit on the northern shore of Lake Erie. Black Americans had begun to settle in Canada West as early as the 1820s. Because slavery was illegal in the British Empire after 1833, fugitive slaves were safe there. The stronger fugitive slave law that Congress passed as part of the Compromise of 1850 (see Chapter 10) made Canada an even more important refuge for African Americans. Between 1850 and 1860, the number of black people in Canada West rose from approximately 8,000 to at least 20,000.

There were several communal black settlements in Canada West, including the Refugee Home Society, the Buxton Community at Elgin, and the Dawn Settlement. But most black immigrants lived and worked in Toronto and Chatham. Most of them found work as craftsmen and laborers, although a few became entrepreneurs or professionals.

The chief advocate of **black migration** to Canada West—and the only advocate of migration who also supported racial integration—was Mary Ann Shadd Cary. She edited the *Provincial Freeman*, an abolitionist paper in Toronto, between 1854 and 1858, and lectured in northern cities promoting emigration to Canada. Yet, although African Americans enjoyed security in Canada, by the 1850s they also faced the same sort of segregation and discrimination there that existed in the northern United States.

 Reading Check How did abolitionism become more aggressive during the 1840s and 1850s?

▶ **Reading Check**

The underground railroad was a system of organized groups who helped slaves escape along a predetermined route to the North. Once they arrived in the North, fugitive slaves were smuggled to Canada.

▶ **Reading Check**

A number of factors contributed to the increasing militancy of abolitionism. As the AASS disintegrated, a number of new organizations rose to take its place, some of them more radical than the AASS. Second, in the face of deteriorating conditions in the border states, minor rebellions and slave escapes increased. Finally, the cases of the *Amistad* and the *Creole* encouraged rising militancy in the North.

▶ How did the views of Frederick Douglass differ from those of Henry Highland Garnet?

▶ What were the causes of the rise of black militancy in the 1840s?

▶ What led a minority of black leaders to consider migration in the 1840s?

KEY WORDS

▶ Philadelphia Vigilance Association, p. 301

▶ slave catchers, p. 301

▶ integrationist, p. 303

▶ nationalism, African-American, p. 303

▶ **Guide to Reading/Key Terms**

For answers, see the *Teacher's Resource Manual.*

▶ **Document**

9-4 *Garnet's "Call to Rebellion," 1843*
In a stirring speech at Buffalo, New York, Garnet shocked delegates at the National Convention of Colored Citizens with a call for violence as an answer to slavery. In his speech he encouraged slaves to turn on their masters and warned black people that white pacifism would take too long. Frederick Douglass protested against Garnet's call for physical violence. Garnet then responded to Douglass' speech, but he could not persuade the convention to support his methods of abolition.

Section 5

Resistance and Nationalism

Black Militancy

During the 1840s growing numbers of black abolitionists were willing to consider forceful action against slavery. The rise in black militancy had several causes. The breakup of the AASS had weakened abolitionist loyalty to the national antislavery organizations. All abolitionists, black and white, were exploring new types of antislavery action. Many black abolitionists had become convinced that most white abolitionists enjoyed debate and theory more than action against slavery.

Influenced by the examples of Cinque, Madison Washington, and other rebellious slaves, many black abolitionists in the 1840s and 1850s wanted to do more to encourage slaves to resist and escape. This militancy inspired Garnet's "Address to the Slaves." A willingness to act rather than just talk helped make the Liberty Party—especially its radical New York wing—attractive to African Americans. However, black abolitionists, like white abolitionists, approached violence and slave rebellion with caution. As late as 1857, Garnet and Frederick Douglass described slave revolt as "inexpedient."

The Antislavery Struggle Intensifies

JUNE 1839	Joseph Cinque leads a successful revolt of enslaved Africans aboard the Spanish schooner *Amistad*.
APRIL 1840	The Liberty Party nominates James G. Birney for U.S. president.
NOVEMBER 1841	Madison Washington leads a successful revolt of American slaves aboard the *Creole*.
MARCH 1842	Charles T. Torrey and Thomas Smallwood organize an underground railroad network to help slaves escape from Washington, D.C., and its vicinity.
AUGUST 1843	Henry Highland Garnet in Buffalo, New York, delivers his "Address to the Slaves."
DECEMBER 1843	Smallwood flees to Canada to avoid arrest.
JUNE 1844	Torrey is arrested in Baltimore on multiple charges of having helped slaves escape.
MAY 1846	Torrey dies in the Maryland penitentiary.

The black abolitionist desire to go beyond rhetoric found its best outlet in the local vigilance organizations. The most famous of these is William Still's **Philadelphia Vigilance Association**, which was active during the late 1840s and 1850s. But such associations were first organized during the late 1830s and often had white as well as black members. As the 1840s progressed, African Americans formed more such associations and began to lead those that already existed. In this they were reacting to a facet of the growing violence in the United States—the use of force by **slave catchers** in northern cities to recapture fugitive slaves.

Another aspect of black militancy during the 1840s was a willingness to charge publicly that white abolitionists were not living up to their own advocacy of racial justice. Economic slights rankled African Americans the most. At the annual meeting of the AFASS in 1852, a black delegate demanded to know why Lewis Tappan did not employ a black clerk in his business. In 1855 Samuel Ringgold Ward denounced Garrison and his associates for failing to have an African American "as clerk in an antislavery office, or editor, or lecturer to the same extent . . . as white men of the same calibre." These charges reflected factional struggles between the AASS and the AFASS. But they also represented real grievances among black abolitionists and real inconsistencies among their white counterparts.

▶ **Living Words Audio Clip**

Track 10 *If There is No Struggle, There is No Freedom,* excerpt from a speech by Frederick Douglass; read by Ossie Davis

▶ **Retracing the Odyssey**

Frederick Douglass National Historic Site, Washington, D.C. This is Douglass's Cedar Hill home, which he purchased in 1878. It contains materials related to his career as an abolitionist and advocate of black rights.

Frederick Douglass

The career of Frederick Douglass illustrates the impact of the failure of white abolitionists to live up to their egalitarian ideals. Douglass was born a slave in Maryland in 1818. Intelligent, ambitious, and charming, he resisted brutalization, learned to read, and acquired a trade before escaping to New England in 1838. By 1841 he had, with Garrison's encouragement, become an antislavery lecturer, which led to the travels with William White discussed earlier.

But as time passed, Douglass, who had remained loyal to Garrison during the 1840s when most other black abolitionists had left the AASS, suspected his white colleagues wanted him to continue in the role of a fugitive slave. In fact, he was becoming one of the premier American orators of his time. "People won't believe you ever was a slave, Frederick, if you keep on this way," a white colleague advised him.

Finally, Douglass decided he had to free himself from the AASS. In 1847 he asserted his independence by leaving Massachusetts for Rochester, New York, where he began publishing the *North Star.* This decision angered Garrison and his associates but permitted Douglass to chart his own course as a black leader. Although Douglass continued to work closely with white abolitionists, especially Gerrit Smith, he could now do it on his own terms and be more active in the black convention movement, which he considered essential to gaining general emancipation and racial justice. In 1851 he completed his break with

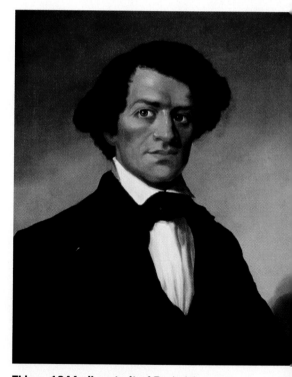

This c. 1844 oil portrait of Frederick Douglass is attributed to E. Hammond. Douglass escaped from slavery in 1838. By the mid-1840s, he had emerged as one of the more powerful speakers of his time.

Martin R. Delany Describes His Vision of a Black Nation

This excerpt comes from the appendix of Martin R. Delany's The Condition, Elevation, Emigration and Destiny of the Colored People of the United States, Politically Considered, *which he published in 1852. It embodies Delany's black nationalist vision.*

Every people should be the originators of their own designs, the projectors of their own schemes, and creators of the events that lead to their destiny—the consummation of their desires.

Situated as we are in the United States, many, and almost insurmountable obstacles present themselves. We are four-and-a-half millions in numbers, free and bond; six hundred thousand free, and three-and-a-half millions bond.

We have native hearts and virtues, just as other nations; which in their pristine purity are noble, potent, and worthy of example. We are a nation within a nation. . . .

But we have been, by our oppressors, despoiled of our purity, and corrupted in our native characteristics, so that we have inherited their vices, and but few of their virtues, leaving us in character, really a broken people.

Being distinguished by complexion, we are still singled out—although having merged in the habits and customs of our oppressors—as a distinct nation of people. . . . The claims of no people, according to established policy and usage, are respected by any nation, until they are presented in a national capacity.

To accomplish so great and desirable an end, there should be held, a great representative gathering of the colored people of the United States; not what is termed a National Convention, representing en masse, such as have been, for the last few years, held at various times and places; but a true representation of the intelligence and wisdom of the colored freemen. . . . A Confidential Council. . . .

By this Council to be appointed, a Board of Commissioners. . . to go on an expedition to the EASTERN COAST OF AFRICA, to make researches for a suitable location on that section of the coast, for the settlement of colored adventurers from the United States, and elsewhere.

The whole continent is rich in minerals, and the most precious metals, as but a superficial notice of the topographical and

geological reports from that country, plainly show. . . . The land is ours—there it lies with inexhaustible resources; let us go and possess it. In Eastern Africa must rise up a nation, to whom all the world must pay commercial tribute.

What Do You Think?

▶ What elements of black nationalism appear in this document?

▶ How does Delany perceive Africa?

Source: Herbert Aptheker, ed., *A Documentary History of the Negro People in the United States*, 5th ed. (New York: Citadel, 1968), 1:327–28.

the AASS by endorsing the constitutional arguments and tactics of the New York Liberty Party as better designed to achieve emancipation than Garrison's disunionism.

 Reading Check How did the views of Frederick Douglass differ from those of Henry Highland Garnet?

Black Nationalism

Douglass always believed black people were part of a larger American nation and their best prospects for political and economic success lay in the United States. He was, despite his differences with some white abolitionists, an ardent **integrationist**. He opposed separate black churches and predicted that African Americans would eventually disappear into a greater American identity. Most black abolitionists did not go that far, but they agreed racial oppression in all its forms could be defeated in the United States.

During the 1840s and 1850s, however, an influential minority of black leaders disagreed with this point of view. Prominent among them were Garnet and Douglass's sometime colleague on the *North Star* Martin R. Delany. Although they differed between themselves over important details, Delany and Garnet both endorsed African-American migration and **nationalism** as the best means to realize black aspirations.

Since the postrevolutionary days of Prince Hall, some black leaders had believed African Americans could thrive only as a separate nation. They suggested sites in Africa, Latin America, and the American West as possible places to pursue this goal. But it took the rising tide of racism and violence to induce a respectable minority of black abolitionists to consider migration. Almost all of them staunchly opposed the African migration scheme of the ACS, which they continued to characterize as proslavery and racist. Nevertheless, Garnet conceded in 1849 that he would "rather see a man free in Liberia [the ACS colony], than a slave in the United States."

▶ **What Do You Think?**

· Elements of black nationalism include the notion that black men in the U.S. were largely outnumbered and this presented many obstacles for them, that black men have native hearts and that currently they are a nation within a nation, and lastly that colored men should commission an expedition to Africa to research a suitable location for black settlement.

· Delany perceives Africa as a land of opportunity for black people. He feels the continent is rich in natural resources, and that it belongs to African Americans.

▶ **Reading Check**

Douglass was an integrationist. He believed that, in the long run, blacks would be absorbed into a greater American identity. In contrast, Garnet did not believe white Americans would ever grant equal rights to blacks. Thus, he supported black migration and nationalism.

NEW YORK CITY.—DEPARTURE OF COLORED EMIGRANTS FROM THE SOUTH FOR THE LIBERIAN REPUBLIC, ON JANUARY 2D.

Freed slaves set sail from New York City for the Liberian Republic.

Douglass and most black abolitionists rejected this outlook, insisting the aim must be freedom in the United States. Nevertheless, emigration plans developed by Garnet and Delany during the 1850s were a significant part of African-American reform culture. Delany, a physician and novelist, was born free in western Virginia in 1812. He grew up in Pennsylvania and by the late 1840s was a champion of black self-reliance. To further this cause, he promoted mass black migration to Latin America or Africa. "We must MAKE an ISSUE, CREATE an EVENT, and ESTABLISH a NATIONAL POSITION for OURSELVES," he declared in 1852.

In contrast, Garnet welcomed white assistance for his plan to foster Christianity and economic development in Africa by encouraging *some*— not all—African Americans to migrate there under the patronage of his African Civilization Society. In 1858 he wrote, "Let those who wished to stay, stay here—and those who had enterprise and wished to go, go and found a nation, if possible, of which the colored Americans could be proud."

Little came of these nationalist visions, largely because of the successes of the antislavery movement. Black and white abolitionists, although not perfect allies, awoke many in the North to the brutalities of slavery. They helped convince most white northerners that the slave-labor system and slaveholder control of the national government threatened their economic and political interests. At the same time, abolitionist aid to escaping slaves and their defense of fugitive slaves from recapture pushed southern leaders to adopt policies that led to secession and the Civil War. The northern victory in the war, general emancipation, and constitutional protection for black rights made most African Americans—for a time—optimistic about their future in the United States.

Supporting a Position

When you take a position on an issue, you have a better chance of winning others to your side if you can back up your argument with solid reasons and evidence.

In his famous speech on the celebration of Independence Day, Frederick Douglass outlines his position on the humanity of slaves.

LEARN THE SKILL

Use the following steps to support a position:

1. **State your position clearly in a sentence.** To take a position on any issue, you must be clear as to what that position is. Writing it out in a sentence forces you to organize your thoughts.

2. **Identify at least three reasons for your position.** To be convincing, you must do more than say what you believe; you must say why you believe it. Think of reasons for your side—or against the opposing position. Pointing out the weakness of an opposing idea can be very effective. Also consider your audience. Think of what reasons will be most effective with those you are trying to persuade.

3. **Support each reason with evidence.** To build a solid case for your position, use facts to support each reason.

4. **Add a conclusion.** This is your chance to sum up and drive your point home.

PRACTICE THE SKILL

Answer the following questions:

1. **(a)** What is the issue on which Douglass is stating his position? **(b)** What is his position? **(c)** What part of his speech states this position? **(d)** Restate Douglass's position in your own words, as if you were using it to begin an essay or a speech.

2. **(a)** What reasons does Douglass give for his position? **(b)** How does Douglass treat the opposing position? **(c)** Does this strengthen or weaken his argument? Explain your reasoning.

3. **(a)** What evidence does Douglass give for each of his reasons? **(b)** Is the evidence factual, or opinion masquerading as fact?

4. **(a)** Which part of the address states Douglass's conclusion? **(b)** In a short paragraph, write your own conclusion to Douglass' position.

But I fancy I hear someone of my audience say, "It is just in this circumstance that you and your brother abolitionists fail to make a favorable impression on the public mind. Would you argue more and denounce less, would you persuade more and rebuke less, your cause would be much more likely to succeed." But, I submit, where all is plain, there is nothing to be argued. What point in the antislavery creed would you have me argue? On what branch of the subject do the people of this country need light? Must I undertake to prove that the slave is a man? That point is conceded already. Nobody doubts it. The slaveholders themselves acknowledge it the enactment of laws for their government. They acknowledge it when they punish disobedience on the part of the slave. There are seventy-two crimes in the state of Virginia which, if committed by a black man (no matter how ignorant he be), subject him to the punishment of death, while only two of the same crimes will subject a white man to the like punishment. What is this but the acknowledgement that the slave is a moral, intellectual, and responsible being? The manhood of the slave is conceded. It is admitted in the fact that the Southern statute books are covered with enactments forbidding, under severe fines and penalties, the teaching of the slave to read or to write. When you can point to any such laws in reference to the beasts of the field, then I may consent to argue the manhood of the slave. When the dogs in your streets, when the fowls of the air, when the cattle on your hills, when the fish of the sea and the reptiles that crawl shall be unable to distinguish the slave from a brute, then will I argue with you that the slave is a man!

—Frederick Douglass, excerpt from *Independence Day Speech*, 1852

Chapter Timeline

AFRICAN-AMERICAN EVENTS	NATIONAL EVENTS

1830

1831
Publication of *Liberator* begun by William Lloyd Garrison

1832
Andrew Jackson reelected president

1833
Formation of AASS

1833
End of Nullification Controversy

1835

1835
Abolitionist Postal Campaign

1836
Martin Van Buren elected president; Texas independence

1839
Amistad mutiny

1840

1840
Breakup of AASS

1840
William H. Harrison elected president

1841
Creole revolt

1844
James K. Polk elected president

1843
Henry Highland Garnet's "Address to the Slaves"

AFRICAN-AMERICAN EVENTS		NATIONAL EVENTS
	1845	
1847 Publication of the *North Star* begun by Frederick Douglass		**1845** Annexation of Texas
1849 Harriet Tubman's career begins		**1846** War against Mexico begins
		1848 Annexation of Mexico's California and New Mexico Provinces
	1850	
1851 Start of resistance to the Fugitive Slave Act of 1850		**1850** Compromise of 1850
Black migration advocated by Martin Delany		
	1855	

Chapter Review and Assessment

SUMMARY

Section 1 A Rising Tide of Racism and Violence, p. 285

- Antiblack riots gained in frequency and intensity as abolitionism gathered momentum.
- Philadephia experienced the worst race riots of the period.
- Under President Polk, war and annexation led to an expansion of the territory in which slavery could spread. This, in turn, raised fears in the North of political domination by the slaveholding South.

Section 2 The Response of the Antislavery Movement, p. 288

- William Lloyd Garrison's decision to create a new, more radical movement was a turning point in the abolitionist cause.
- Garrison's American Anti-Slavery Society (AASS) was the most important abolitionist organization of its time.
- Black men, black women, and white female abolitionists formed their own auxiliaries to the AASS.
- Local, state, and national black conventions created forums for prominent black abolitionists, as well as providing a setting for the development of the abolionist movement.

Section 3 Black Community Institutions, p. 293

- Black churches played a key role in the anti-slavery movement.
- The vast majority of black abolitionist leaders were ministers.
- By the 1840s, black newspapers were an important element of the movement, particularly Frederick Douglass's *North Star* and *Frederick Douglass's Paper*.

Section 4 The Changing Abolitionist Movement

- During the 1830s the AASS pursued a strategy based on moral suasion.
- In the 1840s the AASS splintered in the face of limited success, the issue of slave unrest, and the role of women in the organization.
- New organizations were formed including the American and Foreign Anti-Slavery Society (AFASS) and the Liberty Party. Slave revolts on the *Amistad* and the *Creole* encouraged rising militancy among northern abolitionists.

- The underground railroad served as a conduit for slaves escaping from the South, many of them hoping to make it to Canada West, present-day Ontario.

Section 5 Resistance And Nationalism

- During the 1840s, growing numbers of black abolitionists were willing to consider the use of force to end slavery.
- The career of Frederick Douglass illustrates the gradual separation of black abolitionists from white abolitionist organizations.
- During the 1840s and 1850s, an important minority of black leaders disagreed with Douglass's emphasis on integration, instead endorsing migration and black nationalism.

REVIEWING KEY TERMS

Write a brief explanation of the following terms.

1. manifest destiny, p. 283
2. nativism, p. 283
3. annexation, p. 284
4. American Anti-Slavery Society (AASS), p. 286
5. Free Produce Association, p. 289
6. *Freedom's Journal*, p. 292
7. *North Star*, p. 292
8. moral suasion, p. 293
9. Great Postal Campaign, p. 293
10. Gag Rule, p. 294
11. American and Foreign Anti-Slavery Society, p. 294
12. Liberty Party, p. 294
13. disunion, p. 295
14. *Amistad*, p. 296
15. underground railroad, p. 297
16. Canada West, p. 299
17. black migration, p. 299
18. Philadelphia Vigilence Association, p. 301
19. slave catchers, p. 301
20. integrationist, p. 303
21. nationalism, African-American, p. 303

REVIEWING MAIN IDEAS

22. What was the historical significance of Henry Highland Garnet's "Address to the Slaves"?

23. How did Garnet's attitude toward slavery differ from that of William Lloyd Garrison?

24. Evaluate Frederick Douglass's career as an abolitionist. How was he consistent? How was he inconsistent?

25. Discuss the contribution of black women to the antislavery movement. How did participation in this movement alter their lives?

26. Compare and contrast the integrationist views of Frederick Douglass with the nationalist views of Martin Delany and Henry Highland Garnet.

27. Why did black abolitionists leave the AASS in 1840?

ANALYZING DOCUMENTS

Frederick Douglass Describes an Awkward Situation

In the summer of 1843, I was traveling and lecturing in company with William A. White, Esq., through the state of Indiana. Anti-slavery friends were not very abundant in Indiana . . . and beds were not more plentiful than friends. . . . At the close of one of our meetings, we were invited home with a kindly-disposed old farmer, who, in the generous enthusiasm of the moment, seemed to have forgotten that he had but one spare bed, and that his guests were an ill-matched pair. . . . White is remarkably fine looking, and very evidently a born gentleman; the idea of putting us in the same bed was hardly to be tolerated; and yet there we were, and but the one bed for us, and that, by the way, was in the same room occupied by the other members of the family. . . . After witnessing the confusion as long as I liked, I relieved the kindly-disposed family by playfully saying, "Friend White, having got entirely rid of my prejudice against color, I think, as proof of it, I must allow you to sleep with me to-night." White kept up the joke, by seeming to esteem himself the favored party, and thus the difficulty was removed.

—From Michael Meyer, ed., *Frederick Douglass: The Narrative and Selected Writings* (New York: Modern Library, 1984), 170–71.

 Thinking Critically: What does Douglass reveal about his own character?

WRITING ACTIVITY

In a short report or research paper, consider these questions:

 Compare and contrast the attitudes of black and white antislavery activists. What tensions existed within the antislavery movement?

STUDY ONLINE!

www.prenhall.com/aah

Additional study resources are available for this chapter on the *Companion Website*.

▶ Review and Assessment

Section 4

Abraham Lincoln and Black People

GUIDE TO READING

▶ What was the impact of John Brown's raid on Harpers Ferry?

▶ What were Lincoln's views on racial equality?

KEY TERMS

▶ Secret Six, p. 332

▶ secession, p. 335

The Lincoln-Douglas Debates

In 1858 Senator Stephen Douglas of Illinois, a Democrat, ran for reelection to the Senate against Republican Abraham Lincoln. The main issues in the campaign were slavery and race, which the two candidates addressed in a series of debates around the state. In carefully reasoned speeches and responses, these experienced and articulate lawyers focused almost exclusively on slavery's expansion and its future in the Union. At Freeport, Illinois, Lincoln, a former Whig congressman, attempted to trap Douglas, the incumbent, by asking him if slavery could expand now that the Dred Scott decision had ruled slaves were property whom their owners could take into any federal territory. In reply, Douglas, who wanted to be president and had no desire to offend either northern or southern voters, cleverly defended "popular sovereignty" and the Dred Scott decision. He insisted that slave owners could indeed take their slaves where they pleased. But, he contended, if the people of a territory failed to enact slave codes to protect and control slave property, a slave owner was not likely to settle there with his or her slaves.

The Lincoln-Douglas debates did not always turn on the fine points of constitutional law or on the fate of slavery in the territories. Douglas accused Lincoln and the Republicans of promoting the interests of black people over those of white people. The debates sometimes degenerated into crude and savage exchanges about which candidate favored white people more and black people less. Douglas proudly advocated white supremacy. "The signers of the Declaration [of Independence] had no reference to the negro . . . or any other inferior or degraded race when they spoke of the equality of men." He later charged that Lincoln and the Republicans wanted black and white equality. "If you, Black Republicans, think the negro ought to be on social equality with your wives and daughters, . . . you have a perfect right to do so. . . . Those of you who believe the negro is your equal . . . of course will vote for Mr. Lincoln."

Lincoln did not believe in racial equality, and he made that plain. In exasperation, he explained that merely because he opposed slavery did not mean he believed in equality.

> I am not, nor ever have been in favor of bringing about in any way the social and political equality of the white and black races—that I am not

▶ **Guide to Reading/Key Terms**

For answers, see the *Teacher's Resource Manual*.

nor ever have been in favor of making voters or jurors of negroes, nor of qualifying them to hold office, nor to intermarry with white people; and I will say in addition to this that there is a physical difference between the races which I believe will forever forbid the two races living together on terms of social and political equality.

But without repudiating these views, Lincoln later tried to transcend this blatant racism. "Let us discard all this quibbling about this man and the other man—this race and that race and the other race being inferior." Instead, he added, let us "unite as one people throughout this land, until we shall once more stand up declaring that all men are created equal." Lincoln stated unequivocally that race had nothing to do with whether a man had the right to be paid for his labor. He pointed out that the black man, "in the right to eat the bread, without leave of anybody else, which his own hand earns, he is my equal and the equal of Judge Douglas, and the equal of every living man."

Lincoln may have won the debate in the minds of many, but Douglas won the Senate election. Lincoln, however, made a name for himself that would work to his political advantage in the near future.

John Brown and the Raid on Harpers Ferry

While Lincoln and Douglas were debating, John Brown was plotting the violent overthrow of slavery in the South itself. In May 1858, accompanied by eleven white followers, he met thirty-four black people led by Martin Delany at Chatham in Canada West (now the province of Ontario) and appealed for their support. Brown was determined to invade the South and end slavery. He hoped to attract legions of slaves as he and his "army" moved down the Appalachian Mountains into the heart of the plantation system.

Planning the Raid

Only one man at the Chatham gathering agreed to join the raid. Brown returned to the United States and garnered financial support from prosperous white abolitionists. Contributing money rather than risking their lives seemed more realistic to these men. They preferred to keep their identities confidential and thus came to be known as the **Secret Six**: Gerrit Smith, Thomas Wentworth Higginson, Samuel Gridley Howe, George L. Stearns, Theodore Parker, and Franklin Sanborn.

Brown also asked Frederick Douglass and Harriet Tubman to join him. They declined. By the summer of 1859, at a farm in rural Maryland, Brown had assembled an "army" consisting of seventeen white men (including three of his sons) and five black men. The black men who enlisted were Osborne Anderson, one of the Chatham participants; Sheridan Leary, an

▶ **Retracing the Odyssey**

Chatham, Ontario, Canada: The First Baptist Church. On May 28, 1858, John Brown met with members of Chatham's black community—many of whom had fled to Canada to escape the fugitive slave law. Brown appealed for support to begin an armed uprising of slaves in the South. Fire destroyed the original structure in 1907, and the current church was built in 1908.

Harpers Ferry National Park, West Virginia. Picturesquely situated in the Blue Ridge mountains at the confluence of the Shenandoah and Potomac rivers, this is where John Brown and his "army" in October 1859 attempted to secure weapons to begin a slave rebellion.

JOHN BROWN AT HARPER'S FERRY.

John Brown was captured in the Engine House at Harpers Ferry on October 18, 1859.

escaped slave who had become a saddle and harness maker in Oberlin, Ohio; Leary's nephew John A. Copeland, an Oberlin College student; and two escaped slaves, Shields Green and Dangerfield Newby. Newby was determined to rescue his wife, Harriet, and their seven children who were about to be sold.

PROFILE ❖ Martin Delany

"I thank God for making me a man, but Delany thanks Him for making him a black man."
—*Frederick Douglass on Martin Delany*

Martin Delany (1812–1885) was one of the first individuals to insist that people of African descent in the United States should control their own destiny. In speeches, articles, and books, he evoked pride in his African heritage. He stressed the need for black people to rely on themselves and not on the white majority.

Delany was a medical doctor, a journalist, an explorer, an anthropologist, a military officer, and a political leader. He was born free in Charlestown, Virginia (now West Virginia). In 1831 Martin went west to Pittsburgh where he spent most of the next twenty-five years.

Delany was active in the Pittsburgh Anti-Slavery Society and helped slaves escape on the underground railroad. In 1843 he married Catherine Richards, the daughter of a well-to-do black butcher. By 1860 they had had seven children.

In 1843 Delany began publishing *The Mystery*, a four-page weekly newspaper devoted to abolition. It did not thrive. In 1847 he joined Frederick Douglass briefly as the coeditor of the *North Star*. In 1850 Delany was admitted to the Harvard Medical School with two other black students for formal training, but they were forced to leave after one term because of the protests of white students.

In 1852 he wrote and published *The Condition, Elevation, Emigration and Destiny of the Colored People of the United States*—the first major statement of black nationalism. Delany observed,

"We are a nation within a nation." He recommended that people of African descent abandon the United States and migrate to Central America, South America, or Hawaii. Delany was the key figure in organizing the National Emigration Convention in Cleveland in 1854.

He and his family left the United States for Canada and lived in Canada West. He organized a meeting there of black people and John Brown in 1858. He also managed to find time to write a novel, *Blake*, the fictional account of a West Indian slave who promotes revolution in the United States and leads a black rebellion in Cuba.

Once the United States began to enlist black troops in the Civil War, Delany helped recruit black men. His son Toussaint joined the famed 54th Massachusetts Regiment. Delany himself became one of the few black men to be commissioned an officer.

After the war, he remained in South Carolina, where he entered politics. He ran for lieutenant governor on a reform party ticket, but he was not elected. In 1876, he astounded many black people when he supported white Democrats who favored the restoration of white political control over South Carolina. When Democrats won the election, the new governor, Wade Hampton, rewarded Delany by naming him to a minor political office.

After he failed to win an appointment to a federal position in Washington, D.C., Delany went to Xenia, Ohio, and Wilberforce University, where his family had lived since the late 1860s. He died there in 1885.

Delany

The Raid

Brown's invasion began on Sunday night October 16, 1859, with a raid on Harpers Ferry, Virginia, and the federal arsenal there. Brown hoped to secure weapons and then advance south. But the operation went awry from the start. The dedication and devotion of Brown and his men were not matched by their strategy or his leadership. The first man Brown's band killed was ironically a free black man, Heyward Shepard, who was a baggage handler at the train station. The alarm then went out, and opposition gathered.

Even though they had lost the initiative, Brown and his men neither advanced nor retreated. Instead they remained in Harpers Ferry while Virginia and Maryland militia converged on them. Fighting began, and two townspeople, the mayor, and eight of Brown's men, including Sheridan Leary, Dangerfield Newby, and two of Brown's sons, were killed. Brown managed to seize several hostages, among them Lewis W. Washington, the great grandnephew of George Washington.

By Tuesday morning, Brown, with his hostages and what remained of his "army," was holed up in an engine house. A detachment of U.S. Marines under the command of Robert E. Lee arrived, surrounded the building, and demanded Brown's surrender. He refused. The Marines broke in. Brown was wounded and captured.

The raid was an utter failure. No slaves were freed. Shields Green and John A. Copeland fled but were caught. Osborne Anderson eluded capture and later fought in the Civil War. Virginia quickly tried Brown, Green, and Copeland for treason. They were found guilty and sentenced to hang.

The Reaction

The raid failed, but Brown and his men succeeded in intensifying the deeply felt emotions of those who supported and those who opposed slavery. At first regarded as crazed zealots and insane fanatics, they showed they were willing—even eager—to die for the antislavery cause. The dignity and assurance that Brown, Green, and Copeland displayed as they awaited the gallows impressed many black and white Northerners.

Black teacher and abolitionist Frances Ellen Watkins Harper wrote to John Brown's wife two weeks before Brown was executed to express compassion and admiration for both husband and wife:

> Belonging to the race your dear husband reached forth his hand to assist, I need not tell you that my sympathies are with you. I thank you for the brave words you have spoken. A republic that produces such a wife and mother may hope for better days. Our heart may grow more hopeful for humanity when it sees the sublime sacrifice it is about to receive from his hands. Not in vain had your dear husband periled all, if the martyrdom of one hero is worth more than the life of a million cowards.

▶ **Living Words Audio Clip**

Track 12 *John Brown: An Address*, by Frederick Douglass; pamphlet excerpt

▶ **Document**

10-9 *An Abolitionist is Given the Death Sentence in 1859*
After his conviction, John Brown gave this speech, which was printed in several newspapers.

James A. Copeland wrote home to his family that he was proud to die:

> I am not terrified by the gallows, which I see staring me in the face, and upon which I am soon to stand and suffer death for doing what George Washington was made a hero for doing. . . . Could I die in a manner and for a cause which would induce true and honest men more to honor me, and the angels more ready to receive me to their happy home of everlasting joy above? . . . I imagine that I hear you, and all of you, mother, father, sisters and brothers, say—"No, there is not a cause for which we, with less sorrow, could see you die."

Brown eloquently and calmly announced his willingness to die as so many had died before him. "Now, if it is deemed necessary that I should forfeit my life for the furtherance of the ends of justice, and mingle my blood further with the blood of my children and with the blood of millions in this slave country whose rights are disregarded by wicked, cruel, and unjust enactments, I say, let it be done."

For many Northerners, the day Brown was executed, December 2, 1859, was a day of mourning. Church bells tolled, and people bowed their heads in prayer. One unnamed black man later solemnly declared: "The memory of John Brown shall be indelibly written upon the tablets of our hearts, and when tyrants cease to oppress the enslaved, we will teach our children to revive his name, and transmit it to the latest posterity, as being the greatest man in the 19th century."

White Southerners felt differently. They were terrified and traumatized by the raid, and outraged that Northerners made Brown a hero and a martyr. A wave of hysteria and paranoia swept the South as incredulous white people wondered how Northerners could admire a man who sought to kill slave owners and free their slaves.

Brown's raid and the reaction to it further divided a nation already badly split over slavery. Although neither he nor anyone else realized it at the time, Brown and his "army" had propelled the South toward **secession** from the Union—and thereby moved the nation closer to his goal of destroying slavery.

Abolitionist leader John Brown's raid and execution were considered heroic by many.

 Reading Check What was the impact of John Brown's raid on Harpers Ferry?

▶ **Reading Check**

The raid intensified the feelings of Americans on both sides of the slavery debate. The willingness of Brown and his fellow raiders to die for the antislavery cause impressed many in the North. On the other hand, southerners were shocked that Brown had become a hero in the North and could not understand the attitude of northern whites to a man they saw as a murderer.

GUIDE TO READING

► What were the key factors in Abraham Lincoln's victory in 1860?

► How did African Americans and white Southerners react to the election of Abraham Lincoln in 1860?

KEY TERMS

► Constitutional Union Party, p. 336

► Confederate States of America, p. 337

► **Guide to Reading/Key Terms**

For answers, see the *Teacher's Resource Manual.*

► **Recommended Reading**

Leon Litwack. *North of Slavery: The Negro in the Free States, 1790–1860.* Chicago: University of Chicago Press, 1961. A story of black Northerners and the discrimination that they encountered.

Section 5

The Election of Abraham Lincoln

With the country fracturing over slavery, four candidates ran for president in the election of 1860. The Democrats split into a northern faction, which nominated Stephen Douglas, and a southern faction, which nominated John C. Breckenridge of Kentucky. The **Constitutional Union Party**, a new party formed by former Whigs, nominated John Bell of Tennessee. The breakup of the Democratic Party assured victory for the Republican candidate, Abraham Lincoln (see Map 10–3).

Lincoln's name was not even on the ballot in most southern states. His candidacy was based on the Republican Party's adamant opposition to the expansion of slavery into any western territory. Although Lincoln took pains to reassure white Southerners that slavery would continue in states where it already existed, they were not in the least persuaded. A South Carolina newspaper was convinced Lincoln would abolish slavery. "[Lincoln] has openly proclaimed a war of extermination against the leading institutions of the Southern States. He says that there can be no peace so long as slavery has a foot hold in America."

A Georgia newspaper preferred a bloody civil war to a Lincoln presidency. "Let the consequences be what they may—whether the Potomac is crimsoned in human gore, and Pennsylvania Avenue is paved ten fathoms deep with mangled bodies . . . the South will never submit to such humiliation and degradation as the inauguration of Abraham Lincoln."

Black People Respond to Lincoln's Election

Although they were less opposed to Lincoln than white Southerners, black Northerners and white abolitionists were not eager to see Abraham Lincoln become president. Dismayed by his contradictions and racism—he opposed slavery, but he tolerated it; he was against slavery's expansion, but he condemned black Americans as inferiors—many black people refused to support him or did so reluctantly. The New York *Anglo-African* opposed both Republicans and Democrats in the 1860 election, telling its readers to depend on each other. "We have no hope from either [of the] political parties. We must rely on ourselves, the righteousness of our cause, and the advance of just sentiments among the great masses of the . . . people."

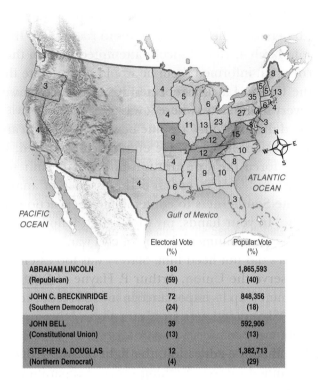

	Electoral Vote (%)	Popular Vote (%)
ABRAHAM LINCOLN (Republican)	180 (59)	1,865,593 (40)
JOHN C. BRECKINRIDGE (Southern Democrat)	72 (24)	848,356 (18)
JOHN BELL (Constitutional Union)	39 (13)	592,906 (13)
STEPHEN A. DOUGLAS (Northern Democrat)	12 (4)	1,382,713 (29)

MAP 10–3 The Election of 1860

The results reflect the sectional split over slavery. Lincoln carried the election although he won only in northern states.

 How was Lincoln able to win without getting any electoral votes from the South?

Abolitionists such as William Lloyd Garrison and Wendell Phillips believed Lincoln was too willing to tolerate slave-holding interests. But Frederick Douglass wrote, "Lincoln's election will indicate growth in the right direction" and his presidency "must and will be hailed as an anti-slavery triumph."

After Lincoln's election, black leaders almost welcomed the secession of southern states. H. Ford Douglas urged the southern states to leave the Union. "Stand not upon the order of your going, but go at once. . . . There is no union of ideas and interests in this country, and there can be no union between freedom and slavery." Frederick Douglass was convinced that there were men prepared to follow in the footsteps of John Brown's "army" to destroy slavery. "I am for dissolution of the Union—decidedly for a dissolution of the Union! . . . In case of such a dissolution, I believe that men could be found . . . who would venture into those states and raise the standard of liberty there."

 Reading Check How did African Americans and white southerners react to the election of Abraham Lincoln in 1860?

Disunion

When South Carolina seceded on December 20, 1860, it began a procession of southern states out of the Union. By February 1861 seven states—South Carolina, Mississippi, Alabama, Florida, Louisiana, Georgia, and Texas—had seceded and formed the **Confederate States of America** in Montgomery, Alabama. Before there could be the kind of

Map 10-3

The electoral votes won by Lincoln from the northern states represented the majority of all electoral votes.

Reading Check

Many African Americans were wary of Lincoln and unhappy with his many contradictions on the issues of slavery and race. White southerners did not believe that he would limit his opposition to slavery to halting its expansion. They believed he meant to end it. This belief fueled the process of secession.

Black men in New York formed their own military companies and began to drill. In Boston, they drew up a resolution modeled on the Declaration of Independence and appealed for permission to go to war:

> Our feelings urge us to say to our countrymen that we are ready to stand by and defend our Government as equals of its white defenders; to do so with "our lives, our fortunes, and our sacred honor," for the sake of freedom, and as good citizens; and we ask you to modify your laws, that we may enlist—that full scope may be given to patriotic feelings burning in the colored man's breast.

Black men in Philadelphia volunteered to infiltrate the South to incite slave revolts but were turned down. In Washington, Jacob Dodson, a black employee of the U.S. Senate, wrote a letter to Secretary of War Simon Cameron shortly after the fall of Fort Sumter volunteering the services of local black men. "I desire to inform you that I know of some 300 reliable colored free citizens of this city who desire to enter the service for the defense of the city." Cameron curtly replied, "This Department has no intention at the present to call into the service of the government any colored soldiers."

 Reading Check Why did black men volunteer to fight?

Union Policies toward Confederate Slaves

Slaves started to liberate themselves as soon as the war began, but Union political and military leaders had no coherent policy for dealing with them. To the deep disappointment of black Northerners and white abolitionists, Union military commanders showed more concern for the interests of Confederate slave owners than for the people in bondage. In May 1861 General George B. McClellan reassured Virginia slave owners: "Not only will we abstain from all interferences with your slaves, but we will, with an iron hand, crush any attempt at insurrection on their part."

General Henry Halleck ordered slaves who escaped in the Ohio Valley returned to their owners, and General Winfield Scott, the army's chief of staff, asked that Confederate slave owners be permitted to recover slaves who crossed the Potomac River to what they believed was the freedom of Union lines. In Tennessee in early 1862, General Ulysses S. Grant returned runaway slaves to their owners if the owners supported the Union cause, but Grant put black people to work on fortifications if their owners favored secession.

▶ **Reading Check**

Black people felt an obligation to fight in the war because they recognized that the defeat of the South was essential to their freedom.

▶ **Reading Check**

Black men in New York formed military companies and began to drill. In Boston they drew up a formal declaration asking for permission to fight. In Philadelphia they volunteered to infiltrate the South and incite slave revolts. All of these overtures were rejected.

These African-American troops served as teamsters for the Union Army in Virginia.

Not all Union commanders were as callous as these generals. A month after the war began, three bondmen working on Confederate fortifications in Virginia escaped to the Union's Fortress Monroe on the coast. Their owner, a Confederate colonel, appeared at the fortress the next day under a flag of truce and demanded the return of his slaves under the 1850 Fugitive Slave Act. The incredulous Union commander, General Benjamin Butler, informed him that because Virginia had seceded from the Union, the fugitive slave law was no longer in force. Butler did not free the three slaves, but he did not reenslave them either. He declared them **contraband**—enemy property—and put them to work for the Union. Soon, over a thousand slaves fled to Fortress Monroe. The white authorities may have thought of them as contraband, but that is not how they viewed themselves.

On August 6, 1861, Congress clarified the status of runaway slaves when it passed the **First Confiscation Act**. Any property that belonged to Confederates used in the war effort could be seized by federal forces. Any slaves used by their masters to benefit the Confederacy—and only those slaves—would be freed. Almost immediately, Union general John C. Fremont (the 1856 Republican presidential candidate) exceeded the strict limits of the act by freeing all the slaves belonging to Confederates in Missouri. President Lincoln quickly countermanded the order and told Fremont that only slaves actively used to aid the Confederate war effort were to be freed. Lincoln worried that Fremont would drive Missouri or Kentucky into the Confederacy.

Black leaders were—to put it mildly—displeased with Lincoln and with federal policies that both prohibited the enlistment of black troops and ignored the plight of the enslaved. To fight a war against the South without fighting against slavery, the institution on which the South was so thoroughly dependent, seemed absurd. Frederick Douglass stated the argument cogently: "To fight against slaveholders, without fighting against slavery, is but a half-hearted business, and paralyzes the hands engaged in it. . . . Fire must be met with water. . . . War for the destruction of liberty must be met with war for the destruction of slavery."

Others were less charitable. Joseph R. Hawley, a white Connecticut Republican, thought Lincoln was foolish to worry about whether the border states might leave the Union. "Permit me to say damn the border states. . . . A thousand Lincolns cannot stop the people from fighting slavery." Lincoln did not budge. Union military forces occupied an enclave on South Carolina's southern coast and the Sea Islands in late 1861. On May 9, 1862, General David Hunter ordered slavery abolished in South Carolina, Georgia, and Florida. Lincoln quickly revoked Hunter's order and reprimanded him. Nevertheless, thousands of slaves along the South Carolina and Georgia coast threw off their shackles and welcomed Union troops as plantation owners fled to the interior.

 Reading Check How did African Americans respond as the Civil War began in 1861?

A Ride for Liberty—The Fugitive Slaves, 1862. On March 23, 1862, artist Eastman Johnson witnessed a family of three fleeing slavery and commited the episode to canvas.

Oil on board, The Brooklyn Museum, Gift of Miss Gwendolyn O.L. Conkling.

▶▶ **Recommended Readings**

James McPherson. *Battle Cry of Freedom: The Civil War Era*. New York: Oxford University Press, 1988. A superb one-volume account of the Civil War.

Dudley Taylor Cornish. *The Sable Arm: Negro Troops in the Union Army, 1861–1865*. New York: Norton, 1956. The best single study of black men in the military during the war.

▶▶ **Teaching Notes**

In the New York *Anglo-African*, a letter writer who identified himself as "Ivanhoe" urged Northern black men to decline any request to serve in Union military forces until the slaves were freed and black Northerners received treatment equal to that of white people. "And suppose we were invited [to enlist]," he asked, "what duty would we then owe to ourselves and our posterity?_ Our enslaved brethren must be made freedmen_. We of the North must have all of the rights which white men enjoy; until then we are in no condition to fight under the flag [which] gives us no protection."

GUIDE TO READING

▶ What was Lincoln's initial position on slavery?

▶ How did Lincoln's policies on slavery change as the Civil War continued?

▶ How did African Americans respond to Lincoln's advocacy of colonization?

▶ Why did Lincoln support colonization?

KEY TERMS

▶ compensated emancipation, p. 354

▶ **Guide to Reading/Key Terms**

For answers, see the *Teacher's Resource Manual.*

▶ **Recommended Reading**

Lerone Bennett. *Abraham Lincoln's White Dream.* Chicago: Johnson Publishing Co., 2000. Bennett is critical of Lincoln's attitudes and actions in the popular account.

Section 2
Lincoln and Emancipation

Lincoln's Initial Position

For more than a year, Lincoln remained reluctant to strike decisively against slavery. He believed the long-term solution to slavery and the race problem in the United States was the **compensated emancipation** of slaves followed by their colonization outside the country. That is, slave owners would be paid for their slaves; the slaves would be freed but forced to settle in the Caribbean, Latin America, or West Africa.

As a Whig congressman in 1849, Lincoln voted for a bill that would have emancipated slaves and compensated their owners in the District of Columbia if it had passed. In 1861 he tried—but failed—to persuade the Delaware legislature to support compensated emancipation. Then in April 1862, at Lincoln's urging, Republicans in Congress (against almost unanimous Democratic opposition) voted to provide funds to "any state which may adopt gradual abolishment of slavery." Lincoln wanted to eliminate slavery from the border states with the approval of slave owners there and thus diminish the likelihood that those states would join the Confederacy.

But leaders in the border states rejected the proposal. Lincoln brought it up again in July. This time he warned congressmen and senators from the border states that if their states opposed compensated emancipation they might have to accept uncompensated emancipation. They ignored his advice and denounced compensated emancipation as a "radical change in our social system" and an intrusion by the federal government into a state issue.

To many white Americans, Lincoln's support for compensated emancipation and colonization was a misguided attempt to link the war to the issue of slavery. But to black Americans, abolitionists, and an increasing number of Republicans, Lincoln's refusal to abolish slavery immediately was tragic. Antislavery advocates regarded Lincoln's willingness to purchase the freedom of slaves as an admission that he considered those human beings to be property. They deplored his seeming inability to realize the Union would not win the war unless slaves were liberated.

Lincoln Moves Toward Emancipation

However, by the summer of 1862, after the border states rejected compensated emancipation, Lincoln concluded that victory and the future of the Union were tied directly to the issue of slavery. Slavery became the instrument Lincoln would use to hasten the end of the war and restore the Union. He told Secretary of the Navy Gideon Welles:

> We must free the slaves or be ourselves subdued. The slaves were undeniably an element of strength to those who had their service, and we must decide whether that element should be with us or against us.

Emancipation, Lincoln stressed, would "strike at the heart of the rebellion."

In cabinet meetings on July 21 and 22, 1862, Lincoln discussed abolishing slavery. Except for Postmaster General Montgomery Blair, the cabinet supported emancipation. Blair feared that eliminating slavery would cost the Republicans control of Congress in the fall elections. Secretary of State William H. Seward supported abolition but advised Lincoln not to issue a proclamation until the Union Army won a major victory. Otherwise emancipation might look like the desperate gesture of the leader of a losing cause. Lincoln accepted Seward's advice and postponed emancipation.

Lincoln Delays Emancipation

Nevertheless, word circulated that Lincoln intended to abolish slavery. But weeks passed, and slavery did not end. Frustrated abolitionists and Republicans attacked Lincoln. Frederick Douglass was exasperated with a president who had shown inexcusable deference to white Southerners who had rebelled against the Union:

> Abraham Lincoln is no more fit for the place he holds than was [previous president] James Buchanan. . . . The country is destined to become sick of both [General George B.] McClellan and Lincoln, and the sooner the better. The one plays lawyer for the benefit of the rebels, and the other handles the army for the benefit of traitors. We should not be surprised if both should be hurled from their places before the rebellion is ended.

In his *Prayer of Twenty Millions*, Horace Greeley, editor of the New York *Tribune*, expressed his disappointment that the president had not moved promptly against slavery, the issue that had led the southern states to leave the Union and go to war:

> We ask you to consider that Slavery [is the] inciting cause and sustaining base of treason. . . . We think timid counsels in such a crisis [are] calculated to prove perilous, probably disastrous.

Greeley insisted that Lincoln should have long ago warned white Southerners that their support of secession would endanger slavery.

⏵ **Documents**

11-1 *The Working Men of Manchester, England Write to President Lincoln on the Question of Slavery in 1862*
While the government of Great Britain was sympathetic to the South, most working people in England favored the Union because of their opposition to slavery. On December 31, 1862, an assembly of factory workers in Manchester urged President Lincoln to go the full distance and make emancipation the law of the entire land.

11-2 *President Lincoln Responds to the Working Men of Manchester on the Subject of Slavery in 1863*
On January 19, 1863, two weeks after the Emancipation Proclamation had taken effect, Lincoln replied to the Manchester workers. His letter is an effective summary statement of his position on the prosecution of the war.

On August 22, 1862, Lincoln replied to Greeley and offered a masterful explanation of his priorities. Placing the preservation of the Union before freedom for the enslaved, Lincoln declared,

> My paramount object in this struggle is to save the Union, and is not either to save or destroy slavery. If I could save the Union without freeing any slave I would do it; and if I could save it by freeing all the slaves, I would do it; and if I could do it by freeing some and leaving others alone, I would also do that.

Lincoln concluded, "I have here stated my purpose according to my view of *official* duty, and I intend no modification of my oft-expressed *personal* wish that all men, everywhere, could be free."

▶ **Reading Check**

After 1862, Lincoln was convinced that the future of the Union was linked to slavery. He began to discuss the abolition of slavery. Nonetheless, he resisted pressure to take this ultimate step.

✓ **Reading Check** How did Lincoln's policies on slavery change as the Civil War continued?

Abraham Lincoln meets with a free black family on the lawn of the Executive Mansion.

Black People Reject Colonization

Lincoln's policy on emancipation had shifted dramatically, but he remained committed to colonization. On August 14, 1862, Lincoln invited black leaders to the White House and appealed for their support for colonization. After condemning slavery as "the greatest wrong inflicted on any people," he explained that white racism made it unwise for black people to remain in the United States.

> Your race suffer very greatly, many of them, by living among us, while ours suffer from your presence. There is an unwillingness on the part of our people, harsh as it may be, for you free colored people to remain among us. . . . I do not mean to discuss this, but to propose it as a fact with which we have to deal. I cannot alter it if I would.

Lincoln asked the black leaders to begin enlisting volunteers for a colonization project in Central America.

Most black people were unimpressed by Lincoln's words and unmoved by his advice. A black leader from Philadelphia condemned the president.

> This is our country as much as it is yours, and we will not leave it.

Frederick Douglass accused Lincoln of hypocrisy and claimed that support for colonization would lead white men "to commit all kinds of violence and outrage upon the colored people."

Lincoln would not retreat from his support for colonization. Attempts were already under way to put compensated emancipation and colonization into effect. In April 1862 Congress enacted a bill to pay District of Columbia slave owners up to $300 for each slave they freed and to provide $100,000 to support the voluntary colonization of the freed people in Haiti or Liberia. In 1863 the government tried to settle 453 black American colonists at Ile à Vache, an island near Haiti. The settlers suffered terribly from disease and starvation. This attempt at government-sponsored colonization ended in 1864 when the U.S. Navy returned 368 survivors to the United States.

 Reading Check　Why did Lincoln support colonization?

▶ **Reading Check**

Lincoln felt that blacks could not live in the United States without suffering from white racism and that colonization was a way to protect blacks.

▶ **Guide to Reading/Key Terms**

For answers, see the *Teacher's Resource Manual.*

Section 3
Liberation

The Preliminary Emancipation Proclamation

Finally on September 22, 1862 the president issued the **Preliminary Emancipation Proclamation**. It came five days after General George B. McClellan's Army of the Potomac turned back an invasion of Maryland at Antietam by General Robert E. Lee's Army of Northern Virginia. This bloody but less-than-conclusive victory allowed Lincoln to justify emancipation. But this first proclamation freed no people. Instead, it stipulated that anyone in bondage in states or parts of states still in rebellion on January 1, 1863, would be "thenceforward, and forever free." Lincoln's announcement gave the Confederate states one hundred days to return to the Union. If any or all of those states did rejoin the Union, the slaves there would remain in bondage. The Union would be preserved, and slavery would be maintained.

What were Lincoln's intentions? Lincoln knew there was virtually no chance that white Southerners would return to the Union just because he had threatened to free their slaves. Most Confederates expected to win the war, thereby confirming secession and safeguarding slavery. White Southerners ridiculed the preliminary proclamation.

Northern Reaction to Emancipation

In the Union, the Preliminary Emancipation Proclamation was greeted with little enthusiasm. Most black people and abolitionists, of course, were gratified that Lincoln, after weeks of procrastination, had finally issued the proclamation. Frederick Douglass was ecstatic. "We shout for joy that we live to record this righteous decree." In *The Liberator*, William Lloyd Garrison wrote that it was "an act of immense historical consequence." But they also worried that—however remote the possibility might be—some slave states would return to the Union by January 1, denying freedom to those enslaved.

Many white Northerners resented emancipation. A northern newspaper editor vilified Lincoln as a "half-witted usurper" and the Proclamation as "monstrous, impudent, and heinous . . . insulting to God as to man, for it declares those 'equal' whom God created unequal."

Even before the announcement of emancipation, antiblack riots flared in the North. In Cincinnati in the summer of 1862, Irish dock workers invaded black neighborhoods after black men had replaced the striking wharf hands along the city's river front. In Brooklyn, New York, Irish Americans set fire to a tobacco factory that employed black women and children.

Political Opposition to Emancipation

Northern Democrats almost unanimously opposed emancipation. They accused Lincoln and the Republicans of "fanaticism" and regretted that emancipation would liberate "two or three million semi savages" who would "overrun the North" and compete with white working people. The Democratic-controlled lower houses of the legislatures in Indiana and Illinois condemned the Proclamation as "wicked, inhuman, and unholy." Republicans recognized the intense hostility among many white Northerners to black people. Senator Lyman Trumball of Illinois conceded that "there is a very great aversion in the West—I know it to be so in my state—against having free negroes come among us."

And as some Republicans had predicted and feared, the Democrats capitalized on dissatisfaction with the war's progress and with Republican support for emancipation to make significant gains in the fall elections. Democratic governors were elected in New York and New Jersey, and Democrats won thirty-four more seats in the U.S. House of Representatives, although the Republicans retained a majority. Overjoyed Democrats proclaimed, "Abolition Slaughtered." Republicans took solace that their losses were not greater.

The Emancipation Proclamation

On January 1, 1863, Abraham Lincoln issued the **Emancipation Proclamation**. It was not the first step toward freedom. Since 1861 several thousand slaves had already freed themselves. But it was the first significant effort by Union authorities to assure freedom to nearly four million people of African descent who, with their ancestors, had been enslaved for 250 years in North America. The Civil War was now a war to make people free.

Black communities and many white people across the North celebrated. Church bells rang. Poems were written, and prayers of thanksgiving were offered. Many considered it the most momentous day in American history since July 4, 1776. Frederick Douglass had difficulty describing the emotions of people in Boston when word reached the city late on the night of December 31 that Lincoln would issue the Proclamation the next day. "The effect of this announcement was startling beyond description, and

▶ **Document**

11-9   *The Emancipation Proclamation, 1863*

▶ **Recommended Reading**

John Hope Franklin. *The Emancipation Proclamation*. Garden City, NY: Doubleday, 1963. A work written to commemorate the centennial of the Proclamation.

The Emancipation Proclamation was essentially a military directive that freed more than three million people from bondage by 1865.

The Steps to Emancipation

APRIL 1861	Fort Sumter is attacked; Civil War begins
MAY 1861	General Butler refuses to return escaped "contrabands" to slavery
AUGUST 1861	General Fremont orders emancipation of slaves in Missouri; Lincoln countermands him
AUGUST 1861	First Confiscation Act frees captured slaves used by Confederate Army
APRIL 1862	Congress provides funds for compensated emancipation; border states spurn the proposal
MAY 1862	General Hunter's order abolishing slavery in South Carolina, Georgia, and Florida is revoked by Lincoln
SUMMER 1862	Lincoln concludes that Union victory requires emancipation
SEPTEMBER 22, 1862	Lincoln issues Preliminary Emancipation Proclamation after Battle of Antietam
JANUARY 1, 1863	Emancipation Proclamation takes effect

the scene was wild and grand. Joy and gladness exhausted all forms of expression, from shouts of praise to sobs and tears. . . . A Negro preacher, a man of wonderful vocal power, expressed the heartfelt emotion of the hour, when he led all voices in the anthem, 'Sound the loud timbrel o'er Egypt's dark sea, Jehovah hath triumphed, his people were free.' "

Limits of the Proclamation

Despite this excitement, the language of the Emancipation Proclamation was uninspired and unmoving. It lacked the eloquence of the Declaration of Independence or the address Lincoln would deliver after the Union victory at Gettysburg in July 1863. Lincoln dryly wrote that "as a fit and necessary measure for suppressing said rebellion . . . I do order and declare that all persons held as slaves within said designated States, and parts of States, are, and henceforth shall be free."

Moreover, by limiting emancipation to those states and areas still in rebellion, Lincoln did not include enslaved people in the four border states still in the Union or in areas of Confederate states that Union forces had already occupied (see Map 11–1). Hundreds of thousands of people would remain in bondage despite the proclamation. The immediate practical effect of the Proclamation was negligible in the areas it was intended to affect. After all, slave owners in the Confederacy did not recognize Lincoln's authority. They certainly did not free their slaves on January 1 or anytime soon thereafter. Yet the Emancipation Proclamation remains one of the most important documents in American history. It made the Civil War a war to free people, as well as to preserve the Union, and it gave moral authority to the Union cause. And as many black people had freed themselves before the Proclamation, now many more would liberate themselves after.

Effects of the Proclamation on the South

The Emancipation Proclamation destroyed any chance that Great Britain or France would offer diplomatic recognition to the Confederate government. Diplomatic recognition would have meant accepting the Confederacy as a legitimate state equal in international law to the Union, and it would almost surely have led to financial and military assistance for the South. British leaders, who had considered recognizing the Confederacy, now declined to support a "nation" that relied on slavery while its opponent moved to abolish it. In this sense, the Proclamation weakened the Confederacy's ability to prosecute the war.

▶ **Teaching Notes**

Well into the twentieth century, New Year's Day was commemorated as Emancipation Day, a holiday zealously observed by black Americans in churches and with parades and celebrations.

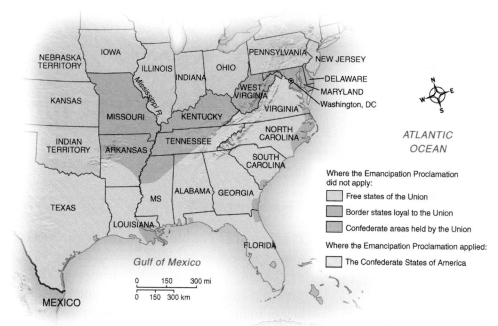

Where the Emancipation Proclamation did not apply:

☐ Free states of the Union

☐ Border states loyal to the Union

☐ Confederate areas held by the Union

Where the Emancipation Proclamation applied:

☐ The Confederate States of America

ATLANTIC OCEAN

Gulf of Mexico

0   150   300 mi
0 150 300 km

MEXICO

MAP 11–1 Effects of the Emancipation Proclamation

When Abraham Lincoln issued the Emancipation Proclamation on January 1, 1863, it applied only to slaves in those portions of the Confederacy not under Union authority.

 Where, according to the map, did slaves reside who were to be freed under the terms of the Proclamation?

 Explore this map online at www.prenhall.com/aah/map11.1

▶▶ **Map 11-1**

Slaves living in those states and areas still in rebellion.

Even more important, it undermined slavery in the South and contributed directly to the Confederacy's defeat. Word of freedom spread rapidly across the South. Black people—aware a Union victory in the war meant freedom—were far less likely to labor for their owners or for the Confederacy. Slave resistance became more likely, although Lincoln cautioned against insurrection in the Proclamation: "And I hereby enjoin upon the people so declared to be free to abstain from all violence, unless in necessary self-defence." The institution of slavery cracked, crumbled, and collapsed after January 1, 1863.

Without emancipation, the United States would not have survived as a unified nation. Abraham Lincoln, after first failing to make the connection between eliminating slavery and preserving the Union, came to understand it fully and also grasped what freedom meant to both black and white people. In his annual message to Congress in December 1862, one month before the Proclamation, Lincoln described the importance of emancipation with a passion and feelings that were absent in the Proclamation itself. "We know how to save the Union. The world knows we do know how to save it. We—even we here—hold the power, and bear the responsibility. In giving freedom to the slave, we assure freedom to the free—honorable alike in what we give, and what we preserve."

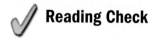 **Reading Check** Why did Lincoln issue the Emancipation Proclamation?

▶▶ **Reading Check**

The Proclamation ended southern hopes that Great Britain or France would offer the Confederacy diplomatic recognition. It undermined slavery in the South contributing to the South's defeat. Most important, as Lincoln himself recognized, the United States could not survive as a unified country if slavery was allowed to continue.

▶ **Guide to Reading/Key Terms**

For answers, see the *Teacher's Resource Manual.*

▶ **Recommended Reading**

George W. Williams. *History of the Negro Troops in the War of the Rebellion.* New York: Harper & Row, 1888. An account of black soldiers in the war by America's first African-American historian.

▶ **Map 11-2, p. 363**

The Union military first worked to fragment the Confederacy along the Mississippi River, and then moved eastward towards the coast in similar fashion to divide the Confederacy.

Section 4

Black Men Fight for the Union

The Union Enlists Black Troops

The Emancipation Proclamation not only marked the beginning of the end of slavery, but it also authorized the enlistment of black troops in the Union Army. Just as white leaders in the North came to realize the preservation of the Union necessitated the abolition of slavery, they also began to understand that black men were needed for the military effort if the Union was to triumph in the Civil War.

By early 1863 the war had not gone well for the all-white Union Army. Although they had won significant battlefield victories in Kentucky and Tennessee and had captured New Orleans, the war in the east was a much different matter (see Map 11–2). The Union's Army of the Potomac faced a smaller but highly effective Confederate Army—the Army of Northern Virginia—led by the remarkable General Robert E. Lee. Confederate troops forced a Union retreat from Richmond during the 1862 Peninsular campaign. Union forces lost at the first and second battles of Bull Run. Their only victory over Lee at Antietam provided Lincoln with the opportunity to issue the Preliminary Emancipation Proclamation. But that was followed by a crushing Union loss at Fredericksburg.

Much like the decision to free the slaves, the decision to employ black troops proceeded neither smoothly nor logically. The commitment to the Civil War as a white man's war was deeply entrenched, and the initial attempts to raise black troops were strongly opposed by many white Northerners. As with emancipation, Lincoln moved slowly from outright opposition to cautious acceptance to enthusiastic support for enlisting black men in the Union Army.

South Carolina Volunteer Regiments

Some Union officers recruited black men long before emancipation was proclaimed and before most white Northerners were prepared to accept, much less welcome, black troops. In May 1862 General David Hunter began recruiting former slaves along the South Carolina coast and the Sea Islands, an area Union forces had captured in late 1861. But some black men did not want to enlist, and Hunter used white troops to force

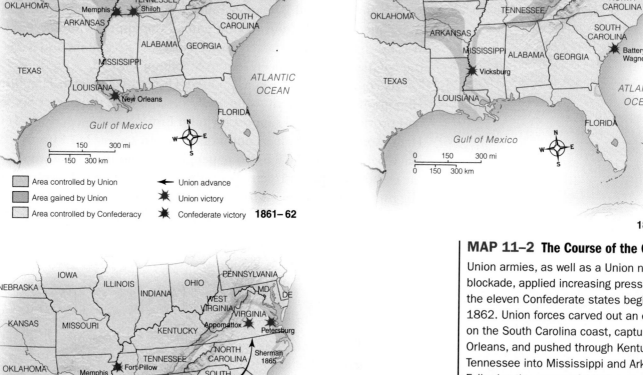

1861–62

☐ Area controlled by Union	← Union advance
☐ Area gained by Union	✶ Union victory
☐ Area controlled by Confederacy	✶ Confederate victory

1863

1864–65

MAP 11–2 The Course of the Civil War

Union armies, as well as a Union naval blockade, applied increasing pressure on the eleven Confederate states beginning in 1862. Union forces carved out an enclave on the South Carolina coast, captured New Orleans, and pushed through Kentucky and Tennessee into Mississippi and Arkansas. Following the successful Union siege of Vicksburg in 1863, the Confederacy was divided along the Mississippi River. In 1864 General Ulysses S. Grant's Army of the Potomac drove General Robert E. Lee's Army of Northern Virginia into entrenchments around Richmond and Petersburg. General William Tecumseh Sherman marched from Atlanta to Savannah and then into the Carolinas. The war ended in April 1865 with Lee's surrender to Grant at Appomattox Court House and Joseph E. Johnston's capitulation to Sherman near Durham, North Carolina.

 Based on an examination of these maps, what appears to have been the strategy of Union military forces to defeat the Confederacy?

black men to "volunteer" for military service. He managed to organize a five-hundred-man regiment—the **First South Carolina Volunteers**.

The former slaves were outfitted in bright red pants, with blue coats and broad-brimmed hats. Through the summer of 1862, Hunter trained and drilled the regiment while awaiting official authorization and funds to pay them. When Congress balked, Hunter reluctantly disbanded all but one company of the regiment that August. The troops were dispersed,

Published in 1868, Keckley began her autobiography soon after the end of the Civil War. It was in those tumultuous years that Elizabeth Hobbs Keckley (ca. 1824–1907) a talented dressmaker and designer to the political elite of Washington, D.C., became a confidante of Mary Todd Lincoln. Born into slavery, Keckley not only provides a rare look at African Americans, free born and fugitive as well, she also offers an important-firsthand—look at northern military and political leaders.

unpaid and disappointed. The surviving company was sent to St. Simon's Island off the Georgia coast to protect a community of former slaves.

Although Congress failed to support Hunter, it did pass the **Second Confiscation Act** and the **Militia Act of 1862**, which authorized President Lincoln to enlist black men. In Louisiana that fall, two regiments of free black men, the Native Guards, were accepted for federal service, and General Benjamin Butler organized them into the Corps d'Afrique. General Rufus Saxton gained the approval of Secretary of War Edwin Stanton to revive Hunter's dispersed regiment and to recall the company that had been sent to St. Simon's Island.

As commander, Saxton appointed Thomas Wentworth Higginson. Higginson was an ardent white abolitionist, one of the Secret Six who had provided financial support for John Brown's raid on Harpers Ferry. Higginson was determined not merely to end slavery but to prove that black people were equal to white people, a proposition most white people regarded as preposterous. Disposing of the unit's gaudy red trousers, Higginson set out to mold this regiment of mostly former slaves into an effective fighting force. On Emancipation Day, January 1, 1863, near

PROFILE ❖ Elizabeth Keckley

Born a slave in 1818, Elizabeth Keckley became a skilled dressmaker for First Lady Mary Todd Lincoln. After President Lincoln's assassination, Keckley wrote one of the first personal accounts of life inside the Lincoln White House, *Behind the Scenes: Or Thirty Years a Slave and Four Years in the White House.*

Elizabeth Keckley had experienced the exploitation and degradation common to thousands of slave women. She was born in Dinwiddie Court House, Virginia, and spent her childhood as a slave of the Burwell family.

During adolescence, she was "loaned" to a North Carolina slave owner and beaten and eventually raped. She was later returned to one of the Burwell daughters, who took Elizabeth and her son George to St. Louis. She became an increasingly skilled dressmaker. As a proficient seamstress, Keckley was able to purchase herself and her son for $1,200. She learned to read and write. In 1860 she moved to Washington and attracted a prosperous clientele that included the wives of prominent politicians, such as Varina Davis, the wife of Mississippi senator Jefferson Davis, soon to be president of the Confederacy.

Shortly after the Lincolns arrived in Washington, Keckley began making dresses for the First Lady and became Mrs. Lincoln's confidante and traveling companion. Keckley helped convert Mrs. Lincoln, whose family owned slaves in Kentucky, to strong antislavery views. With Mrs. Lincoln's assistance, Elizabeth Keckley founded the Contraband Relief Association to provide aid to former slaves in Washington.

Elizabeth Keckley spent the rest of her life living off the pension from her son's service as a Union soldier. She died in Washington in 1907 at the Home for Destitute Women and Children, which she had helped found years earlier.

Beaufort, South Carolina, the First South Carolina Volunteer Regiment was inducted into the U.S. Army.

A month later, the Second South Carolina Volunteers began enrolling ex-slaves, many from Georgia and Florida. James Montgomery, another former financial supporter of John Brown, commanded them. Montgomery was determined that the regiment would wipe out all vestiges of slavery, especially the homes, plantations, and personal possessions of families who owned slaves. But like Hunter, Montgomery found that many former slaves were reluctant to volunteer for military service, so he also used force to recruit them. He concluded that black men responded to the call to arms much the way white men did, except black men were less likely to desert once they joined the army:

> Finding it somewhat difficult to induce Negroes to enlist, we resolved to the draft. The negroes reindicate their claim to humanity by shirking the draft in every possible way; acting exactly like white men under similar circumstances. . . . The only difference that I notice is, the negro, after being drafted does not desert; but once dressed in the uniform with arms in his hands he feels himself a man; and acts like one.

The 54th Massachusetts Regiment

While ex-slaves joined the Union ranks in South Carolina, free black men in the North enlisted in what would become the most famous black unit, the 54th Massachusetts Regiment. In January 1863 governor of Massachusetts John A. Andrew received permission from Secretary of War Stanton to raise a black regiment, but because few black men lived in Massachusetts, Andrew asked prominent black men across the North for help. The **Black Committee**—as it became known—included Frederick Douglass, Martin Delany, Charles Remond, and Henry Highland Garnet.

These black leaders were convinced that by serving in the military, black men would prove they deserved to be treated as equals and had earned the right to be citizens. Frederick Douglass put it succinctly: "Once let the black man get upon his person the brass letters, U.S.; let him get an eagle on his button, and a musket on his shoulder and bullets in his pocket, and there is no power on earth which can deny that he has earned the right to citizenship." Two of Douglass's sons, Charles and Lewis, joined the 54th.

Lincoln, who had opposed emancipation and resisted enlisting black troops, became an enthusiastic supporter of black men in the Union Army. Writing to Andrew Johnson, who was the Union military governor of Tennessee, Lincoln perhaps overoptimistically predicted that "The bare sight of fifty thousand armed, and drilled black soldiers on the banks of the Mississippi, would end the rebellion at once. And who doubts that we can present that sight, if we but take hold in earnest."

▶▶ **Documents**

11-6 *Retaliation in Camp, 1864*
In May 1864, George W. Hatton, sergeant in Company C, First Regiment, United States Colored Troops, and his Union regiment were camped close to Jamestown, Virginia. Hatton had been a slave and now his unit was waiting in an area where some of the soldiers had once toiled as slaves. Hatton witnessed a scene of punishment and revenge and described what he saw in an article published in *The Christian Recorder* on May 28, 1864.

11-8 *Paul Laurence Dunbar–The Colored Soldiers (1896)*
As an African-American writer of the Reconstruction period, Paul Laurence Dunbar used the poetic resonance of folk life and culture in many of his best-known poems. His first book of poems, *Oak and Ivy* (1893) garnered him attention as a promising poet. His poems, such as "Sympathy" and "The Colored Soldiers," emphasize the African-American struggle for dignity and equality.

Governor Andrew selected twenty-five-year-old Robert Gould Shaw to command the 54th Massachusetts Regiment. Shaw was a Harvard graduate from a prominent Massachusetts family, and he had already been wounded at the battle at Antietam. Although not an active abolitionist, he opposed slavery and was determined to prove that black men would fight well. The men the Black Committee recruited came from most of the northern states. Their average age was around twenty-five and virtually all of them were literate. Only one of them had grown up in a slave state. As the ranks of the 54th filled, the 55th Massachusetts Regiment and the all-black 5th Massachusetts Cavalry Regiment were also formed.

Black Soldiers Confront Discrimination

Many white Northerners were willing to accept neither the presence of black troops nor the idea that black men could endure combat. That black troops would serve in separate, all-black units was accepted as a matter of course. No one seriously proposed to integrate black men into previously all-white regiments. In 1863 the War Department created the Bureau of

This young man is Jackson. In the first photo he is shown as a slave who worked as a servant in the Confederate Army. In the second photo he has been freed and has joined the U.S. Colored Troops as a drummer.

Colored Troops, and the Union Army remained segregated throughout the war. The only exception was the officers of the black regiments.

Almost all black troops had white officers. Yet many white officers, convinced their military record would be tainted by such service, refused to command black troops. Others believed black men simply could not be trained for combat. Even those white officers who were willing to command black troops sometimes regarded their men as suited only for work or fatigue duty. When the 110th U.S. Colored Infantry joined General William Tecumseh Sherman's army on its march through Georgia and South Carolina in 1864 and 1865, Sherman kept the black men out of combat.

Black soldiers were paid less than white soldiers. Based on the assumption that black troops would be used almost exclusively for construction, transportation, cooking, and burial details, and not for fighting, the War Department authorized a lower pay scale for them. A white private earned $13 per month; a black private earned $10 per month. This demoralized black soldiers, particularly after they had shown they were more than capable of fighting.

The 54th Massachusetts Regiment refused to accept their pay until they received equal pay. To take no compensation was an enormous sacrifice for men who had wives, children, and families to support. For some, it was more than a monetary loss. Sergeant William Walker insisted—despite orders—that the men in his company take no pay until they received equal pay. He was charged with mutiny, convicted, and shot.

The pay issue festered in Congress for nearly two years. Finally, near the end of the war, Congress enacted a compromise, but many black soldiers remained dissatisfied. The law equalized pay between black and white troops, but made it retroactive only to January 1, 1864—except for black men who had never been slaves. The thousands of black men who had been slaves and had joined the military before January 1, 1864, would not be entitled to equal pay for the entire period of their service.

Black Men in Combat

Once black men put on the Union uniform, they took part in almost every battle that was fought during the rest of the Civil War. Black troops not only faced an enemy dedicated to the belief that the proper place of black people was in slavery, but they also confronted doubts about their fighting abilities among white Northerners. Yet by war's end, black units had suffered disproportionately more casualties than white units.

In October 1862 the first black unit went into combat in Missouri. James H. Lane, a white Free-Soiler, recruited five hundred black men in Kansas. Most were runaway slaves from Missouri and Arkansas. After some hasty training, they advanced against a Confederate position at Island Mountain. The black troops held off an attack until

reinforcements arrived, and the Confederates were pushed back. Soon thereafter, the black unit became the First Kansas Colored Infantry.

On July 17, 1863, at Honey Springs in Indian territory (now Oklahoma), the Kansas soldiers attacked a Confederate force composed of white Texans and Cherokee Indians. After an intense twenty-minute battle, the black troops broke through the southern line and won a victory, capturing the colors of a Texas regiment.

In January 1863 Thomas Wentworth Higginson led the First South Carolina Volunteers on raids on the Georgia and Florida coasts. At one point, they were surrounded at night by Confederate cavalry but managed to fight their way out and escape.

On June 3, 1863, the 54th Massachusetts Regiment arrived in South Carolina and joined the raids in Georgia. Other raids in the Carolina low country devastated rice plantations and liberated hundreds of slaves.

The Assault on Battery Wagner

Since the Confederate capture of Fort Sumter in Charleston harbor that began the Civil War, Union leaders had been determined to retake the fort and occupy nearby Charleston—the heart of secession. In 1863 Union commanders began a combined land and sea offensive to seize the fort. But **Battery Wagner**, a heavily fortified installation on the northern tip of Morris Island, guarded the entrance to the harbor.

On the evening of July 18, 1863, more than six hundred black men attacked heavily fortified Battery Wagner on Morris Island near the southern approach to Charleston harbor.

Frustrated in their initial efforts to enter the harbor, Major General Quincy A. Gilmore and Rear Admiral John Dahlgren decided on a full-scale assault on Wagner. After an unsuccessful attack by white troops, Colonel Shaw volunteered to lead the 54th in a second attack on the battery.

To improve the Union's chances, artillery fired more than nine thousand shells on Wagner on July 18, 1863. Everyone but the fort's Confederate defenders was convinced that no one could survive the bombardment. In fact, only eight of the 1,620 defenders had been killed.

At sunset, 650 men of the first brigade of the 54th prepared to lead more than 5,000 Union troops in storming the battery. The regiment was tired and hungry but eager for the assault. Colonel Shaw offered brief words of encouragement to his troops:

Now I want you to prove yourselves men.

At 7:45 P.M., the 54th charged and was met by heavy rifle and artillery fire. Within minutes, the sand was littered with injured and dying men. Sergeant Major Lewis Douglass (the son of Frederick Douglass) was among those who took part. The 54th reached the walls only to be thrown back in hand-to-hand combat. Shaw was killed.

Sergeant Major William H. Carney, though wounded four times, saved the regiment's flags. Thirty-seven years later, in May 1900, he was awarded the Congressional Medal of Honor for his gallantry that night.

Although white troops fought to support the 54th, the attack could not be sustained, and the battle was over by 1 A.M. But within days, the courage of the 54th was known across the North, putting to rest—for a time—the myth that black men lacked the nerve to fight.

The day after the attack, Shaw and twenty of his men were buried in a trench outside Wagner. Several wounded men had drowned when the tide came in.

Altogether 246 black and white men were killed, 890 were wounded, and 391 were taken prisoner. Forty-two percent of the men of the 54th were killed or injured, and 80 men were taken prisoner.

Union forces never took Wagner. The Confederates abandoned Charleston as the war was ending in February 1865. Black Union troops—the 21st U.S. Colored Infantry and the 55th Massachusetts Regiment—occupied the city. Years later Charles Crowley recalled the scene.

Never, while memory holds power to retain anything, shall I forget the thrilling strain of music of the Union, as sung by our sable soldiers when marching up Meeting Street with the battle stained banners flapping in the breeze.

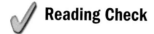 **Reading Check** What led to the formation of the 54th Massachusetts Regiment?

▶ **Reading Check**

In January 1863 John A. Andrew, governor of Massachusetts, was given permission to form a black regiment. Because so few black men lived in Massachusetts, Andrew turned to a group of prominent black men, known as the Black Committee, for help. As a result of their efforts, the 54th Massachusetts Regiment and two other regiments were formed.

Poised with his rifle, this African-American soldier was a member of the Twenty-first U.S. Colored Infantry at the battle of Dutch Gap in Virginia in August, 1864.

reportedly murdered several Confederate prisoners. Captain Charles Francis Adams Jr. reported, "The darkies fought ferociously. . . . If they murdered prisoners, as I hear they did . . . they can hardly be blamed."

Union commanders in the field also retaliated for the Confederate treatment of captured black troops. Captured black men were virtually enslaved and forced to work at Richmond and Charleston on Confederate fortifications that were under Union attack. Union offi-

PROFILE ❖ Harriet Tubman

Long before her death in 1913, Harriet Tubman had achieved legendary status. She was personally responsible for freeing more slaves than any other individual in American history.

Harriet Tubman was born in 1821 or 1822 on Maryland's eastern shore, one of eleven slave children of Harriet Greene and Benjamin Ross. In 1849 she married John Tubman, a free black man. Fearing that she would be sold following the death of her owner, she escaped to Pennsylvania. Her husband refused to go with her. He married another woman and died shortly after the Civil War.

Tubman—like Sojourner Truth—never learned to read or write. She had, however, a deep reservoir of religious faith that sustained her and helped inspire her to return to slave states again and again to free people held in bondage. She made at least fifteen trips south in ten years as a conductor on the Underground Railroad. She led between 70 and 80 people to freedom on 14 trips to Maryland's Eastern Shore between 1849 and 1860. Among them were her sister, her sister's two children, and her parents. Tubman also assisted as many as 200 other people escape slavery. She never lost a passenger.

Aware that she had a hefty reward on her head, Tubman devised detailed plans and elaborate disguises to elude capture. She feigned insanity, she pretended to be feeble, she forged passes, and she acquired real railroad tickets. She also packed a gun, as much to goad any of her charges whose courage might waver as to protect herself.

In 1862, during the Civil War, Tubman journeyed to the South Carolina low country where Union military forces had established a base. She worked as a nurse, cook, scout, and liberator. She made her way up the Combahee River and helped more than seven hundred slaves to freedom. She was on Morris Island in 1863 when the 54th Massachusetts Regiment attacked Battery Wagner.

After the war, she married Nelson Davis, a Union veteran, who died in 1888. She and several of her supporters spent years in a determined effort to gain her federal pension. They finally succeeded in securing an award of $20 a month that was based on her husband's military service rather than her contributions to the Union cause.

Tubman was active in the women's rights movement of the late nineteenth century. She attended several women's rights conventions. She also worked to help elderly ex-slaves who faced insecurity and uncertainty after emancipation. She bought a home in Auburn, New York, and eventually died there.

Many Americans talk about freedom, but not many have done as much to make it a reality for as many people as did Harriet Tubman.

Tubman

cers did the same and put Confederate prisoners to work on Union installations that were under fire. Aware they were not likely to be treated as well as white soldiers if they were captured, black men often fought desperately.

Liberators, Spies, and Guides

Besides serving as soldiers and sailors, black men and women aided themselves and the Union cause as liberators, spies, guides, and messengers. At about 3 A.M. on May 13, 1862, Robert Smalls, a twenty-three-year-old slave, fired the boiler on *The Planter*, a Confederate supply ship moored in Charleston harbor. With the aid of seven black crewmen, Smalls sailed *The Planter* past Confederate fortifications, including Fort Sumter, to the Union fleet outside the harbor and to freedom. Smalls liberated himself and fifteen other slaves, including the families of several crewmen and his own wife, daughter, and son.

In 1863 Harriet Tubman organized a spy ring in the South Carolina low country. In cooperation with the all-black Second South Carolina Volunteer Regiment, she helped organize an expedition that destroyed plantations and freed nearly eight hundred slaves, many of whom joined the Union Army.

In Richmond in 1864, slaves helped more than one hundred escaped Union prisoners of war. Other slaves drew sketches and maps of Confederate fortifications. Others warned Union forces about troop movements. A black couple near Fredericksburg, Virginia, cleverly transmitted military intelligence to Union general Joseph Hooker. The woman washed laundry for a Confederate officer. She hung shirts and blankets in patterns that conveyed information to her husband, who was a cook and groom for Union troops and relayed the information to Union officers.

Mary Elizabeth Bowser was a former slave who worked as a servant at the Confederate White House in Richmond. She overheard conversations by President Jefferson Davis and his subordinates, and—because she was literate—she covertly examined Confederate correspondence. She relayed the information to Union agents until the Confederates became suspicious. Bowser and slave Jim Pemberton managed to flee after unsuccessfully trying to burn down the mansion to distract their pursuers.

In Virginia's Shenandoah Valley, slave John Henry Woodson was a guide for Union general Philip H. Sheridan's cavalry in 1864 and 1865. Woodson was the father of Carter G. Woodson, who would become the "father" of black history in the twentieth century.

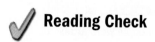 **Reading Check** Besides being soldiers, what other roles did African Americans play in the Union war effort?

Robert Smalls became a successful Republican politician in South Carolina in the decades following the Civil War.

▶ **Living Words Audio Clip**

Track 13 *Harriet Tubman*; read by Jean Brannon

▶ **Retracing the Odyssey**

Auburn, New York: Harriet Tubman Museum. In 1896, the famed liberator of slaves bought this property and made it her home. She died here in 1913. The African Methodist Episcopal Zion Church operates the house as a museum. Harriet Tubman is buried nearby at Fort Hill Cemetery.

▶ **Reading Check**

Black men and women served the Union cause in a variety of ways. They liberated slaves. They acted as spies. Blacks also helped guide Union troops.

▶ **Guide to Reading/Key Terms**

For answers, see the *Teacher's Resource Manual.*

▶ **Document**

11-4 *"If It Were Not for My Trust in Christ I Do Not Know How I Could Have Endured It":* *Testimony from Victims of New York's Draft Riots, July 1863*

Discontented Irish workers took to the streets of New York to protest the draft between July 13 and 16, 1863. Enraged by the prospect of fighting for emancipation as well as the threat of increasing competition from free blacks for jobs, Irishmen rioted for four days. Stunned by the violence, a handful of Wall Street businessmen sought to aid the devastated black community. The Committee of Merchants for the Relief of Colored People Suffering from the Late Riots collected money, distributed funds, and recorded this testimony.

Section 6

Opposition to Black People

The New York City Draft Riot

No matter how well black men fought, no matter how much individual black women contributed, and no matter how many people—black and white—died "to make men free," many white Northerners, both civilian and military, remained bitter and often violently hostile to black people. They used intimidation, threats, and terror to injure and kill people of color.

Irish Catholic Americans, themselves held in contempt by prosperous white Protestants, indulged in an orgy of violence in New York City in July 1863. The **New York draft riot** arose from racial, religious, and class antagonisms. Poor, unskilled Irish workers and other white Northerners were convinced by leading Democrats, including New York governor Horatio Seymour, that the war had become a crusade to benefit black people.

The violence began when federal officials prepared to select the first men to be drafted by the Union for military service. An enraged mob made up mostly of Irish men attacked the draft offices and any unfortunate black people who were in the vicinity. Many of the Irish men were angry because black men had replaced striking Irish stevedores on the

During the draft riot in New York City in July 1863, black people were attacked, beaten, and killed. A mob lynched this black man near Clarkson Street. *Illustrated London News,* August 8, 1863.

city's wharves the month before and because rich white Northerners could purchase an exemption from the draft.

The riot went on for four days. The poorly trained city police could not control it. Black people were beaten and lynched. The Colored Orphan Asylum was burned to the ground, although the children had already fled. The mob attacked businesses that employed black people. Protestant churches were burned. Rioters set fire to Horace Greeley's New York *Tribune*. The houses of Republicans and abolitionists were attacked and destroyed. The violence and destruction did not end until the U.S. Army arrived. Soldiers who had been fighting Confederates at Gettysburg two weeks earlier found themselves firing on New York rioters.

Refugees

Throughout the war, black people took advantage of the hostilities to free themselves. It was not easy. Confederate authorities did not hesitate to reenslave or even execute black people who sought freedom.

As Union armies plunged deep into the Confederacy in 1863 and 1864, thousands of black people liberated themselves and became refugees. When General William Tecumseh Sherman's army of 60,000 troops laid waste to Georgia in 1864, an estimated 10,000 former slaves followed his troops to Savannah, although they lacked adequate food, clothing, and housing. Sherman did not like black people, and his troops tried with little success to discourage the refugees. As one elderly black couple prepared to leave a plantation, Union soldiers as well as their master urged them to remain. They declined in no uncertain terms. "We must go, freedom is as sweet to us as it is to you."

Black People and the Confederacy

As the war went on, the demand for more troops and laborers in the Confederacy increased. Slave owners were first asked and then compelled to contribute their slave laborers to the war effort. In July 1861 the Confederate Congress required the registration and enrollment of free black people for military labor. In the summer of 1862 the Virginia legislature authorized the **impressment** of 10,000 slaves between the ages of eighteen and forty-five for up to sixty days. The owners would receive $16 per month per slave.

The most important factory in the South was the Tredegar Iron Works in Richmond. During the war, more than twelve hundred slaves and free black men worked there in every capacity manufacturing artillery, locomotives, nails, and much more. Other black men across the South loaded and unloaded ships, worked for railroads, and labored in salt works.

In South Carolina in 1863, Confederate officials appealed to slave owners to provide 2,500 slaves to help fortify Charleston. The owners

offered fewer than 1,000. During the Union bombardment of Fort Sumter, 500 slaves were employed in the difficult, dirty, and dangerous work of building and rebuilding the fort. Slaves were even forced into combat. Two Virginia slaves who were compelled to load and fire Confederate cannons near Yorktown were shot and killed.

Many white Southerners who did not own slaves were infuriated when the Confederate **conscription law** in 1862 exempted men who owned twenty or more slaves from military service. This law, later reduced to fifteen, meant that poor white men were drafted while wealthier planters remained home, presumably to supervise and discipline their slaves. One Mississippi soldier deserted the Confederate Army, claiming he "did not propose to fight for the rich men while they were home having a good time." Although the law was widely criticized, planters—always a small percentage of the white southern population—dominated the Confederate government and would not permit the repeal of the exemption.

Confederates Enslave Free Black People

After Lincoln's Emancipation Proclamation, Confederate president Jefferson Davis issued a counterproclamation in February 1863. It declared that free people would be enslaved, "all free negroes within the limits of the Southern Confederacy shall be placed on the slave status, and be deemed to be chattels . . . forever." This directive was not widely enforced. Davis, however, went on to order Confederate armies that invaded Union states to capture free black people in the North and enslave them. "All negroes who shall be taken in any of the States in which slavery does not now exist, in the progress of our arms, shall be adjudged, immediately after their capture, to occupy slave status."

Several hundred northern black people were taken south after Confederate forces invaded Pennsylvania in 1863 and fought at Gettysburg. Robert E. Lee's Army of Northern Virginia at Greensburg, Pennsylvania, captured at least fifty black people. A southern victory in the Civil War could conceivably have led to the enslavement of more than 300,000 free black residents of the Confederate States.

Black Confederates

Most of the labor black people did for the Confederacy was involuntary. A few free black men and women offered their services to the southern cause. In Lynchburg, Virginia, in the spring of 1861, seventy free black people volunteered "to act in whatever capacity may be assigned them." In Memphis in the fall, several hundred black residents cheered for Jefferson Davis and sang patriotic songs. These demonstrations of black support were made early in the conflict before the war became a crusade against slavery.

Black troops were among the first Union military forces to "liberate" the devastated city of Charleston, South Carolina, in the waning weeks of the Civil War.

In Virginia in 1861, impressment laws, like those applying to slaves, compelled free black men to work on Confederate defenses around Richmond and Petersburg. Months before the war, South Carolina considered forcing its free black population to choose between enslavement and exile. The legislature rejected the proposal, but it terrified the state's free black people. Many people of color there had been free for generations. When the war came, many were willing to demonstrate their devotion to the South in a desperate attempt to gain white acceptance before they lost their freedom and property. In early 1861 eighty-two free black men in Charleston petitioned Governor Francis W. Pickens "to be assigned any service where we can be useful." Pickens rejected the petition, but white South Carolinians were pleased at this show of loyalty.

White southern leaders generally ignored offers of free black support unless it was for menial labor. But in Charleston, when the city was under siege between 1863 and 1865, black and white residents were grateful that volunteer fire brigades composed of free black men turned out repeatedly to fight fires caused by Union artillery.

Other black men contributed in different ways to the Confederate military effort. Black musicians in Virginia played for Confederate regiments and received the same pay as white musicians. Well-to-do white men often took their slaves as personal servants when they went off to war. The servants cooked, cleaned uniforms, cared for weapons, maintained horses, and even provided entertainment. Being the personal servant for a soldier was hard and sometimes dangerous work. Those close to combat could be killed or injured. One father warned his son not to take Sam, a valuable slave, into battle. "I write to tell you not to let Sam go into the fight with you. Keep him in the rear. . . ." The father evidently placed a higher value on the slave, "worth a thousand dollars," than on his son.

Black Men Fighting for the South

Approximately 144,000 black men from the southern states fought with the Union Army. Most had been slaves. A much, much smaller number of black men did fight for the Confederacy. White New York troops claimed to have encountered about seven hundred armed black men in late 1861 near Newport News, Virginia. In 1862 a black Confederate sharpshooter positioned himself in a chimney and shot several Union soldiers before he was finally killed. Fifty black men served as pickets for the Confederates along the Rappahannock River in Virginia in 1863.

Some black civilians supported the war effort and stood to profit if the South won. The free black Ellison family grew corn, sweet potatoes, peas, sorghum, and beans to feed Confederate troops on the family plantation. The Ellisons had earned nearly $1,000 by 1863. By 1865 they had paid almost $5,000 in taxes to the Confederacy, nearly one-fifth of their total income. At war's end, the eighty slaves the Ellisons owned—worth approximately $100,000—were free people (see Chapter 6). Other black Southerners also suffered economically from the Confederate defeat. Richard Mack, a South Carolina slave, went off to war as a personal servant. After his master died, he became an orderly for another Confederate officer. He worked hard and accumulated a large sum in Confederate currency. He later joked, "If we had won, I would be rich."

White Southerners effusively praised the few black people who actively supported the South. Several states awarded pensions to black men who served in the war and survived. Henry Clay Lightfoot was a slave in Culpeper, Virginia, who went to war as a body servant of Captain William Holcomb. After the war, he bought a house, raised a family, and was elected to the Culpeper town council. He collected a pension from Virginia, and when he died in 1931, the United Daughters of the Confederacy draped his coffin in a Confederate flag.

The Confederate Debate on Black Troops

By late 1863 and 1864, prospects for the Confederacy had become grim. The Union naval blockade of southern ports had become increasingly effective, and the likelihood of British aid had all but vanished. Confederate armies suffered crushing defeats at Vicksburg and Gettysburg in 1863 and absorbed terrible losses in Tennessee, Georgia, and Virginia in 1864.

As defeat loomed, some white Southerners began to discuss the possibility of arming black men. Several southern newspapers advocated it. In September 1863 the Montgomery (Alabama) *Weekly Mail* admitted black troops had now become necessary to save the white South:

> We are forced by the necessity of our condition—by the insolence and barbarity of the enemy, by his revengeful and demoniacal spirit—to take a step which is revolting to every sentiment of pride, and to every principle that governed our institutions before the war. But the war has made great changes, and we must meet those changes, for the sake of preserving our very existence. It is a matter of necessity, therefore, that we should use every means within our reach to defeat the enemy. One of these, and the only one which will checkmate him, is the employment of negroes in the military service of the Confederacy.

In early 1864 Confederate general Patrick Cleburne recommended enlisting slaves and promising them their freedom if they remained loyal to the Confederacy. Cleburne argued that this policy would gain recognition and aid from Great Britain and would disrupt Union military efforts to recruit black Southerners. Yet most white Southerners considered arming slaves and free black men an appalling prospect. Jefferson Davis ordered military officers, including Cleburne, to cease discussing the issue.

Most white Southerners were convinced that to arm slaves and put black men in gray uniforms defied the assumptions on which southern society was based. Black people were inferior, and their proper status was to be slaves. It was absurd to contemplate black people as soldiers and as free people. Georgia politician Howell Cobb explained that slaves could not be armed. "If slaves will make good soldiers our whole theory of slavery is wrong."

The Civil War for white Southerners was a war to prevent the abolition of slavery. Now white southern voices were proposing abolition to preserve the southern nation. North Carolina senator Robert M. T. Hunter opposed any attempt to enlist slaves and free them.

> If we are right in passing this measure we were wrong in denying to the old government the right to interfere with the institution of slavery and to emancipate slaves. Besides, if we offer slaves their freedom . . . we confess that we were insincere, were hypocritical, in asserting that slavery was the best state for the negroes themselves.

Lee Enlists Black Troops

Nevertheless, as the military situation deteriorated, the South moved toward employing black troops. In November 1864 Virginia governor William Smith enthusiastically supported the idea.

> There is not a man that would not cheerfully put the negro in the Army rather than become a slave himself. . . . Standing before God and my country, I do not hesitate to say that I would arm such portion of our able-bodied slaves population as may be necessary.

In February 1865 Jefferson Davis and the Confederate cabinet conceded, "We are reduced to choosing whether the negroes shall fight for us or against us."

The opinion of General Robert E. Lee was critical to determining whether the Confederacy would decide to arm black men. No Southerner was more revered and respected. Lee announced in February 1865 that he favored both enrolling and emancipating black troops. "My own opinion is that we should employ them without delay." He believed their service as slaves would make them capable soldiers.

> They possess the physical qualities in an eminent degree. Long habits of obedience and subordination, coupled with moral influence which in our country the white man possesses over the black, furnish an excellent foundation for that discipline which is the best guarantee of military efficiency.

Less than a month later in March 1865, the Confederate Congress voted to enlist 300,000 black men. They would receive the same pay, equipment, and supplies as white soldiers. But those who were slaves would not be freed unless their owner consented and the state where they served agreed to their emancipation.

It was a desperate measure by a nearly defeated government and did not affect the outcome of the conflict. Before the war ended in April, authorities in Virginia managed to recruit some black men and send a few into combat. By the end of March, one company of thirty-five black men—twelve free black men and twenty-three slaves—was organized. On April 4, 1865, Union troops attacked Confederate supply wagons that the black troops were guarding in Amelia County. Less than a week later, Lee surrendered to Grant at Appomattox Court House, and the Civil War ended.

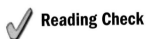 **Reading Check** Why did southern whites consider using black soldiers in the Confederate army?

▶ **Reading Check**

By late 1863, the Confederates faced a grim military situation. With defeat looming, some Confederate leaders suggested that the South enlist black men as soldiers. General Lee finally authorized this step in February 1865, far too late to affect the outcome of the war.

▶ **Document**

11-3 *President Abraham Lincoln Delivers the Gettsyburg Address in 1863*

Reading Biographies and Autobiographies

Biographies and autobiographies are two major sources of evidence about a historical period. A biography is an account of a person's life written by someone else; it is a secondary source. An autobiography, an account of a person's life written by that person, is a primary source. Both offer clues as to what society was like at the time the person lived; they reveal living conditions, people's reactions to those conditions and to events, and prevailing attitudes and values. While both must be evaluated for reliability and bias, autobiographies are especially likely to show the subject in a good light.

The excerpt below is from Elizabeth Keckley's biography, written in 1868. In this passage, she describes her impressions of freedmen and freedwomen and their experience moving North.

LEARN THE SKILL

Use the following steps when you read biographies and autobiographies:

1. **Identify the kind of account and the subject of the profile.** Determine not only who the subject is but also whether the profile covers all or part of the subject's life. If it is a biography, is it by someone who knew or interviewed the subject, or by someone relying on other sources?

2. **Analyze the account's reliability as historical evidence.** Evaluate these accounts as you would other sources: What is the writer's purpose? How objective is the writer? Does the account reveal only certain facts, or does it present some facts in a misleading way?

3. **Search for clues that tell what the historical period was like.** Look for facts about the period, but also for indications of how the subject's or writer's values and assumptions differ from current views.

PRACTICE THE SKILL

Answer the following questions:

1. **(a)** Is the excerpt from an autobiography or a biography? How can you tell? **(b)** What events are Keckley's focus in this part of her book?

SOME of the freedmen and freedwomen had exaggerated ideas of liberty. To them it was a beautiful vision, a land of sunshine, rest, and glorious promise. They flocked to Washington, and since their extravagant hopes were not realized, it was but natural that many of them should bitterly feel their disappointment. The colored people are wedded to associations, and when you destroy these you destroy half of the happiness of their lives. They make a home, and are so fond of it that they prefer it, squalid though it be, to the comparative ease and luxury of a shifting, roaming life. Well, the emancipated slaves, in coming North, left old associations behind them, and the love for the past was so strong that they could not find much beauty in the new life so suddenly opened to them. Thousands of the disappointed, huddled together in camps, fretted and pined like children for the "good old times." In visiting them in the interests of the Relief Society of which I was president, they would crowd around me with pitiful stories of distress. Often I heard them declare that they would rather go back to slavery in the South, and be with their old masters, than to enjoy the freedom of the North. I believe they were sincere in these declarations, because dependence had become a part of their second nature, and independence brought with it the cares and vexations of poverty.

—Elizabeth Keckley, *Behind the Scenes, or, Thirty Years a Slave, and Four Years in the White House*, 1868

2. **(a)** How well acquainted is the writer with the facts she describes? **(b)** Are there other historical sources that could support or challenge her description and interpretation of these events? Explain.

3. **(a)** What do you learn about Keckley from this excerpt? **(b)** What can you learn about the time period from Keckley's excerpt? **(c)** What can you learn about freedmen and freedwomen?

▶ **Skills for Life**

For answers, see *Teacher's Resource Manual.*

Chapter Timeline

AFRICAN-AMERICAN EVENTS   **NATIONAL EVENTS**

1860

November 1860
Abraham Lincoln wins the presidential election

December 1860
South Carolina secedes from the Union

1861

April–May 1861
Black men volunteer for military service and are rejected

August 1861
First Confiscation Act

February 1861
The Confederate States of America is formed

March 1861
Lincoln inaugurated

April 1861
The firing on Fort Sumter begins the Civil War

November 1861
Union military forces capture the Sea Islands and coastal areas of South Carolina and Georgia

1862

May 1862
Robert Smalls escapes with *The Planter* and sixteen slaves

May–August 1862
The First South Carolina Volunteers, an all-black regiment, forms

September 1862
Lincoln announces the Preliminary Emancipation Proclamation

October 1862
Black troops see combat for the first time in Missouri

September 1862
Battle of Antietam is fought

1863

January 1, 1863
Lincoln issues the Emancipation Proclamation

January–March 1863
Troops recruited for the 54th and the 55th Massachusetts Regiments

June 1863
Battle of Milliken's Bend

July 1863
Assault on Battery Wagner; New York City draft riots; Battle at Honey Springs

March 1863
The U.S. government enacts a Conscription Act

July 1863
Battles of Vicksburg and Gettysburg

1864

February 1864
Battle at Olustee

April 1864
Fort Pillow Massacre

November 1864
Lincoln is reelected

November–December 1864
Sherman makes his march to the sea

1865

February 1865
Black troops lead the occupation of Charleston

March 1865
Confederate Congress approves the enlistment of black men

December 1865
Thirteenth Amendment ratified

February 1865
Charleston falls

March 1865
Richmond falls

April 1865
Lee surrenders at Appomatox; Lincoln is assassinated

Chapter Review and Assessment

SUMMARY

Section 1 The Civil War Begins, p. 351

▶ When the Civil War began in 1861, Lincoln's overriding aim was to preserve the Union. All other policies, including policies directed at slavery, were subordinate to that goal.

▶ Blacks responded to the outbreak of war by volunteering to fight on the Union side. Such offers were rejected.

▶ Union policies toward escaped slaves reflected the ambiguity of the Union position.

▶ Its leaders were attempting to fight a war against the South without fighting a war against slavery.

Section 2 Lincoln and Emancipation, p. 354

▶ Lincoln began the war as an advocate of compensated emancipation and colonization.

▶ As the war dragged on, he began to consider the abolition of slavery as a tactic for achieving military victory.

▶ Lincoln continued to advocate colonization, a policy rejected by most African Americans.

Section 3 Liberation, p. 358

▶ On September 22, 1862 Lincoln issued a Proclamation declaring that slaves residing in states still in rebellion on January 1, 1863, would be freed.

▶ On January 1, 1863, he followed through and issued the Emancipation Proclamation.

▶ The Proclamation produced a political backlash against the president. Nonetheless, as Lincoln had hoped, it succeeded in undermining the South's position and contributing to Union victory.

Section 4 Black Men Fight for the Union, p. 362

▶ The Emancipation Proclamation cleared the way for the enlistment of black troops in the Union Army.

▶ The actual recruitment and deployment of black troops did not proceed smoothly or logically.

▶ Black men served before emancipation, notably in the South Carolina Volunteer Regiments.

▶ After emancipation additional units were formed, most famously the 54th Massachusetts Regiment.

▶ Despite considerable discrimination and an abiding belief among many whites that blacks would not make good combat soldiers, African Americans participated in every major battle of the war after emancipation.

Section 5 The Confederate Reaction to Black Soldiers, p. 372

▶ Confederate leaders and soldiers did not recognize black men as legitimate soldiers, going so far as to order the execution of captured black soldiers.

▶ Union leaders promised to retaliate for mistreatment of black soldiers in General Order 11.

▶ Despite the risks, blacks served the Union cause in a variety of ways, acting as soldiers, liberators, spies, and guides.

Section 6 Opposition to Black People, p. 376

▶ Despite their contributions to the war effort, many white Northerners remained resentful and even hostile to African Americans.

▶ The New York City Draft Riots attest to the depth and violence of this hostility.

▶ Throughout the war, slaves took advantage of the fighting to free themselves, creating large numbers of refugees.

▶ The Confederacy relied on the labor of black people to sustain its war effort.

▶ Towards the end of the war, consideration was given to employing black soldiers.

▶ The Confederate Congress did, in fact, vote to authorize the enlistment of black soldiers in March 1865, but by then defeat was inevitable.

REVIEWING KEY TERMS

Write a brief explanation of the following terms.

1. Confederacy, p. 351
2. contraband, p. 353
3. First Confiscation Act, p. 353
4. compensated emancipation, p. 354
5. Preliminary Emancipation Proclamation, p. 358
6. Emancipation Proclamation, p. 359
7. First South Carolina Volunteers, p. 363
8. Second Confiscation Act, p. 364
9. Militia Act of 1862, p. 364

REVIEWING MAIN IDEAS

15. How did the Union's purposes in the Civil War change between 1861 and 1865? What accounts for those changes?

16. How did policies of the Confederate government toward slaves change during the Civil War? What were those changes and when and why did they occur?

17. When the Civil War began, why did northern black men volunteer to serve in the Union army if the war had not yet become a war to end slavery?

18. To what extent did Abraham Lincoln's policies and attitudes toward black people change during the Civil War? Does Lincoln deserve credit as "the Great Emancipator"? Why or why not?

19. What was the purpose of the Emancipation Proclamation? Why was it issued? Exactly what did it accomplish?

20. What did black men and women contribute to the Union war effort? Was it in their interests to participate in the Civil War? Why or why not?

21. Why did at least some black people support the southern states and the Confederacy during the Civil War?

22. Was the result of the Civil War worth the loss of 620,000 lives?

ANALYZING DOCUMENTS

Excerpts from The Emancipation Proclamation

That on the first day of January, in the year of our Lord one thousand eight hundred and sixty-three, all persons held as slaves within any State or designated part of a State, the people whereof shall then be in rebellion against the United States, shall be then, thenceforward, and forever free; and the Executive Government of the United States, including the military and naval authority thereof, will recognize and maintain the freedom of such persons, and will do no act or acts to repress such persons, or any of them, in any efforts they may make for their actual freedom.

▶ Review and Assessment

For answers, see *Teacher's Resource Manual.*

That the Executive will, on the first day of January aforesaid, by proclamation, designate the States and parts of States, if any, in which the people thereof, respectively, shall then be in rebellion against the United States; and the fact that any State, or the people thereof, shall on that day be, in good faith, represented in the Congress of the United States by members chosen thereto at elections wherein a majority of the qualified voters of such State shall have participated, shall, in the absence of strong countervailing testimony, be deemed conclusive evidence that such State, and the people thereof, are not then in rebellion against the United States. . .

. . . I do order and declare that all persons held as slaves within said designated States, and parts of States, are, and henceforward shall be free; and that the Executive government of the United States, including the military and naval authorities thereof, will recognize and maintain the freedom of said persons.

And I hereby enjoin upon the people so declared to be free to abstain from all violence, unless in necessary self-defense; and I recommend to them that, in all cases when allowed, they labor faithfully for reasonable wages.

And I further declare and make known, that such persons of suitable condition, will be received into the armed service of the United States . . .

And upon this act, sincerely believed to be an act of justice, warranted by the Constitution, upon military necessity, I invoke the considerate judgment of mankind, and the gracious favor of Almighty God.

—Abraham Lincoln, September 22, 1862

Thinking Critically: What reasons does Lincoln give in the proclamation for granting freedom to slaves?

WRITING ACTIVITY

In a short report or research paper, consider the following question.

Why were African Americans who wanted to enlist rejected in 1861?

STUDY ONLINE!

www.prenhall.com/aah

Additional study resources are available for this chapter on the *Companion Website.*

The Promise of Reconstruction

1865–1868

A Union soldier reads the Emancipation Proclamation to a group of freed people. In some cases it took weeks for slaves to learn that the U.S. government had declared an end to slavery.

Chapter 12

Witnessing History . . .

Many Thousand Gone

No more auction block for me,
No more, no more,
No more auction block for me,
Many thousand gone.

No more driver's lash for me,
No more, no more,
No more driver's lash for me,
Many thousand gone.

No more peck of salt for me,
No more, no more,
No more peck of salt for me,
Many thousand gone.

No more iron chain for me,
No more, no more.
No more iron chain for me,
Many thousand gone.

—An African American Emancipation Song

 What do you think is the meaning of the line "Many thousand gone"?

TO MY FRIEND DAN SELBY, BUFFALO, N.Y.

I'M GOING HOME TO CLO.

CHARLESTON MT. PLEASANT

S.C. STATE LINE

SONG & CHORUS.

WORDS BY S.N. MITCHELL   MUSIC BY WILLIAM A. HUNTLEY.

BOSTON, MASS.
Published by THOMPSON & ODELL, 177 Washington Street,
Branch Store, 18 Tremont Street.

Many freed blacks returned to the South looking for family who had been sold away.

Chapter Preview

▶ Witnessing History

"Many thousand gone" could refer to the many people who suffered the cruelty of slavery, who died or were killed.

What did freedom mean to a people who had endured and survived 250 years of enslavement in America? What did the future hold for nearly four million African Americans in 1865? Freedom meant many things to many people. But to most former slaves, it meant that families would stay together. Freedom meant that women would no longer be sexually exploited. Freedom meant learning to read and write. Freedom meant organizing churches. Freedom meant moving around without having to obtain permission. Freedom meant that labor would produce income for the laborer and not the master. Freedom meant working without the whip. Freedom meant land to own, cultivate, and live on. Freedom meant a trial before a jury if charged with a crime. Freedom meant voting. Freedom meant citizenship and having the same rights as white people.

Section 1

The End of Slavery

Differing Reactions

With the collapse of slavery, many black people were quick to inform white people that whatever loyalty, devotion, and cooperation they might have shown as slaves had never been a reflection of their inner feelings and attitudes. Near Opelousas, Louisiana, a Union officer asked a young black man why he did not love his master. The youth responded sharply. "When my master begins to lub me, den it'll be time enough for me to lub him. What I wants is to get away. I want to take me off from dis plantation, where I can be free." In North Carolina, planter Robert P. Howell was deeply disappointed that a loyal slave named Lovet fled at the first opportunity.

In contrast, some slaves, especially elderly ones, were fearful and apprehensive about freedom. On a South Carolina plantation, an older black woman refused to accept emancipation. "I is got a marster and mistiss! Dee right dar in de great house. Ef you don' b'lieve me, you go dar an' see."

Emancipation was a traumatic experience for many former masters. A Virginia freedman remembered that "Miss Polly died right after the surrender, she was so hurt that all the negroes was going to be free." Another former slave, Robert Falls, recalled that his master assembled the slaves to inform them they were free. "I hates to do it, but I must. . . . You is free. Just as free as I am. Here I have raised you all to work for me, and now you are going to leave me. I am an old man, and I can't get along without you. I don't know what I am going to do." In less than a year, he was dead. Falls attributed his master's death to the end of slavery. "It killed him."

Reuniting Black Families

As slavery ended, the most urgent need for many freed people was finding family members who had been sold away from them. Slavery had not destroyed the black family. Husbands, wives, and children went to great lengths to reassemble their families after the Civil War. For years and even decades after the end of slavery, advertisements appeared in black

GUIDE TO READING

▶ What steps did African Americans take to reunite families divided by slavery?

▶ What did freedom mean to nearly four million people who had been slaves?

▶ How did most former slaves acquire land of their own?

▶ What was the Freedmen's Bureau and how effective was it?

KEY TERMS

▶ Special Field Order #15, p. 393

▶ Port Royal Experiment, p. 394

▶ Freedmen's Bureau, p. 394

▶ Southern Homestead Act, p. 398

▶ sharecropping, p. 399

⏩ Guide to Reading/Key Terms

For answers, see the *Teacher's Resource Manual.*

⏩ Living Words Audio Clip

Track 14 Remembering Slavery

⏩ Recommended Reading

Leon F. Litwack. *Been in the Storm Too Long: The Aftermath of Slavery.* New York: Alfred A. Knopf, 1979. A rich and detailed account of the transition to freedom largely based on recollections of former slaves.

Eric Foner. *Reconstruction: America's Unfinished Revolution, 1863–1877.* New York: Harper & Row, 1988. The best and most comprehensive account of Reconstruction.

► **Reading Check**

African Americans went to extraordinary lengths to reassemble families divided by slavery. Finding family members was a first priority for many newly freed people. Some walked hundreds of miles to search for loved ones who had been sold away. For years after the end of slavery, newspaper advertisements appeared in black newspapers appealing for help finding missing relatives.

► **Documents**

12-2 *"A Jubilee of Freedom": Freed Slaves March in Charleston, South Carolina, March, 1865*
In Charleston, South Carolina, only days before General Robert E. Lee's surrender at Appomattox, black people held a parade. For the largest African-American communities in the antebellum South, it was a joyous occasion. This report published in the New York Daily Tribune on April 4, 1865 describes the scene as thousands of marchers expressed their joys, hopes, and sheer excitement at being free.

12-3 *William Garrison, "The Governing Passion of My Soul," 1865*
For more than three decades William Lloyd Garrison battled against the South's peculiar institution. In speeches, letters, and newspapers he angered thousands of people, clamoring for immediate abolition. Garrison made this speech marking the end of the Confederacy and the death of slavery.

► **Recommended Readings**

Herbert G. Gutman. *The Black Family in Slavery and Freedom, 1750–1925*. New York: Oxford University Press, 1976. An illustration of how African-American family values and kinship ties forged in slavery endured after emancipation.

Ira Berlin and Leslie Rowland, eds. *Families and Freedom: A Documentary History of African-American Kinship in the Civil War Era*. New York: Cambridge University Press, 1997. A collection of documents that conveys the aspirations and frustrations of freedmen.

newspapers appealing for information about missing kinfolk. The following notice was published in the *Colored Tennessean* on August 5, 1865:

> Saml. Dove wishes to know of the whereabouts of his mother, Areno, his sisters Maria, Neziah and Peggy, and his brother Edmond, who were owned by Geo. Dove of Rockingham County, Shenandoah Valley, Va. Sold in Richmond, after which Saml. and Edmond were taken to Nashville, Tenn., by Joe Mick; Areno was left at the Eagle Tavern, Richmond. Respectfully yours, Saml. Dove, Utica, New York.

In North Carolina a northern journalist met a middle-age black man "plodding along, staff in hand, and apparently very footsore and tired." The nearly exhausted freedman explained that he had walked almost six hundred miles looking for his wife and children who had been sold four years earlier.

There were emotional reunions as family members found each other after years of separation. Ben and Betty Dodson had been apart for twenty years when Ben found her in a refugee camp after the war. "Glory! glory! hallelujah," he shouted as he hugged his wife. Other searches had more heart-wrenching results. Husbands and wives sometimes learned that their spouses had remarried during the separation. Believing his wife had died, the husband of Laura Spicer remarried—only to learn after the war that Laura was still alive. Sadly, he refused to meet with her.

One freedman testified to the close ties that bound many slave families when he replied bitterly to the claim that he had had a kind master who had fed him and never used the whip. "Kind! yes, he gib men corn enough, and he gib me pork enough, and he neber gib me one lick wid de whip, but whar's my wife?—whar's my chill'en? Take away de pork, I say; take away de corn, I can work and raise dese for myself, but gib me back de wife of my bosom, and gib me back my poor chill'en as was sold away."

 Reading Check What steps did African Americans take to reunite families divided by slavery?

Land

As freed people embraced freedom and left their masters, they wanted land. Nineteenth-century Americans of virtually every background associated economic security with owning land. Families wanted to work land and prosper as self-sufficient yeomen. Former slaves believed their future as a free people was tied to the possession of land. But just as it had been impossible to abolish slavery without the intervention of the U.S. government, it would not be possible to procure land without federal assistance. At first, federal authorities seemed determined to make land available to freedmen.

Former slaves assembled in a village near Washington, D.C. Black people welcomed emancipation, but without land, education, or employment, they faced an uncertain future.

Special Field Order #15

Shortly after his army arrived in Savannah—after having devastated Georgia—Union general William T. Sherman announced that freedmen would receive land. On January 16, 1865, he issued **Special Field Order #15**. This military directive set aside a 30-mile-wide tract of land along the Atlantic coast from Charleston, South Carolina, 245 miles south to Jacksonville, Florida. White owners had abandoned the land, and Sherman reserved it for black families. The head of each family would receive "possessory title" to forty acres of land. Sherman also gave the freedmen the use of army mules, thus giving rise to the slogan, "Forty acres and a mule."

Within six months, forty thousand freed people were working 400,000 acres in the South Carolina and Georgia low country and on the Sea Islands. Former slaves generally avoided the slave crops of cotton and rice and instead planted sweet potatoes and corn. They also worked together as families and kinfolk. They avoided the gang labor associated with slavery. Most husbands and fathers preferred that their wives and daughters not work in the fields as slave women had had to do.

The Port Royal Experiment

Meanwhile, hundreds of former slaves had been cultivating land for three years. In late 1861 Union military forces carved out an enclave around Beaufort and Port Royal, South Carolina, that remained under federal authority for the rest of the war. White planters fled to the interior, leaving their slaves behind. Under the supervision of U.S. Treasury officials and northern reformers and missionaries who hurried south in 1862, ex-slaves began to work the land in what came to be known as the **Port Royal Experiment**. When Treasury agents auctioned off portions of the land for nonpayment of taxes, freedmen purchased some of it. But northern businessmen bought most of the real estate and then hired black people to raise cotton.

White owners sometimes returned to their former lands only to find that black families had taken charge. A group of black farmers told one former owner, "We own this land now, put it out of your head that it will ever be yours again." And on one South Carolina Sea Island, white men were turned back by armed black men.

 Reading Check   How did most former slaves acquire land of their own?

The Freedmen's Bureau

In early 1865, Congress created the Bureau of Refugees, Freedmen, and Abandoned Lands—commonly called the **Freedmen's Bureau**. It was created as a temporary agency to assist freedmen to make the transition to freedom. The bureau was placed under the control of the U.S. Army. General Oliver O. Howard was put in command. Howard, a devout Christian who had lost an arm in the war, was eager to aid the freedmen.

The bureau was given enormous responsibilities. It was to help freedmen obtain land, gain an education, negotiate labor contracts with white planters, settle legal and criminal disputes involving black and white people, and provide food, medical care, and transportation for black and white people left destitute by the war. However, Congress never provided sufficient funds or personnel to carry out these tasks.

The Freedmen's Bureau never had more than nine hundred agents spread across the South from Virginia to Texas. Mississippi, for example, had twelve agents in 1866. One agent often served a county with a population of ten thousand to twenty thousand freedmen. Few of the agents were black because few military officers were black. John Mercer Langston of Virginia was an inspector of schools assigned to the bureau's main office in Washington, D.C.; Major Martin R. Delany worked with freedmen on the South Carolina Sea Islands.

▶ **Reading Check**

In the immediate aftermath of the war, the federal government took steps to make land available to freedmen. Special Field Order #15 and the Southern Homestead Act were meant to make land available to former slaves. However, over time, most southern blacks were forced into dependent labor arrangements like sharecropping.

▶ **Document**

12-4   *The Freedmen's Bureau Bill, 1865*
Congress established the Bureau of Refugees, Freedmen, and Abandoned Lands to provide aid for freed people and to oversee free labor arrangements in the South. President Andrew Johnson's policy of liberally pardoning ex-confederates and returning their land frustrated Bureau commissioner General O. O. Howard's efforts to resettle freed people on confiscated lands. Congress extended the life of the Bureau in 1866 over Johnson's veto.

▶ **Interactive Activity**

Reconstruction: The Struggle to Define the Meaning of Freedom
This activity highlights some of the complexities that faced the nation following the Civil War and the emancipation of nearly four million people who had been held as slaves.

OFFICE OF THE FREEDMEN'S BUREAU, MEMPHIS, TENNESSEE.
[See Page 816.]

Freedmen's Bureau agents often found themselves in the middle of angry disputes over land and labor that erupted between black and white Southerners. Too often the Bureau officers sided with the white landowners in these disagreements with former slaves.

The need for assistance was desperate. Thousands of black and white Southerners endured extreme privation in the months after the war ended. The bureau established camps for the homeless, fed the hungry, and cared for orphans and the sick as best it could. It distributed more than thirteen million rations—consisting of flour, corn meal, and sugar—by 1866. The bureau provided medical care to a half million freedmen and thousands of white people who were suffering from smallpox, yellow fever, cholera, and pneumonia. Many more remained untreated.

In July 1865 the bureau took a first step toward distributing land when General Howard issued Circular 13 ordering agents to "set aside" forty-acre plots for freedmen. But the allocation had hardly begun when the order was revoked. It was announced that land already distributed under General Sherman's Special Field Order #15 was to be returned to its previous white owners.

The reason for this reversal in policy was President Andrew Johnson, who had become president after Lincoln's assassination in April 1865. He began to pardon hundreds and then thousands of former Confederates and restore their lands to them. General Howard was forced to tell black people that they had to relinquish the land they thought they had

Freed women washing laundry along a creek near Circleville, Texas, ca. 1866.

Southern Homestead Act

In early 1866 Congress attempted to provide land for freedmen with the passage of the **Southern Homestead Act**. More than three million acres of public land were set aside for black people and southern white people who had remained loyal to the Union. Much of this land, however, was unsuitable for farming and consisted of swampy wetlands or unfertile pinewoods. More than four thousand black families—three-quarters of them in Florida—did claim some of this land. But many of them lacked the financial resources to cultivate it. Eventually southern timber companies acquired much of it, and the Southern Homestead Act largely failed.

Sharecropping

▶▶ **Reading Check p. 399**

The Freedmen's Bureau was established in 1865 to help freedmen make the transition to freedom. The bureau had enormous responsibilities. However, Congress never gave it sufficient funds or personnel to carry out its assigned tasks.

▶▶ **Map 12-1**

This map demonstrates black people's desire to create their own plots of land, and communities, thereby distancing themselves from slavery and white supervision.

By 1866 bureau officials tried to force freedmen to sign labor contracts with white landowners—putting black people once again under white authority. Black men who refused to sign contracts could be arrested. Theoretically, these contracts were legal agreements between two equals: landowner and laborer. But they were seldom freely concluded. Bureau agents usually sided with the landowner and pressured freedmen to accept unequal terms.

Occasionally, the landowner would pay wages to the laborer. But because most landowners lacked cash to pay wages, they agreed to provide the laborer with part of the crop. The laborer, often grudgingly, agreed to work under the supervision of the landowner. The contracts required labor for a full year. The laborer could neither quit nor strike.

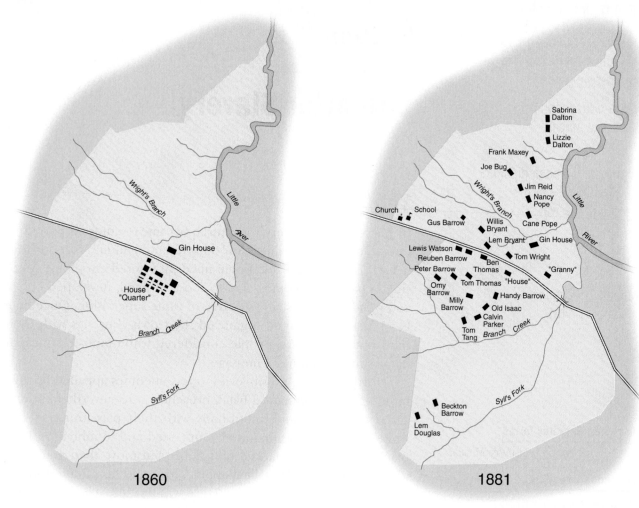

1860

1881

Landowners demanded that the laborers work the fields in gangs. Freedmen resisted this system. They sometimes insisted on making decisions involving planting, fertilizing, and harvesting as they sought to exercise independence (see Map 12–1).

Thus it took time for a new form of agricultural labor to develop. But by the 1870s, the system of **sharecropping** had emerged and dominated most of the South. There were no wages. Freedmen worked land as families—not in gangs—and not under direct white supervision. When the landowner provided seed, tools, fertilizer, and work animals (mules, horses, oxen), the black family received one-third of the crop. There were many variations on these arrangements. Frequently black families were cheated out of their fair share of the crop.

 Reading Check What was the Freedmen's Bureau and how effective was it?

MAP 12–1 The Effect of Sharecropping on the Southern Plantation: The Barrow Plantation, Oglethorpe County, Georgia.

With the advent of sharecropping, black people preferred to have each family cultivate separate plots of land.

 Although many freed people worked the same land that they had as slaves, how does this map suggest the changes experienced by black people in family life, religion, education, and their relationships with white people?

▶ What role did the black church play in African-American life in the post-war decades?

▶ Why was education so important to African Americans?

▶ Describe the violence directed at southern blacks in the aftermath of the war.

KEY TERMS

▶ Savannah Educational Association, p. 402

▶ **Guide to Reading/Key Terms**

For answers, see the *Teacher's Resource Manual*.

▶ **Recommended Readings**

Clarence E. Walker. *A Rock in a Weary Land: The African Methodist Episcopal Church during the Civil War and Reconstruction.* Baton Rouge, LA: Louisiana State University Press, 1982.

Tera W. Hunter. *To 'Joy My Freedom: Southern Black Women's Lives and Labors after the Civil War.* Cambridge, MA: Harvard University Press, 1997. An examination of the interior lives of black women, their work, social welfare, and leisure.

▶ **Retracing the Odyssey**

Wilmington, North Carolina: St. Stephen African Methodist Episcopal Church. Following the Civil War, black members of the Front Street Methodist Church withdrew and founded their own church on Red Cross Street. In 1880, they began construction of the current building. For a time parishioners met in the basement while work continued on the imposing and ornate sanctuary above them.

Section 2

Life after Slavery

The Black Church

In the years after slavery, the church became the most important institution among African Americans other than the family. Not only did it fill deep spiritual and inspirational needs, it offered enriching music, provided charity and compassion to those in need, developed community and political leaders, and was free of white supervision. Once liberated, black men and women organized their own churches with their own ministers. Most black people considered white ministers incapable of delivering a meaningful message.

Northern white missionaries were sometimes appalled by the unlettered and ungrammatical black preachers who nevertheless communicated effectively and emotionally with their parishioners. A visiting white clergyman was genuinely impressed and humbled on hearing a black preacher who lacked education, but more than made up for it with devout faith. "He talked about Christ and his salvation as one who understood what he said. . . . Here was an unlearned man, one who could not read, telling of the love of Christ, of Christian faith and duty in a way which I have not learned."

Church members struggled, scrimped, and saved to buy land and to build churches. Most former slaves founded Baptist and Methodist churches. These denominations tended to be more independent. Their doctrine was usually simple and direct without complex theology. Of the Methodist churches, the African Methodist Episcopal (AME) church made giant strides in the South after the Civil War.

In Charleston, South Carolina, the AME church was resurrected after an absence of more than forty years. In 1822, during the turmoil over the Denmark Vesey plot, the AME church was forced to disband and its leader had to flee (see Chapter 8). But by the 1870s, three AME congregations were thriving in Charleston. In Wilmington, North Carolina, the sixteen hundred members of the Front Street Methodist Church decided to join the AME church soon after the Civil War ended. They replaced the longtime white minister, the Reverend L. S. Burkhead, with a black man.

White Methodists initially encouraged cooperation with black Methodists and helped establish the Colored (now Christian) Methodist Episcopal church (CME). But the white Methodists lost some of their

Hundreds of black churches were founded across the South following the Civil War. This illustration shows a congregation crowded into Richmond's First African Baptist Church in 1874.

fervor after they tried but failed to persuade the black Methodists to keep political issues out of the CME church and to dwell solely on spiritual concerns.

The Presbyterian, Congregational, and Episcopal churches appealed to the more prosperous members of the black community. Their services tended to be more formal and solemn. Black people who had been free before the Civil War were usually affiliated with these congregations and remained so after the conflict. Well-to-do free black people in Charleston organized St. Mark's Protestant Episcopal Church when they separated from the white Episcopal church. But they retained their white minister Joseph Seabrook as rector. Poorer black people of darker complexion found churches like St. Mark's decidedly unappealing.

The Roman Catholic Church made modest in-roads among black Southerners. There were all-black parishes in St. Augustine, Savannah, Charleston, and Louisville after the Civil War. For generations prior to the conflict, large numbers of well-to-do free people of color in New Orleans had been practicing Catholics, and their descendants remained faithful to the church. On Georgia's Skidaway Island, Benedictine monks established a school for black youngsters in 1878 that survived for nearly a decade.

Religious differences among black people notwithstanding, the black churches, their parishioners, and clergymen would play a vital role in Reconstruction politics. More than one hundred black ministers were elected to political office after the Civil War.

▶ **Recommended Reading**

Cyprian Davis. *The History of Black Catholics in the United States.* New York: Crossroad, 1990.

▶ **Document**

12-1 *Charlotte Forten, Life on the Sea Islands, 1864*

Charlotte Forten one of many northern teachers who volunteered to help educate ex-slaves and demonstrate that African Americans were capable of self-improvement. This selection, published in 1864, was compiled from letters she wrote to her friend, the poet John Greenleaf Whittier.

▶ **Retracing the Odyssey**

Charleston, South Carolina: The Avery Research Center for African-American History and Culture. In 1865 the American Missionary Association opened a private school for black youngsters that served the Charleston community until 1954. The renovated structure currently contains an archive, a restored classroom, and exhibits devoted to African-American life in the Carolina low country.

Charlotte Forten came from a prominent Philadelphia family of color. She joined hundreds of black and white teachers who migrated South during and after the Civil War to instruct the freed people.

Education

Freedom and education were inseparable. To remain illiterate after emancipation was to remain enslaved. Almost every freed black person—young or old—desperately wanted to learn. Elderly people were especially eager to read the Bible. Even before slavery ended, black people began to establish schools.

In 1861 Mary Peake, a free black woman, opened a school in Hampton, Virginia. On South Carolina's Sea Islands, a black cabinet-maker began teaching openly after having secretly operated a school for years. In 1862 northern missionaries arrived on the Sea Islands to begin teaching. Laura Towne, a white woman, and Charlotte Forten, a black woman, opened a school on St. Helena's Island as part of the Port Royal Experiment. They enrolled 138 children and 58 adults. By 1863 there were 1,700 students and 45 teachers at 30 schools in the South Carolina low country.

With the end of the Civil War, northern religious organizations in cooperation with the Freedmen's Bureau organized hundreds of day and night schools. Classes were held in stables, homes, former slave cabins, taverns, churches, and even—in Savannah and New Orleans—in the old slave markets. Former slaves spent hours in the fields and then trudged to a makeshift school to learn the alphabet and arithmetic. In 1865 black ministers created the **Savannah Educational Association**, raised $1,000, employed fifteen black teachers, and enrolled six hundred students.

In 1866 the Freedmen's Bureau set aside $500,000 for education. The bureau furnished the buildings while former slaves hired, housed, and fed the teachers. By 1869 the Freedmen's Bureau was involved with 3,000 schools and 150,000 students. Even more impressive, by 1870 black people had contributed $1 million to educate their people.

Black Teachers

Although freedmen appreciated the dedication and devotion of the white teachers affiliated with the missionary societies, they usually preferred black teachers. The Reverend Richard H. Cain, an AME minister who came south from Brooklyn, New York, said that black people needed to learn to control their own futures. "We must take into our own hands the education of our race. . . . Honest, dignified whites may teach ever so well, but it has not the effect to exalt the black man's opinion of his own race, because they have always been in the habit of seeing white men in honored positions, and respected."

Black men and women responded to the call to teach. Hezekiah Hunter, a black teacher from Brooklyn, New York, commented in 1865 on the need for black teachers. "I believe we best can instruct our own people, knowing our own peculiarities—needs—necessities. Further—I believe we that are competent owe it to our people to teach them our speciality." In Malden, West Virginia, when black residents found that a

MAP 12–2 The Location of Black Colleges Founded before and during Reconstruction.

Three black colleges were founded before the Civil War. In Pennsylvania, Cheyney University opened in 1837, and it was followed by the establishment of Lincoln University in 1854. In 1856, Wilberforce University was founded in Ohio. After the Civil War, northern black and white missionary groups fanned out across the South and—frequently with assistance of Freedmen's Bureau officials—founded colleges, institutes, and normal schools in the former slave states.

recently arrived eighteen-year-old black man could read and write, they promptly hired him to teach.

In some areas of the South, the sole person available to teach was a poorly educated former slave equipped primarily with a willingness to teach his or her fellow freedmen. Many northern teachers, black and white, provided more than the basics of elementary education. Black life and history were occasionally read about and discussed. Abolitionist Lydia Maria Child wrote *The Freedmen's Book*, which offered short biographies of Benjamin Banneker, Frederick Douglass, and Toussaint Louverture. More often northern teachers were dismayed at the backwardness of the freedmen. They struggled to modify behavior and to impart cultural values by teaching piety, thrift, cleanliness, temperance, and timeliness.

Black Colleges

Northern churches and religious societies established dozens of colleges, universities, academies, and institutes across the South in the late 1860s and the 1870s (see Map 12–2). Most of these institutions provided elementary and secondary education. Few black students were prepared for actual college or university work. The American Missionary Association—an abolitionist and Congregationalist organization—worked with the Freedmen's Bureau to establish Berea in Kentucky, Fisk in Tennessee, Hampton in Virginia, Tougaloo in Alabama, and Avery in South Carolina. The primary purpose of these schools was to educate black students to become teachers.

▶ **Retracing the Odyssey**

Raleigh, North Carolina: Shaw University and St. Augustine's College. These are two of the many black colleges that were established during Reconstruction. The Baptists founded Shaw in 1865, and its impressive Estey Hall has survived almost 130 years. The Episcopal Church and the Freedmen's Bureau collaborated to found St. Augustine's in 1867.

Nashville, Tennessee: Fisk University. The American Missionary Association established Fisk in 1866. Magnificent Jubilee Hall is the nation's oldest building dedicated to the higher education of black students. It was completed in 1876. There is an impressive collection of European and American art on the campus at the Carl Van Vechten Art Gallery.

Black and white land-grant colleges stressed training in agriculture and industry. These Hampton Institute students learn milk production. The men are in military uniforms, which was typical for males at these colleges. Military training was a required part of the curriculum.

▶ **Teaching Notes**

Most white people were well aware that black people could learn. Otherwise, the slave codes that prohibited educating slaves would have been unnecessary. One planter bitterly conceded in 1870, "Every little negro in the county is now going to school and the public pays for it. This is one hell of [a] fix but we can't help it, and the best policy is to conform as far as possible to circumstances."

▶ **Retracing the Odyssey**

Cheyney University of Pennsylvania, Cheyney, Pennsylvania. Founded in 1837, Cheyney is the oldest of the historically Black Colleges and Universities in America. The university was founded in Philadelphia originally as the Institute for Colored Youth to provide a free classical education. In 1983 Cheyney joined the higher education system of Pennsylvania as Cheyney University.

Lincoln University, Lincoln University, Pennsylvania. The university was chartered in 1854 to provide higher education in the arts and sciences.

In Missouri, the black enlisted men and the white officers of the 62nd and 65th Colored Volunteers raised $6,000 to establish Lincoln Institute in 1866, which would become Lincoln University. The American Baptist Home Mission Society founded Virginia Union, Shaw in North Carolina, Benedict in South Carolina, and Morehouse in Georgia. Northern Methodists helped establish Claflin in South Carolina, Rust in Mississippi, and Bennett in North Carolina. The Episcopalians were responsible for St. Augustine's in North Carolina and St. Paul's in Virginia. These and many other similar institutions formed the foundation for the historically black colleges and universities.

Response of White Southerners

White Southerners considered efforts by black people to learn absurd. For generations, white Americans had looked on people of African descent as inferior. When significant efforts were made to educate former slaves, white Southerners reacted with suspicion, contempt, and hostility. Some white people went out of their way to prevent black people from learning. Countless schools were burned, mostly in rural areas. In Canton, Mississippi, black people collected money to open a school—only to have white residents inform them that the school would be burned and the prospective teacher lynched if it opened. The female

teacher at a freedmen's school in Donaldsonville, Louisiana, was shot and killed. Other white Southerners grudgingly tolerated the desire of black people to acquire an education.

Most white people adamantly refused to attend school with black people. No integrated schools were established in the immediate aftermath of emancipation. Most black people were more interested in gaining an education than in caring whether white students attended school with them. When black youngsters tried to attend a white school in Raleigh, North Carolina, the white students stopped going to it. For a brief time in Charleston, South Carolina, black and white children attended the same school, but they were taught in separate classrooms.

 Reading Check Why was education so important to African Americans?

Violence

In the days, weeks, and months after the end of the Civil War, a wave of brutality and violence swept across the South. Embittered white Southerners lashed out at black people. There were beatings, murders, rapes, and riots, often with little or no provocation.

Black people who demanded respect, wore better clothing, refused to step aside for white people, or asked to be addressed as "mister" or "missus" were attacked. In South Carolina, a white clergyman shot and killed a black man who protested when another black man was removed from a church service. In Texas, one black man was killed because he failed to remove his hat in the presence of a white man and another for refusing to relinquish a bottle of whiskey. A black woman was beaten for "using insolent language," and a black worker in Alabama was killed for speaking sharply to a white overseer. In Virginia, a black veteran was beaten after announcing he had been proud to serve in the Union Army.

There was also large-scale violence. In May 1866 in Memphis, white residents went on a brutal rampage after black veterans forced local police to release a black prisoner. The city was already beset with economic difficulties and racial tensions caused in part by an influx of rural refugees. White people, led by Irish policemen, invaded the black section of Memphis and destroyed hundreds of homes, cabins, and shacks as well as churches and schools. Forty-six black people and two white men died.

On July 30, 1866, in New Orleans, white people—angered that black men were demanding political rights—assaulted black people on the street and in a convention hall. City policemen, who were mostly Confederate veterans, shot down the black delegates as they fled in

▶ **Reading Check**

Freedom and education were inseparable. African Americans understood that to remain illiterate after emancipation was to remain enslaved. As a result, almost every freed black person wanted to learn.

panic waving white flags in a futile attempt to surrender. Thirty-four black people and three of their white allies died. Federal troops eventually arrived and stopped the bloodshed. General Philip H. Sheridan characterized the riot as "an absolute massacre."

Little was done to stem the violence. Most Union troops had been withdrawn from the South and demobilized after the war. The Freedmen's Bureau was usually unwilling and unable to protect the black population. Black people left to defend themselves were usually in no position to retaliate. Instead, they sometimes attempted to bring the perpetrators to justice. In Orangeburg, South Carolina, armed black men brought three white men to the local jail who had been wreaking violence in the community. In Holly Springs, Mississippi, a posse of armed black men apprehended a white man who had murdered a freedwoman.

For black people, the system of justice was thoroughly unjust. Although black people could now testify against white people in a court of law, southern juries remained all white. These juries refused to convict white people charged with harming black people. In Texas in 1865 and 1866, five hundred white men were indicted for murdering black people. Not one was convicted.

▶▶ **Teaching Notes**

In 1865, University of North Carolina students twice attacked peaceful meetings of black people. Near Pine Bluff, Arkansas, in 1866, a white mob burned a black settlement and lynched twenty-four men, women, and children. An estimated two thousand black people were murdered around Shreveport, Louisiana. In Texas white people killed one thousand black people between 1865 and 1868.

PROFILE ❖ Charlotte E. Ray

Charlotte E. Ray became the first African American woman to earn a law degree and the first woman admitted to the practice of law in Washington, D.C. She was born on January 13, 1850, in New York City. One of seven children, her parents were the Reverend Charles B. Ray and his second wife, Charlotte Augusta Burroughs Ray. They were firm believers in the rights of African Americans and in their potential for success.

Charlotte attended Myrtilla Miner's Institution for the Education of Colored Youth in Washington, D.C. Myrtilla Miner, a white educator from upstate New York, was determined to demonstrate that black women were as capable of high moral and mental development as white women.

Charlotte completed high school at Miner's in 1869. She then taught at the Normal and Preparatory Department of recently established Howard University. She also enrolled in law classes at Howard and wrote a thesis analyzing corporations. She graduated from the law school in 1872, and a month later was admitted to the bar in Washington, D.C. She opened an office and planned to practice real estate law. As a real estate lawyer, she could avoid court appearances and the discrimination that women attorneys encountered. She often used her initials, C. E. Ray, so her clients would not suffer because their legal counsel could be identified as a woman.

Because of the Panic of 1873 and the ensuing economic depression and the difficulties of being a black woman in a white male profession, Ray gave up the practice of law. She supported women's rights. In 1876 she attended the annual meeting of the National American Woman Suffrage Association in New York City. By 1879 she had returned to New York and taught school in Brooklyn. Charlotte Ray died of acute bronchitis on January 11, 1911.

Ray

Section 3

The Crusade for Political and Civil Rights

Political Rights

In October 1864 in Syracuse, New York, 145 black leaders gathered in a national convention. Some of the century's most prominent black men and women attended, including Henry Highland Garnet, Frances E. W. Harper, William Wells Brown, Francis L. Cardozo, Richard H. Cain, Jonathan J. Wright, and Jonathan C. Gibbs. They embraced the basic tenets of the American political tradition. They also proclaimed that they expected to participate fully in it.

Even before the Syracuse gathering, northern Republicans met in Union-controlled territory around Beaufort, South Carolina. They nominated the state's delegates to the 1864 Republican national convention. Among those selected were Robert Smalls and Prince Rivers, former slaves who had exemplary records with the Union Army. The probability of black participation in postwar politics seemed promising indeed.

But northern and southern white leaders who already held power would largely determine whether black Americans would gain any political power or acquire the same rights as white people. As the Civil War ended, President Lincoln was more concerned with restoring the seceded states to the Union than in opening political doors for black people. Yet Lincoln suggested that at least some black men deserved the right to vote. On April 11, 1865, he wrote, "I would myself prefer that [the vote] were now conferred on the very intelligent, and on those who serve our cause as soldiers." Three days later Lincoln was assassinated.

Presidential Reconstruction under Andrew Johnson

Vice President Andrew Johnson then became president. He initially seemed inclined to impose stern policies on the white South while befriending the freedmen. In 1864 he had told black people, "I will be your Moses, and lead you through the Red Sea of War and Bondage to a fairer future of Liberty and Peace." Nothing proved to be further from the truth. Andrew Johnson was no friend of black Americans.

Johnson strongly opposed secession and was the only senator from the seceded states to remain loyal to the Union. He had nonetheless acquired five slaves and the conviction that black people were so thoroughly inferior that white men must forever govern them. In 1867 Johnson argued that black people could not exercise political power and they had "less capacity for government than any

PROFILE ❖ Aaron A. Bradley

Aaron Bradley was a major figure in Georgia politics during Reconstruction. He was born a slave in about 1815 in South Carolina. His father was probably white. He belonged to Francis W. Pickens, who was South Carolina's governor when the state seceded. At about age twenty, he escaped and went to Boston where he studied law and met black and white abolitionists.

In 1865, after the war, Bradley moved to Savannah where he took up the cause of the freedmen and opened a school. Bradley demanded that black families keep the land they had occupied under Sherman's Special Field Order #15. He believed black people had to have land to prosper. He criticized the Freedmen's Bureau for attempting to force black people off the land. He argued that President Johnson should be impeached for supporting Confederate landowners rather than black and white people who were loyal to the union.

Bradley also insisted that black people deserved the rights to vote, testify in court, and have jury trials. After he urged black farmers to defend their land by force, federal authorities charged him with advocating insurrection. He was sentenced to a year's confinement but was soon paroled.

He returned to Boston and renewed his pleas for land for the freedmen. In 1867 Bradley returned to Savannah and attacked the system of sharecropping. He complained that freedmen were compelled to work involuntarily and asked that black men be permitted to arm themselves. He also argued that justice would be fairer if the courts included black men. Although the Freedmen's Bureau considered Bradley a troublemaker, he never backed down.

Black farmers and workers elected Bradley to the state constitutional convention that year but he was soon expelled. Then he was elected to the state senate—only to be expelled again along with all the black members of the Georgia legislature.

Meanwhile, Bradley carried on a running battle with Savannah's mayor, a former Confederate colonel affiliated with the Ku Klux Klan. In 1868 Bradley organized black workers to arm themselves to retain the lands they believed belonged to them. For a month, black men controlled parts of Chatham County outside Savannah. Eventually, federal authorities jailed one hundred of them. Bradley again fled north.

He returned to Georgia in 1870 and reclaimed his senate seat after Congress forced the legislature to seat its black members. Democrats regained control of Georgia politics in 1872. Bradley and the Republicans were swept from power. He ran for Congress in South Carolina in 1874 but lost. He supported black migration to Liberia and Florida. He moved to St. Louis and died there in 1881.

Aaron Bradley maintained few close ties to black or white politicians. He was constantly embroiled in factional disputes. He did not cooperate with middleclass black leaders and had no ties with local churches and their clergymen.

He dressed in expensive and flashy clothes. He could be pompous, abrasive, and intemperate. White people universally detested him. Yet Bradley remained exceedingly popular among freedmen.

Bradley

other race of people. No independent government of any form has ever been successful in their hands. On the contrary, wherever they have been left to their own devices they have shown a constant tendency to relapse into barbarism."

Johnson began to placate white Southerners. In May 1865 Johnson granted blanket amnesty and pardons to former Confederates willing to swear allegiance to the United States. The main exceptions were high former Confederate officials and those who owned property in excess of $20,000, a large sum at the time. Yet even these leaders could appeal for individual pardons. And appeal they did. By 1866 Johnson had pardoned more than seven thousand high-ranking former Confederates and wealthier Southerners. Moreover, he had restored land to those white people who had lost it to freedmen.

Johnson's actions blatantly encouraged those who had supported secession, owned slaves, and opposed the Union. He permitted long-time southern leaders to regain political influence and authority only months after the end of America's bloodiest conflict. As black people and radical Republicans watched in disbelief, Johnson appointed provisional governors in the former Confederate states. Leaders in those states then called constitutional conventions, held elections, and prepared to regain their place in the Union. Johnson merely insisted that each Confederate state formally accept the **Thirteenth Amendment** (ratified in December 1865, it outlawed slavery) and repudiate Confederate war debts.

The southern constitutional conventions gave no consideration to the inclusion of black people in the political system or to guaranteeing them equal rights. As one Mississippi delegate explained, "'Tis nature's law that the superior race must rule and rule they will."

Black Codes

After the election of state and local officials, white legislators gathered in state capitals across the South to determine the status and future of the freedmen. With little debate, the legislatures drafted the so-called **black codes**. Southern politicians gave no thought to providing black people with the political and legal rights associated with citizenship.

The black codes sought to ensure the availability of a subservient agricultural labor supply controlled by white people. They imposed severe restrictions on freedmen. Freedmen had to sign annual labor contracts with white landowners. South Carolina required black people who wanted to establish a business to purchase licenses costing from $10 to $100. The codes permitted black children ages two to twenty-one to be apprenticed to white people and spelled out their duties and obligations in detail. Corporal punishment was legal. Employers were designated "masters" and employees "servants." The black codes also

▶ **Recommended Reading**

Steven Hahn. *A Nation Under Our Feet: Black Political Struggles in the Rural South from Slavery to the Great Migration.* Cambridge, MA: Harvard University Press, 2003. In a sophisticated analysis, Hahn explores the ways in which African Americans conceived of themselves as political people and organized from slavery through Reconstruction and disfranchisement to the growth of Marcus Garvey's Universal Negro Improvement Association in the 1920s.

A black man is auctioned off shortly after the Civil War. Under the black codes, black people arrested and fined for vagrancy or loitering could be "sold" if they could not pay the fine.

▶ **Reading Check**

The black codes were laws passed by southern legislatures meant to ensure the availability of a subservient agricultural labor supply. They imposed severe restrictions on freedmen. In essence, they amounted to nothing less than an effort to put black people under the control of whites.

▶ **Document**

12-6 *Address of the Colored State Convention to the People of the State of South Carolina, 1865*
Unwilling to accept white southerners discriminatory attempts, in South Carolina black southerners held a convention to protest the codes and to decide on a plan of action. With the Declaration of Independence as their blueprint for freemen, the delegates asked for no special privileges or favors, only fair treatment and the removal of the new obstructions: the black codes.

restricted black people from loitering or vagrancy, using alcohol or firearms, hunting, fishing, and grazing livestock. The codes did guarantee rights that slaves had not possessed. Freedmen could marry legally, engage in contracts, purchase property, sue or be sued, and testify in court. But black people could not vote or serve on juries. The black codes conceded—just barely—freedom to black people.

 Reading Check   What were the black codes and what did they mean for African Americans?

Black Conventions

Alarmed by these threats to their freedom, black people met in conventions across the South in 1865 and 1866 to protest, appeal for justice, and chart their future. Men who had been free before the war dominated the

conventions. Many were ministers, teachers, and artisans. Few had been slaves. Women and children also attended—as spectators, not delegates. Women often offered comments, suggestions, and criticism. These meetings were hardly militant or radical affairs. Delegates respectfully insisted that white people live up to the principles and rights embodied in the Declaration of Independence and the Constitution.

At the AME church in Raleigh, North Carolina, delegates asked for equal rights and the right to vote. At Georgia's convention they protested against white violence. They appealed for leaders who would enforce the law without regard to color.

> We ask not for a Black Man's Governor, nor a White Man's Governor, but for a People's Governor, who shall impartially protect the rights of all, and faithfully sustain the Union.

Delegates at the Norfolk meeting reminded white Virginians that black people were patriotic.

> We are Americans. We know no other country. We love the land of our birth.

But they protested that Virginia's black code caused "political or legal distinctions, on account of color merely." They requested the right to vote. They added that they might boycott the businesses of "those who deny to us our equal rights."

Two conventions were held in Charleston, South Carolina—one before and one after the black code was enacted. At the first, delegates stressed the "respect and affection" they felt toward white Charlestonians. They even proposed that only literate men be granted the right to vote if it were genuinely applied to both races. The second convention denounced the black code and insisted on its repeal. Delegates again asked for the right to vote and the right to testify in court. They also appealed for public schools and for "homesteads for ourselves and our children." White authorities ignored these and other black conventions and their petitions. Instead they were confident they had effectively relegated the freedmen to a subordinate role in society.

By late 1865 President Johnson's reconstruction policies had aroused black people. One black Union veteran summed up the situation.

> If you call this Freedom, what do you call Slavery?

Republicans in Congress also opposed Johnson's policies toward the freedmen and the former Confederate states.

▶▶ **Guide to Reading/Key Terms**

For answers, see the *Teacher's Resource Manual.*

Section 4

The Radical Republicans

Radical Proposal

Radical Republicans, as more militant Republicans were called, were especially disturbed that Johnson seemed to have abandoned the ex-slaves to their former masters. They considered white Southerners disloyal and unrepentant, despite their military defeat. Moreover, radical Republicans were determined to transform the racial fabric of American society by including black people in the political and economic system.

Among the most influential radical Republicans were Charles Sumner, Benjamin Wade, and Henry Wilson in the Senate and Thaddeus Stevens, George W. Julian, and James M. Ashley in the House. Few white Americans have been as dedicated to the rights of black people as these men. They had fought for the abolition of slavery. They were reluctant to compromise. They were honest, tough, and articulate but also abrasive, difficult, self-righteous, and vain. Black people appreciated them. Many white people despised them.

Stevens was determined to provide freedmen with land. He introduced a bill in Congress in late 1865 to confiscate 400 million acres from the wealthiest 10 percent of Southerners and distribute it free to freedmen. The remaining land would be auctioned off in plots no larger than 500 acres. Few legislators supported the proposal. Even those who wanted fundamental change considered confiscation a gross violation of property rights.

Radical Republicans supported voting rights for black men. They were convinced that black men—to protect themselves and to secure the South for the Republican Party—had to have the right to vote. Moderate Republicans, however, found the prospect of black voting almost as objectionable as the confiscation of land. They preferred to build the Republican Party in the South by cooperating with President Johnson and attracting loyal white Southerners.

The thought of black suffrage appalled northern and southern Democrats. Most white Northerners—Republicans and Democrats—favored denying black men the right to vote in their states. After the war, proposals to guarantee the right to vote to black men were defeated in New York, Ohio, Kansas, and the Nebraska Territory and the District of

With the adoption of radical Republican policies, most black men, women and children eagerly took part in meetings, conventions, speeches, barbecues, and other gatherings.

Columbia. Five New England states as well as Iowa, Minnesota, and Wisconsin did allow black men to vote.

As much as they objected to black suffrage, most white Northerners objected even more strongly to defiant white Southerners. Journalist Charles A. Dana described the attitude of many Northerners. "As for negro suffrage, the mass of Union men in the Northwest do not care a great deal. What scares them is the idea that the rebels are all to be let back . . . and made a power in government again, just as though there had been no rebellion."

In December 1865 Congress created the **Joint Committee on Reconstruction** to determine whether the southern states should be readmitted to the Union. The committee investigated southern affairs and confirmed reports of widespread mistreatment of black people and white arrogance.

The Freedmen's Bureau Bill and the Civil Rights Bill

In early 1866 Senator Lyman Trumball, a moderate Republican from Illinois, introduced two major bills. The first was to provide more financial support for the Freedmen's Bureau and extend its authority to defend the rights of black people.

▶ **Document**

12-7 *The Civil Rights Act of 1866*
Passed over President Johnson's veto in April 1866, the Civil Rights Act provided the first statutory definition of American citizenship. By conferring citizenship rights upon freed people, it negated the Supreme Court's Dred Scott decision of 1857, which had held that a black person could not be a citizen of the United States. The Civil Rights Act proposed that the federal government guarantee the principle of equality before the law, regardless of race.

1865	Freedmen's Bureau established
1865	Thirteenth Amendment passed and ratified
1866	Freedmen's Bureau Bill and the Civil Rights Act of 1866 passed over Johnson's veto
1866	Fourteenth Amendment passed (ratified 1868)
1867	Reconstruction Acts passed over Johnson's veto

The second proposal was the first civil rights bill in American history. It made any person born in the United States a citizen (except Indians) and entitled them to rights protected by the U.S. government. Black people would possess the same legal rights as white people. The bill was clearly intended to invalidate the black codes.

Johnson's Vetoes

Both measures passed in Congress with nearly unanimous Republican support. President Johnson vetoed them. He claimed that the bill to continue the Freedmen's Bureau would greatly expand the federal bureaucracy. It would permit too "vast a number of agents" to exercise arbitrary power over the white population. He insisted that the civil rights bill benefited black people at the expense of white people. "In fact, the distinction of race and color is by the bill made to operate in favor of the colored and against the white race."

The Johnson vetoes stunned Republicans. Although he had not meant to, Johnson drove moderate Republicans into the radical camp and strengthened the Republican Party. The president did not believe Republicans would oppose him to support the freedmen. He was wrong. Congress overrode both vetoes. The Republicans broke with Johnson in 1866, defied him in 1867, and impeached him in 1868 (failing to remove him from office by only one vote in the Senate).

The Fourteenth Amendment

To secure the legal rights of freedmen, Republicans passed the **Fourteenth Amendment**. This amendment fundamentally changed the Constitution. It compelled states to accept their residents as citizens and to guarantee that their rights as citizens would be safeguarded.

Its first section guaranteed citizenship to every person born in the United States. This included virtually every black person. It made

▶ **Document**

12-8 *President Johnson's Veto of the Civil Rights Act, 1866*
The Civil Rights Act was the first major piece of legislation to become law over a president's veto. Johnson's veto message helped make the estrangement between Congress and the President irreparable. Johnson's constitutional arguments induced Congress to enact the Fourteenth Amendment, which forbade individual states to deprive citizens of the "equal protection of the laws."

each person a citizen of the state in which he or she resided. It defined the specific rights of citizens and then protected those rights against the power of state governments. Citizens had the right to due process (usually a trial) before they could lose their life, liberty, or property.

> All persons born or naturalized in the United States, and subject to the jurisdiction thereof, are citizens of the United States and of the State wherein they reside. No State shall make or enforce any law which shall abridge the privileges or immunities of citizens of the United States; nor shall any State deprive any person of life, liberty, or property, without due process of law; nor deny to any person within its jurisdiction the equal protection of the laws.

Eleven years earlier Chief Justice Roger Taney had declared in the Dred Scott decision that black people were "a subordinate and inferior class of beings" who had "no rights that white people were bound to respect." The Fourteenth Amendment gave them the same rights of citizenship other Americans possessed.

The amendment also threatened to deprive states of representation in Congress if they denied black men the vote. The end of slavery had also made obsolete the three-fifths clause in the Constitution, which had counted slaves as only three-fifths (or 60 percent) of a white person in calculating a state's population and determining the number of representatives each state was entitled to in the House of Representatives. Republicans feared that southern states would count black people in their populations without permitting them to vote, thereby gaining more representatives than those states had had before the Civil War. The amendment mandated that the number of representatives each state would be entitled to in Congress (including northern states) would be reduced if that state did not allow adult males to vote.

Democrats almost unanimously opposed the Fourteenth Amendment. Andrew Johnson denounced it, although he had no power to prevent its adoption. Southern states refused to ratify it except for Tennessee. Women's suffragists felt badly betrayed because the amendment limited suffrage to males. Despite this opposition, the amendment was ratified in 1868.

 **Reading Check** What was the purpose of the Fourteenth Amendment?

Radical Reconstruction

By 1867 radical Republicans in Congress had taken control over Reconstruction from Johnson. They then imposed policies that brought black men into the political system as voters and officeholders. It was a

MAP 12–3 Congressional Reconstruction

Under the terms of the First Reconstruction Act of 1867, the former Confederate states (except Tennessee) were divided into five military districts and placed under the authority of military officers. Commanders in each of the five districts were responsible for supervising the reestablishment of civilian governments in each state.

In which states by 1868 did black state legislators have sufficient strength to pass legislation over white opposition?

Explore this map online   at www.prenhall.com/aah/map12.3

dramatic development, second in importance only to emancipation and the end of slavery.

Republicans swept the 1866 congressional elections despite the belligerent opposition of Johnson and the Democrats. With two-thirds majorities in the House and Senate, Republicans easily overrode presidential vetoes. Two years after the Civil War ended, Republicans dismantled the state governments established in the South under President Johnson's authority. They instituted a new Reconstruction policy.

Republicans passed the **First Reconstruction Act** over Johnson's veto in March 1867. It divided the South into five military districts, each under the command of a general (see Map 12–3). Military personnel would protect lives and property while new civilian governments were formed. Elected delegates in each state would draft a new constitution and submit it to the voters.

▶▶ Map 12-3

South Carolina (61%) and possibly Louisiana (50%)

Universal Manhood Suffrage

The Reconstruction Act stipulated that all adult males in the states of the former Confederacy were eligible to vote. Those who had actively supported the Confederacy or were convicted felons were not eligible. Once each state had formed a new government and approved the Fourteenth Amendment, it would be readmitted to the Union with representation in Congress.

The advent of radical Reconstruction was the culmination of black people's struggle to gain legal and political rights. Black leaders had long argued that one of the consequences of the Civil War should be the inclusion of black men in the body politic. The achievement of that goal was due to their persistent and persuasive efforts, the determination of radical Republicans, and, ironically, the obstructionism of Andrew Johnson who had played into their hands.

Black Politics

Full of energy and enthusiasm, black men and women rushed into the political arena in the spring and summer of 1867. Although women could not vote, they joined men at the meetings, rallies, parades, and picnics that accompanied political organizing in the South. For many former slaves, politics became as important as the church and religious activities. Black people flocked to the Republican Party and the new Union Leagues.

The **Union Leagues** had been established in the North during the Civil War, but they expanded across the South as quasi-political organizations in the late 1860s. The Leagues were social, fraternal, and patriotic groups in which black people often, but not always, outnumbered white people. League meetings featured ceremonies, rituals, initiation rites, and oaths. They gave people an opportunity to sharpen leadership skills and gain an informal political education by discussing issues from taxes to schools.

Sit-Ins and Strikes

Political progress did not induce apathy and a sense of satisfaction and contentment among black people. Gaining citizenship, legal rights, and the vote generated more expectations and demands for advancement. For example, black people insisted on equal access to public transportation. After a Republican rally in Charleston, South Carolina, in April 1867, several black men staged a "sit-in" on a nearby horse-drawn streetcar before they were arrested. In Charleston, black people were permitted to ride only on the outside running boards of the cars. They wanted to sit on the seats inside. Within a month, due to the intervention of military authorities, the streetcar company gave in. Similar protests occurred in Richmond and New Orleans.

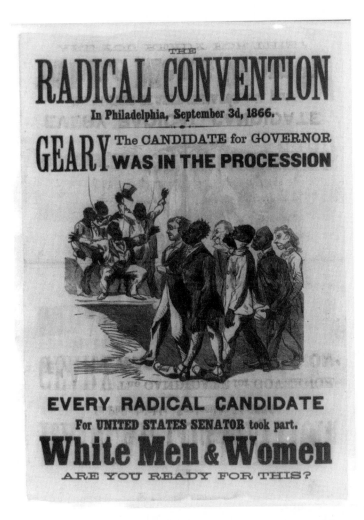

A racist poster attacks Republican gubernatorial candidate John White Geary for his support of black suffrage. The artist purports to show the convention of Radical Republicans held in Philadelphia in September 1866.

▶ Reading Check

The First Reconstruction Act (1867) stipulated that all adult males in the sates of the former Confederacy were eligible to vote with the exception of those who had actively supported the Confederacy or were convicted felons. This act, in combination with the Fourteenth Amendment extended the right to vote to all African American adult men.

Black workers also struck across the South in 1867. Black longshoremen in New Orleans, Mobile, Savannah, Charleston, and Richmond walked off the job. Black laborers were usually paid less than white men for the same work, and this led to labor unrest during the 1860s and 1870s. Sometimes the strikers won, sometimes they lost. In 1869 a black Baltimore longshoreman, Isaac Myers, organized the **National Colored Labor Union**.

Reading Check How did African American men gain the right to vote?

The Reaction of White Southerners

White Southerners grimly opposed radical Reconstruction. They were outraged that black people could claim the same legal and political rights they possessed. Such a possibility seemed preposterous to people who had an abiding belief in the absolute inferiority of black people. A statement by Benjamin F. Perry, whom Johnson had appointed provisional governor of South Carolina in 1865, captures the depth of this racist conviction. "The African," Perry declared, "has been in all ages, a savage or a slave. God created him inferior to the white man in form, color and intellect, and no legislation or culture can make him his equal. . . . His hair, his form and features will not compete with the caucasian race, and it is in vain to think of elevating him to the dignity of the white man. God created differences between the two races, and nothing can make him equal."

Some white people, taking solace in their belief in the innate inferiority of black people, concluded they could turn black suffrage to their advantage. White people, they assumed, should easily be able to control and manipulate black voters just as they had controlled black people during slavery. White Southerners who believed this, however, were destined to be disappointed, and their disappointment would turn to fury.

Using Maps to Show Change Over Time

Historians compare maps to help them identify changes over time. One far-reaching change that took place after the Civil War was the breakup of Southern plantations. The maps below show 2,000 acres of land before and after the Civil War.

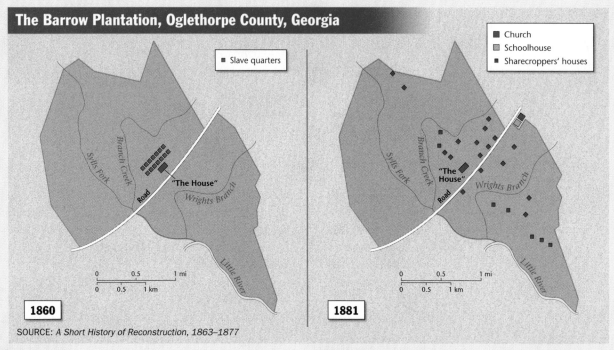

The Barrow Plantation, Oglethorpe County, Georgia

■ Slave quarters

■ Church
■ Schoolhouse
■ Sharecroppers' houses

Skulls Fork
Branch Creek
Road
"The House"
Wrights Branch
Little River

0   0.5   1 mi
0   0.5   1 km

1860

Skulls Fork
Branch Creek
Road
"The House"
Wrights Branch
Little River

0   0.5   1 mi
0   0.5   1 km

1881

SOURCE: *A Short History of Reconstruction, 1863–1877*

LEARN THE SKILL

Use the following steps to analyze maps for evidence of change over time:

1. **Identify the location and time periods of the maps.** Most maps are labeled with the location and subject. If a date is not included, historians can often determine the date based on the style and content of the map.

2. **Identify the subject of the maps.** Maps can include information about geographic features as well as man-made features, such as buildings and roads.

3. **Analyze the map key and scale.** The key identifies what different symbols and colors represent on the map. The scale helps you determine the actual distance between features shown on the map.

4. **Analyze the data on the maps.** Compare the data to draw conclusions about change over the time period the maps indicate. Also use what you already know about events in the time period.

▶ **Skills for Life**

For answers, see *Teacher's Resource Manual*.

PRACTICE THE SKILL

Answer the following questions:

1. **(a)** What specific area of land do both maps show? **(b)** What dates are given on the maps? How long a time period is represented? **(c)** Is there anything unusual about the style of the maps? Explain.

2. **(a)** What geographic features are shown on both maps? **(b)** What man-made features are shown on each map? Are they the same on both maps?

3. **(a)** According to the key, what do the red squares on the 1860 map represent? **(b)** According to the key, what do the blue squares on the 1881 map represent? **(c)** How did the mapmaker show the difference between a church and a schoolhouse on the 1881 map? **(d)** What do you think the label "The House" means on each map? **(e)** On the 1881 map, approximately how far is "The House" from any other dwelling?

4. **(a)** How has the location of dwellings on the plantation changed during this time period? **(b)** What type of dwelling has disappeared? **(c)** What type of dwelling has been added? **(d)** What other new buildings have been added? **(e)** Summarize the changes to this plantation over time. What historical events helped produce these changes?

Chapter Timeline

AFRICAN-AMERICAN EVENTS	NATIONAL EVENTS

1862

March 1862
The beginning of the Port Royal Experiment in South Carolina

February 1862
Julia Ward Howe publishes the first version of "Battle Hymm of the Republic" in the "Atlantic Monthly"

July 1862
Morrell Land-Grant College Act signed into law by Abraham Lincoln

1864

October 1864
Black national convention in Syracuse, New York

November 1864
Abraham Lincoln reelected

1865

January 1865
General Sherman's Special Field Order #15

March 1865
Freedmen's Bureau established

Sept.–Nov. 1865
Black codes enacted

April 1865
Abraham Lincoln is assassinated; Andrew Johnson succeeds to presidency

May 1865
Andrew Johnson begins presidential Reconstruction

June–August 1865
Southern state governments are reorganized

December 1865
Thirteenth Amendment to the Constitution is ratified

1866

February 1866
Southern Homestead Act

March 1866
President Johnson's vetoes of bill to extend the Freedmen's Bureau and the Civil Rights bill

April 1866
Override of Johnson's veto of the Civil Rights bill by Congress

May 1866
Memphis riot

July 1866
New Freedmen's Bureau bill enacted by Congress over Johnson's veto
New Orleans Riot

November 1866
Republican election victories produce greater than two-thirds majorities in House and Senate

1867

Spring–Summer 1867

Union Leagues and the Republican Party organized in southern states

March 1867

The first Reconstruction Act passes over President Johnson's veto

The United States agrees to buy Alaska from Russia

1868

February 1868

House impeaches President Johnson

May 1868

Senate acquits Johnson by one vote

July 1868

Fourteenth Amendment to the Constitution is ratified

November 1868

Ulysses S. Grant elected president

1869

1869

The National Colored Labor Union established under the leadership of Isaac Myers

May 1869

Transcontinental railroad completed

Chapter Review and Assessment

SUMMARY

Section 1 The End of Slavery, p. 391

- The end of slavery meant the end of the pretense of the love and loyalty of slaves for their masters.
- Former slaves wanted to establish their independence, to reunite with family members, and own their own land.
- In the immediate aftermath of the war, the federal government seemed poised to help former slaves achieve this goal.
- Over time, most southern blacks were forced into dependent labor arrangements such as sharecropping.

Section 2 Life after Slavery, p. 400

- In the decades after the Civil War, African Americans sought to build free communities.
- The black church played a central role in this effort.
- Recognizing the connection between freedom and education, blacks aggressively sought educational opportunities.
- Many whites in the South responded to defeat with violence directed at black people.
- Little was done to stop the violence and the southern justice system refused to convict whites accused of attacking blacks.

Section 3 The Crusade for Political and Civil Rights, p. 407

- Under Andrew Johnson, Reconstruction quickly came to mean a return to the status quo in the South.
- Johnson's policies were meant to placate southern elites and to return them to power.
- Southern legislatures passed black codes, laws that severely restricted the freedom of blacks.
- Blacks responded with calls for full civil rights.

Section 4 The Radical Republicans, p. 412

- Radical Republicans resisted Johnson and presidential Reconstruction. Their vision was one in which African Americans would become full participants in American society.

- Johnson's vetoes of Reconstruction legislation strengthened the Republican opposition to his policies.
- Republicans passed the Fourteenth Amendment and the First Reconstruction Act which, together, extended the right to vote to all adult males.
- White Southerners opposed radical Reconstruction. They could not accept a system based on an assumption of racial equality.

REVIEWING KEY TERMS

Write a brief explanation of the following terms.
1. Special Field Order #15, p. 393
2. Port Royal Experiment, p. 394
3. Freedmen's Bureau, p. 394
4. Southern Homestead Act, p. 398
5. sharecropping, p. 399
6. Savannah Educational Association, p. 402
7. Thirteenth Amendment, p. 409
8. black codes, p. 409
9. Radical Republicans, p. 412
10. Joint Committee on Reconstruction, p. 413
11. Fourteenth Amendment, p. 414
12. First Reconstruction Act, p. 416
13. Union Leagues, p. 417
14. National Colored Labor Union, p. 417

REVIEWING MAIN IDEAS

15. How did freedmen define their freedom? What did freedom mean to ex-slaves? How did their priorities differ from those of African Americans who had been free before the Civil War?
16. What did the former slaves and the former slaveholders want after emancipation? Were these desires realistic? How did former slaves and former slaveholders disagree after the end of slavery?
17. Why did African Americans form separate churches, schools, and social organizations after the Civil War? What role did the black church play in the black community?

18. How effective was the Freedmen's Bureau? How successful was it in assisting ex-slaves to live in freedom?
19. Why did southern states enact black codes?
20. Why did radical Republicans object to President Andrew Johnson's Reconstruction policies? Why did Congress impose its own Reconstruction policies?
21. Why were laws passed to enable black men to vote?
22. Why did black men gain the right to vote but not possession of land?
23. Did congressional Reconstruction secure full equality for African Americans as American citizens?

ANALYZING DOCUMENTS

A Northern Black Woman on Teaching Freedmen

I have been in this city now nearly five months. . . . The colored teachers three in number, sent out by the [American Missionary] Association to this city, have been brought down here it is true. And then left to the mercy of the colored people or themselves. The distinction between the two classes of teachers (white and colored) is so marked that it is the topic of conversation among the better class of colored people.

My school is very large, some of them pay and some do not. And from the proceeds I pay the board of my sister and myself, and also for the rent of two rooms; rent as well as board is very high so I have to work quite hard to meet my expenses. I also furnish lights, wood and coal. I do not write this as fault-finding, far from it. I shall be thankful if I can in any way help. I sometimes get discouraged. . . .

I have become very much attached to my school; the interest they manifest in their studies pleases me. I will now tell you how I employ my time. From 8 A.M. until 2 P.M. I teach the children. At 3 P.M. I have a class of adults and at night I have night school.

One afternoon we have prayer meeting, another sewing school. And another singing school. I hope my next letter may be more interesting to you.

Very Respectfully,
Blanche Harris
(23 January 1866, Natchez, Miss.)

—From: Ellen NicKenzie Lawson, ed., *The Three Sarahs: Documents of Antebellum Black College Women*, New York: Edward Mellon Press, 1984.

 Drawing Conclusions: What does Harris's letter suggest about the status and living conditions of black teachers?

WRITING ACTIVITY

In a short report or research paper, consider this question.

 Who supported Radical Reconstruction? Why?

STUDY ONLINE!

www.prenhall.com/aah
Additional study resources are available for this chapter on the *Companion Website*.

▶ Review and Assessment
For answers, see *Teacher's Resource Manual*.

The Promise of Reconstruction   423

13

The Failure of Reconstruction

1868–1877

The first seven African Americans to serve in the U.S. Senate and the U.S. House of Representatives. Three of them—Benjamin S. Turner, Josiah T. Walls, and Jefferson H. Long—were former slaves.

Chapter 13

An African-American attorney confers with white colleagues during an historic session of the Supreme Court in the late 1800s.

Let us with a fixed, firm, hearty, earnest, and unswerving determination move steady on and on, fanning the flame of true liberty until the last vestige of oppression shall be destroyed, and when that eventful period shall arrive, when, in the selection of rulers, both State and Federal, we shall know no North, no East, no South, no West, no white nor colored, no Democrat nor Republican, but shall choose men because of their moral and intrinsic value, their honesty and integrity, their love of unmixed liberty, and their ability to perform well the duties to be committed to their charge.

—From a speech delivered in 1872 by Jonathan J. Wright, Associate Justice of the South Carolina Supreme Court

 How would black judges and lawyers be treated in the late 1800s?

Chapter Preview

In 1868, for the first time in American history, thousands of black men would elect hundreds of black and white leaders to state and local offices across the South. Would this newly acquired political influence enable freedmen to complete the transition from slavery to freedom? Would political power propel black people into the mainstream of American society? Equally important, would white Southerners and Northerners accept black people as fellow citizens?

Events in the decade from 1867 to 1877 generated hope that black and white Americans might learn to live together on a compatible and equitable basis. But these developments also raised the possibility that black people's new access to political power would fail to resolve the racial animosity and intolerance that persisted in American life after the Civil War.

▶▶ **Witnessing History**

Black judges and lawyers would likely be limited to black clients and shunned by their white counterparts.

Section 1

Constitutional Conventions

GUIDE TO READING

▶ How did white Democrats in the South respond to the elections of 1868?

▶ What political offices were black men elected to— and not elected to—during Reconstruction?

▶ What issues most concerned black political leaders?

▶ What steps did black politicians take to deal with the economic problems facing their constituencies?

KEY TERMS

▶ carpetbaggers, p. 427

▶ scalawags, p. 427

▶ ratification, p. 428

▶ Morrill Land-Grant Act, p. 430

▶ stay laws, p. 432

New State Constitutions

Black men as a group first entered politics as delegates to constitutional conventions in the southern states in 1867 and 1868. Each of the former Confederate states, except Tennessee, which had already been restored to the Union, elected delegates to these conventions. Most southern white men were Democrats. They boycotted these elections to protest both Congress's assumption of authority over Reconstruction and the extension of voting privileges to black men. The delegates to the conventions met to frame new state constitutions to replace those drawn up in 1865 under President Johnson's authority. They were mostly Republicans joined by a few conservative southern Democrats. The Republicans represented three constituencies. One consisted of white northern migrants who moved to the South in the wake of the war. They were disparagingly called **carpetbaggers**, because they were said to have arrived in the South with all their possessions in a single carpetbag. A second group consisted of native white Southerners, mostly small farmers in devastated regions of the South who hoped for economic relief from Republican governments. This group was known derogatorily as **scalawags**, or scoundrels, by other southern white people. African Americans made up the third and largest Republican constituency.

Of the 1,000 men elected as delegates to the ten state conventions, 265 were black. Black delegates were a majority only in the South Carolina and Louisiana conventions. In most states, including Alabama, Georgia, Mississippi, Virginia, North Carolina, Arkansas, and Texas, black men made up 10 percent to 20 percent of the delegates. At least 107 of the 265 had been born slaves. About 40 had served in the Union Army. Several were well-educated teachers and ministers; others were tailors, blacksmiths, barbers, and farmers. Most went on to hold other political offices in the years that followed.

These delegates produced impressive constitutions. Unlike previous state constitutions in the South, the new constitutions ensured that all adult males could vote, and except in Mississippi and Virginia, they did not disfranchise large numbers of former Confederates. They gave broad guarantees of civil rights. In several states they provided the first statewide systems of public education. These constitutions

▶▶ **Guide to Reading/Key Terms**

For answers, see the *Teacher's Resource Manual.*

▶▶ **Recommended Reading**

John Hope Franklin. *Reconstruction after the Civil War.* Chicago: University of Chicago Press, 1961. An excellent summary and interpretation of the post-war years.

Eric Foner. *Freedom's Lawmakers: A Directory of Black Officeholders During Reconstruction.* New York: Oxford University Press, 1993. Biographical sketches of every known southern black leader during the era.

Southern black men cast ballots for the first time in 1867 in the election of delegates to state constitutional conventions.

▶ **Recommended Readings**

Howard N. Rabinowitz, ed. *Southern Black Leaders of the Reconstruction Era*. Urbana, IL: University of Illinois Press, 1982. A series of biographical essays on black politicians.

Thomas Holt. *Black Over White: Negro Political Leadership in South Carolina*. Urbana, IL: University of Illinois Press, 1979. A masterful and sophisticated study of black leaders in the state with the most black politicians.

were progressive, not radical. Black and white Republicans hoped to attract support from white Southerners for the new state governments by encouraging state support for private businesses, especially railroad construction.

Elections

Elections were held in 1868 to ratify the new constitutions and elect officials. The white Democratic response varied. In some states, Democrats boycotted the elections. In others, they participated, but voted against **ratification**. In still other states they supported ratification and attempted to elect as many Democrats as possible to office. Congress required only a majority of those voting to ratify the constitutions. In each state a majority of those voting eventually did vote to ratify. In each state black men were elected to political offices.

Black Political Leaders

Over the next decade, 1,465 black men held political office in the South. Black leaders, individually and collectively, enjoyed significant political leverage. However, white Republicans dominated politics during Reconstruction. In general the number of black officials in a state reflected the size of that state's African-American population. Black people were a substantial majority of the population in just Mississippi and South Carolina. Most of the black officeholders came from those two states and Louisiana, where black people were a bare majority. In most states, such as Arkansas, North Carolina, Tennessee, and Texas where black people made up between 25 percent and 40 percent of the population, far fewer black men were elected to office (see Table 13–1).

Initially, black men chose not to run for the most important political offices. They feared their election would further alienate already angry white Southerners. But as white Republicans swept into office in 1868, black leaders reversed their strategy. By 1870 black men had been elected to many key political positions. No black man was elected governor, but Lieutenant Governor P. B. S. Pinchback served one month as governor in Louisiana after the white governor was removed from office. Blanche K. Bruce and Hiram Revels represented Mississippi in the U.S. Senate. Beginning with Joseph Rainey in 1870 in South Carolina, fourteen black men served in the U.S. House of Representatives during Reconstruction. Six men served as lieutenant governors. In Mississippi and South Carolina, a majority of the representatives in state houses were black men, and each of these states had two black speakers of the house in the 1870s. Jonathan J. Wright, quoted at the beginning of this chapter, served seven years as a state supreme court justice in South Carolina. Four black men served as state superin-

African-American Population and Officeholding during Reconstruction in the States Subject to Congressional Reconstruction

	African-American Population in 1870	African Americans as Percentage of Total Population	Number of African-American Officeholders during Reconstruction
South Carolina	415,814	58.9	314
Mississippi	444,201	53.6	226
Louisiana	364,210	50.1	210
North Carolina	391,650	36.5	180
Alabama	475,510	47.6	167
Georgia	545,142	46.0	108
Virginia	512,841	41.8	85
Florida	91,689	48.7	58
Arkansas	122,169	25.2	46
Texas	253,475	30.9	46
Tennessee	322,331	25.6	20

Source: Eric Foner, *Freedom's Lawmakers: A Directory of Black Officeholders during Reconstruction* (1993), xiv; The Statistics of the Population of the United States, Ninth Census (1873), xvii.

tendents of education, and Francis L. Cardozo served as South Carolina's secretary of state and then treasurer. During Reconstruction, 112 black state senators and 683 black representatives were elected. There were also 41 black sheriffs, 5 black mayors, and 31 black coroners. Tallahassee, Florida, and Little Rock, Arkansas, had black police chiefs.

Many of these men were well qualified. Others were not. Of the 1,465 black officeholders, at least 378 had been free before the Civil War, 933 were literate, and 195 were illiterate. Sixty-four had attended college or professional school. In fact, 14 of the leaders had been students at Oberlin College in Ohio, which began admitting both black and female students before the Civil War.

Several black politicians were wealthy, and a few were former slave owners. Former slave Ferdinand Havis became a member of the Arkansas House of Representatives. He owned a saloon, a whiskey business, and two thousand acres near Pine Bluff, where he became known as "the Colored Millionaire."

Black men did not dominate any state politically. A few did dominate districts with sizable black populations. Before he was elected to the U.S. Senate, Blanche K. Bruce all but controlled Bolivar County, Mississippi. He served as sheriff, tax collector, and superintendent of education. Former slave and Civil War hero Robert Smalls was the political "kingpin"

▶▶ **Document**

13-3 *Blanche K. Bruce, Speech in the Senate, 1876*
Bruce won election to the U.S. Senate in 1874, where he was the first African American to serve a full term. In this selection, Bruce protests violent election frauds in his home state.

▶▶ **Teaching Notes**

Black farmers and artisans—tailors, carpenters, and barbers—were well represented among those who held political office. There were also 237 ministers and 172 teachers. At least 129 had served in the Union Army, and 46 had worked for the Freedmen's Bureau.

Hiram R. Revels represented Mississippi in the U.S. Senate from February 1870 until March 1871. He went on to serve as Mississippi's secretary of state.

▶ **Reading Check**

Black men served in a variety of positions, including as congressmen in the U.S. House of Representatives, as lieutenant governors, as representatives in states houses, and in other state offices. However, no black man was elected governor.

in Beaufort, South Carolina. He served successively in the South Carolina house and senate, and in the U.S. House of Representatives. He was also a member of the South Carolina constitutional conventions in 1868 and 1895. He was a major figure in the Republican Party. He served as customs collector in Beaufort from 1889 to 1913.

 Reading Check What political offices were black men elected to—and not elected to—during Reconstruction?

The Issues

Many, but not all, black and white Republican leaders favored increasing the authority of state governments to promote the welfare of all the state's citizens. Before the Civil War, most southern states did not provide schools, medical care, assistance for the mentally impaired, or prisons. Such concerns—if attended to at all—were left to local communities or families.

Education and Social Welfare

Black leaders were eager to increase literacy and promote education among black people. Republican politicians created statewide systems of public education throughout the South. It was a difficult and expensive task, and the results were only a limited success. Schools had to be built, teachers employed, and textbooks provided. To pay for it, taxes were increased in states still reeling from the war.

Some people—black and white—opposed compulsory education laws, preferring to let parents determine whether their children should attend school or work to help the family. Some black leaders favored a poll tax on voting if the funds it brought in were spent on the schools. Thus, although Reconstruction leaders established a strong commitment to public education, the results they achieved were uneven.

Furthermore, white parents refused to send their children to integrated schools. Although no laws required segregation, public schools during and after Reconstruction were segregated. Black parents were usually more concerned that their children should have schools to attend than whether the schools were integrated. New Orleans, however, was an exception; it provided integrated schools.

Reconstruction leaders also supported higher education. In 1872 Mississippi legislators took advantage of the 1862 federal **Morrill Land-Grant Act**, which provided states with funds for agricultural and mechanical colleges. They founded the first historically black state university: Alcorn A&M College. The university was named after a white Republican governor, James L. Alcorn. Former U.S. senator Hiram Revels was its first president. The South Carolina legislature created a similar college and attached it to the Methodist-sponsored Claflin University. Black leaders in the state legislature compelled the University of South Carolina, which

had been all white, to admit black students and hire black faculty. Many, but not all, of the white students and faculty left.

Despite the costs, Reconstruction leaders also created the first state-supported institutions for the insane, the blind, and the deaf in the South. Some southern states during Reconstruction began to offer medical care and public health programs. Orphanages were established. State prisons were built. Black leaders also supported revising state criminal codes, eliminating corporal punishment for many crimes, and reducing the number of capital crimes.

Civil Rights

Black politicians were often the victims of racial discrimination when they tried to use public transportation and accommodations such as hotels and restaurants. Rather than provide separate arrangements for black customers, white-owned businesses simply excluded black patrons. This was true in the North as well as the South. Robert Smalls, for example, the Civil War hero, was unceremoniously ejected from a Philadelphia streetcar in 1864. After protests, the company agreed to accept black riders. In South Carolina, Jonathan J. Wright won $1,200 in a lawsuit against a railroad after he had purchased a first-class ticket but had been forced to ride in the second-class coach.

Black leaders were determined to open public facilities to all people. In the process deep divisions between themselves and white Republicans were revealed. In several southern states they introduced bills to prevent proprietors from excluding black people from restaurants, barrooms, hotels, concert halls, and auditoriums, as well as railroad coaches, streetcars, and steamboats. Many white Republicans and virtually every Democrat attacked such proposals as efforts to promote social equality and gain access for black people to places where they were not welcome. Only South Carolina—with a black majority in the house and many black members in the senate—enacted such a law, but it was not effectively enforced. In Mississippi, the Republican governor James L. Alcorn vetoed a bill to outlaw racial discrimination by railroads. In Alabama and North Carolina, civil rights bills were defeated. Georgia and Arkansas enacted measures that encouraged segregation.

Economic Issues

Black politicians sought to promote economic development in general and for black people in particular. For example, white landowners sometimes arbitrarily fired black agricultural laborers near the end of the growing season and then did not pay them. Some of these landowners were dishonest, but others were in debt and could not pay their workers. To prevent such situations, black politicians secured laws that required laborers to be paid before the crop was sold or at the time when it was sold.

were murdered in 1868 in South Carolina. In 1870 black lawmaker Richard Burke was killed in Sumter County, Alabama, because he was considered too influential among "people of his color."

White men attacked a Republican campaign rally in Eutaw, Alabama, in 1870 and killed four black men and wounded fifty-four other people. After three black leaders were arrested in 1871 in Meridian, Mississippi, for delivering what many white people considered inflammatory speeches, shooting broke out in the courtroom. The Republican judge and two of the defendants were killed. In a wave of violence, thirty black people were murdered, including every black leader in the small community. In the same year, a mob of five hundred men broke into the jail in Union County, South Carolina, and lynched eight black prisoners who had been accused of killing a Confederate veteran.

 Reading Check What was the purpose of the Ku Klux Klan and how effective was it?

The Klan and York County

Nowhere was the Klan more active and violent than in York County, South Carolina. Almost the entire adult white male population joined in threatening, attacking, and murdering the black population. Hundreds were beaten and at least eleven killed. Terrified families fled from their homes into the woods. Appeals for help were sent to Governor Robert K. Scott.

But Scott did not send aid. He had already sent the South Carolina militia into areas of Klan activity, and even more violence had resulted. The militia was made up mostly of black men, and white terrorists retaliated by killing militia officers. Scott could not send white men to York County because most of them sympathized with the Klan. Thus Republican governors like Scott responded ineffectually. Republican-controlled legislatures passed anti-Klan measures that made it illegal to appear in public in disguises and masks. They strengthened laws against assault, murder, and conspiracy. But enforcement was weak.

A few Republican leaders did deal harshly and effectively with terrorism. Governors in Tennessee, Texas, and Arkansas declared martial law and sent in hundreds of well-armed white and black men to stop the violence. Hundreds of Klansmen were arrested. Many fled and three

▶ **Reading Check**

The governor initially sent the militia, which was made up of black men, but more violence erupted. He did not send whites because most white men sympathized with the Klan.

▶ **Reading Check**

The Ku Klux Klan was a terrorist organization aimed at intimidating black people and neutralizing the power of the Republican Party. The Klan succeeded in reducing support for the Republican Party and helped eliminate some of its leaders. They were very effective in terrorizing blacks through intimidation, threats, and physical violence.

Federal Reconstruction Legislation: 1868–1875	
1869	Fifteenth Amendment passed (ratified 1870)
1870	Enforcement Act passed
1871	Ku Klux Klan Act passed
1875	Civil Rights Act of 1875 passed

were executed in Arkansas. But when Governor William W. Holden of North Carolina sent the state militia after the Klan, he succeeded only in provoking an angry reaction. Subsequent Klan violence in ten counties helped Democrats carry the 1870 legislative elections, and the North Carolina legislature then removed Holden from office.

Outnumbered and outgunned, black people in most areas did not retaliate against the Klan. The Klan was rarely active where black people were in a majority and prepared to defend themselves. In the cause of white supremacy, the Klan usually attacked those who could not defend themselves.

 Reading Check Why wouldn't the governor of South Carolina send aid to the blacks of York County?

The West

During the 1830s the U.S. government forced the Five Civilized tribes—the Cherokee, Chickasaw, Choctaw, Creek, and Seminole—from their southern homelands to Indian territory in what is now Oklahoma. By 1860 Native Americans held 7,367 African Americans in slavery. Many of the Indians fought for the Confederacy during the Civil War. Following the war, the former slaves encountered nearly as much violence and hostility from Native Americans as they did from southern white people. Indians were reluctant to share their land with freedmen, and they vigorously opposed policies that favored black voting rights.

Gradually and despite considerable Indian prejudice, some African Americans managed to acquire tribal land. Also, the Creeks and the Seminoles permitted former slaves to take part in tribal government. Black men served in both houses of the Creek legislature—the House of Warriors and the House of Kings. An African American, Jesse Franklin, served as a justice on the Creek tribal court in 1876. In contrast, the Chickasaw and Choctaw were absolutely opposed to making concessions to freed people, and thus the U.S. government ordered federal troops onto Chickasaw and Choctaw lands to protect the former slaves.

Elsewhere on the western frontier, black people struggled for legal and political rights and periodically participated in territorial governments. In 1867 two hundred black men voted—although white men protested—in the Montana territorial election. In the Colorado territory, William Jefferson Hardin, a barber, campaigned with other black men for the right to vote. They persuaded 137 African Americans (91 percent of Colorado's black population) to sign a petition in 1865 to the territorial governor appealing for an end to a white-only voting provision. In 1867 black men in Colorado finally did gain the right to vote. Hardin later moved to Cheyenne and was elected in 1879 to the Wyoming territorial legislature.

 Reading Check What was the experience of black people in the West during Reconstruction?

▶▶ **Reading Check**

By 1860, Native Americans held more than 7,000 African Americans in slavery. Following the war, former slaves encountered considerable hostility and violence from Native Americans. As elsewhere, blacks in the West struggled for political and legal rights.

▶ **Guide to Reading/Key Terms**

For answers, see the *Teacher's Resource Manual*.

▶ **Reading Check**

The Fifteenth Amendment stipulated that a person could not be deprived of the right to vote on the basis of race. The amendment was meant to protect black voting rights and defend Republican governments in the South.

Section 3

Protecting Civil Rights

The Fifteenth Amendment

The federal government under Republican domination tried to protect black voting rights and defend Republican state governments in the South. In 1869 Congress passed the **Fifteenth Amendment**, which was ratified in 1870. It stipulated that a person could not be deprived of the right to vote because of race: "The right of citizens of the United States to vote shall not be denied or abridged by the United States or by any State on account of race, color, or previous condition of servitude." Black people, abolitionists, and reformers hailed the amendment as the culmination of the crusade to end slavery and give black people the same rights as white people.

Northern black men were the amendment's immediate beneficiaries. Before its adoption, black men could vote in only eight northern states. Yet to the disappointment of many, the amendment said nothing about women voting and did not outlaw poll taxes, literacy tests, and property qualifications that could disfranchise citizens.

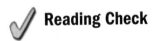 **Reading Check** What was the purpose of the Fifteenth Amendment?

The Enforcement Acts

In direct response to the terrorism in the South, Congress passed the **Enforcement Acts** in 1870 and 1871. The federal government expanded its authority over the states. The 1870 act outlawed disguises and masks and protected the civil rights of citizens. The 1871 act—known as the **Ku Klux Klan Act**—made it a federal offense to interfere with an individual's right to vote, hold office, serve on a jury, or enjoy equal protection of the law. Those accused of violating the act would be tried in federal court. For extreme violence, the act authorized the president to send in federal troops and suspend the **writ of habeas corpus**. (Habeas corpus is the right to be brought before a judge and not be arrested and jailed without cause.) Black congressmen, who had long advocated federal action against the Klan, endorsed the Enforcement Acts.

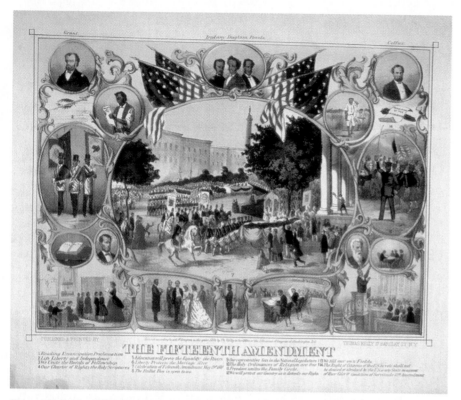

This optimistic 1870 illustration exemplifies the hopes and aspirations generated during Reconstruction as black people gained access to the political system.

Armed with this new legislation, the Justice Department and Attorney General Amos T. Ackerman moved vigorously against the Klan. Hundreds of Klansmen were arrested—seven hundred in Mississippi alone. Faced with a full-scale rebellion in late 1871 in South Carolina's up country, President Ulysses S. Grant declared martial law in nine counties, suspended the writ of habeas corpus, and sent in the U.S. Army. Mass arrests and trials followed. But federal authorities permitted many Klansmen to confess and thereby escape prosecution. The government lacked the human and financial resources to bring hundreds of men to court for lengthy trials. Some white men were tried, mostly before black juries, and were imprisoned or fined. Comparatively few Klansmen, however, were punished severely, especially considering the enormity of their crimes.

The North Loses Interest

The federal government did reduce Klan violence for a time. But white Southerners remained convinced that white supremacy must be restored and Republican governments overturned. Klan violence did not overthrow any state governments. It gravely undermined freedmen's confidence in the ability of these governments to protect them. Meanwhile, radical Republicans in Congress grew frustrated that the South and especially black people continued to demand so much of

▶ **Recommended Reading**

William Gillette. *Retreat from Reconstruction, 1869–1879.* Baton Rouge, LA: Louisiana State University Press, 1979. An analysis of how and why the North lost interest in the South.

An Appeal for Help against the Klan

H. K. Roberts, a black lieutenant in the South Carolina state militia, described Klan terror in York County in late 1870 to Governor Robert K. Scott. Roberts desperately appealed for aid to protect Republicans and defend the black community.

ANTIOCH P.O.
YORK COUNTY
S.C.

Dec. the 6th 1870. To Your Excelency R. K. Scott

Sir I will tell you that on last friday night the 2nd day of this [month] 8 miles from here thier was one of the worst outrages Commited that is on record in the state from 50 to 75 armed men went to the house of Thomas Blacks a colored man fired shots into the house and cald for him he clibed up in the loft of the house they fired up their and he came down jumped out at a window ran about 30 steps was shot down then they shot him after he fell they then draged him about 10 steps and cut his throat from ear to ear their was about 30 bullet holes in his body some 50 to one hundred shots in the house. . . . [They] abused his wife and enquired for one or two more colored men some of the colored people are leaving and a great many lying out in the woods and they reports comes to me evry day that they Ku Kluxs intend to kill us all out and I heard yesterday that they had 30 stands of arms. . . . I wish you would give me 20 or 25 men or let me enroll that many and I will stop it or catch some of them or send some U S Soldiers on for I tell you their must be something don and that quick to for I do believe that they intend to beat and kill out the Radical party in the upper Counties of the state where the vote is close if we was to have the ellection now the Radicals would turn [out] to vote their ticket I leave the matter with you I hope you will wright back to me by return mail and let me heare what you think you can do for us up here I cant tell whether I can hold my own or not I know some men that stay with us at night for safety but if they come as strong as they were the other night they may kill me and all of my men I remain yours truly as ever

H.K. Roberts, Lieut.

Commanding Post

of State Guards Kings Mountain

their time and attention year after year. There was less and less sentiment in the North to continue support for the freedmen and involvement in southern affairs.

Many Republicans in the North lost interest in issues and principles and became more concerned with elections and economic issues. By the mid-1870s there was more discussion in Congress of patronage, veterans' pensions, railroads, taxes, tariffs, the economy, and monetary policy than civil rights or the future of the South.

The American political system was awash in corruption by the 1870s, and that detracted from concerns over the South. Though President Ulysses S. Grant was a man of integrity and honesty, many men in his administration were not. They were implicated in an assortment of scandals involving the construction of the transcontinental railroad, federal taxes on whiskey, and fraud within the Bureau of Indian Affairs. William Marcy "Boss" Tweed and the Democratic political machine that dominated New York City were riddled with corruption as well.

Many Republicans began to question the necessity for more moral, military, and political support for African Americans. Others, swayed by white Southerners' views of black people, began to doubt the wisdom of universal manhood suffrage. Many white people who had nominally supported black suffrage began to believe the exaggerated complaints about corruption among black leaders. And they began to believe the unrelenting claims that freedmen were incapable of self-government. Some white Northerners began to conclude that Reconstruction had been a mistake.

Economic conditions contributed to changing attitudes. A financial crisis—the **Panic of 1873**—sent the economy into a slump for several years. Businesses and financial institutions failed, unemployment soared, and prices fell sharply. In 1874 the Democrats recaptured a majority in the House of Representatives for the first time since 1860. They also took political control of several northern states.

The Freedmen's Bank

One of the casualties of the financial crisis was the Freedmen's Savings Bank, which failed in 1874. Founded in 1865 when hope flourished, the Freedmen's Savings and Trust Company had been chartered by

On January 6, 1874, Robert Brown Elliott delivered a ringing speech in the U.S. House of Representatives in support of the Sumner civil rights bill.

Congress but was not connected to the Freedmen's Bureau. However, the bank's advertising featured pictures of Abraham Lincoln. Many black people assumed it was a federal agency. Freedmen, black veterans, black churches, fraternal organizations, and benevolent societies opened thousands of accounts in the bank. Most of the deposits totaled under $50, and some amounted to only a few cents.

Although the bank had many black employees, its board of directors consisted of white men. They unwisely invested the bank's funds in risky ventures. With the Panic of 1873, the bank lost large sums in unsecured railroad loans. To restore confidence, its directors asked Frederick Douglass to serve as president and persuaded him to invest $10,000 of his own money to help the bank. Douglass lost his money, and African Americans from across the South lost more than $1 million when the bank closed in June 1874. Eventually about half the depositors received three-fifths of the value of their accounts. But many African Americans believed the U.S. government owed them a debt. Well into the twentieth century, they wrote to Congress and the president to retrieve their hard-earned money.

The Civil Rights Act of 1875

Before Reconstruction finally expired, Congress made one final—some said futile—gesture to protect black people from racial discrimination when it passed the **Civil Rights Act of 1875**. Strongly championed by Senator Charles Sumner of Massachusetts, it was originally intended to open public accommodations including schools, churches, cemeteries, hotels, and transportation to all people regardless of race. It passed in the Republican-controlled Senate in 1874 shortly before Sumner died. But House Democrats held up passage until 1875 and deleted bans on discrimination in churches, cemeteries, and schools.

The act stipulated "That all persons . . . shall be entitled to the full and equal enjoyment of the accommodations, advantages, facilities, and privileges of inns, public conveyances on land or water, theaters, and other places of public amusement." After its passage, no attempt was made to enforce these provisions, and in 1883 the U.S. Supreme Court declared it unconstitutional. Justice Joseph Bradley wrote that the Fourteenth Amendment protected black people from discrimination by states but not by private businesses. Black newspapers likened the decision to the Dred Scott case a quarter century earlier.

Section 4

The End of Reconstruction

GUIDE TO READING

▶ What did Democrats mean by "Redemption"?

▶ What was Mississippi's "Shotgun Policy"? Did it work?

▶ How and why did black and white Republican leaders lose control of every Southern state by 1877?

KEY TERMS

▶ Redemption, p. 445

▶ Shotgun Policy, p. 446

▶ Hamburg Massacre, p. 446

Violent Redemption

Reconstruction ended as it began—in violence and controversy. Democrats demanded **Redemption**—a word with biblical and spiritual overtones. They wanted southern states restored to conservative, white political control. By 1875 those Democrats had regained authority in all the former Confederate states except Mississippi, Florida, Louisiana, and South Carolina (see Map 13–1). Democrats had redeemed Tennessee in 1870 and Georgia in 1871. Democrats had learned two valuable lessons. First, few black men could be persuaded to vote for the Democratic Party—no matter how much white leaders wanted to believe former slaves were easy to manipulate. Second, intimidation and violence would win elections in areas where the number of black and white voters was nearly equal. The federal government had stymied Klan violence in 1871, but by the mid-1870s, the government had become reluctant to send troops to the South to protect black citizens.

In Alabama in 1874, black and white Republican leaders were murdered, and white mobs destroyed crops and homes. On Election Day in Eufaula, white men killed seven and injured nearly seventy unarmed black voters. Black voters were also driven from the polls in Mobile. Democrats won the election and redeemed Alabama.

White violence accompanied every election in Louisiana from 1868 to 1876. After Republicans and Democrats each claimed victory in the 1872 elections, black people seized the small town of Colfax along the Red River to protect themselves against a Democratic takeover. They held out for three weeks. On Easter Sunday in 1873, a well-armed white mob attacked the black defenders, killing 105 in the worst single day of bloodshed during Reconstruction. In 1874 the White League almost redeemed Louisiana in an astonishing wave of violence. Black people were murdered, and courts were attacked. White people refused to pay taxes to the Republican state government. Six white and two black Republicans were murdered at Coushatta. In September, President Grant finally sent federal troops to New Orleans after 3,500 White Leaguers attacked and nearly wiped out the black militia and the Metropolitan Police. But the stage had been set for the 1876 campaign.

▶ **Guide to Reading/Key Terms**

For answers, see the *Teacher's Resource Manual.*

▶ **Interactive Activity**

Did Reconstruction Work for the Freed People?
The end of the Civil War was supposed to signal the beginning of a new life for African Americans. This activity asks students to explore this issue and answer questions such as: How did newly freed slaves attempt to build lives for themselves? What were the principal obstacles they faced?

▶ **Recommended Reading**

Michael L. Perman. *Emancipation and Reconstruction, 1862–1879.* Arlington Heights, IL: Harlan Davidson, Inc., 1987. Another excellent survey of the period.

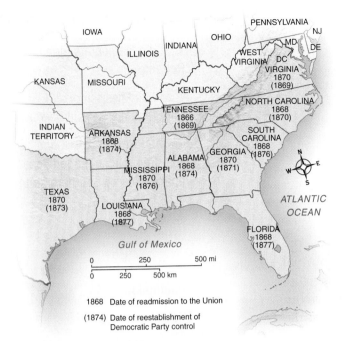

MAP 13–1 Dates of Readmission of Southern States to the Union and Reestablishment of Democratic Party Control

Once conservative white Democrats regained political control of a state government from black and white Republicans, they considered that state "redeemed."

 In which states did black and white Republicans hold political control for the shortest and longest periods of time?

Explore this map online at www.prenhall.com/aah/map13.1

➤➤ **Map 13-1**

Virginia and Georgia were held by Republicans for the shortest period of time, Louisiana and Florida the longest.

The Shotgun Policy

In 1875 white Mississippians, no longer fearful the national government would intervene in force, declared open warfare on the black majority. The masks and hoods of the Klan were discarded. One newspaper publicly proclaimed that Democrats would carry the election, "peaceably if we can, forcibly if we must."

White Mississippi unleashed a campaign of violence known as the **Shotgun Policy** that was extreme even for Reconstruction. Many Republicans fled and others were murdered. In late 1874 an estimated three hundred black people were hunted down outside Vicksburg after black men armed with inferior weapons had lost a "battle" with white men. In 1875 thirty teachers, church leaders, and Republican officials were killed in Clinton. The white sheriff of Yazoo County, who had married a black woman and supported the education of black children, had to flee the state.

Mississippi governor Adelbert Ames appealed for federal help. President Grant refused: "The whole public are tired out with these annual autumnal outbreaks in the South . . . [and] are ready now to condemn any interference on the part of the Government." No federal help arrived. The terrorism intensified. Many black voters went into hiding on Election Day, afraid for their lives and the lives of their families. Democrats redeemed Mississippi and prided themselves that they—a superior race representing the most civilized of all people—were back in control.

In Florida in 1876, white Republicans noted that support for black people in the South was fading. They nominated an all-white Republican slate and even refused to renominate black congressman Josiah Walls.

The Hamburg Massacre

South Carolina Democrats were divided between moderate and extreme factions. They united to nominate former Confederate general Wade Hampton for governor after the **Hamburg Massacre**. The prelude to this event occurred on July 4, 1876—the nation's centennial. Two white men in a buggy confronted the black militia that was drilling on a town street in Hamburg, a small, mostly black town. Democrats demanded the militia be disarmed. White rifle club members from around the state arrived in Hamburg and attacked the armory, where forty black members of the militia defended themselves. The rifle companies brought up a cannon and reinforcements from nearby Georgia. After the militia ran low on ammunition, white men captured the armory. One white man was killed, twenty-nine black men were taken prisoner, and the other eleven fled. Five of the black men identified as leaders were shot down in cold blood. The rifle companies invaded and wrecked Hamburg. Seven white men were indicted for murder. All were acquitted.

As Reconstruction drew to an end in 1876, black men from across the country assembled in Nashville, Tennessee, for the Colored National Convention.

The Hamburg Massacre incited South Carolina Democrats to imitate Mississippi's "Shotgun Policy." It also forced a reluctant President Grant to send federal troops to South Carolina. In the 1876 election campaign, hundreds of white men in red flannel shirts turned out on mules and horses to support Wade Hampton in his contest against incumbent Republican governor Daniel Chamberlain and his black and white allies. When Chamberlain and fellow Republicans tried to speak in Edgefield, they were ridiculed, threatened, and shouted down by six hundred Red Shirts, many of them armed.

Democrats attacked, beat, and killed black people to prevent them from voting. Democratic leaders instructed their followers to treat black voters with contempt. "In speeches to negroes you must remember that argument has no effect on them. They can only be influenced by their fears, superstition, and cupidity. . . . Treat them so as to show them you are a superior race and that their natural position is that of subordination to the white man."

As the election approached, black people in the up country of South Carolina knew it would be exceedingly dangerous if they tried to vote. But in the low country, black people went on the offensive and attacked Democrats. In Charleston, a white man was killed in a racial melee. At a campaign rally at Cainhoy, a few miles outside Charleston, armed black men killed five white men.

A few black men supported Wade Hampton and the Red Shirts. Hampton had a paternalistic view of black people. Although he considered them inferior to white people, he promised to respect their rights.

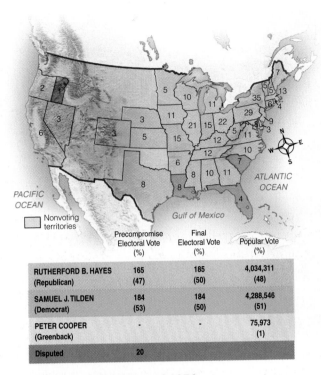

	Precompromise Electoral Vote (%)	Final Electoral Vote (%)	Popular Vote (%)
RUTHERFORD B. HAYES (Republican)	165 (47)	185 (50)	4,034,311 (48)
SAMUEL J. TILDEN (Democrat)	184 (53)	184 (50)	4,288,546 (51)
PETER COOPER (Greenback)	-	-	75,973 (1)
Disputed		20	

MAP 13–2 The Election of 1876

Democrat Samuel Tilden appeared to have won the election of 1876. Rutherford B. Hayes and the Republicans were able to claim victory after a prolonged political and constitutional controversy involving the disputed electoral college votes from Louisiana, Florida, and South Carolina (and one from Oregon).

 What factors explain the loss of political power by southern Republicans?

▶ **Map 13-2**

Violent outbreaks against southern black people to deter voting, and the view of some black men that Republicans were unreliable, contributed to the loss of political power by southern Republicans.

▶ **Reading Check**

Threats, violence, and the indifference of political leaders in the North led to the collapse of Republican power in the South. After the election of 1876, President Hayes withdrew the last federal troops from the South. The Democrats took control of Florida, Louisiana, and South Carolina and redemption was complete.

Martin Delany believed Hampton and the Democrats were more trustworthy than unreliable Republicans. Delany campaigned for Hampton and was later rewarded with a minor political post. A few genuinely conservative black men during Reconstruction also supported the Democrats and curried their favor and patronage. Most black people despised them. When one black man threw his support to the Democrats, his wife threw him and his clothes out, declaring she would prefer to "beg her bread" than live with a Democrat.

The "Compromise" of 1877

Threats, violence, and bloodshed accompanied the elections of 1876, but the results were confusing and contradictory. Samuel Tilden, the Democratic candidate, won the popular vote by more than 250,000, and he had a large lead over Republican Rutherford B. Hayes in the electoral vote. Hayes had won 167, but Tilden had 185. The 20 remaining electoral college votes were in dispute. Both Democrats and Republicans claimed to have won in Florida, Louisiana, and South Carolina, the last three southern states that had not been redeemed. (There was also one contested vote from Oregon.) Whoever took the twenty electoral votes of the three contested states (and Oregon) would be the next president (see Map 13–2).

There was a prolonged controversy. The constitutional crisis over the outcome of the 1876 election was not resolved until shortly before Inauguration Day in March 1877. Although not a formal compromise, an informal understanding ended the dispute. Democrats accepted a Hayes victory, but Hayes let southern Democrats know he would not support Republican governments in Florida, Louisiana, and South Carolina. Hayes withdrew the last federal troops from the South. The Republican administration in those states collapsed. Democrats immediately took control.

Redemption was now complete. Each of the former Confederate states was under the authority of white Democrats. Henry Adams, a black leader from Louisiana, explained what had happened.

The whole South—every state in the South had got into the hands of the very men that held us as slaves.

 **Reading Check** How and why did black and white Republican leaders lose control of every Southern state by 1877?

Analyzing Political Cartoons for Point of View

Political cartoons can tell you a great deal about the past. Political cartoonists try to influence public opinion about issues by exaggerating or highlighting certain details about the facts. A cartoon can often make a point more strongly than words alone. When you look at a political cartoon from the past, however, it is important to remember that there were different points of view when the event took place. To analyze the cartoon, be sure to consider the cartoonist's frame of reference—the place, time, and circumstances when the cartoon was created.

Reconstruction provided a wealth of material for cartoonists at the turn of the nineteenth century.

LEARN THE SKILL

Use the following steps to analyze a political cartoon for point of view:

1. **Identify the symbols used in the cartoon.** Cartoons often use visual images that stand for some other idea or event. For example, a heart is a commonly used symbol for love. A dove is a symbol for peace.

2. **Analyze the meaning of the symbols and words.** Use what you already know about the historical period and the cartoon itself to decide what the symbols refer to and how they are used as shorthand to represent actions or ideas. Summarize what is happening in the cartoon in your own words.

3. **Interpret the cartoon.** Determine what the cartoonist is saying about the political issue. Consider the cartoonist's frame of reference, and compare the cartoonist's representation with other opinions of the time and with the facts. Finally, draw conclusions about the cartoonist's point of view.

RECONSTRUCTION,
OR "A WHITE MAN'S GOVERNMENT".

PRACTICE THE SKILL

Answer the following questions:

1. **(a)** What is the freedman doing in the cartoon? **(b)** What does the tree and the freedman's holding on to the tree represent? **(c)** What is the freedman offering the drowning man?

2. **(a)** What does the drowning man represent? **(b)** What is the reaction of the man watching the attempted rescue? **(c)** Summarize the action in the cartoon; be sure to represent each character.

3. **(a)** What political issue is the cartoon about? **(b)** What is the cartoonist's point of view? **(c)** Is the cartoonist's view typical of the 1860s–1870s? Explain. **(d)** What action is the cartoon advocating? Do you think the cartoon was effective at the time? Explain.

➤ **Skills for Life**

For answers, see the *Teacher's Resource Manual.*

Chapter Timeline

1865

1865
The Freedmen's Savings Bank and Trust Company is established

1865
Freedmen's Bureau established

1866
President Johnson vetoes Freedmen's Bureau bill and civil rights bill. Congress overrides both vetoes

Ku Klux Klan is founded in Pulaski, Tennessee

1867

1867–1868
Ten southern states hold constitutional conventions

1867
Congress takes over Reconstruction and provides for universal manhood suffrage

1867
Howard University established in Washington, DC

1868
Fourteenth Amendment to the Constitution is ratified

1868
Black political leaders elected to state and local offices across the South

Ulysses S. Grant elected president

1869

1870
Hiram R. Revels is elected to the U.S. Senate and Joseph H. Rainey is elected to the U.S. House of Representatives

Congress passes the Enforcement Act

1869
Knights of Labor founded in Philadelphia

1870
Fifteenth Amendment to the Constitution is ratified

John D. Rockefeller incorporates Standard Oil Co. in Cleveland

1871

1871
Congress passes the Ku Klux Klan Act

1871
William Marcy "Boss" Tweed indicted for fraud in New York City

Much of Chicago burns in a fire

1872
Ulysses S. Grant reelected

Yellowstone National Park established

1873

1873
The Colfax Massacre occurs in Louisiana

1873
Financial panic and economic depression begin

1875

1875
Blanche K. Bruce is elected to the U.S. Senate

Congress passes the Civil Rights Act of 1875

Democrats regain Mississippi with the "Shotgun Policy"

1876
Hamburg Massacre occurs in South Carolina

1875
Whiskey Ring exposes corruption in federal liquor tax collections

1876
Presidential election between Samuel J. Tilden and Rutherford B. Hayes is disputed

Gen. George A. Custer and U.S. troops defeated by Sioux and Cheyenne in Battle of Little Big Horn

1877

1877
Last federal troops withdrawn from South

1877
The "Compromise of 1877" ends Reconstruction

Chapter Review and Assessment

SUMMARY

Section 1 Constitutional Conventions, p. 427

▶ In 1867 and 1868 constitutional conventions met in the former Confederate states.

▶ Roughly one quarter of the delegates to these conventions were black.

▶ The constitutions the delegates created were ratified in 1868. At the same time, new state officials were elected.

▶ Black leaders served in a variety of offices. Their priorities were education, civil rights, and economic opportunity.

Section 2 Black Politicians, p. 434

▶ Disagreements among black leaders and, more important, Republican factionalism undermined the power of the Republican party.

▶ The party was further damaged by opposition from white Southerners.

▶ This opposition was willing to use any means to restore white Democratic power, a fact that is attested to by the rise of the Ku Klux Klan.

▶ As elsewhere, blacks in the West struggled for political and legal rights.

Section 3 Protecting Civil Rights, p. 440

▶ In the face of rising violence, Congress passed the Enforcement Acts in 1870 and 1871. These acts had limited success in reducing attacks on black people and Republican officials.

▶ By the early 1870s, many in the North were losing interest in the issues and principles of Reconstruction, turning their attention to elections and economic problems.

▶ The Civil Rights Act of 1875 was the final federal effort to protect the rights of black people. Its provisions were never enforced and it was declared unconstitutional in 1883.

Section 4 The End of Reconstruction, p. 445

▶ Democrats were determined to "redeem" the South, which is to return southern states to conservative white political control.

▶ They were willing to use any means to achieve this end. Mississippi's "Shotgun Policy" epitomized the use of violence to regain political control.

▶ The withdrawal of federal troops from the South following the election of 1876 marked the end of Reconstruction.

REVIEWING KEY TERMS

Write a brief explanation of the following terms.

1. carpetbaggers, p. 427
2. scalawags, p. 427
3. ratification, p. 428
4. Morrill Land-Grant Act, p. 430
5. stay laws, p. 432
6. Ku Klux Klan, p. 436
7. Fifteenth Amendment, p. 440
8. Enforcement Acts, p. 440
9. Ku Klux Klan Act, p. 440
10. Writ of habeas corpus, p. 440
11. Panic of 1873, p. 443
12. Civil Rights Act of 1875, p. 444
13. Redemption, p. 445
14. Shotgun Policy, p. 446
15. Hamburg Massacre, p. 446

REVIEWING MAIN IDEAS

16. What issues most concerned black political leaders during Reconstruction?
17. What did black political leaders accomplish and fail to accomplish during Reconstruction? What contributed to their successes and failures?
18. Were black political leaders unqualified to hold office so soon after the end of slavery?
19. To what extent did African Americans dominate southern politics during Reconstruction? Should we refer to this era as "Black Reconstruction"?
20. Why was it so difficult for the Republican Party to maintain control of southern state governments during Reconstruction?
21. What was "redemption?" What happened when redemption occurred? What factors contributed to redemption?

22. How did Reconstruction end?

23. How effective was Reconstruction in assisting black people to make the transition from slavery to freedom? How effective was it in restoring the southern states to the Union?

ANALYZING DOCUMENTS

Black Leaders Support the Passage of a Civil Rights Act

[James T. Rapier]

I must confess it is somewhat embarrassing for a colored man to urge the passage of this bill, because if he exhibit an earnestness in the matter and expresses a desire for its immediate passage, straightaway he is charged with a desire for social equality, as explained by the demagogue and understood by the ignorant white man. But then it is just as embarrassing for him not to do so, for, if he remains silent while the struggle is being carried on around, and for him, he is liable to be charged with a want of interest in a matter that concerns him more than anyone else, which is enough to make his friends desert his cause. So in steering away from Scylla I may run upon Charybdis. But the anomalous, and I may add the supremely ridiculous, position of the Negro at this time, in this country, compel me to say something. Here his condition is without comparison, parallel alone to itself. Just that the law recognizes my right upon this floor as a lawmaker, but that there is no law to secure to me any accommodations whatever while traveling here to discharge my duties as a Representative of a large and wealthy constituency. Here I am the peer of the proudest, but on a steamboat or car I am not equal to the most degraded. Is not this most anomalous and ridiculous?

[Robert Brown Elliott]

The results of the war, as seen in Reconstruction, have settled forever the political status of my race. The passage of this bill will determine the civil status, not only of the Negro but of any other class of citizens who may feel themselves discriminated against. It will form the capstone of that temple of liberty begun on this continent under discouraging circumstances, carried on in spite of the sneers of monarchists and the cavils of pretended friends of freedom, until at last it stands in all its beautiful symmetry and proportions, a building the grandest which the world has ever seen, realizing the most sanguine expectations and the highest hopes of those who in the name of equal, impartial and universal liberty, laid the foundation stone.

—From: *Congressional Record*, vol. II, part 1, 43d Congress, 1st session, pp. 565–7; Peggy Lamson, *The Glorious Failure*, p. 181.

 Drawing Conclusions: If black men had the right to vote and serve in Congress, why was a civil rights law needed?

WRITING ACTIVITY

In a short report or research paper, consider this question.

 Why did so many whites in the North lose interest in the situation of blacks in the South?

STUDY ONLINE!

www.prenhall.com/aah

Additional study resources are available for this chapter on the *Companion Website*.

Higher Education for African Americans Begins

Three black colleges were founded before the Civil War. In Pennsylvania, Cheyney University opened in 1837, followed by the establishment of Lincoln University in 1854. In 1856, Wilberforce University was founded in Ohio. After the Civil War, northern black and white missionary groups fanned out across the South and—frequently with the assistance of Freedmen's Bureau officials—founded colleges, institutes, and normal schools in the former slave states in the late 1860s and the 1870s. Most of these institutions provided elementary and secondary education. Few black students were prepared for actual college or university work. Even so, black colleges soon offered academic and trade courses and professional and military training. A comprehensive list of current black colleges and universities is included on page 924.

▶ The faculty of Tuskegee Institute poses for a portrait with Mr. and Mrs. Booker T. Washington and Andrew Carnegie, the industralist (all seated in the front row.)

▲ Students perform experiments in the biological laboratory at Agricultural and Mechanical College in Greensboro, North Carolina, which began in 1892 as a land-grant college.

◀ The choir of Fisk University, Nashville, Tennessee, poses in front of the school's organ. Founded in 1866 as a liberal arts college and affiliated with the United Church of Christ, Fisk was also the home of the famed Jubilee singers, who performed in fund-raising concerts in the United States and Europe in the 1870s.

A class learns the craft ▶ of woodworking at Claflin University, Orangeburg, South Carolina, circa 1899. The university was founded in 1869 and affiliated with the United Methodist Church.

This 1850s lithograph offers a view of the buildings that comprised Wilberforce University in Xenia, Ohio, founded as a black college in 1856 by the Methodist Episcopal Church and named after the abolitionist, William Wilberforce.

These classes in dressmaking and capillary physics at Hampton Institute, (now University) in Virginia illustrate the range of studies available. Hampton was founded as a private university in 1868.

The Howard University law graduating class of 1900 poses on the campus in formal attire.

Students gathered on the campus of Berea College, in Berea, Kentucky, which was founded after the Civil War. Established by the Reverend John G. Fee in 1865, the college provided educational opportunities to black and white students, both men and women.

Howard University in Washington, D.C. provided education for African Americans in many professions, including dentistry. Howard first opened its doors in 1867 as a public university.

VISUALIZING THE PAST

	1860–1900	1900–1910

Religion

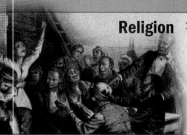

1880s–1890s Holiness Movement and Pentecostal churches spread among African Americans

1886 Augustus Tolten ordained first African-American Roman Catholic priest in Rome

1890 Baptist churches count 1.3 million southern black members, making them the largest African-American denomination

Culture

1887 Black players banned from major league baseball

1890s–1920s Emergence of jazz and the blues among southern blacks

1899 Scott Jopin writes the "Maple Leaf Rag"

1900 James W. Johnson writes "Lift Every Voice and Sing"

1901 Booker T. Washington publishes *Up From Slavery*

1903 W.E.B. DuBois publishes *The Souls of Black Folk*

1905 *The Defender* begins publication in Chicago

1908 Jack Johnson wins heavyweight championship in boxing

Politics & Government

1869–1889 Four black regiments stationed on the Western frontier

1881 First Jim Crow law segregates trains in Tennessee

1882 South Carolina disenfranchises black voters

1892 Populist Party attracts many black voters

1896 *Plessy v. Ferguson* upholds "separate but equal" doctrine of racial segregation

1898 First black officers command black troops in the Spanish-American War

1899–1901 George H. White serves as the South's last black congressman until 1972

Society & Economy

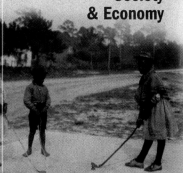

1867 Independent Order of St. Luke founded

1868 Hampton Institute founded

1870 Howard University Law School founded

1881 Tuskegee Institute founded

1886 Washington County, Texas, race riot

1887 National Colored Farmers' Alliance formed

1892 155 African Americans lynched in the U.S.

1895 Booker T. Washington addresses the Cotton States Exposition in Atlanta

1896 National Association of Colored Women founded

1903 St. Luke Penny Savings Bank established in Richmond

1904 Boule (Sigma Phi Beta) formed

1905 Niagara Movement begins

1906 Brownsville Affair
Atlanta Riot

1908 Springfield Riot
National Association of Colored Graduate Nurses founded

1909 NAACP established

Zora Neale Hurston

Countee Cullen

Jack Johnson

1910–1920

1920–1940

Key People

1920 Baseball's Negro League organized

1922 Claude McKay publishes *Harlem Shadows*

1924 Jessica R. Faucet publishes *There is Confusion*

1925 Countee Cullen publishes *Color*
Alain Locke publishes *The New Negro*

1926 Carter Woodson organizes Negro History Week
Langston Hughes publishes *The Weary Blues*

1927 James W. Johnson publishes *God's Trombones*

1928 Duke Ellington debuts at the Cotton Club
Claude McKay publishes Home to Harlem

1929 Fats Waller's "Ain't Misbehavin" opens on Broadway

1930 James W. Johnson publishes *Black Manhattan*

1933 James W. Johnson publishes his autobiography
Along the Way

1937 Zora Neale Hurston publishes *Their Eyes Were Watching God*

1914 President Woodrow Wilson defends racial segregation

1917–1918 Over 1,000 black men serve as officers in World War I

1920 Nineteenth Amendment grants female suffrage with support from black women

1921 Tulsa riot

1923 Rosewood, Florida destroyed

1910 Urban League founded
Negro Fellowship League founded

1914 Universal Negro Improvement Association founded

1915 Reemergence of the Ku Klux Klan

1917 East St. Louis riot
Houston riot

1919 Chicago riot
Elaine, Arkansas riot
Pan-African Congress meets in Paris
Marcus Garvey founds the Black Star Line

1925 National Bar Association founded
A. Philip Randolph founds the Brotherhood of Sleeping Car Porters

1927 *Nixon v. Herndon* strikes down the white primary laws

After the Civil War southern whites used terror and mob violence to repress African-American demands for political rights and social equality.

Witnessing History . . .

The supremacy of the white race of the South must be maintained forever, and the domination of the negro race resisted at all points and at all hazards—because the white race is the superior race. This is the declaration of no new truth. It has abided forever in the marrow of our bones, and shall run forever with the blood that feeds Anglo-Saxon hearts.

—Henry Grady, Editor of the Atlanta *Constitution,* 1887

I remember a crowd of white men who rode up on horseback with rifles on their shoulders. I was with my father when they rode up, and I remember starting to cry. They cursed my father, drew their guns and made him salute, made him take off his hat and bow down to them several times. Then they rode away. I was not yet five years old, but I have never forgotten them.

—Benjamin E. Mays on his childhood in Epworth, South Carolina, in 1898

 How does Mays' recollection of the incident with his father illustrate white supremacy?

Chapter Preview

▶ Witnessing History

It illustrates the power exerted over blacks by whites through the humiliation of Mays' father at gunpoint.

▶ Recommended Reading

Benjamin E. Mays. *Born to Rebel: An Autobiography.* New York: Charles Scribner, 1971. Eloquent and graphic recollection of what it was like to grow up black in the rural South at the turn of the century.

Congress, the president, and especially the Supreme Court abandoned the commitment to protect civil and legal rights of African Americans. Political and judicial leaders would not intervene to safeguard the rights of black citizens. The Supreme Court interpreted the Fourteenth Amendment to protect corporations from government regulation, but it failed to protect the basic rights of black people.

The conservative white Democrats had regained political power in the South. They were no more than mildly fearful that the U.S. government or Republicans would intrude as white authority expanded over virtually every aspect of the lives of southern African Americans. Between 1875 and 1900, black people in the South were gradually excluded from politics. They were segregated in public life and denied equal, even basic, rights. Most of them were limited to doing menial agricultural and domestic jobs that left them poor and dependent on white landowners and merchants. They were often raped, lynched, and beaten.

Unwilling and unable to tolerate such conditions, some African Americans left the South for Africa or the American West. However, most black people remained in the South where many acquired a semblance of education, some managed to purchase land, and a few even prospered.

Section 1

Politics

Black Leaders

In the late nineteenth century, black people remained important in southern politics. Black men served in Congress, state legislatures, and local governments. They received federal patronage appointments to post offices and custom houses. But as southern Democrats steadily disfranchised black voters in the 1880s and 1890s, the number of black politicians declined until the political system was virtually all white by 1900 (see Figure 14–1).

When Reconstruction ended in 1877 and the last Republican state governments collapsed, black men who held major state offices were forced out. In South Carolina, Lieutenant Governor Richard H. Gleaves resigned in 1877, but not without a protest. "I desire to place on record, in the most public and unqualified manner, my sense of the great wrong which thus forces me practically to abandon rights conferred on me, as I fully believe by a majority of my fellow citizens of this State."

For a time, some conservative white Democrats accepted limited black participation in politics as long as no black leader had power over white people and black participation did not challenge white domination. South Carolina's governor Wade Hampton even assured black people that he respected their rights and would appoint qualified black men to minor political offices.

Paternalistic Democrats like Hampton did appoint black men to lower-level positions. Hampton, for example, appointed Richard Gleaves and Martin Delany trial justices. In turn, some black men supported the Democrats. A few black Democrats were elected to state legislatures in the 1880s. Some had been Democrats throughout Reconstruction; others had abandoned the Republican Party.

Most black voters, however, remained loyal Republicans even though the party had become a hollow shell of what it had been during Reconstruction. Its few white supporters usually shunned black Republicans. The party rarely fielded candidates for statewide elections, limiting itself to local races in regions where Republicans remained strong.

GUIDE TO READING

▶ How did many black political leaders manage to remain in office after Reconstruction ended in 1877?

▶ What was the Colored Farmers' Alliance and why was it formed?

▶ What were the goals of the Populist Party?

KEY TERMS

▶ yeoman farmer, p. 464

▶ Grange, p. 464

▶ farmers alliances, p. 464

▶ Colored Farmers' Alliance, p. 464

▶ Populist Party, p. 465

▶ Subtreasury system, p. 465

▶ **Guide to Reading/Key Terms**

For answers, see the *Teacher's Resource Manual.*

▶ **Recommended Reading**

Edward L. Ayers. *The Promise of the New South: Life after Reconstruction.* New York: Oxford University Press, 1992. An excellent overview of how people lived in the late nineteenth-century South.

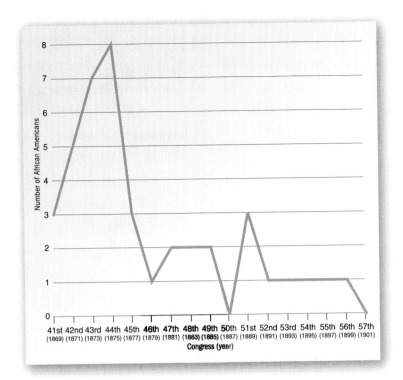

Black Congressmen

Democrats skillfully created oddly shaped congressional districts to confine much of the black population of a state to one district, such as Mississippi's third district, South Carolina's seventh, Virginia's fourth, and North Carolina's second. A black Republican usually represented these districts while the rest of the state elected white Democrats to Congress. This diluted black voting strength, and it reduced the number of white people represented by a black congressman. Thus Henry Cheatham of North Carolina, John Mercer Langston of Virginia, Thomas E. Miller of South Carolina, and George H. White of North Carolina were elected to the House of Representatives long after Reconstruction had ended (see Table 14–1).

But like their predecessors during Reconstruction, these black men wielded only limited power in Washington. They could not persuade their white colleagues to enact significant legislation to benefit their black constituents. They did, however, get Republican presidents to appoint black men and women to federal positions in their districts—including post offices and custom houses. They spoke out about the plight of African Americans.

FIGURE 14–1 African-American Representation in Congress, 1867–1900

Black men served in the U.S. Congress from Joseph Rainey's election in 1870 until George H. White's term concluded in 1901. All were Republicans.

Explore this figure online at www.prenhall.com/aah/figure14.1

✓ **Reading Check** How did many black political leaders manage to remain in office after Reconstruction ended in 1877?

Democrats

Black involvement in politics survived Reconstruction, but it did not survive the nineteenth century. Divisions within the Democratic Party and the rise of a new political party—the Populists—accompanied successful efforts to remove black people entirely from southern politics.

Militant Democrats opposed the more moderate and paternalistic conservatives who took charge after Reconstruction. In the eyes of the militants, these redeemers seemed too willing to tolerate even limited black participation in politics while showing little interest in the needs of white yeoman farmers. Dissatisfied independents, "readjusters," and other disaffected white people resented the domination of the Democratic Party by former planters, wealthy businessmen, and lawyers. They often favored limited government and reduced state support for schools, asylums, orphanages, and prisons while encouraging industry and railroads. Nor did the redeemer and paternalistic Democrats always agree among themselves. Some did favor agricultural education, the establishment of boards of health, and even separate colleges for black

▶ **Reading Check**

For a time, white Democrats accepted limited black participation in politics since black leaders no longer had power over white people and did not challenge white domination. However, the steady disfranchisement of blacks led to a political system that was virtually all white by 1900.

TABLE 14–1 Black Members of the U.S. Congress, 1870–1901

Dates	Name	State	Occupation	Prewar Status
1. 1870–1879	Joseph H. Rainey	South Carolina	Barber	Slave, then free
2. 1870–1873	Jefferson Long	Georgia	Tailor, storekeeper	Slave
3. 1870–1873	Hiram Revels*	Mississippi	Barber, minister, teacher, college president	Free
4. 1871–1877	Josiah T. Walls	Florida	Editor, planter, teacher, lawyer	Slave
5. 1871–1873	Benjamin Turner	Alabama	Businessman, farmer, merchant	Slave
6. 1871–1873	Robert C. DeLarge	South Carolina	Tailor	Free
7. 1871–1875	Robert B. Elliott	South Carolina	Lawyer	Free
8. 1873–1879	Richard H. Cain	South Carolina	AME minister	Free
9. 1873–1875	Alonzo J. Ransier	South Carolina	Shipping clerk, editor	Free
10. 1873–1875	James T. Rapier	Alabama	Planter, editor, lawyer, teacher	Free
11. 1873–1877, 1882–1883	John R. Lynch	Mississippi	Planter, lawyer, photographer	Slave
12. 1875–1881	Blanche K. Bruce*	Mississippi	Planter, teacher, editor	Slave
13. 1875–1877	Jeremiah Haralson	Alabama	Minister	Slave
14. 1875–1877	John A. Hyman	North Carolina	Storekeeper, farmer	Slave
15. 1875–1877	Charles E. Nash	Louisiana	Mason, cigar maker	Free
16. 1875–1887	Robert Smalls	South Carolina	Ship pilot, editor	Slave
17. 1883–1887	James E. O'Hara	North Carolina	Lawyer	Free
18. 1889–1893	Henry P. Cheatham	North Carolina	Lawyer, teacher	Slave
19. 1889–1891	Thomas E. Miller	South Carolina	Lawyer, college president	Free
20. 1889–1891	John M. Langston	Virginia	Lawyer	Free
21. 1893–1897	George W. Murray	South Carolina	Teacher	Slave
22. 1897–1901	George H. White	North Carolina	Lawyer	Slave

*Revels and Bruce served in the Senate, and the twenty remaining black legislators served in the House of Representatives.

students. This lack of redeemer unity permitted insurgent Democrats and even Republicans sometimes to exploit economic and racial issues to undermine Democratic solidarity.

Farmer Discontent

Many farmers felt betrayed as the industrial revolution transformed American society. They fed and clothed America, but large corporations, banks, and railroads increasingly dominated economic life. Wealth was concentrated in the hands of big industrialists and financiers. Farmers were no longer self-sufficient, admired for their hard work and self-reliance. They now depended on banks for loans, were exploited when they bought and sold goods. They found themselves at the mercy of railroads when they shipped their agricultural commodities. As businessmen got richer, farmers got poorer.

▶ Document

13-5 *"When We Worked on Shares, We Couldn't Make Nothing": Henry Blake Talks About Sharecropping after the Civil War*
Henry Blake, an African-American farmer, described the difficulties black farmers faced under sharecropping. During the Great Depression, teams of writers went south searching for exslaves to interview between 1936–1938. Known as the "Slave Narratives" it was created under the New Deal's Federal Writers Project and is an unequaled resource of first person accounts of slave life, emancipation, and Reconstruction.

This promotional print for Grange members shows scenes of farming and farm life that did not include black farmers.

Small independent (**yeoman**) farmers in the South suffered from a sharp decline in the price of cotton between 1865 and 1890. Overwhelmed by debt, many lost their land and were forced into tenant farming and sharecropping. By 1890 most farmers, both black and white—between 58 percent and 62 percent in each state in the deep South—worked land they did not own.

In response to their economic woes and political weakness, farmers organized. In the 1870s they formed the Patrons of Husbandry, or **Grange**. Initially a social and fraternal organization, the Grange promoted the formation of cooperatives and involvement in politics. Grangers especially favored government regulation of the rates railroads charged to transport crops. By the early 1880s, many hard-pressed small farmers turned to **farmers' alliances**. The first of these was the Southern Farmers' Alliance, which formed in Texas. Alliances soon spread throughout the South and northward into the states of the Great Plains and westward to the Pacific coast. These organizations further encouraged farmers to buy and sell products cooperatively and to unite politically. They favored railroad regulation, currency inflation (to increase crop prices and ease debt burdens), and support for agricultural education. By 1888 many of them joined in the National Farmers' Alliance.

The Colored Farmers' Alliance

Although the alliances were radical on economic issues, they were conservative on racial issues. The Southern Alliance did not include black farmers, who instead formed their own **Colored Farmers' Alliance**. It spread from Texas across the South in 1888 and 1889 and claimed over one million members. Even if it did not have that many supporters, the Colored Farmers' Alliance was one of the largest black organizations in American history. The alliances maintained strict racial distinctions but promised to cooperate to resolve their economic woes.

However, black and white alliance members did not always see their economic difficulties from the same perspective. Some of the white farmers owned the land that the black farmers lived on and worked. Black men saw their alliance as a way of getting a political education. In 1891, sixteen black men organized a branch of the Colored Farmers' Alliance in St. Landry Parish in Louisiana. Their purpose was to help their race and their families and to acquire enough information to vote effectively. "This organization is for the purpose of trying to elevate our race, to make us better citizens, better husbands, better fathers and sons, to educate ourselves so that we may be able to vote more intelligently on questions that are of vital importance to our people."

But white people were less certain that they wanted black men to vote at all—intelligently or otherwise. Many white alliance members harbored serious doubts about the right of black men to vote, and they opposed electing black men to office. Paradoxically, they also encouraged black

THE MILITARY OCCUPATION OF BALTIMORE—MAJOR-GENERAL BUTLER'S ENCAMPMENT ON FEDERAL HILL.—PHOTOGRAPHED BY WEAVER.—[SEE P

CITY OF MONTGOMERY, ALABAMA.—DRAWN BY OUR SPECIAL AGENT TRAVELING WITH W. H. RUSSELL, LL.D.—[SEE PAGE 341.]

Black farmers work the fields in Montgomery, Alabama in 1861.

men to vote as long as the black voters supported candidates the alliances backed. By the late 1880s, alliance-backed candidates in the South were elected to state legislatures, to Congress, and to four governorships.

 Reading Check What was the Colored Farmers' Alliance and why was it formed?

The Populist Party

By 1892 many alliance farmers threw their political support to a new political party—the People's Party. Generally known as the **Populist Party**—that mounted a serious challenge to the Democrats and Republicans. They were convinced that neither of the traditional parties cared about the plight of American farmers and industrial workers. The Populists hoped to wrestle political control of the nation's economy from bankers and industrialists and their allies in the Republican and Democratic parties and to let the "people" shape the country's economic destiny. The Populists favored no less than the federal government takeover of railroads, telegraph, and telephone companies. The new party wanted the government to operate a loan and marketing program known as a **Subtreasury system** to benefit farmers. The Populists ran candidates for local and state offices and for Congress. In 1892 they nominated James B. Weaver of Iowa for president. The Populists urged southern white men to abandon the Democratic Party and southern black men to reject the Republican Party and to unite politically to support the Populists.

The foremost proponent of black and white political unity was Thomas Watson of Georgia. He and other Populist leaders believed economic and political cooperation could transcend racial differences. During the 1892 campaign, Watson explained that black and white

▶ **Reading Check**

The Colored Farmer's Alliance was an organization of black farmers that claimed over 1 million members. The group cooperated at times with the white Southern Farmers Alliance and alliance-backed political candidates were elected across the South. It was formed because black farmers were excluded from alliances formed by white farmers.

farmers faced the same economic exploitation, but that they failed to cooperate with each other because of race. "The white tenant," he said,

> lives adjoining the colored tenant. Their homes are almost equally destitute of comforts. Their living is confined to bare necessities. They are equally burdened with heavy taxes. They pay the same high rent for gullied and impoverished land. . . .
>
> Now the Peoples' Party says to these two men, You are kept apart that you may be separately fleeced of your earnings. You are made to hate each other because upon that hatred is rested the keystone of the arch of financial despotism which enslaves you both. You are deceived and blinded that you may not see how this race antagonism perpetuates a monetary system which beggars both.

Despite such remarks, Watson was not calling for improved race relations. He opposed economic exploitation that was disguised by race, but when Democrats accused him of promoting racial reconciliation, he denied it and bluntly supported segregation to a black audience:

> They say I am an advocate of social equality between the whites and the blacks. THAT IS AN ABSOLUTE FALSEHOOD, and the man who utter[s] it knows it, I have done no such thing, and you colored men know it as well as the men who formulated the slander. It is best for your race and my race that we dwell apart in our private affairs. It is best for you to go to your churches, and I will go to mine; it is best that you send your children to the colored school, and I'll send my children to mine; you invite your colored friends to your home, and I'll invite my friends to mine.

Years after the failure of the Populists, Watson warmly and thoroughly supported white supremacy. But in 1892 Watson and the Populists desperately wanted black and white voters to support Populist candidates. The Populists lost the national election that year and again in 1896. They did win several congressional and governor's races. Southern Democrats, furious and outraged at the Populist appeal for black votes, resorted again to fraud, violence, and terror to prevail. When a biracial coalition of black and white Populists succeeded in taking political control of Grimes County in east Texas, Democrats massacred first the black and then the white leaders in 1900.

Nor is it a coincidence that in the elections of 1892, when the Democrats carried every southern state, there was an explosion of violence. Democrats were determined to destroy the Populist challenge. That year 235 people were lynched in the United States, more than in any other year in U.S. history.

The Populist challenge heightened the fears of southern Democrats that black voters could tip the balance of elections if the white vote split. But many black people were suspicious of the Populist appeals and remained loyal to the Republican Party. The Republican Party in the South, however, was a much weaker organization than it had been during Reconstruction. Many of its supporters could no longer vote. Years before the alliances and the Populists emerged, southern Democrats had begun to eliminate the black vote.

Section 2

Disfranchisement

GUIDE TO READING

▶ What methods were used to disfranchise black voters?

▶ What effect did the grandfather clause have on black voting rights?

KEY TERMS

▶ Eight Box Law, p. 467

▶ grandfather clause, p. 469

Evading the Fifteenth Amendment

As early as the late 1870s, southern Democrats had found ways to undermine black political power. Violence and intimidation, so effective during Reconstruction, continued in the 1880s and 1890s. Frightened, discouraged, or apathetic, many black men stopped voting. Black sharecroppers and renters could sometimes be intimidated or bribed by their white landlords not to vote, or to vote for candidates the landlord favored.

There was also simple injustice. In 1890 black congressman Thomas E. Miller ran for reelection and won—or so he thought. But he was charged with using illegal ballots and declared the loser. He appealed to the South Carolina Supreme Court. The court ruled that although his ballots were printed on the required white paper, it was "white paper of a distinctly yellow tinge." He did not return to Congress.

More militant and determined Democrats in the South were not content to rely on an assortment of unreliable methods to curtail the black vote. Some "legal" means had to be found to prevent black men from voting. However, the Fifteenth Amendment to the Constitution was a serious obstacle to this goal. It explicitly stated that the right to vote could not be denied on "account of race, color, or previous condition of servitude."

White leaders worried that if they imposed what were then legally acceptable barriers to voting—literacy tests, poll taxes, and property qualifications—they would disfranchise many white as well as black voters. But resourceful Democrats committed to white supremacy found ways around this problem. In 1882, for example, South Carolina passed the **Eight Box Law**. This primitive literacy test required voters to deposit separate ballots for separate election races in the proper ballot box. Illiterate voters could not identify the boxes unless white election officials assisted them.

Mississippi

Mississippi made the most concerted and successful effort to eliminate black voters without openly violating the Fifteenth Amendment. Black men had continued to vote in Mississippi despite hostility and intimidation. In 1889 black leaders from forty Mississippi counties protested the "violent and criminal suppression of the black vote." In response white men called a constitutional convention to do away with the black vote.

▶▶ **Guide to Reading/Key Terms**

For answers, see the *Teacher's Resource Manual.*

▶▶ **Living Words Audio Clip**

Track 15 *A Republican Textbook for Colored Voters,* an excerpt

Black voters cast their ballots in this historic Washington D.C. municipal election held on June 3, 1867.

With a single black delegate and 134 white delegates, the convention adopted complex voting requirements that—without mentioning race—disfranchised black voters. Voting required proof of residency and payment of all taxes, including a two-dollar poll tax. A person who had been convicted of arson, bigamy, or petty theft—crimes the delegates associated with black people—could not vote. People convicted of so-called white crimes—murder, rape, and grand larceny—could vote.

Above all, the new Mississippi constitution required voters to be literate, but with a notable exception. Illiterate men could still qualify to vote by demonstrating that they understood the constitution if the document was read to them. It was taken for granted that white voting registrars would accept almost all white applicants and fail most black applicants seeking to register under this provision.

South Carolina

Black voting had been declining in South Carolina since the end of Reconstruction. In the 1876 election, 91,870 black men voted. In the 1888 election, only 13,740 did. Unhappy that even so few voters might decide an election, U.S. senator Benjamin R. Tillman won approval for a constitutional convention in 1895. The convention followed Mississippi's lead and created an "understanding clause," but not without a vigorous protest from black leaders.

Six black men and 154 white men were elected to the South Carolina convention. Two of the black men—Robert Smalls and William Whipper (see Chapter 13)—had been delegates to the 1868 constitutional convention. The six black men protested black disfranchisement. Thomas E. Miller explained it was not just a matter of black power, but that the basic rights of citizens were at stake. "The Negroes do not want to dominate. They do not and would not have social equality, but they do want to cast a ballot for the men who make their laws and administer the laws. I stand here pleading for justice to a people whose rights are about to be taken away with one fell swoop."

It was all for naught. Black voters were disfranchised in South Carolina. White delegates did not even pretend that elections should be fair. William Henderson of Berkeley County admitted

> We don't propose to have fair elections. We will get left at that every time. . . . I tell you, gentlemen, if we have fair elections in Berkeley we can't carry it. There's no use to talk about it. The black man is learning to read faster than the white man. And if he comes up and can read you have got to let him vote. Now are you going to throw it out. . . . We are perfectly disgusted with hearing so much about fair elections. Talk all around, but make it fair and you'll see what'll happen.

 Reading Check What methods were used to disfranchise black voters?

The Grandfather Clause

In 1898 Louisiana added a new twist to disfranchisement. Its **grandfather clause** stipulated that only men who had been eligible to vote before 1867—or whose father or grandfather had been eligible before that year—would be qualified to vote. Because virtually no black men had been eligible to vote before 1867—most had just emerged from slavery—the law immediately disfranchised almost all black voters. In Louisiana in 1896, 130,000 black men voted; in 1904, 1,342 voted.

Except for Kentucky and West Virginia, each southern state had enacted elaborate restrictions on voting by the 1890s. As a result, few black men continued to vote, and no black men were elected to office.

The federal government demonstrated a fleeting willingness to protect black voting rights. Republican senator Henry Cabot Lodge of Massachusetts introduced a bill in 1890 to send federal supervisors to states and congressional districts where election fraud was alleged. But southern Democrats blocked it.

The Spread of Disfranchisement

	STATE	STRATEGIES
1889	Florida	Poll tax
	Tennessee	Poll tax
1890	Mississippi	Poll tax, literacy test, understanding clause
1891	Arkansas	Poll tax
1893, 1901	Alabama	Poll tax, literacy test, grandfather clause
1894, 1895	South Carolina	Poll tax, literacy test, understanding clause
1894, 1902	Virginia	Poll tax, literacy test, understanding clause
1897, 1898	Louisiana	Poll tax, literacy test, grandfather clause
1899, 1900	North Carolina	Poll tax, literacy test, grandfather clause
1902	Texas	Poll tax
1908	Georgia	Poll tax, literacy test, understanding clause, grandfather clause

▶ **Reading Check**

Violence and outright fraud were used to prevent blacks from voting. In addition, southern states devised a number of systems, such as literacy tests, to disfranchise black voters without openly violating the Fifteenth Amendment. The grandfather clause, first used in Louisiana in 1898, stipulated that only voters whose father or grandfather had been eligible to vote before 1867 would be eligible to vote.

But black people were even more bitterly opposed to Jim Crow streetcars. During Reconstruction, they had fended off streetcar discrimination with boycotts and sit-ins. Thirty years later, they tried the same techniques. There were streetcar boycotts in at least twenty-five southern cities between 1891 and 1910. Black people refused to ride segregated cars in Atlanta, Augusta, Jacksonville, Montgomery, Mobile, Little Rock, and Columbia. They walked or took horse-drawn hacks. Initially, the boycotts succeeded in Atlanta and Augusta, where segregation was briefly abandoned. The boycotts seriously hurt the streetcar companies. Black people also attempted to form alternative transportation companies in Portsmouth and Norfolk, Virginia, and in Chattanooga and Nashville, Tennessee. In 1905 the black community in Nashville organized a black-owned bus company and committed $25,000 to it. They purchased five buses, but they could not raise enough capital to keep the company going. It failed after a few months.

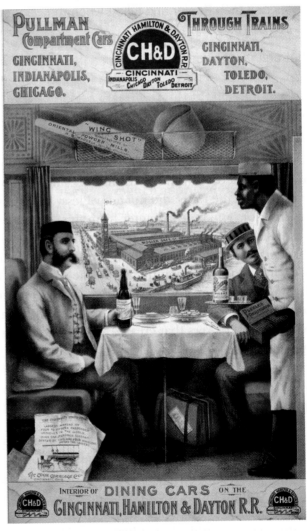

The Pullman Company employed black men to serve and wait on passengers who were usually white people. Black porters and attendants were expected to be properly deferential as they dealt with passengers.

Segregation Proliferates

"White" and "colored" signs appeared in railroad stations, theaters, auditoriums, and rest rooms and over drinking fountains. Southern white people were willing to go to any length to keep black and white people apart. Courtrooms maintained separate Bibles for black and white witnesses "to swear to tell the truth." By 1915 Oklahoma mandated white and colored public telephone booths.

Plessy v. Ferguson required "separate but equal" facilities for black and white people. When facilities were made available to black people, they were inferior to those afforded white people. Often, no facilities at all were provided for people of color. They were simply excluded. Few hotels, restaurants, libraries, bowling alleys, public parks, amusement parks, swimming pools, golf courses, or tennis courts would admit black people. The only exceptions would be black people who accompanied or assisted white people. For example, a black woman caring for a white child could visit a "white-only" public park with the child, but she dare not visit it with her own child.

Racial Etiquette

Since slavery, white people had insisted that black people act in an obedient and subservient manner. Such behavior made white dominance clear. After emancipation, white Southerners sought to maintain that dominance through a complex pattern of **racial etiquette** that determined how black and white people dealt with each other in their day-to-day affairs.

Black and white people did not shake hands. Black people did not look directly into the eyes of white people. They were supposed to stare at the ground when addressing white men and women. Black men removed their hats in the presence of white people. White men did not remove their hats in a black home or in the presence of a black woman. Black people went to the back door, not the front door, of a white house. A black man or boy was never to look at a white woman. A black man in Mississippi observed, "You couldn't smile at a white woman. If you did you'd be hung from a limb." It was a serious offense if a black male touched a white woman, even inadvertently.

White customers were always served first in a store, even if a black customer had been the first to arrive. Black women could not try on clothing in white businesses. White people did not use titles of respect—mister, missus, miss—when addressing black adults. They used first names, or "boy" or "girl," or sometimes even "nigger." Older black people were sometimes called "auntie" or "uncle." But black people were expected to use mister, missus, and miss when addressing white people, including adolescents. "Boss" or "cap'n" might do for a white man.

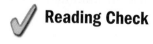 **Reading Check** How, where, and why did segregation of the races begin?

▶ **Reading Check**

In the decades following the Civil War, segregation gradually evolved into a system of white control and domination. The first segregation laws involved passenger trains. *Plessy v. Ferguson* established the legal principle of "separate but equal" public facilities, clearing the way for further legal segregation.

GUIDE TO READING

▶ Why was political violence common in the South of the 1880s and 1890s?

▶ Who were the primary targets of lynching?

▶ Why did the abuse of black women go unpunished in the late nineteenth-century South?

KEY TERMS

▶ lynching, p. 478

▶ **Guide to Reading/Key Terms**

For answers, see the *Teacher's Resource Manual.*

Section 4

Violence

Riots and Mob Violence

In the late nineteenth century, the South was a violent place. Political and mob violence, so prevalent during Reconstruction, continued unabated into the 1880s and 1890s as Democrats often used armed force to drive the dwindling number of black and white Republicans out of politics.

Washington County, Texas

In 1886 in Washington County in eastern Texas, Democrats were determined to keep the political control that they had only won in 1884 through fraud. Masked Democrats tried to seize ballot boxes in a Republican precinct. But armed black men resisted and, with a shotgun blast, killed one of the white men. Eight black men were arrested. A mob of white men in disguise broke into the jail, kidnapped three of the black men, and lynched them. Three white Republicans fled for their lives, but convinced federal authorities to investigate. The U.S. Attorney twice tried to secure convictions for election fraud. The first trial ended in a hung jury, the second in acquittal. The white Democratic sheriff did not investigate the lynching. But the black man charged with firing the shotgun was sentenced to twenty-five years in prison.

The Phoenix Riot

In the tiny South Carolina community of Phoenix in 1898, a white Republican candidate for Congress urged black men to fill out an affidavit if they were not permitted to vote. This produced a confrontation with Democrats. Words were exchanged, shots were fired, and the Republican candidate was wounded. White men then went on a rampage through rural Greenwood County. Black men were killed—how many is unknown. Others, including Benjamin Mays's father, as related in one of the quotes that opens this chapter—had to humiliate themselves by bowing down and saluting white men.

The Wilmington Riot

While white men roamed Greenwood County in search of black victims, an even bloodier riot erupted in Wilmington, North Carolina. Black and white men shared power as Republicans and Populists in Wilmington's city government, and white Democrats bitterly resented it. The Democrats were determined to drive the legitimately elected political leaders from power and would not hesitate to use violence to do so.

In the midst of this tense situation, the young editor of a local black newspaper, Alex Manly, published an editorial condemning white men for the sexual exploitation of black women. Manly also suggested that black men had sexual liaisons with rural white women, which infuriated the white community.

A white mob that included some of Wilmington's business and professional leaders destroyed the newspaper office. Black and white officials resigned in a vain attempt to prevent further violence. But at least a dozen black men—and perhaps many more—were murdered. Some 1,500 black residents of Wilmington fled. White people then bought up black homes and property at bargain rates. Black congressman George H. White, who represented Wilmington and North Carolina's second district, served the remainder of his term and then moved north. He ruefully remarked, "I can no longer live in North Carolina and be a man." White was the last black man to serve in Congress from the South until the election of Andrew Young in Atlanta in 1972.

Black men fought unsuccessfully to defend themselves in the Wilmington, North Carolina riot in November 1898.

The New Orleans Riot

Robert Charles was a 34-year-old literate laborer who had migrated to New Orleans from rural Mississippi. Infuriated by lynching, he was tantalized by the prospect of emigration to Liberia promoted by AME Bishop Henry M. Turner. On July 23, 1900, Charles and a friend were harassed by white New Orleans police officers. One of the officers attempted to beat Charles with a nightstick. Failing to subdue the large black man, the officer then drew a gun. Charles pulled out his own gun, and each man wounded the other. Charles fled and for a time evaded authorities. He was tracked down to a rooming house. He had secluded himself with a Winchester rifle with which he proceeded to shoot his tormentors. Eventually, a white mob that numbered as many as twenty thousand gathered. In the meantime, Charles—an expert marksman—methodically shot twenty-seven white people, killing seven, including four policemen. Finally, burned out of the dwelling, Charles was shot and his corpse stomped beyond recognition by enraged white people. Four days of rioting ensued in which at least a dozen black people were killed and many more injured.

⏩ **Document**

14-5 *Alex Manly and the 1898 Wilmington "Race Riot"*

This article by Alex Manly, editor of the *The Daily Record*, denounced white men who seduced black women and suggested to his readers that rural white women willingly met black men for sexual encounters. Two days after the article appeared, a mob descended on the newspaper office, destroying its press and setting fire to the building. Manly ran for his life. The mob then turned on black people, terrorizing and killing indiscriminately.

Lynching

Lynching had become common in the South by the 1890s. Between 1889 and 1932, 3,745 people were lynched in the United States (see Figure 14–2). An average of two to three people were lynched every week for thirty years. Most lynchings happened in the South, and black men were usually the victims. Sometimes white people were lynched. In 1891 in New Orleans eleven Italians were lynched for alleged involvement with the Mafia and for the murder of the city's police chief. For black Southerners, violence was an ever-present possibility. Rarely did a sheriff or police officer protect a potential victim, and even if one did, that protection was often not enough.

The people who carried out the lynchings were never apprehended, tried, or convicted. Prominent community members frequently encouraged and even participated in lynch mobs. White political leaders, journalists, and clergymen rarely denounced lynching in public. The Atlanta *Constitution* dismissed lynching as relatively inconsequential. "There are places and occasions when the natural fury of men cannot be restrained by all the laws in Christendom."

There was no such thing as a civilized lynching. Lynchings were barbaric, savage, and hideous. Such mob brutality was another manifestation of white supremacy. Black people were murdered, beaten, burned, and mutilated for trivial reasons—or for no reason. Most white Southerners justified lynching as a response to the raping of white women by black men. But many lynchings involved no alleged rape, and even when they did, the victims often had no connection to the alleged offense.

During the early 1900s the NAACP waged a battle against the lynching of black people in the South. One method used was to hang a flag outside NAACP headquarters reporting each incident of lynching that occurred.

▶▶ **Living Words Audio Clip**

Track 17 *Lynch Law in Georgia by Ida B. Wells Barnett, pamphlet excerpt*

▶▶ **Document**

14-3 *Ida B. Wells, A Red Record, 1895*
During the 1890s, Wells began speaking out and writing about the taboo subject of lynching. Wells was convinced that lynching formed a critical part of the system of racial oppression in the South, often as tool against successful black businesses. Her carefully researched anti-lynching crusade drew international attention to the issue.

FIGURE 14–2 Lynching in the United States: 1889–1932

Depending on the source, statistics on lynching vary. It was difficult to assemble information on lynching, particularly in the nineteenth century. Not every lynching was recorded.

Source: *The Negro Year Book*, 1931-32, p. 293.

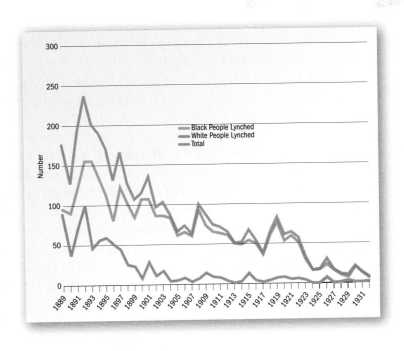

Mobs often attacked black people who had achieved economic success. In Memphis, Thomas Moss with two friends opened the People's Grocery Company in a black neighborhood. The store flourished, but it competed with a white-owned grocery. "[T]hey were succeeding too well," one of Moss's friends observed. After the white grocer had had the

PROFILE ❖ Ida Wells Barnett

Ida Wells Barnett began life as a slave in 1862 and grew up during Reconstruction. As a young woman, she saw the worst indignities and cruelties that the Jim Crow South could inflict. She fought back as a journalist, agitator, and reformer.

Ida Wells was one of eight children born to Jim and Lizzie Wells in Holly Springs, Mississippi. After the Civil War, she attended a school for freed people with her mother, and they learned to read and write. She attended Shaw University in Holly Springs (now Rust College) and taught school in Mississippi and Tennessee.

In 1884 a railroad conductor removed Wells from a first-class car. She sued the railroad and won a $500 settlement. But a higher court reversed the decision.

Wells took up journalism. She wrote a weekly column for *The Living Way*. In 1889 she bought a one-third interest in the Memphis *Free Speech and Headlight*. She wrote about racial issues and criticized black educators for the quality of black schools. In 1892 her friend Thomas Moss was lynched with two other men for the crime of running a successful grocery store. Wells expressed her rage and horror in a fiery editorial, thus beginning a lifelong crusade against lynching. Wells pointed out that more black men were lynched for challenging the myth of white superiority than for allegedly raping a white woman. She blamed white clergymen and their parishioners for tolerating lynching.

Wells moved to Chicago and wrote a pamphlet criticizing the racism at the 1893 World's Fair: *The Reason Why the Colored American Is Not in the Columbian Exposition*. In 1895 she married Ferdinand Barnett, the owner of the Chicago *Conservator*.

After a white journalist from Missouri wrote that black women were immoral, "having no sense of virtue and altogether without character," black women including Wells Barnett founded the National Association of Colored Women in 1896.

In 1909 Wells Barnett was one of two black women who supported the founding of the National Association for the Advancement of Colored People (NAACP). She later broke with the group because of its mostly white board of directors and what she considered its cautious stands. She also helped organize the Negro Fellowship League in 1910.

Wells Barnett became an ardent supporter of black voting rights. In 1913 she helped found the Alpha Suffrage Club, the first black women's suffrage organization in Illinois. She was a delegate to the National American Woman's Suffrage Association meeting in Washington, D.C.

She continued to write, campaign, speak out, and organize. She was directly involved in protesting the execution of black soldiers after the 1917 Houston riot. She took the lead in exposing the injustice 12 poor black farmers experienced after the Elaine riot and massacre in 1919. She supported A. Phillip Randolph and the formation of the Brotherhood of Sleeping Car Porters. In 1928 she ran as a Republican for the state Senate. Only death from kidney failure in 1931 ended her efforts to secure justice for black Americans.

Barnett

479

three black men indicted for conspiracy, black people organized a protest and violence followed. The three black men were jailed. A white mob attacked the jail, lynched them, and then looted their store. Ida B. Wells, a newspaper editor and a friend of Moss, was heartbroken. "A finer, cleaner man than he never walked the streets of Memphis." She considered his lynching an "excuse to get rid of Negroes who were acquiring wealth and property and thus keep the race terrorized and keep the nigger down." Responding to the incident in her paper, Wells began a lifelong crusade against lynching. Responding to the incident in her paper, Wells began a lifelong crusade against lynching. Although less often than men, black women were also lynched.

 Reading Check Who were the primary targets of lynching and why?

Abuse of Black Women

White people often justified lynching as a response to the presumed threat black men posed to the virtue of white women. White men routinely harassed and abused black women. There are no statistics on such abuse. Like lynching, rape inflicted pain and suffering, and it demonstrated the power of white men over black men and women.

Black men tried to keep their wives and daughters away from white men. They refused to permit black women to work as maids and domestics in homes where white men were present. One black man commented in 1912, "I believe nearly all white men take, and expect to take, undue liberties with their colored female servants, not only the fathers, but in many cases the sons also." A black man could not easily protect a black woman. He might be killed trying to do it. An Alabama clergyman pointed out, "[W]hite men on the high ways and in their stores and on the trains will insult our women and we are powerless to resent it as it would only be an invitation for our lives to be taken."

Many white people believed black women "invited" white males to take advantage of them. Black women were considered inferior and immoral. White people reasoned it was impossible to defend the virtue of black women because they had none. Governor Coleman Blease of South Carolina pardoned black and white men found guilty of raping black women. "I am of the opinion," he said in 1913, "as I have always been, and have very serious doubts as to whether the crime of rape can be committed upon a negro."

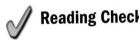 **Reading Check** Why did the abuse of black women go unpunished in the late nineteenth-century South?

▶ **Reading Check**

Most lynchings took place in the South and black men were the most frequent targets. Most white Southerners justified lynching as a response to the raping of white women by black men. However, many lynchings involved no alleged rape or targeted victims who had no connection to the alleged crime or who had achieved economic success. Lynching was another way to assert power over African Americans.

▶ **Reading Check**

Many whites believed that black women "invited" white women to take advantage of them. White people reasoned that it was impossible to defend the virtue of black women because, in their minds, they had none.

Section 5
Migration

GUIDE TO READING

▶ Why did African Americans begin to leave the South?

▶ Who were the Exodusters?

▶ Describe the economic situation of blacks in the South in the late nineteenth century.

KEY TERMS

▶ Liberian Exodus, p. 481

▶ Exodusters, p. 482

▶ 1862 Homestead Act, p. 484

▶ lien, p. 486

▶ peonage, p. 486

The Liberian Exodus

In 1900 AME minister Henry M. Turner despaired for black people in America. "Every man that has the sense of an animal must see that there is no future in this country for the Negro. [W]e are taken out and burned, shot, hanged, unjointed and murdered in every way. Our civil rights are taken from us by force, our political rights are a farce."

It is, therefore, not surprising that thousands of African Americans fled poverty, powerlessness, and brutality in the South. What is perhaps surprising is that more did not leave. The Great Migration to the northern industrial states did not begin until about 1915. Emigrants of the 1870s, 1880s, and 1890s were more likely to strike out for Africa, move west to Kansas, Oklahoma, and Arkansas, or move from farms to southern towns or cities.

When white Democrats redeemed Mississippi in 1875 with the "Shotgun Policy," a group of black people from Winona, Mississippi, wrote to Governor Adelbert Ames "to inquire about the possibility of moving to Africa. [W]e the colored people of Montgomery County are in a bad fix for we have no rights in the county and we want to know of you if there is any way for us to get out of the county and go to some place where we can get homes . . . so will you please let us know if we can go to Africa?"

They did not go to Africa, but some black Georgians and South Carolinians did. In 1877 black leaders in South Carolina, including AME minister and congressman Richard H. Cain, probate judge Harrison N. Bouey, and Martin Delany urged black people to migrate to Liberia. Many black communities and churches caught "Liberia Fever." Black people in upper South Carolina still felt the trauma of the political terror that had ended Reconstruction.

A white journalist described the situation in Chester County: "At some places in this county the desire to shake off the dust of their feet against this Democratic State is so great, that they are talking of selling out their crops and their personal effects, save what they would need in their new home." They were given promising although sometimes inaccurate information about Liberia: one potato in Liberia, they were told, could feed an entire family.

Several black men organized the **Liberian Exodus** Joint Stock Steamship Company. They raised $6,000 and hired a ship, the *Azor*, for

▶▶ **Guide to Reading/Key Terms**

For answers, see the *Teacher's Resource Manual.*

▶▶ **Teaching Notes**

In the 1910s, 90 percent of black Americans still lived in the southern states. And of those who left the South, most did not head north along the old Underground Railroad.

Milking a goat in Liberia.

the trip to Africa. The ship left Charleston in April 1878 with 206 migrants aboard. With inadequate food and fresh water and no competent medical care, twenty-three migrants died at sea. The ship arrived in Liberia on June 3.

Once settled in Liberia, several of the migrants prospered. Sam Hill established a seven hundred-acre coffee plantation. C. L. Parsons became the chief justice of the Liberian Supreme Court. But others did less well. Some returned to the United States. The Liberian Exodus Company experienced financial difficulties and could not pay for further voyages.

The Exodusters

In May 1879 black delegates from fourteen states met in a convention in Nashville presided over by Congressman John R. Lynch of Mississippi. The convention resolved to support migration. The delegates declared that "the colored people should emigrate to those States and Territories where they can enjoy all the rights which are guaranteed by the laws and Constitution of the United States." They also asked Congress—in vain—to appropriate $500,000 for this venture.

Nevertheless, black people headed west. Between 1865 and 1880, 40,000 black people known as **Exodusters** moved to Kansas. Several hundred were persuaded to migrate by Benjamin "Pap" Singleton, a charismatic ex-slave and cabinetmaker from Tennessee. Six black men were instrumental in founding the Kansas town of Nicodemus in 1877. Named after an African prince who bought his freedom, Nicodemus thrived for a few years in the 1880s. Edwin P. McCabe, a black native of

▶▶ **Retracing the Odyssey**

Nicodemus National Historic Site, Nicodemus, Kansas:. W.R. Hill was a black real estate agent who founded Nicodemus in 1877. By 1887 over 250 people lived in the town. The absence of a railroad led to a prolonged decline of what had been a small, thriving community. Most of the town's original structures have not survived.

With their meager belongings, these African Americans await the arrival of a steamboat in about 1878 to transport them to Kansas or perhaps another western location.

Troy, New York, settled for a time in Nicodemus. In 1882 Kansas voters elected him state auditor.

By 1890, however, Nicodemus went into a decline from which it never recovered. Three separate railroads were built across Kansas, but each avoided Nicodemus, spelling economic ruin for the community. Edwin McCabe moved to Oklahoma and helped found the black town of Langston. Eventually more black people settled in Oklahoma than in Kansas. By 1900 African Americans possessed 1.5 million acres in Oklahoma worth $11 million. In 1889 Congress had enacted legislation eliminating Indian Territory in Oklahoma, dispossessing the Five Civilized tribes of their land and dismantling tribal government. More than two dozen black towns including Boley and Liberty were founded in Oklahoma. There were nearly fifty black towns in the west by the early twentieth century including Allensworth, California; Blackdom, New Mexico; and Dearfield, Colorado. Other black migrants settled in rural and isolated portions of Nebraska, the Dakotas, Colorado as well as elsewhere on the Great Plains and in the Rocky Mountains (see Map 14–1).

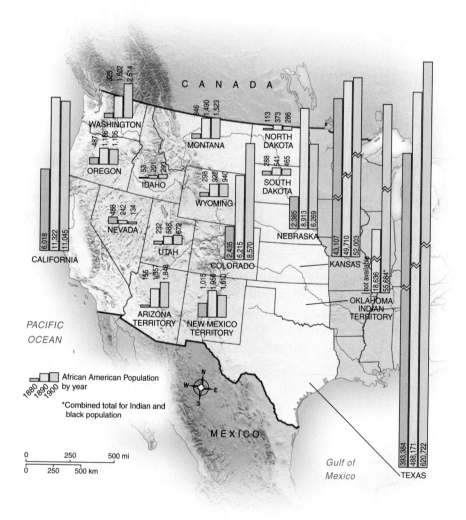

MAP 14–1 legend:
African American Population by year
1880 1890 1900
*Combined total for Indian and black population

0 250 500 mi
0 250 500 km

▶ Retracing the Odyssey

Great Plains Black Museum, Omaha, Nebraska. Contains information and artifacts on black homesteaders and on the role that black women played in migration and settlement on the Plains.

Langston, Oklahoma and Langston University. Langston was one of the many all-black towns established after the Civil War. In 1897 the town set aside forty acres to create a black land-grant university. The town and university are named for John Mercer Langston, a prominent nineteenth-century black leader and congressman from Virginia.

Historic District, Boley, Oklahoma. Boley was an all-black town incorporated in 1905. Many of the town's residents left when the economy collapsed during the Great Depression. Some of the historic black businesses and buildings still stand.

Black American West Museum and Heritage Center, Denver, Colorado. Founded by Paul Stewart, this museum is dedicated to the black pioneers of the frontier west including cowboys, soldiers, barbers, and homesteaders. It has artifacts, photographs, recordings, and other memorabilia of nineteenth- and early twentieth-century African Americans. It is located in the former home of Dr. Justina Ford, a pioneer and black woman physician, who delivered seven thousand babies of virtually every ethnic background.

MAP 14–1 African-American Population of Western Territories and States, 1880–1900
Although most African Americans remained in the South following the Civil War, thousands of black people moved west and settled on farms and ranches.

Many black and white people who moved west after the Civil War took advantage of the **1862 Homestead Act** that provided 160 acres of federal land free to those who would settle on it and farm it for at least five years. (Alternatively, a settler could buy the land for $1.25 per acre and possess it after six months' residency.) Life on the frontier was often a bleak, dreary, and lonely existence where trees were few and rain infrequent. People lived in sod houses and relied on cow (or buffalo) chips for heat and cooking fuel as they struggled to endure.

Railroads encouraged migration by offering reduced fares. Some western farmers and agents were eager to sell land, but some of it was of little value. Some of the white residents of Mississippi and South Carolina, which had large black majorities in their population, were glad to see the black people go. Others were alarmed at the loss of cheap black labor.

Some black leaders opposed migration and urged black people to stay put. In 1879 Frederick Douglass insisted that more opportunities existed for black people in the South than elsewhere. Robert Smalls urged black people to come to his home county of Beaufort, South Carolina, "where I hardly think it probable that any prisoner will ever be taken from jail by a mob and lynched."

Migration Within the South

Many black people left the poverty and isolation of farms and moved to nearby villages and towns in the South. Others went to larger southern cities including Atlanta, Richmond, and Nashville, where they settled in growing black neighborhoods. Urban areas offered more economic opportunities than rural areas. Although black people were usually confined to menial labor city work paid cash on a fairly regular basis. Rural residents received no money until their crops were sold. Towns and cities also afforded more entertainment and religious and educational activities. Black youngsters in towns spent more time in school than rural children, who had to help work the farms.

Black women had a better chance than black men of finding regular work in a town, although it was usually as a domestic or cleaning woman. This economic situation adversely affected the black family. Before the increase in migration, husband and wife headed 90 percent of black families. But with migration, many black men remained in rural areas where they could get farm work while women went to urban communities. Often these women became single heads of households.

Reading Check Why did African Americans begin to leave the South?

▶ **Reading Check**

In the face of violence, discrimination, and poverty, thousands of blacks decided to leave the South. Emigrants in the 1870s, 1880s, and 1890s tended to move to Africa, to the West, or to southern town or cities.

▶ **Document**

14-4 *Anna Julia Cooper, From A Voice from the South: By a Black Woman of the South, 1892* Born in Raleigh, North Carolina, Anna Julia Cooper was the daughter of a slave. Cooper gave a voice to the disenfranchised black women of the nineteenth century while anticipating the feminist movement of the twentieth century.

Black Farm Families

Most black people did not leave the South or move to towns. They remained poverty-stricken sharecroppers and renters on impoverished land white people owned. They were poorly educated. They lacked political power. They were always in debt. Many rural black families remained precariously close to involuntary servitude in the decades after Reconstruction.

Sharecroppers

Most black farm families (and many white families as well) were sharecroppers. Sharecropping had emerged during Reconstruction as landowners allowed the use of their land for a share of the crop. The landlord also usually provided housing, horses or mules, tools, seed, and fertilizer as well as food and clothing. Depending on the agreement or contract, the landowner received from one-half to three-quarters of the crop.

Sharecropping lent itself to cheating and exploitation. By law, verbal agreements were considered contracts. In any case, many sharecroppers were illiterate and could not have read written contracts. The landowner informed the sharecropper of the value of the product raised—typically cotton—as well as the value of the goods provided to the sharecropping family. Black farmers who disputed white landowners put themselves in peril. Although many sharecroppers were aware the proprietor's calculations were wrong, they could do nothing about it. Also, cotton brokers and gin owners routinely paid black farmers less than white farmers per pound for cotton.

First as slaves, then as sharecroppers, renters, and landowners, generations of black people toiled in the cotton fields.

▶▶ **Document**

13-4 *The New Slavery in the South—An Autobiography*
This autobiographical account of one former slaves experience from slavery to sharecropping appeared in *The Independent* in 1904.
14-1 *A Sharecrop Contract, 1882*
This contract typifies the sort of formal arrangements that many thousands of poor black and white farmers made with local landowners.

Black men were forced to accept the white man's word. One Mississippi sharecropper explained, "If we ask any questions we are cussed, and if we raise up we are shot, and that ends it."

Renters

When they could, black farmers preferred renting to sharecropping. As tenants, they paid a flat charge to rent a given number of acres. Payment would be made in either cash—perhaps $5 per acre—or, more typically, in a specified amount of the crop—two bales of cotton per twenty acres. Tenants usually owned their own animals and tools.

Crop Liens

In addition to the landowner, many sharecroppers and renters were also indebted to a local merchant for food, clothing, tools, and farm supplies. The merchant advanced the merchandise but took out a **lien** on the crop. If the sharecropper or renter failed to repay the merchant, the merchant was legally entitled to all or part of the crop once the landowner had received his payment. Merchants tended to charge high prices and high interest rates. They usually insisted that farmers plant cotton before they would agree to a lien. Cotton could be sold quickly for cash.

Peonage

Many farmers fell deeply into debt to landowners and merchants. They were cheated. Bad weather destroyed crops. Crop prices declined. Farmers who were in debt could not leave the land until the debt was paid. If they tried to depart, the sheriff pursued them. This was called **peonage**. It amounted to enslavement, holding thousands of black people across the South in a state of perpetual bondage. Peonage violated federal law, but the law was rarely enforced. When landowners and merchants were prosecuted for keeping black people in peonage, white juries acquitted them.

Black Landowners

Considering the incredible obstacles against them, black farm families acquired land at an astonishing rate after the Civil War. Many white people refused to sell land to black buyers, preferring to keep them dependent. Black people also found it difficult to save enough money to purchase land even when they could find a willing seller. Still, they steadily managed to accumulate land.

Some black families had kept land that had been distributed in the Carolina and Georgia low country under the Port Royal Experiment and Sherman's Special Field Order #15 (see Chapter 11). In 1880 black people on South Carolina's Sea Islands held ten thousand acres of land worth $300,000.

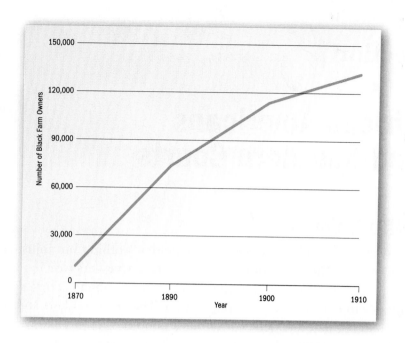

FIGURE 14–3 Black Farm Owners in Alabama, Arkansas, Florida, Georgia, Louisiana, Mississippi, South Carolina, and Texas: 1870–1910

It was very difficult for black families to acquire land. Many former slaves had barely enough money to survive, and saving money to buy land was almost impossible. Moreover, many white people would not sell land to black people. Thus it is remarkable that so many black families purchased land in the decades after emancipation.

Source: Loren Schweninger, *Black Property Owners in the South, 1790–1915*, p. 164.

By 1900 more than 100,000 black families owned their own land in the eight states of the deep South (see Figure 14–3). Black land ownership increased more than 500 percent between 1870 and 1900. Most black people possessed small farms of about twenty acres. In many cases these small plots of land were subsequently subdivided among sons and grandsons, making it more difficult for their families to prosper. But some black farmers owned impressive estates. Prince Johnson had 360 acres of excellent Mississippi Delta land. Freedman Leon Winter was the richest black man in Tennessee, with real estate worth $70,000 in 1889. Florida farmer J. D. McDuffy had an 800-acre farm near Ocala and raised cantaloupes, watermelons, cabbages, and tomatoes. Texas freedman Daniel Webster Wallace had a 10,000-acre cattle ranch. Few black people inherited large estates. Most of these landowners had been born into slavery. In the decades after emancipation, they managed to accumulate land—usually just a few acres at a time.

White Resentment of Black Success

Many white Southerners found it difficult to tolerate black economic success. They resented black progress and lashed out at those who had achieved it. When one rural black man built an attractive new house, local white people told him not to paint it—lest it look better than theirs. He accepted the advice and left the dwelling bare.

When automobiles arrived in the early twentieth century, Henry Watson, a well-to-do black farmer in Georgia, drove a new car to town. Enraged white people surrounded the car, forced Watson and his daughter out at gunpoint, and burned the vehicle.

Section 6

African Americans and Southern Courts

Segregated Justice

The southern criminal justice systems yielded nothing but injustice to black people who ran afoul of it. Southern lawmakers worried about what they considered the growing black crime problem. They worked diligently to control the black population. They enacted laws and ordinances to regulate the behavior of black people. Vagrancy laws made it easy to arrest any idle black man or one who was passing through a community. Contract evasion laws ensnared black people who attempted to escape **peonage** and perpetual servitude.

The legal system also became increasingly white after Reconstruction. Black police officers were gradually eliminated. White policemen acquired a deserved reputation for brutality. Fewer and fewer black men served on juries, which were all white by 1900. (No women served on southern juries.) When black men were accidentally called for jury duty, they were rejected. In Alabama, a black man called for a local grand jury insisted on serving until he was beaten and forced to step down. Judges were white men. Most attorneys were white. The few black lawyers faced daunting hurdles. Some black defendants believed—correctly—that they would be found guilty and sentenced to a longer term if they retained a black attorney rather than a white one. Court personnel treated black plaintiffs, defendants, and witnesses with contempt. A black defendant could not get justice. Black men and women were more often charged with crimes than white people. They were almost always convicted, regardless of the strength of the evidence or the credibility of witnesses.

Race was always the priority with jurors. Even when black people were the victims of crime, they were punished. In 1897 in Hinds County, Mississippi, a white man beat a black woman with an axe handle. She took him to court only to have the justice of the peace rule that he knew of "no law to punish a white man for beating a negro woman."

Juries rarely found white people guilty of crimes against black people. In a Georgia case in 1911, the evidence against several white people for holding black families in peonage was so overwhelming that the judge virtually ordered the jury to return a guilty verdict. Nonetheless, after five minutes of deliberation, the jury found the defendants not guilty. Many black and white people were, therefore, astonished in 1898 in

Shreveport, Louisiana, when a jury actually found a white man guilty of murdering a black man. He was sentenced to five years in prison.

Black people could receive leniency from the judicial system, but it was not justice. They were much less likely to be charged with a crime against another black person than against a white person. Black people often were not charged with crimes such as adultery and bigamy because white people considered such offenses typical of black behavior.

PROFILE ❖ Johnson C. Whittaker

Johnson C. Whittaker was born a slave in 1858 on Mulberry Plantation near Camden, South Carolina. He was the son of a house slave and a free man. In 1876 white Republican congressman Solomon L. Hoge nominated Whittaker to West Point.

During his first year at the academy, Whittaker roomed with the only other black cadet, Henry O. Flipper. But Flipper graduated in 1877, the first black man to graduate from the academy. Whittaker spent the next four years as the only remaining black cadet. White cadets refused to associate or room with him. Quiet and studious, he established a creditable academic record. But when he failed an exam in 1878, he was required to repeat a year.

Shortly after 6 A.M. on April 6, 1880, Whittaker was found lying unconscious on the floor of his room in the barracks. He was splattered with blood. His hands were tied together, and his feet were tied to the bed. Whittaker claimed he had been assaulted by three masked men after receiving a warning note the day before. A Court of Inquiry, however, declared that he had mutilated himself. Whittaker insisted on a court martial to prove his innocence. In February 1881, that court martial convened in New York City.

Whittaker was charged with conduct unbecoming an officer and with lying. After four months of testimony, the court found him guilty. The court determined that Whittaker was "shamming"—making it all up to avoid failing an exam.

The court ordered Whittaker dishonorably discharged, fined one dollar, and sentenced to a year's hard labor. In March 1882 President Chester Arthur overturned the verdict. But on the same day, the secretary of war, Robert Lincoln (Abraham's son), ordered Whittaker discharged from West Point.

Whittaker spent most of the rest of his life working with young black people at South Carolina State College and at Douglass High School in Oklahoma City. He died in South Carolina in 1931 at age 72. Whittaker had two sons. Both were commissioned officers and served in all-black units in World War I.

Whittaker summed up the meaning of his experience at West Point in a speech after the court martial found him guilty.

> West Point has tried to take from me honor and good name, but West Point has failed. I have honor and manhood still left me. I have an education which none can take from me. That education has come to me at fearful cost. The government may not wish me to use it in her service, but I shall use it for the good of my fellow men and for the good of those around me . . .

In July 1995 President Bill Clinton posthumously awarded Johnson C. Whittaker his commission in the U.S. Army.

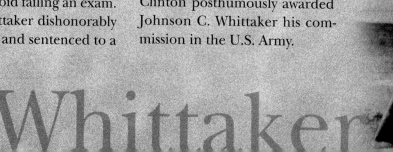

Whittaker

Black defendants who had some personal or economic connection to a prominent white person were less likely to be treated or punished the same way as black people who had no such relationship.

Black people received longer sentences and larger fines than white people. In Georgia, black convicts served much longer sentences than white convicts for the same offense—five times as long for larceny, for example. In New Orleans, a black man was sentenced to ninety days in jail for petty theft. According to a local black newspaper, it was "three days for stealing and eighty-seven days for being colored."

 **Reading Check** What was justice like for black people in the South?

The Convict Lease System

Conditions in southern prisons were indescribably wretched. Black prisoners—many incarcerated for vagrancy, theft, disorderly conduct, and other misdemeanors—spent months and years in oppressive conditions. They were subjected to the unrelenting abuse of white authorities. But conditions could and did get worse.

Southern politicians devised the **convict lease system** in the late nineteenth century. Businesses and planters leased convicts from the state to build railroads, clear swamps, cut timber, tend cotton, and work mines. The company or planter had to feed, clothe, and house the prisoners. Of course, the convicts were not paid. The state and local community was not only freed of the burden of maintaining prisons and jails but also received revenue. For example, South Carolina was paid three dollars per month per prisoner. Some states and counties found this very profitable. Law enforcement officials were encouraged to charge even more black men with assorted crimes so they could contribute to this lucrative enterprise.

Leased convicts endured appalling treatment and conditions. They were shackled and beaten. They were overworked and underfed; they slept on vermin-infested straw mattresses and received little or no medical care. They sustained terrible injuries on the job and at the hands of guards. Diseases proliferated in the camps. Hundreds died, meaning they had, in effect, been sentenced to death for their petty crimes.

Businessmen and planters found such cheap labor almost irresistible. Black prisoners found it "nine kinds of hell." It was worse than slavery because these black lives had no value to either the government or the businesses involved in this sordid system. The inhumanity of convict leasing became such a scandal that states outlawed it by the early twentieth century. Convicts were returned to state-operated penitentiaries.

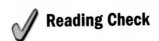 **Reading Check** How did the convict lease system make life even more difficult for black prisoners?

▶ **Reading Check**

The legal system became increasingly white after Reconstruction. Blacks who ran afoul of the legal system could have no expectation of justice. Blacks were almost always convicted. In contrast, whites accused of crimes against blacks were almost never convicted. Worried about what they considered a growing black crime problem, white officials passed laws to control and regulate the behavior of black people.

▶ **Reading Check**

Prisoners who were leased were treated worse than slaves because they were viewed as having no value (whereas slaves had value). They were supposed to be paid, cared for, and fed, but were not. Living conditions were inhumane. Many prisoners were seriously injured and hundreds died of disease or from injuries.

Expressing Problems Clearly

Expressing a problem clearly is the first step toward understanding and solving it. Problems often arise out of situations that have many elements; this makes them complex or puzzling. Other problems are difficult because there are clearly several possible solutions; this makes these problems open to debate. The ability to express a problem clearly means being able to describe a complex situation or body of information so that possible solutions can be evaluated, and the problem can be solved.

In 1877, the United States was in the midst of a depression. On July 14, the Baltimore and Ohio Railroad announced a 10 percent wage cut. The passage below is from an editorial, "The Railroad Strike," which appeared in a business journal.

LEARN THE SKILL

Use the following steps to express problems clearly:

1. **Analyze the information.** Identify the difficulties faced by the persons or groups involved. Consider what led to the problem, including the historical context. Be aware of the point of view of those who are describing the problem.

2. **Identify the basic concepts involved.** Problems usually arise out of a specific set of circumstances. However, they often revolve around a general principle, such as fairness. To identify this concept, try to express the problem in terms of what each side wants for itself.

3. **Identify the function of the supporting details.** Note details that are not basic to the problem. Eliminating them from consideration can help you see the problem more clearly.

4. **Express the problem as simply and completely as possible.** Once you have identified the main area of dispute and have stripped away irrelevant details, you are ready to express the problem clearly.

PRACTICE THE SKILL

Answer the following questions:

1. **(a)** What difficulty were the railroad companies facing? What actions did they take? **(b)** What difficulty were the workers facing? What action did they take? **(c)** Who else may have been affected by the problem? Why? **(d)** How does the historical context affect this situation? **(e)** What is the point of view of the writer of this editorial?

2. **(a)** Explain what each party wants for itself. **(b)** Do you think the writer is interested in fairness, or unfairly favors one side? Explain.

"The present strike among the employees of most of our principal railroad lines, is an illustration of errors in judgment . . . committed by the employers as well as by the employees of the railroad companies. None can deny, as a fundamental principle, the absolute necessity of . . . 'making both ends meet.' This principle is as applicable to every line of business, whether small or large, as to every family, whether poor or rich. Now, the railroad companies, in order to make ends meet, had the choice of three different means: 1st, to pay less dividends to the stockholders, in case dividends are paid; 2d, to raise the rates of freight; 3d, to reduce expenses. . . .

Of these three ways to make ends meet, the railroad companies, or rather those who are supposed to have sound judgment enough to be entrusted with their management . . . chose the latter means; and this was unjust to the employees and unfortunate for the stockholders, and especially unfortunate for the community at large, which is highly interested in reliable railroad transportation. . . .

It should not be lost sight of that the railroad on which the strike began (the Baltimore & Ohio) has been paying, and has thus far continued to pay, 10 per cent dividends to its stockholders. We ask if it would not be more just all around to pay only 8 or 9, or even 6 or 7 per cent dividend, and thus, instead of reducing the already too scanty wages of their employees, enable the railroad company to increase their pay. They forget that the interest on the capital invested must be earned by the men they employ, without whom they could not earn anything. . . ."

—*The Manufacturer and Builder*, August 1877

3. **(a)** Is the detail that the Baltimore & Ohio Company is paying 10 percent to its stockholders important to understanding the problem? Explain. **(b)** Are there any details in this excerpt that are irrelevant to the problem? Explain.

4. **(a)** Describe the problem caused by the railroad strike. **(b)** Evaluate the editorial's proposed solution. **(c)** What other solutions might be possible?

▶ **Skills for Life**

For answers, see *Teacher's Resource Manual*.

Several hundred African-American cowboys participated in the development of the western cattle empire in the decades after the Civil War.

The Anglo-Saxon said to the negro, in most haughty tones: "in this great 'battle for bread,' you must supply the brute force while I will supply the brain." . . . He will contribute the public funds to educate the negro and then exert every possible influence to keep the negro from earning a livelihood by means of that education.

They pay our teachers poorer salaries than they do their own; they give us fewer and inferior school buildings and they make us crawl in the dust before the very eyes of our children in order to secure the slightest concessions. . . .

In school, they are taught to bow down and worship at the shrine of men who died for the sake of liberty, and day by day they grow to disrespect us, their parents[,] who have made no blow for freedom. But it will not always be thus!—

—Black novelist Sutton E. Griggs in *Imperium in Imperio*, 1899.

Young African-American children being taught washing and ironing at a primary school in Hampton, Virginia in the 1890s.

 What do these quotes suggest about the education of African Americans in the late 1800s?

Chapter Review

> ►► **Witnessing History**
>
> African Americans were not being given the same level of education as whites; educational opportunities were not well funded or supported, and black students were being taught to be subservient and trained for menial jobs.
>
> ►► **Recommended Reading**
>
> James D. Anderson. *The Education of Blacks in the South, 1860–1931.* Chapel Hill, NC: University of North Carolina Press, 1988. Anderson is highly critical of the education and philosophy promoted and provided by Hampton Institute and Tuskegee Institute.

Industrialization and the rise of large, powerful corporations transformed the American economy in the late nineteenth century. Millions of European immigrants crowded into the cities of the North and Midwest to find jobs in the nation's new factories. Agriculture production increased and prices declined, impoverishing many rural Southerners. Most black people—nearly eight million—remained in the southern states, where they struggled to confront the malignant effects of white supremacy. By the late nineteenth century black Americans relied mostly on each other and the people and institutions in their own communities to sustain themselves. They established businesses and sometimes formed labor unions and went on strike. They founded their own hospitals. They expressed themselves in music by creating ragtime, jazz, and blues. At times they were allowed to participate with white people in organized sports such as professional boxing, baseball, and college football. More often, they formed their own athletic teams. African Americans refused to allow white supremacy to prevent them from creating a meaningful place for themselves in American society.

Section 1

Educating African Americans

GUIDE TO READING

▶ What kinds of educational opportunities were available to African Americans by the late nineteenth century?

▶ How was social Darwinism used to justify social and economic disparities?

▶ What was the experience of black nurses?

▶ What was the Tuskegee Model? What criticisms were made of it by W. E. B. Du Bois and others?

KEY TERMS

▶ social Darwinism, p. 499

▶ the white man's burden, p. 499

▶ talented tenth, p. 504

Social Darwinism

Pseudoscientific evidence and academic scholarship bolstered the conviction of many Americans that white people, especially those of English and Germanic descent—Anglo-Saxons—were culturally and racially superior to nonwhites and even other Europeans. Sociologists Herbert Spencer and William Graham Sumner drew on Charles Darwin's theory of evolution and concluded that life in modern industrial societies mirrored life in the animal kingdom. This theory was called **social Darwinism**. It held that through a process of natural selection, the strong would thrive, prosper, and reproduce while the weak would falter, fail, and die. Life was a struggle; only the fittest survived.

Social Darwinism applied to both individuals and "races." It conveniently justified great disparities in wealth. It suggested that men such as John D. Rockefeller and Andrew Carnegie were rich because they were "fit," whereas many European immigrants and most African Americans were poor and unlikely to succeed because they were "unfit." Many Americans and Europeans came to believe they had a responsibility to introduce the values of Western cultures to the "less advanced" and usually darker peoples of the globe. This presumed responsibility was summed up in the words of the English poet Rudyard Kipling as "**the white man's burden**."

Social Darwinism increasingly influenced the way most Protestant white Americans perceived their society. It led them to believe people could be ranked from superior to inferior based on their race, nationality, and ethnicity. Black people were invariably ranked at the bottom of this hierarchy. The eastern and southern European immigrants who were flooding the country were only slightly above them. Black people were capable, so the reasoning went, of no more than a subordinate role in a complex and advanced society as it rushed into the twentieth century. And if their position was biologically determined, why should society devote substantial resources to their education?

Education and Schools

A black youngster who wanted an education in the late nineteenth century faced formidable obstacles. Most black people were poor farmers who had few opportunities for an education and even fewer prospects

▶▶ **Guide to Reading/Key Terms**

For answers, see the *Teacher's Resource Manual*.

▶▶ **Living Words Audio Clip**

Track 18 *The Primary Needs of the Negro Race,* by Kelly Miller, excerpt

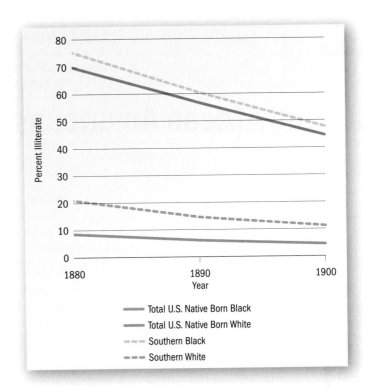

FIGURE 15–1 Black and White Illiteracy in the United States and the Southern States, 1880–1900

Although more than half of adult black Southerners were still illiterate in 1900, black people had made substantial progress in education during the last two decades of the nineteenth century.

Explore this figure online at www.prenhall.com/aah/figure15.1

for a career in business or one of the professions. It is remarkable—and a testimony to black perseverance—that so many black people did manage to acquire some education and to free themselves from illiteracy (see Figure 15–1).

Gaining even a rudimentary education was not easy. Rural schools for black children rarely operated for more than thirty weeks a year. Because of the demands of fieldwork, most black youngsters could not attend school on a regular basis.

Schools were often dilapidated shacks. They lacked plumbing, electricity, books, and teaching materials. Some schools were in churches and homes. Teachers were poorly paid and often poorly prepared.

Segregated Schools

Although southern states could not afford to support even one first-rate public school system, each of them operated separate schools for black and white children (see Table 15–1). The South had almost no public black high schools. In 1915 in 23 southern cities with populations of more than 20,000, including Tampa, New Orleans, Charleston, and Charlotte, there was not one black public high school. But these 23 cities had 36 high schools for white youngsters. In 1897 over the vehement protests of the black community, white school officials in Augusta, Georgia, closed Ware High School, the black secondary school, and transformed it into a black

TABLE 15–1 South Carolina's Black and White Public Schools, 1908–1909

Black Schools		White Schools
2,354	Public Schools	2,712
894	Men Teachers	933
1,802	Women Teachers	3,247
181,095	Total Pupils	153,807
123,481	Average Attendance	107,368
77	Pupils per School	55
63	Pupils per Teacher	35
14.7	Average Number of Weeks of School	25.2
$118.17	Average Yearly Salary for Men Teachers	$479.79
$91.45	Average Yearly Salary for Women Teachers	$249.13
$308,153.16	Total Expenditures	$1,590,732.51

School for most southern black students and teachers was a part-time activity. Because of the demands of agriculture, few rural students, black or white, attended school more than six months a year. Very few teachers were graduates of four-year college programs. The situation was better in urban communities and upper South schools, where the school year lasted longer and education was better financed. But all public schools were segregated in the South.

Source: Department of Education Annual Report, South Carolina, 1908–09, pp. 935, 961.

primary school. The U.S. Supreme Court in 1899 in *Cumming v. Richmond County* [*Georgia*] *Board of Education* unanimously refused to accept the contention of black parents that the elimination of the black high school violated the "separate but equal" doctrine announced in the *Plessy v. Ferguson* case three years earlier. Augusta was left with two white high schools—one for males and one for females, and none for black people.

Young black people who sought more than a primary education often had to travel to a black college or university that offered a high school program. In many communities, black people, with the assistance of churches and northern philanthropists, operated private academies and high schools to fill the void created by the lack of public schools. Typically students were charged a modest tuition, and those who attended came from the more prosperous families of the black community. In 1890 the number of black youngsters between the ages of fifteen and nineteen attending black public or private high schools in the South was 3,106. By 1910 that number had risen to 26,553.

▶ **Document**

15-1 *Booker T. Washington, The Atlanta Exposition Address, 1895*

▶ **Living Words Audio Clip**

Track 19 *Nineteenth Annual Report of the Principal of the Tuskegee Normal and Industrial Institute, by Booker T. Washington, excerpt*

The Hampton Model

Some black people and many white people regarded education for black youngsters a pointless exercise. In 1911 South Carolina's governor Coleman Blease was even more blunt: "Instead of making an educated negro, you are ruining a good plow hand and making a half-trained fool."

Many of those who did value schooling were convinced the most appropriate education for a black child was industrial or domestic training. Black youngsters, these people maintained, should learn skills they could teach others and use to make themselves productive members of the community.

Hampton Normal and Agricultural Institute was founded in 1868 in Virginia. It was dominated for decades by Samuel Chapman Armstrong, a white missionary with strong paternalistic inclinations. Hampton trained legions of African Americans and Native Americans to teach skills and to embrace the importance of hard work, diligence, and Christian morality. Armstrong stressed learning trades, such as shoemaking, carpentry, tailoring, and sewing. Hampton placed little emphasis on critical or independent thinking. Students were taught to conform to middle-class values. Armstrong cautioned against black involvement in politics. He acquiesced in Jim Crow racial practices. The chapel walls at Hampton featured pictures of Robert E. Lee and Andrew Johnson.

Washington and the Tuskegee Model

Armstrong's prize student and Hampton's foremost graduate was Booker T. Washington. He became the nation's leading apostle of industrial training and one of the preeminent leaders and most remarkable men— black or white—in American history. Washington was born a slave in western Virginia in 1856. His father was a white man whose identity is unknown. He was raised by his mother, Jane, in an unimpressive, but tidy, cabin of split logs on a small farm. As a child, he was employed at a salt works and in coal mines. He was also a houseboy for a prominent white family. He attended a local school where he learned to read and write.

Intensely ambitious, Washington set off for Hampton Institute in 1872. While there, he was much affected by Armstrong and his curriculum and method of instruction. He worked his way through school and taught for two years at Hampton after graduating. In 1881 he accepted an invitation to found a black college in Alabama—Tuskegee Institute. The result was an institution, which he forged almost single-handedly, that reflected his experience at Hampton and the influence of Armstrong.

Washington worked tirelessly to persuade black and white people that the surest way for black people to advance was by learning skills and demonstrating a willingness to do manual labor. Washington believed that if black people acquired skills and became prosperous small farmers, artisans, and shopkeepers, they would in time earn the respect and

Booker T. Washington was the most influential black leader in America by 1900.

acceptance of white Americans. They would eventually eradicate the race problem—all without unseemly protest and agitation.

Washington's message earned accolades from white political leaders and philanthropists. They were more inclined to support the promotion of trades and skills among black people than an academic and liberal education. Steel magnate Andrew Carnegie, impressed by Washington, financed the construction of twenty-nine buildings on the campuses of black schools and colleges. White railroad executive William H. Baldwin provided millions of dollars for black industrial education, and the John F. Slater Fund poured large sums of money into vocational education. Disciples of Washington and graduates of Tuskegee fanned out across the South as industrial and agricultural educational training for black youngsters proliferated.

The Morrill Act, which Congress passed in 1862, entitled each state to the proceeds from the sale of federal land (most of it in the West) for establishing land-grant colleges to provide agricultural and mechanical training. However, southern states did not admit black students to their A&M (Agricultural and Mechanical) schools. A second Morrill Act passed in 1890 permitted states to establish and fund separate black land-grant colleges. By 1915 there were sixteen black land-grant colleges.

Most of the institutions were not actually colleges. Few of their students graduated with bachelor's degrees. Many of them were enrolled in primary and secondary programs. Virtually all the students at the black land-grant schools had to take courses in trades, agriculture, and domestic sciences. Most of the schools required students to do manual labor for which they were paid small sums. Students built and maintained the campuses, and they raised the food served in the school cafeteria. Some of the students were in the "normal" curriculum, which prepared them to teach at a time when most states did not require a college degree for a teaching certificate.

Critics of the Tuskegee Model

Not everyone shared Washington's stress on industrial and agricultural training for young black men and women to the near exclusion of the liberal arts, including literature, history, philosophy, and languages. Washington's program, some critics charged, seemed to be designed to train black people for a subordinate role in American society. Black people, they worried, would continue to labor much as they had in slavery, and not far removed from it.

W. E. B. Du Bois, a Fisk- and Harvard-trained scholar, and AME Bishop Henry M. Turner believed education went beyond mere training and the acquisition of skills. It involved intellectual growth and development. It would confront racial problems. It would create wise men. According to Du Bois, "The function of the Negro college, then, is clear, it must maintain standards of popular education, it must seek the social regeneration of the Negro, and it must help in the solution of problems of race contact and cooperation. And finally, beyond all this, it must develop men."

▶▶ **Retracing the Odyssey**

Tuskegee Institute National Historic Site, Tuskegee, Alabama. What is now Tuskegee University opened in 1881 and remained under the leadership of Booker T. Washington until his death in 1915. His home—The Oaks—was built by students and is now a museum. His grave and memorial are also on the campus as is the George Washington Carver Museum.

Many private black colleges resisted the emphasis on agricultural and mechanical training. American Missionary Association schools such as Fisk, Talladega, and Tougaloo; AME schools such as Allen, Paul Quinn, and Morris Brown; and Methodist institutions such as Claflin, Bennett, and Rust still promoted the liberal arts and taught Latin, Greek, mathematics, and natural sciences. Henry L. Morehouse of the American Baptist Home Missionary Society explained the purpose of education was to develop strong minds. He believed gifted intellectuals—a **"talented tenth"** as he characterized them in 1896—could lead people forward. Du Bois likewise stressed the need for the best educated 10 percent of the black population to promote progress and to advance the race.

Washington did not deny the importance of a liberal arts education. He believed industry was the foundation to progress:

> On such a foundation as this will grow habits of thrift, a love of work, economy, ownership of property, bank accounts. Out of it in the future will grow practical education, professional education, and positions of public responsibility. Out of it will grow moral and religious strength. Out of it will grow wealth from which alone can come leisure and the opportunity for the enjoyment of literature and the fine arts.

Ultimately, however, Washington was wrong to believe education for black people that focused on economic progress would earn the respect of most white Americans. As Du Bois explained, most white people preferred ignorant and unsuccessful black people to educated and prosperous ones:

> If my own city of Atlanta had offered it to-day the choice between 500 Negro college graduates—forceful, busy, ambitious men of property and self-respect—and 500 black cringing vagrants and criminals, the popular vote in favor of the criminals would be simply overwhelming. Why? Because they want Negro crime? No, not that they fear Negro crime less, but that they fear Negro ambition and success more. They can deal with crime by chain gang and lynch law, or at least they think they can, but the South can conceive neither machinery nor place for the educated, self-reliant, self-assertive black man.

As Chapter 16 discusses, the conflict among black leaders over the most suitable form of education would expand by the early twentieth century into a larger controversy. What began as a disagreement over the value of practical education would become a passionate debate among Washington, Du Bois, and others over the most effective strategy—accommodation or confrontation—for overcoming Jim Crow and white supremacy.

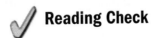 **Reading Check** What kinds of educational opportunities were available to African Americans by the late nineteenth century?

▶ **Reading Check**

It was difficult for most African Americans to gain even a basic education. Rural schools did not operate for more than thirty weeks a year and were often run down and short of supplies. Public school opportunities beyond grade school were even scarcer. Many black communities tried to fill this void by supporting private high schools and academies.

▶ **Document**

15-5 *W.E.B. DuBois The Talented Tenth, 1903*
The concept of "The Talented Tenth," conceived by W.E.B. Du Bois called for the need for higher education among the most talented of the African American community. This group would in turn "inspire the masses."

▶ **Retracing Odyssey**

Hampton University, Hampton, Virginia.
Founded by Samuel Chapman Armstrong with the assistance of the American Missionary Association, Hampton Normal and Agricultural Institute opened in 1868 to train former slaves (and later Native Americans) in agricultural and mechanical skills. Virginia Hall (1874), Memorial Church (1886), the Hampton Museum, and the giant Emancipation Oak are all located on this picturesque campus overlooking Chesapeake Bay and Hampton Roads.

Section 2
Church and Religion

GUIDE TO READING

▶ Why were religious beliefs and activities so important to so many African Americans?

▶ What was the appeal of the Holiness movement and Pentacostal churches?

KEY TERMS

▶ Holiness movement, p. 507

The church had long been the most important institution—after the family—that African Americans controlled for themselves. After the Civil War, black people organized their own churches and religious denominations, which grew and thrived as sources of spiritual comfort and centers of social activity. Black clergymen were often the most influential members of the black community.

In 1890 the South had more black Baptists than all other denominations combined. Baptist congregations were more independent and under less supervision by church hierarchy than other denominations. Bishops, for example, in the African Methodist Episcopal Zion church and the African Methodist Episcopal (AME) church exercised considerable authority over congregations, as did Methodist and Presbyterian leaders. Many black people (and many southern white people as well) preferred the independence of the Baptist churches (Figure 15–2).

But whatever the denomination, the church was integral to the lives of most black people. It fulfilled spiritual needs through sermons and music. It gave black people the opportunity, free from white interference, to plan, organize, and lead. It was especially a sanctuary for black women, who immersed themselves in church activities. Although church members usually had little money to spare, they helped the sick, the bereaved, and people displaced by fires and natural disasters. Black congregations also helped thousands of youngsters attend school and college.

The church service itself was the most important aspect of religious life for most black congregations. Parishioners were expected to participate in the service and not merely listen quietly to the minister's sermon. Black people had long considered white church services too sedate. In most black churches, members punctuated the minister's call with many an "Amen." They testified, shouted, laughed and cried, and sometimes fainted. Choirs provided joyful music and solemn songs.

Many black ministers had little or no education. Poorly prepared and unqualified clergymen who relied on ungrammatical and rhetorical appeals disturbed some black leaders. In 1890 Booker T. Washington claimed that "three-fourths of the Baptist ministers and two-thirds of the Methodists are unfit, either mentally or morally, or both, to preach the Gospel to any one or to attempt to lead any one." W. E. B. Du Bois wanted black churches free of "the noisy and unclean leaders of the

▶▶ **Guide to Reading/Key Terms**

For answers, see the *Teacher's Resource Manual.*

▶▶ **Recommended Reading**

Clarence E. Walker. *A Rock in a Weary Land: The African Methodist Episcopal Church during the Civil War and Reconstruction.* Baton Rouge, LA: Louisiana State University Press, 1982.

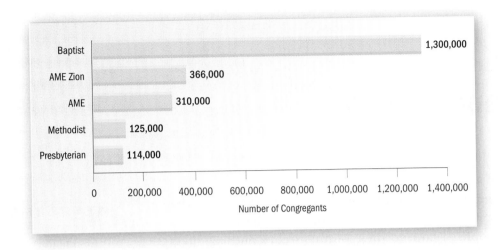

FIGURE 15–2 Church Affiliation among Southern Black People: 1890

The vast majority of black Southerners belonged to Baptist, Methodist, and Presbyterian congregations in the late nineteenth century, although there were about 15,000 black Episcopalians and perhaps 200,000 Roman Catholics.

Source: Edward L. Ayers, *The Promise of the New South*, pp. 160–61.

thoughtless mob" and the clergy replaced by thoughtful "apostles of service and sacrifice."

Although infrequently, black women sometimes led congregations. Nannie Helen Burroughs established Women's Day in Baptist churches. Women delivered sermons and guided the parishioners. But Burroughs complained that Women's Day quickly became more an occasion to raise money than to raise women.

Nannie Helen Burroughs and other black women came together at the Banner State Woman's National Baptist Convention in the early twentieth century. In addition to her involvement with the Baptist woman's movement, Burroughs was devoted to industrial education as well as voting rights for black men and women. She was also active with the National Association of Colored Women, serving as the chair of its anti-lynching committee.

The Church as Solace and Escape

For many black people, the emotional involvement and enthusiastic participation in church services was an escape from their dreary and oppressive daily lives. Growing up in rural Greenwood County, South Carolina, Benjamin E. Mays admitted that his Baptist preacher, James F. Marshall, who barely had a fifth-grade education, "emphasized the joys of heaven and the damnation of hell" and that the "trials and tribulations of the world would all be over when one got to heaven." But Mays understood the need for such messages to assuage the impact of white supremacy. "Beaten down at every turn by the white man, as they were, Negroes could perhaps not have survived without this kind of religion."

Black clergymen refused to challenge white supremacy. Even veiled comments might invite retaliation or even lynching. When a visiting minister began to criticize white people to Marshall's congregation, Marshall immediately stopped him. Despite the reluctance of many black clergymen to advocate improvement in race relations, many white people still viewed black religious gatherings as a threat. Black churches were burned and black ministers assaulted and killed with tragic regularity in the late-nineteenth-century South.

Black clergymen, like their white counterparts, often stressed middle-class values to their congregations. They suggested that many black people found themselves in shameful situations because of their sinful ways. They urged them to improve their behavior. The black clergyman at Mount Ever Rest Colored Church in rural Mississippi warned his congregation to quit their "cussin; lyin; stealin; crap shootin; whisky drinkin, and backbiting one another to de white folks." Black people who had acquired sinful reputations sometimes received funeral sermons that consigned them to eternal damnation in a fiery hell. As Benjamin Mays recalled, "The church was usually full at funerals, especially if the deceased had been well known; and when a man of bad reputation died the church was jammed."

There were black religious leaders who publicly and vigorously opposed white supremacy and insisted that black people stand up for their rights. AME Bishop Henry M. Turner persistently spoke out on racial matters. In 1883 after the U.S. Supreme Court declared the 1875 Civil Rights Act unconstitutional, Turner called the Constitution "a dirty rag, a cheat, a libel and ought to be spit upon by every Negro in the land."

The Holiness Movement and the Pentecostal Church

Not all black people belonged to mainline denominations. The **Holiness movement** and the emergence of Pentecostal churches affected Methodist and Baptist congregations. Partly in reaction to the elite domination and stiff authority of white Methodism, the Holiness movement gained a foothold among white people and then spilled over

▶▶ **Recommended Readings**

Iain MacRobert. *The Black Roots and White Racism of Early Pentecostalism in the USA.* Basingstoke, United Kingdom: Macmillan, 1988.

Benjamin E. Mays. *Born to Rebel.* New York: Scribner, 1971. Mays's autobiography includes penetrating insights into religion and education among rural black Southerners.

▶ **Recommended Reading**

Stephen W. Angell. *Bishop Henry McNeal Turner and African American Religion in the South.* Knoxville, TN: University of Tennessee Press, 1992.

among black Southerners. Holiness churches ordained women such as Neely Terry to lead them. Holiness clergy preached that sanctification allowed a Christian to receive a "second blessing" and to feel the "perfect love of Christ." Believers thus achieved an emotional reaffirmation and a new state of grace.

PROFILE ❖ Henry McNeal Turner

Henry McNeal Turner was born to free black parents in Newberry, South Carolina, in 1834. He worked in cotton fields and learned to be a blacksmith and a carriage maker. He also learned to read and write while working for a white lawyer. Drawn to religion, he was licensed to preach by the Methodist Episcopal church, a white denomination. In 1859 he was ordained in the AME church. He then became pastor of Union Bethel Church, the largest black congregation in Washington, D.C. During the Civil War, he served as a chaplain with the First Regiment of U.S. Colored Troops.

After the war, he briefly worked for the Freedmen's Bureau in Georgia. In an Emancipation Day address in Savannah in 1866, he praised the American flag and predicted that white people would soon accept black people.

Turner became active in Republican politics and was elected to the 1867–1868 Georgia constitutional convention. He was the only black delegate to favor a literacy requirement for voting. He also supported a measure to help white planters who had not paid their taxes to keep their land.

In 1868 Turner was elected to the Georgia House of Representatives. When white legislators voted to remove the thirty-two black representatives, he objected: "I am here to demand my rights, and to hurl thunderbolts at the men who dare to cross the threshold of my manhood." The black lawmakers were reinstated.

In 1880 he was elected one of the twelve bishops in the AME church and became president of Morris Brown College in Atlanta, where he served until 1900. He also became an advocate of emigration to Africa and supported the Liberian Exodus of 1877. Turner supported women's suffrage and ordained a woman as a deacon in the AME church in 1888, but the AME Council of Bishops withdrew the appointment.

He helped establish and edited a monthly AME newspaper, the *Voice of Missions.* In its pages he took a progressively Black Nationalist stance. He criticized white supremacy and lynching. Growing older and angrier, he told black readers of the *Voice of Missions* to get guns and attack white predators.

He denounced black soldiers who fought to suppress the Philippine Insurrection. "I boil over with disgust when I remember that colored men from this country . . . are there fighting to subjugate a people of their own color . . . I can scarcely keep from saying that I hope the Filipinos will wipe such soldiers from the face of the earth. . . . "

Embittered and tired, Turner lost faith in the intentions of white people and no longer praised the flag. "I used to love what I thought was the grand old flag, . . . but to the Negro in this country the American flag is a dirty and contemptible rag. . . . Without multiplying words, I wish to say that hell is an improvement on the United States where the Negro is concerned."

Bishop Henry McNeal Turner died of a heart attack in 1915. He was married four times, outliving three Courtesy of the Library of Congress wives and all but two of his children.

Turner

The Church of God in Christ (COGIC) became the leading black Holiness church. After a series of successful revivals in Mississippi and Memphis, two black former Baptists—Charles Harrison Mason and C. P. Jones—founded COGIC in 1907. However, Mason was expelled after reporting that "a flame touched [his] tongue," and his "language changed." He had spoken in tongues. Mason then organized the Pentecostal General Assembly of the Church of God in Christ. He assigned several black men to serve as bishops in Mississippi, Arkansas, Texas, Missouri, and California. In 1911 Mason appointed Lizzee Woods Roberson to lead the Woman's Department, a post she held until 1945. She transformed that department into a financial powerhouse for COGIC.

In the meantime, Charles Fox Parham, a dynamic white minister, had founded the Pentecostal church in the early twentieth century in the Houston-Galveston area of Texas. William J. Seymour, who was born a slave in Louisiana, played a key role in the development of the church. After hearing black people speak in tongues in Houston, he went to Los Angeles where he and others also began to speak in tongues. There he founded the highly evangelistic church that became the Pentecostal church. It attracted enormous interest and grew rapidly.

Charles Harrison Mason joined the Pentecostal movement. Under his leadership the Reorganized Church of God in Christ became the leading Pentecostal denomination. It soon spread across the South among black and white people. Although there were tensions between black and white believers, the Pentecostal church was the only movement of any significance that crossed the racial divide in early twentieth-century America.

 Reading Check What was the appeal of the Holiness movement and Pentecostal churches?

Roman Catholics and Episcopalians

Most African Americans belonged to one of the Baptist or Methodist churches. Booker T. Washington reportedly observed that "If a black man is anything but a Baptist or Methodist, someone has been tampering with his religion." Nevertheless, black people also belonged to other churches and denominations—or occasionally belonged to no organized religious group.

▶▶ **Recommended Reading**

James M. O'Toole. *Passing for White: Race, Religion, and the Healy Family, 1820-1920.* Amherst, MA: University of Massachusetts Press, 2002.

▶▶ **Reading Check**

Not all African Americans were satisfied with Methodist and Baptist churches. The Holiness movement developed first among whites, partly in response to the elite authoritarianism of white Methodism, and then spread to blacks. Pentecostal churches offered an emotional, highly evangelical religious experience.

Although he rarely mentioned it, James A. Healy's mother was black and a slave. He became the Bishop of Portland, Maine, in 1875.

As many as 200,000 African Americans were Roman Catholic in 1890. They were rarely fully accepted by the church or white Catholics. They were segregated in separate churches with separate parish schools in the South.

The most prominent black Catholics in nineteenth-century America came from the Healy family. Eliza Clark was a slave who had nine children by Michael Healy, an Irish-Catholic plantation owner in Georgia. Unlike many white men, Healy genuinely cared for Eliza and their children, although by law he could not marry a black woman. The children were educated in northern schools. James A. Healy graduated from the Jesuit-run Holy Cross College in Massachusetts and was ordained a priest at Notre Dame Cathedral in Paris in 1854. He later became a bishop in Portland, Maine.

Patrick Healy also attended Holy Cross and became the first black Jesuit priest in the United States. He served eight years as president of Georgetown University in Washington. Eliza Healy took vows as a nun and was the headmistress of a Catholic school in Vermont. Most white people were unaware of the racial ancestry of the Healys. Members of the family did not openly acknowledge being African American even when other black Catholics asked for their support. Bishop James Healy, for example, refused on three occasions to speak to the Congress of Colored Catholics, an association of black Catholics. Its members were mainly concerned with the discrimination they faced in the Roman Catholic Church and with the educational opportunities that were available—or more often that were not available—to black Catholic children in church schools.

Augustus Tolton was another African-American priest, and there was no question about his color. Because no American seminary would accept him, he was educated and ordained in 1886 in Rome. For a time, he presided over a parish in Quincy, Illinois, made up mainly of Irish and German Catholics.

Mother Mathilda Beasley came from a prominent free black family in Savannah. Her efforts to establish a community of Franciscan sisters in rural Georgia ultimately failed. In New Orleans, where there were sizable numbers of black Catholics of French and Spanish descent, the Sisters of Blessed Sacrament established a black high school in 1915 that became Xavier University in 1925.

Fairly or unfairly, most African Americans identified black Episcopalians with wealth and privilege. Many of those Episcopalians traced their heritage to free black families before the Civil War. By 1903 approximately 15,000 members of black Episcopal parishes worshipped in Richmond, Raleigh, Charleston, and other urban communities in the North and South.

 **Reading Check** Why were religious beliefs and activities so important to so many African Americans?

▶ **Reading Check**

Aside from the family, the church was the most important institution controlled by African Americans themselves. It fulfilled spiritual needs, gave black people an opportunity to plan, organized and lead, and was a sanctuary for many black women. Finally, for many black people, church services were an escape from the harsh conditions of their daily lives.

gangs,
1860s t
hostile
attacke
Colorac
rescued
and 10t
Mexico
slipped
Texas. I
10th kil
Mexico
Cavalry
dogged
rugged
In 1
children
Chickas
Comanc
On
Sioux a
erupted
were kil
next day
the aid
the bitte
Prather,
the last t

Several bla
St. Mary's,

Section 3

Black Troops

GUIDE TO READING

- Why did black men in the U. S. Army engage in combat against Native Americans, the Spanish, and Filipinos?
- What was the Philippine Insurrection?
- Why did many African American leaders oppose U.S. occupation of the Philippines?

KEY TERMS

- buffalo soldiers, p. 512
- Brownsville affair, p. 514
- Spanish-American War, p. 516
- Philippine Insurrection, p. 516
- immune regiments, p. 516
- smoked yankees, p. 517
- Rough Riders, p. 517

The Buffalo Soldiers

After the Civil War, the U.S. Army was reduced to fewer than 30,000 troops. Congressional Democrats tried to eliminate black soldiers and their regiments from this small force. But radical Republicans, led by Massachusetts senator Henry Wilson, prevailed to keep the military open to black men. The Army Reorganization Act of 1869 maintained four all-black regiments: the 9th and 10th Cavalry Regiments and the 24th and 25th Infantry Regiments. These four regiments spent most of the next three decades on the western frontier. Nearly 12,500 black men served during the late nineteenth century in these segregated units commanded—as black troops had been during the Civil War—by white officers. Unlike in the Civil War, however, many of these white officers were Southerners, and all too frequently, they held black men in low regard.

Military service in the West was wretched for white troops and worse for black soldiers. Too often officers considered black troops lazy, undisciplined, and cowardly. Black regiments were assigned mainly to the New Mexico and Arizona territories and to west Texas. The army thought black people tolerated heat better than white people did. Most black soldiers were compelled to endure the hot, dry, and dusty Southwest desert. Still some black troops were sent to Kansas, Colorado, and the Dakotas, where they confronted howling blizzards, subzero temperatures, and frostbite (see Map 15–1).

Discrimination in the Army

Black troops faced more than adverse weather. The army routinely provided them inferior food and inadequate housing. In 1867 white troops at Fort Leavenworth in Kansas lived in barracks while black troops were forced to sleep in tents on wet ground. Black regiments were allotted used weapons and equipment. The army sent its worst horses—often old and lame—to the black cavalry.

Long stretches of boredom, tedious duty, and loneliness marked army life for black and white men in the West. Weeks and months might pass without combat. Commanders constantly had to deal with desertion and alcoholism. Black soldiers were much less likely to desert or turn to drink than were white troops. For example, in 1877 eighteen men deserted

Guide to Reading/Key Terms

For answers, see the *Teacher's Resource Manual.*

Living Words Audio Clip

Track 21 *The Negro as Soldier by Christian A. Fleetwood; pamphlet excerpt*

Recommended Reading

William H. Leckie. *The Buffalo Soldiers: A Narrative of the Negro Cavalry in the West.* Norman, OK: University of Oklahoma Press, 1967.

Civilian Hostility to Black Soldiers

Despite the gallant performance of the buffalo soldiers, civilians frequently treated them with hostility. In southern Texas in 1875, Mexicans ambushed five black soldiers and killed two of them. The next day the infuriated white commander of the 9th Cavalry, Colonel Edward Hatch, rode out with sixty soldiers and apprehended the Mexicans. A local grand jury indicted nine of them for murder, but the only one tried was acquitted. The other eight were released without a trial. Hatch, another white officer, and three buffalo soldiers were then indicted for breaking into and burglarizing the shack where the Mexicans had sought refuge. The charges were eventually dropped.

In 1877 fifty-four black troops from the 9th Cavalry intervened successfully in a tense political and ethnic dispute between white and Mexican residents of El Paso, Texas. The 9th also found itself dispatched to police the so-called Johnson County War in Wyoming between big and small ranchers in 1890. The black troops deployment was arranged by one of the state's U.S. senators, who favored the big ranchers. The presence of black soldiers angered small ranchers, as it was intended to do.

Brownsville

One of the worst examples of hostility to black troops, the so-called **Brownsville affair**, also occurred in Texas. In 1906 the 1st Battalion of the 25th Infantry was transferred from Fort Niobrara, Nebraska, to Fort Brown in Brownsville, Texas, along the Rio Grande. The black soldiers immediately encountered discrimination from both white people and Mexicans in this border community. More than four out of five of Brownsville's residents were Hispanic. Black people were not permitted in public parks, and white businesses refused to serve them. Several times civilians provoked and attacked individual black soldiers.

Shortly after midnight on August 14, shooting erupted in Brownsville. About 150 shots were fired. One man died. An Hispanic policeman and the editor of a Spanish-language newspaper were injured. Black troops were blamed for the violence when clips and cartridges from the army's Springfield rifles were found in the street. Two military investigations concluded that black soldiers did the shooting. The army could not identify the specific soldiers responsible because no one would confess or name the alleged perpetrators.

With no hearing or trial, President Theodore Roosevelt dismissed three companies of black men—167 soldiers—from the army. They were barred from rejoining the military and from government employment. They were denied veterans' pensions or benefits. The black community, which had supported Roosevelt, reacted angrily. Booker T. Washington, a Roosevelt supporter, privately wrote, "There is no law, human or divine, which justifies the punishment of an innocent man."

Republican senator James B. Foraker of Ohio later led a Senate investigation that upheld Roosevelt's dismissals. But Foraker, a strong opponent

MAP 1
Troops S

Black tro
and the
Infantry
western
Civil War

▶▶ **Living Words Audio Clip**

Track 20 What the Government is Doing for Our Colored Boys. The New Slavery in the South; delivered at the Israel C.M.E. Church, Washington, D.C.; excerpt from a pamphlet by S.B. Wallace

▶▶ **Recommended Reading**

John M. Carroll, ed. *The Black Military Experience in the American West.* New York: Liveright, 1973.

of Roosevelt, questioned the guilt of the black men. The clips and cartridges that served as evidence were apparently planted. After Roosevelt left office in 1909, the War Department reinstated fourteen of the soldiers. In 1972 the Justice Department determined that an injustice had occurred. The black soldiers were posthumously awarded honorable discharges. The only survivor of the Brownsville affair—Dorsie Willis—received $25,000 from Congress and the right to treatment at veterans' facilities.

African Americans in the Navy

Naval service was even more unappealing than life in the army. In the late nineteenth century, as the navy made the transition from timber and sail to steam and steel, approximately one sailor in ten was a black man. The navy's ships were technically integrated. Black and white sailors served on them together. But white sailors were still hostile to black sailors. They would not eat or bunk with them or take orders from them. Black sailors were restricted to stoking boilers in the bowels of naval vessels and to cooking and serving food to white sailors.

Although several black men enrolled as midshipmen at the Naval Academy in the 1870s, they faced social ostracism and none of them graduated. Not until 1949 did a black man graduate from the academy.

The Black Cowboys

Black men before, during, and after the Civil War were familiar with horses and mules. As slaves, they tended and cared for animals. Some black men served with the 9th and 10th U.S. Cavalry Regiments and gained experience with horses. By the 1870s and 1880s, black men joined several hundred Mexicans, Native Americans, and white men on the long cattle drives from Texas to Kansas, Nebraska, and Missouri. There were probably no more than a few hundred black cowboys in the late nineteenth and early twentieth centuries.

Black cowhands sometimes endured discrimination and abuse. They had to tame the toughest horses, work the longest hours. They faced hostility in saloons, hotels, brothels, and shops in towns like Dodge City, Abilene, or Cheyenne. Still, many black cowboys earned the respect of white ranchers and cattle barons. Bose Ikard had been born a slave in Mississippi and went to work for Texas cattleman Charles Goodnight after the Civil War. Goodnight praised Ikard: "He was my detective, banker, and everything else in Colorado, New Mexico, and the other wild country I was in. . . . We went through some terrible trials during those four years on the trail. . . . [Ikard] was the most skilled and trustworthy man I had."

▶ **Retracing the Odyssey**

Black American West Museum and Heritage Center, Denver, Colorado. Founded by Paul Stewart, this museum is dedicated to the black pioneers of the frontier west including cowboys, soldiers, barbers, and homesteaders.

▶ **Recommended Reading**

Paul W. Stewart and Wallace Yvonne Ponce. *Black Cowboys*. Broomfield, CO: Phillips Publishing, 1986.

THE NORMAN FILM MFG. CO.
PRESENTS

BILL PICKETT
WORLD'S COLORED CHAMPION IN
'THE BULL-DOGGER'
Featuring The Colored Hero of the Mexican Bull Ring in Death Defying Feats of Courage and Skill.

Bill Pickett was an authentic cowboy who became one of the first black movie stars. "The Bull-Dogger" was a 1922 black and white, silent film aimed at attracting black audiences. No copies of the film are known to have survived. Pickett's skill as a bull-dogger was legendary. He would ride alongside a steer, jump off his horse, and grab the animal by the horns. He then wrestled it to the ground by sharply biting the animal's upper lip or nose. Pickett was the hit of the 1904 Cheyenne Frontier Days rodeo in Wyoming.

The Spanish-American War

With the western frontier subdued by 1890, many Americans concluded that the United States should expand overseas. European nations had already carved out extensive colonies in Africa and Asia. Many, but by no means all, Americans favored the extension of U.S. political, economic, and military authority to Latin America and the Pacific. In 1893 the U.S. Navy and American businessmen toppled the monarchy in Hawaii, and the United States annexed that chain of islands in 1898.

The same year, the United States went to war to liberate Cuba from Spanish control. As in the Civil War, black men enlisted, fought, and died. Twenty-two black sailors were among the 266 men who died when the battleship USS *Maine* blew up in Havana harbor, the event that helped trigger the war. Many black Americans were convinced, as they had been in previous wars, that the willingness of black people to support the war against Spain would impress white Americans sufficiently to reduce or even eliminate white hostility.

Many black and white Americans, however, questioned the American cause. Some black people saw the war as an effort to extend American influence and racial practices, including Jim Crow, beyond U.S. borders. The Reverend George W. Prioleau, chaplain of the Ninth Cavalry, wondered why black Americans supported what he considered a hypocritical war:

> Talk about fighting and freeing poor Cuba and of Spain's brutality. . . . Is America any better than Spain? Has she not subjects in her very midst who are murdered daily without a trial of judge or jury? Has she not subjects in her own borders whose children are half-fed and half-clothed, because their father's skin is black. . . . Yet the Negro is loyal to his country's flag.

Whether or not they harbored doubts, black men by the thousands served in the **Spanish-American War** and in the **Philippine Insurrection** that followed it. Shortly before war was declared, the army ordered its four black regiments of regular troops transferred from their western posts to Florida to prepare for combat in Cuba. President William McKinley also appealed for volunteers. The War Department designated four of the black volunteer units **immune regiments**. It believed black men would tolerate the heat and humidity of Cuba better than white troops, and black people were immune or at least less susceptible to yellow fever, which was common in Cuba. (Yellow fever was carried by mosquitoes, but this was unknown in 1898. Most people believed the disease was caused by the tropical Caribbean climate.)

State militia (national guard) units were also called into federal service, and several states, including Alabama, Ohio, Massachusetts, Illinois, Kansas, Virginia, Indiana, and North Carolina, sent all-black militias, as well as white units. But Georgia's governor refused to permit

▶▶ **Teaching Notes**

E. E. Cooper, editor of the Washington *Colored American*, declared that the war would bring black people and white people together in "an era of good feeling the country over and cement the races into a more compact brotherhood through perfect unity of purpose and patriotic affinity." The war, he asserted, would help white Americans "unloose themselves from the bondage of race prejudice."

that state's black militia to serve. New York would not permit black men to enlist in its militia. The states typically followed the federal example and kept black men confined to all-black units commanded by white officers, but there were exceptions.

Black Officers

The buffalo soldiers of the 9th and 10th Cavalry and the 24th and 25th Infantry remained under the leadership of white officers. But the men of several volunteer units insisted they be led by black officers: "No officers, no fight." So for the first time in American military history, black men commanded all-black units: the 8th Illinois, the 23rd Kansas, and the 3rd North Carolina. Mindful that many people doubted the ability of black men to lead, the colonel of the 8th Illinois cautioned his men, "If we fail, the whole race will have to shoulder the burden." The War Department also permitted black men to serve as lieutenants with other black volunteer units, but all higher ranking officers were white men.

Most of the black units never saw combat. White military authorities considered black men unreliable and inadequately trained for combat. Black volunteer units stayed behind in Florida when white units embarked for Cuba. However, the four regiments of regular black troops, the buffalo soldiers, did go to Cuba, where they performed well despite the doubts and persistent criticism of some white men. The Spanish troops were impressed enough to give the black men the nickname **smoked yankees**.

A Splendid Little War

In the summer of 1898, U.S. troops arrived in Cuba. Black men of the 10th Cavalry fought alongside Cuban rebels, many of whom were themselves black. Four black American privates earned the Congressional Medal of Honor for their part in an engagement in southwestern Cuba. Black and white troops were best remembered for their role in the assault on San Juan and Kettle Hills overlooking the key Cuban port of Santiago in eastern Cuba. Santiago was the main Spanish naval base in Cuba and its capture would break Spain's hold over the island.

In this assault, black soldiers from the 24th Infantry and the 9th and the 10th Cavalry Regiments fought alongside white troops including Theodore Roosevelt's volunteer unit, the **Rough Riders**. In the fiercest fighting of the war and amid considerable confusion, black and white men were thrown together as they encountered withering Spanish fire. Although for a time the outcome was in doubt, they took the high ground overlooking Santiago harbor. White soldiers praised the performance of the black troops. One commented, "I am not a negro lover. My father fought with Mosby's Rangers [in the Confederate Army] and I was born in the South, but the negroes saved

IN THEIR OWN WORDS . . .

Black Men in Battle in Cuba

On October 1, 1898, a letter appeared in the Illinois Record, *a black newspaper, from one of the men in the 10th Cavalry. The author was probably John E. Lewis. Lewis described the enthusiastic reaction of the Rough Riders to the 9th and 10th Cavalry, but he complained the contributions of the black soldiers were too often overlooked and ignored.*

The Rough Riders were mustered out on the 12th and 13th [of September], and when Colonel Roosevelt bade the regiment good-bye he paid a glowing tribute to the 9th and 10th Cavalry, especially in saving them from ambush.

Mr. Editor, if your readers could have heard the Rough Riders yell when the 10th Cav. was mentioned as the 'Smoked Yankees' and that they were of a good breed, they would have been doubly proud of the members of their race who rendered such signal service on the battle field. . . .

When a troop of the 10th made their famous charge of 3,000 yards under the command of Capt. [William J.] Beck, the non-commissioned officers, all colored, distinguished themselves in a manner that will redound to the glory of the race. Among those who distinguished themselves are Carter Smith, acting 1st Sergeant, Sgts. Geo. Taylor, James F. Cole, James H. Williams, Smith Johnson and Corpl. Joseph G. Mitchell who was wounded at San Juan.

All are soldiers whose names should go down in history. They never faltered in the thickest of the battle; they encouraged on in a rain of shot and shell and showed by their actions that they were the leaders. They did not hesitate to take the lead, and when that charge was made it was "save your cartridges, don't waste a shot."

The half will never be told of their deeds upon the battlefield. All deserve praise from the private up, but the praise has been given those who should have been in the lead instead of laying in the rear under cover. And yet they say that the black is not fit to lead.

If our war reports would only give credit where credit is due there would be no need writing these poorly composed lines that your readers might know of the deeds and hardships their dear ones have passed through.

You will read that colored troops, or companies did so and so, but the white papers never mention a name and the world only knows one who has done an act of bravery as a Negro soldier, nameless and friendless. It was never mentioned how, at that famous charge of the 10th Cav. And the rescue of the Rough Riders at San Juan Hill, the yell was started by a single trooper of C Troop, 10th Cav. and was carried down the line.

Brave 1st Sgt. Adam Huston at the head of his troop commanded "forward" which seemed into almost certain death. In him the troop found an able leader; Lieut. [E. D.] Anderson who was in command and fell to the rear and when the command "Forward March," was given, the brave Major [Theodore J.] Wint only smiled, for he admired bravery and did not change the command although he knew that the troops was in a desperate position. The troops were carried safely through. . . .

Will it ever be known how Sgt. Thomas Griffith of Troop C cut the wire fence along the line so that the 10th Cav. and Rough Riders could go through?

Never once did these brave men give thought to danger. . . .

The Spaniard would have sent our army home in disgrace had it not been for the daring and almost reckless charge of the Negro regiments. God was with them in that charge and no man who has ever seen the place will say that it was possible to make the charge without being slaughtered. . . .

[Unsigned]

What Do You Think?

▶ What is the source of the bitterness revealed in this letter?

▶ What motivated black men to risk their lives in combat in the Spanish-American War?

▶ Do any portions of this account seem strained, exaggerated, or unreliable? Why or why not?

Source: Willard B. Gatewood Jr., *Smoked Yankees and the Struggle for Empire: Letters from Negro Soldiers, 1898–1902*, Urbana: University of Illinois Press, 1971, pp. 76–78.

that fight." In his campaign for vice president in 1900, Theodore Roosevelt stated that black men saved his life during the battle. Later, however, Roosevelt reversed himself and accused several black men of cowardice.

As hostilities concluded, men of the 24th Infantry agreed to work in yellow fever hospitals after white regiments refused the duty. About half the black soldiers—some 471 men—contracted yellow fever. Other black troops arrived in Cuba after the war to serve garrison duty. The 8th Illinois and the 23rd Kansas built roads, bridges, schools, and hospitals. The black men were especially pleased at the lack of discrimination and absence of Jim Crow in Cuba. Some black soldiers discussed the possibility of organizing emigration to Cuba, but nothing came of it. Still other black troops from the 6th Massachusetts joined in the invasion of Puerto Rico as the United States took that island from Spain.

▶▶ **What Do You Think?**

· The author is bitter that people did not feel that black men were fit to lead and yet the white soldiers were cowardly and held back, while the black men were courageous and put themselves in harm's way.

· These black men risked their lives in combat as they did not want the Spanish to send their army home in disgrace.

· Answers will vary.

The Philippine Insurrection

With the resounding victory in the Spanish-American War, many Americans decided their nation had an obligation to uplift those less fortunate peoples who had been part of the Spanish Empire. Thus, President William McKinley and American diplomats insisted the United States acquire Guam, Puerto Rico, and the Philippines from Spain in the Treaty of Paris that ended the war in December 1898. The Filipinos, like the Cubans, had long opposed Spanish rule and fully expected the American government to support their independence. Instead, they were infuriated to learn that the United States intended to annex the Philippines. The Filipinos, under Emilio Aguinaldo, switched from fighting the Spanish to fighting the occupying U.S. forces.

Many black and white Americans denounced the U.S. effort to take the Philippines. They were unconvinced the Filipinos would benefit from American benevolence. AME Bishop Henry Turner termed it an "unholy war of conquest." Booker T. Washington believed the Filipinos "should be given an opportunity to govern themselves."

Opposition to U.S. involvement in the Philippines notwithstanding, black men in the military served throughout the campaign in the Pacific islands. The black troops included the regular 25th Infantry and 24th Infantry, the 9th Cavalry, and the 48th and 49th Volunteer Regiments. Through propaganda, the Filipino rebels attempted to convince black troops to abandon the cause. Posters reminded "The Colored American Soldier" of injustice and lynching in the United States. Although many black soldiers had reservations about the fighting, they remained loyal. By the time the conflict ended with an American victory in 1902, only five black men had deserted. David Fagen of the 24th Infantry joined Filipino forces and became an officer, fighting American troops for two years before he was killed. Two black men from the 9th Cavalry were executed for desertion; fifteen white soldiers who deserted had their death sentences commuted.

Although black men had served with distinction as professional soldiers for forty years after the Civil War—on the frontier, in Cuba, and in the Philippines—the army little valued their achievements and sacrifice, as the Brownsville affair showed. White military and political leaders persistently relied on passions and prejudices over evidence of achievement. Time and again, these circumstances dashed the hopes of those black civilians and soldiers who believed the performance of black troops would challenge white supremacy and demonstrate that black citizens had earned the same rights and opportunities as other Americans.

 Reading Check Why did black men in the U.S. Army engage in combat against Native Americans, the Spanish, and Filipinos?

▶ **Reading Check**

Black troops knew that life in the army was harsh and dangerous. However, the civilian world offered few genuine opportunities and army pay was regular. Moreover, black soldiers took immense pride in themselves as professional soldiers.

Section 4

Business and the Professions

Black Businesspeople and Entrepreneurs

Well-educated black men and women stood no chance of gaining employment with any major business or industrial corporation at the turn of the century. White males monopolized management and supervisory positions. They also occupied nearly every job that did not involve manual labor.

White supremacy and the proliferation of Jim Crow severely restricted opportunities for educated black people. Those same limitations enabled enterprising black men and women to open and operate businesses that served black clientele. By the early twentieth century, black Americans had established banks, newspapers, insurance companies, retail businesses, barbershops, beauty salons, and funeral parlors. Virtually every black community had its own small businesses, markets, street vendors, and other entrepreneurs.

Some black men and women established thriving and substantial businesses. In Atlanta, Union Army veteran Alexander Hamilton was a successful building contractor. He supervised construction of the Good Samaritan Building, oversaw the erection of buildings on the Morris Brown College campus, and built many of the impressive houses on Peachtree Street. Hamilton employed both black and white workmen on his projects.

Alonzo Herndon was a former slave who also achieved financial success in Atlanta. He operated a fashionable barbershop on Peachtree Street that served well-to-do white men. Herndon expanded and opened two other shops, eventually employing seventy-five men. He also founded the Atlanta Life Insurance Company, the largest black stock company in the world.

In Richmond, Virginia, Maggie Lena Walker—the secretary–treasurer of the Independent Order of St. Luke, a mutual benefit society, and a founder of the St. Luke's Penny Savings Bank—became the wealthiest black woman in America. Also in Richmond, former slave John Dabney owned an exclusive catering business that served wealthy white Virginians. He catered two state dinners for President Grover Cleveland. He used his earnings to purchase several houses and to invest in real estate.

GUIDE TO READING

► What kinds of businesses did black men and women own and operate?

► What was the relationship between black and white union members?

► What opportunities existed for African American men and women in the legal and medical professions?

KEY TERMS

► Knights of Labor, p. 523

► American Federation of Labor, p. 524

► United Mine Workers, p. 524

► Industrial Workers of the World, p. 524

► National Colored Labor Union, p. 524

► stevedores, p. 524

▶▶ **Guide to Reading/Key Terms**

For answers, see the *Teacher's Resource Manual*.

▶▶ **Retracing the Odyssey**

Alonzo F. Herndon Home, Atlanta, Georgia. Herndon was the founder of the Atlanta Life Insurance Company and was one of the wealthiest black men in America by the early 1900s. His fifteen-room mansion with immense white pillars was finished in 1910 and is open to the public. It is furnished with antiques, Roman and Venetian glass, as well as ornate artwork.

Maggie L. Walker National Historic Site, Richmond, Virginia. Built in 1883, this twenty-two-room Victorian mansion was home to the Walker family from 1904 to 1934 and is now open for tours. There is a visitor center that contains exhibits on the life of Maggie Lena Walker and the Jackson Ward community.

Madam C. J. Walker

The most successful black entrepreneur of them all may have been Madam C. J. Walker. Born Sarah Breedlove in 1867 on a Louisiana cotton plantation, she married at age fourteen. She was a widowed single parent by age twenty. She spent the next two decades struggling to make ends meet. In 1905 with $1.50, she developed a formula to nourish and

PROFILE ❖ Maggie Lena Walker

Maggie Lena Walker was born Maggie Mitchell in Richmond, Virginia, on July 15, 1867, to Elizabeth Draper, a laundress. Her mother married William Mitchell in 1870. Young Maggie was much influenced by the determination, fortitude, and hard work of her mother.

Maggie Mitchell graduated from a normal school in 1883 and taught primary school. She was active in the First African Baptist Church and remained a committed member for life. In 1886 she married Armstead Walker. Her views on marriage were progressive. Explaining the responsibilities she shared with her husband, she wrote, "Since marriage is an equal partnership, I believe that the woman and the man are equal in power and should by consultation and agreement, mutually decide as to the conduct of the home and the government of the children."

Walker became active in the Independent Order of St. Luke at the age of fourteen in 1881. The order was one of many black mutual aid societies that flourished in the nineteenth century. She was elected Grand Matron and became the Right Worthy Grand Secretary in 1899. When she assumed her duties, the order had $31.61 in funds and 1,080 members. She proved to be a dynamic leader and an inspirational speaker. By the early twentieth century under Walker's guidance, the order operated in twenty-two states. Its membership had increased. Its financial standing had improved. In 1924 the Independent Order of St. Luke had funds totaling $3,480,540.

The order ran a newspaper, the *St. Luke Herald,* and a bank with Maggie Lena Walker as president. She was the first black woman to serve as the chief executive of a bank in the United States. The bank subsequently merged with two other banks and became the Consolidated Bank and Trust Company with Walker as president. She was especially pleased that the bank enabled black customers to purchase homes.

Walker was deeply concerned with the plight of black women. She made certain the order employed black women in significant positions.

Maggie Lena Walker became a wealthy woman and lived in a twenty-two-room house. She was deeply involved in community affairs and organizations. She supported Virginia Union University, which later awarded her an honorary degree, and the Industrial School for Colored Girls. She worked with the Piedmont Tuberculosis Sanitarium for Negroes. She served on Richmond's Council for Colored Women and with the Virginia Federation of Colored Women's Clubs. She was among the prominent women who helped organize the Council of Women of the Darker Races. She joined the National Association of Colored Women in 1912 and was active in the NAACP. She was also a committed Republican. She ran unsuccessfully for state superintendent of public instruction. She died on December 15, 1934.

enrich the hair of black women. She insisted it was not a process to straighten hair.

She sold the product door to door in Denver but could not keep up with the demand. The business rapidly expanded and became a thriving enterprise that employed hundreds of black women. She established the company's headquarters in Indianapolis. In the meantime, she married Charles Joseph Walker and took his name and the title Madam. As she accumulated wealth, she shared it generously with Bethune Cookman College, Tuskegee Institute, and the NAACP. She was a major contributor to the NAACP's antilynching campaign. When she died of a stroke at age fifty-one in 1919, she was reportedly a millionaire.

Despite such successes, most black people who went into business had difficulty surviving, and many failed. Too often they depended on black customers who were themselves poor. White-owned banks were unlikely to provide credit to aspiring black businesspeople. And even the wealthiest black entrepreneurs did not come close to possessing the wealth the richest white Americans accumulated.

 Reading Check What kinds of businesses did black men and women own and operate?

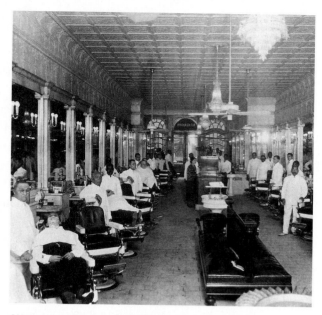

Alonzo Herndon's palatial barbershop on Atlanta's Peachtree Street was unlike most black-owned businesses in that its customers were exclusively white men.

▶ **Reading Check**

The same limitations that restricted opportunities for black men and women in white businesses, created the opportunity for black business people to build businesses catering to a black clientele. Blacks established businesses of almost every kind. Despite some success stories, many black-owned businesses struggled to survive.

African Americans and Labor

Thousands of black Southerners worked in factories, mills, and mines. Although most textile mills refused to hire black people except for janitorial duties, many black laborers toiled in tobacco and cigarmaking facilities, flour mills, coal mines, sawmills, turpentine camps, and on railroads. Black women worked for white families as cooks, maids, and laundresses. Black workers usually were paid less than white men employed in the same capacity. Conversely, white working people frequently complained they were not hired because employers retained black workers who worked for less pay. In 1904 in Georgia white railroad firemen went on strike in an unsuccessful attempt to compel railroad operators to dismiss black firemen. There was persistent antagonism between black and white laborers.

Unions

When white workers formed labor unions in the late nineteenth century, they usually excluded black workers. The **Knights of Labor**, however, founded in 1869, was open to all

Thousands of black people toiled in factories, mills, and mines. Here black women stem tobacco in a Virginia factory.

workers (except whiskey salesmen, lawyers, and bankers). By the mid-1880s it counted 50,000 women and 70,000 black workers among its nearly 750,000 members. But by the 1890s, after unsuccessful strikes and a deadly riot in Chicago, the Knights had lost influence to a new organization, the **American Federation of Labor** (AFL). Founded in 1886, the AFL was open to all skilled workers, but most of its local craft unions barred women and black tradesmen. In contrast, the **United Mine Workers** (UMW), formed in 1890, encouraged black coal miners to join the union rather than serve as strikebreakers. By 1900 approximately 20,000 of the 91,000 members of the UMW were black men. The **Industrial Workers of the World** (IWW), a revolutionary labor organization founded in 1905, brought black and white laborers together in, among other places, the Brotherhood of Timber Workers in the Piney Woods of east Texas.

In 1869 a Baltimore ship caulker, Isaac Myers, organized the **National Colored Labor Union**, which lasted for seven years. It discouraged strikes and encouraged its members to work hard and be thrifty. It lost whatever effectiveness it had when it was largely taken over by Republican leaders during Reconstruction.

Strikes

During the late nineteenth and early twentieth centuries, some strikes by unions won concessions from business owners. Most failed because owners could rely on strikebreakers and the police or national guard to intervene and bring the strikes to an often violent end. For a time, black shipyard workers in southern ports did achieve some success. Black **stevedores** who loaded and unloaded ships endured oppressive conditions and long hours for low pay. They periodically went on strike in Charleston, Savannah, and New Orleans. The Longshoremen's Protective Union in Charleston won several strikes in the 1870s. In Nashville in 1871 black dockyard workers went on strike, demanding twenty cents an hour. Steamboat owners broke the strike by hiring state convicts for fifteen cents an hour.

Black and white laborers who toiled in the Louisiana sugarcane fields earned an average of $13 a week in the 1880s. They were paid in scrip—not cash—that was redeemable only in stores the planters owned where prices were exorbitant. Workers lived in 12′ × 15′ cabins that they rented from the planters. In some ways, it was worse than slave labor.

Although the state militia had broken previous strikes, 9,000 black and 1,000 white workers responded to a call for a new strike in 1887 by organizers from the Knights of Labor. They quit the sugar fields in four parishes (as Louisiana counties are called) to demand more pay. The strike was peaceful, but planters convinced the governor to send in the militia. The troops fired into a crowd at Pattersonville and killed four people. The next day local officials killed several strikers who had been taken prisoner. In the town of Thibodaux, "prominent citizens" organized and armed themselves and had martial law declared. More than

thirty-five unarmed black people, including women and children, were killed in their homes and churches. Two black strike leaders were lynched. The strike was broken.

Black washerwomen went on strike in Atlanta in 1881. The women, who did laundry for white families, refused to do any more until they were guaranteed $1 per twelve pounds of laundry. The strike was well organized through black churches. It spread to cooks and domestics. Some three thousand black people joined the strike. White families went two weeks without clean clothes. However, Atlanta's white community broke the strike. Police arrested strike leaders for disorderly conduct. Several black women were fined from $5 to $20. The city council threatened to require each member of the Washer Women's Association of Atlanta to purchase a city business license for $25. Although the strike gradually ended without having achieved its goal, it did demonstrate that poor black women could organize effectively.

 Reading Check What was the relationship between black and white union members?

Black Professionals

Like business and labor, the medical and legal professions were strictly segregated. Most black physicians, nurses, and lawyers attended all-black professional schools in the late nineteenth century. Black people in need of medical care were either excluded from white hospitals or confined to all-black wards. Black physicians were denied staff privileges at white hospitals. Thus black people in many communities formed their own hospitals. Most were small facilities with fifty or fewer beds.

Medicine

In 1891 Dr. Daniel Hale Williams established Provident Hospital and Training Institute in Chicago, the first black hospital operated solely by African Americans. In 1894 the Freedmen's Hospital was organized in Washington, D.C. It later affiliated with Howard University. Frederick Douglass Memorial Hospital and Training School was founded in Philadelphia in 1895. Dr. Alonzo McClennan in cooperation with several other black physicians established the Hospital and Training School for Nurses in Charleston, South Carolina, in 1897.

In 1900 Williams, explaining why black medical institutions were necessary, wrote

> In view of this cruel ostracism, affecting so vitally the race, our duty seems plain. Institute Hospitals and Training Schools. Let us no longer sit idly and inanely deploring existing conditions. Let us not waste time trying to effect changes or modifications in the institutions unfriendly to us, but rather let us seek to promote the doctrine of helping and stimulating our race.

▶▶ **Reading Check**

There was persistent antagonism between black and white laborers. When white workers formed unions, they usually excluded blacks. However, some unions, notably the Knights of Labor and the United Mine Workers, welcomed black members.

▶▶ **Retracing the Odyssey**

Detroit, Michigan: Dunbar Hospital. This red brick structure was built in 1892 and served as a hospital for Detroit's black community from 1918 to 1928. It is currently operated by the Detroit Medical Society, and it has exhibits, medical devices, photographs, and papers documenting the medical care available to black Detroit.

By 1890 there were 909 black (most of whom were male) physicians practicing in the United States. They served a black population of 7.5 million people. Barred from membership in the American Medical Association, black doctors organized the National Medical Association in Atlanta in 1895. Most black doctors had been educated at seven black medical schools that included Leonard Medical School at Shaw University in Raleigh, North Carolina; Flint-Goodridge Medical College in New Orleans; Meharry Medical School in Nashville; and the Howard University School of Medicine in Washington, D.C.

In 1910, in a report issued by the Carnegie Foundation for the Advancement of Teaching, Abraham Flexner recommended improving medical education in the United States by eliminating weaker medical schools. He suggested raising admission standards and expanding laboratory and clinical training in the stronger schools. As a result of the implementation of these recommendations, 60 of 155 white medical schools closed. Among black medical schools, only Howard and Meharry survived.

By 1920 there were 3,885 black physicians. The number of black women physicians was declining. In 1890 there were ninety black women practicing medicine, and by 1920 there were sixty-five. The number of medical schools had decreased. Most black and white men considered medicine an inappropriate profession for women. Black women also had to contend with the opposition of white women. Isabella Vandervall was a 1915 graduate of New York Medical College and Hospital who was accepted for an internship at the Hospital for Women and Children in Syracuse. When she appeared in person, however, the hospital's female administrator rejected Vandervall because she was black.

Nursing was another matter. By 1920 there were 36 black nurse training schools and 2,150 white nursing schools. White nurses resented the competition from black nurses for positions as private duty nurses. Black physicians who ran nurse training schools exploited their students by hiring them out, as part of their training, for private duty work. They required them to relinquish their pay to the schools. Moreover, many people—black and white—regarded black nurses more as domestics than as trained professionals. Unlike white nurses, for example, black nurses were usually addressed by their first names. To confront such obstacles, fifty-two black nurses met in New York City in 1908 and formed the National Association of Colored Graduate Nurses (NACGN). By 1920 the NACGN had five hundred members.

Black physicians and nurses struggled to provide medical care to people who were often desperately ill and sought treatment only as a last resort. Disease and sickness flourished among people who were ill nourished, poorly clad, and inadequately housed. Bessie Hawes, a 1918 graduate of Tuskegee Institute's Nurse Training program, described the kind of situation she faced in rural Alabama:

> A colored family of ten were in bed and dying for the want of attention. No one would come near. I was glad of the opportunity. As I entered the

little country cabin, I found the mother in bed. Three children were buried the week before. The father and the remainder of the family were running a temperature of 102–104. Some had influenza, others had pneumonia. No relatives or friends would come near. I saw at a glance I had work to do. I rolled up my sleeves and killed chickens and began to cook. . . . and did everything I could to help conditions. I worked day and night trying to save them for seven days. . . . I only wished that I could have reached them earlier and been able to have done something for the poor mother.

 Reading Check   What was the experience of black nurses?

The Law

Black lawyers were permitted to practice in what was essentially a white male court system. But white judges and attorneys did not welcome them. Rather than create additional problems for themselves, black defendants and plaintiffs often retained white lawyers in the hope that white legal counsel might improve their chances of receiving justice. As a result, many black attorneys had a hard time making a living from the practice of law.

The American Bar Association (ABA) would not admit black attorneys to membership. Attorney William H. Lewis, a graduate of Amherst College and the Harvard Law School who was appointed an assistant U.S. attorney general by President William Howard Taft in 1911, was expelled by the ABA in 1912 when its leaders discovered he was black. The leaders defended his expulsion by claiming the association was mainly a social organization. In 1925 black lawyers—led by Howard Law School graduate George H. Woodson—organized the National Bar Association.

In 1910 the United States had about eight hundred black lawyers. Some, like Lewis, had attended white law schools, such as Harvard or the University of South Carolina during Reconstruction in the 1870s. Others attended black law schools such as Howard or Allen University's law school in South Carolina. Still other black men (and white men) learned the law by reading and working in the law offices of practicing attorneys.

Very few black women were lawyers. Charlotte Ray was the first (see p. 406). In 1900 there were ten black women practicing law. There were over 700 black men and 112,000 white men engaged in the legal profession. Lutie A. Lytle, who graduated from Central Tennessee Law School in 1879, later returned to that black institution and became the first black woman to be a law professor in the United States.

 **Reading Check**   What opportunities existed for African American men and women in the legal and medical professsions?

▶▶ **Reading Check**

Black nurses were trained at black nursing schools. They were resented by white nurses, hired out during training for private nursing duties and required to give their pay to the school, and treated overall like domestics.

▶▶ **Reading Check**

The medical and legal professions were strictly segregated. Most black physicians and lawyers attended all-black professional schools. Black physicians were denied staff privileges at white hospitals. Black lawyers were allowed, but not welcomed, in the white judicial system.

GUIDE TO READING

▶ What kinds of music did African Americans develop in the late nineteenth and early twentieth century?

▶ Who were some of the prominent African Americans in music and sports by the early twentieth century?

KEY TERMS

▶ ragtime, p. 528

▶ jazz, p. 529

▶ blues, p. 529

▶ Negro Leagues, p. 532

Section 5

Music and Sports

Music

In the half century after the Civil War, music created and performed by black people evolved into the uniquely American art forms of ragtime, jazz, and blues. The roots of these extraordinary musical innovations are obscure and uncertain. Some late-nineteenth-century music can be traced to African musical forms and rhythms. One source is slave work songs; another is the spirituals of the slavery era.

Traveling groups of black men, some of them ex-slaves, put on minstrel shows that featured "coon songs" after the Civil War. Many black Americans resented these popular shows as caricatures and exaggerations of black behavior. At least six hundred "coon songs" that attracted a predominantly white audience were published by 1900.

Most black people did not perform in or enjoy the demeaning minstrel shows. They had other forms of musical entertainment. "The Civil Rights Juba," published in 1874, was a precursor to ragtime. In 1871 the Fisk University Jubilee Singers began the first of many fund-raising concert tours that entertained black and white audiences in the United States and Europe for years thereafter with slave songs and spirituals. Other black colleges and universities also sent choirs and singers on similar trips.

Ragtime

Ragtime, which emerged in the 1890s, was composed music, written down for performance on the piano. Ragtime pieces were not accompanied by lyrics and not meant to be sung. The creative genius of the form, Scott Joplin, was born in Texarkana, Texas, in 1868. He learned to play on a piano his mother bought from her earnings as a maid. He may have had some training in classical music. Joplin subsequently learned to transfer complex banjo syncopations to the piano as he fused European harmonies and African rhythms. He traveled to Chicago in 1893 and played at the Columbian Exposition. He soon began to write ragtime sheet music that sold well. In 1899 he composed his best-known tune, the "Maple Leaf Rag," named after a social club (brothel) in Sedalia, Missouri. It sold an astonishing one million copies.

▶ Guide to Reading/Key Terms

For answers, see the *Teacher's Resource Manual*.

▶ Living Words Audio Clips

Track 22 *I Couldn't Hear Nobody Pray; sung by the Fisk Jubilee Singers*
Track 28 *Maple Leaf Rag* by Scott Joplin

Jazz

Jazz gradually replaced ragtime in popularity in the early twentieth century. Unlike ragtime, jazz was mostly improvised, not composed, and it was not confined to the piano. Jazz incorporated African and European musical elements drawn from such diverse sources as plantation bands, minstrel shows, riverboat ensembles, and Irish and Scottish folk tunes. The first jazz bands emerged in and around New Orleans where they played at parades, funerals, clubs, and outdoor concerts. Instead of the banjos, pipes, fifes, and violins of earlier black musical groups, these bands relied more on brass, reeds, and drums.

Ferdinand J. La Menthe, regarded as the first prominent jazz musician, was born in 1890 and grew up in a French-speaking family in New Orleans. Young La Menthe played several musical instruments before settling on the piano. He was also a superb composer and arranger. Later he changed his name to Morton and came to be known as Jelly Roll Morton. He played in the "red light" district of New Orleans known as Storeyville where he was also a pool shark and gambler. He moved to Los Angeles in 1917 and to Chicago in 1922 where he subsequently led and recorded with "Morton's Red Hot Peppers." He died in 1941.

The Blues

In rural, isolated areas of the South, poor black people composed and sang songs about their lives and experiences. W. C. Handy, the father of the **blues**, later recalled, "Southern Negroes sang about everything. Trains, steamboats, steam whistles, sledge hammers, fast women, mean bosses, stubborn mules." They accompanied themselves on anything from a guitar, to a harmonica, to a washboard. They played in juke joints (rural nightclubs), at picnics, lumber camps, and urban nightclubs.

Handy, who was born in Florence, Alabama, in 1873, took up music despite the opposition of his devoutly Christian parents. He learned to play the guitar, although his mother and father regarded it as the "devil's plaything." He later led his own nine-man band. In the Mississippi Delta in 1903, Handy encountered "primitive," or "boogie," music unlike anything he had heard before. Handy was not initially impressed by the mostly unskilled and itinerant musicians whose lives swirled around cheap whiskey, gambling, prostitution, and violence. "Then I saw the beauty of primitive music. They had the stuff people wanted. It touched the spot. Their music wanted polishing, but it contained the essence. People would pay money for it." Handy went on to compose many tunes including "Memphis Blues" and "St. Louis Blues."

Handy was not the only musician to "discover" the blues. Gertrude Pridget sang in southern minstrel shows. In 1902 she heard a young black woman in a small Missouri town sing forlornly about a lover who had left her. Pridget took the song and included it in her shows. In 1904 she married William "Pa" Rainey and became "Ma" Rainey. Rainey proceeded to create other "blues" songs based on ballads,

Scott Joplin (1868–1917) was one of America's most prolific composers, and his name is indelibly linked with ragtime. Although ragtime's popularity faded by the 1920s, Joplin's reputation and compositions were resurrected in 1974 when the Hollywood film, *The Sting*, relied on Joplin's 1902 rag, "The Entertainer," for its soundtrack. In 1976 Scott Joplin was posthumously awarded the Pulitzer Prize for music.

An early jazz band arrives in a small Texas town in about 1915 for a performance at a black fair.

hymns, and the experiences of black people. As "Mother of the Blues," she recorded extensively and continuously in the 1920s and 1930s.

By 1920 two forms of American music were well along in their evolution—jazz and the blues. Both drew on African and American musical elements as well as on European styles. But most of all, jazz and the blues represented the experiences of African Americans and the creativity of the exceptional musicians who developed and performed the music.

Sports

While talented black men and women were making dramatic musical innovations, black athletes found that white athletes and sports entrepreneurs were increasingly opposed to the presence of black men in the boxing ring and on the playing field. In boxing, black men regularly fought white men through the end of the nineteenth century. But many white people, especially Southerners, were offended by the practice. In 1892 George Dixon, a black boxer, won the world featherweight title. Some white men cheered his victory, distressing a Chicago journalist. "It was not pleasant," he complained, "to see white men applaud a negro for knocking another white man out. It was not pleasant to see them crowding around 'Mr.' Dixon to congratulate him on his victory, to seek an introduction with 'the distinguished colored gentleman' while he puffed his cigar and lay back like a prince receiving his subjects." Despite such opinions, there was never any official prohibition of interracial bouts.

Jack Johnson

The success of another black boxer, heavyweight Jack Johnson, angered many white Americans. Johnson was born in Galveston, Texas, in 1878 and became a professional boxer in 1897. Between 1902 and 1907 he

won fifty-seven bouts against black and white fighters. In 1908 he badly beat the white heavyweight champion, Tommy Burns, in Australia. Many white boxing fans were unwilling to accept Johnson as the champion and looked desperately for "a great white hope" who could defeat him. Jim Jeffries, a former champion, came out of retirement to take on Johnson. In a brutal fight under a scorching sun in Reno, Nevada, in 1910, Johnson knocked Jeffries out in the fifteenth round.

Johnson's personal life, as well as his prowess in the ring, provoked white animosity. Having divorced his black wife, he married a white woman in 1911. Several months later, overwhelmed by social ostracism, she committed suicide. After Johnson married a second white woman, he was convicted of violating the Mann Act, which made it illegal to transport a woman across state lines for immoral purposes. In Johnson's case the "immorality" was his marriage to white women. Sentenced to a year in prison and fined $1,000, Johnson fled to Canada and then to France to avoid punishment. He lost his title to Jesse Willard in 1915 in Havana in the twenty-sixth round in a fight many people believe that Johnson threw. He returned to the United States in 1920 and served ten months in Leavenworth Prison.

Baseball

Baseball was a relatively new sport that became popular after the Civil War. As professional baseball developed in the 1870s and 1880s, both black and white men competed to earn money playing the game. It was not easy. They were the nation's first professional athletes, but professional baseball was unstable. Teams were formed and dissolved with depressing regularity. Players moved from team to team. Some thirty black men played professional baseball in the quarter century after the Civil War.

White players led by Adrian Constantine "Cap" Anson of the Chicago White Stockings tried to get baseball club owners to stop signing black men to contracts. Anson, who was from Iowa, bitterly resented having to play against black men. In 1887 International League officials rescinded a rule that had permitted them to sign black baseball players. One black player, Weldy Wilberforce Walker, protested the exclusion in a letter to *Sporting Life*. He insisted black men be judged by their skills, not by their color. "There should be some broader cause—such as lack of ability, behavior, and intelligence—for barring a player, rather than his color. It is for these reasons and because I think ability and intelligence should be recognized first and last—at all times and by everyone—I ask the question again, 'Why was the law permitting colored men to sign repealed, etc.?'" There was no intelligent answer to Walker's question. But Jim Crow was now on the baseball diamond. Moses Fleetwood Walker—Weldy's brother—was the last black man to play major league baseball in the nineteenth century as a catcher with Toledo of the American Association. No black men would be allowed to play with white men in major league baseball until Jackie Robinson joined the Brooklyn Dodgers in 1947.

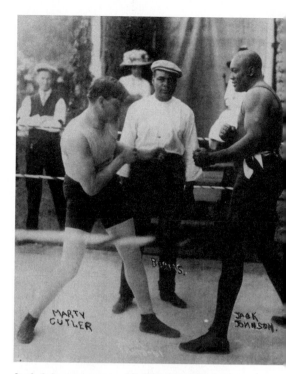

Jack Johnson spars with Marty Cutler in the early twentieth century. Johnson was a superb fighter whose ability to defeat white boxers rankled many white men. But Johnson's involvement with white women infuriated them even more and led to his imprisonment.

▶▶ **Recommended Readings**

Randy Roberts. *Papa Jack: Jack Johnson and the Era of White Hopes.* New York: The Free Press, 1983.

Neil Lanctot. *Negro League Baseball: The Rise and Ruin of a Black Institution.* Philadelphia, PA: University of Pennsylvania Press, 2004.

In reaction to their exclusion, black men formed their own teams. By 1900 there were five black professional teams including the Norfolk Red Stockings, the Chicago Unions, and the Cuban X Giants of New York. The **Negro Leagues** would be an integral (but not integrated) part of sports for the next half century.

Basketball and Other Sports

James Naismith invented basketball in 1891 in Springfield, Massachusetts. Black youngsters were playing organized basketball by 1906 in New York City, Philadelphia, and Washington, D.C. By 1910–1911 Howard University and Hampton Institute had basketball teams. In horse racing, black jockeys regularly won major races. Willie Simms won the Kentucky Derby in 1894, 1895, 1896, and 1898. Bicycling and bicycle racing were enormously popular by the 1890s, and in 1900 a black rider, Marshall W. "Major" Taylor, won the U.S. sprint championship.

College Athletics

Generally, white colleges and universities in the North that admitted black students would not let them participate in intercollegiate sports. (Southern colleges and universities did not admit black students.) There were, however, exceptions. In 1889 W. T. S. Jackson and William Henry Lewis played football for Amherst College. Lewis was the captain of the team in 1890. As a law school student, Lewis played for Harvard and was named to the Walter Camp All-American team in 1892. White institutions with black players often encountered the racism so rampant during the era. In 1907 the University of Alabama baseball team canceled a game with the University of Vermont after learning the Vermont squad had two black infielders. Moreover, black players were frequently subjected to abuse from opposing teams and their fans.

Intercollegiate athletics emerged at black colleges and universities in the late nineteenth century. White schools occasionally played black institutions. The Yale Law School baseball team, for example, played Howard in 1898. But black college teams were far more likely to play each other. The first football game between two black colleges took place on December 27, 1892, when Biddle University (today Johnson C. Smith University) defeated Livingston College in Salisbury, North Carolina.

Eventually black athletic conferences were formed. The Central Intercollegiate Athletic Association (CIAA) was organized in 1912 with Hampton, Howard, Virginia Union, and Shaw College in Raleigh, North Carolina, among its early members. The Southeastern Conference was established in 1913 and consisted of Morehouse, Fisk, Florida A&M, and Tuskegee among others. In Texas, in 1920, five black colleges founded the Southwestern Athletic Conference: Prairie View A&M, Bishop College, Paul Quinn College, Wiley College, and Sam Houston College.

 Reading Check Who were some of the prominent African Americans in music and sports by the early twentieth century?

▶▶ **Reading Check**

Scott Joplin was a prolific composer of ragtime music. Jelly Roll Morton was the first prominent jazz musician. W. C. Handy is considered by many to be the father of the blues. Jack Johnson was a dominant heavyweight boxer in the early twentieth century. Willie Simms won the Kentucky Derby in 1894.

Evaluating Advertisements

Advertisements offer more than evidence of the consumer goods and services produced in a historical period. They often hold clues to widely held ideas, attitudes, and values. However, when using advertisements as historical evidence, keep in mind that their stated or unstated messages may reflect what the advertisers want readers to believe, value, or desire—rather than the reality for most people of the time.

Advertisements often depicted not only products and what they did, but also the ways these products might enhance the lives of typical consumers. One such ad from the 1900s is shown at right.

LEARN THE SKILL

Use the following steps to evaluate historical advertisements:

1. **Identify the subject of the advertisement.** What product or service does the advertisement promote?

2. **Analyze the advertisement's reliability as historical evidence.** Consider both the product itself and the way it is advertised.

3. **Study the advertisement to learn more about the historical period.** Consider the product and its purpose, the situation depicted in the advertisement, the text, and the visuals.

PRACTICE THE SKILL

Answer the following questions:

1. **(a)** What product or service does this advertisement promote? **(b)** What facts about the product does it provide? **(c)** What "problem" would this product solve for women who use it? **(d)** What strategy does this advertisement use to appeal to women?

2. **(a)** Do you think the woman depicted in the advertisement represents typical African-American consumers of the time? Explain. **(b)** In this ad, what is the unstated message that the advertiser is using to persuade people to buy the product?

3. **(a)** What social or cultural values are promoted in the advertisement? **(b)** What clues to the time period are given in the photograph? **(c)** Do you think this advertisement reflects consumers' desires for this product? Explain your reasoning.

This advertisement for a line of hair products created and manufactured by Madame C.J. Walker, one of the first African-American millionaires. The ad promises "fascinating beauty" to users of its products.

➤ **Skills for Life**

For answers, see *Teacher's Resource Manual.*

Although Tuskegee Institute stressed agricultural and vocational subjects, students did enroll in math, science, and English courses. These students are in a U.S. history class.

Chapter 16

The first issue of *The Crisis* monthly magazine edited by W. E. B. Du Bois, was published in November 1910.

Witnessing History . . .

The wisest among my race understand that the agitation of questions of social equality is the extremest folly, and that progress in the enjoyment of all privileges that will come to us must be the result of severe and constant struggle rather than of artificial forcing. No race that has anything to contribute to the markets of the world is long in any degree ostracized. It is important and right all privileges of the law be ours, but it is vastly more important that we be prepared for the exercises of these privileges.

—Booker T. Washington, Atlanta Cotton States and International Exposition, September 18, 1895

Mr. Washington distinctly asks that black people give up, at least for the present three things,—
First, political power,
Second, insistence on civil rights,
Third, higher education of Negro youth,—
and concentrate all their energies on industrial education, the accumulation of wealth, and the conciliation of the South.

—W. E. B. Du Bois, *The Souls of Black Folk*, 1903

 How do the opinions of Washington and Du Bois differ on social equality for blacks?

Chapter Preview

▶ Witnessing History

Washington believed that social equality could not be forced, whereas Du Bois favored a frontal assault on discrimination and inequality as well as a rigorous pursuit of political power.

As the twentieth century dawned, black and white Americans had profoundly different views on the future of black people in America. Black scholar W. E. B. Du Bois announced in 1903 that race would be the century's most critical issue. "The problem of the twentieth century is the problem of the color line—the relation of the darker to the lighter races of men in Asia and Africa, in America and the islands of the sea." Black people refused to accept the inferiority to which they had been consigned. They devised strategies and organized institutions to enable them to prosper in a hostile society.

One of the most important episodes in American history was a vast and prolonged migration of hundreds of thousands of rural black Southerners to northern cities. This migration began in earnest after 1910. Drawn mainly by economic opportunities, black people moved to New York, Philadelphia, Cleveland, Chicago, and other urban centers.

Section 1

Race and Social Change

The Progressive Movement

By the first decade of the twentieth century, many Americans were concerned and even alarmed about the rapid economic and social changes that confronted the United States. Industrialization, the rise of powerful corporations, the explosive growth of cities, and the influx of millions of immigrants fueled their concern. Their apprehensions spawned various efforts at reform known as the **progressive movement**. Progressives believed America needed a new social awareness to deal with new social and economic problems. Most of the middle- and upper-class white people who formed the core of the movement showed little interest in white racism and its impact. Indeed, many were racists themselves. They were primarily concerned with the concentration of wealth in monopolies such as Standard Oil, with pervasive political corruption in state and local governments, and with the plight of working-class immigrants in American cities. They cared deeply about the debilitating effects of alcohol, tainted food, and prostitution, but little about the grim impact of white supremacy. When Upton Sinclair wrote his novel *The Jungle* to expose the exploitation of European immigrants in Chicago meatpacking houses, he depicted black people as brute laborers and strikebreakers.

The reforms of the progressive movement offered at least a glimmer of hope that racial advancement was possible. If efforts were made to improve America, was it not possible that there be some advances achieved in policies and conditions affecting black Americans? But how much militancy or forbearance was necessary to achieve significant racial progress?

Booker T. Washington's Approach

Booker T. Washington's commitment to agricultural and industrial education served as the basis for his approach to "the problem of the color line." By the beginning of the twentieth century, Washington was convinced that black men and women who had mastered skills acquired at

GUIDE TO READING

▶ On what issues did Booker T. Washington and W. E. B. Du Bois agree and disagree in their efforts to promote the advancement of African Americans?

▶ What was the Niagara Movement and why was it formed?

▶ What stand did members of the Niagra Movement take on racial issues in America?

KEY TERMS

▶ progressive movement, p. 541

▶ The Tuskegee Machine, p. 543

▶ Afro-American League, p. 545

▶▶ Guide to Reading/Key Terms

For answers, see the *Teacher's Resource Manual.*

▶▶ Living Words Audio Clip

Track 23 *Address at the Atlanta Exposition, Booker T. Washington*

▶▶ Recommended Reading

Booker T. Washington. *Up from Slavery.* New York: Doubleday, 1901.

Booker T. Washington had access to and influence among the most powerful political and business leaders in the United States. Here he shares the podium with President Theodore Roosevelt.

▶▶ **Recommended Reading**

Louis R. Harlan. *Booker T. Washington: The Making of a Black Leader, 1856–1901.* New York: Oxford University Press, 1972 and *Booker T. Washington: The Wizard of Tuskegee, 1901–1915.* New York: Oxford University Press, 1983. The definitive two-volume biography of Washington.

▶▶ **Retracing the Odyssey**

The Booker T. Washington National Monument, Hardy, Virginia. Booker T. Washington lived his first nine years on this farm. A museum and restored schoolhouse depict rural life in nineteenth-century America, especially for slaves.

institutions like Tuskegee and Hampton would be recognized, if not welcomed, as productive contributors to the southern economy. Washington believed economic acceptance would lead in due course to political and social acceptance.

The Tuskegee leader eloquently outlined his philosophy in the speech he delivered at the opening ceremonies of the Cotton States Exposition in Atlanta in 1895. Black people, he told his segregated audience, would find genuine opportunities in the South. "[W]hen it comes to business, pure and simple, it is in the South that the Negro is given a man's chance in the commercial world." Washington added that black people should not expect too much but should welcome menial labor as a first step in the struggle for progress. Ever optimistic, he looked for opportunities while deprecating those who complained. He told white listeners that the lives of black and white Southerners were historically linked and black people were far more loyal and steadfast than newly arrived immigrants.

> "[I]n our humble way, we shall stand by you with a devotion that no foreigner can approach, ready to lay down our lives, if need be, in defence of yours, interlacing our industrial, commercial, civil, and religious life with yours in a way that shall make the interests of both races one."

Washington reassured white people that cooperation between the races in the interest of prosperity did not endanger segregation. Washington implied that black people need not protest because they were denied rights white men possessed. Instead, he urged his black listeners to struggle steadily rather than make defiant demands.

> "The wisest among my race understand that the agitation of questions of social equality is the extremest folly, and that progress in the enjoyment of all the privileges that will come to us must be the result of severe and constant struggle rather than of artificial forcing."

Washington was convinced that as African Americans became productive and made economic progress, white people would concede them their rights.

The speech was warmly received by both white and black listeners and by those who read it when it was widely reprinted. T. Thomas Fortune, the black editor of the New York *Age*, told Washington he had replaced Frederick Douglass (who died in 1895) as a leader. "It looks as if you are our Douglass, the best equipped of the lot of us to be the single figure ahead of the procession."

But not everyone was complimentary. The black editor of the *Washington Bee*, W. Calvin Chase, complained, "He said something that was death to the Afro-American and elevating to white people." Bishop Henry M. Turner of the AME church added that Washington "will have to live a long time to undo the harm he has done our race."

White people regarded Washington's speech as moderate, sensible, and altogether praiseworthy. Almost overnight he was designated the spokesman for African Americans. Washington accepted the recognition and took full advantage of it.

Washington's Influence

Booker T. Washington was a complex man. Many people found him unassertive, dignified, and patient. Yet he was ambitious, aggressive, and opportunistic as well as shrewd, calculating, and devious. He had an uncanny ability to determine what he might say to other people that would elicit a positive response from them. He became extraordinarily powerful. In the words of his assistant, Emmett J. Scott, Washington was "the Wizard of Tuskegee."

After the Atlanta speech, Washington's influence soared. He received extensive and mostly positive coverage in black newspapers. Some of that popularity stemmed from admiration for his leadership and agreement with his ideas. But Washington also cultivated and flattered editors, paid for advertisements for Tuskegee, and subsidized struggling journalists.

He was especially effective in dealing with prominent white businessmen and philanthropists. William H. Baldwin, vice president of the Southern Railroad, was so impressed with Washington's management of Tuskegee that Baldwin agreed to serve as the chairman of Tuskegee's board. Washington developed support among the nation's industrial elite including steel magnate Andrew Carnegie and Julius Rosenwald, the head of Sears, Roebuck, and Company. They trusted Washington's judgment. They invariably consulted him before contributing to black colleges and universities. Washington assured them of the wisdom of investing in the training of black men and women in agricultural and mechanical skills. These students, he repeatedly reminded donors, would be self-sufficient and productive members of southern society.

The Tuskegee Machine

Washington advised black people to avoid politics, but he ignored his own advice. Although he never ran for office or was appointed to a political position, Washington was a political figure to be reckoned with. His connections to white businesspeople and politicians gave him enormous influence. Critics and admirers alike referred to him as "the Wizard of Tuskegee." With his influence, his connections, and his organizational skills, Washington operated what came to be known as **The Tuskegee Machine**.

Most of Washington's political activities were not public. He secretly helped finance an unsuccessful court case against the Louisiana grandfather clause. (The statute disfranchised those voters—black men—

whose grandfathers had not possessed the right to vote; see Chapter 14.) Washington provided funds to carry two cases challenging Alabama's grandfather clause to the U.S. Supreme Court, which ultimately rejected both on a technicality. He tried to persuade railroad executives to improve the conditions on segregated coaches and in station waiting rooms. He worked covertly with white attorneys to free a black farm laborer imprisoned under Alabama's peonage law. In many of these secret activities, Washington used code names in correspondence to hide his involvement. In the Louisiana case he was identified only as X.Y.Z.

Washington was a conservative leader who did not directly or publicly challenge white supremacy. He was willing to accept literacy and property qualifications for voting if they were equitably enforced regardless of race. He also opposed women's suffrage. He attacked lynching only occasionally. But he did write an annual letter to white newspapers filled with data on lynchings that had been compiled at Tuskegee. Washington let the grim statistics speak for themselves rather than denounce the injustice himself.

Washington founded the National Negro Business League in 1900 and served as its president until he died in 1915. The league brought together merchants, retailers, bankers, funeral directors, and other owners and operators of small enterprises. It helped promote black businesses in the black community and brought businessmen together to exchange information. Moreover, the league's annual meetings allowed Washington to develop support for the Tuskegee Machine from black businessmen who were community leaders from across the nation. Similarly, he worked closely with leaders in black fraternal orders such as the Odd Fellows and Pythians.

Washington and Roosevelt

In 1896 Washington supported winning Republican presidential candidate William McKinley over the Democratic and Populist William Jennings Bryan. Washington got along superbly with McKinley's successor, Theodore Roosevelt. Although Roosevelt subscribed to social Darwinism (see Chapter 15) and regarded black Americans as inferiors, he liked and respected Washington.

In 1901 Roosevelt invited Washington to dinner at the White House, where Roosevelt's wife, daughter, three sons, and a Colorado businessman joined them. Black people applauded, but the white South, alarmed by such a flagrant breach of racial etiquette (black people did not dine with white people), recoiled in disgust. Roosevelt was unmoved. A few days later the two men dined again together at Yale University. Still, Roosevelt never invited Washington for another meal at the Executive Mansion.

Washington and Roosevelt regularly consulted each other on political appointments. In the most notable case, Washington urged Roosevelt to appoint William D. Crum, a black medical doctor, as the collector of customs for the port of Charleston, South Carolina. White Southerners, led by Senator Benjamin R. Tillman, a South Carolina Democrat, opposed Crum's appointment and delayed final confirmation by the Senate for nearly three years. With Washington's assent, Roosevelt appointed black attorney and former all-American football player William Lewis to be U.S. district attorney in Boston. Several years later, President William Howard Taft appointed Lewis assistant attorney general of the United States. (For more details on Lewis, see Chapter 15.)

Opposition to Washington

Years before Washington rose to prominence, there were black leaders who favored a direct challenge to racial oppression. In 1889 delegates representing twenty-three states met to form the **Afro-American League** in Chicago. The league's main purpose was to press for civil and political rights guaranteed by the U.S. Constitution. "The objects of the League are to encourage State and local leagues in their efforts to break down color bars, and in obtaining for the Afro-American an equal chance with others in the avocations of life . . . in securing the full privileges of citizenship." But the league did not flourish, and it was eventually displaced by the Niagara Movement.

Opposition to Washington's conciliatory stance on racial matters steadily intensified. William Monroe Trotter became the most vociferous critic of Booker T. Washington and the Tuskegee Machine. Trotter was the Harvard-educated editor of the Boston *Guardian*. He savagely attacked Washington as "the Great Traitor," "the Benedict Arnold of the Negro Race," and "Pope Washington." At a 1903 meeting of the National Negro Business League in Boston, Trotter stood on a chair and interrupted a speech by Washington, defiantly asking, "Are the rope and the torch all the race is to get under your leadership?" Washington ignored him. The police arrested the editor for disorderly conduct. He spent thirty days in jail for what newspapers labeled "the Boston Riot."

W. E. B. Du Bois

William Edward Burghardt Du Bois, who was twelve years younger than Booker T. Washington, would eventually exceed the influence and authority of the Wizard of Tuskegee. Du Bois emerged as the most significant black leader in America during the first half of the twentieth century. Washington's life had been shaped by slavery, poverty, and the

▶ **Recommended Reading**

W. E. B. Du Bois. *The Souls of Black Folk*. New York: Library of America, 1903. An essential collection of superb essays.

W. E. B. Du Bois was a key figure in opposing Booker T. Washington's Tuskegee Machine. Du Bois helped found the NAACP and edited its publication, *The Crisis*, for two decades.

W. E. B. Du Bois on Being Black in America

W. E. B. Du Bois's The Souls of Black Folk (1903) contained perhaps the most eloquent statement ever written on being black in white America. The difficulties of their circumstances, Du Bois believed, create a double consciousness among Americans of African descent.

After the Egyptian and Indian, the Greek and Roman, the Teuton and Mongolian, the Negro is a sort of seventh son, born with a veil, and gifted with second-sight in this American world,—a world which yields him no true self-consciousness, but only lets him see himself through the revelation of the other world. It is a peculiar sensation, this double-consciousness, this sense of always looking at one's self through the eyes of others, of measuring one's soul by the tape of a world that looks on in an amused contempt and pity. One ever feels his two-ness,—an American, a Negro; two souls, two thoughts, two unreconciled strivings; two warring ideals in one dark body, whose dogged strength alone keeps it from being torn asunder.

The history of the American Negro is the history of this strife,—this longing to attain self-conscious manhood, to merge his double self into a better and truer self. In this merging he wishes neither of the older selves to be lost. He would not Africanize America, for America has too much to teach the world and Africa. He would not bleach his Negro soul in a flood of white Americanism, for he knows that Negro blood has a message for the world. He simply wishes to make it possible for a man to be both a Negro and an American, without being cursed and spit upon by his fellows, without having the doors of Opportunity closed roughly in his face.

What Do You Think?

▶ Why, in the judgment of W. E. B. Du Bois, is it impossible for a black person to be simply an American?

▶ Would Du Bois agree, based on his concept of double consciousness, that African Americans have a separate identity and separate culture from other Americans?

Source: Du Bois, *The Souls of Black Folk*, pp. 8–9.

▶ **What Do You Think?**

· As both black and American, African Americans cannot view themselves one without the other.

· Answers will vary.

industrial work ethic fostered at Hampton Institute. Du Bois was born and raised in the largely white New England town of Great Barrington, Massachusetts. It was a small community where he encountered little overt racism and developed a passion for knowledge.

Du Bois possessed, as he put it, "a flood of Negro blood, a strain of French, a bit of Dutch, but, thank God! no Anglo-Saxon." He graduated from Great Barrington High School at a time when few white and still fewer black youngsters attended more than primary school. He went south to Fisk University in Nashville and graduated at age twenty. He was the first black man to earn a Ph.D. (in history) at Harvard in 1895. He pursued additional graduate study in Germany.

Du Bois was perhaps the greatest scholar-activist in American history. He was an intellectual, at ease with words and ideas. He wrote sixteen nonfiction books, five novels, and two autobiographies. He was a fearless activist determined to confront disfranchisement, Jim Crow, and lynching. Washington solicited the goodwill of powerful white leaders. He was comfortable with a gradual approach to the eradication of white supremacy. Du Bois was impatient with white people who accepted or ignored white domination. Moreover, he had little tolerance for black people who were unwilling to demand their civil and political rights. Du Bois was well aware that he and Washington came from dissimilar backgrounds.

> I was born free. Washington was born a slave. He felt the lash of an overseer across his back. I was born in Massachusetts, he on a slave plantation in the South. My great-grandfather fought with the Colonial Army in New England in the American Revolution. I had a happy childhood and acceptance in the community. Washington's childhood was hard. I had many more advantages: Fisk University, Harvard, graduate years in Europe. Washington had little formal schooling.

The Souls of Black Folk

Du Bois was not always critical of Washington. Following Washington's speech at the Cotton States Exposition in 1895, Du Bois, then a young Harvard Ph.D. teaching at Ohio's Wilberforce University, wrote to praise him. "Let me heartily congratulate you upon your phenomenal success at Atlanta—it was a word fitly spoken." But in 1903 Du Bois, by then an Atlanta University professor, published *The Souls of Black Folk*. One of the major literary works of the twentieth century, it contained the first formal attack on Washington and his leadership.

In a provocative essay, "Of Booker T. Washington and Others," Du Bois conceded it was painful to challenge Washington, a man so highly praised and admired. "One hesitates, therefore, to criticize a life which, beginning with so little, has done so much. And yet the time is come when one may speak in all sincerity and utter courtesy of the mistakes and shortcomings of Mr. Washington's career, as well as the

▶▶ **Documents**

15-5 *W.E.B. Du Bois The Talented Tenth, 1903*
The concept of "The Talented Tenth," conceived by W.E.B. Du Bois called for the need for higher education among the most talented of the African American community.

16-1 *W. E. B. Du Bois, from The Souls of Black Folks, 1903*
In chapter three of *The Souls of Black Folks* (1903), Du Bois takes Washington to task for his apparent passivity in the face of white domination.

▶▶ **Recommended Reading**

David Levering Lewis. *W. E. B. Du Bois: Biography of a Race, 1868-1919*. New York: Henry Holt and Co., 1993; *W. E. B. Du Bois: The Fight for Equality and the American Century, 1919-1963*. New York: Henry Holt and Co., 2001. A magisterial and exhaustive account of the 95-year life and times of Du Bois.

The founders of the Niagara Movement posed in front of a photograph of the falls when they met at Niagara Falls, Ontario, Canada, in 1905. W. E. B. Du Bois is second from the right in the middle row.

▶ **Reading Check**

Washington believed that agricultural and industrial education was the key to solving "the problem of the color line." He believed that economic acceptance would lead to political and social acceptance. He did not challenge segregation or urge blacks to vocal protest. Du Bois attacked Washington for failing to stand up for political and civil rights for black Americans. He accused Washington of, in essence, apologizing for injustice and accepting the idea of black inferiority.

▶ **Documents**

15-5 *W.E.B. Du Bois The Talented Tenth, 1903* The concept of "The Talented Tenth," conceived by W.E.B. Du Bois called for the need for higher education among the most talented of the African American community.

triumphs." Du Bois attacked Washington for failing to stand up for political and civil rights and higher education for black Americans. Du Bois found even more infuriating Washington's willingness to compromise with the white South and his apparent agreement with white Southerners that black people were not their equals. "Mr. Washington represents in Negro thought the old attitude of adjustment and submission . . . and Mr. Washington's programme practically accepts the alleged inferiority of the Negro races."

Du Bois stressed that he agreed with Washington on some issues but disagreed even more about significant ones. He believed that on these issues it was vital to oppose Washington:

> So far as Mr. Washington preaches Thrift, Patience, and Industrial Training for the masses, we must hold up his hands and strive with him. . . . But so far as Mr. Washington apologizes for injustice, North or South, does not rightly value the privilege and duty of voting, belittles the emasculating effects of caste distinctions, and opposes higher training and ambition of our brighter minds,—so far as he, the South, or the Nation, does this,—we must unceasingly and firmly oppose them.

Washington worried the opposition of Trotter, Du Bois, and others would jeopardize the flow of funds from white philanthropists to black colleges and universities. In an effort to reconcile with his opponents, he organized a meeting with them, funded by white philanthropists, at Carnegie Hall in New York City in 1904. But Du Bois and other opponents of Washington came to the gathering determined to adopt a radical agenda. When Washington loyalists monopolized the proceedings, Du Bois left in disgust.

 **Reading Check** On what issues did Booker T. Washington and W. E. B. Du Bois agree and disagree in their efforts to promote the advancement of African Americans?

The Talented Tenth

Du Bois, joined by a small group of black intellectuals, then set out to organize an aggressive effort to secure the rights of black citizens. He was convinced that the advancement of black people was the responsibility of the black elite, those he called the Talented Tenth, meaning the upper 10 percent of black Americans. Education, he believed, was the key:

> Work alone will not do it unless inspired by the right ideals and guided by intelligence. Education must not simply teach work—it must teach Life. The Talented Tenth of the Negro race must be made leaders of

thought and missionaries of culture among people. No others can do this work, and Negro colleges must train men for it. The Negro race, like all other races, is going to be saved by its exceptional men.

The Niagara Movement

In 1905 Du Bois carried the anti-Washington crusade a step further. He invited a select group to meet at Niagara Falls, in Canada. The twenty-nine delegates to this meeting insisted that black people no longer quietly accept the loss of the right to vote.

We believe that [Negro] American citizens should protest emphatically and continually against the curtailment of their political rights.

They also demanded an end to segregation, declaring, "All American citizens have the right to equal treatment in places of public entertainment." They appealed for better schools, health care, and housing. They protested the discrimination endured by black soldiers and criticized the racial prejudice of most churches. Perhaps most important, the Niagara gathering insisted that white people did not know what was best for black people.

We repudiate the monstrous doctrine that the oppressor should be the sole authority as to the rights of the oppressed.

The Niagara Movement that emerged from this meeting attracted four hundred members and remained active for several years. Du Bois composed annual addresses to the nation designed to arouse black and white support. But the Niagara Movement was no match for the powerful, efficient, and well-financed Tuskegee Machine. Washington used every means at his disposal to undermine the movement. Black newspaper editors like the *Washington Bee*'s W. Calvin Chase, who had earlier attacked Washington's Atlanta Compromise address, were paid to attack Du Bois and to praise Washington. Washington dispatched spies to Niagara meetings to report on the organization's activities.

There were also internal problems among Niagara members. Du Bois was an inexperienced leader, and difficulties developed between Du Bois and Trotter. In 1908 the Niagara Movement virtually collapsed. Most black and white Americans were not prepared to support an organization that seemed so uncompromising in its demands.

 Reading Check What was the Niagra Movement and why was it formed?

▶▶ **Reading Check**

Led by W. E. B. Du Bois, a group of African American leaders who convened at Niagara Falls in the summer of 1905 to develop a more militant racial strategy as an alternative to Washington's.

▶▶ **Document**

16-2 *The Niagara Movement, Declaration of Principles, 1905*
In 1909, their declaration of principles found concrete institutional expression when a group of African Americans and white Progressives founded the National Association for the Advancement of Colored People.

GUIDE TO READING

▶ What were the purposes and aims of the NAACP?

▶ How did black women foster progress among African Americans?

▶ What were the defining characteristics of the black upper class?

KEY TERMS

▶ National Association for the Advancement of Colored People (NAACP), p. 550

▶ Dyer bill, p. 551

▶ Urban League, p. 552

▶ New Era Club, p. 553

▶ National Association of Colored Women, p. 554

▶ Nineteenth Amendment, p. 555

▶ American Negro Academy, p. 556

▶ Ugly Club, p. 558

▶ Boulé, p. 558

⟫ **Guide to Reading**

For answers, see the *Teacher's Resource Manual.*

⟫ **Document**

16-6 *"Our Reason for Being": A. Philip Randolph Embraces Socialism, 1919* A. Philip Randolph rejected the NAACP and urged black and white workers to embrace socialism to achieve political and economic goals. Randolph saw racial militancy as the only antidote available for black Americans against white treatment.

Section 2

New Black Organizations

The NAACP

As the Niagara Movement expired, the **National Association for the Advancement of Colored People** (**NAACP**) came to life. There was no direct link between the demise of the Niagara Movement and the rise of the NAACP. But the relatively small numbers of people—black and white—who felt comfortable with the Niagara Movement's assertive stance on race were inclined to support the NAACP. In its early years the NAACP was a militant organization dedicated to racial justice. White leaders dominated it and white contributors largely financed it.

A few white progressives were deeply concerned about the rampant racial prejudice manifested so graphically in lynchings, Jim Crow, black disfranchisement, and a vicious riot in 1908 in Springfield, Illinois—Abraham Lincoln's hometown. After a gathering of leaders in January 1909 in New York City, Oswald Garrison Villard issued a call on February 12—Lincoln's Birthday—to "all believers in democracy to join a national conference to discuss present evils, the voicing of protests, and the renewal of the struggle for civil and political liberty."

Villard was the president and editor of the New York *Evening Post* and the grandson of abolitionist William Lloyd Garrison. Prominent progressives endorsed the call, including social workers Lillian Wald and Jane Addams, literary scholar Joel E. Spingarn, and respected attorneys Clarence Darrow and Moorfield Storey. W. E. B. Du Bois, Ida Wells Barnett, and Mary Church Terrell were the black leaders most involved in the formation of the NAACP.

The NAACP was determined that black citizens should fully enjoy the civil and political rights the Constitution guaranteed to all citizens. It relied on the judicial and legislative systems in what would be a persistent and decades-long effort to secure those rights. The NAACP won its first major legal victory in 1915 when the Supreme Court overturned Oklahoma's grandfather clause in *Guinn v. United States.* But poll taxes and literacy tests continued to disfranchise black citizens.

In 1917, in a case brought by the Louisville NAACP branch and argued before the Supreme Court by Moorfield Storey, the court struck down a local law that enforced residential segregation. The law prohibited black people and white people from selling real estate to people of

The Emergence of National African-American Organizations

1889 Afro-American League organized in Chicago

1892 Colored Women's League of Washington formed

1893 New Era Club founded in Boston

1895 National Federation of Afro-American Women organized in Boston

1896 National Association of Colored Women (NACW) formed in Washington

1897 American Negro Academy founded in Washington

1897 First Phillis Wheatley home established in Detroit

1900 National Negro Business League established in Boston

1905 Niagara Movement organized in Niagara Falls, Ontario, Canada

1909 National Association for the Advancement of Colored People (NAACP) founded in New York City

1910 National League on Urban Conditions among Negroes (Urban League) formed in New York City

the other race. The NAACP also tried in 1918 to secure a federal law prohibiting lynching. With the assistance of Congressman Leonidas Dyer, a white St. Louis Republican, the antilynching measure—the **Dyer bill**—passed in the House of Representatives in 1922 over vigorous Democratic opposition. But the Senate blocked it, and it never became law.

Du Bois and *The Crisis*

W. E. B. Du Bois was easily the most prominent black figure associated with the NAACP during its first quarter century. He became director of publicity and research and edited the NAACP publication, *The Crisis*. He largely left leadership and administrative tasks to others.

With *The Crisis*, Du Bois the scholar became Du Bois the propagandist. In the pages of *The Crisis*, he denounced white racism and atrocities. He demanded that black people stand up for their rights. "Agitate, then, brother; protest, reveal the truth and refuse to be silenced. . . . A moment's let up, a moment's acquiescence, means a chance for the wolves of prejudice to get at our necks." He would not provoke violence, but he would not tolerate mistreatment either. "I am resolved to be quiet and law abiding, but to refuse to cringe in body or in soul, to resent deliberate insult, and to assert my just rights in the face of wanton aggression." These were not the even-tempered, cautious words of Booker T. Washington to which so many Americans had grown accustomed. *The Crisis* became required reading in many black homes. By 1913 it had thirty thousand subscribers when the membership of the NAACP was only three thousand.

▶▶ **Living Words Audio Clip**

Track 24 *Crisis Magazine, by W.E.B. Du Bois*

Washington versus the NAACP

In 1909, with the founding of the NAACP, Oswald Garrison Villard tried to reassure Washington the organization posed no threat and to gain his support for the new association. "It is not to be a Washington movement, or a Du Bois movement. The idea is that there shall grow out of it, first, an annual conference . . . for the discussion by men of both races of the conditions of the colored people, politically, socially, industrially and educationally."

Many black leaders and members of the NAACP, however, despised Washington and his ideology. Washington returned the sentiment. With the assistance of his followers, he worked to subvert the new organization. Washington looked on Du Bois as little more than the puppet of white people, who dominated the leadership of the NAACP. The Tuskegee leader declined to debate Du Bois.

Charles Anderson, a Tuskegee loyalist in New York City, wrote to Washington in 1909 that the NAACP was meeting secretly and he would attempt to disrupt its efforts. Washington relied again on allies who were editors of black newspapers to criticize the NAACP. He also wrote Clark Howell, the white editor of the Atlanta *Constitution*, to attack Du Bois. Washington later told an alumnus of Tuskegee that the main aim of the NAACP was to destroy Washington and Tuskegee.

Washington became so obsessed with the NAACP that he was not above manipulating white supremacists to damage those connected with the association. He learned that a group of black and white progressives associated with the NAACP were going to gather at the Café Boulevard in New York City in 1911. He allowed Charles Anderson to alert the hostile white press. They gleefully described the multiracial dinner in the most inflammatory terms.

Ultimately, Washington's efforts to ruin the NAACP and to reduce the influence of its supporters failed. By the time of his death in 1915, the NAACP had grown steadily to over six thousand members and fifty local branches. Its aggressive campaign for civil and political rights replaced Washington's strategy of progress through conciliation and accommodation.

 Reading Check   What were the purposes and aims of the NAACP?

The Urban League

In 1910 the National League on Urban Conditions among Negroes was founded in New York City. The goal of this social welfare organization, soon known simply as the **Urban League**, was to alleviate conditions black people encountered as they moved into large cities in ever-increasing numbers in the early twentieth century. Like the NAACP, the Urban

▶ **Reading Check**

The NAACP was dedicated to racial justice. Its members were determined that blacks should enjoy the same civil and political rights as whites. They relied on the persistent use of the legal system to achieve these aims.

League was created by black and white progressives. It worked to improve housing, medical care, and recreational facilities among black residents who lived in segregated neighborhoods in New York, Philadelphia, Atlanta, Nashville, Norfolk, and other cities. The league also assisted youngsters who ran afoul of the law. It helped establish the Big Brother and Big Sister movements.

▶ **Living Words Audio Clip**

Track 25 *The Progress of Colored Women by Mary Church Terrell; excerpt*

PROFILE ❖ Mary Church Terrell

Mary Church Terrell lived from the year of the Emancipation Proclamation (1863) to the year that the U.S. Supreme Court declared segregated schools unconstitutional (1954). Mary Church was born in Civil War Memphis and raised during Reconstruction. She went to Oberlin College where she studied classics, became proficient in languages, and earned an M.A. In 1891 she married Robert H. Terrell, a Harvard graduate who had earned a law degree at Howard. He was an auditor in the U.S. Treasury Department and later became a District of Columbia municipal judge.

Mary Church Terrell immersed herself in literary, social, and political activities. She spearheaded the creation of the Colored Women's League and became the first president of the National Association of Colored Women in 1896. Terrell was an inspirational speaker. She spoke in 1904 at the International Congress of Women in Berlin—in German, French, and English.

Terrell was devoted to the NAACP and its program. She served on its board, and spoke forcefully on civil rights. She risked the wrath of President Theodore Roosevelt after she criticized his dismissal of three companies of black soldiers following the Brownsville incident (see Chapter 15). She presented President William Howard Taft with NAACP petitions against lynching. She wrote articles attacking chain gangs, peonage, disfranchisement, and lynching. She worked with progressive organizations, such as the Women's International League for Peace and Freedom. She supported women's suffrage and the Nineteenth Amendment.

The Terrells were active in Washington's black elite—the Four Hundred. They attended balls, concerts, and parties, traveled extensively. They belonged to Washington's most exclusive black congregation, the Lincoln Temple Congregational Church.

Terrell consistently opposed racial discrimination. She protested to Oberlin College officials when her daughters encountered more prejudice as students than she had. A lifelong Republican, she opposed Democratic president Franklin Roosevelt's inaction on civil rights in the 1930s. At the age of eighty-seven she demonstrated against Thompson's Restaurant, an all-white establishment in Washington, D.C.

Mary Church Terrell summed up her legacy in her 1940 autobiography, *A Colored Woman in a White World.*

"This is the story of a colored woman living in a white world. It cannot possibly be like a story written by a white woman. A white woman has only one handicap to overcome—that of sex. I have two—both sex and race. I belong to the only group in this country which has two such huge obstacles to surmount."

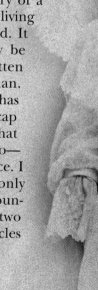

Terrell

553

Black Women and the Club Movement

Years before the Urban League and the NAACP were founded, black women began creating clubs and organizations. The local groups that began forming in the 1870s and 1880s were mainly concerned with cultural, religious, and social matters. But many of the mostly middle-class women active in these clubs eventually became less interested in tea and gossip and more involved with community problems. In 1893 black women in Boston founded the **New Era Club**. They published a monthly magazine, *Woman's Era*, that featured articles on fashion, health, and family life.

In 1895 a New Era Club member, Josephine St. Pierre Ruffin was enraged by white journalist James W. Jack's vilification of black women as "prostitutes, thieves, and liars" who were "altogether without character." She issued a call to "Let Us Confer Together" that drew 104 black women to a meeting in Boston. The result was the formation of the National Federation of Afro-American Women, which soon included thirty-six clubs in twelve states. The Colored Women's League of Washington, D.C., which had been founded in 1892, published an appeal in *Woman's Era* for black women to organize a national association. At that gathering, representatives from several local black women's clubs organized the National Colored Woman's League.

The two groups—The National Federation of Afro-American Women and the National Colored Woman's League—merged in 1896 to form the **National Association of Colored Women** (NACW) with Mary Church Terrell elected the first president. The NACW adopted the self-help motto "Lifting as We Climb." They stressed moral, mental, and material advancement. By 1914 there were fifty thousand members of the NACW in one thousand clubs nationwide.

There were sometimes unpleasant disagreements and conflicts among the club women. Margaret Murray Washington—Booker T. Washington's wife—served as NACW president from 1912 to 1916. The organization's *National Notes* was published at Tuskegee until 1922. Not everyone was fond of this arrangement. Ida Wells Barnett claimed that the Tuskegee Machine censored the publication. There were also regional rivalries and ideological disputes.

More important than these internal struggles were the efforts of black women to confront the problems black people encountered in urban areas. The NACW clubs worked to eradicate poverty, end racial discrimination, and promote education, including the formation of kindergartens and day nurseries. Members cared for older people, especially former slaves. They aided orphans; assisted working mothers by providing nurseries, health care, and information on child rearing; and established homes for delinquent and abandoned girls.

Phillis Wheatley Clubs

Black women also formed Phillis Wheatley clubs and homes across the nation (named in honor of the eighteenth-century African-American poet). The residences offered living accommodations for single, black working women in many cities where they were refused admittance to YWCA facilities. Some Phillis Wheatley clubs also provided nurseries and classes in domestic skills. In Cleveland, nurse Jane Edna Hunter organized a residence for single, black working women who could not find comfortable and affordable housing. In 1911 she formed the Working Girls' Home Association for cleaning women, laundresses, and private duty nurses. With association members contributing five cents a week, Hunter opened a twenty-three-room residence in 1913 that expanded to a seventy-two-room building in 1917.

Anna Julia Cooper and Black Feminism

"Only the BLACK WOMAN can say 'when and where I enter, in the quiet, undisputed dignity of my womanhood, without violence and without suing or special patronage, then and there the whole Negro race enters with me.'" Anna Julia Cooper was convinced that black women would play a decisive role in shaping the destiny of their people. She labored to dispel the stereotype that black women lacked refinement, grace, and morality.

Cooper was born a slave in Raleigh, North Carolina, in 1858 and graduated from St. Augustine's School. She then earned a bachelor's degree from Oberlin College in 1884. Speaking and writing with increasing confidence and authority, she published *A Voice from the South by a Black Woman of the South* in 1892. In this collection of essays she stressed the pivotal role that black women would play in the future. She chastised white women for their lack of support. In 1900 she addressed the Pan African Conference in London.

Cooper was principal of Washington's famed M Street Colored High School (later Paul Laurence Dunbar High School) from 1901 to 1906. She was forced out in 1906. Supporters of the powerful Tuskegee Machine resented Cooper's emphasis on academic preparation over vocational training. She went on to teach for four years at Missouri's Lincoln University before returning to M Street High as a teacher. She earned a Ph.D. at the Sorbonne in Paris. She was active with the NACW, the NAACP, and YWCA. She died in 1964 at age 105.

Women's Suffrage

Historically, many black women had supported women's suffrage. Before the Civil War, many abolitionists, including Mary Ann Shadd Cary, Sojourner Truth, and Frederick Douglass, had also backed women's suffrage. Cary and Truth tried unsuccessfully to vote after the

▶▶ **Document**

14-4 *Anna Julia Cooper, From A Voice from the South: By a Black Woman of the South,1892* Born in Raleigh, North Carolina, Anna Julia Cooper was the daughter of a slave. Her speeches and essays were collected in *A Voice from the South: By a Black Woman of the South* (1892). Cooper gave a voice to the disenfranchised black women of the nineteenth century while anticipating the feminist movement of the twentieth century.

▶▶ **Interactive Activity**

The Struggle for Women Suffrage

In this activity students explore some of the different ideas and goals of the suffragists, and how they shaped women's efforts to gain the right to vote.

▶▶ **Recommended Reading**

Deborah Gray White. *Too Heavy a Load: Black Women in Defense of Themselves*. New York: Norton, 1999. An exploration of the contours of black women's history in the twentieth century.

war. Black women, such as Caroline Remond Putnam of Massachusetts, Lottie Rollin of South Carolina, and Frances Ellen Watkins Harper of Pennsylvania, attended conventions of the mostly white American Woman's Suffrage Association in the 1870s.

Black women were also involved in the long struggle for women's suffrage on the state level. Ida Wells Barnett was a leader in the Illinois suffrage effort. By 1900 Wyoming, Utah, Colorado, and Idaho permitted women to vote. By 1918 women in seventeen northern and western states had gained the vote. But as more women won voting rights, women's suffrage became more controversial. The proposed **Nineteenth Amendment** to the U.S. Constitution drove a wedge between black and white advocates of women's political rights. Many opponents of women's suffrage, especially white Southerners, warned that granting women the right to vote would increase the number of black voters. Some white women advocated strict literacy and educational requirements for voting in an effort to limit the number of black voters, both women and men.

As it turned out, only two southern states—Kentucky and Tennessee—ratified the Nineteenth Amendment before its adoption in 1920. Black suffragists understood that the right to vote meant political

▶ **Recommended Reading**

Willard Gatewood. *Aristocrats of Color: The Black Elite, 1880–1920.* Bloomington, IN: Indiana University Press, 1990. An examination of the lives and activities of well-to-do black people.

Lawrence Otis Graham. *One Kind of People: Inside America's Black Upper Class.* New York: HarperCollins, 1999. An informative history and analysis of black America's wealthiest families and organizations.

James Van der Zee was a prominent black photographer in Harlem whose photos frequently depicted the community's well-to-do residents. This is a wedding party in 1926.

power. Political power could be exercised to acquire civil rights, improve education, and gain respect. White Southerners also grasped the importance of voting rights. Thus despite the Nineteenth Amendment, large numbers of black people in the South—both men and women—remained unable to vote.

The Black Elite

Many of the black leaders described by W. E. B. Du Bois as the Talented Tenth formed protest organizations, joined reform efforts, and organized self-help groups. The leaders were middle- and upper-class black people who were better educated than most Americans—black or white.

PROFILE ❖ Lewis Latimer, Black Inventor

Lewis H. Latimer (1848–1928) was a draftsman, inventor, and pioneer in the electrical industry. During his lifetime, Latimer was awarded eight patents for his inventions. He was born in Chelsea, Massachusetts, in 1848. His parents had fled from slavery and settled in Boston. Abolitionists including William Lloyd Garrison and Frederick Douglass raised funds to purchase their freedom.

After a year in the Union Navy during the Civil War, Latimer worked as an office boy for the patent solicitor firm of Crosby and Gould. There he taught himself drafting. As a draftsman, Latimer worked closely with inventors and began to tinker with ideas for inventions. In 1874 he received his first patent for improving the toilet on passenger railroad cars. He developed a flushing mechanism that prevented the upflow of sewage and cinders. He also executed drawings for Alexander Graham Bell's patent application for the telephone. Latimer later worked on electric lights. In 1882 he received a patent for producing carbon filaments that made electric lighting more practical.

Latimer became superintendent of the incandescent lamp department of the United States Electric Lighting Company. He supervised the installation of lights for buildings in the United States and Canada. In 1883 Thomas A. Edison hired Latimer as an engineer, chief draftsman, and expert witness in patent infringement cases. In 1890 Latimer published a book entitled *Incandescent Lighting: A Practical Description of the Edison System.* He served as chief draftsman for General Electric/Westinghouse Board of Patent Control when it was established in 1896.

Men who had worked with Thomas A. Edison joined together in 1918 as the Edison Pioneers to preserve memories of their early days working together and to honor Edison's genius and achievements. Latimer was a founding member and the only African-American Edison Pioneer. He died in Flushing, New York, on December 11, 1928.

races as a means to avoid friction. Trotter vehemently disagreed. Wilson became visibly irritated. The president warned that he would no longer meet with the group if Trotter remained their spokesman.

Black Men and the Military in World War I

In 1915–1916 Wilson faced more than problems with dissatisfied black people. United States–Mexican relations had steadily deteriorated after a revolution and civil war in Mexico. War in Europe threatened to draw the United States into conflict with Germany.

In 1914 war almost broke out between the United States and Mexico when U.S. marines landed at Vera Cruz after an attack on American sailors. Then, in March 1916, Francisco "Pancho" Villa, one of the participants in Mexico's civil war, led a force of Mexican rebels across the border into New Mexico in an effort to provoke war between Mexico and the United States. Fifteen Americans were killed, including seven U.S. soldiers. In response, Wilson dispatched a **punitive expedition** that eventually numbered 15,000 U.S. troops under the command of General John J. "Black Jack" Pershing. Pershing acquired the nickname "Black Jack" after commanding black troops in Cuba during the Spanish-American War.

United States forces, including the black 10th Cavalry (see Chapter 15), spent ten months in Mexico in a futile effort to capture Villa. The 10th Cavalry was, as had been the case with black troops since the Civil War, commanded by white men. But Lieutenant Colonel Charles Young, an 1889 black graduate of the U.S. Military Academy at West Point, helped lead the regiment. Young led the black troops against a contingent of Villa's rebels who had ambushed an element of the 13th Cavalry, a white unit, at Santa Cruz de Villegas. U.S. troops were withdrawn from Mexico in 1917 as the probability increased that the United States would enter World War I against Germany.

World War I

When World War I erupted in Europe in August 1914, Woodrow Wilson and most Americans had no intention and no desire to participate. Wilson promptly issued a proclamation of neutrality. Running for reelection in 1916 on the appealing slogan "He Kept Us Out of War," Wilson narrowly defeated Republican candidate Charles Evans Hughes. Repeated German submarine attacks on civilian vessels and the loss of American lives infuriated Wilson and many Americans as a gross violation of U.S. neutral rights. On April 6, 1917, Congress declared war on Germany. Most African Americans supported the war effort. As in previous conflicts, black people sought to demonstrate their loyalty and devotion to the country through military service.

Some white leaders were less enthusiastic about the participation of black men. One southern governor wondered about the wisdom of having the military train and arm thousands of black men at southern camps and

▶ Reading Check

A scholarly organization made up of black men publish works on histor science. In addition to concepts, the academy women's suffrage (ever could not be members)

▶ Recommended F

Lawrence C. Ross, Jr. *Th of African-American Sororities*. New York 2000.

▶ Retracing the O

The George Washingto Monument. Diamond, Washington Carver wa 1864 or 1865 in a cal The 210-acre park has exhibits on Carver's life about his boyhood. Th and the Carver Scienc

▶ Recommended Reading

Arthur E. Barbeau and Florette Henri. *Black American Troops in World War I*. Philadelphia: Temple University Press, 1974.

Bernard C. Nalty. *Strength for the Fight: A History of Black Americans in the Military*. New York: The Free Press, 1986.

▶ Retracing the Odyssey

The 369th Historical Society, New York, New York. The 369th all-black regiment distinguished itself during World War I in combat alongside French units. Previously it had been the 15th Infantry Regiment of the New York National Guard. The 369th armory contains a museum that features weapons, equipment and photos of black troops from World War I to Operation Desert Storm of 1991.

posts. General Pershing argued for the use of black troops, but insisted on white leadership. "Under capable white officers and with sufficient training, Negro soldiers have always acquitted themselves creditably."

Black Troops and Officers

There were about 10,000 black regulars in the U.S. Army in 1917: the 9th and 10th Cavalry regiments and the 24th and 25th Infantry regiments. There were more than 5,000 black men in the navy. Virtually all of them were waiters, kitchen attendants, and stokers for the ships' boilers. The Marine Corps did not admit black men. During World War I, the newly formed Selective Service system drafted more than 370,000 black men—13 percent of all draftees—although none of the local draft boards had black members. Several all-black state National Guard units were also incorporated into federal service.

The military remained rigidly segregated. There was political pressure from black newspapers and the NAACP to commission black officers to lead black troops. The War Department created an officer training school at Fort Des Moines, Iowa. Nearly 1,250 black men enrolled. Over 1,000 received commissions. Black officers, however, were confined to the lower ranks. None of these new black officers were promoted above captain, and the overall command of black units remained in white hands.

Lieutenant Colonel Charles Young was eligible to lead black and white troops in World War I. He had already served in Cuba, the Philippines, Haiti, and Mexico. Several white soldiers complained, however, that they did not want to take orders from a black man. Over Young's protests, military authorities forced him to retire by claiming he had high blood pressure. Young insisted he was in good health, and he rode a horse from his home in Xenia, Ohio, to Washington, D.C., to prove it. But Young remained on the retired list until he was given command of a training unit in Illinois five days before the war ended.

Discrimination and Its Effects

As in earlier American wars, black troops were discriminated against, abused, and neglected. Some were compelled to drill with picks and shovels rather than rifles. At Camp Hill, Virginia, black men lived in tents with no floors, no blankets, and no bathing facilities through a cold winter. White men failed to salute black officers. Black officers were denied admission to officers' clubs. Morale among black troops was low. Their performance sometimes reflected it.

Military authorities did not expect to use black troops in combat. The army preferred to employ black troops in labor battalions, as stevedores, in road construction, and as cooks and bakers. Of more than 380,000 black men who served in World War I, only 42,000 went into combat. The army did not prepare black soldiers adequately for combat.

▶ **Living Words Audio Clip**

Track 31 *"Swing Low, Sweet Chariot"; traditional; sung by Paul Robeson*

Lieutenant Colonel Charles D. Young, an 1889 graduate of the U.S. Military Academy at West Point who served in Cuba, the Philippines, Haiti, and Mexico, was not permitted to command troops during World War I.

Military leaders complained when black soldiers who did face combat performed poorly in battle.

The 368th Infantry Regiment of the 92nd Division came in for especially harsh criticism. Fighting alongside the French in September 1918, the second and third battalions fell back in disorder. Some black officers and enlisted men ran. The white regimental commander blamed black officers. Thirty of them were relieved of command. Five officers were court-martialed for cowardice; four were sentenced to death and one to life in prison. All were later freed. Black Lieutenant Howard H. Long agreed that the perceptions of white officers caused the poor performance. "Many of the [white] field officers seemed far more concerned with reminding their Negro subordinates that they were Negroes than they were in having an effective unit that would perform well in combat."

Even the white commander of the 92nd Division, General Charles C. Ballou, identified white officers as the main problem. "It was my misfortune to be handicapped by many white officers who were rabidly hostile

African-American troops on the march near Verdun in France in 1918.

to the idea of a colored officer, and who continually conveyed misinformation to the staff of the superior units, and generally created much trouble and discontent."

White officials stressed the weaknesses of the 368th Infantry Regiment and mostly ignored the commendable records of the 369th, 370th, 371st, and 372nd Regiments. The 369th compiled an exemplary combat record. Sent to the front for ninety-one consecutive days, these **Men of Bronze**—as they came to be known—consisted mainly of soldiers from the 15th New York National Guard. They fought alongside the French and were given French weapons, uniforms, helmets, and food. They had an outstanding military band led by Jim Europe, one of the finest musical leaders of the early twentieth century. The 369th lived up to their motto, "Let's Go," as they took part in some of the war's heaviest fighting. They never lost a trench or gave up a prisoner. By June 1918 French commanders were asking for all the black troops the Americans could send.

Most French civilians and troops praised the conduct of black soldiers and accepted them as equals. Following the triumph of the Allies in World War I, French authorities awarded the Croix de Guerre, one of France's highest military medals, to the men of the 369th, the 371st, and the 372nd Regiments. Black troops returned to America on segregated ships. The 15th New York National Guard Unit from the 369th Regiment and its famed band were not permitted to join the farewell parade in New York City.

Du Bois's Disappointment

Black leaders who had supported American entry in the war were embittered at the treatment of black soldiers. During the war in 1918, Du Bois appealed to black people in *The Crisis* to "close ranks" and support the war.

> We of the colored race have no ordinary interest in the outcome. That which the German power represents today spells death to the aspirations of Negroes and all darker races for equality, freedom and democracy. Let us not hesitate. Let us, while this war lasts, forget our special grievances and close ranks with our own white fellow citizens and the allied nations that are fighting for democracy.

Du Bois's support may well have been connected to his effort to secure an officer's commission in military intelligence. Du Bois did not get his commission. What he did get was criticism for his "close ranks" editorial. His former ally, William Monroe Trotter, said that Du Bois had "finally weakened, compromised, deserted the fight, [and] betrayed the cause of his race." To Trotter, Du Bois was "a rank quitter in the cause for equal rights."

In 1930 Du Bois confessed that he should not have supported U.S. intervention in the war.

> I was swept off my feet during the world war by the emotional response of America to what seemed to be a great call to duty. The thing that I did not understand is how easy and inevitable it is for an appeal to blood and force to smash to utter negation any ideal for which it is used. Instead of a war to end war, or a war to save democracy, we found ourselves during and after the war descending to the meanest and most sordid of selfish actions.

By the end of World War I, Du Bois could see that black loyalty and sacrifice had not eroded white racism. He wrote defiantly in *The Crisis* that black people were determined to make America yield to its democratic ideals:

> But by the God of heaven, we are cowards and
> jackasses if now that the war is over, we do not
> marshal every ounce of our brain and brawn to fight
> a sterner, longer, more unbending battle against the
> forces of hell in our own land.
>   We return.
>   We return from fighting.
>   We return fighting.
>   Make way for Democracy! We saved it in France,
> and by the Great Jehovah, we will save it in the
> United States of America, or know the reason why.

 **Reading Check** How did African Americans contribute to U.S. participation in World War I?

▶ **Reading Check**

Most African Americans supported the war effort. Blacks demonstrated their loyalty and devotion to the United States by volunteering for military service. By the end of the war, 370,000 black men were drafted into the military. Black men were trained as officers, but were confined to the lower ranks.

▶ **Teaching Notes**

Even when white Americans offered praise, it was riddled with racist stereotypes. The Milwaukee *Sentinel* offered a typical compliment. "Those two colored regiments fought well, and it calls for special recognition. Is there no way of getting a cargo of watermelons over there?"

Section 4

Racial Violence

GUIDE TO READING

▶ Why was there so much racial violence in the early twentieth century?

▶ What factors contributed to the racial violence in Chicago in 1919?

KEY TERMS

▶ race riots, p. 567

Race Riots

Despite the reformist impulse of the progressive era, most white Americans clung to social Darwinism and white supremacy. White people reacted with contempt and violence to demands by black people for fairer treatment and equal opportunities in American society. The campaigns of the NAACP, the efforts of the black club women, and the services and sacrifices of black men in the war not only failed to alter white racial perceptions but were sometimes accompanied by a backlash against African Americans.

Many white Americans agreed with Mississippi senator James K. Vardaman when he declared in 1914 that white people would not accept black claims for a meaningful political and legal role in America.

> God Almighty never intended that the negro should share with the white man in the government of this country. . . . Do not forget that. It matters not what I may say or others may think; it matters not what constitutions may contain or statutes provide, wherever the negro is in sufficient numbers to imperil the white man's civilization or question the white man's supremacy the white man is going to find some way around the difficulty. And that is just as true in the North as it is in the South.

The racial violence that had permeated southern life in the late nineteenth century expanded into northern communities. Many white Americans were hostile to the arrival of black migrants from the South. Black people defended themselves, and casualties among both races escalated in **race riots** that occurred from 1900 to 1923. (see Map 16–1).

Atlanta 1906

In 1906 white mobs attacked black residents in Atlanta. Several factors aggravated white racial apprehensions in the city. Many rural black people, attracted by economic opportunities, had moved to Atlanta. White residents considered the newcomers more lawless and immoral than the longtime black residents. The Atlanta newspapers—*The Constitution, The Journal,* and *The Georgian*—ran inflammatory accounts about black crime and black men who brutalized white women. Many of these stories were false or exaggerated. Two white Democrats—Hoke Smith and Clark Howell—were engaged in a divisive campaign for a U.S. Senate

▶ **Guide to Reading**

MAP 16–1 Major Race Riots, 1900–1923

In the years between 1900 and 1923, race conflicts and riots occurred in dozens of American communities as black people migrated in increasing numbers to urban areas.

 Were the causes of each of these riots similar, or were the reasons for the upsurge in racial violence unique to each situation?

▶ Map 16-1

These riots were caused primarily by white Americans who, through violence, attempted to prevent black Americans from assuming a more equitable role in American society

seat in 1906. Both candidates stirred up racial animosity. There were also determined and ultimately successful efforts under way to disfranchise black voters in Georgia.

On a warm Saturday night, September 22, 1906, a white man jumped on a box on Decatur Street, one of Atlanta's main thoroughfares, and waved an Atlanta newspaper emblazoned with the headline THIRD ASSAULT. He hollered, "Are white men going to stand for this?" The crowd roared, "No! Save our women!" A five-day orgy of violence followed.

The mayor, police, and fire departments vainly tried to stop the mob. Thousands of white people roamed the streets in search of black victims. Black people were indiscriminately tortured, beaten, and killed. White men pulled black passengers off streetcars. They destroyed black businesses. As white men armed themselves, the police disarmed black men. Black men and women who surrendered to marauding white mobs in hopes of mercy were not spared. Black men who fought back only further infuriated the crazed white crowd. Twenty-five black people and one white person died, and hundreds were injured in the riot.

Du Bois hurried home to Atlanta from a trip to Alabama to defend his wife and child. He waited on his porch with a shotgun for a mob that never came. He later explained, "I would without hesitation have sprayed their guts over the grass."

Booker T. Washington looked for a silver lining in the awful affair by noting that "while there is disorder in one community there is peace and harmony in thousands of others." He said that black resistance would merely result in more black fatalities. Washington went to Atlanta and appealed for racial reconciliation.

A Committee of Safety of ten black and ten white leaders was formed. Charles T. Hopkins, an influential white Atlantan, warned in strong paternalist terms, "If we let this dependent race be butchered before our eyes, we cannot face God in the judgement day." But little real racial cooperation resulted. No members of the white mob were brought to justice. Black Georgia voters were disfranchised. Atlanta's streetcars were segregated. The city had no public high school for black youngsters. The Carnegie Library did not admit black people, and the Atlanta police force had no black officers.

Springfield 1908

Two years later in August 1908, white citizens of Springfield, Illinois, attacked black residents in an episode that led to the creation of the NAACP in 1909. George Richardson, a black man, was falsely accused of raping a white woman. The sheriff managed to save Richardson by getting him out of town. But an angry mob tore into Springfield's small black population. Six black people were shot and killed, two were lynched, dozens were injured, and damage in the thousands of dollars was inflicted on black homes and businesses. About two thousand black people were driven out of the community.

There was even more violence in the second decade of the twentieth century as major racial conflicts occurred between 1917 and 1921 in East St. Louis, IL; Houston, TX; Chicago; Elaine, AR; and Tulsa, OK. Smaller violent confrontations occurred at Washington, D.C.; Charleston, SC; Knoxville, TN; Omaha, NE; and Waco and Longview, TX. Although different incidents sparked each riot, the underlying causes tended to be similar. White residents were concerned that recently arrived black migrants would compete for jobs and housing.

East St. Louis 1917

East St. Louis, Illinois, was a gritty industrial town of nearly sixty thousand across the Mississippi River from St. Louis, Missouri. About 10 percent of the inhabitants were black. The town's schools, public facilities, and neighborhoods were segregated. Racial tensions increased in February 1917 after 470 black workers were hired to replace white members of the American Federation of Labor who had gone on strike against the Aluminum Ore Company. On July 1 several white people drove through a black neighborhood firing guns. Shortly after, two white plainclothes police officers drove into the same neighborhood and were

▶▶ **Recommended Reading**

Roberta Senechal. *The Sociogenesis of a Race Riot: Springfield, Illinois, in 1908.* Urbana, IL: University of Illinois Press, 1990.

On July 28, 1917, the NAACP organized a silent march in New York City to protest the East St. Louis, Illinois, race riot in which thirty-five black people died as well as to denounce the ongoing epidemic of lynchings.

▶ **Recommended Reading**

Robert V. Haynes. *A Night of Violence: The Houston Riot of 1917.* Baton Rouge, LA: Louisiana State University Press, 1976.

shot and killed by residents who may have believed the drive-by shooters had returned.

Angry white mobs then sought revenge. Black people were killed, and their bodies were thrown into the river. Black homes, many of them little more than cabins and shacks, were burned. Hundreds of black people were left homeless. The police joined the rioters. Thirty-five black people and eight white people died in the violence.

The NAACP sent W. E. B. Du Bois and Martha Gruening to East St. Louis. They compiled a twenty-four-page report, "Massacre at East St. Louis," that documented instance after instance of brutality. "Negroes were 'flushed' from the burning houses, and ran for their lives, screaming and begging for mercy.

A Negro crawled into a shed and fired on the white men. Guardsmen started after him, but when they saw he was armed, turned to the mob and said: `He's armed boys. You can have him. A white man's life is worth the lives of a thousand Negroes.'"

To protest the riot, the NAACP organized a silent march in New York City and thousands of well-dressed black people marched to muffled drums down Fifth Avenue.

Houston 1917

A month after the East St. Louis riot, black soldiers in Houston attacked police officers and civilians. The Third Battalion of the 24th Infantry recently had been transferred from Wyoming and California to Camp Logan near Houston. The black troops came face to face with Jim Crow. Streetcars and public facilities were segregated. Local white and Hispanic people regularly called the black troops "niggers."

On August 23 a black soldier tried to prevent a police officer, Lee Sparks, from beating a black woman. Sparks clubbed the soldier and hauled him off to jail. Corporal Charles W. Baltimore later attempted to determine what had happened. He was also beaten and incarcerated. Both soldiers were later released. But a rumor circulated that Baltimore had been slain. Led by Sergeant Vida Henry, black men sought revenge.

About one hundred armed black soldiers mounted a two-hour assault on the police station. Fifteen white residents—including five policemen—one Mexican American, four black soldiers, and two black civilians were killed. The army arrested 118 black soldiers, 63 of whom were charged with mutiny. Three separate courts martials were held over the next several months. The NAACP retained the son of Texas legend Sam Houston to help defend them. Eight black men, however, agreed to testify against the defendants. Thirteen black troops were hanged (including Corporal Baltimore) after the first court-martial. Later seven more were executed and seven others were acquitted. The remainder were sentenced to prison terms ranging from two years to life.

The Houston violence prompted some political and military leaders to call for the abolition of the black regiments. W. E. B. Du Bois eulogized the first 13 black soldiers to be executed: "Thirteen young men, strong men, soldiers who have fought for a country which never was wholly theirs; men born to suffer ridicule, injustice and, at last, death itself." In the meantime, Lee Sparks remained on the Houston police force and killed two black people later that year.

Chicago 1919

Between 1916 and 1919, the black population of Chicago doubled as migrants from the South moved north in search of jobs, political rights, and humane treatment. Many encountered a violent reception. A severe housing shortage strained the boundaries between crowded, segregated black neighborhoods and white residential areas. In the months after

▶ **Recommended Readings**

William Tuttle. *Chicago in the Red Summer of 1919.* New York: Atheneum, 1970.

Lee E. Williams. *Anatomy of Four Race Riots: Racial Conflict in Knoxville, Elaine (Arkansas), Tulsa, and Chicago, 1919–1921.* Hattiesburg, MS: University and College Press of Mississippi, 1972.

World War I ended in November 1918, racial tensions increased as black men were hired to replace striking white workers in several industries in Chicago.

The Chicago riot began on Sunday, July 27, 1919—one day after black troops were welcomed home with a parade down the city's Michigan Avenue. Eugene Williams, a young black man, was swimming in Lake Michigan and inadvertently crossed the invisible boundary that separated the black and white beaches and bathing areas. He was stoned by white people and drowned. Instead of arresting the alleged perpetrators, the police arrested a black man who complained about police inaction.

Williams's death set off a week of violence that left twenty-three black people and fifteen white people dead. More than five hundred were injured. Nearly one thousand were left homeless after fire raged through a Lithuanian neighborhood. Not only did police fail to stem the violence, they often joined roaming white mobs as they attacked black pedestrians and streetcar passengers. Black men formed a barrier along State Street to stop the advance of white gangs from the stockyard district. Three regiments of the Illinois National Guard were sent into the streets. The violence ended on Saturday, August 1, as heavy rains kept people indoors. During the riot, the Chicago *Defender*, the city's black newspaper, reported many violent incidents.

 Reading Check What factors contributed to the racial violence in Chicago?

▶ **Reading Check**

Between 1916 and 1919, the black population of Chicago doubled. Housing shortages strained the boundaries between segregated neighborhoods. Tensions were further increased by the hiring of blacks to replace striking white workers.

▶ **Retracing the Odyssey**

Tulsa, Oklahoma: The Greenwood Cultural Center. The Greenwood Cultural Center has a permanent exhibit of forty-five photos taken during the 1921 riot that devastated the Greenwood community. There is also a replica of one of the houses that was destroyed. The center maintains exhibits on other aspects of local black history as well, and is home to a Jazz Hall of Fame.

This is the Greenwood neighborhood of Tulsa, Oklahoma, in flames during the riot in June 1921.

Elaine 1919

In the fall of 1919, black sharecroppers in and around Elaine, Arkansas, attempted to organize a union. They withheld their cotton from the market until they received a higher price. Deputy sheriffs tried to break up a union meeting in a black church. One of the deputies was killed. In retaliation, white people killed dozens of black people. No white people were prosecuted, but twelve black men were convicted of the deputy's murder. They were sentenced to death. Sixty-seven other black men received prison terms of up to twenty years. Many were tortured and beaten while they were held in jail. Ida Wells Barnett and the Equal Rights League generated enormous publicity about the case. The NAACP appealed the convictions, and in 1923 the Supreme Court overturned them. The court agreed with NAACP attorney Moorfield Storey that the defendants had not received a fair trial.

Tulsa 1921

Violence erupted in Tulsa, Oklahoma, on May 31, 1921. Dick Rowland allegedly assaulted a white woman elevator operator. Rumors circulated that white men intended to lynch him. To protect Rowland, who was later found innocent, black men assembled at the courthouse jail where white men also gathered. Angry words were exchanged, and shooting erupted. Several black and white men died in the chaos that ensued.

Black men retreated to their neighborhood, known as Greenwood, to protect their families and homes. The governor dispatched the National Guard. The sheriff removed Rowland from the jail to an unknown location. By the morning of June 1, some five hundred white men confronted about one thousand black men across a set of railroad tracks. White men in sixty to seventy automobiles were also cruising around the black residential area.

Approximately fifty armed black people defended themselves in a black church as white men advanced on them. The attackers set fire to the church. As black people fled the burning building, they were shot. More fires were set. About two thousand black residents managed to escape to a convention hall. Forty square blocks and more than one thousand of Greenwood's homes, churches, schools and businesses went up in flames. White men even utilized aircraft for reconnaissance and to drop incendiary devices on Greenwood. As many as three hundred black people and twenty white people may have perished in what was perhaps the worst episode of civilian violence in American history until September 11, 2001.

Following a three and a half year investigation, an eleven-member commission in 2001 made a series of recommendations to the Oklahoma legislature to offer a measure of restitution. The legislators declined to set aside funds for survivors, but they did appropriate

▶ **Recommended Readings**

Scott Ellsworth. *Death in a Promised Land: The Tulsa Race Riot of 1921.* Baton Rouge, LA: Louisiana State University Press, 1982.

Sherry Sherrod Dupree. *The Rosewood Massacre at a Glance.* Gainesville, FL: Rosewood Forum, 1998.

$750,000 to formulate plans for a museum and memorial. They also created a Greenwood Redevelopment Authority and instituted a scholarship program.

Rosewood 1923

During the first week of January 1923, the small town of Rosewood, Florida, was destroyed. Its black residents were driven out or killed. Rosewood was a mostly black community located in the pinewoods of west central Florida not far from the Gulf of Mexico. On New Year's Day, Fannie Taylor, a married white woman from a nearby town, claimed she had been assaulted and beaten by a black man. Many white people quickly assumed Jessie Hunter was responsible. Other white people believed Mrs. Taylor wanted to divert attention from herself because she was having an affair.

White men sought Hunter and vengeance. Unable to locate him, they brutally beat Aaron Carrier. The mob shot and killed Samuel Carter after savagely mutilating him. Tensions dramatically escalated.

On January 4 a band of angry white men invaded Rosewood. Black people were prepared to defend themselves. Led by Sylvester Carrier and his mother Sarah, many townspeople had congregated in the Carrier home. The mob unleashed a hail of gunfire into the residence, killing Sarah Carrier. Two white men who attempted to gain entry into the home were shot and killed. Shooting continued until the mob's supply of ammunition was depleted on January 5.

The following day a mob of 250, including Ku Klux Klan members from Gainesville, invaded, burned, and destroyed Rosewood. The community's black residents fled to the nearby woods and swamps with little more than the clothes on their backs, never to return. Rosewood was no more.

The precise number of black people who died will never be known. It may have been well over one hundred. In 1994 the Florida legislature appropriated $2.1 million to survivors of Rosewood and to families who lost property in the assault. Although seven decades had elapsed, ten survivors were still alive and collected $150,000 each. But it proved impossible for many black people to verify they had been in Rosewood in 1923 or that they were related people who had owned property in the town. Much of the money was not disbursed.

 **Reading Check** Why was there so much racial violence in the early twentieth century?

▶▶ **Reading Check**

Many whites reacted angrily to black calls for fairer treatment and equal opportunities. In fact, the actions of the NAACP, black women's clubs, and the sacrifices of black men during World War I were accompanied by a backlash against African Americans. Racial violence was also fueled by the migration of blacks to the North.

Section 5

The Great Migration

GUIDE TO READING

▶ Why did so many African Americans leave the South in the 1910s and 1920s?

▶ How did Harlem come to be the "Negro Capital of the World"?

KEY TERMS

▶ great migration, p. 575

▶ Harlem, p. 580

The **great migration** of African Americans from the rural South to the urban North began as a trickle of people after the Civil War and became a flood of human beings by the second decade of the twentieth century (see Table 16–1). Between 1910 and 1940, 1.75 million black people left the South. Most of the initial wave of migrants were younger people born in the 1880s and 1890s had no recollection of slavery. They anticipated a better future for themselves and their families in the North.

TABLE 16–1   Black Population Growth in Selected Northern Cities, 1910–1920

	1910		1920		
	Number	Percentage*	Number	Percentage*	Percentage Increase
New York	91,709	1.9%	152,467	2.7%	66.3%
Chicago	44,103	2.0	109,458	4.1	148.2
Philadelphia	84,459	5.5	134,229	7.4	58.9
Detroit	5,741	1.2	40,838	4.1	611.3
St. Louis	43,960	6.4	69,854	9.0	58.9
Cleveland	8,448	1.5	34,451	4.3	307.8
Pittsburgh	25,623	4.8	37,725	6.4	47.2
Cincinnati	19,739	5.4	30,079	7.5	53.2
Indianapolis	21,816	9.3	34,678	11.0	59.0
Newark	9,475	2.7	16,977	4.1	79.2
Kansas City	23,566	9.5	30,719	9.5	30.4
Columbus	12,739	7.0	22,181	9.4	74.1
Gary	383	2.3	5,299	9.6	1,283.6
Youngstown	1,936	2.4	6,662	5.0	244.1
Buffalo	1,773	.4	4,511	.9	154.4
Toledo	1,877	1.1	5,691	2.3	203.2
Akron	657	1.0	5,580	2.7	749.3

*"Percentage" refers to percentage of city's population; "Percentage Increase" refers to growth of black population.

Source: U.S. Department of Commerce.

▶ **Guide to Reading**

For answers, see the *Teacher's Resource Manual.*

▶ **Document**

16-5 *Letters from the Great Migration, 1916–1917*
These letters were written primarily to the Chicago Defender and reflect concerns of would-be immigrants.

▶ **Recommended Readings**

Florette Henri. *Black Migration, 1900–1920.* Garden City, NY: Anchor Press, 1975.

Carole Marks. *Farewell—We're Good and Gone: The Great Black Migration.* Bloomington, IN: Indiana University Press, 1989.

Why Migrate?

People moved for many reasons. Often they were both pushed from their rural circumstances and pulled toward urban areas. The push resulted from disasters in southern agriculture in the 1910s. The boll weevil destroyed cotton crops across the South from Mexico to the Carolinas. Floods devastated Mississippi and Alabama in 1915. The pull resulted from labor shortages created by World War I in northern industry and manufacturing. The war all but ended European immigration to the United States, eliminating a main source of cheap labor. At the same time, European governments and the United States placed huge orders for war material with northern factories. Thousands of jobs became available in steel mills, railroads, meatpacking plants, and the automobile industry. Northern businessmen sent labor agents to recruit southern workers.

Many southern white people reacted ambivalently to the loss of black residents. They welcomed the departure of people they held in such low regard. They also worried about the loss of tenants and sharecroppers. Southern states and municipalities required labor agents to obtain licenses to recruit workers. Angry white landowners and businessmen threatened some of these agents and forced them to leave southern towns.

Black newspapers, such as the Pittsburgh *Courier* and especially the Chicago *Defender*, encouraged black Southerners to move north. Black railroad porters and dining car employees distributed thousands of copies of the *Defender* throughout the South. One unnamed black man wrote in the *Defender* that sensible men would leave the poverty, injustice, and violence of the South for the cold weather of the North. "To die from the bite of frost is far more glorious than that of the mob. I beg of you, my brothers, to leave that benighted land. You are free men."

Black people who departed the South escaped the most blatant forms of Jim Crow and the injustice in the judicial system. Black people in the North could vote. The North offered better public schools. In the early twentieth century the South had almost no public high schools for black youngsters. The longer school year in the urban North was not tied to the demands of planting and harvesting crops. Some black people migrated to escape the dull, bleak, impoverished life and culture of the rural South.

The decision to migrate could take years of pondering and planning. To depart was to leave family, friends, and familiar surroundings behind for the uncertainty, confusion, and rapid pace of urban communities. Migrants often first moved to southern towns or cities and then headed for a larger city. Poet and writer

Jacob Lawrence (1917–2000) had an abiding interest in the lives and history of African Americans. He painted sixty panels depicting the migration of black people from the South to the North. In *Migration of the Negro, Panel 1* (1940–41) he shows black Southerners bound for northern cities.

Langston Hughes was born in Joplin, Missouri, in 1902 and moved to Lincoln, Illinois.

> I had no sooner graduated from grammar school in Lincoln than we moved from Illinois to Cleveland. My stepfather sent for us. He was working in a steel mill during the war, and making lots of money. But it was hard work, and he never looked the same afterwards.

Some people made the decision to move impulsively.

Most migrants maintained a genuine fondness for their southern homes and kinfolk. They returned regularly for holidays, weddings, and funerals. Thousands of black migrants routinely sent money home to the South. Over the years, several million dollars earned in the North flowed into southern communities.

Destinations

Although many black Southerners went to Florida, most migrants from the Carolinas and Virginia settled in Washington, Philadelphia, and New York (see Map 16–2). Black people who left Georgia, Alabama, and Mississippi tended to move to Pittsburgh, Cleveland, and Detroit.

MAP 16–2 The Great Migration and the Distribution of the African-American Population in 1920

Several hundred thousand black Southerners migrated north in the second and third decades of the twentieth century in the largest internal migration in American history.

 Why did most African Americans stay in the South if so many opportunities beckoned in the North?

▶ **Map 16-2**

Many stayed in the South, as migrating North meant leaving their families, friends, and familiar surroundings for uncertainty, confusion and the rapid pace of urban communities.

Migrants from Louisiana, Mississippi, and Arkansas often rode the Illinois Central Railroad to Chicago. Once they experienced a large city, many black people then resettled in smaller communities. Migrants to Philadelphia, for example, moved on to Harrisburg or Altoona, Pennsylvania, or to Wilmington, Delaware.

Few black Southerners moved west to California, Oregon, or Washington. There were only 22,000 black residents of California in 1910. Substantial black migration west did not occur until the 1930s and 1940s.

Most black migrants found their destination was neither near heaven nor the Promised Land. Black people congregated in all-black neighborhoods—Harlem in New York City, Chicago's South Side, Paradise Valley in Detroit, Cleveland's East Side, and the Hill District of Pittsburgh—that later would be called ghettoes. White property owners resisted selling or renting real estate to black people outside the confines of these neighborhoods. And many southern black migrants themselves, wary of white hostility, preferred to live among black people, often friends and family who had preceded them north.

Migration from the Caribbean

Many descendants of Africans who had been slaves in the sugarcane fields of the West Indies joined the migration of black Southerners to towns and cities in the North. Between 1900 and 1924, 102,000 West Indians came to the United States. Most came from British colonies including Jamaica, Barbados, and Trinidad and Tobago. People also arrived from French-held Guadaloupe and Martinique; Dutch colonies of Aruba, Curacao, and Montserrat; and the Danish Virgin Islands (which the United States acquired in 1917). Some of these migrants were middle-class professionals and skilled workers. A sizable number were black men from Barbados, Jamaica, and elsewhere who had been employed as laborers on the construction of the Panama Canal from 1904 until 1914.

White Americans tended to lump all people of color together, regardless of their complexion or origin. The West Indians often did not mix easily or comfortably with African Americans. Some spoke Dutch and French. Those who came from British islands were usually members of the Anglican Church and not Baptists or Methodists. Moreover, many of the Caribbean arrivals were temporary residents. As many as one-third would return to the West Indies. In 1924 Congress imposed rigid restrictions on immigration to the United States. Migration from the Caribbean dropped drastically.

Northern Communities

Even before the Civil War, most northern cities had small free black populations. By the late nineteenth century, southern migrants began to gravitate to these urban areas and make their presence felt. Black resi-

dents established churches, social organizations, businesses, and medical facilities. They gained representation in community and political affairs.

There was less overt segregation in the North. Most northern states, as well as California, had enacted laws in the late nineteenth century that prohibited racial discrimination in public transportation, hotels, restaurants, theaters, and barbershops. Most of these states also forbade segregated schools. However, passage of such laws and their enforcement were two different matters. Many white businesses and communities ignored the statutes and embraced Jim Crow, especially in areas along the Ohio River in southern Ohio, Indiana, and Illinois.

Chicago

As early as 1872, Chicago had a black policeman. In 1876 John W. E. Thomas became the first black man elected to the Illinois Senate. Black physician Daniel Hale Williams established African-American-staffed Provident Hospital on Chicago's South Side in 1891. By 1900 black Chicagoans were the twelfth largest ethnic group in the city, behind such European immigrant groups as the Irish, Poles, and Germans.

Chicago's black population surged during the first three decades of the twentieth century as migrants poured into the city. Black institutions flourished. In 1912 an NAACP branch was established. By 1920 black Chicago had 80 Baptist and 36 Methodist churches. The Olivet Baptist Church grew from 3,500 members in 1916 to 9,000 by 1922. Because the downtown YMCA barred black men, black people raised $50,000 and Julius Rosenwald of Sears, Roebuck, and Company contributed $25,000 to build the Wabash YMCA for the black community in 1913. Many black Chicagoans considered this a surrender to segregation and insisted that black men should be admitted to the white YMCA.

The Chicago *Defender* was the city's leading black newspaper. Its founder, Robert S. Abbott, the son of slaves, began publishing the *Defender* in 1905. By 1920 it had a nationwide circulation of 230,000. Chicago's first black bank, Jesse Binga's State Bank, was established in 1908. In 1919 Frank L. Gillespie organized the Liberty Insurance Company.

In 1915 black Chicago's political influence expanded when Oscar DePriest was elected second ward alderman. Two other black men were elected to the city council by 1918. DePriest was then elected to the U.S. House of Representatives as a Republican in 1928, becoming the first black congressman since North Carolina's George White left the House in 1901.

As the number of black people in Chicago swelled, racial tensions increased and exploded in the 1919 race riot. Competition for jobs was a critical issue. White employers, such as the meatpacking companies, regularly replaced white strikers with black workers. Black men usually did not hesitate to take such jobs because most labor unions would not admit them. But a few weeks before the riot in 1919, the Amalgamated Meatcutters Union tried to sponsor a unity parade of black and white stockyard workers.

The police prohibited it because, some observers believed, the meatpacking companies feared that black and white workingmen might unite.

Housing was an even more divisive issue than employment. Chicago's black population was almost entirely confined to an eight-square-mile area on the South Side east of State Street. Prosperous black people who could afford more expensive housing outside the area could not purchase it because of their race. As the black population grew, housing became more congested, and crime and vice increased.

Harlem

Harlem was a white community in upper Manhattan that had declined by the late 1800s. It then enjoyed an incredible building boom in anticipation of the construction of the subway that would link upper Manhattan to downtown New York City by the early twentieth century. But real estate speculators overbuilt. They were left with empty houses and apartments. Facing foreclosure, many white property owners sold or rented to black people in Harlem. In 1904 Philip A. Payton formed the Afro American Realty Company that sold homes and rented apartments to black clients before it failed in 1908.

Harlem's white residents opposed the influx of black people. Some of them formed the Harlem Property Owners' Improvement Corporation in 1910 to block black settlement. Its founder, John G. Taylor, warned in 1913, "We are approaching a crisis, it is a question of whether the white man will rule Harlem or the Negro." However, many white property owners—eager for a profit—preferred to sell to black people than to maintain white unity.

As thousands of black people moved to Harlem, many left the "Tenderloin" and "San Juan Hill" areas of Manhattan's West Side where New York's black residents had lived in the nineteenth century. The construction of Pennsylvania Station forced many to vacate the "Tenderloin." Black churches took the lead in the "On to Harlem" movement as they occupied churches formerly used by white denominations. Some of the black churches were among the largest property owners in Harlem.

St. Philip's Protestant Episcopal Church, the wealthiest black church in the United States, moved from West 25th Street in 1910 to Harlem. In 1911 St. Philip's purchased ten apartment houses on West 135th Street between Lenox and Seventh Avenues for $640,000. The Abyssinian Baptist Church, St. Mark's Episcopal Church, and the African Methodist Episcopal Zion Church ("Mother Zion") also moved to Harlem and acquired extensive real estate holdings there. The black churches helped make Harlem a black community.

As the black population increased in Harlem, large houses and apartments were often subdivided among working families that could not rent or buy in other areas of New York. They paid higher prices for real estate than white people did. The average Harlem family paid $9.50

▶▶ Map 16-3, p. 581

African Americans settled in Harlem and not elsewhere as a strong black community developed here, and black people felt united.

African-American Population
1911
1920
1930

Polo Grounds

Harlem River

145 ST

135 ST

St Nicholas Park

Grant's Tomb

Hudson River

125 ST

EIGHTH AVE

SEVENTH AVE

LENOX AVE

Mount Morris Park

MADISON AVE

LEXINGTON AVE

THIRD AVE

ST NICHOLAS AVE

Columbia University

St John's Cathedral

Central Park

a room per month; white working families paid $6.50 for similar accommodations elsewhere in New York.

By 1920, 75,000 black people lived in Harlem (see Map 16–3). Harlem became the "Negro Capital of the World." Black businesses and institutions, including the Odd Fellows, Masons, Elks, Pythians, the NAACP, the Urban League, and the YMCA and YWCA moved to Harlem. Black newspapers—the *New York News* and *Amsterdam News*—opened in Harlem to compete with the older *New York Age*. One resident observed, "If my race can make Harlem, good lord, what can't it do?"

Families

Migration placed black families under enormous strains. Relatives frequently moved north separately. Fathers or mothers would leave a spouse and children behind as they sought employment and housing.

MAP 16–3 The Expansion of Black Harlem, 1911–1930

Before the American Revolution, Harlem was a small Dutch village located at the northern end of Manhattan Island. In the early twentieth century, African Americans transformed it into a thriving black metropolis.

Adapted from Steven Watson, *The Harlem Renaissance* (New York: Pantheon Books, 1996).

? **Why did African Americans settle in Harlem and not elsewhere in New York City?**

Explore this map online at www.prenhall.com/aah/map16.3

Children might be left with grandparents for extended periods. In other instances, extended family members—cousins, in-laws, brothers and sisters—crowded into limited living space.

Men generally found more opportunities for work in northern industries than women did. There was a huge demand for unskilled labor during and after World War I. In 1915 Henry Ford astounded industrial America when he began to pay employees of the Ford Motor Company in Detroit the unprecedented sum of $5 per day. That included black men and occasionally black women. Rarely, however, would a black man be promoted beyond menial labor. Except for some opportunities in manufacturing during the war, black women were confined to domestic and janitorial work. Mary Ellen Washington recalled the experience in her family. "In the 1920s my mother and five aunts migrated to Cleveland, Ohio from Indianapolis and, in spite of their many talents, they found every door except the kitchen door closed to them."

Black women employed as domestics lived with white families, worked long hours, and saw more of their white employer's children than they did their own. One maid explained her dreary and unhappy situation:

> I am now past forty years of age and am the mother of three children. My husband died nearly fifteen years ago. . . . For more than thirty years—or since I was ten years old—I have been a servant in one capacity or another in white families.
> I frequently work from fourteen to sixteen hours a day. I am compelled . . . to sleep in the house. I am allowed to go home to my own children, the oldest of whom is a girl of 18 years, only once in two weeks, every other Sunday afternoon—even then I'm not permitted to stay all night. . . . I don't know what it is to go to church; I don't know what it is to go to a lecture or entertainment of any kind; I live a treadmill life. . . . You might as well say that I'm on duty all the time—from sunrise to sunrise, every day in the week. I am the slave, body and soul, of this family.

Some vulnerable younger women were lured into prostitution in the intimidating urban environment. Black women's organizations worked to prevent newly arrived migrants from falling prey to sexual exploitation. They did not always succeed.

Despite the stresses and pressures, most black families survived intact. Most northern black families, although hardly well to do, were two-parent households. Women headed comparatively few families. Fathers were present in seven of ten black families in New York City in 1925. But the great migration transformed southern peasants into an urban proletariat.

 Reading Check Why did so many African Americans leave the South in the 1910 and 1920s?

▶ **Reading Check**

African Americans moved for many reasons. They pushed by the disasters that struck southern agriculture in the 1910s. They were pulled to cities by the economic opportunities created by a labor shortage in the industrial North. Blacks also hoped to find greater equality in the North.

Identifying and Analyzing Alternatives

Identifying alternatives means finding one or more possible ways to achieve a goal or to solve a problem. The excerpts from Booker T. Washington and W.E.B. Du Bois illustrate their differing views on how African Americans should approach the struggle for equality.

LEARN THE SKILL

Use the following steps to identify and analyze alternatives:

1. **Identify the nature of the problem under discussion.** Before you can identify alternative solutions to a problem, you must understand what the problem is.

2. **Note the solutions proposed.** Write down the main points of each proposed solution.

3. **Evaluate the potential effectiveness of each solution.** Consider the strengths and weaknesses of each proposal.

4. **Consider other alternatives.** Recall the nature of the problem under discussion. Then, using the insights you gained by following the preceding steps, think of other possible solutions.

PRACTICE THE SKILL

Answer the following questions:

1. **(a)** What is the issue that both passages address? **(b)** What do you already know about this issue from your reading?

2. **(a)** What does Passage A suggest is the proper approach to the struggle for equality? **(b)** What does Passage B suggest is the proper response?

3. **(a)** What benefits do you see in Washington's approach? What are the difficulties? **(b)** Why does Du Bois oppose Washington's view? **(c)** Does Du Bois explain what his alternative approach might be in this excerpt?

4. Based on what you have read, what other alternatives to achieving social equality might have been considered? Explain.

A

THE wisest among my race understand that the agitation of questions of social equality is the extremest folly, and that progress in the enjoyment of all privileges that will come to us must be the result of severe and constant struggle rather than of artificial forcing. No race that has anything to contribute to the markets of the world is long in any degree ostracized. It is important and right all privileges of the law be ours, but it is vastly more important that we be prepared for the exercises of these privileges.

—Booker T. Washington, Atlanta Cotton States and International Exposition, September 18, 1895

B

So far as Mr. Washington preaches Thrift, Patience, and Industrial Training for the masses, we must hold up his hands and strive with him. . . . But so far as Mr. Washington apologizes for injustice, North or South, does not rightly value the privilege and duty of voting, belittles the emasculating effects of caste distinctions, and opposes higher training and ambition of our brighter minds,—so far as he, the South, or the Nation, does this,—we must unceasingly and firmly oppose them.

—W. E. B. Du Bois, *Of Booker T. Washington and Others,* 1903

▶ **Skills for Life**

For answers, see *Teacher's Resource Manual.*

Chapter Timeline

1895

1895
Frederick Douglass dies;
Booker T. Washington delivers Cotton States Exposition address

1896
Plessy v. Ferguson is decided

1898
Riot erupts in Wilmington, N.C.

1896
William McKinley is elected president

1898
Spanish-American War begins

1899
Philippine insurrection begins

1900

1900
New Orleans riot

1903
W. E. B. Du Bois publishes *The Souls of Black Folk*

1900
William McKinley reelected

1901
McKinley is assassinated;
Theodore Roosevelt becomes president

1903
Boston defeats Pittsburgh in the first World Series

1904
Theodore Roosevelt is elected president

1905

1905
Niagara Movement is founded at Niagara Falls, Ontario; The *Defender* is founded in Chicago

1906
Brownsville affair occurs; Atlanta riot occurs

1908
Springfield riot occurs

1909
NAACP is founded

1905
Thomas Dixon publishes *The Clansman*. The film *Birth of a Nation* is based on the novel.

1906
Upton Sinclair publishes *The Jungle*
The San Francisco earthquake kills nearly 700 people

1908
William Howard Taft is elected president

1909
Robert E. Peary and Matthew Henson, an African American, reach the North Pole with four Eskimos

1910

1910
National Urban League is founded in New York City

1912
W. E. B. Du Bois endorses Woodrow Wilson for President

1910
The Mann Act prohibits the transporation of a woman across state lines for immoral purposes

1912
Woodrow Wilson is elected president

1914
World War I breaks out in Europe

1915

1915
Guinn v. United States overturns the Oklahoma grandfather clause
Booker T. Washington dies

1917
East St. Louis riot occurs; Houston riot occurs

1919
Chicago riot occurs; Elaine, Arkansas, riot occurs

1915
A German submarine sinks the British liner, *The Lusitania*

1916
United States sends punitive expedition in Mexico; Woodrow Wilson is reelected

1917
United States enters World War I

1918
World War I ends

1919
Treaty of Versailles is negotiated

1920

1920
Harlem becomes "The Negro Capital of the World"

1921
Tulsa riot occurs

1923
Rosewood destroyed

1920
Nineteenth Amendment (Women's Suffrage) is ratified; Warren Harding is elected president

1925

Chapter Review and Assessment

SUMMARY

Section 1 Race and Social Change, p. 541

▶ In the late nineteenth century white progressives were pushing for a series of social and economic reforms.

▶ At the same time, black leaders searched for ways for African Americans to overcome the challenges they faced in American society.

▶ Some, like Booker T. Washington, urged blacks to concentrate on industrial and agricultural education, arguing that economic inclusion would lead to political and social inclusion.

▶ Others, like W. E. B. Du Bois, believed that blacks needed to stand up and demand political and legal equality.

Section 2 New Black Organizations, p. 550

▶ In 1909 the National Association for the Advancement of Colored People (NAACP) was founded by a coalition of whites and blacks committed to taking an assertive stance on racial issues.

▶ Despite Booker T. Washington's efforts to undermine the NAACP, the organization grew steadily.

▶ Black women formed clubs that focused on community issues, providing help to urban blacks. Black women were also active in the women's suffrage movement.

▶ Like their white counterparts, black elites were conscious of their status and took steps to reinforce their position at the top of black society.

Section 3 Politics and the Military, p. 561

▶ Woodrow Wilson's victory in the presidential election of 1912 gave hope to some black leaders. However, once in office, Wilson pursued segregationist policies.

▶ When the U.S. entered World War I in 1917, most African Americans supported the war effort. Blacks demonstrated their loyalty and devotion to the United States by volunteering for military service.

▶ Blacks endured discrimination and mistreatment in the army and their service did not have the positive impact on white views of blacks that Du Bois and others hoped it would.

Section 4 Racial Violence, p. 567

▶ The hopes of many black leaders that the twentieth century would begin a new era in American race relations were disappointed.

▶ Instead, the new century brought a backlash against African Americans. This backlash, combined with the migration of blacks to the North, contributed to widespread racial violence in both the North and the South.

Section 5 The Great Migration, p. 575

▶ Between 1910 and 1940, 1.75 million African Americans moved from the rural South to the urban North. They were both pushed by poor conditions in the South and pulled by the hope of better lives in the North.

▶ The population shift contributed to the development of vibrant black communities in Chicago and New York.

▶ Migration was not without costs. Relocation placed enormous strains on black families.

REVIEWING KEY TERMS

Write a brief explanation of the following terms.

1. progressive movement, p. 541
2. The Tuskegee Machine, p. 543
3. Afro-American League, p. 545
4. National Association for the Advancement of Colored People (NAACP), p. 550
5. Dyer bill, p. 551
6. Urban League, p. 552
7. New Era Club, p. 553
8. National Association of Colored Women, p. 554
9. Nineteenth Amendment, p. 556
10. American Negro Academy, p. 558
11. Ugly Club, p. 558
12. Boulé, p. 558
13. Progressive Party, p. 561
14. punitive expedition, p. 562
15. Men of Bronze, p. 565
16. race riots, p. 567

REVIEWING MAIN IDEAS

19. Compare and evaluate the strategies promoted by Booker T. Washington with those of W. E. B. Du Bois and the NAACP.

20. On which issues did Booker T. Washington and W. E. B. Du Bois agree and disagree?

21. Assess Booker T. Washington's contributions to the advancement of black people.

22. To what extent did middle-class and prosperous black people contribute to progress for their race? Were their efforts effective?

23. Why did most African Americans support U.S. participation in World War I? Was that support justified?

24. What factors contributed to race riots and violence in the World War I era?

25. Why did many black people leave the South in the 1920s? Why didn't this migration begin earlier or later?

26. What factors affected the decision to migrate or stay?

ANALYZING DOCUMENTS

A Migrant to the North Writes Home

Philadelphia, Pa., Oct. 7, 1919

Dear Sir:

I take this method of thanking you for yours early responding and the glorious effect of the treatment. Oh. I do feel so fine. Dr. the treatment reach me almost ready to move I am now housekeeping again I like it so much better than rooming. Well Dr. with the aid of God I am making very good I make $75 per month. I am carrying enough insurance to pay me $20 per week if I am not able to be on duty. I don't have to work hard. dont have to mister every little white boy comes along I havent heard a white man call a colored nigger you no now—since I been in the state of Pa. I can ride in the electric street and steam cars any where I get a seat. I dont care to mix with white what I mean I am not crazy about being with white folks, but if I have to pay the same fare I have learn to want the same accomidation. and if you are the first in a place here shoping you dont have to wait until the white folks get thro tradeing yet amid all this I shall ever love the good old South and I am praying that God may give every well wisher a chance to be a man regardless of his color, and if my going to the front [World War I] would bring about such conditions I am ready any day—well Dr. I dont want to worry you but read between the lines; and maybe you can see a little sense in my weak statement the kids are in school every day I have only two and I guess that all. Dr. when you find time I would be delighted to have word from the good old home state. Wife join me in sending love you and yours.

—From: Emmett J. Scott, ed., "Letters of Negro Migrants of 1916–1918," *Journal of Negro History*, 4 (1 July 1919) in Fishel and Quarles, *The Negro American: A Documentary History*, pp. 398–99.

 Making Comparisons How would the writer's life in the north as described in his letter compare to the life he left in the South?

WRITING ACTIVITY

In a short report or research paper, consider this question.

Compare and contrast W.E.B. Du Bois's and Booker T. Washington's approach to the position of black Americans in early twentieth-century society. What were the key differences in the two men's positions?

STUDY ONLINE!

www.prenhall.com/aah

Additional study resources are available for this chapter on the *Companion Website*.

17

African Americans and the 1920s

1915–1928

The fight to stop lynchings was one of the NAACP's most important campaigns in the early twentieth century. Demonstrations and protests like this one at the Crime Conference in Washington, D.C. kept the issue in the public arena.

I, Too

I, too, sing America.
I am the darker brother.
They send me to eat in the kitchen
When company comes.
But I laugh,
And eat well,
And grow strong.
To-morrow
    I'll sit at the table
    When company comes
  Nobody'll dare
  Say to me,
  "Eat in the kitchen"
  Then.
    Besides, they'll see how beautiful I am
     And be ashamed,—
I, too, am America.
—Langston Hughes, 1926

Jim Crow racism was a fact of life throughout the South.

 What is Hughes's message to white America in this poem?

Chapter Preview

Many Americans had difficulty adjusting to life after World War I. The Allied victory brought little long-term satisfaction or security. Many Americans were disillusioned. Labor agitation at home heightened fears and increased anxiety. Racial and ethnic intolerance escalated.

Enthusiasm for progressive reforms faded as middle-class Americans became preoccupied with making money and with acquiring automobiles, radios, and home appliances.

Many native white Americans were convinced that black people and immigrants—especially Jewish and Catholic immigrants—posed a threat to their Anglo-Saxon ethnic purity. White Americans joined the revived Ku Klux Klan in the 1920s as it promoted white supremacy, American patriotism, and Protestant values.

African Americans denounced injustice and pressed for inclusion in society. Black workers organized. The 1920s also saw African Americans enthusiastically support Marcus Garvey and the Universal Negro Improvement Association. The 1920s also saw black culture blossom and flourish.

Section 1

Fighting Racism

GUIDE TO READING

▶ What was "scientific racism"? What fears did it reflect?

▶ Why was the Ku Klux Klan so popular and powerful in the 1920s?

KEY TERMS

▶ Reds, p. 591

▶ aliens, p. 591

▶ xenophobia, p. 591

▶ anarchists, p. 591

Strikes and the Red Scare

In 1919 and 1920, Americans were bewildered and angered by labor unrest and afraid the communists (or **Reds**) in the new Soviet Union would try to incite a revolution in America. There were 3,600 strikes in 1919 as workers who had deferred demands during the war for pay raises and improved working conditions walked off their jobs. More than 300,000 steel workers in Pittsburgh and Gary, Indiana, struck, including 7,000 unskilled black steel workers in Pittsburgh. In a demonstration of solidarity with striking shipyard workers, most of Seattle's working people shut the city down in a general strike. Americans were even more alarmed when police officers in Boston went on strike. Many worried that labor agitation was a prelude to revolution.

Political leaders warned that communists and foreign agents were plotting to overthrow the government. Woodrow Wilson's attorney general A. Mitchell Palmer warned Americans of the Red menace and the threat **aliens** posed. He ordered 249 aliens deported and some 6,000 arrested and imprisoned in gross violation of their rights. Evidence indicates that some business leaders supported the Palmer raids as a means of discouraging workers from forming and joining labor unions and participating in strikes.

Prompted in part by the Red Scare, **xenophobia** (fear of foreigners) swept the nation in the 1920s. Two Sicilian immigrants, Nicola Sacco and Bartolomeo Vanzetti, who were **anarchists**, were charged in 1920 with a murder that had occurred during a payroll robbery near Boston. They were found guilty. After a prolonged controversy, they were executed in 1927. But their supporters believed the guilty verdict was due more to their foreign origins and radical beliefs than to conclusive proof they had committed the murder.

Varieties of Racism

The entrenched racism of American society found continued expression in more than one form in the 1920s. There was the sophisticated racism associated with supposedly scholarly studies that reflected the

▶▶ **Guide to Reading/Key Terms**

For answers, see the *Teacher's Resource Manual.*

▶▶ **Teaching Notes**

Palmer's deportation and arrest of aliens was an action that many Americans warmly approved. Palmer went too far, however, when he predicted that the Red revolution would begin in the United States on May 1, 1920. There was no revolution, and confidence in Palmer waned. There were, however, several terrorist bombings, including one on Wall Street in September 1920 that killed thirty-three people.

ideology of social Darwinism. There was also the raw bigotry in various aspects of popular culture and in the ideology of the increasingly popular Ku Klux Klan.

Scientific Racism

Many white Americans believed the United States was under siege as European immigrants and black migrants flooded American cities. Pseudoscholars gravely warned about the peril these "inferior" peoples posed. In 1916 Madison Grant published *The Passing of the Great Race.* Grant warned that America was committing "race suicide." Northern Europeans and their descendants—the Great Race—were being diluted by inferior people from eastern and southern Europe.

These racist claims were presented as legitimate scholarship. They strengthened the cause of white supremacy in the 1920s and helped "protect" America from the "threat" of immigration. In 1921 and in 1924, Congress imposed quotas that severely restricted immigration from southern and eastern Europe, Latin America, and the Caribbean, and prohibited it entirely from Asia.

The Birth of a Nation

In 1915 D. W. Griffith released *The Birth of a Nation,* a cinematic masterpiece and historical travesty based on Thomas Dixon's 1905 novel *The Clansman.* Both the book and the film purported to depict Reconstruction in South Carolina authentically. In this account, immoral and ignorant Negroes joined by shady mulattoes and greedy white Republicans ruthlessly seize control of state government. The heroic and honorable Ku Klux Klan saves the state and rescues its white womanhood. The film distorted public perceptions about Reconstruction and black Americans.

The NAACP was enraged by *The Birth of a Nation* and fought to halt its presentation. The motion picture unleashed racist violence. After seeing the film in Lafayette, Indiana, an infuriated white man killed a young black man. In Houston, white theatergoers shouted, "Lynch him!" during a scene in which a white actor in blackface pursued the film's star, Lillian Gish. In front of a St. Louis theater, white real estate agents passed out circulars calling for residential segregation.

Thanks largely to NAACP opposition, the film was banned in Pasadena, California; Wilmington, Delaware; and Boston. With an election looming in Chicago, Republican mayor "Big Bill" Thompson appointed AME bishop Archibald Carey to the board of censors, which temporarily banned the film there. When the sound version of *The Birth of a Nation* was released in 1930, the NAACP renewed its opposition. Ironically, the NAACP campaign may have provided publicity that attracted more viewers to the film. By the same token, however, the campaign also helped increase NAACP membership.

The Ku Klux Klan

The Ku Klux Klan (KKK), which disappeared after Reconstruction, was resurrected a few months after *The Birth of a Nation* was released. On Thanksgiving night in 1915, William J. Simmons and thirty-four other men gathered at Stone Mountain near Atlanta. In the flickering shadows of a fiery cross, they brought the Klan back to life.

The Ku Klux Klan that rose to prominence and power in the 1920s stood for white supremacy and more. Klansmen styled themselves as "100 percent Americans" who opposed perceived threats from immigrants as well as black Americans. The Klan claimed to represent white, Anglo-Saxon, Protestant America. With European immigrants flocking to America, William Simmons announced the United States was no melting pot. "It is a garbage can! . . . When the hordes of aliens walk to the ballot box and their votes outnumber yours, then that alien horde has got you by the throat."

The Klan found enormous support among apprehensive white middle-class Americans in the North and West. Many of these people believed the liberal, immoral, and loose lifestyles they associated with urban life, immigrants, and African Americans threatened their religious beliefs and conservative cultural values. The KKK opposed Jews, Roman Catholics, and black people. Klansmen often used violent intimidation to convey their patriotic, religious, and racial convictions. They burned synagogues and Catholic churches. They beat, branded, and lynched their opponents.

By 1925 the Klan had an estimated 5 million members, and 40,000 of them marched in Washington, D.C., that year. The Klan attracted small businessmen, shopkeepers, clerks, Protestant clergymen, farmers, and professional people. It was open only to native-born white men. But it also had a Women's Order, a Junior Order for boys, and a Tri K Klub for girls. The Klan was active in Oregon, Colorado, Illinois, and Maine. It became a strong political force in Indiana, Oklahoma, and Texas. In those three states in particular, candidates for public office who refused to support or join the Klan stood little chance of election.

The Klan was also a highly effective moneymaking machine. Its leaders collected millions of dollars in initiation fees, membership dues, and income from selling Klan paraphernalia. The Klan declined rapidly in the late 1920s when its leaders fought among themselves. Its claim to uphold the purity of white womanhood was damaged when one of its leaders, D. C. Stephenson, was arrested in Indiana and charged with raping a young woman who subsequently committed suicide. Stephenson was sentenced to life in prison, and the Klan never fully recovered.

 **Reading Check** Why was the Ku Klux Klan so popular and powerful in the 1920s?

The glorification of the Ku Klux Klan in D. W. Griffith's *The Birth of a Nation* outraged African Americans. The NAACP protested when the silent film was first distributed in 1915 and again when a sound version was released in 1930.

▶▶ **Reading Check**

The Klan claimed to represent white, Anglo-Saxon, Protestant America. The Klan found enormous support among white middle-class Americans who believed that immigrants and African Americans threatened their values.

▶▶ **Recommended Reading**

Nancy MacLean. *Behind the Mask of Chivalry: The Making of the Second Ku Klux Klan.* New York: Oxford University Press, 1994. This is the most recent study of the revived KKK.

GUIDE TO READING

▶ How did the NAACP change in the 1920s?

▶ Why did the Universal Negro Improvement Association and Marcus Garvey appeal to so many African Americans?

▶ **Guide to Reading/Key Terms**

For answers, see the *Teacher's Resource Manual.*

▶ **Recommended Reading**

Charles F. Kellogg. *NAACP: A History of the National Association for the Advancement of Colored People.* Baltimore: Johns Hopkins University Press, 1967.

▶ **Teaching Notes**

African Americans responded to racism and to larger cultural and economic developments in the 1920s in several ways. The NAACP forged ahead with its efforts to secure constitutional rights and guarantees by advocacy in the political and judicial systems. Many working-class black people who had migrated to northern cities were attracted to the racial pride promoted by Marcus Garvey and the Universal Negro Improvement Association. There were also ongoing attempts to foster racial cooperation among peoples of African descent and to exert diplomatic influence through the work of several Pan-African congresses that were held during the first three decades of the twentieth century.

Section 2

Black Organizations in the 1920s

The NAACP

During its second decade, the NAACP expanded its influence and increased its membership. In 1916 James Weldon Johnson (who wrote "Lift Every Voice and Sing") joined the NAACP as field secretary. He played a pivotal role in the organization's development and in its growth from 9,000 members in 1916 to 90,000 in 1920. Johnson traveled tirelessly, recruiting members and establishing branches. He journeyed to rural southern communities, to northern cities, and to the West Coast.

Johnson impressed both black and white people. He was an excellent diplomat. He methodically reported the gruesome details of lynchings. When some NAACP directors complained in 1921 that these graphic descriptions offended people, Johnson stood his ground. "What we need to do is to root out the thing which makes possible these horrible de-tails. I am of the opinion that this can be done only through the fullest publicity."

In 1918 Johnson hired Walter White to assist him. White was from Atlanta and, like Johnson, a graduate of Atlanta University. White's very fair complexion permitted him to move easily among white people to investigate racial discrimination and violence. White devoted his life to the organization and to racial justice.

Johnson and the NAACP fought hard in Congress to secure passage of the Dyer anti-lynching bill in 1921 and 1922 (see Chapter 16). The legislation ultimately failed, but the NAACP succeeded in publicizing the persistence of barbaric behavior by mobs in a nation supposedly devoted to fairness and the rule of law. It was the first campaign by a civil rights organization to lobby Congress.

Johnson blamed the Dyer bill's failure on Republican senators. He charged that the Republican Party took black support for granted: "The Republican Party will hold the Negro and do as little for him as possible, and the Democratic Party will have none of him at all." He warned, however, that black voters in the North would abandon the Republicans. Johnson pointed out that black voters in Harlem had elected a black Democrat to the state legislature.

The NAACP continued to rely on the judicial system to protect black Americans and enforce their civil rights. By the 1920s the Democratic Party in virtually every southern state barred black people from membership, which excluded them from voting in Democratic primary elec-

tions. The result was what was known as **white primaries**. The Republican Party had almost ceased to exist in most of the South. Victory in the Democratic primary elections led to victory in the general election. In 1924 the NAACP, in cooperation with its branch in El Paso, filed suit over the exclusion of black voters from the Democratic primary in Texas. In 1927 the Supreme Court ruled in *Nixon v. Herndon*

PROFILE ❖ James Weldon Johnson

James Weldon Johnson was born in 1871 in Jacksonville, Florida. His father was a waiter in a fashionable hotel, and his mother was a schoolteacher. He received his secondary and collegiate education at Atlanta University where he also earned a master's degree. In 1902 he moved to New York City.

With his brother John Rosamond and black entertainer Robert Cole, he became part of a successful songwriting team. They contributed two musical numbers to Theodore Roosevelt's 1904 presidential campaign: "You're All Right Teddy" and "The Old Flag Never Touched the Ground." Johnson spent seven years as a consul in Venezuela and Nicaragua. In 1910 he married Grace Neal, the sister of a prominent New York real estate broker.

Johnson became an editorial writer for the *New York Age*. He also published anonymously *The Autobiography of an Ex-Colored Man*. In 1916 Joel Spingarn, the president of the NAACP, asked Johnson to take a leadership role with that organization. Johnson became its field secretary.

Johnson spent the next fourteen years with the NAACP. In 1920 he became chief executive. He had organized the silent march on Fifth Avenue on July 28, 1917, to protest the East St. Louis riot (see Chapter 16). He publicized lynchings. He recruited members and established new branches. In 1920 in *The Nation*, he documented the mistreatment of Haitians by U.S. troops who had occupied that Caribbean nation. He supported black workers and A. Philip Randolph and the Brotherhood of Sleeping Car Porters.

Johnson also managed to write prolifically and imaginatively. In 1920 he wrote "The Creation: A Negro Sermon." He wrote many other works of prose and poetry. In 1930 he finished *Black Manhattan*, which traced the cultural contributions of black people in music, poetry, and theater to New York City from the seventeenth to the twentieth centuries.

Like so many civil rights leaders, Johnson could be inconsistent in his stands on racial issues. He was dedicated to the proposition that black and white people should enjoy equal access to public facilities. But he supported an all-black YMCA in Harlem and the separate training of black military officers during World War I. He appreciated Marcus Garvey's emphasis on black pride. But he considered the back-to-Africa movement to be an attempt to escape from America's racial problems rather than as a solution to them.

In 1930 Johnson left the NAACP to become a professor of creative writing at Fisk University in Nashville. He left the NAACP a far more visible and stronger organization than he had found it in 1916. At Fisk, he worked with some of the twentieth century's leading black scholars, including Horace Mann Bond, Alrutheus A. Taylor, and E. Franklin Frazier. Historian John Hope Franklin was one of his students. Johnson's autobiography, *Along the Way*, was published in 1933. He died in an automobile accident in 1938.

Johnson

that the Democratic primary was unconstitutional. This was the first victory in what would become a twenty-year legal struggle to permit black men and women to vote in primary elections across the South.

"Up You Mighty Race": Marcus Garvey and the UNIA

With several million loyal and enthusiastic followers, Marcus Garvey's **Universal Negro Improvement Association (UNIA)** became the largest mass movement of black people in American history. The UNIA enabled people to celebrate one another and their heritage and to anticipate a glorious future. Garvey was an energetic, charismatic, and flamboyant leader. He wove racial pride, Christian faith, and economic cooperation into a black nationalist organization throughout the United States by the early 1920s.

Garvey was born in 1887 in the British colony of Jamaica, the eleventh child in a rural family. He quit school at age fourteen and became a printer in Kingston, the island's capital. He was promoted to foreman before he was fired in 1907 for prolabor activities during a strike. He traveled to Costa Rica, Panama, Ecuador, and Nicaragua. He became increasingly disturbed over the conditions black workers endured in fields, factories, and mines. He returned to Jamaica. With a growing appreciation of the power of the written and spoken word, he set out to educate himself. He spent two years in London where he sharpened his oratorical and debating skills discussing the plight of black people with Africans and people from the Caribbean.

He returned to Jamaica and founded the UNIA in 1914. With the slogan "One God! One Aim! One Destiny!" he stressed the need for black people to organize for their own advancement. Garvey had read Booker T. Washington's *Up from Slavery*. He was much impressed with Washington's emphasis on self-help and on progress through education and the acquisition of skills. Garvey also—like Washington—criticized black people for their lack of progress: "The bulk of our people are in darkness and are really unfit for good society." They had no right to aspire to equality because they had "done nothing to establish the right to equality."

▶▶ Recommended Readings

Judith Stein. *The World of Marcus Garvey: Race and Class in Modern Society*. Baton Rouge, LA: Louisiana State University Press, 1991. This is an effective examination of Garvey and the Universal Negro Improvement Association.

Randall K. Burkett. *Garveyism as a Religious Movement: The Institutionalization of a Black Civil Religion*. Metuchen, NJ: Scarecrow Press, 1978.

E. David Cronon. *Black Moses: The Story of Marcus Garvey and the Universal Negro Improvement Association*. Madison, WI: University of Wisconsin Press, 1955.

The UNIA in America

Garvey came to the United States in 1916 just as thousands of African Americans were migrating to cities. A dynamic speaker whose message resonated among the disaffected urban working class, Garvey quickly built the UNIA into a major movement. He urged his listeners to take pride in themselves as they restored their race to its previous greatness.

"We must canonize our own saints, create our own martyrs, and elevate to positions of fame and honor black men and women who have made their distinct contributions to our racial history."

He reminded people that Africa had a remarkable past. "Africa was peopled with a race of cultured black men, who were masters in art, science and literature; men who were cultured and refined; men, who, it was said, were like the gods. . . . Black men, you were once great; you shall be great again." He insisted that his followers change their thinking. "We have outgrown slavery, but our minds are still enslaved to the thinking of the Master Race. Now take these kinks out of your mind, instead of out of your hair."

With the formation of the New York division of the UNIA in Harlem in 1917, Garvey exhorted, "Up you mighty race!" as he commanded black people to take control of their destiny. Still, he blamed them for their predicament. "That the Negro race became a race of slaves was not the fault of God Almighty . . . it was the fault of the race." Their salvation would result from their own exertion and not from concessions by white people.

Garvey's message and the UNIA spread to black communities large and small. He regularly couched his rhetoric in religious terms. He came to be known as the Black Moses, a messiah. Garvey dwelled on Christ's betrayal as he identified himself with Jesus. "If Garvey dies, Garvey lives." "Christ died to make men free, I shall die to give courage and inspiration to my race."

Garvey's followers enjoyed the pageantry, ceremonies, and titles that were a part of the UNIA. The African Legionnaires and the Black Cross Nurses, resplendent in their uniforms, assembled in New York's Liberty Hall, and they paraded through Harlem. They prayed from The Universal Negro Catechism and reflected on their connection to Africa: "O Blessed Lord Jesus, redeem Africa from the hands of those who exploit and ravish her."

Garvey and the UNIA established businesses that employed nearly one thousand black people. The weekly newspaper, *Negro World*, promoted Garvey's ideology. In New York City, the Negro Factories Corporation operated three grocery stores, two restaurants, a printing plant, a steam laundry, and a factory that turned out uniforms, hats, and shirts for UNIA members. The association also owned buildings, vehicles, and facilities in other cities. Garvey proudly declared to white Americans that the UNIA "employs thousands of black girls and black boys. Girls who could only be washerwomen in your homes, we made clerks, stenographers. . . . You will see from the start we tried to dignify our race."

Although Garvey and the UNIA are most frequently associated with urban communities in the North, the UNIA also spread rapidly through the rural South in the 1920s. Black farmers and sharecroppers established UNIA chapters from Virginia to Louisiana.

A member of Marcus Garvey's United Negro Improvement Association stands outside a UNIA club in New York City.

➤ **Document**

17-2 "If You Believe the Negro Has a Soul": "Back to Africa" with Marcus Garvey, 1921 Garvey's speech denounces as hopeless interracial coexistence while stressing the inevitability of racial antagonisms in 1921. He championed racial purity, economic self-sufficiency, and black separatism and instilled a mounting pride in millions of black Americans who enjoyed the pomp, ceremony, and titles of the UNIA.

Marcus Garvey Appeals for a New African Nation

Marcus Garvey and the UNIA offered hope to African Americans in the 1920s. In the following words, Garvey passionately calls for African Americans and West Indians to support the creation of a new African nation.

For five years the Universal Negro Improvement Association has been advocating the cause of Africa for the Africans—that is, that the Negro peoples of the world should concentrate upon the object of building up for themselves a great nation in Africa. . . .

It is only a question of a few more years when Africa will be completely colonized by Negroes, as Europe is by the white race. What we want is an independent African nationality, and if America is to help the Negro peoples of the world establish such a nationality, then we welcome the assistance.

It is hoped that when the time comes for American and West Indian Negroes to settle in Africa, they will realize their responsibilities and duty. It will not be to go to Africa for the purpose of exercising an over-lordship over the natives, . . .

It will be useless, as stated before, for bombastic Negroes to leave America and the West Indies to go to Africa, thinking that they will have privileged positions to inflict upon the race that bastard aristocracy that they have tried to maintain in this Western world at the expense of the masses. Africa shall develop an aristocracy of its own, but it shall be based upon service and loyalty to race. Let all Negroes work toward that end. . . .

The time has really come for the Asiatics to govern themselves in Asia, as the Europeans are in Europe and the Western world, so also is it wise for the Africans to govern themselves at home, and thereby bring peace and satisfaction to the entire human family.

So Negroes, I say, through the Universal Negro Improvement Association, that there is much to live for. I have a vision of the future, and I see before me a picture of redeemed Africa, with her dotted cities, with her beautiful civilization, with her millions of happy children going to and fro. Why should I lose hope, why should I give up and take a back place in this age of progress? . . .

Africa shall reflect a splendid demonstration of the worth of the Negro, of the determination of the Negro, to set himself free and to establish a government of his own.

What Do You Think?

► On what logical basis does Garvey rest his call for a black homeland in Africa? How realistic was this call in the 1920s for nationhood in Africa?

► Who does Garvey believe should lead (or should not lead) the new African nation? What are the qualifications for such leadership?

► What vision does Garvey offer for what the globe will look like in the future? Does he suggest how peoples of various colors will coexist?

Source: David Levering Lewis, ed., *The Portable Harlem Renaissance Reader* (Viking Penguin, 1994), 17, 19, 20, 21, 25.

►► What Do You Think?

· Garvey feels that Africans should have their own homeland to foster loyalty to their race. In the 1920s, it would likely prove difficult for African Americans to assimilate with native Africans.

· Garvey feels that the African nation should be lead by black people who are loyal to their race, and it should not merely be lead by African Americans.

· Garvey feels that nations across the globe will govern themselves separately by their own distinct races.

Back to Africa

Garvey may be best remembered for his proposal to return black people to Africa by way of the Black Star Line, a steamship company he founded in 1919. Garvey sold stock in the company for five dollars a share. He hoped to establish a fleet with black officers and crew members. In 1920 the company purchased the *Yarmouth*, a dilapidated vessel that became the first ship in the fleet. Garvey raised enough capital to buy two additional ships, the *Kanawha* and the *Booker T. Washington*. But he lacked the financial resources to maintain them or to transport anyone to Africa.

Garvey knew it was unrealistic to expect several million black residents of the Western Hemisphere to join the back-to-Africa enterprise. But he genuinely believed the UNIA could liberate Africa from European colonial rule. "Wake up Ethiopia! Wake up Africa! Let us work towards the one glorious end of a free, redeemed and mighty nation." The UNIA adopted a red, green, and black flag for the proposed African republic that represented the blood, land, and race of the people of the continent.

The UNIA attempted to establish a settlement on the Cavalla River in southern Liberia. Garvey also petitioned the League of Nations to permit the UNIA to take possession of the former German colony of Tangaruyka (today's Tanzania) in East Africa. But the major colonial powers in Africa—Britain and France—and the United States thwarted Garvey's plans. The UNIA never gained a foothold on the continent.

Jamaican-born Marcus Garvey in a 1924 parade in Harlem attired in a uniform similar to those worn by British colonial governors in Jamaica, Trinidad, and elsewhere.

The End of the UNIA

The U.S. government and several black American leaders also undermined the UNIA and Garvey. J. Edgar Hoover and the Bureau of Investigation (the predecessor of the FBI) considered Garvey a serious threat to the racial status quo. Hoover employed black agents to infiltrate the UNIA and compile information that could be used to deport Garvey, who had never become an American citizen.

Garvey had few friends or admirers among African-American leaders because he and they differed fundamentally on strategy and goals. Garvey deplored efforts to gain legal and political rights within the American system. By appealing to the black masses, he rejected Du Bois's notion that the Talented Tenth would lead the race to liberation. He mocked the NAACP:

> [Y]ou had to be as near white as possible, otherwise there was no place for you as stenographer, clerk or attendant in the office of the National Association for the Advancement of 'Colored' People.

Unlike African-American leaders, Garvey believed black and white people had separate destinies. He regarded interracial cooperation as absurd. Thus Garvey considered a meeting he had with Ku Klux Klan leaders in Atlanta in 1922 consistent with his racial views. He praised the white supremacist organization.

> They are better friends to my race, for telling us what they are, and what they mean, thereby giving us a chance to stir for ourselves.

He added that "every whiteman is a Klansman . . . and there is no use lying about it."

In 1922 Garvey and three other UNIA leaders were arrested and indicted on twelve counts of fraudulent use of the U.S. mail to sell stock in the Black Star Line. Eight African-American leaders wrote to the U.S. attorney general to condemn Garvey and insist on his prosecution. Garvey was guilty of no more than mismanagement and incompetence. He was eventually found guilty and sent to the federal penitentiary in Atlanta in 1925. President Calvin Coolidge commuted his sentence in 1927, and he was deported.

The UNIA barely survived the loss of its inspirational leader. It declined steadily in the late 1920s and the 1930s. The various UNIA businesses closed, and its property—including the *Yarmouth*—was sold. Garvey was never permitted to return to the United States. He died in London in 1940. However, his legacy persisted. The Reverend Earl Little, a Baptist minister and the father of Malcolm X, belonged to the UNIA and much admired Garvey. Malcolm X recalled his father's association with Garvey.

> I remember hearing that he had black followers not only in the United States but all around the world, and I remember how the meetings always closed with my father saying, several times, and the people chanting after him, 'Up, you mighty race, you can accomplish what you will!'

Pan-Africanism

Garvey and Du Bois shared an abiding interest in Africa. Garvey, Du Bois, and other black leaders believed people of African descent from around the world should come together. They would share their heritage, discuss their ties to the continent, and explore ways to moderate—if not eliminate—colonial rule in Africa.

By 1914 Britain, France, Germany, Portugal, Belgium, Spain, and Italy had established colonies across almost all of Africa. Only Liberia and Ethiopia (then called Abyssinia) remained independent. The Europeans assumed the "white man's burden" in their "scramble" for Africa. Christian missionaries sought to convert Africans. European companies exploited Africa's human and natural resources. As they gained control over the continent, the European powers confirmed their conviction that they represented a superior race and culture.

The first **Pan-African Congress** had convened in London in 1900. It was organized principally by Henry Sylvester Williams, a lawyer from Trinidad who had resided in Canada and then London. Du Bois attended and chaired the Committee on the Address to the Nations of the World. He called for the creation of "a great central Negro state of the world." But Du Bois did not insist on the immediate withdrawal of the European powers from Africa. Instead he offered a modest recommendation that would provide "as soon as practicable the rights of responsible self-government to the black colonies of Africa and the West Indies."

The second Pan-African Congress met in Paris for three days in February 1919, near Versailles, where the peace conference ending World War I was assembled. There were fifty-eight delegates from sixteen nations. Du Bois was among the sixteen African Americans in attendance. (None of them had been to Africa.) Marcus Garvey did not attend. The delegates took seriously the **Fourteen Points** that U.S. president Woodrow Wilson had proposed to fashion the postwar world. They were especially interested in the fifth point, which called for the interests of colonial peoples to be given "equal weight" in the adjustment of colonial claims after the war. The congress recommended that the League of Nations assume authority over the former German colonies in East Africa. The League later established mandates over those colonies but delegated authority to administer those mandates to Britain, France, and Belgium. Two more Pan-African Congresses in the 1920s met in Brussels and London but also failed to influence the policies of the colonial powers.

Reading Check Why did the Universal Negro Improvement Association and Marcus Garvey appeal to so many African Americans?

► **Reading Check**
The UNIA promoted the celebration of black culture and presented a vision of a much better future for black people everywhere. Garvey himself was a charismatic leader who combined racial pride, Christian faith, and economic cooperation into an attractive vision of Black Nationalism.

▶ What was the attitude of most labor unions to black workers in the 1920s?

▶ Why did the Pullman Porters form their own union?

▶ What role did A. Philip Randolph play with the Brotherhood of Sleeping Car Porters?

KEY TERMS

▶ Brotherhood of Sleeping Car Porters (BSCP), p. 604

▶ Guide to Reading

For answers, see the *Teacher's Resource Manual.*

▶ Recommended Reading

David E. Bernstein. *Only One Place of Redress: African Americans, Labor Regulations and the Courts from Reconstruction to the New Deal.* Durham, NC: Duke University Press, 2001.

Section 3

Uniting Black Workers

Labor

The arrival of thousands of black migrants in American cities during and after World War I changed the composition of the industrial workforce. Their arrival also intensified pressure on labor unions to admit black members. By 1916 twelve thousand of the nearly fifty thousand workers in the Chicago stockyards were black people. In Detroit, black laborers made up nearly 14 percent of the workforce in the automobile industry. The Ford Motor Company employed 50 black people in 1916 and 2,500 by 1920.

Yet even with the industrial revolution and the great migration, more than two-thirds of black workers in 1920 were employed in agriculture and domestic service (see Figure 17–1). Less than 20 percent were engaged in manufacturing. Those who were part of industrial America worked in the dreary, dirty, and sometimes dangerous unskilled jobs that paid the least. Still, work in the factories, mills, and mines paid more than agricultural labor.

Most of the major labor unions would not admit black workers. Since its founding in 1886, the American Federation of Labor (AFL) officially prohibited racial discrimination. But most of its local unions were all white and all male. The AFL was made up of skilled laborers, and less than 20 percent of black workers were skilled (see Figure 17–2). But even those with skills were usually not admitted to the local craft unions that made up the AFL. More than fifty trade unions within the AFL had no black members. Unions that did admit black workers included those representing cigar makers, coal miners, garment workers, and longshoremen.

By the World War I years, the NAACP and the Urban League regularly appealed to employers and unions to accept black laborers. The Urban League attempted to convince business owners that black employees would be efficient and reliable. But many employers preferred to divide black and white workers by hiring black men and women as strikebreakers, thereby enraging striking white workers. In 1918 Urban League officials met with Samuel Gompers, the longtime president of the AFL. He agreed to bring more black people into the federation, but there were few tangible results. The Urban League did succeed in persuading the U.S. Department of Labor to establish a Division of Negro Economics to advise the secretary of labor on issues involving black workers.

made with the police who looked the other way as the music and alcohol continued through the night. Musicians from "legal" clubs drifted into the after-hours joints and played until dawn.

Another popular—and sometimes necessary—form of entertainment among Harlemites was the **rent party**. Housing costs in Harlem were extravagant. White people and real estate agents refused to rent or sell to black people in most other areas of New York City. To make the steep monthly rent payments, apartment dwellers would push the furniture aside and begin cooking chicken, chitterlings, rice, okra, and sweet potatoes. They would distribute a few flyers and hire a musician or two. The party was usually on a Saturday or a Thursday night. (Most domestic servants had Thursdays off.) Partygoers paid ten cents to fifty cents admission. Food and liquor were sold. With a decent crowd, the month's rent was paid.

Song, Dance, and Stage

Black women became popular as singers and dancers in Harlem. They often appeared in Broadway shows and revues. Florence Mills entranced audiences in several Broadway productions including *Plantation Review, Dixie to Broadway*, and *Blackbirds* before she died of appendicitis in 1927. Adelaide Hall also appeared in *Blackbirds* and later opened her own nightclubs in London and Paris. Ethel Waters worked her way up from smoky gin joints in Harlem basements to Broadway shows and then to films. Many years later she toured with Billy Graham's religious crusades and revivals.

White men wrote many of the popular Broadway productions that starred black entertainers. In 1921, however, Eubie Blake and Noble Sissle put on *Shuffle Along*, which became a major hit. Its most memorable tune was "I'm Just Wild about Harry." Sissle and Blake wrote several more shows, including *Chocolate Dandies* in 1924. It was created especially for a thin, lanky, dark, and funny young lady named Josephine Baker. In 1925 Baker left New York and moved to Paris. She starred in the *Revue Nègre*, which created a sensation in the French capital. She remained in France for the rest of her life.

White playwright Eugene O'Neill wrote serious drama involving black people. Charles Gilpin and then Paul Robeson appeared in O'Neill's *Emperor Jones*. Robeson went on to an illustrious performing career. He was a graduate of Rutgers University where he was an all-American football player. He earned a law degree at Columbia University but abandoned the law for the stage. He appeared in numerous productions, including O'Neill's *All God's Chillun Got Wings*, Shakespeare's *Othello*, Gershwin's *Porgy and Bess*, and Kern and Hammerstein's *Showboat*. He often sang spirituals in his magnificent, rich voice and later recorded many of them.

▶ **Living Words Audio Clip**
Track 31 " *Swing Low, Sweet Chariot";
traditional; sung by Paul Robeson*

Bessie Smith was born in poverty on April 15, 1894, in Chattanooga, Tennessee. She was one of seven children of a Baptist preacher, William Smith, and his wife, Laura. Bessie's parents and two brothers died while she was still a child. The surviving children were raised by an older sister, Viola.

With her brother Andrew on the guitar, Bessie began to sing on Chattanooga street corners to earn money for the family. The experience helped shape her career. In 1912 she toured briefly with a musical group that featured Gertrude "Ma" Rainey. In 1913 she worked in Atlanta for ten dollars a week plus tips. Her fame spread and soon she was touring the South. By the 1920s she was singing in Philadelphia and Atlantic City.

In 1923 Frank Walker signed her to a contract with Columbia Records. She recorded what were known in the 1920s as "race" records, produced for black audiences by white recording companies. Her second recording, "Tain't Nobody's Business If I Do," sold an astonishing 780,000 records within months.

In 1925 she recorded "St. Louis Blues" and "Careless Love" with Louis Armstrong—their only recordings together. She toured major cities in a private railroad coach. Huge crowds lined up at clubs and theaters to hear her.

She had a striking and appealing voice that conveyed the depths of her emotions and experiences. Smith's blues tore at the raw feelings that sociologists and academics missed when they discussed poverty, unemployment, alcoholism, or sexual relationships. Her blues were firmly grounded in African-American oral and musical traditions.

Bessie Smith was married twice. Her first husband, Earl Love, died shortly after they married. Her second marriage, to Jack Gee, was marked by jealousy, drinking, and physical conflict and ended in separation in 1930. Her warmest and most enduring relationship was with Richard Morgan, a Chicago bootlegger.

People did not trifle with Bessie Smith. A large lady, over two hundred pounds, she ate, drank, and fought to excess. She could be mean, difficult, and violent. She physically attacked others and was herself attacked. But she also had a sweet and loyal side and could be helpful, generous, and compassionate. However, she seemed fond of some of the sleaziest, most dangerous nightclubs in America. She admitted wanting to go where "the funk was flying."

She continued to record even after record sales declined during the Depression. Her last recording session included "Nobody Knows You When You're Down and Out." Bessie Smith died at age forty-three in 1937 in a car accident near Clarksdale, Mississippi. Perhaps Louis Armstrong summed up her musical legacy best. "She used to thrill me at all times, the way she could phrase a note with a certain something in her voice no other blues singer could get. She had music in her soul and felt everything she did."

Smith

Section 5

Sports

GUIDE TO READING

▶ Why was it so difficult for professional black athletes to earn a living in the 1920s?

▶ What role did black athletes play in college sports in the 1920s?

KEY TERMS

▶ Negro National League, p. 617

Baseball

Sports flourished in America in the 1920s. Americans worshiped their athletic heroes. Babe Ruth and Jack Dempsey were as well known as President Calvin Coolidge. Professional athletics, especially baseball and boxing, expanded dramatically. Professional football and basketball emerged later. Black men had been banned from major league baseball in 1887 (see Chapter 15). Nevertheless, in 1901 New York Giants' manager John J. McGraw signed a black man, Charlie Grant, to play second base. McGraw claimed that Grant was "Chief Tokohoma," a full-blooded Cherokee Indian. Chicago White Sox owner Charles Comiskey knew otherwise. Grant did not play in the major leagues.

Playing among themselves, black baseball players barely made a living as they moved from team to team. Teams came and went with regularity. No leagues functioned effectively for the black teams and players. Owners of the black teams were sometimes involved in organized crime. William A. Greenlee, for example, was the proprietor of the Pittsburgh Crawfords. He made most of his money from the numbers racket.

Black players crisscrossed the country on trains and in automobiles. They played each other in small towns and large cities for meager amounts of money shared from gate receipts. The black clubs kept few individual or team statistics. Their financial records were frequently in disarray.

Rube Foster

Andrew "Rube" Foster was the father of black baseball in twentieth-century America. He was a crafty pitcher from Texas who combined athletic skills with mental dexterity. In 1911 he founded the Chicago American Giants. He pitched with them regularly until 1915 and then mainly managed after that. As fine an athlete as Foster was, he was an even more talented organizer and administrator.

In 1919 in the *Chicago Defender*, he argued for the establishment of a Negro baseball league. In 1920 he was the force in the formation of the eight-team **Negro National League**. He became its president and secretary. It was the first stable black league, with franchises in Kansas City, St. Louis, Indianapolis, Detroit, Dayton, and two teams in Chicago. The eighth team was the Cuban Stars.

▶▶ **Guide to Reading/Key Terms**

For answers, see the *Teacher's Resource Manual*.

▶▶ **Retracing the Odyssey**

Kansas City, Missouri: The Negro Leagues Baseball Museum. Devoted to the history of African Americans and baseball from the 1860s to the 1950s, the museum opened in 1991 and contains films, exhibits, and interactive computer stations. Its Field of Legends features twelve life-sized bronze sculptures that honor the men who contributed the most to black baseball.

Andrew "Rube" Foster was the father of black baseball. He was elected to the Baseball Hall of Fame in 1981.

Foster and the new league took advantage of the migration of black people to northern cities. The black ball clubs usually played late in the afternoon or in the early evening so fans could attend after a day's work. Sunday doubleheaders in Chicago or Kansas City might draw eight thousand to ten thousand people. Players were paid regularly, and athletes on Foster's Giants earned at least $175 a month. The biggest obstacle black teams faced was the lack of their own fields or stadiums. They were forced to rent, often at exorbitant rates, from major league clubs, which frequently kept the profits from concessions.

Black baseball thrived—more or less—in the 1920s, thanks mostly to Foster's personality and dedication. He was a tireless worker and strict disciplinarian, but the pressure may have been too much. In 1926 he suffered a mental breakdown and died in 1930. Foster's loss—combined with the impact of the Depression—severely disrupted the league system.

College Sports

Football, baseball, basketball, and track and field were popular at the collegiate level. Amateur sports were not as rigidly segregated as professional baseball. Black men continued to play for white northern universities. Few teams had more than one black player. Paul Robeson was on the Rutgers football team in 1916 that played against Frederick Douglass "Fritz" Pollard and Brown University. Pollard was the first black man to play in the Rose Bowl where his Brown team lost to Washington State in 1916.

Black players on white teams encountered discrimination when the teams traveled. Spectators taunted and threatened them. The Big Ten had an unwritten agreement that basketball coaches would not accept black players. All-white college teams sometimes refused to play against schools with black players. In 1920 Virginia's Washington and Lee University canceled a football game against Washington and Jefferson College of Pennsylvania. Charles West, a black man, played in the Washington and Jefferson backfield.

Sports in black colleges and universities thrived in the 1920s. Baseball and football were the most popular spectator events. Traditional rivalries attracted large crowds. Several schools played baseball religiously each Easter Monday. In 1926 Livingstone College defeated Biddle University (now Johnson C. Smith University) before a crowd of six thousand in Charlotte, North Carolina. With the migration of black people to the North, black colleges began to play football in northern cities. Howard and Lincoln played to a scoreless tie before eighteen thousand people in Philadelphia on Thanksgiving in 1925. Hampton and Lincoln played at New York's Polo Grounds on the edge of Harlem in 1929 in a game won by Lincoln 13–7 before ten thousand spectators.

 Reading Check Why was it so difficult for professional black athletes to earn a living in the 1920s?

▶ **Reading Check**

Blacks were banned from white professional sports. Black leagues were often poorly run and produced little revenue for either the teams or the players. Andrew "Rube" Foster's Negro National League was an exception to this trend.

✓ Examining Photographs

Photographs are a form of visual evidence that can provide valuable information about an event or a historical period. Photographers, however, like other observers of events, have their own points of view. By their choice of subject, lighting, and camera angle, photographers can influence what is seen and how it is perceived. They may also distort the appearance of objects in their photographs to create an illusion or to convey a particular mood. For these reasons, you should always analyze photographs carefully.

LEARN THE SKILL

Use the following steps to examine photographs:

1. **Study the photograph to identify the subject.** Look at the photograph as a whole; then study the details. If a title and a caption are provided, refer to them for more information.

2. **Analyze the reliability of the photograph as a source of information.** Note how the photograph conveys information and how it creates a mood or an emotion. Think about other ways the event or scene might have been photographed.

3. **Study the photograph to learn more about the historical period.** Think about how the photograph fits with what you already know. Consider what the photograph adds to your understanding of the historical period.

PRACTICE THE SKILL

Answer the following questions:

1. **(a)** What do you see in the picture? **(b)** How does the caption help you understand the photograph? **(c)** What visual details help you understand why the men are protesting?

2. **(a)** Do you think the photograph depicts the situation accurately? Explain. **(b)** What mood or emotion do you think the

The fight to stop lynchings was one of the NAACP's most important campaigns in the early twentieth century. Demonstrations and protests like this one at the Crime Conference in Washington, D.C. kept the issue in the public arena.

photographer wanted viewers to feel? **(c)** What aspects of the photograph help to create this feeling? **(d)** What choices might the photographer have made before taking this picture?

3. **(a)** Briefly summarize what you already know about lynching and violence against African Americans. Does this photograph in any way contradict what you already know, or does it add to your understanding? Explain. **(b)** What can photographs like this contribute to your knowledge of an event that written sources cannot?

▶ **Skills for Life**

For answers, see *Teacher's Resource Manual.*

Chapter 18

The Great Depression pushed many black Americans to the edge of despair.

Witnessing History . . .

The Depression brought everyone down a peg or two. And the Negro had but a few pegs to fall.

—Langston Hughes

The only thing that we not only can, but must do, is voluntarily and insistently to organize our economic and social power, no matter how much segregation it involves. Learn to associate with ourselves and to train ourselves in methods of democratic control within our own group. Run and support our own institutions.

—W. E. B. Du Bois

 What does Du Bois see as the way to black economic power?

Chapter Preview

▶ **Witnessing History**

Blacks must work within their own communities to create and support economic and political institutions to develop true economic and social power.

For African Americans, the Great Depression was an era of suffering. The horrors and burdens of American racism, profound political change, demographic shifts, and social activism would lay the foundation for the progress of coming decades. At the beginning of the economic collapse, most African Americans were trapped in the already failing southern agricultural system. Others were barely existing in the booming urban economy. The fall of the economy pushed many black Americans to the edge of starvation, throwing them off the land and out of the small niches they had carved out in other occupations. Coming out of the southern-dominated Democratic Party, President Franklin Roosevelt's New Deal program for fighting the Depression might have simply reinforced existing racism, as in fact it did to some extent. The emerging political power of African-American voters in the North, the continuing development of civil rights organizations, and the growth of an antiracist agenda and labor unions created the preconditions for a profound change in American politics. Amid economic despair, peonage, lynchings, and labor conflict, black men, women, and their children saw glimmers of hope in protests against racial segregation and radical critiques of capitalist exploitation. Their protests helped shape the policies and programs of the New Deal.

Section 1

The Great Depression 1929–1933

Causes of the Depression

The **Great Depression** was catastrophic. National income fell from $81 billion in 1929 to $40 billion in 1932. Americans lost faith in banks. The resulting panic deepened the despair. Overnight millions of Americans lost their life savings in bank closings and foreclosures. Individual Americans responded by buying fewer consumer goods. In turn, businesses cut back production, investment, and payrolls. The result was a downward spiral of economic activity made worse by increasing numbers of unemployed. According to the American Federation of Labor (AFL), the number of unemployed people increased from 3,216,000 in January 1930 to 13,689,000 in March 1933 (see Figure 18–1). The standard of living of nearly everyone from farmers to small businessmen and entrepreneurs to wage laborers dropped to a fraction of what it had been before 1929.

Most people blamed the stock market crash and Republican president Herbert Hoover for the hard times. But the explanation is more complicated. Although still a hotly debated issue, the Great Depression was probably caused by a combination of factors. These factors included rampant speculation, corporate capitalism's drive for markets and profits unchecked by federal regulation, the failure of those in the government or private sector to understand the workings of the economy and a weak international trading system. Most important, the great inequality of wealth and income limited the purchasing power of millions of Americans.

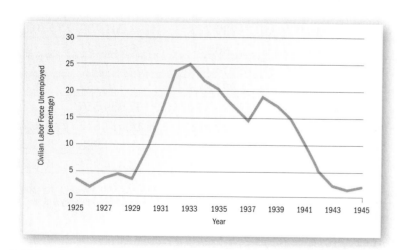

GUIDE TO READING

▶ What factors caused the Great Depression of the 1930s?

▶ How did the Depression affect African Americans?

▶ What steps did Herbert Hoover take in response to the economic crisis?

KEY TERMS

▶ The Great Depression, p. 631

▶ Hoovervilles, p. 637

▶▶ **Guide to Reading/Key Terms**

For answers, see the *Teacher's Resource Manual.*

▶▶ **Recommended Reading**

Raymond Wolters. *Negroes and the Great Depression: The Problem of Economic Recovery.* Westport, CT: Greenwood Publisher Group Incorporated, 1974. A solid survey of African Americans in the Depression that covers the impact of the Depression on African Americans, the workings of the Black Cabinet, and the effects of the New Deal agencies on the lives of black Americans.

▶▶ **Retracing Odyssey**

Wright Museum of African-American History

Detroit, Michigan. The largest African-American history museum in America. The Field to Factory exhibit documents the Great Migration of African Americans from the rural South to the industrial North during the twentieth century. It sponsors a variety of educational programs throughout the year.

FIGURE 18–1 Unemployment, 1925–1945

With the collapse of the American economy, unemployment soared in the 1930s.

Explore this figure online at www.prenhall.com/aah/figure 18.1

Harder Times for Black America

The collapse of the American economy hit African Americans particularly hard. Most black people remained in the rural South in an increasingly exploitive agricultural system. The Depression worsened the key problems affecting cash-crop production in the 1920s. Consumer demand for cotton and sugar fell with the economy. As farmers grew more of these crops to make ends meet, the supply of these staples increased. The result was prices for cotton—still the mainstay of the southern economy—plunging from eighteen cents a pound in 1929 to six cents in 1933. Families of black sharecroppers and tenant farmers, nearly powerless in the rural South, found themselves reduced to starvation or thrown off the land.

The hard times also struck those 1.5 million African Americans who had escaped the South for northern urban communities (see Table 18–1). Even during the height of the prosperous 1920s, black Americans suffered layoffs and witnessed a steady decline in their living standards. After 1929 the same forces that impoverished those in the countryside affected those in urban areas. Waves of refugees from the farms crowded into the cities (see Table 18–2). By 1934, the federal government noted that 17 percent of white citizens could not support themselves. The figure for black Americans had increased to 38 percent overall. In Chicago the jobless rate for African-American men was 40 percent, in Pittsburgh 48 percent, in Harlem 50 percent, in Philadelphia 56 percent, and in

▶ Interactive Activity

Dealing with Hard Times

The exercises in this activity look at ways in which people coped with the hard times of the Depression and at some of the alternatives that were proposed to change the political and economic system that had led to the Depression.

TABLE 18–1 Demographic Shifts: The Second Great Migration, 1930–1950

Year	Region	Black Population	Total Population	% Black
1930	Northeast	1,146,985	34,427,091	3.33
	Midwest	1,262,234	38,594,100	3.27
	Southeast	7,079,626	25,680,803	27.57
	South Central	2,281,951	12,176,830	18.74
	Mountain	30,225	3,701,789	0.82
	Pacific	90,122	8,622,047	1.05
1950	Northeast	2,018,182	39,477,986	5.11
	Midwest	2,227,876	44,460,762	5.01
	Southeast	7,793,379	32,659,516	23.86
	South Central	2,432,028	14,517,572	16.73
	Mountain	66,429	5,074,998	1.31
	Pacific	507,043	15,114,964	3.35

Source: U.S. Bureau of the Census Release, 1991 and Statistical Abstract, 1990. Also see Schomburg Center, The New York Public Library: African American Desk Reference (New York: John Wiley & Sons, 1999), 100-1.

TABLE 18–2 Median Income of Black Families Compared to the Median Income of White Families for Selected Cities, 1935–1936

City and Type of Family	Black	White	Black Income as a Percentage of White Income
Husband–Wife Families			
New York	$980	$1,930	51%
Chicago	$726	$1,687	43%
Columbus	$831	$1,622	51%
Atlanta	$632	$1,876	34%
Columbia	$576	$1,876	31%
Mobile	$481	$1,419	34%
Other Families			
Atlanta	$332	$940	35%
Columbia	$254	$1,403	18%
Mobile	$301	$784	38%

Source: Gunnar Myrdal et al., *An American Dilemma* (New York: Harper and Brothers, 1944).

Detroit 60 percent. The figures were even worse for black workers in southern cities. In Atlanta, Georgia, 65 percent of black workers needed public assistance. In Norfolk, Virginia, a stunning 80 percent had to apply for welfare.

African Americans lost jobs in those parts of the economy where they had gained a tenuous foothold. Before 1929 jobs in low-status or poorly paid occupations such as garbage collection, foundries, or domestic service had been regarded as "Negro work." They were generally immune from white competition. As desperation set in, white Southerners competed for these jobs. They also used the old tactics of terror and intimidation to compel employers to fire black people. Unions, north and south, continued to exclude African Americans from membership. They pressured manufacturers to hire white people.

Black women workers, overwhelmingly concentrated in domestic service and laundry work, were affected even more than black men. There were fewer jobs because many families could no longer afford domestic help. Those white people with the money to hire help found they could pay almost nothing and still employ these desperate women. In 1935 two black women, Marvel Cooke and Ella Baker, published an exposé of the exploitation of these women laborers in *The Crisis*. They entitled the article "The Bronx Slave Market." The buying and selling of labor reminded them of the old slave marts in the antebellum South. Cooke and Baker described how the street corner market worked: "The Simpson avenue block exudes the stench of the slave market at its worst.

A market woman in the 1930s with burdens on her head and in her arms. Black women drew upon proven strategies of self-help, hard work, and communal sharing to survive the Great Depression.

Not only is human labor bartered and sold for a slave wage, but human love also is a marketable commodity." The black women gathered on particular street corners and waited as well-to-do white women selected them for a day's labor. They received "wages as low as 15 to 25 cents an hour, some working only two or three hours a day." Some black people were hired but never paid.

African Americans were no strangers to adversity. Many used the survival strategies developed through centuries of hardship to eke out an existence during the first years of the Great Depression. Survival demanded that black women pool their resources. In Chicago, for example, women and their families lived in crowded tenements in which they shared bathrooms and other facilities including hot plates, stoves, and sinks. They bartered and exchanged goods and services because money was so scarce. One woman might dress the hair of a neighbor in return for permission to borrow her dress or use her pots and pans. Another woman might trade bread and sugar or some other household staple for milk, beans, or soap. Grandmothers watched over children as their mothers went to look, often without success, for a domestic job. They helped each other as best they could.

Rural black women, like their urban sisters, had to rely on their individual and collective ingenuity to survive. As one observer of black women household heads in rural Georgia noted, "In their effort to maintain existence, these people are catching and selling fish, reselling vegetables, sewing in exchange for old clothes, letting out sleeping space, and doing odd jobs. They understand how to help each other." The depth and duration of this downturn pressed these mutual aid strategies to the breaking point. By 1933 the clock seemed to have been turned back to 1865 when many African Americans could claim to own little more than their bodies.

 Reading Check   What factors caused the Great Depression of the 1930s?

▶ **Reading Check**

The Depression was caused by a combination of factors. Among these factors were: rampant speculation, a lack of effective regulation, limited understanding of the workings of the economy, a weak international trading system, and the limited purchasing power of most Americans.

Black Businesses in the Depression: Collapse and Survival

Members of the black business and professional class also experienced economic losses. African Americans who had built successful businesses and professional practices in medicine and law, for example, faced the same Depression-borne problems as other businesses. They suffered

even more because the communities on which they depended were poorer. A description of two kinds of business, banking and insurance, illustrates how black enterprises stood or fell during the economic crisis.

Banking and Insurance

The Binga Bank, Chicago's first black-owned-and-operated financial institution, had been founded in 1908 by its president Jesse Binga (1865–1950). Binga had managed the bank so effectively that by 1930 its deposits had grown to more than $1.5 million. The Binga Bank was, during its early years, an important symbol of successful black capitalism. As such, it represented the hopes and aspirations of Chicago's black people. But the bank's assets were too heavily invested in mortgage loans to black churches and fraternal societies, many of which could not meet their payments after their members lost their jobs. Binga refused to seize the properties of these community institutions. His restraint, coupled with financial improprieties, led to the bank's failure. On July 31, 1930, Illinois state bank auditors padlocked the institution and filed a federal misuse-of-funds charge against the once proud financier. Sentenced to prison in 1932, Binga was pardoned by President Franklin Delano Roosevelt a year later. However, he never rebuilt his bank or his fortune.

Some black businesses did survive the economic cataclysm, although often in a much weakened state. Among the fortunate businesses still standing when prosperity finally returned in the 1940s were the leading insurance companies, such as Atlanta Life, Supreme Life, Golden State, and the North Carolina Mutual Life Insurance Company. Atlanta Life Insurance Company, for example—founded by a former Georgia slave, Alonzo Franklin Herndon, in 1905—not only survived the Depression but recorded substantial profit. Between 1931 and 1936, the company's assets increased by more than $1 million. Insurance companies such as Atlanta Life provided an essential service for African Americans, particularly in an era before government provided social security. These companies could thus depend on a continued flow of premiums. And unlike Binga Bank, the officers of the Atlanta Life Insurance Company drastically reduced the percentage of their investment capital that secured mortgage loans in the black community.

The North Carolina Mutual Life Insurance Company, in Durham, weathered the Great Depression under the astute leadership of Charles Clinton Spaulding (1874–1952), a former manager of a black cooperative grocery store. In 1899 Spaulding joined with two other African Americans to transform the insurance company into the nation's largest black business. His partners were John Merrick, a former slave and leading realtor and barber and his uncle, Dr. Aaron McDuffie Moore, Durham's only black physician. Merrick owned six barbershops—three for whites and three for blacks. Following on the heels of the great migration to the North, Spaulding expanded the company's territory into Virginia, Maryland, and the District of Columbia. The company adhered to the

thrift, hard work, and self-help philosophy so strongly expressed by Booker T. Washington. It remains today one of the three largest black-owned insurance companies in the United States.

 Reading Check What was the fate of black-owned businesses during the Depression?

Healthcare

Many of the 250 black hospitals, clinics, and nursing training schools were unable to survive the ravages of the Depression. Confronting a diminishing clientele and worsening health among black people, some black physicians began encouraging their patients to demand admission to the segregated government-operated hospitals and clinics. At the outset of the Depression, Dr. Matilda A. Evans (1872–1935) of Columbia, South Carolina, an 1897 graduate of the Woman's Medical College in Philadelphia, mobilized a diverse group of people to persuade the state board of health to allocate money to provide free inoculations and immunization shots to black schoolchildren. Other healthcare professionals volunteered to conduct free medical and dental examinations.

When Evans's Columbia Clinic opened in July 1930, over seven hundred patients showed up. This short-lived clinic reflected Evans's belief that health care was a state responsibility just as important as the provision of free public education. The black South Carolina newspaper, the *Palmetto Leader*, declared in October 1930 that

> evidence keeps on piling on top of evidence to the effect that the Columbia Clinic is just proving to be, and will yet stand as the most important effort sponsored for our group in Columbia within the last half century.

The deteriorating economic conditions of both the state of South Carolina and its people made it impossible to sustain this effort. But the Columbia Clinic movement taught black people a powerful lesson about how to mobilize to achieve change. As Evans anticipated it would, black consciousness was raised about the need to apply pressure on the state to gain greater access to public resources.

The Failure of Relief

Before Franklin Roosevelt's New Deal, private charities or, as a last resort, state and local governments were responsible for providing relief from economic hardships. Even in good times these institutions provided too little for all those in need. African Americans had a much

Dr. Matilda A. Evans (1872–1935) believed in the importance of establishing institutions and organizations that would enable black people to survive and from which they could fight to end racial segregation and discrimination.

▶ **Recommended Reading**

Darlene Clark Hine, "The Corporeal and Ocular Veil: Dr. Matilda A. Evans (1872-1935) and the Complexity of Southern History," *The Journal of Southern History*, Vol. LXX, No. 1, February 2004, 1-34. A case study of the strategies pursued by a black woman physician to provide health care for impoverished African Americans in Columbia, South Carolina during the opening decades of the twentieth century.

▶ **Teaching Notes**

Dr. Matilda Evans established two hospitals and founded a nursing training school. She organized the Good Health Association of South Carolina, edited The Negro Health Journal, and served a term as president of the Palmetto Medical Association.

harder time getting aid than white people and were given less when they did get it. The Depression made it impossible for the nation's charitable organizations to meet the needs of more than a small portion of the hungry, homeless, and unemployed millions. State and local governments could not or would not provide unemployment insurance or increased welfare benefits to ease the pain and suffering of those most vulnerable to the economic disaster. Even when these governments wanted to help, the magnitude of the economic collapse had lowered tax receipts. It was nearly impossible for relief agencies to act.

Despite the great need to alleviate the economic disaster, President Herbert Hoover hesitated to act. He believed government should do little to interfere with the workings of the economy. Nevertheless, he did more to counteract a depression than any previous president had done. Hoover tried to convince businesses to retain employees and not to cut wages. He believed companies would understand that by doing so they would contribute to the health of the general economy and promote their own long-term interests. The president also approved loans to banks, railroads, and insurance companies by the Reconstruction Finance Corporation, a federal agency set up to rescue large corporations. He hoped these businesses would reinvigorate production, create new jobs, and restore consumer spending. His faith was misplaced. Businesses, seeking to save themselves, took the government loans and still laid off workers.

Hoover's reluctance to use the federal government to intervene in the economy extended to providing relief. He suggested that local governments and charities should address the needs of the unemployed, the homeless, and the starving masses. Hoover was not a callous person. He was trapped in a rigid ideology. He watched with dismay the wandering groups of men, women, and children who began settling into what they called **Hoovervilles**, sordid clusters of shacks made of tin, cardboard, and burlap adjacent to railroad tracks and dumps. Still, he refused to allow the federal government to provide relief directly.

Hoover's inactivity was bad enough, but his politics were as racist as that of the Democratic Party. He wanted to create a white Republican Party in the South. He cultivated white Southerners by attempting to appoint judge John Parker of North Carolina to the U.S. Supreme Court. Parker believed in "separate but equal." He displaced black Republican Party leaders. Hoover's policy was not new. For decades the national Republican Party had treated black voters with contempt and often declined to reward them with patronage appointments. This policy took on a different meaning during the early 1930s against the backdrop of black suffering.

 **Reading Check** What steps did Herbert Hoover take in response to the economic crisis?

▶ **Reading Check, p. 636**

Successful blacks businesses and professionals suffered the same problems during the Depression as whites. Some were able to survive, namely black insurance companies. These companies not only survived, but also thrived, due to the fact that premiums for policies continued to be paid even during the Depression.

▶ **Reading Check**

In the face of economic crisis, President Hoover did very little. He believed that government should not interfere in the economy and stuck by this belief even as the Depression deepened. Moreover, he believed that it was the place of local government and charities, not the federal government, to provide relief to those hit hardest by the crisis.

▶▶ **Guide to Reading/Key Terms**

For answers, see the *Teacher's Resource Manual.*

▶▶ **Recommended Reading**

John Egerton. *Speak Now against the Day: The Generation before the Civil Rights Movement in the South.* New York: Knopf, 1994. An excellent survey of the period before the southern civil rights era, with chapters on the Depression in the South and black and white Southerners' reactions to it.

Section 2

Black Protest during the Great Depression

The NAACP and Civil Rights Struggles

During the 1930s the NAACP developed a new effectiveness as an advocate for African-American civil rights. The **biracial** organization took the lead in pressing the government to protect African-American rights and to eliminate blatant racism in government programs. Part of the reason for this new dynamism was the astute leadership of Walter White. He became an insistent voice of protest, personally investigating forty-two lynchings and eight race riots. He was an ardent lobbyist for civil rights legislation and racial justice. Throughout the 1930s African Americans moved into leadership positions in the NAACP and added their names to the membership roles of its many branches.

The new dynamism of the NAACP became apparent in 1930 when Walter White took a prominent role in the successful campaign to defeat Hoover's nomination of John J. Parker of North Carolina to the U.S. Supreme Court. Parker had infuriated the organization because he openly embraced white supremacy. He stated, for example, that the "participation of the Negro in politics is a source of evil and danger to both races." The NAACP formed a coalition with the American Federation of Labor to stop the Parker nomination. Although the NAACP could take only part of the credit, White trumpeted the victory. He let it be known that African Americans would not be silent while "the Hoover administration proposed to conciliate southern white sentiment by sacrificing the Negro and his rights."

Du Bois Ignites a Controversy

The NAACP had critics, even within its own ranks. Many younger black people criticized its focus on civil liberties and deplored it for ignoring the economic misery of most African Americans. In 1934 W. E. B. Du Bois, editor of the NAACP's journal *The Crisis*, joined the critics. Du Bois advocated a program of self-determination he hoped would permit black people to develop "an economic nation within a nation." Du Bois acknowledged that this internal economy could only meet part of the needs of the African-American community. But he insisted it could be developed and expanded in many ways: "This smaller part could be so important and wield so much power that its influence upon

the total economy of Negroes and the total industrial organization of the United States would be decisive for the great ends towards which the Negro moves."

The black intellectual community quickly attacked Du Bois for advocating "voluntary segregation." Sociologist E. Franklin Frazier, for example, called the idea of black businesses succeeding within a segregated economy a black upper-class fantasy and social myth. Nevertheless, Du Bois held fast to his position that the NAACP should continue to oppose legal segregation yet combine that opposition with vigorous support to improve segregated institutions as long as discrimination persisted. He was eventually forced from the editorship of *The Crisis*, but his resignation did not end the controversy. By the late 1930s the NAACP had developed, alongside its older activities, a much greater emphasis on economic policy and worked to develop stronger ties to the burgeoning labor movement.

Challenging Racial Discrimination in the Courts

A dramatic expansion of its legal campaign against racial discrimination enhanced the NAACP's effectiveness. Central to this project was the hiring of Charles Hamilton Houston, a Harvard-trained African-American lawyer and scholar, to lead it. Houston had been vice dean of Howard University Law School. He had transformed the school into a powerful institution for training black attorneys in the intricacies of civil rights law. At the NAACP, Houston laid out a plan for a legal program to challenge inequality in education and the exclusion of black people from voting in the South. Houston used lawsuits both to force state and local governments to live up to the Constitution and to inspire community organization.

Houston did not focus directly on eliminating segregation. Instead, he sought to force southern states to equalize their facilities. Studies by the NAACP had revealed great disparities in per capita expenditures for white and black students, and huge differences in salaries paid to white and black teachers. Houston was no supporter of segregation. He hoped to use litigation to secure judgments that would so increase the cost of separate institutions that states would be forced to abandon them.

To execute his agenda, Houston convinced Walter White to hire his former student, Thurgood Marshall, in 1936. Marshall was born in Baltimore in 1908. His father was a dining-car waiter and club steward. His mother had been a teacher. During the 1930s Marshall and Houston focused on bringing greater parity between

▶▶ **Recommended Readings**

Harvard Sitkoff. *A New Deal for Blacks: The Emergence of Civil Rights as a National Issue, Vol. I: Depression Decade.* New York: Oxford University Press, 1978. An important work that covers the New Deal era and presents it as a period when the groundwork for the civil rights movement was laid.

Patricia Sullivan. *Days of Hope: Race and Democracy in the New Deal Era.* Chapel Hill, NC: University of North Carolina Press, 1996. An invaluable study showing how the ideas of civil rights and democracy were forged in the New Deal South.

▶▶ **Teaching Notes**

NAACP studies on per capita expenditures for white and black students showed that in Georgia, for example, the average annual per pupil expenditure for white students was $36.29, compared with $4.59 for black students. White teachers' salaries averaged $97.88 per month, while black teachers received only $49.41.

In 1935, attorneys Thurgood Marshall and Charles Hamilton Houston handled Donald Murray's suit against the University of Maryland Law School. In 1938 Murray became the first African American to graduate from a southern state school. Thus began the attack against segregated education in America.

black and white teachers. They hoped this would increase NAACP membership among teachers, their students, and parents.

The two men worked with a remarkable network of African-American attorneys. They attempted to end discrimination against black men and women in professional and graduate schools. Inequalities were obvious here because many southern states offered no graduate facilities of any kind to black students.

Graduate Education

Like other campaigns, the focus on graduate education was intended to establish precedents that might be used to gain equality in other areas. The first significant accomplishment in the NAACP's legal campaign against segregation in graduate and professional education was the U.S. Supreme Court's 1938 decision in *Gaines v. Canada*. The Supreme Court ordered the state of Missouri to provide black citizens an opportunity to study law in a state-supported institution. Failure to do so, the Court held, would violate the equal protection of the law clause of the Fourteenth Amendment to the U.S. Constitution. Lloyd Gaines, the prospective student for whom the case was brought, disappeared before the final resolution of this challenge. But, Missouri hastily established a law school for African Americans at the historically black Lincoln University. In the 1940s several southern states, including North Carolina, Texas, Oklahoma, and South Carolina, followed Missouri's lead and established law schools for their black citizens.

"Separate But Equal"

Thurgood Marshall and the NAACP were encouraged by the *Gaines* decision to persist in challenging the constitutionality of the **separate but equal doctrine**. The case of *Sipuel v. Board of Regents of the University of Oklahoma* (1947) was another such effort. In this case Ada Lois Sipuel sought admission to the law school of the University of Oklahoma at Norman. In accordance with state **statutes** she was refused admission but granted an out-of-state tuition award. Thurgood Marshall argued that this arrangement failed to meet the needs of the state's black citizens. The Supreme Court declared that Oklahoma was obliged under the equal protection clause of the Fourteenth Amendment to provide a legal education for Sipuel. The case established the principle that the state had to provide a separate law school for African-American students in their home states.

Heman Sweatt, a black mail carrier, tested this principle in a suit against the University of Texas Law School. In *Sweatt v. Painter* (1950), the U.S. Supreme Court again sided with the NAACP lawyers. In response to Sweatt's initial challenge, Texas had created a separate law school that had inadequate library facilities, faculty, and support staff. It was separate but hardly equal. Marshall and local Texas black lawyers argued that the legal education offered Sweatt at the black law school

was so inferior it violated the equal protection clause of the Fourteenth Amendment. Marshall declared,

> "whether the University of Texas Law School is compared with the original or new law school for Negroes, we cannot find substantial equality in the educational opportunities offered white and Negro law students by the state. In terms of number of the faculty, variety of courses and opportunity for specialization, size of the student body, scope of the library, availability of law review and similar activities, the University of Texas Law School is superior."

The victories registered in these early cases laid the legal foundation for the 1954 *Brown v. Topeka Board of Education* decision.

Disfranchisement

The fight against political disfranchisement also helped mobilize local and state communities and branches. Nowhere was this more apparent than in Texas. In 1923 the Texas legislature enacted the **Terrell law**, which expressly declared, "In no event shall a Negro be eligible to participate in a Democratic primary election . . . in . . . Texas." In the one-party South, the primary elections were more important than the general elections, which often merely rubber-stamped the choice made in the primary. Thus to be denied the right to vote in Democratic Party primary elections was to be disfranchised. The NAACP developed a case to test the constitutionality of the Terrell law and commenced a twenty-year battle through the courts. The Texas branches of the NAACP raised money and coordinated local involvement in the campaign to overthrow the Democratic white primary that disfranchised so many black Texans.

The Texas white primary fight was the most sustained and intense effort that any NAACP chapter undertook at that time. It began in the 1920s and won its first victory when the Supreme Court ruled in 1927 in *Nixon v. Herndon* that the Texas Democratic primary was unconstitutional (see Chapter 17). At the national headquarters, Charles H. Houston and Thurgood Marshall orchestrated the assault. Their efforts were rewarded in subsequent decisions that further chipped away at the legal basis for the white primary. Finally, in 1944 the U.S. Supreme Court issued a ruling in *Smith v. Allwright* that ended the white primary altogether. It was the NAACP's greatest legal victory to that time. Many more would soon follow.

Black Women and Community Organizing

Black women made exceptional contributions to the NAACP during the 1930s through their successful fund-raising and membership drives. Three agitators for racial justice were Daisy Adams Lampkin (c. 1884–1965), Juanita Mitchell (1913–1992), and Ella Baker (1903–1986). These women worked closely with White and the NAACP throughout the Depression and World War II.

Daisy Lampkin

In 1915 Lampkin, a native of Washington, D.C., became the president of the **Negro Women's Franchise League**, a group dedicated to fighting for the vote. During World War I she directed Liberty Bond sales in the black community of Pennsylvania's Allegheny County and in Pittsburgh, selling some $2 million worth of government securities. In 1930 Walter White enlisted her as regional field secretary of the NAACP. She was made national field secretary in 1935. She continued raising funds for the NAACP and played leading roles within organized black womanhood.

Juanita E. Jackson

Juanita E. Jackson was born in Hot Springs, Arkansas, and raised in Baltimore, Maryland. She earned a degree in education from the University of Pennsylvania in 1931. She returned to Baltimore, and helped found the City-Wide Young People's Forum. This organization encouraged young people to discuss and plan attacks on such issues as unemployment, segregation, and lynching. The success of the group, which she headed from 1931 to 1934, attracted Walter White's attention. He offered her the leadership of the NAACP's new youth program. From 1935 to 1938 she served as NAACP national youth director. In 1950 she received a law degree from the University of Maryland. She was the first black woman admitted to practice law in Maryland. She embarked on a series of cases that helped destroy racial segregation on the state's public beaches and in its public schools.

The NAACP in the 1930s and 1940s depended on the formidable fund-raising talents of black women like Daisy Lampkin (shown here in a black Baptist church), Ella Baker, and Juanita Mitchell. These women played a major role in building NAACP membership.

Ella Baker

Ella Baker became one of the most important women in the civil rights movement of the 1950s and 1960s. She began her life's work during the Depression. Born in Norfolk, Virginia, Baker moved to New York City in 1927 and worked as a waitress and as an organizer involved in radical politics. She was also on the staff of two local newspapers, *The American West Indian News* and the *Negro National News*. Within two years after her arrival she had cofounded with George Schuyler the Young Negroes' Cooperative League in Harlem. The group practiced collective decision making and attempted to involve all segments of the community in the cooperatives. As she worked with the young men and women, Baker developed a strong belief in grassroots mobilization. She worked with women's and labor groups. She served as publicity director of the Sponsoring Committee of the National Negro Congress

and worked with the WPA. Walter White was impressed with her relentless organizing and management skills.

After much persuasion Baker accepted, in 1941, White's offer to become an assistant field secretary of the NAACP. This position enabled her to travel across the country and throughout the South, making friendships that would serve her well in the coming decades. From 1943 to 1946 Baker worked as director of NAACP branches and measurably enhanced the membership of the organization. After resigning from the NAACP she joined the staff of the New York Urban League.

Housewives' Leagues

Other black women organized outside the NAACP. Black women in Detroit provide a good example of this kind of activity. On June 10, 1930, fifty black women responded to a call issued by Fannie B. Peck, wife of Reverend William H. Peck, pastor of the two-thousand-member Bethel African Methodist Episcopal Church and the president of the Booker T. Washington Trade Association. Out of this initial meeting emerged the Detroit Housewives' League, an organization that combined economic nationalism and black women's self-determination to help black families and businesses survive the Depression. Peck had been inspired by M. A. L. Holsey, secretary of the National Negro Business League. Holsey described the directed spending campaigns that enabled housewives in Harlem to consolidate their economic power to persuade businesses to hire black women and children. Peck became convinced that such an organization would be equally as successful in Detroit. An admirer recalled that Peck effectively "focused the attention of women on the most essential, yet most unfamiliar factor in the building of homes, communities, and nations, namely, 'The Spending Power of Women.'"

The Detroit organization grew rapidly. By 1934 ten thousand black women belonged to it. According to Peck, the black woman had finally realized "that she has been traveling through a blind alley, making sacrifices to educate her children with no thought as to their obtaining employment after leaving school." The only requirement for membership was a pledge to support black businesses, buy black products, and patronize black professionals, thereby keeping money in the community. The league quickly spread to other cities. Housewives' leagues in Chicago, Baltimore, Washington, Durham (North Carolina), Harlem, and Cleveland used boycotts of merchants who refused to sell black products and employ black children as clerks or stock persons to secure an estimated 75,000 new jobs for black people.

 **Reading Check** What role did African-American women play in the NAACP in the 1930s?

▶ **Reading Check**

Black women made exceptional contributions to the NAACP in the 1930s. Fund-raising and membership drives and helping youth and black families with employment, legal challenges to segregation, among other activities, led by women such as Daisy Lampkin, Ella Baker, and Juanita Mitchell, helped advance the organization's cause.

▶ **Guide to Reading/Key Terms**

For answers, see the *Teacher's Resource Manual.*

Section 3

The New Deal

African Americans and the New Deal

In 1932, the third year of the Great Depression, voters elected New York governor Franklin Delano Roosevelt to the presidency with a total of nearly 23 million votes. Roosevelt's lopsided victory over Hoover demonstrated the country's loss of faith in the Republican Party and its economic philosophy. The new president appealed to the Democratic Party's base of support in the white South, but to this group he added a coalition of western farmers, industrial workers, urban voters from the white ethnic groups in northern cities, and reform-minded intellectuals. For the time being, however, black Americans still clung to the Republican banner. In Chicago, for example, less than 25 percent of black voters cast their ballots for Roosevelt. But this was the last election in which the party of Lincoln could take them for granted. In his first term Roosevelt inaugurated a multitude of programs to counter the Depression—collectively known as **the New Deal**—which would shift the allegiance of African Americans. Initially his programs continued past patterns of discrimination against African Americans. But by 1935 the New Deal was providing more equal benefits and prompting profound social changes. The result was a new political order that ultimately undermined key portions of the edifice of American racism.

Roosevelt and the First New Deal, 1933–1935

During his first one hundred days in office, Franklin Roosevelt pressed through Congress bold new economic initiatives that came to be known as **the first New Deal**. To combat the Depression, Roosevelt, unlike Hoover, followed no predetermined plan. Instead he favored experimentation over ideology as the guide to federal action. With little resistance Congress passed the president's sprawling and complex laws aimed at overhauling the nation's financial, agricultural, and industrial systems. Most hoped, vainly as it turned out, that these changes would eventually bring a return to prosperity. In the meantime Roosevelt moved forcefully to counter the immediate suffering of the unemployed

with a massive emergency federal relief effort. Many of the first New Deal's programs benefited both white and black people. The strength of white Southerners in the Democratic Party and the nearly complete lack of African-American political power in the South caused much of this early program to be unfairly administered.

The **Agricultural Adjustment Act (AAA)** was designed to protect farmers by giving them subsidies to limit production and thereby stabilize prices. It illustrates the key benefits and problems African Americans experienced during the first New Deal. The theory underlying the AAA was that creating scarcity would increase agricultural prices. So farmers would be paid to grow less. The program provided for sharecroppers and tenant farmers to get part of the subsidies and allowed new rural relief agencies to dispense supplementary income to off-season wageworkers.

This program helped many African Americans. It pumped billions of dollars into an economic sector on which over 4.5 million black people relied for their livelihood. The flow of money from the AAA did, for a time, slow the exodus of black people from farming. During the 1930s only 4.5 percent of African Americans abandoned farming, compared with 8.6 percent who did so during the 1920s.

But the AAA was often administered unfairly and corruptly. Local control of the AAA resided in the hands of the Extension Service and County Agricultural Conservation Committees, which were supposed to represent all farmers. The county agents, however, were often the planters themselves. The committees mirrored southern politics by excluding black people. During the first two years of the AAA, black farmers complained bitterly that white landlords simply grabbed and pocketed the millions of dollars of benefit checks they were supposed to forward to tenants. To compound the injury, some planters then evicted the sharecroppers and tenants from the land.

The experience of African Americans with the **National Industrial Recovery Act (NIRA)** was similar to the problems with the AAA. The NIRA was intended to promote the revival of manufacturing. The act allowed various industries to cooperate in establishing codes of conduct governing prices, wage levels, and employment practices. These were to be overseen by a **National Recovery Administration (NRA)**. The NRA oversaw the drafting of the codes but faced tremendous resistance from employers and unions in eliminating racial disparities in wage rates and working conditions. Even when African-American advocates did win wage increases for occupations in which black people predominated, the result was often a shift to white labor. To the relief of many African-American advocates and workers, the U.S. Supreme Court declared the NIRA unconstitutional in spring 1935.

The New Deal's national welfare programs included the Federal Emergency Relief Administration (FERA), the Civilian Conservation Corps (CCC), Public Works Administration (PWA), and Civil Works Administration (CWA). Although inadequate and unfairly administered

▶ Document

18-4 *Luther C. Wandall, A Negro in the CCC, 1935*
A favorite of many, and the brainchild of FDR, the Civilian Conservation Corp was created to employ young men from urban areas. By 1945, when the CCC was abolished, more than 200,000 black youths had participated in the program. The CCC was tightly segregated, with separate camps for black and white workers.

18-5 *E. E. Lewis, Black Cotton Farmers and the AAA, 1935*

▶ Teaching Notes

The AAA was designed to remedy the problems of those farmers disproportionately African American—who were over-reliant on such cash crops as cotton. By 1929 three out of four black farmers, compared with two out of five white farmers, received at least 40 percent of their gross income from cotton.

All these relief programs included substantial numbers of African Americans and helped many through the worst parts of the Depression. But the programs also tended to be less helpful to black people than they were to whites. In its early days, the CCC, for example, was a tightly segregated institution, with only about 5 percent of its slots going to black youths during its first year. Likewise, although FERA tended to be administered fairly in northern cities, in the South it reached few of those in need.

Black Officials in the New Deal

The first New Deal was not completely bleak for African Americans. In addition to the benefits that they derived from New Deal relief programs, African Americans also gained new influence and allies within the Roosevelt administration. Their experience reflected both the growing availability of highly trained African Americans for government service and the emerging consciousness among white liberals about the problems—and potential electoral power—of black people.

Black people found a staunch ally in First Lady Eleanor Roosevelt. She was revered for her relentless commitment to racial justice. She arranged meetings at the White House for some black leaders. She cajoled her husband to consider legislation on behalf of black rights. She personally defied Jim Crow laws by refusing to sit in a "white only" section while attending a meeting in the South. Moreover, she wrote newspaper columns calling for "fair play and equal opportunity for Negro citizens." Roosevelt further

African Americans greatly revered First Lady Eleanor Roosevelt (1884–1962). Mrs. Roosevelt consistently used her influence to fight against racial discrimination and segregation.

endeared herself to black Americans when she resigned her membership in the Daughters of the American Revolution after that organization refused to allow a young black opera singer, Marian Anderson, to perform at its Constitution Hall in Washington in 1939.

Eleanor Roosevelt was joined by other liberals to press the cause of racial justice and to seek the appointment of African Americans throughout the government. Early in 1933 President Roosevelt gave in to their request that he appoint someone in his administration to assume responsibility for ensuring that African Americans received fair treatment. He asked Harold Ickes, a former president of the Chicago chapter of the NAACP, and a white man whom most black Americans recognized as a tried and true friend, to make this happen. Ickes invited Clark Foreman, a young white Georgian who had rejected his region's racism, to handle the assignment. Foreman recognized the irony of a white man representing black people in the government and immediately began to recruit highly trained African Americans.

Similar efforts to bring African Americans into government positions were made by Eleanor Roosevelt, Ickes, and other administration officials such as Daniel Roper, secretary of commerce, and Harry Hopkins, FDR's relief administrator. The result was that doors to the government began opening in an unprecedented way. For the first time, the government employed professional black architects, lawyers, engineers, economists, statisticians, interviewers, office managers, social workers, and librarians. The Department of Commerce hired Eugene K. Jones, on leave from the National Urban League. The National Youth Administration brought in Mary McLeod Bethune, and the Department of Interior employed William H. Hastie and Robert Weaver. Ira De A. Reid joined the Social Security Administration, and Lawrence W. Oxley worked for the Department of Labor, with Ambrose Caliver serving in the Office of Education.

▶▶ **Teaching Notes**

Bethune played a powerful role in Roosevelt's black cabinet, but this was only one of the many forums in which she exercised consummate leadership and diplomatic skill. Bethune's life and work are major links connecting the social reform efforts of post-Reconstruction black women to the civil rights protest activities of the generation emerging after World War II. All the various strands of black women's struggle for education, political rights, racial pride, and sexual autonomy are united in Bethune's writings, speeches, and organizational work.

▶▶ **Retracing the Odyssey**

Bethune Museum and Archives Washington, D.C. Mary McLeod Bethune, born in 1875 in Mayesville, South Carolina was one of the most politically engaged black women in the first half of the twentieth century. The Bethune Museum and Archive Center was her home and headquarters of the NCNW from 1943 to 1966. It contains exhibits and sponsors programs that emphasize the contributions of African-American women to American society. The Archive contains important manuscript collections and other research materials pertaining to the NCNW and to black women's history.

Roosevelt's "Black Cabinet." Mary McLeod Bethune is in the center of the front row. The advisers included Robert Weaver, Eugene Kinckle Jones, Ambrose Caliver, and William H. Hastie, among many others.

A core of highly placed African Americans became linked in a network called the Federal Council on Negro Affairs, more loosely known as Roosevelt's **Black Cabinet**. Mary McLeod Bethune was the undisputed leader of this body, which consisted primarily of "New Deal race specialists." It numbered twenty-seven men and three women working mostly in temporary emergency agencies such as the Works Progress Administration (WPA) and included such stalwarts as housing administrator Robert Weaver. This group of advisers pres-

PROFILE ❖ Mary McLeod Bethune

Mary McLeod Bethune was born on July 10, 1875, near Mayesville, South Carolina. She graduated from Scotia Seminary in 1894 and entered Dwight Moody's Institute for Home and Foreign Missions in Chicago. After teaching in mission schools, she founded the Daytona Educational and Industrial Institute for Training Negro Girls. Eventually, she agreed to merge with Cookman Institute, an educational facility for black boys under the auspices of the Methodist Church. In 1923 the now coeducational institution was renamed Bethune-Cookman College.

During the 1920s Bethune became the leader of the National Association of Colored Women, a federation of women's clubs. As the NACW's president she attempted to turn the organization away from its previous focus on self-help and moral uplift and toward broader goals. Although she made progress, by 1935 she had become frustrated by the NACW's caution. She founded the National Council of Negro Women (NCNW). The women present at the creation of the NCNW were the who's who of black women's activism. They included Charlotte Hawkins Brown, Mary Church Terrell, Colored Graduate Nurses Mabel K. Staupers, Daisy Lampkin, and Addie W. Hunton. Eventually, the NCNW included twenty national affiliates and ninety local councils across the country. Club engagement provided safe space for them to develop the skills and networks that proved critical in the post-World War II civil rights movement.

With the New Deal Bethune became a Democratic Party activist and a government official. She and Eleanor Roosevelt persuaded the president that the National Youth Administration (NYA) needed a Negro division to assure that benefits would be distributed fairly. When the organization started, Bethune was named the NYA's director of Negro affairs. She was the first African-American woman to hold a high position in the government. Bethune supported the administration during the 1936 campaign by helping convince African Americans that their best interests lay with the Democratic rather than Republican Party.

One of Bethune's many noteworthy accomplishments was the 1937 conference held by the Department of Labor on the Problems of the Negro and Negro Youth, at which Eleanor Roosevelt delivered a key speech. During the session entitled "Security of Life and Equal Protection under the Law," the conference called for a federal antilynching law, equal access to the ballot in federal elections, and elimination of segregation and discrimination on interstate carriers. This was a virtual blueprint of the agenda of the civil rights movement.

Bethune

The Works Progress Administration offered African Americans numerous opportunities for vocational training from experienced craftsmen.

sured the president and the heads of federal agencies to adopt and support color-blind policies and lobbied to advance the status of black Americans.

Black Social Scientists and the New Deal

Many black intellectuals, scholars, and writers believed the social sciences could be used to adjudicate race relations in the country during the New Deal they found greater receptiveness to their work than ever before. Nearly two hundred African Americans received Ph.D.s during the 1930s, more than four times the combined total from the first three decades of the century. Several of these young scholars reached the top ranks of the social sciences studying the economic, political, and sociological problems of black people with a depth of experience and theoretical sophistication lacking in earlier generations of scholars. In sociology E. Franklin Frazier and Charles S. Johnson took the lead. Frazier's pioneering studies of black families, although now dated, placed him at the forefront of debates on social policy. As the editor of *Opportunity*, the journal of the Urban League, throughout the 1930s, Johnson published insightful critiques of American racial practices and policies, as well as the work of emerging black novelists, poets, and

playwrights. Meanwhile Ralph Bunche became well known within the field of political science, and Abram Harris and Robert Weaver gained renown in economics.

Historians such as Carter G. Woodson, Lorenzo Greene, Benjamin Quarles, and John Hope Franklin advanced the idea that black people had been active agents in the past and not simply the passive objects of white people's actions. Through the Association for the Study of Negro Life and History as well as Negro History Week, Woodson and his coworkers Greene, Alrutheus Taylor, and Monroe Work used their scholarship to dismiss claims of black inferiority. Their scholarly emphasis on racial pride, achievement, and autonomy helped raise black morale.

The increasing importance of black scholars became apparent late in the 1930s. The Carnegie Corporation, a philanthropic foundation sponsored a major study of black life. The study was led by Gunnar Myrdal, a Swedish social scientist. Nearly half the large staff of scholars were African Americans, and several, particularly Bunche, had a major impact on the work. Published in 1944 as *An American Dilemma,* this massive study profoundly affected public understanding of how racism undermined the progress of African Americans. It helped set the agenda for the civil rights movement.

African Americans and the Second New Deal

By late 1935, after two years marked by a slow recovery, much of the first New Deal lay in shambles. The U.S. Supreme Court had invalidated major parts of it, and a conservative backlash was emerging against the Roosevelt administration. In response Roosevelt pressed for a second round of legislation marked by the passage of the Social Security Act (SSA), the National Labor Relations Act (NLRA), the creation of the Works Progress Administration (WPA), and other measures considerably more radical than those that had come in 1933. The NLRA, for example, helped unions get established and grow. The SSA provided the basics of a social welfare system as well as unemployment and retirement insurance. This new set of laws, known as the **second New Deal**, survived legal challenges and changed the United States, particularly by strengthening the role of the federal government.

The Changing Democratic Party

Roosevelt's leftward political shift helped him win the 1936 presidential election in a landslide. This election cemented a new electoral coalition. The southern wing of the Democratic Party included more liberal farmers and working-class voters who were labor union members in the

▶ **Document**

18-2 *National Labor Relations Act, 1935*
The National Labor Relations Act guaranteed the right of workers to collective bargaining. It established the National Labor Relations Board to oversee elections in which workers could choose whether they wanted union representation and, if so, which specific bargaining unit they preferred. One of the most popular New Deal measures, the Act contributed substantially to the Democratic landslide of 1936 and to the successful organizing drives of the Committee for Industrial Organization (CIO).

North and West. The Democratic Party began to win the votes of the large African-American populations in the great cities of the North. The great migration had effectively relocated tens of thousands of prospective black voters in northern urban centers, traditional strongholds of Democratic Party machines, such as in Chicago. Institutionalized housing segregation combined with the often conscious choice to live in their own neighborhoods concentrated the black electorate and increased its political power. This power had already appeared in the 1928 election of Republican Oscar De Priest to the U.S. House of Representatives, the first African-American congressman from the North. In 1934, reflecting a shift in partisan allegiance, Chicago's black voters elected Democrat Arthur W. Mitchell to Congress to replace De Priest. Mitchell, a registered Republican at the outset of the Great Depression, switched to the Democratic Party. He became the first black Democrat ever to win a seat in the House of Representatives.

Mitchell's election was only the beginning of the change in black people's political party identification. The powerful black press fanned the shifting winds. Many more black urban dwellers developed an intense interest in politics. They began to connect political power with the prospect of improving their economic conditions. By the end of the decade, black urban voters gained noteworthy influence in key states such as Illinois, Ohio, Pennsylvania, and New York. This political consciousness led to the election of black state legislators in California, Illinois, Indiana, Kansas, Kentucky, New Jersey, New York, Ohio, Pennsylvania, and West Virginia.

In another indication of change, some Democrats began supporting antilynching legislation. Congressman Mitchell gave a strong speech printed in the *Congressional Record* in 1935 supporting President Roosevelt as an antilynching advocate. "No President," he declared, "has been more outspoken against the horrible crime of lynching than has Mr. Roosevelt. In speaking of lynching some time ago he characterized it as 'collective murder' and spoke of it as a crime which blackens the record of America." Mitchell told black audiences, "Let me say again, the attitude of the administration at the White House is absolutely fair and without prejudice, insofar as the Negro citizenry is concerned."

There are many complex reasons for the revolutionary transformation in black political allegiance. The shift to the Democratic Party did not occur without anxiety. Some black people feared that by joining the party they would open the door for even more white southern Democrats to assume national political power and thwart black advancement. But by 1936 most African-American voters were willing to take the risk.

The increased participation of African Americans in the Democratic Party sent chills down the spines of the white southern elite. The tension between black Democrats and white conservative Democrats erupted at the party's 1936 convention in Philadelphia. The seating of thirty-two

black Democratic Party delegates provoked the wrath of southern politicians. The selection of a black Baptist minister to open one session with a prayer especially outraged South Carolina senator Ellison D. "Cotton Ed" Smith. Accompanied by Mayor Burnet Maybank of Charleston, South Carolina, and one or two other delegates, he marched off the floor proclaiming that they refused to support "any political organization that looks upon the Negro and caters to him as a political and social equal." Undaunted, the black minister simply observed that "Brother Smith needs more prayer."

The South Carolina delegation subsequently adopted a protest resolution denouncing the appearance of black men on the convention's program. The protests of southern white politicians, however, had no effect on the political decisions of black men and women. Heeding the advice of the NAACP, they voted their personal interests.

 Reading Check Why did African Americans shift their political allegiance to the Democratic party?

The Works Progress Administration

Despite the rise of black people in the Democratic Party, southern congressmen succeeded in excluding many African Americans from key government programs. For example, they insisted on denying the benefits of the National Labor Relations Act and Social Security Act to agricultural laborers and domestic servants. These white Southerners could not, however, stop the tilt toward fairer administration of programs or the revival of the push for equal rights, which had lain all but dormant since the end of the Reconstruction era.

An examination of the **Works Progress Administration (WPA)** illustrates the changes brought about by the second New Deal and the increasing shift of African Americans to the Democratic Party. The WPA, with Harry Hopkins (1890–1946) as its head, was created to employ the unemployed. Under Hopkins's direction, and sustained with $1.39 billion in federal funds, the WPA put thousands of men and women to work building new roads, hospitals, city halls, courthouses, and schools. Under the WPA, American citizens built bridges, ports, and local water-supply systems. Larger scale projects included the Lincoln Tunnel under the Hudson River connecting New York and New Jersey, the Triborough Bridge system linking Manhattan to Long Island, and the Bonneville and Boulder Dams. (Boulder Dam was later renamed the Hoover Dam by a Republican-controlled Congress in 1946.)

The WPA was administered far more fairly than were the first New Deal programs. The national government explicitly rejected racial discrimination and worked to make sure local officials complied. Although far from perfect, by 1939 it provided assistance to one million black families on a far more equitable basis than ever before.

▶ **Reading Check**

As Roosevelt shifted leftward, he gained the support of large numbers of African American voters. Moreover, some Democrats began to support anti-lynching legislation. The movement of African Americans toward the Democratic Party created tensions within the party.

The same pattern prevailed in the WPA's four arts programs—the Federal Art Project, the Federal Music Project, the Federal Theater Project, and the Federal Writers Project. These programs employed thousands of musicians, intellectuals, writers, and artists. A fifth program, the Historical Records Survey, created in 1937, sent teams of writers, including Zora Neale Hurston, to collect folklore and study various ethnic groups. One team collected the life histories and reminiscences of some two thousand former slaves.

Between 1935 and 1943, the WPA helped artists display their talents and made their work widely available. Among the black artists hired to adorn government buildings, post offices, and public parks were Aaron Douglas, Charles Alston, Richmond Barthe, Sargent Johnson, Archibald Motley Jr., and Augusta Savage. Savage was a sculptor who worked in clay, marble, and bronze. She became the first director of the Harlem Community Art Center in 1937. Her students included Jacob Lawrence, William Artis, Norman Lewis, and Elton Fax.

The **Federal Theater Project** established sixteen black theater units. Among their most notable productions was a version of *Macbeth* set in Haiti with an all-black cast. White actor John Houseman and black actress Rose McClendon directed the Harlem Federal Theater Project. This project—more than the others—proved controversial due to the fear of communist influence and the leftist political views of some African-American writers and performers.

Organized Labor and Black America

The relationship of African Americans to labor unions changed profoundly during the 1930s. The New Deal, especially after 1935, did much to transform the labor movement. The National Labor Relations Act and the militancy of workers provided the opportunity to organize the nation's great mass production industries. Still, leaders of the AFL dragged their feet, unwilling to incorporate into their unions the masses of unskilled workers, many of whom were African American or recent European immigrants. Frustrated by this situation, in 1935 John L. Lewis (1880–1969), head of the United Mine Workers, and his followers formed the **Committee for Industrial Organization** (CIO) to take on the task.

Unlike the AFL, the CIO was committed to interracial and multiethnic organizing and so enabled more African Americans to participate in the labor movement. Its leaders knew it was in organized labor's best interest to admit black men and women to membership. As one black union organizer said, "We colored folks can't organize without you and you white folks can't organize without us." But it took a massive change in outlook to achieve this unity. By 1940 the CIO had enlisted approximately 210,000 black members.

▶▶ **Document**

18-1 *Lester B. Granger, Negro Workers and Recovery, 1934*
Until the 1930s, most labor unions connected to the AF of L barred black workers. Not until John L. Lewis organized the Committee for Industrial Organization (CIO) in 1935 did African Americans and recent European immigrants find a voice in support of their participation in the labor movement. In five years, black membership swelled to more than 200,000. This article describes the obstacles black workers in St. Louis faced and the gains they made.

▶▶ **Teaching Notes**

Unions that valued and sustained interracial cooperation included the International Mine, Mill and Smelter Workers; the Food, Tobacco, and Agricultural Workers Union, and the United Farm Equipment and Metal Workers.

Photographer Lewis Hines captured the tedious work as these women roll tobacco leaves in a cigar factory.

A. Philip Randolph's Brotherhood of Sleeping Car Porters (BSCP) remained with the AFL, but it also benefited from New Deal legislation. In 1934 Congress had amended the **Railway Labor Act** in a way that helped the BSCP overcome the opposition of the Pullman Company. The law required that corporations bargain in good faith with unions if the unions could demonstrate through elections monitored by the National Mediation Board that they genuinely represented the corporations' employees. The Pullman Company resisted, but in 1937, long after an election certified the BSCP as the workers' representative, the company finally recognized the brotherhood. Then—and only then—did the AFL grant the BSCP full membership as an international union. After more than twelve years, A. Philip Randolph and thousands of black men won their struggles against a giant corporation and a powerful labor organization. These were no small victories.

Although most black people in unions were men, some unions also represented and helped improve the lives of black working women. For example, there had been a rigid hierarchy among workers in the tobacco industry since the early nineteenth century. It was one of the few areas of the economy outside agriculture or domestic service that employed many black women. Jobs were assigned on the basis of race and gender, with black women receiving the most difficult and tedious job, that of "stemmer." In 1939 stemmer Louise "Mama" Harris instigated a series of walkouts at the I. N. Vaughn Company in Richmond. The strikes were supported by CIO affiliates, including the white women of the International Ladies Garment Workers Union. They led to the formation of the Tobacco Workers Organizing Committee, another CIO affiliate. In 1943 black women union leaders and activists, including Theodosia Simpson and Miranda Smith, were involved in a strike against the R. J. Reynolds tobacco company to force it to the negotiating table. Smith later became southern regional director of the Food, Tobacco, Agricultural, and Allied Workers of America. It was the highest position held by a black woman in the labor movement up to that time.

▶ **Reading Check**

New Deal programs helped large numbers of African Americans, but whites tended to receive disproportionate benefits. African Americans gained influence and allies in the Roosevelt administration. Black scientists and scholars found greater receptiveness to their work than had previously been the case. The New Deal did much to help African Americans gain a new place in the national labor movement.

 Reading Check   How did the New Deal affect African Americans?

Section 4

The Communist Party and African Americans

GUIDE TO READING

▶ What was the Scottsboro case and what were its consequences?

▶ What role did the Communist Party and organized labor play in radicalizing black Americans during the 1930s?

KEY TERMS

▶ International Labor Defense (ILD), p. 658

▶ National Negro Congress (NNC), p. 661

Throughout the 1930s the Communist Party intensified its support of African Americans' efforts to address unemployment and job discrimination and to seek social justice. Some African Americans were attracted to the party because of its militant antiracism and its determination to be interracial. The party expelled members who exhibited racial prejudice and gave black men key leadership positions. James Ford, an African American, ran as the party's vice-presidential candidate in the election of 1932. Although few black men and women actually joined the Communist Party, some became increasingly sympathetic to left-wing ideas and prescriptions as the Depression wore on.

Many black workers were drawn to the Communist Party because it criticized the refusal of organized white labor to include them. The communists maintained that "the low standard of living of Negro workers is made use of by the capitalists to reduce the wages of the white workers." They chided "the mis-leaders of labor, the heads of the reformist and reactionary trade union organizations" for refusing to organize black workers. They insisted "this anti-Negro attitude of the reactionary labor leaders helps to split the ranks of labor, allows the employers to carry out their policy of 'divide and rule,' frustrates the efforts of the working class to emancipate itself from the yoke of capitalism, and dims the class-consciousness of the white workers as well as of the Negro workers." Indeed, much of the push for racial equality within the CIO emanated from those connected with the party.

The International Labor Defense and the "Scottsboro Boys"

The Scottsboro case brought the Communist Party to the attention of many African Americans. The case began when nine black youths who had caught a ride on a freight train in Alabama were tried, convicted, and sentenced to death for allegedly raping two white women. Their ordeal began on the night of March 25, 1931, when they were accosted by a group of young white hobos. A fight broke out. The black youths threw the white youths off the train. The losers filed a complaint with the Scottsboro, Alabama, sheriff, charging that black hoodlums had

▶▶ Guide to Reading/Key Terms

For answers, see the *Teacher's Resource Manual.*

▶▶ Recommended Reading

Robin D. G. Kelley. *Hammer and Hoe: Alabama Communists during the Great Depression.* Chapel Hill, NC: University of North Carolina Press, 1990. A splendid study of the radicalizing activism of working people in the steel industry and on the farm during the thirties. Kelley does an excellent job of showing why the Communists appealed to black workers.

viciously assaulted them. The sheriff ordered his deputies to round up every black person on the train. The sweep netted the nine young black men: Ozie Powell, Clarence Norris, Charlie Weems, Olen Montgomery, Willie Robertson, Haywood Patterson, Eugene Williams, Andy Wright, and Roy Wright. The police also discovered two young white women: nineteen-year-old Victoria Price and seventeen-year-old Ruby Bates.

Afraid of being arrested, and perhaps ashamed of being hobos, Price and Bates falsely claimed that the nine black youths had sexually assaulted them. On the basis of that accusation, the "Scottsboro Boys" (ranging in ages from thirteen to twenty) were given a hasty trial. Three days after the trial started, and fifteen days after their arrest, the jurors found all of them guilty. Eight received the death sentence, and the youngest, a thirteen-year-old, was sentenced to life imprisonment, even though medical examinations of Price and Bates proved that neither had been raped.

While other organizations either dawdled or refused to intervene, the Communist Party's **International Labor Defense (ILD)** rushed to the aid of the "boys" by appealing the conviction and death sentence to the U.S. Supreme Court. The case produced two important decisions that reaffirmed black people's right to the basic protections that all other American citizens enjoyed. In *Powell v. Alabama* (1932), the Court ruled that the nine Scottsboro defendants had not been given adequate legal counsel and the trial had taken place in a hostile and volatile

The "Scottsboro Boys," a case of southern justice gone awry, attracted international attention and fueled competition between the NAACP and the Communist Party. In this 1937 photograph the NAACP's Juanita E. Jackson Mitchell visits with the Scottsboro Boys. Nine unemployed black young men accused of raping two white women mill workers on a Southern Railroad freight car on March 25, 1931, were sentenced to death, with one exception. Eugene Williams's life was spared because he was only thirteen. Victoria Price and Ruby Bates recanted their stories, but it made no difference. The United States Supreme Court overturned the death convictions and sentences in two landmark cases, one of which established the right of the accused to competent legal counsel.

atmosphere. Asserting the youths' right to due process as set forth in the Fourteenth Amendment had been violated, the Court ordered a new trial. Alabama did as instructed, but the new trial resulted in another guilty verdict and sentences of death or life imprisonment. The ILD promptly appealed, and in *Norris v. Alabama* (1935) the Supreme Court decided that all Americans have the right to a trial by a jury of their peers. The systematic exclusion of African Americans from the Scottsboro juries, the Court held, denied the defendants equal protection under the law, which the Fourteenth Amendment guaranteed. Chief Justice Charles Evans Hughes pointed out that no black citizens had served on juries in the Alabama counties for decades, even though many were qualified to serve. The Court noted that the exclusion was blatant racial discrimination and called for yet another trial.

PROFILE ❖ Angelo Herndon

In the South, the Communist Party gravitated toward those areas where black and white laborers were grossly exploited. The party's efforts in Georgia, Alabama, and Mississippi produced black organizers such as Hosea Hudson, Nate Shaw, and Angelo Herndon, who by virtue of their activism became targets of white supremacists.

In 1932 a young organizer, Angelo Herndon, was arrested, tried, and convicted in Atlanta for inciting insurrection. One of thirteen children, Herndon was born May 6, 1913, in Ohio. Seeking better opportunities, Herndon at age thirteen escaped the poverty of his home region to work in the coal mines in Alabama. At eighteen he was already a seasoned worker but deeply disillusioned and angry at the exploitation of coal miners. He attended a meeting called by the Communist Party and was impressed by its commitment to equality, both racially and socially. He joined the party and poured enormous energy into organizing and recruiting members from among the mine workers and the unemployed.

The party sent Herndon to Atlanta, Georgia, where he organized an interracial relief group and staged peaceful demonstrations against hunger. This was to prove his undoing. One week later, while picking up his mail at the post office, he was arrested on the charge that he had violated an old ordinance forbidding black and white people from mingling together. Herndon's trial and conviction made him the best-known African-American communist in the nation. The case underscored the fear that white Southerners had concerning the specter of social equality across racial lines. The Communist Party assigned a young black attorney, Benjamin Davis Jr. of Atlanta, to represent Herndon. Davis challenged the constitutionality of the ordinance as well as Atlanta's jury system, which excluded African Americans from service. Davis's defense was unsuccessful, and the judge sentenced Herndon to twenty years on a chain gang. The severity of the sentence sparked a nationwide movement to free Herndon as black organizations, labor unions, and religious groups joined with the Communist Party to fight for Herndon's immediate release. After four years of appeals, in 1937 the U.S. Supreme Court, in a five-to-four decision, declared Georgia's slave insurrection law unconstitutional and ordered the state to let him go.

Herndon

659

Despite these stunning defeats and increasing evidence that the "boys" had been falsely convicted, Alabama still pursued the case. Even when Ruby Bates publicly admitted the rape charge had been a hoax, white Alabamians ignored her. Finally, in 1937 Alabama dropped its charges against five of the nine men, and in the 1940s the state released those still in jail. Altogether, nine innocent black men had collectively served some three-quarters of a century in prison. Clarence Willie Norris, however, escaped and fled to Michigan, returning decades later to receive a ceremonious pardon from Governor George Wallace. When a reporter asked Norris how he felt, he declared, "I'm just glad to be free." The experience had taught him "to stand up for your rights, even if it kills you. That's all life consists of."

Debating Communist Leadership

Throughout the Scottsboro case, the NAACP tried unsuccessfully to wrest control from the Communist Party. Indeed, as the case evolved, tensions and competition between the Communist Party and the NAACP for leadership of black America flared into open hostility. At first, the NAACP had hesitated to defend accused rapists, but it moved more decisively after the Communist Party had taken the lead.

The contest between the NAACP and the communists reveals the differences between the two groups. The party organized protest marches and demonstrations and used its press to denounce more cautious middle-class organizations. The NAACP countered with a carefully orchestrated campaign that questioned the sincerity and effectiveness of the communists and sought to repair its own reputation as a respectable and effective advocate for African Americans.

Black public opinion divided in its evaluation of the party. Some black men and women applauded the communists. Historian Carter G. Woodson praised the Communist Party in the *New York Age*:

> I have talked with any number of Negroes who call themselves Communists, and I have never heard one express a desire to destroy anyone or anything but oppression. . . . Negroes who are charged with being Communists advocate the stoppage of peonage, equality in employment of labor. . . . If this makes a man 'Red,' the world's greatest reformers belong to this class, and we shall have to condemn our greatest statesmen, some of whom have attained the presidency of the United States.

But other African Americans ridiculed the party. George Schuyler, a columnist for the Pittsburgh *Courier*, used his razor-sharp wit to castigate the party and persuade black people that its claim to champion African Americans was a lie. Schuyler objected to the communists' "campaign of vilification . . . against the NAACP":

> No Ku Kluxer ever denounced the latter organization more vigorously and unfairly. The Communists know they are lying when they assert time

and time again that the NAACP wants to see the boys convicted and is betraying the race. They have quite the same sort of grooved mentality as Ku Kluxers, Garveyites and other race fanatics, black and white. The course they tentatively pursue is held the only true one and whoever takes exception is denounced as an enemy of humanity, even though they may have to change that course in a few months.

Although most African Americans applauded the antiracist work that the Communist Party supported and performed, there was no chance they would defect from the traditional American political system.

The National Negro Congress

The infighting between the Communist Party and other groups doomed a major attempt to unite all the disparate African-American protest groups into the **National Negro Congress** (**NNC**). John P. Davis, a Washington-based economist, organized the NNC, modeling it on his experience as the executive secretary of the Joint Committee on National Recovery (JCNR). The JCNR was a coalition of black groups that pressed for fairness in the early New Deal. The NNC was to be a federation of organizations on a national scale supported by regional councils. Over 800 delegates representing 585 organizations attended its first meeting, held in Chicago in 1936. However, prominent black activists, leaders, and intellectuals, notably those associated with the NAACP, were absent. A. Philip Randolph was elected president, and Davis became the executive secretary. The group resolved not to be dominated by any one political faction and to build on the strength of all parts of the black community. Although handicapped by lack of funds, the NNC initially worked effectively at the local or community level. With branches in approximately seventy cities, the organization gained for its members increased employment opportunities, better housing, and adequate relief work. The NNC also prodded labor unions, in particular the CIO, to fight for better conditions and higher wages for black workers.

At the NNC's second meeting in Philadelphia in 1937, a skeptical Davis maintained that the Democratic Party would never allow black people to benefit justly and fairly from the New Deal. Eventually the increasing importance of communists in the NNC alienated most other groups and reduced the organization's ability to speak for the majority of black people. By 1940 it was greatly weakened. Randolph was voted out of office, and the once-promising NNC became little more than a front group for the Communist Party.

 **Reading Check** What role did the Communist Party and organized labor play in radicalizing black Americans during the 1930s?

▶ **Reading Check**

Throughout the 1930s, the Communist Party supported African American's efforts to seek social and economic justice. The Party appealed to many blacks because it criticized the refusal of white organized labor to include them. Black public opinion split in its evaluation of the Party. In the end, most African Americans were unwilling to abandon the traditional American political system.

▶ **Recommended Reading**

Mark Naison. *Communists in Harlem during the Depression*. Urbana, IL: University of Illinois Press, 1983. A well-researched and clear-sighted study of the Communist party in Harlem and the history of the National Negro Congress.

Chapter 19

Witnessing History . . .

He would not Africanize America, for America has too much to teach the world and Africa. He would not bleach his Negro soul in a flood of white Americanism, for he knows that Negro blood has a message for the world. He simply wished to make it possible for a man to be both a Negro and an American, without being cursed and spit upon by his fellows, without having the doors of opportunity closed roughly in his face. This, then, is the end of his striving: to be a co-worker in the kingdom of culture, to escape both death and isolation, to husband and use his best powers and his latent genius.

—W. E. B. Du Bois, *The Souls of Black Folk: Essay and Sketches*

 How does Leroy Satchel Paige exemplify the message in this excerpt?

Pitching great Leroy Satchel Paige warms up at New York's Yankee Stadium in 1942.

Chapter Preview

▶ Witnessing History

Paige achieved success in a white-dominated field and as the quote suggests was able to do so with dignity as an African American.

▶ Teaching Notes

W. E. B. Du Bois commented often on the gifts black people had made to America. Even before he wrote the passage that opens this chapter, Du Bois had proclaimed, "We are the first fruits of this new nation. . . . We are the people whose subtle sense of song has given America its only American music, its only American fairy tales, its only touch of pathos and humor amid its money-getting plutocracy." African-American "destiny is not a servile imitation of Anglo-Saxon culture, but a stalwart originality which shall unswervingly follow Negro ideals."

A key theme in black life during the 1930s and 1940s was the many strategies African Americans devised to protest segregation, discrimination, and disfranchisement, and to resist the negative racial stereotypes and the appropriation of black culture by white entrepreneurs. At heart this was a quest to shape the representation of black people in American society and create a viable black culture for a rapidly urbanizing people. A central issue in this chapter is the extent to which black culture during the 1930s and 1940s became a source of strength—cultural power—that helped African Americans define and assert themselves within American society.

Cultural power allowed African Americans to define and create new images that replaced the distortion of the true appearance, intellect, religious practice, and family values of black people in American society. The new black cultural power had to fight the well-worn stereotypes of the dumb, lazy black man; the selfless mammy, and the promiscuous dark Venus. As we have seen throughout this book, black people were disfranchised and socially and economically marginalized. But in the arts, black people drove a small wedge into the wall of racism through which they could explode onto America's center stage. The 1930s and 1940s was, ironically a time when most black people were suffering from the combined effects of the Depression and the entrenched Jim Crow regime. It was also a fertile period in the history of black expressive culture.

Section 1

Black Culture

Black Culture in a Midwestern City

During the 1930s and 1940s, black migrants flocked to St. Louis, swelling its population to make it the fifth largest city in the United States. Yet because of segregation and discrimination, the black community in St. Louis developed institutions to address their own educational and cultural needs. Attention has usually focused on St. Louis's contributions to popular culture. There was also considerable interest in the city in classical music. Black community residents had to struggle to secure training in this genre of music and for opportunities to perform it.

St. Louis is in the heart of a region often considered remote from the nation's cultural centers. Yet it has produced outstanding jazz musicians. Chuck Berry virtually invented rock and roll there. A closer look at black support for classical music in St. Louis during the 1930s and 1940s reveals the interior diversity of black community life; even though white St. Louisians marginalized or ignored the contributions of black artists in the city.

Schools, churches, labor, and media within the St. Louis black community had to create opportunities for black children to study, appreciate, and perform classical music. The two largest black newspapers, the St. Louis *Argus* and the St. Louis *American,* publicized recitals and concerts. Two all-black institutions supported classical music education: Lincoln University in Jefferson City (founded in 1866 as a school created by and for black Civil War veterans and their families) and Sumner High School (founded in 1875 as the first secondary school for black people west of the Mississippi).

By the 1940s Lincoln University had become the institution for training St. Louis musicians. Its music instructors were active in the black community's cultural affairs. Sumner High School had orchestras, bands, choirs, and glee clubs. Many of its music teachers had advanced degrees from prestigious music departments. The most influential teacher was Kenneth Billups, an arranger, composer, and founding director of the **Legend Singers,** a black professional chorus.

The Legend Singers appeared with the St. Louis Symphony and with the Municipal Opera Company (MUNY) in productions of Showboat, where they dressed in demeaning slave costumes. Billups's response to

GUIDE TO READING

▶ How did black institutions support classical music in St. Louis in the 1930s and 40s?

▶ How did African Americans merge a distinct aesthetic with a demand for social justice?

▶ What national and international forces shaped the evolution of jazz?

KEY TERMS

▶ Legend Singers, p. 671

▶ Diaspora, p. 672

▶ territorial bands, p. 673

▶ swing, p. 674

▶ bebop, p. 675

▶▶ **Guide to Reading/Key Terms**
For answers, see the *Teacher's Resource Manual.*

▶▶ **Recommended Reading**

Samuel A. Floyd Jr. *The Power of Black Music: Interpreting Its History from Africa to the United States.* New York: Oxford University Press, 1995. An excellent overview of the history of black music with an insightful comparison of the Harlem and Chicago flowerings.

▶▶ **Retracing Odyssey**

Harold Washington Library Center, Chicago, Illinois. Named in honor of Chicago's first African American Mayor, Harold Washington, the ten-story library, art, and computer reference center features the Harold Washington Archives and Collections (on the 9th floor), and the Chicago Blues Archive, and the work of several African-American artists. Jacob Lawrence contributed a mural-sized mosaic entitled "Events in the Life of Harold Washington," on the north wall of the Library.

criticism of these appearances indirectly addressed the dilemma of black artists in a racially restrictive environment:

> I've seen situations where I felt inwardly . . . I might have had to do some things; for example, let's take this Showboat thing at MUNY Opera. There is the need of a black chorus to go there, and I had the privilege of doing that with my Legend Singers, simply because one of the first requirements was to have a black chorus.

Black churches, including Antioch Baptist, Central Baptist, and Berea Presbyterian, sponsored religious programs highlighting the works of both black and white composers. Local 197 of the American Federation of Musicians and the St. Louis Music Association, which was the local branch of the National Association of Negro Musicians, promoted black performing organizations and training. These groups sponsored choirs, orchestras, and other musical organizations and devoted part of their members' dues to scholarships and summer choirs for boys and girls.

The Black Culture Industry and American Racism

Black American artists had to confront institutional racism in the culture industry. Individual black creative artists could rarely afford to produce and distribute their work. This power often resided in the hands of record companies, publishers, and the owners of radio stations and film studios. Yet black artists in the 1930s and 1940s were shaping a new black consciousness that would erupt in the 1950s as the modern civil rights movement. Paul Robeson, a graduate of Rutgers University and Columbia University Law School won acclaim as a great performing artist. But he also established friendships with African freedom fighters such as Kwame Nkrumah in Ghana, Jomo Kenyatta in Kenya, and Dr. Nnamdi Azikiwe of Nigeria. He received the NAACP's most prestigious award, the Spingarn Medal, in 1945. The U.S. government, however, revoked Robeson's passport in 1950 because of his support for radical social and economic reform, and his advocacy of black internationalism.

The political content of black art provoked heated debates among black artists. Many black Americans insisted that music, the visual and performing arts, literature, and oratory serve both a functional and an aesthetic purpose. They expected black artists not only to create beauty, but also to use their art to further black freedom from white oppression across the black **Diaspora**. African-American artists and intellectuals joined with people of African descent throughout the Diaspora in support of Ethiopian resistance against Italian aggression in 1935. Still, the involvement of white people in the marketing and use of black culture created tension among black artists during these

Paul Robeson (1898–1976) as "Othello" in 1943. A man of astonishing magnetism and creative power, Paul Robeson became, in 1943, the first black actor to play "Othello" in the United States.

decades. Although many white Americans had long appreciated black culture, some had also appropriated it for their own profit.

During the late 1930s and 1940s, corporate America recognized the money that could be made in producing and marketing black culture. Black artists had to be made "acceptable" if they were to be successfully marketed to affluent white consumers. These artists had to compromise, mask, and subordinate their true feelings and expressiveness if they wanted to earn income from their work. Artists who exhibited the right combination of showmanship, charm, and talent could reap some of the financial rewards their creativity generated. The paradox of the black performer—using your art to entertain your oppressor—was nowhere more apparent than in music.

 Reading Check How did African Americans merge a distinct aesthetic with a demand for social justice?

The Music Culture from Swing to Bebop

Ironically, the very creativity that white Americans valued and often appropriated depended on the artists' ability to preserve some intellectual and emotional independence. Black artists had to juxtapose the requirements of earning a living with the need to remain true to their art. Black musicians continuously had to refine, expand, and perfect their art not only for themselves and each other but also for a white-dominated marketplace. In many respects black music is virtually synonymous with black culture. Segregation or self-imposed separation often made possible the creation of new cultural expressions. Music reflects the core values and underlying tensions and anxieties in black communities. In black music we witness cultural producers developing strategies of resistance against white domination.

The Great Depression wrought havoc on the vibrant black culture industry of the 1920s. Record sales in 1932 were only a sixth of those in 1927. Black musicians like Louis Armstrong had enjoyed a golden age of creativity during the 1920s. The record companies had their separate black music labels and sold thousands of records to southern migrants to the big cities. New bands sprouted up from Kansas City to Chicago; Memphis to Detroit; Washington, D.C., to New York. Los Angeles, San Francisco, and Seattle had their own black music enthusiasts and performers. The **territorial** (traveling) **bands** took the music to the outposts of black America. The big bands under Fletcher Henderson, Duke Ellington, Count Basie, and Cab Calloway played in white urban dance halls and ballrooms that admitted black people only as staff or entertainers.

New York was where black musicians felt they had to go to prove themselves. After entertaining affluent white people or providing backup music for the Apollo Theater in Harlem, black musicians discarded their masks of docility and deference and made a different sound in their own space and on their own time in late-night jam ses-

▶ **Reading Check**

Black artists in the 1930s and 1940s helped shape a new black consciousness that would erupt in the 1950s civil rights movement. The political content of black art stirred debate in the black community. However, black artists who wanted to reap financial rewards from their creativity had to compromise and adapt their work to make it acceptable to a white audience.

▶ Recommended Reading

Scott DeVeaux. *BeBop: A Social and Musical History*. Berkeley, CA: University of California Press, 1997. A perceptive study of the creative artistry and lives of the pivotal black professional musicians in the jazz world during the 1930s and 1940s and how they made bebop into a commercially successful art movement.

sions. The small clubs, such as Monroe's Uptown House and Minton's Playhouse in Harlem became the most fertile sites for innovation in melody, tempo, and dexterity. In them a new kind of jazz was born.

Swing

The big band swing style that became popular in the 1930s transformed white American culture. **Swing** emerged as white bands reduced the music of the more innovative black bandleaders to a broadly appealing formula based on a swinging 4/4 beat, well-blended saxophone sections, and pleasant-sounding vocals. The big swing bands of the 1930s

---

PROFILE ❖ Charlie Parker

Charlie Parker was one of the most innovative and influential of all American musicians. He was one of the architects of modern jazz, or "bebop." His playing challenged his contemporaries. He profoundly influenced subsequent generations of jazz musicians and helped transform jazz from entertainment to one of America's most respected art forms. But Parker was also troubled by drug addiction, mental instability, and tumultuous personal relationships.

Charles Parker, Jr. was born on August 29, 1920, in Kansas City, Kansas. He had little formal musical instruction. Young Parker became a fixture at many of the local clubs. In 1939, Parker left Kansas City, Missouri, for New York, then the jazz capital of the country. In New York, Parker began to sit in, or "jam," at Harlem nightclubs such as Monroe's and Minton's. In 1942 he was back in Kansas City playing as a member of Jay McShann's band, a popular "territory band." The band traveled as far north as Lincoln, Nebraska, and as far south as New Orleans, Louisiana. During this time he acquired the nickname "Bird."

Parker left the McShann Band in 1942 to join pianist Earl Hines's band in New York. In March and April 1943, all the following musicians were in the band with Parker: "Little" Benny Harris, Bennie Green, Wardell Gray, and vocalists Billy Eckstine and Sarah Vaughan. This collection of talent reflected a musical environment that fostered innovation.

It was from the close collaboration between Parker and Dizzy Gillespie in this period that bebop emerged. Parker joined the first bebop big band, formed by Billy Eckstine in 1944. In the same year a recording of Parker's composition, "Red Cross," the first to be copyrighted in his name, was released on the Savoy label.

Parker and Gillespie first recorded together commercially in 1945. Also in 1945, Parker led an expanded group at the Spotlite club that included trumpeter Miles Davis, tenor saxophonist Dexter Gordon, bassist Leonard Gaskin and drummer Stan Levey. During a disastrous trip to California, Parker had a nervous breakdown and spent several months at Camarillo State Hospital.

In 1947, when Parker returned to New York, he formed his "classic" quintet, with trumpeter Miles Davis, drummer Max Roach, pianist Duke Jordan, and Tommy Potter on bass. The recordings produced by this quintet, four sides on the Savoy label, are the foundation on which much of Parker's reputation rests.

In 1949, in a fitting tribute to his genius by his contemporaries, a New York nightclub, "Birdland," was named for him. Charlie Parker died in New York on March 12, 1955.

played written-out, completely arranged music. The popularity of swing helped boost the careers of black and white bandleaders. It also led to a creative slump that disheartened many of the younger black musicians. Tired of swing's predictability, they began improvising in the jazz clubs, sharpening their reflexes, ears, and minds.

Bebop

In the 1940s at least seven musicians were among the men most responsible for making a revolution in jazz, ushering in a new sound and dimension that became known as **bebop**. These musicians were Charlie Parker, Dizzy Gillespie, Thelonious Monk, Bud Powell, Kenny Clarke, Max Roach, and Ray Brown. Bebop featured complex rhythms and harmonies and highlighted improvisation. Gillespie (1917–1993) said that Kansas City–born Charlie "Yardbird" and then just "Bird" Parker (1920–1955) was "the architect of the style."

Bebop met resistance from white America. The nation was about to enter World War II and was too preoccupied to switch from the big band swing ballroom dancing music to bebop. Moreover, because jazzmen played in small, intimate clubs, not big bands, they had more freedom from the expectations of white society. Bebop music was of such enduring quality, however, that it shaped the contours of American popular culture and style for two generations. Before long, bebop became the principal musical language of jazz musicians around the world.

Bebop was a way of life and had its own attendant styles whose nuances depended on class status and, perhaps, age. Gillespie helped create one side of bebop style in dress, language, and demeanor. He began to wear dark glasses on stage to reduce the glare from lights after he had cataract surgery. He grew a goatee because shaving every day irritated his bottom lip. He wore pegged pants, jackets with wide lapels, and a beret when men were still wearing hats with brims. Other bebop musicians emulated and modified this attire. Beboppers also created their own slang, hip Black English that mingled colorful and obscene language.

Bebop was the dominant black music of the war decade, but after 1945 returning veterans preferred a slower-paced music, simple love songs, and melodies. This contributed to bebop's waning and led to more transformations. All artistic innovation comes with a high price. Bebop was no exception. Many of the most talented musicians, like Billie Holiday, discussed later in this chapter, paid that price in lives decimated by drugs, poverty, sickness, and broken relationships. Few black musicians received the respect, recognition, and financial rewards from white America that their creativity warranted. Ultimately, white Americans wanted the art, but not the artists.

 **Reading Check** What national and international forces shaped the evolution of jazz?

▶ **Reading Check**

By the 1930s, big band swing had become the dominant form of American popular music. Swing helped boost the careers of black and white composers, but also contributed to a creative slump in American music. Black jazz musicians playing small clubs created a new jazz form in the 1940s, bebop. The preoccupation of the nation with World War II slowed the acceptance of bebop, but it also allowed the form to develop without the pressure to reach a mainstream audience.

▶ **Document**

19-2 *W.C. Handy, How the Blues Came to Be, 1941*

Born in Alabama in 1873, William Christopher Handy first heard the primitive rhythms and "simple declarations" that would eventually earning him the title "Father of the Blues," in the Mississippi Delta. The son and grandson of Baptist ministers, Handy taught music at A & M College in Huntsville, Alabama and toured the countryside with his nine man band.

GUIDE TO READING

▶ What place did black performers have in radio and film in the 1930s and 1940s?

▶ How did African Americans create and employ popular culture to counteract negative stereotypes of black people?

KEY TERMS

▶ race films, p. 678

▶ Mammy, p. 678

▶ Fair Play Committee, p. 679

▶ **Guide to Reading**

For answers, see the *Teacher's Resource Manual.*

▶ **Retracing the Odyssey**

DuSable Museum of African-American History
Artist Margaret Goss Burroughs opened the Ebony Museum in 1961 in her home. She moved it in 1973 to its present location at Washington Park and renamed it the DuSable Museum of African-American History. The DuSable Museum honors the accomplishment of Jean Baptiste Pointe DuSable, a Haitian-born immigrant who arrived in Chicago in 1779 and was the first non-Indian to settle in the area. The Museum houses an extensive collection of artifacts, art, books, civil rights documents and sponsors a diverse array of cultural and educational programs and exhibits.

Section 2
Popular Culture for the Masses

The Comics

African Americans quickly noted the difference between the fun that black people made of each other and the mockery white people made of them. These differences were reflected in tone, intent, and sympathetic versus derisive laughter. During the Depression, comic strips in newspapers and comic books featuring superheroes diverted millions of Americans. Comic strips in black newspapers entertained, but also affirmed, the values and ideals of black people. They portrayed humorous situations and elaborated tales of intrigue and action.

The Philadelphia *Independent,* a black paper, ran a serial in the 1930s called "The Jones Family." This strip, drawn by an editorial cartoonist named Branford, was a good example of the dual function of entertaining and affirming. The strip emphasized black people's desire for achievement and respectability. The plot centered around the young Jones boy's search for the "good life" of money, success, love, and a happy marriage. But at every turn he confronts a harsh environment. Unable to get a job because of the Depression, he becomes an outlaw and narrowly escapes jail. He is constantly "on the run" from oppression. His only consolations are his family and his beautiful, ever-faithful girlfriend.

"The Jones Family" illuminates the gray areas that most African Americans, regardless of their class, faced when attempting to live rational and coherent lives in the northern cities. Although they espoused and cherished middle-class values, they often had to live among poverty, crime, and racial oppression. The black comic strips sought to provide entertaining, nonjudgmental prescriptions and blueprints for middle-class life. To more cynical and alienated black people they seemed to be promoting unattainable values and lifestyles.

Radio and Race

Although there were individual exceptions, during the Depression black performers in radio and film were marginalized, exploited, or excluded. Commercial radio operated to deliver an audience of white consumers to white advertisers, and it denied black people jobs as announcers, broadcast journalists, or technicians. White entertainers schooled in

blackface minstrelsy portrayed black radio characters. The major labor unions involved in the entertainment side of the radio industry restricted membership to white people. Still—with its offerings of vaudeville, big bands, drama, and comedy—radio provided relief from the miseries of the Depression to all Americans, black as well as white.

Amos 'n' Andy

The most popular comedy radio program in the early 1930s was *The Amos 'n' Andy Show*. The inauguration of this program was a significant moment in radio history. The title roles were played by two white performers, Charles Correll and Freeman Gosden. Skillful showmen, Correll and Gosden ingratiated themselves in Chicago's black community, appearing at parades and posing with black children. The Chicago *Defender* endorsed them. They received standing ovations at the Regal Theater in Chicago's black South Side. Part of the amusement they generated derived from their mispronounced words, garbled grammar, and their show's minstrel ambience. Each episode highlighted an improbable situation involving the black cab driver (Amos) and his gullible overweight friend (Andy). Other characters included the scheming con artist Kingfish, his overbearing wife Sapphire, and his domineering mother-in-law, Mama. The characters and their humor reinforced unflattering racial and gender stereotypes, but the show was not mean spirited. Some of the characters conducted themselves with dignity, modeling such positive values as marital fidelity, strong families, hard work, and economic independence.

Black audiences recognized the minstrel stereotyping in *Amos 'n' Andy*, yet many among them still enjoyed the show. A vocal component of the black population, however, complained that this show, and other radio programs, reinforced negative images—of black women as bossy Sapphires or Mammies and black men as childish clowns—in the nation's consciousness. Educator and activist Nannie Helen Burroughs considered the show demeaning. Robert L. Vann, editor of the Pittsburgh *Courier*, argued that it exploited African Americans for white commercial gain. Vann sponsored a petition to the Federal Communications Commission to ban the show, but his efforts were futile. By the 1940s *The Amos 'n' Andy Show* was less popular. In the early 1950s, it had a brief life as a television series, this time with black actors.

For almost two decades, *Amos 'n' Andy* was the only depiction of black people on the nation's airwaves. Its negative stereotypes of African Americans supported white people's notions of their own superiority. The show never demonstrated how the characters' race affected their lives or the psychological or economic costs of racism. It taught white America that it was permissible to laugh at striving black men and women.

The best-known and most successful African American on network radio in the late 1930s was Eddie Anderson, who played Jack Benny's sidekick Rochester in NBC's *The Jack Benny Show*. Like the characters in

"Food for Thought," editorial cartoon by Rosie Nelson, illustrated by Branford. Comic strips provided humor and distraction and operated as a public space for commentary on important personal and political issues.

⏵ **Recommended Readings**

William Barlow. *Voice Over: The Making of Black Radio*. Philadelphia: Temple University Press, 1999. A lucidly written, informative cultural history of the evolution of black radio and the personalities who made it a powerful instrument for disseminating black music, culture, language, and politics, and for constructing an African-American public sphere.

Melvin Patrick Ely. *The Adventures of Amos 'n' Andy: A Social History of an American Phenomenon*. New York: Free Press, 1991. A subtle and penetrating examination of the complexities of racial stereotyping in one of the most influential and controversial radio and television programs in the history of media race relations.

Amos 'n' Andy, Anderson's character reinforced negative racial stereotypes. Anderson rationalized his role in a way that suggests discomfort with it:

> I don't see why certain characters are called stereotypes. The Negro characters being presented are not labeling the Negro race any more than "Luigi" is labeling the Italian people as a whole. The same goes for "Beulah," who is not playing the part of thousands of Negroes, but only the part of one person, "Beulah." They're not saying here is the portrait of the Negro, but here is "Beulah."

Race, Representation, and the Movies

In the 1930s and 1940s—after the introduction of sound in motion pictures—black and white producers began to make what were known as **race films** for African-American audiences. Since the beginning of the film industry, white film executives had cast black men and women in roles designed to comfort, reassure, and entertain white audiences. Continuing this trend, African Americans in Hollywood movies of the 1930s were usually cast in servile roles and often portrayed as buffoons. The first black actor to receive major billing in American films, Stepin Fetchit (1902–1985, born Lincoln Theodore Monroe Perry), purportedly earned $2 million in ten years playing a servile, dim-witted, slow-moving character.

Black performers appeared as servants in many other box office successes during the Depression era. Among them were Gertrude Howard and Libby Taylor, who played servants to Mae West's characters in *I'm No Angel* (1933) and *Belle of the Nineties* (1934). In *Imitation of Life* (1934), Louise Beavers played a black servant whose light-skinned daughter, played by Fredi Washington, tries to pass for white. The black tap dancer and stage performer Bill "Bojangles" Robinson was featured in four popular films—*The Little Colonel* (1935), *The Littlest Rebel* (1935), *Just around the Corner* (1938), and *Rebecca of Sunnybrook Farm* (1938)—as a servant to white child star Shirley Temple.

The film that most firmly cemented the role of black Americans as servants in the American consciousness was *Gone With the Wind* (1939). Hattie McDaniel and Butterfly McQueen were the black "stars" in this epic adaptation of Margaret Mitchell's romanticized literary salute to the Old South. McDaniel had played servant or **Mammy** roles throughout the 1930s. The image of Mammy, the headscarf-wearing, obese, dutiful black woman who nurtured white families, appealed to white America. But in *Gone With the Wind*, McDaniel gave the performance of a lifetime. In 1940 she became the first African American to win an Oscar. Many in the black community criticized her for playing "female Tom" roles. Defensively, McDaniel retorted she would rather play a maid and earn $700 a week than be one and earn only $7 a week. Some

▶ Document

19-4 *Ethel Waters, On Black Movies*
Conceived in a violent attack on her thirteen year-old mother, Ethel Waters grew up in a hostile environment in and around Philadelphia. She never knew a mother's love and longed for affection and kindness. She suffered hunger and often stole food. As a small child, she grew up in a world of parasites, whores, pimps, and thieves looking for victims. Waters was a survivor with a deep faith in God. As a gifted singer, she made such songs as "St. Louis Blues" and "Stormy Weather" favorites. In 1929, she became one of the first black women to make "talkies." In this selection Waters discusses her feelings regarding a film with an African-American cast and crew, *Tales of Manhattan*.

Louise Beavers (1908–1962) was a splendid actress whose talent was largely restricted to "mammy" roles. Here she appears with Claudette Colbert in a scene from the melodramatic film *Imitation of Life* (1934), which deals with the theme of black people passing for white.

black actors such as McDaniel, dismayed by their relegation to demeaning roles, formed the **Fair Play Committee** (FPC). The FPC lobbied the white-dominated movie industry for more substantial roles, to get rid of dialect speech, and to ban the term *nigger* from the screen. But in the *Beulah* radio show, which premiered in 1947, McDaniel again played a wise but subservient maid who provides the family that employs her with advice, guidance, and direction.

 Reading Check What place did black performers have in radio and film in the 1930s and 1940s?

Black Filmmakers

Eventually, during and after World War II, Hollywood developed more sophisticated race-directed movies. Of particular significance was the positive, even romanticized, portrayal of black Americans in a movie financed by the War Department to gain support among African Americans for the U.S. role in World War II. *The Negro Soldier*, directed by Frank Capra in 1944, played to vast audiences of enthusiastic black people. But even before the *The Negro Soldier*, some motion pictures had displayed African Americans positively. Paul Robeson made two movies, *The Emperor Jones* (1933) and *Show Boat* (1936), in which he attempted to change how black

▶ **Reading Check**

Black performers were marginalized, exploited, and excluded from radio and film. In an effort to appeal to white audiences, commercial radio and mainstream film kept most blacks out of the industry. White entertainers portrayed black radio characters.

▶ **Living Words Audio Clip**

Track 31 *Swing Low, Sweet Chariot traditional; sung by Paul Robeson*

▶ **Document**

19-1 *Paul Robeson "Welcome Home Rally," June 19, 1949*
During the Cold War of the 1950s, Robeson's passport was revoked and his ability to earn a livelihood was sharply curtailed. A Supreme Court decision in 1958 resulted in the return of his passport.

▶ **Recommended Reading**

Manthia Diawara, ed. *Black American Cinema.* New York: Routledge, 1993. A collection of provocative essays. Three examine the work of filmmaker Oscar Micheaux. Others provide fresh interpretations of the recent independent cinema movement.

men and women were represented on screen. He proclaimed in 1934, "In my music, my plays, my films I want to carry always this central idea: to be African. Multitudes of men have died for less worthy ideals; it is even more eminently worth living for." Robeson's films, however, were not box office successes. He left the United States to pursue his career in Europe. There his commitment to communism and leftist politics made him a target of the anticommunist hysteria that gripped the United States as the Cold War took hold in the late 1940s (see Chapter 20).

To succeed commercially, African-American filmmakers had to disguise their dissent or create art purely for other black people. One of the most enterprising black filmmakers was Oscar Micheaux (1884–1951). He made films aimed primarily at the black public, a group that Hollywood directors and producers of race movies ignored or insulted with stereotypical representations. Unlike the dominant Hollywood stereotypes, the black men and women in Micheaux's films were often educated, cultured, and prosperous. Micheaux endowed black Americans with cinematic voice and subjectivity.

Micheaux produced more than thirty feature films between 1919 and 1948. In 1932, he released *The Exile*, the first sound motion picture to be made by, with, and for black Americans. The following year he produced *Veiled Aristocrats*, about passing for white among Chicago's black professional class. The characters in the film are considered "aristocrats" because they are descended from the white gentry of the Old South and Europe. They are "veiled" because of their color. The plot turns on the revelation that the wealthy "white" heroine is actually "colored," which enables her to marry the talented mulatto hero.

Micheaux tried to transform Hollywood without changing it, much as members of the black bourgeoisie struggled to be included in American society. His films capture the dilemma of black double consciousness. Black culture existed within and was shaped by, while simultaneously transforming, American culture. To the degree that black Americans had been assimilated, white American culture was their culture as well.

The white ethnic immigrants who created Hollywood were determined to help marginal and excluded groups like Jews and Italians assimilate into the American mainstream. Hollywood sought to create the illusion that these groups belonged to the power elite. However, these Hollywood entrepreneurs did not do the same for African Americans. Their films during the Depression represented black people as unassimilable. A small group of black filmmakers and actors created independent films and showed them in cinema houses exclusively for black patrons. Following the lead of pioneers like Micheaux, they created an alternative cinema in which they introduced nuanced and fully human characters.

 **Reading Check** How did African Americans create and employ popular culture to counteract negative stereotypes of black people?

▶ **Reading Check**

Comic strips in black newspapers affirmed the ideals and values of black people. Black filmmakers made movies aimed primarily at black audiences. Filmmakers like Oscar Micheaux presented positive images of African Americans in their movies, avoiding the stereotypes that were the staple of the mainstream film industry.

Section 3

The Black Chicago Renaissance

Black Writers

Chicago was the center of black culture during the 1930s and 1940s. In contrast to some of the artists of the "Harlem Renaissance," the leading writers in Chicago harbored no illusions that art would solve the problems caused by white supremacy and black subordination. The Chicago writers of the 1930s and 1940s emphasized the idea that black art had to combine aesthetics and function. It had to serve the cause of black freedom.

Arna Bontemps (1902–1973) was to the Chicago Renaissance what Alain Locke had been to the Harlem Renaissance. Born in Louisiana, Bontemps migrated in 1935 from California to Chicago where he met Richard Wright. He joined the South Side Writers Group, which Wright founded in 1936. The Group included poet Margaret Walker and playwright Theodore Ward. It offered criticism and moral support to black writers. Bontemps's own writing was influenced by his association with the group. After 1935 his novels and short stories reflected a militant restlessness and revolutionary spirit. In 1936 he published *Black Thunder* about the nineteenth-century slave conspiracy led by Gabriel and in 1939 *Drums at Dusk* about the Haitian Revolution and Toussaint L'Ouverture (1746–1803). Richard Wright's writings also celebrated resistance, but with more nuance. He published *Uncle Tom's Children* in 1938 and his masterpiece, *Native Son*, in 1940.

Margaret Walker attracted widespread attention when her collected poems appeared as the book *For My People* in the Yale Series of Younger Poets. Willard Motley worked with a radio group while writing his powerful novel *Knock on Any Door* (1947), which depicted the transformation of an Italian-American altar boy into a criminal headed for the electric chair. The novel invited comparisons with Wright's *Native Son*.

Chicago and Black Culture

Before the 1930s several black intellectuals misjudged the potential of Chicago to become a vibrant center of black culture. In the late 1920s, black social scientists Charles S. Johnson and E. Franklin Frazier expressed disdain for black Chicago's artistic and intellectual prospects.

GUIDE TO READING

▶ How did the Chicago Renaissance differ from the Harlem Renaissance of the 1920s?

▶ What contributions to black music were represented in Chicago?

▶ What place did dance have in the Chicago Renaissance?

KEY TERMS

▶ Bronzeville, p. 682

▶ Black Metropolis, p. 683

▶ gospel, p. 684

▶▶ **Guide to Reading/Key Terms**

For answers, see the *Teacher's Resource Manual*.

▶▶ **Retracing the Odyssey**

Carter G. Woodson Regional Library This branch of the Chicago Public Library, named in honor of the "Father of Black History," Carter G. Woodson, contains a wealth of photographs, books, documents, and manuscript collections concerning the artists and authors, women's clubs, and social institutions that detail the Black Chicago Renaissance. The Vivian Harsah Collection of Afro-American History and Literature contains over 70,000 volumes by Langston Hughes, Richard Wright, Gwendolyn Brooks, and Arna Bontemps among others.

Frazier proclaimed that "Chicago has no intelligentsia." In 1923 Johnson asked rhetorically,

Who can write of lilies and sunsets in the pungent shadows of the stockyards? . . . It is no dark secret why literary societies fail, where there are no Art exhibits or libraries about, why periodicals presuming upon an I.Q. above the age of 12 are not read, why so little literature comes out of the city. No, the kingdom of the second ward [the black neighborhood] has no self-sustaining intelligentsia, and a miserably poor acquaintance with that of the world surrounding it.

Johnson did, however, admit one saving grace in Chicago's cultural wasteland: "[I]t leads these colored United States in its musical aspirations with, perhaps, the best musical school in the race, as these go."

Johnson and Frazier were too harsh. Chicago's industrial economy attracted working-class black people. It also nurtured artists who drew inspiration from and reflected black people who wanted to transgress class and geographical lines. These working-class people wanted to enjoy the middle-class life of accomplishment and consumption. A critical pulse point on Chicago's South Side came to be known as **Bronzeville**. It measured and reflected the reality of the lives of ordinary working-class people. As Harlem had its 125th Street, Chicago had 35th and State Street and 47th and South Park (now Martin Luther King Jr. Drive).

Chicago was heir to the Harlem Renaissance. In 1930 Langston Hughes published *Not without Laughter*, the first major novel about the

Archibald Motley (1891–1981) captures in *Barbecue* (1934) the exuberance and vitality of nightlife in Chicago's Bronzeville. Motley was a major artistic talent during Chicago's Black Renaissance during the 1930s and 1940s. Oil on canvas, 36¼ × 40⅛ in. The Howard University Gallery of Art, Washington, D.C.

black experience in Chicago. Hughes moved to the city himself in 1941 and wrote often for the widely read Chicago *Defender*. The city epitomized urban industrial America. It had long attracted displaced agricultural workers from the southern cotton fields. By 1930 it had a black population of 233,903. The migrants arrived eager to absorb Chicago's hard-driving blues and jazz culture.

During the 1920s a discernible class structure among African Americans emerged in Chicago, fueled in part by the new migrants. These men and women expanded the consumer base and gave rise to educated professionals and entrepreneurs who developed an appreciation for the arts. The **Black Metropolis**, as social scientists St. Clair Drake and Horace R. Cayton designated Chicago's South Side, became a black city within a city. Black businesses, such as banks and insurance companies, formed the financial foundation. Entrepreneur Walter L. Lee started Your Cab Company. Each day he put on the streets a half-dozen chauffeur-uniformed drivers of vehicles. In the late 1940s, John Johnson would launch a publishing empire with such magazines as *Negro Digest*, *Jet*, and *Ebony*. These businesses depended on black support. It was in their best interest to support the arts and provide venues for performances.

Black Music

Chicago was a pioneering center both for recording and performing music. As black music became a commodity, influential black disk jockeys like Al Benson appeared on radio in Chicago. Benson proved to be as skilled a businessman as he was a cultural impresario. Music was the primary inspiration for the creativity that characterized black cultural movements in America. Avant-garde developments in black music preceded black cultural activity in the visual arts, poetry, drama, dance, literature, film, and sports. Cultural creativity was a potent force for black liberation and occurred simultaneously in different locations in America.

Jazz in Chicago

Within the confines of the South Side of Chicago, black musical giants, such as trumpeter Louis Armstrong (1898–1971) and his wife, Lillian Hardin Armstrong (1898–1971), performed and nurtured a distinct jazz culture. "Lil" Armstrong, a well-known and respected jazz pianist, was born in Memphis, Tennessee, and received formal music training at Fisk University, the Chicago College of Music, and the New York College of Music. "Lil" Hardin Armstrong led her own band and was talented at arranging, composing, and singing. She played with great performers of the day. She befriended Louis Armstrong when he arrived in Chicago, and they were married in 1924. Lil Armstrong eventually encouraged her husband to leave King Oliver's Creole Jazz Band and to join Fletcher Henderson in New York. The Armstrongs were divorced in 1938. She continued her recording career with Decca records under the name Lil Hardin.

Duke Ellington in his autobiography, *Music Is My Mistress*, remarked,

> Chicago always sounded like the most glamorous place in the world to me when I heard the guys in Frank Holliday's poolroom talking about their travels. . . . They told very romantic tales about nightlife on the South Side. By the time I got there in 1930, it glittered even more . . . the Loop, the cabarets . . . city life, suburban life, luxurious neighborhoods—and the apparently broken-down neighborhoods where there were more good times than any place in the city.

At this point Ellington was recording some of his best jazz, such as *Mood Indigo* (1930) and *Ko-Ko* (1940).

The seeds that blossomed into full-bodied jazz culture were planted across America at the turn of the century. The most famous musicians, however, all went to or passed through Chicago. As the Chicago Jazz Age came into its own, the beguiling tune *Pretty Baby* became the city's theme song. It was written by Tony Jackson. Jelly Roll Morton (the self-proclaimed "inventor of jazz") called Jackson "maybe the best entertainer the world has ever seen." The South Side, specifically along State Street between 31st and 35th, was the beating heart of the city's Jazz Age. Although Chicago did not replace New York as the major location for the aspiring jazz musician, it was the place you went to prove you had what it took to make a name for yourself.

Gospel in Chicago: Thomas Dorsey

The term **gospel** designates the traditional religious music of the black church. It was nurtured and flourished in Chicago's churches, in storefronts, or large edifices. Gospel music became the backbone of urban and contemporary black religion and is deeply entrenched in worship. The use of instruments—tambourines, drums, pianos, horns, guitars, and Hammond organs—characterizes gospel and distinguishes it from the earlier spiritual and black folk music. During the 1930s and 1940s, it developed its own idioms and performance techniques. The doctrines of black "folk churches" encourage free expression, group participation, spontaneous testimonies, prayers, witnessing, and music. Singers and choirs rarely perform the same songs in the same way more than once.

In Chicago, Thomas Dorsey (1899–1993)—one of Chicago's leading composers of the blues since the mid-1920s—was most responsible for developing black urban gospel. Dorsey's genius lay in his ability to synthesize elements of the blues with religious hymns to create a gospel blues. His gospel pieces, performed with a ragtime-derived, boogie-woogie piano accompaniment, radiated an urban religious spirit. In 1930 Dorsey gained widespread attention when gospel singer Willie Mae Ford Smith (1904–1994) performed his "If You See My Savior, Tell Him That You Saw Me" at the National Baptist Convention meeting in Chicago. Two years later, in 1932, Dorsey's place in musical history was assured when Theodore Frye, with Dorsey at the piano, performed in the Ebenezer Baptist Church in Chicago his now classic gospel song, "Take

My Hand, Precious Lord." The song had a profound impact on gospel performers and their audiences. Dorsey's abundant works provided a foundation for shout worship in the urban Protestant churches formed by transplanted black Southerners in the 1930s and succeeding decades.

One of the greatest gospel singers, Chicago-based Mahalia Jackson (1911–1972), sang and promoted Dorsey's songs all over the country on the church circuit and at religious conventions between 1939 and 1944. Jackson once said of the music, "Gospel songs are the songs of hope. When you sing them you are delivered of your burden." During the Depression and World War II, gospel became big business.

▶ **Living Words Audio Clip**

Track 33 *I Sing Because I'm Happy; sung by Mahalia Jackson*

Track 34 *Backwater Blue from Leadbelly's Last*

Chicago in Dance and Song

Dance has always been an integral part of African-American life, and the dances of black people have always been important in the American theater. The first performances by black dancers given within and taken seriously by the concert dance world occurred in the 1930s. The first "Negro Dance Recital in America" was performed in 1931 by the New Negro Art Theater Dance Company, co-founded by Edna Buy and Hemsley Winfield.

Katherine Dunham

In that same year, Katherine Dunham (1909–) founded the Negro Dance Group in Chicago. As Dunham later recalled, "Black dancers were not allowed to take classes in studios in the '30s. I started a school because there was no place for blacks to study dance. I was the first to open the way for black dancers and I was the first to form a black dance company."

Dunham was unique. Trained in anthropology, she studied African-based ritual dance in the Caribbean. In 1938 her troupe stunned an audience with the sexual vitality of its performance of one of her works. When the company, now renamed the Katherine Dunham Dance Company, performed in February 1940, audiences and critics were awed. The *New York Times* declared, "With the arrival of Katherine Dunham on the scene the development of a substantial Negro dance Art begins to look decidedly bright." The reviewer continued,

> Her performance with her group at the Windsor Theater may very well become a historic occasion, for certainly never before in all efforts of recent years to establish the Negro dance as a serious medium has there been so convincing and authoritative approach. . . . The potential greatness of the Negro dance lies in its discovery of its own roots and the crucial nursing of them into growth and flower. . . . It is because she has showed herself to have both the objective quality of the student and the natural instinct of the artist that she has done such a truly important job.

Katherine Dunham founded one of the first black dance companies. She was an outspoken critic of Jim Crow segregation.

What kept audiences returning to Dunham dance performances, however, was the dancer's bold sensuality. A reviewer of *Tropical Revue*, for example, wrote that it was "likely to send thermometers soaring to the bursting point. . . . Tempestuous and torrid, raffish and revealing." *The New York Sun* marveled, "Shoulders, midsections and posteriors went

PROFILE ❖ Billie Holiday

Billie Holiday was born Eleanora Fagan in Philadelphia, Pennsylvania, on April 7, 1915 to teenagers Sadie Fagan and Clarence Holiday. She grew up in Baltimore, Maryland. She became perhaps the greatest jazz singer ever recorded, a unique improviser and soloist. Much attention has focused on the tragic and destructive dimensions of her private life. It is her musical talent that compels interest and admiration. Holiday used her talent to do more than to entertain. She challenged and often disturbed her listeners, especially with her soul-shattering rendition of "Strange Fruit."

"Strange Fruit," which Billie Holiday first performed in 1929, became her signature piece. It was written by a white schoolteacher who went by the name of Lewis Allan (his real name was Abel Meerpol). The lyrics speak of "black bodies" hanging like "strange fruit" from Southern trees with "bulging eyes and twisted mouth," and capture the sickening brutality of lynching in the South. Holiday's incomparable vocal style and delivery gave the song its political, emotional, and cultural power.

"Every time she sang that song," recalled Barney Josephson, a New York nightclub owner, it was unforgettable. . . . I made her do it as her last number. . . . When she sang "Strange Fruit" she never moved. Her hands were down. She didn't even touch the mike. With the little light on her face. The tears never interfered with her voice, but the tears would come and just knock everybody in that house out.

"Strange Fruit" remains a harrowing song even today.

Saxophonist Lester Young, who began recording with Holiday in 1937, gave her the nickname, Lady Day. By the late 1940s, Holiday's addiction to drugs was hurting her career. In 1947 she entered a private clinic, but was unable to stay clean. Following her discharge, the police arrested her for possession of heroin, and she served nine and one-half months at the Federal Reformatory for Women at Alderson, West Virginia. New York officials revoked her cabaret card and prohibited her from performing in night clubs in the city. She gave concerts in other cities and went on international tours.

In 1958, a year before her death at age forty-four, Holiday recorded her most popular album, "Lady in Satin." By this time her voice had become older, less flexible, grainier. But many would argue that it had also become richer, full of the sad wisdom of a great artist whom life had not treated kindly. Billie Holiday died in New York City on July 17, 1959. Thousands of friends and fans attended the funeral at Saint Paul the Apostle Cathedral. She was buried in Saint Raymond's Catholic Cemetery in the Bronx.

◀ Between 1935 and 1938, Billie Holiday released some eighty titles on the Brunswick label for marketing to the black jukebox audience.

round and round. Particularly when the cynosure was Miss Dunham, the vista was full of pulchritude."

Dunham explained her motivation:

> I felt a new dance form was needed for black people to be able to appear in any theater in the world and be accepted and exciting. One of the prerequisites of art is uniqueness. Rather than taking years to build a classical ballet company for blacks, I decided to create a dance with an authentic base for black people. Through my anthropological work, I studied primitive and folk dances and created the Dunham dance from them.

The success in New York led to film offers. The producers of the all-black musical extravaganza *Cabin in the Sky* hired the dance troupe and gave the feature role of Georgia Brown to Dunham. The role gave Dunham, as the *Times* dance critic wrote, the chance "to sizzle." But it also undermined her seriousness, allowing white audiences to view her as the stereotypical sultry black sexpot.

In 1943 Dunham moved to New York and opened the Katherine Dunham School of Arts and Research. The school trained artists not only in dance, but in theater, literature, and world cultures.

Dunham was not afraid to protest racial segregation, even though it hurt her popularity. In the early 1940s, she denounced discrimination. In 1944 in Louisville, Kentucky, after a performance, Dunham announced, "We are glad we have made you happy. We hope you have enjoyed us. This is the last time I shall play Louisville because the management refuses to let people like us sit by people like you. Maybe after the war we shall have democracy and I can return." Dunham is important for two reasons. First, she was a gifted and talented pioneer in dance whose choreography inspired future generations. Second, she underscored the responsibility that a black artist had to the black community to fight racism.

Billie Holiday

Billie Holiday (1915–1959) was another great performer whose career took shape during the Depression. She also used her art to challenge the oppression of black people. Holiday, popularly known as "Lady Day," began singing at age fifteen and was discovered three years later by John Hammond, a Chicago jazz producer and promoter. In 1933 Hammond arranged for Holiday's first recording session, and in 1934 she made her debut at the Apollo Theater in Harlem. An incomparable singer known for subtle and artful improvisation, she left a wealth of recordings.

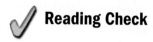 **Reading Check** How did the Chicago Renaissance differ from the Harlem Renaissance of the 1920s?

▶ **Reading Check**

In contrast to some of the artists of the Harlem Renaissance, that art would solve the problem of racism in America. Chicago writers of the 1930s and 1940s emphasized that black art had to combine aesthetics and functions. The artists of the Chicago Renaissance drew inspiration from the African American who migrated to Chicago looking for a better life.

GUIDE TO READING

▶ How did black graphic artists of the 1930s fuse politics and art in their work?

▶ What was the impact of the work of Richard Wright and Ralph Ellison?

⇒ **Guide to Reading/Key Terms**

For answers, see the *Teacher's Resource Manual*.

⇒ **Recommended Readings**

Richard J. Powell. *Black Art and Culture in the 20th Century*. New York: Thames and Judson, 1997.

Henry Louis Gates and Nellie Y. McKay, eds. *Norton Anthology of African American Literature*. New York: W. W. Norton, 1997.

⇒ **Document**

19-5 *Richard Wright, "Are We Solving America's Race Problem?"* 1945
Born in Mississippi, Richard Wright lived in Tennessee and Arkansas, where he experienced first hand hostility and hatred. Wright's work explored racism and its impact on all of society.

Section 4

Black Art and Literature

Black Graphic Art

Chicago artists, such as Charles White, Elizabeth Catlett, and Eldzier Cortor, and Harlem's Jacob Lawrence, celebrated both rural and urban working-class black people while implicitly criticizing the racial hierarchy of power and privilege. Their art belonged to the **social realism school** that flourished in the United States in the 1930s. Social realist art was intensely ideological. It strove to fuse propaganda—both left wing and right wing—to art to make it socially and politically relevant.

As the Depression worsened, black artists became even more determined to use their art to portray the crisis in capitalism. This involved depicting social and racial inequality. Chicago's Charles White wrote that "paint is the only weapon I have with which to fight what I resent. If I could write I would write about it. If I could talk I would talk about it. Since I paint, I must paint about it."

Defense Worker, a painting by Dox Thrash, reflects these concerns. Completed in 1942, just after the United States had entered World War II, it shows an isolated black worker looming over the horizon. The heroic imagery alludes to the dream of a racially integrated labor force, equal opportunity, and social reform in the wake of the New Deal and the sudden demand for labor triggered by the war.

The Harmon Foundation sponsored five juried exhibitions (1926–1931, 1933) of the work of black artists. The William E. Harmon Awards for Distinguished Achievement among Negroes celebrated black artists in the hope they would serve as role models for others. William E. Harmon, a real estate investor from Iowa, established the New York–based foundation in 1925. In the 1930s the WPA established art workshops and community art centers in black urban communities to teach art to neighborhood young people and provide work for artists. Sculptor Augusta Savage, as the first director of the Harlem Community Art Center, presided over more than 1,500 students enrolled in day and evening classes in drawing, painting, sculpture, printmaking, and design. Among the teachers was Selma Burke (1900–1995), who sculpted the relief of Franklin D. Roosevelt that appears on the dime.

One of the initiatives of the **Federal Arts Project**, another New Deal agency, was to sponsor the creation of murals in public buildings, such as post offices and schools, that celebrated American ideals. Murals by

black artists celebrated the heritage, contributions to society, and struggles of African Americans. Aaron Douglas was a leading painter of such public art. Douglas and other black artists pressed the WPA to appoint more African Americans to its local boards and to hire them for more projects. The Harlem Artists Guild and the Arts and Crafts Guild in Chicago provided forums where black artists could meet and plan strategies to foster the visual arts and support the social and political issues that affected black people's lives.

Black Literature

Black literature, like black art, has been assessed in terms of what it reveals about the social, cultural, and political landscape at a given historical moment. Black literature, like all black cultural production, is valued both for aesthetic reasons on its own and for the way it represents the struggles of black people to attain freedom. In their work black writers in the 1930s and 1940s felt obliged to address questions of identity and to define and describe urban life to the dispossessed and impoverished black migrants to the cities. They tried to delineate the dimensions of a shared American heritage by portraying the specific contributions that African Americans had made to American society. Finally, black writers explored the issue of the rights African Americans were entitled to as Americans and the demands they could and should make on the state and society.

Richard Wright's *Native Son*

In 1940 Richard Wright (1908–1960) published *Native Son,* the first of many important novels by Depression-generation black authors. Reviewers hailed it as "the new American tragedy." Its tale of the downfall of the young Bigger Thomas could be read as a warning about how economic hardship combined with segregation and discrimination could lead young black men to lash out in violence and rage. Setting out for an interview for a job as a chauffeur, Bigger meets with his neighborhood friends who want him to help them rob a grocery store. Bigger's fear of whites prevents him from going along. Instead, he picks a fight to camouflage his fear and avoid committing the crime. Bigger gets the chauffeur's job, which requires him to drive the wealthy Dalton family. On his first assignment, he is supposed to drive young Mary Dalton to a university lecture. But she talks him into picking up her boyfriend, Jan—a communist—and taking them to a restaurant in the black neighborhood. Jan and Mary are oblivious to the offensively patronizing way they treat Bigger. After dinner

▶▶ **Recommended Readings**

Michael Fabre. *The Unfinished Quest of Richard Wright.* Iowa City: University of Iowa Press, 1973.

Joyce Ann Joyce. *Richard Wright's Art of Tragedy.* New York: Warner Books, 1986.

▶▶ **Teaching Notes**

The most distinguishing feature of black literature may be the way that black writers have attempted to create spaces of freedom in their work, to liberate place, a trait that also marks black religious culture and folk cultural practices, such as storytelling.

Richard Wright (1908–1960) The first black writer to command serious attention in mainstream American literature. In *Native Son* (1940) and *Black Boy* (1945) Richard Wright provided incisive critiques of American racism. In his early works he poignantly portrayed the pathos of black southern migrants to the urban industrial north.

Bigger drives them around the city while they drink and make love in the back seat.

When Jan leaves, Bigger takes an intoxicated Mary home. Because Mary is too drunk to walk, Bigger carries her to her room and is putting her to bed when blind Mrs. Dalton comes to check on her daughter. Bigger panics. He covers Mary's head with a pillow to keep her quiet. When Mrs. Dalton leaves, Bigger discovers he has inadvertently smoth-

PROFILE ❖ Langston Hughes

Langston Hughes was born in Joplin, Missouri, in 1902 and was raised by his maternal grandmother, Mary Langston. His father, James Hughes emigrated to Mexico, and his mother, Carrie Langston, remarried. Hughes became fascinated by black urban folk culture, which had been transplanted from the rural South by the great migration. He joined his mother in Cleveland in 1916, attended an integrated high school, and began to publish. He dropped out of Columbia University in 1922, lived in Harlem, and traveled to Europe and Africa. With the publication of *The Weary Blues* in 1926, his career took off. Hughes was enraptured by the language of the blues.

Langston Hughes identified with poor and working class black people. He used his poetry, prose, and playwriting skills to make the dignity and beauty of black people visible and known.

Hughes once referred to himself as "a literary sharecropper." Admirers called him a range of names—"Poet Laureate of the Negro People," for starters. During his career he produced fifteen volumes of poetry, two collections of short stories, one novel, two volumes of autobiography—*The Big Sea* (1940) and *I Wonder as I Wander* (1956)—and fifteen plays, along with

librettos, scripts, essays, songs, translations, anthologies, children's stories, biographies and histories for the young, and two decades of weekly newspaper columns. He recorded the humor, wisdom, dialects, moods, and music of black people. One of the best examples of his social poetry was "The Negro Speaks of Rivers":

I've known rivers:
I've known rivers ancient as the world and older
    than the flow of human blood in human veins.
My soul has grown deep like the rivers.
I bathed in the Euphrates when dawns were young.
I built my hut near the Congo and it lulled me to
    sleep.
I looked upon the Nile and raised the pyramids above
    it.
I heard the singing of the Mississippi when Abe
    Lincoln went down to New Orleans, and I've seen
    its muddy bosom turn all golden in the sunset.
I've known rivers:
Ancient, dusky rivers.
My soul has grown deep like the rivers.

In 1932 Hughes visited Moscow, where he felt comfortable and appreciated. He was impressed by the absence of Jim Crow segregation and discrimination and ignored Stalin's oppression and murders. But Hughes was never a member of the Communist Party. He eventually became disillusioned with the Soviet Union. Hughes remains an enduring symbol of the artist who championed black folk culture as authentic American culture.

Source: Poem from *Collected Poems* by Langston Hughes. © 1994 by the Estate of Langston Hughes. Used by permission of Alfred A. Knopf, a division of Random House, Inc.

Hughes

ered Mary. He then burns her body in the basement furnace. Not fully grasping what he has done, Bigger writes a ransom note signed with a phony name to make it seem that Mary has been kidnapped. When Mary's remains are discovered, Bigger flees. Fearing she might betray him, Bigger then murders his girlfriend, Bessie. Bigger is captured, tried, and condemned. The remainder of the novel explores the hysteria and bigotry that envelop the case, the harsh criminal justice system, the insensitivity of the Communist Party, which seeks to exploit Bigger's plight, and the poverty and social ills that plagued Chicago's African-American communities during the Depression.

At the center of the drama is Wright's exploration of how Bigger comes to terms with his murder of Mary and Bessie. In conversations with Max, his communist lawyer, he realizes his irrational fear of white people had caused him to kill the two women. Bigger realizes he was in fact a product of his experiences in the ghetto. At the end of the novel he says, "What I killed for I am."

Wright's novel poignantly and chillingly thrust the impact of urbanization and racism on black men and women into the collective consciousness of the American people. One white critic declared,

> "Speaking from the black wrath of retribution, Wright insisted that history can be punishment. He told us the one thing even the most liberal whites preferred not to hear: that Negroes were far from patient or forgiving, that they were scarred by fear, that they hated every moment of their suppression even when seeming most acquiescent, and that often enough they hated us the decent and cultivated white men who from complicity or neglect shared in the responsibility of their plight."

In his closing arguments, the lawyer, Max, describes the psychological conditions that led Bigger to kill and warns of the destructive potential of suppressed black rage:

> The hate and fear which we have inspired in him, woven by our civilization into the very structure of his consciousness and into his blood and bones, into the hourly functioning of his personality, have become the justification of his existence. . . . Kill him and swell the tide of pent up lava that will some day break loose, not in a single, blundering crime, but in a wild cataract of emotion that will brook no control.

Native Son was an immediate success. It became a Book-of-the-Month Club selection and has sold millions of copies.

James Baldwin Challenges Wright

Wright's influence on American literature has been immense. He was the first African-American writer to enjoy an international reputation and showed that success and militancy were not mutually exclusive. A younger generation of black writers, however, especially James Baldwin (1924–1987), took issue with Wright. African Americans, they argued, need not all be portrayed as hapless victims of American racism. In a

famous short essay, "Everybody's Protest Novel," in 1949, Baldwin argued that Bigger's tragedy was not that he was black, poor, and scared. It was that he had accepted "a theology that denies him life, that he admits the possibility of his being sub-human and feels constrained, therefore, to battle for his humanity according to those brutal criteria bequeathed him at his birth." Baldwin concluded, "The failure of the protest novel lies in its rejection of life, the human being, the denial of his beauty, dread, power, in its insistence that it is his categorization alone which is real and which cannot be transcended." In turn, Wright accused Baldwin of trying to destroy his reputation and of betraying all African-American writers who wrote **protest literature**. "What do you mean, protest!" Wright demanded. "All literature is protest. You can't name a single novel that isn't protest."

Baldwin answered Wright in a second essay in 1951 entitled, "Many Thousand Gone." "Wright's work," Baldwin declared, "is most clearly committed to the social struggle. . . . [T]hat artist is strangled who is forced to deal with human beings solely in social terms; and who has, moreover, as Wright had, the necessity thrust on him of being the representative of some thirteen million people. It is a false responsibility (since writers are not congressmen) and impossible, by its nature, of fulfillment."

The controversy ended the budding friendship between Wright and Baldwin. Baldwin, whose work would soon include many powerful and revealing novels and insightful essays, inherited the mantle of "best-known black American male writer" (see Chapter 22).

Ralph Ellison and *Invisible Man*

The most intricate novel about the black experience in America written during this era was Ralph Ellison's (1914–1994) *Invisible Man,* which won the National Book Award for fiction in 1952. Partially autobiographical, it traces the life of a young black man from his early years in a southern school (a thinly disguised Tuskegee Institute) through his migration to New York City. The novel explores class tensions within American society and within the black community. It illuminates the interaction between white and black Americans with a balanced incisive perspective.

Although he wrote many essays, *Invisible Man* was Ellison's only completed novel. He argued that the black tradition teaches one "to deflect racial provocation and to master and control pain. . . . It is a tradition which abhors as obscene any trading on one's own anguish for gain or sympathy. . . . It takes fortitude to be a man and no less to be an artist. Perhaps it takes even more if the black man would be an artist." He concluded, "It would seem to me, therefore, that the question of how the 'sociology of his existence' presses upon the Negro writer's work depends upon how much of his life the individual writer is able to transform into art."

 Reading Check What was the impact of the work of Richard Wright and Ralph Ellison?

▶ **Reading Check**

Like other black writers of their time, Richard Wright and Ralph Ellison explored black identity and to describe the reality of black urban life in America. Wright's *Native Son* looked at the root causes of violence and anger in young black men. Ellison's Invisible Man explored class tensions within the black community and in American society as a whole. Wright and Ellison's work brought these issues to the attention of the general reading public.

▶ **Teaching Notes**

Echoing Du Bois's now classic characterization of the "twoness" of the African-American character, Ellison observed, "[Black people] are an American people who are geared to what is and who yet are driven by a sense of what it is possible for human life to be in this society."

Section 5

African Americans in Sports

GUIDE TO READING

▶ What was the significance of the achievements of Jesse Owens and Joe Louis in sports for African Americans?

▶ What made Jackie Robinson such a good candidate to break the color barrier in baseball?

KEY TERMS

▶ Aryan race, p. 963

▶ Negro American League, p. 694

Jesse Owens and Joe Louis

It is in the arena of professional sports that black Americans have demonstrated what human life can achieve when unconstrained by racism. The experiences of black men and women in American sports are a microcosm of their lives in American society. The privileges whites enjoyed in sports in this era paralleled the disadvantages and exclusions that were a constant part of black life. In the 1930s two black athletes, Jesse Owens and Joe Louis, captured the world's attention and inspired African Americans with pride, hope, and pleasure.

Jesse Owens (1913–1980) was born on an Alabama sharecropping farm but grew up in Cleveland, Ohio. A talented runner, he studied at Ohio State University and prepared for the 1936 Olympics, which were to be held in Berlin, the capital of Nazi Germany. Many African-American leaders objected to participating in the games because they believed this would help legitimate the Nazi myth of the superiority of the so-called **Aryan race**. Owens participated to debunk that myth. He

African-American Milestones in Sports

1934 The Negro National League is revived.

1936 Jesse Owens wins four gold medals at Berlin Olympics.

1937 Joe Louis defeats James J. Braddock to win world heavyweight title. The Negro American League is formed.

1938 Joe Louis defeats the German Max Schmeling.

1947 Jackie Robinson signs with the Brooklyn Dodgers to become the first black major-league baseball player. Dodgers win the National League Pennant.

1948 Alice Coachman wins a gold medal in the high jump to become the first black woman Olympic champion.

Larry Doby joins the Cleveland Indians, becoming the first black player in the American League.

Brooklyn Dodgers hire their second black player, Roy Campanella.

1949 Jackie Robinson wins the National League's Most Valuable Player Award.

▶▶ Guide to Reading/Key Terms

For answers, see the *Teacher's Resource Manual.*

▶▶ **Recommended Readings**

Richard Bak. *Joe Louis: The Great Black Hope.* New York: Da Capo Press, 1998.

Jackie Robinson. *I Never Had It Made.* New York: G. P. Putnam's Son, 1972.

Publicity photo of a young Joe Louis who rose from sharecropping roots to become a heavyweight boxing champion.

succeeded, becoming the first Olympian ever to win four gold medals. Hitler left the stadium to avoid congratulating Owens. His snub meant little to African Americans who relished Owens's victory over racism.

Joe Louis Barrow (1914–1981), like Owens, was the son of Alabama sharecroppers. His family migrated to Detroit, Michigan, when he was twelve. Although his mother wanted him to be a violinist, Joe Louis—he dropped the name Barrow—had other interests. As a youth, Louis displayed impressive boxing ability and won a string of local victories. In 1935 he faced former heavyweight champion Primo Carnera. A record crowd of 62,000 attended the fight in New York. The fight had political overtones. Louis was fighting an Italian-American at a time when Benito Mussolini, the Fascist dictator of Italy, was about to invade Ethiopia. Ethiopia was the oldest black independent nation in Africa, whose ruler, Emperor Haile Selassie, many black Americans admired. Sports writers and police were amazed to observe everybody cheering when Louis beat Carnera in the sixth round.

Louis won the world heavyweight title against James J. Braddock in 1937 and beat the German Max Schmeling in a symbolic victory over Nazism in 1938. Louis retained the world heavyweight title until 1949.

 Reading Check What was the significance of the achievements of blacks in sports for African Americans?

Breaking the Color Barrier in Baseball

Although African Americans were integrated in track and in boxing, professional baseball remained strictly segregated until after World War II. Despite the hardships of the Depression, however, virtually every major black community tried to field its own baseball team. The Negro National League, which had folded in 1932, was revived in 1934, and a second league, the **Negro American League**, formed in 1937. Many of the players in the Negro leagues, including such legends as Josh Gibson, Satchel Paige, Leon Day, and Cool Papa Bell, would have equaled or excelled their white counterparts in the major leagues. Except for Paige, they never had the chance.

In 1947, however, major-league baseball, which had been a white man's game since the departure of Fleetwood Walker in 1887, became integrated again when Jackie Robinson signed to play with the Brooklyn Dodgers. In 1945 Branch Rickey, the general manager of the Dodgers, decided to sign a black ball player to improve the Dodgers' chances of winning the National League pennant and the World Series. After scouting the Negro Leagues, he signed twenty-six-year-old Jackie Robinson.

▶ **Reading Check**

Athletes like Jesse Owens, Joe Louis, and Jackie Robinson inspired African Americans with pride and hope. They demonstrated to the general public that, when unconstrained by racism, blacks could compete at the highest levels.

Jackie Robinson (1919–1972) broke baseball's color barrier when he joined the Brooklyn Dodgers in 1947. He silently endured considerable hostility and threats from angry white citizens.

Robinson was the ideal choice. He was a superb athlete and a man of fortitude and immense determination. Born in Georgia and raised in southern California, he had been an All-American running back in football at UCLA. He had played baseball for the legendary Kansas City Monarchs of the Negro leagues. Robinson was also committed to black people and racial progress. Robinson played the 1946 season for the Brooklyn Dodgers minor-league team in Montreal where he and his wife Rachel were warmly received by the Canadians. But spring training in segregated Florida was difficult to endure.

Robinson broke the color barrier when he opened at first base for the Dodgers in April 1947. Taunted, ridiculed, and threatened by some spectators and players, he responded by playing spectacular baseball. He won the Rookie of the Year honors in 1947. The Dodgers won the National League pennant. Robinson retired in 1957 but remained outspoken on racial issues until his death from diabetes in 1972.

In July 1947 Larry Doby became the first black player in the American League when he joined the Cleveland Indians. As other major-league teams also signed black players, the once-popular Negro Leagues withered.

 Reading Check What made Jackie Robinson a good candidate to break the color barrier in baseball?

▶ **Reading Check**

Robinson was a great athlete. He was a man of fortitude and determination and had a college education. Moreover, he was committed to the cause of racial equality. This background allowed him to excel even under the enormous pressure and difficult conditions he faced.

GUIDE TO READING

▶ How did black churches help African-American migrants adjust to urban life?

▶ What were the alternative religious movements and how did they help African Americans?

KEY TERMS

▶ proletariat, p. 696

▶ Nation of Islam, p. 697

▶ Peace Mission Movement, p. 697

➤ **Guide to Reading/Key Terms**

For answers, see the *Teacher's Resource Manual.*

Section 6

Black Religious Culture

The Black Church

The black church helped hundreds of thousands of migrants adjust to urban life while affirming an enduring set of core values consisting of freedom, justice, equality, and an African heritage. There was of course, no single "black church." The term is a shorthand way of referring to a collection of institutions. It includes most prominently seven independent, historic, and black-controlled denominations: the African Methodist Episcopal Church, the African Methodist Episcopal Zion Church; the Christian Methodist Episcopal Church; The National Baptist Convention, Incorporated; the National Baptist Convention of America, Unincorporated; the Progressive National Baptist Convention; and the Church of God in Christ. Together, these denominations account for more than 80 percent of all black Christians.

The black church helped black workers make the transition from being southern peasants to being part of a northern urban **proletariat**. Yet the relationship between black religious tradition and the secular lives of black people was always changing. The blues and jazz performed in nightclubs were transformed into urban gospel music. Many of the nightclub musicians and singers received their training and first public performances in their churches. During the Depression, the black church helped black people survive by enabling them to pool their resources and by offering inspiration and spiritual consolation.

Alternative Black Religions

Alternative religious groups became prominent during the 1930s and 1940s. They addressed specific needs growing out of the Depression and the traumatic experience of relocating to alien and often hostile northern cities. Elijah Muhammad's Nation of Islam and Father Divine's Peace Mission Movement combined secular concerns with sacred beliefs. Both strengthened a sense of identity, affirmation, and community among their members.

The Nation of Islam

The **Nation of Islam** emerged in 1929, the year Timothy Drew died. Drew, who took the name Nobel Drew Ali, was founder of the Moorish Science Temple of America, which flourished in Chicago, Detroit, and other cities in the 1920s. After his death, a modified version of the Moorish Science Temple emerged in 1930 in Detroit. It was led by a mysterious door-to-door peddler of silks and other items that supposedly originated in Africa, known variously as Wallace D. Fard, Master Farad Muhammad, or Wali Farad. He wrote two manuals of instruction, *The Secret Ritual of the Nation of Islam* and *Teaching for the Lost-Found Nation of Islam in a Mathematical Way*. His teachings that black people were the true Muslims attracted many poor residents in Depression-era Detroit. In addition to the beliefs of Nobel Drew Ali, Fard's Nation of Islam also taught a mixture of Koranic principles, the Christian Bible, his own beliefs, and those of nationalist Marcus Garvey.

In 1934, after establishing a Temple of Islam, Fard disappeared. One of his disciples, Elijah Poole (1897–1975), renamed Elijah Muhammad by Fard, became leader of the Detroit temple and then of a second temple in Chicago. The Nation attracted the attention of federal authorities during World War II when its members refused to serve in the military. Muhammad was arrested in May 1942 on charges of inciting his followers to resist the draft and was imprisoned in Milan, Michigan, until 1946. After his release he settled in Chicago and began to expand his movement.

The Nation of Islam taught that black people were the earth's original human inhabitants who had lived, according to Elijah Muhammad, in the Nile Valley. Approximately six thousand years ago, a magician named Yakub produced white people. These white people proved so troublesome that they were banished to Europe where they began to spread evil. Their worst crime was their enslavement of black people. Elijah Muhammad taught that white supremacy was ending and black people would rediscover their authentic history and culture. To prepare for the coming millennium, he instructed members to adhere to a code of behavior that included abstaining from many traditionally southern black foods, especially pork. Members subscribed to a family-centered culture in which women's role was to produce and rear the next generation. The Nation also demanded part of the South for a black national state.

Father Divine and the Peace Mission Movement

Father Major Jealous Divine (ca. 1877–1965) was born George Baker in Savannah. Little is known about his early life. He captured attention in 1919 when he settled with twenty followers in Sayville, New York, and began what became known in the 1930s as the **Peace Mission Movement**. Divine secured domestic jobs for many of his followers on

Chapter 20

Witnessing History . . .

The treatment that the Negro soldier has received has been resented not only by the Negro soldier but by the Negro civilian population as well. In fact, any straight-thinking person with a sense of justice and right, without any respect to color or race, must realize the dangers inherent in the evil practices that have been permitted to exist in the Army. It is not a pleasant thought for Negroes to ponder that their tax money is being spent to help maintain an army that has little regard for the real principles of democracy.

—David H. Bradford, *The Louisville Courier Journal*, September 2, 1941

? How does the quote show the irony of military segregation for African Americans?

Chapter Preview

▶ **Witnessing History**

The irony is that the tax dollars of African Americans support an army that did not permit black soldiers to serve with dignity and respect.

▶ **Teaching Notes**

The Cold War also had a tremendous impact on African Americans and their struggle for freedom. The two sides of this conflict avoided direct confrontation with each other. Instead, to a great degree, they enlisted the peoples of Africa, Asia, and Latin America as proxies. U.S. leaders, seeking to convince these peoples of America's virtues as a democracy, were pressed to address the segregation and racial discrimination that remained firmly imbedded in the basic fabric of American life. The U.S. Department of State sponsored worldwide tours of outstanding black jazz musicians to represent the positive dimensions of American culture.

International events replaced the Great Depression as the defining force in the lives of African Americans. In preparing for and in fighting World War II, America finally emerged from the Depression and laid the basis for an era of unprecedented prosperity. Industrial and military mobilization resulted in the movement of millions of people, many of them African American, from agriculture into the cities. This population shift substantially increased black voting strength in the North and West. The moral recoil from the savage racial policies of the Nazis drove the issue of black equality to the forefront of national politics. Moreover, hundreds of thousands of black men and women learned new skills and ideas while serving in the armed forces. Many resolved to come home and claim their rights. Events abroad and in the United States during the 1940s heightened black consciousness and led to a more aggressive militancy among local leaders and black citizens in southern states.

The advocacy groups and black press that had come of age during the 1930s and 1940s focused attention on fighting racism and demanded the full rights and responsibilities of citizens for all people. The result was a powerful movement for civil rights that many liberal white Americans and, increasingly, key institutions in the national government supported.

These favorable developments, however, provoked strong resistance. White Southerners used all the power at their command to defend segregation. The push for a new democracy, on one hand, and the Cold War mentality, on the other would indelibly place their stamp on the emerging civil rights movement.

Section 1

World War II

On the Eve of War, 1936–1941

As the world economy wallowed in the Great Depression, the international order collapsed in Europe and Asia. Germany under the dictatorship of Adolf Hitler (1889–1945) and Italy under the dictatorship of Benito Mussolini (1883–1945) created an alliance, known as the **Axis**. They aimed to take economic and political control of Europe. These fascist dictators advocated a political program based on extreme nationalism. They brutally suppressed internal opposition and used violence to gain their will abroad. Germany was the dominant partner in the Axis. Hitler was driven by a virulent form of racism and Anglo-Saxon supremacy. Unlike racists in the United States, he focused his hatred on Jews, blaming them for all Germany's social and economic problems. But the Nazis also despised black people and considered them inferior human beings. They discriminated against Germans with African ancestors and banned jazz music. Through the late 1930s, the Germans and Italians embarked on a series of military campaigns that placed much of Central Europe under their power. In August 1939 Germany signed a nonaggression pact with the Soviet Union, a prelude to a September 1 attack on Poland by Germany, which the Soviets joined a few weeks later. Britain and France reacted to the invasion by declaring war on Germany, thus beginning World War II.

As Germany and Italy pursued their plans in Europe during the 1930s, the Empire of Japan sought to extend its power and territory in Asia. The Japanese wanted to drive out Britain, France, the Netherlands, and the United States, which had extensive economic interests and colonial possessions in Asia. (The United States controlled the Philippines, Hawaii, Guam, and other Pacific islands.) Japan's aggressive and expansionist policies also led to conflict with the Soviet Union in Manchuria and with the Nationalist regime in China. The Japanese had become involved against China in a long and bloody struggle in the 1930s. The United States supported China. The U.S. encouraged the European powers to resist Japanese demands for economic and territorial concessions in their Asian colonies. Japan's alliance with Nazi Germany and Fascist Italy further aggravated United States–Japanese relations. These tensions led to war on December 7, 1941, when the Japanese bombed American warships at Pearl Harbor, Hawaii, and launched a massive offensive against British, Dutch, and American holdings throughout the Pacific.

GUIDE TO READING

▶ How did African Americans use the World War II crisis to protest racial discrimination?

▶ What was Executive Order #8802 and how effective was it?

KEY TERMS

▶ Axis, p. 707

▶ fascism, p. 708

▶ Double V campaign, p. 709

▶ March on Washington Movement (MOWM), p. 709

▶ Executive Order #8802, p. 711

▶ Fair Employment Practices Committee (FEPC), p. 711

▶▶ **Guide to Reading/Key Terms**

For answers, see the *Teacher's Resource Manual.*

▶▶ **Living Words Audio Clips**

Track 35 *Roosevelt and Hitler: Buster Ezell's Wartime Song, or, Strange Things Are Happenin' in the Land performed by Buster Ezell*
Track 36 *Pearl Harbor; performed New York, Georgia Singers*

▶▶ **Teaching Notes**

President Franklin D. Roosevelt watched the events in Europe and Asia with growing concern, but had only a limited ability to react. Despite its large economy, America was not a preeminent military power at the time. FDR had trouble convincing Congress to enlarge the Army and Navy, because Isolationists believed that the United States had been hoodwinked into fighting World War I and should avoid again becoming entangled in a foreign war. During the late 1930s the president had managed to overcome some of this opposition. By early 1940 the United States had instituted its first peacetime draft to provide men for the U.S. Army and Navy.

African Americans and the Emerging World Crisis

Many African Americans responded to the emerging world crisis with growing activism. When Ethiopia was invaded by Italy in 1935, it was, along with Liberia and Haiti, one of three black-ruled nations in the world. Black communities throughout the United States organized to send it aid. Mass meetings in support of the embattled Ethiopians were held in New York City. Similar rallies occurred in other large cities while reporters from black newspapers brought the horror of this war home to their readers. Although it was a violation of American law for its citizens to engage in active combat in Ethiopia, over seventeen thousand African Americans indicated a desire to help Emperor Haile Selassie (r. 1930-1974) resist the Italian invasion. Despite fierce resistance, the Italians won the war, in part, by using poison gas. The conflict alerted many African Americans to the dangers of **fascism**. It also reawakened interest in, and identification with, Africa, and fanned the flames of black internationalism.

A civil war in Spain had stimulated renewed activism among leftist African Americans. In 1936 the left-leaning Spanish Republic became embroiled in a civil war against a Fascist movement led by General Francisco Franco (1892–1975) whom Germany and Italy supported. About a hundred African Americans traveled to Spain in 1936–1937 to serve with the Abraham Lincoln Battalion, an integrated fighting force of three thousand American volunteers. Support of the Abraham Lincoln Battalion reflected a commitment by a few African Americans to the communists' vision of internationalism. Mobilization for war, however, would soon bring most black people and their organizations into the fight against fascism abroad and for equality and justice in the United States.

A. Philip Randolph and the March on Washington Movement

In 1939 and 1940, the American government, along with the governments of France and Britain, spent so much on arms that the U.S. economy was finally lifted out of the Depression. But the United States mobilized its economy for war and rebuilt its military in keeping with past practices of discrimination and exclusion. As unemployed white workers streamed into aircraft factories, shipyards, and other centers of war production, most jobless African Americans were left waiting at the gate. Most aircraft manufacturers would hire black people only in janitorial positions no matter what their skills. Many all-white AFL unions enforced closed-shop agreements that prevented their employers from hiring black workers who were not members of the labor organization. Government-funded training programs regularly rejected black applicants. They often reasoned that training them would be pointless given their poor prospects of finding skilled work. The

▶ **Teaching Notes**

Among the 100 African Americans who traveled to Spain were two women: Salaria Kee, who actually nursed the wounded on the battlefield, and Chicagoan Thyra Edwards, who participated in the Medical Bureau and North American Committee to Aid Spanish Democracy.

▶ **Recommended Reading**

William R. Scott. *The Sons of Sheba's Race: African-Americans and the Italo-Ethiopian War, 1935–1941*. Bloomington, IN: Indiana University Press, 1993. A detailed and illuminating account of African American responses to the Italian invasion of Ethiopia and the growth of black internationalism.

Paula F. Pfeffer. *A. Philip Randolph, Pioneer of the Civil Rights Movement*. Baton Rouge, LA: Louisiana State University Press, 1990. A richly insightful biography of a pioneering labor leader and activist who's March on Washington Movement in 1941 was essential to the formation of the first Fair Employment Practices Committee and the integration of the armed services.

United States Employment Service (USES) filled "whites-only" requests for defense workers. The military itself made it clear that it would accept black men in their proportion to the population, about 11 percent at the time. It would put them in segregated units and assign them to service duties. The navy limited black servicemen to menial positions. The Marine Corps and the Army Air Corps refused to accept them altogether.

When a young African-American man wrote the Pittsburgh *Courier* and suggested a **Double V campaign**—victory over fascism abroad and over racism at home—the newspaper adopted his words as the battle cry for the entire race. Fighting this struggle in a nation at war would be difficult, but the effort led to the further development of black organizations and transformed the worldview of many African-American soldiers and civilians.

African-American protest groups and newspapers criticized discrimination in the defense program. Two months before the 1940 presidential election, the NAACP, Urban League, and other groups pressed President Roosevelt to take action. The president listened to their protests. Aside from a few token gestures—appointing Howard University Law School dean William Hastie as a "civilian aide on Negro affairs" in the Department of War and promoting Benjamin O. Davis, the senior black officer in the army, to brigadier general—he responded with little of substance. As a result, during late 1940 the NAACP and other groups staged mass protest rallies around the nation. With the election safely won, the president, anxious not to offend white southern politicians he needed to back his war program, refused even to meet with black leaders.

A. Philip Randolph, who was president of the Brotherhood of Sleeping Car Porters had been working with other groups to get Roosevelt's attention. In January 1941 he called on black people to unify their protests and direct them at the national government. He suggested that ten thousand African Americans march on Washington under the slogan "We loyal Negro-American citizens demand the right to work and fight for our country." In the coming months Randolph helped create the **March on Washington Movement (MOWM)**, which soon became the largest mass movement of black Americans since the activities of Marcus Garvey's Universal Negro Improvement Association of the 1920s. The MOWM's demands included a presidential order forbidding companies with government contracts from engaging in racial discrimination, eliminating race-based exclusion from defense training courses, and requiring the USES to supply workers on a nonracial basis. Randolph also wanted an order to abolish segregation in the armed forces and the president's support for a law withdrawing the benefits of the National Labor Relations Act from unions that refused to grant membership to black Americans. Departing from the leadership tactics of most other African-American protest groups of the time, Randolph

Horace Pippins's (1888–1946) *Mr. Prejudice* (1943) is a powerful expression of black Americans' ongoing struggle against racial discrimination, segregation, and violence even within a nation at war against facism, Nazism, and the spread of communism. Oil on canvas. 18 × 14 inches. Philadelphia Museum of Art, gift of Dr. and Mrs. Matthew T. Moore. Photo by Graydon Wood. 1984-108-1.

▶▶ **Document**

20-4 *Jim Crow In The Army Camps, 1940, and Jim-Crow Army, 1941*
Despite their patriotism, commitment, and a reputation as exemplary fighting men in past wars, African-American soldiers were segregated. Government policies mirrored racism found in civilian life and accepted the doctrine of "separate but equal."

▶▶ **Recommended Readings**

John Morton Blum. *V Was for Victory: Politics and American Culture during World War II*. New York: Harcourt Brace Jovanovich, 1996.

Herbert Garfinkel. *When Negroes March: The March on Washington Movement in the Organizational Politics for FEPC*. New York: Atheneum, 1973.

WHY SHOULD WE MARCH?

What Are Our Immediate Goals?

1. To mobilize five million Negroes into one militant mass for pressure.

2. To assemble in Chicago the last week in May, 1943, for the celebration of

"WE ARE AMERICANS – TOO" WEEK

And to ponder the question of Non-Violent Civil Disobedience and Non-Cooperation, and a Mass March On Washington.

15,000 Negroes Assembled at St. Louis, Missouri
20,000 Negroes Assembled at Chicago, Illinois
23,500 Negroes Assembled at New York City
Millions of Negro Americans all Over This Great
Land Claim the Right to be Free!

FREE FROM WANT!
FREE FROM FEAR!
FREE FROM JIM CROW!

"Winning Democracy for the Negro is Winning the War for Democracy!" — A. Philip Randolph

440

Posters like this sought both to attract black support for A. Philip Randolph's March on Washington Movement and to convince political leaders of the strength of the movement.

▶ **Reading Check**

Many African Americans responded to the growing crisis of World War II with greater activism. A. Philip Randolph organized a march on Washington to demand that blacks have right to work and fight for their country. The march was eventually called off, but only after the federal government acknowledged the validity of the marchers' demands.

prohibited white participation and encouraged the participation of the black working class.

Randolph's powerful appeal captured the support of many African Americans who had not before taken part in the activities of middle-class-dominated groups like the NAACP. Soon he alarmed the president by raising the number expected to march to fifty thousand. Roosevelt feared the protest would undermine America's democratic message and provide fuel for German propaganda. He dispatched First Lady Eleanor Roosevelt and New York City mayor Fiorello La Guardia to dissuade Randolph from marching. Their pleas for patience fell on deaf ears. Roosevelt and his top military officials were forced to meet with Randolph and other black leaders. African Americans stood firm and raised the stakes by increasing their estimate of black marchers coming to Washington to 100,000. By the end of June 1941, the president had his aides draft Executive Order #8802, prompting Randolph to call off the march. It was a grand moment.

NAACP leader Roy Wilkins wrote in his autobiography,

> To this day, I don't know if he would have been able to turn out enough marchers to make his point stick . . . but, what a bluff it was. A tall, courtly black man with Shakespearean diction and the stare of an eagle had looked the patrician Roosevelt in the eye—and made him back down.

 Reading Check How did African Americans use the World War II crisis to protest racial discrimination?

Executive Order #8802

On the surface at least, the president's order marked a significant change in the government's stance. It stated in part:

> I do hereby affirm the policy of the United States that there shall be no discrimination in the employment of workers in the defense industry or government because of race, creed, color, or national origin.

Executive Order #8802 instructed all agencies that trained workers to administer such programs without discrimination. To ensure full cooperation with these guidelines, Roosevelt created the **Fair Employment Practices Committee** (**FEPC**) with the power to investigate complaints of discrimination. The order said nothing about desegregation of the military, but private assurances were made that the barriers to entry in key services would be lowered.

Executive Order #8802 was the first major presidential action countering discrimination since Reconstruction, but it was no new Emancipation Proclamation. Black excitement with the order soon soured as many industries, particularly in the South, evaded its clear intent and engaged in only token hirings. The black community learned in this instance and would witness repeatedly in the decades to come were that merely stating antidiscrimination principles and establishing commissions and committees did not erase inequalities. Moreover, the order did not mention union discrimination. Nonetheless, the threat of the march, the issuance of the executive order, and the creation of the FEPC marked the formal acknowledgment by the federal government that it bore some responsibility for protecting black and minority rights in employment. Black activists and their allies would have to continue their fight if the order was to have any meaning. Randolph sought to lead them but would find it difficult to do so because of the opposition of key government agencies—notably the military—the political power of southern congressmen, and a belief among white people that winning the war took precedent over racial issues.

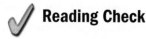 **Reading Check** What was Executive Order #8802 and how effective was it?

▶ **Reading Check**

Executive Order #8802 affirmed that it was the policy of the United States that there should be no discrimination in the employment of workers in the defense industry or government. To ensure compliance, President Roosevelt created the Fair Employment Practices Committee (FEPC). Despite this, many industries, particularly in the South, evaded the intent of the order.

▶ **Document**

20-1 *Executive Order 8802, 1941*
Executive Order 8802 abolished discrimination and required full participation in defense programs.

GUIDE TO READING

▶ What was the basis of the armed forces' racial policy?

▶ What role did African-American physicians and nurses play in the struggle to desegregate the U.S. military during World War II?

▶ What kinds of discrimination did blacks in the military face?

KEY TERMS

▶ National Medical Association, p. 712

▶ December 7, 1941, p. 713

▶ **Guide to Reading/Key Terms**

For answers, see the *Teacher's Resource Manual.*

Section 2

Race and the U.S. Armed Forces

Institutional Racism in the American Military

The demands to end segregation in the armed forces initially met stiffer resistance than pleas for change in the civilian sector. Black men were expected to serve their country. But at the beginning of the war, most were assigned to segregated service battalions, relegated to noncombat positions and kept out of the more prestigious branches of the service. They faced tremendous obstacles to appointment as commissioned officers.

During the prewar mobilization period, 1940–1941, black physicians and leaders of their black professional organization, the **National Medical Association** (**NMA**), queried the War Department about their status. In a new war, would black physicians be integrated into the medical corps or required to practice in separate facilities for sick and wounded black soldiers? In a 1940 speech, Dr. G. Hamilton Francis underscored the concerns of black doctors: "Our nation is again preparing to defend itself against aggression from without. Today, we are ready and willing to contribute all of our skill and energy and to wholeheartedly enlist our services as members of the medical profession, but we must be permitted to take our right places, as evidenced by our training, experience, and ability."

Much of the armed forces' racial policy derived from negative attitudes and discriminatory practices common in American society. Reflecting this ingrained racism, a 1925 study by the American War College concluded that African Americans were physically unqualified for combat duty. It stated that blacks were by nature subservient and mentally inferior, believed themselves to be inferior to white people, were susceptible to the influence of crowd psychology, could not control themselves in the face of danger, and did not have the initiative and resourcefulness of white people.

Based on this and later studies, the War Department laid out two key policies in 1941 for the use of black soldiers. Although they would be taken into the military at the same rate as white inductees, African Americans would be segregated and would serve primarily in noncombat units.

In creating these policies, the army and navy ignored evidence of the fighting ability that African Americans had shown in previous wars,

such as the heroism of Dorie Miller during the attack on Pearl Harbor. Miller was the son of Texas sharecroppers who had enlisted in the navy in 1938. Like all black sailors in the navy at the time, he had been assigned to mess attendant duty. In other words, he was a cook and a waiter. When the Japanese air force attacked the naval base on **December 7, 1941**, the twenty-two-year-old Miller was below decks on the battleship *Arizona.* When his captain was seriously wounded, Miller braved bullets to help move him to a more protected area of the deck. He then took charge of a machine gun, shooting down at least two and perhaps six enemy aircraft before running out of ammunition. Miller had never before fired the gun. On May 27, 1942, the navy cited him for "distinguished devotion to duty, extraordinary courage and disregard for his own personal safety" and awarded him a Navy Cross. The navy then sent Miller back to mess duty without a promotion.

The Costs of Military Discrimination

Although the War and Navy Departments held to the fiction of "separate but equal" in their segregation program, their policies gave black Americans inferior resources or excluded them entirely. Sick and injured black soldiers received treatment in segregated wards in hospitals located on military bases. Black physicians were allowed only to treat black military personnel. Segregation at army camps most often meant that black soldiers were placed in the least desirable spots and denied the use of officers' clubs, base stores, and recreational areas. Four-fifths of all training camps were located in the South, where black soldiers were harassed and discriminated against off base as well as on.

For southern African Americans, even going home in uniform could be dangerous. For example, when Rieves Bell of Starkville, Mississippi, was visiting his family in 1943, three young white men cornered him on a street and attempted to strip off his uniform. Bell fought back and injured one of them with a knife. The army could not save him from the wrath of local civilian authorities. They tried and sentenced Bell to three and a half years in the notorious Parchman state penitentiary for the crime of self-defense.

German prisoners of war were accorded better treatment than African-American soldiers. Dempsey Travis of Chicago recalled his experiences at Camp Shenango, Pennsylvania: "I saw German prisoners free to move around the camp, unlike black soldiers who were restricted. The Germans walked right into the doggone places like any white American. We were wearin' the same uniform, but we were excluded." In 1944 black servicemen stationed at Fort Lawton in Washington State objected to living and working conditions that were inferior to those granted to Italian prisoners of war. Some Italian POWs were allowed to go to local bars that

"above and beyond the call of duty"

DORIE MILLER
Received the Navy Cross at Pearl Harbor, May 27, 1942

This World War II War Department recruitment poster recognizes the heroism of Dorie Miller (1919–1943) at Pearl Harbor. His bravery, however, did not alter the navy's policy of restricting black sailors to the kitchens and boiler rooms of navy vessels.

▶ **Recommended Reading**

Laura Wexler, *Fire in a Canebrake: The Last Mass Lynching in America.* New York: Scribners, 2003. A riveting and sobering account of the lynching by a white mob of four victims on July 25, 1946 in Walton County, Georgia, at Moore's Ford Bridge. The book is a poignant study of the pernicious power of racism in the wake of the global holocaust of World War II.

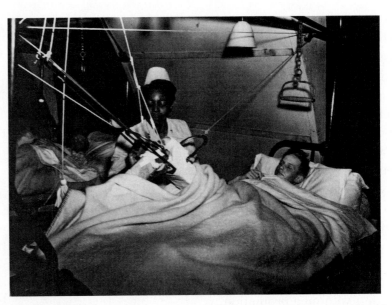

African-American women nurses served at station hospitals at home and abroad. Black nurses such as Lt. Florie E. Grant provided expert care for prisoners-of-war.

refused to admit African Americans. The tension and resentment erupted into a full-scale riot on August 14, 1944, when black soldiers stoned the barracks housing Italian prisoners. One prisoner was killed and 24 others injured. A court-martial convicted 23 black servicemen.

Most of the nearly one million African Americans who served during World War II did so in auxiliary units, notably in the transportation and engineering corps. Soldiers in the transportation corps, almost half of whom were black, loaded supplies and drove them in trucks to the front lines. As they drove toward Germany in 1944 and 1945, African Americans braved enemy fire and delivered the fuel, ammunition, and other goods that made the fight possible. Black engineers built camps and ports, constructed and repaved roads, and performed many other tasks to support frontline troops.

Black soldiers performed well in these tasks but were often subject to unfair military discipline. In Europe, black soldiers were executed in vastly greater numbers than whites even though African Americans made up only 10 percent of the total number of soldiers. One of the most glaring examples of unfair treatment was the navy's handling of a "mutiny" at its Port Chicago base north of San Francisco. On July 17, 1944, in the worst home-front disaster of the war, an explosion at the base killed 320 American sailors, of whom 202 were black ammunition loaders. In the following month 328 of the surviving ammunition loaders were sent to fill another ship. When 258 of them refused to do so, they were arrested. Eventually the Navy charged fifty men with mutiny, convicted them, and sentenced them to terms of imprisonment ranging from eight to fifteen years at Terminal Island in Southern California. The NAACP's Thurgood Marshall filed a brief on behalf of the fifty men arguing that they had been railroaded into prison because of their race, but to no avail.

Soldiers and Civilians Protest Military Discrimination

Black American leaders identified a formidable but vulnerable target in military segregation. Employing a variety of strategies they mobilized the black civilian workforce, black women's groups, college students, and an interracial coalition to participate in resistance to this blatant inequality. They provoked a public dialogue with government and military officials at a pivotal moment when America's leaders most desired to present a united democratic front to the world.

Examples of black protest abound. In 1942 the NAACP's *Crisis*, and *Opportunity*, the organ of the National Urban League, published numerous editorials denouncing the army's segregation policy. Walter White traveled across the country and throughout the world visiting camps and making contacts with black soldiers and their white officers. He inundated the War Department and the president with letters citing examples of improper, hostile, and humiliating treatment of black servicemen by military personnel and in the white communities in which bases were located. Frustration with continued military intransigence, however, forced William Hastie into a dramatic protest. He tendered his resignation as an adviser on Negro affairs on January 5, 1943.

William H. Hastie became the first black American to serve as a federal judge. He sat on the Third Circuit Court of Appeals until 1971.

 Reading Check What was the basis of the armed forces' racial policy?

Black Women in the Struggle to Desegregate the Military

The role of black women in the struggle to desegregate the military has often been overlooked, but their militancy contributed to the effort. A 1942 editorial in the *Crisis* suggested why:

> [T]he colored woman has been a more potent factor in shaping Negro society than the white woman has been in shaping white society because the sexual caste system has been much more fluid and ill-defined than among whites. Colored women have worked with their men and helped build and maintain every institution we have. Without their economic aid and counsel we would have made little if any progress.

The most prominent example of black women's struggle is found in the history of the National Association of Colored Graduate Nurses (NACGN). Mabel K. Staupers, its executive director, led an aggressive fight to eliminate quotas established by the U.S. Army Nurse Corps. Although many black nurses volunteered their services during World War II, they were refused admittance into the navy, and the army allowed only a few to serve. To draw attention to the unfairness of

▶ **Reading Check**

Much of the armed forces' racial policies reflected the racism in American society as a whole. A 1925 American War College study concluded that blacks were unfit for combat duty. Based on this and other study, the War Department decided in 1941 that African American soldiers would be segregated and serve primarily in non-combat units.

▶ **Recommended Reading**

Darlene Clark Hine, "Black Professional and Race Consciousness: Origins of the Civil Rights Movement, 1890–1950." Vol. 89. No. 4 *The Journal of American History*. March 2003, 1279–1294. A detailed discussion of the struggle of black physicians and nurses to end the racial segregation of medicine in the armed forces during World War II.

quotas, Staupers requested a meeting with Eleanor Roosevelt. In November 1944 the First Lady and Staupers met, and Staupers described black nurses' troubled relationship with the armed forces. She informed the First Lady that 82 black nurses were serving 150 patients at the all-black station hospital at Fort Huachuca, Arizona, at a time when the army was complaining of a dire nursing shortage and debating the need to draft nurses. Staupers expounded on the practice of using black women to care for German prisoners of war. She asked, rhetorically, if this was to be the special role of the black nurse in the war? Staupers elaborated, "When our women hear of the great need for nurses in the Army and when they enter the service it is with the high hopes that they will be used to nurse sick and wounded soldiers who are fighting our country's enemies and not primarily to take care of these enemies."

Soldiers and sailors also resisted segregation and discrimination while in the service. Their action included well-organized attempts to desegregate officers' clubs. At Freeman Field, Indiana, for example, one hundred black officers refused to back down when their commanders threatened to arrest them for seeking to use the officers' club. In other bases African-American soldiers responded with violence to violence, intimidation, and threats. Their actions, although put down with dispatch, prompted the army brass to reevaluate their belief in the military efficiency of discrimination.

 Reading Check   What role did African-American physicians and nurses play in the struggle to desegregate the U.S. military during World War II?

These African American Army engineers were sent to serve in Liberia in 1942.

▶▶ **Reading Check**

As the United States mobilized for war black physicians and the leaders of the National Medical Association questioned the War Department about their status. They called for the integration of black physicians and nurses in the medical corps.

Section 3

The Beginning of Military Desegregation

The Government's Response

In response to the militancy of black officers, civil rights leaders, and the press, the War Department made changes and began to take on the challenge of reeducating soldiers, albeit in a limited fashion. The Advisory Committee on Negro Troop Policies was charged with coordinating the use of black troops and developing policy on social questions and personnel training. In 1943 the War Department also produced its own propaganda film—*The Negro Soldier*, directed by Frank Capra—to alleviate racial tensions. This patronizing film emphasized the contributions black soldiers had made in the nation's wars since the American Revolution and was designed to appeal to both black and white audiences.

The War Department also attempted to use propaganda to counter black protest groups and the claims of discrimination found in the black press. The key to this effort was fighter Joe Louis, whom the army believed was "almost a god" to most black Americans. "The possibilities for using him," a secret internal report stated, "are almost unlimited,

GUIDE TO READING

▶ What steps did the government take to counter claims of discrimination in the armed forces?

▶ Who were the Tuskegee Airmen?

▶ How did military experience shape African-American soldiers?

KEY TERMS

▶ *The Negro Soldier*, p. 727

▶ Tuskegee Airmen, p. 721

William Baldwin became the first African-American recruit for general services in the U.S. Navy on June 2, 1942.

▶▶ Guide to Reading/Key Terms

For answers, see the *Teacher's Resource Manual.*

Separate but Equal Training for Black Army Nurses?

In August 1944 Mabel Staupers received this reply from Under Secretary of War Robert Patterson in response to her query about a segregated training center the army had established at Fort Huachuca, Arizona, for black nurses:

August 7, 1944
Mrs. Mabel K. Staupers R.N.,
Executive Secretary,
National Association
of Colored Graduate Nurses, Inc.,
1790 Broadway,
New York 19, N.Y.

Dear Mrs. Staupers:

Thank you for your letter of July 19 with reference to the establishment of the first basic training center for Army Negro nurses at Fort Huachuca.

In establishing the first basic training center for Army Negro nurses at Fort Huachuca, the War Department desired that these nurses receive the best possible training and the most valuable experience for the type of service they would be required to render as Army nurses. It is the policy of the War Department to assign Negro nurses to those hospitals where there is a substantial number of Negro troops in relation to the personnel of the entire installation. The trainee at Fort Huachuca will therefore have the advantage of serving in a facility and under conditions parallel to those under which she will serve as an Army nurse.

You may be assured that the facilities for training afforded Negro nurses at Fort Huachuca will in no way be inferior to those of other similar establishments, and in their subsequent assignments these nurses will have full opportunity to render valuable service to the Army.

Sincerely yours,

(Signed) ROBERT P. PATTERSON

ROBERT P. PATTERSON,

Under Secretary of War

such as touring the army camps as special instructor on physical training; exhibition bouts, for use in radio or in movies; in a movie appearance a flashback could be shown of Louis knocking out Max Schmeling, the champion of the Germans." The same report also mentioned other prominent black men and women who had "great value in any propaganda programs. Other athletes like Ray Robinson, also track athletes, etc.; name bands like Cab Calloway, [Jimmy] Lunceford; stage, screen and concert stars like Ethel Waters, Bill Robinson, Eddie Anderson, Paul Robeson, etc." The effect of this propaganda barrage is impossible to gauge. It did little to counter the real incidents of prejudice and discrimination that most black people experienced in their daily lives.

Racism remained strong throughout the war, but the persistent push of protest groups and the military's need for soldiers gradually loosened its grip. After the attack on Pearl Harbor, nearly all the services had to relax their restrictions on African Americans. The navy, previously the most resistant service, began to accept black men as sailors and noncommissioned officers. By 1943 it allowed African Americans into officer training schools. The Marine Corps, exclusively white throughout its history, began taking African Americans in 1942. Black officers were trained in integrated settings in all services except the Army's Air Corps. The War Department even acted to compel commanding officers to recommend black servicemen for admission to the officer training schools. Soon, over two thousand a year were graduated.

Many African Americans also saw combat, although under white officers. Several African-American artillery, tank destroyer, antiaircraft, and combat engineer battalions fought with distinction in Europe and Asia. Military prejudice seemed to be borne out by the poor showing of the all-black 92nd Combat Division. Investigation revealed that its failure was the result of poor training and leadership by a white officer with no confidence in his men. After the Battle of the Bulge, a massive late-1944 German counterattack, 2,500 black volunteers fought in integrated units. The experiment would not be repeated during the war, but its success laid the groundwork for later changes. Although subject to many of the same kinds of discrimination as African-American men,

African-American women also found expanded opportunities in the military. Approximately four thousand black women served in the Women's Army Auxiliary Corps (WAACs).

Mabel Staupers's efforts also bore fruit in early 1945. When the War Department claimed there was a shortage of nurses, Staupers mobilized nursing groups of all races to write letters and send telegrams protesting the discrimination against black nurses in the Army and Navy Nurse Corps. There was an immediate groundswell of public support to

PROFILE ❖ Mabel K. Staupers

Mabel K. Staupers was born in Barbados, in the British West Indies, on February 27, 1890 to Thomas Clarence and Pauline (Lobo) Doyle. Mother and daughter emigrated to New York in 1903, her father joined them later. In 1917 Mabel became a naturalized citizen of the United States. Mabel received her RN diploma from Freedmen's Hospital School of Nursing in Washington, DC. She worked as a private duty nurse in Washington, DC, and in New York City. She helped to organize the Booker T. Washington Sanatorium, an inpatient clinic for African Americans with tuberculosis. She served as the superintendent from 1920 to 1922.

Staupers further honed her organizing and leadership skills when she became executive secretary of the Harlem Committee of the New York Tuberculosis and Health Association, serving from 1922 to 1934. In 1935, Staupers joined with Mary McLeod Bethune to found the National Council of Negro Women. Staupers also accepted the challenge of revitalizing the National Association of Colored Graduate Nurses (NACGN). She became its first executive director in 1934 and its president in 1949. Under her stewardship the NACGN, in 1951, officially dissolved, and black nurses gained membership in the American Nursing Association.

Staupers's organizing and leadership talent was put to its greatest test during World War II. She mobilized wide-ranging support to end quotas that limited the numbers of black nurses accepted into the Armed Forces Nurse Corps. The Army initially indicated that it would accept fifty-six black nurses to work in the hospital units at Camp Livingston in Louisiana and Fort Bragg in North Carolina. The Navy refused to accept any black women nurses.

When, in January 1945, President Franklin D. Roosevelt announced his support of legislation to draft nurses, Staupers was appalled that the government would entertain such a notion when hundreds of black women nurses were available and eager to serve. She led the struggle to end quotas and discrimination against black women nurses in the armed forces.

In 1961 Staupers published her account of this struggle in a book entitled, *No Time for Prejudice: A Story of the Integration of Negroes in Nursing in the United States* (New York: Macmillan, 1961). In recognition of her courageous and relentless struggle against racial discrimination, the NAACP awarded Staupers the Spingarn Medal in 1951. An array of honors followed. In 1967, New York Mayor John V. Lindsay gave her a citation of appreciation, which read, "To an immigrant who came to the United States and by Individual Effort through Education and Personal Achievement has become an Outstanding American Leader and Distinguished Citizen of America." She died of pneumonia at her home in Washington, DC, in 1989.

Staupers

remove quotas. Buried beneath an avalanche of telegrams from an inflamed public, the War Department declared an end to quotas and exclusion. On January 10, 1945, the army opened its Nurse Corps to all applicants without regard to race. Five days later the navy followed suit. Within a few weeks, Phyllis Daley became the first black woman inducted into the navy's Nurse Corps. Over three hundred black nurses were eventually accepted into the Army Nurse Corps.

The Tuskegee Airmen

The most visible group of black soldiers served in the Army Air Force. In January 1941 the War Department announced the formation of an all-black Pursuit Squadron and the creation of a training program at Tuskegee Army Air Field, Alabama, for black pilots.

Unlike all other units in the army, the 99th Squadron and the 332nd Group, made up of the 100th, 301st, and 302nd Squadrons, had black officers. The 99th went to North Africa in April 1943 and flew its first combat mission against the island of Pantelleria on June 2. Later the squadron participated in the air battle over Sicily, operating from its base in North Africa, and supported the invasion of Italy. The squadron regularly engaged German pilots in aerial combat. General Benjamin O. Davis Jr. commanded the 332nd Group when it was deployed to Italy in January 1944. In July the 99th was added to the 332nd and the Group participated in campaigns in Italy, France, Germany, and the Balkans.

The **Tuskegee Airmen** amassed an impressive record. They flew over 15,500 sorties and completed 1,578 missions. During the two hundred missions in which they escorted heavy bombers deep into Germany's Rhineland, not one of the "heavies" was lost to enemy fighter opposition. They destroyed 409 enemy aircraft, sank an enemy destroyer, and knocked out numerous ground installations. They were well regarded and recognized for their heroism. They accumulated 150 Distinguished Flying Crosses, a Legion of Merit, a Silver Star, 14 Bronze Stars, and 744 Air Medals. Tuskegee pilot Coleman Young (1919–1997; mayor of Detroit 1973–1993) recalled, "once our reputation got out as to our fighting ability, we started getting special requests for our group to escort their group, the bombers. They all wanted us because we were the only fighter group in the entire air force that did not lose a bomber to enemy action. Oh, we were much in demand."

The Transformation of Black Soldiers

A new generation of African Americans became soldiers during World War II. Many would emerge from the experience with an enhanced sense of themselves and a commitment to the fight for black equality. They returned home with a broader perception of the world and a

The distinguished World War II record of the "Tuskegee Airmen," pilots who trained and fought in all-black fighter squadrons, confounded the expectations of white officers who doubted that black men had the ability or nerve to pilot fighter aircraft.

▶ **Recommended Readings**

Charles W. Dryden. *A-Train: Memoirs of a Tuskegee Airman.* Tuscaloosa, AL: University of Alabama Press, 1997.

Alan M. Osur. *Blacks in the Army Air Forces during World War II: The Problem of Race Relations.* Washington, DC: Office of Air Force History, 1977.

▶ **Retracing the Odyssey**

National Museum of the Tuskegee Airmen at Historic Fort Wayne This museum documents the achievements of the combat aviators who served as a segregated unit of the U.S. Armed Forces in World War II. They received their training at the Army Air Corps base in Tuskegee, Alabama. During World War II these black aviators shot down enemy aircraft, bombed barges and enemy power stations, and successfully escorted other fighter pilots to their missions across Europe.

transformed consciousness. Unlike the black soldiers in World War I, a greater percentage of those drafted at the outset of World War II had attended high school and more were either high school or college graduates. Some black soldiers brought so-called radical ideas with them as they were drafted and sent to segregated installations. The urban and northern black servicemen and women and many of the southern rural recruits had a strong sense of their own self-worth and dignity.

In their study of Chicago, sociologists St. Clair Drake and Horace Cayton noted the following:

> At least half of the Negro soldiers—and Bronzeville's men fall into this class—were city people who had lived through a Depression in America's Black Ghettoes, and who had been exposed to unions, the Communist movement, and to the moods of racial radicalism that occasionally swept American cities. Even the rural southern Negroes were different this time—for the thirty years between the First and Second World War has seen a great expansion of school facilities in the South and distribution of newspapers and radios.

Serving in the armed forces first exposed many African Americans to a world outside the segregated South and nurtured a budding internationalism among them. Haywood Stephney of Clarksdale, Mississippi, recalled that when he first encountered segregation in the military he simply thought it was supposed to be that way. He explained,

> Because you grow up in this situation you don't see but one side of the coin. Having not tasted the freedom or the liberty of being and doing like other folks then you didn't know what it was like over across the street. So we accepted it.

Like many others, his experiences during the war quickly removed him from "total darkness" and raised fundamental questions about the racial system of the nation.

Douglas Conner, a Mississippi veteran, captured the collective understanding of the social and political meaning of the war shared by the men in his unit, the 31st Quartermaster Battalion stationed in Okinawa:

> The air people in Tuskegee, Dorie Miller, and the others gave the blacks a sense that they could succeed and compete in a world that had been saying that 'you're nothing.'

Conner insisted that "because of the world war, I think many people, especially blacks, got the idea that we're going back, but we're not going back to business as usual. Somehow we're going to change this nation so that there's more equality than there is now." The personal transformation that Conner and others experienced, combined with a number of international, national, and regional forces, laid the foundation for a modern movement for freedom of opportunity.

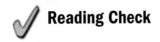 **Reading Check** What steps did the government take to counter claims of discrimination in the armed forces?

▶ **Reading Check**

Black soldiers in World War II were better educated (through high school), less inclined to accept the segregation of the military, had a larger world experience, and were more committed to racial equality.

Section 4

Black People on the Home Front

Black Workers: From Farm to Factory

Just as they did in the military, African Americans on the home front fought a dual war against the Axis and discrimination. Black workers and volunteers helped staff the factories and farms that produced goods for the fight while also purchasing war bonds and participating in other defense activities. The changes brought on by the war also created new points of conflict while exacerbating preexisting problems and occasionally igniting full-scale riots. Throughout the war, protest groups and the black press continued to fight employment discrimination and political exclusion.

The war accelerated the migration of African Americans from rural areas to the cities. Even though the farm economy recovered during the war, the lure of high-paying defense jobs and other urban occupations tempted many black farmers to abandon the land. By the 1940s the bitter experiences of the previous decades had made it clear there was little future in the cotton fields. Boll weevils, competition from other parts of the world, and mechanization reduced the need for black labor. Indeed, by the end of the war, only 28 percent of black men worked on farms, a decline of 13 percent since 1940. More than 300,000 black men left agricultural labor between 1940 and 1944 alone.

The wartime need for workers, backed by pressure from the government, helped break down some of the barriers to employing African Americans in industry. During the war the total number of black workers in nonfarm employment rose from 2,900,000 to 3,800,000. Nearly all industries relaxed their resistance to hiring African-American workers, and thousands moved into previously whites-only jobs.

With so many of their men away at war, black women increasingly found work outside the laundry and domestic service that had previously been their lot. Nationally 600,000 black women—400,000 of them former domestic servants—shifted into industrial jobs. As one aircraft worker wryly put it, "Hitler was the one that got us out of the white folks' kitchen." Even those women who stayed in domestic work often saw their wages improve as the supply of competing workers dwindled.

The abundance of industrial jobs helped spur and direct the migration of African Americans during and after World War II. Some 1.5 million migrants, nearly 15 percent of the population, left the South, swelling the black communities in northern and western cities that had

GUIDE TO READING

▶ How did the war contribute to accelerated black migration to the cities?

▶ How did the war worsen tensions and competition over housing and jobs between black and white Americans?

▶ How did the tactics of the Congress of Racial Equality (CORE) differ from those of existing civil rights groups?

KEY TERMS

▶ Executive Order #9346, p. 724

▶ Southern Regional Council (SRC), p. 726

▶ Congress of Racial Equality, p. 727

▶▶ Guide to Reading/Key Terms
For answers, see the *Teacher's Resource Manual.*

With so many men in the armed forces, women were recruited for jobs in shipyards and airplane factories like this aircraft worker. Between 1940 and 1944, the percentage of black women in the industrial workforce increased from 6.8 percent to 18 percent.

▶ **Recommended Reading**

Herbert Garfinkel. *When Negroes March: The March on Washington Movement in the Organizational Politics for FEPC.* New York: Atheneum, 1973.

significant war industries. By 1950 the proportion of the nation's black population living in the South had fallen from 77 percent to 68 percent. The most dramatic rise in black population was in southern California. Because of its burgeoning aircraft industry and the success of civil rights groups and the federal government in limiting discrimination, Los Angeles saw its relatively small African-American community increase by more than 340,000 during the war.

During the war many unions became more open to African-American workers. Between 1940 and 1945, black union membership rose from 200,000 to 1.25 million. Those unions connected to the CIO, particularly the United Automobile Workers, were the most open to black membership. AFL affiliates were the most likely to treat African Americans as second-class members or to continue to exclude them altogether. Some white unionized workers continued to oppose hiring black workers, even going on strike to prevent it. Their resistance was often deflected by the union leadership, the government, or employers. The growth in black membership did not end racism in unions, even in the CIO. It did provide African Americans a stronger foundation upon which to protest continuing discrimination in employment.

The FEPC During the War

After President Roosevelt issued the executive order banning job discrimination in defense industries with government contracts, thousands of impoverished black southerners rushed to cities in the Pacific Northwest, especially to Seattle. Wartime Seattle had offered jobs in its shipyards, in logging-truck manufacturing, and at the Boeing aircraft production plants. By the end of World War II, Boeing had employed over twelve hundred black workers, approximately 3 percent of its labor force. African Americans also accounted for 7 percent of Seattle's shipyard workers. By 1948 black families in Seattle boasted a median income of $3,314, a mere 10 percent lower than the median for the nation's white families. But the economic good fortune of black workers on the West Coast was not typical of other regions of the country.

In the Middle West and on the East Coast, many African Americans criticized industry's failure to heed the call to end economic discrimination. Responding to the ineffectiveness of the Fair Employment Practices Committee during the first years of the war, in May 1943 President Roosevelt issued **Executive Order #9346**. The order established a new Committee on Fair Employment Practice, increased its budget, and placed its operation directly under the Executive Office of the President. Roosevelt appointed Malcolm Ross, a combative white liberal, to head the committee. Ross proved to be more effective than

the committee's previous leadership. He initiated nationwide hearings of cases concerning discrimination in the shipbuilding and railroad industries. These proceedings caused embarrassment for companies and brought some compliance with the FEPC's orders. Resistance, however was more common. In Mobile, Alabama, for example, the white employees of the Alabama Dry Dock and Shipbuilding Company opposed the FEPC's efforts to pressure the company to promote 12 of the 7,000 African Americans it employed in menial positions to racially mixed welding crews. The white workers went on a rampage, assaulting 50 African Americans. The FEPC thereupon withdrew its plan and agreed in the traditional Jim Crow arrangements for all work assignments. White workers retained their more lucrative positions. The committee failed to redress most of the grievances of black workers. A concerted effort to continue the committee after the war was defeated.

Anatomy of a Race Riot: Detroit, 1943

One of the bloodiest race riots in the nation's history took place in 1943 in Detroit, Michigan, where black and white workers were competing fiercely for jobs and housing. Relations between the two communities in the city had been smoldering for months, with open fighting in the plants and on the streets. White racism, housing segregation, and economic discrimination were part of the problem. The brutality of white police officials was an especially potent factor. Tensions were so high that weeks before the riot NAACP leader Walter White had warned the city could explode in violence at any moment.

The immediate trigger for the riot was a squabble on June 20 between groups of white and black bathers at the segregated city beaches on Belle Isle in the Detroit River. Within hours, two hundred white sailors from a nearby base joined the white mob that pursued and attacked individual black men and women. A rumor that white citizens had killed a black woman and thrown her baby over the bridge spread across the city. The riot spread quickly along Woodward Avenue, the city's major thoroughfare, into Paradise Valley where some 35,000 southern black migrants had, in the spring of 1943, joined the city's already crowded black population. By Monday morning downtown Detroit was overrun with white men roaming in search of more victims. At first the mayor refused to acknowledge that the situation had gotten out of hand, but by Tuesday evening he could no longer deny the crisis.

Six thousand federal troops had to be dispatched to Detroit to restore order. When the violence ended, 34 people had been killed (25 black and 9 white people) and more than 700 injured. Of the 25 black people who died, the Detroit police killed 17. The police did not kill any of the white men who assaulted African Americans or committed arson. Property damage exceeded $2 million and one million man-hours were lost in war production.

▶ **Recommended Reading**

Dominic Capeci and Martha Wilkerson. *Layered Violence: The Detroit Rioters of 1943*. Jackson, MS: University Press of Mississippi, 1991.

Robert Shogan and Tom Craig. *The Detroit Race Riot: A Study in Violence*. New York: Chilton Books, 1964.

In the aftermath, the city created the Mayor's Interracial Committee, the first permanent municipal body designed to promote civic harmony and fairness. Despite the efforts of labor and black leaders, many white people in Detroit, including Wayne County prosecutor William E. Dowling, blamed the black press and the NAACP for instigating the riot. Dowling and others accused the city's black citizens of pushing too hard for economic and political equality and insisted that they operated under communist influence. One of many commissioned reports concluded that black leaders provoked the riot because they had compared "victory over the axis . . . [with] a corresponding overthrow in the country of those forces which . . . prevent true racial equality." In contrast, black leaders, radical trade unionists, and members of other ethnic organizations, especially Jewish groups, blamed, "the KKK, the Christian Front, the Black Dragon Society, the National Workers League, the Knights of the White Camelia, the Southern Voters League, and similar organizations based on a policy of terror and . . . white supremacy."

Old and New Protest Groups on the Home Front

The NAACP grew tremendously during the war. By the end of the war, it stood poised for even greater achievements. Under the editorial direction of Roy Wilkins, the circulation of the NAACP's *Crisis* grew from 7,000 to 45,000. During the war, the *Crisis* was one of the most important sources for information on the status of black men and women. The NAACP's membership increased from 50,000 in 1940 to 450,000 at the end of the war. Even more important, much of this growth occurred in the South, which had more than 150,000 members by 1945. Supreme Court victories and especially close monitoring of the "Double V" campaign help explain these huge increases.

With success, however, came conflict and ambivalence. Leaders split over the value of integration versus self-segregation. They questioned the benefit of relying so heavily on legal cases rather than paying more attention to the concerns and needs of working-class black men and women. Wilkins acknowledged the organization's uncertainty and indecisiveness:

> The war was a great watershed for the NAACP. We had become far more powerful, and now the challenge was to keep our momentum. Everyone knew the NAACP stood against discrimination and segregation, but what was our postwar program to be? Beyond discrimination and segregation, where would we stand on veterans, housing, labor-management relations, strikes, the Fair Employment Practices Commission, organizations at state levels, education? What would we do to advance the fight for the vote in the South? . . . We had a big membership . . . but we didn't know how to use them.

In 1944 southern white liberals joined with African Americans to establish the **Southern Regional Council** (SRC). This interracial coali-

tion was an important example of the local initiative of private citizens. It was devoted to expanding democracy in a region better known for the political and economic oppression and exploitation of its black citizens. The SRC conducted research and focused attention on the political, social, and educational inequalities of black life in the South. Although its patient, gradualist program would soon be overtaken by the events of the 1950s and 1960s, the SRC challenged the facade of southern white supremacy.

▶ **Recommended Reading**

John D'Emilio. Lost Prophet: *The Life and Times of Bayard Rustin*. New York: Simon & Schuster, 2003. A first rate, well-written, thoughtful biography of a key, though often under appreciated, leader in the long struggle for social justice for all Americans.

Congress of Racial Equality

In 1942 a far more strident group called the **Congress of Racial Equality** (**CORE**) had been formed. It pursued different tactics from those of the NAACP, Urban League, and other existing civil rights groups. CORE began in Chicago when an interracial group of Christian pacifists gathered to find ways to make America live up to the ideals of equality and

PROFILE ❖ Bayard Rustin

Bayard Rustin, the preeminent strategist of nonviolent resistance, was born on March 17, 1910, in West Chester, Pennsylvania. Rustin worked behind the scenes to give shape and coherence to the modern civil rights movement. During his youth he belonged to the Young Communist League. But in the 1940s he, along with Pauli Murray and James Farmer, became staff members of the pacifist organization Fellowship of Reconciliation (FOR) and experimented with Gandhian techniques of nonviolent resistance to racial injustice. In 1942 Rustin and Farmer were active in founding the Congress of Racial Equality (CORE). A year later, Rustin refused to be drafted. Convicted of violating the Selective Service Act, he served three years in a federal penitentiary in Ashland, Kentucky.

Upon release from prison, Rustin became race relations secretary for FOR and participated in countless protest organizations. He organized a Free India Committee and directed A. Philip Randolph's Committee against Discrimination in the Armed Forces. He orchestrated CORE's 1947 Journey of Reconciliation, a precursor to the Freedom Rides of 1961, in which sixteen black and white men traveled by bus through the upper South to test new federal laws prohibiting segregated services in interstate transportation. In the late 1950s Rustin served as an important adviser to Martin Luther King Jr. He was one of the key figures in nearly all phases of the civil rights movement of the 1950s and 1960s.

Rustin, who was gay, fought oppression all his life. After the civil rights movement he shifted his attention to combating homophobia. He declared shortly before his death on August 24, 1987, that "the barometer of where one is on human rights questions is no longer the black community, it's the gay community. Because it is the community which is most easily mistreated."

Rustin

justice on which it based its war program. Activists James Farmer and Bayard Rustin were key in getting the group off the ground. Unlike the NAACP, CORE was a decentralized, intensely democratic organization. CORE dedicated itself to the principles of nonviolent direct action as expounded by Indian leader Mohandas Gandhi. Over the course of the war this pacifist organization expanded to other cities and challenged segregation in the North with sit-ins and other protest tactics that the civil rights movement would later adopt.

Black Women

African Americans found many ways to fight discrimination. Women were central to these efforts. Throughout the 1940s, in countless communities across the South and the Middle West, black women organized women's political councils and other groups to press for integration of public facilities—hospitals, swimming pools, theaters, and restaurants—and for the right to pursue collegiate and professional studies. Others were galvanized by the war and took advantage of the limited social and political spaces afforded them to create lasting works in the arts, literature, and popular culture. Women whose names would become virtually synonymous with the modern civil rights movement in the 1950s and 1960s helped lay its foundation in the World War II era. Ella Baker was accumulating contacts and sharpening her organizing skills as she served as the NAACP field secretary. Rosa Parks began resisting segregation laws on Montgomery, Alabama, buses in the 1940s.

Black Students

Black college students also began protesting segregation in public accommodations. The spark that ignited the Howard University campus civil rights movement came in January 1943. Three sophomore women, Ruth Powell from Massachusetts and Marianne Musgrave and Juanita Morrow from Ohio, sat at a lunch counter near the campus and were refused service. They demanded to see the manager and vowed to wait until he came. Instead of the manager, two policemen arrived who instructed the waitress to serve them. When the check arrived the trio learned they had been charged 25 cents each instead of the customary 10 cents. They placed 35 cents on the counter, turned to leave, and were arrested. Ruth Power later reported that "the policemen who arrested us told us we were being taken in for investigation because he had no proof that we weren't 'subversive agents.'" In fact, no charges were lodged against the women. The purpose of their arrest had been to intimidate them. Instead the incident fanned the smoldering embers of resentment in the Howard University student body.

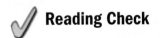 **Reading Check** How did the war worsen tensions and competition over housing and jobs between black and white Americans?

▶ **Reading Check**

As black migration accelerated, tensions over housing and jobs intensified. These tensions could, and did, erupt into violent confrontations such as the 1943 race riot in Detroit, Michigan.

Section 5

The Transition to Peace

The Cold War and International Politics

After the German surrender in May 1945 and the Japanese surrender in August 1945, the United States began the transition to peace. Many of the gains of black men and women were wiped away as the armed forces demobilized. Factories began reinstituting the discriminatory hiring systems in place before the conflict. It was clear segregation and discrimination would face a huge challenge in the coming years. The African-American community was ready, willing, and able to fight in ways undreamed of in earlier eras.

In early 1945, the United Nations began planning for peace. Within a short time, however, the opposing interests of the Soviet Union and the United States led to a long period of intense hostility that became known as the **Cold War**. This conflict soon led to a division of Europe into two spheres, with the Soviets dominating part of Germany and the nations to its east and a coalition of democratic capitalist regimes allied with the United States in the west. Thereafter the overriding goal of the United States and its allies was the "containment" of communism. To this end, the **North Atlantic Treaty Organization** (**NATO**) was formed in 1949 to provide a military counterforce to Soviet power in Europe while American dollars helped rebuild Western Europe's war-shattered economy. The United States forged a similarly close relationship with Japan. Much of the rest of the world, however, became contested terrain during the Cold War.

As the nations of Asia and Africa gained independence from colonial domination over the ensuing decades, the United States struggled to keep them out of the Soviet orbit. It did so through foreign aid, direct military force, and, occasionally, through clandestine operations run by the Central Intelligence Agency (CIA). These military interventions were matched by a rising diplomatic and propaganda effort to convince the emerging nations of the world that the United States was a model to be emulated and an ally to be trusted.

The Cold War had an enormous influence on American society precisely when the powerful movement for African-American rights was beginning to emerge. The long conflict resulted in the rise of a permanent military establishment in the United States. Small in scope before World War II, the reorganized American military enlisted

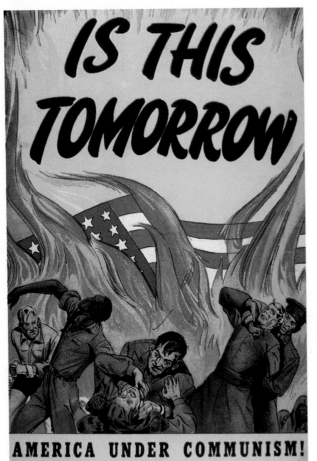

America's Cold War propaganda targeted all citizens, black and white. This anticommunism poster was one of many designed to remind Americans of threats to their freedom and to fan the flames of patriotism.

millions of men and women by the early 1950s and claimed most of the national budget. The federal government also grew in power during the war and provided a check on the control that white Southerners had so long exercised over race relations in their region. American policy makers also became concerned about the nation's ability to win the allegiance of Africans and other nonwhite people who formed the population of the emerging nations. The Soviet Union possessed a powerful propaganda advantage because it could discredit American sincerity by pointing to the deplorable state of race relations within the United States. Hence, during the Cold War, external pressures reinforced efforts to change American racial policy.

African Americans in World Affairs: W. E. B. Du Bois and Ralph Bunche

The Cold War gave new importance to the voices of African Americans in world affairs. Two men, W. E. B. Du Bois and Ralph Johnson Bunche (1904–1971), represent alternative strategies for responding to this opportunity. Du Bois took a highly critical approach to American policy. For half a century he had linked the fate of African Americans with that of Africans. By 1945 he was widely hailed as the Father of Pan-Africanism. In that year he directed the Fifth Pan-African Congress, which met in Manchester, England. The Africans who had been radicalized by World War II dominated the conference and encouraged it to denounce Western imperialism. Du Bois considered the United States a protector of the colonial system and opposed its stance in the Cold War. On returning from the Manchester congress, he declared,

> We American Negroes should know . . . until Africa is free, the
> descendants of Africa the world over cannot escape their chains. . . .
> The NAACP should therefore put in the forefront of its program
> the freedom of Africa in work and wage, education and health,
> and the complete abolition of the colonial system.

In contrast to Du Bois, scholar diplomat Ralph Bunche opted to work within the American system. Bunche held a Harvard doctorate in government and international relations. He had spent much of the 1930s studying the problems of African Americans. During World War II the American government found his expertise on Africa of tremendous value. Bunche became one of the key policy makers for the region. Bunche's analysis of events and changes in Africa and the Far East after World War II led to his appointment as adviser to the U.S. delegation at the San Francisco conference that drafted the United Nations (UN)

Charter. In 1948 he served as acting mediator of the UN Special Committee on Palestine, and in 1949 he negotiated an armistice between Egypt and Israel. He received the Spingarn Medal of the NAACP in 1949, and in 1950 he became the first African American to receive the Nobel Peace Prize. Bunche was committed to winning independence for African nations and freedom for his own people. As he wrote,

> Today, for all thinking people, the Negro is the shining symbol of the true significance of democracy. He has demonstrated what can be achieved with democratic liberties even when grudgingly and incompletely bestowed. But the most vital significance of the Negro . . . to American society . . . is the fact that democracy which is not extended to all of the nation's citizens is a democracy that is mortally wounded.

Anticommunism at Home

The rising tensions with the Soviet Union affected all aspects of domestic life in the United States. Conservatives used fears of communist subversion to attack anyone who advocated change in America. This included people who were, or had been, members of the **Communist Party**, union members, liberals, and people who had fought for African-American rights. The Truman administration (1945–1952) responded to fears of subversion by instituting government loyalty programs. Government employees were dismissed for the merest suspicion of disloyalty. Militant American anticommunism reached a feverish peak in the immediate postwar years. It gave rise to an explosion of hysteria that led to the rise of Wisconsin Republican senator Joseph McCarthy (1909–1957) and the **House Un-American Activities Committee (HUAC)**. The relentless pursuit of "communist sympathizers" by McCarthy and HUAC ruined many lives. HUAC in particular hounded people in the media and in the entertainment industry. Even so prominent a figure as W. E. B. Du Bois was ripe for attack. On February 8, 1951, HUAC indicted him for allegedly serving as an "agent of a foreign principal" in his work with the Peace Information Center. In November a federal judge dismissed all charges against Du Bois. The government had been unable to prove he was an agent of communism. Despite Du Bois's past contributions, fear and personal malice prevented most African-American leaders from defending him.

Paul Robeson

Paul Robeson was one of the most tragic victims of these anticommunist witch-hunts. Robeson had always been an advocate for the rights of African Americans and workers. During the 1930s he worked closely with the Communist Party (although he was never a member), becoming one of the most famous defenders of the Soviet Union. Many leftists of the

▶ **Document**

19-1 *Paul Robeson "Welcome Home Rally," June 19, 1949*

Paul Robeson was a scholar, collegiate athlete, Columbia Law School graduate, consummate performer, and a star of stage and screen.

time became disaffected with the USSR after its 1939 pact with Hitler and after its brutal repressiveness became clear. Robeson, however, doggedly stuck to his belief in Soviet communism.

In the late 1940s, Robeson's pro-Soviet views and inflammatory statements aroused the ire of the U.S. government and its red hunters. A statement he made at the communist-dominated World Congress of the Defenders of Peace in Paris in 1949 provoked particular outrage. "It is unthinkable," Robeson said, "that American Negroes would go to war on behalf of those [the United States] who have oppressed us for generations against a country [the Soviet Union] which in one generation has raised our people to full human dignity of mankind."

Throughout the 1940s Robeson consistently linked the struggles of black America with the struggles of black Africa, brown India, yellow Asia, the black men and women of Brazil and Haiti, and oppressed workers throughout Latin America. Robeson also refused to sign an affidavit concerning past membership in the Communist Party. In response, the U.S. State Department revoked his passport in 1950, explaining "the action was taken because the Department considers that Paul Robeson's travel abroad at this time would be contrary to the best interest of the United States." The travel ban remained in effect until ruled unconstitutional by the Supreme Court in 1958.

Robeson had combined his art and his politics to launch a sustained attack against racial discrimination, segregation, and the ideology of white supremacy and black inferiority as practiced in American society. During the Cold War the state would tolerate no such dissent by even a world-acclaimed black artist.

Henry Wallace and the 1948 Presidential Election

Robeson's struggles illustrate how conservative attacks choked off left-wing involvement in the struggle for black equality. The attacks destroyed Robeson's brilliant singing career. The increasing importance of black votes to Democrats, however, meant that key elements of the African-American liberation struggle remained at the center of national politics. Nowhere was this more apparent than in the 1948 presidential election.

President Harry S Truman was not expected to win this election because he faced a strong challenge from Thomas Dewey, the popular and well-financed Republican governor of New York. Truman's problems were compounded by a challenge from his former secretary of commerce Henry Wallace, who had been Roosevelt's vice president from 1941 to 1945. Wallace ran on the ticket of the communist-backed Progressive Party, which sought to take the votes of liberals, leftists, and civil rights advocates disappointed by Truman's moderation. Wallace also supported

▶ **Document**

20-5 Henry Wallace, Radio Address, 1948
This speech was given for the Progressive Party on NBC in New York City on September 13, 1948.

a peaceful accommodation with the Soviet Union. To undercut Wallace's challenge, Truman began to press Congress to pass liberal programs.

Black votes in key northern states were central to Truman's strategy for victory. African Americans in these tightly contested areas could make the difference between victory and defeat. To retain their allegiance, Truman sought to demonstrate his administration's support of civil rights. In January 1948 he embraced the findings of his biracial Committee on Civil Rights and called for their enactment into law. The committee's report, "To Secure These Rights," was a blueprint for changing the racial caste system in the United States. It recommended passage of federal antilynching legislation, ending discrimination at the ballot box, abolishing the poll tax, desegregating the military, and a whole range of other measures.

The reaction of white southern politicians was swift and threatening, causing Truman to pause. But as the election neared, fear of black abandonment at the polls became so great that the Democratic convention passed a strong pro–civil rights plank. Many white Southerners, led by South Carolina's governor Strom Thurmond, bolted the convention and formed their own States' Rights, or **Dixiecrat, party**. The Dixiecrats carried South Carolina, Alabama, Mississippi, and Louisiana in the election. Wallace carried no state. The failure of the bulwark of white supremacy to prevent the Democratic Party from advocating African-American rights, and Truman's ultimate victory despite the defection of hard-line racists, represented a profound turning point in American politics.

Desegregating the Armed Forces

The importance of the black vote, the fight for the allegiance of the emerging nations, and the emerging civil rights movement hastened the desegregation of the military. In February 1948 a communist coup in Czechoslovakia raised the possibility of war between the United States and the Soviet Union and heightened concerns among military leaders about the willingness of African Americans to serve yet again in a Jim Crow army. When President Truman reinstated the draft in March 1948, A. Philip Randolph, who had formed the League for Non-Violent Civil Disobedience against Military Segregation in 1947, warned the nation that black men and women were fed up with segregation and Jim Crow and would not take a Jim Crow draft lying down. New York congressman Adam Clayton Powell Jr. also supported this stance. He declared there weren't enough jails in America to hold the black men who would refuse to bear arms in a Jim Crow army. On June 24, 1948, the Soviet Union heightened tensions even further when it imposed a blockade on West Berlin. On July 26 Truman, anticipating war between the superpowers and hoping to shore up his support among black voters for the approaching November elections, issued **Executive Order #9981**, officially desegregating the armed forces.

▶▶ **Document**

20-6 *Executive Order 9981: Desegregation of the Armed Forces, 1948*
President Harry Truman issued Executive Order 9981 on July 26, 1948 and officially desegregated the armed forces. The order required "equality of treatment and opportunity" for everyone in the armed forces.

▶▶ **Recommended Reading**

Richard Dalfiume. *Desegregation of the U.S. Armed Forces: Fighting on Two Fronts 1939–1953*. Columbia, MO: University of Missouri Press, 1969.

The NAACP Detroit branch's 1944 "Parade for Victory" featured pallbearers with caskets as they marched behind a sign that proclaimed "here lies JIM CROW." It conveyed the sentiment, if not the reality. But Jim Crow's days were numbered.

▶ **Reading Check**

Truman needed black votes in northern states to secure victory in 1948. In an effort to secure these votes, he embraced the findings of the Committee on Civil Rights and pushed for the adoption of a strong civil rights plank in the Democratic party platform. In addition, he ordered the official desegregation of the armed forces on July 26, 1948.

▶ **Recommended Reading**

William C. Berman. *The Politics of Civil Rights in the Truman Administration.* Columbus, OH: Ohio State University Press, 1970.

▶ **Skills for Life, p. 735**

For answers, see *Teacher's Resource Manual.*

Executive Order #9981 mandated "equality of treatment and opportunity for all persons in the armed services without regard to race, color, religion, or national origin." It signaled the victorious culmination of a decades-long struggle by black civilians and soldiers to win full integration into the nation's military. After Truman signed the order, Randolph and Grant Reynolds, a former minister and co-chair of the League for Nonviolent Civil Disobedience against Military Segregation, disbanded the organization and called off marches planned for Chicago and New York.

Not until 1950 and the outbreak of the Korean War, however, was Truman's order fully implemented. The war reflected the American Cold War policy of containment, which was intended to stop what American leaders believed to be a worldwide conspiracy orchestrated by Moscow to spread communism. In 1950 North Koreans, allied to the Soviets, attacked the American-supported government in South Korea and launched the "hot war" in the midst of the Cold War. After the North Koreans invaded South Korea, the United States under UN auspices intervened. Heavy casualties early in the war depleted many white combat units. Thus, early in 1951, the army acted on Truman's executive order and authorized the formal integration of its units in Korea. By 1954 the army had disbanded its last all-black units, and the armed forces became one of the first sectors of American society to abandon segregation.

✓ **Reading Check** What role did the 1948 campaign and politics have in President Truman's decision to order the military desegregated?

Analyzing Trends in Electoral College Maps

As you recall, votes in a presidential election are not cast directly for a presidential candidate but rather for presidential electors—the members of the electoral college. Each state has as many electoral votes as it has members of Congress: two for its two Senate seats, plus at least one more based on its representation in the House, which is in turn determined by the state's population. In all states but Maine and Nebraska, it's "winner take all": The candidate with the most popular votes gets *all* of a state's electoral votes. Therefore, it's not surprising that states and regions with the largest population—and most electoral votes—get the most attention from presidential candidates.

Electoral college maps show shifts in population—and political clout. Maps that also show election results reveal where the strength of a candidate or a party lies.

LEARN THE SKILL

Use the following steps to analyze trends shown in electoral college maps:

1. **Determine what information the maps provide.** In some electoral college maps, population size determines the size of each state on the map. Other maps just use the number of electoral votes. Still others show election results.

2. **Look for differences between the maps.** Note differences in population and electoral votes for particular states and for regions over time.

3. **Draw conclusions about population shifts and party strengths.** Relate what you know from other sources to what you see on the maps.

PRACTICE THE SKILL

Answer the following questions:

1. **(a)** What kind of information does Map A provide? How does the map present the information? **(b)** Does Map B provide more, less, or the same kind of information as Map A? Explain. **(c)** How is Map C different from Map A?

2. Between 1948 and 1980: **(a)** Which two states gained the most population? **(b)** Which two states lost the most population? **(c)** Which region(s) gained political clout?

3. **(a)** If you had been a candidate in 1948, where would you have concentrated your resources? **(b)** In 1980, what regions would you have concentrated on? **(c)** What conclusions can you draw about the changes in the political landscape between 1948 and 1980?

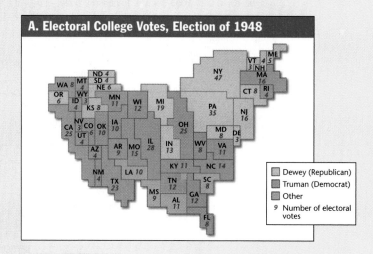

A. Electoral College Votes, Election of 1948

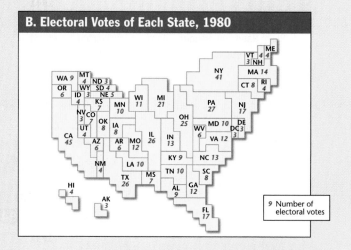

B. Electoral Votes of Each State, 1980

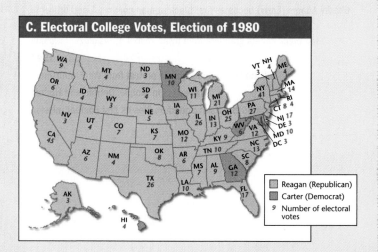

C. Electoral College Votes, Election of 1980

UNIT 6 — The Black Revolution

CHAPTERS

21. The Freedom Movement
22. The Struggle Continues
23. Black Politics, White Backlash
24. African Americans in the New Millennium

	1950–1965	1965–1975
Religion	1954 Malcolm X becomes minister of Harlem's Temple 7 1963 Malcolm X founds the Muslim Mosque, Inc.	
Culture	1959 Miles Davis records "Kind of Blue" 1960 Louis Armstrong's jazz band tours Africa 1963 James Baldwin publishes *The Fire Next Time* 1965 Alex Haley publishes *The Autobiography of Malcolm X* LeRoi Jones founds the Black Arts Repertory Theater	1966 San Francisco State University sets up nation's first black studies program 1968 Eldridge Cleaver publishes *Soul on Ice* 1969 Harvard University's African-American Studies program established Robert Chrisman and Nathan Hare start "The Black Scholar" 1970 Imamu Amiri Baraka organizes the Congress of African Peoples 1974 National Council for Black Studies formed
Politics & Government	1954 Brown v. Board of Education ends "separate but equal" 1955 Brown II decision calls for schools to desegregate with "all deliberate speed" 1957 Federal troops enforce school desegregation in Little Rock, AR 1963 Federal government forces Governor George Wallace to desegregate University of Alabama 1964 Equal Employment Opportunity Commission established	1965 President Lyndon Johnson first uses the term "affirmative action" Voting Rights Act of 1965 enacted by Congress 1966 Edward Brooke of Massachusetts elected the first black U.S. senator since Reconstruction Black Panther party founded 1967 Thurgood Marshall becomes first black Supreme Court Justice 1968 Kerner Report released
Society & Economy	1955 Rosa Parks arrested for refusing to give up her seat on a bus in Montgomery, AL 1958 Southern Christian Leadership Conference organized 1960 Black students launch the sit-in movement SNCC founded 1961 Freedom Riders attacked in Alabama 1962 James Meredith admitted to the University of Mississippi 1963 Medgar Evers assassinated Martin Luther King, Jr. delivers "I Have a Dream" speech Baptist church bombed in Birmingham, AL 1964 Mississippi Freedom Summer Project Civil rights workers murdered in Mississippi Martin Luther King Jr. awarded Nobel Peace Prize	1965 Watts Riot Selma March 1967 Riots in Detroit, Newark, and other cities 1968 Poor People's Campaign Martin Luther King assassinated 1969 Chicago police kill Black Panther leaders Fred Hampton and Mark Clarke 1970 Jackson State killings 1971 Jesse Jackson founds PUSH 1973 National Black Feminist Organization founded

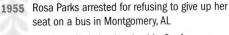

Barbara Jordan

Eldridge Cleaver

Nikki Giovanni

1975–1990

1978	Louis Farrakhan becomes leader of the Nation of Islam
1989	Barbara Harris first African-American woman elected bishop of the Episcopal Church
1990	Black Baptists constitute the fourth largest U.S. religious group with 8.7 million members

1979	Sugar Hill Gang records "Rapper's Delight"
1980	Toni C. Bambara's *Salt Eaters* wins American Book Award
	Molete Kete Asante publishes *Afrocentricity*
1982	Alice Walker's *The Color Purple* wins Pulitzer Prize
1984	Prince films "Purple Rain"
1986	*The Oprah Winfrey Show* becomes nationally syndicated
1987	Rita Dove wins Pulitzer Prize for poetry
1988	Temple University becomes first college to offer a Ph.D. in African-American studies
1989	N.W.A. records "Straight Outta Compton"

1977	Randall Robinson founds TransAfrica
	Patricia Harris becomes the first black woman to serve in the Cabinet
1983–1984	Jesse Jackson runs for president
1989	L. Douglas Wilder of Virginia becomes first African-American governor since Reconstruction

1990–2001

1991	George A. Stallings consecrated a Roman Catholic bishop
1993	Pope John Paul II apologizes for the Catholic Church's support of slavery
2000	Vashti M. McKenzie first woman elected bishop of AME church
2001	Bishop Wilton D. Gregory elected president of the United States Conference of Catholic Bishops

1990	August Wilson's *The Piano Lesson* wins Pulitzer Prize
1993	Rita Dove becomes Poet Laureate
	Toni Morrison becomes the first African American to win Nobel Prize for Literature
1999	Hip-hop performer Lauryn Hill wins five Grammy Awards

1991	Clarence Thomas nominated to the Supreme Court
1996	California approves Proposition 209
2001	Colin Powell becomes first African-American secretary of state
	Condoleezza Rice becomes national security adviser to President Bush

1991	Los Angeles riot after police officers who beat Rodney King are acquitted
1995	Million Man March
1997	Million Woman March
2000	Census records large gains in income and education by African Americans

Key People

Ella Baker (1903–1986)
Fannie Lou Hamer (1917–1977)
Rosa Parks (1918–)
James Farmer (1920–1999)
Alex Haley (1921–1992)
Medgar Evers (1925–1963)
Malcolm X (1925–1965)
Ralph Abernathy (1926–1990)
Miles Davis (1926–1991)
Coretta Scott King (1927–)
Carl Stokes (1927–1996)
Maya Angelou (1928–)
Martin Luther King, Jr. (1929–1968)
Toni Morrison (1931–)
James Brown (1933–)
James Meredith (1933–)
Vernon Jordan (1935–)
Eldridge Cleaver (1935–1998)
Bobby Seale (1936–)
Barbara Jordan (1936–1996)
Colin Powell (1937–)
Maxine Waters (1938–)
Marian W. Edelman (1939–)
John Lewis (1940–)
Jesse Jackson (1941–)
Stokely Carmichael (1941–1998)
Muhammed Ali (1942–)
Molefe Kete Asante (1942–)
Aretha Franklin (1942–)
Randall Robinson (1942–)
Huey Newton (1942–1989)
Terri McMillan (1943–)
Angela Davis (1944–)
Alice Walker (1944–)
August Wilson (1945–)
Clarence Thomas (1948–)
Jamaica Kincaid (1949–)
Henry L. Gates (1950–)
Cornell West (1953–)
Condeleezza Rice (1954–)
Oprah Winfrey (1954–)
Anita Hill (1956–)
Spike Lee (1957–)

This black student at the University of Oklahoma was not allowed to sit in a classroom with white students. It took two Supreme Court decisions to end such segregation at the University of Oklahoma.

Chapter 21

Witnessing History . . .

When the history books are written in the future, somebody will have to say, "There lived a race of people, black people, fleecy locks and black complexion, people who had the moral courage to stand up for their rights. And thereby they injected a new meaning into the veins of history and of civilization." And we're gonna do that. God grant that we will do it before it's too late.

—Martin Luther King, Jr., December 5, 1955

 What point is Martin Luther King making about African Americans?

Mary McLeod Bethune pickets outside a drugstore in Washington, D.C.

Chapter Preview

▶ **Witnessing History**

King is saying that history will recognize the efforts black people made to claim their rightful place in America.

▶ **Recommended Readings**

Henry Hampton and Steve Fayer, eds. *The Voices of Freedom: An Oral History of the Civil Rights Movement from the 1950s through the 1980s.* New York: Bantam Books, 1990. A remarkable and indispensable oral history of all the participants in the civil rights movement, from the least well known to the internationally celebrated.

Steven F. Lawson. *Running for Freedom: Civil Rights and Black Politics in America since 1941.* Philadelphia: Temple University Press, 1991. A succinct analysis of the politics, legislative measures, and individuals that figured in the successes and failures of the civil rights movement.

Between 1954 and 1965, the civil rights movement achieved a revolutionary transformation in the legal and social status of African Americans. The long struggle to overthrow the "separate but equal" doctrine in public schools, the Montgomery bus boycott, and massive protests throughout the South, changed the face of race relations in the United States. Legally sanctioned segregation, racial discrimination, and disfranchisement fell before a mighty coalition of civil rights groups and their allies. Demonstrations and the pressures of the Cold War compelled high government officials to abandon their early caution. Racism remained powerful in American life after 1965, and African Americans continued to suffer from economic disadvantages. But the significant enlargement of freedom of opportunity and recognition of African-Americans' full citizenship rights transformed America and radiated across the globe.

The modern civil rights movement is the remarkable courage and tenacity people in their own communities showed in their determination to attack segregation and exclusion from the political process. Ordinary citizens initiated protests, formulated strategies and tactics, and garnered other essential resources that made collective action work. The people's actions were made effective through their families, churches, voluntary associations, political organizations, women's clubs, labor unions, and college organizations and facilities. The sacrifices and experience gained in the previous one hundred years of struggle had, by the mid-1950s, accumulated sufficiently to permit an all-out attack on white supremacy. The civil rights movement would be long and bloody. It would not lead to the Promised Land, but it would profoundly change America.

Section 1

The 1950s

Prosperity and Prejudice

For most white Americans, the 1950s ushered in an era of unparalleled prosperity, heightened consumer consumption, and a patriarchal business culture. Affluent white Americans fled to the suburbs, and by 1960 52 percent of Americans owned their own homes. The decade is remembered nostalgically as a time of large stable nuclear families, wives and mothers who stayed at home, and communities untroubled by drugs and juvenile delinquency.

For most black Americans, however, the 1950s were less blissful. American society remained rigidly segregated in housing and in education. Despite the gains African Americans made during the World War II era, Jim Crow still reigned. Jim Crow restrictions and the ever-present threat of white violence kept millions of African Americans from voting in the deep South. Violence and extralegal practices still made housing integration a distant dream.

More importantly, most African Americans did not benefit from the economic boom of the 1950s that allowed so many white Americans to purchase homes in the suburbs. Moving into urban centers just as the number of factories and jobs there began to decline, they suffered a higher unemployment rate than any other segment of the population. White workers, fearing for their jobs, felt threatened by competition from unemployed black workers. As urban neighborhoods deteriorated, conditions ripened for a massive explosion.

The Road to *Brown*

In 1954, with the U.S. Supreme Court's decision in *Brown v. Board of Education of Topeka, Kansas,* progress in the desegregation of American society moved from the military into the civilian realm. Ultimately, the *Brown* decision would undermine state-sanctioned segregation in all aspects of American life. The NAACP's legal program of the 1920s and 1930s was largely responsible for this turn of events. In 1940 the NAACP set up the **Legal Defense and Educational Fund (NAACP-LDEF)** to pursue its assault on the legal foundations of race inequality in American education. Thereafter, NAACP-LDEF fought segregation and discrimination

GUIDE TO READING

▶ How did the experience of the 1950s differ for white and black Americans?

▶ Why is the *Brown v. Board of Education of Topeka* one of the most important U.S. Supreme Court decisions of the twentieth century?

▶ How did white southerners' strategy of massive resistance affect the modern civil rights movement?

KEY TERMS

▶ Legal Defense and Educational Fund (NAACP-LDEF), p. 747

▶ *Briggs v. Elliott,* p. 751

▶ *Brown v. Board of Education of Topeka,* p. 752

▶ *Brown II,* p. 753

▶ The Southern Manifesto, p. 754

▶▶ **Guide to Reading/Key Terms**

For answers, see the *Teacher's Resource Manual.*

in education, housing, employment, and politics. In the first years of its existence, attorneys for the fund won stunning victories including a 1944 U.S. Supreme Court decision, *Smith v. Allwright*, declaring white primaries unconstitutional, and the *Shelley v. Kramer* (1948) decision outlawing restrictive residential covenants. The life and career of one of the NAACP-LDEF lawyers, Constance Baker Motley, symbolizes the struggle that black professionals, both men and women, waged to overcome racial and gender exclusion and the coalescence of disparate forces that carried the seeds of the coming revolution. Motley is our guide on the road to *Brown*.

Constance Baker Motley

Constance Baker Motley was born in 1921 to immigrant parents, Rachel Huggins and Willoughby Alva Baker, from Nevis, in the British West Indies. She grew up in a tightly knit West Indian community in New Haven, Connecticut. The members of New Haven's black community, including Baker's parents, worked as domestics or in service jobs for Yale University. Baker attended integrated schools and experienced episodic racism, including being refused admission to a local beach or to a roller-skating rink. Baker developed a strong racial consciousness. She recalled, "[M]y interest in civil rights [was] a very early interest which developed when I was in high school. The fact that I was a Black, a woman, and a member of a large, relatively poor family was also the base of this great ambition [to enter the legal profession]."

The most important event in her early life was the lecture that George Crawford, a 1903 Yale Law School graduate, who worked as an NAACP lawyer in New Haven, gave at the local Dixwell Community Center. The talk concerned the Supreme Court decision in *State of Missouri ex rel. Gaines v. Canada.* Crawford explained that the University of Missouri's law school had denied Gaines admission but had offered to pay his tuition expenses to an out-of-state school. After *Gaines*, states were required to furnish within their borders facilities for legal education for black people equal to those offered white citizens.

Baker desperately wanted to go to law school, but her family could not even afford to send her to college. For a year and a half after graduation from high school in 1939, Baker earned $50 a month varnishing chairs for a building restoration project under the auspices of the National Youth Administration. In 1940, however, Baker came to the attention of Clarence Blakeslee, a local white businessman and philanthropist. After hearing her speak at a meeting of black and white community residents, Blakeslee offered to finance her education. She attended Fisk University until 1942 and then transferred to New York University. She earned a bachelor's degree in economics in 1943. She then became the second black woman ever to attend Columbia

▶ **Document**

20-3 *Thurgood Marshall, "The Legal Attack to Secure Civil Rights," 1942*
In this speech before the NAACP Wartime Conference, Thurgood Marshall discusses the obstacles and general plan to achieve full citizenship.

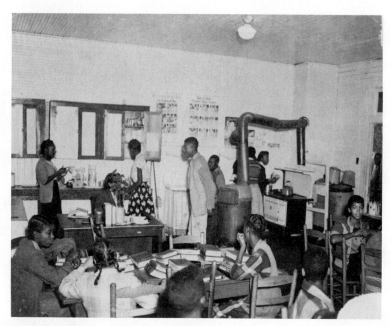

The glaring inequalities between black and white schools underscored the need for social change in American race relations.

University Law School. In 1946, shortly after she finished her legal training she married former New York University law student Joel Motley and went to work with the NAACP's LDEF.

Constance Baker Motley first met Thurgood Marshall in October 1945 when he hired her as a law clerk during her second year in law school. Marshall assigned her to work on the hundreds of army court-martial cases filed after World War II. Motley recalled, "From the first day I knew that this was where I wanted to be. I never bothered interviewing anywhere else." She added, "But for this fortuitous event, I do not think that I would have gotten very far as a lawyer. Women were simply not hired in those days."

Black lawyers in the South handling civil rights cases were frequently assaulted. On February 27, 1942, for example, NAACP attorney Leon A. Ransom was attacked by a former deputy sheriff in the hall of the Davidson County Courthouse in Nashville, Tennessee. At Ransom's death in 1954, Thurgood Marshall eulogized,

> Negro Americans, whether they know it or not, owe a great debt of gratitude to Andy Ransom and men like him who battled in the courts down a span of years to bring us to the place we now occupy in the enjoyment of our constitutional rights as citizens, in helping to build up the NAACP legal program step by step, in the skill which he gave to individual cases and to the planning of strategy, Dr. Ransom left a legacy to the whole population.

It was no less difficult for a black woman lawyer to venture into the South in search of justice. Constance Motley was keenly aware of her precarious situation. "Often a southern judge would refer to men attorneys as Mister, but would make a point of calling me 'Connie,' since

Constance Baker Motley endured many hardships and even assaults as she tried school desegregation cases in the South. Here she leaves the federal court in Birmingham after an unsuccessful attempt to force the University of Alabama to accept a black student.

traditionally Black women in the South were only called by their first name." Housing was another problem. Motley recalled that when in a southern town for a long trial, "I knew that it was going to be impossible to stay in a decent hotel." These lawyers had to depend on the good graces and courage of local people. Motley explained, "Usually in these situations a Black family would agree to put you up. But there was so much publicity involved with civil rights cases that no Black family dared have us—they were too afraid."

The Challenge to "Separate but Equal"

In the late 1940s, the NAACP-LDEF's attack on inequality in graduate education provided the basis for a full-scale assault on segregation. No longer would the organization be satisfied only to push for fulfillment of the promise of "separate but equal" facilities. In 1948 Ada Lois Sipuel was denied admission to the University of Oklahoma Law School because she was black. The U.S. Supreme Court ordered Oklahoma, in *Sipuel v. Board of Regents of the University of Oklahoma*, to "provide [a legal education] for [Sipuel] in conformity with the equal protection clause of the Fourteenth Amendment and provide it as soon as it does for applicants of any other group."

Another case, *Sweatt v. Painter*, which the Supreme Court decided in 1950, began when the University of Texas at Austin attempted to circumvent court orders to admit Heman Sweatt into its law school. The

University created a separate facility consisting of three basement rooms, a small library, and a few instructors who would lecture to him alone. The court ruled that the University of Texas had deprived Sweatt of intangibles such as "the essential ingredient of a legal education . . . the opportunity for students to discuss the law with their peers and others with whom they would be associated professionally in later life." On the same day the justices ruled in *Sweatt*, they also declared illegal the University of Oklahoma's segregation of George W. McLaurin from white students attending the Graduate School of Education. The University of Oklahoma had admitted McLaurin but made him sit in the hallway at the classroom door, study in a private part of the balcony of the library, and eat in a sequestered part of the lunch room. When he finally gained a seat in the classroom, it was marked "reserved for colored." In these precedent-setting cases, the U.S. Supreme Court signaled a readiness to reconsider the "separate but equal" doctrine and to redefine the meaning of the "equal protection of the laws" clause. These cases were important stepping-stones on the road to *Brown*.

A year after the *Sweatt* and *McLaurin* decisions, black parents and their lawyers filed suits in Kansas, South Carolina, Virginia, Delaware, and the District of Columbia. They asked the courts to apply the qualitative test of the *Sweatt* case to elementary and secondary schools and to declare the "separate-but-equal" doctrine invalid in public education.

Brown and the Coming Revolution

In the late 1940s, the black parents of Scott's Branch School in Clarendon County, South Carolina, approached Roderick W. Elliott, the chairman of the school board, with a modest request. There were 6,531 black students and only 2,375 whites students enrolled in the county's schools. Although the county had thirty buses to convey the white students to their schools, not one bus was available to black schoolchildren. Some of the black students had to walk eighteen miles round trip each day. Once they arrived they entered buildings heated by wood stoves and lit by kerosene lamps. For a drink of water or to go to the toilet they had to go outdoors.

With the encouragement of AME pastor and schoolteacher, Reverend Joseph Armstrong DeLaine, the parents mustered the courage and resolve to petition the school board for buses. In 1949 DeLaine went to the NAACP officials in Columbia, and Thurgood Marshall was there. On December 20, 1950, Harry Briggs, a navy veteran, and twenty-four other Clarendon County residents sued the Summerton School District (Clarendon District 22). The case, ***Briggs v. Elliott***, was the first legal challenge to elementary school segregation to originate in the South. Meanwhile, however, four other cases in different parts of the country were advancing through the federal courts. These would be combined into one case that would decide the fate of the *Plessy* doctrine of "separate but equal."

▶ **Document**

20-7 *McLaurin v. Oklahoma State Regents, 1950*
Though admitted to the University of Oklahoma graduate school, George McLaurin was required by Oklahoma statute to receive instruction "upon a segregated basis." Consequently, he was assigned a seat outside the classroom, a special table in the library and cafeteria as well as a different time to eat. This selection outlines the Court's decision.

➡ **Document**

20-2 Brown v. Board of Education, 1954
This historic case involved a class action suit
filed against the Board of Education of Topeka
Public Schools. The Court's decision was
delivered by Chief Justice Earl Warren.

➡ **Recommended Reading**

Richard Kluger. *Simple Justice: The History of
"Brown v. Board of Education" and Black
America's Struggle for Equality*. New York: Knopf,
1976, New ed. 2004. An excellent treatment
of the historical events leading up to *Brown*
and the local individuals whose lives were
forever changed because of their resistance
to Jim Crow segregation. The new edition
includes an illuminating assessment of the
fifty years since Brown.

The years of preparation and hardship paid off. Motley worked with the dream team of black lawyers and academics. An inner circle of advisers included Louis Redding from Wilmington, Delaware; James Nabrit from Washington, D.C.; Robert Ming from Chicago; psychologist Kenneth Clark from New York; and historian John Hope Franklin to prepare the case, ***Brown v. Board of Education of Topeka***, and argue it before the U.S. Supreme Court. In 1950, the all-white Sumner School in Topeka, Kansas, refused to admit Linda Brown (1943–). Her father, Oliver Brown, filed a lawsuit and testified in court that his daughter had to travel an hour and twenty minutes to attend a black school. The Sumner School was only seven blocks away but practiced racial exclusion. Linda became the "named plaintiff" in this landmark case, in which the court declared laws mandating public school segregation unconstitutional.

Motley, Robert Carter, Jack Greenberg, and Marshall also sought assistance from Spottswood Robinson and Oliver Hill of Richmond, Virginia, and read papers prepared by historians C. Vann Woodward and Alfred Kelly about the original equalitarian intentions of the post–Civil War amendments and other legislation. In his argument, Marshall appealed to the U.S. Supreme Court to meet the *Plessy* doctrine head on and declare it erroneous.

> It (*Plessy*) stands mirrored today as a legal aberration, the faulty conception of an era dominated by provincialism, by intense emotionalism in race relations . . . and by the preaching of a doctrine of racial superiority that contradicted the basic concept upon which our society was founded. Twentieth century America, fighting racism at home and abroad, has rejected the race views of *Plessy v. Ferguson* because we have come to the realization that such views obviously tend to preserve not the strength but the weakness of our heritage.

By the time Marshall made this argument, black intellectuals, scholars, and activists and their progressive white allies had closed ranks in support of integration.

During late 1953 and early 1954, Chief Justice Earl Warren brought the court in support of Marshall's position. On May 17, 1954, the court ruled unanimously in favor of the NAACP lawyers and their clients that a classification based solely on race violated the Fourteenth Amendment to the U.S. Constitution. In a stirring passage Warren declared,

> We come then to the question presented: Does segregation of children in public schools solely on the basis of race, even though the physical facilities and other 'tangible' factors may be equal, deprive the children of the minority group of equal educational opportunities? We believe that it does. . . . To separate them from others of similar age and qualifications solely because of their race generates a feeling of inferiority as to the status in the community that may affect their hearts and minds in a way unlikely ever to be undone. . . . We conclude that

Linda Brown, who was at the center of the landmark
Supreme Court case that challenged segregated schools,
sits in an all black classroom in 1950.

in the field of public education the doctrine of "separate but equal" has no place. Separate educational facilities are inherently unequal.

The *Brown* decision would eventually lead to the dismantling of the entire structure of Jim Crow laws that regulated important aspects of black life in America. The *Brown* decision, more than any other case, signaled the emerging primacy of equality as a guide to constitutional decisions. This and subsequent decisions helped advance the rights of other minorities and women. As Motley reflected, "In the *Brown* case and in the decisions that followed, we blazed a trail for others by showing the competence of Black lawyers."

 Reading Check Why is the Brown v. Board of Education of Topeka one of the most important U.S. Supreme Court decisions of the twentieth century?

Brown II

A year after the 1954 *Brown* decision, the Supreme Court issued a second ruling, commonly known as ***Brown II***, which addressed the practical process of desegregation. The Court underscored that the states in the suits should begin prompt compliance with the 1954 ruling, but that this should be done with "all deliberate speed." Many black Americans interpreted this to mean "immediately." White Southerners hoped it meant a long time, or never. Ominously, President Eisenhower seemed displeased with the Court's rulings and refused to put the moral authority of his office behind their enforcement.

Nevertheless, in 1955 and early 1956, desegregation proceeded without hindrance in Maryland, Kentucky, Delaware, Oklahoma, and Missouri. Alabama governor Jim Folsom declared that his state would obey the courts. Initially, many other moderate white southern politicians counseled calm and worked to head off a full-scale conflict between their region and the federal government.

Massive White Resistance

White moderates, however, soon found themselves a shrinking minority. Extremists, determined to maintain white supremacy at any cost, prepared for mass resistance to the Court's decisions. The rhetoric of these extremists bordered on hysteria but found a receptive audience among many white people. A young minister from Virginia named Jerry Falwell, for example, explained that black people were the descendants of Noah's son Ham and destined to be servants because of a curse God had put on him. Falwell also claimed the Supreme Court's decisions were inspired by Moscow. In 1955 leading businessmen, white-collar professionals,

➤➤ **Reading Check**

Brown v. Board of Education of Topeka overturned the doctrine of "separate but equal" established by *Plessy v. Ferguson.* The *Brown* decision would eventually lead to the dismantling of the entire structure of Jim Crow laws.

➤➤ **Retracing the Odyssey**

Brown v. Board of Education National Historic Landmark. Topeka, Kansas. The Sumner and Monroe Elementary Schools composed the *Brown v. Board of Education* National Historic Landmark. *Brown* was the culmination of a long struggle waged by the NAACP's team of lawyers headed by Thurgood Marshall and dozens of ordinary citizens in local communities.

and clergy began organizing White Citizens' Councils in virtually every southern city. These were groups dedicated to preserving the southern way of life and the South's "sacred heritage of freedom." The councils used their economic and political power to intimidate black people who challenged segregation. They fired people from their jobs, evicted them from their homes, and refused them credit.

Many white politicians took up the banner of massive resistance. Senator James O. Eastland, from Mississippi, called the *Brown* decision a "monstrous crime." The Virginia legislature closed all public schools in Prince Edward County to thwart integration. Most dramatically, on March 12, 1956, ninety-six southern congressmen led by North Carolina's senator Sam Ervin Jr. and South Carolina's senator Strom Thurmond issued **The Southern Manifesto**, vowing to fight to preserve segregation and the southern way of life. The manifesto called the *Brown* decisions an "unwarranted exercise of power by the court, contrary to the Constitution." The only southern senators who refused to sign the "Manifesto" were Albert Gore Sr. of Tennessee and Lyndon B. Johnson of Texas.

The NAACP came under siege after the *Brown* decision as southern states tried to wipe it out of existence. By 1957 nine southern states had filed suit to eradicate the organization. Some states, alleging the NAACP was linked to a worldwide communist conspiracy, made membership illegal. Membership plummeted from 128,716 to 79,677, and the association lost 246 branches in the South.

Under these pressures, desegregation ground to a halt. By 1958 thirteen school systems had been desegregated. By 1960, two years later, the total had risen to only seventeen. Massive resistance successfully challenged the possibility of achieving change through court action alone.

The Lynching of Emmett Till

The violent reaction of white Southerners to the growing assertiveness of black people found expression in the summer of 1955 in the lynching of fourteen-year-old Emmett Till of Chicago, an event that helped galvanize the emerging civil rights movement. Till was visiting relatives in the small town of Money, Mississippi. On a dare from his friends, he entered Bryant's grocery store, bought candy, and said "Bye, baby" to Carolyn Bryant, the wife of the owner, as he left. Till was unaware how far white people in the town would go to avenge this small breach of white supremacy's racial etiquette. In the middle of the night a few days after the incident, Bryant's husband and brother-in-law arrived at the small home where Till was staying and kidnapped him at gunpoint. His body was subsequently found in the Tallahatchie River tied to a heavy cotton gin

Emmett Till's murder helped demonstrate the horrors of racial hatred. In May, 2004, almost fifty years after his death, federal authorities reopened their investigation of the crime.

The lynching of Emmet Till and the subsequent acquittal of his murderers reflected the low regard in which black life was held in the Jim Crow South and the extent to which whites were determined to maintain the racial status quo.

fan. Till had a bullet in his head and had been tortured before his murder. Despite overwhelming evidence and the brave testimony of Mose Wright, Till's uncle, and other local black people, an all-white jury acquitted the two men who lynched Till. In early 1956 the murderers sold their confession to *Look* magazine and gloated over their escape from justice. In 2004, new evidence surfaced indicating that ten people may have been involved in the Till lynching.

The Till lynching shaped the consciousness of an entire generation of young African-American activists. Partly this was due to the efforts of Till's mother, Mamie Bradley. Unwilling to let America turn away from this crime, Till's mother had her son's mangled body displayed in an open casket in Chicago. Thousands of mourners paid their respects, and many committed themselves to fighting the system that made this crime possible. Bradley also traveled around the nation speaking to groups on whom her grief had a profound impact.

In May 2004, the Justice Department reopened the investigation into the lynching of Emmett Till, fifty years after two suspects were tried and acquitted of his murder. Federal and Mississippi state and local authorities, believing that others may have been involved, continued through June, 2005 to look for further evidence to help bring the case to a just conclusion.

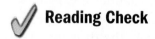 **Reading Check** How did white southerners' strategy of massive resistance affect the modern civil rights movement?

▶ **Reading Check**

Brown v. Board of Education of Topeka polarized southern whites, with extremists coming to the forefront of a resistance movement. The NAACP was key target of this movement. The early success of resistance made it clear that desegregation would not be accomplished by court action alone.

GUIDE TO READING

▶ What was the Montgomery Bus Boycott and what events ignited it?

▶ What role did black women and children play in the challenges to segregation and discrimination in their communities?

▶ What role did white northerners play in the boycott?

KEY TERMS

▶ Women's Political Council (WPC), p. 756

▶ Rosa Parks, p. 757

▶ Montgomery Improvement Association (MIA), p. 757

▶ *Gayle v. Browder*, p. 761

▶ **Guide to Reading/Key Terms**

For answers, see the *Teacher's Resource Manual.*

▶ **Recommended Reading**

Vickie Crawford, Jacqueline Rouse, and Barbara Woods, eds. *Women in the Civil Rights Movement: Trailblazers and Torchbearers.* Brooklyn, NY: Carlson Publishing, 1990. An anthology of essays presented at a symposium. The meeting was designed to draw attention to the women whose contributions to the freedom struggle of the 1950s and 1960s are often overlooked or neglected.

Section 2

The Montgomery Bus Boycott

The Roots of Revolution

Strong local communities formed the core of the civil rights movement and they were often sparked to action by the deeds of brave and committed individuals. The first and one of the most important expressions of this process occurred in Alabama's small capital city of Montgomery.

The movement in Montgomery was the result of years of organization and planning by protest groups. In addition to its numerous churches, two black colleges, and other social organizations, the Alabama capital had a strong core of protest groups. One, the **Women's Political Council (WPC)**, had been founded in 1946 by Mary Frances Fair Burks, chair of Alabama State College English Department, after the all-white League of Women Voters had refused to allow black women to participate in its activities. Although the WPC had only forty members, all middle-class women, its courageous and competent leaders were willing to stand up to powerful white people. The WPC was joined by a chapter of the NAACP led by E. D. Nixon, a Pullman train porter and head of the Alabama chapter of the Brotherhood of Sleeping Car Porters. In 1943 Nixon had founded the Montgomery Voters League, an organization dedicated to helping African Americans navigate Alabama's tortuous voter registration process. In the decade after 1945 these groups searched for a way to mobilize the black community to challenge white power.

The 1954 *Brown* decision seemed to provide a means to destroy segregation and discrimination in the city. Four days after it was announced, Jo Ann Robinson, a professor at Alabama State College, wrote a letter to Montgomery's mayor on behalf of the WPC. In it she reiterated the complaints of the black community concerning conditions on the city's buses and ended, "Please consider this plea, for even now plans are being made to ride less, or not at all, on our buses." The mayor ignored the warning and the buses remained as segregated as before. Montgomery's black lawyers and NAACP chapter began laying the groundwork for a test case challenging segregation of the city's bus lines.

On March 2, 1955, a fifteen-year-old girl, Claudette Colvin, was arrested for refusing to give up her seat on a bus to a white person. The WPC was ready to use this incident to initiate the threatened bus

boycott, but Nixon dissuaded them. He felt that Colvin, who was unmarried and pregnant, would not be an appropriate symbol around which to organize. He and other activists resolved to wait for another chance.

Rosa Parks

On Thursday, December 1, 1955, **Rosa Parks**, a forty-three-year-old department store seamstress and civil rights activist, boarded a city bus and moved to the back where African Americans were required to sit. All seats were taken so she sat in one toward the middle of the bus. When a white man boarded the bus, the driver ordered Parks to vacate her seat for him. On this fateful day, Rosa Parks refused to move. She had not planned to resist on that day, but, as she later said, she had "decided that I would have to know once and for all what rights I had as a human being and a citizen. . . . I was so involved with the attempt to bring about freedom from this kind of thing . . . I felt just resigned to give what I could to protest against the way I was being treated, and felt that all of our meetings, trying to negotiate, bring about petitions before the authorities . . . really hadn't done any good at all." At the time Parks was portrayed as someone who was simply tired, but she had been training for just this kind of challenge for years. When her moment came, she seized it. This act of resistance launched the Montgomery bus boycott movement and inspired the modern civil rights struggle for freedom and equality.

The plans of the WPC and NAACP came into play after Parks's arrest for violating Montgomery's transportation laws. She was ordered to appear in court on the following Monday. Meanwhile, E. D. Nixon bailed her out of the city jail and began mobilizing the leadership of the black community behind her. Working in tandem with Nixon, Robinson wrote and circulated a flyer calling for a one-day boycott of the buses followed by a mass meeting of the community to discuss the matter. Robinson took the flyer to the Alabama State College campus, stayed up all night, and, with the help of a colleague, mimeographed thirty thousand copies of it. The WPC had planned distribution routes months earlier, and the next day, Robinson and nearly two hundred volunteers distributed bundles of flyers through-out black neighborhoods.

Montgomery Improvement Association

On December 5, 1955, the black community did not ride the buses, and the movement had begun. Nixon and other community leaders decided to form a new organization, the **Montgomery Improvement Association** (MIA), to coordinate the protest. They also selected a twenty-six-year-old

▶▶ **Document**

21-1 Digest Of Jim-Crow Laws Affecting Passengers in Interstate Travel
In 1955, the black people in Montgomery, Alabama, boycotted the city's segregated bus system, and in 1956, the Supreme Court struck another blow against segregation laws when it ruled that Alabama's statutes requiring segregated buses were unconstitutional.
21-2 Jo Ann Gibson Robinson, Bus Boycott
This selection offers an intimate look at Rosa Parks.

▶▶ **Recommended Reading**

Jo Ann Gibson Robinson, with David Garrow. *The Montgomery Bus Boycott and the Women Who Started It.* Knoxville, TN: University of Tennessee Press, 1987.

Aldon D. Morris. *The Origins of the Modern Civil Rights Movement: Black Communities Organizing for Change.* New York: Free Press; London: Collier Macmillan, 1984. An important and insightful analysis of the mobilization and organizing strategies pursued by diverse communities for social change that paved the way for the modern civil rights movement.

▶▶ **Retracing the Odyssey**

Southern Poverty Law Center Civil Rights Memorial, Montgomery, Alabama. The Civil Rights Memorial captures the history of the freedom struggle while ensuring that we do not forget the costs so many paid in the ongoing struggle against racism and social inequality.

minister, Martin Luther King Jr., to act as its president. That evening there was an overflowing mass meeting of the black community at the large Holt Street Baptist Church to decide whether to continue the boycott. King, with barely an hour to prepare, spoke to the crowd and delivered a message that would define the goals of the boycott and the civil

PROFILE ❖ Rosa Louise McCauley Parks

Rosa McCauley Parks was born on February 4, 1913, to James and Leona (Edwards) McCauley, a carpenter and school teacher, of Tuskegee, Alabama. Her father migrated north when his daughter was two years old. When she was eleven, Rosa attended the Montgomery Industrial School for Girls while living with a widowed aunt. In 1932 Rosa married Raymond Parks, a socially aware young man who worked in the Atlas Barber Shop in Montgomery. Rosa Parks enjoyed a full and busy life, working as a self-employed seamstress and serving as the secretary of the Montgomery branch of the NAACP (1943–1956) and as a member of the African Methodist Episcopal Church. In the 1950s she worked as a seamstress at Montgomery Fair, a department store in downtown Montgomery.

On December 1, 1955, Rosa Parks had had enough. When she refused to give up her seat on that fateful day in Montgomery, little could she have anticipated that she would become a living symbol of the African-American quest for freedom, justice, and equality of opportunity. With great dignity and little fanfare, Parks chose to be arrested rather than to comply with the white bus driver's order to move to the back-of-the-bus section reserved for black people. Her defiance on this occasion was part of a larger pattern of personal and public resistance. In the 1940s Parks had participated in voter registration campaigns. In 1954 she attended the Highlander Folk School, a training center for social change in Monteagle, Tennessee.

As soon as word of Parks's arrest spread through the Montgomery community, Jo Ann Robinson and members of the Women's Political Council (WPC), swung into action. On December 2, 1955, Robinson wrote and circulated thirty thousand copies of a flyer, declaring that "Another Negro woman has been arrested and thrown in jail because she refused to get up out of her seat on the bus for a white person to sit down. It is the second time since the Claudette Colvin case that a Negro woman has been arrested for the same thing. This has to be stopped. Negroes have rights too, for if Negroes did not ride the buses, they could not operate. . . ." Robinson and the WPC asked the community to stay off the buses for a day to show their opposition to bus segregation and their solidarity with Rosa Parks.

The success of the one-day boycott aroused the community and motivated thousands to attend the first mass meeting at the Holt Street Baptist Church. Under the leadership of Reverend Martin Luther King Jr., they founded the Montgomery Improvement Association. A year later, December 20, 1956, the U.S. Supreme Court ruled Alabama's state and local segregation laws unconstitutional. In retaliation, the department store fired Parks from her seamstress job.

Parks's resistance ignited the civil rights movement of the 1950s and 1960s. In 1957, Parks, her husband, and mother moved to Detroit, Michigan, where her brother resided. For a quarter of a century, Rosa Parks worked as a special assistant to Michigan U.S. congressman John Conyers. In 1979 the NAACP awarded Parks its Spingarn Medal. Rosa Parks continues to inspire countless Americans.

Parks

rights movement that followed. In his dramatic voice he connected the core values of America and of the Judeo-Christian tradition to the goals of African Americans nationwide as well as in Montgomery. "We are here this evening," he began,

> for serious business. We are here in a general sense because first and foremost we are American citizens, and we are determined to apply our citizenship to the fullness of its means. . . . You know, my friends, there comes a time when people get tired of being trampled over by the iron feet of oppression. There comes a time, my friends, when people get tired of being flung across the abyss of humiliation, when they experience the bleakness of nagging despair. . . . We are not wrong in what we are doing. If we are wrong, the Supreme Court of this nation is wrong. If we are wrong, the Constitution of the United States is wrong. If we are wrong, God Almighty is wrong. If we are wrong, Jesus of Nazareth was merely a utopian dreamer that never came down to earth. If we are wrong, justice is a lie. Love has no meaning. And we are determined here in Montgomery to work and fight until justice runs down like water, and righteousness like a mighty stream.

Martin Luther King Jr.

King's speech electrified the meeting, which unanimously decided to stay off the city's buses until the MIA's demands were met. The speech also marked the beginning of King's role as a leader of the civil rights movement. King had been raised in a prominent ministerial family with a long history of standing up for African-American rights. King's grandfather had led a protest to force Atlanta to build its first high school for African Americans. King's father spoke out for African-American rights as pastor of Ebenezer Baptist Church. At age fifteen, King had entered Morehouse College but did not embrace the ministry as his profession until he came under the influence of its president, Dr. Benjamin E. Mays. By age twenty-five, King had been awarded a Ph.D. in theology from Boston University. He moved to Alabama with his wife, Coretta Scott King, to become pastor of Dexter Avenue Baptist Church in Montgomery.

In addition to his verbal artistry, King had the ability to inspire moral courage and to teach people how to maintain themselves under excruciating pressure. King merged Gandhian nonviolence with black Christian faith and church culture to create a unique ideology well suited for the civil rights struggle. King declared that the boycott would continue with or without its leaders because the conflict was not "between the white and the Negro" but "between justice and injustice." He explained to the boycotting community, "If we are arrested every day, if we are exploited every day, if we are trampled over every day, don't ever let anyone pull you so low as to hate them. . . . We must realize so many people are taught to hate us that they are not totally responsible for their hate." King's faith was severely tested. As the boycott proceeded, his home was bombed.

▶▶ **Living Words Audio Clip**

Track 37 *Mass Meeting; speech by Martin Luther King, Jr.*

▶▶ **Retracing the Odyssey**

The Martin Luther King, Jr. Center for Nonviolent Social Change. Founded by Mrs. Coretta Scott King in 1968 as a living memorial dedicated to the preservation and advancement of the work of her husband, The Martin Luther King, Jr. Center for Nonviolent Social Change features exhibits that detail the life and legacy of Martin Luther King, Jr. It contains a unique exhibit of his personal memorabilia. The King Library and Archives contain the world's largest existing collection of civil rights materials.

Martin Luther King, Jr., spoke to an overflow crowd at a mass meeting at the Holt Street Baptist Church in Montgomery, Alabama during the boycott of city busses.

Segregationists also bombed Nixon's home and those of two other black clergymen and MIA leaders, Ralph Abernathy and Fred Shuttlesworth, and inflicted violence on many other boycott participants.

Walking for Freedom

Although men occupied the top leadership positions in the boycott, women were the key to its effectiveness. The boycott lasted more than a year—381 days—and over its course nearly all the black women previously dependent on the buses to get to work refused to ride them. Some walked twelve miles a day. Others had the support of their white women employers, who provided transportation. And many helped organize an efficient car pool of two hundred vehicles that proved critical to sustaining the boycott. The community at large participated in mass meetings held nightly in local churches. Robinson edited the MIA newsletter. Other women supported the boycott in dozens of ways. Some organized bake sales, and others made door-to-door solicitations to raise the $2,000 per week needed to keep the car pools going.

The boycott took 65 percent of the bus company's business, forcing it to cut schedules, lay off drivers, and raise fares. White merchants also suffered. The bus company, however, could scarcely afford to break the laws of the city that chartered it, and despite the company's losses, the city government refused to capitulate. Officials would not even accede to such a modest demand as a "first come, first served" seating arrangement—like that proposed by the Montgomery Women's Political Council before the boycott began—in which black riders would sit from back to front and white riders from front to back.

Impressive as it was, the boycott by itself could not end segregation on the buses. Black Montgomery needed a two-pronged strategy of mass local pressure and legal recourse through the courts. The legal backing of the federal government was necessary to end Jim Crow. Thus NAACP lawyers and MIA's lawyer Fred Gray filed a suit in the names of Claudette Colvin, Mary Louise Smith, and three other women.

 Reading Check What was the Montgomery Bus Boycott and what events ignited it?

Friends in the North

The Montgomery movement was not without allies outside the South. Money poured into the MIA's coffers from concerned Americans. Many northern activists who had long been hoping black Southerners would begin just this kind of resistance also swung into action to help. Two people were particularly important at this juncture: Bayard Rustin and liberal Jewish lawyer Stanley Levison. Two and a half months into the boycott, Montgomery officials indicted King and one hundred other leaders on

▶ **Reading Check**

The Montgomery Bus Boycott was boycott of the Montgomery bus system by the city's black residents. The boycott was sparked by Rosa Parks' arrest for refusing to give up her bus seat to white man. However, it is important to note that years of planning and organizing preceded the actual boycott.

▶ **Interactive Activity**

The Civil Rights Movement A close look at the ideas, events, and people involved in the struggle to end discrimination based on race.

charges of conspiracy to disrupt the bus system. At this juncture Bayard Rustin arrived in Montgomery and immediately encouraged the leaders to follow Gandhian practice and submit freely to arrest. Rustin continued working behind the scenes as one of King's most trusted advisers on non-violent principles and tactics. Stanley Levison and Ella Baker created a group called In Friendship, which raised money for the boycott.

Levison was a wealthy attorney committed to social justice. He had worked with the Communist Party. Rustin had a long history of association with radical groups. Their influence soon attracted the attention of the Federal Bureau of Investigation, which had long been obsessed with black leaders and organizations. King was not a communist, but FBI director J. Edgar Hoover developed an intense hatred of him and other black leaders. At one point Hoover called King "the most dangerous man in America." He pressed his subordinates to prove King was a communist and that the civil rights movement was a Moscow-inspired conspiracy. Hoover and his men began tapping King's telephone and hotel rooms and even threatened to expose his extramarital affairs if he did not commit suicide. By the early 1960s, the FBI had stopped warning King when it uncovered threats to his life.

Victory

As the bus boycott reached the one-year mark, it was obvious that the all-white city government would not budge, no matter how long the boycott lasted. Any white politician who hoped to remain in office had to defend segregation. King and all the others who suffered through the ordeal grew discouraged and their hopes seemed to fade in November 1956 when it became clear the state courts would soon move to declare the car pools illegal.

Salvation for the movement came from the cases local women and the NAACP had taken to the federal courts. In keeping with the *Brown* precedent, on November 13, 1956, the Supreme Court ordered an end to Montgomery's bus segregation. The *Gayle v. Browder* decision, unlike the *Brown* decision, expressly overturned the 1896 *Plessy v. Ferguson* decision, because like *Plessy* it applied to transportation. Ironically, the ruling was handed down on the same day that the city of Montgomery finally secured a state court injunction to end the MIA car pool. The bus company agreed not only to end segregation but also to hire African-American drivers and to treat all passengers with equal respect.

The city's black community rejoiced. On the morning of December 21, 1956, black citizens of Montgomery boarded the buses and sat wherever they pleased.

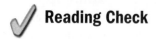 **Reading Check** What role did black women and children play in the challenges to segregation and discrimination in their communities?

> ⟩⟩ **Reading Check**
> Women and children played key roles in the fight for civil rights, as evidenced by their role in the Montgomery Bus boycott. The Women's Political Council had a central role leadership role in the boycott. Moreover, many black women relied on the bus system. Their participation in the boycott was essential.

GUIDE TO READING

▶ What role did the Southern Christian Leadership Council (SCLC) play in the civil rights movement of the late 1950s?

▶ What did the Civil Rights Act of 1957 accomplish?

▶ How did black students play a significant role in advancing the cause of civil rights?

KEY TERMS

▶ Southern Christian Leadership Council (SCLC), p. 762

▶ Civil Rights Act of 1957, p. 762

▶ sit-in, p. 764

▶ Student Nonviolent Coordinating Committee, (SNCC), p. 766

▶ Freedom Rides, p. 766

▶ **Guide to Reading/Key Terms**

For answers, see the *Teacher's Resource Manual.*

▶ **Recommended Reading**

Taylor Branch. *Parting the Waters: America in the King Years, 1954–63.* New York: Simon & Schuster, 1988. Richly researched, lively study that places King at the center of American politics during a critically transformative decade.

Section 3

No Easy Road to Freedom: 1957–1960

Martin Luther King and the SCLC

By the end of the campaign in Montgomery, Martin Luther King Jr. had emerged as a moral leader of national stature. On the advice of Levison, Rustin, and Ella Baker, he helped create a new organization, the **Southern Christian Leadership Council** (**SCLC**), to provide an institutional base for continuing the struggle. The SCLC was a federation of civil rights groups, community organizations, and churches that sought to coordinate all the burgeoning local movements. King assumed leadership of the SCLC, crisscrossing the nation in the ensuing years to build support for the organization and to raise money to fund its activities. Members of the organization also began training black activists, particularly on college campuses, in the tactics of nonviolent protest. Because the ballot was deemed the critical weapon needed to complete school desegregation and secure equal employment opportunity, adequate housing, and equal access to public accommodations, the SCLC focused on securing voting rights for black people. In the three years after the Montgomery bus boycott, the SCLC also aided black communities in applying the lessons of that struggle to challenge bus segregation in Tallahassee (Florida) and Atlanta.

The NAACP's leadership doubted the effectiveness of the protest tactics favored by the SCLC. They resented having to divert resources away from work on important court cases to defend people arrested in protests and were troubled by the left-wing connections of King's advisers. Despite their differences, the SCLC and the NAACP worked together, but the tensions over tactics were never far from the surface.

Civil Rights Act of 1957

Despite President Eisenhower's lukewarm response to *Brown*, Congress proved willing to take a modest step toward ending racial discrimination. It enacted the **Civil Rights Act of 1957**, the first such legislation since the end of Reconstruction. In a departure from the past, liberals in the Senate were able to end a filibuster by Southerners, but the bill they passed was, for all its symbolic import, weak. It created a commission to monitor violations of black civil

rights and to propose remedies for infringements on black voting. It upgraded the Civil Rights Section into a division within the Justice Department and gave it the power to initiate civil proceedings against those states and municipalities that discriminated on the basis of race. This act disappointed black activists because it was not strong enough to counter white reaction and because they felt the Eisenhower administration would not enforce it.

Little Rock, Arkansas

Eisenhower may have had little inclination to support the fight for black rights, but the defiance of Arkansas governor Orville Faubus would soon force him to. At the beginning of the school year in 1957, Faubus posted 270 soldiers from the Arkansas National Guard outside Little Rock Central High School to prevent nine black youths from entering. Faubus was determined to ignore the *Brown* ruling and to maintain school segregation. A federal district court order forced the governor to allow the children into the school. He simply withdrew the state guard and left the children alone to face a hate-filled mob.

To defend the sovereignty of the federal court and the Constitution, Eisenhower had to act. He sent in 1,100 paratroopers from the 101st Airborne to Little Rock and put the state national guard under federal authority. It was the first time since Reconstruction that troops had been

Elizabeth Eckerd, one of nine black students who sought to enroll at Little Rock Central High School in September 1957, endures the taunts of an angry white crowd as she tries to make her way to the school.

 Document

21-4 *Executive Order 10730: Desegregation of Central High School, 1957*

▶ **Recommended Reading**

Numan V. Bartley. *The Rise of Massive Resistance: Race and Politics in the South during the 1950's*. Baton Rouge, LA: Louisiana State University Press, 1969.

sent to the South to protect the rights of African-American citizens. The troops remained in Little Rock Central High School for the rest of the school year. Governor Faubus closed the Little Rock public schools in 1958–1959. Eight of the nine black students valiantly withstood the abuse, harassment, and curses of segregationists both inside and outside the facility and eventually desegregated the high school. Other young African Americans throughout the South would show similar courage.

Sit-Ins: Greensboro, Nashville, Atlanta

Beginning in 1960 motivated black college students adapted a strategy that CORE had used in the 1940s—the **sit-in**—and emerged as the dynamic vanguard of the civil rights movement. Their contributions to the black protest movement accelerated the pace of social change.

Early on the morning of February 1, 1960, Ezell Blair Jr., Joseph McNeil, Franklin McCain, and David Richmond, all freshmen at North Carolina Agricultural and Technical College (A & T), decided to desegregate local restaurants by sitting at the lunch counter of Greensboro, North Carolina's Woolworth five-and-dime store. Black people were welcome to spend their money in the store. But they were not permitted to dine at the lunch counter, making it a painful symbol of white supremacy. At 4:30 in the afternoon the students sat at the counter. They received no service that day but sat quietly doing their school work until the store

Joseph McNeil, Franklin McCain, Billy Smith, and Clarence Henderson sit patiently at Woolworth's lunch counter on February 2, 1960, the second day of the sit-in in Greensboro, North Carolina.

closed. The action of these four young men electrified their fellow students, and the next day many others joined them. Soon, black women students from Bennett College and a few white students from the University of North Carolina Women's College joined the protest. By the fifth day hundreds of young, studious, neatly dressed African Americans crowded the downtown store demanding their rights.

The students in Greensboro had long debated how they could best participate in the desegregation movement. All four of the black students had been members of NAACP college or youth groups and were aware of the currents of change flowing through the South. Although they began the sit-in on their own, it quickly gained the support of the black community. Many people in the North and West—both black and white—also joined the campaign by picketing local stores of the national chains that approved of segregation in the South. After facing the collective power of the black community and their allies for many months, white businessmen and politicians finally gave in to the black community's demands.

The students at Greensboro were not alone in their desire to strike out at discrimination. Indeed, at Fisk University in Nashville, Tennessee, Diane Nash, John Lewis, Marion Barry, James Bevel, Curtis Murphy, Gloria Johnson, Bernard Lafayette, and Rodney Powell had begun organizing nonviolent workshops before the Greensboro sit-in. Even better organized than their comrades in North Carolina, they had been undergoing intensive training for a sit-in campaign. Twelve days after the first sit-ins began, the Nashville group swung into action. Hundreds were arrested, and those who sat suffered insults, mob violence, beatings, arrest, and torture while in jail. Nonetheless, they compelled major restaurants to desegregate by May 1960.

Atlanta spawned an even more dramatic movement. It began after Spelman College freshman Ruby Doris Smith persuaded her friends and classmates to launch sit-ins in the city. On March 15, 1960, at Atlanta University, two students, Julian Bond and Lonnie King, executing a carefully orchestrated plan, deployed two hundred sit-in students to ten different eating places. They targeted government-owned property and public places, including bus and train stations and the state capitol, that should have been willing to serve all customers. At the Federal Building, Bond and his classmates attempted to eat in the municipal cafeteria and were arrested. After hours of incarceration they were released. The Atlanta sit-in students broadened their campaign demands to include desegregation of all public facilities, black voting rights, and equal access to educational and employment opportunities. On September 27, 1961, the Atlanta business and political elite gave in.

By April 1960 more than two thousand students from black high schools and colleges had been arrested in seventy-eight southern towns and cities. Local people demonstrated their allegiance to them in numerous ways, but their most effective tactic was the economic boycott. When business began to suffer as a result of the protests, white leaders

James Farmer was one of the driving forces behind the creation of the Congress of Racial Equality (CORE) and the 1961 Freedom Rides.

▶▶ **Document**

21-5 *Julian Bond, Sit-ins and the Origins of SNCC, 1960*
The Student Nonviolent Coordinating Committee (SNCC) was founded in 1960 by student protestors. SNCC accepted the non-violent principles and the principles of civil disobedience espoused by Martin Luther King, Jr. while involving itself in social, economic, and political issues. By 1965, SNCC had challenged segregation and had commenced voter registration projects across the South.

▶▶ **Recommended Reading**

Clayborne Carson. *In Struggle: SNCC and the Black Awakening of the 1960s.* Cambridge, MA: Harvard University Press, 1981. One of the best historical studies of SNCC and the contributions students made to galvanize the civil rights movement.

proved willing to negotiate the racial status quo. By the summer, more than thirty southern cities had set up community organizations to respond to the complaints of local black citizens.

The Student Nonviolent Coordinating Committee

Recognizing the significance of the regionwide student action and fearing it would soon melt away, the SCLC's Ella Baker organized a conference for 150 students at her alma mater, Shaw University, in Raleigh, North Carolina. Baker, who managed operations in the SCLC's Atlanta headquarters, chafed under the rigid male leadership of the organization. In contrast, she advocated decentralized leadership and celebrated participatory democracy. Her skepticism about the SCLC struck a chord with the students.

On April 15–17, 1960, delegates representing over fifty colleges and high schools from thirty-seven communities in thirteen states arrived and began discussing how to keep the movement going. Baker addressed the group in a speech entitled "More Than a Hamburger" and became the midwife of a new organization named the **Student Nonviolent Coordinating Committee** (**SNCC**). The newest addition to the roster of civil rights associations adhered to the ideology of nonviolence. It also acknowledged the possible need for increased militancy and confrontation. More accommodating black leaders, even some of those in the SCLC, objected to the students' use of direct confrontational tactics that disrupted race relations and community peace.

Freedom Rides

The sit-in movement paved the way for the **Freedom Rides** of 1961. CORE's James Farmer and Bayard Rustin resolved it was time for a reprise of their 1947 mission to ride interstate buses and trains in the upper South. That early effort—a planned bus trip from Washington, D.C., to Kentucky—reached only as far as Chapel Hill, North Carolina. There the group of interracial riders met violent resistance, were arrested, and were sentenced to thirty days on a road gang. This new journey tested the Justice Department's willingness to protect the rights of African Americans to use bus terminal facilities on a nonsegregated basis.

The Freedom Rides showed the world how far some white Southerners would go to preserve segregation. The first ride ran into trouble on May 4, 1961. John Lewis, one of the seven black riders, tried to enter the white waiting room of the Greyhound bus terminal in Rock Hill, South Carolina. He was brutally beaten by local white people in full view of the police. The interracial group continued through Alabama toward Jackson, Mississippi, but repeated acts of white violence made

On May 14, in Anniston, Alabama, a white mob firebombed this Freedom Riders' bus and attacked passengers as they escaped the flames.

escape from Alabama difficult. At Anniston, Alabama, a mob firebombed the bus and beat the escaping riders. A group of local African Americans led by the Reverend Fred Shuttlesworth took many of the shocked and injured riders to Birmingham.

With the police offering no protection, CORE abandoned the Freedom Rides, and all but a few of the original riders left Alabama. But SNCC activists and students in Nashville refused to let the idea die. At least twenty civil rights workers went to Birmingham where they vowed on May 20 to ride on to Montgomery. John Lewis remained with the group that arrived in Montgomery. Awaiting them was another angry mob of more than a thousand white people, and not a policeman in sight. This time Lewis was knocked unconscious, and all the riders had to be hospitalized. Even a presidential aide assigned to monitor the crisis was injured.

News services flashed graphic images of the violence around the world, and the federal government resolved to end the bloodletting. Attorney General Robert Kennedy sent four hundred federal marshals to restore law and order. Martin Luther King Jr. and Ralph Abernathy joined the conflict on May 21, as 1,200 men, women, and children met at Abernathy's church. The federal marshals averted further bloodshed by surrounding the building. Only then did Governor John Patterson order the National Guard and state troopers to protect the protesters. When the group arrived in Jackson, Mississippi, white authorities promptly arrested them. By summer's end, more than three hundred Freedom Riders had served time in Mississippi's notorious prisons.

 Reading Check How did black students play a significant role in advancing the cause of civil rights?

▶▶ **Reading Check**

Students played an active role in sit-ins and other demonstrations. In 1960, students from more than fifty colleges and high schools met to discuss the movement and form the SNCC, the Student Nonviolent Coordinating Committee.

▶▶ **Guide to Reading/Key Terms**

For answers, see the *Teacher's Resource Manual.*

▶▶ **Teaching Notes**

Between 1960 and 1963 the civil rights movement developed the techniques and organization that would finally bring America face to face with the conflict between its democratic ideals and the racism of its politics. Day after day the movement squared off against the die-hard resistance of the white South and created a situation that demanded that the president and Congress take action.

Section 4

The Movement at High Tide

The Election of 1960

One of the persistent fears of white Southerners was that black Americans, if armed with the ballot, would possess the balance of political power. The presidential election of 1960 proved this to be the case. Initially, many African Americans favored the Republican Party's nominee, Richard Nixon, who had advocated strong civil rights legislation. Baseball star Jackie Robinson was a Nixon supporter as were many other well-known African Americans. It seemed as if the New Deal coalition had weakened and black citizens would reverse their move into the Democratic Party. The Democratic nominee, Massachusetts senator John F. Kennedy, in contrast, had done little to distinguish himself to black Americans in the struggles of the 1950s. As the campaign progressed, however, Kennedy made more sympathetic statements in support of black protests. Meanwhile, Nixon attempted to strengthen his position with white southern voters and remained silent about civil rights issues, even though the Republican Party had a strong pro–civil rights record.

Shortly before the election, Martin Luther King was sentenced to four months in prison for leading a nonviolent protest march in Atlanta. Kennedy seized the opportunity to telephone King's wife, Coretta Scott King, to offer his support while his brother Robert F. Kennedy used his influence to obtain King's release. These acts impressed African Americans and won their support. African-American voters in key northern cities provided the crucial margin that elected John F. Kennedy. In Illinois, for example, with black voters casting 250,000 ballots for Kennedy, the Democrats carried the state by merely 9,000 votes.

The Kennedy Administration and the Civil Rights Movement

Early in his administration John F. Kennedy grew concerned about the mounting violence occasioned by the civil rights movement. As the Freedom Rides continued across the deep South, the activists provoked crises and confrontations and forced the federal government to inter-

vene in their behalf. Kennedy's primary interest at this point was to prevent disorder from getting out of hand and to avoid compromising America's position with the developing nations. But Kennedy had little room to maneuver given the continued power of white Southerners in his party and in Congress.

Despite these limitations, Kennedy did aid the cause of civil rights. He issued **Executive Order 11063**, which required government agencies to discontinue discriminatory policies and practices in federally supported housing. He named Vice President Lyndon B. Johnson to chair the newly established Committee on Equal Employment Opportunity. Kennedy also pleased black Americans when he nominated Thurgood Marshall to the Second Circuit Court of Appeals on September 23, 1961. Opposition in the Senate blocked Marshall's confirmation until September 11, 1963. He named journalist Carl Rowan deputy assistant secretary of state. More than forty African Americans took positions in the new administration, including Robert Weaver, director of the Housing and Home Finance Agency; Mercer Cook, ambassador to Norway; and George L. P. Weaver, assistant secretary of labor. Moreover, Kennedy's brother Robert put muscle into the Civil Rights Division of the Justice Department by hiring an impressive team of lawyers headed by Washington attorney Burke Marshall.

When President Kennedy felt that southern governors were challenging his authority, he acted decisively. On June 25, 1962, one year after James Meredith had filed a complaint of racial discrimination against the University of Mississippi, the U.S. Circuit Court of Appeals for the Fifth Circuit ruled that the university had to admit him. Mississippi governor Ross Barnett vowed to resist the order, but Kennedy sent three hundred federal marshals to uphold it. Thousands of students rioted at the campus. Two people died, two hundred were arrested, and nearly half the marshals were injured. Kennedy did not back down. He federalized the Mississippi National Guard to ensure Meredith's admission. Although isolated and harassed throughout his time at the university, Meredith eventually graduated. Likewise, in June 1963, the Kennedy administration compelled Governor George Wallace of Alabama to allow the desegregation of the University of Alabama.

Voter Registration Projects

On June 16, 1961, Robert Kennedy met with student leaders and urged them to redirect their energies to voter registration projects and to lessen their concentration on direct-action activities. He and the Justice Department aides persuaded the students that the free exercise of the ballot would result in profound and significant social change. James Foreman, SNCC's executive director, followed Kennedy's lead. By October 1961 SNCC had joined forces with the NAACP, SCLC, and CORE in the voter education project funded by major philanthropic

▶▶ **Recommended Reading**

Steven F. Lawson. *Running for Freedom: Civil Rights and Black Politics in America since 1941.* Philadelphia: Temple University Press, 1991. A succinct analysis of the politics, legislative measures, and individuals that figured in the successes and failures of the civil rights movement.

▶ **Recommended Reading**

Eric R. Burner. *And Gently He Shall Lead Them: Robert Parris Moses and Civil Rights in Mississippi.* New York: New York University Press, 1994.

foundations and administered by the Southern Regional Council. SNCC was responsible for Alabama and Mississippi. Drawing heavily on the expertise of Robert Moses and working closely with local leaders like Amzie Moore, head of the NAACP in Mississippi's Cleveland county, and Fannie Lou Hamer of Ruleville, SNCC opened a series of voter registra-

PROFILE ❖ Robert Parris Moses

Bob Moses was born in 1935 in Harlem, Moses was an excellent student. He attended Hamilton College in New York State. From his reading in philosophy there, including works on Buddhism and existentialism, he developed a sophisticated understanding of nonviolent protest.

When Moses learned of the sit-ins in 1960, he immediately went south to participate. It was a fateful trip during which he met Amzie Moore, one of the World War II veterans who had returned home to make Mississippi safe for democracy. Moore was the vice president of the state conferences of the NAACP branches. The two men developed a deep-seated appreciation for each other's strengths. Moore soon convinced Moses to center his work in Mississippi. By August 1961 Moses was a SNCC organizer in the small town of McComb, Mississippi. There his group registered black voters. In early 1962 the SNCC activist became the program director of the Council of Federated Organizations (COFO) and remained in the center of the struggle in Mississippi for the next three years.

The violence of white people and the courage of local black people had a profound effect on Moses. In McComb he was arrested, jailed, beaten, and threatened with death. One of the local black people who helped his group was murdered in cold blood by a state senator who was subsequently acquitted of the crime by an all-white jury. He sought to give local people the tools to continue to control their lives long after movement organizers had left.

Although Moses refused to become a formal leader of the SNCC forces in Mississippi, he profoundly affected the movement. The young civil rights worker set an example of nonviolent resistance for other members of SNCC. In late 1963 Moses became the driving force behind the Freedom Summer project and played a central role in persuading SNCC to accept white volunteers from the North.

In 1965 Moses began to drift away from the civil rights movement and toward active opposition to the war in Vietnam. Exhausted from his ordeal in the South and seeking to avoid the draft, he emigrated first to Canada and then to the African nation of Tanzania. Moses returned soon after President Jimmy Carter offered amnesty to draft resisters in 1977. He began teaching math and science to inner-city black children. After receiving a MacArthur Foundation "genius grant," he developed the Algebra Project. The program uses many of the empowerment strategies pioneered during the civil rights era to help children and their families gain the education they need in the emerging computer-oriented economy.

tion schools. The "graduates" thereupon attempted to register to vote. These attempts unleashed a wave of white violence and murder across Mississippi.

The Albany Movement

In Albany, Georgia, the burgeoning civil rights movement met sophisticated resistance and experienced its most profound defeat up to that time. The movement in Albany began in the summer of 1961 when SNCC members moved into the city to conduct a voter registration project. Soon representatives of various local groups decided to form a coalition called the **Albany Movement** and elected William G. Anderson as its president. The movement's goal quickly expanded from securing the vote to the total desegregation of the town.

In Laurie Pritchett, Albany's police chief, the movement faced an uncommonly sophisticated opponent. Pritchett studied the past tactics of SNCC and King and resolved not to confront the federal government directly and to avoid the kind of violence that brought negative media attention. When students from a black college decided to begin demonstrations by desegregating the bus terminal, Pritchett immediately arrested them after they entered the white waiting room and attempted to eat in the bus terminal dining room. Shrewdly, he charged the students with violating a city ordinance for failing to obey a law enforcement officer. They were not arrested on a federal charge.

The Albany Movement decided to invite King and the SCLC to aid them and to overwhelm the police department by filling the jails with protesters. King answered the call. On December 16, 1961, he and more than 250 demonstrators were arrested, joining the 507 people already in jail. The plan was to stay in jail in order to, as Charles Sherrod explained, "break the system down from within. Our ability to suffer was somehow going to overcome their ability to hurt us." King vowed to remain in jail until the city desegregated. Sheriff Pritchett, however, made arrangements to house almost two thousand people in surrounding jail facilities and trained his deputies in the use of nonviolent techniques. Thus Pritchett avoided confrontation, violence, and federal intervention.

On December 18, 1961, two days after King's arrest, the city and the Albany Movement announced a truce. King returned to Atlanta, and the city refused to implement the terms of the agreement. When King and Ralph Abernathy returned to Albany in July 1962 for sentencing on their December arrests, they chose forty-five days in jail rather than admit guilt by paying a fine. The mass marches resumed, but again Pritchett thwarted King by having him released from jail to avoid negative publicity. The city's attorney then secured a federal injunction to prevent King and the other leaders from demonstrating. Given his dependence on the federal government, King felt he could not violate the injunction and

Bernice Johnson Reagon on How to Raise a Freedom Song

Civil rights activists created a special culture in which black music helped communicate a sense of common purpose, strengthen the resolve to endure hardship and pain, and overcome despair and fear. One of the great singers to emerge out of the Albany Movement was Bernice Johnson Reagon, who today is known internationally as the founder of the a cappella group Sweet Honey in the Rock. During the 1960s she and Cordell Reagon and others formed the SNCC Freedom Singers and traveled the country performing freedom songs. In this statement Reagon describes the significance of song to the civil rights participants.

If you cannot sing a congregational song at full power, you cannot fight in any struggle. . . . It is something you learn.

In congregational singing you don't sing a song—you raise it. By offering the first line, the song leader just offers the possibility, and it is up to you, individually, whether you pick it up or not. . . . It is a big personal risk because you will put everything into the song. It is like stepping off into space. A mini-revolution takes place inside you. Your body gets flushed, you tremble, you're tempted to turn off the circuits. But that's when you have to turn up the burner and commit yourself to follow that song wherever it leads. This transformation in yourself that you create is exactly what happens when you join a movement. You are taking a risk—you are committing yourself and there is no turning back. . . .

Organizing is not gentle. When you organize somebody, you create great anxiety in that person because you are telling them to risk everything. Put yourself in the place of a woman getting by as a hairdresser. You spend your day curling and frying hair, curling and frying. Somebody asks you to put up some civil rights workers in your home. You have to imagine what is going to happen: there may be people shooting up your home; you have to picture the check you get, the car you drive; everything you own, going on the block. You decide to take that risk because this is important enough. . . .

When you get together at a mass meeting you sing the songs which symbolize transformation, which make that revolution of courage inside you. . . . You raise a freedom song.

abandoned the protest. For King, the Albany Movement was a failure, his most glaring defeat, and one that called into question the future of the movement.

 Reading Check What kinds of resistance did white authorities put up against the Albany movement?

The Birmingham Confrontation

By early 1963 the movement appeared to be stalled. Black communities in many parts of the South were strong and well organized, but their enormous efforts had achieved only modest changes. It was impossible to overcome the power of southern state and local governments without the intervention of the federal government. National politicians, including President Kennedy, remained reluctant to act unless faced with open defiance by white people or televised violence against peaceful protesters. King and other black leaders knew that if city governments throughout the South followed the model of Sheriff Pritchett in Albany, the civil rights movement might lose momentum. To rejuvenate the movement, the SCLC decided to launch a massive new campaign during 1963, the year of the one hundredth anniversary of the Emancipation Proclamation.

Birmingham, Alabama, a large, tightly segregated industrial city, was chosen as the site for the action. The city was ripe for such a protest, in part because its black community suffered from severe police brutality as well as economic, educational, and social discrimination. The Ku Klux Klan terrorized people with impunity. The black community had, however, developed a strong group of protest organizations called the **Alabama Christian Movement for Human Rights** (ACMHR) led by the Reverend Fred Shuttlesworth. The ACMHR and SCLC planned a campaign of boycotts, pickets, and demonstrations code-named **Project C** for Confrontation. Their program would be far more extensive than any before, with demands to integrate public facilities, for guarantees of employment opportunities for black workers in downtown businesses,

▶ **Reading Check**

Shrewd tactics by Albany's police chief, Laurie Pritchett, stymied the Albany Movement. Pritchett avoided the kind of violence that attracted media attention. He also tried hard not to directly confront the federal government. In so doing, he headed off federal intervention in the city.

▶ **What Do You Think?**

· Both require an emotional and personal commitment, a willingness to take a risk without turning back.

· Ordinary people became involved in the movement despite the dangers because it was the only way to bring about change.

▶ **Retracing the Odyssey**

Birmingham Civil Rights Institute. Exhibits depict the history of the black freedom struggle. The museum chronicles the dramatic and often violent activities that occurred in Birmingham during the 1960s as black protest confronted massive white resistance.

Violence and the Civil Rights Movement

MAY 7, 1955	The Reverend George Lee killed for leading voter registration drive, Belzoni, MS
AUGUST 13, 1955	Lamar Smith murdered for organizing black voters, Brookhaven, MS
AUGUST 28, 1955	Emmett Louis Till murdered for speaking to white woman, Money, MS
OCTOBER 22, 1955	John Earl Reese slain by night riders opposed to black school improvements, Mayflower, TX
JANUARY 23, 1957	Willie Edwards Jr. killed by Klan, Montgomery, AL
SEPTEMBER 24, 1957	President Eisenhower orders federal troops to enforce school desegregation, Little Rock, AR
APRIL 27, 1959	Mack Charles Parker taken from jail and lynched, Popularville, MS
MAY 14, 1961	Freedom Riders attacked in Alabama while testing compliance with bus desegregation laws
SEPTEMBER 25, 1961	Voter registration worker Herbert Lee killed by a white legislator, Liberty, MS
APRIL 1, 1962	Civil rights groups join forces to launch voter registration drive
APRIL 9, 1962	Roman Ducksworth Jr. taken from bus and killed by police, Taylorsville, MS
SEPTEMBER 30, 1962	Riots erupt when James Meredith, a black student, enrolls at the University of Mississippi. Paul Guihard, European reporter, killed
APRIL 23, 1963	William Lewis Moore slain during one-man march against segregation, Attalla, AL
MAY 3, 1963	Birmingham police attack marching children with dogs and fire hoses
JUNE 12, 1963	Medgar Evers, civil rights leader, assassinated, Jackson, MS
SEPTEMBER 15, 1963	Schoolgirls Addie Mae Collins, Denise McNair, Carole Robertson, and Cynthia Wesley die in the bombing of the 16th St. Baptist Church, Birmingham, AL
SEPTEMBER 15, 1963	Virgin Lamar Ware killed during racist violence, Birmingham, AL
JANUARY 31, 1964	Louis Allen, witness to the murder of a civil rights worker, assassinated, Liberty, MS
APRIL 7, 1964	The Reverend Bruce Klunder killed protesting construction of segregated school, Cleveland, OH
MAY 2, 1964	Henry Hezekiah Dee and Charles Eddie Moore killed by Klan, Meadville, MS
JUNE 21, 1964	Civil rights workers James Chaney, Andrew Goodman, and Michael Schwerner abducted and slain by Klan, Philadelphia, MS

JULY 11, 1964	Lt. Col. Lemuel Penn killed by Klan while driving north, Colbert, GA
FEBRUARY 26, 1965	Jimmie Lee Jackson, civil rights marcher, killed by state trooper, Marion, AL
MARCH 11, 1965	Selma to Montgomery march volunteer, the Reverend James Reeb, beaten to death, Selma, AL
MARCH 25, 1965	Viola Gregg Liuzzo killed by Klan while transporting marchers, Selma Highway, AL
JUNE 2, 1965	Oneal Moore, black deputy, killed by night riders, Varnado, LA
JULY 18, 1965	Willie Wallace Brewster killed by night riders, Anniston, AL
AUGUST 20, 1965	Jonathan Daniels, seminary student, killed by deputy, Hayneville, AL
JANUARY 3, 1966	Samuel Younge Jr., student civil rights activist, killed in dispute over whites-only rest room, Tuskegee, AL
JANUARY 10, 1966	Vernon Dahmer, black community leader, killed in Klan bombing, Hattiesburg, MS
JUNE 10, 1966	Ben Chester White killed by Klan, Natchez, MS
JULY 30, 1966	Clarence Triggs slain by night riders, Bogalusa, LA
FEBRUARY 2, 1967	Wharlest Jackson, civil rights leader, killed when police fired on protesters, Jackson, MS
FEBRUARY 8, 1968	Students Samuel Hammond Jr., Delano Middleton, and Henry Smith killed when highway patrolmen fire on protesters, Orangeburg, SC
APRIL 4, 1968	Dr. Martin Luther King Jr. assassinated, Memphis, TN

to desegregate the schools, to improve services in black neighborhoods, and to provide low-income housing. Organizers hoped to provoke the city's public safety commissioner Eugene T. "Bull" Connor, who, unlike Sheriff Pritchett, had a reputation for viciousness. Civil rights leaders believed Connor's conduct would horrify the nation and compel Kennedy to act.

Project C began on the third of April with college students conducting sit-ins. Days later, marches began, and Connor, following the lead of Pritchett, arrested all who participated but avoided overt violence. When the state courts prohibited further protests, King and Abernathy, among others, violated the ruling. They were arrested and jailed on Good Friday, April 12, 1963.

While in jail, King received a letter from eight local Christian and Jewish clergymen who objected to what they considered the "unwise and untimely" protest activities of black citizens. King had smuggled a

▶▶ **Document**

21-6 *Martin Luther King, Jr.: Letter from Birmingham City Jail, 1963*
After King was arrested and while serving time in jail, he penned a letter in response to eight African-American clergymen who had denounced African-American activism.

▶▶ **Recommended Reading**

Taylor Branch. *Pillar of Fire: America in the King Years, 1963–65.* New York: Simon & Schuster, 1998.

pen into jail and on scraps of paper, including toilet paper and the margins of the Birmingham *News*, he wrote an eloquent treatise on the use of direct action. His **"Letter from Birmingham Jail"** was widely published in newspapers and magazines. In it, King dismissed those who called for black people to wait: "I guess it is easy for those who have never felt the stinging darts of segregation to say, 'Wait.'" But, he declared, "freedom is never voluntarily given by the oppressor; it must be demanded by the oppressed." In the letter King also explained,

> "Nonviolent direct action seeks to create such a crisis and foster such a tension that a community which has constantly refused to negotiate is forced to confront the issue. It seeks so to dramatize the issue that it can no longer be ignored. . . . Any law that degrades human personality is unjust. All segregation statutes are unjust because segregation distorts the soul and damages the personality. It gives the segregator a false sense of superiority and the segregated a false sense of inferiority."

King's letter had a powerful national impact, but the Birmingham movement was beginning to lose momentum because many of the protesters were either in jail or could not risk new arrests. At this juncture James Bevel of the SCLC proposed using schoolchildren to continue the protests. Many observers criticized this idea, as did some of those in the movement. But King and other leaders believed it was necessary to risk harm to children in order to ensure their freedom. Thus, on May 2 and 3, 1963, a **children's crusade** involving thousands of youths, some as young as six, marched. This tactic enraged "Bull" Connor and his officers. The police not only arrested the children but flailed away with nightsticks and set vicious dogs on them. On Connor's order, firefighters aimed their powerful hoses at the youngsters, ripping the clothes from backs, cutting flesh, and tumbling children down the street. In the ensuing days many of the children and their parents began to fight back, hurling bottles and rocks at their uniformed tormentors. As the violence escalated, white businessmen became concerned, and the city soon came to the bargaining table.

President Kennedy deployed Assistant Attorney General for Civil Rights Burke Marshall to negotiate a settlement. On May 10, 1963, white businessmen agreed to integrate downtown facilities and to hire black men and women. The following night the KKK bombed the A. G. Gaston Motel, where the SCLC had its headquarters, and the house that belonged to King's brother, the Reverend A. D. King. Black citizens in turn burned cars and buildings and attacked the police. Only intervention by King and other movement leaders prevented a riot. White moderates delivered on the promises and the agreement stuck.

Although the SCLC did not win on every demand, Birmingham was a major triumph and a turning point in the movement. The summer of 1963 saw a massive upsurge in protests across the South with nearly

Young protestors huddle against a wall for protection as firefighters spray them with fire hoses.

eight hundred marches, demonstrations, and sit-ins. Ten civil rights protesters were killed and twenty thousand arrested as the white South desperately sought to stem the tide. In one of the most tragic losses for the movement, white extremist Byron de la Beckwith gunned down Medgar Evers in the driveway of his home on June 12, 1963, in Jackson, Mississippi. Evers had been the executive secretary of the NAACP's Mississippi organization and the center of a powerful movement in that city. His cold-blooded murder dramatized the depth of hatred among some white Southerners and the lengths to which they would go to prevent change.

 Reading Check How did the federal government support, and at times thwart, the freedom movement?

▶ Reading Check

The Kennedy administration took action in support of the civil rights movement. Over forty African-Americans took positions in the administration. On the other hand, the administration's desire to avoid unrest and disorder in the South and the continuing power of white Southerners in the Democratic party limited the federal government's commitment to the movement.

▶ **Guide to Reading/Key Terms**

For answers, see the *Teacher's Resource Manual.*

Section 5

A Hard Victory

The March on Washington

The lingering image of Birmingham and the growing number of demonstrations throughout the South compelled action from President Kennedy. He proposed the strongest civil rights bill the country had yet seen. Despite the public's heightened awareness of discrimination, he still could not muster sufficient support in Congress to counter the powerful southern bloc within his own party.

To demonstrate their support for Kennedy's civil rights legislation, a coalition of civil rights organizations—SCLC, NAACP, CORE, SNCC, and the National Urban League—and their leaders resurrected the idea of organizing a **march on Washington** that A. Philip Randolph had first proposed in 1941. In 1962 Randolph and Bayard Rustin had proposed a march to protest black unemployment. Their call received a lukewarm response, but after Birmingham many of the major civil rights organizations reconsidered. Reflecting renewed hope, Randolph christened it a march for "Jobs and Freedom."

In August 1963 nearly 250,000 marchers gathered before the Lincoln Memorial to show their support for the civil rights bill and the movement at large. Throughout the day they sang freedom songs and listened to speeches from civil rights leaders. Finally, late in the afternoon, Martin Luther King Jr. arose, and casting aside his prepared remarks, he delivered an impassioned speech. Most powerfully, King spoke of this vision of the future:

I say to you today, my friends, that in spite of the difficulties and frustrations of the moment I still have a dream. It is a dream deeply rooted in the American dream. I have a dream that one day this nation will rise up and live out the true meaning of its creed: "We hold these truths to be self-evident; that all men are created equal." I have a dream that one day on the red hills of Georgia the sons of former slaves and the sons of former slave owners will be able to sit down together at the table of brotherhood. I have a dream that one day even the state of Mississippi, a desert state sweltering with the heat of injustice and oppression, will be transformed into an oasis of freedom and justice. I have a dream that my four children will one day live in a nation where they will not be judged by the color of their skin but by the content of their character. I have a dream today. I have a dream that one day the state of Alabama, whose

governor's lips are presently dripping with the words of interposition and nullification, will be transformed into a situation where little black boys and black girls will be able to join hands with little white boys and white girls and walk together as sisters and brothers. I have a dream today . . .

King's words did not still the angry opposition of some white Southerners. On September 15, 1963, only days after the march on Washington, white racists bombed the 16th St. Baptist Church in Birmingham and killed four little girls attending Sunday school: Addie Mae Collins, Denise McNair, Carole Robertson, and Cynthia Wesley. Chris McNair, the father of the youngest victim, pleaded for calm out of the depth of his own pain: "We must not let this change us into something different than who we are. We must be human." In a similar vein, Martin Luther King sadly intoned, "The innocent blood of these little girls may well serve as the redemptive force that will bring new light to this dark city. . . . Indeed, this tragic event may cause the white South to come to terms with its conscience." The event shook the nation, and combined with the reaction to the assassination of John F. Kennedy in November 1963, set the stage for real change.

The Civil Rights Act of 1964

Kennedy's successor Lyndon B. Johnson lobbied hard to secure passage of the landmark Civil Rights Act. Many in the civil rights movement feared that Johnson, a Southerner, would back his region's defiance. Nonetheless, only four days after taking the oath of office, Johnson told the nation he planned to support the civil rights bill as a memorial for the slain president. A master politician, Johnson pushed the bill through Congress despite a marathon filibuster by its opponents.

The **Civil Rights Act of 1964** was the culmination of the civil rights movement to that time. The act banned discrimination in places of public accommodation, including restaurants, hotels, gas stations, and entertainment facilities, as well as schools, parks, playgrounds, libraries, and swimming pools. The desegregation of public accommodations irrevocably changed the face of American society. The issue of legally mandated racial separation was now settled. The act also banned discrimination by employers, of labor unions on the basis of race, color, religion, national origin, and sex in regard to hiring, promoting, dismissing, or making job referrals. The act had strong provisions for enforcement. Most important, it allowed government agencies to withhold federal money from any program permitting or practicing discrimination. This provision had particular import for the desegregation of schools and colleges across the country. The act also gave the U.S. attorney general the power to initiate proceedings against segregated facilities and schools on behalf of people who could not do so on their own. Finally it created the **Equal Employment Opportunity Commission** to monitor discrimination in employment.

MARCH ON WASHINGTON FOR JOBS AND FREEDOM
AUGUST 28, 1963

LINCOLN MEMORIAL PROGRAM

1.	The National Anthem	Led by Marian Anderson.
2.	Invocation	The Very Rev. Patrick O'Boyle, Archbishop of Washington.
3.	Opening Remarks	A. Philip Randolph, Director March on Washington for Jobs and Freedom.
4.	Remarks	Dr. Eugene Carson Blake, Stated Clerk, United Presbyterian Church of the U.S.A.; Vice Chairman, Commission on Race Relations of the National Council of Churches of Christ in America.
5.	Tribute to Negro Women Fighters for Freedom Daisy Bates Diane Nash Bevel Mrs. Medgar Evers Mrs. Herbert Lee Rosa Parks Gloria Richardson	Mrs. Medgar Evers
6.	Remarks	John Lewis, National Chairman, Student Nonviolent Coordinating Committee.
7.	Remarks	Walter Reuther, President, United Automobile, Aerospace and Agricultural Implements Wokers of America, AFL-CIO; Chairman, Industrial Union Department, AFL-CIO.
8.	Remarks	James Farmer, National Director, Congress of Racial Equality.
9.	Selection	Eva Jessye Choir
10.	Prayer	Rabbi Uri Miller, President Synagogue Council of America.
11.	Remarks	Whitney M. Young, Jr., Executive Director, National Urban League.
12.	Remarks	Mathew Ahmann, Executive Director, National Catholic Conference for Interracial Justice.
13.	Remarks	Roy Wilkins, Executive Secretary, National Association for the Advancement of Colored People.
14.	Selection	Miss Mahalia Jackson
15.	Remarks	Rabbi Joachim Prinz, President American Jewish Congress.
16.	Remarks	The Rev. Dr. Martin Luther King, Jr., President, Southern Christian Leadership Conference.
17.	The Pledge	A Philip Randolph
18.	Benediction	Dr. Benjamin E. Mays, President, Morehouse College.

"WE SHALL OVERCOME"

A. Philip Randolph, John Lewis, James Farmer, Whitney Young, Roy Wilkins, and Martin Luther King Jr., the leaders of the organizations that spearheaded the modern civil rights movement, came together in one of the great mass marches in American history to address issues of jobs and freedom.

▶▶ **Document**

Excerpts from the *Civil Rights Act of 1964* are included in the *Teacher's Resource Manual*.

▶▶ **Retracing the Odyssey**

The Lincoln Memorial. The Lincoln Memorial was built to celebrate President Abraham Lincoln and the Civil War (1861–1865) to preserve the union. It possesses a particular relevance and meaning to African Americans. The Lincoln Memorial was the site of the August 1963 March on Washington during which Martin Luther King delivered his powerful "I Have a Dream" speech.

Mississippi Freedom Summer

While Congress considered the Civil Rights Act, movement activists renewed their focus on voter registration in the deep South. In the fall of 1963, many CORE and SNCC workers saw segregation crumbling, but they knew that without the ballot, African Americans could never drive racist politicians from office, gain a fair hearing in court, reduce police and mob violence, or get equal services from state and local governments. CORE took responsibility for running registration campaigns in Louisiana, South Carolina, and Florida while SNCC took on the two most repressive states, Alabama and Mississippi. Mississippi was widely known in the movement as the "toughest nut to crack"—the symbolic center of American racism and white violence. By the summer of 1964, national attention had shifted from Alabama to Mississippi, the site of a massive project known as **Freedom Summer**.

The voter registration campaign in Mississippi began in late 1963 when Robert "Bob" Moses mobilized the **Council of Federated Organizations (COFO)**, which had been established in 1961 to aid imprisoned freedom riders. Moses convinced the members of COFO (CORE, SNCC, SCLC, and the NAACP) to sponsor a mock Freedom Election in Mississippi. On Election Day, eighty-thousand disfranchised black people cast ballots for COFO candidates. Impressed with the turnout, Moses and other COFO members believed a massive effort to register voters during the summer of 1964 might break the white monopoly on the ballot box.

After much debate, COFO decided to invite northern white students to participate in the Mississippi project. These students, about one thousand in all, were to be drawn primarily from the nation's most prestigious universities. This move contradicted the movement's emphasis on black empowerment. But COFO leaders calculated that the presence of elite white students in the Magnolia State would attract increased media attention and pressure the federal government to provide protection.

Shortly after the project began, three volunteers, two white New Yorkers—twenty-four-year-old Michael Schwerner and twenty-one-year-old Andrew Goodman—and a black Mississippian, twenty-one-year-old James Chaney, disappeared. Unknown at the time, Cecil Price, deputy sheriff of Philadelphia, Mississippi, had arrested the three on a trumped-up speeding charge. That evening the young men were delivered to a deserted road where three carloads of Klansmen waited. Schwerner and Goodman were shot to death. Chaney was beaten with chains and then shot.

These events were not publicly known until Klan informers, enticed by a $30,000 reward, led investigators to the earthen dam in which Goodman, Schwerner, and Chaney had been buried. The disappearance of the three nonetheless focused national attention on white terrorism. During the summer, approximately thirty homes and thirty-seven churches were bombed, thirty-five civil rights workers were shot

At the height of his moral authority, Martin Luther King Jr. (1929–1968) delivers the memorable "I Have A Dream" speech at the 1963 March on Washington.

▶ **Recommended Reading**

Doug McAdam. *Freedom Summer.* New York: Oxford University Press, 1988.

at, eighty people were beaten, six were murdered, and more than one thousand were arrested. In the face of this violence, uncertainty, and fear, many SNCC activists rejected Martin Luther King's commitment to nonviolence, the inclusion of white activists in the movement, and the wisdom of integration. Divisions over these issues greatly increased tensions among the groups that made up the movement.

Despite the problems it encountered, the Freedom Summer organized dozens of Freedom Schools and community centers throughout Mississippi. Its efforts mobilized the state's black people to an extent not seen since the first Reconstruction. Many communities began to develop the rudiments of a political movement, one that would grow in coming years.

The Mississippi Freedom Democratic Party

Freedom Summer intersected with national politics at the Democratic Party's national convention in August 1964 in Atlantic City, New Jersey. White Mississippians routinely excluded African Americans from the political process. Robert Moses encouraged COFO to set up the **Mississippi Freedom Democratic Party** (MFDP) to challenge the state's regular Democratic delegation at the convention. Under the leadership of veteran activists Fannie Lou Hamer, Victoria Gray, Annie Divine, and Aaron Henry, the MFDP held its first state convention on August 6. Approximately eighty thousand citizens put their names on the rolls. The convention elected sixty-four delegates who traveled to the national convention to present their credentials.

The MFDP challenge caused considerable difficulty for the Democratic Party. Many liberals wanted to seat the civil rights delegation. But President Lyndon Johnson, who was running for reelection, did not want to alienate white Southerners, fearing they would vote for Barry Goldwater, his Republican opponent. Liberal Democratic senator Hubert H. Humphrey, from Minnesota, worked out a compromise calling for Mississippi regulars to be seated if they swore loyalty to the national party and agreed to cast their forty-four votes accordingly. The compromise also provided for the creation of two "at-large" seats to be filled by MFDP members Aaron Henry and Ed King. The rest of the Freedom Democrats could attend the convention as nonvoting guests.

Martin Luther King Jr., Bayard Rustin, and other black leaders counseled acceptance of this compromise. Johnson and the Democrats, they argued, had achieved much of the legislative program favored by the movement. If the party were returned to power they could do much more. But most of the MFDP delegation, fed up with the violence of Mississippi and unwilling to settle for token representation, rejected the compromise. Many members of SNCC, bitter and angry, turned their backs on liberalism and cooperation with white people of any political persuasion.

▶ **Recommended Reading**

Frank R. Parker. *Black Votes Count: Political Empowerment in Mississippi after 1965.* Chapel Hill, NC: University of North Carolina Press, 1990.

Fannie Lou Hamer found the moral courage to challenge an unjust system. She worked for voting rights and was one of the leaders in the Mississippi Freedom Democratic Party (MFDP). Denied participation in the political process, the MFDP held elections and sent 64 delegates to the Democratic National Convention to challenge the all-white Democratic delegation.

Selma and the Voting Rights Act of 1965

The Civil Rights Act of 1964 contained provisions for helping black voters to register, but white resistance in the deep South had rendered them ineffective. In Alabama, for example, at least 77 percent of black citizens were unable to vote. Their cause was taken up by businesswoman Amelia P. Boynton, owner of an employment and insurance agency in Selma, along with her husband and a high school teacher, the Reverend Frederick Reese, who also led the Dallas County Voters League. These three, with others, fought for black enfranchisement and an end to discriminatory treatment. Their struggle would help pass the

PROFILE ❖ Fannie Lou Hamer

Fannie Lou Hamer (1917–1977) emerged from the ranks of "local people" in Mississippi to become one of the most powerful leaders and orators of the civil rights movement. Unlike many major leaders, Hamer, the youngest of twenty children, had grown up in extreme poverty and had only a few years of education. She worked and lived as a timekeeper on a plantation in Ruleville, Mississippi. When SNCC workers came to the community for a voting rights campaign, Hamer was one of the first to participate.

On August 1, 1962, Hamer attempted to register to vote in Indianola, Mississippi. In response, she was fired from her plantation job and evicted from her land. Still, she refused to give in. She accepted full-time employment as a field secretary for SNCC where she worked on the Voter Education Project. This aroused even more police hostility. On June 9, 1963, she and eight other women on their way back from a workshop in South Carolina were arrested by the police in Winona, Mississippi. Hamer was beaten and never fully recovered from the injuries she suffered.

Despite her lack of education, Hamer was a spellbinding orator who had the ability to move not only her friends and neighbors but the nation as well. Her televised testimony before the 1964 Democratic Convention won national support for the MFDP's challenge to the party regulars from Mississippi. The next year Hamer, who had run for the House of Representatives, challenged the seating of the Mississippi congressional delegation. Although unsuccessful, her action helped reduce tolerance for disfranchisement and paved the way for the Voting Rights Act of 1965.

After 1965 Hamer continued to fight for her people. Although basic civil and voting rights had been won by then, most black people in the Mississippi Delta still lived in deep poverty. In 1968 Hamer sought to address this problem by setting up the nonprofit Freedom Farms Corporation as an agricultural cooperative. With help from northern supporters, the enterprise had some success, but the problems it confronted proved overwhelming. The mixed results of this last campaign, however, cannot diminish the profound changes that Fannie Lou Hamer was so instrumental in bringing about. She died in 1977.

Voting Rights Act of 1965, which finally ended the systematic exclusion of African Americans from southern politics.

Selma's sheriff James G. Clark worked to block the voter registration activity sponsored by the Boyntons, Reese, and SNCC suffrage workers. By 1964 fewer than four hundred of the fifteen thousand eligible African Americans had registered to vote in Dallas County. President Lyndon Johnson refused requests to deploy federal marshals to the county to protect voter registration workers. Seeking reinforcements, the workers sent a call to Martin Luther King Jr. and the SCLC. King came and was promptly arrested. In mid-February 1965, during a night march in neighboring Perry County, twenty-six-year-old Jimmie Lee Jackson was shot in the stomach as he tried to shield his mother from a beating by a state trooper. His death and the thrashing of several reporters attracted the national media.

The SCLC announced plans for a mass march from Selma to Montgomery, the state capital, to begin on Sunday, March 7, 1965. At the forefront of six hundred protesters were King; one of his aides, Hosea Williams; and the chairman of SNCC, John Lewis. As the marchers approached the Edmund Pettus Bridge, state troopers and Sheriff Clark's county police, in a shocking display of aggression, teargassed and beat the retreating marchers while their horses trampled the fallen. Captured in graphic detail by television cameras, this battle became known as **Bloody Sunday**. Seizing the moment, King and the activists rescheduled a pilgrimage for March 9. The SCLC leader soon found himself in a dilemma. A federal judge, who was normally supportive of civil rights, had issued an injunction against the march. Moreover, President Johnson and many other key figures in the government urged King not to go through with it. King was reluctant to violate a federal injunction, and he knew he needed Johnson's support to win strong voting rights legislation. But the people of Selma and the hundreds of young SNCC workers would probably march even if King did not.

When the day of the march came, 1,500 protesters marched to the bridge singing "Ain't Gonna Let Nobody Turn Me 'Round" and other freedom songs. To their surprise, King crossed the Pettus Bridge, prayed briefly, and turned around. He had privately made a face-saving compromise with the federal authorities. SNCC workers felt betrayed, and King's leadership suffered. That evening a white Unitarian minister from Boston, James Reeb, was clubbed to death by local white people. His martyrdom created a national outcry and prompted Johnson to act. On March 15 the president, in a televised address to Congress, announced he would submit voter registration legislation. In his address he praised civil rights activists, electrifying them when he invoked the movement's slogan to declare, in his Texas drawl, "We shall overcome."

The protests at Selma and the massive white resistance spurred Congress to pass the **Voting Rights Act of 1965**, which President Johnson signed on August 6. The act outlawed educational requirements for

On March 25, 1965, more than two weeks after "Bloody Sunday," when police brutalized civil rights marchers trying to cross Selma's Edmund Pettus Bridge, a second march finally completed the 53-mile trek to Montgomery.

Chapter 22

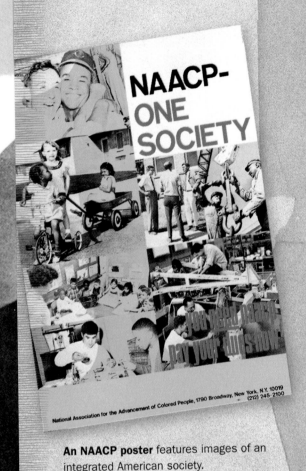

An **NAACP poster** features images of an integrated American society.

We must work on two levels. In every city we have a dual society. . . . In every city, we have two economies. In every city, we have two housing markets. In every city, we have two school systems. This duality has brought about a great deal of injustice. . . . Black Power in the positive sense is a psychological call to manhood . . . and a sense of dignity. . . . Black Power is pooling black political resources in order to achieve our legitimate goals. . . . Black Power in its positive sense is a pooling of black economic resources in order to achieve legitimate power. . . . What is necessary now is to see integration in political terms. . . . [T]here are times when we must see segregation as a temporary way-station to the ultimate goal which we seek . . . a truly integrated society where there is shared power
—Martin Luther King Jr.

Black Power . . . a call for black people in this country to unite, to recognize their heritage, to build a sense of community . . . to define their own goals, to lead their own organizations . . . to reject the racist institutions and values of this society. The concept of Black Power rests on a fundamental premise: *Before a group can enter the open society, it must first close ranks.* [emphasis in the original]
—Stokely Carmichael and Charles V. Hamilton

 How are these two views of the meaning of Black Power similar?

Chapter Preview

President Lyndon Johnson brought to the office determination to reconcile the racial, social, and economic disparities dividing black from white Americans. Johnson's escalation of America's involvement in Vietnam, however, undermined his domestic social policies. In the face of a white backlash against the gains of the civil rights movement, many leaders and scholars—like Stokely Carmichael and Charles Hamilton—argued for black power and black separatism. King remained ambivalent about black power, preferring to define it as a temporary strategy for black solidarity in the struggle for an integrated society. A. Philip Randolph called black power a "menace to peace and prosperity" and added, "No Negro who is fighting for civil rights can support black power, which is opposed to civil rights and integration." These opposing ideologies represent a generational shift, and the tensions between them frame many of the key events of the post–civil rights movement years.

▶ **Witnessing History**

Both view Black power as black people coming together to develop their own unity, economic resources, and values before they can become part of the larger society.

Section 1

Racial Integration

Black Nationalism and White Backlash

Even though President Johnson easily defeated Republican senator Barry Goldwater, the 1964 election was hardly a mandate for civil rights. When, in 1966, Johnson asked Congress for federal legislation to ban discrimination in housing, a weakened version of his bill died in the Senate. In elections that year, white opposition to civil rights helped elect Republicans, including former movie actor Ronald Reagan as governor of California.

Meanwhile, Alabama governor George Wallace, an outspoken opponent of racial integration and civil rights legislation, was emerging as a national political figure. Heartened by the favorable response he received from northern white voters, Wallace was planning a full-scale presidential race in 1968.

With many white Americans increasingly reluctant to support the goals of the civil rights movement, many black Americans began searching for new approaches to their problems. The reign of terror experienced by COFO (Council of Federated Organizations) workers in Mississippi had undermined the commitment to integration and nonviolence of the civil rights movement and would help radicalize a new, younger generation of activists. Men like Floyd McKissick of the Congress of Racial Equality (CORE) and Stokely Carmichael of the Student Nonviolent Coordinating Committee (SNCC) became disillusioned, rejecting King's moderation, nonviolence, and universalism. The differences between King's SCLC (Southern Christian Leadership Conference) and Carmichael's SNCC grew with each confrontation. Carmichael had argued after the 1964 failure of the Mississippi Freedom Democratic party that it was time to form an independent black political party. In 1965, after the Selma-to-Montgomery march, he helped found the **Lowndes County** (Mississippi) **Freedom Organization** (**LCFO**). It became the first political organization in the civil rights movement to adopt the symbol of the black panther.

Black residents of northern and western cities also lost patience with the slow pace of change. Increasing numbers of young black churchmen criticized mainstream white religious groups for their complicity with racism, demanded reparations, and agitated for substantive power or leadership roles within the governing structures of the

GUIDE TO READING

▶ Why did many African Americans become more militant during the 1960s?

▶ What effect did black power have on white and black religious leaders in the 1960s?

▶ What were the goals of the Black Panther Party?

KEY TERMS

▶ Lowndes County Freedom Organization (LCFO), p. 793

▶ Black Power, p. 796

▶ prisoners' rights movement, p. 801

▶ Soledad Brothers, p. 802

▶▶ **Guide to Reading/Key Terms**

For answers, see the *Teacher's Resource Manual*.

▶▶ **Teaching Notes**

In California voters gave Johnson a decisive victory, but also approved an amendment to the state constitution that not only repealed all existing legislation prohibiting discrimination in the sale or rental of housing, but prevented such legislation from ever being enacted in the future. Although the amendment was later struck down by the Supreme Court, its passage suggested that white opposition to racial integration was not confined to the South.

National Council of Churches. Out of the interracial conflict and tension emerged a black theology that critiqued racism within white religious groups. It was followed by a black feminist theology that offered searing critiques of sexism within the black church. Leaders in the development of Black Theology and the expression of a black nationalist Christianity were theologians James H. Cone, and the Reverend Albert Cleage Jr. of Detroit who was pastor of the Shrine of the Black Madonna and a passionate advocate of black liberation theology. Black Christian nationalism argued for black symbols of religious faith. Jesus Christ was, as Reverend Cleage expounded, a black messiah. Black liberation theology asserted the importance of conjoining religious practice and faith with political activism and social change. Growing numbers of young African Americans, along with diverse black religious leaders, dismayed by the great political and economic disparities between themselves and white Americans, became catalysts for an increasingly radical turn in the civil rights movement.

Malcolm X

After 1965, the year in which he was assassinated, no one had more influence on young black activists and the residents of America's ghettoized inner cities than Malcolm X. The son of a Baptist preacher, he was born Malcolm Little in Omaha, Nebraska, and grew up in Lansing, Michigan. His family's home was burned by Klan terrorists. His father was murdered two years later. His mother was subsequently committed to a mental institution, and welfare agencies separated the children. Malcolm was sent to a juvenile detention home, quit school after the eighth grade, and moved to Boston to live with his sister. There he became involved in the street life of gambling, drugs, and burglary. He was arrested and sentenced to a ten-year prison term in 1946. During the six and a half years he spent in prison, he embraced the teachings of Elijah Muhammad of the Nation of Islam. He renounced what he considered his "slave name" to become Malcolm X. In 1954 he became minister of Harlem's Temple Number 7. Articulate, charismatic, and forceful, Malcolm did not believe in nonviolence or advocate integration. His was the voice of the northern urban "second ghettoes." In 1961 he began publishing *Muhammad Speaks*, the official newspaper of the Nation.

Malcolm X attracted black people's attention. His dismissal of the goal of racial integration and King's message of redemption through brotherly love resonated with many younger civil rights workers disillusioned by white violence. "The day of nonviolent resistance is over," Malcolm insisted. And in 1964 he declared, "Revolutions are never based upon love-your-enemy, and pray-for-those-who-despitefully-use-you. And revolutions are never waged by singing 'We Shall Overcome.' Revolutions are based on bloodshed."

▶▶ **Living Words Audio Clip**

Track 45 *Message to the Grassroots; speech by Malcolm X, excerpt*

▶▶ **Recommended Readings**

Henry Hampton and Steve Fayer, eds. *The Voices of Freedom: An Oral History of the Civil Rights Movement from the 1950s through the 1980s.* New York: Bantam Books, 1990. A remarkable and indispensable oral history of all the participants in the civil rights movement, from the least well known to the internationally celebrated.

Steven F. Lawson. *Running for Freedom: Civil Rights and Black Politics in America since 1941.* Philadelphia: Temple University Press, 1991. A succinct analysis of the politics, legislative measures, and individuals that figured in the successes and failures of the civil rights movement.

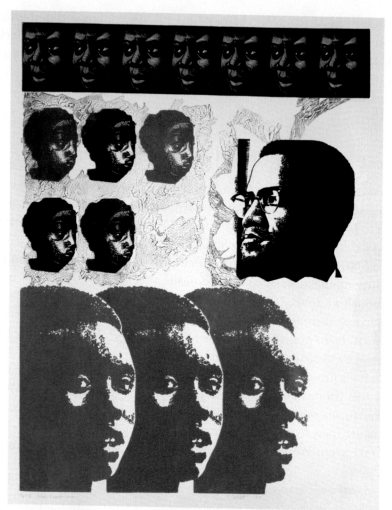

Elizabeth Catlett (1919–) created *Malcolm X Speaks for Us* (1969), a linoleum block print, as part of her series on African-American heroes.

Malcolm X's New Departure

Malcolm X's popularity created tensions between himself and the leadership of the Nation of Islam. He grew disillusioned with Elijah Muhammad's aversion to political activism. Elijah Muhammad grew jealous of Malcolm's success. When Malcolm described the Kennedy assassination as a case of "the chickens coming home to roost" (meaning Kennedy was a victim of the same kind of violence that afflicted black people), Elijah Muhammad suspended him. In 1964 Malcolm broke with the Nation of Islam and founded his own organization, the Muslim Mosque, Inc. That same year he went on a pilgrimage to Mecca that profoundly influenced him. He changed his name to El-Hajj Malik El-Shabazz. He founded the Organization for Afro-American Unity (after the Organization of African Unity) and repudiated the Nation of Islam doctrine that all white people are evil. He began lecturing on the connection between the civil rights struggle in the South and the struggle against

colonialism in Africa. On February 14, 1965, assassins associated with the Nation of Islam killed Malcolm X as he addressed an audience in Harlem.

Malcolm's militant advocacy of self-defense, of "overturning systems" that deprive African Americans of basic human rights, helped radicalize other black leaders of the civil rights movement.

Stokely Carmichael and Black Power

In 1966 Stokely Carmichael, a native of Trinidad who had been raised in New York City and educated at Howard University, became chairman of SNCC. By then he had given up on the ideal of interracial collaboration and was determined to move SNCC toward black nationalism. He dismissed SNCC's few white staffers, including Bob Zellner, who had been with the organization since its inception.

About this time, James Meredith began a one-man "march against fear" from Tennessee to Jackson, Mississippi, to encourage black Southerners to register and vote. On this march, he was shot and wounded by white gunmen. In June 1966, after this incident, SNCC and Carmichael joined with other organizations to complete the march. It was at this time that Carmichael popularized the slogan **Black Power** that was to become SNCC's rallying cry. "The only way we gonna stop them white men from whippin' us," he announced to a cheering crowd, "is to take over. We been saying freedom for six years and we ain't got

▶ **Document**

22-1 *Stokely Carmichael and "Black Power,"* *1966*

▶ **Recommended Readings**

Stokely Carmichael and Charles V. Hamilton. *Black Power: The Politics of Liberation in America.* New York: Vintage Books, 1967. One of the most important books of the era of black power, by Carmichael, who popularized the slogan, and political scientist Hamilton.

Theodore Cross. *The Black Power Imperative: Racial Inequality and the Politics of Nonviolence.* New York: Faulkner Books, 1984. Provides a useful critique of the black power movement and explores the persistence of racial inequality.

Stokely Carmichael (1941–1998) changed his name to Kwame Ture, a combination of the names of two major African leaders, Kwame Nkrumah and Ahmed Sekou Toure. After he settled in Guinea in 1969, he founded the All-African People's Revolutionary Party.

nothin'. What we gonna start saying is Black Power." Carmichael was specific about what black power meant to black Southerners:

> In Lowndes County [Mississippi], for example, black power will mean that if a Negro is elected sheriff, he can end police brutality. If a black man is elected tax assessor, he can collect and channel funds for the building of better roads and schools serving black people—thus advancing the move from political power into the economic arena. . . . Politically, black power means what it has always meant to SNCC: the coming-together of black people to elect representatives and to force those representatives to speak to their needs. It does not mean merely putting black faces into office.

Critics accused advocates of black power of reverse racism. Carmichael argued on the contrary that they were promoting positive self-identity, racial pride, and the development of independent political and economic power. All of the organizations suffered internal problems. As the leaders became more disillusioned about the slow pace of social change, some questioned whether white people belonged in their organizations. In 1968 CORE followed SNCC's example and ejected its white members with a resulting loss of financial resources. For various reasons both organizations began to decline, and by the end of the 1960s, SNCC had virtually disappeared.

Martin Luther King had mixed feelings about the ideology of black power. He welcomed its promotion of black political and economic strength, psychological assertiveness, and cultural pride. But when black power degenerated into a mantra of taunts against white people, King denounced it as "a nihilistic philosophy born out of the conviction that the Negro can't win." King also objected to black power's "implicit and often explicit belief in black separatism" and the assertion of its proponents that "there can be a separate Black road to power and fulfillment."

In May 1967 Hubert G. Brown followed Carmichael as head of SNCC. "H. Rap" Brown, as he became known, raised the militancy of the black power movement's rhetoric to a new level, calling white people "honkies" and the police "pigs." "Violence," he said, was "as American as apple pie." In August 1967 Brown told enthusiastic listeners in the black neighborhood of Cambridge, Maryland, that "black folks built America, and if America don't come around, we're going to burn America down." When a few hours later, a fire erupted in a dilapidated school in the heart of the city's black community, white firemen refused to fight it. Police charged Brown with inciting a riot and committing arson, but he posted bail and fled. Later he was arrested on other charges.

The National Council of Churches

Black and white leaders of mainstream religious organizations were transformed by black power. In 1946 the Federal Council of Churches, composed of Protestants, Catholics, and Jews, pledged to work for "a

▶ **Recommended Reading**

James F. Finley, Jr. *Church People in the Struggle: The National Council of Churches and the Black Freedom Movement, 1950–1970.* New York: Oxford University Press, 1993.

non-segregated church and a non-segregated society." Between 1963 and 1965, the National Council of Churches (NCC) contributed financial and moral support to the civil rights movement. In 1963 the NCC founded its Commission on Religion and Race to support the black freedom movement. Although a white-controlled and managed operation, three of the eight staff members of the commission were African American: Anna Hedgeman, J. Oscar Lee, and James Breeden. The NCC supported events such as the March on Washington and lobbied for passage of the Civil Rights Act of 1964 and the Voting Rights Act of 1965.

In 1965 the NCC appointed Benjamin Payton as director of the Commission on Religion and Race. Payton, a native of Orangeburg, South Carolina, had been educated at Harvard Divinity School and had earned a Ph.D. at Yale. Payton had taught at Howard University and he was a member of the National Baptist Convention, U.S.A., the largest African-American denomination.

Payton had his own views about how organized religion could help address racial problems. He viewed the economic development of black people and their communities as the critical prerequisite to improving national racial relations. In July 1966 he convened a small group of men that included Gayraud S. Wilmore, who served as the director of the United Presbyterian's Commission on Religion and Race. Out of this gathering emerged the National Commission of Black Churchmen (NCBC), which advocated black power concepts and strategies throughout the rest of the 1960s. In May 1967, however, the NCC's Department of Social Justice lost some of its momentum and direction when Payton left to become president of Benedict College, a black Baptist-affiliated college in Columbia, South Carolina.

The black power movement spurred the creation of black caucuses within the predominantly white churches. In February 1968 James Lawson headed the Black Methodists for Church Renewal, a caucus that crystallized within the United Methodist Church. In the same year, the United Presbyterian Church witnessed the formation of the Black Presbyterian United that replaced the Presbyterian Interracial Council. The Episcopal Society for Racial and Cultural Unity, an interracial group, was replaced by an Episcopal Union of Black Clergy and Laity. By the early 1970s, there were nine such caucuses. Within the Roman Catholic Church, black Catholics insisted that the church demonstrate more respect for African-American patterns of worship. All these black religious groups pressed for more black leadership within the denominations. Thus the stage was set for James Forman's black manifesto.

In April 1969 James Forman, a former Chicago schoolteacher renowned for his work with SNCC, addressed the National Black Economic Development Conference in Detroit, sponsored by the Interreligious Foundation for Community Organizations (which was supported by predominantly white churches). Forman demanded that white churches pay $500 million in reparations for their participation in and benefit from American slavery and racial exploitation. His sharply

secular critique of American religion precipitated the withdrawal of mainstream white religion groups from active participation in the civil rights movement. These white groups were offended by Forman's black power rhetoric and revolutionary Marxist ideology. Black and other minority groups wanted to share real power within the white-dominated churches. Relations between Blacks and Jews also deteriorated as countercharges circulated of "Jewish racism" and "Black anti-Semitism."

The Black Panther Party

The most institutionalized expression of the new black militancy was the Black Panther Party for Self-Defense created by Huey P. Newton and Bobby Seale in Oakland, California, in October 1966. Newton and Seale took the name of the party from the black panther symbol of the Lowndes County Freedom Organization (LCFO). The Black Panthers combined Black Nationalist ideology with Marxist-Leninist doctrines. Working with white radicals, they hoped to fashion the party into a revolutionary vanguard dedicated to overthrowing capitalist society and ending police brutality. For a few months Stokely Carmichael, who had become estranged from SNCC, aligned himself with the Panthers and was named the party's prime minister. Eldridge Cleaver, the Panthers' minister of education, helped formulate the party's ideology. Cleaver spent most of his youth in prison, where he became a follower of Malcolm X and began writing the autobiographical essays that would be published as *Soul on Ice* in 1968. Black people, Cleaver maintained, were victims of colonization, not just disfranchised American citizens. Thus integrationism could not meet their needs. They needed, instead, like other colonized peoples, to be liberated. "To achieve these ends," he wrote, "we believe that political and military machinery that does not exist now and has never existed must be created. We need functional machinery that is able to deal with these two interrelated sets of political dynamics which, strictly speaking, make up the total political situation on the North American continent." Cleaver and other top Panther leaders were arrested after a shoot-out with Oakland police in 1968. Cleaver escaped and fled into exile. While abroad, he abandoned his radicalism and became involved with the Republican Party and fundamentalist Christianity after his return to the United States in 1975.

Police Repression and the FBI's COINTELPRO

The Panthers alarmed white Americans when they took up arms for self-defense and patrolled their neighborhoods to monitor the police. A series of bloody confrontations and shoot-outs in Oakland distracted attention from the Panthers' broader political objectives and community service projects. In Oakland and Chicago, the Panthers arranged free breakfast and health-care programs, worked to instill racial pride, lectured and

▶ **Recommended Reading**

Toni Morrison, ed. *To Die for the People: The Writings of Huey P. Newton.* New York: Writers and Readers Publishing, 1995.

The Black Panther Party Platform

Huey Newton and Bobby Seale's Ten-Point Program reflects their determination to move from the pursuit of civil rights to a radical restructuring of American society along socialist lines, with work and rewards equally shared.

October 1966

BLACK PANTHER PARTY, PLATFORM AND PROGRAM
WHAT WE WANT, WHAT WE BELIEVE

1. We want freedom. We want power to determine the destiny of our Black Community . . .
2. We want full employment for our people . . .
3. We want an end to the robbery of the capitalists of our Black Community . . .
4. We want decent housing fit for shelter of human beings . . .
5. We want education for our people that exposes the true nature of this decadent American society. We want education that teaches us our true history and our role in present-day society . . .
6. We want all Black men to be exempt from military service . . .
7. We want an immediate end to POLICE BRUTALITY and MURDER of Black people . . .
8. We want freedom for all Black men held in federal, state, county and city prisons and jails . . .
9. We want all Black people when brought to trial to be tried in court by a jury of their peer group or people from their Black communities, as defined by the Constitution of the United States . . .
10. We want land, bread, housing, education, clothing, justice, and peace. And as our major political objective, a United Nations supervised plebiscite to be held throughout the Black colony in which only Black colonial subjects will be allowed to participate, for the purpose of determining the will of Black people as to their national destiny.

What Do You Think?

▶ In what ways is the Panthers' Ten-Point Program similar to the Bill of Rights in the United States Constitution? How do they differ?

▶ How did the Panthers propose to achieve black liberation? Why did they emphasize studying history? How did the Panthers' program conflict with that of the older civil rights organizations?

Source: Clayborne Carson et al., eds., *The Eyes on the Prize Civil Rights Reader: Documents, Speeches, and Firsthand Accounts from the Black Freedom Struggle, 1954–1990* (New York: Viking Penguin, 1991), 346–47.

▶▶ **What Do You Think?**

· The Ten-Point Program is similarly to the Bill of Rights in that it focuses on civil liberties and freedom. The Program is unlike the Bill of Rights in that is proposes socialist measures to ensure black prosperity.

· Panthers proposed to achieve black liberation by creating black military and political organizations. They emphasized studying the history of other colonized peoples, as this supported their view that they needed to be liberated. The Panthers' program conflicted with that of older civil rights organizations in that they did not believe in integrationism, and instead supported black militancy.

wrote about black history, and launched some of the earliest drug education programs. These activities were captured in the slogan "Power to the People."

FBI director J. Edgar Hoover was determined to infiltrate, harass, destabilize, and destroy all nationalist groups and their leaders. The FBI cooperated with local law enforcement officials to ridicule and discredit leaders and to undermine and weaken the Black Panther Party. In August 1967 Hoover distributed an explanatory memorandum that detailed the FBI's Counterintelligence Program directed toward black nationalist groups. The purpose, according to the memo, of this new "counterintelligence (COINTELPRO) endeavor is to expose, disrupt, misdirect, discredit, or otherwise neutralize the activities of black nationalist, hate-type organizations and groupings, their leadership, spokesmen, membership, and supporters, and to counter their propensity for violence and civil disorder." Undercover agents infiltrated the Panthers and provoked violence and criminal acts. The FBI and its counterintelligence agents may have provoked much of the mayhem and violence that became associated with the Black Panther Party. Certainly, COINTELPRO helped shape negative public opinion of black nationalist ideology.

In their effort to destroy the party, law enforcement officials killed an estimated 28 Panthers and imprisoned 750 others. In perhaps the most egregious incident, police in Chicago killed Fred Hampton and Mark Clark in their sleep in a predawn raid on the Illinois Black Panther Headquarters on December 4, 1969. While the police fired hundreds of rounds, only two shots were fired from within the apartment.

The Black Panther Party advocated a radical economic, social, and educational agenda that made it the target of a determined campaign of suppression by the police and the FBI.

 Reading Check   What were the goals of the Black Panther Party?

Prisoners' Rights

Despite such repression, black militancy survived in many forms, including the **prisoners' rights movement**. One of the Black Panthers' social programs had focused on the conditions of black prisoners. By 1970 more than half the inmates in U.S. prisons were African American. In New York State, black Americans were around 70 percent of the prison population. Black activists argued that many African Americans were in jail for political reasons and suffered from unfair sentences and deplorable conditions because of racism and class exploitation.

Angela Davis, an assistant professor of philosophy at the University of California at Los Angeles, became the first black woman to be listed on the FBI's Ten Most Wanted list because of her involvement in prisoners' rights. In 1969 UCLA's board of regents refused to renew her contract citing her lack of a Ph.D., but in fact they objected to her membership in the Communist Party. During the late 1960s, she had worked on

▶ **Reading Check**

The Black Panthers hoped to be the vanguard of a movement that would overthrow capitalism and end police brutality.

▶ **Recommended Reading**

Kenneth O'Reilly. *Racial Matters: The FBI's Secret File on Black America, 1960–1972*. New York: Free Press, 1989.

Angela Davis continues her forceful advocacy for the rights of prisoners. She serves on the advisory board of the Prison Activist Resource Center and teaches in the History of Consciousness Department at the University of California, Santa Cruz.

▶ **Reading Check**

In the mid-1960s, with many white Americans increasingly reluctant to support the civil rights movement, many black Americans began to look for new approaches to their problems. Black residents of northern and western cities were frustrated with the slow pace of change and community leaders reflected this frustration in more militant rhetoric and tactics.

▶ **Living Words Audio Clip**

Track 40 *Angela Davis, interview from prison*

behalf of the **Soledad Brothers**, three prisoners—George Jackson, John Clutchette, and Fleeta Drumgo—accused of murdering a white guard at Soledad Prison. On August 7, 1970, George Jackson's younger brother, seventeen-year-old Jonathan Jackson, staged a one-man raid on the San Rafael courthouse in Marin County, California, to try to seize hostages to trade for the Soledad Brothers. In the ensuing shoot-out, Jonathan Jackson, two prisoners, and a judge were killed. Angela Davis, accused of supplying the weapons for the raid, was charged with murder, kidnapping, and conspiracy. She escaped and lived as a fugitive. She was eventually captured and spent over a year in jail. After a long ordeal and a national "Free Angela" campaign, a jury acquitted Davis. On August 21, 1971, George Jackson was shot and killed at San Quentin Prison by guards who claimed he was trying to escape.

Across the country, prisoners at Attica, a maximum-security prison in northern New York State, began a fast in memory of George Jackson that within days erupted into a full-scale rebellion. On September 9, 1971, 1,200 inmates seized control of half of Attica and took hostages. Four days later, state police and prison guards suppressed the uprising. Tom Wicker, a columnist for *The New York Times*, filed this report:

> A task force consisting of 211 state troopers and corrections officers retook Attica using tear gas, rifles, and shotguns. After the shooting was over, ten hostages and twenty-nine inmates lay dead or dying. At least 450 rounds of ammunition had been discharged. Four hostages and eighty-five inmates suffered gunshot wounds that they survived. After initial reports that several hostages had died at the hands of knife-wielding inmates, pathologists' reports revealed that hostages and inmates all died from gunshot wounds. No guns were found in the possession of inmates.

A state commission, assembled in October 1971 to reconstruct the events at Attica, concluded:

> With the exception of Indian massacres in the late nineteenth-century, the State Police assault which ended the four-day prison uprising was the bloodiest one-day encounter between Americans since the Civil War.

 Reading Check Why did many African Americans become more militant during the 1960s?

Section 2

The Great Society

GUIDE TO READING

▶ What were the causes of the urban riots of the late 1960s?

▶ What were the sources of opposition to the Great Society programs?

▶ How did the Vietnam War affect the Great Society and African Americans?

KEY TERMS

▶ The Great Society, p. 806

▶ Economic Opportunity Act of 1964, p. 806

▶ War on Poverty, p. 806

▶ Community Action Programs (CAPS), p. 806

▶ Education Act, p. 807

▶ Vietnam, p. 807

▶ Project 100,000, p. 809

▶ Tet Offensive, p. 813

Inner-City Rebellions

The militant nationalism of Malcolm X and Stokely Carmichael and the radicalism of the Panthers reflected growing alienation and anger in America's impoverished inner cities. In 1965, 29.1 percent of black households, compared with only 7.8 percent of white households, lived below the poverty line. Almost 50 percent of nonwhite families lived in substandard housing compared with 18 percent of white families. Despite a drop in the number of Americans living in poverty from 38.0 million in 1959 to 32.7 million in 1965, the percentage of poor black people increased from 27.5 percent to 31 percent. In 1965 the black unemployment rate was 8.5 percent, almost twice the white unemployment rate of 4.3. For black teenagers the unemployment rate was 23 percent compared with 10.8 percent for white teenagers. As psychologist Kenneth Clark declared in 1967, "The masses of Negroes are now starkly aware of the fact that recent civil rights victories benefited a very small percentage of middle-class Negroes while their predicament remained the same or worsened."

The passage of civil rights legislation did not resolve these disparities or diminish inner-city alienation. As jobs moved increasingly to suburbs to which inner-city residents could neither travel nor relocate. Inner-city neighborhoods sank deeper into poverty. School dropout rates reached epidemic proportions. Crime and drug use increased. Fragile family structures weakened. It was these conditions that led militants like the Panthers to liken their neighborhoods to exploited colonies kept in poverty by repressive white political and economic institutions. Few white Americans understood the depths of the black despair that flared into violence each summer between 1965 and 1969, beginning with the Watts rebellion of 1965.

Watts

In the summer of 1965, a section of Los Angeles called Watts exploded. Watts was 98 percent black. Its residents suffered from overcrowding, unemployment, inaccessible health-care facilities, inadequate public transportation, and increasing crime and drug addiction. Almost 30 percent of the black male population was unemployed. The poverty, combined with

▶▶ **Guide to Reading/Key Terms**

For answers, see the *Teacher's Resource Manual.*

▶▶ **Recommended Reading**

William Julius Wilson. *The Truly Disadvantaged: The Inner City, the Underclass, and Public Policy.* Chicago: University of Chicago Press, 1987.

Martin Gilens. *Why Americans Hate Welfare: Race, Media, and the Politics of Antipoverty Policy.* Chicago: University of Chicago Press, 1999.

Michael Katz. *The Undeserving Poor: From the War on Poverty to the War on Welfare.* New York: Pantheon Books, 1989.

The first major urban uprising of the 1960s was in the Watts neighborhood of East Los Angeles in August 1965. It lasted nearly a week and left thirty-four people dead.

anger at the often-brutal behavior of Los Angeles's police force in Watts, proved to be an explosive combination. On August 11, 1965, a policeman pulled over a young black man to check him for drunk driving. The man was arrested, but not before a crowd gathered. The policeman called for reinforcements. When they arrived, the crowd pelted them with stones, bottles, and other objects. Within a few hours, Watts was in a total riot.

Governor Pat Brown, a Democrat, sent in the National Guard to restore order. By the sixth day, Watts had been reduced to rubble and ashes. Thirty-four people had been killed; more than 900 injured; and 4,000 arrested. Total property damage was more than $35 million, equivalent to hundreds of millions of dollars today. The Watts rebellion was the beginning of four summers of uprisings that would engulf cities in the North and Midwest. There were riots in the summer of 1966, but even worse ones erupted in Newark and Detroit in 1967.

Newark

Newark, New Jersey, had more than 400,000 inhabitants in 1967. As was true in many other urban areas, white flight to the suburbs in the 1950s and 1960s made Newark a majority black city, but one that operated on an inadequate tax base and under white political control. The city lacked the means to meet its inhabitants' social needs. The school system deteriorated as unemployment had increased. In 1967 Newark had the highest unemployment rate among black men in the entire nation. As tensions flared and police brutality escalated, white officials paid little attention to black people's complaints. On July 12, after a black cab driver in police custody was beaten, protesters gathered at the police station near the Hayes Homes housing project. When a firebomb hit the wall of the station house, the police charged, clubbing the crowd. This triggered one of the most destructive civic rebellions of the period. During four days of rioting, the police and National Guard killed twenty-five black people—most of them innocent bystanders, including two children. A white policeman and fireman were also killed. Widespread looting and arson caused millions of dollars in property damage.

Detroit

When Detroit erupted a few days after Newark, it caught everyone by surprise except the residents of its inner-city neighborhoods. On the surface Detroit seemed like a model of prosperity and interracial accord. Some of the country's most dynamic popular music flowed from Detroit's Motown recording company. Owned by the astute Berry Gordy, Motown was a classic up-by-the-bootstraps success story. Gordy and his wife Raynoma and their extended family had, by 1967, produced such stars as Diana Ross and Mary Wells. "Before Motown," said Wells, "there were three careers available to a black girl in Detroit—babies, the factories or daywork."

But success like Gordy's was rare among the black migrants and their children, who poured into Detroit during and after World War II. The parents held their disappointment in check, but the children, particularly young men aged between seventeen and thirty-five, sought an outlet for their anger and alienation. Some joined the Nation of Islam; others embraced the Panthers or formed even more radical organizations calling for an all-black nation.

On the night of Saturday, July 23, police raided an after-hours drinking establishment in the center of the black community where more than eighty people were celebrating the return of two veterans from Vietnam. Police efforts to clear the club triggered five days of rioting. Congressman John Conyers, the black U.S. representative for Michigan's First District, knew many of the people in the area and tried to get them to disperse, but they refused. Later, Conyers said, "People were letting feelings out that had never been let out before, that had been bottled up. It really wasn't that they were that mad about an after-hours place being raided and some people being beat up as a result of the closing down of that place. It was the whole desperate situation of being black in Detroit."

Of the fifty-nine urban rebellions that occurred in 1967, Detroit's was the deadliest. Forty-three black people died, most of them shot by members of the National Guard, which had been sent in by Republican governor George Romney. But even the National Guard, combined with 200 state police and 600 Detroit police, could not restore order. A reluctant President Johnson had to order 4,700 troops of the elite 82nd and 101st Airborne units to Detroit.

The Kerner Commission

On July 29, 1967, in the wake of the Newark and Detroit riots, Johnson established the National Advisory Commission on Civil Disorders, headed by Illinois governor Otto Kerner. The commission included two black members, Republican senator Edward W. Brooke of Massachusetts (elected in 1966 and the first black senator since Reconstruction) and Roy Wilkins, executive director of the NAACP. In a speech explaining why he had set up the commission, Johnson declared,

> The only genuine, long-range solution for what has happened lies in an attack—mounted at every level—upon the conditions that breed despair and violence. All of us know what those conditions are: ignorance, discrimination, slums, poverty, disease, not enough jobs. We should attack these conditions—not because we are frightened by conflict, but because we are fired by conscience. We should attack them because there is simply no other way to achieve a decent and orderly society in America.

In its final report, released in 1968, the Kerner Commission indicted white racism as the underlying cause of the riots. It warned that America was "moving towards two societies, one white, one black—separate and unequal." The commission emphasized that "Negroes firmly believe

▶ **Document**

22-3 *"Our Nation Is Moving Toward Two Societies, One Black, One White-Separate and Unequal": Excerpts from the Kerner Report, 1968*
The 1968 Kerner Report blamed "white society" for isolating and neglecting the problems confronting African Americans and urged legislation that promoted integration.

▶ **Teaching Notes**

Republicans criticized Johnson's order to send troops into Detroit as designed to embarrass George Romney, who was a contender for the Republican presidential nomination in 1968. Johnson vehemently denied the charge. Others argued that Johnson's social welfare policies had raised expectations beyond the country's ability or desire to fulfill them and had subsidized the rioters.

that police brutality and harassment occur repeatedly in Negro neighborhoods. This belief is unquestionably one of the major reasons for intense Negro resentment against the police." The report added, "Physical abuse is only one source of aggravation in the ghetto. In nearly every city surveyed, the Commission heard complaints of harassment of interracial couples, dispersal of social street gatherings and the stopping of Negroes on foot or in cars without objective basis." The report called for massive government aid to the cities, including funds for public housing, better and more integrated schools, two million new jobs, and funding for a "national system of income supplementation." None of its major proposals was enacted.

 Reading Check What were the causes of the urban riots of the late 1960s?

Creating the Great Society

The urban riots of the late 1960s undercut support for the broadest attack the federal government had yet waged on the problems of poor Americans, what President Lyndon Johnson in his election campaign in 1964 had called **the Great Society.** Much of the legislation Johnson pushed through Congress in 1964 and 1965—the Medicare program, for example, which provided medical care for the elderly and disabled or federal aid to education—remained popular. But the most ambitious Great Society programs—what Johnson called "an unconditional war on poverty"—were controversial and tested the limits of American reform.

Johnson's concern for the disadvantaged showed itself in the cornerstone of his War on Poverty, the **Economic Opportunity Act of 1964.** This act created an Office of Economic Opportunity that administered several programs: Head Start to help disadvantaged preschoolers, Upward Bound to prepare impoverished teenagers for college, and Volunteers in Service to America (or VISTA) to serve as a domestic peace corps to help the poor and undereducated across the country. These programs included community-governing boards on which black men and women gained representation, learning such essential political skills as bargaining and organizing.

The **War on Poverty** was the first government-sponsored effort to involve poor African Americans directly in designing and implementing programs to serve low-income communities. For example, in the New Careers program, residents of poor neighborhoods found jobs as community organizers, day care workers, and teacher aides. The program provided meaningful work, access to education, and critical material resources to poor people, so they would become leaders in their own communities and run for office. The **Community Action Programs (CAPs)** insisted on "maximum feasible participation" by the poor. On

▶ **Reading Check**

Poverty, frustration, and white racism contributed to the riots of the late 1960s. The Kerner Commission, set up in the aftermath of the riots, concluded that America was moving toward two separate and unequal societies.

▶ **Teaching Notes**

Lyndon Johnson was a savvy politician. He had to be to rise from Stonewall, Texas, to the pinnacle of power. But he never lost a deep sympathy for the disadvantaged and the powerless. Entering the House of Representatives in 1937, he had been an enthusiastic New Dealer. Elected to the Senate in 1948, he had refused to sign the Southern Manifesto (see Chapter 21) and, as majority leader, had overcome southern filibusters to win passage of the 1957 and 1960 Civil Rights Acts. As president, he pushed the 1964 Civil Rights Act and the 1965 Voting Rights Act through Congress.

▶ **Recommended Reading**

Robert Dalleck. *Flawed Giant: Lyndon B. Johnson and His Times 1961–1973.* New York: Oxford University Press, 1998. A definitive biography of President Lyndon Johnson with fresh insights, grounded in exhaustive research.

another level, the **Education Act** increased federal funding to colleges and universities and provided low-interest student loans. This initiative increased college enrollments and put higher education within the reach of many more Americans than before.

Johnson faced considerable opposition to CAPs and other Great Society programs. Local politicians, fearing the federal government was subsidizing their opponents and undercutting their power, were especially threatened by programs that empowered the previously disfranchised and dispossessed. Others, reflecting persistent white stereotypes of African Americans, complained that Johnson was rewarding lawlessness and laziness with handouts to the undeserving poor. The black residents of America's inner cities, for their part, had their expectations raised by the promises of the Great Society only to be frustrated by white backlash and minimal gains. They felt as betrayed by its programs as Johnson's white critics felt robbed by them.

No one will ever know whether Lyndon Johnson could have won his War on Poverty had he been given the resources to do so. As it turned out, the nation's resources were increasingly going into his other war, the war in Vietnam. Statistics tell the story. Government spending, including spending for domestic programs, increased dramatically under Johnson. But most of the money spent on domestic programs during Johnson's presidency, $44.3 billion, went to social security benefits, which now included Medicare. Appropriations for the War on Poverty came to only $10 billion. The war in Vietnam, in contrast, consumed $140 billion.

One of the most prominent programs of President Johnson's War on Poverty was the Job Corps, which provided occupational training for poor Americans. In this photo, Johnson speaks with James Truesville at a Job Corps center in Camp Catoctin, Maryland.

Johnson and the War in Vietnam

Vietnam was a French colony from the 1860s until the Japanese seized it during World War II. After the war the Vietnamese communists, led by Ho Chi Minh, declared independence. The French, with massive U.S. financial aid, fought to reassert their control from 1945 until they were finally defeated in 1954. With the French pulling out, the Americans arranged a temporary division of the country into a communist-controlled North Vietnam and a U.S.-supported South Vietnam (which, however, contained many communist guerrillas, called "Viet Cong" by the Americans). The United States ignored the possibility that it would replace the French as targets for those Vietnamese who were determined to end white colonial domination and unify their country.

For nine years, under Presidents Eisenhower and Kennedy, American aid and advisers propped up the corrupt and incompetent South Vietnamese government in Saigon. By the time Johnson became president, only the dramatic escalation of American involvement could keep the South Vietnamese government in power. Johnson himself doubted the advisability of a wholesale American commitment. He did not want a foreign war to distract the public's attention or take away

▶ **Recommended Reading**

Wallace Terry. *Bloods: An Oral History of the Vietnam War by Black Veterans.* New York: Ballantine Books, 1984. One of the best sources for firsthand accounts of the Vietnam War as experienced by black soldiers.

resources from the Great Society programs about which he cared so much. "I knew from the start," Johnson claimed later,

> that I was bound to be crucified either way I moved. If I left the woman I really loved—the Great Society—in order to get involved with that bitch of a war on the other side of the world, then I would lose everything at home. All my programs. All my hopes to feed the hungry and shelter the homeless. All my dreams to provide education and medical care to the browns and the blacks and the lame and the poor. But if I left that war and let the Communists take over South Vietnam, then I would be seen as a coward and my nation would be seen as an appeaser and we would both find it impossible to accomplish anything for anybody anywhere on the entire globe.

Determined to slug through it, Johnson intervened in Vietnam.

After an incident involving an alleged North Vietnamese attack on U.S. Navy destroyers in the Gulf of Tonkin in August 1964, Johnson pushed a resolution through Congress that gave him authority to escalate American involvement in Vietnam. In the spring of 1965, he authorized the bombing of selected North Vietnamese targets. The bombing failed to stop the North Vietnamese from resupplying and reinforcing their forces in the south. The American military presence in South Vietnam then grew rapidly. By the end of 1966, more than 385,000 U.S. troops were there, and by 1968 more than 500,000.

Black Americans and the Vietnam War

In the mid-1960s, black Americans made up 10 percent of the armed forces. This percentage increased during America's involvement in the Vietnam War. (In the Persian Gulf War in 1991, African Americans were

Black men served in disproportionately high numbers in Vietnam. Black and white troops fought together but tended mostly to keep to themselves behind the lines.

25 percent of the troops deployed.) Black overrepresentation among the U.S. troops in Vietnam resulted, in large part, from draft deferments for college and graduate students who were predominantly white and middle class. Black men and women entered the military for many compelling reasons, in addition to the draft. One was patriotism. Another was that the military offered educational and vocational opportunities that the children of the working black poor could not otherwise obtain. Still another was Project 100,000.

Project 100,000

In 1966 the U.S. Defense Department launched **Project 100,000** to reduce the high rejection rate of African Americans by the military. The project enabled recruitment officers to accept applicants whom they otherwise would have rejected because of criminal records or lack of skills. The project supplied more than 340,000 new recruits for Vietnam, 136,000 of whom were African Americans. As some have argued, this made the Vietnam War a white man's war but a black man's fight. Although the recruits were promised training and "rehabilitation," they saw more combat duty than regular recruits.

Vietnam Destroys the Great Society

By the end of 1967, the nation seemed to be heading toward total racial polarization. In their rage against economic exploitation and police brutality, some inner-city black people had destroyed many of their own neighborhoods. Frightened white people, unable to comprehend black anger, rallied behind those who promised to restore order by any means. The two men who, only a few years before, had seemed the most effective advocates of racial reconciliation—Lyndon Johnson and Martin Luther King Jr.—were both trying to regain the initiative. Each, tragically, ended by alienating himself from the other.

By 1967 Johnson had escalated the war in Vietnam without convincing many Americans it was worth fighting. With misleadingly optimistic claims about the progress of the war, his administration had opened what journalists called "the credibility gap." Johnson hoped that, with more bombing and more troops, the Vietnamese communists would give up. He knew that if Congress had to choose between spending on the war and spending on domestic programs, it would choose the war. After Johnson asked for a tax increase, his Great Society programs met increasing resistance.

A dramatic example of the ugly mood on Capitol Hill was the House of Representatives expulsion in 1967 of the most prominent African-American politician in the United States, Adam Clayton Powell Jr. (1908–1972). Pastor of the Abyssinian Baptist Church in

Adam Clayton Powell, Jr.'s (1908–1972) Harlem constituency elected him to eleven successive terms in the U.S. House of Representatives. His brilliant leadership of the Education and Labor Committee proved crucial to the successful passage of social reform legislation in the 1960s.

They Called Each Other "Bloods"

Captain Joseph B. Anderson Jr. of Topeka, Kansas, served as a platoon leader at An Khe, from June 1966 to June 1967, and as company commander in Cambodia, Phouc Vinh, from May 1970 to April 1971, 1st Cavalry Division, U.S. Army. His unit was the subject of THE ANDERSON PLATOON, *a 1967 French documentary film.*

Shortly after I got to Vietnam, we got into a real big fight. We were outnumbered at least ten to one. But I didn't know it. I had taken over 1st Platoon of B Company of the 12th Cav. We were up against a Viet Cong battalion. There may have been 300 to 400 of them. And they had just wiped out one of our platoons. At that time in the war, summer of 1966, it was a terrible loss. A bloody massacre.

I was an absolute rarity in Vietnam. A black West Pointer commanding troops. One year after graduation, I was very aggressive about my role and responsibilities as an Army officer serving in Vietnam. I was there to defend the freedom of the South Vietnamese government, stabilize the countryside, and help contain Communism. The Domino Theory was dominant then, predominant as a matter of fact. I was gung ho. And I thought the war would last three years at the most.

There weren't many opportunities for blacks in private industry then. And as a graduate of West Point, I was an officer and a gentleman by act of Congress. Where else could a black go and get that label just like that?

Throughout the Cav, the black representation in the enlisted ranks was heavier than the population as a whole in the United States. One third of my platoon and two of my four squad leaders were black. For many black men, the service, even during a war, was the best of a number of alternatives to staying home and working in the fields or bumming around the streets of Chicago or New York.

There were only a very few incidents of sustained fighting during my tours. Mostly you walked and walked, searched and searched. If you made contact, it would be over in thirty or forty minutes. One burst and then they're gone, because they didn't want to fight or could not stand up against the firepower we could bring with artillery and helicopter gunships.

I had a great deal of respect for the Viet Cong. They were trained and familiar with the jungle. They relied on stealth, on ambush, on their personal skills and wile, as opposed to firepower. They knew it did not pay for them to stand and fight us, so they wouldn't. . . .

What was very clear to me was an awareness among our men that the support for the war was declining in the United States. The gung ho attitude that made our soldiers so effective in 1966, 67, was replaced by the will to survive. They became more security conscious. They would take more defensive measures so they wouldn't get hurt. They were more scared. They wanted to get back home.

Career officers and enlisted men like me did not go back to a hostile environment in America. We went back to bases where we were assimilated and congratulated and decorated for our performance in the conduct of the war.

Personally it was career enhancing. A career Army officer who has not been to war during the war is dead, careerwise. I had done that. I received decorations. Two Silver Stars, five Bronze Stars, eleven Air Medals. . . . But in 1978 I decided I did not want to cool my heels for the next eight to ten years to become a general. . . . I resigned my commission, worked a year as a special assistant to the U.S. Secretary of Commerce, and joined General Motors as a plant manager.

The Anderson Platoon won both an Oscar and an Emmy. As time passes, my memory of Vietnam revolves around the film. I have a print, and I look at it from time to time. And the broadness and scope of my two-year experience narrows down to sixty minutes.

What Do You Think?

▶ How do the experiences of this Vietnam veteran compare with those of black soldiers in World War II?

▶ Why were African-American men attracted to military service? What benefits did they derive from the military, and what does their disproportionate representation in the military suggest about social and economic conditions in black communities?

Source: "Captain Joseph B. Anderson Jr.," in Wallace Terry, *Bloods: An Oral History of the Vietnam War by Black Veterans* (New York: Ballantine Books, 1984), 219–28.

Harlem and a longtime civic activist, Powell had first been elected to represent his Harlem district in 1944 and became the foremost champion of civil rights in the House. Because of his seniority he became chairman of the Education and Labor Committee in 1961 and had been instrumental in passing Johnson's education and antipoverty legislation.

Powell gave ammunition to his enemies. He mismanaged the committee's budget, and took numerous trips abroad at government expense. He was exiled from his district when threatened with arrest

▶ **What Do You Think?**

· During World War II, black soldiers served in segregated battalions, were relegated to noncombat positions, and faced tremendous obstacles to appointment as commissioned officers. In Vietnam, segregation was eliminated, black soldiers served in combat, and appointment as commissioned officers was possible.

· African-American men were attracted to the military as there were not many opportunities for blacks in private industry. The military provide black men with an escape from the social and economic conditions prevalent in black communities.

GUIDE TO READING

▶ What lessons did Martin Luther King learn from his actions in Chicago in 1966?

▶ Why did Martin Luther King oppose the war in Vietnam?

▶ How did black Americans respond to the assassination of Martin Luther King?

KEY TERMS

▶ Poor People's Campaign, p. 814

▶ Civil Rights Act of 1968, p. 816

▶ **Guide to Reading/Key Terms**

For answers, see the *Teacher's Resource Manual*

▶ **Retracing the Odyssey**

The Martin Luther King, Jr. National Historic Site, Atlanta, Georgia. The district is composed of Martin Luther King's birthplace and gravesite. The Ebenezer Baptist Church where three generations of King men served as pastors, along with an informative National Park Service Visitors Center provides a detailed overview of King's life. Also in the district is the Martin Luther King, Jr., Center for Non-Violent Social Change, which contains King's personal papers and the records of the Southern Christian Leadership Conference in addition to an oral history collection.

Section 3

Martin Luther King

Searching for a New Strategy

Like President Johnson, Martin Luther King was attacked on many fronts. Many white people considered him a dangerous radical. Black militants considered him an ineffectual moderate. His first response to the urban rebellions in 1965 and 1966 had been to move his campaign to the North to demonstrate the national range of the civil rights movement. In 1966 King and the SCLC set up operations in Chicago at the invitation of the Chicago Freedom Movement. King was confident he would receive the support of the city's white liberals and the entire black community. James Bevel, King's Chicago lieutenant, declared, "We are going to create a new city. . . . Nobody will stop us." His optimism proved unwarranted.

Chicago's powerful, wily mayor Richard Daley viewed King suspiciously from the outset. He treated him with respect and cautioned the police not to use violence against King's civil rights demonstrators. Because King's movement depended on provoking confrontation, not much happened until King attempted to march into the white ethnic enclave of Marquette Park and the all-white suburb of Cicero.

The ensuing violence attracted the nation's television cameras. Chicago's white liberals joined with King and Daley in negotiating the Summit Agreement on housing. It amounted to a hasty retreat by King in the face of virulent white rage and black militancy. The Chicago strategy was a dismal failure.

But Chicago reinforced two important lessons for King. First, racial discrimination was more than a southern problem. In Chicago he witnessed an intensity of hatred and hostility that surpassed even that of Birmingham. Second, racial discrimination was intertwined with the country's economic structure. He began to think more critically about the need not only to eradicate poverty but to end systemic economic inequality. "What good is it to be allowed to eat in a restaurant," he remarked, "if you can't afford a hamburger?" In the fall of 1967, he announced plans for his most ambitious and militant project, an integrated, nonviolent **Poor People's Campaign** the following spring. According to the plan, tens of thousands of the nation's dispossessed would descend on Washington to focus attention on the disadvantaged members of American society. Among other things, King and his aides wanted a federally guaranteed income policy.

King on the Vietnam War

While planning the Poor People's Campaign, King began to attack the war in Vietnam. King rejected what he considered the hypocrisy of the federal government's determination to send black and white men to Vietnam "to slaughter, men, women, and children" while failing to protect black American civil rights protesters in places like Albany, Birmingham, and Selma. His statements that the president was more concerned about winning in Vietnam than winning the "war against poverty" in America turned Johnson against him. It also further alienated King from many of Johnson's black supporters, including the more traditional civil rights leaders who supported the war in Vietnam. At the same time, the young militants in SNCC, who had already condemned the war, did not rush to embrace him. But King persisted. By 1968 he had become one of the war's most vocal critics.

King's Murder

His search for a new strategy led King to a closer involvement with labor issues. In February 1968, attempting to gain union recognition for municipal workers in Memphis, 1,300 members of a virtually all-black sanitation workers local went on strike and together with the local black community boycotted downtown merchants. But Memphis mayor Henry Loeb refused to negotiate. On March 18, 1968, responding to a call from James Lawson, a longtime civil rights activist and the minister of Centenary Methodist Church in Memphis, King went to Memphis to address the striking sanitation workers.

Martin Luther King in Memphis on the balcony of the Lorraine Motel. King's assassination in 1968 ignited a reign of urban rebellions and riots across America. For many black people King's death signaled the end of the modern civil rights movement.

▶ **Document**

22-2 *Martin Luther King, Jr., "Conscience and the Vietnam War," 1967*
This sermon was aired by the Canadian Broadcasting Corporation in December, 1967.

A mule drawn wagon carries the casket of Martin Luther King Jr. through the thronged streets of Atlanta, Georgia, April 9, 1968.

The occasion was marked by violence. Nevertheless, King returned to Memphis on April 3 and delivered his last and perhaps most prophetic speech:

> I would like to live a long life. Longevity has its place. But I'm not concerned about that now. I just want to do God's will. And He's allowed me to go up to the mountaintop, and I've looked over. And I've seen the promised land. I may not get there with you. But I want you to know tonight that we as a people will get to the promised land. So I'm happy tonight. I'm not worried about anything. I'm not fearing any man. "Mine eyes have seen the glory of the coming of the Lord."

The next day King was murdered by James Earl Ray as he stood on the balcony of the Lorraine Motel in Memphis. His assassination unleashed a torrent of civic rage in black communities. More than 125 cities experienced uprisings. By April 11, forty-six people were dead, 35,000 were injured, and more than 20,000 had been arrested.

In what seemed to many a belated gesture of racial reconciliation, within days of King's assassination, Congress passed the **Civil Rights Act of 1968**. Proposed by Johnson two years before, the act outlawed discrimination in the sale and rental of housing and gave the Justice Department authority to bring suits against such discrimination.

King's assassination also boosted support for the SCLC's faltering Poor People's Campaign. The campaign began in May when more than two thousand demonstrators settled into a shantytown they called Resurrection City in Washington, D.C. For more than a month, they marched daily to various federal offices and took part in a mass demonstration on June 19. On June 24, police evicted them, and the campaign ended, leaving an uncertain legacy.

▶▶ **Reading Check**

King believed that the government was more interested in winning in Vietnam than winning the war against poverty. His position created a split between himself and President Johnson. By 1968, King was one of the war's most vocal critics.

 Reading Check Why did Martin Luther King oppose the war in Vietnam?

Section 4

The Arts and Education

GUIDE TO READING

▶ How did the Black Power movement stimulate black culture?

▶ What characterized the second phase of the black student movement?

▶ What are the generally accepted goals of black studies?

KEY TERMS

▶ black arts movement, p. 817

▶ Eurocentric, p. 822

▶ black studies, p. 824

The Black Arts Movement and Black Consciousness

The years between 1967 and 1975 witnessed some of the most intense political and cultural discussions in the history of the black freedom struggle. Black power stimulated debate about both the future of black politics in the post–civil rights era and the role of black art and artists in the quest for black liberation. Creative people revisited the long-standing issue of whether black art is political or aesthetic. For a decade, discussion about black culture and identity focused on the relationship between art and the artist, and the political movement within the black community. This period became known as the **black arts movement**.

Among the outstanding poets who helped shape the revolutionary movement, introducing new forms of black writing and delivering outspoken attacks on "the white aesthetic" while stressing black beauty and pride, were Sonia Sanchez, Nikki Giovanni, and Don L. Lee (Haki Madhubuti). Sanchez captured the violence and turbulence of the era. In 1970 she published a major collection of poetry entitled, *We a BaddDDD People*. Of equal significance in the development and evolution of this creative flowering was playwright and poet LeRoi Jones.

The formal beginning of the movement was the founding in 1965 of the Black Arts Repertory Theater by LeRoi Jones, who changed his name to Imamu Amiri Baraka in 1967. Jones was the bridge that linked the political and cultural aspects of black power. He had been closely associated with the white avant-garde poets in New York in the 1950s and early 1960s. He began to change in 1965 from an integrationist to a black cultural nationalist.

The guiding ethos of the black arts movement was the determination of black artists to produce black art for black people and thereby to accomplish black liberation. Baraka declared, "The Black man must seek a Black politics, an ordering of the world that is beneficial to his culture, to his interiorization and judgment of the world. The Black Artist . . . is desperately needed to change the images his people identify with, by asserting Black feeling, Black mind, Black judgment." In 1968 he coedited with Larry Neal the anthology *Black Fire*, which revealed the extent to which black writers and thinkers had rejected the premises of

▶ **Guide to Reading/Key Terms**

For answers, see the *Teacher's Resource Manual*

▶ **Recommended Reading**

Michael D. Harris. Colored Pictures: Race and Visual Representation. Chapel Hill: University of North Carolina Press, 2003. A splendid study of how race has been represented and visualized with insigtful analyses of arts movements and informative discussions of black painters.

Imamu Amiri Baraka means "spiritual leader, prince, blessed" in Swahili and is the chosen name of LeRoi Jones, the celebrated "father of the black arts movement."

integration in favor of a new black consciousness and nationalist political engagement.

Larry Neal, who was part of the revolutionary action movement, offered a succinct definition of this important dimension of the freedom struggle:

> The Black Arts Movement is radically opposed to any concept of the artist that alienates him from his community. Black Art is the aesthetic and spiritual sister of the Black Power concept. As such, it envisions an art that speaks directly to the needs and aspirations of Black Americans. In order to perform this task, the Black Arts Movement proposes a radical reordering of the western cultural aesthetic. It proposes a separate symbolism, mythology, critique, and iconography. The Black Arts and the Black Power concept both relate broadly to the Afro-American's desire for self-determination and nationhood. Both concepts are nationalistic. One is concerned with the relationship between art and politics; the other with the art of politics.

The black arts movement was criticized because of its celebration of black maleness, its racial exclusivity, and its homophobia. It was never a unified movement in the sense of all black artists speaking in one voice. There was creative dissent and competing visions of freedom. In 1970 Maya Angelou published an autobiographical novel, *I Know Why the Caged Bird Sings*, that unveiled her experience with sexual abuse and the silencing of black women within black communities. Other black women writers would follow suit and in the 1970s create a black women's literary renaissance. Still, prominent integrationist writers agreed with some of the black arts movement's fundamental beliefs and were converted to its principles.

James Baldwin

The works of Langston Hughes, Lorraine Hansberry, Gwendolyn Brooks, and James Baldwin linked the black cultural renaissances of the 1930s, 1940s, and 1950s to the black arts movement. Brooks, for example, stressed the commitment of artist to community and the importance of the relationship between the artist and her audience. She had consistently supported community-based arts programs. It seemed natural that she should "convert" to a Black Nationalist perspective during the 1960s and join forces with younger artists.

But the most popular black writer of the era, especially among white audiences, was James Baldwin. Baldwin was an integrationist. In his work he had resisted the simple inversion of racial hierarchies that characterized some parts of the black power and black arts movements. He wrote, "I think all theories are suspect, that the finest principles may have to be modified, or may even be pulverized by the demands of life, and that one must find therefore, and move through the world hoping that center will guide one aright." Yet in many ways, Baldwin was as alienated and angry as some of the artists identified with black arts.

In *The Fire Next Time* (1963), he concluded with a phrase that echoed through discussions of the rebellions in Watts, Newark, and Detroit. "If we do not now dare everything, the fulfillment of that prophecy, recreated from the bible in song by a slave, is upon us: 'God gave Noah the rainbow sign, No more water, the fire next time!'"

Baldwin was also an unflinching commentator on white racism and had a major impact on public discourse. At one point he told his white readers, "There appears to be a vast amount of confusion on this point, but I do not know many Negroes who are eager to be 'accepted' by white people, still less to be loved by them; they, the blacks, simply don't wish to be beaten over the head by the whites every instant of our brief passage on this planet." And in *No Name in the Street*, Baldwin declared, "I agree with the Black Panther position concerning black prisoners: not one of them has ever had a fair trial, for not one of them has ever been tried by a jury of his peers." He explained: "White middle-class America is always the jury, and they know absolutely nothing about the lives of the people on whom they sit in judgment: and this fact is not altered, on the contrary it is rendered more implacable by the presence of one or two black faces in the jury box."

Poetry and Theater

The black arts movement had its greatest and most significant impact in poetry and theater. The movement had three geographical centers: Harlem, Chicago and Detroit, and San Francisco.

The Chicago-based *Negro Digest/Black World*, edited by Hoyt Fuller and published by John Johnson, promoted many of the works of the new generation of creative artists. Fuller, a well-connected intellectual with an exhaustive command of black literature, became editor of the monthly magazine in 1961. In 1970 he changed the name of the magazine to *Black World* to signal the rejection of "Negro" and the adoption of "black" to designate people of African descent. The name change identified African Americans with both the African Diaspora and Africa itself.

In Detroit, Naomi Long Madgett's Lotus Press and Dudley Randall's Broadside Press republished the previous generation of black poets, notably Gwendolyn Brooks, Margaret Walker, and Sterling Brown. In Chicago, poet and literary critic Don L. Lee, who changed his name to Haki Madhabuti, launched Third World Press, which published many of the black arts poets and writers.

The Chicago-Detroit publishing houses promoted new poets like Nikki Giovanni, Etheridge Knight, and Sonia Sanchez. These and other poets produced some of the most accomplished and experimental work of the black arts movement. It resonated with the sounds of the African-American vernacular, combining the rhythmic cadences of sermons with popular music and black "street speech" into a spirited new form of poetry that was free, conversational, and militantly cool.

▶ **Recommended Reading**

Brian Ward. *Just My Soul Responding: Rhythm and Blues, Black Consciousness, and Race Relations.* Berkeley, CA: University of California Press, 1998. An excellent study of black popular culture during the civil rights and black power movement era.

▶ **Living Words Audio Clips**

Track 41 Song of the Front Yard; poem and reading by Gwendolyn Brooks

Track 42 liberation/poem; poem and reading by Sonia Sanchez

Track 43 Woman; poem and reading by Nikki Giovanni

Theater was another prominent genre of the black arts movement. Playwright Ed Bullin edited a special issue of the journal *Drama Review* in the summer of 1968 that featured essays and plays by most of the major activists in black arts, including Sonia Sanchez, Ron Milner, and Woodie King Jr. This volume became the textbook of black arts. In his plays Bullins was greatly influenced by Baraka. He portrayed ordinary black life and explored the inner forces that prevented black people from realizing their own liberation and full potential. He showed how racism had deformed the black experience and consciousness. Across the country local black communities formed their own theater groups, including Val Gray Ward's Kuumba Workshop in Chicago and Baraka's Spirit House Theater in New Jersey. These groups reached out to people by hosting seminars, guest appearances, fashion shows, art exhibits, dance recitals, parades, and mass media parties.

On the West Coast, in 1969, Robert Chrisman and Nathan Hare launched *The Black Scholar*, the first serious journal to promote black studies. Chrisman compared the black arts movement with the renaissance in Harlem during the 1920s: "More so than the Harlem Renaissance, in which Black artists were always on the leash of white patrons and publishing houses, the Black Arts movement did it for itself. Black people going out nationally, in mass, saying we are an independent Black people and this is what we produce."

Music

The cultural nationalists in the black arts movement cultivated an appreciation for modern jazz musicians, making them icons of the quest for black freedom. Baraka argued that jazz and other black music was the language that black people developed to give uncensored accounts of their experiences. He and other cultural nationalists believed music could promote black identity and encourage the pride that was vital for political struggle. The music of the jazzmen was often dense and austere, but it could also be powerfully primitive and dazzlingly complex. Above all, the music appeared to challenge Western conceptions of harmony, rhythm, melody, and tone. In jazz you have to improvise, to create your own form of expression by using whatever information inspires you. The emphasis is not on the original, but on individual articulation.

Cultural nationalists perceived jazz to be a self-consciously engaged, economically independent, politically useful art form. Novelist Ralph Ellison put it most succinctly:

> True jazz is an art of individual assertion within and against the group. Each true jazz moment (as distinct from the uninspired commercial performance) springs from a contest in which each artist challenges all the rest; each solo flight, or improvisation, represents (like the successive canvases of a painter) a definition of his identity: as individual, as member of the collectivity and as a link in the chain of tradition.

▶▶ **Recommended Reading**

Craig Hansen Werner. *Playing the Changes: From Afro-Modernism to the Jazz Impulse.* Urbana, IL: University of Illinois Press, 1994. An insightful study of the gospel, blues, and jazz impulse in the writings of key black writers, including James Baldwin and Leon Forrest, during the post-civil rights movement era.

This outlook explains why Miles Davis's legendary album *Kind of Blue* (1959), one of the most progressive jazz albums ever produced, also became one of the most popular. Davis showed that art could be accessible without sacrificing excellence and rigor. Davis, in the words of one admirer, was able to "dance underwater and not get wet." For black cultural nationalists, Davis projected an image of uncompromising and uncompromised black identity.

Among other intensely celebrated jazzmen were Charlie Parker, Archie Shepp, Ornette Coleman, Pharoah Sanders, Eric Dolphy, Thelonious Monk, and John Coltrane. Playwright Ronald Milner described Coltrane as "a man who through his saxophone before your eyes and ears completely annihilates every single western influence." Coltrane also played the deep, and deeply political, blues of "Alabama" written in response to the Birmingham church bombings.

Jazz, however, tended to appeal to intellectuals. Most black people preferred rhythm and blues, gospel, and soul. During the height of the black consciousness movement, black popular musicians gave performances and concerts to raise funds and to assert racial pride. Aretha Franklin and Ray Charles, for example, allowed SNCC workers to attend their concerts free. Just as the freedom songs had done, the soul music of the black power era helped unify black people.

No history of the era would be complete without mentioning the performances of the "Godfather of Soul," James Brown, the "Queen of Soul," Aretha Franklin's powerful rendition of the song "R.E.S.P.E.C.T.," and the financial contributions of Berry Gordy of Motown. James Brown's "Say It Loud, I'm Black and I'm Proud" became an anthem for the era. Brown linked sound commercial marketing to social commentary, confronting American racism with racial pride and righteous indignation. Brown was "totally committed to black power, the kind that is achieved not through the muzzle of a rifle but through education and economic leverage."

Berry Gordy contributed to black freedom struggles both artistically and financially. To support King's Chicago movement, Gordy arranged for Stevie Wonder to give a benefit concert at Soldier Field in Chicago. He made cash contributions to black candidates, to the NAACP and its Legal Defense and Educational Fund, and to the Urban League.

During the late 1960s and early 1970s, the musical and lyrical innovations of the Temptations, Stevie Wonder, and Marvin Gaye reflected Motown's politicization. In an address to one of the sessions launching Jesse Jackson's People United to Save Humanity (PUSH) in 1971, Gordy declared, "I have been fortunate to be able to provide opportunities for young people. . . . Opportunities are supposed to knock once in a lifetime, but too often we have to knock for an opportunity. The first obligation we (as black businessmen) have is to ourselves and our own employees, the second is to create opportunities for others."

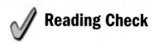 **Reading Check**   How did the Black Power movement stimulate black culture?

▶ **Reading Check**

Black power stimulated debate about the future of black politics and the role of black art and black artists in the quest for black liberation. Painters, actors, musicians, writers. and poets all participated in the black arts movement. The dominant ethos of the movement was the determination of black artists to produce black art for black people.

▶ **Recommended Reading**

Samuel A. Hay. *African American Theater: An Historical and Critical Analysis*. Cambridge, MA: Cambridge University Press, 1994.

▶ **Retracing the Odyssey**

Motown Museum, Detroit, Michigan. Birthplace of Berry Gordy's Motown Record Corporation, founded in 1957. The "Motown Sound" exemplified the music of such performers as The Jackson Five, Gladys Knight and the Pips, Marvin Gaye, Stevie Wonder. A sign hangs on the front of the structure, "Hitsville U.S.A." acknowledging the importance of this state historic site. The museum is composed of two adjoining houses filled with memorabilia of gold record awards, album covers, costumes, and musical instruments. Visitors are able to view in Studio A the original control booth where hits by the Temptations, Supremes, and other artists were recorded.

▶ **Recommended Readings**

Jack Bass and Jack Nelson. *The Orangeburg Massacre*. Cleveland, OH: Word Publishing, 1970.

William H. Exum. *Paradoxes of Protest: Black Student Activism in a White University*. Philadelphia, PA: Temple University Press, 1985.

The Second Phase of the Black Student Movement

The most dramatic expression of militant assertiveness after 1968 occurred among black college students. The black power generation of students was committed to transforming society. Those on predominantly white campuses often, but not always, seemed to be more reformist than revolutionary. Some observers describe the period of activism between 1968 and 1975 as the "second phase" of the black students' movement.

The Orangeburg Massacre

The first phase, in this view, was launched by students at southern black colleges in the early 1960s. It began with the sit-ins in Greensboro, North Carolina, and the Freedom Rides, and it culminated in the Mississippi Freedom Summer of 1964. By 1968, however, many of the student organizations that had grown out of the civil rights movement, notably SNCC, were in decline. The massacre of black students at South Carolina State College in Orangeburg on February 8, 1968, marks the end of the first phase and the beginning of the second. Students attending the historically black institution had protested a local bowling alley's whites-only admission policy. When the tension and protests escalated, state officials deployed the highway patrol and National Guard. On the evening of February 8, the students assembled at the front of the campus and taunted the officers; some threw rocks, bricks, and bottles. One officer was hit by a piece of lumber. Later, without warning, nine highway patrolmen opened fire on the students with shotguns. The officers killed three young men and wounded twenty-seven. Most of them were shot in the back. All the officers involved were later acquitted. A young black activist and SNCC leader, Cleveland Sellers, was convicted of rioting and served nearly a year in prison. He was pardoned in 1993. On February 8, 2001, South Carolina governor James Hodges apologized to a group of survivors who had assembled in Orangeburg.

South Carolina State College Massacre, 1968, Orangeburg, South Carolina. The three young men killed in the Orangeburg Massacre were Henry Smith and Samuel Hammond, both 18, and a 17-year-old high school student, Delano Middleton.

Black Studies

The second phase owed much of its inspiration to the black power and black arts movements. It began when significant numbers of black students enrolled in predominantly white institutions for the first time. The black students at the white campuses demanded courses in black history, culture, literature, and art as alternatives to the **Eurocentric** bias of the average university curriculum. Many black students also formed all-black organizations, such as the Black Allied Students' Association at New York University and the Black Organization of Students at Rutgers University.

Black students understood that education was essential to empowerment. In 1967 black students accounted for only 2 percent of the total enrollment at predominantly white colleges and universities. This meant that only 95,000 African Americans were among the approximately 5 million full-time undergraduates at these schools. Federal legislation—especially the Civil Rights Act of 1964 and the Higher Education Act of 1965—outlawed discrimination or segregation in higher education. By instituting an array of financial aid programs, it spurred colleges and universities to take affirmative action to recruit black students.

On the national level, the overall status of black people in education reflected the accomplishments of the classic phase of the civil rights movement, but the black power generation was determined to make its own mark on the struggle. In 1960 only 227,000 black Americans attended the nation's colleges (including those at predominantly black institutions). By the end of the 1960s, enrollments had increased by 100 percent, and in 1977, 1.1 million black students attended America's universities. This was an almost 500 percent increase over 1960. There was wide political diversity among this generation of students, but they shared the sense of being strangers in a white-controlled environment. Many found the campuses hostile, alien places and discovered little there with which they could identify. They resolved to change this situation.

At San Francisco State College, Nathan Hare, formerly a professor at Howard University, and black students demanded not only curriculum changes but the structural transformation of the college. In the 1966–1967 academic year, the Black Student Union (BSU) orchestrated a strike that involved thousands of students of diverse ethnic and racial backgrounds. The students deliberately chose to strike, rather than take over buildings, so they could circulate freely on the campus, increasing their support and maintaining their momentum. Among their demands were the creation of an autonomous degree-granting black studies department and the admission of more black students. The college ultimately did create the first black studies department in 1968, with Hare as its head.

Black students also took over administration buildings at other institutions, demanding not only that the schools offer more black studies courses and programs and hire more black faculty, but often that classrooms and facilities also be made available to local black communities. The upheavals that shut down Columbia University in 1968, for example, began when black student members of the Students Afro-American Society and Students for a Democratic Society at Columbia University demonstrated to block plans to construct a university gymnasium in nearby Morningside Park. The demonstrators argued the gym would impinge on one of the few parks located in Harlem and that it was being built over strenuous objections from the Harlem community.

Degree Programs

In 1968 Yale University's Black Student Alliance sponsored a symposium to discuss the need, status, and function of Afro-American Studies. Conference organizer Armstead Robinson saw it as the first attempt to create a viable program of Afro-American Studies. In December 1968 the faculty voted to make Yale one of the first major universities in the country to institute a degree-granting African-American Studies program. In 1969 Harvard University created an Afro-American Studies Department, and other schools soon followed. In 1969 the Institute of the Black World in Atlanta conducted a project to define the methods and purpose of black studies and then sponsored a black studies directors' seminar. Maulena Karenga wrote what remains a major textbook for the new field, *Introduction to Black Studies*. By 1973 some two hundred black studies programs existed in the United States. By the late 1980s, several of the programs, such as those at Cornell, Yale, and UCLA, offered master's degrees in African-American studies. In 1988 Temple University, under the leadership of Molefi Kete Asante, became the first university to offer a Ph.D. in African-American Studies. In 2002, Michigan State University became the sixth to offer the doctorate in the discipline.

Still, there was no universally accepted definition of **black studies**. James E. Turner, founder of Africana Studies at Cornell, viewed it as a collective, interdisciplinary scholarly approach to the experiences of people of African descent throughout the world. History, in black studies, constituted the foundation for the analysis of common patterns of life that reflected the social conditions of black people. Africana studies or black studies theoreticians have generally agreed on four goals for this new scholarly field:

1. It should develop solutions to the problems facing black people in the African Diaspora;
2. it should provide an analysis of black culture and life that challenges and replaces preexisting Eurocentric models;
3. it should promote social change and educational reform throughout the academy; and
4. it should institutionalize the study of black people as a field with its own theories, methods, ideologies, symbols, language, and culture.

In short, the first generation of advocates envisioned black studies as a revolutionary, historically grounded educational reform movement that sought to make the study of African descendants—their culture, problems, worldviews, and spirituality—a serious scholarly endeavor with practical implications for improving black people's lives.

 Reading Check What are the generally accepted goals of black studies?

▶▶ **Reading Check**

It should develop solutions to problems facing black people. It should challenge and replace Eurocentric models of black life and culture. It should promote social and educational reform throughout academia. It should institutionalise the study of black people.

Section 5

Politics

GUIDE TO READING

▶ What were the contradictions in President Nixon's policies toward African Americans and civil rights?

▶ What policies did President Nixon pursue with respect to the Vietnam War between 1969 and 1973?

KEY TERMS

▶ Southern Strategy, p. 826

▶ Moynihan Report, p. 826

▶ Family Assistance Plan (FAP), p. 827

The Election of 1968

In the presidential campaign of 1968, the Democrats provided the excitement but lost the election. In late 1967 Senator Eugene McCarthy of Minnesota entered the race as the antiwar alternative to Lyndon Johnson. Few politicians took him seriously, even though he won several primaries. Robert Kennedy, U.S. senator from New York, was taken seriously. By the time he entered the race in mid-March, most of the convention delegates were already pledged to Johnson. After Johnson's withdrawal, they quickly transferred their allegiance to Vice President Hubert Humphrey. Whether Kennedy could have gained the nomination will never be known because—in the second traumatic assassination of 1968—he was murdered in June. Grief over his death, bitterness over the war, and personal rivalries spilled over to produce the most tumultuous political convention in modern American history, with Chicago policemen clubbing and gassing antiwar demonstrators.

In November, Republican Richard Nixon narrowly defeated Humphrey 43.1 percent to 42.7 percent in the popular vote and 301 to 191 in the electoral vote. George Wallace, the segregationist ex-governor of Alabama, in his first serious bid for the presidency, won 13.5 percent of the popular vote and forty-six electoral votes. Running as the candidate of the American Independent Party, Wallace denounced civil rights legislation and court-ordered desegregation. He also endorsed the repression of demonstrators and rioters and promised to stamp out communism in Southeast Asia.

The Nixon Presidency

Of all modern presidents, Richard Nixon is probably the hardest to pin down with neat ideological labels. By the standards of the early twenty-first century, much of his record seems progressive. He created the Environmental Protection Agency, endorsed an equal rights amendment to the Constitution that would have prohibited gender discrimination, and signed more regulatory legislation than any other president. His willingness to innovate in policy affecting African Americans can be illustrated by his naming of Daniel Patrick Moynihan, one of Johnson's

▶▶ **Guide to Reading/Key Terms**

For answers, see the *Teacher's Resource Manual*.

experts on social policy, to be his domestic policy adviser. But Nixon also pursued a **Southern Strategy** that realigned the Republican Party with the white southern backlash to civil rights and weakened the New Deal coalition.

The "Moynihan Report" and FAP

Moynihan first attracted national attention as assistant secretary of labor in the Johnson administration. A confidential memorandum he wrote—loosely organized and full of sweeping generalizations—was leaked to the press. It would later be published as "The Negro Family: The Case for National Action" and is popularly known as the **Moynihan Report**. Moynihan's guiding assumption was that civil rights legislation, necessary as it was, would not address the problems of the inner city. There, he argued, the breakdown of the "lower-class" black family had led to the juvenile delinquency, illegitimacy, drug addiction, and poor performance in school. He attributed the vulnerability of the black family to "three centuries of almost unimaginable treatment" by white society: exploitation under slavery, the strain of urbanization, and persistent unemployment.

These forces, he argued, weakened the role of black men and resulted in a disproportionate number of dysfunctional female-headed families. In the most-often repeated passage in the report, Moynihan declared that the black community had been forced into "a matriarchal structure, [which] because it is so out of line with the rest of American society, seriously retards the progress of the group as a whole, and imposes a crushing burden on the Negro male. . . . Obviously, not every instance of social pathology afflicting the Negro community can be traced to the weakness of family structure . . . [but] once or twice removed, it will be found to be the principal source of most of the aberrant, inadequate, or anti-social behavior that did not establish, but now serves to perpetuate the cycle of poverty and deprivation."

Although based on the work of earlier black scholars, such as E. Franklin Frazier, Moynihan's condemnation of "matriarchy" drew fire. Black social scientists, such as Joyce Ladner, Andrew Billingsley, and Carol Stack, countered that the structure of the black family reflected a functional adaptation that black people had made to survive in a hostile and racist American society. Historians Herbert Gutman and John Blassingame argued that Moynihan underestimated the prevalence of two-parent black families in the past. Although many of the criticisms of the report were deserved, they diverted attention from its positive thrust. Moynihan wanted to eliminate poverty and unemployment in the black community. He recommended vigorous enforcement of the civil rights laws to achieve equality of opportunity. Setting himself apart from other Johnson administration policy makers, Moynihan was one of the first to appreciate how white resentment of the Community Action Program (CAP) and the expansion of the welfare rolls would make both programs politically unfeasible.

Intrigued with Moynihan's independence, Nixon told him to develop a plan to assist poor families. Under the **Family Assistance Plan** (FAP) that Nixon unveiled in the summer of 1969, each family of four with no wage earner would receive an annual payment of $1,600 plus $800 of food stamps. With its across-the-board guarantee of income, the plan eliminated an oppressive welfare bureaucracy.

Had it passed, FAP would have preserved and promoted two-parent families by removing the prohibition against assistance to dependent children whose fathers were alive, well, and living at home. It would also have encouraged work by requiring able-bodied recipients to accept jobs or vocational training and by providing benefits to those accepting low-paying jobs. But although the House approved the plan, the Senate, under pressure both from conservatives who objected to any government programs for the poor and from welfare-rights advocates who complained the payments were too low, killed it. Arguably, at least until President Clinton's failed health-care plan in the 1990s, Nixon's FAP was the most significant failed initiative in the history of American social policy.

Busing

Yet however flexible he might have been on many issues, Nixon was acutely aware that he moved in a changed political environment and particularly in a far more conservative Republican Party than he had when he ran against and lost to John F. Kennedy in 1960. In 1968 an influx of southern segregationists whom Barry Goldwater had attracted to the Republican Party in 1964 had to be appeased. Now Nixon chose to court closer relations with South Carolina senator Strom Thurmond, a Republican who had abandoned the Democratic Party in 1964. Thurmond and his allies had demanded that, if elected, Nixon would slow down the process of court-ordered school desegregation in the South. Finally, Nixon could hardly ignore George Wallace, with his racist appeals. In another three-way race in 1972, Wallace might ensure Nixon's defeat.

As a result of these pressures, the Nixon administration perfected its southern strategy and embarked on a collision course with civil rights organizations such as the NAACP, which supported busing to achieve school integration. Thus the major battle over civil rights in the early 1970s was over the federal courts' willingness to implement desegregation goals by busing students across district lines. Nixon used the busing controversy to lure Wallace voters. In 1971 he had advised federal officials to stop pressing to desegregate schools

African American schoolchildren board school buses before a police escort outside a school in Boston, Massachusetts.

through "forced busing." He argued that such efforts were ultimately "counterproductive, and not in the interest of better race relations."

Educational segregation in the North reflected residential segregation. In Boston, site of some of the most vicious busing protests, schools in black neighborhoods received less funding than their white counterparts. Buildings were derelict, seriously overcrowded, and deficient in supplies and equipment, even desks. In 1974 U.S. district judge W. Arthur Garrity ruled in favor of a group of black parents who had filed a class action suit against the Boston School Committee. The ruling found the school committee guilty of violating the equal protection clause of the Fourteenth Amendment. To achieve racial balance in the Boston schools, the judge ordered the busing of several thousand students between mostly white South Boston, Hyde Park, and Dorchester, and mostly black Roxbury.

White people who opposed busing organized demonstrations and boycotts to prevent their children from being bused into black communities and black children from being bused into white schools. During the first week of busing to achieve desegregation, white students and their mothers clashed with police officers outside South Boston High School. Violence and hostilities continued for weeks despite the arrests of dozens of people and the closing of bars and liquor stores. Sporadic violence persisted for another two years in Boston.

 Reading Check What were the contradictions in President Nixon's policies toward African Americans and civil rights?

Nixon and the War

Meanwhile, the war in Vietnam seemed to drag on endlessly, with the peace negotiations that had begun in Paris in May 1968 making no apparent progress. Nixon realized that what most Americans disliked about the war was that it was killing their sons and husbands. So in 1969 he began to phase out direct U.S. involvement in the war. This "Vietnamization," he claimed, was made possible by the growing ability of the South Vietnamese to fight for themselves. What Nixon did not say was that another reason for troop withdrawals was that the morale of American soldiers was plunging rapidly. Drug abuse among troops was widespread, some soldiers had killed their officers, and some of those incidents had racial overtones. Along with his domestic record, Nixon's promise to "wind down the war" was widely popular and assured his reelection. In 1972 he defeated South Dakota senator George McGovern in a landslide.

Few in the Nixon administration, however, took South Vietnamese military capability seriously. Nixon, just as much as Johnson, was unwilling to "lose" Vietnam. Between 1969 and 1971, Nixon stepped up the war. Even as American soldiers were being sent home, he escalated the air war dramatically. In the bombing of Cambodia in 1969–1970, for example—which was kept secret from Congress and the public—the United States dropped more bombs than it had on all of Asia in the Second World War.

▶ **Reading Check**

On the one hand, Nixon supported an equal rights amendment to the Constitution and to pursue innovative policies affecting African Americans. On the other, he pursued a "Southern Strategy" that aligned the Republican Party with the white backlash to civil rights.

But each time Nixon escalated the war opposition to it grew. Antiwar demonstrations kept Nixon off balance and may have deterred him from further escalation. The most dramatic response to Nixon's escalation in the Vietnam War came after the invasion of Cambodia in April 1970. The invasion triggered antiwar protests on many campuses. In one such protest, on May 4, Ohio National Guardsmen shot and killed four white students at Kent State University. The response of students across the country was electric: the first nationwide student strike in American history. Ten days later in Mississippi, the shooting and killing of two black students at Jackson State University attracted much less attention from either white students or the media. Three years later, at the beginning of 1973, the United States and North Vietnam signed a peace agreement. Congress then prohibited the reintroduction of American troops and the resumption of bombing. In 1974 Congress began cutting off military aid to the South Vietnamese government. The result of this loss of American support was predictable: in 1975 the communists launched their final offensive, and South Vietnam collapsed.

Nixon's Downfall

If Nixon assumed the presidency in 1969 with any popular mandate, it was to restore law and order. The disorder that irritated the American public included many things: the inner-city riots, the antiwar demonstrations and campus protests, and the rise in crime. Responding to this mood, Nixon pushed legislation through Congress that gave local law enforcement officials expanded power to use wiretaps and enter premises without advance warning.

But Nixon's personality—a combination of paranoia and ruthlessness—pushed him beyond what the public would tolerate, and even beyond the law itself. He increasingly confused ordinary criminals with principled protesters and his political opponents, and he decided to punish them all. One method was to create an extralegal ring of burglars, operating out of the White House to gather incriminating information. In June 1972 they were discovered breaking into Democratic National Committee headquarters in the Watergate apartment complex in Washington. Full details emerged in a Senate investigation in 1973–1974. On August 9, 1974, threatened with impeachment, Nixon resigned. His downfall, however, left no one of his stature or with his flexible attitude toward public policy to resist the takeover of the Republican Party by more ideologically dogmatic conservatives. One early intimation of this was the difficulty Nixon's successor, Gerald Ford, had in securing the 1976 Republican presidential nomination against the right's new hero, former California governor Ronald Reagan.

 Reading Check What policies did President Nixon pursue with respect to the Vietnam War between 1969 and 1973?

▶ **Reading Check**

Despite campaign promises to "wind down the war," President Nixon stepped up the war between 1969 and 1971. Nixon's actions sparked increasing opposition to the war. In 1973, the United States began the process that would lead to U.S. withdrawal from Vietnam.

► What political gains did black Americans make during the 1970s?

► What was the overall economic status of African Americans in the 1970s?

► What contributed to President Carter's support among black people?

KEY TERMS

► Voting Rights Act of 1965, p. 830

► Gary convention, p. 830

► **Guide to Reading/Key Terms**

For answers, see the *Teacher's Resource Manual.*

► **Recommended Reading**

Robert C. Smith. *We Have No Leaders: African Americans in the Post-Civil Rights Era.* New York: State University of New York Press, 1996. A thoughtful critique of the successes and failures of black politics beginning with the National Black Political Convention in Gary, Indiana, in 1972.

Section 6

Black Elected Officials

Winning Political Office

Just as King searched for a new strategy after the victories of the early phase of the civil rights movement, other black leaders mobilized the newly enfranchised black electorate to win political office. After the adoption of the **Voting Rights Act of 1965**, Vernon Jordan, director of the Voter Education Project, coordinated registration drives and workshops across the South.

By 1974 there were 1,593 black elected officials outside the South. By 1980 the number had risen to 2,455. Although black people in northern cities had been able to vote for a century, they had not been able to command an equal voice in city governance. The rise of black power and the inspiration of the Voting Rights Act, however, signaled a new departure. People now eagerly engaged in the electoral process to achieve a political influence to which their numbers entitled them. In 1967 in Cleveland, where the black population had skyrocketed after World War II, Carl Stokes became the first black mayor of a major American city, winning election with the support of white business leaders and the solid backing of the black community. In the same year prosecutor Richard G. Hatcher became mayor of Gary, Indiana, where the black population had also increased greatly after the war. Hatcher won by a mere 1,389 votes, garnering 96 percent of the black vote and 14 percent of the white vote.

The Gary Convention and the Black Political Agenda

These victories made possible one of the most significant events of recent black political history, the **Gary convention** of 1972. The cochairs of the convention were Detroit congressman Charles Diggs, Hatcher, and writer and cultural nationalist Amiri Baraka of Newark, New Jersey. Political scientist Ronald Walters, who helped plan the convention, recalled that various ideological factions had to be placated to make the convention work: "The most important thing about 1972 was the fact that it was an election year, so it provided the environment for the politics taking place. So you had two groups of people who saw this as an opportunity to make some very important state-

The National Black Convention Movement of the Black Power Era

1965 Maulena Karenga founds the US (as opposed to them) Organization in Los Angeles, California. Advocates cultural nationalism.

1966 Amiri Baraka founds Spirit House Movers and Players in Newark, New Jersey. Advocates cultural nationalism.

1966 Huey P. Newton and Bobby Seale found the Black Panther Party.

1966 Stokely Carmichael coins the term "black power."

1966 Representative Adam Clayton Powell Jr. hosts the first Black Power Conference.

1967 Second Black Power Conference, held in Newark, New Jersey, calls for partitioning the United States into separate black and white nations.

1968 Third Black Power Conference is held in Philadelphia, Pennsylvania.

1969 National Black Economic Development Conference held in Detroit, Michigan.

1969 Last Black Power Conference, held in Bermuda, ends in disarray.

1970 Congress of Afrikan Peoples, led by Amiri Baraka, is organized in Atlanta, Georgia. Adopts the slogan, "It's nation time."

1971 The Reverend Jesse Jackson founds People United to Save Humanity (PUSH) in Chicago, Illinois.

1972 National Black Political Convention is held in Gary, Indiana.

1973 National Black Feminist Organization is founded by Eleanor Holmes Norton and Margaret Sloan.

1974 Last National Black Political Convention is held in Little Rock, Arkansas.

ments. One of these, of course, was the black nationalist movement led by Amiri Baraka, Maulana Karenga, and others at that time." The nationalists interpreted "black power" to mean that black people should control their own communities and create separate cultural institutions distinct from those of white society. These views clashed with the ideas espoused by the black elected officials represented by Stokes and Hatcher. According to Walters, "It was this body of people who really were contending for the national leadership of the black community in the early seventies. And in the seventies this new group of black elected officials joined the civil rights leaders and became a new leadership class, but there was sort of a conflict in outlook between them and the more indigenous, social, grass roots-oriented nationalist movement."

Hatcher observed that "people had come to Gary from communities all over the United States where they were politically impotent, but . . . they went back home and rolled up their sleeves and dived into the political arena." Approximately eight thousand people gathered to develop an agenda for black empowerment. The discussions about bloc voting, the efficacy of coalitions, and the feasibility of a third party inspired scores of individual African Americans to run for local office. The convention was not homogeneous, however, and no unified black consensus emerged.

Several discussions over strategies to secure common interests revealed deep-seated internal divisions that allowed ancillary issues to provoke even more impassioned disagreement. Coleman Young and other Michigan delegates walked out to protest a proposal calling for African Americans to reject "discriminatory" unions and form their own. Others walked out over a resolution condemning Israel for its "expansionist policy" toward the Palestinians. Others opposed "forced racial integration of schools" through busing, arguing that such practices insulted black students and would cost black teachers their jobs.

The Gary convention was important because it signaled a shift in the political focus of the black community toward electoral politics and away from mass demonstrations and protest measures. Unity continued to elude subsequent conventions, however, and delegates attending the last National Black Convention at Little Rock, Arkansas, in 1974 abandoned the idea of a black political party. Deep ideological differences and institutional cleavages precluded coalitions and cooperation between black nationalists and the rising numbers of black elected officials. These same differences prevented some nationalists and elected officials from taking seriously the 1972 Democratic Party presidential bid of New York congresswoman Shirley Chisholm.

Black People Gain Local Offices

Despite the demise of the National Black Convention movement, African Americans continued to register impressive gains in electoral politics. A few statistics indicate the success of black politicians. When the leaders first convened the Gary convention, there were 13 African-American members of Congress; by 1997 there were 40. In 1972 there were 2,427 black elected officials; by 1993 there were 8,106. An amendment to the Voting Rights Act in 1975 enabled minorities to mount court challenges to at-large voting practices that diluted the impact of bloc voting; this helped increase the number of black elected officials. Districts were redrawn with race as the predominant factor in their reconfiguration. On November 5, 1985, state senator L. Douglas Wilder was elected lieutenant governor in Virginia, the first African-American lieutenant governor in a southern state since

L. Douglas Wilder of Virginia was the first black governor in the United States.

Coleman A. Young served as mayor of Detroit for five terms.

Reconstruction. In 1989 he was elected governor, the first black governor of any state since Reconstruction.

Between 1971 and 1975, the number of African-American mayors rose from 8 to 135, leading to the founding of the National Conference of Black Mayors in 1974. In 1973 Coleman Young in Detroit and Thomas Bradley in Los Angeles became the first African-American mayors of cities of more than a million citizens. Bradley won in Los Angeles even though black people made up only 15 percent of the city's electorate. Ten years later, in 1983, Chicago swore in its first black mayor, Harold Washington. The era of the black elected official had arrived.

 Reading Check   What political gains did black Americans make during the 1970s?

Economic Downturn

The 1970s were a decade of recessions and economic instability. Many black people experienced this economic downturn as a depression. During the 1970s, as the gap between the incomes of the upper 20 percent of African Americans and their white counterparts narrowed, the gap between black men and women at the bottom of the economic ladder and their counterparts expanded. Poor black people were losing

▶ **Reading Check**

Blacks made impressive gains in electoral politics in the 1970s. African Americans were elected to public office in growing numbers at almost every level of government. Moreover, an amendment to the Voting Rights Act in 1975 allowed court challenges to voting practices that diluted the strength of black votes.

▶ **Documents**

22-5 *"The Bottom of the Economic Totem Pole":* *African American Women in the Workplace* Despite the fact that Title VII of the landmark Civil Rights Act of 1964 prevented sex discrimination in employment, African-American women as a class remained "at the bottom of the economic totem pole" because of "their dual victimization by race and sex-based discrimination," in the words of Dr. Paul Murray. Dr. Murray, an African-American professor of American studies advocated the position that all antidiscrimination legislation should explicitly prohibit sex descrimination.

22-6 *Affirmative Action in Atlanta, "Can Atlanta Succeed Where America Has Failed?"* In 1974 Maynard Jackson became Atlanta, Georgia's first black mayor. Jackson was part of growing trend that sent African Americans to city hall in record numbers. With a new city charter that enhanced the mayor's power, Jackson implanted a series of sweeping changes. His early programs called for increasing the number of black municipal employees and black contractors.

22-7 *Presidential candidate Jimmy Carter speaks of growing up behind an Invisible Wall of Racial Segregation," Los Angeles, CA, June 1, 1976*

ground. In 1969 approximately 10 percent of white men and 25 percent of black men earned less than $10,000 (in 1984 constant dollars). In 1984 about 40 percent of black men between twenty-five and fifty-five earned less than $10,000 compared with 20 percent of comparable white men. Put a different way, between 1970 and 1986, the proportion of black families with incomes of less than $10,000 grew from 26.8 to 30.2 percent. Still, there were some improvements. The black middle class grew. In 1970, 4.7 percent of black families had incomes of more

PROFILE ❖ Eleanor Holmes Norton

Eleanor Holmes was born in Washington, D.C., on April 8, 1938, to Coleman and Vela Holmes. Her father worked in the housing department of the District of Columbia and earned a law degree. Her mother was a teacher. Holmes attended Dunbar High School and Antioch College in Yellow Springs, Ohio. In 1963 and 1964, she earned an M.A. in American Studies and a law degree from Yale University. While clerking for a federal judge in Philadelphia, she met her husband, Edward Norton, and married him in October 1965. From that time to the present she would combine marriage, career, and motherhood with a commitment to social struggle for justice and equity for workers, women, and minorities.

After completing her clerkship she became an advocate for human rights. Norton also placed her expertise at the service of the Mississippi Freedom Democratic Party when it challenged the all-white Mississippi delegation at the Democratic National Convention of 1964.

Committed to preserving constitutional guarantees of the freedom of speech for all Americans, she represented Vietnam War protesters, activists from civil rights organizations, and even white klansmen. Norton was also able to put aside her personal feeling and successfully defend Alabama governor George Wallace's rights to express his racist ideas in public facilities in New York City as the candidate of the American Independent Party. Her defense of Wallace attracted both critics and admirers. In 1970 Mayor John V. Lindsay appointed her chair of New York's Human Rights Commission, the city's most powerful antidiscrimination agency. Again she impressed people with her mastery of legal questions and articulate commitment to battle racism and sexism, and to preserve free speech.

Norton, in 1973, helped cofound the National Black Feminist Organization, to mobilize black women against the interwoven race, class, and sex exploitation and discrimination they face in finding employment. In 1975 she coauthored *Sex Discrimination and the Law: Causes and Remedies.*

Jimmy Carter named Norton head of the Equal Employment Opportunity Commission (EEOC). From 1977 to 1982 she was largely responsible for enforcement of Title VII of the Civil Rights Act of 1972 and the Equal Employment Act of 1972. She cut the backlog of cases in half and increased the productivity of EEOC area offices by 65 percent. Norton firmly supported affirmative action. In 1990, after serving as professor of law at the Georgetown University Law Center, Norton was elected the nonvoting representative to Congress from the District of Columbia.

Norton

than $50,000; by 1986 the number had almost doubled to 8.8 percent. But in general, the relative economic status of black workers did not improve.

 Reading Check What was the overall economic status of African Americans in the 1970s?

Black Americans and the Carter Presidency

In 1976 the United States celebrated its bicentennial. For African Americans, it was an important year, but for another reason. For the first time since 1964, the man most of them voted for was elected president—Jimmy Carter, a former governor of Georgia. Ninety percent of African-American voters favored the soft-spoken, religious Georgia Democrat over incumbent president Gerald Ford. As in 1960 their votes were crucial; without them, Carter could not have even carried his native South.

Black Appointees

Carter acknowledged his debt to the black electorate by appointing African Americans to highly visible posts. He named Patricia Harris secretary of Housing and Urban Development, making her the first black woman to serve in the Cabinet. Carter appointed Andrew Young, former congressman from Georgia and a longtime political ally, ambassador to the United Nations. (Young was forced to resign in 1979.) Clifford Alexander Jr. became the secretary of the army. Eleanor Holmes Norton became the first woman to chair the Equal Employment Opportunity Commission (EEOC). Ernest Green, who had been one of the nine students to desegregate Little Rock's Central High School, was appointed assistant secretary of the Department of Labor. Wade McCree was appointed solicitor general in the Justice Department. Drew Days III became assistant attorney general for civil rights. Historian and former University of Colorado chancellor Mary Frances Berry was appointed assistant secretary for education. Carter also named Louis Martin his special assistant, making him the first African American in a position of influence on the White House staff.

Carter's Domestic Policies

There are many ways to judge the significance of the Carter presidency to African Americans. Carter's black appointments were practically and symbolically important. Never had so

▶ **Reading Check**

Recessions and economic instability which characterized the 1970s were particularly difficult for many blacks. Income gaps between African Americans and whites at the bottom of the economic ladder increased, as well as the percentage of black families earning less than $10,000. There was some growth between 1970 and 1986 in the percentage of middle class African Americans. Overall, however, black economic status did not improve in the 1970s.

Andrew Young, former mayor of Atlanta, Georgia, served in the Carter Administration as ambassador to the United Nations.

many black men and women occupied positions that had direct and immediate impact on the day-to-day operations of the federal government. Carter also helped cement gains for civil rights. When Congress passed legislation to stop busing for schoolchildren as a means of integrating the schools, Carter vetoed it. He tried to improve fair employment practices by strengthening the enforcement powers of the EEOC. His Justice Department chose cases to prosecute under the Fair Housing Act that involved widespread discrimination, to make the greatest possible impact.

Yet Carter's overall record proved unsatisfactory to most African Americans. Despite a Public Works Employment Act that directed 10 percent of public works funds to minority contractors and helped spur the creation of 585,000 jobs, Carter failed to help Democrats in Congress pass either full-employment or universal health-care bills. He also cut social welfare programs in an attempt to balance the budget, including school lunch programs and financial aid to black students.

Although the sluggish economy undermined Carter's popularity, the event that proved his undoing was the Iran hostage crisis that began in the fall of 1979. For many black people, however, Carter had become a disappointment long before that. They believed he had done little to help them achieve social justice and economic advancement. Still, the nomination of the conservative Ronald Reagan by the Republicans left black voters no alternative to Carter. In the election of 1980, 90 percent of black voters again supported him, but this time they could not prevent his defeat. Carter pulled down scores of Democrats with him, and the Republicans regained the Senate for the first time since 1954.

Still, some black intellectuals chose a long view in their assessment of the significance of the post–World War II decades of struggle. Historian and theologian Vincent Harding put it most eloquently:

> It may be that the greatest discovery . . . was the fact that there is no last word in the human struggle for freedom, justice, and democracy. Only the continuing word, lived out by men, women, and children who dance and rest, who wrestle with alligators and stand firm before tanks, and presidents, and drug lords and deep, deep, fears. We learn again that the continuing word remains embedded in those who determined not to be moved, who know, against all odds, that they will overcome, will continue to create a more perfect union, a more compassionate world. The world remains with those who discover, in the midst of unremitting struggle, deep amazing powers within their own lives, power from, power for, the planet.

 Reading Check What contributed to President Carter's support among black people?

▶ **Reading Check**

Blacks played a key role in the election of President Carter. He acknowledged this debt by naming African Americans to important and highly visible positions within his administration. Carter also supported efforts to cement gains for civil rights. However, the poor economy of the late 1970s undermined his support among black and white voters alike.

Exploring Oral History

Oral history is made up of people's verbal accounts and recollections of former times and events. Historians collect oral history through interviews, which may take place at the time of an event or at some later date, perhaps even decades later. These interviews are primary sources that record not only facts about the past, but also people's opinions, feelings, and impressions—all important for putting together a picture of the past.

The excerpt below is from an interview with John Lewis on the twentieth anniversary of President Kennedy's death. In 1963, Lewis was chairperson of the Student Nonviolent Coordinating Committee and one of the leaders of the civil rights March on Washington.

LEARN THE SKILL
Use the following steps to analyze an oral history:

1. **Identify the nature of the oral account.** Determine who was interviewed, that person's relationship to the event, and any factors that might have influenced the person's recollection of the event.

2. **Determine the reliability of the evidence.** Consider whether the person was in a position to observe events first-hand, or to judge events impartially. Also consider the length of time between the event and the interview.

3. **Study the evidence to learn more about the historical event.** Note any new facts you learn from the interview, as well as new insights into people's attitudes at the time of the event.

PRACTICE THE SKILL
Answer the following questions:

1. **(a)** Who was interviewed? **(b)** When did the interview take place? **(c)** What was Lewis's attitude toward Kennedy at the time of his death? Why? **(d)** Did that attitude change in any way over time?

2. **(a)** What was Lewis's relationship to the event he is describing? **(b)** How might Lewis's role in the civil rights movement have affected his interpretation of the event? **(c)** How might events after Kennedy's death have affected the account? **(d)** What do Lewis's views reveal about his political perspective?

An Interview with John Lewis: Remembering President Kennedy's Assassination

"I was living in Atlanta then, but I had gone back to Nashville for a trial. I was getting into a car to go to the Nashville airport when I heard it on the radio. And to me, it was the saddest moment in my life. I had grown up to love and to admire President Kennedy. I remember crying on the plane.

I saw him as a sort of guy that listened. Sincere. Caring. People argue and say that he didn't really do anything. But he did listen, and during that period from 1961 to 1963, I'll tell you, I think probably for the first time in modern American history, we felt, 'Well, we have a friend in the White House.' On some things we disagreed. We'd call them up and argue and debate with them on some issue, and we said a lot of different things, and sometimes it was harsh. But we saw the Kennedy administration during that period as a sympathetic referee in the whole struggle for civil rights.

His campaign had created a sense of hope, a sense of optimism for many of us. When someone asked him about the civil rights sit-ins that year, he said, 'By sitting down, these young people are standing up for the very best in American tradition.' "

—*Newsweek*, November 28, 1983

3. **(a)** What impact does Lewis think Kennedy's presidency had on government policy and the nation? **(b)** What can you learn about Kennedy's presidency from Lewis's account?

APPLY THE SKILL
See the Chapter Review and Assessment for another opportunity to apply this skill.

▶▶ **Skills for Life**

For answers, see *Teacher's Resource Manual*.

CHAPTER

23

Black Politics

1980–2004

U.S. Senator Barack Obama of Illinois electrified the 2004 Democratic Convention with a powerful reminder of the as yet unfulfilled promises of American democracy while expressing abiding hope for a better future.

Witnessing History . . .

Many were lost in the struggle for the right to vote: Jimmie Lee Jackson, a young student, gave his life; Viola Liuzzo, a White mother from Detroit, called nigger lover, had her brains blown out at point blank range; [Michael] Schwerner, [Andrew] Goodman and [James] Chaney—two Jews and a Black—found in a common grave, bodies riddled with bullets in Mississippi; the four darling little girls in a church in Birmingham, Alabama. They died that we might have a right to live.

Dr. Martin Luther King Jr. lies only a few miles from us tonight. Tonight he must feel good as he looks down upon us. We sit here together, a rainbow, a coalition—the sons and daughters of slavemasters and the sons and daughters of slaves, sitting together around a common table, to decide the direction of our party and our country. His heart would be full tonight.

We meet tonight at the crossroads, a point of decision. Shall we expand, be inclusive, find unity and power; or suffer division and impotence?

—Address by the Reverend Jesse Louis Jackson to the Democratic National Convention, July 19, 1988

 What is Jesse Jackson's message in this excerpt?

A delegate to the 1988 Democratic National Convention holds a sign supporting Jesse Jackson for president.

Chapter Preview

► **Witnessing History**

Many people lost their lives in the struggle for equality and now people of all races have come together to bring about change. Jackson is suggesting that people need to decide whether they want to work in unity to make change happen or be weakened by divisiveness.

Despite the hardships and setbacks of the 1980s, African Americans hoped the election in 1992 of William Jefferson (Bill) Clinton to the presidency represented the rise of the rainbow coalition of progressive forces championed in the 1980s by Jesse Jackson. Clinton was undoubtedly a friend to African America, but these hopes were only partly fulfilled. Despite the conservative triumph in the 2000 elections, the NAACP and other organizations crafted a broad national and international political agenda during the 2004 presidential race, and a generation of new black politicians, such as Barack Obama of Illinois, addressed the economic, health-care, education, and security concerns of black and white America in a healing new centrist voice.

This chapter explores the complexity, contradictions, ironies, and tensions between race-conscious progressive politics and conservative backlash politics from 1980 to the opening years of the new millennium.

Section 1

The Conservative Reaction

Dismantling the Great Society

Beginning in the late 1970s, American politics took a hard turn to the right. This shift profoundly affected African Americans, particularly the poor. With the election of Ronald Reagan (1911–2004) to the presidency in 1980, the executive branch ceased to support expanded civil rights. It also sought to reduce welfare programs. It staffed key agencies and the federal judiciary with opponents of affirmative action. The now overwhelmingly white Republican Party became increasingly entrenched in the South, ending the Democratic Party's long dominance in that region. The political landscape of the 1980s and 1990s was thus marked by a realignment and ideological conflict between liberal and progressive Democrats on one side and conservative Republicans on the other.

Ronald Reagan's defeat of Jimmy Carter in the 1980 presidential election marked the emergence of the **New Right** as the dominant force in American politics. Reagan possessed charm and the ability to communicate his vision to the American people. His election was the result of more than personal charisma, however. Over the previous decade, many groups unhappy with the changes of the 1960s had developed powerful political organizations that found a home in the Republican Party. These groups included those opposed to equal rights for women, to abortion rights, to the Supreme Court's decisions protecting the rights of the accused and banning compulsory prayer from the public schools, and a range of other issues. White Southerners opposed to the changes wrought by the civil rights movement, and white Northerners angry at school busing, affirmative action programs, and the tax burden they associated with welfare were a key part of this coalition.

One of the New Right's goals was to reverse the growth of social welfare programs created during and after the New Deal. To this end, from 1981 to 1992, Reagan and his Republican successor George H. W. Bush cut federal grants to cities in half and terminated programs crucial to the stability of many black families. As a result, inner-city neighborhoods, where 56 percent of poor residents were African American, became more unstable.

Reagan advanced a **trickle-down theory** of economics. He believed if the financial position of the wealthiest Americans improved, their

GUIDE TO READING

▶ How did Reagan and Bush try to dismantle the "Great Society" and undermine social welfare programs?

▶ What role did black conservatives play in the Republican Party in the 1980s and 1990s?

KEY TERMS

▶ New Right, p. 845

▶ trickle-down theory, p. 845

▶ archconservative, p. 849

▶▶ **Guide to Reading/Key Terms**

For answers, see the *Teacher's Resource Manual*.

▶▶ **Document**

23-2 *Richard Viguerie, Why the New Right is Winning, 1981*

Richard Viguerie represents the right-wing, ultra conservative movement. This document is an excerpt from his book on the New Right.

increased prosperity would filter down through the middle and working classes to the poor. Unemployment statistics soon challenged this theory. By December 1982, the unemployment rate had risen to 10.8, and the rate for African Americans was twice that of white Americans. The real income of the highest paid 1 percent of the nation, meanwhile, increased from $312,206 to $548,970 during the 1980s.

Reagan and Bush often masked their intent to undermine rights-oriented policies by appointing black conservatives to key administrative positions. Reagan chose William Bell, for example, to replace Carter appointee Eleanor Holmes Norton as chair of the Equal Employment Opportunity Commission (EEOC). Because Bell was a conservative with few qualifications for the post, civil rights leaders and organizations immediately protested his appointment. Reagan simply replaced Bell the following year with yet another black conservative, Clarence Thomas, who strongly opposed affirmative action. Thomas reduced the commission's staff and allowed the backlog of affirmative action cases to grow to 46,000 and processing time to increase to ten months.

Reagan similarly tried to change the direction of the U.S. Commission on Civil Rights (CCR), but in this case he met with resistance. Since its creation in 1957, the commission had served as a civil rights watchdog. It had no real enforcement powers but had considerable influence on public opinion. Soon after Reagan took office, the CCR began to issue reports critical of his civil rights policies. Reagan responded by trying to load the commission with members sympathetic to his perspective. He replaced the commission's chair, Arthur S. Flemming, who was white, with a black Republican, Clarence Pendleton, former executive director of the San Diego Urban League. The vice chair, however, was Mary Frances Berry, a well-respected, long-time civil rights activist and historian. She had been appointed by Carter and frequently clashed with the new president. In 1984 Reagan tried to remove Berry from the CCR. She resisted, suing successfully in court to retain her position. Even with Berry, however, the CCR declined to virtual insignificance under Pendleton during the Reagan years.

Black Conservatives

Men like Bell, Thomas, and Pendleton were part of a vocal group of black, middle-class, conservative intellectuals, professionals, and politicians who gained prominence during the Reagan years. To strengthen their influence in the Republican Party, these conservatives cultivated a small, well-educated, articulate group of black men and women intellectuals in addition to black politicians. Prominent black proponents of conservative ideology include Thomas Sowell, Walter Williams, Shelby Steele, Armstrong Williams, Ward Connerly, and, until he broke with

▶ **Document**

23-1 *William Julius Wilson, The Urban Underclass*
In 1978 sociologist and urban researcher, William Julius Wilson argued that race was not as important as class and economics in regards to the black urban poor. In 1987 he continued his discourse on government welfare programs that would ameliorate urban poverty.

▶ **Retracing the Odyssey**

The *Amistad* Research Center. Tilton Hall, Tulane University, New Orleans. The *Amistad* Center contains manuscripts and art that illuminate the history and culture of diverse ethnic groups and race relations in the United States. Approximately 90 percent of its holdings document the history and records of African Americans' community organizations and struggles. The Center also houses records related to religious denominations—Protestant, Catholic, and Jewish. Its art gallery frequently exhibits the work of early black artists, such as Aaron Douglas.

the others in the late 1990s, Glenn Loury. There was a critical difference, however, between elite black Republicans and the black politicians in the Democratic camp. Black Republican politicians rarely exercised meaningful power within the party. They were expected to embrace the existing values and goals set down by the white party leaders. In contrast, elite black Democratic politicians could, and often did, make their influence felt. Moreover, they represented a large and essential constituency within the party.

The Thomas–Hill Controversy

The role of black conservatives acquired its greatest visibility when, in 1991, President George H. W. Bush nominated Clarence Thomas to the U.S. Supreme Court. The symbolism of Thomas, who opposed the expansion of civil rights, replacing Thurgood Marshall, the greatest civil rights lawyer of the twentieth century, could not have been more dramatic.

As a justice on the United States Supreme Court Clarence Thomas has staunchly adhered to conservative values in all of his opinions.

George Bush's nomination of Thomas began the most public exposure of gender conflict within the black community in history. Marshall had been one of the Court's great liberals and a staunch defender of civil rights. Thomas was a black conservative whose record on civil rights did not endear him to white liberals, or to many within the black community. His credentials for the position were also open to question. He had served only fifteen months as an appellate court judge. However, he was a black man, and the black community was loath publicly to contest his nomination or to challenge the tokenism of the Bush administration. Still, civil rights organizations expressed grave reservations about the Thomas nomination. The anticipated easy confirmation process derailed when black law professor Anita Hill agreed to appear before the Senate Judiciary Committee, which heard testimony on Thomas's confirmation. Hill accused Thomas of sexually harassing her when she worked for him at the Equal Employment Opportunity Commission.

Both Anita Hill and Clarence Thomas were conservative Republicans, and both had earned law degrees at Yale. Hill did not volunteer to testify about Thomas's sexual harassment of her. She had answered questions put to her in a confidential investigation. When her answers were leaked to the press, she agreed to appear before the committee. Some senators questioned her own character and integrity. Thomas countered her charges with charges of his own. He declared he was a victim of a "high-tech lynching" in the media and that Hill's accusations were false. Although many in the black community supported Thomas, progressive feminists, white liberals, and some black people supported Hill. Activist black

Anita Hill's testimony about her experience of sexual harassment brought considerable controversy.

Black Women in Defense of Themselves

Within days after Anita Hill appeared before the Senate Judiciary Committee, a group of black women led by Elsa Barkley Brown, Barbara Ransby, and Deborah King raised more than $50,000 to purchase a three-quarter-page ad in the New York Times *to print this statement, "In Defense of Ourselves." Appearing on November 17, 1991, it was signed by 1,603 black women. Five black newspapers—the* San Francisco Sun Reporter, *the* Los Angeles Sentinel, *the* New York Sun, *the* Atlanta Inquirer, *and the* Chicago Defender—*also published the statement.*

As women of African descent, we are deeply troubled by the recent nomination, confirmation and seating of Clarence Thomas as an Associate Justice of the U.S. Supreme Court. We know that the presence of Clarence Thomas on the Court will be continually used to divert attention away from the historic struggles for social justice through suggestions that the presence of a Black man on the Supreme Court constitutes an assurance that the rights of African Americans will be protected. Clarence Thomas's public record is ample evidence that this will not be true. Further, the consolidation of a conservative majority on the Supreme Court endangers the working class people and the elderly. The seating of Clarence Thomas is an affront not only to African American women and men, but to all people concerned with social justice.

We are particularly outraged by the racist and sexist treatment of Professor Anita Hill, an African American woman who was maligned and castigated for daring to speak publicly of her own experience of sexual abuse. The malicious defamation of Professor Hill insulted all women of African descent and sent a dangerous message to all women who might contemplate a sexual harassment complaint.

We speak here because we recognize that the media are now portraying the Black community as prepared to tolerate the dismantling of affirmative action and the evil of sexual harassment in order to have any Black man on the Supreme Court. We want to make clear that the media have ignored and distorted many African American voices. We will not be silenced.

Many have erroneously portrayed the allegations against Clarence Thomas as an issue of either gender or race. As women of African descent, we understand sexual harassment as both. We further understand that Clarence Thomas outrageously manipulated the legacy of lynching in order to shelter himself from Anita Hill's allegations. To deflect attention away from the reality of sexual abuse in African American women's lives, he trivialized and

misrepresented this painful part of African American people's history. This country, which has a long legacy of racism and sexism, has never taken the sexual abuse of Black women seriously. Throughout U.S. history Black women have been sexually stereotyped as immoral, insatiable, perverse, the initiators in all sexual contacts—abusive or otherwise. The common assumption in legal proceedings as well as in the larger society has been that Black women cannot be raped or otherwise sexually abused. As Anita Hill's experience demonstrates, Black women who speak of these matters are not likely to be believed. In 1991, we cannot tolerate this type of dismissal of any one Black woman's experience or this attack upon our collective character without protest, outrage, and resistance.

As women of African descent, we express our vehement opposition to the policies represented by the placement of Clarence Thomas on the Supreme Court. The Bush administration, having obstructed the passage of civil rights legislation, impeded the extension of unemployment compensation, cut student aid and dismantled social welfare programs, has continually demonstrated that it is not operating in our best interests. Nor is this appointee. We pledge ourselves to continue to speak out in defense of one another, in defense of the African American community and against those who are hostile to social justice no matter what color they are. No one will speak for us but ourselves.

What Do You Think?

▶ Why did the African-American women who signed this letter feel the need to defend themselves?

▶ Why did they oppose the confirmation of Clarence Thomas to the Supreme Court?

▶ Why were they unsympathetic to Thomas's claim that he had been a victim of a "high-tech" lynching?

Source: *New York Times*, November 17, 1991 p. 53.

women were especially incensed by the treatment that Hill received from the Senate. They were determined to voice their opposition to Thomas's political views. Despite the opposition, Clarence Thomas won confirmation to the U.S. Supreme Court by a narrow 52 to 48 majority. On the Court, Thomas has proved to be an **archconservative** who consistently votes against progressive or liberal causes such as affirmative action.

 Reading Check   How did Reagan and Bush try to dismantle the "Great Society" and undermine social welfare programs?

▶ **What Do You Think?**

· They felt the need to defend themselves as they believed the media had ignored and distorted African American voices on this matter.

· They opposed the confirmation of Thomas to the Supreme Court as they feel he is an affront to all people concerned with social justice.

· They were unsympathetic to Thomas's claim that he had been a victim of a "high-tech" lynching as they felt he had intentionally used this metaphor to shelter himself from the allegations by deflecting attention away from the issues at hand.

▶ **Reading Check**

Reagan and Bush cut federal grants to cities and terminated programs crucial to the stability of many black families. They supported trickle-down economics, a theory that focused on improving the financial position of America's wealthiest people. And, they did what they could to undermine rights-oriented policies.

▶ **Recommended Readings**

Deborah Gray White. *Too Heavy a Load: Black Women in Defense of Themselves, 1894–1994.* New York: W. W. Norton, 1998. A brilliant study by a black woman historian of black women and the organizations they founded to fight for the ballot, against segregation, and against the sexism and misogyny of contemporary Black Nationalism.

▶ **Guide to Reading/Key Terms**

For answers, see the *Teacher's Resource Manual.*

▶ **Recommended Reading**

James F. Finley, Jr. *Church People in the Struggle: The National Council of Churches and the Black Freedom Movement, 1950–1970.* New York: Oxford University Press, 1993.

Section 2

Civil Rights

Debating the "Old" and the "New" Civil Rights

The Reagan and Bush administrations distinguished between what might be called the "old civil rights law," which they claimed to support, and the "new civil rights law," which they opposed. Developed in the decade between the *Brown* decision and the Voting Rights Act of 1965, the old civil rights law prohibited intentional discrimination, be it legal segregation in the schools, informal discrimination in the workplace, or racially biased restrictions on voting. The new civil rights law is concerned with discriminatory outcomes, as measured by statistical disparities, rather than with discriminatory intent. If, for example, black children overall are disproportionately in all-black schools, or if the workforce in a given firm, compared with the community in which it is located, is disproportionately white (or male), or if elected officials in a multiracial state or municipality are disproportionately white, discrimination is assumed.

The remedies for such historic discrimination, collectively labeled **affirmative action**, tend to be statistical in nature. They include increasing the number of minority pupils, minority employees, or (by redrawing the districts from which they were elected) minority elected officials to correspond to the percentage of the relevant minority population. In employment (and in admissions to colleges and universities), the methods used in reaching these goals became known as affirmative action "guidelines." Sometimes guidelines were imposed by court order; more often they were the result of voluntary efforts by legislatures, government agencies, business firms, and colleges and universities to comply with civil rights laws and court rulings.

Affirmative Action

Few civil rights policies in the twentieth century have proved more persistently controversial than affirmative action. Many white Americans oppose affirmative action, arguing it runs contrary to the concept of achievement founded on objective merit and amounts to reverse racial or sexual discrimination. Ironically, because gender discrimination in employment was made illegal in the 1964 Civil Rights Act, prompting

federal agencies to scrutinize the percentage of women in a given work-force, white women have been among the major beneficiaries of affirmative action. But the major advocates of affirmative action have been African Americans, most of whom see it as a remedy for centuries of discrimination. The debate over affirmative action has led to racial polarization. It even divided the black community.

Supreme Court Cases on Affirmative Action in Employment

1979 *United Steelworkers v. Weber* upholds preferential treatment in hiring and training by private firms

1980 *Fullilove v. Klutznick* upholds government programs that reserve places for minorities

1984 *Memphis Firefighters v. Stotts* rejects a judicial order for retaining less-senior black employees over white employees during layoffs

1986 *Wygant v. Jackson Board of Education* rejects school board's plan for laying off white teachers while retaining less senior black teachers, but it also rejects Reagan administration position that affirmative action be limited to actual victims of discrimination, thus broadly upholding affirmative action

1986 *Local 93 of International Association of Firefighters v. City of Cleveland* upholds promotion of minorities ahead of white applicants with higher test scores and greater seniority

1986 *Local 28 of Sheet Metal Workers v. EEOC* upholds order that union meet minority quota for membership

1987 *U.S. v. Paradise* upholds judicial order imposing racial quotas in hiring and promotions of Alabama state troopers

1987 *Johnson v. Transportation Agency of Santa Clara County* upholds plan that promoted women over men

1987 *American Tobacco Co. v. Patterson* upholds seniority plans in place before 1964 unless discriminatory intent can be shown

1989 *Martin v. Wilks* rules that employees may challenge affirmative action plan after it has gone into effect. This decision is overruled by Congress in the Civil Rights Act of 1991

1989 *Richmond v. J. Croson and Co.* rules that Fourteenth Amendment prohibits set-asides for minority contractors, thus going against spirit of *Weber* and against the letter of *Fullilove v. Klutznick* and implying that all such plans face "strict scrutiny"

1990 *Metro Broadcasting v. FCC* upholds affirmative action plan increasing minority broadcasting owners, returning to *Fullilove*

1995 *Adarand Constructors v. Pena* strikes down a congressional statute requiring 10 percent of federal highway money to go to minority contractors and broadly asserts that any such programs using racial classifications are constitutionally suspect

2003 *Grutter v. Bollinger* upholds the University of Michigan Law School's use of racial preferences in admissions to achieve a more diverse student body

▶ **Document**

22-6 *Affirmative Action in Atlanta, "Can Atlanta Succeed Where America Has Failed?"*
In 1974 Maynard Jackson became Atlanta, Georgia's first black mayor. Jackson was part of growing trend that sent African Americans to city hall in record numbers. With a new city charter that enhanced the mayor's power, Jackson implanted a series of sweeping changes. His early programs called for increasing the number of black municipal employees and black contractors.

The term affirmative action was first used by President Lyndon Johnson in a 1965 executive order. It required federal contractors to "take affirmative action" to guarantee that job seekers and employees "are treated without regard to their race, color, religion, sex, or national origin." Much of the credit for compliance with affirmative action belongs to conservative Republican president Richard Nixon. In 1969 Arthur A. Fletcher, a black assistant secretary of labor in the Nixon administration, developed the **Philadelphia Plan**. Firms with federal government contracts in the construction industry would have to set and meet hiring goals for African Americans or be penalized. The plan became a model for subsequent **set-aside programs** that reserved some contracts for minority-owned businesses or that favored the hiring of women and minorities. The process of setting goals and timetables to achieve full compliance with federal civil rights requirements appealed to large corporations and accounted for the early success of affirmative action initiatives.

The Backlash

Although it has produced more litigation, affirmative action in employment has been less controversial than affirmative action in college and university admissions. State higher education institutions have been at the center of the controversy. They are narrowly bound by the Fourteenth Amendment's prohibitions on racial discrimination, and they represent the gateways to upward mobility for millions of Americans, white and black. As the 1970s progressed, in the interest both of aiding disadvantaged minorities and of increasing racial and cultural diversity on campus, admissions offices began using different criteria for white and minority admissions. Conservatives called these criteria **racial preferences**. They argued that such policies did more harm than good and created new unfairness and white resentment of African Americans.

Negative reaction to affirmative action mushroomed in the late 1970s. The case of *Regents of the University of California v. Bakke* was a key part of this backlash. The medical school at the University of California, as a form of affirmative action, had set aside sixteen of its one hundred places in each entering class for disadvantaged and minority students. They were considered for admission in a separate system. A white male student named Alan Bakke sued the university for discrimination after it rejected his application for admission. In 1976 the California Supreme Court ruled he should be admitted to the university. The university appealed the ruling to the U.S. Supreme Court, which also ruled in Bakke's favor in 1978. Of the nine justices, five agreed the university violated Bakke's rights.

California remains the center of the affirmative action storm because of its multiracial population. In 1995 Republican governor Pete Wilson ended affirmative action in state employment. In 1996 California voters approved Proposition 209, the so-called California Civil Rights Initiative, which banned all state agencies from implementing affirma-

Black, Asian, Hispanic, and white women protest in support of affirmative action at a meeting of the University of California's board of trustees at UCLA in 1994.

tive action programs. The campaign for the proposition was led by Ward Connerly, a conservative black entrepreneur who had received over $140,000 from state contracts set aside for minority businesses. Nonetheless, Connerly maintained that affirmative action exacerbated the negative stereotyping of African Americans. He and his supporters insisted moreover that affirmative action had failed to address problems of poverty, unemployment, and inadequate education. Instead, it had merely elevated to higher status those least in need of assistance, especially middle-class white women. Finally, Connerly accepted the broader argument that affirmative action assaulted the concept of individual merit and violated core American values of equality and opportunity.

Fifty-four percent of California voters agreed with Connerly, and after the U.S. Supreme Court upheld Proposition 209, it went into effect. Its effect and that of similar laws or court rulings around the nation are now known. The number of African Americans and other protected minorities admitted to the whole University of California system dropped since the proposition was upheld by the U.S. Supreme Court, and the numbers at Berkeley, U.C.'s most prestigious campus, fell precipitously. In both California and Texas, which abandoned affirmative action in its university system after a court challenge, administrators have attempted to assure a diverse student body by other means. Both states now offer admission to their top schools to all students in the top ranks of their high school class.

On June 23, 2003, the U.S. Supreme Court, in two separate decisions, handed the University of Michigan both a major victory, when it upheld the law school's practice of using race as a criterion in admissions procedures to create a diverse student body, and a defeat, when it banned the university from awarding points based on race as a criterion for admitting undergraduates. In the first case, *Grutter v. Bollinge*, a 5–4 decision declared that the University of Michigan Law School could use race to achieve diversity, thus firmly endorsing the long-standing *Bakke* decision written by Justice Powell. Justice Sandra Day O'Connor's majority opinion declared that the Equal Protection Clause of the Fourteenth Amendment to the U.S. Constitution did not prohibit the law school's narrowly tailored use of race in admissions decisions. She was persuaded that the law school acted out of a compelling interest to obtain the educational benefits that accrued from a diverse student population and meaningful integration. However, writing for the majority in the second case, *Gratz v. Bollinger*, Chief Justice Rehnquist appeared to contradict O'Connor's opinion. Rehnquist maintained that in admitting undergraduates the university crossed the line of what was permissible by giving points to black applicants: "The university's policy, which automatically distributed 20 points, or one-fifth of the points needed to guarantee admission, to every single 'underrepresented minority' applicant solely because of race, is not narrowly tailored to achieve the interest in educational diversity that respondents claim justifies their program."

Black Political Activism in the Age of Conservative Reaction

Presidents Reagan and Bush did not completely reverse or halt the advancement of the civil rights agenda. The increased participation of black men and women in the upper echelons of the Democratic Party reflected the extent to which they had overcome political exclusion. In 1964 there were only 103 black elected officials in the nation; by 1994 there were nearly 8,500. Forty-one African Americans were serving in Congress by 1996. In 1988 Representative William H. Gray of Pennsylvania became chair of the House Democratic caucus, making him the first African American to reach the top ranks of congressional leadership. In June 1989 Gray became majority whip of the House of Representatives. In February 1989 Ronald H. Brown became the first African American to lead a major national political party when he was elected chairman of the Democratic Party. That same year, David Dinkins was elected the first black mayor of New York City. In 1990 Sharon Pratt Dixon (Kelly) was elected mayor of Washington, D.C., becoming the first woman and the first District of Columbia native to serve in that position. By the mid-1990s, black men and women held the mayor's office in four hundred towns and cities. Clearly, the days of black political powerlessness had ended. Or had they?

During the Reagan–Bush era, one house of Congress—and often both—was in the hands of the Democratic Party. Reflecting the importance of African-American voters to the party, that house used its power to pass many equal rights laws. Among the most important of these statutes were the Voting Rights Act of 1982, the Civil Rights Restoration Act of 1988, and the Fair Housing Act of 1988. The Civil Rights Restoration Act of 1988 authorized the withholding of federal funds from an entire institution if any program within it discriminated against women, racial minorities, the aged, or the disabled. The Fair Housing Act of 1988 provided for enforcing fair housing laws. It stipulated that either an individual or the Department of Housing and Urban Development (HUD) could bring a complaint of housing discrimination and authorize administrative judges to investigate housing complaints, issue injunctions and fines, and award punitive damages. With both laws, Congress was responding to Supreme Court decisions that had narrowed the scope of earlier legislation. The Civil Rights Act of 1991 was likewise a response to a spate of restrictive Supreme Court decisions. In it, Democrats secured the protection of many of the defenses of civil rights the court had called into question.

The King Holiday

Many African Americans invested symbolic importance in an effort to make Martin Luther King Jr.'s birthday a national holiday, elevating him to the stature of Presidents George Washington and Abraham Lincoln, both of whom are honored with a holiday. At first Reagan resisted the

effort, but he eventually gave in to pressure from African Americans and their white allies. On November 2, 1983, Reagan signed a law designating the third Monday in January to honor the great civil rights leader. On January 20, 1985, the United States officially observed Martin Luther King Jr. Day for the first time. In 1988 more than sixty thousand people made the pilgrimage to Washington, D.C., to commemorate the twenty-fifth anniversary of the 1963 March on Washington and to remember Martin Luther King Jr.'s "I Have a Dream" speech.

TransAfrica and the Antiapartheid Movement

Black activism persisted on the international as well as the national front. Much of this effort focused on ending the oppressive conditions of **apartheid**—the complete social, political, and economic isolation of black people—in South Africa. A particularly detestable aspect of apartheid was its glorification of white racial supremacy, an ideology reminiscent of Adolf Hitler's Germany and the American South before the late 1960s.

Randall Robinson worked as an assistant for Michigan congressman Charles Diggs. He sought to link African-American liberation struggles with those waged by Africans in South Africa and elsewhere. In 1977 he founded **TransAfrica** to lobby for black political prisoners in South Africa, chief among them Nelson Mandela. In 1984 Robinson was joined by Mary Francis Berry of the U.S. Commission on Civil Rights, Eleanor Holmes Norton, and others for a year-long series of sit-ins at the South African Embassy in Washington, D.C., during which hundreds were arrested.

The **antiapartheid movement** became a major priority for African-American activists. They were able to enlist the sympathy and help of white Americans on college campuses and to pressure many universities into divesting their investments in South Africa. Similar pressures were put on corporations, especially those vulnerable to consumer boycotts. In 1986 the Black Congressional Caucus persuaded their colleagues to enact a U.S. trade embargo against South Africa and sustain it over President Reagan's veto.

In 1990, bowing to international pressure and a souring domestic economy, South African president F. W. de Klerk removed the ban on the African National Congress, the key opposition party, and a few days afterward ended the twenty-eight-year prison term of its leader, Nelson Mandela. Soon thereafter, South Africa was transformed into a multiracial democracy, and Mandela was elected its president.

 **Reading Check** What were the focal points of black activism during the Reagan and Bush years?

Nelson Mandela's release from prison was celebrated around the globe as the event that signaled the final days of South Africa's system of racial apartheid.

⮞ **Reading Check**

In the 1980s, African Americans used their power in the Democratic Party to promote civil rights legislation, including the Voting Rights Act of 1982, the Civil Rights Restoration Act of 1988, and the Fair Housing Act of 1988. African-American activists also pushed to make Martin Luther King Jr.'s birthday a national holiday and focused attention on apartheid in South Africa.

▶ **Guide to Reading/Key Terms**

For answers, see the *Teacher's Resource Manual.*

▶ **Documents**

23-3 *Jesse Jackson, Address before the Democratic National Convention, July 18, 1984* Late in the evening of July 17, 1984, Jesse Jackson spoke to the delegates at Democratic National Convention in San Francisco. For the better part of an hour, Rev. Jackson converted the convention hall into a great tent revival. Jackson's emotional oration, reminiscent of an old-time gospel preacher, galvanized his audience in the name of party unity. Throughout the speech, the television audience kept increasing—reaching 33 million viewers by the end. Many compared the speech to one of the greatest ever delivered at a nominating convention. "If you are a human being and weren't affected by what you just heard, you may be beyond redemption," declared Florida Governor Bob Graham.

23-5 *Jesse Jackson, Common Ground, 1988* Jesse Jackson delivered this speech at the 1988 Democratic National Convention.

Section 3

Jesse Jackson and the Rainbow Coalition

As Reagan's first term ended, Jesse Jackson made history by announcing he would campaign for the presidency of the United States. The first African American to seek the presidential nomination of a major political party was congresswoman Shirley Chisholm, in 1972. Chisholm had little money and only a small campaign organization, and she was never taken as a serious candidate by her male competitors or the press. Her campaign had nonetheless helped raise the visibility of African-American voters. She captured more than 150 votes on the first ballot at the Democratic National Convention. In the thoroughly male world of presidential politics, however, a black man was a more credible contender.

Jesse Jackson's preparation for political battle was not the traditional climb from one elective office to another. Rather, he came up through the ranks of the civil rights movement, working alongside Martin Luther King Jr. in the Southern Christian Leadership Conference (SCLC) and heading Operation Breadbasket, an organization that attempted to mobilize Chicago's black poor. After King's death, Jackson founded **People United to Save (later Serve) Humanity (PUSH)**. This Chicago-based organization induced major corporations with large markets in the black community to adopt affirmative action programs. PUSH-EXCEL, which focused on education, succeeded in raising students' test scores and was given a large grant by the Carter administration.

In 1983, angered by the effects of Reagan's social welfare and civil rights rollbacks, Jackson and PUSH began a successful drive to register black voters. Jackson's charismatic style engendered enthusiasm, especially as the Democratic Party searched for a presidential candidate who could challenge Reagan's popularity.

On November 4, 1983, Jackson declared his candidacy for the Democratic nomination and honed an already effective style of grassroots mobilization. He began by appealing to what he would call a "rainbow coalition" of people who felt politically marginalized and underrepresented. The **Rainbow Coalition** was composed of diverse groups, including black people, white workers, liberals, Latinos, feminists, students, and environmentalists. Jackson developed a comprehensive eco-

Section 4

Policing the Black Community

GUIDE TO READING

▶ What is police profiling and how did it affect African Americans?

▶ What was the Rodney King episode and why was it important?

KEY TERMS

▶ Amnesty International, p. 860

The Rodney King Incident

In March 1991 Los Angeles police pulled Rodney Glen King from his car after a high-speed chase and beat him with nightsticks. A bystander, George Holliday, captured the incident on videotape. Television newscasts broadcast the videotape repeatedly, increasing long-simmering anger over police brutality among African Americans in Los Angeles. When a jury of eleven white Americans and one Hispanic American acquitted the four police officers involved in the incident of all but one of the charges brought against them, south-central Los Angeles burst into flames of protest. The verdict highlighted the gulf between the perceptions of white and black Americans about the police and the criminal justice system. Where the mostly white jury had seen the police imposing justice and maintaining law and order, black Americans saw proof of injustice, police repression, and racism. Fifty-two people were killed in the outbreak that followed the verdict. Arsonists and looters devastated much of the community. Thousands of people were injured, four thousand were arrested, and an estimated half-billion dollars worth of property was damaged or destroyed. The four officers were later retried in federal court on charges of violating King's civil rights. This time juries found two of them guilty and acquitted the other two. Meanwhile, a jury in King's civil suit ordered the city of Los Angeles to pay him $3.8 million in damages.

The Rodney King episode resonated with many black men across the country. Writer Earl Ofari Hutchinson suggested why:

> Black professionals or business owners still tell harrowing tales of being spread-eagle over the hoods of their expensive BMW's or Porsches while the police ran makes on them and tore their cars apart searching for drugs. In polls taken after the Rodney King beating, blacks were virtually unanimous in saying that they believed any black person could have been on the ground that night being pulverized by the police. These were eternal reminders to the "new" black bourgeoisie that they could escape the hood, but many Americans still considered them hoods.

Several such high-profile cases focused public attention on the relation of black communities to police authorities throughout the 1980s and 1990s. In a sense the issue of police repression remained a constant. On November 16, 1992, two Detroit police officers were formally

▶▶ **Guide to Reading/Key Terms**

For answers, see the *Teacher's Resource Manual.*

▶▶ **Recommended Reading**

Mary Pattillo, David Weiman, and Bruce Western, editors. *Imprisoning America: The Social Effects of Mass Incarceration.* New York: Russel Sage Foundation, 2004. Important essays that explore the sociological, political, and economic consequences of the mass incarceration of African-American men and other minorities. These studies demonstrate the need for new policies to deal with ex-prisoners, their families, and communities.

revealed that as many as two-thirds remained unemployed. As for the bill's effect on families, it is true that most women on welfare had their first children when they were unmarried teenagers. But little evidence indicates that cutting welfare prevents teenage pregnancies. There is evidence that reforms targeted at improving the collection of child support payments for divorced mothers would reduce welfare costs far more effectively and humanely.

Clinton's support of the welfare act was consistent with his centrist ideology. It also protected him from Republican attacks on the issue and had little impact on his support among African Americans. Clinton endorsed other policies that had negative impact on African Americans but seemed, at least symbolically, to reassure white moderates. He signed a crime bill that allowed local communities to hire more police officers, build more prisons, and implement the **three strikes policy** of stiffer penalties for those who had at least two prior criminal convictions. He also failed, in the face of intense Republican opposition, to enact comprehensive health-care legislation. Yet black support for him remained strong. Clinton easily defeated his Republican opponent, Senator Robert Dole of Kansas, in the election of 1996.

The preliminary results of the new welfare reform provisions indicated that within a couple of years half of those who had taken jobs had returned to lives of unemployment, poverty, and quiet desperation. As the economy took a downturn in the closing months of Clinton's second term and in the opening years of the new millennium, conditions of poor mothers and children deteriorated steadily. The debate over welfare policy receded to the back burner during the 2000 election campaign. It disappeared completely after George W. Bush took office, replaced by the emphasis on tax cuts for the wealthy.

 Reading Check What were the results of the Personal Responsibility Act of 1996?

Republicans Challenge Clinton

Congressional Republicans and radical conservatives hated Clinton's presidency and many of them hated Clinton himself. They vowed to take back the White House. Early on, Republicans began raising huge sums of money and energetically organized local constituencies, especially in the South. The Democrats seemed demoralized and did little to mobilize their base, especially in the black community. Many African Americans did not vote in the midterm congressional elections in 1994, and the Democrats lost control of Congress. For the first time in forty years, the Republicans could implement their conservative legislative agenda, which included rolling back environmental protection policies, reducing the capital gains tax for the rich, and cutting benefits for the elderly. Some younger Democratic Party leaders began to fight back. In 1994 thirty-year-old Jesse Jackson Jr. won a seat in Congress representing a southside Chicago district. Jackson outlined a comprehensive social

▶ Reading Check

The program promised to move poor people from welfare to work. However, preliminary results indicated that half of those who had taken jobs had returned to unemployment and poverty within a couple of years. As the economy took a downturn in late 2000, conditions for poor mothers and children deteriorated.

▶ Document

23-6 *Elaine Bell Kaplan, "Talking to Teen Mothers"*
Sociologist Kaplan discusses the problems of teenage pregnancy.

The Congressional Black Caucus of the 106th Congress assemble for an official photograph on the steps of the Capitol building. (James Clyburn, William Clay, Maxine Waters, Earl Hilliard, Corrine Brown, John Lewis, Sheila Jackson Lee, Stephanie Tubbs Jones, Juanita Millender McDonald, Barbara Lee, William Jefferson, Donna Christian Christensen, Gregory Meek, Julian Dixon, Cynthia McKinney, Edolphus Towns, Danny Davis, Charles Rangel).

democratic agenda for black America that included full employment, health care, high quality public education, decent and affordable housing, a safe and sustainable encvironment, the right to vote, and equality of sexes before the law. But Democrats were now in a minority.

Republicans drew further strength from the appointment of Kenneth Starr as an independent counsel to investigate allegations surrounding Bill and Hillary Clinton's investment in an Arkansas land development deal known as Whitewater. Although no proof was found that the Clintons had broken the law, Starr relentlessly pursued every hint or rumor of misdeed. As the investigations escalated, Clinton made the tactical mistake of denying sexual involvement with a White House intern, Monica Lewinsky. On December 19, 1998, the Republican majority in the House of Representatives narrowly voted to impeach Clinton for perjury and obstruction of justice for tampering with witnesses to conceal his relationship with Lewinsky. But the Senate refused to convict him. He remained in office. In the midst of the turmoil, Clinton had the unwavering support of black people, the Congressional Black Caucus, and his friends, including Vernon Jordan and Jesse Jackson.

 Reading Check Why were African Americans so supportive of Bill Clinton's presidency and attached to the Democratic Party?

▶ **Reading Check**

Most black people considered Clinton, despite major disappointments, the best president on race issues since President Johnson. Clinton appointed African Americans to important positions throughout his administration, not just to positions that had something to do with race. He supported economic policies that decreased unemployment and helped the poor and the working-poor.

GUIDE TO READING

▶ How did George W. Bush win the presidential election in 2000?

▶ What were the key issues in the election of 2004?

KEY TERMS

▶ *Gore v. Bush*, p. 868

▶ No Child Left Behind Act, p. 871

▶ **Guide to Reading/Key Terms**

For answers, see the *Teacher's Resource Manual*

▶ **Teaching Notes**

The Chair of the Commission, Mary Frances Berry, wrote in an essay in *The Journal of American History* (Vol. 88, no. 2, September 2001), "The United States Supreme Court helped undermine the pursuit of equal opportunity by African Americans for most of our history. . . . *Bush v. Gore* was so striking, in part, because the 5-4 majority has been assiduous about deference to state courts and states' rights in general. What the Court has done is to remind us that judges have social and political views that are reflected in their decisions. Each side has used the equal protection clause of the Fourteenth Amendment to convey its policy preferences. But, unlike the majority, in cases involving African American voting and the outcome of the 2000 election, the justices in dissent have remained consistent."

Section 6
The Bush Years

The Contested 2000 Presidential Election

The election of 2000 focused largely on economic issues—social security, taxes, health care (HMO reform and a prescription-drug benefit for seniors), and education. Black community leaders and organizations worked hard to register voters and to increase turnout for the 2000 election. The NAACP, for example, spent $9 million on Operation Big Vote. Organizers even registered more than eleven thousand inmates in county jails in the South.

In a hotly contested election, the outcome hung on one state: Florida. In the end, the U.S. Supreme Court, in a 5-to-4 ruling [*Bush v. Gore*, 121 S. Ct. 525 (2000)], decided the issue by halting the recount of ballots in Florida. The Court's majority based its ruling on the Fourteenth Amendment's prohibition of states denying citizens equal protection of the law. The Court insisted the recount had to be stopped because the Florida Supreme Court, which had authorized it, had failed to provide uniform standards for determining the intent of the voters. Bush was declared the winner in Florida by fewer than six hundred votes, which gave him a four-vote majority in the electoral college.

Bill Clinton called *Gore v. Bush* "an appalling decision." He compared its impact on African Americans to the infamous Dred Scott and *Plessy v. Ferguson* decisions of the nineteenth century. Indeed, African Americans reported serious discrimination and interference with their voting in Florida. A lawsuit filed in Jacksonville, Florida, claimed that many votes were thrown out as "undervotes" or "overvotes," especially in four districts with the highest concentration of African Americans in the state. According to the lawsuit, 26,000 ballots were not counted in Duval County. More than 9,000 of those were cast in largely African-American precincts where Gore had captured more than 90 percent of the vote. Indeed, the U.S. Civil Rights Commission found that tens of thousands of African Americans were disfranchised in Florida. In a draft report, it declared, "African American voting districts were disproportionately hindered by antiquated and error-prone equipment like the punch card ballot system." This meant that more

black and low-income voters, who tended to vote Democratic, had their ballots invalidated.

 Reading Check How did George W. Bush win the presidential election in 2000?

Republican Triumph

In the 2000 elections, Republicans also retained narrow majorities in both the House and the Senate. Gore v. Bush thus not only put George W. Bush in the White House. It also meant that for the first time since the early 1950s, the Republican Party was in control of the presidency and of both houses of Congress.

President Bush was aware that few African Americans had voted for him. But this did not prevent him from appointing black men and women to key posts within his administration. Such appointments tended to mute black criticism. They also satisfied white swing voters who disdained racial exclusion. Bush named the highly regarded General Colin L. Powell to be secretary of state. Powell had served as chairman of the Joint Chiefs of Staff (1989–1993), the highest military position in the Department of Defense. During his tenure he oversaw Operation Desert Storm, the

▶ **Reading Check**

The hotly contested election of 2004 came down to one state, Florida. In a 5-4 decision, the Supreme Court ruled in Bush v. Gore that the recount of ballots in that state should be halted. Bush was declared the winner in Florida by fewer than six hundred votes, which gave him an electoral college majority. Many observers believed that voting improprieties in Florida disfranchised substantial numbers of African Americans, denying Gore votes that would have resulted in his victory.

PROFILE ❖ Donna Brazile

In a history-making move, Gore selected the first African-American woman to head a major presidential campaign, Donna Brazile. Born in 1960 in Louisiana, she graduated from Louisiana State University and worked on the presidential campaigns of Jesse Jackson, Michael Dukakis, and Bill Clinton. Recalling Jesse Jackson's bid for the Democratic Party's presidential nomination in her memoir, *Cooking with Grease: Stirring the Pot in American Politics*, Brazile declared, "Reverend Jackson was at the time the best at mobilization and politics, and he understood the marriage between electoral politics and grassroots progressive movements. He created a coalition of conscience, bringing together white women, Hispanics, environmentalists, peace activists, gays, lesbians, and organized labor."

Brazile took what she had learned from Jackson and deployed her own skill as a political organizer to turn out the black vote. George W. Bush, she said, would "rather take pictures with black children than feed them." Brazile understood her role inside the campaign and the larger political picture. " I knew how to organize on the ground. . . . I was fighting for prosperity, health care, job security, freedom and equality for all. I was cooking with grease." Her efforts to get out the vote succeeded. Although the U.S. Supreme Court eventually awarded Bush the presidency, Gore won the popular vote, including 90 percent of the African-American vote.

Brazile

869

Colin Powell and Condoleezza Rice occupied high-ranking positions within George W. Bush's first administration.

victorious 1991 Persian Gulf War. Secretary Powell not only assisted in the formulation of foreign policy, but he also "represented the race."

Bush also tapped a black woman, Condoleezza Rice, to be his national security adviser. Rice was the first African American and the first woman to hold this post. During the 2000 election, Rice had formed a strong personal bond with Bush. This relationship became the foundation of her power in his administration.

An expert on European affairs, especially the Soviet Union, Rice had been sharply critical of the Clinton administration's policies and peace-keeping efforts in Bosnia and Haiti. Foreign policy under Clinton, she charged, had "assiduously failed" to separate "the important from the trivial . . . we don't need to have the 82nd Airborne escorting kids to kinder-garten." But Rice should have paid closer attention to Samuel Berger, Clinton's national security adviser, when he warned, "America is in a deadly struggle with a new breed of anti-Western jihadist—nothing less than a war . . . as a nation . . . we are engaged in a wholly new battle against an inter-national terrorist network in dozens of countries, which is deeply commit-ted to injuring and destroying the United States and its allies. This is one of the most serious threats the next administration will face." As September 11, 2001, was to show, Rice should have heeded Berger's warning.

Education Reform: Leave No Child Behind

Bush had made many pledges during the 2000 presidential campaign, none more important than his vow to reform public education. This was an issue of vital importance to both black and white families. Black

parents were especially alarmed over the resegregation of black children in urban schools. Thus many were heartened when Bush selected black fellow Texan Rod Paige as the secretary of education.

As secretary, Paige introduced the **No Child Left Behind Act**, an education reform that Bush ardently embraced. This legislation spoke directly to the concerns of white working- and middle-class Americans. It underscored their demand for student and teacher competency testing, that is, the use of testing as an assessment tool to measure performance. The legislation required all schools to test students at regular intervals in reading, math, and science. States also have to publish the test results and sanction schools whose students fail to do well on the tests. Implicitly the measure rejected integration as a primary social policy objective and retreated from mandatory busing while promoting parents' freedom to enroll their children in the schools of their choice through voucher programs.

Some African Americans, such as Anthony Williams, the mayor of Washington, D.C., supported the school voucher program. He argued that competition with strong schools would force weaker schools to improve their performance. However, Reginald Weaver, the black president of the National Educational Association, argued the voucher program ignored the needs of most of the students in poor schools. No Child Left Behind was soon mired in controversy. Critics, including many conservatives, blasted the measure for setting unrealistic goals and for not including sufficient federal funding to help schools meet the higher standards.

Reparations

While party politics attracted attention, many African Americans shifted their focus to specific issues including **reparations** (compensation) for slavery and the spread of HIV/AIDS in the United States and in Africa. In 1969 James Foreman, in his "Black Manifesto," called on America's churches and synagogues to collect $500 million as "a beginning of the reparations due us as a people who have been exploited and degraded, brutalized, killed, and persecuted." Although Foreman's call was widely publicized, churches made no serious effort to respond to his demand. Four years later, Boris Bittker, a Yale Law School professor, raised the issue again. He argued in *The Case for Black Reparations* that slavery and the persistence of government-sanctioned racial discrimination justified the creation of a program to provide compensation to black Americans. Since 1993 John Conyers, a black Democratic congressman from Detroit, has introduced a bill in every session of Congress—not to pay reparations, but to establish a federal commission to investigate slavery and the legacy of racial discrimination. The bill has never come to the floor of the House of Representatives for a vote.

In 2000 the issue of reparations for slavery was resurrected and finally received widespread attention when Randall Robinson, founder and president of TransAfrica, published *The Debt: What America Owes to*

▶ **Recommended Reading**

Martha Biondi, "The Rise of the Reparations Movement." *Radical History Review*, 87 (Fall 2003): 5-18. A superb historical overview of the black reparations movement from the Civil War to the present.

Blacks. Robinson reasoned that because Jews and Japanese Americans have been compensated for the indignities and horrors they experienced in World War II, African Americans were also due financial indemnification for slavery, for "246 years of an enterprise murderous both of a people and their culture." Robinson maintained that many African Americans still bear the scars of slavery in terms of poor housing, inadequate health care, and insufficient educational opportunities. He insists that reparations would remedy the effect of such inequalities. Temple University professor and Afrocentrist Molefi Asante proposed that instead of "a one-time cash payout" that the American government make long-term commitments for "educational, health care, land or property grants, and a combination of such grants." He elaborated, "What I have argued for is the establishment of some type of organization that would evaluate how reparations would be determined and distributed: the National Commission of African Americans (NCAA) would be the overarching national organization to serve as the clearinghouse for reparations."

Some black writers and journalists adamantly reject arguments that reparations are a realistic resolution of the nation's slave and racist legacy. Two black journalists, William Raspberry and Juan Williams, object to the very idea of reparations. Instead, Raspberry favors a greater investment in education for African Americans, "not because of debts owed to or incurred by our ancestors, but because America needs its citizens to be educated and productive." Williams declared, "The suffering of long-dead ancestors is not a claim check for a bag full of cash. I don't want any money that belongs to any slave. That is obscene. The struggle of African-Americans for civil rights is not about selling out for a check."

HIV/AIDs in America and Africa

Jesse Jackson, along with scholars, health-care professionals, social activists, and others, drew attention to the HIV/AIDs epidemic and its disastrous impact on black America and in Africa. Jackson believed HIV/AIDs was as much a political issue as it was a matter of health care. His words reflected a mature black internationalism that emphasized the bonds of health and disease across the African Diaspora. He declared,

> As it is in Africa, AIDS is now the leading cause of death for African Americans between twenty-five and forty-four in the United States. Almost two-thirds (63 percent) of all women reported with AIDS are African American; 62 percent of all reported pediatric cases are African-American children; 1 in 50 African-American men and 1 in 160 African-American women are estimated to be HIV infected. Like Africans, many African Americans do not know their HIV status; like Africans, many African Americans cannot access care or afford adequate treatment. Like Africans, many African Americans

▶ **Recommended Reading**

Cathy J. Cohen. *The Boundaries of Blackness: AIDS and the Breakdown of Black Politics.* Chicago: University of Chicago Press, 1999. A black political scientist provides a sophisticated and provocative exploration into the social, political, and cultural impact of the AIDS epidemic on the African-American community.

are in poverty, and many of their communities lack the infrastructure needed to meet the needs of those infected and afflicted by AIDS. Simply speaking, as we begin to understand our commonalities, our differences will no longer be a continent away.

Of the fifteen leading causes of death, African Americans have the highest incidence rates in thirteen. Paraphrasing Martin Luther King Jr., Rodney Hood, former president of the National Medical Association, concluded, "Of all forms of inequity, injustice in health care is the most shocking and inhumane." (For more on African Americans and health care, see Chapter 24.)

September 11, 2001

Americans were stunned on a Tuesday morning in September 2001, when four commercial airliners were commandeered by terrorists and crashed into New York's World Trade Center, the Pentagon in Washington, and rural Pennsylvania. Several hundred African Americans perished among the three thousand people who died that day.

If the debate over reparations dramatized the separate pasts that black and white Americans have experienced, then the tragedy of September 11, 2001, reminded them of their common future. But the sense of national unity did not last. Less than two years later, as the United States prepared to invade Iraq, activist and scholar Manning Marable wrote of the lessons he had learned from the 9/11 tragedy: "No political ideology, no crusade, no belief in a virtuous cause, can justify the moral bankruptcy of terror. Yet, because of the military actions of our own government, any claims to moral superiority have now disintegrated, in the minds of much of the black and brown world."

The War in Iraq

Following September 11, Americans expected President Bush to devise an effective strategy against the Taliban regime in Afghanistan and to destroy Osama bin Laden and the al-Qaeda network. The president and Secretary of Defense Donald Rumsfeld pledged retribution, and the war in Afghanistan began on October 7, 2001. The Taliban government was easily overthrown, but bin Laden and the Taliban leader, Mullah Omar, proved elusive, even though tens of thousands of American troops hunted them in the mountains of Afghanistan.

Still, the Bush administration called its Afghan war a success even though the Taliban soon launched a new guerrilla war. Much of Afghanistan remained in the control of warlords and insurgents. However, critics argued that the Bush adminstration's real target after 9/11 was not Afghanistan and al-Qaeda but Saddam Hussein's Iraq and that Bush and National Security Adviser Condoleezza Rice had failed to take seriously the reports of a planned terrorist attack before September

▶▶ **Recommended Readings**

Condoleezza Rice. "Why We Know Iraq is Lying," *The New York Times*, January 23, 2003.

Andrea Y. Simpson. *The Tie That Binds: Identity and Political Attitudes in the Post–Civil Rights Generation.* New York: New York University Press, 1998.

11, 2001. Al-Qaeda, which claimed responsibility for the bombing of U.S. embassies in Kenya and Tanzania in 1998 and for an attack on the USS *Cole* in Yemen in 2000, should have been the national security priority. Rice strenuously denied these charges, but early in 2002 the administration began to shift the nation's attention from Afghanistan to war with Iraq.

The prospect of war aroused mass protests at home and strong opposition abroad. The United Nations refused to back the United States despite strenuous diplomatic lobbying led by Secretary of State Colin Powell. In a speech before the UN Security Council in February 2003, Powell argued, based on what turned out to be misleading intelligence reports, that Saddam not only had weapons of mass destruction, but he also had ties to international terrorist networks, including al-Qaeda. The Security Council was not convinced and voted against the invasion. The United States invaded Iraq anyway on March 19, 2003. Only Britain gave it significant support.

As in Afghanistan, victory in Iraq appeared to come quickly. Bush declared the mission had been accomplished when Baghdad was occupied after a few weeks of fighting. However, it proved easier to overthrow Saddam than to secure peace in Iraq. Much of the country quickly descended into chaos. By August 2004 over nine hundred U.S. service men and women had died, Iraq remained in turmoil, and there were renewed threats of terror attacks against U.S. cities. Critics blasted the administration for failing to develop an effective and coherent peace plan. The war, they charged, had actually strengthened terrorism. The failure to secure UN support or to find weapons of mass destruction or establish ties between Saddam and al-Qaeda had damaged America's reputation and credibility and weakened the fabric of international cooperation.

The 2004 Presidential Election

Massachusetts senator John F. Kerry won the Democratic Party's nomination to be its presidential candidate. Kerry selected Senator John Edwards from North Carolina to be his running mate against incumbents George W. Bush and Dick Cheney. While these men campaigned, African Americans registered an important, but subtle, shift in their status within the Democratic Party. It became clear that they would play a key role in determining the outcome of the 2004 presidential election.

The process of political transformation begun in the 1960s peaked in the 2004 presidential primaries. In these contests African Americans emerged as the most reliable base of the Democratic Party. They made their views heard and their power acknowledged. They wanted Americans to understand that little divided black and white Americans when it came to regaining the White House. In so doing,

African-American leaders skillfully moved from being considered spokespersons for a small special interest group. In 2004 they demanded acknowledgment of their central role as Democratic Party standard-bearers. Two of the nine contenders for the Democratic Party's nomination were African Americans: Carol Moseley Braun, former U.S. senator from Illinois, and Reverend Al Sharpton of New York. Braun and Sharpton participated in all of the primary debates before throwing their support to Kerry.

In the spirit of presenting a united front, Braun, Sharpton, and Jesse Jackson addressed the delegates at the Democratic National Convention in Boston. While praising Kerry and attacking Bush, they reiterated their concerns about high black unemployment, the lack of national health-care insurance, and the deteriorating physical plant of the nation's schools, especially those that served the poor and inner-city residents. And they emphatically expressed their objections to the war in Iraq.

The star of the convention, however, was the little known forty-two-year-old state senator from Illinois, Barack Obama, who was running for the U.S. Senate. Obama's keynote speech, claiming that good and efficient government would improve the life chances of all Americans, catapulted him into the nation's limelight. The *Chicago Tribune*'s black columnist Clarence Page called Obama "the quintessential crossover candidate, a Colin Powell for the party of the Revs. Jesse Jackson and Al

Al Sharpton raised important issues of racial and social justice and addressed the problems of the poor and uninsured during the 2004 Democratic Party primary.

Sharpton." In the passage of his speech that received the most sustained applause, Obama asserted,

> Yet even as we speak, there are those who are preparing to divide us, the spin masters and negative ad peddlers who embrace the politics of anything goes. Well, I say to them tonight, there's not a liberal America and a conservative America; there's the United States of America. There's not a black America and white America and Latino America and Asian America; there's the United States of America.

Obama underscored the essential oneness of America:

> The pundits like to slice and dice our country into red states and blue states; red states for Republicans, blue states for Democrats. But I've got news for them too. We worship an awesome God in the blue states and we don't like federal agents poking around our libraries in the red states. We coach Little Leagues in the blue states and, yes, we've got some gay friends in the red states. There are patriots who opposed the war in Iraq and patriots who supported it. We are one people, all of us pledging allegiance to the Stars and Stripes, all of us defending the United States of America.

Obama's personal history captures the complexity of identity in new millennium America. As he reminded his listeners, "I live in the African-American community but I am not limited by it." Obama's father was an immigrant from Kenya who married a white American from Kansas. Obama was raised in Hawaii, attended Harvard Law School, and taught law at the University of Chicago before entering the political arena. As a state senator, Obama voted to ban racial profiling and supported increased funding for child health care, among other issues of great importance to African Americans. In 2004 he won the Democratic primary for the U.S. Senate. When a scandal forced his white Republican opponent to withdraw from the race, the Republican state committee selected black conservative Alan Keyes to run against Obama. For the first time in American history, both major candidates in a U.S. Senate race were African Americans.

On November 4, 2004, Americans reelected George W. Bush by a 3 million vote margin. After the election Secretary of State Colin Powell tendered his resignation. In repayment for her loyalty and experience in international affairs, President Bush appointed Condoleezza Rice to replace Powell as Secretary of State. Significant developments also occurred on the state level. Few in Illinois were surprised that Barack Obama emerged triumphant over Republican challenger Allan Keyes. The wildly popular "rising star" of the Democratic Party, Obama became the second African American to serve in the Senate from Illinois; the first had been Carol Mosely Braun. As 2004 faded into 2005, politics in America had become even more important and outcomes difficult to anticipate. All would agree, however, that these were interesting times.

▶▶ **Living Words Audio Clip**

Track 46 *The Audacity of Hope; speech by Barack Obama, 2004, excerpt*

Predicting Consequences

Predicting consequences means studying what has happened in the past, and using this knowledge to try to forecast what might happen in the future. Social scientists use this skill to predict trends. They study data from the census and other statistical sources and then relate patterns in the data to historical events. For example, what has the rate of population growth been over recent decades? What does this suggest about the rate of population growth in the next few years? What events have affected this growth? Which groups are likely to grow faster and which groups are likely to grow more slowly? The table at right answers some of these questions.

Change in Number of Families and Median Income,* by Selected Ethnic Groups, 1980–2000

	Year	Number of Families (in thousands)	Percent Change (from preceding census)	Median Income (in dollars)	Percent Change (from preceding census)
White Families	1980	52,710	—	43,583	—
	1990	56,803	+7.8	47,398	+8.8
	2000	60,222	+6.0	53,256	−12.4
African American Families	1980	6,317	—	25,218	—
	1990	7,471	+18.3	27,506	+9.1
	2000	8,814	+18.0	34,192	+24.3
Latino Families	1980	3,235	—	29,281	—
	1990	4,981	+54.0	30,085	+2.7
	2000	7,728	+55.1	35,054	+16.5

* In 2000 dollars. Median income represents the center of the income distribution—half of the families in the group earn more and half earn less than the median income.

SOURCE: *Statistical Abstract of the United States*

LEARN THE SKILL

Use the following steps to predict consequences from a table:

1. **Identify the kinds of information in the table.** Determine what is being measured by the data in the table. Note the time span of the table and the time intervals it shows.

2. **Analyze the rate of change.** Compare the rate, or percent, of change of different ethnic groups at different time periods.

3. **Use your knowledge of history and the trends you have noted in the data to predict future trends.** Determine whether some of the changes and trends you have found in the data were the consequences of particular historical events. In this case, consider the Immigration Act of 1965, which allowed more people from places other than Europe to immigrate to the United Sates, and the Immigration Act of 1990, which further increased immigration quotas by 40 percent.

APPLY THE SKILL

See the Chapter Review and Assessment for another opportunity to apply this skill.

PRACTICE THE SKILL

Answer the following questions:

1. **(a)** What does this table tell you about the number of families in various ethnic groups in the United States? **(b)** What periods of time does the table cover? **(c)** By what percentage did the number of Latino families increase between 1990 and 1995? **(d)** What does it mean if one group has a lower median income than another group?

2. **(a)** Which group of families is growing at the fastest rate? **(b)** Which group's median income has grown at the fastest rate? **(c)** Which group seems the most economically vulnerable—that is, which has the least stable median income?

3. **(a)** How might the table illustrate the effects of the 1965 law? **(b)** What consequences might the 1990 law have by the year 2010? **(c)** What might explain the significant increases in median income among all three groups in the decade of the 1990s? **(d)** What effects do you think a long recession would have on the number of families and on the median income? Why?

▶ **Skills for Life**

For answers, see *Teacher's Resource Manual*.

Chapter Timeline

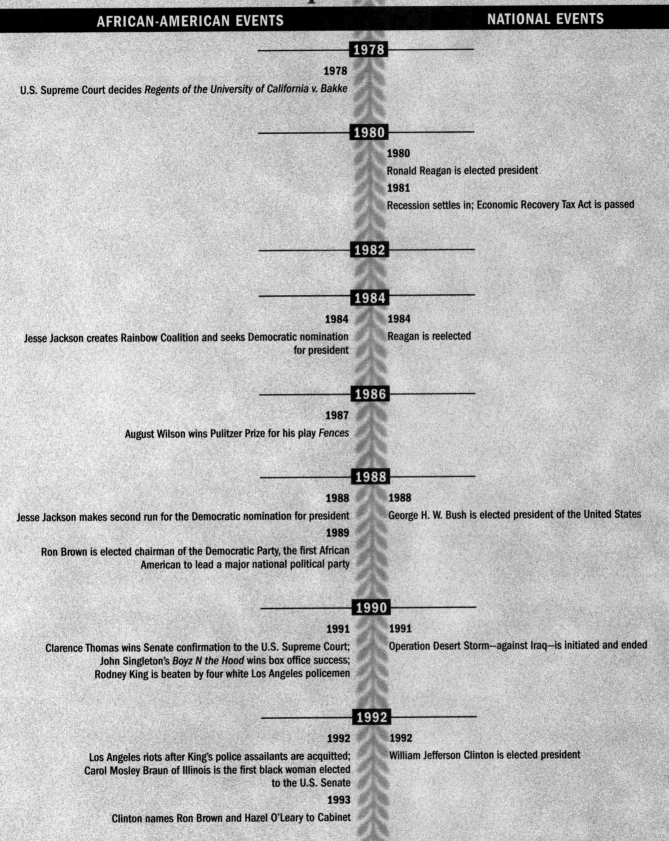

1978

1978
U.S. Supreme Court decides *Regents of the University of California v. Bakke*

1980

1980
Ronald Reagan is elected president

1981
Recession settles in; Economic Recovery Tax Act is passed

1982

1984

1984
Jesse Jackson creates Rainbow Coalition and seeks Democratic nomination for president

1984
Reagan is reelected

1986

1987
August Wilson wins Pulitzer Prize for his play *Fences*

1988

1988
Jesse Jackson makes second run for the Democratic nomination for president

1989
Ron Brown is elected chairman of the Democratic Party, the first African American to lead a major national political party

1988
George H. W. Bush is elected president of the United States

1990

1991
Clarence Thomas wins Senate confirmation to the U.S. Supreme Court; John Singleton's *Boyz N the Hood* wins box office success; Rodney King is beaten by four white Los Angeles policemen

1991
Operation Desert Storm—against Iraq—is initiated and ended

1992

1992
Los Angeles riots after King's police assailants are acquitted; Carol Mosley Braun of Illinois is the first black woman elected to the U.S. Senate

1993
Clinton names Ron Brown and Hazel O'Leary to Cabinet

1992
William Jefferson Clinton is elected president

1994

1994

Jesse Jackson Jr. elected to Congress

1994

Midterm elections give Republican Party control of Congress

1996

1996

Clinton is reelected; Clinton signs welfare reform legislation

1998

1998

Clinton is impeached by the House of Representatives

1999

The U.S. Senate acquits Clinton

2000

2000

Donna Brazile manages the presidential campaign of Al Gore

2000

George W. Bush becomes president of the United States

2001

Bush names Condoleezza Rice National Security Adviser and Colin Powell Secretary of State

Sept. 11

Terrorists demolish the World Trade Center in New York City and attack the Pentagon in Washington

United States invades Afghanistan

No Child Left Behind Act becomes law

2002

2003

Supreme Court upholds use of racial preferences in admission to University of Michigan Law School

2003

United States invades Iraq

2004

2004

Carol Mosely Braun and Al Sharpton run for president

Barack Obama elected to U.S. Senate

Condoleezza Rice appointed Secretary of State

2004

George W. Bush reelected president of the United States

2005

2005

Federal authorities reopen investigation into lynching of Emmett Till 50 years after his murder

Ex-Klansman convicted in 1963 murder of three civil rights workers— Michael Schwerner, Andrew Goodman and James Chaney

Chapter Review and Assessment

SUMMARY

Section 1 The Conservative Reaction, p. 845

- Ronald Reagan's victory in the election of 1980 reflected a shift to the right in American politics that began in the late 1970s.
- Reagan and his allies were determined to dismantle the programs established by the New Deal and the Great Society.
- Black conservatives played a role in the Republican Party, but had little real power.

Section 2 Civil Rights, p. 850

- The Reagan and Bush administrations opposed what they called "new civil rights law," especially affirmative action programs.
- Affirmative action was a focal point for debate about inequality in America and the role of the government in its elimination.
- In the 1980s, African Americans used their power in the Democratic Party to promote civil rights legislation.

Section 3 Jesse Jackson and the Rainbow Coalition, p. 856

- Jackson formed People United to Save Humanity (PUSH).
- Backed by a grassroots organization, Jackson competed for the Democratic presidential nomination in 1984. appealed to a "rainbow coalition" of people for support. He ran for president again in 1988.
- In the 1988 election George Bush used an ad that played on the general white perception of young black men as criminals.

Section 4 Policing the Black Community, p. 859

- The initial verdict in the Rodney King case and the subsequent riots touched off new debates about race and criminal justice in America.
- Many African Americans pointed to numerous incidents in which it appeared that police profiling and bias against black men played a role in police conduct.
- The appointment of black police chiefs has helped change the behavior of law enforcement.

Section 5 The Clinton Years, p. 863

- Clinton appointed African Americans to important positions throughout his administration, not just to positions that had something to do with race.
- He supported economic policies that decreased unemployment and helped the poor.
- Republicans challenged Clinton by focusing on taking control of Congress and by launching investigations into alleged improprieties.

Section 6 The Bush Years, p. 868

- After a 5-4 Supreme Court ruling, George W. Bush was declared the winner in Florida which gave him an electoral college majority.
- Many observers believed that voting improprieties in Florida disfranchised substantial numbers of African Americans.
- Once in office, Bush launched a controversial education reform program called No Child Left Behind.
- Many African Americans shifted their political focus to specific issues, including the spread of HIV/AIDS and reparations for slavery.
- The events of September 11, 2001 and the subsequent war in Iraq dominated political debate in 2004.

REVIEWING KEY TERMS

Write a brief explanation of the following terms.

1. New Right, p. 845
2. trickle-down theory, p. 845
3. archconservative, p. 849
4. affirmative action, p. 850
5. Philadelphia Plan, p. 852
6. set-aside programs, p. 852
7. racial preferences, p. 852
8. apartheid, p. 855
9. TransAfrica, p. 855
10. antiapartheid movement, p. 855
11. People United to Save Humanity (PUSH), p. 856
12. Rainbow Coalition, p. 856
13. Amnesty International, p. 860
14. centrist, p. 863
15. mandate, p. 863

REVIEWING MAIN IDEAS

22. To what extent and in what key areas did the Reagan and Bush presidencies nullify or dismantle Great Society legislation?

23. What was the significance of Jesse Jackson's campaigns for the Democratic presidential nomination?

24. Compare and contrast the effects on African Americans of the welfare reform legislation passed during Clinton's administration and the education reform policies of George W. Bush's No Child Left Behind Act.

25. Why did affirmative action become one of the most contested issues of the 1990s?

26. How did affirmative action in the workplace differ from affirmative action in education?

27. How did the Rodney King case illuminate the different perceptions black and white Americans have of the police and the justice system?

28. What were some of the major concerns of black Americans during the 2004 presidential campaigns?

29. What are the main arguments of black conservative ideology?

ANALYZING DOCUMENTS

Jesse Jackson, Common Ground, 1988

Common ground. America is not a blanket woven from one thread, one color, one cloth. When I was a child growing up in Greenville, South Carolina my grandmama could not afford a blanket, she didn't complain and we did not freeze. Instead she took pieces of old cloth—patches, wool, silk, gabardine, crockersack—only patches, barely good enough to wipe off your shoes with. But they didn't stay that way very long. With sturdy hands and a strong cord, she sewed them together into a quilt, a thing of beauty and power and culture.

Now, Democrats, we must build such a quilt.

Farmers, you seek fair prices and you are right—but you cannot stand alone. Your patch is not big enough. Workers, you fight for fair wages, you are right—but your patch of labor is not big enough. Women, you seek comparable worth and pay equity, you are right—but your patch is not big enough.

Women, mothers, who seek Head Start, and day care and prenatal care on the front side of life, relevant jail care and welfare on the back side of life—you are right—but your patch is not big enough. Students, you seek scholarships, you are right—but your patch is not big enough. Blacks and Hispanics, when we fight for civil rights, we are right — but our patch is not big enough . . .

But don't despair. Be as wise as my grandmama. Pull the patches and the pieces together, bound by a common thread. When we form a great quilt of unity and common ground, we'll have the power to bring about health care and housing and jobs and education and hope to our Nation. (Standing ovation)

We, the people, can win! . . .

—From: 1988 Democratic Convention Speech.

 Making Connections: What was Jackson's theme and how does he connect it to the larger social and political issues of the time? What did Jackson challenge people to do?

WRITING ACTIVITY

In a short report or research paper, consider this question.

 What role did racism play in the politics of the 1980s?

STUDY ONLINE!

www.prenhall.com/aah

Additional study resources are available for this chapter on the *Companion Website*.

▶ **Review and Assessment**

For answers, see *Teacher's Resource Manual.*

24

African Americans
in the New
Millennium

The Million Man March and the Million Woman March
reflected the determination to redefine black identity.

Chapter 24

African Americans protesting for gay marriage rights.

What demanding respect for people as *blacks* or as *gays* requires is that there be some scripts that go with being an African-American or having same-sex desires. There will be proper ways of being black and gay: there will be expectations to be met; demands will be made. It is at this point that someone who takes autonomy seriously will want to ask whether we have not replaced one kind of tyranny with another. If I had to choose between Uncle Tom and Black Power, I would, of course, choose the latter. But I would like not to have to choose. I would like other options. The politics of recognition requires that one's skin color, one's sexual body, should be politically acknowledged in ways that make it hard for those who want to treat their skin and their sexual body as personal dimensions of the self. And "personal" does not mean "secret" but "not too tightly scripted," "not too constrained by the demands and expectations of others."

—K. Anthony Appiah, "Racial Identity and Racial Identification" in K. Anthony Appiah and Amy Gutmann, *Color Conscious: The Political Morality of Race* (Princeton, N.J.: Princeton University Press, 1996).

How does the writer see the question of identity?

Chapter Preview

In his 1901 book *The Souls of Black Folk*, W. E. B. Du Bois dreamed of a nation in which black people could be both African and American, embracing their own rich cultural heritage and sharing it with America while becoming full-fledged citizens. This merging of the "two-ness" of the African and American "souls" did not happen in Du Bois's lifetime. Had Du Bois lived to the dawn of the twenty-first century, he would have been both pleased by the progress made toward fulfilling his dream and saddened by how far the ideals of that dream remain unfulfilled.

A two-ness thus remains a century after Du Bois wrote. It is complicated both by the successes African Americans have achieved in recent decades and by changes in the nation and in global society. Now, just as Du Bois found two-ness, current observers, such as scholar Anthony Appiah, applaud the possibility of embracing multiple identities linked to sexual preference, religious affiliation, immigration status, and political philosophy, along with the soul of black folk. Reconciling all of these self-understandings within a larger racial identity is the defining struggle of the next phase of the African-American odyssey.

▶ **Witnessing History**

Appiah sees identity as not having to choose between being black and being gay.

Section 1

Progress and Poverty

GUIDE TO READING

▶ What explains African Americans' growing economic security?

▶ Why are so many African Americans less wealthy and less healthy than white Americans?

KEY TERMS

▶ white-collar, p. 886

▶ incarceration, p. 889

Income, Education, and Health

After the triumphs of the civil rights era, many African Americans made great strides in overcoming the economic and educational disadvantages that had plagued their ancestors. Partly as a result of this progress, they also lived longer, healthier lives. Yet the disparities between the levels of wealth, schooling, and health of African Americans and the white majority, although narrowed, have persisted.

The years after 1970 witnessed the consolidation of black economic, civic, and political progress. In part, this was exemplified by the prominence of such visible African Americans as entertainer Oprah Winfrey, Bill Clinton's secretary of commerce Ronald Brown, chairman of the Joint Chiefs of Staff and later secretary of state Colin Powell, professional golfer Tiger Woods, and public intellectual Henry Louis Gates. These people, and many other African Americans, rose to the top of their fields.

As with the American population as a whole, the ultrarich remain rare in the black community, but their ranks have grown. Oprah Winfrey, Bill Cosby, Michael Jackson, and Michael Jordan acquired immense fortunes as entertainers or athletes. Others in this fortunate few include businessman Robert L. Johnson, founder of Black Entertainment Television (BET), who became the first African American to own a professional basketball team, the Charlotte, North Carolina, Hornets; John H. Johnson, publisher of *Ebony* and *Jet* magazines; Berry Gordy, founder of Motown Records; and Russell Simmons, a recording and fashion entrepreneur.

The career of Reginald Lewis illustrates the possibilities open to black people in other industries. Armed with a degree from Harvard Law School, he first purchased the McCall Pattern Company, and then in 1987 bought Beatrice Foods, an international packaged goods company, for $2.5 billion. At the time it was the largest leveraged buyout in U.S. history. Lewis became the wealthiest African American. Before his death in 1993, Lewis demonstrated an understanding of the need to give back to his community by donating millions of dollars to Howard University and the NAACP.

▶▶ **Guide to Reading/Key Terms**

For answers, see the *Teacher's Resource Manual*.

Oprah Winfrey with Michael Jordan on her television show in 1996.

African Americans' Growing Economic Security

The achievements of the most successful African Americans are impressive, but more significant is the increase in job opportunities, income, and wealth for a broad cross section of working African Americans. Before the 1960s nearly all black men worked in the lower rungs of agriculture, construction, transportation, and manufacturing. Black women were predominantly caged in domestic and food service jobs. Few black men or women had a chance to move to higher paid and more prestigious skilled or managerial positions. The wages for all African Americans remained low.

Antidiscrimination laws and affirmative action programs allowed millions of black people to begin climbing off the bottom rungs of career ladders. In 1940, for example, only 5.2 percent of black men and 6.4 percent of black women worked in **white-collar** occupations. By 2000

PROFILE ❖ Oliver Harrington & Aaron McGruder

Although born more than six decades apart, Oliver Harrington and Aaron McGruder were the two most creative and controversial black comic artists to emerge in the twentieth century. By combining artistic skill with the written word, each man offered incisive and clever commentary on modern America. Many readers were amused by Harrington's and McGruder's comic offerings. Others were annoyed and even outraged at what they believed to be their unfair depictions of black and white people.

Harrington was born in Westchester County, New York, in 1912. His family moved to the South Bronx when he was about seven. His father was black and his mother was white. He was attracted to drawing at an early age. He received a degree in fine arts from Yale University in 1940. In the meantime, he spent time in Harlem, absorbing its life, energy, and culture. He began contributing drawings to the *Amsterdam News* in the mid-1930s and then switched to the Pittsburgh *Courier.* He also contributed comic art to *The People's Voice*, a weekly newspaper founded in Harlem by Adam Clayton Powell, Jr., and Charles Buchanan. During World War II, Harrington covered black troops in North Africa and Europe as a war correspondent for the *Courier.*

After the war, Harrington increasingly associated with causes and individuals, including Paul Robeson, who were allegedly connected to subversive activities and the Communist Party. He contributed cartoons to *Freedom*, a journal that the FBI and its director, J. Edgar Hoover, regarded with suspicion.

In 1951 Harrington left the United States and spent most of the remainder of his life in Europe. After living for ten years in Paris, he went to East Germany in 1961 and became a cartoonist for the communist newspaper, the *Daily Worker* (later the *Daily World*). He never became a communist himself. He occasionally returned to the United States but preferred to comment on American society from abroad. His artwork featured the Vietnam War, the Watergate scandal, the Iran-Contra controversy, the U. S. invasion of Grenada, apartheid in South Africa, and racism in America. Oliver Harrington died in Berlin in 1995.

those figures had risen to 35.3 percent for black men and 62.3 percent for black women. Black people moved in large numbers into jobs in government, education, finance, and such professions as the law and medicine, which had largely excluded them.

As a result of these changes, black family income has increased dramatically. In 1940 only 1 percent of black families, compared with 12 percent of white families, had incomes at least twice as high as the government's poverty line. By 1998, 50 percent of black families did, compared with 73 percent of white families. The disparity of income between similar families also decreased. In 1960 two-parent black families earned 61 percent as much as two-parent white families, but by 1998 they earned 87 percent as much. This figure is even more impressive when one considers that a larger proportion of black people live in the low-wage South than do white people. On average black women now make 94 percent of what white women earn. The economic boom of the Clinton years from

Harrington's most enduring character was Bootsie, a fat, bald, middle-aged black man who commented dryly on white people, made caustic observations about American society, dealt (mostly unsuccessfully) with black women, and fell victim to his own weaknesses and foibles. After the 1943 race riot in Detroit, Harrington drew a cartoon that featured a little white boy showing a friend his father's hunting trophies that included the heads of a moose, tiger, walrus, and a black man. The caption read: "Dad got that one in Detroit last week."

Aaron McGruder's comic strip *The Boondocks* first appeared nationally in 1996, one year after Harrington's death. McGruder was born in Chicago in 1974 but spent his youth in a middle-class suburb of Washington, D.C. He majored in African-American studies at the University of Maryland where his first comic strip appeared in the campus newspaper, *The Diamondback*.

By 2004 *The Boondocks* appeared in 230 newspapers including the *Los Angeles Times*, the *Chicago Tribune*, and the *Washington Post*. Published seven days a week, it reaches far more people and has created far more controversy than Bootsie ever did.

McGruder's comic strip is set in the fictional and mostly white Chicago suburb of Woodcrest—The Boondocks—that is inhabited by the Freemans: two brothers, Huey and Riley, and their grandfather. Appropriately, Huey and Riley attend J. Edgar Hoover Elementary School. The Freemans offer a running commentary on life in contemporary America that is invariably critical and often savage. Speaking mainly through Huey, McGruder does not hesitate to attack those black and white people he regards with contempt. The strip has featured yearly "Most Embarrassing Black People Awards," and McGruder has referred to Black Entertainment Television (BET) as Butts Every Time.

Recently McGruder stopped doing the artwork for *The Boondocks*, but he still writes the dialogue and is preparing a television series based on the strip.

& McGruder

TABLE 24–1 Median Income of Black and White Households, 1992–2001

	1992	2001	Change	Percentage Increase
White	$39,825	$44,517	$4,692	11.6
Black	$23,190	$29,470	$6,280	27.0

Source: U.S. Census Bureau Historical Income Tables–Households

1993 to 2000 particularly benefited black people. Although the median income of black families remains substantially below that of white families, it rose at more than twice the rate over this period (see Table 24–1).

Although many African-American families have made progress in closing the income gap, their average wealth remains far behind that of whites. This is due partly to the centuries-long heritage of poverty during which most black people accumulated little property or other forms of wealth to hand on to their children. It is also closely tied to differences in the proportions of blacks and whites who own their own homes because home ownership is most American families' primary asset. Only 35 percent of African-American families owned their homes in 1950. This was partly due to low incomes but also to systematic discrimination. By the end of the twentieth century, 48 percent of African Americans owned their own homes, and government programs were helping more do so. Still, in the year 2000, black households on average held only about $7,500 of assets compared to nearly $80,000 in assets for the average white household.

The Persistence of Black Poverty

Most African Americans enjoyed greater absolute and relative increases in income. Many remained mired in poverty. The poverty rate (in 2001 this meant having an annual income below $18,104 for a family of four) for blacks dipped to a low of 22.7 percent during the Clinton boom. It climbed back to 24.1 percent during the first years of George W. Bush's presidency. Most poor black people are trapped in inner-city neighborhoods plagued by gang warfare, crime, drug and alcohol addiction, and high rates of HIV/AIDS infection. There they are cut off from meaningful participation in the social and economic life of the nation and experience fewer educational and other opportunities that might allow them to escape from poverty. A second large concentration of black poverty is found in depressed rural areas, especially in the South. Mechanization and declining commodity prices for crops have long limited African-American opportunities. Despite cherished myths about rural life, these areas see many of the same social problems as the inner cities.

▶ **Recommended Reading**

Christopher Jencks. *Rethinking Social Policy: Race, Poverty, and the Underclass.* Cambridge, MA: Harvard University Press, 1992.

The high rate of poverty in the black community disproportionately affects children. In the year 2000, 53.3 percent of all African Americans under age eighteen lived in families with only one parent, generally with their mother. Partly for this reason, 55.6 percent of black children lived in families at or near the poverty level. Many, if not most, single-parent families headed by females suffer from limited earning capacity, meager public assistance, poor housing, and inferior schools. These conditions often handicap children for the rest of their lives, helping perpetuate poverty from generation to generation. Given their proportion among African-American youth, this is an ominous sign for the future.

Poverty persists among urban African Americans in part because of the national economic restructuring that has been under way since the 1960s. Deindustrialization, relentless advances in laborsaving technology, and the development of low-wage offshore production have wiped out many jobs that African Americans with limited education and skills once held.

Racial Incarceration

The growth in criminal activity in inner-city districts during the 1980s and 1990s and an overwhelming national shift toward aggressive policing and harsher sentencing for those convicted of breaking the law led to a vast increase in the imprisonment rates of African-American men. **Incarceration** is an increasingly common experience for poor young black men, compounding the barriers to advancement they already face. (For more on black imprisonment, see Chapter 23.)

Education One-Half Century after Brown

Educational attainment is the key factor that distinguishes the African Americans who achieve economic success from those who do not. Black rates of school completion have advanced tremendously in the past half century. Many more black youths graduate from high school than ever before. In 1960 only 37.7 percent of African Americans between ages twenty-five and twenty-nine had completed high school. By 2000, 86.8 percent had, which is close to the 94 percent for white Americans. Black enrollment in college also rose from a mere 136,000 in 1960 to 1,548,000 in 2000. Although still behind white Americans, these rates of achievement place African Americans among the most highly educated groups of people in the world. African Americans between the ages of twenty-five and thirty-four are now more likely than young adults in Canada, France, Italy, and the United Kingdom to have completed high school. They are more likely than those in Italy, the United Kingdom, Germany, and France to have completed college.

▶ Recommended Readings

Douglas G. Glasgow. *The Black Underclass: Poverty, Unemployment, and Entrapment of Ghetto Youth.* New York: Random House, 1981.

Jonathan Kozel. *Savage Inequalities: Children in America's Schools.* New York: Crown, 1991.

Robin D.G. Kelley. *Yo' Mama Is DysFunkshional!* Boston: Beacon Press, 1998. Insightful essays about America's culture wars and an excellent critique of scholarship about black working-class culture by one of this generation's finest historians.

Black students in Mississippi reflect both the challenges and the obstacles to quality education. Barbara Gauntt/Clarion-Ledger

IN THEIR OWN WORDS . . .

A Vision for America

Martin Luther King, Jr. delivered one of the most famous speeches of the twentieth century on the steps of the Lincoln Memorial in Washington, D.C. on August 28, 1963. Thousands gathered to support the civil rights movement and civil rights laws. King passionately described his vision for the future. Over 40 years later, his historic words still speak to the issues faced by African Americans in the new millenium.

Five score years ago, a great American, in whose symbolic shadow we stand signed the Emancipation Proclamation. This momentous decree came as a great beacon light of hope to millions of Negro slaves who had been seared in the flames of withering injustices. It came as a joyous daybreak to end the long night of captivity. But one hundred years later, we must face the tragic fact that the Negro is still not free.

One hundred years later, the life of the Negro is still sadly crippled by the manacles of segregation and the chains of discrimination. One hundred years later, the Negro lives on a lonely island of poverty in the midst of a vast ocean of material prosperity. One hundred years later, the Negro is still languishing in the corners of American society and finds himself an exile in his own land.

So we have come here today to dramatize an appalling condition. In a sense we have come to our nation's captial to cash a check. When the architects of our republic wrote the magnificent words of the Constitution and the Declaration of Independence, they were signing a promissory note to which every American was to fall heir.

This note was a promise that all men would be guaranteed the inalienable rights of life, liberty, and the pursuit of happiness. It is obvious today that America has defaulted on this promissory note insofar as her citizens of color are concerned. Instead of honoring this sacred obligation, America has given the Negro people a bad check which has come back marked "insufficient funds." But we refuse to believe that the bank of justice is bankrupt. We refuse to believe that there are insufficient funds in the great vaults of opportunity of this nation.

So we have come to cash this check—a check that will give us upon demand the riches of freedom and the security of justice. We have also come to this hallowed spot to remind America of the fierce urgency of now. This is no time to engage in the luxury of cooling off or to take the tranqualizing drug of gradualism. Now is the time to rise from the dark and desolate valley of segregation to the sunlit

path of racial justice. Now is the time to open the doors of opportunity to all of God's children. Now is the time to lift our nation from the quicksands of racial injustice to the solid rock of brotherhood.

What Do You Think?

▶ How do King's words reflect the struggle of African Americans in the 21st century?

▶ What does King mean when he says America has given blacks a 'bad check'? Has America come closer to paying that debt in the new millenium? Why or why not?

▶ How does King's vision compare to that expressed by Barack Obama in his speech excerpted on page 919?

Excerpt from *I Have a Dream*, speech delivered by Martin Luther King on August 28, 1963 in Washington, D.C.

Yet despite these encouraging figures, black people who want an education, particularly those in poor inner-city and rural areas, still face severe problems. Schools starved of funds by regressive tax policies and the movement of wealthier people—both black and white—to the suburbs are almost predestined to fail. Affirmative action programs that made a place for African-American students have been cut in California, Texas, and elsewhere, resulting in declining enrollments among black students at the top schools. For impoverished black youth, the combined effect of failing schools and few opportunities results in dropout rates sharply higher than for more affluent African Americans.

 Reading Check What educational gains have African Americans made since the *Brown* decision of the 1950s?

The Health Gap

As in income and education, African Americans have made significant progress toward living longer, healthier lives, but they still suffer greater incidence of disease and mortality for most major illnesses. In 1970, the first year for which we have statistics, life expectancy was 60 years for black men and 68.3 years for black women. By 2000 it had risen to 68.3 and 75.2 years, respectively. Improvements in the quality of care accessible to blacks are partly responsible for these increases. Higher infant mortality rates and greater numbers of deaths from diseases kept them well below the 74.9-year life span for white men and 80.1 years for white women.

Cancer and HIV/AIDS infections are currently among the greatest threats to black health. African-American men are significantly more likely than white men to develop cancer and to die from the disease

▶ **Reading Check**

The percentage of African Americans completing high school has increased substantially to 86.8%, although still behind white Americans. Over 1.5 million blacks enroll in college. There are still gaps for those in poor and rural areas with failing schools and few opportunities, which result in high dropout rates.

▶ **What Do You Think?**

· Although African Americans have made significant gains since King gave this speech in 1960, his words are still true today regarding continued inequalities and injustices in the 21st century.

· He means that America has made promises that it has not fulfilled. There are still inequities and opportunities denied to African Americans.

· Like King, Obama describes an America that is united by people with common interests and desires that should not be determined by the color of their state on a map or their skin.

within five years of diagnosis. Black women have a somewhat lower incidence of cancer than do white women. Those black women who do get the disease die at a higher rate from it than white women do. Cancer is a complicated disease caused by a variety of factors. Some of the higher rate of its incidence among African Americans is related to risky behaviors common to all impoverished people. These include smoking, heavy drinking, obesity, and a general lack of knowledge about health. A lack of access to health insurance or quality providers compounds the impact of these behaviors. Evidence also indicates that many African Americans mistrust the health-care system. On the other side, medical workers tend to treat black cancer patients less aggressively than white patients.

HIV/AIDs

African Americans are more likely to have HIV/AIDS than any other group in the United States. Black people comprise 38 percent of all HIV/AIDS cases despite making up less than 13 percent of the U.S. population. For new cases of the disease, the disparity is even greater: 47 percent of all reported new cases of HIV/AIDS were among African Americans, and 63 percent of the American women newly diagnosed with the disease were black. Although HIV/AIDS first spread in the United States primarily among gay men, and unprotected sex between men is still the primary form of transmission, only about one-third of African Americans contract the disease in this manner. More acquire HIV/AIDS through intravenous drug use and unprotected heterosexual sex.

Although African Americans have had high rates of HIV infection from the beginning of the epidemic, consciousness that this was an important black problem only began to rise in the 1990s. At first the disease was perceived by many black leaders to affect only gay white men and to be relatively less important than the many other crises affecting their community during the 1980s. This began to change when Los Angeles Lakers' star Earvin "Magic" Johnson told the world he had HIV. The deaths of tennis star Arthur Ashe and the young rapper Eric "Eazy-E" Wright also shocked the black community into action.

Identity issues that concerned sexual orientation, feminine and masculine roles, and male/female relationships acquired a new urgency when 2003 reports indicated that African-American women registered more new cases of HIV/AIDS than any other sector of the population. Clearly, heterosexual African-American women sought testing to a greater extent than men. While women received treatment and understanding, their male partners remained in denial and avoided such active engagement in programs that could prolong their lives. The future of the black community in the new millennium demands open conversation and creative measures to address the HIV/AIDS crisis.

Reading Check Why are so many African Americans less wealthy and less healthy than white Americans?

⯈ **Reading Check**

Despite the gains made by most African Americans, many remained in poverty. Many poor black people are trapped in violent, dysfunctional neighborhoods. A second large concentration of black poverty is found in rural areas, especially the South. Cancer and HIV/AIDS are currently among the greatest threats to black health. Both occur more frequently in the black population than in the population as a whole.

⯈ **Recommended Reading**

Cathy J. Cohen. *The Boundaries of Blackness: AIDS and the Breakdown of Black Politics.* Chicago: University of Chicago Press, 1999. A black political scientist provides a sophisticated and provocative exploration into the social, political, and cultural impact of the AIDS epidemic on the African-American community.

Section 2

African Americans at the Center of Art and Culture

GUIDE TO READING

▶ Why has rap music achieved international popularity?

▶ What is the main philosophy of Afrocentricity?

▶ What types of academic programs have emerged for the study of African Americans?

KEY TERMS

▶ poet laureate, p. 895

▶ rap, p. 895

▶ hip-hop nation, p. 895

▶ gangsta rap, p. 897

▶ Afrocentricity, p. 899

▶ assimilation, p. 900

Cultural triumphs are among the most positive recent developments for black Americans. Beginning in the 1980s, a cultural renaissance emerged in every American community with a substantial African-American presence. Black consciousness institutions proliferated and flourished. They included black history and culture museums, festivals, expositions, publishing houses, bookstores and boutiques, concerts, theaters, and dance troupes. In 1996 *Publishers Weekly* reported that bookstores specializing in African-American books had increased from a dozen a few years earlier to more than two hundred. By 1994 there were seventy-five African-American publishing companies. In 1998 the National Literary Hall of Fame for Writers of African Descent opened at Chicago State University. Black painters used outdoor murals to celebrate the black experience.

Theater and Film

Black playwrights helped revitalize the American theater. August Wilson had begun writing overtly political work in the 1960s and 1970s but focused on broader themes of race and personality as his work matured. His first great success came in 1984 with the Broadway production of *Ma Rainey's Black Bottom* that explored the impact of racism in the music industry. He won praise for his powerful use of the rhythmic and symbolic power of black speech. He has since had four other plays on Broadway, two of which won Pulitzer Prizes—*Fences* in 1987 and *The Piano Lesson* in 1990. Charles Fuller has also made race the center of his plays, attacking stereotypes and exploring the complexity of racial identity in modern America. His most well-known play was the 1982 *A Soldier's Play* that also won a Pulitzer Prize. George C. Wolfe is a playwright, director, and producer whose achievements helped demolish racial barriers in the theater. His plays, such as *The Colored Museum* and *Jelly's Last Jam,* have won critical acclaim. He received a Tony Award as best director for *Angels in America* in 1994. His talent and energy are credited with returning the New York Shakespeare Festival to its former glory after his appointment as its director. Anna Deavere Smith has pioneered new forms of theater with her powerful one-woman plays derived from interviews. Her first major success was *Fires in the Mirror* about tensions between blacks and Jews in Brooklyn's Crown Heights

▶▶ **Guide to Reading/Key Terms**

For answers, see the *Teacher's Resource Manual.*

▶▶ **Recommended Readings**

Ismael Reed. *Airing Dirty Laundry.* Reading, MA: Addison-Wesley, 1993. Provocative, iconoclastic, and entertaining essays by an insightful cultural critic.

Terry McMillan. *Five for Five: The Films of Spike Lee.* New York: Stewart, Tabori & Chang, 1991.

neighborhood. This was followed by *Twilight: Los Angeles 1992,* a powerful portrayal of the Rodney King riots. Smith's achievements in drama and her gifted teaching were rewarded with a MacArthur genius grant in 1996.

The new cultural renaissance differed from the black arts movement of the 1960s and 1970s. The contemporary flowering was more inclusive and more appreciative of women artists. It included the work of openly gay and lesbian artists, such as documentary filmmaker Marion Riggs, dance choreographer Bill T. Jones, and novelist E. Lynn Harris. Whereas poets and dramatists dominated earlier movements, novelists took center stage in the 1980s. Much of the new work in all fields appeals to white as much as to black audiences, providing new insights into the lives of people of African heritage in a predominantly **Eurocentric** society.

Black Writers

There were signs of the emergence of a new wave of African-American novelists as early as 1977 when Toni Morrison's *Song of Solomon* became a Book-of-the-Month-Club selection, the first by a black author since Richard Wright's *Native Son* in 1940. Then Barbara Chase-Riboud made waves with *Sally Hemings* (1979), a fictional treatment of a woman who was both slave to and mistress of President Thomas Jefferson. In 1980 Toni Cade Bambara won the American Book Award for *The Salt Eaters.* At least as significant as these individual books was the founding in 1981 of a new publishing house, Kitchen Table: Women of Color Press. Then, in 1982, Alice Walker won the Pulitzer Prize and the American Book Award for *The Color Purple.* In 1987 poet Rita Dove won the Pulitzer Prize for poetry.

▶▶ **Recommended Reading**

Patricia Liggins Hill, gen.ed. *Call and Response: The Riverside Anthology of the African American Literary Tradition.* New York: Houghton Mifflin, 1969.

One of the most acclaimed writers in the history of U.S. literature, Toni Morrison's novels are, as a Nobel Prize press release put it, "characterized by visionary force and poetic import, [that] gives life to an essential aspect of American reality."

In 1993 she became America's **poet laureate**. In the same year Toni Morrison became the first African American to win the Nobel Prize for Literature.

Critics were not the only ones to take an interest in these works. In 1992 novels by three African-American women—Morrison, Walker, and Terry McMillan—made the *New York Times* best-seller list at the same time. In 2001 the works of four African Americans made the *Times* best-seller list and revealed the expanding readership and growing appreciation of black literature across the racial spectrum.

Origins of a New Music: A Generation Defines Itself

Rap is the most recent musical genre to arise out of black urban communities. Since the 1980s it has been emblematic of the younger generation of African Americans, known collectively as the **hip-hop nation**. Rap is a form of rhythmic speaking in rhyme: hip-hop refers to the backup music for rap that is often composed of excerpts or "samples" from other songs. Rap's roots lie in long traditions of street boasting, in the preaching style of black clergy, and in Afro-Caribbean rhythmic traditions.

The rap musical style arose in the early 1970s in poverty-stricken South Bronx neighborhoods in New York City. Its original purpose was to substitute musical and dance competition for gang violence. Rap pioneer Kool Herc (aka Clive Campbell) began using simple raps to cover a mix of beats played from two turntables. At the same time, former gang leader Afrika Bambaataa developed a political version of rap by merging the ideology of the Nation of Islam with the Black Panthers' cultural nationalism. Bambaataa's Zulu Nation promoted competition in break dancing, rapping, and graffiti art and helped spread rap among poor black and Latino neighborhoods.

The first commercial rap hit, *Rapper's Delight* by the Sugar Hill Gang, came out in 1979 and popularized the term *hip-hop*. This was followed by the rise to stardom of Grandmaster Flash and the Furious Five, which grew out of 1970s funk but added rap vocals and the technique of *scratching*—moving a record back and forth under a needle to produce a rhythmic, jarring sound, and manipulating turntable speeds. Much of this music was made primarily for entertainment in the club scene. Some rappers, following the early lead of the leftists Gil Scott-Heron and The Last Poets, offered a political critique of American society wrapped in taunting humor.

Hip-hop music provided African American youths with a creative medium in which they could discuss the things that mattered most to them, especially their lives in cities burdened by racial poverty and all that that entailed. In the Reagan years (1981–1989), few middle-class Americans cared to acknowledge the millions left behind in urban decay. Conditions in inner cities worsened during this period when crack flooded

▶ **Recommended Reading**

Tricia Rose. *Black Noise: Rap Music and Black Culture in Contemporary America*. Hanover, N.H.: Wesleyan University Press, 1994.

▶ **Retracing the Odyssey**

Rock and Roll Hall of Fame and Museum. Cleveland, Ohio. Among the museum's permanent collection of the 500 songs that most influenced the development of rock and roll are ones by early blues singers, Otis Redding, Chuck Berry, James Brown, Ray Cook, Ray Charles, Marvin Gaye, and Aretha Franklin.

neighborhoods and gang warfare erupted over drug turfs. The "keeping it real" lyrics of hip-hop artists helped forge a sense of community and common destiny among members of an often-ignored generation.

Rap Music Goes Mainstream

Ironically, white indifference allowed the first hip-hop entrepreneurs to take control of the production, dissemination, and profits connected with this new musical genre. Russell Simmons saw the potential of rap street music in the mid-1970s and recognized that the mainstream entertainment industry was not aware of it. He became a concert promoter, encouraging early rap groups to stay close to the dress styles and language of the inner-city African-American community. In 1984 he and a partner formed Def Jam Records. Their bands, such as RunDMC

PROFILE ❖ Bob & Ziggy Marley

During the 1970s and 1980s, many African Americans relished the music of Bob Marley of Jamaica (1945–1981), embraced his Rastafarian beliefs, and grew dreadlocks like those he wore. Marley shaped reggae music to liberate the minds of his people from neocolonial oppression. Marley attracted international audiences and followers at a time when issues affecting black Americans aroused little outside interest. His music also deepens our understanding of the birth of hip-hop or rap music that emerged from the inner-city neighborhoods of New York in the 1980s. Hip-hop's subsequent spread around the world signaled the internationalization of African America and helped unite the black Diaspora.

Marley was a son of the urban ghetto of Trench Town in Kingston, Jamaica's capital city. As a young man he became a Rastafarian, the Jamaican cultural and religious movement that held the black Emperor Haile Selassie of Ethiopia (r. 1930–1974) to be divine. By 1968 Marley was fully engaged in writing and performing music that merged culture, religion, and politics. Especially noteworthy were Marley's three concept albums: *Survival*, *Uprising*, and *Confrontation*, which brought together the themes that framed his life and work—celebrating black survival, challenging mental slavery, and constructing new visions for the future through defiance and hope. According to scholar Anthony Bogues, "one not only dances to Marley, but one has to LISTEN to Marley since he is both singing and engaging in social criticism." The lyrics, combined with Marley's conversational style and use of poetry, chants, biblical imagery, and hypnotic offbeats, reach across boundaries of class, race, gender, and region.

After Marley's untimely death in 1981, his musical mission was taken up by his son Ziggy. Born in 1968 David Marley, nicknamed "Ziggy" by his father, grew up in Jamaica and the United States. Ziggy Marley carried on the reggae tradition but incorporated other sounds from the African Diaspora, including roots rock and hip-hop. In doing so he continues his father's tradition of international engagement and politically informed music.

Marley

and Public Enemy, became enormously popular. Many of their albums sold millions of copies. Simmons expanded his business to include marketing hip-hop clothing under the label Phat Pharm and promoting poetry and comedy acts. In 2000 he sold his share of Def Jam for over $100 million. Like Simmons, P. Diddy (aka Sean "Puff Daddy" Combs) found success by working within the mainstream recording industry. Raised in a suburban neighborhood, P. Diddy dropped out of Howard University in 1990 to work for Uptown Records where his knowledge of the rap scene and instinct for hits fueled a rapid rise to vice president. In 1993 he formed his own company, Bad Boy Records, which was an immediate success.

Commercial success brought new groups to the fore. The genre changed and grew tremendously during the 1980s and 1990s. Hard-core rap bands such as RunDMC, which dominated the charts in the mid-1980s, brought the sound to MTV and to a larger public, which soon came to include white suburban teens. Hip-hop culture quickly spread beyond New York to other African-American urban centers. Each developed a distinctive, and often more graphic, variant of the original. With the music came changes in clothing style, such as baggy, loose-fitting jeans, that trend-hungry fashion designers quickly adopted.

White suburban youths had always been the wealthiest consumers of hip-hop music and its cultural artifacts. By the turn of the century, hip-hop had become a global culture force and the source of astonishing profits for men such as Russell Simmons and Sean "P. Diddy" Combs—and for white-owned business and music companies. Not surprisingly, the recurrence of the age-old tension between black creativity and white profits fueled new debate. As cultural studies analyst Gregg Tate put it, "Our music, our fashion, our hairstyles, our dances, our anatomical traits, our bodies, our souls continue to be considered ever ripe for the picking and the biting by the same crafty devils who brought you the African slave trade and the Middle Passage."

Gansta Rap

The southern California group NWA was one of the most successful of the new rap bands coming out in the late 1980s. Their 1988 release of the album *Straight Outta Compton* heralded the rise of **gangsta rap**. Its song "Gansta, Gansta" shocked many observers with its sexist and violent lyrics. Particularly troubling, however, is the persistent portrayal of black women as objects and commodities to be used by men—as something less than human—that bears an all-too-close resemblance to racist characterizations of black women from the era of slavery.

Gansta rap, however, is only part of the story. The rap genre is so broad that it includes many bands that explicitly reject hard-core obscenity and violence. Artists like Queen Latifah, for example, avoid putting down other African Americans even as they put forward a message of empowerment for black women and men. Other black

▶ **Recommended Reading**

Michael Eric Dyson. *Between God and Gangsta Rap: Bearing Witness to Black Culture*. New York: Oxford University Press. 1996.

Queen Latifah is the best-known black woman rapper in America and has amassed a distinguished record of awards for her work in movies.

female hip-hop artists were also in the game. Many, such as Lil' Kim, resolved to make sexuality their signature in ways that left little to the imagination.

Hip-hop quickly moved beyond the shores of the United States and has influenced music worldwide, particularly across the African Diaspora. France, for example, has a thriving rap music scene. Most of its artists are of Arab, African, or Spanish descent whose music focuses on ethnic and racial discrimination and social criticism. Africa, the Caribbean, and Latin America have also developed rap that builds on indigenous traditions of African music. The ability of rap to combine with other musical forms to create compelling hybrids and the global penetration of American popular culture ensures that it will continue to thrive and evolve.

 Reading Check   Why has rap music achieved international popularity?

▶ **Reading Check**

Rap music influenced music worldwide, particularly across the African Diaspora. Musicians around the world found ways to develop rap that builds on indigenous traditions of African music. This ability of rap to combine with other forms explains, in part, its global appeal.

▶ **Recommended Reading**

Joan Morgan. *When Chickenheads Come Home to Roost: My Life as a Hip-Hop Feminist.* New York: Simon & Schuster, 1999.

African-American Intellectuals

The struggles of the civil rights and black power movements forced predominantly white academic and cultural institutions to open their doors to African Americans. With a beachhead established, a number of black scholars gained a level of prominence as public intellectuals unknown in earlier eras. These individuals go beyond their roles as academics to participate in public debate on major issues. In the past most public intellectuals were white males. Some African Americans, like the formidable W. E. B. Du Bois and novelists Richard Wright, James Baldwin, and Ralph Ellison, were exceptions. The voices of most black intellectuals were seldom heard in the mainstream before the 1960s. In the past four

decades, however, many of the most prominent public intellectuals to emerge have been African American. Among them are Cornel West, Henry Louis Gates Jr., Molefi Kete Asante, Shelby Steele, William Julius Wilson, Michele Wallace, Ishmael Reed, Stanley Crouch, Charles Johnson, Vonnie McLoyd, John Edgar Wideman, Manning Marable, Adolph Reed, Thomas Sowell, Robin D. G. Kelley, Michael Eric Dyson, Nell Irvin Painter, bell hooks, and Anthony Appiah. Their views range from Marxist to extreme conservative. They all strive to define black identity in the United States and to explore the role of race in its social, economic, and political life. Their emergence and the acclaim accorded to them mark the end of America's long refusal to acknowledge the intellectual accomplishments of African Americans.

Many African-American scholars are connected to the black studies programs founded in the late 1960s and early 1970s. Initially marginalized and few in number, these programs now exist in nearly every major university or college. They have become institutionalized—even prized—by institutions that once resisted them. Doctoral degrees are now offered at Temple University, the University of Massachusetts at Amherst, Harvard, Michigan State University, and the University of California at Berkeley. Yale and Cornell offer masters' degrees in the field.

There are several main approaches to understanding the path of African Americans through U.S. history and in contemporary society. Three broad approaches predominate: Afrocentrist, what might be loosely termed "integrationist" or "inclusionist," and approaches emphasizing class, gender, and international comparisons.

Molefi Kete Asante served as professor and chair of the Department of African American Studies at Temple University from 1984 to 1996.

Afrocentricity

In the 1980s and 1990s, a philosophy of culture referred to as **Afrocentricity** captured widespread media and academic attention. The philosophy and practice of Afrocentricity had been a prominent feature in the political movement that created black studies. The emergence of Temple University professor Molefi Kete Asante gave it a presence and a personality. In the 1980s Asante published three books, *Afrocentricity, Kemet, Afrocentricity and Knowledge,* and *The Afrocentric Idea* in which he argued that an African-centered perspective was needed to re-orient African Americans from the Eurocentric periphery to a centered place in their own history. In its most extreme form, Afrocentrists argue that much of European civilization arose out of African origins, particularly the culture of ancient Egypt. They also point to evidence of advanced cultures in other parts of the continent to refute assertions of African cultural inferiority.

Many black educators enthusiastically embraced Afrocentricity as a way to celebrate and reclaim a positive African identity and to unite the

▶ **Recommended Readings**

Molefi Kete Asante. *The Afrocentric Idea.* Philadelphia: Temple University Press, 1987.

Tsehloane Keto. *Vision, Identity and Time: The Afrocentric Paradigm and the Study of the Past.* Dubuque, IA: Kendall/Hunt Publishing Co., 1995.

Wilson Jeremiah Moses. *Afrotopia: The Roots of African American Popular History.* Cambridge, MA: Cambridge University Press, 1998.

peoples of the African Diaspora. Afrocentrists rejected the idea of America as a melting pot. **Assimilation**, they argued, meant a rejection of their African cultural heritage. At the heart of this position is an indictment of American ideas and institutions for their complicity in the long oppression of black people.

Afrocentrists have strongly defended their perspective. Asante explained to his critics,

> Afrocentricity is a terribly maligned concept. Afrocentricity is the idea that African people and interests must be viewed as actors and agents in human history, rather than as marginal to the European historical experience—which has been institutionalized as universal.

Black historians and social scientists, Afrocentrists argue, have to place Africa and its descendants at the center of their studies to increase appreciation of the contributions of black people in world history.

Many black scholars, however, insist that Afrocentricity is regressive and fosters self-segregation. Writer Earl Ofari Hutchinson, for example, agrees that Asante's ideas merit attention. Still, he is skeptical about the claims of some Afrocentrist academics. "In their zeal to counter the heavy handed 'Eurocentric imbalance of history', some have crossed the line between historic fact and fantasy. They've constructed groundless theories in which Europeans are 'Ice People', 'suffer genetic defects,' or are obsessed with 'color phobias.' They've replaced the shallow European 'great man' theory of history with a feel good interpretation of history." White and black critics alike caution that the Afrocentrist desire to fabricate "a glorious past" for black people did a disservice to the truth and fostered a narrow notion of race ill suited as a platform for pursuing the study of Africans in America.

 Reading Check What is the main philosophy of Afrocentricity?

African-American Studies Matures

The African-American studies department at Temple was the first in the nation. It is the center of the Afrocentric approach and remains one of the largest black studies programs. Many other programs adopt a more ideologically flexible approach. Under the leadership of literary scholar Henry Louis Gates Jr., Harvard University now has the premier program in the integrationist tradition. Gates took charge of the department and the W. E. B. DuBois Institute in 1991 and has since attracted some of the leading lights of African-American studies from universities around the nation. His goals for the department focus less on recovering a usable past and more on the rigor-

Literary scholar and Harvard University professor Henry Louis Gates Jr. directs the multidisciplinary African-American studies program at Harvard.

ous multidisciplinary study of the black experience. Gates defines his project in this way:

> We're eager to demonstrate that Afro-American studies is an academic department. It is not a place for ethnic cheerleading; it is not a place for a 12-step recovery program to restore your sense of identity. It is a place where one studies an academic discipline in a fashion as rigorous as the study of mathematics or physics, English or history.

Apart from intellectual rigor, what binds the department together is a belief that race is a category of identity to be analyzed critically. Effective scholarship in the area is not fundamentally limited by the racial identity of the scholar.

As with American intellectual life as a whole, African-American studies has been influenced by the emergence of scholarship that questions prevailing gender assumptions. Just as the black studies movement challenged racial ideology, women's studies have forced a reconsideration of deeply held gender beliefs and raised historical and social science questions that went unasked in an earlier era. African-American scholars in *womanism* studies, a term popularized by Alice Walker to describe the intellectual project of women of color, have paid particular attention to the intersections of gender with racial and class hierarchies in shaping the lives of black women. They started journals such as *SAGE* and organizations such as the Association of Black Women Historians, founded by Rosalyn Terborg-Penn and Eleanor Smith. Gradually, their scholarly, literary, historical, and polemical works found readers in the general public and a place in women's studies curricula. As more black women enrolled in college, courses with titles like "Black Women Writers" and "Black Women's History" became part of black studies curricula. The field of black women's history has grown rapidly: scholarly monographs, reference works, anthologies, conferences, and exhibitions have all been devoted to the contribution black women have made to the political struggles and artistic accomplishments of African Americans. These historians have productively explored the role of race, class, and gender in the oppression of marginalized people in American society.

Perhaps most importantly, scholars have begun to flesh out the larger picture of the black Diaspora. Building on the important work of Philip Curtin, Colin Palmer, and others who have studied the development of the Atlantic slave-labor economy, scholars have begun serious comparisons of the centuries-old African-descended communities throughout the New World and those of more recent African immigrants to Europe. This project is enriching our understanding of African-American history by placing it in the context of a larger global story.

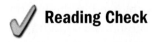 **Reading Check** What types of academic programs have emerged for the study of African Americans?

▶▶ **Reading Check**

African-American studies programs focus on an Afrocentric approach, as at Temple University, a multidisciplinary approach as at Harvard University, women's studies focusing on Black women's history, and the black Diaspora, understanding African-American history in a larger global context.

GUIDE TO READING

▶ How has African-American religious life changed in the last several decades?

▶ What are the strengths and tensions within the black church today?

KEY TERMS

▶ Nation of Islam, p. 905

Section 3
Religion

Black Religion in the Millennium

Religion remains at the heart of the African-American experience. Black churches, claiming over 25 million members, remain by far the largest black-controlled institutions in the nation. The major denominations remain those with ties going back to the nineteenth century. Among the largest are the African American National Baptist Convention of America, Inc., Progressive National Baptist Convention, Inc., African Methodist Episcopal Church, National Missionary Baptist Convention of America, Churches of Christ, and the African Methodist Episcopal Zion Church. Due to immigration from the Caribbean and Africa, African Americans are becoming a larger part of some predominantly white denominations. For example, black worshippers make up more than 9 percent of the American Catholic Church and over 10 percent of the Episcopal Church. Many African-American Catholics and Episcopalians attend predominantly black churches.

Black Religious Leaders

African-American men and women have had great success in occupying leadership positions within a variety of predominantly white denominations since the 1960s. Harold R. Perry was consecrated a bishop in the American Roman Catholic Church in 1966, and Bishop Wilton Gregory became the first African American to head the American Catholic bishops in 2002. Recognizing the importance of Africans and African Americans to the future of the church, in 1993 Pope John Paul II apologized for the Catholic Church's support of slavery. African-American John M. Burgess was installed as the first black bishop to head an Episcopal diocese in America in Massachusetts in 1970, followed by John T. Walker in Washington, D.C., in 1977. African Americans made similar gains in other denominations as churches worked to rid themselves of racist practices.

Despite this continuity with the past and the successes of black religious leaders, African-American religious life has changed in the last several decades. Most African Americans remain Protestants. Demographic and social changes within the community have challenged the mainline denominations. One difficulty is the move of middle-class parishioners

out of the close-knit urban communities that once supported churches with people from many different walks of life. Greater levels of education and different life experiences combine with geographical distance to create large suburban mega churches with a distinct character and worship practice. Often Pentecostal, these churches follow a theology that emphasizes the individual's relationship to God. Their ministers speak to the tensions and anxiety of people with stressful lives and careers or with specific problems such as substance abuse or difficulty with relationships. They also provide community institutions with tremendous services for their parishioners.

Perhaps the best-known minister of this new African American religious tradition is Bishop T. D. Jakes. Starting in 1980 with a ten-member storefront church in Charleston, West Virginia, he built Potter's House, an enormous ministry with a 28,000-member interracial congregation and 5,000-seat church in Dallas, Texas. In the 1990s Jakes began writing best-selling books such as *Woman, Thou Art Loosed*, which focused on using religion to heal the psychological wounds of modern society. His message is distributed through national seminars, television broadcasts, and the Internet.

Black Christians on the Front Line

Faced with the problems of the black community in the United States and with a changing population, African-American Christians in both traditional and nontraditional religious institutions have developed outreach programs to create supportive communities for the embattled and vulnerable. Some of the new mega churches are located in or near the black inner-city communities and retain a commitment to local action. The Salem Baptist Church in Chicago is a good example. It has over seventeen thousand members, many of whom are organized to patrol neighborhoods to discourage prostitutes and drug dealers. Reverend James T. Meeks led a political campaign for an antiliquor referendum as a response to the ravages of alcoholism in the community. Similar ministries, often with radio and television broadcasts of services, exist in many other predominantly black communities.

Reverend Eugene Rivers has developed a different approach from that of the mega churches. Along with like-minded former students at Harvard University, he founded the small Azusa Christian Community in a crime-plagued neighborhood in Boston. An evangelical Christian, Rivers believes "the church is the last best hope that black people have." He turned a former crack house into a Christian settlement named Ella J. Baker House. Its primary goal, Rivers says, is to keep children from killing one another. He and fellow black clergy formed the 10-Point Coalition and entered into a partnership with the police. The collaboration helped eliminate juvenile murders for two-and-a-half years. Rivers advocates a pragmatic black nationalism aimed at developing a rich, viable black civil society centered on the church.

Tensions in the Black Church

Tensions have arisen within many black churches over their socially conservative message, patriarchal structure, staid ritual, and lack of social engagement. Gender and sexuality are two key areas in which this has been expressed. The black church has long been in accord with other conservative Christian churches in advocating the subordination of women to men. Although most black churchgoers are women, men overwhelmingly dominate visible church leadership. Some African-American women, particularly of the younger generations, have left the church because of marginalization. Others have stayed to challenge sexism in individual churches and the denominations.

The African Methodist Episcopal (AME) Church has been at the forefront of this movement for reform. Although it has ordained women since 1898, the number of women ministers has only recently grown significant. Now 3,000 of its 8,000 ministers are female. In 2000 it elected Reverend Vashti M. McKenzie bishop of its Southern African district. She took the post after a successful ten-year stint as pastor of Baltimore, Maryland's Payne Memorial Church, whose membership she increased from 300 to 1,700. She connected her achievement to the past efforts of other women. "I stand here tonight, she told the AME convention, "on the shoulders of the unordained, women who serve without affirmation or appointment. I don't stand here alone, but there is a cloud of wit-

▶ **Teaching Notes**

Although a few voices, both male and female, have always challenged patriarchal assumptions in the churches, only in recent decades has the chorus grown too loud to ignore. As Howard University professor and ordained Baptist minister Cheryl Townsend Gilkes puts it, "[t]he cultural maxim 'If it wasn't for the women, you wouldn't have a church,' rises up against male attempts to exclude, ignore, trivialize, or marginalize women in a number of capacities."

Vashti Murphy McKenzie became the first woman to be appointed a bishop in the history of the AME Church.

Black churches continue to play a significant role in the social, political, and economic struggles of African Americans.

nesses who sacrificed, died and gave their best." The achievements of women in the churches have not come without conflict. This promises to be at the center of the black religious life in the twenty-first century.

Black Muslims

Although still a relatively small phenomenon in African America, Islam has been gaining a significant number of converts. The **Nation of Islam** is the best known of the many groups comprising African-American Muslims. Its 20,000 to 40,000 members make up only a small percentage of the estimated 1.5 million black American Muslims. After the death of founder Elijah Muhammad in 1975, the Nation of Islam was led by his son Wraith Deen Muhammad, who rejected the racialist aspects of his father's theology for more orthodox, mainstream Sunni Muslim beliefs. He eventually left the organization to found the Muslim American Society, the largest group of African-American Muslims with perhaps 500,000 members. Many black Muslims have rejected Christianity for what they perceive as its Eurocentric bias and for its former tolerance of slavery, although Islam also had a long history of slave trading in Africa. The clarity and discipline of the Muslim faith and the solidarity they feel with Muslims around the world also attract converts, estimated at about 18,000 per year in the United States.

With growing immigration from Islamic countries, African Americans have become more closely connected to the larger trends of the religion. This is evident in the rise of more orthodox Islam among American blacks. Tensions have arisen between African-American and immigrant Muslims, who make up three-quarters of all American Muslims.

▶▶ **Teaching Notes**

Ordained Baptist minister and University of Pennsylvania professor Michael Eric Dyson lists a number of the challenges for black Christians regarding sexuality: "[t]he guilt and shame that result from unresolved conflicts about the virtues of black sexuality... The Role of eroticism in a healthy black Christian sexuality. The revulsion to and exploitation of homosexuals. The rise of AIDS in black communities. The sexual and physical abuse of black women and children by black male church members. The resistance to myths of super black sexuality."

Louis Farrakhan achieved the greatest feat in the history of black mass mobilization October 16, 1995: the Million Man March.

The aftermath of the attacks on the World Trade Center and the Pentagon on September 11, 2001, has left many African-American Muslims conflicted. On the one hand, most deplore the attacks and the ideology that led to them. On the other hand, many African Americans are troubled by what they perceive to be an indiscriminate anti-Muslim feeling in the United States and are concerned the nation's war on terror might become a holy war against Islam.

Louis Farrakhan and the Nation of Islam

Beginning in the 1980s, the Nation of Islam's minister Louis Farrakhan became a potent source of racial division in the United States. Farrakhan was the younger of two sons of immigrant parents from the West Indies. As a young man, Farrakhan attended a black teachers' college in Winston-Salem, North Carolina, but he dropped out to become a Calypso singer known as the Charmer. In 1955, while performing in Chicago, he heard Elijah Muhammad preach at the Nation of Islam's mosque. This marked a turning point in his life. Farrakhan joined the Nation and quickly ascended within its hierarchy in the wake of Malcolm X's break with Elijah Muhammad and subsequent murder in February 1965. Farrakhan became minister of the Harlem Mosque No. 7 and Muhammad's national representative. Farrakhan opposed Wraith Muhammad's move to a more orthodox Islam and was able to take leadership of the Nation of Islam by 1978. In 1982 he purchased a building to publish the Nation of Islam's newspaper, *The Final Call.* Under Farrakhan's direction, the Nation developed a number of economic enterprises, including media ventures, restaurants, clothing stores, and companies to provide security for apartment buildings, distribute soap and cosmetics, and manufacture pharmaceuticals. Farrakhan recruited among poor and marginalized urban African Americans and within the black prison population. The national

move to the right during the Reagan era complemented the reconstituted Nation's conservative social ideas, which harked back to those advanced by Booker T. Washington at the turn of the century. Like Elijah Muhammad, Farrakhan downplayed the struggle for political rights.

 Reading Check What are the strengths and tensions within the black Church today?

Millennium Marches

In recent years Farrakhan has attempted to move beyond his extremist ideas and reach out to a broader group of African Americans. To this end he called for a **Million Man March** in Washington, D.C. Farrakhan framed this march as a "Holy Day of Atonement and Reconciliation," meant "to reconcile our spiritual inner beings and to redirect our focus to developing our communities, strengthening our families, working to uphold and protect our civil and human rights, and empowering ourselves through the Spirit of God, more effective use of our dollars, and through the power of the vote."

The estimated 400,000-strong crowd at the October 16, 1995, march made it a symbolic success and generated positive coverage even in the mainstream media. It inspired many black men to become more engaged with their communities and to speak out more forcefully against oppression. Many marchers reported that even though they did not support the Nation of Islam's program, they drew hope from the peaceful solidarity of the gathering.

Yet the goodwill dissipated when, three months after the march, Farrakhan embarked on a World Friendship Tour to Africa and the Middle East. To the consternation of many, he met with the leader of the brutally

Participants of the historic Million Man March in Washington, October 1995.

▶ **Reading Check**

African-American men and women have risen to leadership positions within mainline denominations and black churches have taken an active role in responding to the problems and challenges of their communities. At the same time, tensions exist in many black churches over issues related to such subjects as gender and sexuality.

Hundreds of thousands of black women stood shoulder to shoulder at the Woman March in Philadelphia to show their solidarity and to draw attention to issues important to African Americans.

repressive military regime in Nigeria, General Sani Abacha. At home, Farrakhan's intemperate rhetoric continued to attract attention. In the wake of the Million Man March, however, he failed to forge a coherent strategy to resolve African America's continuing social problems.

The Million Man March inspired women to organize their own march. Initiated by two Philadelphia women—Phile Chionesu, a small-business owner, and Asia Coney, a public housing activist—on October 25, 1997, an estimated 300,000 black women gathered in Philadelphia to listen to speeches by California congresswoman and president of the Congressional Black Caucus Maxine Waters, rapper Sister Souljah, and South African activist Winnie Mandela. The march was a celebration, a call to unity, and a forum for black women to speak out against domestic violence, and inadequate access to quality health care and educational opportunities. The march did not garner nearly as much media attention as the Million Man March, perhaps because the organizers were relatively unknown. The March nonetheless symbolized the ongoing struggle of black women to be seen and heard in American society and to counter negative stereotypes and derogatory images of black womanhood. As Detroit real estate agent Gloria Graves put it, "I thought that it was very important that we as black women come together in prayer and unity and the belief that we can bring back the family unit that has been lost. I wanted to meet other strong black women who had the same agenda and be united. It has been just great."

Section 4

Black Identity in the Twenty-First Century

Classifying Race

The 2000 U.S. census counted 281,421,906 Americans, a 13.2 percent increase from 1990. African-American numbers stood at 34.7 million, or about 12 percent of the total. For the first time in U.S. history, African Americans were no longer the largest minority group: the 35.3 million Americans who identified themselves as Hispanic slightly outnumbered them.

As in the past, most black Americans, 54 percent, live in the South with about 19 percent in the Midwest, 18 percent in the Northeast, and 10 percent in the West. New York City had the largest black population of any urban area at 2.3 million, followed by Chicago at 1.1 million, with Detroit, Philadelphia, and Houston all in the 500,000 to 1 million range. Looking beyond these raw numbers, however, reveals important information about the evolving nature of African-American identity in an increasingly multiethnic nation.

One of the most important changes in the census was the ability of respondents to choose more than one racial designation for themselves. Since the first census, such classifications have been shaped by the politics of race. During the early civil rights movement, some groups like the ACLU attempted to remove racial classifications altogether from the census data, reasoning that the only purpose of such distinctions was to disadvantage black people.

The civil rights laws of the 1960s changed the purpose of gathering data by racial classification. It was now necessary to have reliable statistics on racial characteristics of people to combat discrimination. With the rise of affirmative action programs, an individual's identity as an African American could actually be a benefit. The black power movement led many to embrace their identity as African Americans and reject the assimilation implied by abandoning racial categories.

In 1977 the Office of Management and Budget addressed the U.S government's need for standard racial categories with its **Statistical Policy Directive 15**. This set up the familiar racial classifications: white, black, Asian and Pacific Islander, and Native American. "Hispanic" was chosen to denote an ethnicity and could be chosen in addition to one of the four racial categories. There is no scientific backing for any biological racial distinctions. These categories are bureaucratic approximations

GUIDE TO READING

▶ Why has black identity become more complicated at the dawn of the twenty-first century?

▶ What were the accomplishments of Second Wave Feminism and what role did black women play in the movement?

KEY TERMS

▶ Statistical Policy Directive 15, p. 909

▶ ethnicity, p. 910

▶ antimiscegenation laws, p. 910

▶ 1965 Hart-Cellar Act, p. 911

▶ autocratic, p. 912

▶ rights revolution, p. 912

▶ feminism, p. 913

▶ Educational Amendments Act, p. 913

▶ Equal Rights Amendment, p. 913

▶▶ **Guide to Reading/Key Terms**

For answers, see the *Teacher's Resource Manual*

▶▶ **Recommended Reading**

Tsehloane Keto. *Vision, Identity and Time: The Afrocentric Paradigm and the Study of the Past.* Dubuque, IA: Kendall/Hunt Publishing Co., 1995.

of socially relevant distinctions designed to serve administrative needs. They were not necessarily meant to reflect the complex identities of many individuals included in them. For example, "Asian and Pacific Islander" encompasses individuals from nations with vastly different histories and cultures. The white category included people descended from Arabs and Turks as well as Europeans. In terms of **ethnicity**, people now called Hispanic had formerly thought of themselves in terms of national identities, such as Mexican American, Cuban American, and so on, and overlapped with the "black" category for Dominicans and other African-descended people from the former Spanish colonial regions. Over the quarter century after its adoption, these categories became incorporated into identities and social understandings and, in important ways, influenced business and government programs.

Two groups sought to change the categories. The first group saw an end to racial categories as the true legacy of the civil rights movement. These advocates point to the rhetoric of Martin Luther King Jr. and the plain language of the Civil Rights Act of 1964, which forbade any discrimination on the basis of race, as evidence of the need to eliminate racial classifications by the government. Some adherents to this view want to do away with the notion of race altogether. Their goal is a color-blind society that they believe will not be achieved until an individual's race ceases to have a positive or negative impact on access to education, government programs, or employment. Others who advocate this position, however, are ideologically driven conservatives who want to limit the power of the federal government to redress inequality. They have bankrolled state referendums and court cases to end racial classifications and see this as a way to roll back the gains of the civil rights era.

Biracial and Multiracial Identity

Those who are biracial form a second group opposed to the old classification scheme. Racial mixing is nothing new in America. Under slavery many black women were compelled to bear children to their white masters. There have also been consensual relationships and marriages between African Americans and other ethnic and racial groups. The number of such unions and their social acceptance as legitimate relationships have grown precipitously, however, since the civil rights movement destroyed many of the old racial barriers and the U.S. Supreme Court cast down the last **antimiscegenation laws** in *Loving v. Virginia* in 1967. Although still a small percentage of the total, there are now more than 1.5 million mixed-race marriages in the United States and an increasing number of children growing up in these households. The proportion of mixed-race marriages is much higher among younger generations and seems likely to increase rapidly in the future.

The debate over biracial and multiracial identities rages in the African-American community. One of the most significant concerns is that to make fundamental changes in the classification system will

undermine the project they were designed to advance. As poverty researcher John A. Powell put it, "Without racial statistics, we will not know how distributions of resources affect racial and ethnic groups. Without them, racism, which is still very much a part of our society, will be that much more difficult to eradicate, and that much more likely to remain a societal norm." The programs that use these statistics include the Equal Employment Opportunity Act, the Civil Rights Act of 1964, the Voting Rights Act of 1965, the Public Health Act, the Job Partnership Training Act, the Equal Credit Opportunity Act, the Fair Housing Act, and many others. Some argue that offering mixed-race people the option of not being black might undermine the racial solidarity that has been the basis for black advances. As historian Ibrahim K. Sundiata puts it, "[t]he disaggregation of Blacks would drive a wedge into the community that would only increase the isolation of its most disadvantaged members."

Although only 1.8 million Americans opted for the biracial designation in the 2000 census, its existence does bring into question the nature of racial identity itself. Clearly black Americans experienced centuries of discrimination that distinguishes them from other groups. At the same time, many who would have been considered black under the American system of racial classification no longer think of themselves in the same way and may be increasingly able to assert a multiple identity. The larger pattern of recent immigration that the United States is undergoing undermines what had once been a largely biracial dynamic.

Immigration and African Americans

Because of immigration restrictions and the general oppression of people of African descent in America, few blacks, either from the Western Hemisphere or Africa, immigrated to the United States before the last few decades. Changes in immigration laws, particularly the landmark **1965 Hart-Cellar Act**, which abandoned the racially exclusive restrictions of the past, helped open the door. Military, economic, health, and environmental crises in Africa and the Caribbean have pushed substantial numbers from these regions through it. These new African Americans often do not fit their identity neatly into the traditional African-American category.

Black people from the West Indies have a long history of immigration to the United States, but their numbers increased dramatically since the 1960s. During the entire decade of the 1950s, only 123,000 Caribbean people immigrated. During the 1990s nearly one million did so. The Caribbean islands were one of the main areas of importation for African slaves. The islands' sugar production served as the economic engine of the Spanish, French, and British New World empires well into the nineteenth century. These empires all abandoned slavery by the late 1800s. The retreat of colonialism from the Caribbean in the twentieth century

Immigration of peoples of African descent increased dramatically in the 1990s further complicating racial identity issues in black and white America.

has left a number of micro-nations largely populated by people of African descent. Their cultures have remained more influenced by Africa than was true of the United States. Hence African cultural practices were fused with those of the British in Jamaica, the French in Haiti, and the Spanish in Santo Domingo and Cuba. Although a racial hierarchy is not unknown in these societies, racial identity is less important than class and merit-based achievement. Upon immigration to mostly New York, Florida, and other parts of the East Coast, immigrants from the Caribbean soon learn the importance of race in the United States. At the same time they have carved out a separate identity from other African Americans. First-generation West Indians tend to have more economic success than native African Americans, in part because employers often favor them. The second generation has tended to have a more difficult time as the effects of racial discrimination and poor schools take their toll.

Voluntary immigrants from Africa once came in very small numbers. Before 1980 they were mainly European colonials or from North African nations such as Egypt. In the 1950s only 14,000 Africans came over. During the 1990s over 350,000 arrived. Most of these new immigrants are men, and they tend to be among the most highly educated of all immigrants. Part of their reason for coming to the United States was the destabilization of many African nations and the persecution of **autocratic** regimes.

Black Feminism

The feminist and gay rights movements have challenged traditional ideas of racial identity in recent decades. Both arose as part of the broader **rights revolution** that began with the civil rights movement.

Each highlights a different aspect of an individual's identity—gender or sexuality—in addition to race.

A new wave of **feminism** emerged on the American political landscape in the 1960s and 1970s and transformed gender relations. This movement arose, in part, out of the successes of the African-American civil rights struggle. The 1964 Civil Rights Act outlawed sexual as well as racial discrimination in employment. Although this had not been a goal of the civil rights movement at that time, its inclusion was meant in part to lessen the law's chance of passage. It helped open discussions of gender oppression. Many white women activists in SNCC and other civil rights groups assumed leading roles in the emerging feminist movement, often using the same strategies and tactics that had worked in the fight against racism.

Second Wave Feminism achieved many important changes as it gathered adherents in the 1960s and 1970s. The National Organization for Women (NOW), founded in 1966, spearheaded efforts to end job discrimination against women, to expand access to safe and effective birth control, to legalize abortion, and to secure federal and state support for child care. One of the movement's most important early successes was Title IX of the **Educational Amendments Act of 1972**, which required colleges and universities to ensure equal access for women. Another was the Supreme Court's decision in *Roe v. Wade*, legalizing abortion. Beyond these legislative and judicial victories, the feminist movement has opened up choices for women on nearly every aspect of their lives that traditional gender roles had precluded. It has also engendered a backlash as conservative men and women organized to fight against passage of the **Equal Rights Amendment** to the Constitution, access to abortion, sex education in schools, and a variety of related issues. This fight has driven much of the political conflict in the United States since the 1970s.

Black women were involved from the start in shaping modern feminism. The core of black feminist thinking is a dual critique of the women's and black liberation movements' core ideology. Black women scholars and writers argued that analyzing patriarchy was incomplete without attention to race and class. Whereas white leaders of the women's movement were silent on race, many male leaders in the African-American freedom movement were all too forthright about their views on gender. Many believed racial oppression was the primary evil to be fought. Feminism was either a distraction or, by encouraging women to be strong and self-reliant, actually undermined the efforts of black men to overcome the emasculating effects of white male power.

Responding to sexism in the black power movement, many black women writers and activists sought to make the struggle against it as important as that against racism. Between 1973 and 1975, the National Black Feminist Organization (NBFO) articulated many of the concerns specific to black women, from anger with black men for dating and marrying white women, to internal conflict over skin color, hair texture, and facial features, to sexual violence and harassment against black women,

"For Colored Girls who Have Considered Suicide When the Rainbow Is Enuf," a poster by Paul Davis for the ground-breaking play about African-American women by Ntozake Shange (1975).

▶ **Recommended Readings**

Patricia Hill Collins. *Black Feminist Thought: Knowledge, Consciousness, and the Politics of Empowerment.* Boston: Unwin Hyman, 1990. A classic text on black feminist theory and practice by one of black studies' foremost sociologists.

Leith Mullings. *On Our Own Terms: Race, Class, and Gender in the Lives of African American Women.* New York: Routledge, 1997.

Jonathan Betsch Cole and Beverly Guy Sheftall. *Gender Talk: The Struggle for Women's Equality in African-American Communities.* New York: Ballantine Books, 2003.

Epilogue

"A Nation Within a Nation"

Since the first Africans were brought to these shores in the seventeenth century, black people have been a constant and distinct presence in America. During the prolonged course of the Atlantic slave trade, approximately 600,000 Africans were sold into servitude in what became the United States. By the outbreak of the Civil War in 1861 there were nearly four million African Americans in this country. Today black people number over 30 million and make up slightly over 10 percent of the nation's population.

Initially regarded merely as an enslaved labor force to produce cash crops and not as a people who would or could enjoy an equal role in the political and social affairs of American society, African Americans constituted a separate ethnic, racial, and cultural group. For more than two centuries they remained outcasts.

People of African descent developed decidedly ambivalent relationships with the white majority in America. Never fully accepted and never fully rejected, black people relied on their own resources as they created their own institutions and communities. In 1852 Martin Delany declared, "We are a nation within a nation." A half century later W. E. B. Du Bois observed that the black man wanted to retain his African identity and to be an American as well. "He would not Africanize America, for America has too much to teach the world and Africa. He would not bleach his Negro soul in a flood of white Americanism, for he knows that Negro blood has a message for the world. He simply wishes to make it possible for a man to be both a Negro and an American, without being cursed and spit upon by his fellows, without having the doors of Opportunity closed roughly in his face."

Sometimes in desperation or disgust, some black people have been willing to abandon America or reject assimilation. The slaves who engaged in South Carolina's 1739 Stono rebellion attempted to reach Spanish Florida. As early as 1773, slaves in Massachusetts pledged to go to Africa after emancipation. From the 1790s to the start of the Civil War, visions of nationhood in Africa attracted a minority of African Americans. During the 1920s, Marcus Garvey and the Universal Negro Improvement Association glorified Africa while seeking black autonomy in the United States. By the 1950s, Elijah Muhammad, Malcolm X, and the Nation of Islam attracted black people by emphasizing a separate black destiny.

Yet in spite of the horrors of slavery, the indignity and cruelty of Jim Crow, and the unrelenting violence and discrimination inflicted on people of color, most African Americans have not rejected America but worked and struggled to participate fully in the American way of life. African slaves accepted elements of Christianity, and their descendants found solace in their spiritual beliefs. Black Americans have embraced American principles of brotherhood, justice, fairness, and equality before the law that are embedded in the Declaration of Independence and the Constitution. Again and again, African Americans have insisted that America be America, that the American majority live up to its professed ideals and values.

The nation within a nation has never been homogeneous. There have been persistent class, gender, and color divisions. There have been tensions and ideological conflicts among black leaders and organizations as they sought strategies to overcome racial inequities and white supremacy. Some leaders, such as Booker T. Washington, have emphasized self-reliance and economic advancement while others, including W. E. B. Du Bois and leaders of the NAACP, have advocated full inclusion in the nation's political, economic, and social fabric.

Furthermore, African Americans have been far more than victims, than an exploited labor force, than the subjects of segregation and stereotypes. They have contributed enormously to the development and character of American society and culture. As slaves, they provided billions of hours of unrequited labor to the

American economy. Black people established churches, schools, and colleges that continue to thrive. Black people demonstrated a willingness to fight and die for a country that did not fully accept or appreciate their sacrifices. African Americans have made remarkable and innovative contributions to art, music, folklore, science, politics, and athletics that have shaped and enriched American society.

America is no longer what it was in 1700, 1800, or 1900. Chattel slavery ended in 1865. White supremacy is no longer fashionable or openly acceptable. Legal segregation was prohibited a generation ago. The capacity and willingness of Americans of diverse backgrounds and origins to live together in harmony has vastly improved in recent decades. Though we are now in the twenty-first century, the long odyssey of people of African descent has not ended nor will it end in the immediate future. Black people will continue to help mold and define this society, and they will continue to be "a nation within a nation."

Historically Black Four-Year Colleges and Universities

Institution and Location	Year Founded	Land-Grant, Public, or Church Affiliated Denomination
Alabama A&M University, Normal, Alabama	1875	Land-grant
Alabama State University, Montgomery, Alabama	1867	Public
Albany State University, Albany, Georgia	1903	Public
Alcorn State University, Lorman, Mississippi	1871	Land-grant
Allen University, Columbia, South Carolina	1870	AME
Arkansas Baptist College, Little Rock, Arkansas	1884	Baptist
Barber-Scotia College, Concord, North Carolina	1904	Presbyterian
Benedict College, Columbia, South Carolina	1870	Baptist
Bennett College, Greensboro, North Carolina	1873	United Methodist
Bethune-Cookman College, Daytona Beach, Florida	1904	United Methodist
Bluefield State College, Bluefield, West Virginia	1895	Public
Bowie State University, Bowie, Maryland	1865	Public
Central State University, Wilberforce, Ohio	1887	Public
Cheyney University, Cheyney, Pennsylvania	1837	Public
Claflin College, Orangeburg, South Carolina	1869	United Methodist
Clark Atlanta University, Atlanta, Georgia	1988	United Methodist
Concordia College, Selma, Alabama	1922	Lutheran
Coppin State University, Baltimore, Maryland	1900	Public
Delaware State University, Dover, Delaware	1891	Land-grant
Dillard University, New Orleans, Louisiana	1930	Congregational/ United Methodist
Edward Waters College, Jacksonville, Florida	1866	AME
Elizabeth City State University, Elizabeth City, North Carolina	1891	Public
Fayetteville State University, Fayetteville, North Carolina	1867	Public
Fisk University, Nashville, Tennessee	1866	United Church of Christ
Florida A&M University, Tallahassee, Florida	1887	Land-grant
Florida Memorial College, Miami, Florida	1879	Baptist
Fort Valley State College, Fort Valley, Georgia	1895	Land-grant
Grambling State University, Grambling, Louisiana	1901	Public
Hampton University, Hampton, Virginia	1868	Private
Harris-Stowe State College, St. Louis, Missouri	1857	Public
Howard University, Washington, DC	1867	Public
Huston-Tillotson College, Austin, Texas	1952	United Church of Christ/ United Methodist
Jackson State University, Jackson, Mississippi	1877	Public
Jarvis Christian College, Hawkins, Texas	1913	Disciple of Christ Christian Church
Johnson C. Smith University, Charlotte, North Carolina	1867	Presbyterian
Kentucky State University, Frankfort, Kentucky	1886	Land-grant
Knoxville College, Knoxville, Tennessee	1875	Presbyterian
Lane College, Jackson, Tennessee	1882	Christian Methodist Episcopal
Langston University, Langston, Oklahoma	1897	Land-grant
LeMoyne-Owen College, Memphis, Tennessee	1870	United Church of Christ
Lincoln University, Jefferson City, Missouri	1866	Land-grant

Institution and Location	Year Founded	Land-Grant, Public, or Church Affiliated Denomination	Institution and Location	Year Founded	Land-Grant, Public, or Church Affiliated Denomination
Lincoln University, Lincoln, Pennsylvania	1854	Public	Southern University at New Orleans, New Orleans, Louisiana	1956	Public
Livingstone College, Salisbury, North Carolina	1879	AME	Southwestern Christian College, Terrell, Texas	1949	Church of Christ
Miles College, Birmingham, Alabama	1908	Christian Methodist Episcopal	Spelman College, Atlanta, Georgia	1876	Presbyterian
Mississippi Valley State University, Ita Bena, Mississippi	1946	Public	Stillman College, Tuscaloosa, Alabama	1876	Presbyterian
Morehouse College, Atlanta, Georgia	1867	Baptist	Talladega College, Talladega, Alabama	1867	United Church of Christ
Morgan State University, Baltimore, Maryland	1867	Public	Tennessee State University, Nashville, Tennessee	1912	Land-grant
Morris Brown College, Atlanta, Georgia	1881	AME	Texas College, Tyler, Texas	1894	Christian Methodist Episcopal
Morris College, Sumter, South Carolina	1908	Baptist	Texas Southern University, Houston, Texas	1947	Public
Norfolk State University, Norfolk, Virginia	1935	Public	Tougaloo College, Tougaloo, Mississippi	1869	United Church of Christ/United Missionary Society
North Carolina A&T St. U, Greensboro, North Carolina	1892	Land-grant	Tuskegee University, Tuskegee, Alabama	1881	Land-grant
North Carolina Central University, Durham, North Carolina	1909	Public	University of Arkansas at Pine Bluff, Pine Bluff, Arkansas	1873	Land-grant
Oakwood College, Huntsville, Alabama	1896	Seventh Day Adventist	University of the District of Columbia, Washington, DC	1977	Public
Paine College, Augusta, Georgia	1882	United Methodist	University of Maryland, Eastern Shore, Princess Anne, Maryland	1886	Land-grant
Paul Quinn College, Dallas, Texas	1872	AME			
Philander Smith College, Little Rock, Arkansas	1877	United Methodist	University of the Virgin Islands, St. Thomas, United States Virgin Islands	1962	Public
Prairie View A&M University, Prairie View, Texas	1878	Land-grant			
Rust College, Holly Springs, Mississippi	1866	United Methodist	Virginia State University, Petersburg, Virginia	1882	Land-grant
Saint Augustine's College, Raleigh, North Carolina	1867	Episcopal	Virginia Union University, Richmond, Virginia	1865	Baptist
Saint Paul's College, Lawrenceville, Virginia	1888	Episcopal	Voorhees College, Denmark, South Carolina	1897	Episcopal
Savannah State College, Savannah, Georgia	1890	Public	West Virginia State College, Institute, West Virginia	1891	Public
Selma University, Selma, Alabama	1878	Baptist	Wilberforce University, Wilberforce, Ohio	1856	AME
Shaw University, Raleigh, North Carolina	1865	Baptist	Wiley College, Marshall, Texas	1873	United Methodist
Sojourner-Douglass College, Baltimore, Maryland	1980	Private	Winston-Salem State University, Winston-Salem, North Carolina	1892	Public
South Carolina State University, Orangeburg, South Carolina	1896	Land-grant			
Southern University and A&M College, Baton Rouge, Louisiana	1880	Land-grant	Xavier University of New Orleans, New Orleans, Louisiana	1925	Roman Catholic

Glossary

A

abolitionism Movement to abolish slavery.

abolitionist An advocate of the abolition of slavery.

acculturation The modification of a culture as the result of contact with another culture.

affirmative action Policies intended to actively remedy historical discrimination and racial inequality.

African Dorcas Associations Societies that distributed used clothing to the poor.

Afro-American League Organization formed in 1889 to press for civil and political rights for African Americans.

Afrocentricity Philosophy of culture with an African-centered perspective.

Agricultural Adjustment Act (AAA) A federal program that provided subsidies to farmers to grow less to help stabilize prices.

Aid to Families with Dependent Children Program providing aid to poor families with dependent children, created as part of the New Deal.

Alabama Christian Movement for Human Rights (ACMHR) Civil rights coalition formed in Birmingham, Alabama.

Albany Movement Civil rights coalition formed in Albany, Georgia in 1961.

aliens Non-citizen residents of the United States.

American and Foreign Anti-Slavery Society (AFASS) Group formed after the AASS splintered in the 1840s.

American Anti-Slavery Society (AASS) Organization formed by William Lloyd Garrison in 1833 to work for immediate emancipation and equal rights for African Americans.

American Colonization Society (ACS) White organization that supported the migration of African Americans to Africa.

American Colonization Society Organization founded in 1816 to promote the migration of African Americans to Africa.

American Federation of Labor Labor federation founded.

American Negro Academy Scholarly organization for men of African descent formed in 1897.

American Party Nativist party also known as the Know-Nothing Party.

Amistad A Spanish slave schooner that was the site of a successful slave uprising in 1839.

Amnesty International International human rights organization.

anarchists Supporters of the theory that all forms of government are undesirable and should be abolished.

Ancient Egypt The earliest civilization in Africa, which emerged in the Nile valley in the fourth millennium BCE .

annexation To incorporate territory into an existing political entity.

antebellum Pre-Civil War.

antiapartheid movement Movement to end apartheid in South Africa.

antimiscegenation laws Laws outlawing interracial relationships and marriages.

antislavery movements The two main movements, one in the North and one in the South, dedicated to ending slavery.

antislavery societies Societies formed under Quaker leadership to promote the abolition of slavery.

apartheid An official policy of racial segregation.

archconservative Highly conservative.

Articles of Confederation The constitution from which the Congress derived its authority between 1781 and 1789.

Asiento Monopolies over the slave trade granted by the Spanish government to private companies.

assimilation The adoption by a minority group of the customs and norms of the majority culture.

Atlantic slave trade The trade begun by the Portuguese in the late fifteenth century in which Europeans bought slaves in Africa and shipped them to the Americas.

autocratic Acting with unlimited power or authority.

Axis Alliance that included Germany, Italy, and Japan.

B

Bacon's rebellion Failed rebellion led by Nathaniel Bacon against Virginia's tobacco-planting elite.

Battle of New Orleans Battle fought in January 1815, one month after a peace treaty had been negotiated.

bebop A new style of jazz music developed in the 1940s.

Beecher's Bibles Term for firearms used by antislavery forces in Kansas.

Benevolent Empire A network of church-related voluntary organizations.

benign institution An institution with generally beneficial effects.

Berbers The indigenous people of western North Africa.

biracial Group or organization with members of two races.

black arts movement Artistic movement reflecting the determination of black artists to produce black art for black people.

Black Brigade Brigade made up of African-Americans formed by James Forten, Richard Allen, and Absalom Jones during the War of 1812.

Black Cabinet A group of highly placed African Americans that made up the Federal Council on Negro Affairs.

black codes Laws passed by southern legislatures that imposed severe restrictions on freedmen.

The Black Committee Committee of elite black men formed to help raise a black regiment.

Black laws Laws designed to restrict the migration of blacks.

Black Metropolis Term used by St. Clair Drake and Horace R. Cayton for Chicago's South Side.

black migration The movement of African Americans from the United States to other countries, particularly Canada.

black nationalist tradition Belief that a separate nation was in the best interests of African Americans.

Black Power Slogan popularized by Stokely Carmichael.

black studies Scholarly study of the experiences of people of African descent throughout the world.

Bleeding Kansas Term for Kansas during the violence that followed the passage of the Kansas-Nebraska Act.

Bloody Sunday March 7, 1965 attack on civil rights marchers by Clark county police.

blues Musical form developed by poor black people in the South.

bondage The condition of enslavement.

Border Ruffians Proslavery forces that entered Kansas from Missouri to attack antislavery settlers and vote illegally in Kansas elections.

Boston Massacre 1770 event in which British troops fired into an angry crowd, killing five Bostonians.

Boulé Exclusive organization founded by two wealthy Philadelphia physicians in 1904.

Briggs v. Elliott The first legal challenge to elementary school segregation to originate in the South.

Bronzeville A neighborhood on Chicago's South Side.

Brookes Ship frequently used to illustrate a slaver's capacity for human cargo.

Brotherhood of Sleeping Car Porters (BSCP) Union of Pullman porters formed under the leadership of A. Philip Randolph in 1925.

Brown II Second set of Supreme Court rulings that addressed the practical problem of desegregation.

Brown v. Board of Education of Topeka Landmark court ruling that overturned the doctrine of "separate-but-equal."

Brownsville affair The dismissal of three companies of black soldiers for their alleged involvement in a shooting incident.

buffalo soldiers Term used by Plains Indians for black soldiers.

C

Cahokia The largest center of the Mississippian culture.

Canada West Present-day Ontario and the ultimate destination for many on the underground railroad.

carpetbaggers White northern migrants to the South.

centrist One who positions him or herself in the middle of the political mainstream.

chattel slavery A system of slavery in which slaves were legal property on a level with livestock.

chattel The personal property of a particular person, in the case of a slave, his or her master.

children's crusade Birmingham civil rights march involving thousands of young people.

Civil Rights Act of 1875 Act intended to open public accommodations to all people regardless of race.

Civil Rights Act of 1957 First civil rights act passed by Congress since the end of Reconstruction.

Civil Rights Act of 1964 Act banning segregation in places of public accommodation and establishing the Equal Employment Opportunity Commission.

Civil Rights Act of 1968 Act outlawing discrimination in the sale and rental of housing.

coffles A group of slaves chained or roped together.

Cold War The decades long conflict between the United States and the Soviet Union.

colonization The establishment of colonies outside of the United States for African Americans.

Colored Farmers' Alliance Organization of black farmers that claimed over 1 million members.

Committee for Industrial Organization (CIO) Labor organization that was committed to inter-racial and multiethnic organizing.

Communist Party Political party formed to promote communism.

Community Action Programs (CAPS) Anti-poverty programs involving "maximum feasible participation" by the poor themselves.

compensated emancipation Emancipation accompanied by the monetary compensation of former slave owners.

Compromise of 1850 Compromise introduced by Henry Clay that would allow California to enter the Union as a free state at the same time as it strengthened the Fugitive Slave Law.

Confederacy Association of slave states that left the Union in 1861.

Confederate States of America Alliance of the seven states that seceded in February 1861.

Congress of Racial Equality Protest group committed to nonviolent direct action.

Congressional Black Caucus (CBC) Caucus of African-American members of Congress.

conscription law 1862 Confederate law defining who was required to provide military service.

conservatives Individuals who tend to support traditional views and values and to oppose change.

Constitutional Union Party A party formed by former Whigs which nominated John Bell of Tennessee for president in 1860.

Continental Congress Organization of patriot leaders that, in July 1776, declared the colonies to be independent states.

contraband Goods that may be seized or confiscated.

convict lease system System in which businesses and planters leased convicts from the state.

Cotton Club Harlem's most exclusive and fashionable nightspot in the 1920s.

cotton culture The area in which cotton was a predominant crop.

cotton gin Machine for the removal of seeds from cotton.

Council of Federated Organizations Civil rights organization active in 1964's Freedom Summer.

Creoles Slaves born in the Americas.

creolization The process of cultural exchanges that led African parents to produce African-American children.

D

December 7, 1941 The date on which Pearl Harbor was attacked by Japanese forces.

Declaration of Independence Document adopted by the Continental Congress on July 4, 1776 that called for independence from Britain.

Democratic Party Party created Andrew Jackson's supporters, led by Martin Van Buren.

diaspora dispersion of a people from their original homeland.

disfranchisement To deprive of the right to vote.

disunion The separation of the North from the South.

Dixiecrat party Splinter party formed after the Democratic party adopted a strong civil rights platform plank at its convention.

domestic slave trade The interstate market for slaves.

Double V campaign Slogan during World War II that stood for victory over fascism abroad and over racism at home for blacks.

drivers Overseers, almost always black, who directed the activities of work gangs.

Dyer bill 1918 anti-lynching measure sponsored by Leonidas Dyer.

Economic Opportunity Act of 1964 Act creating the Office of Economic Opportunity and a number programs aimed at poor communities.

E

Education Act Act that increased federal funding to colleges and universities and provided low-interest loans to students.

Educational Amendments Act Act requiring colleges and universities to ensure equal access for women.

Eight Box Law A primitive literacy test used in South Carolina to disfranchise black voters.

1862 Homestead Act Act providing 160 acres of federal land to anyone willing to settle and farm on it for five years.

Eighteenth Amendment Amendment to the U.S. Constitution that, along with the Volstead Act, prohibited the manufacture, distribution, and sale of alcoholic beverages.

Emancipation Proclamation Proclamation issued on January 1, 1863 declaring all slaves residing in states in rebellion free.

emancipation The freeing of enslaved African Americans.

Enforcement Acts Acts of 1870 and 1871 meant to respond to terrorism in the South.

Enlightenment Eighteenth-century intellectual movement that stressed the ability of human reason to discover the "natural laws" of the universe.

Equal Employment Opportunity Commission Agency established to monitor discrimination in employment.

Equal Rights Amendment Proposed amendment to the Constitution ending discrimination on the basis of sex.

Erie Canal Canal that opened a water route from New York City to the Old Northwest.

ethnicity Ethnic background.

Eurocentric Centered or focused on Europe.

Executive Order #11063 Order requiring government agencies to end discrimination in federally supported housing.

Executive Order #8802 Order that affirmed that it was the policy of the United States that there should be no discrimination in the employment of workers in the defense industry or government.

Executive Order #9346 Order establishing a new Committee on Fair Employment Practices, with greater resources, and direct oversight by the Executive Office of the President.

Executive Order #9981 Order officially desegregating the armed services.

Exodusters Black migrants to Kansas between 1865 and 1880.

expansionism The drive to expand the territory of the United States.

expatriation Forced removal of African Americans to Africa.

F

factories Fortified structures in which slaves were held in preparation for transport to the Americas.

Fair Employment Practices Committee A committee created by Franklin Roosevelt to investigate complaints of discrimination.

Fair Play Committee Organization formed to promote black actors in the movie industry and improve the image of blacks in film.

Family Assistance Plan (FAP) Plan giving financial assistance to families with no wage earner.

farmers alliances Alliances formed by small farmers across the country in the 1880s.

fascism An authoritarian political system stressing the merger of big business and the state.

Federal Arts Project New Deal agency created to promote the creation of public art.

Federal Theater Project WPA arts project that employed actors, writers, and other theater professionals.

Federalist One of United States' first political parties.

feminism Belief in the social, political, and economic equality of the sexes.

fictive kin relationships Fictional relationships created by enslaved Africans intended to help provide mutual support.

Fifteenth Amendment Amendment to the U.S. Constitution stipulating that a person cannot be deprived of the right to vote on the basis of race

Fifth Amendment Amendment to the U.S. Constitution that protects individuals from the loss of life, property, or liberty without due process of law.

First Confiscation Act 1861 Act that stated that any slaves used by their masters to benefit the Confederacy would be freed.

First New Deal Economic initiatives enacted in the first one hundred days of the Roosevelt administration.

First Reconstruction Act 1867 Act that implemented the radical Republican vision of Reconstruction.

First South Carolina Volunteers Black regiment organized by General David Hunter in May of 1862.

forest region The area of West Africa that extends along the Atlantic coast from Senegambia to the former kingdom of Benin.

Forty-Niners Americans who went to California in 1849 to search for gold.

Fourteen points Woodrow Wilson's principles for the fashioning of the post-World War I world.

Fourteenth Amendment Amendment to the U.S. Constitution compelling states to accept their residents as citizens and to guarantee their rights as citizens.

franchise The right to vote.

Free African Society A famous mutual aid society established in 1787 by Richard Allen and Absalom Jones.

free labor Free men and women working for their own gain.

free papers Documents free blacks in the upper South had to carry at all times and which were subject to periodic renewal.

Free Produce Association Quaker-led effort to boycott agricultural products produced by slaves.

Freedmen's Bureau Temporary agency set up to assist freedmen to make the transition to freedom.

Freedom Rides Travel by civil rights advocates on buses and trains in the South.

Freedom Summer 1964 civil rights campaign in Mississippi.

Freedom's Journal The first black newspaper.

freemasonry Fraternal organization featuring rationalism, secrecy, and obscure ritual.

Free-Soil Party Party formed in 1848 to prevent the expansion of slavery.

Freetown A refuge established in Sierra Leone in 1787 for former slaves.

Fugitive Slave Act Act of 1793 that allowed masters or their agents to pursue slaves across state lines.

Fugitive Slave Law of 1793 Extended into the northern states the power of southern slaveholders to enslave African Americans

Fugitive Slave Law of 1850 Strengthened law for the recovery of runaway slaves.

G

Gabriel's conspiracy 1800 abortive effort to launch a slave revolt.

Gag Rule Rule stating that no petition related to slavery could be introduced in the House of Representatives.

gang system System of collective agricultural labor that existed on most plantations.

gangsta rap Form of rap that focuses on the experience of gang life.

Gary convention 1972 meeting of black political groups and leaders.

Gayle v. Browder Supreme Court ruling that segregation of public transportation was unconstitutional.

General Order 11 Order threatening retaliation for the mistreatment of black soldiers by Confederate forces.

Gore v. Bush Supreme Court decision halting the recount of ballots in Florida.

gospel The traditional religious music of the black church.

grandfather clause Louisiana law that stipulated that only voters whose father or grandfather had been eligible to vote before 1867 would be eligible to vote.

Grange A social and fraternal organization founded in the 1870s that promoted the formation of cooperatives and involvement in politics.

Great Awakening Eighteenth-century religious revival that grew out of growing dissatisfaction among white Americans with a deterministic and formalistic style of Protestantism.

The Great Depression Economic downturn that began in 1929 and lasted throughout the 1930s.

great gang The group of male slaves who did the heavy work of planting and harvesting.

great migration The migration of African Americans from the rural South to the urban North between 1910 and 1940.

Great Postal Campaign Campaign to send antislavery material to southern post offices and individual slaveholders.

The Great Society Programs created in response to the problems of poor Americans championed by President Johnson.

griots Self-employed poets who travelled from place to place and used their trained memories to recall historical events and precise genealogies.

H

Hamburg Massacre Violent confrontation between black militiamen and whites in Hamburg, South Carolina.

Harlem Renaissance The intellectual, artistic, and cultural flowering of Harlem in the 1920s and 1930s.

Harlem Section of New York City that became the intellectual and cultural center of black society in the 1920s.

hemp A plant used to make rope and bagging for cotton bales.

hip-hop nation Term for younger generation of African Americans.

Holiness movement Religious movement offering an alternative to mainline denominations.

hominids The biological family to which humans belong.

homo erectus An advanced human that appeared in Africa 1.6 million years ago.

Hoovervilles Makeshift camps inhabited by poor men, women, and children.

House of Burgesses Virginia's governmental body empowered to enact legislation for the colony.

house slaves House slaves were slaves who worked as cooks, maids, butlers, nurses, and gardeners.

House Un-American Activities Committee (HUAC) Congressional committee formed to investigate the activities of communists and "communist sympathizers" in America.

I

immigrant A person who leaves one country to settle in another.

immune regiments Name given to black units by the War Department due to the supposed immunity of blacks to the heat and humidity of Cuba.

impressment The forced seizure of men for labor or military service.

incarceration Imprisonment.

indentured servant Person who lost their freedom for a specified period of time, either because they sold it or as punishment for debt or crime.

Indians The diverse peoples called Indians as a result of Christopher Columbus's mistaken belief that in 1492 he had landed in the "Indies."

indigenous peoples Populations originating in an area or environment.

indigenous Originating in an area or environment.

industrial slavery The use of slaves in industrial work.

Industrial Workers of the World Revolutionary labor organization founded in 1905.

industrialization The development of industrial modes of production.

integrationist Proponent of the racial integration of society.

internal slave trade Interstate trade in slaves, particularly between the old tobacco-growing regions and the new cotton-growing regions.

International Labor Defense (ILD) Communist Party organization that provided legal support to the "Scottsboro boys."

J

Jacksonian reform Reform movement launched by the Benevolent Empire.

jazz Mostly improvised music that supplanted ragtime in the early twentieth century.

Jim Crow Term associated with segregated public spaces and amenities.

Joint Committee on Reconstruction Congressional committee formed in 1865 to determine whether the southern states should be readmitted to the Union.

jumping the broom A common part of the slave wedding ceremony.

K

Kansas-Nebraska Act 1854 Act granting residents of Kansas the right to vote on whether or not slavery should be allowed in the territory.

Knights of Labor Labor union formed in 1869 that welcomed both black and white members.

Know-Nothings Members of a nativist party also know as the American Party.

Ku Klux Klan Act 1871 Act that made it a federal offense to interfere with the right to vote, hold office, serve on a jury, or enjoy equal protection under the law.

Ku Klux Klan Terrorist organization founded in 1866 with the goal of neutralizing the power of the Republican party.

L

lactose intolerance The inability to properly digest milk and milk products.

Legal Defense and Educational Fund (NAACP-LDEF) Fund set up by the NAACP to support the attack on the legal foundations of race inequality in American education.

Legend Singers Black professional chorus directed by Kenneth Billups.

"Letter from Birmingham Jail" Influential letter written by Martin Luther King Jr. while in prison in Birmingham, Alabama.

The Liberator Abolitionist newspaper established by William Lloyd Garrison in 1831.

Liberia Colony of free African Americans founded on the West African coast.

Liberian Exodus Company organized to ship 206 black migrants to Liberia in 1878.

Liberty Party Group formed after the AASS splintered in the 1840s.

lien Security for payment of a debt.

Louisiana Rebellion 1811 slave revolt led by Deslondes, a Haitian native and slave driver on a plantation north of New Orleans.

low country The coastal plain of Carolina and Georgia.

Lowndes County Freedom Organization (LCFO) Political organization founded in 1965 by Stokely Carmichael.

Loyalist A citizen of the American colonies who remained loyal to the British government during the War for Independence.

lynching Executions without due process of law.

M

Mammy Stereotype of the dutiful black woman who nurtures white families.

mandate Authorization or approval of the electorate.

manumission The legal freeing of slave.

manumit The freeing of slave by his or her master.

March on Washington Movement (MOWM) Movement created by A. Philip Randolph to pressure the federal government to end discrimination in the defense industry and government.

March on Washington Civil rights demonstration in August 1963 that drew 250,000 marchers.

market revolution The transformation of the North into a modern industrial society.

maroons A word for escaped slaves derived from the Spanish word *cimarron*, meaning wild.

matrilineal Relating to, based on, or tracing descent through the female line.

Men of Bronze Name given to soldiers of the 369th regiment for their exemplary combat record in World War I.

middle passage The section of the triangular trade in which slaves were transported from Africa to the Americas.

Militia Act of 1862 1862 Act authorizing Lincoln to enlist black soldiers.

Militia Act Act of 1792 that eliminated armed black participation in all state militias except that of North Carolina.

miscegenation Interracial sexual contact.

Mississippi Freedom Democratic Party (MFDP) Party set up to challenge Mississippi's regular Democratic delegation to the 1964 national convention.

Missouri Compromise 1820 compromise that permitted Missouri to enter the Union as a slave state and Maine to enter the Union as a free state.

Missouri Territory Portion of the Louisiana Territory that applied for admission to the Union in 1819 as a slave state.

money power According to the Democrats, a conspiratorial alliance of bankers and businessmen that worked against the interests of workers and farmers.

Montgomery Improvement Association (MIA) Organization formed to coordinate the Montgomery bus boycott.

moral suasion The appeal to Americans to support abolition on the basis of their Christian consciences.

Morrill Land-Grant Act 1862 Act which provided states with funds for agricultural and mechanical colleges.

Moynihan Report Report attributing many of the problems of poor black communities to the breakdown of the "lower-class" black family.

mulattoes Individuals of mixed African and European ancestry.

mutual aid societies Societies that provided for their members' medical and burial expenses and helped support widows and children.

N

Nation of Islam Religious movement that fused Islam and black nationalism.

National Association for the Advancement of Colored People (NAACP) Militant organization formed by W. E. B. Du Bois dedicated to racial justice.

National Association of Colored Women Group formed by the merger of the National Federation of Afro-American Women and the National Colored Women's League in 1896.

National Colored Labor Union Union formed by black Baltimore longshoreman, Isaac Myers, in 1869.

National Industrial Recovery Act (NIRA) An Act intended to promote the revival of manufacturing by allowing for cooperation among industries.

National Medical Association Black physician's professional organization.

National Negro Congress (NNC) Organization intended to unite African-American protest groups.

National Recovery Administration (NRA) Organization responsible for overseeing the NIRA.

nationalism African-American Movement for the creation of separate African-American nations.

nativist A political philosophy favoring the rights of established citizens over new immigrants.

natural laws Basic laws that governed all natural events, including human social organization and interactions.

Negro Leagues Professional baseball leagues for black players.

Negro National League Black baseball league formed in 1920 under the leadership of Andrew "Rube" Foster.

The Negro Soldier Film produced by the War Department designed to reduce racial tensions in the military.

Negro Women's Franchise League Group led by Daisy Lampkin and dedicated to fighting for the vote for African Americans.

negroes A word used for black people, derived from the Spanish word for black.

new Africans Slaves who had just survived the middle passage.

New Deal Set of policies proposed by the Roosevelt administration in response to the Great Depression.

New Era Club Club formed in 1893 by black women in Boston

New Right Emergent conservative political force marked by the election of Ronald Reagan in 1980.

New York draft riot Riot by mostly Irish mob in response to the Union draft.

1965 Hart-Cellar Act Act ending racially exclusive restrictions of immigration.

Nineteenth Amendment Amendment to the United States Constitution granting women the right to vote.

No Child Left Behind Act Education reform act that required schools to regularly test students' progress toward defined goals.

North Atlantic Treaty Organization Military alliance formed to counter the threat posed by the Soviet Union and its allies.

North Star Influential black newspaper published in the 1840s and 1850s by Frederick Douglass.

Northwest Ordinance Ordinance that provided for the formation of new states in the Old Northwest and the banning of slavery in that region.

Nullification Crisis 1832–1833 crisis over South Carolina's effort to nullify the collection of the U.S. tariff on imports within the state.

O

Olaudah Equiano Writer and antislavery activist who born in 1745 in Nigeria, captured and enslaved when he was ten years old, and wrote a book about his experience as a slave after he purchased his own freedom.

outliers Escaped slaves who lived nearby their master's estate.

P

Pan-African Congress Congress convened to promote the connection and cooperation of people of African descent around the world.

Panic of 1873 Financial crisis that sent the U.S. economy into a slump that lasted several years.

paternalism The treatment or governing of people in a fatherly manner.

patriarchy A social system or government based on the rule of fathers.

patrilineal Relating to, based on, or tracing descent through the male line.

patriot Advocate of the colonies' separation from Britain.

Peace Mission Movement Religious movement led by Father Major Jealous Divine.

peculiar institution A euphemism for slavery.

peonage The virtual enslavement of a debtor farmer.

People United to Save Humanity (PUSH) Organization founded by Jesse Jackson after Martin Luther King's assassination.

per capita tax Tax calculated on the basis of the number of people residing in a state.

Personal Responsibility Act Welfare reform act of 1996.

pharaoh The title given to Egypt's kings.

Philadelphia Female Anti-Slavery Society Society formed in 1833 by black and white women dedicated to ending slavery.

Philadelphia plan Plan in which federal government contracts in the construction industry would have to set or meet hiring goals for African Americans.

Philadelphia Vigilance Association Group formed in response to the use of force by slave catchers to recapture fugitive slaves.

Philippine Insurrection Filipino uprising led by Emilio Aguinaldo against the American occupation of the Philippines.

placebo An inactive substance used as a control in an experiment.

planters White plantation owners who controlled large plots of agricultural land.

Plessy v. Ferguson Supreme Court ruling that established the principle of "separate but equal" public accommodations.

poet laureate Poet appointed to an honorary position.

polygynous Having more than one wife at a time.

Poor People's Campaign Project supported by Martin Luther King involving the march of tens of thousands of poor people on Washington.

popular sovereignty The principle that each state should decide major issues, such as slavery, on its own.

Populist Party Party formed in 1892 with the support of many alliance farmers.

Port Royal Experiment Enclave around Beaufort and Port Royal, South Carolina, where freedmen farmed under federal supervision.

positive good Something that produces an unambiguous benefit.

practical abolitionists People who, while not members of formal abolitionist organizations, nonetheless took action to oppose slavery and help slaves.

practical Christianity Evangelical emphasis on action and on a form of Christianity that helped others.

Preliminary Emancipation Proclamation Proclamation issued on September 22, 1862 declaring that slaves residing in states still in rebellion on January 1, 1863, would be freed.

Prince Hall Masons Members of the Masonic lodge founded by Prince Hall.

prisoners' rights movement Movement in support of prisoners' rights backed by the Black Panthers and others.

privateers Merchants vessels armed and authorized by the government to raid enemy shipping.

Proclamation Line Act of 1763 that forbid American settlement west of the crest of the Appalachian Mountains.

progressive movement Late nineteenth-century reform movement dedicated to the creation of a new social awareness in America.

Progressive Party Political party that stood for social reform and which nominated Theodore Roosevelt for president in 1912.

Project 100,000 Military project with the goal of reducing the number of African Americans rejected by the military.

Project C Campaign of civil rights activities planned by the ACMHR and the SCLC.

proletariat Industrial wage earners.

protest literature Literature intended to call attention to injustice.

punitive expedition 1916 U.S. intervention in Mexico launched in response to Francisco "Pancho" Villa's incursion into New Mexico.

Put-in-Bay 1813 naval engagement on Lake Erie in which one quarter of the U.S. sailors were black.

R

race films Films made for African-American audiences.

race riots Violent confrontations between whites and blacks sparked by racial tensions.

racial etiquette Complex social code that determined how blacks and whites interacted.

racial preferences Preferences based on race.

Radical Republicans Militant Republicans who opposed Andrew Johnson and presidential Reconstruction.

ragtime Form of composed music written for piano that emerged in the 1890s.

Railway Labor Act Act defining the legal rights of railway owners and workers.

Rainbow Coalition Coalition of people who felt politically marginalized and underrepresented, founded by Jesse Jackson in 1983.

rap Form of rhythmic speaking in rhyme.

ratification To approve or give formal sanction.

Redemption The return of southern states to conservative white political control.

Reds Derogatory term for communists and communist sympathizers.

rent party Party thrown to help raise money for rent.

Republican One of United States first political parties.

revivalism Movement to "revive" the place of Christianity in American life.

rights revolution Collective term for emergence of movements for rights for women and minorities.

Rosa Parks African-American woman whose refusal to give up her bus seat sparked the Montgomery Bus boycott.

Rough Riders Theodore Roosevelt's volunteer unit involved in the invasion of Cuba.

S

Savannah Educational Association Association created by black ministers in Savannah to help create a school for black students.

savannah A flat grassland of tropical or subtropical regions.

scalawags White Southerners who hoped for assistance from Republican governments.

seasoning A period of up to two years of acculturating slaves and breaking them into plantation routines.

secession Withdrawal from the United States.

Second Confiscation Act 1862 Act freeing all slaves of rebel owners.

Second Great Awakening Evangelical religious movement that lasted from the late eighteenth century to the 1830s.

Second New Deal Roosevelt's second burst of legislation that included the Social Security Act and the National Labor Relations Act.

Secret Six The six men who secretly financed John Brown's raid on Harpers Ferry.

segregation The practice of separating people on the basis of race.

"separate but equal" doctrine The doctrine that "separate but equal" public institutions and facilities satisfied the requirements of the U.S. Constitution.

set-aside programs Programs that reserved some contracts for minority-owned businesses or that favored the hiring of women and minorities.

Seven Years' War War between France and Britain that began in North America in 1754, spread to Europe in 1756, and forced France to withdraw from North America in 1763.

sharecropping Agricultural labor arrangement in which landowners supplied seed and equipment to farmers in return for two-thirds of the crop.

Shays's Rebellion Armed uprising of the farmers of Western Massachusetts that began in 1786 and ended in 1787.

Shotgun Policy A campaign of violence directed at blacks and Republican officials in Mississippi in 1875.

sickle cell anemia A fatal disease more common in people of African than Europan descent.

sit-in The act of occupying the seats or an area of a segregated establishment to protest racial discrimination.

skilled slaves Skilled slaves worked as carpenters, blacksmiths, millwrights, and at other skilled labor.

slave catchers Individuals who recaptured escaped slaves and returned them to their masters.

slave codes Laws governing the practice of slavery in a given region.

slave pens Holding areas used by slave traders.

slave power According to the Democrats' opponents, a conspiratorial alliance that included the Democrats that worked to expand and strengthen slavery.

slavers Small and narrow ships used to transport slaves to the Americas.

smoked Yankees Name given to black troops by Spanish soldiers.

social Darwinism A misapplication of Darwin's theory of evolution to human societies.

social realism school A form of naturalistic realism focusing specifically on social problems and the hardships of everyday life.

Soledad Brothers Three black prisoners accused of killing a white guard.

Southern Christian Leadership Council (SCLC) Organization created to provide an institutional base for the civil rights movement.

Southern Homestead Act 1866 Act which set aside 3 million acres for black people and southern whites who had remained loyal to the Union.

Southern Regional Council (SRC) Organization that conducted research and focused attention on social, political, and educational inequality in the South.

The Southern Manifesto Statement issued by Strom Thurmond vowing to preserve segregation.

Southern Strategy President Nixon's strategy to attract southern white voters.

sovereignty The concept under which each state retained control over its internal affairs.

Spanish-American War 1898 war between the United States and Spain sparked by the destruction of the USS *Maine*.

Special Field Order #15 Military directive setting aside a strip of land along the Atlantic coast for freedmen.

Stamp Act Act of 1765 designed to raise revenue for the British government that levied duties on paper products.

Statistical Policy Directive 15 Directive that set up standard racial categories for federal government use.

statutes A law enacted by a legislature.

stay laws Laws which prohibited the seizure of property to satisfy debts.

stevedores Workers who loaded and unloaded ships.

Student Nonviolent Coordinating Committee (SNCC) Civil rights organization formed in 1960 at the instigation of Ella Baker.

Subtreasury system A loan and marketing system to be run for the benefit of farmers.

Sudan The huge grassland region south of the semidesert region known as Sahel.

suffrage The right to vote.

Sugar Act Act of 1764 designed to raise revenue for the British government that levied duties on sugar.

swing A style of dance music popular in the 1930s and 1940s.

T

talented tenth According to W. E. B. Du Bois, the best educated 10 percent of the black population who should advance the cause of African Americans.

Tea Act Act that gave the British East India Company a monopoly over all tea sold in the American colonies.

temperance Abstinence from the use of alcoholic beverages.

tenant farmers Farmers who cultivated rented land.

term slavery Slavery for a defined period of time, rather than for life.

Terrell law The Terrell law was Texas law banning African American participation in the Democratic primary.

territorial bands Traveling musical groups.

Tet Offensive 1968 offensive by North Vietnamese forces.

Thirteenth Amendment Amendment to the U.S. Constitution that outlaws slavery.

three strikes policy Policy of stiffer penalties for individuals with at least two prior criminal convictions.

three-caste system System that developed in the deep South that divided the population into whites, free blacks, and slaves.

Three-Fifths Clause Clause in the Constitution that provided that a slave be counted as three-fifths of a free person in determining a state's representation in the House of Representatives in the electoral college.

Toussaint Louverture Leader of the Haitian independence movement.

Townshend Acts Act of 1767 that taxed glass, lead, paint, paper, and tea imported into the colonies from Britain.

Trail of Tears The 1838 forced migration of the Cherokee to Oklahoma.

TransAfrica Organization founded to lobby for black political prisoners in South Africa.

transatlantic immigration The immigration of white laborers from Europe to America.

triangular trade systems Three-sided trade in which European goods were exchanged in West Africa for slaves, who were, in turn, traded for New World products in the Americas, which, in turn, were traded for European goods in Europe.

trickle-down theory Economic theory that financial gains by the wealthiest Americans would trickle down to less affluent Americans.

Tuskegee Airmen All-black combat air unit.

The Tuskegee Machine The name given to Booker T. Washington's political influence, connections, and organizational skills.

Tuskegee Study A study of the effects of syphilis on 622 black men, all of whom were given placebos.

U

Ugly Club Social organization initially made up of New York's wealthiest black men.

Uncle Tom Derogatory term for a subservient black.

underground railroad Organizations and individuals that aided escaped slaves in their journeys to the North.

Union Leagues Quasi-political organizations in which members gained political skills and education.

United Mine Workers Union formed in 1890 that encouraged black membership.

Universal Negro Improvement Association (UNIA) Black nationalist organization founded by Marcus Garvey in 1914.

Urban League Social welfare organization formed to help alleviate conditions black people encountered in large cities.

urban slaves Slaves who lived and worked in urban environments.

U.S. Constitution The formal basis of U.S. government since 1789.

V

Vietnam Southeast Asian country that was site of sustained American military intervention in the 1960s and early 1970s.

Volstead Act Act that, along with the Eighteenth Amendment, prohibited the manufacture, distribution, and sale of alcoholic beverages.

voluntary colonization The expressed position that black colonization of Africa should be voluntary.

Voting Rights Act of 1965 Act extending and supporting voting rights.

W

War on Poverty Term for President Johnson's approach to the problems of low-income communities.

Whig Party Party formed by Henry Clay and others in the early 1830s in opposition to Andrew Jackson and the Democrats.

white primaries Democratic party primaries in the South in the 1920s.

White-collar Work that does not involve manual labor.

the white man's burden The presumed responsibility of "superior" races for "inferior" ones.

Wilmot's Proviso An 1846 measure to prohibit slavery in lands captured from Mexico.

Women's Political Council (WPC) Civil rights organization founded by Mary Frances Fair Burks in 1946.

Works Progress Administration (WPA) Government organization created to employ the unemployed.

Writ of habeas corpus Writ requesting the right to be brought before a judge and not arrested and jailed without cause.

X

xenophobia Fear or contempt for all things foreign, especially foreign people.

Y

yeoman farmer Small independent farmers in the South.

Photo and Text Credits

CHAPTER 1: Photos: British Museum, London/Bridgeman Art Library, London/SuperStock, 4; © The British Museum, 6; The Cleveland Museum of Natural History, 9; Timothy Kendall, 12; © Werner Forman/Art Resource, NY, 13; The Granger Collection, New York, 17; Nigeria, Nok head, 900BC–200AD, Rafin Kura, Nok. Prehistoric West African sculpture from the Nok culture. Terracotta, 36 cms high. © Werner Forman/Art Resource, NY, 19; Roderick J. McIntosh, Rice University, 20; Head of a king, from Ife. c.13th century ce. Brass, height 11-7/16″ (29 cm). © Frank Willett, 20; Yoruba Offering Bowl from Ekiti Efon-Alaye, (BON46967) Bonhams, London, UK/Bridgeman Art Library, London/New York, 22; Christie's Images Ltd., 2005, 27.

CHAPTER 2: Photos: Courtesy of the Library of Congress, 34; Library of Congress, 36; Albrecht Durer (1471–1528), "Portrait of the Moorish Woman Katharina." Drawing. Uffizi Florence, Italy. Photograph © Foto Marburg/Art Resource, NY, 38; Art Resource, N.Y., 39; The Granger Collection, New York, 42; Courtesy of the Library of Congress, 43; Culver Pictures, Inc., 46; Courtesy of the Library of Congress, 47; AP Wide World Photos, 50; © The British Museum, 57; Courtesy of the Library of Congress, 59; The Granger Collection, New York, 61; Courtesy of the Library of Congress, 63; Text: Elizabeth Donnan, ed., Documents Illustrative of the History of the Slave Trade to America, 4 vols. Washington, DC: Carnegie Institute, 1930–35. pp. 1, 141–145, 52.

CHAPTER 3: Photos: Courtesy of the Library of Congress, 68; Getty Images Inc.—Hulton Archive Photos, 70; The South Carolina Historical Society, 72; The Granger Collection, New York, 80; Courtesy, American Antiquarian Society, 84; Thomas Coram, "View of Mulberry Street, House and Street." Oil on paper, 10 × 17.6 cm. Gibbes Museum of Art/Carolina Art Association. 68.18.01, 86; Abby Aldrich Rockefeller Folk Art Museum, Colonial Williamsburg Foundation, VA., 89; John Wollaston, "George Whitefield," ca.1770. National Portrait Gallery, London, 90; Corbis/Bettmann, 91; John F. Watson, "Annals of Philadelphia," being a collection of memiors, anecdotes, & incidents of Philadelphia. The London Coffee House. The Library Company of Philadelphia, 97; Jack W. Dykinga/Jack Dykinga Photography, 98; Arizona State Library, Archives and Public Records, Archives Division, Phoenix, Neg. # 99–9996, 99; Text: Figure 3–1: Reproduced from *The American Colonies: From Settlement to Independence* by R.C. Simmons (Copyright © R.C. Simmons 1976) by permission of PFD (**www.pfd.co.uk**) on behalf of Professor Richard C. Cummins, 82; Dorothy Porten, ed. *Early Negro Writing, 1760–1837*. 1971 reprint. Baltimore: Black Classic Press, 1995. Reprinted by permission, 93; Figure 3–2: Adaptation of "Figure 4 on page 21," from *Time on the Cross: The Economics of American Negro Slavery* by Robert William Fogel and Stanley L. Engerman. Copyright © 1974 Robert William Fogel and Stanley L. Engerman. Used by permission of W. W. Norton & Company, Inc., 96.

CHAPTER 4: Photos: William Ranney, "The Battle of Cowpens," oil on canvas. Photo by Sam Holland. Courtesy South Carolina State House, 108; Courtesy of the Library of Congress, 110; Courtesy of the Library of Congress, 117; Courtesy of the Library of Congress, 120; The Maryland Historical Society, Baltimore, Maryland., 122; University of Virginia Library, 125; The Granger Collection, New York, 126; Anne S.K. Brown Military Collection, John Hay Library, Brown University, 128; Courtesy, American Antiquarian Society, 130; Text: Maps 4–2 and 4–3: Adapted from *The Atlas of African-American History and Politics*, First Edition, by A. Smallwood and J. Elliot, © 1998 The McGraw-Hill Companies. Reprinted with permission of The McGraw-Hill Companies, 124 and 129.

CHAPTER 5: Photos: The Granger Collection, 138; Courtesy of the Library of Congress, 140; The Library Company of Philadelphia, 144; 2001-196-1

Krimmel, John Lewis Pepper Pot, A Scene in the Philadelphia Market Philadelphia Museum of Art: Gift of Mr. & Mrs. Edward B. Leisenring, Jr. in honor of the 125th Anniversary of the Museum, 2001. Sumpter Priddy III, Inc., 148; Schomburg Center for Research in Black Culture, The New York Public Library, 155; The Library Company of Philadelphia, 158; The Granger Collection, 159; Delaware Art Museum, 162; Stock Montage, 163; © Curt Teich Postcard Archives, Lake County Discovery Museum, 167; Text: Table 5–1: Philip S. Foner, *History of Black Americans, from Africa to the Emergence of the Cotton Kingdom*, Vol. 1, p. 374. Reproduced with permission of Greenwood Publishing Group, Inc., Westport, CT, 145.

CHAPTER 6: Photos: © Collection of The New-York Historical Society. Negative number 37628, 179; Library of Congress, 180; The Granger Collection, New York, 188; The Historic New Orleans Collection, assecion no. 1975.93.1, 191; Chicago Historical Society, 193; National Archives and Records Administration, 196; Courtesy of the Library of Congress, 196; Courtesy of the Library of Congress, 197; "Remains of Slave Quarters, Fort George Island, Florida," ca. 1865. Stereograph. © Collection of The New York Historical Society. Negative no. 48163, 200; Abby Aldrich Rockefeller Folk Art Museum, Williamsburg, VA, 201; Getty Images Inc.—Hulton Archive Photos, 204; John Antrobus, "Negro Burial." Oil painting. The Historic New Orleans Collection. #1960.46, 206; Text: Map 6–1: Reprinted by permission of Louisiana State University Press from *Atlas of Antebellum Southern Agriculture* by Sam Bowers Hilliard. © 1984 by Louisiana State Press, 183; Table 6–1: Copyright © 1974 *Slaves Without Masters: The Free Negro in the Antebellum South*, by Ira Berlin. Reprinted by permission of The New Press. www.thenewpress.com, 184; Map 6–2: Reprinted by permission of Louisiana State University Press from *Atlas of Antebellum Southern Agriculture* by Sam Bowers Hilliard. © 1984 by Louisiana State Press, 185; Map 6–4: Faragher, John Mack; Bible, Mari Jo; Czitrom, Daniel; Armitage, Susan H.; *Out of Man: A History of the American People*, Combined Volume, 4th Edition, © 2003. Reprinted by permission of Pearson Education, Inc. Upper Saddle River, NJ.

CHAPTER 7: Photos: Courtesy of the Library of Congress, 214; Manigault Papers, Southern Historical Collection, The Library of the University of North Carolina at Chapel Hill, 216; Three Sisters of the Copeland Family, 1854; William Matthew Prior, American (1806–1873). Oil on canvas; 26-7/8 × 36-1/2 in. (68.3 × 92.7 cm). Bequest of Martha C. Karolik for the M. and M. Karolik Collection of American Paintings, 1815–1865, 48.467, 222; The Granger Collection, 225; The Granger Collection, New York, 228; Nantucket Historical Association, 229; Photographs and Prints Division. Schomburg Center for Research in Black Culture/Art Resource. The New York Public Library. Astor, Lenox and Tilden Foundations. Photo by H. Rocher, 231; Photographs and Prints Division. Schomburg Center for Research in Black Culture/Art Resource, The New York Public Library. Astor, Lenox and Tilden Foundations, 233; Courtesy of the Library of Congress, 234; Courtesy of the Library of Congress, 236; Photographs and Prints Division. Schomburg Center for Research in Black Culture/Art Resource, The New York Public Library. Astor, Lenox and Tilden Foundations, 237; The Maryland Historical Society, Baltimore Maryland, 243; Thomas Waterman Wood, American, 1823–1903, Market Woman, 1858, Oil on canvas, 23-3/8 × 14-1/2 in. Fine Arts Museum of San Francisco, Museum Purchase, Mildred Anna Williams Collection, 1944.8, 245; Text: Table 7–1: Black Population in the States of the Old Northwest, 1800–1840, p. 104, from *In Hope of Liberty: Culture, Community and Protest Among Northern Free Blacks, 1700–1860* by James O. Horton and Lois E. Horton, copyright © 1996 by Oxford University Press, Inc. Used by permission of Oxford University Press, Inc., 223; Table 7–2, Adapted from *The Free Black in Urban America 1800–1850: The Shadow of a Dream* by Dr. Leonard P. Curry, p. 250.

CHAPTER 8: Photos: North Wind Picture Archives, Royal Albert Memorial Museum, Exeter, 252; © Bettmann/CORBIS, 254; Boston Public Library/ Rare Books Department. Courtesy of the Trustees, 256; Robert Lindneux, "The Trail of Tears" (the removal of the Cherokee Indians to the west in 1838). Oil on canvas. © The Granger Collection, New York, 257; Courtesy of the Library of Congress, 262; Virginia Historical Society, Richmond, Virginia, 264; This item is reproduced by permission of The Huntington Library, San Marino, California, 266; National Portrait Gallery, Smithsonian Institution, Art Resource, NY, 269; Boston Anthenaeum, 271; Courtesy of the Library of Congress, 273; The Granger Collection, New York, 274; top and bottom: Courtesy of the Library of Congress, 275; Text: Herbert Aptheker, ed., *A Documentary History of the Negro People in the United States, 1933–1945*, 7 vols. 1951; reprint, New York: Citadel, 1990, pp. 1–89, 270.

CHAPTER 9: Photos: Theo. Kaufmann, "On to Liberty," 1867, Oil on canvas. The Metropolitan Museum of Art. Gift of Erving and Joyce Wolf, 1982 (1982.443.3) Photograph © 1982 The Metropolitan Museum of Art, 280; Corbis/Bettmann, 282; Sophia Smith College, Smith College, 288; The Granger Collection, 295; Savery Library Archives, Talladega College, Talladega, Alabama, 296; Courtesy of the Library of Congress, 297; Sophia Smith Collection, Smith College, 299; Frederick Douglass (1817?–95). Oil on canvas, c1844, attr. to E. Hammond. The Granger Collection, 301; Getty Images Inc.—Hulton Archive Photos, 304; Text: Herbert Aptheker, ed., *A Documentary History of the Negro People in the United States, 1933–1945*, 5th ed. New York: Citadel, 1968, pp. 1, 327–328, 302.

CHAPTER 10: Photos: Courtesy of the Library of Congress, 310; Getty Images Inc.—Hulton Archive Photos, 312; Courtesy of the California History Room, California State Library, Sacramento, California, 314; Courtesy of the Library of Congress, 317; Getty Images, Inc.—Liaison, 321; © Ohio Historical Society, 324; Courtesy of the Library of Congress, 324; The Newberry Library, 325; © CORBIS, 327; The Granger Collection, 332; Courtesy of the Library of Congress, 338; Text: Victor Ullman, Martin R. Delaney: *The Beginnings of Black Nationalism.* Boston: Beacon Press, 1971, pp. 112, 318.

CHAPTER 11: Photos: Courtesy of the Library of Congress, 348; Dave King/ Dorling Kindersley © Confederate Memorial Hall, New Orleans, 350; Courtesy of the Library of Congress, 352; Eastman Johnson, A Ride for Liberty—The Fugitive Slaves, 1862, oil on board. The Brooklyn Museum, Gift of Miss Gwendolyn O.L. Conkling, 353; Corbis/Bettmann, 356; Courtesy of the Library of Congress, 359; Massachusetts Commandery Military Order of the Loyal Legion and The U.S. Army Military History Institute, 366; Courtesy of the Library of Congress, 368; Corbis/Bettmann, 369; The Granger Collection, 373; Photographs and Prints Division. Schomburg Center for Research in Black Culture. The New York Public Library. Astor, Lenox and Tilden Foundations, 375; Culver Pictures, Inc., 376; Harper's Weekly, March 18, 1865. Courtesy of William C. Hine, 379.

CHAPTER 12: Photos: Courtesy of the Library of Congress, 388, 390, 393, 395, 397; Austin History Center, Austin Public Library/PICA 05496, 398; The Granger Collection, 401; Moorland-Spingarn Research Center, 402; Courtesy of Hampton University Archives, 404; The Granger Collection, New York, 410; Library of Congress, 413; Text: Ira Berlin, Steven Hahn, Steven F. Miller, Joseph P. Reidy, and Leslie S. Rowland, "The Terrain of Freedom: The Struggle over the Meaning of Free Labour in the U.S. South," *History Workshop*, No. 22 (Autumn 1986); pp. 108–109. Reprinted by permission of Oxford University Press, 396.

CHAPTER 13: Photos: The Granger Collection, 424; Courtesy of the Library of Congress, 426; The Granger Collection, New York, 428, 430; Rutherford B. Hayes Presidential Center, 437; From The Henry Clay Warmoth Papers # 752, Southern Historical Collection, Wilson Library, University of North

Carolina at Chapel Hill, 437; Courtesy of the Library of Congress, 441; P.S. Duval and Son, Come and join us brothers; Civil War; Philadelphia, Pa.; ca. 1863. Chicago Historical Society ICHi-22051, 444; CORBIS—NY, 447; The New York Public Library Prints Division, 449.

CHAPTER 14: Photos: Solomon D. Butcher Collection, 458; Library of Congress, 460; Culver Pictures, Inc., 468; Corbis/Bettmann, 471; © Collection of The New-York Historical Society, Negative # : 51391, 474; North Carolina Department of Cultural Resources, 477; University of Illinois at Chicago, 478; Courtesy of the Library of Congress, 482; Corbis/Bettmann, 485; Text: Quote: Goldfield, David; Abbott, Carl; Anderson, Virginia DeJohn: Argersinger, Jo Ann E.; Argersinger, Peter H.; Barney, William L.; Weir, Robert M., *American Journey, The: Combined*, 3rd Edition, © 2004. Reprinted by permission of Pearson Education, Inc., Upper Saddle River, NJ, 469; Figure 14–3: Loren Schweninger, *Black Property Owners in the South, 1790–1915*, p. 164. © 1997 University of Illinois Press. Reprinted by permission, 487.

CHAPTER 15: Photos: The Erwin E. Smith Collection of the Library of Congress on deposit at the Amon Carter Museum, Fort Worth, Texas, 496; Courtesy of the Library of Congress, 498; The Granger Collection, New York, 502; Courtesy of the Library of Congress, 506; © College of the Holy Cross and Special Collections, 509; Montana Historical Society, Helena, 513; Museum of the American West Collection, Autry National Center, 515; Courtesy of the Herndon Foundation, 523; Valentine Richmond History Center, 523; © 2000 Bettmann/CORBIS, 529; Erwin E. Smith, "Part of a Parade of the Negro Fair in Bonham, Texas." Home Town of the Photographer. Bonham, Texas. nitrate negative, 1910–1915. LC.S611.790 The Erwin E. Smith Collection of the Library of Congress on deposit at the Amon Carter Museum, Fort Worth, Texas, 530; Courtesy of the Library of Congress, 531; Text: Willard B. Gatewood, Jr., *Smoked Yankees and the Struggle for Empire: Letters from Negro Soldiers, 1898–1902.* University of Arkansas Press. Reprinted by permission of the author, 518.

CHAPTER 16: Photos: Courtesy of the Library of Congress, 538; Corbis/Bettmann, 540; Brown Brothers, 542; The Granger Collection, New York, 545; Photographs and Prints Division, Schomburg Center for Research in Black Culture, The New York Public Library, Astor, Lenox and Tilden Foundations, 548; James VanDerZee, The Wedding Party. Copyright © Donna Mussenden VanDerZee, 556; Courtesy of the Library of Congress, 564, 565, 570; Research Division of the Oklahoma Historical Society, 572; © 2004 Estate of Gwendolyn Knoght Lawrence/Artists Rights Society (ARS), New York, 576; Text: Map 16–3: From *The Harlem Renaissance* by Steven Watson, copyright © 1995 by Steven Watson. Used by permission of Pantheon Books, a division of Random House, Inc.

CHAPTER 17: Photos: Courtesy of the Library of Congress, 588, 590; The Granger Collection, 593; Getty Images Inc.—Hulton Archive Photos, 597; Corbis/Bettmann, 599; Betsy G. Reyneau. A. Philip Randolph. National Archives, 604; Aaron Douglas, "Aspects of Negro Life: From Slavery Through Reconstruction, 1934", oil on canvas, 60 × 139″, Schomburg Center for Research in Black Culture, Art & Artifacts Division, The New York Public Library, Astor, Lenox and Tilden Foundation, 609; Beinecke Rare Book and Manuscript Library, Yale University, 611; © Frank Driggs/CORBIS, 614; Maryland Historical Society, Baltimore, MD, 614; Frank Driggs Collection, 615; National Baseball Hall of Fame Library, Cooperstown, N.Y., 618; Courtesy of the Library of Congress, 619; Text: "I, Too" from *The Collected Poems of Langston Hughes* by Langston Hughes. Copyright © 1994 by The Estate of Langston Hughes. Used by permission of Alfred A. Knopf, a Division of Random House, Inc., 590.

CHAPTER 18: Photos: Margaret Bourke-White/LIFE Magazine © TimePix, 628; Corbis/Bettmann, 630; Schomburg Center for Research in Black Culture/Art Resource, 634; From "A True Likeness: The Black South of Richard Samuel Roberts, 1920–1936 (Bruccoli Clark Layman, 1986), 636; Courtesy of the Library of Congress, 639; Courtesy Mary McLeod Bethune

Council House National Historic Site, Washington, DC, 642; Courtesy of the Library of Congress, 648; Scurlock Studios, 649; Courtesy of the Library of Congress, 651; Courtesy of the Library of Congress, 658; Text: Table 18–2: "Median Incomes of Black Families . . ." from *An American Dilemma: The Negro Problem and Modern Democracy* by Gunnar Myrdal. Copyright © 1944, 1962 by Harper & Row Publisher, Inc. Reprinted by permission of HarperCollins Publishers, Inc., 633; Herbert Aptheker, ed. *A Documentary History of the Negro People in the United States, 1933–1945*. New York: Citadel, 1990. pp. 58–60, 646; "Hoboing in Alabama" from *Going to the Territory* by Ralph Ellison, copyright © 1986 by Ralph Ellison. Used by permission of Random House, Inc., 667.

CHAPTER 19: Photos: Bettmann/Corbis, 668; AP Wide World Photos, 670; Courtesy of the Library of Congress, 672, 675; © International Negro Press, 1936, 677; MGM/Archive Photos, 678; Getty Images Inc.—Hulton Archive Photos, 679; Archibald Motley, Jr., "Barbeque," 1934. Oil on canvas, 36-1/4 × 40-1/8". The Howard University Gallery of Art, Washington, D.C., 682; Courtesy of RCA Records. A Unit of BMG Entertainment, 684; © David Lees/CORBIS, 685; Courtesy of the Library of Congress, 689; Corbis/Bettmann, 694; © CORBIS/Bettmann, 695; Text: "I've Known Rivers," from *The Collected Poems of Langston Hughes* by Langston Hughes, copyright © 1994 by The Estate of Langston Hughes. Used by permission of Alfred A. Knopf, division of Random House, Inc., 690.

CHAPTER 20: Photos: National Archives and Records Administration, 704; Courtesy of the Library of Congress, 706; Horace Pippin (1888–1946), "Mr. Prejudice," 1943. Oil on canvas, 18 × 14 inches. Philadelphia Museum of Art, Gift of Dr. and Mrs. Matthew T. Moore. Photo by Graydon Wood. 1984-108-1, 709; Courtesy of the Library of Congress, 710, National Archives and Records Administration, 714; Hon. William H. Hastie, Oil. By Sarah Belchetz-Swenson, 715; National Archives and Records Administration, 716, 717; Courtesy of the Library of Congress, 721; National Archives and Records Administration, 724; Michael Barson, 730; Courtesy of the Library of Congress, 731; Courtesy of the Library of Congress, 734; 713; Text: William H. Hastie. Excerpt from "Why I Resigned," *Chicago Defender*, February 6, 1943. Reprinted by permission of the Chicago Defender, 739.

CHAPTER 21: Photos: Corbis/Bettmann, 744; Moorland-Spingarn Research Center, 746; © NAACP/Library of Congress, 749; Corbis/Bettmann, 750; Getty Images, Inc., 752; Corbis/Bettmann, 754, 755; AP Wide World Photos, 759; AP Wide World Photos, 763; News & Record Library, 764; Corbis/Bettmann, 766, 767, 777; John F. Kennedy Library, 779; AP Wide World Photos, 780; Take Stock-Images of Change, 783; Text: Witnessing History: Reprinted by arrangement with the Estate of Martin Luther King, Jr., c/o Writers House as agent for the proprietor New York, NY. Copyright 1955 Martin Luther King, Jr., copyright renewed 1991 Coretta Scott King, 746; Excerpt from Montgomery Improvement Association Speech, December 5, 1955: Reprinted by arrangement with the Estate of Martin Luther King, Jr., c/o Writers House as agent for the proprietor New York, NY. Copyright 1955 Martin Luther King, Jr., copyright renewed 1991 Coretta Scott King, 759; Excerpt from "We'll Never Turn Back" by Bernice Johnson Reagan, edited by Pete Seeger & Bob Reiser, from *Everybody Says Freedom: A History of the Civil Rights Movement in Songs and Pictures* by Pete Seeger & Bob Reiser. Used by permission of W.W. Norton & Company, Inc., 772; Excerpt from "I Have a Dream" Speech. Reprinted by arrangement with the Estate of Martin Luther King, Jr., c/o Writers House as agent for the proprietor New York, NY. Copyright 1963 Martin Luther King, Jr., copyright renewed 1991 Coretta Scott King, 778.

CHAPTER 22: Photos: Photograph by Marilyn Nance, used by permission. Courtesy of the Library of Congress. Copyright © 1986 by Marylin Nance, 790; Courtesy of the Library of Congress, 792; Elizabeth Catlett, Malcolm X Speaks for Us, 1969. Lithograph, 95 × 70 cm. Art © Elizabeth Catlett/Licensed by VAGA, New York, NY, 795; © Bettmann/Corbis, 796; Leonard Freed/MAGNUM PHOTOS, 801; Courtesy of the Library of Congress, 802; AP Wide World Photos, 804; Getty Images Inc.—Hulton Archive Photos, 807; Mark Jury, The Vietnam Photo Book, 808; Courtesy of the Library of Congress, 809; Paul S. Conklin/PhotoEdit, 813; AP/Wide World Photos, 815; Corbis/Bettmann, 816; Courtesy of the Library of Congress, 818; AP/Wide World Photos, 822, 827, 832; Office of the Mayor, Detroit, Michigan, 833; Mayor's Office, Atlanta, 835; Text: "Captain Joseph B. Anderson, Jr." in Wallace Terry, *Bloods, An Oral History of the Vietnam War by Black Veterans*. New York: Ballentine Books, 1984, pp. 219–228, 810; Exerpt from Memphis Speech: Reprinted by arrangement with the Estate of Martin Luther King, Jr., c/o Writers House as agent for the proprietor New York, NY. Copyright 1968 Martin Luther King, Jr., copyright renewed 1991 Coretta Scott King, 816.

CHAPTER 23: Photos: AP Wide World Photos, 842; S.M. Wakefield/Pearson Education/PH College, 844; Mike Theiler/Reuters/Corbis/Bettmann, 847; Reuters/Rick Wilking/Corbis/Bettmann, 847; Damian Dovarganes/AP Wide World Photos, 852; © Peter Turnley/Corbis, 855; Paul Conklin/PhotoEdit, 857; Rob Crandall/Stock Boston, 860; AP Wide World Photos, 862; Agence France Presse/Getty Images, 864; © Stephen Jaffe/Agence France Presse/Corbis, 870; © Mary Altaffer/Pool/Reuters/Corbis, 875; Text: "Taking Sides Against Ourselves," Rosemary L. Bray, New York Times Magazine, November 17, 1991, p. 53. Reprinted by permission of Elaine Markson Agency, 848.

CHAPTER 24: © Najlah Feanny-Hicks/Corbis SabaMill, 882; Chuck Nacke/Woodfin Camp & Associates, 884; Steve Green/AP Wide World Photos, 885; Barbara Gauntt/The Clarion-Ledger, 889; AP Wide World Photos, 894; © Tim Mosenfelder/Corbis, 898; Courtesy Molefi Kete Asante. Photo © Joseph V. Labolito, 899; AP/Wide World Photos, 900, 904; © Jacques M. Chenet/Corbis, 906; James Leynse/Corbis/SABA Press Photos, Inc., 907; Michelle Alaimo/AP Wide World Photos, 908; © Tony Arruza, 912; © Paul Davis, 913; National Gay and Lesbian Task Force, 914; Text: Witnessing History: K. Anthony Appiah and Amy Gutmann, *Color Conscious: The Political Morality of Race* (Princeton, NJ: Princeton University Press, 1996), 884; Excerpt from "I Have a Dream" Speech. Reprinted by arrangement with the Estate of Martin Luther King, Jr., c/o Writers House as agent for the proprietor New York, NY. Copyright 1963 Martin Luther King, Jr., copyright renewed 1991 Coretta Scott King, 890.

Index

Family life
    clans/extended, 24
    during the Depression, 633–34
    on farms, 485–486
    free blacks (1820–to start of Civil War), 229–36
    impact of migration on, 484, 581–82
    Moynihan Report, 826–27
    patrilineal versus matrilineal, 826–27
    reuniting families following Civil War, 391–92
    slave, 88–90, 131
    in West Africa, 24–25
Family names, preservation of, 89
Farad, Wali, 697
Fard, Wallace D., 697
Farmer, James, 727, 766
Farrakahn, Louis, 905–07
Faubus, Orville, 763–64
Fauset, Jessie, 607, 609–11, 613
Fax, Elton, 655
Federal Arts Project, 654
Federal Bureau of Investigation (FBI), 761, 860
    See also Hoover, J. Edgar
    Counterintelligence (COINTELPRO), 801
    Ten Most Wanted list, first black woman on, 801–2
Federal Communications Commission (FCC), 677–78
Federal Council of Churches, 797
Federal Council on Negro Affairs, 649–54
Federal Emergency Relief Administration (FERA), 644–48
Federal Music Project, 654–54
Federal Theater Project, 654–55
Federal Writers Project, 649–54
Federalist Party, 167, 221
Female Anti-Slavery Society, 269, 290–92
Female Benevolent Society of St. Thomas, Philadelphia, 154
Female Literary Society of Philadelphia, 244
Feminism, 912–14
Fences (Wilson), 893
Ferebee, Dorothy, 560
Ferraro, Geraldine, 857
Fetchit, Stepin, 678–79
Fictive Kin relationships, 88
Fifteenth Amendment, 440, 467
Fifteenth New York National Guard, 565
Fifth Amendment, 330
5th Massachusetts Cavalry Regiment, 368
54th Massachusetts Regiment, 367–72, 374, 376
55th Massachusetts Regiment, 368, 372
Filmore, Millard, 323
Filmmakers, 678–80
Final Call, The, 906
Fine Clothes to the Jew (Hughes), 607
Finney, Charles G., 258
Fire, 607, 610–11
Fire in the Flint, The (White), 610
Fire Next Time, The (Baldwin), 818
Fires in the Mirror (Smith), 893
First American president to visit Africa, 864
First black person born in English America, 75
First Confiscation Act (1861), 355
First Kansas Colored Infantry, 370
First Reconstruction Act (1867), 416
First South Carolina Volunteers, 365
Fisk, Pomp, 125
Fisk University, 403, 504, 532, 547, 748
    Jubilee Singers, 528
Fitzgerald, F. Scott, 606
Flash and Furious Five, Grandmaster, 895
Fleming, Arthur S., 852
Flexner, Abraham, 526
Flint-Goodridge Medical College, 525
Flipper, Henry O., 489
Florida
    Bush v. Gore, 868–69
    disfranchisement in, 469
    first segregation laws in, 471
    Rosewood riot (1923), 573–74
    secession from the Union, 339
    slaves in, 96–98, 101
    violence against black voters, 446, 780–84
    voting violations in, 868
Florida A&M University, 432, 532
Folk remedies, 53–54, 206
Folsom, Jim, 753
Food, Tobacco, Agricultural and Allied Workers of
        America, 656
Football, 532, 618
For My People (Walker), 681
Foraker, James B., 514–15
Ford, Gerald, 829
Ford, Henry, 581
Ford, James, 657
Ford Motor Co., 581, 602

Forest, Nathan Bedford, 374–75
Forest region, of West Africa, 19–21
Foreman, Clark, 649
Forman, James, 769, 798, 871
Forrest, Nathan Bedord, 436
Forten, Charlotte, 269, 402
Forten, Harriet, 29
Forten, James, 267–268, 285, 288–89
Forten, Margaretta, 269
Forten, Sarah, 269, 290
Fort Pillow Massacre (1864), 374–75
Fort Sumter, 342, 370, 372, 377
Fortune, T. Thomas, 542
"Forty acres and a mule," 393
Forty-eighth Volunteer Regiment, 520
Forty-Niners, 316–317
Forty-ninth Volunteer Regiment, 520
Foster, Andrew "Rube", 617–18
Fourteenth Amendment, 414–415, 472, 641, 659, 828, 853
Fourteen Points, 600–601
France, 37, 43, 64, 97, 111
    Colonization in Africa, 600
Francis, G. Hamilton, 712
Franco, Francisco, 708
Franklin, Aretha, 821
Franklin, Benjamin, 115, 128, 262
Franklin, John Hope, 652, 752–53
Fraternities, 558–560
Frazier, E. Franklin, 639, 651, 681–682, 826
Frederick Douglass Memorial Hospital and Training
        School, 525
Frederick Douglass' Paper, 294
Free African Society (Philadelphia), 154–55
Free Benezet, 155
Free black communities
    emergence of, 154–155
    in the urban North (1820–to start of Civil War), 223–36
Free blacks
    See also Emancipation
    emergence of, in the South, 148, 152, 218
    following the American Revolution, 128–31, 141–46,
        242–50
    charts / maps, 128, 129, 132–33, 142
Free blacks (1820–start of Civil War), 223–36
    See also Emancipation
    Black Laws, 224–25, 247
    Demographics, 222, 229–30
    disfranchisement, 225–26
    Jacksonian era, 221–22, 257–58
    in the North, 229–41
    segregation, 226–29
    in the South (deep), 246–47
    in the South (upper), 242–43
    statistics, 229, 246
Freedmen's Book, The (Child), 403
Freedmen's Bureau, 394–97, 402, 413, 454
Freedmen's Hospital, 525, 720
Freedmen's Savings and Trust Company, 443–44, 443
Freedom, 886
Freedom movement. See Civil rights movement
Freedom Rides, 766–67
Freedom's Journal 218, 267, 294
Freeman, Elizabeth, 140, 142–43
Freemasonry, 155
Free papers, 242–43
Free Produce Association, 292–92
Free Soil Party, 228, 316–17, 329–30, 369
Freetown, 162
Fremont, John C., 329, 355
French and Indian War / Seven Years War (1754–1763),
        111
French Revolution, 153, 165, 262, 264
Frye, Theodore, 684
Fugitive Slave Act (1793), 150, 223
Fugitive Slave Law (1850), 223, 355
Fugitive slave stories of, 319–24, 376
Fuller, Charles, 893
Fuller, Hoyt, 819
Fulton, Robert, 221
Funerals, 11, 89

G

Gabriel, 163, 162–164, 262–63
Gabriel's Conspiracy, 163, 262–63
Gag Rule, 296
Gaines, Lloyd, 640, 748
Gaines v. Canada, 640, 748
Gangsta Rap, 897–98
Galloway, Abraham, 433
Gandhi, Mohandas, 727, 759–60
"Gansta, Gansta," 897
Gao, 38
Garner, Cornelius, 209
Garner, Margaret, 323–24

Garnet, Henry Highland, 266, 284, 289, 292, 297, 305,
        308, 367, 407
Garrett, Thomas, 301
Garrison, William Lloyd, 265, 269, 271, 273–75, 278,
        288, 292, 296, 303, 339, 360
Garrity, W. Arthur, 828
Garvey, Marcus, 596–601, 709
Gary Convention, 830
Gary, Indiana, first black mayor of, 830
Gates, Henry Louis, Jr., 885, 899, 900–901
Gaye, Marvin, 821
Gay and lesbian life, 914, 890–91
Gayle v. Browder, 761
Gay rights, 727
Genius of Universal Emancipation, 271–73
Genovese, Eugene E., 209
Georgia
    Albany movement, 771, 773
    cotton in, 151
    Cotton States Exposition (1895), 540, 542
    disfranchisement in, 469
    education in, 500
    first segregation laws in, 473
    rice in, 188–89
    riot of 1906, 567–69
    secession from the Union, 339
    sit-ins, 764–66
    slavery in, 84
    strike by washerwomen, 525
Georgian, The, 567
Germany, colonization in Africa, 600
Gettysburg Address, 362, 380
Ghana, ancient, 14–17, 20
Gibbs, Jonathan C., 407, 432
Gibbs, Mifflin W., 432
Gibson, Josh, 694
Gibson, Kenneth, 862
Gillespie, John Birks (Dizzy), 674–75
Gillespie, Frank L., 579
Gilmore, Quincy A., 372
Gilpin, Charles, 616
Giovanni, Nikki, 817, 819
Gleaves, Richard H., 461
Gloucester, John, 158
God's Trombones: Seven Negro Sermons in Verse (Johnson), 607
Gold trade, 15, 20, 38
Golden State, 635
Goldwater, Barry, 781, 793
Gompers, Samuel, 602
Goncalvez, Antam, 38
Gone with the Wind, 678
Goodman, Andrew, 774, 780–81
Goodman, Robert, 857
Good Samaritan Building, 521
Goodnight, Charles, 515
Gordy, Berry, 804–5, 821, 885
Gore, Albert, Jr., 868–69
Gore, Albert, Sr., 754
Gorsuch, Edward, 322
Gosden, Freeman, 677–78
Gospel in Chicago, 684–85
Government appointees
    George W. Bush administration and, 868–69
    Carter administration and, 834–35
    Clinton administration and, 863–64
    Kennedy administration and, 769
    Roosevelt administration and, 648–51
Government positions, blacks in during 1870s, 579–80
Grady, Henry, 460
Graham, Billy, 615
Grandfather clause, 469, 543
Grange, 464
Grant, Charlie, 617
Grant, Florie, 714
Grant, Madison, 592
Grant, Ulysses S., 354, 365, 441, 445–47
Gratz v. Bollinger, 853
Gray, Fred D., 662, 760
Gray, Victoria, 781
Gray, William H., 854, 863
Great Awakening, 90–91,119
    Second Great Awakening, 256
Great Bridge, battle of (1775), 124
Great Depression. See Depression (1929–1933)
Great Migration. See Migration, great
Great Postal Campaign, 295
Great Pyramids, 11–12
Great Society, 806–7, 845–47
Greek Civilization, 10
Greeley, Horace, 357, 379
Green, Ernest, 835
Green, Malice, 860
Green, Shields, 335
Green, William, 605

Plessy, Homer A., 471–73, 868
Plessy v. Ferguson, 471–73, 751–52
Plum Bun (Fauset), 607
Poet laureate, 894–95
Poems on Various Subjects (Harper), 236
Poems on Various Subjects, Religious and Moral (Wheatley), 120
Poetry, black arts movement, 690, 819–20
Police brutality, in the 1990s, 859–62, 894–95
Politics (1867–1877)
  See also under name of party
  black leaders, 407–12 416, 428–29
  business and industry issues, 433
  civil rights, 407–9, 414–15, 431
  constitutional conventions, 427–28
  educational and social welfare issues, 394, 402–4, 430–31
  elections, 428–29
  land issues, 392–99, 433
  opposition, 436
  Reconstruction, 391–420
  timeline / chronology / maps, 416, 446, 448–49
Politics (1875–1900)
  black congressmen, 462–63
  colored Farmers' Alliance, 464
  Democrats and farmer discontent, 462–63
  Disfranchisement, 467–69
  Populist party, 465–66
Politics (1900–)
  blacks in government positions, 650
  Kennedy administration and the civil rights movement, 768–71
  Mississippi Freedom Democratic Party (MFDP), 781–82, 834
  National Black Convention movement, 831–33
  1936 election, 652–53
  1948 election, 732–33
  1960 election, 768
  1964 election, 793
  1968 election, 825
  1988 election, 857
  1992 election, 863
  1996 election, 865
  2000 election, 868–69
  2004 election, 874–76
  political activism (1980s–1990s), 854–55
  Rainbow Coalition, 856–58
  rise of black elected officials, 653–54, 830–36
  women politicians (1970s), 834–35
Polk, James K., 286
Poll tax, 468–69
Pollard, Frederick Douglass "Fritz," 618
Poole, Elijah. See Elijah Muhammad
Poor People's Campaign, 814
Poor, Salem, 125–26
Popular sovereignty, 327
Populist party, formation of, 465–66
Porgy and Bess, 616
Poro, 25
Port Royal Experiment, 394, 486
Portugal
  Atlantic slave trader and, 19, 37–39, 42–43
  Christianity, 23
  exploration/colonization by, 19, 21, 600
Potter House, 903
Pound, Ezra, 606
Powell, Adam Clayton, Jr., 809
Powell, Bud, 674–675
Powell, Colin L., 869–70, 874–76, 885
Powell, John A., 911
Powell, Lewis F., 853
Powell, Ozie, 657–61
Powell, Rodney, 765
Powell, Ruth, 728
Powell v. Alabama, 658–59
"Power to the People," 801
Prairie View A&M, 532
Prather, W. H., 513
Prayer of Twenty Millions (Greeley), 357
Preliminary Emancipation Proclamation, 360–61
Presbyterian churches, 158, 400–401
Presbyterian Evangelical Society, 158
Pretty Baby, 684
Price, Cecil, 780–81
Price, Victoria, 657–61
Prince Hall Masons, 155, 241, 246
Prince, Lucy Terry
Principia Mathematica (Newton), 116
Prioleau, George W., 516
Prison life, 492
  incarceration, 989
  reform movements, 801–2, 859
Pritchet, Jack, 264
Pritchett, Laurie, 771

Privateers, 126
Proclamation line, 112
Professionals (1820–to start of Civil War), 233
Progressive movement, 541
Progressive National Baptist Convention, 696, 902
Progressive party, 561
Project 100,000, 808–9
Proletariat, 696
Proposition 209 (California Civil Rights Initiative), 853
Protest literature, 692
Providence, antiblack riots in (1812–1849), 285
Provident Hospital and Training Institute, 525, 579
Provincial Freeman, 301
Public Enemy, 897
Public Works Administration (PWA), 645, 647–48
Public Works Employment Act, 835
Publishers Weekly, 893
Pulitzer Prizes, 893–94
Pullman, George, 606
Pullman Palace Car Co., 604–5, 655–56
Puritans, 95
Purvis, Robert, 288–90
Putnam, Caroline Remond, 555
Pyramids, 11–12
Pythians, 544, 580

Q
Quakers, 95, 127–128, 146, 148, 150, 158, 161, 238, 290
Quarles, Benjamin, 652
Quicksand (Larsen), 607, 611
Quota system, immigration, 592

R
Race, classification, 909–11
  biracial and multiracial identity, 910–11
  ethnicity, 910
  Statistical Policy Directive, 909–10
Race films, 678–79
Race riots, 567–74
Racial etiquette, 474–75
Racial preferences, 852–53
Racism, in the 1920s, 591–93
  See also Civil rights movement
  Birth of a Nation, The 592–93
  Ku Klux Klan, 592–93, 780–81
Racism, used to justify slavery, 152–53
Radical Republicans
  Freedmen's Bureau bill and Civil Rights bill, 413–14
  Johnson's vetoes, 414
  members of, 412
  proposals, 412–13
Radio, 676–77, 683
Ragtime, 528
Railroads
  Brotherhood of Sleeping Car Porters (BSCP), 604–5
  segregation on, 471–73
Railway Labor Act, 655–56
Rainbow Coalition, 844, 856–58, 863
Rainey, Joseph, 428, 463
Rainey, Ma, 529–30
Rainey, William "Pa," 529–30
Ram's Harm, 294
Randall, Dudley, 819
Randolph, Benjamin F., 437
Randolph, A. (Asa) Philip, 604–5
  Brotherhood of Sleeping Car Porters (BSCP), 604–5, 655–56
  League for Non-Violent Civil Disobedience against Military Segregation, 733–34
  March on Washington Movement, 708–10
  Joint Committee on National Recovery (JCNR), 661
Randolph, Benjamin F., 437
Randolph, John, 165, 365
Ransby, Barbara, 848–49
Ransier, Alonzo J., 463
Ransom, Leon A., 748
Rap music, 895–98
Rape, 480, 657, 848–49
Rapier, James T., 463
Rapper's Delight, 895
Raspberry, William, 871
Rastafarian, 896
Ray, Charles B., 294
Ray, Charlotte, 406, 527
Ray, James Earl, 815–16
Re (or Ra), Sun god, 11
Reason, Patrick, 233
Rebecca of Sunnybrook Farm, 678
Reagan, Ronald, 829, 835, 845–47, 855, 895
  affirmative action and, 850–52
  conservative reaction in administration of, 854
  King holiday, 854–55
Reagon, Bernice Johnson, 772
Rebellions / uprisings

Brown raid on Harpers Ferry, 334–37
Gabriel (Prosser) conspiracy, 163, 262–63
Slave, 100–101, 104
  on slave ships, 55–56
Turner rebellion, 275, 278
Vesey conspiracy, 263–64
Reconstruction (1865–1868)
  Churches, 400–401
  civil rights, 414–15, 431
  economic issues, 431–33
  education, 402–4, 430–31
  end of, 445–50
  Freedmen's Bureau, 394–96
  freedom, what it meant, 391–92
  land, issues of, 392–93
  legislation, 409–10, 433
  radical, 415–16
  Radical Republicans, 412–14
  reactions of former slaves, 391
  reactions of white Southerners, 404–6, 417, 420
  reuniting of black families, 391–92
  sharecropping, 398–99
  timeline / chronology / maps, 399, 416, 418–19, 429
  violence, 405–406, 476–80
Reconstruction Act First (1867), 416
Reconstruction Finance Corp, 636
Red Scare, 591–92
Redding, Louis, 752–53
Reeb, James, 775, 783
Reed, Adolph, 899
Reed, Ishmael, 899
Reese, Frederick, 782
Reese, John Earl, 774
Regimento, 23
Rehnquist, William H., 853
Reid, Ira De A., 649
Religion
  See also under name of church or faith
  Affiliation statistics among southern black people (1890), 506
  churches, in antebellum years, 237–38, 258–60
  churches, in Reconstruction years, 400–401
  churches, origins of independent black, 156–58
  Egyptian, 11
  from 1890–1900, 505–10
  in the forest region, 26
  gospel music in Chicago, 684–85
  Great Awakening, 90–91
  Holiness Movement and the Pentecostal Church, 507–9
  Indigenous, 19
  Islam, 26–27
  National Council of Churches (NCC), 797–99
  Nation of Islam, 695–97, 794–96, 905–7
  in the 1930s and 1940s, 696–98
  in the 1990s, 904–7
  Roman Catholics and Episcopalians, 509–10, 902
  Second Great Awakening, 258–60
  slaves and, 90–91
  in the twenty-first century, 902–7
  West Africa, 26–27
Remond, Charles Lenox, 231–232, 367
Reorganized Church of God in Christ, 509
Reparations, 871–872
Republican party, 561, 637, 644, 869, 875–76
  See also Radical Republicans
  archconservative, 849
  blacks in (1880s), 434–36
  factionalism, 434–35
  formation of, 167, 222
  in the 1920s, 594
  New Right, 845
  Southern strategy, 826
  split in 1912, 561
"R.E.S.P.E.C.T," 821
Resurrection City, 816
Revels, Hiram, 428, 430, 463
Revivalists, 90–91, 258
Revue Nègre, 616
Reynolds, Grant, 734
Rhode Island
  emancipation / abolition of slavery in, 142–45
  slaves in, 95
  voting in, 226
Rice, Condoleeza, 870, 873–74, 876
Rice, slave labor and, 85, 188–89
Rice, Thomas "Daddy," 470
Richardson, George, 569
Richmond
  emergence of free black communities in, 154
  free blacks in, 154
Richmond, David, 764–66
Rickey, Branch, 694
Riggs, Marion, 894
Rights revolution, 912–14